1) a
2) b

University Casebook Series

Cases and Problems

on

REMEDIES

By

ELAINE W. SHOBEN
Edward W. Cleary Professor of Law
University of Illinois

WILLIAM MURRAY TABB
Professor of Law
University of Oklahoma

SECOND EDITION

Westbury, New York
THE FOUNDATION PRESS, INC.
1995

Library of Congress Cataloging-in-Publication Data

Shoben, Elaine W., 1948–
    Cases and problems on remedies / by Elaine W. Shoben, William Murray
Tabb. — 2nd ed.
    ISBN 1–56662–262–X
    1. Remedies (Law)—United States—Cases.   I. Tabb, William Murray,
1952–   .   II. Title.   III. Series.
KF9010.A7S47   1995
347.73'77—dc20
[347.30777]   95–4752

 TEXT IS PRINTED ON 10% POST
CONSUMER RECYCLED PAPER

1st Reprint–1996

To our supportive families

*

PREFACE

Few casebooks are prepared to accommodate a well-established fact about law professors: They never teach a book from start to finish, nor do they always teach it in the order and manner that the authors intend. This practice in part reflects differences in the curriculum at schools, such as the number of units assigned to the course and the degree of students' legal knowledge from other courses. It also reflects professors' independence of thought—the very quality that brought their entry into the teaching profession. It therefore seems likely that strict adherence to a text is more a fantasy of authors than a practical reality.

This casebook is designed to provide law teachers with a flexible book to accommodate that reality. Each chapter and section can be used selectively or rearranged without damaging the development of the central themes. A similar philosophy of flexibility is reflected in the internal design of each section. The most important coverage comes first so that any topic can be covered on a "once over lightly" basis by assigning only the material through the first case or two.

Several other features also define the character of this casebook: (1) The overall organization is by the major groups of remedies: Injunctions & Specific Performance, Damages, and Restitution. (2) The book seeks to achieve a balanced coverage of these areas as well as to provide introductory text and problems for discussion, and concluding materials on jury trials, attorneys' fees and declaratory relief. (3) There are complex problems for class discussion integrated with the case materials to provide a daily choice of teaching style. (4) The cases are generally very recent ones, often decided within the past few years, in addition to the classic cases that are traditional to the course. (5) The book provides a broad coverage of the field, with more extended coverage in certain areas that are rarely mentioned in other courses, such as contempt.

Integration of Cases and Problems

This book features a thorough integration of problems with related cases. The problems are ones without solutions provided by existing caselaw; instead they are constructed with elements of several cases or issues uniquely combined. Only future litigation of such a case would provide an "answer" to the problems, although the text provides guidance on the relative strength of the parties' positions under existing law.

The problems can be used flexibly. An entire class session could be focused around one of them; on such days the class can accomplish case coverage indirectly by relating the cases to the problem. Alternatively, the professor can pass quickly over the problem and focus on the surrounding cases. Complex problems are a wonderful tool for teaching Remedies, but teaching from them constantly is difficult for everyone on both sides of the podium. Their frequent appearance throughout the book allows daily choice of teaching style.

Each section of the book begins with a textual introduction and a "model case" that gives a factual reference point for established principles. The model case offers a simple example to contrast with the cases and complex problems later in the section. It also encourages students to work with factual comparisons when dealing with abstract concepts. The overall purpose of this approach is to provide students with an early foundation of knowledge that allows quick progression to more difficult issues.

Structure

The structure of this book was designed to provide law teachers with maximum flexibility in arranging the course to meet individual needs and preferences. Each chapter and section is designed such that selective use or rearrangement of them would not damage the overall structure of the course. Although the remedial themes occur throughout the book, the sections and chapters are not interwoven so strongly that rearrangement of the order would be confusing to the students. This book was designed for professors who want flexibility.

This book also adapts well to the necessity of last minute coverage changes as the semester progresses. The core material is presented in the earliest chapters of each major subject so that the professor can decide if there is enough time for the more extended coverage that comes at the end of each subject area. For example, if the budgeted class time for the chapters in the Part on Injunctions & Specific Performance is exceeded before the subject is completed, it is possible to omit the long chapter on "Special Issues in Equity" without doing serious damage to the coverage of the general subject area. The same organizational structure allows early termination of Damages to move easily on to Restitution.

The book achieves this flexibility with the use of the "Special Issues" chapters at the end of both the Part on Injunctions & Specific Performance and the one on Damages. These chapters contain interesting materials that are not essential to the course and that invite selective use.

A similar philosophy is reflected in the design of each section. The most important coverage comes first so that a topic could be covered quickly by assigning the earliest material. Conversely, if a professor wishes to dwell at greater length on a topic, there is more extended coverage at the end. Everyone has a favorite area in which greater depth of coverage can bring a greater depth of the students' understanding of the overriding principles. This approach allows maximum choice of that area.

Coverage

The book seeks to achieve a balanced coverage of injunctions, damages, and restitution. Within those broad areas, we further attempted to provide a balanced coverage of the topics as well. Professors who have a clear and strong preference for one area or another already have other excellent choices for their courses. This book is for a traditional survey course on Remedies.

In addition to the rule of balance that governed the structure of the book, there was a second guiding principle: Special attention was given to areas that are rarely covered even briefly elsewhere in the curriculum. For example, most students receive exposure to general damages issues in other courses, but contempt is rarely studied or even mentioned. Similarly, the equitable defenses such as unclean hands are unlikely to cross the consciousness of most law students except as a joke in the student newspaper.

There are several other Remedies topics that we identified as ones to which students typically lack any prior introduction. There are interlocutory injunctions, structural injunctions, inflation and prejudgment interest, punitive damages, attorneys' fees, and declaratory judgments. Whereas the goal in other areas, such as contract damages, is to build upon the students' basic knowledge from other courses, the goal in these areas is to provide a broad exposure to the issues.

Case Selection

We have kept in mind two goals in our case selection. First, we have attempted to use recent cases whenever possible. In our experience students enjoy modern cases mixed with the old classic gems. Second, we have tried to limit the number of cases in which the holding states the minority position on a topic or in which the dissent takes the apparently better position. When such cases are best for the topic we use them, but excessive use deadens their provocative effect. Some cases include excerpts from dissenting opinions when the effect is to illustrate why the issue presented is more difficult than the majority opinion makes it appear.

The philosophy of this book is to teach the well established principles quickly with the textual materials at the beginning of every section. The cases then function to present the troublesome issues in the area rather than to illustrate some basic point.

The authors wish to thank Pat Estergard for her tireless efforts typing this book.

ELAINE W. SHOBEN
WILLIAM MURRAY TABB

June 1995

*

ACKNOWLEDGMENTS

Appreciative acknowledgment is made to the following for permission to reprint copyrighted materials:

The American Law Institute
Indiana University Press
The University of Pittsburgh Law Review

*

SUMMARY OF CONTENTS

SUMMARY OF CONTENTS

TABLE OF CONTENTS

PART III. DAMAGES

TABLE OF CASES

Principal cases are in italic type. Non-principal cases are in roman type. References are to Pages.

TABLE OF CASES

*

Cases and Problems
on
REMEDIES

*

Part I

INTRODUCTION

Chapter 1

BASIC REMEDIAL TOOLS

A. TYPES OF REMEDIES

The study of remedies is concerned principally with the nature and the measurement of relief to which a party may be entitled. An appreciation of the nature of each legal and equitable remedy includes an understanding of the prerequisites for entitlement to it. It is not sufficient to establish the violation of a substantive right; a plaintiff must also establish the basis for any desired remedy.

A remedies course is a unique combination of substance and procedure because the subject focuses upon declaration and enforcement of rights, compensation for past violations of rights, and prevention of future threatened harms. As the name suggests, Remedies is a multi-faceted field that draws principles from many legal disciplines. The study is simultaneously practical and theoretical because the subject examines unifying themes and problems with relief across many substantive areas of the law while always focusing upon the important "bottom line" for parties in litigation.

Multiple substantive claims may spring from a single core of facts and several choices of remedies may arise from a single claim. There are four basic types or classifications of remedies: (1) coercive remedies, (2) damages, (3) restitution, and (4) declaratory relief. The processes and principles by which the most effective remedies are selected, and the relationship of alternative remedies to each other, are the central themes of this casebook.

Coercive Remedies. A coercive remedy, such as an injunction or specific performance order, is available from a court sitting in equity. The judge determines whether the plaintiff is entitled to the "extraordinary relief" of an order commanding the defendant to do or refrain from doing specific acts. (Chapters 3 and 4) These remedies, like all equitable ones, are subject to the equitable defenses, including unclean hands, laches, estoppel, and unconscionability. (Chapter 5)

Upon a compelling showing, a plaintiff may receive injunctive relief even before full trial on the merits. A preliminary injunction gives the plaintiff temporary relief pending trial on the merits. Similarly, a temporary restraining order affords immediate relief pending the hearing on the preliminary injunction. The principle behind both of these

1

types of interlocutory relief is to preserve the *status quo* to prevent irreparable harm. The plaintiff must make a strong showing of the necessity for such relief. (Chapter 6)

A coercive remedy is backed by the contempt power. A disobedient defendant can be jailed or fined or required to compensate the plaintiff for losses incurred by the willful disobedience of the order. (Chapter 7)

In modern law there are three types of injunctions in addition to preventive ones: restorative injunctions, prophylactic injunctions, and structural ones. A restorative injunction principally operates to correct the present by undoing the effects of a past wrong. The notion of "restoring" means that it focuses not only prospectively, as does the traditional preventive injunction, but also retroactively. A prophylactic injunction seeks to safeguard the plaintiff's rights by directing the defendant's behavior so as to minimize the chance that wrongs might recur in the future. A structural injunction, such as a school desegregation order, derives its name from the involvement of the courts in the institutional policies and practices of the defendant entities. (Chapter 8)

Special problems with fashioning injunctive relief arise in cases involving prior restraints of speech, abatement of nuisances orders, and injunctions of crimes. In addition to the common law limitations that have evolved in such areas, the legislature occasionally affects the process of judicial discretion in these areas and others. Statutes may prohibit some remedies in some contexts; or they may provide for some remedies but not others; or some rare statutes mandate particular relief, such as an injunction, in circumstances that would otherwise be left to the court's discretion. (Chapter 9)

Damages. The purpose of the damages remedy is to compensate plaintiffs for losses sustained in violation of their rights. Once a plaintiff has established both the claim in substantive law and the entitlement to a particular type of damages, the problem of measurement remains. For example, if a car is severely damaged in an automobile accident, is the appropriate measure of damages the cost of repair or the diminution in fair market value of the car? (Chapters 10 and 11) Similarly, certain adjustments may be made to the award, such as to account for the use and changing value of money in the awards for personal injury victims with permanent injuries. (Chapter 12)

The common law imposes certain limitations on damages. They cannot be too remote, speculative, or uncertain. (Chapter 13) Other forms of limitation come from rules such as the collateral source rule and the avoidable consequences rule. (Chapter 14)

There are limitations on the types of losses that a plaintiff can claim; not all losses are compensable ones. Substantive law imposes restrictions on certain types of losses, such as the restrictions on the recovery of mental distress damages in the absence of physical injury and the limitations on recovery of purely economic losses. Similarly, liquidated damages provided by contract are not always recoverable. (Chapter 14)

The only exception to the compensation goal of damage law is punitive damages. These damages, which are also called exemplary damages, are designed to punish and deter wrongdoers in cases involving egregious conduct. (Chapter 15)

Restitution. The goal of restitution is to restore property to its rightful owner by returning the plaintiff to a position held before a wrong, or to disgorge from a defendant any unjust enrichment occasioned by the wrong to the plaintiff. The recovery may or may not involve money, but its goal is not a compensatory one. The measurement of restitution is the defendant's gains rather than the plaintiff's losses. For example, an embezzler who purchases land with the misappropriated money is not allowed to keep any profit from the investment in the land. A plaintiff may receive the land itself by imposition of a constructive trust. If money profits can be traced, those profits can be received. The plaintiff thus may receive more than was lost in the original embezzlement, but the defendant wrongdoer is prevented from being enriched by his own intentional wrong. Other types of restitutionary remedies include equitable liens, rescission, and suits in assumpsit for quasi-contract.

A distinction must be made between substantive restitution and remedial restitution. Substantive restitution concerns the entitlement to a restitutionary remedy: courts evaluate whether the defendant has acquired or holds a benefit which, if retained, would constitute unjust enrichment. Remedial restitution concerns the measurement of that remedy. (Chapters 16 and 17)

Declaratory Remedies. The purpose of a declaratory remedy is to obtain a declaration of the rights or legal relations between the parties. This remedy is often used to determine the constitutionality of a statute or to construe a private instrument so that the interested parties may obtain a resolution of the dispute at an early stage. Federal and state statutes provide that declaratory relief is to be liberally administered, but the parties must demonstrate a justiciable controversy rather than one of a hypothetical or advisory nature. (Chapter 20)

Other areas important to the study of remedies are jury trial rights and attorneys' fees. Under the Seventh Amendment there is a right to a jury trial in legal cases but not equitable ones. Although this amendment does not apply to the states, the states generally follow that same distinction. Differences between federal and state law occur in some areas, however, such as cases where there are mixed claims of law and equity. (Chapter 18)

The American Rule on attorney fees is that parties bear their own costs of litigation. There are a few common law exceptions to this rule, and several important statutory ones. The major area of statutory change is in the area of civil rights. Further statutory changes have been proposed, including a "loser pays" model. (Chapter 19)

B. REMEDIES AT LAW AND IN EQUITY

The term "to do equity" in everyday speech implies that a decision-maker has reached a fair and impartial result in a conflict. An "equitable result" usually means a resolution that does not come from established principles but simply derives from common sense and socially acceptable notions of fair play. In the judicial system this popular concept of "equity" is not the essence of equitable jurisprudence; equity refers to a system of jurisprudence distinguishable from the system "at law." Although the judge sitting in equity has discretion whether to allow a particular remedy, that process is guided by principles established by *stare decisis*.

Equity was originally a separate court system that afforded relief to petitioners who had no adequate remedy at law because of some harsh legal doctrine. Sometimes a remedy at law was unavailable because the cause of action was not one recognized at law, such as shareholders' derivative actions. Sometimes petitioners came to equity for protection from the legal enforcement of contracts. Equity was the original source of concepts such as promissory estoppel and unconscionability. Today those historically equitable doctrines have been incorporated into legal jurisprudence as well. Indeed, in most American jurisdictions there has been a merger of law and equity such that one no longer thinks of two separate systems of justice.

Despite the diminished importance of recognizing the substantive contributions of equity, the concept of equitable remedies distinct from legal ones remains important. Equitable remedies include flexible coercive orders such as injunctions and specific performance orders. Some restitutionary remedies are equitable, such as constructive trusts or rescission and restitution in contract.

The most prevalent legal remedy is damages. Some restitutionary remedies are also legal, such as quasi-contract. In a merged system of law and equity, a plaintiff may seek both legal and equitable remedies in the same claim. The importance of the distinction between legal and equitable remedies, however, lies with the availability of a jury trial.

The Seventh Amendment of the Constitution provides that there is a right to trial by jury for causes "at law." There is no similar right to trial by jury for actions in equity. In the federal system, this constitutional right has been interpreted to mean that causes of action seeking legal remedies as opposed to equitable ones must be afforded trial by jury. An action seeking only equitable remedies may be tried by the judge without a jury, although an advisory jury can be impaneled.

The United States Supreme Court has held that it is the type of remedy that controls jury trial rights rather than the historical origin of the substantive right. Moreover, if a plaintiff presents a mixed claim of law and equity, the legal issues must be tried first by the jury and any remaining equitable issues may be tried by the judge in a manner not inconsistent with the jury verdict.   Both plaintiffs and defendants possess jury trial rights, which may be waived.

In the state court systems the right to trial by jury is often different. The Seventh Amendment has not been held to apply to the states.   Some states have constitutional provisions of their own affecting the right, but others rely entirely upon historical precedent.   Cases in which the plaintiff seeks only legal remedies usually entitle the parties to trial by jury;   cases seeking only equitable remedies do not.   In a merged state court system, a mixed claim of legal and equitable remedies may not entitle the parties to a jury trial if the primary character of the case is equitable.   The doctrine of "equitable clean-up" may control whereby the judge as trier of fact in equity may decide also any incidental damages issues.

C. INTRODUCTORY REMEDIES PROBLEMS

Consider the following problem concerning the injury or possible destruction of a farm's productivity.   At the end of the problem there are a number of questions concerning appropriate remedies.   The notes that follow give capsule summaries of how related problems have been resolved by the law in the past.   The purpose of these problems is to illustrate recurring remedial problems;   future chapters will provide greater depth on these issues.

PROBLEM: THE WASTE LAGOON

Jim and Joan Pollard own a farm on which they grow feed corn.   A few years ago Krystal Refining Co. constructed wastewater lagoons on the land adjacent to the Pollards' farm land.   Last year the Pollards began experiencing crop losses on the strip of land immediately adjacent to the Krystal Refining lagoons.   Although the crops on other fields did very well that year, the corn in the field adjacent to the lagoons did very poorly.   The Pollards hired a soil analyst who informed them that a new chemical recently introduced into Krystal's refining process has seeped from the wastewater lagoons into the soil on the Pollards' land.   This chemical was responsible for the poor crop last year.   Moreover, the expert informed the Pollards that the increased presence of this chemical may now have irreversibly precluded that strip for any farm cultivation. Only expensive additional testing could determine the permanency of the damage.

Legal Remedies.   Assuming that the Pollards can establish a cause of action against Krystal Refining, what should be the available remedies?   First consider that the damage to the land may be reversible, but only at enormous cost.   Should the high cost of restoration be the measure of damages?   What if that amount exceeds the fair market value of the land?   Would it matter if the Pollards depended upon farming for their livelihood and there were no other acres for sale in the vicinity? If the court rejects the cost of restoration as the measure of damages, what are alternative measures?

Now consider the result if the chemical has caused irreversible injury. What should be the measure of damages? Is it appropriate to award the fair market value of the land when the land itself—as opposed to its productivity—has not been destroyed?

What measure of damage should be used for the injury to last year's crops? Consider both the appropriate measure of damages and the kind of evidence that the plaintiffs should have to produce to support their claim.

Who should have to pay for the expensive test in anticipation of litigation to determine the permanency of the damage to the soil? What if the Pollards do not pay for the test but simply plant again the next year to let the new crop itself be the "test" of the soil's productivity while litigation is pending? Should they recover damages for losses to this new crop as well?

Equitable Relief. Should a court issue an injunction against Krystal to prevent future use of the waste lagoons? Should there be an injunction limiting the use by prohibiting the injurious chemical? Should Krystal be required to drain the lagoons currently in existence? Would it matter if a state or federal environmental protection statute expressly prohibited the discharge of the chemicals into water bodies such as the lagoon? Conversely, what if a zoning ordinance permitted the operation of the chemical plant as it is presently being conducted? Consider, with respect to these questions, whether it would matter if the cost of draining the lagoon or seeking alternative disposal of the waste would exceed the value of the Pollards' land.

———

1. The Restatement (Second) of Torts § 929 * concerns harm to land from past invasions. It summarizes the common law rule:

(1) If one is entitled to a judgment for harm to land resulting from a past invasion and not amounting to a total destruction of value, the damages include compensation for

(a) the difference between the value of the land before the harm and the value after the harm, or at his election in an appropriate case, the cost of restoration that has been or may be reasonably incurred,

(b) the loss of use of the land, and

(c) discomfort and annoyance * * *

2. In the Comments to the Restatement § 929,* it is noted:

* * * [T]he reasonable cost of replacing the land in its original position is ordinarily allowable as the measure of recovery. Thus if a ditch is wrongfully dug upon the land of another, the other normally is entitled to damages measured by the expense of filling the ditch, if he wishes it filled. If, however, the cost of replacing the land in its original position is disproportionate to the diminution in the value of the land caused by the trespass, unless there is a reason personal to the owner for restoring the original condition, damages are measured only by the difference between the value of the land before and after the harm. This would be true, for example, if in trying the effect of explosives, a person were to create large pits upon the comparatively worthless land of another.

3. The Restatement (Second) of Torts § 930 * concerns damages for future invasions of land. It provides that if future invasions are not enjoined because of public interest in the defendant's enterprise, the court may allow the plaintiff to recover damages for both past and future invasions in the single action. Section (3) provides:

(3) The damages for past and prospective invasions of land include compensation for

(a) the harm caused by invasions prior to the time when the injurious situation became complete and comparatively enduring, and

(b) either the decrease in the value of the land caused by the prospect of the continuance of the invasion measured at the time when the injurious situation became complete and comparatively enduring, or the reasonable cost to the plaintiff of avoiding future invasions.

4. Comments to the Restatement (Second) of Torts § 930(3)* say:

Depreciation in the value of the damaged land is the usual standard of compensation when the injured person recovers full damages for the continuance of the invasions. * * * Manifestly, this element of depreciation is distinct from the loss in value brought by the actual effects of past invasions such as damage by floods to the soil's fertility.

5. Comments on Restatement (Second) of Torts § 929(2)* say:

For the destruction of or damage to houses, buildings, crops or mature timber trees that have a market value or a value distinguishable from the value of the land, the owner can, at his election, recover for the loss or diminution of the value of the thing injured or destroyed, in substitution for the diminution in value of the land as a whole. The value of a growing crop at the time of injury or destruction is the value of the yield that at that time would reasonably have been anticipated, less the prospective cost of further cultivation and marketing and a deduction for such hazards as hail and flood.   * * *

6. Should Krystal be enjoined against future use of the waste lagoons? Consider the famous New York case *Boomer v. Atlantic Cement Co.,* reprinted *infra* in Chapter 3. The defendant in that case was a multi-million dollar cement plant sued by neighbors who were victimized by its air pollution. Although the usual remedy for nuisance in New York was an injunction, the court in this 1970 case declined to issue one. Rather than enjoining the operation of the plant, the court required the defendant to pay permanent damages to the plaintiff in exchange for a "servitude on the land" for the company. An injunction was denied because of the harsh result on the defendant compared with the relatively small loss in the plaintiffs' property value. The dissenting opinion complained that the majority view in effect was licensing a continuing wrong. The dissenting judges thought that the majority allowed the defendant to engage in inverse condemnation of the plaintiffs' land. Where does the public interest lie in such cases?

7. Should Krystal be required to return the Pollards' land to its pre-tort condition? A related issue was presented in the now famous environmental case *Puerto Rico v. The SS Zoe Colocotroni,* reprinted *infra* in Chapter 11. This 1980 Fifth Circuit opinion concerned an oil spill from a tanker. The tanker was stuck on a reef off the coast of Puerto Rico and the captain ordered some 5,000 tons of crude oil to be dumped in the surrounding waters in order to refloat the vessel. The resulting oil slick damaged an isolated peninsula owned by the Commonwealth of Puerto Rico. Severe environmental harm resulted to plant and marine animal life on the peninsula. The injured land and marine life did not have a significant market value, however.

An environmental protection statute permitted recovery of the "total value" of the damages, which the court interpreted to mean that the Commonwealth was not restricted to common law damages. Nonetheless, the court refused to uphold the district court's award of damages based upon the replacement value of the marine creatures. There was no actual restoration plan to replace these lost animals, even though experts testified that they were available at an ascertainable market price. The $5.5 million judgment based upon this measure was reversed. The case was remanded to reopen the possibility of damages based on an alternative-site restoration plan or other appropriate measures of damages.

D. ADDITIONAL INTRODUCTORY PROBLEMS

Consider the following problems that present issues to be covered later in this course. Although you have not yet studied the manner in which the law to date has resolved these problems, consider the issues presented in these problems and the ways in which you think they ought

to be resolved. These problems are intended to introduce future material, but they would also be useful for your review at the end of the course.

INTRODUCTORY PROBLEM: THE STUDENT PROTESTER

Assume that you have recently graduated from law school, passed
the bar exam, and opened a law office with some friends in a small
university town. You hear the following story on the six o'clock local
news:

"Students at the University are protesting the quality of dormitory
food. There was a noon rally on this subject today which became a
rather rowdy demonstration." The camera then showed a taped interview with the student who organized the rally, Ken Maxwell, who
announced that a second demonstration was planned for that evening.
He said that a protest march would happen and that all students should
assemble with tonight's dinner tray of dormitory food. Maxwell said
that they would march on the home of the University president and
leave their evidence (the trays of food) on the lawn.

Immediately after you see this story on the news, the telephone
rings and the caller is Maxwell. He tells you that he was just served
with an order signed by a state court judge which forbids him from
holding the rally, encouraging others to demonstrate tonight, and from
"contributing to or inciting any breaches of the peace" in the town in
the future. His answers to your questions lead you to the conclusion
that the city and University successfully sought an ex parte injunction
against Maxwell.

Maxwell says that he has had an undergraduate course in constitutional law and knows perfectly well that "they" cannot keep him from
speaking and petitioning the president of the University. Nonetheless,
Maxwell says that a friend urged that he call a lawyer before running off
to the rally. The rally is due to take place in a few minutes. What do
you say? Who else may be bound by the court's order? What if
Maxwell's friends demonstrated and he stayed at home?

INTRODUCTORY PROBLEM: THE LOTTERY WINNER

You are engaged in a law practice with an office that hires several
part-time workers. One of the part-time workers was out of cash
immediately before payday and wrongfully took some money from petty
cash to buy lunch and to purchase a lottery ticket at the restaurant. As
luck would have it, the lottery ticket was a big winner.

Assume that the theft is proven and that the use of the office money
for the purchase of the lottery ticket is clearly traced. Should the law

partnership be able to recover only the amount taken from petty cash or the full amount of the lottery winnings?

Would it make a difference if the money used to purchase the lottery ticket was an embezzlement by a partner from a client's account? Should the client be reimbursed the embezzled funds or the lottery winnings?

INTRODUCTORY PROBLEM: THE ANXIOUS CLIENT

The town council of the city of Brookfield recently decided to crack down on pornography. It passed an ordinance that prohibited the sale of obscene books within one mile of churches and schools. The ordinance defines obscenity, in part, as "anything which may contribute to the corruption or debauchery of the morals of youth." The ordinance carries stiff criminal and civil penalties for its violation.

You have a client, Pat Caruthers, who owns a popular full-line bookstore called The Bookplace. Caruthers telephones you after reading about the ordinance in the local newspaper, and is concerned that the ordinance may be applied to several of the books sold by The Bookplace. Caruthers is also not certain whether the store is located within one mile of any church or school.

What remedy, if any, might be available to Pat Caruthers to obtain a determination as to whether the ordinance is unconstitutionally vague and overbroad? Would it make any difference if the local prosecuting attorney had already mentioned the possibility that criminal proceedings might be instituted against Caruthers unless The Bookplace stopped selling several "art" books?

INTRODUCTORY PROBLEM: THE LEMON

Your client, Chris Engle, recently purchased a used car from an established used car dealer. The car has needed frequent repair and never has run completely satisfactorily. Engle wishes to force the dealer to take this "lemon" back, but there is no provision for such return in the sales contract. In your initial client meeting with Engle a few weeks ago you explored any possible claim for fraud or other basis under state law that would support rescission, but you find nothing wrong with the transaction.

Engle just called you with a new piece of information discovered when a garage was changing the car's oil. The mechanic discovered an old oil-change sticker on the inside of the front door, and that sticker indicated a mileage greater than the current mileage on the odometer. Apparently someone, either the dealer or a former owner, turned back the odometer after the date of that prior oil change.

A state statute provides that a used car dealer cannot sell a car in which the odometer has been turned back. The statute does not require scienter, but an affirmative defense is the lack of knowledge by the dealer that someone previously had rolled back the odometer. The remedies provided in this statute are "actual damages or other relief as the court deems appropriate."

If Engle successfully sues the dealer under this statute, should rescission be an available remedy? Note that Engle's desire for rescission was formed on grounds other than the incorrect representation of mileage.

Does the reference to "actual damages" in the statute suggest that only damage remedies are appropriate? If so, how should such damages be measured? If scienter is proven, should punitive damages also be allowed?

Chapter 2

SCOPE OF LEGAL AND EQUITABLE REMEDIES

A desired remedy does not automatically follow from the violation of any particular right. A plaintiff must first establish the substantive entitlement to relief and then must establish a legal basis for the desired remedy. For example, a winning case may show that the defendant violated specific statutory rights and that the remedy sought is provided expressly by the statute. The plaintiff then must establish factually the requirements for the desired remedy. Damages require proof of loss, for example, and an injunction requires a showing of irreparable harm. Future chapters examine such requirements. This chapter focuses upon the legal basis for particular remedies and the limitations imposed by the source of the remedy. It also examines briefly the significance of whether that basis is legal or equitable in nature.

A. LIMITATIONS ON REMEDIES

Section Coverage:

There are three sources of remedial rights: statutes, federal and state constitutions, and common law. One or all of these sources may establish a basis for one or more remedies in a particular case. The source of a plaintiff's desired remedies is important because (1) the plaintiff must establish that a particular remedy is permissible, and (2) the source may place some limitations upon the remedy. It is axiomatic that a right is only as great as the remedy that accompanies it. The materials in this section illustrate this principle and provide practical applications of it.

Model Case:

A state statute prohibits retailers from posting customer checks that have been returned as uncollectible from the bank. This "bad checks" bill was designed to curb the growing practice of stores to make a prominent public display of uncollected checks.

The statute provides that the State's Attorney may seek an injunction against any retailer in wilful violation of the act. It also provides a civil action for individuals whose checks have been posted in violation of the act. The civil remedy provision allows $500 damages per violation and attorney's fees.

Baxter is a consumer who was the victim of a wrongfully denied check. The bank erroneously returned for insufficient funds a check

12

that Baxter had written to a store. The retailer did not contact Baxter, but simply posted the check with other "bad checks" on the front wall. A sign over the checks read: "Look Who Took Me Now!"

Baxter's boss saw the returned check on the retailer's wall and summarily discharged the luckless Baxter. Baxter's suit under the act seeks actual damages and a corrective notice of equal prominence to explain the true facts.

Courts are not in agreement whether it is permissible ever to expand the damage remedy beyond its statutory dollar limitation. Therefore Baxter's recovery of actual damages beyond $500 is uncertain.

There is also disagreement whether courts should interpret statutes to allow wholly different types of remedies. The statutory remedy here is damages, whereas Baxter seeks affirmative equitable relief as well. Equitable relief is provided specifically to the State's Attorney, but not to private claimants. Most courts are unlikely to grant plaintiff's request for a corrective statement under statutory authority, but some may do so if the order were consistent with the overall legislative purpose of the act.

Baxter may have separate claims for defamation and privacy. Remedies for these claims would come from common law. If Baxter brings an action with mixed statutory and common law claims in a court with proper jurisdiction, the court may grant separate remedies for violations of the different rights. Two limitations are noteworthy: (1) a plaintiff cannot get a double recovery of the same damages simply because there are two sources of remedies; and (2) the statute may address its relationship to any common law rights. If the statute eliminates an existing right at common law, it may not be constitutional under some state law. If the statute only limits the remedies available for the common law right and substitutes other remedies, it will probably pass muster under state and federal constitutional law.

ORLOFF v. LOS ANGELES TURF CLUB

30 Cal.2d 110, 180 P.2d 321 (1947).

CARTER, JUSTICE:

Plaintiff commenced this action for injunctive relief, alleging in his complaint that defendant Los Angeles Turf Club, a corporation, is engaged in operating a horse racing course and enterprise and a gambling establishment in connection therewith, and invites the public to attend. In January, 1946, plaintiff, an adult, purchased a ticket for admission to the defendant's place of business and was admitted thereto. Thereafter plaintiff was ejected from the establishment by defendant and its employees. In February he was again admitted thereto and was again ejected. The ousting of plaintiff was without cause, he being of good moral character and having conducted himself properly at all times. At the time of the ejections above mentioned "defendants and each of them unlawfully ordered plaintiff not to return to said race course thereafter, and unlawfully threatened to thereafter refuse to admit plaintiff thereto, or if admitted to forcibly remove and eject plaintiff therefrom." By reason of defendant's conduct, plaintiff was humiliated and embarrassed and sustained mental anguish.

* * *

* * * [T]here are specific statutory mandates which are here applicable. "It is unlawful for any corporation, person, or association, or the proprietor, lessee, or the agents of either, of any opera-house, theater, melodeon, museum, circus, caravan, *race-course,* fair or other place of public amusement or entertainment, to refuse admittance to any person over the age of twenty-one years, who presents a ticket of admission acquired by purchase, or who tenders the price thereof for such ticket, and who demands admission to such place. Any person under the influence of liquor, or who is guilty of boisterous conduct, or any person of lewd or immoral character, may be excluded from any such place of amusement." [Emphasis added.] Civil Code, sec. 53. The following section reads: "Any person who is refused admission to any place of amusement contrary to the provisions of the last preceding section, is entitled to recover from the proprietor, lessee, or their agents, or from any such person, corporation, or association, or the directors thereof, his actual damages, and one hundred dollars in addition thereto." Civil Code, sec. 54. And it is that section which is invoked by defendant as establishing the exclusive remedy for the violation of section 53. It is argued that the right established by section 53 was unknown at common law (a question we do not decide); that it is therefore in derogation of the common law, and thence must be strictly construed to the end that the remedy provided by section 54 is exclusive. Thus preventative or specific relief such as injunction or mandamus is not available in the instant case inasmuch as $100 and compensatory damages are the only remedies available.

Defendant relies upon the rule of statutory construction, that where a new right,—one not existing at common law, is created by statute and a statutory remedy for the infringement thereof is provided, such remedy is exclusive of all others. * * * The rule of statutory interpretation here invoked is a corollary of, a consequence flowing from, or a specific application of, the general common-law rule of statutory construction that statutes in derogation of the common law will be strictly construed. [Citations.] But that rule does not prevail in this state, at least, as to the provisions of the four original codes. The statute in the instant case is in the Civil Code and it is provided therein: "The rule of the common law, that statutes in derogation thereof are to be strictly construed, has no application to this code. The code establishes the law of this state respecting the subjects to which it relates, and its provisions are to be liberally construed with a view to *effect its objects and to promote justice.*" [Emphasis added.] Civil Code, sec. 4.

A factor of importance in interpreting the statute and in applying the above-mentioned rule of statutory construction is the adequacy of the remedy provided by the statute. It has been intimated in regard to the rule of statutory interpretation here discussed, that it should not apply when the remedy provided by statute is inadequate. [Citations.] A recovery of compensatory damages and $100 is plainly inadequate relief in a case of this character. [Citations.] Compensable damages would be extremely difficult if not impossible to measure and prove. The sum of $100 is a relatively insignificant recovery when we consider that a positive and unequivocal right has been established and violated. * * * If the objects of the Civil Code are to be effectuated, and justice promoted as required by section 4 thereof, certainly specific relief should be available where the object is to prevent the exclusion of persons from certain places and there are no valid reasons why such relief should be denied.

* * *

We conclude, therefore, that the statutes here involved do not purport to exclude all other remedies for the violation of the right conferred. * * *

The positive declaration of the personal right and the importance of its preservation together with the inadequacy of the remedy by way of damages and the $100 penalty furnish sufficient reason for injunctive relief.

The judgment is reversed.

_____

1.   The California legislature amended this statute subsequent to the *Orloff* decision. The amended statute raises the statutory recovery from $100 to $250, in addition to any actual damages. The legislature did not see fit to add equitable remedies to the act. Should future enforcements of the act include injunctions under appropriate circumstances, or should California courts now consider the *amended* statutory remedies exclusive? If there is no legislative history commenting on *Orloff,* is the legislative action approving or disapproving of the opinion? Is there any reason to believe that individual legislators were even aware of the opinion? Would it matter if this act were one among many with specific dollar damages that were all amended simultaneously upward? What if the legislature considered only this statute and discussed it specifically in relation to its remedies? Is this level of scrutiny into legislative intent desirable?

2.   Some acts providing for civil remedies have criminal counterparts. A defendant thus may be subject to more than one proceeding for the same wrong. Should the availability of criminal sanctions affect a court's implementation of remedies under the civil statute? *See* Fletcher v. Coney Island, Inc., 165 Ohio St. 150, 134 N.E.2d 371 (1956) (rejecting *Orloff* and refusing to expand legislative remedies).

3. *Orloff* involved the creation of a new statutory right with a specific remedial provision which the court expanded in an effort to reflect the underlying legislative purpose. What if a legislature instead wishes to eliminate rights or remedies?

Some legislatures have changed remedies in tort reform acts, especially in the area of medical malpractice. The California legislature, responding to the rise in malpractice insurance premiums, established a dollar limit on non-pecuniary losses such as pain and suffering. The California Supreme Court upheld the constitutionality of this change in the common law. Fein v. Permanente Medical Group, 38 Cal.3d 137, 211 Cal.Rptr. 368, 695 P.2d 665 (1985). The United States Supreme Court denied certiorari, with a dissenting opinion by Justice White who found serious constitutional questions when a legislature alters common law remedies without creating a reasonable alternative scheme. 474 U.S. 892, 106 S.Ct. 214, 88 L.Ed.2d 215 (1985).

The state courts have divided on the constitutionality of such damages limitations. *See* Lucas v. United States, 757 S.W.2d 687 (Tex.1988) (medical malpractice statutory cap on damages violated "open courts" provision of Texas Constitution); Wright v. Central Du Page Hospital Association, 63 Ill.2d 313, 347 N.E.2d 736 (1976) ($500,000 ceiling in malpractice cases constituted "special law" in contravention of Illinois Constitution); Carson v. Maurer, 120 N.H. 925, 424 A.2d 825 (1980) (limit on noneconomic damages violated equal protection guarantee of New Hampshire Constitution). *But see* Johnson v. St. Vincent Hospital, Inc., 273 Ind. 374, 404 N.E.2d 585 (1980) ($500,000 damages ceiling upheld; legislature had created a patient compensation fund as an alternative remedy).

4. Distinguish the alteration or elimination of existing rights versus existing remedies. An interesting example of this distinction occurred in Illinois when the legislature decided to eliminate the old common law cause of action for alienation of affections. Like many other states, Illinois passed a "Heart Balm" statute eliminating several torts relating to domestic relations. Heck, a soldier returning from World War II, wished to sue the man who had an affair with Heck's wife Henrietta. The defendant cited the state statute that eliminated the cause of action, but did not prevail. Although courts in other jurisdictions have upheld Heart Balm Acts as an appropriate exercise of state police power, the Illinois Supreme Court found the act in violation of a state constitutional provision: "Every person ought to find a certain remedy in the laws for all injuries and wrongs which he may receive in his person, property or reputation * * *." Heck v. Schupp, 394 Ill. 296, 68 N.E.2d 464 (1946).

After the Illinois Supreme Court held that a state statute could not eliminate an existing common law right, the legislature tried a different approach. A new act preserves the existing right but restricts the remedy to allow only "actual damages." This term is defined as *excluding* mental anguish, shame, humiliation, sorrow, mortification, or loss in reputation.   The excluded elements would usually be the major components of such claims, so the restriction on the remedy severely curtails the right.   Nonetheless, the Illinois Supreme Court upheld the constitutionality of the new act as a mere alteration of the remedy rather than an elimination of a common law right.   Siegall v. Solomon, 19 Ill.2d 145, 166 N.E.2d 5 (1960).

PROBLEM: THE FIRED NURSE

Susan Kaye is a nurse who was formerly employed by Southside Clinic.   Nurse Kaye is a very religious person and she does not want to perform certain nursing tasks that conflict with her religious beliefs. She carefully inquired about the nature of the tasks she would have to perform before she accepted the job at the clinic.

The clinic reorganized after her employment and Nurse Kaye was reassigned.   The new assignment put her in a position where she could be required occasionally to perform tasks that conflicted with her religious beliefs.   She expressed her concern to her supervisor and the supervisor provided reassurance that other nurses would always do any procedure that Nurse Kaye could not do for religious reasons.

Despite this reassurance, Nurse Kaye was fired for insubordination one day when she refused a doctor's direct order to perform a task offensive to her religious principles.   The incident was humiliating to Nurse Kaye.   She told the doctor of her supervisor's promise and explained that other nurses were available, but the doctor was highly insulting about it and berated her loudly in front of co-workers and patients.   Another nurse then volunteered to perform the task.

Nurse Kaye suffered great embarrassment.   Moreover, the doctor secured her discharge later that day.   Her distress resulting from this episode caused her to be unable to seek any employment for a short time.   She then obtained a job with a private doctor who shares her religious views.

The state in which Southside Clinic is located has a Right of Conscience Act.   That Act provides: "No person engaged in the delivery of medical services may be discriminated against by reason of refusal to act contrary to individual conscience."   Conscience is defined to include sincerely held religious convictions such as those held by Nurse Kaye. The remedial portion of the Act contains only the following provision: "The court may enjoin discrimination prohibited by the Act, and may order such affirmative relief as may be appropriate, which may include, but is not limited to reinstatement or hiring of employees, with or without back pay, or any other equitable relief as the court deems appropriate."

Nurse Kaye does not want to be reinstated because she prefers her present job.   She does not want any affirmative order or equitable relief for herself, but she would like an order that the Southside Clinic may not violate anyone else's rights under the Act in the future.   Kaye wants damages for her humiliation and emotional distress. She also wants damages for the brief period of time she was out of work between jobs, and she would like attorney fees to cover the major cost of bringing the suit under the Right of Conscience Act. Should a court grant any of the relief sought by Nurse Kaye?

COWIN EQUIPMENT CO. v. GENERAL MOTORS CORP.

734 F.2d 1581 (11th Cir.1984).

RONEY, CIRCUIT JUDGE:

Plaintiff Cowin Equipment Co., Inc. sued General Motors Corporation (GMC) for damages on the ground that the terms of its dealer sales and service agreement were unconscionable under § 2–302 of the Uniform Commercial Code. The district court held the provision was unconscionable as a matter of law and denied defendant's motion for summary judgment. * * * We reverse on the ground that U.C.C. § 2–302, which concerns unconscionable contracts, does not create a cause of action for damages.

* * *

Briefly, the facts are as follows: In early 1978, GMC and its dealers anticipated an increase in demand for Terex heavy equipment, which GMC manufactured and Cowin sold. GMC responded * * * by requiring Cowin and other dealers handling Terex equipment to place non-cancellable orders in advance for equipment to be shipped between September 1, 1978 and August 1, 1979. Formerly GMC had permitted liberal cancellation. * * *

Cowin ordered forty-four machines in the months following. Due to a downturn in the economy, however, Cowin later attempted to cancel some of the orders. GMC refused to permit cancellation and delivered all of the machines as ordered, leaving Cowin with excess inventory. Cowin sued in December, 1980 seeking damages on grounds that the [contract terms] were unconscionable. Specifically, plaintiffs sought compensation for (1) interest incurred on loans necessary in order to buy equipment which defendant would not allow cancellation on; (2) insurance on the equipment; (3) storage and maintenance fees on the equipment; (4) loss incurred from sale of certain equipment sold for less than its purchase price.

The district court viewed the case as a "Uniform Commercial Code unconscionability action for damages" based upon what it found to be unconscionable terms in the sales and service agreement between the parties. Our review of the Code provisions and the relevant cases persuades us that U.C.C. § 2–302 was not intended to create a cause of action, and cannot be used as a basis for damages in the instant case.

The language of § 2–302 and the Official Comment which follows it make no mention of damages as an available remedy for an unconscionable contract. This is consistent with traditional common law unconscionability theory. When the equity courts found contracts to be unconscionable, they refused specific enforcement. [Citations.] The remedies available to modern courts under § 2–302 are of similar equitable nature:

> (1) If the court as a matter of law finds the contract or any clause of the contract to have been unconscionable at the time it was made the court may refuse to enforce the contract, or it may enforce the remainder of the contract without the unconscionable clause, or it may so limit the application of any unconscionable clause to avoid any unconscionable result.

U.C.C. § 2–302 (1983).

* * *

Reversed and remanded.

---

1. Was Cowin not injured or not injured in a manner that would give a remedy under U.C.C. § 2–302? Would you characterize the problem in this case as substantive or remedial? Is there a meaningful difference between right and remedy here?

2. Title VII of the Civil Rights Act of 1964 is another example of a statute that limits remedies. That Act prohibits employment discrimination on the basis of race, sex, ethnicity, color or religion. The original remedial provision in the Act, before its amendment in 1991, provides: "The court may enjoin the respondent from engaging in such unlawful employment practice, and order such affirmative act as may be appropriate, which may include, but is not limited to, reinstatement or hiring of employees, with or without back pay (payable by the employer, employment agency, or labor organization, as the case may be, responsible for the unlawful employment practice), or any other equitable relief as the court deems appropriate." 42 U.S.C. § 2000e–5(g).

Courts have interpreted this remedial provision to preclude compensatory and punitive damages. Back pay is considered restitutionary, and the reference to "other equitable relief" has been held to preclude legal damages. *See, e.g.* Pearson v. Western Electric Co., 542 F.2d 1150 (10th Cir.1976) (no "compensatory damages" for humiliation and loss of credit rating).

Congress held hearings in 1989 to determine, among other things, the effect of the remedial limitation. The result was the Civil Rights Act of 1991 which amended Title VII in several respects. One provision of the new Act was to expand the remedies to include compensatory and punitive damages, but again with limitation. First, such damages are permissible only in cases proving intentional discrimination. Second, the Act provides for caps on damage recovery, scaled to the size of the defendant employer.

JURISDICTIONAL REMEDY LIMITATIONS:
The Norris–LaGuardia Act

Statutes may limit the availability of remedies by the language used in the remedial provisions of acts, as illustrated by the acts involved in the two preceding cases and problem. Legislators have occasionally sought to control the remedies available to a court by imposing a jurisdictional limitation. The Norris–LaGuardia Act, passed by the U.S. Congress in 1932, provides a good example. The relevant portions of the Act are:

"No court of the United States shall have jurisdiction to issue any restraining order or temporary or permanent injunction in any case involving or growing out of any labor dispute to prohibit any person or persons participating or interested in such dispute (as these terms are herein defined) from doing, whether singly or in concert, any of the following acts:

"(a) Ceasing or refusing to perform any work or to remain in any relation of employment; * * *

"(e) Giving publicity to the existence of, or the facts involved in, any labor dispute, whether by advertising, speaking, patrolling, or by any other method not involving fraud or violence;

"(f) Assembling peaceably to act or to organize to act in promotion of their interests in a labor dispute;

"(i) Advising, urging, or otherwise causing or inducing without fraud or violence the acts heretofore specified * * *." § 4, 47 Stat. 70, 29 U.S.C. § 104.

The history and purpose of the Norris–LaGuardia Act are explained in the 1970 Supreme Court case *Boys Markets, Inc. v. Retail Clerks Union.* The issue in the case was whether a federal district court could enjoin a strike in breach of a no-strike obligation under a collective bargaining agreement. The contract required the parties to take their grievance to binding arbitration. An act of Congress passed after Norris–LaGuardia, but making no reference to it, allowed federal courts to enforce the arbitration agreement by injunction. The question before the Court was whether the Norris–LaGuardia Act still operated to deprive the district court of jurisdiction to issue an injunction against the strike in order to enforce the arbitration agreement under the subsequent act. Justice Brennan wrote for the Court:

* * *

"The Norris–LaGuardia Act was responsive to a situation totally different from that which exists today. In the early part of this century, the federal courts generally were regarded as allies of management in its attempt to prevent the organization and strengthening of labor unions; and in this industrial struggle the injunction became a potent weapon that was wielded against the activities of labor groups.   The result was a large number of sweeping decrees, often issued *ex parte,* drawn on an *ad hoc* basis without regard to any systematic elaboration of national labor policy.   [Citation.]

"In 1932 Congress attempted to bring some order out of the industrial chaos that had developed and to correct the abuses that had resulted from the interjection of the federal judiciary into union-management disputes on the behalf of management.   See declaration of public policy, Norris–LaGuardia Act, § 2, 47 Stat. 70.   Congress, therefore, determined initially to limit severely the power of the federal courts to issue injunctions 'in any case involving or growing out of any labor dispute * * *.' § 4, 47 Stat. 70.   Even as initially enacted, however, the prohibition against federal injunctions was by no means absolute.   *See* Norris–LaGuardia Act, §§ 7, 8, 9, 47 Stat. 71, 72.   Shortly thereafter Congress passed the Wagner Act, designed to curb various management activities that tended to discourage employee participation in collective action.

"As labor organizations grew in strength and developed toward maturity, congressional emphasis shifted from protection of the nascent labor movement to the encouragement of collective bargaining and to administrative techniques for the peaceful resolution of industrial disputes.   This shift in emphasis was accomplished, however, without extensive revision of many of the older enactments, including the anti-injunction section of the Norris–LaGuardia Act. Thus it became the task of the courts to accommodate, to reconcile the older statutes with the more recent ones.

"A leading example of this accommodation process is Brotherhood of Railroad Trainmen v. Chicago River & Ind. R. Co., 353 U.S. 30, 77 S.Ct. 635, 1 L.Ed.2d 622 (1957).   There we were confronted with a peaceful strike which violated the statutory duty to arbitrate imposed by the Railway Labor Act.   The Court concluded that a strike in violation of a statutory arbitration duty was not the type of situation to which the Norris–LaGuardia Act was responsive, that an important federal policy was involved in the peaceful settlement of disputes throughout the statutorily mandated arbitration procedure, that this important policy was imperiled if equitable remedies were not available to implement it, and hence that Norris–LaGuardia's policy of nonintervention by the federal courts should yield to the overriding interest in the successful implementation of the arbitration process."   398 U.S. 235, 250–252, 90 S.Ct. 1583, 1591–1593, 26 L.Ed.2d 199 (1970).

TREISTER v. AMERICAN ACADEMY
OF ORTHOPAEDIC SURGEONS

78 Ill.App.3d 746, 33 Ill.Dec. 501, 396 N.E.2d 1225 (1979).

MCGILLICUDDY, JUSTICE:

On November 3, 1976, the plaintiff, Michael R. Treister, M.D., filed a three-count complaint against the defendant, American Academy of Orthopaedic Surgeons, challenging the academy's denial of his initial application for membership in the academy. The academy filed a motion to dismiss plaintiff's complaint on various grounds which included the failure to state a cause of action because the decision of a private professional association rejecting an application for membership is not subject to judicial review. The plaintiff filed a motion to strike the motion to dismiss. On January 24, 1977, the trial court denied the academy's motion to dismiss count I. * * *

Count I of the complaint states that the plaintiff is an orthopaedic surgeon licensed to practice medicine and surgery in the State of Illinois and has been certified by the American Board of Orthopaedic Surgery. The plaintiff is a member of numerous professional associations, holds several teaching positions, is the author of numerous papers relating to the field of medicine and is a member of the attending staff of seven Chicago hospitals.

The plaintiff asserts that the American Academy of Orthopaedic Surgeons, a not-for-profit corporation, admits board-certified orthopaedic surgeons to fellowship and membership in the academy on the basis of standards and rules adopted by the academy and published in their by-laws. The plaintiff claims that active fellowship in the academy is a factor relied upon by hospitals in the granting of orthopaedic surgical privileges, by insurance companies in the establishment of malpractice rates, by courts in determining the expertise of an orthopaedic surgeon whose testimony is offered as expert and by young physicians selecting a clinic in which to practice. The plaintiff characterizes membership in the academy as "a practical necessity for an orthopaedic surgeon who wishes to realize maximum potential achievement and recognition in his specialty."

In November 1974 the plaintiff applied for membership in the academy by submitting an application form. According to the plaintiff, the academy prepared a list of applicants for active fellowship and broadly distributed it to physicians throughout the United States together with a request for information concerning the reputation and qualifications of the persons named thereon.

In 1976 the plaintiff was interviewed by Dr. Louis Kolb, who informed him that there was adverse information in the plaintiff's file. Dr. Kolb predicted that this information would result in the rejection of his application. Although Dr. Kolb informed the plaintiff of the general nature of the charges, the plaintiff asserts that Dr. Kolb did not provide sufficient detail to enable him to rebut the charges. When the plaintiff requested that Dr. Kolb permit him to examine the file, the doctor replied that academy regulations forbade such an examination. Dr. Kolb also denied the plaintiff's request that he further specify the nature of the charges and that he identify the persons making the charges. In addition, Dr. Kolb refused to cite any authority for denying the plaintiff's request to see his file and to be informed of the charges and the identity of his accusers.

The plaintiff states that, at the suggestion of Dr. Kolb, he wrote a letter to the academy attempting to rebut the charges as well as possible under the circumstances and requesting all available appeal rights and the right to be represented by counsel. The plaintiff received no communication from the academy until October 1976 when he received a letter notifying him that his application had been rejected, that the matter was closed and that he could not reapply for admission for three years.

* * *

In his prayer for relief the plaintiff asks for a declaration that he is entitled to be informed of any charges against him; to be informed of the identity of his accusers; to have a fair hearing before an impartial adjudicator, and to have conclusions of fact fairly supported by evidence of record. In addition, the plaintiff asks for a declaration that the rejection of his application was void.

* * *

The academy argues that the trial court lacked jurisdiction of matters alleged in count I and maintains that the traditional rule is that judicial review is not available to examine a decision by a private professional association to reject an application for initial membership. [Citation.] The plaintiff contends that in recent years courts have decided that an applicant to professional associations has a right to a fair hearing on his application and to reasonable standards for admission.
* * *

In determining whether we should permit judicial review of the denial of the plaintiff's membership application, we must weigh the importance of two values which are in conflict in this situation. On the one hand, we recognize the necessity of judicial restraint from interfering with or regulating the affairs and decisions of a private, voluntary association. However, we also find it unconscionable that a private association could deprive an individual of the right to pursue his or her profession because of a personality conflict, his or her race or religion, or, as the plaintiff suggests in his brief, testimony on behalf of plaintiffs in malpractice actions.

Balancing these two interests, we hold that our courts can review the application procedures of a private association when membership in the organization is an economic necessity. We approve of the opinions in *Falcone* [*v. Middlesex County Medical Society*, 34 N.J. 582, 170 A.2d 791 (1961)] and *Blende* [*v. Maricopa County Medical Society*, 96 Ariz. 240, 393 P.2d 926 (1964)] which hold that a medical society cannot arbitrarily deny membership to an applicant when the society controls access to local hospital facilities and thus can deprive the applicant of his ability to practice medicine.

We find, however, that the plaintiff has not alleged that membership in the American Academy of Orthopaedic Surgeons is an economic necessity. Membership is not a requisite to hospital staff privileges as evidenced by the fact that the plaintiff is a member of the attending staff at seven Chicago hospitals. In addition, the plaintiff was board-certified and licensed by the State without academy membership.

* * *

Although in this case we sympathize with the plaintiff's frustration with the academy's refusal to give him the courtesy of an explanation of the denial of his application, we believe the courts must refrain from interfering in the affairs of a private association absent a showing of economic necessity.

* * * [Reversed and action dismissed.]

SIMON, PRESIDING JUSTICE, dissenting: * * *

I believe the majority understates Dr. Treister's interest. At the same time, it overestimates the Academy's legitimate interests, and by focusing on the effects of exclusion on Dr. Treister personally, obscures an essential aspect of this case, the nature of the Academy. The public interest at stake is also slighted. * * *

Apart from any established law, I believe that logically the majority's strict economic necessity test is too stringent, and that Count I of the complaint should be sustained. The Academy is not simply a private body, accepting and rejecting applicants according to its private needs and desires. It would no doubt deny indignantly that it exists primarily to fatten its members' wallets and egos. Rather, it aspires to a more exalted function, as guardian of the profession and of the public generally. It purports to be judicious rather than exclusive. The Academy holds itself out as the sole legitimate organization of its kind in the profession, and is widely recognized as such. It is a monopoly; and it is affiliated with the A.M.A., itself a monopoly, and no doubt with many local groups. * * *

The majority underrates the Academy's capacity to harm Dr. Treister. It is true that he has so far done quite well without Academy membership; but that is because until recently his inexperience has made him obviously unripe for membership, so that his nonmembership has been perceived as routine, temporary, and insignificant. From now on, things will be different. Count I of the complaint alleges that hospitals and insurance companies rely on Academy membership. Some of these institutions require disclosure of membership status in professional organizations like the Academy, and, in addition, specifically require disclosure of rejections from such organization. Hospitals, insurance companies, and others know that almost all Board-certified orthopaedic surgeons become members of the Academy 2 years after Board certification. A questionnaire or application form filled out by an orthopaedic surgeon who has not been admitted to Academy membership

2 years after this certification raises serious questions and can substantially impair the practitioner's career.

The revelation that Dr. Treister has been rejected by the Academy is going to "red-flag" every application for staff privileges or insurance that he will ever make, subjecting him to close scrutiny, and making every one of his applications a major event when it would otherwise be approved as a matter or routine. Particularly because Dr. Treister is known to meet every formal requirement for Academy membership, hospitals and insurers can logically conclude that he must have been excluded for incompetence or unethical conduct. It will be difficult for Dr. Treister to rebut this inference with the facts, since the Academy refuses to particularize any accusation.

Also, it is well-known that medical malpractice insurance rates have rocketed and are now a large part of the cost of practice. Although Dr. Treister is now considered a prime risk, paying the lowest rate, his premium is almost $20,000 per year. Even a modest percentage surcharge is substantial.

The more subtle effects of rejection could prove even more crippling. The emerging pattern of medical care distinguishes between internists, who have a stable patient pool, and other specialists, who rely on referrals. Because a single patient is likely to see an orthopaedic surgeon only rarely over the course of a lifetime, while he might see an internist many times, the surgeon is peculiarly dependent on referrals. Referring doctors often use Academy membership to verify their impression of specialists, and may even find a doctor for a referral by examining the Academy membership list. New associates, necessary for the growth of a medical practice, also rely on Academy membership in evaluating an orthopaedic surgeon who seeks to employ them. Finally, many attorneys prefer Academy members as expert witnesses.

* * *

On the other side of the balance, the Academy's legitimate interest is lighter than the majority supposes. It is important to note how modest is Dr. Treister's prayer for relief. He does not seek to compel the Academy to admit him to membership. He asks only that it consider his application fairly, in accordance with its own bylaws and the principles of ethics established by the Academy's affiliate the A.M.A.—a set of principles the Academy requires every member to adhere to. There should be nothing directly offensive to the Academy about doing in fact what it publicly professes to do.

* * *

The Academy's unjust rejection of applicants, resulting from unfair admissions standards and procedures, could have pernicious effects on society. The rejection of qualified applicants injures the public—whom, after all, physicians are licensed to serve—by disabling physicians who might otherwise have been able to perform great public service. Also, applicants who were accepted for membership according to unfair procedures based on arbitrary or biased standards might advance to positions of trust and importance they otherwise would not attain—and for which they were not qualified. Thus, the public has a strong and often-ignored stake in the membership practices of such societies. A professional society that uses its membership policies in the following ways does the public a grave disservice: (i) to enforce a "conspiracy of silence" by excluding doctors who truthfully testify against other members of their professions in instances of malpractice [citation]; (ii) to unreasonably exclude physicians who criticize sacred cows of the profession, thereby stifling creative thought and constructive criticism [citation]; (iii) to deny membership privileges to doctors because of their race, etc. In fact, a professional society using admission and rejection to produce such results betrays the trust of a public it exists to benefit. And it abuses the power it has acquired, advancing some to positions they do not merit, and retarding other, more worthy, orthopaedic surgeons. I find it unconscionable that an association might engage in such conduct, even if it does not thereby succeed in driving the victims entirely out of the profession.

* * *

I believe Dr. Treister is entitled to a fair hearing on the application, to be judged by standards reasonably related to the Academy's purposes, and to be informed of the reasons for his rejection. I would affirm the circuit court's order sustaining Count I of the complaint and permit Dr. Treister to have a trial on the merits of that count. * * *

———

1. What if an influential medical organization that previously chose members on the basis of skill and ethics suddenly began to use secret criteria unrelated to medicine? Would judicial intervention be appropriate to prevent a fraud on the public? Does it matter if the organization concerns services other than medicine: lawyers, architects, plumbers, or real estate developers?

2. Did the plaintiff in the principal case fail to state a cause of action, or fail to establish a basis for the relief he desired? If the complaint had asked also for damages, might the court have awarded at least nominal damages to declare the right?

3. At one time courts said equitable relief was available only to preserve rights in "property." Is there any reason why equity should protect some rights more vigorously than others?

PULLIAM v. ALLEN
466 U.S. 522, 104 S.Ct. 1970, 80 L.Ed.2d 565 (1984).

JUSTICE BLACKMUN delivered the opinion of the Court.

This case raises issues concerning the scope of judicial immunity from a civil suit that seeks injunctive and declaratory relief under § 1 of the Civil Rights Act of 1871, as amended, 42 U.S.C. § 1983. * * *

Petitioner Gladys Pulliam is a state Magistrate in Culpeper County, Va. Respondents Richmond R. Allen and Jesse W. Nicholson were plaintiffs in a § 1983 action against Pulliam brought in the United States District Court for the Eastern District of Virginia. They claimed that Magistrate Pulliam's practice of imposing bail on persons arrested for nonjailable offenses under Virginia law and of incarcerating those persons if they could not meet the bail was unconstitutional. The District Court agreed and enjoined the practice. * * *

Respondent Allen was arrested in January 1980 for allegedly using abusive and insulting language, a Class 3 misdemeanor under Va. Code § 18.2–416 (1982). The maximum penalty for a Class 3 misdemeanor is a $500 fine. Petitioner set a bond of $250. Respondent Allen was unable to post the bond, and petitioner committed Allen to the Culpeper County jail, where he remained for 14 days. He was then tried, found guilty, fined, and released. The trial judge subsequently reopened the judgment and reversed the conviction. Allen then filed his § 1983 claim, seeking declaratory and injunctive relief against petitioner's practice of incarcerating persons waiting trial for nonincarcerable offenses.

Respondent Nicholson was incarcerated four times within the 2–month period immediately before and after the filing of Allen's complaint. His arrests were for alleged violations of Va. Code § 18.2–388 (1982), being drunk in public. Section 18.2–388 is a Class 4 misdemeanor for which the maximum penalty is a $100 fine. Like Allen, respondent Nicholson was incarcerated for periods of two to six days for failure to post bond. He intervened in Allen's suit as a party plaintiff.

The District Court found it to be petitioner's practice to require bond for nonincarcerable offenses. The court declared the practice to be a violation of due process and equal protection and enjoined it. * * *

Although injunctive relief against a judge rarely is awarded, the United States Courts of Appeals that have faced the issue are in agreement that judicial immunity does not bar such relief. This Court, however, has never decided the question.

The starting point in our own analysis is the common law. Our cases have proceeded on the assumption that common-law principles of legislative and judicial immunity were incorporated into our judicial system and that they should not be abrogated absent clear legislative intent to do so. [Citations.] Accordingly, the first and crucial question is whether the common law recognized judicial immunity from prospective collateral relief.

At the common law itself, there was no such thing as an injunction against a judge. Injunctive relief was an equitable remedy that could be awarded by the Chancellor only against the parties in proceedings before other courts. *See* 2 J. Story, Equity Jurisprudence ¶ 875, p. 72 (11th ed. 1873). This limitation on the use of the injunction, however, says nothing about the scope of judicial immunity. And the limitation derived not from judicial immunity, but from the substantive confines of the Chancellor's authority.

Although there were no injunctions against common-law judges, there is a common-law parallel to the § 1983 injunction at issue here. That parallel is found in the collateral prospective relief available against judges through the use of the King's prerogative writs. A brief excursion into common-law history helps to explain the relevance of these writs to the question whether principles of common-law immunity bar injunctive relief against a judicial officer.

The doctrine of judicial immunity and the limitations on prospective collateral relief with which we are concerned have related histories. Both can be traced to the successful efforts of the King's Bench to ensure the supremacy of the common-law courts over their 17th–and 18th–century rivals. *See* 5 W. Holdsworth, A History of English Law 159–160 (3d ed. 1945).

A number of courts challenged the King's Bench for authority in those days. Among these were the Council, the Star Chamber, the Chancery, the Admiralty, and the ecclesiastical courts. In an effort to assert the supremacy of the common-law courts, Lord Coke forbade the interference by courts of equity with matters properly triable at common law. * * *

The King's Bench exercised significant collateral control over inferior and rival courts through the use of prerogative writs. The writs included habeas corpus, certiorari, prohibition, mandamus, quo warranto, and *ne exeat regno.* 1 Holdsworth, at 226–231 (7th ed. 1956). Most interesting for our current purposes are the writs of prohibition and mandamus.[9] The writs issued against a judge, in theory to prevent him from exceeding his jurisdiction or to require him to exercise it. In practice, controlling an inferior court in the proper exercise of its jurisdiction meant that the King's Bench used and continues to use the writs to prevent a judge from committing all manner of errors, including departing from the rules of natural justice, proceeding with a suit in which he has an interest, misconstruing substantive law, and rejecting legal evidence. [Citations.]

* * *

The relationship between the King's Bench and its collateral and inferior courts is not precisely paralleled in our system by the relationship between the state and federal courts. To the extent that we rely on the common-law practice in shaping our own doctrine of judicial immunity, however, the control exercised by the King's Bench through the

---

9. The writ of prohibition appears to have been used more than the writ of mandamus to control inferior courts. Mandamus could issue to any person in respect of anything that pertained to his office and was in the nature of a public duty. *See* 1 Halsbury's Laws of England ¶ 81 (4th ed. 1973). The other prerogative writs are also of some relevance here. The writ of certiorari, for instance, issued to remove proceedings from an inferior tribunal to ensure that the court was keeping within its jurisdiction and effectuating the rules of the common law. Once a writ of certiorari was delivered to a judge, he was forbidden to proceed further in the case. Failure to suspend proceedings amounted to a contempt. *See* R. Pound, Appellate Procedure in Civil Cases 61 (1941).

prerogative writs is highly relevant. It indicates that, at least in the view of the common law, there was no inconsistency between a principle of immunity that protected judicial authority from "a wide, wasting, and harassing persecution," *Taaffe v. Downes,* 13 Eng.Rep., at 18, n. (a), and the availability of collateral injunctive relief in exceptional cases. * * *

Our own experience is fully consistent with the common law's rejection of a rule of judicial immunity from prospective relief. We never have had a rule of absolute judicial immunity from prospective relief, and there is no evidence that the absence of that immunity has had a chilling effect on judicial independence.

* * *

For the most part, injunctive relief against a judge raises concerns different from those addressed by the protection of judges from damages awards. The limitations already imposed by the requirements for obtaining equitable relief against any defendant—a showing of an inadequate remedy at law and of a serious risk of irreparable harm, [citation]—severely curtail the risk that judges will be harassed and their independence compromised by the threat of having to defend themselves against suits by disgruntled litigants. Similar limitations serve to prevent harassment of judges through use of the writ of mandamus. Because mandamus has "the unfortunate consequence of making the judge a litigant, obliged to obtain personal counsel or to leave his defense to one of the litigants before him," the Court has stressed that it should be "reserved for really extraordinary causes." [Citation.] Occasionally, however, there are "really extraordinary causes" and, in such cases, there has been no suggestion that judicial immunity prevents the supervising court from issuing the writ.[19]

* * *

We conclude that judicial immunity is not a bar to prospective injunctive relief against a judicial officer acting in her judicial capacity. In so concluding, we express no opinion as to the propriety of the injunctive relief awarded in this case. Petitioner did not appeal the award of injunctive relief against her. The Court of Appeals therefore had no opportunity to consider whether respondents had an adequate remedy at law, rendering equitable relief inappropriate,[22] or whether the

---

19. In *Hall v. West,* 335 F.2d 481 (CA5 1964), a petition for writ of mandamus was filed by Negro plaintiffs in a civil rights case that had been pending before the District Court more than 11 years. Although two other District Courts, affirmed by this Court, had declared unconstitutional the Louisiana segregated school system and the state statute passed to allow the school board to close public schools to avoid desegregation, the board had made clear that it intended to take no action to change the segregated system without a further order from the District Court. The court, however-er, refused to act. The Court of Appeals therefore issued a writ of mandamus, compelling the District Court to order the defendants to submit a plan for the commencement of desegregation of the schools under their control. * * *

22. Virginia provides, for instance, for appellate review of orders denying bail or requiring excessive bail, *see* Va.Code § 19.2–124 (1983), and for state habeas corpus relief from unlawful detention, *see* Va. Code § 8.01–654 (Supp.1983). On the other hand, the nature and short duration of

order itself should have been more narrowly tailored. On the record before us and without the benefit of the Court of Appeals' assessment, we are unwilling to speculate about these possibilities. * * *

JUSTICE POWELL, with whom THE CHIEF JUSTICE, JUSTICE REHNQUIST, and JUSTICE O'CONNOR join, dissenting.

The Court today reaffirms the rule that judges are immune from suits for damages, but holds that they may be sued for injunctive and declaratory relief. * * *

* * * A review of the common law reveals nothing that suggests—much less requires—the distinction the Court draws today between suits for prospective relief (with the attendant liability for costs and attorney's fees) and suits for damages.

* * *

The prerogative writs of mandamus and prohibition are simply not analogous to suits for injunctive relief from the judgments of common-law courts, and the availability of these writs against judicial officials has nothing to do with judicial immunity. It has long been recognized at common law that judicial immunity protects only those acts committed within the proper scope of a judge's jurisdiction, but provides no protection for acts committed in excess of jurisdiction. Because writs of prohibition and mandamus were intended only to control the proper exercise of jurisdiction, they posed no threat to judicial independence and implicated none of the policies of judicial immunity. Thus, the judges of England's inferior courts were subject to suit for writs of mandamus and prohibition, but judicial immunity barred all suits attacking judicial decisions made within the proper scope of their jurisdiction. There is no allegation in this case that petitioner exceeded her jurisdiction. The suit for injunctive relief is based solely on an erroneous construction and application of law. It is precisely this kind of litigation that the common-law doctrine of judicial immunity was intended to prohibit.

* * *

B. CONSEQUENCES OF REMEDY CHARACTERIZATIONS

Section Coverage:

As discussed in Chapter 1, remedies are broadly categorized as legal or equitable depending upon their historical origin. Remedies are further classified functionally into types, such as injunctive relief, damages, declaratory and restitutionary relief. This section explores the problems involved in the characterization of remedies and focuses on some of the consequences that can flow from those remedial labels.

The process of remedial characterization is often complex because no single test may be employed in all situations. For example, money can

the pretrial detention imposed by petitioner was such that it may have been impossible for respondents to avail themselves of these remedies. * * *

pass from a defendant to a plaintiff under several different types of remedies both at law and in equity; however, in one instance the payment may be classified as "damages" and yet in another it may be viewed as equitable relief. The significance of a given remedial label is that it can affect matters such as insurance coverage, right to jury trial, and method of judicial enforcement of the remedy.

Model Case:

Defendant company dumped large slabs of broken concrete pieces at the back of a neighboring homeowner's yard. The neighbor's suit for trespass seeks both an injunction to remove the slabs and damages for injury done to the land. The availability of a jury trial for these mixed claims of law and equity varies by state law. Under the federal system, also followed in some states, the legal issue must be tried first by a jury unless the parties waive this right. The court then decides the equitable issue in a manner consistent with the findings of fact for the legal claim. Therefore, the parties in this trespass case would have a jury trial right for the damages claim. The judge then would decide the equitable issue whether to issue an injunction.

In many states the jury trial right rests with the judge's determination of whether the claim is predominantly legal or equitable. If the claim is characterized as predominantly equitable, then there is no right to a jury trial for any of the issues. If it is considered predominantly legal, the parties have a right to a jury trial on the legal issues.

The defendant company in this trespass case has insurance to cover "damages" arising out of the business operation, so the policy will cover any money liability to the neighbor if no exceptions apply. The insurance policy may not cover all losses associated with the suit, however. If the court grants the injunction, the policy may not cover the cost of compliance with it because costs expended to comply with court orders are not legal damages and therefore may not be "damages" within the meaning of the contract.

MARYLAND CASUALTY CO. v. ARMCO, INC.

822 F.2d 1348 (4th Cir.1987), *cert. denied,* 484 U.S.
1008, 108 S.Ct. 703, 98 L.Ed.2d 654 (1988).

CHAPMAN, CIRCUIT JUDGE:

The appellee, The Maryland Casualty Company, sought a declaratory judgment concerning its liability to its insured, Armco, Inc., arising out of a suit brought against Armco by the United States. The underlying suit is a claim against Armco for reimbursement and injunctive relief because of an alleged endangerment to the environment at a hazardous waste site in Missouri. The question presented is whether the claim brought against Armco in Missouri constitutes a claim for "damages" as defined in the insurance agreement between Armco and Maryland Casualty. We hold that the claim seeking compliance with regulatory directives of a federal agency, which compliance takes the form of obedience to injunctions and reimbursement of remedial costs, does not constitute a claim for "damages" under the insurance policy. We affirm the decision of the district court that Maryland Casualty is not obligated to indemnify nor defend Armco in the Missouri litigation.

At issue is a general comprehensive liability policy first negotiated between Maryland Casualty and Armco in 1966. Modified periodically, it remained in effect until June 1, 1983. Totaling one hundred and fifty-eight pages, the policy is "manuscript" in several instances: that is, some provisions are negotiated and specifically written for this insured. In pertinent part, the policy obligates Maryland Casualty:

> [T]o pay on behalf of the insured all sums which the insured shall become legally obligated to pay as damages because of injury to or destruction of property, including the loss of use thereof, caused by an occurrence; [and]

> [To] defend any suit against the insured alleging such injury, sickness, disease or destruction and seeking damages on account thereof, even if such suit is groundless, false, or fraudulent....

In the Missouri litigation, *United States v. Conservation Chemical Company*, 653 F.Supp. 152 (W.D.Mo.1986) ("CCC"), the United States brought suit against both the owners of the waste storage facility and the "original waste generator" defendants, which latter group included Armco. The complaint alleged that improper maintenance techniques utilized in storing the hazardous waste resulted in the seepage of toxic chemicals into the soil and groundwater surrounding the site and surface flows off the site and onto adjoining property. The complaint also alleged that the chemicals have migrated from the site as leachate into the Missouri and Blue Rivers and thus pose a threat to persons living in communities downriver who use the rivers for crop irrigation, livestock and wildlife watering, boating, industrial water supply and as a source of drinking water.

The suit was brought pursuant to the Resource Conservation and Recovery Act of 1976, *as amended*, 42 U.S.C. §§ 6901–91, and the Comprehensive Environmental Response, Compensation and Liability Act of 1980, Pub.L. No. 96–510, 94 Stat. 2767 (1980) ("CERCLA"). Among its CERCLA claims the government sued under § 106 and under § 107, 42 U.S.C. § 9607(a)(4)(A) seeking to compel the responsible parties to implement a comprehensive remedial action program and seeking reimbursement for all of its investigatory and other response costs and enforcement activities related to the site and for the costs incurred or to be incurred in cleaning up the affected area.

CERCLA § 107, 42 U.S.C. § 9607 reads in pertinent part:

> (4) any person who accepts or accepted any hazardous substances for transport to disposal or treatment facilities or sites selected by such person, from which there is a release, or a threat-

ened release which causes the incurrence of response costs, of a hazardous substance, shall be liable for—

(A) all costs of removal or remedial action incurred by the United States Government or a State not inconsistent with the national contingency plan;

(B) any other necessary costs of response incurred by any other person consistent with the national contingency plan; and

(C) damages for injury to, destruction of, or loss of natural resources, including the reasonable costs of assessing such injury, destruction, or loss resulting from such a release.

* * * "Damages," as distinguished from claims for injunctive or restitutionary relief, includes "only payments to third persons when those persons have a legal claim for damages. . . ." [Citations.] * * * Maryland law, which governs the construction of this agreement, has similarly adopted the somewhat narrow, technical definition of damages. *See, e.g.,* Haines v. St. Paul Fire and Marine Insurance Company, 428 F.Supp. 435 (D.Md.1977) (holding that a claim for restitution of illgotten profits was an action for "traditional equitable relief and cannot be considered damages within the policy coverage").

The best approach in construing the term "damages" as contained in this insurance contract is to afford it the legal, technical meaning. * * * If the term "damages" is given the broad, boundless connotations sought by the appellant, then the term "damages" in the contract between Maryland Casualty and Armco would become mere surplusage, because any obligation to pay would be covered. The limitation implied by employment of the phrase "to pay as damages" would be obliterated. We thus proceed to examine whether the claim for relief in the *CCC* litigation involves a claim for "damages" properly defined, or whether it asserts claims for equitable relief.

In the *CCC* litigation, the government sought both injunctive relief and restitution in the form of reimbursement of costs, including engineering and clean-up costs, in connection with the allegedly hazardous waste contamination in Missouri. The claim for the reimbursement element arises under CERCLA § 107(a), and it is clear that the form of relief requested in *CCC* pursuant to CERCLA § 107(a) is not "damages" in the legal sense, but rather is a form of equitable, remedial relief. * * * [W]e find the claims raised in *CCC* are not within the coverage of the insurance contract. The general comprehensive liability policy between the parties covers "damages," but not the expenditures which result from complying with the directives of regulatory agencies.

Armco and its *amici* proffer the creative argument that an action for restitution which arises from the fulfillment of one's legal obligation by another is an action in quasi-contract, and therefore is an action at law, and not in equity. This argument, however, misperceives the focus of the inquiry. In defining "damages," and distinguishing "damages" from equitable remedies, we focus not on the *nature* of the underlying action, but rather on the form of *relief* sought. In other words, whether a particular cause of action has historically been considered a "legal" or "equitable" proceeding, with the differing procedural and substantive rights thereto appertaining, is irrelevant. The insurance contract, which controls the obligations between the parties and therefore centers the focus of this court, is written in terms of the relief sought, and not in terms of the form of the cause of action. The contract describes "damages" to be paid, and not liabilities arising out of "legal," rather than "equitable" proceedings.

The appellant relies upon two decisions that have held that a claim for apparent equitable relief for reimbursement of environmental clean-up expenses is a claim for "damages" as used in the standard general comprehensive liability policy. We find these decisions unpersuasive. In United States Aviex Company v. Travelers Insurance Company, 125 Mich.App. 579, 336 N.W.2d 838 (1983), the court held that the term "damages" included monies recovered to reimburse the government for costs incurred in investigating and correcting chemical contamination of percolating waters. * * * [T]he court in *Aviex* reasoned that the "merely fortuitous" event that the state had chosen to clean the contamination itself and then sue for reimbursement, rather than suing straightforwardly for damages, should not excuse the insurer from liability on its policy. According to the *Aviex* court the measure of damages to natural resources is measured simply as the costs of restoration, and whether a plaintiff sues for the damages or the costs should not determine the coverage under the insurance policy.

We think this reasoning is faulty for two reasons. First, it is not necessarily correct that the measure of relief is unrelated to whether the government sues for reimbursement or for damages. Damages is a form of substitutional redress which seeks to replace the loss in value with a sum of money. Restitution, conversely, is designed to reimburse a party for restoring the status quo. It might very well cost far more to restore a contaminated marsh than it would to pay damages for its loss. *See, e.g., Peevyhouse v. Garland Coal & Mining Co.,* 382 P.2d 109 (Okla. 1962), *cert. denied,* 375 U.S. 906, 84 S.Ct. 196, 11 L.Ed.2d 145 (1963) (where the cost of restoring strip-mined land was more than quadruple its potential value in the restored condition).

Second, even assuming that the costs to the defendant are the same regardless of whether the government sues for restitution or for damages, thus in some sense rendering the decision by the government regarding whether to sue for damages or restitution a "mere fortuity," it is a great step, and a dangerous one, for courts to begin to construe insurance policies to encompass costs of compliance with injunctive and reimbursement relief.

Insurance policies, probably for reasons of certainty and economy, traditionally reimburse only damages arising from actual, tangible injury. Insurers are very reluctant to cover what are essentially prophylactic measures, such as safety precautions, for the obvious reason that such expenditures are subject to the discretion of the insured, and are not connected with any harm to specific third parties. * * *

From an insurer's perspective, investigative and remedial action taken by the government respecting potential environmental hazards constitutes a prophylactic measure. In the *CCC* litigation which underlies this case, the government, choosing not to wait and learn whether the environmental spill in Missouri created a hazard which would cause harm to the wildlife and humans in the Missouri River and Blue River region, has intervened immediately upon learning of the toxic contamination. The case thus presents no instance of harm to human or animal life, but merely the prevention of such harm. Even if some such harm had occurred, the fundamental nature of the government's intervention is the same: the government seeks to prevent or mitigate the occurrences or reoccurrences of hazardous contamination. This action is fundamentally prophylactic, and is not of the sort that Maryland Casualty contracted to cover.

* * *

Maryland Casualty has contracted with Armco to reimburse only where Armco is obligated to pay damages which result from injury, which in the insurance context means damages in the legal sense. In the absence of clear contract language or specific Congressional authorization in CERCLA, we decline to extend the obligations of insurance carriers beyond the well-illumined area of tangible injury and into the murky and boundless realm of injury prevention. We hold that the costs to Armco of complying with the directives of a regulatory agency are not covered within the terms of the insurance policy.

* * * [Affirmed.]

---

1. Compare the principal case with Jaffee v. United States, 592 F.2d 712 (3d Cir.1979), where the plaintiff alleged that he had developed cancer as a result of radiation exposure while in the army. The court affirmed the district court's denial of a preliminary injunction which would have required the government to pay medical expenses. The opinion characterized the plaintiff's request for such expenditures as traditional tort damages rather than a proper subject for equitable relief. Accordingly, the court viewed the plaintiff's claim as an attempt to collect money damages rather than a request for an injunction. This difference was relevant procedurally because an injunction would have been appealable under 28 U.S.C. § 1291(a)(1).

The court also considered the legal or equitable nature of the plaintiff's request that the government be required to warn members of plaintiff's class about medical risks from their radiation exposure. On that issue it held: "The payment of money cannot satisfy this claim. Although providing the warning will impose an expense on the Government, the creation of expense does not necessarily remove a form of relief from the category of equitable remedies." This aspect of the appeal was considered a petition for an injunction such that its denial would be properly appealable.

2. In United States v. Price, 688 F.2d 204 (3d Cir.1982), the plaintiffs sought the funding of a diagnostic study. The study would concern the threat to a public water supply posed by toxic chemicals emanating from a landfill and the provision of an alternate water supply. The court held these remedies were permissible forms of preliminary equitable relief at common law and under certain federal environmental statutes. The court reasoned that although the study would require the payment of money, it would be preventive rather than compensatory in character. It nonetheless failed on procedural grounds.

3. The *Price* opinion, *supra,* articulated the distinction that compensating for past harm is a "damages" remedy and protecting against further harm is an "equitable" one. This distinction also played a determining role in Penn Terra Ltd. v. Department of Environmental Resources, 733 F.2d 267 (3d Cir.1984). In this case the Commonwealth obtained a consent decree requiring Penn Terra to perform reclamation work of coal surface mines to correct violations of certain state environmental protection statutes. Penn Terra, however, failed to take the mandated remedial measures and filed a bankruptcy petition. The government, before receiving notice of the bankruptcy filing, obtained a preliminary injunction in state court to enforce the terms of the consent decree.

The issue presented to the bankruptcy court involved an interpretation of several sections of the automatic stay provisions of the bankruptcy code. The sections operate to halt the commencement or continuation of legal proceedings against the debtor while the bankruptcy administration is pending. Specifically, the controversy involved whether the government's injunction to correct the environmental violations constituted an exception to the stay as a valid exercise of its police power or was merely a veiled attempt to enforce a "money judgment" which would be susceptible to the automatic stay. The court of appeals recognized that compliance with the injunction would necessitate the expenditure of the debtor's funds, but held that it was not a money judgment because (1) the compensation was not payable to the government, (2) the reclamation obligation was not reduced to a sum certain, and (3) it was aimed at the prevention of future harm.

Was the court correct? The reclamation of the soil certainly would result in prospective benefits, yet the order would also rectify the past injuries to the environment. Competing policies may be readily seen in the court's decision. If a governmental unit can, through the form of an injunction, require a bankruptcy debtor to expend money to correct past harms several effects will necessarily follow: (a) the total funds in the debtor's estate otherwise available to compensate general creditors will be reduced or perhaps exhausted, (b) the government's position vis-a-vis other creditors may be viewed as a "super-priority" above the statutory scheme of payment priorities, and (c) it depletes the pool of assets which the debtor might have utilized to effect a successful reorganization and have a "fresh start." Conversely, the public interest, as expressed in the environmental protection statutes, deserves to be recognized and fully enforced. Where should the line be drawn?

4. Consider the relationship of interlocutory equitable relief and damages after trial. For example, in Crawford v. University of North Carolina, 440 F.Supp. 1047 (M.D.N.C.1977), the district court issued a preliminary injunction ordering the university to procure and pay an interpreter for the benefit of a deaf student. What difference would it make to the student that the remedy take the form of an injunction as opposed to receiving a money judgment?

BRUNECZ v. HOUDAILLE INDUSTRIES, INC.

13 Ohio App.3d 106, 468 N.E.2d 370 (1983).

BROGAN, JUDGE:

Plaintiff-appellant, Thomas Brunecz, on August 7, 1980 brought an action in the Court of Common Pleas of Cuyahoga County, against defendant-appellee, Houdaille Industries, Inc., for wrongful discharge under R.C. 4123.90.

Plaintiff alleged that he was injured at his place of employment, and that defendant wrongfully discharged him because he filed a claim for compensation with the Bureau of Workers' Compensation. Plaintiff demanded reinstatement, back pay and reasonable attorney fees. He also made a demand for a jury trial. After an answer was filed by defendant, plaintiff moved for leave to amend his complaint, which was granted. The amendment deleted from the prayer the request for reinstatement. Defendant again answered with a general denial.

After a motion for summary judgment filed by defendant was overruled, the trial court referred the claim of plaintiff to arbitration. The board of arbitrators found for plaintiff in the sum of $1838, plus attorney fees. Defendant appealed to the trial court for a hearing *de novo*. Defendant also moved to strike the plaintiff's jury demand, * * * [asserting that] no jury trial right exists where a claim pursuant to R.C. 4123.90 is made. Plaintiff opposed said motion on the basis that * * * since the complaint was for money damages only, a jury trial existed under R.C. 2311.04. The trial was conducted without a jury and the trial court found for defendant.

* * *

Appellant brought his action against appellee for wrongful discharge under R.C. 4123.90 which reads in pertinent part:

"No employer shall discharge, demote, reassign, or take any punitive action against any employee because such employee filed a claim or instituted, pursued or testified in any proceedings under the workers' compensation act for an injury or occupational disease which occurred in the course of and arising out of his employment with that employer. Any such employee may file an action in the common pleas court of the county of such employment in which the relief which may be granted *shall be limited to reinstatement with back pay, if the action is based upon discharge,* or an award for wages lost if based upon demotion, reassignment, or punitive action taken, offset by earnings subsequent to discharge, demotion, reassignment, or punitive action taken * * * " (Emphasis added.)

* * *

There is a conspicuous absence of any reference to a jury trial in R.C. 4123.90 because the remedy provided is essentially equitable in nature, *i.e.,* reinstatement. The back pay is merely a matter of arithmetic computation and ancillary to restoration of the claimant's job.

While we can find no Ohio case wherein a court has addressed the issue of a right to a jury trial in an R.C. 4123.90 action, federal case law has clearly indicated that employer discrimination claims brought under Title VII of the Civil Rights Act of 1964, which like R.C. 4123.90 limits relief to reinstatement and back pay, are clearly equitable in nature and that no right to a jury trial exists. For example, the Sixth Circuit Court of Appeals noted:

"A key dividing line between law and equity has historically been that the former deals with money damages and the latter with injunctive relief. *This distinction has been blurred by court decisions indicating that not all money damages claims will be deemed 'legal.'* * * * A common example is an employment discrimination claim brought under Title VII of the Civil Rights Act of 1964, 42 U.S.C. § 2000e *et seq. which seeks injunctive relief (i.e.* reinstatement) *and back pay.* Although the Supreme Court has never directly addressed this question, the courts of appeals have uniformly held *that no jury trial right exists.* * * * " [Citations.]

In *Great American Fed. S. & L. Assn. v. Novotny* (1979), 442 U.S. 366, at 374–375, 99 S.Ct. 2345, at 2350, 60 L.Ed.2d 957, the Supreme Court in dicta commented on the right to a jury trial in an action pursuant to Title VII of the Civil Rights Act of 1964:

"The Act provides for injunctive relief, specifically including back pay relief. * * * Because the Act expressly authorizes only equitable remedies, the courts have consistently held that neither party has a right to a jury trial."

* * * We find the federal cases interpreting the Title VII discrimination suits to be persuasive. Relief under R.C. 4123.90 is equitable in nature. The fact that appellant amended his complaint to give up his claim for reinstatement does not convert his claim under R.C. 4123.90 into a legal one triable to a jury. The assignment of error is overruled.

The judgment of the trial court is affirmed.

———

1.   The entitlement to a jury is different under state and federal law.   The Seventh Amendment of the federal Constitution provides a right to a jury in all cases "at law," but the Supreme Court has applied the right only to federal courts; it does not apply to the states.   States thus are free to interpret their own state constitutional and common law rights.   The right to a trial by jury is covered more extensively in Chapter 18.

2.   As the principal case reflects, the most common method used to determine the right to a trial by jury is whether the remedy sought is considered a legal or equitable remedy.   Historically there was a right to a trial by jury at law, but not in equity.   This historical approach, sometimes called the analogical approach, requires courts to analogize a cause of action to historical counterparts.

When statutes are involved, courts pay close attention to the remedial provisions to determine the essential nature of the remedy sought.   If it is legal, there is a right to a jury trial.   If it is equitable, there is no jury right.   What if there are mixed legal and equitable remedies sought? *See* Chapter 18.

3.   The court in the principal case analogizes to federal employment discrimination law where parties are not entitled to a jury trial when only equitable relief is sought.   In cases claiming intentional discrimination, federal employment discrimination plaintiffs with a claim under Title VII may now recover compensatory and punitive damages.   When such damages are claimed, either party may demand a jury trial.   When the claim is not one for intentional discrimination, or when the plaintiff seeks only equitable relief for whatever reason, there is no right to a jury trial.

Part II

INJUNCTIONS AND SPECIFIC PERFORMANCE

Chapter 3

PREVENTIVE INJUNCTIONS

A preventive injunction is a court order designed to avoid future harm to a plaintiff by controlling a defendant's behavior. The injunction is "preventive" in the sense of avoiding harm; the term does not refer to the wording of the order. The wording may be either prohibitory ("Do not trespass") or mandatory ("Remove the obstruction"). A preventive injunction is traditional equitable relief in private law, such as an injunction against trespass. Chapter 8 covers other types of injunctions that are more recent developments of public law, such as structural injunctions for institutional reform. The present chapter begins the study of injunctive relief with traditional equity considerations: inadequacy of the remedy at law, irreparable harm, relative hardships, practicality, and public interest.

A. INADEQUACY OF REMEDY AT LAW

Section Coverage:

Courts traditionally cite the maxim that equity will not grant relief when the remedy at law, usually damages, is adequate. History explains the rule better than logic, but the rule still has force to restrict the availability of equitable remedies. Although it is rare for opinions to contain lengthy considerations of the abstract proposition of "adequacy," courts frequently invoke the rule as a shorthand explanation for granting or denying equitable relief. In cases involving interests in real property, as one example, courts often say that the uniqueness of each parcel of land makes damages inadequate to compensate losses. If the threatened loss concerned a contract for the purchase of land a judge could grant specific performance, as studied in the next chapter.

The present chapter examines injunctions to protect non-contractual interests, such as invasions of land. A court may enjoin a trespass if damages would be too speculative, if multiple damage actions would be necessary, or if special circumstances warrant extraordinary relief. Other groups of interests typically covered by the inadequacy at law standard are intangible business interests, nuisances, and civil rights.

40

Model Case:

Plaintiff CompuGame is in the business of selling computer games. Defendant PC–Fun is a competitor that maliciously tries to hurt the plaintiff's reputation for quality games. A clever programmer at PC–Fun devised a devious method for doing so. The PC–Fun games contain a secret code that does its work whenever a consumer installs a new PC–Fun game on a personal computer. The code searches for other programs on the computer that are CompuGame programs. When one is found, the secret code scrambles just a little of the CompuGame program so that it will malfunction every fourth time it is played.

The defendant's purpose is to gain a competitive advantage. Because many of PC–Fun's customers also purchase CompuGame products, the effect is to make the PC–Fun games appear better than those of the rival. Consumers are annoyed to find that CompuGame products malfunction periodically. They conclude that CompuGame makes worse games than PC–Fun ones, which rarely malfunction.

This practice was discovered when a disgruntled PC–Fun employee quit and told CompuGame of the malicious practice. CompuGame sues PC–Fun. A court of equity would enjoin the defendant from engaging in the practice in the future because the plaintiff's remedy at law is inadequate. First, damages for lost customers and future sales would be very speculative. Second, even if damages were ascertainable, the plaintiff would have to return to court repeatedly to sue for future losses caused by Defendant's continuing conduct. Courts enjoin conduct if a multiplicity of suits would otherwise be necessary for redress.

THURSTON ENTERPRISES, INC. v. BALDI

128 N.H. 760, 519 A.2d 297 (1986).

Batchelder, Justice. * * *

Thurston operated a marina. On adjoining property, Baldi operated a drive-in movie theater. In 1978, Baldi sold part of his land to Thurston. The transferred land was rocky, steep, and covered with slash. Baldi knew Thurston planned to develop the land into parking and boat storage facilities for the marina. Although there is now an alternative access, the only way vehicles could reach it at the time Baldi sold the land was to travel over Baldi's drive-in theater. Consequently, Baldi deeded Thurston an easement across the theater.

The easement is a fifty foot wide specified course. It begins at the theater entrance on Route 3, passes under the theater marquee, continues past the ticket booth, which sits roughly in the center of the right-of-way, and crosses the theater lot to Thurston's parcel. * * *

In the spring of 1979, Thurston began using the easement to truck fill into his parcel. The light paving was not designed for heavy truck traffic. * * * The ten-wheel trucks were too high to pass under the marquee and too wide to stay on the right-of-way as it deflected around the ticket booth.   Consequently, Thurston's trucks swung around the marquee and deviated from the right-of-way into speaker aisles 1–3. The trucks destroyed the pavement and caused deep ruts in the earth, both in the right-of-way and in the speaker aisles.   * * *

The master concluded that, at the time of the conveyance, neither party contemplated such extensive use of heavy trucks. He found that Thurston had caused the destruction of the surface and sub-surface of the right-of-way by using the easement unreasonably and by enlarging upon the granted easement. Accordingly, he ordered Thurston to repave the right-of-way.   * * * Thurston was ordered to repair the speaker aisles, limit his trucks to no more than five per day, and to rebuild the rutted right-of-way.   * * *

* * * The grantee of the easement, who is the possessor of the dominant estate, must use the easement reasonably, [citation.], so as not to damage the possessory interest of the grantor, who is the possessor of the servient estate upon which the easement lies, [citation]. Injunctive actions, such as the present claim and counterclaim, look to prevent future conduct rather than to remedy past conduct. [Citation.] Thus, injunctions issue only to prevent imminent irreparable harm. [Citation.] Because the separation between law and equity is not sharp, courts in New Hampshire have broad discretion in exercising equity jurisdiction. [Citation.] Nonetheless, equitable jurisdiction lies only when there is no plain and complete remedy at law. Applying these jurisdictional rules to easements, in an equitable action to determine the scope of rights in an easement, the remedy will ordinarily be limited to future conduct affecting the reasonable use of the easement and possession of the servient estate.

Thus, because the orders to repair look to remedy the effects of past conduct, we vacate them. Those issues involve legal questions of damage. * * * We respectfully advise the superior court to allow the parties to litigate these damage issues in the severed action, with leave to amend their pleadings if necessary. We emphasize, however, that our decision to vacate these rulings does not mean Thurston has no prospective duty to maintain the right-of-way.

[Remanded.]

----

1.   Whether at law or in equity, the defendant in the principal case will have to pay for the cost of repairing the drive-in. Does it matter whether the court makes an equitable order to repair or gives a legal damage remedy equal to the cost? One practical difference is the greater use of judicial resources in an equitable decree because the court retains jurisdiction of the case while the defendant complies with the order. Other differences between law and equity include the availability of a jury trial (*see* Chapter 18) and the method of enforcement (*see* Chapter 7). If the court issues an injunction and the defendant does not

arrange for satisfactory repairs, the plaintiff returns to court with evidence that the defendant disobeyed the order. In contrast, a damages remedy gives the plaintiff money to undertake the necessary repairs as the plaintiff sees fit, without further interaction with the defendant or the court unless the plaintiff encounters difficulty with obtaining satisfaction of the judgment.

2. *Multiplicity of lawsuits.* Damages for past losses is the province of law, but prevention of a multiplicity of future suits for damages is a ground for equitable relief. For example, in Berin v. Olson, 183 Conn. 337, 439 A.2d 357 (1981), the plaintiff sued for water damage caused by the discharge of surface water onto his land by the adjoining landowner. The plaintiff received damages for past losses plus an injunction prohibiting future diversions of water onto his land. The court rejected the defendant's argument that the damage recovery proves the adequacy at law because the basis for the injunctive relief was the probable multiplicity of future suits. *Id.* at 360. *See also* 4 Pomeroy, Equity Jurisprudence (5th ed. Symonds) § 1357.

3. *Inadequacy for Remedial Equity.* The inadequacy limitation applies only to remedial equity, not to substantive equity. Substantive equity, distinguished previously in Chapter 1, allows a cause of action for certain types of interests—like trusts, mortgages, and stockholders' derivative actions—without consideration of adequacy. The Supreme Court noted this distinction in the context of Seventh Amendment rights to jury trials. Ross v. Bernhard, 396 U.S. 531, 90 S.Ct. 733, 24 L.Ed.2d 729 (1970).

PROBLEM: THE BORROWED LOT

A commercial trucking company named Wheelco does not have a big enough parking lot. Wheelco's owner has instructed employees to park trucks on the vacant lot next door when the Wheelco lot is full. That lot belongs to Landry, who is keeping the property for a long-term investment. Landry is not using the lot and has no immediate plans to use it.

Wheelco engaged in this practice for several months without Landry's knowledge. Landry eventually discovered the trespass and contacted Wheelco's owner to complain. The owner offered Landry a rental fee which Landry rejected as low. Since then Wheelco has continued to use Landry's lot when needed. Other calls from Landry to Wheelco have produced only insincere promises to stop and repetition of the offer to rent. Landry has countered with an offer to rent at a high rate. Wheelco rejects the high rate and simply ignores the request to stop trespassing.

Landry has contacted you to see if you could get a court order to keep Wheelco off the lot. Would an injunction be appropriate? Consider the case and notes that follow.

WHEELOCK v. NOONAN

108 N.Y. 179, 15 N.E. 67 (1888).

FINCH, J. The findings of the trial court establish that the defendant, who was a total stranger to the plaintiff, obtained from the latter a license to place upon his unoccupied lots, in the upper part of the city of New York, a few rocks for a short time, the indefiniteness of the period having been rendered definite by the defendant's assurance that he would remove them in the spring. Nothing was paid or asked for this permission, and it was not a contract in any just sense of the term, but merely a license which by its terms expired in the next spring. During the winter, and in the absence and without the knowledge of plaintiff, the defendant covered six of the lots of plaintiff with "huge quantities of rock," some of them 10 or fifteen feet long, and piled to the height of 14 to 18 feet. This conduct was a clear abuse of the license, and in excess of its terms, and so much so that if permission had been sought upon a truthful statement of the intention it would undoubtedly have been refused. In the spring the plaintiff, discovering the abuse of his permission, complained bitterly of defendant's conduct, and ordered him to remove the rocks to some other locality. The defendant promised to do so, but did not, and in the face of repeated demands has neglected and omitted to remove the rocks from the land. The court found as a matter of law from these facts that the original permission given did not justify what was done, either as it respected the quantity of rock or the time allowed; that after the withdrawal of the permission in the spring, and the demand for the removal of the rock, the defendant was a trespasser, and the trespass was a continuing one which entitled plaintiff to equitable relief; and awarded judgment requiring defendant to remove the rocks before March 15, 1886, unless for good cause shown the time for such removal should be extended by the court.

The sole question upon this appeal is whether the relief granted was within the power of the court, and the contention of the defendant is mainly based upon the proposition that the equitable relief was improper since there was an adequate remedy at law. * * * [P]arol license, founded upon no consideration, is revocable at pleasure, even though the licensee may have expended money on the faith of it. [Citation.] And this was a continuing trespass. So long as it lasted it encumbered the lots, prevented their use and occupation by the owner, and interfered with the possibility of a sale. It is now said that the remedy was at law, that the owner could have removed the stone and then recovered of the defendant for the expense incurred. But to what locality could the owner remove them? He could not put them in the street; the defendant presumably had no vacant lands of his own on which to throw the burden; and it would follow that the owner would be obliged to hire some vacant lot or place of deposit, become responsible for the rent, and advance the cost of men and machinery to effect the removal. * * *

But it is further said that he could sue at law for the trespass. That is undoubtedly true. * * * [But there is] abundant authority that in such action only the damages to its date could be recovered, and for the subsequent continuance of the trespass new actions following on in succession would have to be maintained. But in a case like the present, would that be an adequate remedy? In each action the damages could not easily be anything more than the fair rental of the lot. It is difficult to see what other damages could be allowed, not because they would not exist, but because they would be quite uncertain in amount and possibly somewhat speculative in their character. The defendant, therefore, might pay those damages, and continue his occupation, and if there were no other adequate remedy, defiantly continue such occupation, and in spite of his wrong make of himself in effect a tenant who could not be dispossessed. * * * [W]hile, ordinarily, courts of equity will not wield their power merely to redress a trespass, yet they will interfere under peculiar circumstances, and have often done so where the trespass was a continuing one, and a multiplicity of suits at law was involved in the legal remedy. * * *

[Affirmed.]

---

1. Is the availability of damages a meaningful test for whether to issue an injunction? Would such an absolute test make all injunctions theoretically impossible?

What if the defendant were willing to pay the amount of damages in order to continue use of plaintiff's land? He would then become the forced tenant of an unwilling landlord with the "rent" being the damages imposed by the court. If the damages are measured as the "fair rental value" of the land, the defendant has no incentive to remove the rocks. Only a high damage award would create the incentive to move. Should a court choose a measure of damages to affect the defendant's future conduct or to measure the plaintiff's past loss?

2. *Future infringements.* The plaintiff must establish the probability that the defendant will make future infringements of the plaintiff's rights. A *continuing* trespass, such as the one in the main case, requires a showing that the defendant will not follow a demand to vacate. *See, e.g.*, Lucy Webb Hayes National Training School of Deaconesses and Missionaries v. Geoghegan, 281 F.Supp. 116 (D.D.C.1967) (patient at private hospital no longer needed medical care but husband refused hospital's repeated demands to arrange transfer of patient to nursing home).

A pattern of *repeated* trespasses requires a showing that the defendant is likely to continue to repeat the invasions in knowing violation of the plaintiff's rights. *See, e.g.*, Thomas v. Weller, 204 Neb. 298, 281 N.W.2d 790 (1979) (duck hunter enjoined from annual trespasses on neighboring land); Phillips v. Wertz, 546 S.W.2d 902 (Tex.Civ.App.1977) (hedge repeatedly knocked down by neighbor during construction).

3. *Trespass by trash.*   The remedy at law is considered adequate if the defendant simply littered the plaintiff's land with trash; the plaintiff can pay for someone to remove the trash and then sue the defendant for the cost incurred.   *See* Connor v. Grosso, 41 Cal.2d 229, 259 P.2d 435 (1953) (liability is limited to costs to remove defendant's trash, not a general clean-up).   What if the "trash" dumped is snow shoveled off the defendant's land onto plaintiff's neighboring property?   *Compare* Marder v. Realty Construction Co., 43 N.J. 508, 205 A.2d 744 (1964) (damages for use of land by dumping snow, parking cars, and placing trash cans on neighbor's property).

4. *Waste.*   Injunctive relief is appropriate to prevent ongoing waste, even though there are legal remedies available, if the injunction is necessary to halt immediate serious injury to the detriment of the inheritance.   *See, e.g.,* Allegheny Development Corp. v. Barati, 166 W.Va. 218, 273 S.E.2d 384 (1980) (removing top soil, rock, and road building material).

5.   The court in the principal case refers to the "old rule" that an oral license without consideration can be revoked even if the licensee has incurred expenses in good faith.   Should every trespass resulting from such revocation support an injunction, or should the court consider the relative hardships of the parties?   Should the good or bad faith of either party be relevant to the equity determination?   These issues are addressed by the materials in sections C and D of this chapter, *infra.*   The substantive law may affect the result by finding that the good faith reliance has created an easement.   *See* Stoner v. Zucker, 148 Cal. 516, 83 P. 808 (1906) (oral license allowing defendant to construct ditch on plaintiff's land could not be revoked because defendant's expenditures in reasonable reliance created an easement).

Should good faith and relative hardship affect the substantive right, the available remedy, or both?   Do you think that the apparent lack of good faith by the defendant in the principal case affected the court's determination of the inadequacy of the damage remedy at law for the cost of removing the stones?

B.   IRREPARABLE HARM

Section Coverage:

Courts frequently say that equity will aid a suitor only if the threatened future harm would be "irreparable."   This requirement is usually just an alternative phrasing of the inadequacy rule; the harm is irreparable because the damage remedy is inadequate.   In some jurisdictions, however, irreparable harm is considered a separate requirement and the plaintiff must show not only that the remedy at law is inadequate but that the harm threatened is great.   Arguably this test avoids burdening the courts with trivialities, although in practice the irreparable harm rule overlaps significantly with the inadequacy of the remedy at law requirement.

Model Case:

Plaintiff homeowner is annoyed that Defendant neighbor's dog Rover makes a practice of trotting across plaintiff's yard when going to and from defendant's house. Plaintiff's petition for an injunction should be denied because the harm done by the dog's repeated trespasses is not great and irreparable. The Plaintiff's use and enjoyment of the land is not substantially impaired, unless special circumstances are shown. The adequate remedy at law is nominal damages or sanctions provided by a leash law ordinance.

COMPUTE–A–CALL, INC. v. TOLLESON

285 Ark. 355, 687 S.W.2d 129 (1985).

DUDLEY, JUSTICE.

The appellees filed a complaint in chancery court stating that they had suffered irreparable damage because the appellant did not pay money due under the terms of a contract. * * * [The judge granted an] injunction ordering that appellants pay $40,760.13 into the registry of the court and to make future payments under the terms of the contract. We reverse and remand. * * *

The prospect of irreparable harm or lack of an otherwise adequate remedy is at the foundation of the power to issue injunctive relief. Harm is normally only considered irreparable when it cannot be adequately compensated by money damages or redressed in a court of law. [Citation.] Money damages are the only damages asked in this case. The remedy at law is adequate. The chancellor erred in refusing to transfer the case to circuit court and erred in granting an injunction for money damages.

The complaint does state that appellees suffered irreparable damage. However, such a conclusory allegation, with no statement of fact, is not sufficient to give equity jurisdiction. [Citation.]

This case is reversed and remanded with directions to dissolve the injunction. * * *

———

1. *Equity Jurisdiction.* Courts have often used the phrase "equity jurisdiction" to refer simply to the propriety of granting equitable relief. *See, e.g., Lashe v. Northern York County School Dist.,* 52 Pa.Cmwlth. 541, 417 A.2d 260 (1980) (equity jurisdiction describes remedies available whereas subject matter jurisdiction concerns the power of the court to act at all). The inadequacy rule was originally applied by the Chancellor in the sixteenth century to determine whether to take a case or to leave the petitioner to go to the law courts with a writ for relief. *See* W. Blackstone, *Commentaries* *46–*55; F. Maitland, *Equity* 7 (1930).

Although there was some historical justification for the term "juris-diction," the use of the word in modern law is unduly confusing. The phrase "equity jurisdiction" does not refer to the power of the court in the sense that subject matter jurisdiction and personal jurisdiction concern the court's power. Instead the concept refers to the appropri-ateness of equitable relief in light of the adequacy of the remedy at law, the irreparability of future harm to the plaintiff, the relative hardships of the parties, and the public interest. If a court erroneously concludes that equitable relief should be granted, a defendant must appeal the case and cannot collaterally attack the order by disobedience on the ground that the court lacked "jurisdiction." *See* Z. Chafee, Jr., *Some Problems of Equity* 296–336 (1950).

2. The trial judge has sole discretion in deciding whether a case is appropriate for equitable relief. The parties cannot by contract waive or confer "equity jurisdiction." *See* Sherrer v. Hale, 248 Ga. 793, 285 S.E.2d 714 (1982).

K–MART CORP. v. ORIENTAL PLAZA, INC.

875 F.2d 907 (1st Cir.1989).

SELYA, CIRCUIT JUDGE.

Concerned that its landlord's word was somewhat shy of its bond, plaintiff-appellee K–Mart Corporation (K–Mart), a tenant at the Oriental Plaza Shopping Center (the Center) in Humacao, Puerto Rico, brought suit in federal district court against the Center's owner, defendant-appellee Oriental Plaza, Inc. (OPI). K–Mart asserted that OPI had perpetrated a breach of the lease agreement (the Lease) between the two corporations. At the bottom line, the question presented on appeal is whether the court below erred in ordering mandatory injunctive relief in plaintiff's favor. Seeing nothing amiss, we affirm.

The parties entered into the Lease on September 21, 1983. During the negotiations, both sides were concerned with possible future con-struction of retail space in areas of the Center reserved for parking. The Lease resolved these concerns by the inclusion of two key covenants: OPI would build no more than 10,000 sq. ft. of retail space in the parking area north of K–Mart's store (*i.e.*, between its premises and the neighboring Pueblo Supermarket), and any such new construction would not deviate from an agreed site plan without K–Mart's express written consent.

* * *

[As promised in the lease, the defendant presented K–Mart with a site plan for the development of the rest of the shopping center. After considerable discussion and alteration of the plans, K–Mart eventually approved a plan. Construction began, however, according to an earlier version of the plan that K–Mart had rejected. It took eleven weeks for

K–Mart to realize the deviation. At that point the construction was nearly complete.]

K–Mart's verified complaint and motion for preliminary injunction were docketed on June 22, 1988. The complaint asserted that the development violated the Lease and harmed plaintiff in that parking near its store would be reduced; traffic congestion would be increased; plaintiff's store and signage would be obstructed; and in the bargain, the chances of impulse shopping were lessened. * * *

A written decision was soon issued. The court held that defendant had breached the Lease. It concluded that injunctive relief was merited, emphasizing that "K–Mart cannot recoup, even through legal damages, the injury to its goodwill caused by the visual obstruction of its store." In settling upon remediation, the court ordered OPI to raze the southernmost structure under construction and to replace it with no fewer than 30 parking spaces within 60 days. The court allowed completion of the two restaurant buildings, but permanently enjoined further development in the parking area except in strict compliance with the Lease.

* * *

[The court affirmed the district court's finding that K–Mart was not at fault for failure to discover for eleven weeks that the construction was the plan that it had disapproved rather than the one that it had approved.]

Appellant's last line of defense is that, even if K–Mart was entitled to some relief, money damages would have been an adequate anodyne. Although the question may be arguable, we believe that the lower court acted within its proper province.

A district court may grant injunctive relief to a prevailing plaintiff to correct an injury which would, absent an injunction, be irreparable. The irreparability of the injury is of paramount concern. [Citation.] The necessary concomitant of irreparable harm is the inadequacy of traditional legal remedies. The two are flip sides of the same coin: if money damages will fully alleviate harm, then the harm cannot be said to be irreparable.

* * *

Here, the district court found OPI guilty of a breach of the Lease and found the harm to K–Mart from construction of the southernmost building irremediable. It stated that "K–Mart cannot recoup, even through legal damages, the injury to its goodwill caused by the visual obstruction of its store." The court went on to explain that the harm did not consist merely of lost sales (in themselves difficult to calculate and monetize), but also involved a detriment in "presentation of the store to the public," detracting from the desired uniformity in appearance among K–Mart's stores across the nation. These factual findings may not be inevitable, but they derive acceptable support from the record. The court below received photographic and testimonial evidence that the offending construction blocked public view of K–Mart's building from the highway, that it interfered with the store's "presence" (an item bargained for in the lease negotiations), that it lessened available parking, and that it interfered with both vehicular maneuverability and pedestrian safety.

* * * Real estate has long been thought unique, and thus, injuries to real estate interests frequently come within the ken of the chancellor. Then, too, harm to goodwill, like harm to reputation, is the type of harm not readily measurable or fully compensable in damages—and for that reason, more likely to be found "irreparable." * * *

PROBLEM: THE WANDERING GOLF BALLS

The Williams family owns a home next to a country club golf course. The location of the ninth green is such that errant golf balls daily intrude onto their property. The Williams erected a fence, but the balls sail over it. The family's frequent complaints to the country club have not abated the problem. The Williams seek an injunction against the club to require relocation of the ninth green. Is relief appropriate? Consider the case and notes that follow.

MUEHLMAN v. KEILMAN
257 Ind. 100, 272 N.E.2d 591 (1971).

HUNTER, JUDGE.

* * * The action was brought by appellees, Paul A. Keilman and Lorraine Keilman, for an injunction and damages against appellants, Carl F. Muehlman, Jr. and Janice I. Muehlman. Appellees claimed appellants, over a period of four months, maliciously ran, started and raced the diesel engines of their two semi-trailer trucks at all times during the day and night immediately adjacent to the appellees' residence property and in close proximity to appellees' bedroom. It was further alleged that the noise and fumes were destructive to the health and comfort of appellees and their family in the use and occupation of their dwelling house and that it had rendered the use of said real estate unhealthy, undesirable, and annoying. It was asserted that such actions of the appellants constituted a nuisance, and appellees sought an injunction to have this nuisance permanently abated, claiming, in addition, damages in the amount of ten thousand dollars ($10,000.00). * * * The trial court found for appellees and granted a temporary injunction against appellants, enjoining and restraining them from starting, idling, and revving their trucks between the hours of 8:30 P.M. and 7:00 A.M. until a further hearing could be had on the permanent injunction. Appeal is taken from this injunction.

* * *

We cannot agree with appellants' contention that these actions cannot constitute a nuisance. Noise, in and of itself, has been held to sufficiently constitute a nuisance. * * *

Appellants next contend that there was a failure to show irreparable harm. * * * The general rule in Indiana is that if there is great injury and no adequate remedy at law then an injunction can be issued. [Citations.] Appellants cite the case of *Spurgeon v. Rhodes* (1906), 167 Ind. 1, 78 N.E. 228, which apparently requires that the harm be irreparable. However, this is essentially an exercise in semantics. Definitions of "irreparable injury" are somewhat sparse, but we agree with that found in Black's Law Dictionary 924 (4th ed. 1951):

"This phrase does not mean such an injury as is beyond the possibility of repair or beyond possible compensation in damages, or necessarily great damage, but includes an injury, whether great or small, which ought not to be submitted to, on the one hand, or inflicted, on the other; and which, because it is so large or so small, or is of such constant and frequent occurrence, or because no certain pecuniary standard exists for the measurement of damages, cannot receive reasonable redress in a court of law."

Thus, it can be seen that a standard of "irreparable injury" would be nearly synonymous with a standard of great harm coupled with no adequate remedy at law. In fact, the former might require a *less* stringent standard than the latter.

If plaintiff can show great damage and no adequate remedy at law, he is entitled to injunctive relief. A definition of "great damage" is difficult and will depend on the individual circumstances of each case. In the instant case, appellants' conduct has deprived appellees of their sleep which, if allowed to continue over an extended period could be extremely injurious to their health. Appellants' action clearly interfered with appellees' comfortable enjoyment of their property. We consider this sufficient to be considered great damage. Appellees too must show that they have no adequate remedy at law.

"The power of a court of equity, in a proper case, to enjoin a nuisance is of long standing, and apparently has never been questioned since the earlier part of the eighteenth century. As in other cases of equity jurisdiction, it must appear that recovery of damages at law will not be an adequate remedy; but since equity regards every tract of land as unique, it considers that damages are not adequate where its usefulness is seriously impaired." William L. Prosser, Law of Torts 624 (3d ed. 1964).

In this instance, appellees' enjoyment has been substantially impaired. If their health is damaged it is difficult to perceive of a truly adequate remedy at law by which they could receive reparation for the injury done. Such conduct is of a continuing nature so that damages would then become a continuing occurrence and require repeated court actions for the complainant to receive reparation. It is extremely difficult to establish a fixed sum as damages for an injury of this sort; such matters as good health and enjoyment of one's property transcend material wealth and defy attempts to affix a price tag to them. * * * Clearly, in a case such as the one at bar, injunctive relief is a proper remedy.

* * * Evidence was presented by appellees that on numerous occasions they were awakened from their sleep by the noise from Muehlman's truck. Appellees testified as to the damaging effect this was having on their household. There was also testimony by other neighbors as to the interference with the enjoyment of their property caused by appellants' conduct and their annoyance with the manner in which Muehlman operated his trucks. Upon appellants' request, the trial judge himself viewed one of the trucks in front of the courthouse to discern the nature of the noise and fumes. This evidence is sufficient to uphold the trial court's judgment. * * *

Appellants' second contention is that the relative inconvenience, damage, and injury to them cannot be balanced by any benefit to the appellees under the circumstances. Appellants claim irreparable harm will result from the injunction if enforced; however, there is no evidence on the record to support this. Mr. Muehlman merely said he normally started work between 6:00 A.M. and 9:00 A.M. There was no testimony that he would be injured by precluding him from starting until 7:00 A.M., only that he sometimes started at 6:00 A.M. No showing was made that an occasional one hour delay would cause any harm at all. The time restrictions of the injunction seem a fairly reasonable compromise. * * *

Appellants rely on [Owen v. Phillips, 73 Ind. 284 (1881)]. * * * In the *Owen* case, appellants were trying to prevent a flour mill from rebuilding so that to allow the injunction would be to deny appellees' livelihood altogether. The court in that case recognized there must be a weighing of equities and interests when it said,

> "A lawful and useful business is not to be *destroyed* by injunction unless the necessity for doing so be strong, clear and urgent." (our emphasis) 73 Ind. at 290–291.

In the instant case, appellants have not shown that any extensive injury will result, much less a destruction of their livelihood. * * * [Affirmed.]

---

1. *Irreparability and Inadequacy.* The principal case suggests that irreparability may be a necessary component of inadequacy, but nonetheless accepts the historical characterization that there is a two-pronged test: inadequacy and great harm. Compare the observation of Judge Sobeloff: "In one sense, of course, the inadequate remedy requirement is indistinguishable from the irreparable injury requirement. The very thing which makes an injury 'irreparable' is the fact that no remedy exists to repair it." Bannercraft Clothing Co. v. Renegotiation Board, 466 F.2d 345, 356, n.9 (1972), *rev'd on other grounds*, 415 U.S. 1, 94 S.Ct. 1028, 39 L.Ed.2d 123 (1974). He finds that there is a distinction, however, because "the irreparable injury rubric is intended to describe the quality or severity of the harm * * * [whereas] the inadequate

remedy test looks to the possibilities of alternative modes of relief, however serious the initial injury." *Id.*

2. *Nuisance.* Courts frequently enjoin private nuisances, such as the one in the principal case, if the loss in the use or enjoyment of the property is great. If the interference is slight, equity will not intervene. For example, in Nussbaum v. Lacopo, 27 N.Y.2d 311, 317 N.Y.S.2d 347, 265 N.E.2d 762 (1970), the court denied relief to homeowners who sued a neighboring golf course. The proof showed that only "once or twice a week" errant golf balls were found in the bushes and fence area of the plaintiff's property. The court characterized these invasions as minimal intrusions not worthy of relief.

A number of cases have involved roots from trees or hedges protruding underground into neighboring property. Injunctive relief is available to abate the nuisance only if there is a "sensible injury," such as poisoning of other plants from roots of noxious trees. Otherwise equity will not grant relief even if there is a technical trespass cognizable at law. *See, e.g.,* Cannon v. Dunn, 145 Ariz. 115, 700 P.2d 502 (1985); Smith v. Holt, 174 Va. 213, 5 S.E.2d 492 (1939).

3. There are problems in drafting an injunction when the nuisance arises from the conduct of third parties over whom the defendant has only indirect control. What if a line of customers waiting to see a movie completely block the sidewalk, thus interfering with access to a neighboring store? How should a court word an injunction against the theater owner? *See, e.g.,* Tushbant v. Greenfield's Inc., 308 Mich. 626, 14 N.W.2d 520 (1944) (restaurant ordered to have employees handle the lining up of customers outside).

4. *Intangible Business Interests.* Irreparable harm sufficient to support an injunction is often found in cases involving intangible business interests, such as unauthorized use of customer lists. *See* Merrill Lynch, Pierce, Fenner & Smith, Inc. v. Stidham, 658 F.2d 1098 (5th Cir.1981).

C. BALANCING INTERESTS AND PRACTICALITY CONSIDERATIONS

Section Coverage:

Injunctions are discretionary, not a matter of right. A judge may appropriately weigh the relative hardships of the parties in the matter and may consider any problems of practicality in enforcing an order. The factors of practicality and hardship can affect the case in two ways: the judge may consider them both in deciding whether to issue an injunction at all as well as in choosing the scope of the order.

Model Case:

Douglas, a former employee of Parker's health spa, quits work and establishes a rival spa in a near-by community that happens to be across the state line. The original employment contract contained a clause concerning post-employment conduct: Douglas could not compete against Parker in a wide geographic radius for a period of five years. The court could appropriately consider the relative hardships of the parties in deciding whether to enforce the noncompetition clause by injunction. Alternatively, the judge could narrow the scope of the order by changing the time period or radius of noncompetition. Another relevant consideration is the practical problem of enforcing an order that would operate out-of-state.

TRIPLETT v. BEUCKMAN

40 Ill.App.3d 379, 352 N.E.2d 458 (1976).

JONES, JUSTICE.

Plaintiffs appeal from a judgment for defendants rendered in a bench trial in plaintiffs' action for a mandatory injunction requiring defendants to remove a causeway access to an island and replace it with a bridge. * * *

On March 10, 1971, Susan Triplett, as executrix of the estate of Francis L. Wortman, and defendants entered into a written contract for the sale of certain real property from the Wortman estate to defendants. The property conveyed consisted of an island, with residential improvements, except for a riparian ten foot circumferential strip, which was retained by the grantor. Defendants were granted the right to use and cross that ten foot strip of land but not to improve it. The lake in which the island was located and all of the land surrounding the lake were also part of the estate of Francis L. Wortman. Defendants were granted "the right to recreational use" of the lake "jointly with the owners of said lake." They were also granted an easement "for roadway purposes" across a described portion of the land surrounding the lake to a bridge, "thence North across said bridge a distance of 60 feet more or less to the island."

The bridge referred to provided the only above-water access to the island. It was wooden; and at the time of the conveyance was in need of repair. According to his uncontradicted testimony, defendant Fred Beuckman attempted to obtain the assistance of plaintiffs in repairing the bridge not long after defendants began to occupy the island residence. However, in response to this request Susan Triplett had stated "that's not my baby, it's all yours." Thereafter defendants repaired the bridge by resurfacing it with concrete and iron reinforcing rods. These repairs proved unsuccessful when a portion of the bridge "gave way." Consequently, defendants removed the bridge, filled the same area with soil, rock, and concrete, paved the surface with asphalt, and covered the sides of the fill with stone.

According to the testimony of Susan Triplett and William Wortman, the removal of the bridge and construction of the causeway deprived the plaintiffs of the fastest or most convenient water access from some points along the lake to other points and cut off plaintiffs' ability to take advantage of the circular nature of the lake for boating and water-skiing activities. Plaintiffs introduced evidence that prior to the construction of the causeway they were able to boat and water-ski completely around the island by passing under the bridge. Accordingly the causeway constituted a severe restriction on the recreational use of their lake. In the opinion of Susan Triplett the property surrounding the lake would decrease in value as a consequence of the construction of the causeway.

Fred Beuckman, on the other hand, testified that at the time the bridge was removed "there was hardly any water underneath the bridge to start with. It was all dried up." In Beuckman's opinion it would not have been possible to water-ski under the bridge "unless you put wheels on the bottoms of the skis, cause there was no water there at all hardly."

Joan Beuckman testified that the causeway was "[m]uch more attractive" than the bridge. Additionally an engineer and two iron workers testified that they had advised defendants prior to the removal of the bridge that the bridge could not be sufficiently repaired and would have to be replaced.

Based upon the testimony and the trial court's personal viewing (by stipulation of the parties) of the causeway, the court found "[t]he entire result is a practical result to an unusual problem and presents a reasonably attractive access to the 'island' [now 'peninsula']." The court also found that any injury to plaintiffs because of the construction of the causeway "was occasioned by plaintiffs' joint and several acts of disinterest or refusal to cooperate," and refused to issue the requested injunction.

We are of the opinion that the trial court erred in refusing to issue a mandatory injunction requiring the removal of the causeway and reconstruction of the bridge. The easement in this case was determined by express grant. The grant fixed the passage over the water or lakebed as being "across" a bridge then in existence at a described location. * * * In light of the fact that the lake was and is used primarily for recreation, the limitation to access by bridge cannot be ignored. * * *

It is well settled that, in the absence of an agreement to the contrary, the owner of the easement has not only the right but the duty to keep the easement in repair, while the owner of the servient tenement has no duty to either put or keep the easement in repair. * * *

* * * Moreover, although the owner of the dominant estate has the duty to maintain and repair the easement, he cannot make a material alteration in the character of the easement, even though it be more to his convenience to do so, if the alteration places a greater burden upon the servient estate or interferes with the use and enjoyment of the servient estate by its owner. [Citations.]

In light of the above authorities, it is apparent that the duty to maintain and repair the bridge in the instant case was that of defendants, the Beuckmans. In destroying the bridge and constructing a causeway, defendants materially altered the character of the easement and increased the burden on the servient tenement. Plaintiffs are unable to use and enjoy that portion of the lake or lakebed which was previously accessible under the bridge, but which now is covered by the causeway. Plaintiffs had the right to have the bridge maintained and are entitled to injunctive relief; and the court below erred in refusing to grant that relief.

We expressly decline to conclude, however, that defendants should be required to reconstruct a bridge 60 feet in length. A court of chancery can balance the hardships involved and grant relief upon whatever terms it deems equitable when the owner of either the dominant or the servient estate interferes with the rights of the other, under a mistaken belief that he owns the area or structure in dispute. [Citation.] In the instant case both Susan Triplett and Fred Beuckman testified that they had thought that the Beuckmans owned the bridge as a result of the conveyance discussed above. It was under this mistaken belief that Fred Beuckman had the bridge removed.

* * *

We, of course, do not have, and cannot have, the benefit of a personal examination of the lake to determine what amount of water may have been in that part of the lake at the time the bridge was destroyed or at the time of the decision of the trial court. Nor do we know what amount of water may have been under the bridge at times prior to its removal or what amount might have been there in the future. The trial court had the opportunity of personal examination. Based upon that examination, the trial court should be able to determine the length of the bridge span necessary for the reasonable use of the water that can reasonably be expected to be in that portion of the lake. It may very well be that use can be made of some of the causeway and that a bridge of less than 60 feet is sufficient for recreational use of that portion of the lake. If so, the trial court, acting in equity, should frame the relief granted in such terms as will take those factors into account.

We, therefore, reverse the judgment of the trial court with respect to plaintiffs' complaint and remand for further proceedings consistent with this opinion.

Reversed and remanded with directions.

EBERSPACHER, JUSTICE (dissenting).

I agree, as the majority states, "A court of chancery can balance the hardships involved and grant relief upon whatever terms it deems equitable when the owner of either the dominant or the servient estate interferes with the rights of the other, under a mistaken belief that he owns the area or structure in dispute." That, however, is not the function of an intermediate reviewing court.

It appears that the trial court has applied that principle, after hearing the testimony and examining the premises. It has obviously balanced the hardships involved and granted relief upon terms it deemed equitable. The majority is saying, balance the hardships again and grant relief upon different terms which we consider equitable. If the principle is to be here applied, the uncontradicted testimony that there is and was at the point where the bridge existed, an inadequate amount of water to boat, ski or swim, has to be, and obviously was, taken into consideration.

---

1. *Balance of Hardships:* A plaintiff is not entitled to an injunction simply upon proof that an interest has been invaded and that the harm is great and irreparable. Proof of the wrong supports a damage recovery, but equitable relief is always at the discretion of the court. The relative hardship that the injunction would place on each party is an important consideration. The judge weighs how much the plaintiff would benefit by the injunction against the burden to the defendant. After the plaintiff shows irreparable harm from the defendant's conduct, the defendant may show the harm that would be caused by an order to change conduct. *See* Muehlman v. Keilman, *supra* (curtailment of trucking business during certain hours).

2. The burden on the defendant is often economic, as in the principal case, but it need not be a dollar loss. In a 1926 opinion by Justice Cardozo, Yome v. Gorman, the petitioner sought an injunction to disinter the bodies of several relatives in order to move them to another cemetery with a different religious affiliation. The interests balanced in that case were the consciences of the deceased as expressed in their lifetimes, the motives and feelings of the survivors, and the sentiments and usages of the religious body which conferred the original right of burial. The opinion concluded that it is not possible to formulate a rule in such an opinion, but only "to exemplify a process." 242 N.Y. 395, 403, 152 N.E. 126, 129 (1926).

3. *Nuisance:* To obtain an injunction against a private nuisance, a plaintiff must establish more than the existence of an intentional nuisance. The unreasonableness of the activity must be established because it is an undue hardship to stifle a useful enterprise at a reasonable location by injunction. If there is sufficient social value to the activity, then it should continue to operate while it pays its way with damages to those privately harmed. *See Prosser and Keeton on Torts,* 5th edition, 1984, sec. 88A. This subject is treated more extensively as a special issue in equity in Chapter 9.

PROBLEM: THE HARASSING SUITOR

Linda Chandler is a twenty-two year old university student who is seeking legal advice about a problem she is having with a man named Evan Woodward. He is a former student whom she met in a class last year and now he is harassing her. She chatted with him a few times on campus last year, but otherwise she has never dated him nor encouraged him to have further social contact. Nonetheless he persistently calls her on the telephone with professions of love; he sends her unsolicited gifts and flowers; he has contacted her friends and relatives to ask them questions about her; and he frequently follows her around.

At first Chandler was just annoyed by Woodward's attentions, but now she is frightened. Woodward knows her schedule and he often waits for her outside her apartment and near her classroom exits. She either ignores him or tells him to leave her alone, but he follows her to her next destination. She says he is "giving her the creeps" and she is becoming depressed and nervous about it.

Chandler has come to your office for legal help. Upon your questioning Chandler reveals that Woodward has grabbed her arm on a few occasions, and once he blocked her way so as to trap her in a corner while he spoke to her. These incidents were minor, but they fit into the pattern of his aggressive attempts to prove his devotion to her.

Chandler says that Woodward is ruining her life at this point, and she desperately wants him to leave her alone. She contacted the university authorities and the local police, but they both said they could not help her. She wants to sue Woodward and to get a court order for him to leave her alone.

Assume that on the basis of these facts Chandler would have one or more tort claims for damages. Would it be possible to get an injunction against Woodward? How could it be worded? Consider the case and notes that follow.

GALELLA v. ONASSIS
353 F.Supp. 196 (S.D.N.Y.1972).

COOPER, DISTRICT JUDGE.

In the fall of 1970, plaintiff, a professional free-lance photographer, instituted an action against defendant Onassis and three agents of the United States Secret Service (Agents)—Walsh, Kalafatis and Connelly. The verified complaint seeks damages for alleged false arrest and malicious prosecution and damages for, and an injunction against, the interference with his business by the alleged acts of defendant Onassis in resisting his efforts to photograph her, and by the alleged acts of defendant Agents in obstructing these efforts at the contended behest and inducement of defendant Onassis. The damage claims aggregated $1.3 million.

The answer of defendant Onassis was filed March 8, 1971 with a counterclaim seeking compensatory and punitive damages of $1.5 million and injunctive relief, based on claimed violations of her common law, statutory and constitutional rights of privacy and intentional infliction of emotional distress, assault, harassment and malicious prosecution.
* * *

On July 6, 1971 Judge McLean of this Court granted a motion by the United States Government (Government) to intervene. The complaint in intervention, filed October 20, 1971 sought injunctive relief (pursuant to 18 U.S.C. § 3056) against the plaintiff for alleged interference with the protective duties of the United States Secret Service (Secret Service) toward the minor children of defendant Onassis and her late husband John F. Kennedy, a former President of the United States. * * *

[The court examined the plaintiff photographer's evidence and found it baseless. The opinion states that Galella committed blatant perjury for publicity and that the purpose of filing suit was to induce by harassment the payment of money and to obtain publicity from the action.

The court then gives several examples of the photographer's "typical callous behavior" such as jumping out of hiding in front of Onassis and her children in his effort to obtain pictures showing expressions of surprise, fear or anger in the faces of the Presidential widow and the children.]

* * * In addition to these episodes, twenty further episodes are summarized in our supplemental findings of fact. These include instances where the children were caused to bang into glass doors, school parents were bumped, passage was blocked, flashbulbs affected vision, telephoto lenses were used to spy, the children were imperiled in the water, a funeral was disturbed, plaintiff pursued defendant into the lobby of a friend's apartment building, plaintiff trailed defendant through the City hour after hour, plaintiff chased defendant by automobile, plaintiff and his assistants surrounded defendant and orbited while shouting, plaintiff snooped into purchases of stockings and shoes, flashbulbs were suddenly fired on lonely black nights—all accompanied by Galella jumping, shouting and acting wildly. Many of the incidents were repeated time after time; all preceded our restraining orders.

He was like a shadow: everywhere she went he followed her and engaged in offensive conduct; nothing was sacred to him whether defendant went to church, funeral services, theater, school, restaurant, or board a yacht in a foreign land. * * *

Outside of movieland, reporters do not normally hide behind restaurant coat racks, sneak into beauty parlors, don "disguises", hide in bushes and theater boxes, intrude into school buildings and, when ejected, enlist the aid of schoolchildren, bribe doormen and romance maids. * * *

Galella's objective? To establish himself as the peerless photographer who could capture the comings and goings and doings of Mrs. Onassis and her children, and by frightening them, to obtain unusual photographs which bring him handsome returns—financial and otherwise. He made it a world venture. His renown would take him into other fields, other subjects. * * *

[The court found that Galella had committed several torts against Onassis, and that she had not committed any torts against him.] * * *

Intervenor complaint. The Government is entitled to an injunction against interference with the protective duties of the United States Secret Service. 18 U.S.C. § 3056.[53]

* * *

Injunctive relief appears appropriate either as implicit in the statute or on common law principles of equity. The manifold threats to which the minor children of a former president may be exposed requires the most flexible legal tools to protect them, a task for which equity has traditionally been well suited. * * *

Private injunctive relief. Permanent injunctive relief is available where there is no adequate remedy at law, where the balance of the equities favor the moving party, and where success on the merits (probability of success for a preliminary injunction) have been demonstrated. As we have already dealt with the merits, we confine the present analysis to the first two points. [Citation.]

No adequate remedy at law. We conclude there is no adequate remedy at law because of: the recurrent nature of plaintiff's invasions of defendant's rights; the need for a multiplicity of damage actions to assert defendant's rights; the imminent threat of continued emotional and physical trauma; and the difficulty of evaluating the injuries in this case in monetary terms. * * *

In Clemons v. Board of Education, 228 F.2d 853 (6th Cir.), *cert. denied,* 350 U.S. 1006, 76 S.Ct. 651, 100 L.Ed. 868 (1956), the Sixth Circuit adopted Pomeroy's formulation:

> "In determining whether an injunction will be issued to protect any right of property, to enforce any obligation, or to prevent any wrong, there is one fundamental principle of the utmost importance. * * * Wherever a right exists or is created, by contract, by the ownership of property or otherwise, cognizable by law, *a violation of that right will be prohibited,* unless there are other considerations of policy or expediency which forbid a resort to this prohibitive remedy. * * * This jurisdiction of equity to prevent the commission of wrong is, however, modified and restricted by considerations of expediency and of convenience which confine its application to those cases in which the legal remedy is not full and adequate. * * * The incompleteness and inadequacy of the legal remedy is the criterion which, under the settled doctrine, determines the right to the equitable remedy of injunction." 4 Pomeroy, Equity Jurisprudence § 1338, at 935–36 (5th ed.).

53. 3056. Secret Service Powers

(a) * * * [T]he United States Secret Service, Treasury Department, is authorized to protect the person of the President of the United States, the members of his immediate family, * * * the person of a former President and his wife during his lifetime, the person of the widow of a former President until her death or remarriage, and minor children of a former President until they reach sixteen years of age, unless such protection is declined; * * *

* * *

The record demonstrates that Galella's surveillance and harassment of Mrs. Onassis has already gone on for a number of years and will continue, by his own account, for "another four or five years." Hence, Mrs. Onassis' legal remedies are inadequate on this ground alone.

Balance of the equities. The equities clearly balance in favor of defendant, particularly in view of our order which is addressed to protecting Galella's ability to continue his livelihood. * * *

We regarded the portion of the proposed order which would have completely prevented Galella from photographing Mrs. Onassis or her children to be clearly overbroad, struck it, and will not include it in a final order. Galella's occupation is lawful and the objective of the order is to modify his conduct, not to prevent his photography.

For practical reasons, the injunction cannot be couched in terms of prohibitions upon Galella's leaping, blocking, taunting, grunting, hiding and the like. Nor have abstract concepts—harassing, endangering— proved workable. No effective relief seems possible without the fixing of proscribed distances.

We must moreover make certain plaintiff keeps sufficiently far enough away to avoid problems as to compliance with the injunction and injurious disobedience. Disputes concerning his compliance may be frequent, thereby necessitating repeated application to the Court. Hence, the restraint must be clear, simple and effective so that Galella's substantial compliance cannot seriously be disputed unless a violation occurs.

* * *

The permanent injunction * * * shall enjoin plaintiff, his agents, servants, employees and all persons in active concert and participation with him from, *inter alia,* approaching within 100 yards of the home of defendant and her children, 100 yards of the schools attended by the children; at all other places and times 75 yards from the children and 50 yards from defendant; from performing surveillance of defendant or her children; from commercially appropriating defendant's photograph for advertising or trade purposes without defendant's consent; from communicating or attempting to communicate with defendant or her children.

* * *

---

1. This order was modified by the Circuit Court upon appeal. The court noted that injunctive relief was appropriate because of Galella's stated intention to continue his coverage of Onassis, but found the injunction broader than necessary to protect her rights. The order was modified to prohibit only (1) any approach within twenty-five feet or any

touching of Jacqueline Onassis; (2) any blocking of her movement; (3) any act foreseeably or reasonably calculated to place her life or safety in jeopardy; and (4) any conduct which would reasonably be foreseen to harass, alarm or frighten her.   487 F.2d 986, 998 (2d Cir.1973).   Why make these changes?   Did the trial judge balance interests incorrectly? Are there other considerations, such as Constitutional protections, that could affect the availability of the injunction or at least its wording?

2.   Will Galella's wrongful conduct necessarily stop because the court orders him to stop?   The materials on contempt in Chapter 7 consider the means available to punish a contemnor for disobedience or to compensate the victim for noncompliance with the order.

3.   Does the statute providing for Secret Service Powers, printed in footnote 53 of the case, contemplate judicial enforcement?   Why does the opinion state that injunctive relief is appropriate "either as implicit in the statute or on common law principles of equity"?   Is injunctive relief "implicit" in this statute?   Compare Orloff v. Los Angeles Turf Club, 30 Cal.2d 110, 180 P.2d 321 (1947), *supra* in Chapter 2.

4.   Compare the principal case with Portland Feminist Women's Health Center v. Advocates for Life, Inc., 859 F.2d 681 (9th Cir.1988).   A women's clinic obtained a preliminary injunction against right-to-life demonstrators.   The order provided that the defendants were prohibited from "shouting, screaming, chanting, or yelling during on-site demonstrations."   They were further enjoined from "producing noise by any other means which substantially interferes with the provision of medical services within the Center."   The Court of Appeals found that the injunction was not impermissibly vague even though the order did not include a specific decibel level or other objective standard.

D. PUBLIC INTEREST AND TRIBUNAL INTEGRITY

Section Coverage:

The public interest is another relevant consideration for the issuance of an injunction.   A court does not ignore the overall public context of a lawsuit.   Conversely, courts are resistant to prayers for comprehensive relief in the name of public interest in areas that more properly are within the province of the legislature.   Nonetheless, courts often need to use broad equitable powers to resolve immediate threats of harm to important private rights or public interests.

The public interest affects the decision whether to grant an equitable remedy as well as the scope and nature of any relief granted.   A related factor is whether the relief sought threatens the integrity of the court by being impossible to enforce or unlikely to be enforced.   A judge can consider the practical problem of whether enforcement by contempt will be possible when, for example, an order requires performance out of the court's jurisdiction.   Another appropriate consideration is the effect of an injunction on the relative bargaining position of the parties. Consider the plaintiff who really wants to make a favorable monetary arrangement with a defendant but asserts to the court that the damage remedy cannot adequately compensate for the threatened future harm. An injunction would afford the plaintiff an unfairly strong negotiating position for a settlement. Conversely, the court may also consider whether the defendant deliberately took liberty with the plaintiff's rights on the assumption that equity would not interfere later. The integrity of the court requires careful deliberation on these issues.

Model Case:

A major manufacturing company announces a new plant location in an economically depressed town. Construction of the plant begins. A neighboring landowner sues to enjoin construction because it interferes with a minor easement. In evaluating the merits of an injunction, a court may properly consider the public interest in the construction in addition to the factors of adequacy at law and relative hardships.

The landowner may have no intention of demanding enforcement of an injunction against construction even if it were granted. The purpose of the suit may be to delay construction and force the defendant to pay an unreasonably large price to eliminate the easement. The court may consider these factors, including the good faith of both parties with respect to the controversy.

UNITED STATES v. RAINBOW FAMILY

695 F.Supp. 314 (E.D.Tex.1988).

JUSTICE, CHIEF JUDGE. * * *

On May 6, 1988, the government filed its original complaint, demanding a permanent injunction, as well as a temporary restraining order and a preliminary injunction. The complaint named a number of defendants, including the Rainbow Family (also termed the Rainbow Nation, the Rainbow Family of Living Light, and the Gathering of the Tribes), the Rainbow Family Vision Council, the Rainbow Family Tribal Council, and the Rainbow Family Scout Council. These defendants comprise one form or another of a loosely-knit but identifiable association of persons who, for want of a better name, shall be referred to herein as the Rainbow Family. Among the activities of the Rainbow Family are various meetings, "councils," or gatherings, often held in the United States National Forests, for the purposes of "celebrating life," worship, expressing ideas and values, and associating with like-minded persons. The largest of these is the Rainbow Family Summer Gathering, which is held annually and has attracted as many as 20,000 people in the past. The Summer Gatherings typically begin in late May or June of each year, building to a climax over the July 4th holiday weekend. The 1988 Rainbow Family Summer Gathering has been set to take place in a National Forest in the State of Texas, and is the subject of this litigation.

* * * The plaintiff contends that such gatherings pose threats of irreparable harm to public health and safety, and to Forest Service lands and property, and that they will entail numerous instances of offensive or criminal conduct, such as public nudity, public disturbances, or use of illicit drugs.

* * *

The government has alleged several bases for the requested permanent injunctive relief, under both federal and state law, * * * however, final injunctive relief is authorized, only to the extent that the 1988 Summer Gathering constitutes a public nuisance, for the reason that it poses a threat to the public health.

* * * [T]he government contends that the 1988 Summer Gathering will pose a public nuisance in various ways: by threatening public health and safety, through the spread of communicable diseases arising from unsanitary conditions; by traffic congestion on public roads; by the prospect of disorderly conduct, public nudity, and use of illicit drugs; and through the potential damage or destruction of public lands and property. The plaintiff, therefore, demands that the gathering be permanently enjoined altogether, or that defendants be enjoined to comply with various public health and Forest Service regulations.

* * *

The government undoubtedly has the authority—indeed, the burden—of regulating activities on the National Forest lands, pursuant to its proprietary powers as landowner and as conservator of the lands for the public interest. [Citations.] Where necessary to protect its proprietary interests in public lands, or where there is some other genuine interest to protect or defend, such as preserving the public health and safety, the federal government may justifiably seek equitable intervention of the courts to forestall irreparable damage or some other public nuisance. [Citations.]

* * * [T]he evidence presented by the government credibly showed that thousands of persons attending the 1987 Rainbow Family Summer Gathering in North Carolina contracted shigellosis. * * * Although certain conditions present at the North Carolina gathering appear to have been conducive to the spread of the bacteria (heavier than usual rains, for instance), it is clear from the record that the Rainbow Family's failure to observe proper sanitary conditions, in many respects, were substantial contributing conditions to the outbreak. These omissions included their failure systematically to use boiled or chlorinated water for drinking, eating, and cleaning; improper disposal of human and solid wastes; swimming or bathing in contaminated streams; and unhygienic conditions in some communal kitchens.

It is equally clear from the record, however, that the gathering in North Carolina, and other past gatherings, have not resulted in serious or irreparable harm or damage to the environment or to public property, as the government contends. For example, after the 1984 Summer

Gathering in northern California, Forest Service officials themselves stated that no damage to the gathering site could be discerned, and that the land was fully capable of "multiple use" utilization by ranchers, hunters, and others within a short time after the gathering ended. Similarly, Forest Service officials testified that the North Carolina gathering site has not been irreparably damaged after last year's gathering, even though they felt that the Rainbow Family had failed adequately to clean and restore the site, as promised. Thus, the government has failed sufficiently to demonstrate the likelihood of irreparable harm to the environment or to public property as a result of the 1988 Summer Gathering, in order to justify the total exclusion of the event.

Regarding the environment, the evidence in the record does reveal that—at the North Carolina gathering, at least—garbage was left at the gathering site, automobiles were abandoned, pit latrines were not properly closed, and rehabilitation work on the site was not done effectively. Forest Service officials testified that it is common practice to require those disturbing a location, such as for logging or drilling, to clean or repair it. Thus, a limited permanent injunction, to require the Rainbow Family to comply with reasonable requirements for cleaning and rehabilitating any gathering site, will be entered.

As to the alleged nudity, disorderly conduct, or use of illicit drugs which the government alleges will occur at the gathering, it is manifest from the circumstances of this litigation that the government can—and intends to—rigidly enforce the criminal statutes applicable to such behavior. In other cases, a "general fear" that narcotics or other laws will be broken by some participants of a gathering has been held to be an insufficient basis for the issuance of an injunction against the entire gathering, particularly where, as here, the gathering is for significant expressive purposes. [Citations.] Since plaintiff has an adequate remedy at law for any feared criminal violations, no injunction is warranted on these grounds.

Finally, the plaintiff's fears that traffic congestion will occur, or that the local populace will react negatively to the influx of substantial numbers of Rainbow Family adherents, as shown by the evidence presented at the hearing, do not warrant complete abridgement of the defendants' First Amendment rights to participate in the gathering, especially since the government has made no effort to demonstrate why reasonable restrictions cannot be employed to ameliorate these conditions without wholly banning the gathering. However, the defendants plainly may not obstruct Forest Service or health officials, or law enforcement authorities, in their access into and out of any gathering site, notwithstanding a claim that it would inhibit their exercise of First Amendment liberties. [Citations.]

Therefore, based upon the preponderance of the evidence in the record, it is found that the plaintiff has sufficiently proven the likelihood of such a threat to the public health, posed by possible unsanitary and unhygienic conditions at the 1988 Summer Gathering, as to constitute a potential public nuisance. The government has failed, however, to prove that the gathering is likely to result in irreparable harm to the environment or to public property, or that the criminal laws and federal regulations are inadequate remedies for other violations which may occur at the gathering.

Moreover, even if such alleged harms as traffic congestion or public nudity are likely to occur, a balancing of the equities involved leaves little doubt that the gathering cannot be entirely enjoined. It must be taken into account that a permanent injunction against the 1988 Summer Gathering, which the government seeks, would operate as a prior restraint on the defendants' exercise of First Amendment rights to speak, worship, and associate. * * * This concern weighs heavily against granting the comprehensive exclusion of the defendants that the government demands. Moreover, in view of the lack of evidence of irreparable injury in any area other than public health, a total proscription of the gathering would be unjustified.

Conversely, the interests of the parties and of the public are sufficient grounds for a grant of partial permanent injunctive relief, specifically directed toward health and sanitation concerns. It is a reasonable time, place, and manner restriction to require that the defendants' First Amendment activities not threaten the public health or welfare. [Citations.] In requiring that the defendants observe sanitary and hygienic practices at the gathering, they will not be unduly burdened. In fact, the defendants themselves should be healthier as a result.

"Courts of equity may, and frequently do, go much farther both to give and withhold relief in furtherance of the public interest than they are accustomed to go when only private interests are involved." [Citations.] However, "an order issued in the area of First Amendment rights must be couched in the narrowest terms that will accomplish the pin-pointed objective permitted by the constitutional mandate and the essential needs of the public order. . . . In other words, the order must be tailored as precisely as possible to the exact needs of the case." Carroll v. President of Princess Anne, 393 U.S. 175, 183–84, 89 S.Ct. 347, 352–53, 21 L.Ed.2d 325 (1968). Permanent injunctive relief, in such circumstances, "must be specific and reasonably detailed. . . ." [Citations.]

Thus, the defendants will be enjoined, as a class, to comply with discrete health and sanitation provisions appropriate for an outdoor gathering of large numbers of persons, as provided in the permanent injunction, entered herewith.[5] The defendants will be limited to 5,000

---

5. Expert witnesses testifying at the hearing on the motion for permanent injunction indicated that sanitary criteria required for field military encampments or for refugee camps would be appropriate for the Rainbow Family gathering in the National Forests. Hence, in conformity with F.R.Evid. 201(c) and 902(5), judicial notice is taken, *sua sponte,* that certain portions of Department of the Army Field Manual No. 21–10 (FM 21–10), Headquarters, Department of the Army, Washington, D.C., 22 December 1983, entitled *Field Hygiene and Sanitation,* and Department of the Army Training Circular No. 8–30 (TC 8–3), Headquarters, Department of the Army, Wash-

persons at any one gathering site, so that governmental authorities may retain sufficient control over the persons gathering at the site. The defendants also will be required to establish, in advance of occupying any site, that basic health and sanitation measures will be met; and regular inspections will be required to ensure that such measures are maintained during the course of the gathering. A neutral agency, the United States Public Health Service, will be designated to inspect the gathering sites and certify that minimum health and sanitation standards are met. The Forest Service will be authorized to order the closure of any site in the event that the defendants fail to comply with the terms of the permanent injunction; but, as long as the injunction is complied with, the government may not unreasonably restrict the defendants in their access to or participation in the 1988 Rainbow Family Summer gathering. * * *

———

1. What sanctions will be available to the court if the defendants in the principal case disregard the injunction? Contempt, the subject of Chapter 7, is the tool by which courts punish violations of equitable orders. Under criminal contempt the court can fine or imprison disobeying parties. With civil contempt the plaintiff can seek damages for losses caused by the disobedience. If the defendants cannot pay for the damage caused by the gathering, however, this remedy is not helpful.

Should the court have considered the financial condition of the defendants before deciding whether to prohibit the gathering? If the defendants repeat their North Carolina behavior despite the court order, should the next gathering be prohibited?

2. Under the Federal Rule of Civil Procedure 65(d), an injunction binds the parties enumerated in the order and those in "active concert or participation" with them when such persons receive actual notice of the decree "by personal service or otherwise." Although personal service on each member of the Rainbow Family is not practical, what steps might satisfy the "otherwise" language of the alternative notice requirement in Rule 65(d)?

3. The court noted in the principal case that some of the threatened conduct that worried the plaintiff government was criminal. Injunctions against crimes, studied in Chapter 9, pose special due process considerations. Nonetheless, courts do enjoin crimes when the conduct is a public nuisance if the balance of hardships favors the order. Contempt sanctions for disobedience of the order then can be greater than the maximum fine or jail term set for the criminal violation. Are these powerful means to compel conformity with the law justified in the name of public interest?

ington, D.C., 15 September 1978, entitled *Field Sanitation Team Training,* are suitable standards for sanitary measures at the Rainbow Family gathering. The standards set forth in Exhibit A to the permanent injunction are drawn from these manuals.

BOOMER v. ATLANTIC CEMENT COMPANY

26 N.Y.2d 219, 257 N.E.2d 870, 309 N.Y.S.2d 312 (1970).

BERGAN, JUDGE.

Defendant operates a large cement plant near Albany. These are actions for injunction and damages by neighboring land owners alleging injury to property from dirt, smoke and vibration emanating from the plant. A nuisance has been found after trial, temporary damages have been allowed; but an injunction has been denied.

* * * The threshold question raised by the division of view on this appeal is whether the court should resolve the litigation between the parties now before it as equitably as seems possible; or whether, seeking promotion of the general public welfare, it should channel private litigation into broad public objectives.

A court performs its essential function when it decides the rights of parties before it. Its decision of private controversies may sometimes greatly affect public issues. Large questions of law are often resolved by the manner in which private litigation is decided. But this is normally an incident to the court's main function to settle controversy. It is a rare exercise of judicial power to use a decision in private litigation as a purposeful mechanism to achieve direct public objectives greatly beyond the rights and interests before the court.

Effective control of air pollution is a problem presently far from solution even with the full public and financial powers of government. In large measure adequate technical procedures are yet to be developed and some that appear possible may be economically impracticable.

It seems apparent that the amelioration of air pollution will depend on technical research in great depth; on a carefully balanced consideration of the economic impact of close regulation; and of the actual effect on public health. It is likely to require massive public expenditure and to demand more than any local community can accomplish and to depend on regional and interstate controls.

A court should not try to do this on its own as a by-product of private litigation and it seems manifest that the judicial establishment is neither equipped in the limited nature of any judgment it can pronounce nor prepared to lay down and implement an effective policy for the elimination of air pollution. This is an area beyond the circumference of one private lawsuit. It is a direct responsibility for government and should not thus be undertaken as an incident to solving a dispute between property owners and a single cement plant—one of many—in the Hudson River valley.

* * *

The ground for the denial of injunction, notwithstanding the finding both that there is a nuisance and that plaintiffs have been damaged substantially, is the large disparity in economic consequences of the nuisance and of the injunction. This theory cannot, however, be sustained without overruling a doctrine which has been consistently reaffirmed in several leading cases in this court and which has never been disavowed here, namely that where a nuisance has been found and where there has been any substantial damage shown by the party complaining an injunction will be granted.

The rule in New York has been that such a nuisance will be enjoined although marked disparity be shown in economic consequence between the effect of the injunction and the effect of the nuisance.

* * *

Although the court at Special Term and the Appellate Division held that injunction should be denied, it was found that plaintiffs had been damaged in various specific amounts up to the time of the trial and damages to the respective plaintiffs were awarded for those amounts. The effect of this was, injunction having been denied, plaintiffs could maintain successive actions at law for damages thereafter as further damage was incurred.

The court at Special Term also found the amount of permanent damage attributable to each plaintiff, for the guidance of the parties in the event both sides stipulated to the payment and acceptance of such permanent damage as a settlement of all the controversies among the parties. The total of permanent damages to all plaintiffs thus found was $185,000. * * *

This result at Special Term and at the Appellate Division is a departure from a rule that has become settled; but to follow the rule literally in these cases would be to close down the plant at once. This court is fully agreed to avoid that immediately drastic remedy; the difference in view is how best to avoid it.[1]

One alternative is to grant the injunction but postpone its effect to a specified future date to give opportunity for technical advances to permit defendant to eliminate the nuisance; another is to grant the injunction conditioned on the payment of permanent damages to plaintiffs which would compensate them for the total economic loss to their property present and future caused by defendant's operations. For reasons which will be developed the court chooses the latter alternative.

If the injunction were to be granted unless within a short period— *e.g.*, 18 months—the nuisance be abated by improved methods, there would be no assurance that any significant technical improvement would occur.

The parties could settle this private litigation at any time if defendant paid enough money and the imminent threat of closing the plant

---

1. Respondent's investment in the plant is in excess of $45,000,000. There are over 300 people employed there.

would build up the pressure on defendant. If there were no improved techniques found, there would inevitably be applications to the court at Special Term for extensions of time to perform on showing of good faith efforts to find such techniques.

Moreover, techniques to eliminate dust and other annoying by-products of cement making are unlikely to be developed by any research the defendant can undertake within any short period, but will depend on the total resources of the cement industry nationwide and throughout the world. The problem is universal wherever cement is made.

For obvious reasons the rate of the research is beyond control of defendant. If at the end of 18 months the whole industry has not found a technical solution a court would be hard put to close down this one cement plant if due regard be given to equitable principles.

On the other hand, to grant the injunction unless defendant pays plaintiffs such permanent damages as may be fixed by the court seems to do justice between the contending parties. All of the attributions of economic loss to the properties on which plaintiffs' complaints are based will have been redressed.

The nuisance complained of by these plaintiffs may have other public or private consequences, but these particular parties are the only ones who have sought remedies and the judgment proposed will fully redress them. The limitation of relief granted is a limitation only within the four corners of these actions and does not foreclose public health or other public agencies from seeking proper relief in a proper court.

It seems reasonable to think that the risk of being required to pay permanent damages to injured property owners by cement plant owners would itself be a reasonable effective spur to research for improved techniques to minimize nuisance.

The power of the court to condition on equitable grounds the continuance of an injunction on the payment of permanent damages seems undoubted. * * *

The orders should be reversed, without costs, and the cases remitted to Supreme Court, Albany County to grant an injunction which shall be vacated upon payment by defendant of such amounts of permanent damage to the respective plaintiffs as shall for this purpose be determined by the court.

JASEN, JUDGE (dissenting).

I agree with the majority that a reversal is required here, but I do not subscribe to the newly enunciated doctrine of assessment of permanent damages, in lieu of an injunction, where substantial property rights have been impaired by the creation of a nuisance.

It has long been the rule in this State, as the majority acknowledges, that a nuisance which results in substantial continuing damage to neighbors must be enjoined. [Citations.] To now change the rule to permit the cement company to continue polluting the air indefinitely upon the payment of permanent damages is, in my opinion, compounding the magnitude of a very serious problem in our State and Nation today.

* * *

I see grave dangers in overruling our long-established rule of granting an injunction where a nuisance results in substantial continuing damage. In permitting the injunction to become inoperative upon the payment of permanent damages, the majority is, in effect, licensing a continuing wrong. It is the same as saying to the cement company, you may continue to do harm to your neighbors so long as you pay a fee for it. Furthermore, once such permanent damages are assessed and paid, the incentive to alleviate the wrong would be eliminated, thereby continuing air pollution of an area without abatement.

* * *

This kind of inverse condemnation * * * may not be invoked by a private person or corporation for private gain or advantage. Inverse condemnation should only be permitted when the public is primarily served in the taking or impairment of property. [Citations.] The promotion of the interests of the polluting cement company has, in my opinion, no public use or benefit.

Nor is it constitutionally permissible to impose servitude on land, without consent of the owner, by payment of permanent damages where the continuing impairment of the land is for a private use. [Citations.] This is made clear by the State Constitution (art. I, § 7, subd. [a]) which provides that "[p]rivate property shall not be taken for *public use* without just compensation" (emphasis added). It is, of course, significant that the section makes no mention of taking for a *private* use.

* * *

I would enjoin the defendant cement company from continuing the discharge of dust particles upon its neighbors' properties unless, within 18 months, the cement company abated this nuisance.

It is not my intention to cause the removal of the cement plant from the Albany area, but to recognize the urgency of the problem stemming from this stationary source of air pollution, and to allow the company a specified period of time to develop a means to alleviate this nuisance.

* * *

In a day when there is a growing concern for clean air, highly developed industry should not expect acquiescence by the courts, but should, instead, plan its operations to eliminate contamination of our air and damage to its neighbors.

Accordingly, the orders of the Appellate Division, insofar as they denied the injunction, should be reversed, and the actions remitted to Supreme Court, Albany County to grant an injunction to take effect 18 months hence, unless the nuisance is abated by improved techniques prior to said date.

———

1. Problems arise when the conduct that adversely affects the plaintiff simultaneously confers a societal benefit. To what extent should a court consider that the polluting factory employs hundreds of workers in the community, provides a sizable tax base, and cost millions of dollars to build? Should it make a difference that the factory is validly operating within the requirements of a local zoning ordinance, yet has the ancillary negative consequences on the surrounding property?

2. Nuisance cases often require a court to exercise a quasi-legislative role. Judges are called upon to decide whether to allow a factory in one locale to discharge pollutants that adversely affect others, often in adjoining communities or even in other states. When, in the absence of state or federal legislative guidance, should courts act? Nuisance decisions have other political ramifications; if courts in state A historically allow factories to pollute and pay damages for their harm as a cost of doing business, while state B courts tend to enjoin such conduct, this difference could affect the location of new plants. Are such considerations properly weighed in a suit between two private parties?

3. Did the court in the principal case effectively license a wrong simply because of the potentially disparate economic consequences? Has the court essentially granted a power of inverse condemnation? If damages are awarded, should the court measure the harm based only on past conduct or should compensation be given also for future injury?

4. It is noteworthy that *Boomer* was decided in 1970, at the beginning of what became an explosion of legislative action at both the state and federal level to address environmental concerns.

The Environmental Protection Agency [EPA] was created in 1970 and charged with the responsibility of establishing national ambient air quality standards for air pollutants which endanger public health or welfare. Congress further enacted a series of amendments in 1972 and 1977 to the forerunner of the Clean Water Act. In 1971 the EPA administrator, in response to a court order, cancelled and suspended certain pesticides, DDT 2, 4 5–T and aldrin-dieldrin, and in the so-called "18th of March Statement" declared that pesticides would no longer be given perfunctory review regarding registration and enforcement. Additional key federal legislation was passed to combat the serious risks posed by hazardous waste products. The Resource Conservation Recovery Act of 1976 (RCRA), 42 U.S.C. §§ 6901 et seq., and the "Superfund" statute, the Comprehensive Environmental Response, Compensation and Liability Act of 1980 (CERCLA), 42 U.S.C. §§ 9601 et seq., reflect a toughened approach to enforcement by adding more stringent liability provisions for violators. The effectiveness of these various statutory

schemes is disputed; nonetheless, there is a clearly identifiable movement toward increased legislative intervention to solve pollution. *See
generally* "Developments in the Law—Toxic Waste Litigation," 99 Harv.
L.Rev. 1458 (1986).

5. Can health concerns be accurately balanced against economic
costs, particularly when those who bear the health risks are not necessarily the same persons as the ones who would enjoy the economic gains?
The essence of nuisance law involves a balancing of costs and benefits in
a private market system. That market functions well, however, only to
the extent that prices reflect the costs and benefits to society. One
problem when dealing with the sort of environmental issues involved in
Boomer is that several factors distort the efficient operation of that
private system of property rights.

The manufacturer who owns and operates the polluting factory has
an economic interest in forcing the costs of production onto someone
else, normally by passing along the costs of production to the consuming
public. An economist's model postulates that resources should be allocated efficiently to maximize total production. Therefore, where costs
exceed the benefits, production is considered inefficient. A manufacturer has no economic incentive to install costly pollution control equipment
because it does not translate into higher productivity gains for the
manufacturer. Rather, the persons who stand to benefit from pollution
reduction—the general public—would not directly pay for that benefit.
The notion that the public receives the collective goods in pollution
abatement, yet does not pay the costs directly, further distorts the
economist's model of an efficient private market system. *See generally*
Coase, The Problem of Social Cost, 3 Journal of Law and Econ. 1 (1960);
Farber, Contract Law and Modern Economic Theory, 78 Nw.U.L.Rev.
303 (1983); Sagoff, Economic Theory and Environmental Law, 79 Mich.
L.Rev. 1393 (1981).

6. *Boomer* reflects in part the tension between efficient economic-
based decisions predicated upon a cost-benefit analysis and the public
interest in enjoying a pollution-free environment. Part of the solution
has been direct public intervention by legislation where the private
market system fails to provide a sufficient incentive to manufacturers to
clean up the waste that they generate.

Direct regulation has flaws as well. The regulatory schemes typically have gaps in coverage and normally carry high administrative costs to
gather information, set standards, and monitor compliance. The information necessary to regulate effectively is largely in the hands of
industry—those with the least incentive to disclose it. Furthermore,
scientific evidence is often inconclusive regarding "safe" levels of human
exposure to certain pollutants.

PROBLEM: THE ENCROACHMENT

Stone constructed his vacation home on a large wooded site. Stone owns the property under most of the house, but six inches extended onto the property of the adjoining landowner, Blanzy. Blanzy's property is also a large wooded lot, and Blanzy has not constructed anything on it.

Stone offers to pay Blanzy a reasonable price for the sale of enough land to move the boundary between the two large lots and thus to accommodate the house. Blanzy counteroffers at a price ten times higher. Stone refuses to pay it and Blanzy will not negotiate further. Blanzy sues Stone to enjoin the encroachment of the house.

Should the court grant the injunction? Would it matter if Stone had made an innocent mistake about the boundary when the house was constructed as opposed to making an intentional encroachment?

Notes

1. If Blanzy is willing to sell the property at some price, then would damages be the appropriate remedy? What would Blanzy do with an injunctive order if Blanzy is willing to sell to Stone at some price? Should a court take such factors into account in deciding whether to issue the injunction?

Reconsider *K-Mart Corp. v. Oriental Plaza, Inc.*, reproduced *supra* at p. 48. Does it matter whether K–Mart would use the injunction to settle the case for more favorable terms in its lease rather than having the offending buildings moved?

2. Should the good or bad faith of the defendant matter to the court in deciding whether to issue an injunction? In Welton v. 40 East Oak St. Bldg. Corp., 70 F.2d 377 (7th Cir.1934), the court ordered the reconstruction of a twenty story apartment building to meet zoning set back requirements. The defendants had obtained a variance which the plaintiffs were appealing. During the appeal the defendants continued to build the structure. In granting the injunction, the court observed:

> It is impossible for a court or jury to correctly say that a building erected in the face of a city ordinance and in spite of litigation which sought to prevent its erection was nevertheless undertaken in good faith and so carried through. * * * [T]he company and its officers * * * acted knowingly, defiantly, and in reckless disregard of the warnings which the pending litigation effectively proclaimed.

* * *

Pomeroy, in dealing with the subject of balancing conveniences where the wrongdoer deliberately erects the offending building with notice of the pendency of a suit or an appeal, puts it thus:

> They (the cases) all agree in one particular, however, viz., that the defendant who would claim its consideration in his favor

must have committed the tort innocently; a willful wrong-doer is entitled to claim no favor. * * * It is hard to see how anyone can claim any immunity for a tort on the ground that it was innocently done, when at the time of doing it he knew his right to do it was disputed by the person affected. Pomeroy, Equity Jurisprudence § 1966.

3.   In Jerome v. Ross, 7 John.Ch.R. 315 (1823), a court of equity denied an injunction against a continuing trespass to land. The trespasses were made to lots near the Hudson River and the trespassers were building a dam on the river. The land consisted of an extensive ledge of stone and mass of rock, and the construction workers needed such rock for building the dam. The dam was needed for the construction of the Champlain canal. The rock was needed urgently for the completion of the canal at this point, and the public interest was at stake in the swift completion of the canal.

Ross was the owner of the rock and it appeared that the rock had no value except for its use in the construction of this dam. Ross sued at law for the trespass and conversion when the first load of rock was removed. He received very small damages. When the trespass and conversion of the rock was repeated, Ross sought an injunction.

The court denied the injunction. One of the grounds for the denial was that Ross was not suffering an irreparable injury. The trespass was not considered so grievous as to cause a loss that could not be remedied at law. The court also referred to the public interest in completing the canal.

Is this result correct? If the injunction had been granted, would Ross have been in a position to demand an unconscionable price for the rock? Should it matter to the dignity of the court if the injunction would have that effect? What is the economically efficient result in such a situation?

Chapter 4

SPECIFIC PERFORMANCE

The remedy of specific performance is a specialized form of injunctive relief that functions to ensure enforcement, as far as is practicable, of otherwise valid contractual obligations. A court of equity exercises its discretion in determining whether specific performance is an appropriate remedy by considering the following factors: the inadequacy of available legal remedies, the likelihood of future performance by the party seeking enforcement of the contract, the ability of the breaching party to render performance, the balance of interests and relative hardships of the contracting parties, and any potential difficulties in supervision or enforcement of the decree. These determinations affect both the availability of the order and its scope.

This equitable remedy is an *in personam* order that is punishable by contempt if disobeyed. The specific performance remedy is available both at common law and, in a liberalized form, under the Uniform Commercial Code with respect to transactions involving the sale of goods. The equitable defenses, like laches and unclean hands, may preclude specific performance (*see* Chapter 5). If specific performance is denied, the non-breaching party may still seek any available legal remedies.

A. ENTITLEMENT

Section Coverage:

Specific performance, as a discretionary equitable remedy, traditionally would not be ordered if the court determined that an award of damages at law would adequately protect the interests of the injured party. "Adequacy" in this equitable application has taken on a qualitative or relative meaning rather than being viewed purely in a quantitative sense. When the subject matter of the dispute has involved unique or non-fungible items, such as heirlooms or land, courts typically have considered substitutionary relief of money to be inadequate. Thus, a court's evaluation of legal remedies involves the difficulty of proving damages with reasonable certainty or the availability of an appropriate substitute in the market.

Courts traditionally have refused to decree specific performance of contracts that involve rendering personal services, such as contracts with professional athletes or artistic performers. Various reasons support this refusal including the difficulties of enforcement and supervision, the pragmatic need for loyalty and cooperation in the workplace, and the constitutional prohibition of involuntary servitude. Similarly, employers are rarely compelled to accept services tendered under contract unless there is a statutory basis for the order, such as in fair employment acts.

The common law refusal to compel acceptance of unwanted services is derived partly from public policy and partly on the basis of "lack of mutuality." The mutuality of remedy rule in pure form requires perfect symmetry of remedies for whichever party to a contract might breach. In the employment context this rule means that because an employer cannot have specific performance to compel a breaching employee to work, an employee should be denied that remedy against a breaching employer. The lack of mutuality defense, however, has been diminishing steadily in vitality; cases have created numerous exceptions and sometimes have rejected it outright. Under modern contract law there is no general requirement of perfect symmetry of remedies for contracting parties, particularly when the expectation of benefits differ.

Although specific performance may be denied, a court may still prohibit a person under contract with an employer from performing such services for anyone other than the plaintiff. The judge will issue such an injunction upon a showing that the services are unique or involve special skills. This inquiry is simply revisiting the role of equity to provide relief when the damages remedy is inadequate to protect an employer's interests.

Model Case:

On January 1, Owens contracted to sell Blackacre, a 160 acre tract of land, to Farmer Brown for a total purchase price of $100,000. In accordance with the contract Farmer Brown paid to Owens $10,000 as earnest money, with the balance to be paid on July 1, upon Owens' delivery of the deed. On February 1, however, Owens repudiated and refused to convey Blackacre.

Farmer Brown will be entitled to a decree for specific performance immediately, although Owens' delivery of the deed will not be required until July 1, conditioned upon Farmer Brown's payment of the remaining $90,000. The court will rely upon the rationale that each parcel of land is unique, thus making substitutionary relief of damages inadequate to compensate Farmer Brown.

WALGREEN CO. v. SARA CREEK PROPERTY CO.

966 F.2d 273 (7th Cir.1992).

POSNER, CIRCUIT JUDGE.

* * * Walgreen has operated a pharmacy in the Southgate Mall in Milwaukee since its opening in 1951. Its current lease, signed in 1971 and carrying a 30–year, 6–month term, contains, as had the only previous lease, a clause in which the landlord, Sara Creek, promises not to lease space in the mall to anyone else who wants to operate a pharmacy or a store containing a pharmacy. Such an exclusivity clause [is] common in shopping-center leases[.] * * *

In 1990, fearful that its largest tenant—what in real estate parlance is called the "anchor tenant"—having gone broke was about to close its store, Sara Creek informed Walgreen that it intended to buy out the anchor tenant and install in its place a discount store operated by Phar–Mor Corporation, a "deep discount" chain, rather than, like Walgreen, just a "discount" chain. Phar–Mor's store would occupy 100,000 square feet, of which 12,000 would be occupied by a pharmacy the same size as Walgreen's. The entrances to the two stores would be within a couple of hundred feet of each other.

Walgreen filed this diversity suit for breach of contract against Sara Creek and Phar–Mor and asked for an injunction against Sara Creek's letting the anchor premises to Phar–Mor. After an evidentiary hearing, the judge found a breach of Walgreen's lease and entered a permanent injunction against Sara Creek's letting the anchor tenant premises to Phar–Mor until the expiration of Walgreen's lease. He did this over the defendants' objection that Walgreen had failed to show that its remedy at law—damages—for the breach of the exclusivity clause was inadequate. Sara Creek had put on an expert witness who testified that Walgreen's damages could be readily estimated, and Walgreen had countered with evidence from its employees that its damages would be very difficult to compute, among other reasons because they included intangibles such as loss of goodwill.

Sara Creek reminds us that damages are the norm in breach of contract as in other cases. Many breaches, it points out, are "efficient" in the sense that they allow resources to be moved into a more valuable use. [Citation.] Perhaps this is one—the value of Phar–Mor's occupancy of the anchor premises may exceed the cost to Walgreen of facing increased competition. If so, society will be better off if Walgreen is paid its damages, equal to that cost, and Phar–Mor is allowed to move in rather than being kept out by an injunction. That is why injunctions are not granted as a matter of course, but only when the plaintiff's damages remedy is inadequate. [Citation.] Walgreen's is not, Sara Creek argues; the projection of business losses due to increased competition is a routine exercise in calculation. Damages representing either the present value of lost future profits or (what should be the equivalent) the diminution in the value of the leasehold have either been awarded or deemed the proper remedy in a number of reported cases for breach of an exclusivity clause in a shopping-center lease. [Citations.]. Why, Sara Creek asks, should they not be adequate here?

Sara Creek makes a beguiling argument that contains much truth, but we do not think it should carry the day. For if, as just noted, damages have been awarded in some cases of breach of an exclusivity clause in a shopping-center lease, injunctions have been issued in others. [Citations.] The choice between remedies requires a balancing of the costs and benefits of the alternatives. * * *

The plaintiff who seeks an injunction has the burden of persuasion—damages are the norm, so the plaintiff must show why his case is abnormal. * * *

The benefits of substituting an injunction for damages are twofold. First, it shifts the burden of determining the cost of the defendant's conduct from the court to the parties. If it is true that Walgreen's damages are smaller than the gain to Sara Creek from allowing a second pharmacy into the shopping mall, then there must be a price for dissolving the injunction that will make both parties better off. Thus, the effect of upholding the injunction would be to substitute for the costly processes of forensic fact determination the less costly processes of private negotiation. Second, a premise of our free-market system, and the lesson of experience here and abroad as well, is that prices and costs are more accurately determined by the market than by government. A battle of experts is a less reliable method of determining the actual cost to Walgreen of facing new competition than negotiations between Walgreen and Sara Creek over the price at which Walgreen would feel adequately compensated for having to face that competition.

That is the benefit side of injunctive relief but there is a cost side as well. Many injunctions require continuing supervision by the court, and that is costly. * * * A more subtle cost of injunctive relief arises from the situation that economists call "bilateral monopoly," in which two parties can deal only with each other: the situation that an injunction creates. [Citation.] The sole seller of widgets selling to the sole buyer of that product would be an example. But so will be the situation confronting Walgreen and Sara Creek if the injunction is upheld. Walgreen can "sell" its injunctive right only to Sara Creek, and Sara Creek can "buy" Walgreen's surrender of its right to enjoin the leasing of the anchor tenant's space to Phar–Mor only from Walgreen. The lack of alternatives in bilateral monopoly creates a bargaining range, and the costs of negotiating to a point within that range may be high. Suppose the cost to Walgreen of facing the competition of Phar–Mor at the Southgate Mall would be $1 million, and the benefit to Sara Creek of leasing to Phar–Mor would be $2 million. Then at any price between those figures for a waiver of Walgreen's injunctive right both parties would be better off, and we expect parties to bargain around a judicial assignment of legal rights if the assignment is inefficient. R.H. Coase, "The Problem of Social Cost," 3 J. Law & Econ. 1 (1960). But each of the parties would like to engross as much of the bargaining range as possible—Walgreen to press the price toward $2 million, Sara Creek to depress it toward $1 million. With so much at stake, both parties will have an incentive to devote substantial resources of time and money to the negotiation process. The process may even break down, if one or both parties want to create for future use a reputation as a hard bargainer; and if it does break down, the injunction will have brought about an inefficient result. All these are in one form or another costs of the injunctive process that can be avoided by substituting damages.

The costs and benefits of the damages remedy are the mirror of those of the injunctive remedy. The damages remedy avoids the cost of continuing supervision and third-party effects, and the cost of bilateral monopoly as well. It imposes costs of its own, however, in the form of diminished accuracy in the determination of value, on the one hand, and of the parties' expenditures on preparing and presenting evidence of damages, and the time of the court in evaluating the evidence, on the other.

The weighing up of all these costs and benefits is the analytical procedure that is or at least should be employed by a judge asked to enter a permanent injunction, with the understanding that if the balance is even the injunction should be withheld. The judge is not required to explicate every detail of the analysis and he did not do so here, but as long we are satisfied that his approach is broadly consistent with a proper analysis we shall affirm; and we are satisfied here. The determination of Walgreen's damages would have been costly in forensic resources and inescapably inaccurate. [Citations.] The lease had ten years to run. So Walgreen would have had to project its sales revenues and costs over the next ten years, and then project the impact on those figures of Phar–Mor's competition, and then discount that impact to present value. * * *

* * * Sara Creek presented evidence of what happened (very little) to Walgreen when Phar–Mor moved into other shopping malls in which Walgreen has a pharmacy, and it was on the right track in putting in comparative evidence. But there was a serious question whether the other malls were actually comparable to the Southgate Mall, so we cannot conclude, in the face of the district judge's contrary conclusion, that the existence of comparative evidence dissolved the difficulties of computing damages in this case. Sara Creek complains that the judge refused to compel Walgreen to produce all the data that Sara Creek needed to demonstrate the feasibility of forecasting Walgreen's damages. Walgreen resisted, on grounds of the confidentiality of the data and the cost of producing the massive data that Sara Creek sought. Those are legitimate grounds; and the cost (broadly conceived) they expose of pretrial discovery, in turn presaging complexity at trial, is itself a cost of the damages remedy that injunctive relief saves.

Damages are not always costly to compute, or difficult to compute accurately. In the standard case of a seller's breach of a contract for the sale of goods where the buyer covers by purchasing the same product in the market, damages are readily calculable by subtracting the contract price from the market price and multiplying by the quantity specified in the contract. But this is not such a case and here damages would be a costly and inaccurate remedy; and on the other side of the balance some of the costs of an injunction are absent and the cost that is present seems low. The injunction here, like one enforcing a covenant not to compete (standardly enforced by injunction), is a simple negative injunction—Sara Creek is not to lease space in the Southgate Mall to Phar–Mor during the term of Walgreen's lease—and the costs of judicial supervision and enforcement should be negligible. There is no contention that the injunction will harm an *unrepresented* third party. It may harm Phar–Mor but that harm will be reflected in Sara Creek's offer to Walgreen to dissolve the injunction. (Anyway Phar–Mor is a party.)

The injunction may also, it is true, harm potential customers of Phar–Mor—people who would prefer to shop at a deep-discount store than an ordinary discount store—but their preferences, too, are registered indirectly. The more business Phar–Mor would have, the more rent it will be willing to pay Sara Creek, and therefore the more Sara Creek will be willing to pay Walgreen to dissolve the injunction.

The only substantial cost of the injunction in this case is that it may set off a round of negotiations between the parties. In some cases, illustrated by Boomer v. Atlantic Cement Co., 26 N.Y.2d 219, 309 N.Y.S.2d 312, 257 N.E.2d 870 (1970), this consideration alone would be enough to warrant the denial of injunctive relief. The defendant's factory was emitting cement dust that caused the plaintiffs harm monetized at less than $200,000, and the only way to abate the harm would have been to close down the factory, which had cost $45 million to build. An injunction against the nuisance could therefore have created a huge bargaining range (could, not would, because it is unclear what the current value of the factory was), and the costs of negotiating to a point within it might have been immense. If the market value of the factory was actually $45 million, the plaintiffs would be tempted to hold out for a price to dissolve the injunction in the tens of millions and the factory would be tempted to refuse to pay anything more than a few hundred thousand dollars. Negotiations would be unlikely to break down completely, given such a bargaining range, but they might well be protracted and costly. There is nothing so dramatic here. Sara Creek does not argue that it will have to close the mall if enjoined from leasing to Phar–Mor. Phar–Mor is not the only potential anchor tenant. * * *

To summarize, the judge did not exceed the bounds of reasonable judgment in concluding that the costs (including forgone benefits) of the damages remedy would exceed the costs (including forgone benefits) of an injunction. We need not consider whether, as intimated by Walgreen, exclusivity clauses in shopping-center leases should be considered presumptively enforceable by injunctions. Although we have described the choice between legal and equitable remedies as one for case-by-case determination, the courts have sometimes picked out categories of case in which injunctive relief is made the norm. The best-known example is specific performance of contracts for the sale of real property. [Citations.] The rule that specific performance will be ordered in such cases as a matter of course is a generalization of the considerations discussed above. Because of the absence of a fully liquid market in real property and the frequent presence of subjective values (many a homeowner, for example, would not sell his house for its market value), the calculation of damages is difficult; and since an order of specific performance to convey a piece of property does not create a continuing relation between the parties, the costs of supervision and enforcement if specific performance is ordered are slight. The exclusivity clause in Walgreen's lease relates to real estate, but we hesitate to suggest that every contract involving real estate should be enforceable as a matter of course by injunctions. Suppose Sara Creek had covenanted to keep the entrance to Walgreen's store free of ice and snow, and breached the covenant. An injunction would require continuing supervision, and it would be easy enough if the injunction were denied for Walgreen to hire its own ice and snow remover and charge the cost to Sara Creek. [Citation.] On the other hand, injunctions to enforce exclusivity clauses are quite likely to be justifiable by just the considerations present here—damages are difficult to estimate with any accuracy and the injunction is a one-shot remedy requiring no continuing judicial involvement. So there is an argument for making injunctive relief presumptively appropriate in such cases, but we need not decide in this case how strong an argument.

Affirmed.

VAN WAGNER ADVERTISING CORP. v. S & M ENTERPRISES

67 N.Y.2d 186, 492 N.E.2d 756, 501 N.Y.S.2d 628 (1986).

Kaye, Judge.

Specific performance of a contract to lease "unique" billboard space is properly denied when damages are an adequate remedy to compensate the tenant and equitable relief would impose a disproportionate burden on the defaulting landlord. * * *

By agreement dated December 16, 1981, Barbara Michaels leased to plaintiff, Van Wagner Advertising, for an initial period of three years plus option periods totaling seven additional years space on the eastern exterior wall of a building on East 36th Street in Manhattan. Van Wagner was in the business of erecting and leasing billboards, and the parties anticipated that Van Wagner would erect a sign on the leased space, which faced an exit ramp of the Midtown Tunnel and was therefore visible to vehicles entering Manhattan from that tunnel.

In early 1982 Van Wagner erected an illuminated sign and leased it to Asch Advertising, Inc. for a three year period commencing March 1, 1982. However, by agreement dated January 22, 1982, Michaels sold the building to defendant S & M Enterprises. [Michaels sent Van Wagner a letter purporting to cancel the lease.] * * * Van Wagner abandoned the space under protest and in November 1982 commenced this action for declarations that the purported cancellation was ineffective and the lease still in existence, and for specific performance and damages.

* * * Trial Term declared the lease "valid and subsisting" and found the "demised space is unique as to location for the particular advertising purpose intended by Van Wagner and Michaels, the original parties to the Lease." However, the court declined to order specific performance in light of its finding that Van Wagner "has an adequate remedy at law for damages." Moreover, the court noted that specific performance "would be inequitable in that its effect would be disproportionate in its harm to the defendant and its assistance to plaintiff."
* * *

Given defendant's unexcused failure to perform its contract, we next turn to a consideration of remedy for the breach: Van Wagner seeks specific performance of the contract, S & M urges that money damages are adequate but that the amount of the award was improper.[2]

Whether or not to award specific performance is a decision that rests in the sound discretion of the trial court, and here that discretion was not abused. Considering first the nature of the transaction, specific performance has been imposed as the remedy for breach of contracts for the sale of real property [citations], but the contract here is to lease rather than sell an interest in real property. While specific performance is available, in appropriate circumstances, for breach of a commercial or residential lease, specific performance of real property leases is not in this State awarded as a matter of course. [Citations.]

Van Wagner argues that specific performance must be granted in light of the trial court's finding that the "demised space is unique as to location for the particular advertising purpose intended." The word "uniqueness" is not, however, a magic door to specific performance. A distinction must be drawn between physical difference and economic interchangeability. The trial court found that the leased property is physically unique, but so is every parcel of real property and so are many consumer goods. Putting aside contracts for the sale of real property, where specific performance has traditionally been the remedy for breach, uniqueness in the sense of physical differences does not itself dictate the propriety of equitable relief.

By the same token, at some level all property may be interchangeable with money. Economic theory is concerned with the degree to which consumers are willing to substitute the use of one good for another (*see*, Kronman, *Specific Performance*, 45 U.Chi.L.Rev. 351, 359), the underlying assumption being that "every good has substitutes, even if only very poor ones", and that "all goods are ultimately commensurable". Such a view, however, could strip all meaning from uniqueness, for if all goods are ultimately exchangeable for a price, then all goods may be valued. Even a rare manuscript has an economic substitute in that there is a price for which any purchaser would likely agree to give up a right to buy it, but a court would in all probability order specific performance of

---

2. We note that the parties' contentions regarding the remedy of specific performance in general, mirror a scholarly debate that has persisted throughout our judicial history, reflecting fundamentally divergent views about the quality of a bargained-for promise. While the usual remedy in Anglo–American law has been damages, rather than compensation "in-kind" (*see,* Holmes, *The Path of the Law,* 10 Harv.L.Rev. 457, 462 [1897]; Holmes, The Common Law, at 299–301 [1881]; and Gilmore, The Death of Contract, at 14–15), the current trend among commentators appears to favor the remedy of specific performance (*see,* Farnsworth, *Legal Remedies for Breach of Contract,* 70 Colum.L.Rev. 1145, 1156 [1970]; Linzer, *On the Amorality of Contract Remedies—Efficiency, Equity, and the Second Restatement,* 81 Colum.L.Rev. 111 [1981]; and Schwartz, *The Case for Specific Performance,* 89 Yale L.J. 271 [1979]), but the view is not unanimous (*see,* Posner, Economic Analysis of Law § 4.9, at 89–90 [2d ed.1977]; Yorio, *In Defense of Money Damages for Breach of Contract,* 82 Colum.L.Rev. 1365 [1982]).

such a contract on the ground that the subject matter of the contract is unique.

The point at which breach of a contract will be redressable by specific performance thus must lie not in any inherent physical uniqueness of the property but instead in the uncertainty of valuing it: "What matters, in measuring money damages, is the volume, refinement, and reliability of the available information about substitutes for the subject matter of the breached contract. When the relevant information is thin and unreliable, there is a substantial risk that an award of money damages will either exceed or fall short of the promisee's actual loss. * * * In asserting that the subject matter of a particular contract is unique and has no established market value, a court is really saying that it cannot obtain, at reasonable cost, enough information about substitutes to permit it to calculate an award of money damages without imposing an unacceptably high risk of undercompensation on the injured promisee. Conceived in this way, the uniqueness test seems economically sound." (45 U.Chi.L.Rev., at 362.) This principle is reflected in the case law [citations], and is essentially the position of the Restatement (Second) of Contracts, which lists "the difficulty of proving damages with reasonable certainty" as the first factor affecting adequacy of damages (Restatement [Second] of Contracts § 360[a]).

Thus, the fact that the subject of the contract may be "unique as to location for the particular advertising purpose intended" by the parties does not entitle a plaintiff to the remedy of specific performance.

Here, the trial court correctly concluded that the value of the "unique qualities" of the demised space could be fixed with reasonable certainty and without imposing an unacceptably high risk of undercompensating the injured tenant. Both parties complain: Van Wagner asserts that while lost revenues on the Asch contract may be adequate compensation, that contract expired February 28, 1985, its lease with S & M continues until 1992, and the value of the demised space cannot reasonably be fixed for the balance of the term. * * * S & M points out that Van Wagner's lease could remain in effect for the full 10–year term, or it could legitimately be extinguished immediately, [under certain contract conditions not currently existing but possible at any time]. * * * Both parties' contentions were properly rejected.

First, it is hardly novel in the law for damages to be projected into the future. Particularly where the value of commercial billboard space can be readily determined by comparisons with similar uses—Van Wagner itself has more than 400 leases—the value of this property between 1985 and 1992 cannot be regarded as speculative. Second, S & M having successfully resisted specific performance on the ground that there is an adequate remedy at law, cannot at the same time be heard to contend that damages beyond 60 days must be denied because they are conjectural. If damages for breach of this lease are indeed conjectural, and cannot be calculated with reasonable certainty, then S & M should be compelled to perform its contractual obligation by restoring Van Wagner to the premises. * * *

The trial court, additionally, correctly concluded that specific performance should be denied on the ground that such relief "would be inequitable in that its effect would be disproportionate in its harm to defendant and its assistance to plaintiff". [Citations.] It is well settled that the imposition of an equitable remedy must not itself work an inequity, and that specific performance should not be an undue hardship. [Citation.] This conclusion is "not within the absolute discretion of the Supreme Court" [citations]. Here, however, there was no abuse of discretion; the finding that specific performance would disproportionately harm S & M and benefit Van Wagner has been affirmed by the Appellate Division and has support in the proof regarding S & M's projected development of the property. * * * [Affirmed.]

----

1. Courts traditionally have considered a contract for the sale of land to be a proper subject for specific performance. Land is incapable of duplication and therefore each parcel is regarded as unique. Also, valuation problems may exist for certain tracts of land. Damages, then, are viewed as inadequate for a contract to convey an interest in land.

Is this traditional rule with respect to land consistent with the economic view of the inadequacy rule? Is it the difficulty and cost involved in obtaining information about the value of land that distinguishes it from routine consumer goods like appliances? If not, should the rule be changed? *See* Kronman, *Specific Performance,* 45 U.Chi. L.Rev. 351 (1978).

2. What if the purchaser in a land sales contract makes another contract to reconvey the land to a third party? Are damages still inadequate now that the purchaser's expected profit from the resale can be measured precisely? The traditional rule is that the purchaser should receive specific performance for the land even when there is a second contract for reconveyance. The rationale is that courts should routinely grant specific performance for land sales contracts to avoid litigation and damages. Restatement (Second) of Contracts § 360 comment e. Is this rationale satisfactory in terms of theoretical consistency? Does it comport with business reality?

3. Apart from the particular problems existing in land sale contracts, other types of interests present difficulties in estimating the amount of injury with reasonable certainty. For example, equitable relief may be the only appropriate measure to protect an injured party's expectation interest when the subject matter involves family heirlooms. What about the failure to receive a promised job promotion? Would it be sufficient simply to award damages based on the difference in salaries? *See* Clark v. Pennsylvania State Police, 496 Pa. 310, 436 A.2d 1383 (1981).

4. Why should the adequacy of the remedy at law determine whether to award specific performance? Under this rule the discretion of the court to balance the interests of the parties and the circumstances of the contract comes into play only after making the initial determination of adequacy. Is this approach sound? If damages and specific performance are both remedies within the court's power, why should the equitable remedy be subservient to the legal one in a merged system of law and equity in most jurisdictions? Should the court be free to award the remedy that would be most effective and appropriate to achieve a just result? Are there any advantages to the adequacy rule or any practical problems with abandoning it?

NIAGARA MOHAWK POWER CORP. v. GRAVER TANK & MANUFACTURING CO.

470 F.Supp. 1308 (N.D.N.Y.1979).

MUNSON, DISTRICT JUDGE.

Niagara Mohawk Power Corporation ("Niagara Mohawk") and Graver Tank & Manufacturing Co. ("Graver"), a division of Aerojet–General Corporation, entered into a contract on January 4, 1974, for the fabrication and erection by Graver of the reactor primary containment steel plate liner for the Nine Mile Point Unit 2, nuclear power plant, located near Scriba, New York. This plant is owned by Niagara Mohawk and four other New York public utilities as cotenants. * * *

On December 29, 1978, Niagara Mohawk notified Graver that it was terminating, effective two days thereafter, the contract for fabrication and erection of the containment liner for the Nine Mile Point 2 power plant. On the same day, Niagara Mohawk signed a contract with Chicago Bridge & Iron Company ("CB & I") for the completion of the liner and commenced an action in the Northern District of New York against Graver and Aerojet–General Corporation, seeking specific performance of the termination clause of the contract, the recovery of materials fabricated for the project, and the award of damages for faulty performance.

Graver filed an action against Niagara Mohawk, Stone & Webster, Stone & Webster's parent corporation, and CB & I in the Southern District of New York, seeking the entry of an Order enjoining the termination of the contract and directing specific performance of the provisions of the contract, other than the termination clause. * * *

[The termination clause, in article 22B, of the contract, entitled Niagara Mohawk to terminate Graver "at any time for any reason." The trial court denied Graver's preliminary motion for specific performance. It granted Niagara Mohawk's motion for a preliminary order of specific performance of the termination clause and denied an Order of Seizure for materials still held by Graver. The termination rights in the contract already provided for return of the materials.]

* * * Niagara Mohawk decided to terminate the Graver contract, because it believed that the continuation of Graver as the containment liner contractor would result in increased costs and further delays in the scheduled commercial operation date of the Nine Mile Point 2 power plant. The Court observes that Niagara Mohawk had been dissatisfied with Graver's performance over a substantial period of time and had made a number of efforts to resolve the problems. * * *

Graver argues that Niagara Mohawk's demand for specific performance must be denied, because its lawsuit is based upon an irrelevant statute—New York Uniform Commercial Code § 2–716. The Court agrees with Graver that the Uniform Commercial Code, which only applies to the sale of goods, does not govern the contract involved here. The essence of the agreement between Niagara Mohawk and Graver is for the construction and erection of a primary containment liner. The element of service, therefore, predominates and the provision of materials is merely an incidental feature of the transaction. Hence, the contract does not fall within the ambit of the Code. * * *

Since the Code does not govern this case, the Court must look to the common law of New York State to assess the propriety of granting specific performance here. Under the common law, a court may grant a decree of specific performance only if (1) there is a valid contract between the parties; (2) the plaintiff has substantially performed under the contract and is willing and able to perform its remaining obligations; (3) the defendant is able to perform its obligations; and (4) the plaintiff has no adequate remedy at law. [Citations.] When these elements are present, the granting of specific performance is within the sound discretion of the court. [Citations.]

It is clear that there exists a valid contract between the parties in this case. Secondly, the contract has been substantially performed by Niagara Mohawk. Graver's fee claims under the contract have been paid and the power company stands willing and able to perform its obligations under the termination clause—to pay reasonable and proper termination charges, to pay for materials demanded under the terms of Article 22B, and to reimburse the contractor under a cost plus fixed fee format for prior commitments that cannot be cancelled without charge. Any breach that might have previously been committed by Niagara Mohawk is relatively minor, and, therefore, would not bar a decree of specific performance. [Citations.]

Furthermore, it appears that Graver has the ability to perform pursuant to Article 22B. This can be done by Graver's vacating the job site and shipping the materials specially accumulated for the contract. Finally, the record demonstrates that Niagara Mohawk lacks an adequate legal remedy. Monetary damages—the traditional remedy at law—is inadequate in this case, because of the difficulty in computing the amount of such damages. * * *

It might be argued that a decree of specific performance should not be granted with respect to the shipment of materials fabricated for the project, because Niagara Mohawk can avail itself of the legal remedy of replevin. It is apparently for this reason that the power company has moved for an Order of Seizure for those articles that can be physically seized by the United States Marshal.

Graver has raised various questions as to whether Niagara Mohawk has satisfied, in all respects, New York's replevin statute, as recently, amended, CPLR § 7101 *et seq.*, but it is unnecessary to resolve this matter since the Court finds that replevin is not an adequate legal remedy in the circumstances of this case, and that, therefore, it does not have to be exhausted before equitable relief in the nature of specific performance is granted. Many of the materials accumulated by Graver for the Nine Mile Point 2 project are located outside New York State—at Graver's facilities in east Chicago, Indiana, in transit to Scriba, New York, or at various subcontractors' factories. Article 71 of the CPLR appears to apply only to the recovery of chattels located in New York State, [citations], and, therefore, if equitable relief were not granted, an action for replevin would have to be brought in each jurisdiction where the materials are located. The prevention of a multiplicity of suits is recognized as a sufficient basis for equity jurisdiction. * * *

While an Order of Seizure could not be granted with respect to materials located outside New York, this Court, by virtue of the fact that it has personal jurisdiction over Graver, has the authority to grant a decree of specific performance, requiring Graver to ship the materials specially accumulated for the project, no matter where such articles might be located. [Citations.]

Accordingly, * * * Graver is directed to specifically perform under Article 22B of the contract between Niagara Mohawk and Graver, entered into on January 4, 1974 and amended several times thereafter.

———

1. As the principal case reflects, a court's inquiry into the adequacy of the remedy at law is not limited to damages. Other common law remedies are possible, notably replevin and some forms of restitution. These remedies are rarely adequate, however, as a substitution for performance.

The effectiveness of replevin as an effective remedy is reduced by the availability of a bond. Even when there is no jurisdictional problem with the court's power to seize the goods, state law typically provides that a defendant may give a bond in place of surrendering the goods. *See* Chabert v. Robert & Co., 273 App.Div. 237, 76 N.Y.S.2d 400 (1st Dept.1948); Restatement (Second) of Contracts § 359 Comment e; Corbin, Contracts, 5A § 1157.

2. Consider the specific performance order sought by Graver's claim in the principal case—the enforcement of all provisions of the contract other than the termination clause. Would such an order be feasible, even if the court were to resolve the merits in Graver's favor?

During the time needed to complete the container liner, the contractor would need to interact continually with the several subcontractors. Disputes over scheduling and numerous other daily matters would be likely to arise. A court sitting in equity is generally disinclined to grant specific performance if the decree will carry extended burdens of judicial supervision or enforcement. The spectre of extensive judicial involvement may not be fatal to whether specific performance is granted, but it presents another factor for the court to weigh in issuing or framing of the final decree.

3. Is there a public interest element in the principal case? Which side does it favor?

PROBLEM: THE FAMILY CARE CONTRACTS

A couple who retired early in their fifties made a written contract with their child, Pat, who was twenty-two. They agreed to convey the family home to Pat in exchange for a promise of lifetime support. The house was duly conveyed and for several years Pat lived in the house and supported the parents.

Eventually Pat married, sold the family house, and moved. The parents moved to the new house and lived there for a time with the newly wedded couple. A dispute between the new spouse and the parents resulted in Pat asking the parents to move to a nursing home. This arrangement was agreeable to the parents.

Pat paid the nursing home bills for a few months but then stopped making payments. The parents seek to compel Pat to make the monthly payments to the nursing home as fulfillment of the contract. Should the order be granted?

Another couple in their eighties made a contract with their child, Lee, who was fifty. In this contract the parents agreed to convey the family home to Lee "within a reasonable time" in exchange for a promise that Lee would nurse the parents until their death. After three years, however, the parents had not conveyed, although Lee had provided nursing services. A family quarrel resulted in the parents throwing Lee out of the house and hiring another person to provide nursing care. Lee seeks specific performance of the promise to convey the house. What result? Are the ages of the parties in either case relevant to the legal analysis?

HENDERSON v. FISHER

236 Cal.App.2d 468, 46 Cal.Rptr. 173 (1965).

MOLINARI, JUSTICE.

Plaintiffs appeal from a judgment entered after a trial by the court awarding them $381.85 on a *quantum meruit* basis but refusing to grant specific performance of a written contract entered into between plaintiffs and decedent, Marion D. Baker. The sole issue presented on appeal is whether plaintiffs are entitled to specific performance of the subject agreement. We have concluded that they are and that the trial court erred in refusing to grant plaintiffs relief in this form.

On August 11, 1959, plaintiffs and decedent entered into a written contract which provided as follows:

"Whereas, the first party, Marion D. Baker, is 86 years of age and blind and is in need of constant care, the parties of the second part agree to move into the home of Mr. Baker at 717 College Street in the city of Healdsburg, state of California, and to furnish all food necessary or reasonably required by Mr. Baker; and to do all laundry work required by him and to keep the house clean and in good repair and to water the trees and shrubbery and to keep the premises in good condition as long as Mr. Baker lives.

* * *

"It is further agreed that Mr. Baker shall execute and deliver a deed of his interest in the real property, including his home and furniture at 717 College Street in Healdsburg, California, to the second parties, reserving to himself a life estate[.] * * * "

The factual background surrounding the making of this contract was as follows: For about 7 years prior to 1959 plaintiffs had been friends of decedent and his wife. They often referred to the Bakers as Grandma and Grandpa, and they had on numerous occasions helped the Bakers by performing various household chores for them. On July 24, 1959 Mrs. Baker died. About a week after her death and because Mr. Baker, who was blind and 86 years old, could not be left alone, plaintiffs moved into the Baker home. On August 11, 1959, at Baker's request, his attorney, Mr. Sayre, drew up the subject agreement. At this time Baker was in good health. However, 18 days after the execution of this agreement, Baker died. During this 18–day period plaintiffs performed the services set forth in the agreement. Baker did not, however, during this period execute the deed called for in the contract.

Based on these facts, plaintiffs on May 13, 1960 filed a creditor's claim in decedent's estate, demanding specific performance of the agreement or in the alternative $5,000, the reasonable value of the real and personal property which was the subject matter of the contract. This claim was rejected by defendant, the administrator of decedent's estate. [The trial court denied the claim for specific performance but held that plaintiffs were entitled to $381.85 on a *quantum meruit* basis, this being the amount which it determined as the value of the services and supplies which plaintiffs furnished to decedent during his lifetime.] * * *

Beginning with some general principles concerning specific performance, we note that the type of action with which we are involved in the instant case is not truly one for specific performance since Baker, who is now deceased, cannot be compelled to execute the promised conveyance. However, if it is determined that plaintiffs are entitled to the property which Baker promised to convey to them, then the court may declare a constructive trust upon this property in the hands of those who have succeeded to the estate. This is, in effect, the equivalent of specific performance and is sometimes termed "quasi-specific performance." [Citations.]

Although the relief in a "quasi-specific performance" action differs from that in the traditional specific performance action the requisites for relief are identical. They are as follows: The plaintiff must show that his remedy at law is inadequate; the contract must be supported by adequate consideration; there must be a mutuality of remedies, that is, the contract must be subject to specific performance by both of the contracting parties; the terms of the contract must be sufficiently definite for the court to know what to enforce; and the performance which the court is asked to compel must be substantially identical to that promised in the contract. [Citations.]

Proceeding to discuss each of these basic requirements as they specifically apply to the contract before us, we note, first, as to the inadequacy of plaintiffs' remedy at law, it is the general rule that in the case of a contract for the transfer of an interest in land it is presumed that damages would not adequately compensate for the breach. [Citations.] This presumption is based on the historic treatment of land as unique. [Citation.] Therefore, in cases involving the breach of a contract to transfer an interest in land, specific performance will be granted as a matter of course unless some other equitable reason for denial is shown. Accordingly, the party seeking specific performance need not establish inadequacy of the legal remedy and may rely upon this presumption. [Citations.]

Where, as in the instant action, only part of the subject matter of the contract consists of land, specific performance of the whole of the contract may be decreed even though compensation in money would be an adequate remedy for the promisor's failure to perform that part of the contract calling for the transfer of ordinary chattels. [Citations.]

As applied to the instant case, therefore we conclude that the contract between plaintiffs and decedent being one involving the transfer of land, plaintiffs' remedy at law is inadequate. The trial court's statement in its opinion that this contract "is within the class of cases that afford an adequate remedy at law upon quantum meruit" is not a correct articulation of the principle involved. The question, in determining the adequacy of plaintiffs' remedy at law, is not whether they have some remedy at law apart from the contract, but whether their remedy at law upon the contract itself, that is, for damages, is sufficient. Accordingly, the fact that plaintiffs are entitled at law to reimbursement upon a *quantum meruit* theory for the services and supplies which they furnished decedent is not dispositive of the issue of whether their remedy at law upon the contract which they entered into with decedent is adequate.

The second requirement for the specific enforcement of a contract is that the consideration be adequate. The proper time for testing the adequacy of consideration is as of the formation of the contract. [Citations.] And the proper test to apply in determining adequacy of consideration in a contract involving the transfer of property is not whether the promisor received the highest price obtainable for his property, but whether the price he received is fair and reasonable under the circumstances. [Citations.] Moreover, in addition to the value of the property to be conveyed, the court may consider such factors as the relationship of the parties, their friendship, love, affection, and regard for each other, and the object to be obtained by the contract. [Citations.]

In the instant action, the trial court made no specific finding as to adequacy of consideration except insofar as it found that "the services and expenses laid out by plaintiffs for Marion D. Baker during his lifetime were not and are not worth the full value of the aforedescribed real property and personal property, nor any substantial part thereof." While the question of adequacy of consideration is generally considered as a question of fact, the determination of the trial court being final unless totally unsupported by the evidence [citations], it appears in the instant case that the trial court erroneously determined this question as of the date of trial rather than as of the date of execution of the contract. Accordingly, we are not bound by such determination. We are satisfied, moreover, that the evidence adduced at the trial can support no other conclusion than that decedent's promise to convey his property to plaintiffs was amply supported by consideration. At the time the contract was entered into Baker was in good health and the duration of his life was uncertain. * * * The fact that Baker died within a short time after entering into the contract so that plaintiffs' services were of short duration cannot alter this conclusion. * * *

Adverting to the question of mutuality of remedies we first note the applicable rule as stated in [California Civil Code] section 3386 as follows: "Neither party to an obligation can be compelled specifically to perform it, unless the other party thereto has performed, or is compellable specifically to perform, everything to which the former is entitled under the same obligation, either completely or nearly so, together with full compensation for any want or entire performance." In contracts involving the performance of personal services by one of the contracting parties, it is clear that at the inception of the contract specific performance cannot be decreed against this party because of the rule of long standing that a person cannot be compelled to perform personal services. [Citations.] Accordingly, such a contract, at its inception, lacks mutuality of remedies and is, therefore, not specifically enforceable against the other party. [Citations.] The prevailing rule, and that adopted in California in section 3386, is, however, that such contracts which lack mutuality in their inception may be specifically enforced after the want of mutuality is removed by the performance by one party of his obligation under the contract. [Citations.] Thus, although the party who has contracted to perform personal services cannot maintain an action for specific performance while the contract remains executory as to him, if at the time he brings his action for specific performance he has fully carried out his promise to perform such services, then the defense of lack of mutuality can no longer be asserted and the court may properly grant the requested remedy and order the other party to specifically perform his promise. [Citations.]

* * * [I]n making its determination as to mutuality the [trial] court did so on the basis of obligations which existed between Baker and plaintiffs while the latter was still alive. As we have indicated, the trial court should, instead, have considered the problem of mutuality as of the date at which plaintiffs sought enforcement of the contract, that is, after Baker's death. Had the court done so, it is clear that the defense of lack of mutuality would not have been valid since plaintiffs had at this time fully performed their obligation to take care of Baker during his lifetime.

With respect to the requirement for specific performance that the subject contract be certain in its terms, defendant contends that the contract which plaintiffs seek to enforce is uncertain for the reason that it does not indicate a time for performance by Baker. * * *

It is only where the uncertainty or incompleteness of a contract prevents the court from knowing what to enforce that the defense of uncertainty has rationality. [Citations.] No such doubt exists in the instant case where the court was asked to impress a constructive trust in favor of plaintiffs based on a contract which was to be performed at some time during the life of a person who is now deceased and obviously can no longer perform his promise.

* * *

Since the law and undisputed facts require judgment to be entered for plaintiffs, the judgment is reversed. * * *

———

1. *Personal Service Orders.* Equity will not enforce a contract for personal services by an affirmative decree. Tucker v. Warfield, 119 F.2d 12 (D.C. Cir.1941). This rule is based on several policy considerations. First, an adequate remedy at law exists unless the services are unique. Pingley v. Brunson, 272 S.C. 421, 252 S.E.2d 560 (1979). Even if there were no other bar to granting specific performance for personal services, those services must be unique enough to preclude an adequate legal remedy. Bethlehem Engineering Export Co. v. Christie, 105 F.2d 933 (2d Cir.1939) (even though agent's discharge in breach of contract gave rise to an action for damages, equity will not restore him to his position.)

Second, there is inherent difficulty in fashioning an enforceable decree and the subsequent supervision. Bach v. Friden Calculating Machine Co., 155 F.2d 361 (6th Cir.1946). It is essential to fashion a carefully tailored order in order to enforce it by contempt. If a party's conduct does not coincide with the decree, the party may be held in contempt. Thus, it is imperative to meet due process requirements that a clear and precise decree be formed.

There are obvious practical problems with forcing an unwilling employee to work. It is difficult to measure the degree of effort a worker exerts, especially in a hostile environment. Moreover, the constitutional prohibition of involuntary servitude is relevant when the order necessitates direct personal labor. Arthur v. Oakes, 63 Fed. 310 (7th Cir.1894).

2. *Negative Injunctions.* Although equity will not compel personal services, it may prohibit giving services to others in contravention of existing contractual obligations, particularly to competitors of a former employer. Reasonable restrictive covenants, also called negative injunctions, will be enforced if the service involved is unique, the area covered is related to the service involved, and the time period of the restriction is limited. American Broadcasting Companies, Inc. v. Wolf, 52 N.Y.2d 394, 420 N.E.2d 363, 438 N.Y.S.2d 482 (1981). A restrictive covenant may be implied from a contract to render services exclusively for one employer.

The Restatement (Second) of Contracts § 367, comment b, states that the character of a personal service is one which is nondelegable. Thus, the nature of the nursing care contracted for in the principal case typifies personal services which are nondelegable. In contrast, the operation of a retail bakery store, as in *Dover Shopping Center, Inc. v. Cushman's Sons, Inc.,* the next case *infra*, could appropriately be delegated to a hired manager.

3. *Mutuality of Remedy.* Historically, under the mutuality of remedies doctrine, specific performance would not be available to one party unless that remedy was equally available to the other contracting party. Where a land sale contract was bargained for with services rather than money, the mutuality rule prohibited the buyer from obtaining specific performance because constitutional restraints against involuntary servitude would prevent the seller from hypothetically using specific performance to require performance of personal services.

This doctrine was distinguishable from the concept of "mutuality of obligation" as a prerequisite to the formation of a valid bilateral contract, and which itself was expressly rejected by the Restatement (Second) Contracts § 79. The mutuality of remedy doctrine flourished in the late nineteenth century co-existing with the attraction of mirror-image contracting, because it epitomized the distribution of justice with an impartial hand.

4. As the principal case reflects, the common law developed limitations to the rule of mutuality of remedies. Courts did not require mutuality when the contract was fully executed, the party seeking specific performance had substantially performed, or the court was assured of continued performance in the future. Sometimes courts used conditional decrees or required security in order to ensure counterperformance by the party seeking relief. Moreover, mutuality of remedy was required only at the time specific performance was sought rather than when the contract was formed. The rationale behind the rule was to

assure the party against whom enforcement was sought that the non-breaching party would also perform the contract.

5.　Several states, led by California and the Dakotas, enacted statutes which codified the developing common law limitations on the mutuality rule.　The modern view considers the mutuality of remedies requirement a curious historical vestige and, at most, represents just one factor in determining if specific performance is justified.　This philosophy began with the realization that parties typically bargain for different things and, therefore, their respective remedies do not need to correspond precisely.　*See* Restatement (Second) Contracts § 363 comment c.

6.　*Certainty.*　In order for a specific performance decree to be available the contract terms must be definite and certain.　Melaro v. Mezzanotte, 352 F.2d 720 (D.C. Cir.1965).　The requirement of certainty becomes particularly relevant to guide the equity court in framing the order.　For example, if a party contracted to use their best efforts in building a bridge, legal damages for breach would be ascertainable but a court would decline specific performance because no appropriate decree could govern or enforce "best efforts."　The need for certainty of terms, then, dovetails with the consideration of potential difficulties in supervision of the decree.

Although more certainty is required for equitable relief than for damages at law, courts may supply missing subordinate details upon which to predicate the equitable order.　Thus, while an output contract inherently is uncertain as to the final quantity to be produced, an equity court will not hesitate to draft a decree.　*See* U.C.C. § 2–716 comment 2. Similarly, the absence of a time requirement will not necessarily defeat a request for specific performance.　Laclede Gas Co. v. Amoco Oil Co., 522 F.2d 33 (8th Cir.1975).　The court in *Avalon Products v. Lentini,* 98 Cal.App.2d 177, 219 P.2d 485 (1950) stated: "The law leans against the destruction of contracts because of uncertainty and favors an interpretation which will carry into effect the reasonable intention of the parties if it can be ascertained."　Professor Williston has urged that the difficulty surrounding uncertainty has been overemphasized and should not be allowed to restrict equitable relief more than necessary.　11 Williston on Contracts, § 1424.

B.　FASHIONING RELIEF

Section Coverage:

Courts weigh a variety of factors not only to determine the propriety of granting equitable relief but also to fashion the form and scope of the decree.　No single factor is dispositive.　The balancing process goes beyond the threshold issue of the adequacy of legal relief and encompasses the traditional equitable notions of fairness, public policy concerns, and the ability to enforce and supervise the order.　Thus, a court may deny specific performance in situations involving mistake, duress, or unreasonable hardship.　These factors may influence a court in exercising its remedial discretion even if none is sufficiently great to avoid the contract as a matter of substantive law.

A court will try to approximate the balance of contractual rights and duties embodied in the original bargain. A goal of the specific performance remedy is to preserve the respective interests and intentions of the parties in contracting. Sometimes a party cannot deliver the exact performance promised, but the other party still seeks specific performance. For example, a seller in a land sales contract may not have title to the full acreage as represented. A court has several alternatives: (1) decree specific performance with an abatement in the purchase price proportionate to the deficiency; (2) award damages; or (3) give restitution of money already paid. If the defect is sufficiently large, a defendant seller may object on the grounds that specific performance with damages or abatement does not resemble the original contract, or that performance would cause unreasonable hardship outweighing a marginal benefit to the buyer.

Model Case:

Danielson owns a family portrait of his grandparents and their children as they were painted eighty years ago. The artist has since become relatively famous so that the painting has market value. Danielson needed money to help his ailing farm one year, and contracted with Potter for the sale of the painting at $100,000. In anticipation of this sale, Potter arranged for a resale of the portrait to a collector for $110,000. In the meantime, two events affected Danielson: The last surviving member of the family in the portrait died, increasing Danielson's sentimental attachment to the painting, and a government loan bails out the farm. Danielson decides to keep the painting.

Potter sues for specific performance upon Danielson's breach. Although the unique portrait is the proper subject of a specific performance order, such relief is discretionary. The court could balance the interests, including the interest of the third party collector, in deciding whether to grant the order. If specific performance is denied, Potter could recover his $10,000 expectancy damages at law. The collector's rights against Potter will depend upon the terms of that separate contract.

DOVER SHOPPING CENTER, INC. v. CUSHMAN'S SONS, INC.

63 N.J.Super. 384, 164 A.2d 785 (1960).

GOLDMANN, S.J.A.D.

Defendant appeals from a mandatory injunction of the Chancery Division, entered December 3, 1959, ordering it to reopen its retail bakery business at the store premises leased by it from plaintiff * * * and to keep the store open for business during the hours and on the days required by paragraph Third of the lease, with a manager or salesperson in charge and a "Cushman's" sign on the outside of the premises. * * *

On July 16, 1956 the parties entered into a written lease for one of a group of stores in plaintiff's shopping center in Dover which defendant undertook to operate as a retail bakery. The lease, a detailed and comprehensive instrument of some 29 pages, resulted from protracted negotiations between the parties during which defendant was represented by counsel. The printed form, as finally executed, contained numerous typewritten insertions and changes, obviously the result of those negotiations. Among its provisions was paragraph Third:

> "Third: As one of the inducements for the making of this lease, Tenant hereby agrees, beginning as soon after the commencement of the term as is reasonably possible and continuing during the full remaining term of this lease, to operate its business in the demised premises; to keep its store open daily for the regular conduct of its business therein during the same hours at least as are customarily employed by other similar stores in the neighborhood of the demised premises, and to keep and maintain the show window displays in an attractive and dignified manner. * * *"

The lease provided for a minimum annual rental of $7,000 plus a shifting percentage of gross sales in excess of the minimum rent.

Defendant took possession and began business on September 25, 1957, and has continued to pay the minimum rental down to the present time. * * * However, on May 1, 1959 defendant wrote plaintiff that it was permanently ceasing operations, indicating that it had found the enterprise unprofitable and had decided it would be less costly to pay the minimum rent than to resume operations.

Plaintiff subsequently instituted its action for a mandatory injunction directing defendant specifically to perform the covenants contained in paragraph Third of the lease. Defendant answered and by way of separate defenses contended, among other things, that (1) equity should not grant specific performance of a contract relating to personal services or requiring court supervision over a long period of time; (2) defendant had continued to pay its minimum rent down to date, but had not enjoyed sufficient business during its period of operation to April 1, 1959 so as to be required to pay any additional rent over and above the minimum; (3) plaintiff had not suffered any substantial or irreparable injury and had an adequate remedy at law; (4) equity should not grant specific performance where the benefits to plaintiff from the store being open would be slight in comparison to the substantial injury sustained by defendant. * * *

Defendant next contends that plaintiff should have been denied relief since money damages would be adequate, and even if that were not so, a court of equity should not direct the performance of detailed provisions of a lease, such as here, because of the necessity of continued superintendence. In reply, plaintiff cites paragraph Ninth (3) of the lease, which provides that "In the event of a breach or threatened breach by Tenant of any of the covenants or provisions hereof, Landlord shall have the right of injunction * * *." It argues that damages for the breach of a percentage lease arrangement are not readily measurable. Plaintiff also adduced proofs to show that the very nature of the shopping center as a cooperative enterprise, with each store's success dependent on the continued operation of the other stores, requires that defendant's bakery business be maintained in accordance with the lease for the benefit of all involved. Plaintiff further cites recent decisions showing a judicial tendency toward granting specific performance wherever feasible. It argues that the remedy is particularly feasible here because plaintiff has waived judicial superintendence and is willing to rely upon the defendant's self-interest in continuing to preserve its good reputation by conducting its business in a manner which would reflect credit upon its operation.

The mandatory injunction, as we have pointed out, does no more than require defendant to reopen and resume its retail bakery business, to display the name of "Cushman's" on the outside of the premises, to keep the store open as required by paragraph Third of the lease, and to maintain a manager or salesperson in charge.

Courts have recognized the uniqueness of a percentage lease and have generally implied therefrom an obligation on the part of the lessee to occupy the property and to use reasonable diligence in operating the business in a productive manner. [Citations.] But the gravamen of the complaint here is not only the possible loss of additional income by way of a percentage of defendant's increased gross sales, but the difficulty in measuring the harm that would come from the withdrawal of one of the members of a semi-cooperative enterprise like a shopping center. Plaintiff's damages cannot therefore be accurately ascertained, and remedy by way of damages at law would be impractical and unsatisfactory. [Citation.]

We turn to defendant's argument that relief should have been denied because of the necessity of continued superintendence on the part of the court. Equity will not ordinarily order specific performance where the duty to be enforced continues over a long period of time and is difficult of supervision. [Citation.] However, the modern tendency is to grant specific performance in the case of a clear breach, where the difficulties of enforcement are not great, particularly when compared with the inadequacy of damages at law. * * *

The specific performance granted by the court was directed at certain covenants simple of performance and supervision. The judgment expressly provided that except as specifically set forth therein, the court would "make no direction with respect to the method of operating the defendant's business on the demised premises or to the quality of the products sold and services rendered by the defendant therein * * *."

Since the court was careful to limit its order, defendant's objection to it on the ground of required continued supervision is without persuasive force. The judgment as it stands is not so difficult of enforcement that it can be said the difficulties of supervision outweigh the importance of granting specific performance because of the inadequacy of the remedy of damages at law.

Affirmed.

————

1.　If a valid contract has been breached, a court of equity will order specific performance if there is no adequate remedy at law and if the court would not have to undertake a burdensome amount of supervision, such as in building or repair contracts. Although this statement sums up the general rule concerning the applicability of specific performance, courts are becoming more willing to decree specific performance even when supervision by the court is an integral factor. *See generally*, Van Hecke, *Changing Emphases in Specific Performance,* 40 N.C.L.Rev. 1 (1961).

2.　The Restatement (Second) of Contracts § 366 treats the potential problem of supervision as one factor for entitlement to and fashioning of the specific performance decree. Under the Restatement view, a contract will not be specifically enforced if the potential burden to the court is disproportionate to the perceived gain for the plaintiff. Conversely, if the harm from not enforcing the decree would be great, or there is a potential harm to the public, specific performance will be decreed. Thus, where faulty plumbing endangers a family's health, the court will grant specific performance. Fran Realty v. Thomas, 30 Md.App. 362, 354 A.2d 196 (1976). If however, the only harm to the plaintiff is a delay in production, the court may decide against specific performance. Northern Delaware Indus. Dev. Corp. v. E.W. Bliss Co., 245 A.2d 431 (Del.Ch.1968).

The Restatement view also promotes specifically enforcing arbitration clauses since the court is not required to render any direct supervision. Thus, in order to ensure equity, the court will overlook a burden to itself if a serious potential harm to the plaintiff or the public would ensue.

3.　Courts, on the basis of "unfairness," may decline to order specific performance because of inadequate consideration in the agreed exchange. The inadequacy between consideration received and fair market value must amount to a hard, unreasonable, or unconscionable contract, but not necessarily reaching the level of fraud. Humble Oil & Refining v. De Loache, 297 F.Supp. 647 (D.C.S.C.1969). Inadequate consideration is often found in conjunction with separate unconscionable or overreaching conduct to persuade a court to deny specific performance. If the disparity in the value is particularly large it may serve as the sole rationale for disallowing equitable enforcement of the contract. Hodge v. Shea, 252 S.C. 601, 168 S.E.2d 82 (1969).

Valuations are to be made at the time of contracting in order to include the risk inherent in any bargained-for exchange. Craven v. Williams, 302 F.Supp. 885 (D.C.S.C.1969). This rule is occasionally ignored; if the difference is great enough, the court may not allow specific performance even when the bargain was reasonable at the time of contracting. Marks v. Gates, 154 Fed. 481 (C.C.A.9 1907). If one party simply made a bad bargain, the low consideration should not justify denial of specific performance.

WOOSTER REPUBLICAN PRINTING v. CHANNEL 17, INC.

533 F.Supp. 601 (W.D.Mo.1981).

WRIGHT, DISTRICT JUDGE.

Plaintiff, the Wooster Republican Printing Company (Wooster), is a closely-held family corporation which owns and operates daily and weekly newspapers, radio stations, and a commercial printing business. Defendant, Channel Seventeen, Inc., (Channel Seventeen), is a closely-held Missouri corporation which owns and operates a UHF television station in Columbia, Missouri, as an ABC network affiliate under the call letters, "KCBJ–TV." This diversity action was initiated by Wooster, an Ohio corporation, to enforce an alleged contract "to sell the assets, property and business of defendant, excluding bank accounts, cash-on-hand and accounts receivable." Alleging the uniqueness of the business of Channel Seventeen and an anticipatory breach of the contract by repudiation, Wooster primarily seeks specific performance of the alleged agreement. Alternatively, should specific performance be determined inappropriate, Wooster seeks damages in the amount of $912,053.02. Plaintiff also seeks attorneys fees, costs and expenses in conjunction with its claim for specific performance.

* * *

As one expert put it, Channel Seventeen is "a very unique station in itself." It is a UHF station with a national network affiliation which competes with two VHF stations also with national network affiliations. Its network, ABC, had led the industry in audience ratings for several years. The station operates with an exceptionally tall tower which is strategically placed to serve not only Columbia, Missouri, but also Sedalia, Jefferson City, and the surrounding rural areas. It services a market which is youth and government oriented with a high "per family spendable income." One national rating service, Arbitron, has recently upgraded this market from 134th in the nation to 129th. Both Columbia and Jefferson City are stable and growing communities with a high percentage of professionals residing within them.

Despite its strong markets and excellent potential, Channel Seventeen has not achieved the success it could attain. It has "one of the lowest rate cards ... in a market [of its] size," and its potential profitability has not been reached. This failure to achieve full financial potential is the result of a lack of cohesiveness and uniformity in program packaging, an unaggressive sales program and insufficient infusion of working capital. With the proper management, however, the station could achieve a high degree of profitability.

Because of the failure of Channel Seventeen to reach its potential, it is one of the few television stations in the nation which would sell for under $5,000,000. There has been no contention herein that $3,300,000 was not a fair price for the assets of Channel Seventeen on July 18, 1979. To the contrary, the testimony at trial uniformly confirmed that this price was at or above the fair market value of Channel Seventeen at that time. The station has, however, since appreciated in value to approximately $900,000 over the price established by the contract of July 18, 1979. The unrefuted expert testimony at trial established the current fair market value of Channel Seventeen at $4,200,000.

* * *

Wooster primarily seeks specific performance of the contract of July 18, 1979. Defendants, on the other hand, contend that specific performance will not lie because of the impossibility of performance of that contract, mutual mistake as to the material facts by the parties to it, and the adequacy of Wooster's remedy at law.

As an equitable remedy, "[s]pecific performance will not be ordered when the party claiming breach of contract has an adequate remedy at law." * * * In the present case, however, Wooster's remedy at law would not be adequate to afford it the benefit of the agreement which it struck with Channel Seventeen. Uniformly, the expert testimony at trial established that Channel Seventeen, and more specifically station KCBJ–TV, is a "unique" property, unique in the sense that it presents an unusual potential for future growth in a stable and growing market. Because of its potential for expansion with proper management and infusion of capital, its relative position in the local and national markets, its network affiliation, its licensing and frequency, and its physical assets, among other things, Channel Seventeen is unique. Accordingly, Wooster's remedy at law would not provide a certain, prompt, complete or efficient substitute for the specific performance of the contract. [Citations.]

But Channel Seventeen * * * argues that specific performance of the contract is not available to Wooster because of the impossibility of its performance and mutual mistakes of fact regarding certain facts upon which the contract was premised. Performance of the contract is impossible, it urges, because the site upon which the transmitter tower of KCBJ–TV is located was, and still is, owned by a third person who is not a party to this action.

"A thing is impossible in legal contemplation when it is not practicable; and a thing is impracticable when it can be done only at an excessive and unreasonable cost." [Citations.] The contract of July 18, 1979, provided, in part, that Channel Seventeen would "be able to transfer the site or cause it to be transferred in fee to [Wooster] at closing." Because title to that site is held by a third party, the land cannot be conveyed in fee to Wooster upon the closing of the contract. But Wooster states that it is willing to take less; that it is willing to take whatever title Channel Seventeen can convey, if any, with an abatement in the purchase price.

As earlier found herein, Channel Seventeen currently holds a lease to the tower site which will allow it to exercise an option to buy the land for the amount of $10,000 at the end of its term. That lease is, by its terms, assignable to a purchaser of Channel Seventeen. The performance under a decree of specific performance need not be totally identical to that which is provided by the contract as long as the agreement of the parties is substantially performed. [Citations.] Here, the transmitter site, a parcel of one acre of land, is but a minor part of the total agreement of the parties. Since Wooster is willing to accept the leasehold interest with the option to purchase this land at a future date, the impossibility of a present conveyance of the land in fee does not defeat the remedy of specific performance. Nor is the mutual mistake of the contracting parties, if any, sufficient to invalidate the contract or defeat the equitable remedy Wooster now seeks. Under those circumstances, the purchase price of the assets of Channel Seventeen can and should be abated by the amount necessary to exercise the option granted by the lease. [Citation.]

Finally, Channel Seventeen contends that a mutual mistake existed concerning the remedies for breach of the contemplating contract by the parties at the time of its execution. Channel Seventeen asserts that * * * upon breach of contract, Channel Seventeen would only be liable for the amount stated in a liquidated damages clause of the contract. Paragraph 7.1(a) of the contract of July 18, 1979, provides that Channel Seventeen may receive "Fifty Thousand Dollars ($50,000), as liquidated damages" if "closing is not achieved by reason of a breach by [Wooster] prior to closing . . ." On the other hand, Paragraph 7.1(b) of the contract clearly provides that the remedies available to Wooster would include "the right to specific performance, which [Channel Seventeen] acknowledge[d] [was] an appropriate remedy because damages at law would be inadequate." * * * Based upon the testimony at trial, it cannot reasonably be found that a mutual mistake existed at the time of execution of the contract concerning the remedies available to the parties upon its breach.

* * *

For the reasons stated above, it is therefore ordered that judgment be entered in favor of plaintiff Wooster Republican Printing Company and against defendant Channel Seventeen, Inc. * * * and that a Decree of Specific Performance be entered herein.

PROBLEM: THE LAND DEFECT

Brown entered into a written agreement to purchase a 160 acre tract of farm land, Blackacre, from O for $50,000, to be paid in ten equal monthly installments. At the closing of the transaction Brown tendered a check for $5,000 in exchange for a warranty deed to Blackacre from O.

The warranty deed, however, only gave clear title to 157 acres because a 3 acre strip abutting Slippery Creek on the southern part of Blackacre had been taken by the state in eminent domain proceedings. Without the 3 acres Brown had no access to a water supply for irrigating Blackacre. The cost to transport water by pipeline would be approximately $20,000.

Brown further discovered that O lacked the mineral rights to 30 acres of Blackacre. Accordingly, Brown did not make the next scheduled monthly payment but demanded rescission of the agreement and restitution of the $5,000. O counterclaimed and requested specific performance. What result? Would it make a difference if Brown was a dealer in land and had contracted to resell Blackacre to A?

———

1. Equity aims to render more complete relief than that which is available at law. Sometimes that goal is accomplished by rendering to a party the specific thing owed in its original form, but the court will not write for the parties a contract they never made. Floyd v. Segars, 572 F.2d 1018 (5th Cir.1978).

From this general rule springs the practice of awarding specific performance with an abatement in the purchase price. If, for example, a vendor has breached by misrepresenting the acreage in a land sale contract, the vendee may specifically enforce the contract and concurrently obtain an abatement in the purchase price. This practice effectively consolidates an equitable right of specific performance and a legal right to damages for the difference in the expected land and the land received.

Generally, the treatment of specific performance with requested abatement for a breach can be broken down into three categories. If the differential is so minute as not to impair the contract substantially, then arguably no breach occurred and specific performance will lie with no abatement. If the deficiency is sufficient to rise to the level of a breach, the courts are willing to award specific performance with purchase price abatement. This willingness falters, however, when the breach is so substantial that the court would be enforcing not the parties' contract but a contract of the court's own creation. The courts perhaps believe that specific performance of such a small quantity would be "a suit in which the tail wags the dog." *See* Dobbs, Remedies § 12.10.

2. Most cases follow the reasoning that specific performance with abatement is allowed in a title defect or a deficiency in quantity but will not be permitted where the buyer knew the seller would not be able to complete the transaction, or if the breach relates to a collateral promise. A collateral promise relates not to the quantity or quality of the estate, but instead to some non-integral factor such as its earning potential.

At the other end of the spectrum, where the buyer will accept whatever title the seller can offer, without abatement, the court will uphold the contract. *See* Leland v. Kligman, 160 F.2d 27 (D.C.Cir.1947) (vendor not excused from performing contract for the sale of realty on the ground that a third party had a possible interest, because the purchaser was willing to take whatever title vendor had).

3. If a contract is valid and a court is willing to enforce a slightly different performance, why not enforce a widely different one? The general rule—that specific performance will not lie where the breach is so great that the underlying contract is no longer distinguishable—has received a mixed, and often critical reception. *See* Williston, Contracts § 1436; Dobbs, Remedies § 12.10.

4. Consider the abatement issue in light of the following mathematical illustration. Assume that the parties contracted to sell a parcel of land for a price of $+10$. A minor defect (-1) would require an adjustment $(10-1)$ with specific performance for $+9$. This result would satisfy purists who advocate the role of the specific performance remedy to be limited to the enforcement of the parties' original contract.

A major defect (-6) would result in specific performance $(10-6)$ for only $+4$. Certainly the $+4$ figure, when compared to the original contract bargain of $+10$, is not a close approximation. The orthodox view would be to decline specific performance with the -6 reduction and to leave the non-breaching buyer to its legal remedy, if any. If the plaintiff can establish a legal claim for damages, the measure may be $+6$ but it could be less, especially for an innocent misrepresentation. If, however, the plaintiff does receive damages of $+6$, does it make sense to award specific performance for $+10$ and then require the separate suit for damages for -6 for the major defect, with the result still being $+4$? What if the defendant does not have sufficient assets for the $+6$ damages judgment? Are there other practical problems with either approach? Would it be a workable rule to give the court broad discretion to assess hardship, even in a -6 case?

5. A unilateral mistake of fact made by one contracting party may prompt a court to refrain from ordering specific performance if the effect of the order would heavily penalize the mistaken party. *See* Oswald v. Allen, 285 F.Supp. 488 (S.D.N.Y.1968) (contract to sell rare coin collection not specifically enforced where mistake concerned which coins subject to contract); Brooks v. Towson Realty, 223 Md. 61, 162 A.2d 431 (1960) (no specific performance where buyer mistakenly believed contract description included an additional tract of land); Perlmutter v. Bacas, 219 Md. 406, 149 A.2d 23 (1959) (buyer mistake that land could be subdivided justified denial of specific performance). The mistake may not be sufficient to prevent formation of the contract; therefore, the court should award legal relief to which the aggrieved party may be otherwise entitled. The willingness of a court to rely upon a mistake to deny equitable relief is, of course, heightened if it was caused by misrepresentations by the other contracting party. Restatement (Second) Contracts § 364(1)(a).

C. CONTRACTS FOR THE SALE OF GOODS

Section Coverage:

The common law approach to specific performance in the sale of goods focuses upon uniqueness of the subject goods to satisfy the inadequacy at law requirement. A specific performance order is difficult to obtain under common law without a showing that the object of the contract is virtually one-of-a-kind. The Uniform Commercial Code § 2–716(1) changes and expands the specific performance remedy when goods are "unique or in other proper circumstances." Although the contours of "uniqueness" and the "other proper circumstances" provision have not been entirely drawn, the approach in U.C.C. 2–716 is intended to encompass contract matters apart from heirlooms, such as in output and requirements contracts where alternate sources or markets are not readily available.

Model Case:

Parket contracted to purchase from the Fullsail Yacht Co. a customized fiberglass "FX 160" cruising yacht with a special hull design manufactured exclusively by Fullsail. Parket gave the down payment as required under the agreement but Fullsail subsequently repudiated the contract because of a rise in the cost of its materials.

A court is likely to award specific performance of manufacture and delivery of the yacht conditioned upon compliance by Parket with the contract terms. The underlying basis for the order is that Parket cannot obtain substitute goods in the open market because only Fullsail manufactures that particular design of yacht. The inability to cover, according to comment 2 § 2–716 and relevant caselaw, is relevant not only with respect to the uniqueness of the goods but also with respect to the "other proper circumstances" test stated for specific performance under § 2–716(1).

SEDMAK v. CHARLIE'S CHEVROLET, INC.
622 S.W.2d 694 (Mo.App.1981).

Satz, Judge.

This is an appeal from a decree of specific performance. We affirm.

In their petition, plaintiffs, Dr. and Mrs. Sedmak (Sedmaks), alleged they entered into a contract with defendant, Charlie's Chevrolet, Inc. (Charlie's), to purchase a Corvette automobile for approximately $15,000.00. The Corvette was one of a limited number manufactured to commemorate the selection of the Corvette as the Pace Car for the Indianapolis 500. Charlie's breached the contract, the Sedmaks alleged, when, after the automobile was delivered, an agent for Charlie's told the Sedmaks they could not purchase the automobile for $15,000.00 but would have to bid on it.

* * * The record reflects the Sedmaks to be automobile enthusiasts, who, at the time of trial, owned six Corvettes. In July, 1977, "Vette

Vues," a Corvette fancier's magazine to which Dr. Sedmak subscribed, published an article announcing Chevrolet's tentative plans to manufacture a limited edition of the Corvette. The limited edition of approximately 6,000 automobiles was to commemorate the selection of the Corvette as the Indianapolis 500 Pace Car. The Sedmaks were interested in acquiring one of these Pace Cars to add to their Corvette collection. In November, 1977, the Sedmaks asked Tom Kells, sales manager at Charlie's Chevrolet, about the availability of the Pace Car. Mr. Kells said he did not have any information on the car but would find out about it. Mr. Kells said if Charlie's were to receive a Pace Car, the Sedmaks could purchase it.

On January 9, 1978, Dr. Sedmak telephoned Kells to ask him if a Pace Car could be ordered. Kells indicated that he would require a deposit on the car, so Mrs. Sedmak went to Charlie's and gave Kells a check for $500.00. She was given a receipt for that amount bearing the names of Kells and Charlie's Chevrolet, Inc. At that time, Kells had a pre-ordered form listing both standard equipment and options available on the Pace Car. Prior to tendering the deposit, Mrs. Sedmak asked Kells if she and Dr. Sedmak were "definitely going to be the owners." Kells replied, "yes." After the deposit had been paid, Mrs. Sedmak stated if the car was going to be theirs, her husband wanted some changes made to the stock model. She asked Kells to order the car equipped with an L82 engine, four speed standard transmission and AM/FM radio with tape deck. Kells said that he would try to arrange with the manufacturer for these changes. Kells was able to make the changes, and, when the car arrived, it was equipped as the Sedmaks had requested.

Kells informed Mrs. Sedmak that the price of the Pace Car would be the manufacturer's retail price, approximately $15,000.00. The dollar figure could not be quoted more precisely because Kells was not sure what the ordered changes would cost, nor was he sure what the "appearance package"—decals, a special paint job—would cost. * * *

On April 3, 1978, the Sedmaks were notified by Kells that the Pace Car had arrived. Kells told the Sedmaks they could not purchase the car for the manufacturer's retail price because demand for the car had inflated its value beyond the suggested price. Kells also told the Sedmaks they could bid on the car. The Sedmaks did not submit a bid. They filed this suit for specific performance.

* * *

[The court reviewed the evidence and rejected defendant's contention that no contract was made.] Without again detailing the facts, there was evidence to support the trial court's conclusion that the parties agreed the selling price would be the price suggested by the manufacturer. Whether this price accurately reflects the market demands on any given day is immaterial. The manufacturer's suggested retail price is ascertainable and, thus, if the parties choose, sufficiently definite to meet the price requirements of an enforceable contract.

Failure to specify the selling price in dollars and cents did not render the contract void or voidable. [Citation.] As long as the parties agreed to a method by which the price was to be determined and as long as the price could be ascertained at the time of performance, the price requirement for a valid and enforceable contract was satisfied. * * *

Finally, Charlie's contends the Sedmaks failed to show they were entitled to specific performance of the contract. We disagree. Although it has been stated that the determination whether to order specific performance lies within the discretion of the trial court, [citation], this discretion is, in fact, quite narrow. When the relevant equitable principles have been met and the contract is fair and plain, "specific performance goes as a matter of right." [Citation.] Here, the trial court ordered specific performance because it concluded the Sedmaks "have no adequate remedy at law for the reason that they cannot go upon the open market and purchase an automobile of this kind with the same mileage, condition, ownership and appearance as the automobile involved in this case, except, if at all, with considerable expense, trouble, loss, great delay and inconvenience." Contrary to defendant's complaint, this is a correct expression of the relevant law and it is supported by the evidence.

Under the Code, the court may decree specific performance as a buyer's remedy for breach of contract to sell goods "where the goods are unique or in other proper circumstances." § 400.2–716(1) RSMo 1978. The general term "in other proper circumstances" expresses the drafters' intent to "further a more liberal attitude than some courts have shown in connection with the specific performance of contracts of sale." § 400.2–716, U.C.C., Comment 1. This Comment was not directed to the courts of this state, for long before the Code, we, in Missouri, took a practical approach in determining whether specific performance would lie for the breach of contract for the sale of goods and did not limit this relief only to the sale of "unique" goods. *Boeving v. Vandover,* 240 Mo.App. 117, 218 S.W.2d 175 (1949). In *Boeving,* plaintiff contracted to buy a car from defendant. When the car arrived, defendant refused to sell. The car was not unique in the traditional legal sense but, at that time, all cars were difficult to obtain because of war-time shortages. The court held specific performance was the proper remedy for plaintiff because a new car "could not be obtained elsewhere except at considerable expense, trouble or loss, which cannot be estimated in advance and under such circumstances [plaintiff] did not have an adequate remedy at law." Thus, *Boeving,* presaged the broad and liberalized language of § 400.2–716(1) and exemplifies one of the "other proper circumstances" contemplated by this subsection for ordering specific performance. § 400.2–716, Missouri Code Comment 1. The present facts track those in *Boeving.*

The Pace Car, like the car in *Boeving,* was not unique in the traditional legal sense. It was not an heirloom or, arguably, not one of a kind. However, its "mileage, condition, ownership and appearance" did make it difficult, if not impossible, to obtain its replication without considerable expense, delay and inconvenience. Admittedly, 6,000 Pace Cars were produced by Chevrolet. However, as the record reflects, this is limited production. In addition, only one of these cars was available to each dealer, and only a limited number of these were equipped with the specific options ordered by plaintiffs. Charlie's had not received a car like the Pace Car in the previous two years. The sticker price for the car was $14,284.21. Yet Charlie's received offers from individuals in Hawaii and Florida to buy the Pace Car for $24,000.00 and $28,000.00 respectively. As sensibly inferred by the trial court, the location and size of these offers demonstrated this limited edition was in short supply and great demand. We agree, with the trial court. This case was a "proper circumstance" for ordering specific performance.

Judgment affirmed.

PROBLEM: THE JILTED BUYER

Able owns Puppy Acres, a championship dog breeding farm. Able entered into a written requirements contract for a five year term with Chowhound, Inc. ("CI"), manufacturer of a dog food called "Puppy Lite," which provided that CI would deliver between 50 and 100 cartons of Puppy Lite at $1.00 each, every month to Able. The contract contained the following liquidated damages clause:

> "In the event that either party materially breaches this contract, the breaching party shall pay the non-breaching party the sum of $2,500."

The contract further provided that neither party could cancel the contract without obtaining the written consent of the other party.

Puppy Lite is a specially blended dog food which helps dogs have soft and shiny coats, a particularly important factor in dog show judging. A prominent trade journal called Puppy Lite "a unique blend, unmatched in the industry."

The owner of Pups Ltd., and a competitor of Able, induced CI to break the contract with Able, without obtaining the necessary consent, and to begin supplying Pups Ltd. with Puppy Lite.

Able learned of the breach of contract by CI on February 1st. He tried to negotiate with CI to continue supplying him but his efforts were unsuccessful, culminating in a final cancellation letter from CI dated March 10th. During the months of February and March the cost to obtain the closest substitute dog food, Brand X, in the market was $1.05 per carton. However, due to seasonal demand forces, by the time that Able purchased Brand X in April, the cost had risen to $1.20 per carton. Because Brand X was manufactured in Taiwan, Able also had to pay $500 in transportation and insurance costs for each shipment.

Able seeks specific performance of the contract by CI. Should it be granted?

WEATHERSBY v. GORE

556 F.2d 1247 (5th Cir.1977).

CLARK, CIRCUIT JUDGE:

This Mississippi-based diversity action was brought by Frank Weathersby, a Memphis, Tennessee cotton buyer doing business as Weathersby Cotton Company, against Y.B. Gore, a Webster County, Mississippi cotton farmer. Weathersby contended he had a valid contract with defendant Gore which obliged Gore to sell the cotton produced by him on 500 acres of land during the 1973 crop year. Two months after the contract was entered and many months before the cotton was to be picked, Gore gave notice that he was cancelling the contract and indicated his intention of selling his cotton elsewhere. After a jury verdict favoring Weathersby, the district court ordered specific performance of the contract. We reverse and remand.

* * * The genesis of this litigation is to be found in the volatility of the cotton futures market during 1972 and 1973. In 1972 Gore entered into a forward contract for the sale of his cotton, but his experience was not a happy one. The price at the time the cotton was picked was lower than that provided in the contract, and the buyer refused to purchase the cotton. Gore chose to sell at the lower price rather than to bring suit.

* * * As a consequence of his 1972 experience, Gore insisted that any future purchaser provide a performance bond ensuring Gore against loss in the event of a similar breach. The contract in suit was negotiated at a price of 30 cents per pound. Throughout the subsequent months the price rose, until at the time performance was due the price had soared to 80 cents per pound.

* * *

Throughout the period following May 3, and before commencement of suit on September 28, 1973, no attempt was made by Weathersby, Starke Taylor, or Fieldcrest to effect cover. It was stipulated that any party could have purchased other cotton to cover the contract expectancy on the open market.

* * * The parties are in considerable disagreement over the meaning of Miss.Code Ann. § 75-2-716(1) (1973): "Specific performance may be decreed where the goods are unique or in other proper circumstances." Various authorities have been cited to the court indicating that crop contracts historically have been treated as susceptible to specific performance treatment more readily than other types of contracts. [Citations.] However, cotton contracts have not been given such treatment in Mississippi when other cotton was readily available on the open market. In Austin v. Montgomery, 336 So.2d 745 (Miss.1976), the Mississippi Supreme Court permitted without discussion the specific performance of a cotton output contract that had been entered in March

1973 and breached by the farmer-seller in July. The plaintiff buyer contended that it was impossible to obtain cotton elsewhere when notice was given in July that the farmer would refuse to deliver at harvest. The farmer did not attempt to refute this contention. Consequently the seller would have had to default on his contract to deliver the cotton to a textile mill. Since the parties here are in agreement that other cotton was available when the notice of cancellation was sent in May by Gore, the *Austin* decision is not in point.

Far predating Mississippi's adoption of the Uniform Commercial Code, but indicating the reasons why specific performance is not suitable here, is Scott v. Billgerry, 40 Miss. 119 (1866). Billgerry was the purchaser of seventy-five bales of cotton from Scott. The purchase price of $3900 was paid at the time the contract was entered. Upon Scott's subsequent refusal to deliver, Billgerry sought specific performance. Though the court was not referring to an output contract but rather to the simple purchase of cotton bales, the language is equally applicable here:

> It is altogether immaterial whether there was a sale of certain specific bales of cotton, or an agreement to sell and deliver a certain number of bales out of a particular lot, or a general agreement to sell and deliver a certain number of bales, without any designation of the specific bales, or of the particular lot out of which they are to come. All such cases depend upon the same general principle. The rule is, not to entertain jurisdiction in equity for a specific performance of agreements respecting goods, chattels, stock, choses in action, and other things of a personal nature, unless, under the particular circumstances of the case, there can be no adequate compensation in damages at law.

Id. at 140.

The adoption of the Uniform Commercial Code by Mississippi does not suggest the considerations expressed in *Scott v. Billgerry* are now to be rejected. Other than to indicate that the Code is intended to "further a more liberal attitude than some courts have shown in connection with the specific performance of contracts of sale," the comments accompanying UCC § 2–716 are of little guidance. The comments also state that "[o]utput and requirements contracts involving a particularly or peculiarly available source of market present today the typical commercial specific performance situation," but the interpretation of this language appears to range from suggesting all output contracts should be specifically enforceable to a mere observation that output contracts form a suitable factual background in most cases in which specific performance may be sought.

The general rule applicable when specific performance is requested has been stated in Roberts v. Spence, 209 So.2d 623, 626 (Miss.1968): "specific performance of a contract will not be awarded where damages may be recovered and the remedy in a court of law is adequate to compensate the injured party." Considering the reluctance expressed in

Roberts to authorization of the specific performance remedy we hold that the Mississippi Supreme Court would apply a restrictive reading of § 75–2–716. A similar interpretation of the Code provision was adopted by the Georgia Supreme Court in Duval & Co. v. Malcom, 233 Ga. 784, 214 S.E.2d 356 (1975). There a buyer attempted to get specific performance of a cotton output contract entered into with a cotton farmer. Specific performance was rejected with the statement damages would be sufficient unless cotton could not be obtained in the open market. Thus the Georgia court, as did the Mississippi Supreme Court in *Austin,* would have permitted specific performance if the buyer could not otherwise obtain the needed cotton. Absent this fact, specific performance was not an available remedy. The Georgia court gave considerable attention to the Code language that specific performance should be permitted when goods are unique and "in other proper circumstances." The vague language was held not to authorize wholesale granting of the remedy when output contracts were involved. The remedy of damages—the difference between the market price at the time of the breach and the contract price—adequately compensated the buyer for his inability to procure the cotton from the farmer with whom he had contracted. [Citation.] Likewise Weathersby was adequately protected from any damages occasioned by Gore's breach of the contract, if any occurred. He could have acquired additional cotton on the open market when Gore informed him he would no longer perform under the contract. He did not do so and thus, if entitled to damages at all, must settle for the difference between the contract and the market price at the time Gore cancelled. *See* Miss.Code Ann. § 75–2–712 (1973).

* * * Finally, specific performance was not an appropriate remedy in the present case. If Weathersby is successful in proving that Gore improperly cancelled the contract, he is limited to recovery of damages.

Reversed and Remanded.

———

1. The court in *Sedmak, supra,* focused on the uniqueness of the limited edition Corvette automobile in granting specific performance. A similar analysis and result obtained in Fast v. Southern Offshore Yachts, 587 F.Supp. 1354 (D.Conn.1984) and Gay v. Seafarer Fiberglass Yachts, Inc., 1974 WL 21674, 14 U.C.C. 1335 (N.Y.Sup.1974) (customized yachts); Schweber v. Rallye Motors, Inc., 1973 WL 21434, 12 U.C.C. 1154 (N.Y.Sup.1973) (Rolls Royce Corniche convertible); Colorado–Ute Electric Assoc., Inc. v. Envirotech Corp., 524 F.Supp. 1152 (D.Colo.1981) (electrostatic precipitator air pollution control equipment). But compare the following cases in which the subject goods were not considered unique and specific performance was denied: Pierce–Odom, Inc. v. Evenson, 5 Ark.App. 67, 632 S.W.2d 247 (1982) (mobile home); Hilmor Sales Co. v. Helen Neushaefer Division of Supronics Corp., 1969 WL 11054, 6 U.C.C. 325 (N.Y.Sup.1969) (lipsticks and nail polish containers);

Scholl v. Hartzell, 20 Pa.D. & C.3d 304 (Pa.Com.Pl.1981) (1962 Chevrolet Corvette).

2. The court in *Weathersby* denied specific performance because the buyer failed to show the inadequacy of its remedy at law for damages, even though the cotton market was extremely volatile. Similarly, in Duval & Co. v. Malcom, 233 Ga. 784, 214 S.E.2d 356 (1975), and Tower City Grain Co. v. Richman, 232 N.W.2d 61 (N.D.1975), the courts denied specific performance after finding, as a threshold matter, that damages would adequately compensate the aggrieved buyers in an output contract to supply cotton. On the other hand, in R. L. Kimsey Cotton Co. v. Ferguson, 233 Ga. 962, 214 S.E.2d 360 (1975), the Georgia Supreme Court reached a different result than in *Duval* by granting specific performance of a similar cotton output contract because the parties had stipulated that the cotton involved was unique.

3. Section 2–716(1) does not require a finding that available legal remedies are inadequate, but attempts to provide an expanded test for specific performance when the goods are "unique or in other proper circumstances." It is uncertain whether these courts have considered inadequacy of legal remedies as an additional test for entitlement to specific performance or whether it is just another factor to be weighed in the court's equitable discretion. Since the U.C.C. policy was to expand the availability of the specific performance remedy by its "more liberal attitude," the better view is that inadequacy of legal remedies does not present an independent requirement beyond the § 2–716(1) statutory language. A balanced approach is necessary, however, as demonstrated by the *Weathersby* court stating that specific performance would not automatically issue simply because it involved an output contract.

KAISER TRADING CO. v. ASSOCIATED METALS & MINERALS CORP.

321 F.Supp. 923 (N.D.Cal.1970).

LEVIN, DISTRICT JUDGE.

This action was commenced in the Superior Court in Alameda County, California, by the Kaiser Aluminum & Chemical Corporation and its wholly owned subsidiary, The Kaiser Trading Company [hereinafter referred to collectively as "Kaiser"], against the Associated Metal & Minerals Corporation [hereinafter referred to as "Associated"] for breach of contract. Plaintiffs seek a preliminary injunction, specific performance, and money damages. * * * The relevant facts are as follows:

The Kaiser Trading Company is in the business of buying and selling commodities throughout the world. Kaiser Aluminum & Chemical Corporation is a leading manufacturer of aluminum, with plants throughout the United States; through its associates and subsidiaries, it also has interests in aluminum throughout the world. Defendant Associated is in the business of buying and selling metals, minerals, chemicals, and related commodities. One such commodity, which is the subject matter of the contract giving rise to this action, is cryolite, an indispensable chemical compound used in the production of aluminum.[2]

In 1969, Kaiser and Associated entered into an agreement for the sale by Associated to Kaiser of 4,000 metric tons of cryolite produced in Italy by Industrie Chimiche Ing. Bonelli [hereinafter referred to as "ICIB"], from whom Associated has been purchasing cryolite for resale since 1951. This contract was similar to ones that had been entered into annually between Kaiser and Associated since 1964, all of which involved cryolite produced by ICIB. * * * To date, only the first 500 tons have been delivered.

In September, 1970, Associated informed Kaiser that it no longer considered itself obligated under the contract and that it did not intend to make any more deliveries of cryolite. Associated's alleged justification for repudiating the contract was that Kaiser had been surreptitiously negotiating with ICIB during 1969 and 1970 and had concluded a contract with them under which, commencing in 1971, ICIB would supply cryolite directly to Kaiser, thus eliminating Associated's future role as a middleman between Kaiser and ICIB. Associated alleges that the agreement between Kaiser and ICIB violated Associated's agreement with ICIB making Associated the exclusive purchaser of cryolite from ICIB for Kaiser. Associated claims that because Kaiser's dealings with ICIB amounted to tortious interference with Associated's contractual rights and were anticompetitive in effect, it was no longer obligated under its contract with Kaiser to deliver cryolite.

* * *

Specific performance as a buyer's remedy for breach of a contract to sell goods "may be decreed where the goods are unique or in other proper circumstances." Cal.Commercial Code § 2716(1). The enactment of this statutory provision broadened the availability of specific performance from those situations involving "other proper circumstances." Compare Cal.Commercial Code § 2716(1) with Cal.Civil Code § 1788 (repealed Sales Act provision). Moreover, the comments to section 2716 state:

> Specific performance is no longer limited to goods which are already specific or ascertained at the time of contracting. The test of uniqueness under this section must be made in terms of the total situation which characterizes the contract. Output and requirements contracts involving a particular or peculiarly available source or market present today the typical commercial specific performance situation, * * *. However, uniqueness is not the sole basis of the

2. Cryolite is a mineral substance used in the manufacture of primary aluminum. It is found naturally only in one ore body located in Greenland. This source, however, has been effectively exhausted, and consumers of cryolite must rely upon a synthetically produced substitute, which is manufactured in various places throughout the world. In addition to synthetic cryolite, a certain amount of cryolite can be reclaimed from the aluminum manufacturing process itself and then reused.

remedy under this section for the relief may also be granted "in other proper circumstances" and *inability to cover is strong evidence of "other proper circumstances."*

Although no California case has held explicitly that an inability to cover is sufficient justification for decreeing specific performance, the state supreme court in *Bomberger v. McKelvey,* 35 Cal.2d 607, 616, 220 P.2d 729, 734 (1950), did state that scarcity of goods constituting the subject matter of the breached contract is a very significant factor in determining whether to order specific performance. The court in *Bomberger* also noted the " 'growing tendency' to allow specific performance where damages are not the equivalent of the performance."

Courts in other jurisdictions have ruled that specific performance will be decreed when the goods contracted for cannot be purchased on the open market or otherwise covered. [Citations.]

Finally, many cases have noted the trend toward relaxing the requirements for specific performance, particularly those decided since adoption of the Uniform Sales Act and its even more liberal successor, the Uniform Commercial Code. [Citations.]

Despite the absence of California decisions interpreting the "other proper circumstances" phrase of Cal.Commercial Code § 2716(1), the Code comments, in conjunction with prior case law, decisions in other jurisdictions, and the general trend toward a more liberalized availability of specific performance, persuade this court that the remedy should be available when goods cannot be covered or replaced. * * *

[Preliminary injunction granted.]

ACE EQUIPMENT CO., INC. v. AQUA CHEM., INC.

20 U.C.C.Rep.Serv. 392, 73 Pa.D. & C.2d 300 (1975).

GATES, JUSTICE.

This matter comes before the court on defendant's preliminary objections to plaintiff's complaint in equity. The preliminary objections complain that plaintiff has an adequate remedy at law for damages and, in addition, demurs to the complaint for substantially the same reason.

It is defendant's contention that plaintiff has not stated a case for equitable relief in the nature of specific performance of a contract for the sale, inter alia, of a used 6000 KVA General Electric Transformer. Defendant contends that plaintiff has a complete and adequate remedy at law for money damages.

In this posture of the record, the following facts are deemed to be admitted. On or about March 30, 1973, plaintiff's written offer to purchase a used 6000 KVA General Electric Transformer was accepted in writing by defendant for the price of $1,800. * * *

However, plaintiff tells us that on April 12, 1973, the transformer was loaded on board a truck supplied by plaintiff, intending to deliver it to one Frank Lunney with whom plaintiff had an agreement to sell it for the price of $7,500. But plaintiff says that defendant wrongfully, and without prior notice to plaintiff, refused to allow the truck to leave and that defendant has retained possession of the transformer since that time.

Plaintiff further alleges that defendant was made aware of the transaction between plaintiff and Lunney and that defendant is aware that plaintiff is still obligated to perform its contract to Lunney and has not only lost the benefit of the sale, but is subject to consequential damages as a result of the failure to perform.

We agree with defendant that ordinarily a bill for specific performance for the sale of personalty will not be entertained by a court of equity. However, the Uniform Commercial code provides, in pertinent part, as follows:

> "(1) Specific performance may be decreed where the goods are unique or in other proper circumstances." * * *

True it is that, as between the parties, there would be an adequate remedy at law and the measure of damages fixed by the term of the agreement and the content of the complaint. However, in light of the fact that plaintiff has entered into an agreement to sell the transformer to a third party and defendant is aware of that fact, we have a different situation than is ordinarily the case. Here, we are dealing with a huge piece of used equipment. It was purchased at a relatively low price when compared to the resale price plaintiff has contracted to sell it to Lunney. This is unlike the ordinary purchase of goods and merchandise for resale. It is unlikely that there is a substantially identical piece of used equipment which plaintiff could locate in order to perform its contract with a third party.

It is defendant's breach which renders plaintiff unable to perform its contract to the third party. This failure of performance for an item of service equipment may render plaintiff liable to damages, in addition to those for breach of contract, of a consequential nature for failing to perform. [Citation.] The nature of these damages is speculative and conceivably could be extensive. It is this state of affairs which, in our judgment, is the " ... other proper circumstances" contemplated by the Uniform Commercial Code. These facts render a legal remedy inadequate.

Thus, we conclude that plaintiff has stated a case for specific performance and we shall dismiss the preliminary objections.

––––––––––

1. A relative paucity of cases have directly considered the "other proper circumstances" test for specific performance in § 2–716(1). The few courts which have applied the alternate test have been strongly influenced by comment 2 to § 2–716 and have focused on the buyer's inability to cover. Thus, in *Kaiser Trading, supra*, the California court

was persuaded that because the subject matter of the contract was a scarce mineral (cryolite), the buyer could not readily cover and needed specific performance to protect its expectation interest. Similarly, in Eastern Air Lines, Inc. v. Gulf Oil Corp., 415 F.Supp. 429 (S.D.Fla.1975), the court specifically enforced a contract for supplying aviation fuel to an airline company during the 1973 Arab oil embargo. *See also* Copylease Corp. of America v. Memorex Corp., 408 F.Supp. 758 (S.D.N.Y.1976) (specific performance of a contract to supply a certain brand of toner and developer for use in copy machines).

2. In the principal case the court interprets the "other proper circumstances" test in § 2–716 to encompass a contract to buy used equipment at a bargain price with a contract to resell at a higher price to a third party. The court is persuaded by the plaintiff's assertion that, absent equitable relief, plaintiff will incur liability for consequential damages which may be "speculative and conceivably could be extensive." Difficulties in measurement, though, should not necessarily mean that damages would be an inadequate remedy. This result may represent the outer limits of the Code's "more liberal attitude" with respect to granting specific performance.

3. What if the breaching seller in *Ace Equipment* had resold to another party for a still higher price? Proponents of the efficient contract breach theory might suggest that this hypothetical situation is economically sound to all concerned. First, the aggrieved buyer may owe damages on it's third party contract but will be compensated fully by the breaching seller. The seller, although not in a sympathetic role, pays the first buyer his damages but offsets that loss by the profits received on the resale. The ultimate purchaser, willing to pay the highest price for the goods, receives what it bargained for. The view opposing the efficient breach approach is that certainty and confidence in contractual relations is undermined by shifting goods to the highest bidder. Moreover, the transaction costs are difficult to ascertain and are often ignored or arguably underestimated by proponents of efficiency theory. Finally, the moralist view considers that the nonbreaching buyer is not above reproach as he stands to make a tidy profit on an immediate resale.

Which vision of contract law is most persuasive in this context? Are there alternative approaches?

Chapter 5

EQUITABLE DEFENSES

Equitable defenses strongly reflect the origin of equity as the Chancellor's law of conscience. The Chancellor would not give relief to a suitor whose behavior concerning the claims was "tainted" in some respect. The Chancellor would deny equitable relief if the claimant had "unclean hands" or had engaged in unconscionable conduct in securing the right being asserted, or if the defendant had been prejudiced by prior inconsistent conduct or by undue delay by the suitor in pursuing the claim. Even in a case where the defendant's behavior was much worse by comparison, the Chancellor was unsupportive of rights tainted by improper conduct and the plaintiff would be sent away from equity to seek redress from a court of law. Equity would not sully itself by lending aid to a someone who had a questionable moral posture with regard to the claim.

Modern equity preserves the equitable defenses even in the merged system of law and equity. Moreover, the defenses still have a moralistic foundation; a court will not grant equitable relief if the plaintiff has behaved in a way prejudicial to the defendant or offensive to public policy. There is no entitlement to equitable relief in modern law as in the past, and the plaintiff's conduct in the case still affects the court's decision. Equity is guided by principled discretion but its orders still bear the name "extraordinary relief." Whenever the plaintiff seeks equitable remedies, the court may apply the doctrines of laches, estoppel, unconscionability, or unclean hands.

A. LACHES AND ESTOPPEL

Section Coverage:

The equitable defense of laches bars a plaintiff who has not acted promptly in bringing the action. It is reflected in the maxim: "Equity aids the vigilant, not those who slumber on their rights." The essence of the defense is not just delay for a particular length of time like the statute of limitations. Rather, the defense requires proof that the delay was both unreasonable and prejudicial to the defendant.

Even if an applicable statute of limitations has not yet run, the court may deny equitable relief if there was undue delay in filing suit. The plaintiff may still seek legal remedies, however, if there is no other defense to a valid claim. Thus, a plaintiff who is denied specific performance because of laches may still seek contract damages.

The defense of estoppel similarly involves prejudice to the defendant. Whereas laches concerns delay, estoppel involves actions inconsistent with the rights the plaintiff now asserts. The classic example is that a person cannot first stand outside and watch a neighbor build a fence, and then go to equity and demand its removal because the fence is over the property line.

Particular attention should be paid to the nature of laches and estoppel when the government is one of the parties. Even when the government has waived sovereign immunity it is not completely equivalent to a private party. As a defendant, the government more easily shows prejudice to itself when it asserts equitable defenses. As a plaintiff, the sovereign historically could not be estopped; modern cases have made only some modifications to this principle.

Model Case:

A smooth-talking and attractive young stockbroker befriended an elderly person who had little business experience. This elderly client agreed to invest in highly speculative commodities and stocks. The broker and client were in daily personal contact to discuss investments. The client agreed to the transactions recommended by the broker and thus traded very frequently. The heavy trading generated high commissions for the broker. These practices continued for years until a series of bad trades left the client's account depleted. In the end there was barely enough money for this elderly person to live comfortably.

The investor's complaint alleges that the broker took improper advantage of the client's naivete and created a speculative account out of a previously blue-chip portfolio. The broker then allegedly "churned" the speculative account with excessive trades for the purpose of generating high commissions. The broker's defense is that the client knew and approved of every aspect of the account management. Moreover, the broker argues, even if the original conversion of the portfolio from blue-chip to speculative investments was improper, the client has waited for too many years before making this protest.

The defenses of laches and estoppel will turn on a number of factual assessments. Did the plaintiff understand the true nature of the account and approve of the change? Most people in later life do not want to do heavy trading with a speculative portfolio, but some people want to take risks for big gains or big losses at any age. Was this plaintiff such a person? Did the plaintiff's acts of apparent approval prejudice the defendant's position, or was the broker exploiting the plaintiff's lack of business experience to achieve uninformed approvals? Did the plaintiff act promptly to sue as soon as the wrong was discovered, or only when the gamble on big investments was lost?

If the plaintiff did not pursue the claim soon after discovering the broker's misconduct, and if the court finds that the delay prejudiced the defendant, the claim will be barred by laches. If the plaintiff's approvals actually misled the broker into justifiable reliance upon them with resulting detriment to the broker's position, estoppel will bar the claim.

CORNETTA v. UNITED STATES

851 F.2d 1372 (Fed.Cir.1988).

MAYER, CIRCUIT JUDGE.

This is a rehearing in banc of an appeal from the United States District Court for the Western District of Louisiana granting the government's motion for summary judgment and dismissing, because of laches, Ronald J. Cornetta's claim for reinstatement and back pay stemming from his allegedly unlawful discharge from the United States Marine Corps. We * * * reverse the judgment of the district court.

The district court granted summary judgment on the allegations set out in the complaint, so the facts are not now in dispute. After graduation from the United States Naval Academy, Cornetta was commissioned a second lieutenant in the United States Marine Corps. In his early assignments, he was described by his rating officers as an officer with outstanding growth potential, and in September 1968 he was promoted to the rank of first lieutenant. In 1970, he volunteered for duty in the Republic of Vietnam where he flew combat support missions as a helicopter copilot. On four occasions, he participated in the rescue of wounded and stranded soldiers under hazardous flight conditions and hostile fire for which he was decorated in recognition of his superior airmanship and devotion to duty.

Cornetta was promoted to captain shortly after he returned from Vietnam. For the next six years, his superiors consistently reported that he was qualified for promotion and rated him "excellent," "excellent-to-outstanding," or "outstanding" in terms of his growth potential and overall value to the Marine Corps. He was awarded the Navy Achievement Medal for 1974, and in 1975 he was named "Training Air Wing Helicopter Instructor of the Year."

In 1977, Cornetta was assigned to a logistic support unit near San Francisco. His rating officer in this assignment gave him an unfavorable Officer Fitness Report (OFR) covering less than a two-month period, which recognized his limited background and experience in logistics and that this was the primary reason for the low rating. The report included the remark that "within the context of the assignment to the Logistic Support Unit" he was not qualified for promotion. According to Cornetta, "This unfavorable report was prepared, processed and incorporated into [his] naval records in a manner that violated substantive and procedural regulations governing Marine Corps Officer Fitness Reports. . . ."

At his next assignment, Cornetta's rating officer reported that he was an officer of "excellent" value to the Marine Corps and judged him to be qualified for promotion. Shortly thereafter, however, he was passed over for promotion to major. The 1977 San Francisco OFR was part of the file the selection board considered in passing him over.

Cornetta appealed to the Board for the Correction of Naval Records for removal of the 1977 OFR and reversal of the nonselection for promotion. *See* 10 U.S.C. § 1552. The board found that the presence of the 1977 OFR constituted an injustice and that its inclusion in his record "may have substantially prejudiced his promotional opportunity." In accordance with the board's recommendation, the Secretary of the Navy ordered its removal. Instead of setting Cornetta's nonselection for promotion aside, the Secretary ordered that his record be presented to the next selection board as if he were an officer in the promotion zone for the first time. If the second selection board did not select him for promotion, however, his first passover would be counted for purposes of mandatory separation from the service. *See* 10 U.S.C. §§ 627, 632.

Soon thereafter, Cornetta was passed over for promotion again and was considered to have been twice passed over. Accordingly, on May 31, 1979, he was honorably discharged. Following his separation from the Marine Corps, he served three years on active duty as a lieutenant j.g. in the United States Coast Guard Reserve.

On May 20, 1986, Cornetta filed this suit in the district court alleging that his discharge from the Marine Corps was unlawful. * * *

The district court granted the government's motion for summary judgment and dismissed the case. It concluded that Cornetta's delay of nearly seven years from the date of his discharge was unreasonable, and that the government had been prejudiced by the delay. The conclusion of prejudice was not bottomed on defense prejudice, such as loss of records or fading memories, but on the potential recovery of $10,000 in back pay. * * *

The doctrine of laches emerged in an era when equity courts were not bound by statutes of limitations. 2 J. Pomeroy, Equity Jurisprudence §§ 418–19 (5th ed. 1941). It was premised on the maxim *vigilantibus non dormientibus aequitas subvenit,* equity aids the vigilant, not those who slumber on their rights.

The doctrine of laches is based upon grounds of public policy, which require for the peace of society the discouragement of stale demands. And where the difficulty of doing entire justice by reason of the death of the principal witness or witnesses, or from the original transactions having become obscured by time, is attributable to gross negligence or deliberate delay, a court of equity will not aid a party whose application is thus destitute of conscience, good faith and reasonable diligence.

[Citations.]

Because laches is an equitable defense, it has traditionally been unavailable in actions at law brought within the applicable statute of limitations. [Citation.] Based on the twin goals of limiting monetary consequences to the government and compelling the speedy resolutions of disputes, however, it has been applied to claims for back pay by government personnel brought even before the limitations period has run, notwithstanding that these are actions at law, not equity. [Citation.]

* * *

We begin with the first requirement of the laches defense: delay by the claimant. Of course, the mere fact that time has elapsed from the date a cause of action first accrued is not sufficient to bar suit; the delay must be unreasonable and unexcused. [Citation.] Laches must be applied "apart [from] and irrespective of" the statute of limitations. [Citations.] So, for example, while the Soldiers' and Sailors' Civil Relief Act, 50 U.S.C.App. § 525, tolls the running of the limitations period it does not suspend time to be considered in the laches calculation. [Citation.] Here, Cornetta's post-discharge service in the Coast Guard stopped the running of the six-year statute of limitations, but it did not affect the period to be considered in determining whether laches affects his claim.

Cornetta waited nearly seven years from the time he was separated from the Marine Corps to file suit. He says his unanswered discovery requests go to the justification for the delay, so, absent a record, we cannot say now if the district court erred in its summary conclusion that the delay was unreasonable. This is open for consideration on remand.

"Of course, delay alone does not constitute laches." [Citations.] *Gardner v. Panama R.R. Co.,* 342 U.S. 29, 31, 72 S.Ct. 12, 13, 96 L.Ed. 31 (1951) ("where no prejudice to the defendant has ensued from the mere passage of time, there should be no bar to relief"). Even lengthy delay does not eliminate the prejudice prong of the laches test. [Citation.]

There are two types of prejudice that may stem from delay in filing suit. First, the government may be unable to mount a defense. [Citation.] "Defense prejudice" may include loss of records, destruction of evidence, fading memories, or unavailability of witness. This is not an issue here in view of the government's concession [that the claim was based on the face of the administrative record]. The second type, economic prejudice, centers on consequences, primarily monetary, to the government should the claimant prevail. * * *

Equating back pay with prejudice makes a subject of a plaintiff's claim, his request for monetary relief, the focus of the prejudice inquiry. The greater the damages sustained, the less likely the ability to be heard. Accordingly, he is put in the unseemly position of "minimizing" his injury just to get his case before the court. Like a sailor caught between Scylla and Charybdis, a discharged officer is forced to choose between substantially limiting his potential recovery or giving up the right to have his claim heard at all. * * *

Using this as a measure of prejudice is also a waste of judicial resources. Instead of devoting time to the merits of a claim, courts must spend substantial time determining the salary, allowances and other benefits to which a claimant would be entitled should he prevail. * * *

It is more in keeping with the judicial role to reach the merits and give the litigant his day in court than to first spend untold hours deciding how much he might recover should he prevail. [Citation.] We therefore hold that potential receipt of back pay alone is insufficient to show prejudice to the government. * * *

We are not sanguine about the continued vitality of the laches defense in these military cases, particularly within the six years from the accrual of a cause of action normally allowed by the statute of limitations. But we hesitate to be more comprehensive in this case because the record is insubstantial in significant aspects. Specifically, as observed above, this case does not involve defense prejudice, so we cannot confidently decide whether or to what extent the government's handicap in defending a suit because of a claimant's delay is sufficient to bar suit. Similarly, there is no record of nonmonetary, perhaps reliance based, prejudice which might be factored into the laches calculus. And, indeed, this case is not one that was brought within the normal six-year period. All of this is open for consideration on an appropriate record. * * *

Reversed and Remanded.

––––––––

1. The Supreme Court articulated the fundamental premise of laches one hundred years ago:

> The doctrine of laches is based upon grounds of public policy, which requires for the peace of society the discouragement of stale demands. And where the difficulty of doing entire justice by reason of the death of the principal witness or witnesses, or from the original transactions having become obscured by time, is attributable to gross negligence or deliberate delay, a court of equity will not aid a party whose application is thus destitute of conscience, good faith and reasonable diligence.

Mackall v. Casilear, 137 U.S. 556, 566, 11 S.Ct. 178, 181, 34 L.Ed. 776 (1890). These principles guide modern laches law with equal force.

2. Under the Federal Rules of Civil Procedure § 8(c), laches is an affirmative defense; the burden of proving it belongs to the defendant. There are no mechanical rules for proof of unreasonable delay and prejudice to the defendant. It is an equitable doctrine that depends upon the facts of each case, unlike the statute of limitations which is its legal equivalent. Laches "differs from the statute of limitations in that it offers the courts more flexibility, eschewing mechanical rules." Waddell v. Small Tube Products, Inc., 799 F.2d 69, 79 (3d Cir.1986). See also Bott v. Four Star Corp., 807 F.2d 1567 (Fed.Cir.1986).

3. The principal case is unusual in its outright rejection of back pay potential as an element of prejudice to the defendant. Although many cases have considered the potential amount of the claim as relevant to laches, judges are not quick to find significant monetary prejudice. See Yerxa v. United States, 11 Cl.Ct. 110 (1986), aff'd. mem.

824 F.2d 978 (Fed.Cir.1987) ($27,000 potential liability not prejudicial); Park v. United States, 10 Cl.Ct. 790 (1986) ($19,000 potential liability not prejudicial). Do plaintiffs nonetheless have a strong incentive to minimize monetary claims? What equitable relief is likely to be most important to Cornetta?

4. Consider noneconomic prejudice that can result from the passage of time in a case where an employee seeks reinstatement. A discharged employee is normally replaced. Would reinstatement be unduly disruptive of the personnel system? Under what circumstances would such disruption be unduly burdensome? If the plaintiff in *Cornetta* were reinstated as a military officer, how detrimental would it be to the military personnel management system to assign him duties somewhere? To assign him exactly his former duties?

PROBLEM: THE INNOCENT INFRINGER

Poymer, Inc. is a small company whose major asset is a patent on a special catalyst useful in certain types of manufacturing. Poymer has been marketing its patented catalyst to several manufacturers. Several other companies, however, have devised their own similar types of catalysts since the Poymer patent. Poymer claims that the similar catalysts are an infringement of its patent, but these companies maintain that they use additional components in the catalysts to produce a different product, and therefore there is no patent infringement.

Five years ago Poymer sued one of these companies for infringement. At the time the suit was initiated Poymer notified every company known to be using a similar catalyst about this suit. No other company was sued, however, until the first suit was successfully completed. During this five year interim there was no further communication between Poymer and any other alleged infringer. After the success of the first suit, Poymer sued the other companies.

Should a court sitting in equity refuse to grant Poymer injunctive relief against these other companies on the grounds that too many years have passed before filing suit? Should the five year delay be excused by the pending relevant litigation against a different company? What if one of these new defendants is a company that assumed that Poymer had abandoned the claim of infringement because there had been no further communication for five years?

GRUCA v. UNITED STATES STEEL CORPORATION

495 F.2d 1252 (3d Cir.1974).

ALDISERT, CIRCUIT JUDGE. * * *

[The Military Selective Service Act provides that a person who leaves private employment for military service shall be entitled to return to the same position after service. The employer's defenses of impossibility or change of position were not relevant in the case of Mr. Gruca who returned to his employer, U.S. Steel, after his military service from 1960 to 1962. He returned to his position as a general laborer. The principal question raised on appeal concerns whether Mr. Gruca's claims for legal and equitable relief were barred by laches or by the Pennsylvania six year statute of limitations.]

From the position of general laborer a U.S. Steel employee has the choice of following several promotional ladders. One of these ladders is Seniority Unit No. 8—Cranes. To reach the rung of craneman a general laborer must first obtain Crane Extra Board Status. This is achieved by receiving special training in crane operation and passing a test. Once an employee obtains Crane Extra Board Status he is assigned a Crane Extra Board Date, which is essentially a seniority date. Therefore, employees on Crane Extra Board climb to the position of Stockyard Crane Operator, if they bid for the opening, on the basis of the earliest Crane Extra Board Date and if the physical fitness factor is relatively equal.

While Gruca was on active duty, U.S. Steel had, from time to time, advertised openings for crane operators. Four employees responded, each having [initial employment dates] later than plaintiff's. They completed their training, passed the test and were assigned to the Crane Extra Board. Therefore, because of plaintiff's absence from his civilian occupation due to military obligations, employees junior to him had the chance to, and did, hold positions superior to him.

Shortly after his reemployment, plaintiff learned of his plight and took the matter up with his union grievance committeeman. * * * [P]laintiff was told that he "was only guaranteed that he would get his old job back." Because plaintiff thought "it would be useless to try to grieve this matter" and "it would do no good" he neither submitted a grievance nor complained to management.

* * *

Plaintiff did nothing to pursue his veteran's rights until, in April, 1969, he again requested the union to process a grievance on his old claim. This request came approximately seven months after Judge Sorg's decision in *Foremsky v. United States Steel Corporation,* 297 F.Supp. 1094 (W.D.Pa.1968), which held that a returning veteran is entitled to enjoy the seniority status which he would have acquired by virtue of continued employment but for his absence in the military service if, as a matter of foresight, it was reasonably certain that advancement would have occurred, and if, as a matter of hindsight, it did in fact occur. The union denied his grievance request and advised him to seek assistance from the United States Department of Labor, which he did on April 18, 1969. Finally, on August 15, 1972, more than nine years after his being rehired, and three years after he applied to the Department of Labor, plaintiff commenced this action.

[The district court concluded that Gruca was not barred by laches. The judge granted plaintiff's motion for summary judgment, awarded $4,937.66, and ordered U.S. Steel to amend plaintiff's job service date.

Defendant admitted that Gruca was wrongfully denied his seniority status upon his return from the military, but appealed on the ground of laches. The Court of Appeals noted that plaintiff Gruca sought both legal and equitable relief under the Act. The legal claims were barred by the Pennsylvania six year statute of limitations. The equitable claims were not automatically barred, but the statute of limitations created a rebuttable presumption of inexcusable delay and prejudice to the defendant—the two elements of laches.]

* * *

Our starting point is an inquiry into the existence of inexcusable delay. Here, plaintiff was rehired by U.S. Steel on January 18, 1963. He offered no proof of any deception or promise, or any other valid reason for postponing the running of the statute of limitations or the period for delay. * * * Applying the Pennsylvania six year statute by analogy, a presumption of inexcusable delay and prejudice arose. Thus, it became plaintiff's burden to come forward with evidence to rebut the presumption. The district court found * * * that the delay was excusable because the violation was not flagrant and because the defendant "by its own actions, made a substantial contribution to the delay at issue."

Clarity of the violation or uncertainty of the law are not factors which operate to excuse a party's delay. It is the duty of a veteran to promptly pursue his rights in court. [Citation.] The promptness which is demanded is not a naked assertion of a claim but the commencement of an action by the filing of a complaint. One cannot sit back, wait years for someone else to act as his stalking horse, and then ride the coattails of a favorable judicial decision irrespective of the delay involved. This is exactly what plaintiff has done here.

The court also abused its discretion when it concluded that the defendant substantially contributed to the delay. Plaintiff presented no evidence that he was misled by concealment, misrepresentation, unfulfilled promises or any other inequitable conduct on the part of U.S. Steel. * * *

A determination of inexcusable delay does not end the matter. To invoke the laches doctrine, prejudice to the defendant because of the delay must also be shown. Because the plaintiff's delay was in excess of the analogized statute of limitations, prejudice will be presumed. [Citation.] Plaintiff offered no evidence to rebut this presumption. By contrast, defendant offered evidence that it had paid other employees wages to perform the work that plaintiff would have accomplished. By sleeping on his rights plaintiff permitted the defendant to unnecessarily spend money in excess of nine years. The district court rejected this factor as an element of prejudice, viewing it as being created by the defendant's own doing. We disagree.

Pecuniary loss is a very real factor to be considered in determining whether prejudice to the defendant exists. More important is the domino effect precipitated by changing plaintiff's job service dates.

* * * Therefore, we conclude that the district court abused its discretion in concluding that plaintiff had rebutted the presumption of prejudice to the defendant.

* * * [Reversed and complaint dismissed.]

---

1. The laches defense turns on the question of inequity rather than the mere passage of time. The Supreme Court has stated that laches is intended to be flexible and that "no arbitrary or fixed period of time has been, or will be, established as an inflexible rule." The Key City, 81 U.S. (14 Wall.) 653, 660, 20 L.Ed. 896 (1871). The principle has remained unchanged. *See, e.g.,* Costello v. United States, 365 U.S. 265, 81 S.Ct. 534, 5 L.Ed.2d 551 (1961); Lingenfelter v. Keystone Consol. Industries, 691 F.2d 339 (7th Cir.1982).

2. Many cases have held that delay alone is not sufficient for laches; the delay must be prejudicial. *See* Gutierrez v. Waterman S.S. Corp., 373 U.S. 206, 83 S.Ct. 1185, 10 L.Ed.2d 297 (1963) (test of laches is prejudice to the other party); Gardner v. Panama R.R. Co., 342 U.S. 29, 72 S.Ct. 12, 96 L.Ed. 31 (1951) (laches is not a bar if there is no prejudice to the defendant from the passage of time); Tyler v. United States, 600 F.2d 786 (Ct.Cl.1979) (even lengthy delay does not eliminate inquiry into prejudice); Brundage v. United States, 205 Ct.Cl. 502, 504 F.2d 1382 (1974) (delay alone does not constitute laches).

3. What if the delay is caused by an administrative agency? Should a court attribute the inefficiency of a governmental entity to a private plaintiff? *See* Whitfield v. Anheuser–Busch, Inc., 820 F.2d 243 (8th Cir.1987) (ten year delay of Equal Employment Opportunity Commission was unreasonable delay to bar subsequent suit by alleged discrimination victim where defendant's witnesses no longer recalled event); EEOC v. Liberty Loan Corp., 584 F.2d 853 (8th Cir.1978) (four year administrative delay unreasonable, absent any excuse other than heavy workload, if prejudicial to defendant).

4. Compare the treatment of the prejudice issue in *Cornetta, supra,* with *Gruca.* Certainly retroactive promotions will have some negative impact, but is that the test? Is the significant factor that the military was involved in one case and a private sector employer in the other?

UNITED STATES v. VANHORN

20 F.3d 104 (4th Cir.1994).

WILLIAMS, CIRCUIT JUDGE.

On appeal in this civil suit, Dr. Barbara Vanhorn challenges the lower court's determination that she did not fulfill the terms of her National Health Services Corps Scholarship agreement with the Government. After Dr. Vanhorn's testimony, the district court issued judgment as a matter of law for the United States pursuant to Fed.R.Civ.Proc.

50(a) and awarded compensatory damages, interest, and a treble-damage penalty. Concluding that the district court correctly held that contract defenses are not available to relieve Dr. Vanhorn of her statutory liability and correctly applied the Rule 50(a) standard in finding that a reasonable jury could not have decided in favor of Dr. Vanhorn, we affirm.

Between 1977 and 1980, Dr. Vanhorn applied for and received three one-year scholarship awards totaling $26,582.00 from the National Health Service Corps (NHSC) scholarship program. The NHSC program was created in 1976 to address the problem of a decline in the number of doctors available to serve rural areas by providing "a generous scholarship program for students who will undertake service in an area or program into which the Secretary [of Health and Human Services] finds it difficult to attract health professionals...." Through the program, scholarship funds to cover tuition and educational expenses are provided in return for the recipient's agreement to serve for a period of time equivalent to the greater of the number of years of support received or two years. 42 U.S.C.A. § 254l (f)(1)(B)(iv) (West 1991). All scholars in the program must sign written contracts agreeing to serve in an assigned Health Professional Shortage Area (HPSA) as either a commissioned officer of the Public Health Service or in civilian service. The terms of the agreement between the scholar and the Government are specified by statute.

The NHSC Act additionally provides that if the individual funded under the program breaches her contract "by failing (for any reason ...) either to begin such individual's service obligation ... or to complete such service obligation," the United States is entitled to recover three times the amount of scholarship funds awarded, plus interest. The defaulting scholarship recipient must pay this sum within one year of default.

* * * Dr. Vanhorn applied to serve her obligation after [her graduation and residency years] through the Private Practice Option (PPO).[6] Dr. Vanhorn obtained written approval to pursue her PPO at the Howard University Family Health Center, which was located in the North Capital HPSA. The contract provided that she was to serve in a full-time private practice at the Howard Center or at "such other location as may be agreed upon by the Secretary." Dr. Vanhorn completed her residency on schedule and reported to work at the Howard University Center in July 1983. Unfortunately, the Center was unable to pay her salary due to an unanticipated shortage of funds.

After working for six weeks without pay, Dr. Vanhorn left the Center in August 1983. Dr. Vanhorn sought guidance from her Project

---

6. The Private Practice Option requires that the scholar enter a written agreement for a period of service in a full-time private clinical practice in the HMSA (now HPSA) selected by the Secretary. Other statutory provisions limit the amount a PPO scholar may charge patients for services, prohibit discrimination, and allow the Secretary to promulgate other regulations as may be required. If the scholar breaches these requirements, the Secretary may permit her to enter the NHSC to satisfy her obligation.

Officer, James Russo, who was responsible for all direct contact between Dr. Vanhorn and the Public Health Service. Dr. Vanhorn testified that Russo "told me I could set up almost anywhere in Anacostia and be in compliance." Russo did not dispute that he told Dr. Vanhorn this, but testified that he also told her that any move would require formal written approval from the Secretary.

Thereafter, in September 1983, Dr. Vanhorn started a private practice at Good Hope Road in Anacostia in the District of Columbia. The Good Hope Road location was near the Anacostia HPSA, which bordered some of the same census tracts contained in the North Capital HPSA to which Dr. Vanhorn had been assigned. Dr. Vanhorn neither applied for, nor ever received, the required written approval for the move. She claims that Russo's representations led her to believe the move would definitely be approved. * * *

At the close of Dr. Vanhorn's direct testimony, the district court entered judgment as a matter of law for the United States pursuant to Fed.R.Civ.P. 50(a). * * *

Dr. Vanhorn argues that the district court erred in refusing to apply ordinary contract defenses of substantial compliance, estoppel, and economic duress to excuse her noncompliance with the agreements that she signed with the Government. Because we find that the relationship between Dr. Vanhorn and the Government is governed by statute, and ordinary contract principles do not apply, we reject her contentions.

* * *

The damages provision of the statute states that if the scholarship recipient breaches the agreement "for any reason," the recipient may be declared in breach; affirmative defenses are therefore irrelevant. [Citation.] These contracts, governed as they are by a comprehensive statutory scheme that provides not only for the scholarship contract but also for private placement option and forbearance agreements, are simply not subject to the defenses that Dr. Vanhorn attempts to assert. * * *

Dr. Vanhorn did not seek waiver or cancellation of her debt from the Secretary, and therefore we have no agency action to review. Because the contract defenses of substantial compliance, economic duress, and estoppel are not valid defenses in cases under this statutory scheme, and because it is undisputed that Dr. Vanhorn failed to satisfy the written terms of her agreements with the Government, the district court did not err in entering judgment for the United States.[19]

---

19. Dr. Vanhorn claims that she substantially complied with the requirements of a modified PPO, that the Government is estopped from enforcing the original written agreement because it had been modified orally by a Government agent, and that the defense of economic duress applies to excuse her from compliance[.] * * * [S]he contends that the Government modified her PPO contract through the oral representations of James Russo, her program manager, and that she substantially complied with her contract with the Government by serving in her practice on Good Hope Road. Essentially, Vanhorn's argument is that when Russo told her that she could "set up almost anywhere out there," he modified her agreement with the Government and

Dr. Vanhorn's damages were calculated by the district court pursuant to statute. Under the statutory formula, the amount of scholarship monies given and interest on that amount is trebled. * * *

Applying this formula, the district court awarded the Government $183,953.12. Dr. Vanhorn does not challenge the district court's calculation of damages pursuant to the statutory formula. Instead she argues that the disparity between the amount she received in scholarship monies, $26,582, and the amount of damages awarded to the Government, $183,953.12, is unconscionable. We disagree. As the court held in United States v. Swanson, 618 F.Supp. 1231, 1243–44 (E.D.Mich. 1985): To estimate the damages which would be suffered by the loss of the services of a trained ... physician for a three year period in a medically underserved area is difficult, if not impossible, to accurately determine.... [Treble] damages which the government [is] entitled to receive for Defendant's breach of the contract ... [is a] fair and reasonable attempt to fix just compensation in the event of breach. * * *

Affirmed.

---

1. Compare the principal case with Beacom v. Equal Employment Opportunity Comm'n., 500 F.Supp. 428 (D.Ariz.1980). In that case the plaintiff lawyer sought to estop the government from applying a federal hiring freeze to his employment because he had been assured that the freeze would not apply to him. On this assurance he wound down his practice of sixteen years to join the federal agency that had hired him. Only then was he told that he had no job because there had never been a formal appointment and the freeze thus applied. The court noted:

> The Commission's course of dealing with Mr. Beacom permits two estoppel arguments, either of which would provide a basis for relief. The most obvious argument is that the Commission's failure to inform Mr. Beacom that he was not protected by a formal appointment, combined with its misleading confirmation, should estop the Commission from asserting that appointment had not occurred. In addition, it could be argued that, under the circumstances, the Commission's delay in informing Mr. Beacom that the President's freeze would affect his job should estop it from applying [the freeze] to Mr. Beacom.

> In general, the appropriate test of estoppel in this circuit is as follows:

> (1) The party to be estopped must know the facts; (2) he must intend that his conduct shall be acted on or must so act that the party asserting the estoppel has a right to believe it is so intended;

the Government cannot now claim that she owes money. Oral representations by Government officers cannot result in a modification of a statutory contract; such modifications, to be valid, must be in writing. * * *

(3) the latter must be ignorant of the true facts; and (4) he must rely on the former's conduct to his injury. [Citations.]

Where the Government is the party against whom estoppel is being asserted, however, it is clear that the private litigant must do more than meet the general test. Not only must the private litigant make a threshold showing that the Government has engaged in "affirmative misconduct," [citations], he faces the further burden of demonstrating that the injustice caused by the Government's misconduct is sufficiently severe to outweigh the countervailing interest of the public not to be unduly damaged by the imposition of estoppel. [Citations.]

The court held that under these facts the tests for estoppel of the government were satisfied. Can this holding be reconciled with the principal case?

Consider the four-part general test for estoppel, noted above. If the defendant in the principal case had been a private party, would the plaintiff have been able to meet all four parts of this test?

2. The traditional rule was that estoppel applied only to private parties and not to the government. In recent years several cases have eroded the governmental immunity from estoppel under certain circumstances. *Compare* Utah Power & Light Co. v. United States, 243 U.S. 389, 37 S.Ct. 387, 61 L.Ed. 791 (1917) (government cannot be estopped) *with* California Pac. Bank v. Small Business Admin., 557 F.2d 218 (9th Cir.1977) (under appropriate circumstances estoppel is appropriate because the increasing presence of government in the marketplace makes it more like a proprietor and less like a sovereign). What are the competing policy considerations involved in applying equitable estoppel to governmental entities?

3. Should the potential liability of the government for back pay carry more weight than the potential liability of a private employer for back pay? *Compare* Cornetta v. United States, *supra, with* Gruca v. U.S. Steel, *supra.*

JOHN R. v. OAKLAND UNIFIED SCHOOL DIST.

48 Cal.3d 438, 256 Cal.Rptr. 766, 769 P.2d 948 (1989).

ARGUELLES, JUSTICE.

John R., then a 14–year-old junior high school student, allegedly was sexually molested by his mathematics teacher while he was at the teacher's apartment participating in an officially sanctioned, extracurricular program. * * *

At the time of the incidents giving rise to this case, John R. was a ninth grade student at a junior high school in the Oakland Unified School District (district). His mathematics teacher, who had also taught John in the seventh grade, asked John to participate in the school's instructional, work-experience program, under which students received both school credit and monetary payments for assisting teachers by, for example, helping to correct other students' papers. The nature of the tasks would suggest that the program was aimed mainly at high-performing students. John had a history of poor grades in mathematics, but his marks in this teacher's class reflected what his attorney, no doubt ironically, termed "a remarkable increase in his ability to do math. . . ."

Whether legitimately or through artificially inflated grades, John was allowed to participate in the program. Performance of the required work by students at teachers' homes was an option authorized by the district, and the teacher either encouraged or required John to come to his apartment for this purpose. Over the course of many sessions at the teacher's apartment, the teacher sought to develop a close relationship with John as the boy's tutor and counselor, and ultimately endeavored to seduce him. The teacher attempted to convince John that engaging in sex acts with him would be a constructive part of their relationship and, at times, threatened to give John failing grades if John would not go along with his desires and said he would tell people that John had solicited sex from him. [John then agreed to sexual acts.]   * * *

When John protested and told the teacher he would report the incidents to his parents, the teacher threatened to retaliate against him if he revealed what had taken place. As a result of these threats, and his embarrassment and shame at what had happened, John did not disclose the incidents to anyone for a number of months. John finally told his father about the molestation 10 months later in December 1981.

* * *

Before we turn to the [liability] issue, we must first address a threshold question—whether plaintiffs complied in timely fashion with the requirements of the California Tort Claims Act[.] * * *

It is well settled that a public entity may be estopped from asserting the limitations of the claims statute where its agents or employees have prevented or deterred the filing of a timely claim by some affirmative act. [Citations.] Estoppel most commonly results from misleading statements about the need for or advisability of a claim; actual fraud or the intent to mislead is not essential. [Citations.] *A fortiori*, estoppel may certainly be invoked when there are acts of violence or intimidation that are intended to prevent the filing of a claim. [Citations.] And here, the teacher's threats to retaliate against John if the boy reported the incidents of sexual molestation allegedly did just that.

Although the teacher's alleged threats in this case were no doubt motivated largely by self-interest, rather than to prevent John from filing a claim against the district, it would clearly be inconsistent with the equitable underpinnings of the estoppel doctrine to permit the district to benefit to plaintiffs' detriment by such threats. * * * We conclude that, for purposes of applying equitable estoppel, the time for filing a claim against the district was tolled during the period that the teacher's threats prevented plaintiffs from pursuing their claims. * * *

B.   UNCLEAN HANDS AND UNCONSCIONABILITY

Section Coverage:

The conscience defenses—unclean hands and unconscionability—bar plaintiffs whose claims are in some way morally tainted even if they are legally sound.   The foundation of these defenses is that the court will not lower its dignity by granting equitable relief in such cases.   These conscience defenses do not require a showing of prejudice to the defendant, unlike the defenses of laches and estoppel.   It is the interest of the court and the public, rather than relative fairness between the parties that creates the bar.

The unclean hands defense operates when the party seeking relief has behaved inequitably with respect to the rights being asserted in the case.   The maxim accompanying this defense is: "He who comes into a court of equity must come with clean hands."   The uncleanliness that bars relief must be serious yet need not rise to the level of fraud or other actionable wrong.   The "test" is whether the behavior is offensive to the court.   If so, the plaintiff is left only the legal claim and cannot receive equitable relief.

The taint must be specifically related to the matter before the court, not collateral to it.   It is often said that "equity does not require its suitors to lead blameless lives."   In other words, a plaintiff's questionable behavior concerning unrelated matters is not relevant.

Unconscionability is conceptually related to unclean hands, but its history is slightly different.   This defense is limited specifically to contract remedies.   When a judge finds the contractual terms so one-sided as to be oppressive, then the court will not enforce the contract or the objectionable part of it.

Although the concept of unconscionability arose in equity, in modern law its force is primarily at law.   U.C.C. 2–302 adopted the concept as a defense to the legal enforcement of objectionable contracts.   It has been particularly useful with respect to nonfraudulent but shockingly unfair sales practices directed at relatively unsophisticated consumers.

Model Case:

Tina Lee is an aspiring teenage actress who recently came to national attention when an appealing photograph of her won a cereal box contest.   A television network approached her and offered her a contract with very unfavorable terms.   She had no agent and her family was as unsophisticated and star-struck as she was.   She signed the network's contract in which she further promised not to act or model for anyone else for a specific period of time.

Tina Lee appeared in a successful mini-series on this network. She was received very well by the public. When she was at a party after this success, an acquaintance casually commented to her that her contract with the network was invalid because she was underage at the time she signed it. This comment may or may not have been legally correct. There was a significant legal question whether the contract was voidable because she was a minor in the jurisdiction where the contract was to be performed, but not where she signed it. Nonetheless, Tina Lee was unaware of this conflict of laws issue. Without further inquiry into this matter, she believed this casual comment.

A movie studio called her and asked if she were free to contract. She replied that she was, and negotiations began. The network learned this fact and told the studio it would sue if Tina Lee acted for anyone else. The studio then withdrew from negotiations. Tina Lee then filed suit to enjoin the network from asserting its contract claims.

The court in equity need not resolve the conflicts issue if the judge finds that Tina Lee had "unclean hands" when she represented she was "free" to contract. The judge will consider her moral obligation rather than her legal one. Her dealing with the studio would not be "collateral" to the case because they are central to the claim asserted. Denied an injunction, she still could seek a remedy at law.

If the case arises differently, the role of the equitable defenses would change also. If the network had gone to court as plaintiff instead of Tina Lee, then the focus would be on the network's behavior. The conscience defenses relate only to the plaintiff's conduct precisely because they are defenses. Tina Lee might defend enforcement of the network's contract on the grounds that it was unconscionable. If the judge finds the terms of the contract are shockingly oppressive, the court can deny its enforcement for unconscionability.

SENTER v. FURMAN

245 Ga. 483, 265 S.E.2d 784 (1980).

HILL, JUSTICE.

This is suit in equity to declare that a house and lot which Dr. James Senter, a dentist, conveyed by warranty deed to his nursing assistant, Anna Louise Furman, is held by her under a constructive trust. Dr. Senter contends that it was error to grant summary judgment to Ms. Furman on his complaint seeking to have the constructive trust imposed, because, he contends, there were genuine issues of material fact to be tried by a jury.

Dr. Senter executed the warranty deed on his Powers Ferry home, reciting a consideration of "Ten dollars and other good and valuable consideration," when he was 74 and in poor health. He contends that due to his weakened physical and mental condition he was induced to execute the deed by the fraud and undue influence of Ms. Furman at a time when he was facing a malpractice claim which could have cost him all his assets, and that she promised to return the property to him after that exposure was over.[1]

* * *

Regarding the claim of fraud and insofar as Dr. Senter's motive for conveying the property to Ms. Furman in trust is concerned, equity will not enforce the alleged trust arrangement.

* * *

In Whitley v. Whitley, 220 Ga. 471, 139 S.E.2d 381 (1964), plaintiff sought cancellation of contracts and creation of a trust, alleging that he had transferred control of his corporation to his sons to avoid estate taxes but that it was understood that his sons would cancel the contracts at his request. This court denied relief, saying (220 Ga. at 473, 139 S.E.2d at 382): "According to the petitioner's own allegations, he comes into equity with unclean hands. Therefore, he must fail." [Citations.]

The holding of *Whitley v. Whitley, supra,* is equally applicable to conveyances used to conceal assets from creditors. In Bagwell v. Johnson, 116 Ga. 464, 468, 42 S.E. 732, 734 (1902), the court said: " ... this is simply a case where two persons complotted to hinder, delay, and defeat a creditor of one of them, with the result that one of the wrongdoers himself falls a victim to the wiles of the other. In all such cases this court has uniformly held that no relief can be afforded the victimized wrongdoer, but that the parties are to be left as they stand."
* * *

Judgment affirmed.

BYRON v. CLAY

867 F.2d 1049 (7th Cir.1989).

POSNER, CIRCUIT JUDGE.

The question presented is whether the First Amendment entitles the plaintiff, Rudy Byron, who describes himself as "a political hack employed in a make-work position doing virtually nothing in an unnecessary job," to be reinstated to that position, with back pay "to date of reinstatement [and] with all applicable benefits and pay increase to which plaintiff would be entitled had he not been dismissed," because he was fired for political reasons. These quotations from the plaintiff's brief accurately describe the job Byron lost and the relief he requested of the district court, which after a four-day bench trial gave judgment for the defendants and dismissed the suit.

Byron was a friend, political supporter, and protege of Atterson Spann. Spann * * * was one of three members of the Board of Commissioners of Lake County, Indiana. The others were an ally of Spann's,

---

1. Ms. Furman testified that Dr. Senter said he was giving the land to her for her services rendered over the years. However, on motion for summary judgment, we consider the evidence most favorable to the respondent to the motion.

Steve Corey, and an enemy, Ernest Niemeyer; so Spann and Corey controlled the Board. In 1983 Spann hired Byron to work for the Board at an annual salary of $18,700. His job was to inspect three county courthouses and report any maintenance problems that he discovered. Since each courthouse had a building manager able to do any inspecting that needed doing, Byron's job was not taxing (except on the citizens of Lake County). It is uncertain whether he ever visited any courthouse or made any reports; but probably not. He never filled out a time sheet and did not even know who his immediate supervisor was.

In the Lake County Democratic primary held in May 1986, Spann—whose campaign Byron had managed—was defeated for renomination by Rudolph Clay. Clay went on to win the general election in the fall, and having won he formed a coalition with Niemeyer to run the Board of Commissioners. Before the new Board took office, Byron received another job assignment, but he refused to sign in for the new job or to undertake its duties, the nature of which is not specified in the record.

Counseled by attorney Dull, the new Board of Commissioners spent its first day in power, January 2, 1987, firing Byron and other employees. But rather than abolish Byron's make-work job the new Board gave it to Rudolph Clay's son. Clay père had been heard to make comments about finding jobs for his political supporters, and Byron was not the only person fired who had supported Spann. Byron now makes his home in prison, having received a nine-year term for tax evasion. Spann is there too, for the same offense.

Byron brought this suit against Clay and Niemeyer * * * and he presses on us the following syllogism: The First Amendment has been interpreted to forbid a public employer to fire an employee on political grounds unless the employee is either a policy-making employee or a confidential one. [Citations.] Byron was neither, and was fired by his public employer on political grounds. Therefore his rights under the First Amendment were violated.

The magistrate who tried this case with the consent of the parties under 28 U.S.C. § 636(c) did not question the validity of Byron's syllogism but was unwilling to "permit the plaintiff to recover what simply was political payola.... Evidence has demonstrated that Byron already has conducted a raid on the public treasury. He will not be permitted to use the federal courts to pilfer additional county funds." Byron appeals. * * *

The doctrine of unclean hands, functionally rather than moralistically conceived, gives recognition to the fact that equitable decrees may have effects on third parties—persons who are not parties to a lawsuit, including taxpayers and members of the law-abiding public—and so should not be entered without consideration of those effects. * * * For us to order [Byron] reinstated even though he is in prison, and (more important—since he'll be out eventually) even though he does no work and, judging from his reaction to his last job assignment, refuses to do any work, would harm both the criminal justice system and the people of

Lake County, whose tax dollars would pay this parasite's salary. Although a modest salary in absolute terms, it is bountiful in relation to the amount of work Byron is prepared to do for it (zero). True, his successor as supernumerary courthouse inspector may be no improvement. But to give ghost employees a form of job tenure by ordering them reinstated if they are fired on political grounds will encourage them in their efforts to exploit public employment for private enrichment, [citation], thereby vindicating Ambrose Bierce's definition of politics: "A strife of interests masquerading as a contest of principles. The conduct of public affairs for private advantage."

The difference between a bad worker and a no-worker may seem too fine to make a legal difference to a court as concerned as this court is with making the law as clear as possible. But while a bad worker is not a criminal, Indiana has a statute making "ghost employment" a crime. [Citation.] The supremacy clause notwithstanding, a federal court should hesitate to order the commission of a state crime. In arguing that he, not Clay fils, should have the opportunity to defraud the people of Indiana, Byron is like the highwayman who sued his partner in crime for an accounting of the profits—and was hanged for his efforts. *See* Note, The Highwayman's Case, 35 L.Q.Rev. 197 (1893) (Everet v. Williams, Ex. 1725).

Yet unclean hands is an equitable defense, and Byron seeks not only reinstatement, an equitable remedy, but also damages. * * *

But with the merger of law and equity, it is difficult to see why equitable defenses should be limited to equitable suits any more; and of course many are not so limited, [citation], and perhaps unclean hands should be one of these. Even before the merger there was a counterpart legal doctrine to unclean hands—in pari delicto—which forbade a plaintiff to recover damages if his fault was equal to the defendant's. [Citation.] We need not worry about the precise scope of that doctrine. [Citation.] It is enough to observe that a highwayman who decided to sue his partner for common law damages as well as for an equitable accounting for profits would surely have gotten no further with his "legal" claim than with his "equitable" one. Byron's claim to displace the young Clay is of similar character.

* * *

The question posed at the outset of this opinion—the question presented in the plaintiff's own words by this appeal—almost answers itself. It is all very well to speak with Lord Coke of the "artificial reason" of the law, *see* Prohibitions del Roy, 12 Co.Rep. 63, 65, 77 Eng.Rep. 1342, 1343 (1608); but when a court is urged to reach a result that could not be made intelligible—that must seem ridiculous—to educated lay persons, it is a hint that the result may be wrong as a matter of law. It would mock the First Amendment to hold that it entitles a ghost employee to reinstatement with back pay in his sinecure (in violation of state criminal law) because he lost the job as a sequel to the defeat of the patron who had given it to him as a reward for political services.   * * *

[Affirmed.]

PROBLEM: THE COLLEGE STAR'S SECRET

A star senior football player at the University of Metro City enters into a promotional contract with a local car dealer. The contract provides that immediately following any post-season games the dealer will run a series of advertisements featuring this player. The contract provides that the advertisements shall be filmed and appearance fees paid prior to the end of the season, but that no publicity will be made until after the season. Moreover, the contract stipulates that the arrangement shall be entirely secret. The contract further provides that for one year the player may not engage in any other promotional activity for other cars or car dealers.

This contract is in violation of the rules issued by the governing national association of college athletics. Neither the star nor the dealer tell anyone about the contract because of this violation. As provided by the contract, the star films the advertisements secretly.

In a post-season game the team from University of Metro City is a dramatic victor over a more prominent national football team. Overnight the star is a national figure. Because of this new prominence, a major automobile manufacturer offers the star a contract to make advertisements for national distribution. The star accepts this contract, in violation of the first contract with the local car dealer in Metro City.

The dealer sues to enjoin the star from performing the second contract. Should the deceitful conduct of the dealer and the star be relevant in the dealer's suit to enforce the no-competitor endorsement provision in the first contract?

NORTH PACIFIC LUMBER CO. v. OLIVER
286 Or. 639, 596 P.2d 931 (1979).

HOLMAN, JUSTICE.

Plaintiff, North Pacific Lumber Co., is a wholesaler of lumber products. Plaintiff's employees conduct almost all of its trading activities over the telephone from its principal office in Portland, Oregon. In February 1967 plaintiff hired defendant Oliver as a lumber trader in its hardwood division. As part of his employment contract, defendant agreed to refrain from competing with plaintiff for two years following termination of his employment.   * * * In April 1976 defendant voluntarily terminated his employment. Soon thereafter he went to work for Tree Products Company. Tree Products competes with plaintiff, under the terms of the contract.

[North Pacific Lumber Co. promptly filed suit. There was a lengthy trial at which the defendant employee produced considerable evidence concerning the work environment. The trial court found: (1) the traders were paid by an ill-defined salary system whose secrecy produced an atmosphere of restraint and oppressiveness; (2) some managers who had special telephones engaged in eavesdropping which sometimes went beyond the avowed "training" purpose and which was illegal to the extent it was not consented; (3) fictitious names were more than occasionally used for deception, although it is not clear anyone was damaged by this "shoddy practice"; (4) most seriously, department managers encouraged a practice of fraudulent misrepresentation when traders settled disputes between suppliers and customers. The amount of settlement would be misrepresented when possible to leave a difference between the parties which the company kept as undisclosed profit. On the basis of these findings the trial court denied enforcement of the contract on the grounds of unclean hands. The employer appeals.]

* * *

Covenants binding a person not to exercise his trade or profession for a period of time in a particular area are contracts in restraint of trade disfavored at common law. Nonetheless, courts will uphold them where they are reasonably necessary to protect a legitimate interest of the person in whose favor they run, do not impose an unreasonable hardship upon the person against whom they are asserted, and are not injurious to the public interest. * * *

The threshold issue in this case is whether the trial court properly refused plaintiff all requested relief in a suit based on an otherwise valid contract because of what the trial court viewed as plaintiff's unclean hands. * * * It is therefore necessary to have some general understanding of the operation of the clean hands maxim.

In his treatise, Pomeroy describes the concept underlying the clean hands maxim, as follows:

> * * * [T]he principle was established from the earliest days, that while the court of chancery could interpose and compel a defendant to comply with the dictates of conscience and good faith with regard to matters outside of the strict rules of the law, or even in contradiction to those rules, while it could act *upon the conscience* of a defendant and force him to do right and justice, it would never thus interfere on behalf of a plaintiff whose own conduct in connection with the same matter or transaction had been unconscientious or unjust, or marked by a want of good faith, or had violated any of the principles of equity and righteous dealing which it is the purpose of the jurisdiction to sustain. * * * This fundamental principle is expressed in the maxim, He who comes into a court of equity must come with clean hands * * *. 2 Pomeroy, Equity Jurisprudence § 398 at 93–94 (5th ed. 1941).

The maxim is applied for the protection of the court and not for the benefit of the defendant, who may in fact be equally affected with the improper transaction. McClintock, Principles of Equity at 60 (1948). The plaintiff may have a perfectly valid claim, but he will nevertheless be denied relief where the doctrine applies.

* * *

Broad as the principle seems to be in its operation, it still has some reasonable limitations. In quantitative terms, the misconduct must be serious enough to justify a court's denying relief on an otherwise valid claim. Even equity does not require saintliness. Perhaps more importantly, the misconduct must bear a certain kind of relationship to the subject matter of the suit before a court will consider it. * * * Dobbs speaks of the clean hands doctrine, as follows:

> [T]his is not a license to destroy the rights of persons whose conduct is unethical. The rule is that unrelated bad conduct is not to be considered against the plaintiff. It is only when the plaintiff's improper conduct is the source, or part of the source, of his equitable claim, that he is to be barred because of this conduct. "What is material is not that the plaintiff's hands are dirty, but that he dirties them in acquiring the right he now asserts. * * * "Dobbs, Remedies § 2.4 at 46 (1973).

* * *

The critical question here is whether the employer's improper conduct "sufficiently affected the equitable relations between the parties" to justify the trial court's refusal to grant relief. Since this suit arises out of an employment relationship we believe the question can best be answered by seeking to determine whether, under the circumstances, the continued existence of that relationship made it necessary for the defendant to participate with the plaintiff in the improper conduct. We are unwilling to permit an employee to terminate his employment contract without obligation whenever his employer commits some indiscretion and the improper conduct concerns a matter with which the employee is not directly concerned. Such a rule would render many contracts unenforceable in equity. * * *

The trial court felt that the most serious charge against plaintiff was that plaintiff made a practice of making improper profits on the resolution of claims. Plaintiff, as a lumber wholesaler, matched up buyers with sellers. The seller of a lumber product generally bore legal responsibility for any deficiency in an order. When a shipment was unsatisfactory, the buyer would register its complaint with plaintiff's traders. The trader then attempted to negotiate a settlement. By downplaying the seriousness of the deficiency, the trader sought to obtain the buyer's consent to a low settlement figure. The trader could then turn around and tell the supplier that the deficiency was very serious and the buyer demanded a large settlement. Once agreement was reached, plaintiff pocketed the difference between the two figures as additional profit on the transaction.

* * *

It is our conclusion that the trial judge was correct in ruling that this conduct sufficiently affected the relations between the parties to justify invocation of the clean hands rule. The making of profits on customer claims against manufacturers was a common practice in the department in which defendant was employed. It continued over a long period of time during seven and one-half years of which defendant was assistant manager of the department and had responsibility for the supervision of such activities. He derived a personal profit from the misconduct since it affected department earnings and his compensation as assistant manager of the department. Defendant could not occupy the position of assistant manager and avoid participating in his employer's improper practices because he was responsible for carrying out and overseeing department policy. A court of equity should not lend its aid to an employer who attempts to enforce a contract of employment the performance of which involves participation by the employee in such wrongdoing. We do not refuse the court's aid in order to punish plaintiff or reward defendant but only to avoid involving ourselves in settling accounts arising from a tainted relationship.

* * * [Affirmed.]

————

1. The uncleanliness that will bar a plaintiff from equitable relief must concern the claim before the court and not a collateral matter. The problem that often arises is determining what matters directly affect the claim and which are collateral.

2. The problem of identifying direct and collateral matters appeared in a highly political case involving the affairs of a foreign government, in a suit by a foreign government brought in a New York court. In Islamic Republic of Iran v. Pahlavi, 116 Misc.2d 590, 455 N.Y.S.2d 987 (1982), the government of Iran brought an action against the sister of the former shah of that country. The complaint alleged breach of fiduciary obligations, seeking equitable remedies of an accounting, constructive trust, and an injunction.

The defendant asserted that the plaintiff, Iran's then current government, had unclean hands because of its involvement in the seizure of hostages from the personnel in the American embassy shortly after the Shah's necessary departure from the country. The United States historically had supported the Shah and was therefore considered an enemy by the succeeding government, who was the plaintiff in the case. The hostile takeover of the American embassy was not done directly by the government, but it was substantially involved during the many months the hostages were held before their eventual release.

The court agreed that the government's activities concerning the hostages were immoral and unconscionable. Nonetheless, the judge rejected the unclean hands defense on the ground that the Iranian government's conduct concerning the American hostages was unrelated to the subject matter of the lawsuit, specifically the money held by the sister of the former Shah.

3.　The use of the unclean hands defense against a governmental plaintiff also failed in a recent case where the conduct in question occurred during the litigation. In S.E.C. v. Electronics Warehouse, Inc., 689 F.Supp. 53 (D.Conn.1988), the issue was the unclean hands defense asserted against the plaintiff agency which is a part of the United States government. The defendant, an underwriter accused of violating federal securities laws, alleged that the government had unclean hands by harassing the defendant's attorney in connection with a current securities offering. The court rejected the unclean hands argument partly on the rationale that the basis of the defense cannot be conduct which occurs during the litigation of a lawsuit; rather, the conduct must occur during accrual of the action. The court also noted that equitable defenses against governmental agencies are strictly limited to instances where the agency's misconduct is egregious and the resulting prejudice to the defendant rises to a constitutional level.

Is it sound to distinguish improper conduct before litigation and during it? Does the court have other tools for sanctioning conduct during the time the parties are litigating? Could the *Electronics Warehouse* case have been decided instead on the collateral matter exception to the unclean hands defense?

CAMPBELL SOUP CO. v. WENTZ

172 F.2d 80 (3d Cir.1948).

GOODRICH, CIRCUIT JUDGE.

These are appeals from judgments of the District Court denying equitable relief to the buyer under a contract for the sale of carrots. * * *

The transactions which raise the issues may be briefly summarized. On June 21, 1947, Campbell Soup Company (Campbell), a New Jersey corporation, entered into a written contract with George B. Wentz and Harry T. Wentz, who are Pennsylvania farmers, for delivery by the Wentzes to Campbell of all the Chantenay red cored carrots to be grown on fifteen acres of the Wentz farm during the 1947 season. * * * The prices specified in the contract ranged from $23 to $30 per ton according to the time of delivery. The contract price for January, 1948 was $30 a ton.

The Wentzes harvested approximately 100 tons of carrots from the fifteen acres covered by the contract. Early in January, 1948, they told a Campbell representative that they would not deliver their carrots at the contract price. The market price at that time was at least $90 per ton, and Chantenay red cored carrots were virtually unobtainable. The Wentzes then sold approximately 62 tons of their carrots to the defendant Lojeski, a neighboring farmer. Lojeski resold about 58 tons on the open market, approximately half to Campbell and the balance to other purchasers.

On January 9, 1948, Campbell, suspecting that Lojeski was selling it "contract carrots," refused to purchase any more, and instituted these suits against the Wentz brothers and Lojeski to enjoin further sale of the contract carrots to others, and to compel specific performance of the contract. * * *

The reason that we shall affirm instead of reversing with an order for specific performance is found in the contract itself. We think it is too hard a bargain and too one-sided an agreement to entitle the plaintiff to relief in a court of conscience. For each individual grower the agreement is made by filling in names and quantity and price on a printed form furnished by the buyer. This form has quite obviously been drawn by skillful draftsmen with the buyer's interests in mind.

* * * [Paragraph 3 of the contract] allows Campbell to refuse carrots in excess of twelve tons to the acre. The next contains a covenant by the grower that he will not sell carrots to anyone else except the carrots rejected by Campbell nor will he permit anyone else to grow carrots on his land. Paragraph 10 provides liquidated damages to the extent of $50 per acre for any breach by the grower. There is no provision for liquidated or any other damages for breach of contract by Campbell.

The provision of the contract which we think is the hardest is paragraph 9, set out in the margin.[11] It will be noted that Campbell is excused from accepting carrots under certain circumstances. But even under such circumstances the grower, while he cannot say Campbell is liable for failure to take the carrots, is not permitted to sell them elsewhere unless Campbell agrees. This is the kind of provision which the late Francis H. Bohlen would call "carrying a good joke too far." What the grower may do with his product under the circumstances set out is not clear. He has covenanted not to store it anywhere except on his own farm and also not to sell to anybody else.

We are not suggesting that the contract is illegal. Nor are we suggesting any excuse for the grower in this case who has deliberately broken an agreement entered into with Campbell. We do think, howev-

---

11. "Grower shall not be obligated to deliver any Carrots which he is unable to harvest or deliver, nor shall Campbell be obligated to receive or pay for any Carrots which it is unable to inspect, grade, receive, handle, use or pack at or ship in processed form from its plants in Camden (1) because of any circumstance beyond the control of Grower or Campbell, as the case may be, or (2) because of any labor disturbance, work stoppage, slow-down, or strike involving any of Campbell's employees. Campbell shall not be liable for any delay in receiving Carrots due to any of the above contingencies. During periods when Campbell is unable to receive Grower's Carrots, Grower may with Campbell's written consent, dispose of his Carrots elsewhere. Grower may not, however, sell or otherwise dispose of any Carrots which he is unable to deliver to Campbell."

er, that a party who has offered and succeeded in getting an agreement as tough as this one is, should not come to a chancellor and ask court help in the enforcement of its terms. That equity does not enforce unconscionable bargains is too well established to require elaborate citation.

The plaintiff argues that the provisions of the contract are separable. We agree that they are, but do not think that decisions separating out certain provisions from illegal contracts are in point here. As already said, we do not suggest that this contract is illegal. All we say is that the sum total of its provisions drives too hard a bargain for a court of conscience to assist.

* * *

The judgments will be affirmed.

------

1. What remedy may be available to Campbell if the company sues Wentz at law now that it has been rebuffed in equity? If the court awards Campbell the cost of cover, has Wentz gained anything in the end? Are there practical problems with the legal remedy that would have made the equitable remedy more desirable for Campbell? Does this result create higher transaction costs for the parties concerned?

2. Can the court's decision be reconciled with the policy of moving goods to the highest bidder in order to achieve the most efficient allocation of resources? Was the risk of shortage the main reason why Campbell contracted? If so, would the court's analysis have remained the same if the price of carrots had plummeted and the grower was seeking specific performance?

3. Distinguish fraud from unconscionability. Fraud is a tort cause of action that can provide a variety of remedies, such as damages or rescission. Fraud has several specific elements that are difficult to prove. Notably, the seller must make a misrepresentation of a material fact—an element often not present in cases involving overreaching by one party.

Transactions that do not have the elements of fraud nonetheless may be unconscionable. There are no elements of unconscionability; it is present when a judge is so shocked by the oppressive nature of the contract that the court simply will not enforce it. Unconscionability is merely a defense; it provides no relief except to excuse a plaintiff's continued performance under the contract. *See* Cowin Equip. Co. v. General Motors, *supra*, Chapter 2.

PROBLEM: THE GULLIBLE COMPUTER GENIUS

Cory Dexter, an eighteen-year-old student who excells at computers, wrote an excellent program and wished to market it. Distributech is a venture firm that caters to unsophisticated individuals who want to sell their computer programs. Distributech charges a fee to do a "market evaluation" of a program, but promises no results. For most individuals the company collects the fee and does little or no work except to send a standard glossy report that indicates the market is "not quite ready" for the program. The Distributech contract, however, not only provides for this fee but it further provides that the company is entitled to one-third of the gross sales of any program for which it did a market evaluation.

Dexter paid the fee to Distributech and received the standard glossy report. Subsequently Dexter managed to market the program individually with the help of an older friend. The program sold so successfully that Dexter was interviewed by a computer magazine in a feature on successful young programmers. The article alerted Distributech to Dexter's profits from the program.

Distributech sued Dexter to enforce the agreement for one-third of all past and future sales. Could Dexter defend with Distributech's unconscionability? Does it matter if Dexter's claims are legal, equitable, or mixed claims in law and equity?

JONES v. STAR CREDIT CORP.

59 Misc.2d 189, 298 N.Y.S.2d 264 (1969).

Wachtler, Justice.

On August 31, 1965 the plaintiffs, who are welfare recipients, agreed to purchase a home freezer unit for $900 as the result of a visit from a salesman representing Your Shop At Home Service, Inc. With the addition of the time credit charges, credit life insurance, credit property insurance, and sales tax, the purchase price totalled $1,234.80. Thus far the plaintiffs have paid $619.88 toward their purchase. The defendant claims that with various added credit charges paid for an extension of time there is a balance of $819.81 still due from the plaintiffs. The uncontroverted proof at the trial established that the freezer unit, when purchased, had a maximum retail value of approximately $300. The question is whether this transaction and the resulting contract could be considered unconscionable within the meaning of Section 2–302 of the Uniform Commercial Code which provides in part:

(1) If the court as a matter of law finds the contract or any clause of the contract to have been unconscionable at the time it was made the court may refuse to enforce the contract, or it may enforce the remainder of the contract without the unconscionable clause, or it may so limit the application of any unconscionable clause as to avoid any unconscionable result.

(2) When it is claimed or appears to the court that the contract or any clause thereof may be unconscionable the parties shall be afforded a reasonable opportunity to present evidence as to its commercial setting, purpose and effect to aid the court in making the determination. L.1962, c. 553, eff. Sept. 27, 1964.

There was a time when the shield of "caveat emptor" would protect the most unscrupulous in the marketplace—a time when the law, in granting parties unbridled latitude to make their own contracts, allowed exploitive and callous practices which shocked the conscience of both legislative bodies and the courts.

The effort to eliminate these practices has continued to pose a difficult problem. On the one hand it is necessary to recognize the importance of preserving the integrity of agreements and the fundamental right of parties to deal, trade, bargain, and contract. On the other hand there is the concern for the uneducated and often illiterate individual who is the victim of gross inequality of bargaining power, usually the poorest members of the community.

* * *

Section 2–302 of the Uniform Commercial Code enacts the moral sense of the community into the law of commercial transactions. It authorizes the court to find, as a matter of law, that a contract or a clause of a contract was "unconscionable at the time it was made," and upon so finding the court may refuse to enforce the contract, excise the objectionable clause or limit the application of the clause to avoid an unconscionable result. "The principle," states the Official Comment to this section, "is one of the prevention of oppression and unfair surprise." It permits a court to accomplish directly what heretofore was often accomplished by construction of language, manipulations of fluid rules of contract law and determinations based upon a presumed public policy.

* * *

Fraud, in the instant case, is not present; nor is it necessary under the statute. The question which presents itself is whether or not, under the circumstances of this case, the sale of a freezer unit having a retail value of $300 for $900 ($1,439.69 including credit charges and $18 sales tax) is unconscionable as a matter of law. The court believes it is.

* * *

Having already paid more than $600 toward the purchase of this $300 freezer unit, it is apparent that the defendant has already been amply compensated. In accordance with the statute, the application of the payment provision should be limited to amounts already paid by the plaintiffs and the contract be reformed and amended by changing the payments called for therein to equal the amount of payment actually so paid by the plaintiffs.

———

1. *Unconscionability at Law and in Equity. Campbell Soup Co. v. Wentz, supra,* was a case in equity specific performance whereas the principal case, *Jones v. Star Credit Co.,* involved enforcement of a contract at law. The concept of unconscionability is equitable in nature

because of its close relationship to "unclean hands." *Wentz* is an example of unconscionability as a defense in a case arising in equity, but such cases are rare because most sales contracts involve damages at law. The concept has been absorbed into law to affect enforcement of contract damages, most notably through U.C.C. 2–302. Virtually all unconscionability claims arise in claims for legal damages rather than for equitable relief. The rhetoric nonetheless reflects the equitable roots of the concept, as *Star Credit* illustrates.

2. A 1965 case that was decided before the U.C.C. was effective in the District of Columbia found a common law basis for an unconscionability defense at law. *Williams v. Walker–Thomas* held that a court could refuse legal remedies under common law when a contract is unreasonably favorable to one party and when the other party lacks meaningful choice on harsh contract terms. In the *Williams* case there were hidden important terms in a printed consumer form contract. 350 F.2d 445 (D.C.Cir.1965).

3. Unconscionability is only a defense at common law or under the U.C.C. It is not a source of a right for damages suffered because of an unconscionable contract. In Vom Lehn v. Astor Art Galleries, Ltd., for example, a dealer charged $67,000 for jade carvings worth less than $15,000. The purchasers could not use unconscionability as a basis for damages; damages require proof of fraud. The dealer's unconscionable conduct was relevant in his counterclaim for the $18,000 unpaid balance because the court refused to enforce the contract. 86 Misc.2d 1, 380 N.Y.S.2d 532 (1976).

C. ELECTION OF REMEDIES

Section Coverage:

In some instances an injured party may have several available remedies to redress the violation of a single right. A classic example would be where a purchaser of a used car later discovers that the dealer fraudulently misrepresented the condition of the car. The buyer must choose whether to affirm the transaction and seek damages for fraud or to disaffirm the contract and seek restitution. The remedies are necessarily inconsistent; therefore the act of choosing or "electing" one remedy will preclude recovery on the other.

The two policies that gave rise historically to recognition of the doctrine of election of remedies were sensible: to prevent double recovery and to avoid undue prejudice to the defendant. Some courts, however, have applied the doctrine in situations where neither policy concern is furthered and the result appears perfectly insensible. Thus, some courts have allowed the doctrine to extinguish a substantive cause of action even before the plaintiff filed suit and even though the plaintiff never intended to make an election. For example, if the defrauded car purchaser takes the car back to the dealer, that action may be considered an election to rescind the contract. Alternatively, if the car buyer sent a letter to the dealer demanding damages as a consequence of the fraud, a court may characterize the conduct as an election to affirm the contract. Unfortunately for the car purchaser, either "election" may very likely not be upon the advice of counsel and probably does not reflect a meaningful choice. Nonetheless, the buyer may be deemed bound by the election even if the seller would not be unduly prejudiced by a later change of heart.

Critics of the doctrine cite occasions where it worked harsh results upon unwary plaintiffs who unwittingly manifested a choice of remedies by action or delay of action. Some courts have not agreed that the election should be final and irrevocable even though no prejudice would actually accrue to the other party if the plaintiff were allowed to change remedies. Consequently, the Uniform Commercial Code has reacted to the unsubstantiated harshness and inequities of the election of remedies doctrine by rejecting it outright. [U.C.C. § 2–703 Comment 1; § 2–711 and § 2–721]. Similarly, the Restatement (Second) of Contracts § 378 severely circumscribes the common law doctrine by stating that the manifestation of a choice of inconsistent remedies does not bar another remedy unless the other party "materially changes his position in reliance on the manifestation." Thus, although the election of remedies doctrine survives, its vitality has been substantially weakened and its application replaced by the principles of res judicata, merger, and estoppel.

Model Case:

The Beyers are antique dealers who want to purchase a distinctive older home as their personal residence. They own many fine pieces of antique furniture as their personal property and they are quite particular about the kind of house appropriate for them.

One day they saw exactly the house they wanted, but it was not for sale. The Beyers rang the doorbell and spoke to the homeowners, the Owens. At first the Owens refused to sell, but after several days negotiations the two parties reached an agreement. Each couple was represented by counsel and signed a contract for the sale of the property.

A short time later the Owens called the Beyers and said they would not go through with the sale because they had just learned that their daughter was engaged and she wanted the wedding in the family's old home. The Beyers happened to be having marital difficulties at the time and responded, "Fine. You keep it. But you'll be hearing from our lawyer about our costs."

The Owens proceeded to repair the house in anticipation of the wedding. The front porch was removed and completely replaced with an expensive new entrance; a gazebo was built in the backyard; and extensive renovations were made throughout the house. In the meantime the Owens refused to pay the costs claimed by the Beyers, so the attorney for the Beyers filed a complaint in state court. The prayer for relief asked for damages.

After these events the Beyers reconciled their marital difficulties. As a reaffirmation of their marriage, they decided that they wanted to purchase the Owens' house as originally planned. The Beyers' attorney seeks to amend the complaint to ask for specific performance of the land sales contract.

In jurisdictions that strictly apply election of remedies the Beyers' claim may be barred even if the Owens were not prejudiced by the inconsistent demands. The initial demand for damages could be a binding election, since damages and specific performance could not both be recovered. The Restatement (Second) of Contracts has modified the doctrine by basing it on estoppel principles. Jurisdictions following this approach would preclude specific performance if Owens' change in position is material. The extensive renovations are likely to be a sufficient change in position to bar the belated specific performance request.

HEAD & SEEMANN, INC. v. GREGG
104 Wis.2d 156, 311 N.W.2d 667 (1981).

Voss, Presiding Judge. * * *

Defendant Bettye J. Gregg offered to buy a Brookfield home from plaintiff corporation. She represented, verbally and in writing, that she had $15,000 to $20,000 of equity in another home and would pay this amount to plaintiff after selling the other home. She knew, however, that she had no such equity. Relying on these intentionally fraudulent representations, plaintiff accepted defendant's offer to buy, and the parties entered into a land contract. After taking occupancy, defendant failed to make any of the contract payments. Plaintiff's investigation then revealed the fraud.

Plaintiff commenced this action seeking one of two alternative forms of relief. Based on the fraud, plaintiff sought rescission, ejectment and recovery for five months of lost use of the property and out-of-pocket expenses. Alternatively, based on defendant's breach of contract, plaintiff sought rescission, foreclosure and ejectment.

The trial court granted partial summary judgment for plaintiff, rescinding the contract for fraud. The court ordered ejectment but stayed the order for two weeks pending defendant's voluntary removal. The court also obtained plaintiff's stipulation that, if defendant removed herself within the two weeks, the plaintiff's claim for damages would be dismissed. Defendant failed to vacate the property, and the court entered an interlocutory judgment of ejectment.

Defendant later sought dismissal of the damages claim based on the election of remedies doctrine. The court determined that the judgment for ejectment was an election of remedies barring recovery of damages and, therefore, dismissed the cause of action based on fraud.   * * *

Plaintiff contends that it is entitled to recover for the lost use of the property and out-of-pocket expenses during defendant's possession of the property. It contends that recovery for these items, in addition to the rescission and return of the real estate, is necessary to restore plaintiff to his status before the fraud and execution of the contract. Since these "damages" would only restore plaintiff to its previous position and would not give plaintiff the purchase price or the benefit of the bargain, plaintiff argues that the remedies are not inconsistent, and the doctrine of election of remedies should not be applied. We agree.

The election of remedies doctrine is an equitable principle barring one from maintaining inconsistent theories or forms of relief. [Citation.] Its underlying purpose is to prevent double recovery for the same wrong. [Citations.] The label "election of remedies" is frequently used as a cloak for an estoppel or ratification where, for example, it bars a suit for rescission of a contact *subsequent* to some act of affirmance of the contract. [Citation.] Wisconsin courts have been attempting to restrict the doctrine to reduce its harsh effects. [Citations.]

The classic application of the election of remedies doctrine is that a defrauded party has the election of either rescission or affirming the contract and seeking damages. [Citation.] The choice is forced with respect to alternative theories in a single lawsuit because of inconsistency of both rescinding and affirming the contract. [Citation.]

Thus, it superficially appears that if a claimant chooses to seek rescission, he may not sue for damages. But the word "damages," like the label "election of remedies," impedes rather than aids the inquiry into the types of relief appropriate in a given case. Rescission is always coupled with restitution: the parties return the money, property or other benefits so as to restore each other to the position they were in prior to the transaction. * * *

In Carpenter v. Mason, 181 Wis. 114, 193 N.W. 973 (1923), plaintiff entered into a land contract in reliance on defendant's fraudulent statements. The trial court entered judgment of rescission and ordered recovery of the money paid toward the purchase plus $140 for plaintiff's costs in moving from another state as a result of the fraud. The Wisconsin Supreme Court disallowed the moving costs. The court stated that placing the parties *in status quo* "does not mean that the parties are to be restored to the situation which existed previous to their entering into the contract." It means, the court indicated, only that each party must return what he has actually received. Defendants did not receive plaintiff's expenditures for moving. "To require them to restore more than they received would be to permit the plaintiff to recover *damages for breach of the contract.* The plaintiff does not affirm the contract but disaffirms it and seeks rescission. He may not do both." (emphasis added).

* * * *Carpenter v. Mason* has become a somewhat infamous horror story cited as a good reason why the election of remedies doctrine ought to be abolished:

The best example that I can recall to show the need for the fraud statute [abolishing election of remedies in fraud cases in New York] is a case decided in Wisconsin during an earlier boom period. * * *

What substantial reason can be given for such a decision? Did not the defendants' wrong proximately cause the plaintiff all of the losses that he sustained? Did not the plaintiff allege and prove all of the facts necessary to entitle him to all of the items of recovery claimed? Was there any *duplication* of items of recovery? Certainly not. Was the defendant misled prejudicially by the plaintiff's suing to get his money "back," and also his money paid out for moving? No prejudicial reliance appears. Then is not the doctrine of election of remedies here merely a requirement of formal consistency? * * *

Patterson, *Improvements in the Law of Restitution,* 40 Cornell L.Q. 667, 679–80 (1955). * * *

A host of commentators support elimination of the election of remedies doctrine. A common theme is that the doctrine substitutes labels and formalism for inquiry into whether double recovery results in *fact*. The rigid doctrine goes to the other extreme, actually resulting in the undercompensation of fraud victims and the protection of undeserving wrongdoers. * * *

It appears that the commentators and the modern trend of the law support abandonment of the formalistic shell of the doctrine of election of remedies. The law can prevent windfalls to claimants without going overboard by requiring that fraud victims bear part of the loss, absolving defrauding parties of their proper responsibility.

Elimination of the formal doctrine would permit courts to focus on the rule of one satisfaction and deemphasize theoretical consistency of remedies. In the instant case, plaintiff might have its rescission and consequential damages for the *tort* of fraud or deceit. Since the tort system is designed to make one whole to the extent possible through a monetary award, plaintiff would receive such damages in tort which in addition to return of the land would restore it to its preinjury position. [Citation.] No double recovery would result in this case.

* * *

Order reversed.

———

1. A key issue with respect to the election of remedies doctrine is whether several remedies are "inconsistent" with each other. In Villeneuve v. Atlas Yacht Sales, Inc., 483 So.2d 67, 69–70 (Fla.App.1986), for example, the election of remedies doctrine precluded a claim to recover title to a yacht; the facts that supported a judgment for damages for loss of the purchase price were inconsistent with the facts necessary to obtain title.

See also Baker v. Superior Court, 150 Cal.App.3d 140, 197 Cal.Rptr. 480, 483 (1983) (no election of remedies where fraud in the inducement and breach of contract actions involved different obligations and different operative facts); Trahan v. Trahan, 455 A.2d 1307, 1312 (R.I.1983) (action of debt on judgment not inconsistent with contempt proceedings); North American Graphite Corp. v. Allan, 184 F.2d 387, 389 (D.C.Cir. 1950) (no election required between contract and quasi-contract); *contra* Boyd v. Margolin, 421 S.W.2d 761, 768 (Mo.1967) (action on express contract factually dissimilar from quantum meruit, and thus "inconsistent" for election of remedies).

2.   There cannot be an "election" barring an inconsistent remedy unless two or more remedies for the same claim in fact coexist.   In Fitzgerald v. Title Guarantee and Trust Co., 290 N.Y. 376, 49 N.E.2d 489 (1943), the plaintiff sought to rescind the purchase of certain mortgage certificates on the basis of fraudulent misrepresentations allegedly made by the defendant. The lower court granted the defendant's motion for summary judgment because the plaintiff's claim was barred by the applicable statute of limitation. The New York Court of Appeals, though, held that election of remedies did not preclude the plaintiff from amending the complaint to seek a different remedy because, at the time the suit was commenced, the plaintiff did not possess coexisting but inconsistent remedies.

3.   Courts have split over whether the pursuit of a worker's compensation claim constitutes an election which forecloses an employee from subsequently asserting a common law tort cause of action. *Compare* Martinkowski v. Carborundum Co., 108 Misc.2d 184, 437 N.Y.S.2d 237 (1981) (election by filing for and collecting workmens' compensation benefits precludes action against employer for intentional tortious conduct) *with* Flaherty v. United Engineers and Constructors, 213 F.Supp. 835, 838 (E.D.Pa.1961) (suit for personal injuries against employer allowed despite prior acceptance of statutory workmen's compensation benefits); Davis v. Rockwell International Corp., 596 F.Supp. 780, 787–788 (N.D.Ohio 1984) (employer may not be permitted to shield itself from intentional tort claim by asserting election of workmen's compensation remedy). *See also* Velez v. Oxford Development Co., 457 So.2d 1388, 1389 (Fla.App.1984) (election of remedies not applicable where employee's tort action against employer alleged injuries sustained outside course of employment); Hines v. Superior Court, 435 P.2d 149, 151 (Okl.1967) (final order by the State Industrial Court that it lacked subject matter jurisdiction over employee's disability claim not an election barring personal injury claim against the employer).

4.   The common law doctrine of election of remedies has been expressly repudiated by the Uniform Commercial Code with respect to the sale of goods. U.C.C. § 2–703 comment a. The Code's liberal treatment of inconsistent demands is illustrated by Melby v. Hawkins Pontiac, Inc., 13 Wash.App. 745, 537 P.2d 807 (1975). The plaintiff, after several months of repair difficulties following the purchase of a new automobile, filed suit against the dealership claiming damages for breach

of warranty. The trial court granted the plaintiff rescission of the purchase agreement and restitution of amounts paid on the contract. On appeal, the dealership asserted that rescission was an inappropriate remedy because the plaintiff had affirmed the contract by electing to pursue only the damages remedy. The appellate court acknowledged that an affirmance of a contract and a demand for damages is inconsistent with disaffirmance by a claim for rescission, but rejected a "harsh application" of election of remedies. The court reasoned that (1) a harsh application is not necessary to prevent double recovery, and (2) the doctrine as sometimes applied is inconsistent with modern rules of pleading which allow demands for alternative relief and amendments to the pleadings to conform to the evidence. The court added, however, that the doctrine should not be ignored when the defendant has relied detrimentally on the plaintiff's prayer for relief or has been otherwise prejudiced by the plaintiff's actions.

5. Several states have enacted statutes that abrogate the election of remedies doctrine in cases other than those involving the sale of goods. For example, Georgia Code § 3–1.4 provides "A plaintiff may pursue any number of consistent or inconsistent remedies against the same person or different persons until he shall obtain a satisfaction from some of them."

New York Civil Practice Law § 3002(e) (McKinney) rejects the election of remedies doctrine in cases involving fraud or misrepresentation. Similarly, California Civil Code § 1692 provides that a claim for damages is not inconsistent with rescission. The aggrieved party may be awarded "complete relief," including restitution of benefits and any consequential damages as long as there are no duplicate or inconsistent items of recovery.

In Cobian v. Ordonez, 103 Cal.App.3d Supp. 22, 163 Cal.Rptr. 126 (1980), the buyer of an automobile sued the seller demanding rescission, restitution and damages based upon fraudulent misrepresentations. The jury awarded the plaintiff rescission of the contract and damages for fraud. The appellate court rejected the seller's contention that the plaintiff, by electing to rescind, gave up the right to damages. The court stated that the plaintiff's recovery of his down payment did not foreclose the availability of punitive damages, and noted that Civil Code section 1692 provided that a damages claim was not inconsistent with a claim for rescission as long as no double recovery resulted.

PROBLEM: THE FRAUDULENT SALE

Abrams purchased all the shares of stock in a small goldmining company, Klondike King, Inc., from Meyers for $10,000. Several weeks after the sale was completed, Abrams' accountant discovered that the financial disclosures given by Meyers in connection with the transaction substantially understated the liabilities of Klondike. The accountant estimated that the current fair market value of Klondike King was only

$4,500. Based upon the accountant's information, Abrams sent a letter to Meyers demanding $5,500 as damages for the difference in the value of the company as promised and the value actually received.

Negotiations between the parties proved unsuccessful and, six months after the closing date, Abrams filed suit seeking, in the alternative: (a) damages for breach of contract for lost expectancy, (b) tort damages based upon common law fraud, or (c) rescission and restitution.

1. Should the doctrine of election of remedies bar any of Abrams' asserted claims?

2. Assume instead that Abrams initially demanded rescission and restitution rather than damages. Does that make a difference?

3. What if Abrams, during the six months period of ownership of the company, made several personnel changes and instituted a different system of bookkeeping?

4. What if the price of gold declined from $400 per ounce at the time of the transaction to $300 per ounce, resulting in a corresponding decline in the fair market value of Klondike King to approximately $2,000 at the time of trial?

ALTOM v. HAWES

63 Ill.App.3d 659, 20 Ill.Dec. 330, 380 N.E.2d 7 (1978).

JONES, JUSTICE.

* * * [O]n or about February 10, 1976, the plaintiff, Janice Altom, and her then husband, Melvin Altom, entered into a separation agreement which provided that Janice Altom was to have exclusive possession of the marital home and of the household furniture and furnishings, except such items as the parties might agree would be Melvin Altom's. On March 7, 1976, Melvin Altom called Tracy Hawes, a longtime friend, and asked if he wanted to buy some furniture. Tracy Hawes went to the marital residence where he found Melvin Altom and Melvin's brother. He chose several items of furniture, agreed to pay the asking price of $1,500 and took the items away that same afternoon. Mr. Altom gave him a bill of sale. * * *

On March 18, the plaintiff filed a complaint for divorce. A default hearing was held and a decree was entered on May 6, 1976. The decree recited that Melvin Altom had appropriated and sold certain household furniture belonging to Janice Altom in violation of the separation agreement of the value of $1,500 and judgment was entered against Melvin Altom in that amount.

Approximately one month after the entry of the decree of divorce Janice Altom filed her complaint in replevin against the Haweses.

Defendants contend that the granting of the motion for summary judgment was proper in that the plaintiff has elected her remedy in choosing to pursue her claim against Melvin Altom to judgment and may not seek a double recovery by now proceeding against them in replevin. The plaintiff counters that the judgment against Melvin Altom is unsatisfied and further that the doctrine of election of remedies does not apply as the prior judgment and the instant replevin action are not inconsistent remedies.   * * *

Plaintiff's arguments on the issue of election of remedies are two. First, the remedies sought must be inconsistent in order for the doctrine to apply and second, that in order to act as a bar to a subsequent suit the prior suit must be pursued not only to the rendering of a judgment but to full satisfaction of the judgment.

The doctrine of election of remedies has proved to be confusing and difficult of application, no less so to the courts of Illinois than to the courts of other states.   * * *

There is little question here that the remedies pursued by the plaintiff are inconsistent. She initially obtained a judgment for damages against her husband for a tortious sale of her furniture, a judgment that presupposes plaintiff's affirmance of the sale. By this later action of replevin she seeks a return of the furniture, an action in which she necessarily disaffirm the sale. It is this circumstance of inconsistency of remedies that prompted the defendant to advance the election of remedies argument and seek summary judgment.

Although we do not cite them here, many cases can be found which would sustain the granting of summary judgment upon these facts. Too, logic would repel the notion that a litigant could on the one hand say the sale was good but on the other say it was bad.

Research has disclosed to us, however, that the courts of Illinois, as well as those of other jurisdictions, have ameliorated the harsh results that have often flowed from a strict application of the election of remedies doctrine. Rather than follow a literal application of the rule, an approach has been derived whereby courts endeavor to determine not whether by the nature of the remedies invoked they are inconsistent, but whether the party should be estopped to bring the second action. We think the policy is best expressed by Prof. Corbin in his treatise on *Contracts,* Vol. 5A, sec. 1220:

> "The view with respect to election of remedies that is now becoming the prevailing one and that ought to be accepted is that, where a party injured by a breach definitely manifests a choice of a remedy that is actually available to him, in the place of some other alternative remedy, such a manifestation will bar an action for the latter remedy, provided that the party against whom the remedy is asked makes a substantial change of position in reliance on the manifestation of intention before notice of its retraction. This makes the conclusiveness of an 'election' depend upon the existence of facts sufficient to create an 'estoppel.' Cases stating this view are now very numerous and hold either that the remedy asked was not barred because there was no basis for an estoppel, or that an election was conclusive only because such a basis had been proved.

The mere bringing of a suit asking one remedy rather than another practically never affords ground for an estoppel and is not sufficient reason to deny an application for an alternative remedy."

* * *

Of the same import as Prof. Corbin's statement is sec. 381 of the Restatement of the Law, Contracts. Comment b of that section states:

"b. A mere manifestation of intention to pursue one remedy rather than the other is not an irrevocable election; but it becomes such as soon as the other party has materially changed his position in reasonable reliance thereon. The bringing of a suit for one remedy is a manifestation of choice of that remedy; but it does not preclude the plaintiff from seeking the other remedy instead, if he has a reasonable ground for so doing, so long as the defendant has not so altered his position as to make it unjust to permit the change."

* * *

In the case under consideration there is no threat of double recovery (plaintiff's judgment for damages against her husband has not been collectible and, in fact, appears uncollectible), defendant was not misled and did not change his position by reason of plaintiff's action for damages against her husband so that he would suffer some prejudice thereby, and there is nothing about the action for damages that would serve to bar the subsequent action by reason of *res judicata* or collateral estoppel.

For the foregoing reasons, the summary judgment rendered in defendant's behalf is reversed and this cause remanded for trial on the replevin issue.

———

1. A key issue regarding the election of remedies doctrine involves determining at what time a person must elect between existing, inconsistent remedies. Under the modern rules of civil procedure a party should not be barred from asserting alternate counts. F.R.C.P. 8(e)(2). Additionally, F.R.C.P. 15(a) liberally permits a party to amend pleadings.

Despite the liberalization of pleading, some courts may apply the election of remedies doctrine to extinguish a substantive cause of action prior to trial. For example, in Hipp v. Kennesaw Life & Accident Insurance Co., 301 F.Supp. 92, 94 (D.S.C.1968), an insured sent a letter to the insurance company demanding cancellation of a policy and reinstatement of a savings account based on alleged false representations by an agent. After the insurance company complied, the insured instituted suit seeking damages for fraud. The court held that the pretrial letter which demanded rescission was a "decisive act" which indicated an unequivocal election and thus precluded the subsequent suit for fraud.

2. Some jurisdictions have held that a binding election among inconsistent remedies occurs at the time the suit is filed. In Radiophone Service, Inc. v. Crowson Well Service, Inc., 309 So.2d 393 (La.App.1975) a landlord commenced an action to rescind a lease for nonpayment of rent. Before the tenant answered, the landlord sought to amend the complaint to eliminate the rescission claim but the court held that an irrevocable election had occurred. As a consequence, the landlord was denied potential recovery of amounts reflecting subsequently arising delinquencies under the lease agreement.

Similarly, in Morris Plan Leasing Company v. Karns, 197 Kan. 150, 415 P.2d 291 (1966) a lessor repossessed certain equipment and then commenced an action against the lessee to recover amounts for rental due but unpaid. The court held that the presuit actions of the lessor in repossession did not constitute an election of remedies, but determined that the "filing of a petition * * * gives finality to the election." The court further stated that the election upon commencement of a suit would be irrevocable "even though it is later dismissed without prejudice and not prosecuted to a finality." Later authority in Kansas, however, has suggested later stages in the proceedings when an election must be made. Lehigh, Inc. v. Stevens, 205 Kan. 103, 468 P.2d 177, 182 (1970) (plaintiff must elect while case is pending); Scott v. Strickland, 10 Kan.App.2d 14, 691 P.2d 45, 50 (1984) (election required prior to submission of claim to jury).

3. Other jurisdictions have not found an election of remedies based solely upon the commencement of an action, but have followed widely varied approaches as to what stage in the proceeding an election between inconsistent remedies must be made. See Jacobson v. Yaschik, 249 S.C. 577, 155 S.E.2d 601, 607 (1967) (elect at any stage of proceedings but not before defendant answers); Wills v. Regan, 58 Wis.2d 328, 206 N.W.2d 398, 407 (1973) (discretion of the court whether to require election before close of the case); Scott v. Strickland, 10 Kan.App.2d 14, 691 P.2d 45, 50 (1984) (must elect before submission of claim to jury); Coldwell Banker Commercial Group, Inc. v. Nodvin, 598 F.Supp. 853, 856 (N.D.Ga.1984) (elect prior to entry of judgment); Twentieth Century–Fox Film Corp. v. National Publishers, Inc., 294 F.Supp. 10, 12 (S.D.N.Y. 1968) (binding election only where other party detrimentally relies on action); Frazier v. Metropolitan Life Insurance Co., 169 Cal.App.3d 90, 214 Cal.Rptr. 883, 889 (1985) (no election until one of inconsistent rights satisfied by res judicata or estoppel); Taylor Rental Corp. v. J.I. Case Co., 749 F.2d 1526, 1529 (11th Cir.1985) (no election until debt actually satisfied).

4. The court in the principal case treated election of remedies as functionally delimited by the other preclusion doctrines of estoppel, double recovery, and res judicata. This treatment, although gaining many adherents, raises a number of semantic and substantive problems. Notably, if the election of remedies doctrine serves no useful purpose distinct from other preclusion doctrines, it should be expressly rejected

by courts rather than receive "lip service" but never functionally applied.

In Bocanegra v. Aetna Life Insurance Co., 605 S.W.2d 848, 851 (Tex.1980), the court noted that equitable estoppel differs from the election of remedies doctrine because it requires some deception that is relied upon by another resulting in prejudice. The court posited that election of remedies was a viable preclusion doctrine which would constitute a bar to relief when a plaintiff successfully exercises an informed choice between two or more remedies, rights, or states of facts that are so inconsistent as to constitute manifest injustice. The court failed to explain what significance "manifest injustice" has apart from the sort of prejudice involved in traditional estoppel theory.

5. In Roam v. Koop, 41 Cal.App.3d 1035, 116 Cal.Rptr. 539 (1974) a homeowner filed suit against a contractor alleging fraud, unlawful misappropriation of funds, breach of contract, and money had and received. After filing the multiple count complaint, the plaintiff obtained a writ of attachment and levied against various bank accounts, a safety deposit box, and certain real property belonging to the defendant.

The appellate court noted that the plaintiff can plead inconsistent causes of action in tort and in contract, but that obtaining an attachment constituted a positive act in pursuit of his contractual remedy. By levying under the writ, the plaintiff deprived Koop of the use of his property. The court held that because plaintiff was pursuing two inconsistent remedies and took unequivocal action under only one of them whereby he gained an advantage over the defendant the doctrine of election of remedies applied. However, since the appellate court viewed the election of remedies defense as a form of estoppel, the defendant was deemed to have waived the defense by failing to raise it in the trial court. Like estoppel, it could not be raised for the first time on appeal.

6. Some courts have inartfully interchanged the doctrines of res judicata and election of remedies to explain preclusion of claims by judgment. For example, in Family Bank of Commerce v. Nelson, 72 Or.App. 739, 697 P.2d 216 (1985) the court noted that an "election" occurs at the time of judgment. In contrast, in Frazier v. Metropolitan Life Insurance Co., 169 Cal.App.3d 90, 101, 214 Cal.Rptr. 883, 888 (1985), the court differentiated among the doctrines by stating that "A person should be entitled to change his alternative remedies until one of his inconsistent rights is vindicated by application of the doctrines of res judicata or estoppel."

7. The Restatement (Second) of Judgments § 25, comment m (1982) further explains the interrelationship of election of remedies and res judicata:

Sometimes it is held that the mere beginning of an action for one remedy is itself an election preventing recourse to another remedy deemed in some sense "inconsistent." In a mature procedural system the mere commencement of an action for a given remedy should not of itself prevent the granting of a different remedy when warranted by the facts proved (perhaps after amendment in the course of trial). Ordinarily a plaintiff may pursue alternative remedies, however "inconsistent," with final "election" postponed to a late stage of the action—after the proof is in or even after the fact-finder, court or jury, has made its findings on both alternatives. In such circumstances, if the plaintiff seeks but one remedy, and judgment is entered for or against him, he should be precluded from a second action by the rules of merger or bar. This is properly explained on res judicata principles rather than on any notions of election of remedies.

8.   For additional commentary on the election of remedies doctrine *see*: Brill, The Election of Remedies Doctrine in Arkansas, 37 Ark.L.Rev. 385 (1983); Corbin, Waiver of Tort and Suit in Assumpsit, 19 Yale L.J. 221 (1910); Deinard & Deinard, Election of Remedies, 6 Minn.L.Rev. 341 (1922); Dobbs, Pressing Problems for the Plaintiff's Lawyer in Rescission: Election of Remedies and Restoration of Consideration, 26 Ark.L.Rev. 322 (1972); Fraser, Election of Remedies: An Anachronism, 29 Okla.L.Rev. 1 (1976); Hine, Election of Remedies, A Criticism, 26 Harv.L.Rev. 707 (1913); Mendelsohn, Election of Remedies and Settlement—New Lyrics to an Outworn Tune, 12 St. Mary's L.J. 367 (1980); Merrem, Election of Remedies in Texas, 8 Sw.L.J. 109 (1954); Note, Election of Remedies: A Delusion? 38 Colum.L.Rev. 292 (1938); Note, Modern Views of the Election of Remedies, 34 Yale L.J. 665 (1925); Oesterle, Restitution & Reform, 70 Mich.L.Rev. 336 (1980); Patterson, Improvements in the Law of Restitution, 40 Cornell L.Q. 667 (1955); Pray, Election of Remedies: A Judicial Weed?, 16 Okla.L.Rev. 193 (1963); Rothschild, A Remedy for Election of Remedies, 14 Cornell L.Q. 141 (1929); Yerkes, Election of Remedies in Cases of Fraudulent Misrepresentation, 26 S.Cal.L.Rev. 157 (1963).

Chapter 6

INTERLOCUTORY INJUNCTIONS

Interlocutory relief is expedited relief for a short term that a court may give before final adjudication of a case on the merits. This chapter concerns two important forms of interlocutory relief: the temporary restraining order (TRO) and the preliminary injunction. These equitable orders are available in special circumstances when a plaintiff needs immediate court action to avoid irreversible losses while waiting for the trial on the merits.

Courts generally are reluctant to act when there has not been time for careful deliberation of the full facts of a case. Interlocutory injunctions are considered extraordinary relief that require a strong showing of its necessity. Moreover, a plaintiff must be prepared to compensate a wrongfully enjoined defendant for losses caused by the order unless the plaintiff is ultimately victorious in the underlying case. The plaintiff's good faith in seeking the TRO or preliminary injunction is not a defense; a defendant who finally wins the case can recover any proven losses resulting from the interlocutory order. This rule serves to deter plaintiffs who doubt the strength of their claims from asking courts to grant extraordinary relief in advance of trial.

The primary differences between temporary restraining orders and preliminary injunctions are the speed with which they are acquired and their duration. A TRO is a brief stop-gap measure for a truly urgent situation. It can be replaced with a preliminary injunction after the court has had a few days to receive some greater amount of evidence in the case. A preliminary injunction, which is appealable, then lasts until the full trial.

States vary slightly in the names, procedures, and requirements for interlocutory injunctions. They are constrained by Constitutional requirements, and the Supreme Court has held that there are limits on the issuance of an *ex parte* TRO under state law, at least when First Amendment rights are at stake.

The primary focus of this chapter is on common law substantive requirements and the procedures in Federal Rule of Civil Procedure 65. Rule 65 concerns interlocutory relief in federal courts, and many states have identical or similar rules.

A. SUBSTANTIVE REQUIREMENTS

Section Coverage:

The common law has developed several substantive requirements for temporary injunctive orders. Although Federal Rule of Civil Procedure

65 covers only procedural requirements, federal courts have interpreted Rule 65 to incorporate common law substantive requirements.

A plaintiff must convince the court that an interlocutory order is necessary to preserve the *status quo* pending trial because otherwise irreparable harm will result. The plaintiff further must make some showing of the strength of the claim in the underlying suit. This section examines differing formulations for tests combining these elements for relief under federal law. Notably, the rules differ on whether the plaintiff must always show a "probability" of success on the merits of the underlying claim, or whether a lesser standard is appropriate when the degree of potential harm without the order is especially great.

Model Case:

The Tufts own a fruit orchard neighboring on the Jones Chemical Company (Jones). Jones is a repacking plant for various chemicals. The company's business is to transfer chemicals from large containers received from the manufacturers to small packages for consumer distribution. Both the orchard and the Jones plant are lawful activities in the area.

This year the Tufts suddenly have noticed a sharp deterioration in the trees adjacent to the chemical plant. Expert evidence establishes the cause to be chlorine gas and fumes escaping from the Jones plant. The Tufts sue in state court pursuant to a statute modelled after the Federal Rule of Civil Procedure 65 that governs temporary restraining orders and preliminary injunctions. They seek a preliminary and permanent injunction and damages. After a brief hearing the judge determines that continuous and irreparable damage will occur to the orchard unless the plant is enjoined from emitting the fumes.

The substantive legal issue under nuisance law is whether the activity of the defendant constitutes a substantial and unreasonable interference with the use and enjoyment of the plaintiff's property. Although there is insufficient time at a preliminary injunction hearing to determine this issue, each side can present some evidence to give the judge a general idea of the strength of the position of each party. The defendant can also introduce evidence of the degree of hardship that will occur to the plant if a preliminary injunction is issued.

The traditional test for a preliminary injunction is that the judge must find the plaintiff's claim is likely to be successful on the merits and that there will be irreparable harm to a significant portion of the orchard. If the court does not find the strength of the plaintiff's claim to amount to a "probability" of success on the merits at the full trial, then there will be no preliminary relief unless this court follows the alternative test. Under the sliding scale alternative test the court will grant the preliminary injunction for a weak substantive claim only if the showing of irreparable harm is exceptionally strong.

The public interest factor here may favor either side. If the escaping gas threatens people or things in addition to the orchard, it will likely favor the plaintiffs. If the defendant is a large employer and if an injunction will close operations, then it may favor the defendant.

• NARRAGANSETT INDIAN TRIBE v. GUILBERT

934 F.2d 4 (1st Cir.1991).

SELYA, CIRCUIT JUDGE.

This is a civil action commenced by the Narragansett Indian tribe and certain members thereof, as class representatives, to protect tribal rights and property from threatened despoliation.

* * *

The Narragansett Indians have inhabited lands within Rhode Island since time immemorial. Through the negotiated settlement of certain disputes, culminating in a Joint Memorandum of Understanding (JMU) signed in 1978, and the subsequent passage of federal and state statutes, [citations], the Tribe acquired approximately eighteen hundred acres of real estate in or around 1979. The land is not contiguous but lies entirely within the municipal boundaries of Charlestown, Rhode Island. The land comprises what is known colloquially as the Narragansett Indian Reservation.

Defendant-appellee Paul E. Guilbert owns a parcel of land in Charlestown, the dimensions of which are roughly one hundred fifty feet by two hundred forty feet. He purchased the lot from a Narragansett Indian. It is zoned single-family residential. Guilbert wishes to build a house on it. He has received all state and local permits necessary for the planned construction.

The Tribe filed its complaint against Guilbert in federal district court on December 6, 1990, alleging that his property encroaches on the Reservation in various ways and seeking to enjoin the work. At that time, construction was already underway; Guilbert had cleared the site, laid the foundation, installed the septic system, and was about to place a modular home on the foundation. The district court granted an *ex parte* temporary restraining order and scheduled a prompt hearing on preliminary injunction. *See* Fed.R.Civ.P. 65. When the hearing concluded, the court ruled from the bench, denying the preliminary injunction and vacating the temporary restraining order. This appeal followed.

To determine the appropriateness of granting or denying a preliminary injunction, we have instructed trial courts to use a quadripartite test, taking into account: 1. The likelihood of success on the merits; 2. The potential for irreparable injury; 3. A balancing of the relevant equities (most importantly, the hardship to the nonmovant if the restrainer issues as contrasted with the hardship to the movant if interim relief is withheld); and 4. The effect on the public interest of a grant or denial of the restrainer. [Citations.] In turn, "[w]e scrutinize a district court's decision to grant or deny a preliminary injunction under a relatively deferential glass." [Citation.] Unless a mistake of law or an abuse of discretion is made manifest, we will not disturb the ruling below. * * *

Likelihood of Success

Our analysis begins with probability of success, as we have often found this furcula to be critical. [Citations.] We preface our observations by noting that a court's conclusions as to the merits of the issues presented on preliminary injunction are to be understood as statements of probable outcomes. [Citation.] Thus, a party losing the battle on likelihood of success may nonetheless win the war at a succeeding trial on the merits.

* * * [T]he district court, although recognizing certain ambiguities as to the boundaries of the area ceded to the Tribe, found as fact that Guilbert's lot was outside the perimeters of the Reservation and that any aboriginal claims to the land had been extinguished by the settlement. For another thing, neither the relevant exhibit attached to the JMU nor the town assessor's map corroborates the appellants' claim. Lastly, appellants' counsel conceded in this court that he could not yet prove whether Guilbert's land was actually tribal land.

On this chiaroscuro record, the court's findings, abetted by appellants' concession, easily pass Rule 65 muster. Likelihood of success cannot be woven from the gossamer threads of speculation and surmise. The Tribe's claim of a right to exercise civil authority over Guilbert's land is, in this case, largely dependent on the situs of the property. [Citations.] At this juncture, then, the preliminary finding that the land is located beyond the sphere of tribal suzerainty severely undercuts any suggested likelihood of success on the Tribe's encroachment claims.

Irreparable Harm

The district court's alternative ground for denying a preliminary injunction was equally solid. In cases involving real property, we have often found the irreparability of the injury to be of paramount concern. The reason, of course, is that "[r]eal estate has long been thought unique, and thus, injuries to real estate interests frequently come within the ken of the chancellor." [Citation.] Be that as it may, irreparable harm is not assumed; it must be demonstrated. And even where real property is involved, "[s]peculative injury does not constitute a showing of irreparable harm." [Citation.]

In this instance, the court below was satisfied that the possibility of irreparable damage to the Reservation or to any of the other claimed property rights was very faint. There had already been extensive site preparation work on the property, including the cutting of trees and clearing of underbrush, the excavation for the house's foundation, and the invasive work incident to the installation of a septic system. In other words, the parcel of land had already undergone significant transformation. The Tribe failed to particularize in any meaningful way how further progress, up to and including the actual completion, or even occupancy, of the dwelling, would wreak harm less readily repairable than that which had already transpired. Given two additional opportunities, in appellate briefing and at oral argument before us, the Tribe remained wholly unable to make the conceptual case for irreparable injury. Hence, the district court's finding must stand. [3]

    * * * [Affirmed.]

---

    1. The four traditional prerequisites for issuance of a preliminary injunction are: 1) a substantial likelihood that movant will ultimately prevail on the merits; 2) a showing that movant will suffer irreparable injury unless the injunction issues; 3) proof that the threatened injury to movant outweighs whatever damage the proposed injunction may cause the opposing party; and 4) a showing that the injunction, if issued, would not be adverse to the public interest. The burden of proof on each of these four elements rests with the movant.

    2. *Likelihood of success on the merits.* The traditional requirements for granting a preliminary injunction begin with likelihood of success on the merits. As the court in the principal case notes, such a determination indicates only a probability. A different result may obtain after a full trial on the merits. This determination of probability has a tremendous effect on the negotiating positions of the parties with respect to any settlement of the suit, however. Many suits are won or lost as a practical matter at the preliminary injunction stage. Is there any alternative to this approach?

    3. *Irreparable harm.* The presence of irreparable harm is a requirement for a preliminary injunction. The plaintiff in the principal case failed to satisfy this requirement. What kind of evidence might have made a sufficient showing of irreparable harm in this case?

    In Winkle Pontiac Motorsports, Inc. v. Shepherd, 699 F.Supp. 1572 (N.D.Ga.1988), the plaintiff Winkle was in the business of building and racing cars. Winkle contracted with the defendant Shepherd, a professional stock car driver, to drive Winkle's cars in several races. Following a dispute between the parties, Winkle received notice that Shepherd had withdrawn from the contract. Winkle sought to prevent Shepherd from driving a particular car in a specific race because Winkle claimed ownership to that car and Winkle planned to run in that race with another driver. Winkle requested a preliminary injunction on a conversion claim.

    The court found a probability of success on the merits of the conversion claim, but no irreparable harm. The court noted:

> The key word in this consideration is *irreparable*. Mere injuries, however substantial, in terms of money, time and energy necessarily expended in the absence of a stay, are not enough. The possibility

---

    3. Of course, should the plaintiffs ultimately prevail on their claim, the trial court will have available the remedial option of prescribing injunctive relief at that time and ordering that the house be razed and the land restored. [Citation.]

that adequate compensatory or other corrective relief will be available at a later date, in the ordinary course of litigation, weighs heavily against a claim of irreparable harm.

The court held that if plaintiff were to prevail on the merits, money damages would be adequate to compensate him for the cost of replacing the car.

The plaintiff further argued that he would be irreparably injured by having to compete with one less car than expected. The lack of a back-up car would force him to race more conservatively. The court did not find the argument credible because the plaintiff had made no effort to acquire another back-up car.

4.   The inability to wait for monetary relief can occasionally, but rarely, constitute irreparable harm. In DiDomenico v. Employers Coop. Ind. Trust, 676 F.Supp. 903 (N.D.Ind.1987), the plaintiff sought a preliminary order to enjoin the defendant health insurer from denying coverage for a liver transplant operation. The health plan specifically excluded "experimental" liver transplants and said that transplants for patients under the age of twelve were not experimental. Other parts of the insurance plan were ambiguous concerning the coverage of organ transplants for adults. The plaintiff's doctors testified at the preliminary injunction hearing that the contemplated operation was medically necessary for the plaintiff's diseased liver condition and that adult liver transplants recently have become accepted and were no longer considered experimental by the medical community.

The plaintiff could not afford the operation without the insurance coverage that the defendant denied. The district court found that the plaintiff had made a sufficient showing of irreparable harm in addition to the other requirements for a preliminary injunction. Irreparable harm was established because the plaintiff showed that he could not "easily wait" to get relief until the end of a full trial on the merits which might be several years in the future.

5.   For copyright infringement cases, the great majority of federal Courts of Appeal make a presumption of irreparable harm once the plaintiff shows a likelihood of success on the copyright claim. See West Publishing Co. v. Mead Data Central, Inc., 799 F.2d 1219 (8th Cir.1986), cert. denied, 479 U.S. 1070, 107 S.Ct. 962, 93 L.Ed.2d 1010 (1987); Apple Computer, Inc. v. Franklin Computer Corp., 714 F.2d 1240 (3d Cir.1983), cert. dismissed, 464 U.S. 1033, 104 S.Ct. 690, 79 L.Ed.2d 158 (1984). But see Southern Monorail Co. v. Robbins & Myers, Inc., 666 F.2d 185 (5th Cir.1982).

Why should the irreparable harm requirement be different for different types of claims? If the plaintiff in Winkle, supra, had had a claim of copyright infringement rather than a claim for conversion, he would have had the benefit of a presumption of irreparable harm in most federal jurisdictions once he made the showing of likelihood of success on the merits. Is copyright more important to protect than car ownership?

Are the damages more difficult to calculate in one case or the other if the preliminary relief is not granted?

HARDING v. UNITED STATES FIGURE SKATING ASSOCIATION

851 F.Supp. 1476 (D.Or.1994).

PANNER, DISTRICT JUDGE.

Plaintiff Tonya Harding brought this diversity action for breach of contract against defendant United States Figure Skating Association, Inc. I enjoined defendant from holding a planned disciplinary hearing in Colorado on March 10, 1994. When the parties were unable to agree upon a new date for the disciplinary hearing, I extended that injunction to preclude defendant from holding the hearing prior to June 27, 1994. Defendant has now moved for reconsideration of my earlier ruling along with a motion to dismiss this action. I grant both motions, though not for the reasons urged by defendant.

At the time this action was filed, plaintiff was a member of the defendant United States Figure Skating Association. Plaintiff paid her dues, and agreed to comply with the rules of that association. The parties mutually agreed to certain rules that would govern any disciplinary proceeding against a member of the association.

Defendant's bylaws provide that when disciplinary charges are filed against a member, that member has thirty days to file a reply. The bylaws further provide that "upon receipt of the reply, the Hearing Panel shall set a place and date for a hearing that is reasonably convenient for all parties." Article XXVII, § 3(c)(iv). Defendant violated this rule by unilaterally setting a time and date for the hearing that was just three days after the reply was due. Defendant acted contrary to its bylaws by setting the date before it received the reply. Furthermore, in view of the complexity of the charges, March 10 was not a date "reasonably convenient for all parties."

I reviewed in camera the evidence defendant intended to present at the disciplinary hearing. The evidence was complex, involving the actions of several dozen individuals over a period of weeks. The evidence included statements by alleged co-conspirators, each of whom may have had a motive to misrepresent plaintiff's role in this matter. Moreover, because the Rules of Evidence do not apply at this disciplinary hearing, the documents defendant proposed to use were replete with hearsay, newspaper clippings, conclusions, an anonymous letter, forensic opinions, affidavits, media interviews, and similar items that would not be admissible in a court of law. In addition, it was intimated that plaintiff's defense might include a form of the "battered wife" defense, which would require extensive investigation by experts and interviews with persons who have known plaintiff and her former husband over a period of many years. Finally, the Hearing Panel that would decide the charges against plaintiff was the same panel that acted as a de facto grand jury in the decision to file charges against plaintiff in the first place. Based on my fourteen years of experience as a trial judge, and thirty years of experience as a trial lawyer before taking the bench, it was immediately apparent that plaintiff could not possibly prepare a defense to those charges in the time allotted. The hearing date established by defendant was not "reasonably convenient for all parties," as required by defendant's bylaws.

When one party to a contract is given discretion in the performance of some aspect of the contract, that discretion must be exercised in good faith. [Citation.] Colorado, where defendant is incorporated, recently adopted a similar view. [Citation.] The date set by defendant was arbitrary and manifestly unreasonable, and would severely prejudice plaintiff's chances of obtaining a fair hearing. Plaintiff immediately advised defendant that this date was not convenient and requested an extension of time. Defendant denied the request because it wanted to conduct the hearing prior to the World Championships so it could remove plaintiff from the United States delegation for that event. Plaintiff then exhausted her internal appeals within the association before filing this action for injunctive relief.

The courts should rightly hesitate before intervening in disciplinary hearings held by private associations, including the defendant United States Figure Skating Association. Intervention is appropriate only in the most extraordinary circumstances, where the association has clearly breached its own rules, that breach will imminently result in serious and irreparable harm to the plaintiff, and the plaintiff has exhausted all internal remedies. Even then, injunctive relief is limited to correcting the breach of the rules. The court should not intervene in the merits of the underlying dispute.

This is one of those rare cases where judicial intervention was appropriate. It appeared at the time that had defendant not been enjoined from holding the hearing on March 10, plaintiff would have suffered serious irreparable harm. Defendant argued that the matter was not ripe because the outcome of the hearing was unknown. If the only issue was whether plaintiff should have been allowed to skate in the World Championships in Japan later that month, defendant's point might have been well taken, since injunctive relief could still be sought at the conclusion of the disciplinary hearing. In this particular case, however, merely holding the hearing on March 10 would have caused plaintiff to suffer irreparable harm. In order to maintain her right to contest the decision of the Hearing Panel, plaintiff would have been obliged to appear before the panel and prematurely present her defense without having adequate time to prepare for that hearing. If the Hearing Panel found her guilty as charged, the resultant publicity could have severely prejudiced her chances for a fair trial in any future criminal case. Plaintiff would also have been obliged to decide upon and publicly disclose a defense strategy for both the civil and criminal matters before she had time to conduct full discovery and interview witnesses. Finally, the entire testimony, including information that has heretofore not been made public, would inevitably have been leaked to the media, despite defendant's best intentions to maintain the confidentiality of the proceedings, thereby further poisoning plaintiff's chance of obtaining a fair trial in the criminal proceeding. Under the circumstances, plaintiff's attorneys might well have advised their client not to attend the hearing. In that case, plaintiff would likely have forfeited any right to contest the results of the hearing. Her failure to contest the charges would have also resulted in her being found guilty in the court of public opinion.

I rejected plaintiff's suggestion that the disciplinary hearing be postponed until after resolution of the criminal charges against her. Defendant is a private association, not a governmental body. [Citation.] Plaintiff's constitutional right against self-incrimination is not implicated unless she is compelled to testify either before or by a governmental body.

I nonetheless concluded that plaintiff was entitled to additional time to prepare for the hearing. The harm to plaintiff greatly outweighed the harm to defendant from postponing the hearing. Defendant has an interest in enforcing its rules and promptly disciplining violators, and ensuring that only qualified skaters represent the United States at the World Championships. However, the United States Olympic Committee ("USOC") charter requires that resolution of disputes be both swift and equitable. In this case, equity was sacrificed for speed. Plaintiff exhausted all her internal remedies before filing suit. Defendant's bylaws provide for accelerated binding arbitration, but only to review the decision of the Hearing Panel after it finds plaintiff guilty and orders she be expelled from the Figure Skating Association. In most cases that would have been sufficient to protect the member's interests. This case was the exception. Defendant's bylaws do not provide for emergency arbitration of a dispute as to the timing of the disciplinary hearing. Under the unique circumstances of this case, which included the circus atmosphere generated by an international media frenzy, the complexity of the accusations against plaintiff, and the close connection between the disciplinary proceeding and possible criminal charges against plaintiff, defendant's internal remedies were inadequate to prevent the imminent injury to plaintiff.

* * * I did not order defendant to include plaintiff as a member of the United States delegation to the World Championships, or take any position upon the merits of the disciplinary proceeding. I merely ordered defendant to comply with the requirement in its own bylaws that the hearing be set at a time reasonably convenient for all parties, thus ensuring plaintiff could obtain a fair hearing.

Defendant also argues that the Figure Skating Association's bylaws provide an exclusive administrative procedure for resolution of disputes. However, that procedure works only so long as defendant follows it. Defendant's argument boils down to an assertion that plaintiff has no remedy even if defendant refuses to follow its own procedures. * * * [T]he harm to plaintiff did not flow solely from the penalty that might be imposed following the decision of the hearing panel, but rather from the premature hearing itself. Plaintiff exhausted all available remedies with respect to the hearing date.

*   *   *

Although I conclude this court has jurisdiction and the injunction was properly issued, I now grant defendant's motion for reconsideration because the circumstances requiring the injunction no longer exist. Plaintiff has resigned from the Figure Skating Association and pled guilty to the criminal charges. A disciplinary hearing has been set for June 29, a date that is reasonably convenient for all parties in accordance with defendant's bylaws. There is no reason to exercise continued jurisdiction over this matter, or to enjoin defendant any longer than absolutely necessary. Any intervention by the courts in the internal affairs of the Figure Skating Association should be restricted to that necessary to vindicate the rights at issue. Accordingly, the injunction dated March 31, 1994 is vacated, and the action dismissed as moot.

---

1. Reconsider the refusal of the court to review the action of a private association in *Treister v. American Academy of Orthopaedic Surgeons*, in Chapter 2 *supra*. Is that case consistent with the principal case?

2. What would have caused the irreparable harm to Tonya Harding if the defendant had held the hearing on March 10? To the extent that the harm is caused by third parties, such as the press, should the defendant suffer?

3. Irreparable injury is a prerequisite for temporary injunctive relief as it is for permanent orders. Even if the balance of hardships favors the plaintiff, a court should not issue an injunction without a showing of loss beyond economic loss compensable with damages. *See* Frank's GMC Truck Center, Inc. v. General Motors Corp., 847 F.2d 100 (3d Cir.1988) (only economic loss from refusal of manufacturer discontinuing line of trucks to supply parts to retailer losing service business).

4. In Classic Components Supply, Inc. v. Mitsubishi Electronics America, Inc., 841 F.2d 163 (7th Cir.1988), the plaintiff distributor sought an injunction to compel the defendant manufacturer to continue using it as a distributor. The defendant complained to the court that the plaintiff had promised by contract to arbitrate disputes of this character. The trial court ordered the plaintiff to arbitrate and denied the request for a preliminary injunction. The plaintiff appealed and argued that it was being irreparably injured because

> customers have already started to cancel their orders for Mitsubishi products. [Classic's] market development for Mitsubishi products will be totally lost if there is any significant interruption in its Dealership Agreement. This will effect [sic] not only the portion of

[Classic's] business represented by the Mitsubishi line, but its entire customer base which Classic has traditionally serviced by holding itself out as a source for a broad range of its customers' needs.

The Court of Appeals for the Seventh Circuit held for the defendant. Judge Easterbrook, writing for the majority, noted that this assertion of irreparable harm

> shows only that Classic may suffer injury. Injuries of this sort, common consequences of broken contracts, yield damages. Any injury compensable in money is not "irreparable," so an injunction is unavailable. [Citation.] Classic does not acknowledge the existence, let alone the force, of this principle. Classic therefore has not appealed to the exception: that a terminated supply arrangement may create irreparable injury if the interruption bids fair to propel one firm into bankruptcy and frustrate later attempts to compute or collect damages. [Citations.] Classic does not suggest that the injury it confronts is harder to quantify than the injury in any other contract case. Perhaps Classic abjured the exception because it offered no shelter. Classic distributes the lines of about 65 manufacturers; Mitsubishi's semiconductors accounted for only 1.5% of its sales in 1986 and 3.4% in early 1987; Classic can purchase Mitsubishi products (with Mitsubishi's blessing) from its distributors even if not directly from Mitsubishi.

Judge Easterbrook opined that the plaintiff's motive in bringing the appeal was solely for the purpose of delay to avoid its contractual duty to arbitrate. Believing that the plaintiff misused the legal process as "a crowbar for obtaining concessions that the merits of the case do not support," the court found that the action was frivolous and awarded attorneys' fees to the defendant. 841 F.2d 163 (7th Cir.1988).

5. Problems arise not only in interpreting which potential injuries are incapable of redress with damages, but also which are sufficiently ripe to pose a threat of irreparable harm. For example, in Flowers Ind. v. F.T.C., 849 F.2d 551 (11th Cir.1988), the Court of Appeals held that the district court erroneously granted a preliminary injunction against the Federal Trade Commission to bar enforcement of a divestiture order. There was no irreparable harm, the court held on appeal, because the agency did not have the power to divest the plaintiff's assets before a resolution of the underlying dispute with a consent decree. The lawsuit was premature until the parties had completed the administrative process.

6. The standard for review of a district court's grant or denial of a preliminary injunction is whether there was an abuse of discretion by the trial judge. The standard is a very deferential one because the balancing process for issuance of a preliminary injunction is highly discretionary. The question before the appellate court is whether the judge "exceeded the bounds of permissible choice in the circumstances" rather than what the appellate court would have done in the trial court's

place. Adams v. Attorney Registration and Disciplinary Com'n, 801 F.2d 968 (7th Cir.1986).

Abuse of discretion in the issuance of a preliminary injunction can occur in several ways. (1) The trial judge's decision must be based on relevant factors so as not to be a clear error in judgment. Citizens to Preserve Overton Park, Inc. v. Volpe, 401 U.S. 402, 91 S.Ct. 814, 28 L.Ed.2d 136 (1971). (2) The trial court must apply the correct legal standard for the federal circuit. Benda v. Grand Lodge of Int'l Ass'n of Machinists & Aerospace Workers, 584 F.2d 308 (9th Cir.1978), *cert. dismissed,* 441 U.S. 937, 99 S.Ct. 2065, 60 L.Ed.2d 667 (1979). (3) The trial judge must apply the correct law with respect to the underlying issues in the case. Sports Form, Inc. v. United Press Int'l, Inc., 686 F.2d 750 (9th Cir.1982). (4) The findings of fact must not be clearly errone- ous. United States v. United States Gypsum Co., 333 U.S. 364, 68 S.Ct. 525, 92 L.Ed. 746 (1948).

CASSIM v. BOWEN

824 F.2d 791 (9th Cir.1987).

SKOPIL, CIRCUIT JUDGE:

M.M. Cassim is a Medicare participating physician. He argues that as a matter of due process he is entitled to a full evidentiary hearing before the Secretary of Health and Human Services [HHS] can suspend him from Medicare and publish notice of his suspension in a local newspaper. The district court denied Cassim's motion for a preliminary injunction. We affirm.

* * *

Cassim argues that the district court improperly balanced the hard- ships. First, he emphasizes that his livelihood, reputation, and profes- sional career will be irreparably harmed. He contends the stigma of exclusion and publication could not be removed even if the ALJ [Admin- istrative Law Judge] completely exonerated him. Second, he asserts that the district court mistakenly believed he threatened the lives or health of his patients. Instead, he claims, OIG [Office of Inspector General] accused him of skillfully performing excessive surgery.

We reject Cassim's argument even though we recognize the possibili- ty of irreparable harm created by the Secretary's sanctions. Cassim is simply mistaken in asserting that HHS did not believe he threatened the health of his patients. OIG charged Cassim with doing unnecessary surgery in eight cases culled from a six-month period. In those eight cases, Cassim's patients ranged in age from 66 to 86. In each case, OIG concluded that Cassim had placed his patients in "high risk" situations or in "imminent danger." The Secretary persuasively argues that unnecessary surgery on elderly patients endangers their health.

Against the harm Cassim might suffer we must balance the harm his patients might suffer. We affirm the district court's finding that the balance of hardships neither tips sharply in Cassim's favor, nor favors him. * * *

Cassim's interests are substantial. * * * Cassim may still treat Medicare patients. If he prevails in his administrative appeal, he must be reimbursed. A successful appeal would also help restore his reputation and practice. The Secretary would have to reinstate Cassim as a Medicare participating physician, 42 C.F.R. § 1004.120(b) (1986), and give notice of his reinstatement to the public, 42 C.F.R. § 1001.134(a)(2) (1986). On the other hand, even that vindication may not remove all of the stigma associated with the Secretary's sanctions. Some damage might remain. Cassim's patients and members of the public may distrust him.

The Government's interests, however, are compelling. In the judgment of OMPRO [Oregon Medical Profession Review Organization] and OIG, Cassim performed unnecessary surgery. Such surgery wastes public resources and, even more important, threatens the patient's health. * * *

Affirmed.

———

1. Recall that the traditional rule for awarding a preliminary injunction is the four-part test: the plaintiff must show each of the elements of (1) irreparable injury if the relief is denied, (2) a probability of prevailing on the merits, (3) the balance of hardships favoring the plaintiff, and (4) the public interest favoring the relief.

The alternative test, followed in some federal circuits, allows a plaintiff the choice of establishing the four traditional factors or of satisfying a sliding scale test: the greater the potential irreparability of the harm and the clearer the balance of hardships without the order, the lesser the required showing of strength on the merits of the case. *See* Caribbean Marine Services Co. v. Baldrige, the next case *infra*.

2. A 1986 opinion by Judge Posner has introduced an arithmetic explanation of the standard for preliminary injunction in the Seventh Circuit. In *American Hosp. Supply Corp. v. Hospital Products Ltd.* there is a "formula" for assessing preliminary injunction requests: If $[P \times H_p]$ $(1-P) \times H_d$ then the preliminary injunction should be granted. P is the probability that the denial is an error because plaintiff will win on the substance; H_p is the harm to the plaintiff if the injunction is denied; H_d is the harm to the defendant if the injunction is granted. 780 F.2d 589 (7th Cir.1986).

Judge Posner's opinion in *American Hospital* characterized this formula as the procedural counterpart to Judge Learned Hand's famous negligence formula in *United States v. Carroll Towing Co.*, 159 F.2d 169 (2d Cir.1947).

Does this formula make a change? *See* Silberman, Injunctions by the Numbers: Less than the Sum of its Parts, 63 Chicago–Kent L.Rev. 279 (1987).

PROBLEM: THE THREATENED LANDMARK

Riverdale is a small rural town that has one main street with businesses and shops. At the end of this quaint street is an old railroad depot. The depot has been closed for years, but it is a handsome building constructed of limestone. It provides an attractive end to the street and it contributes an essential element to the quaint atmosphere of the town.

The depot is owned by the Rapid Railway Co. [RR]. The empty building has not been used for years, but RR has kept it reasonably maintained. An employee regularly visits the Riverdale depot to inspect and repair it.

Recently RR decided to raze all its closed buildings in order to save maintenance costs. The Riverdale depot was scheduled for demolition on July 14. RR made no public announcement of this plan.

On July 10 a member of the Riverdale town council learned of this secret plan from a relative in Metropolis who works in the RR main office. The town council immediately sought legal advice and formed a plan to save the depot. The council declared it a "landmark" and passed an ordinance prohibiting destruction of town landmarks without council approval.

The lawyer who proposed this plan explained to the council that these ordinances may not be enforceable. There is a substantial question under state law whether the town has the power to restrict land use by such an ordinance without state legislative delegation. There is scant law on the question and, although the law is unclear, existing authority is somewhat unfavorable to the council. When the council asked for an estimate on the probability of success, the lawyer said there is probably one chance in twenty that a court would uphold the validity of such ordinances.

The council decided that, even with that slight chance of success, it was worth paying the lawyer to draft the ordinances immediately. Another council meeting to pass the ordinances was scheduled for July 13. The council notified RR of this impending action in order to prevent the dispatch of the demolition crew. The response of RR was to change secretly the demolition date to July 13. The council member's relative who works for RR in Metropolis learned of this change and spread the news. The Riverdale council and its lawyer then speeded up the process and passed the ordinance just a few hours before the demolition crew arrived.

The council promptly notified RR that the ordinance had been passed, but RR said that the demolition crew should proceed anyway. The council's lawyer drove to the nearest state courthouse and sought an injunction to halt the demolition immediately.   Should the judge grant the order?

CARIBBEAN MARINE SERVICES CO. v. BALDRIGE

844 F.2d 668 (9th Cir.1988).

WALLACE, CIRCUIT JUDGE: * * *

The owners and certain crew members (crew) fish for yellow fin tuna using purse seine nets.   To locate the tuna, they scan the water looking for porpoises, which for unknown reasons often swim with the tuna.   Nets are set around the porpoises, and the tuna swimming beneath them are captured when the net is closed or "pursed" around them.   During this procedure, many porpoises may be caught in the nets and drowned.   In 1970 and 1971, for example more than 600,000 porpoises were killed in the course of such operations.   [Citation.]

In 1972, Congress enacted the Marine Mammal Protection Act (Act), 16 U.S.C. §§ 1361–1406.   One of the declared goals of the Act is to reduce the number of incidental kills and injuries to marine mammals permitted in the course of commercial fishing operations. * * *

Pursuant to section 1373, the Secretary promulgated regulations requiring permit holders to allow an employee of the National Oceanic and Atmospheric Administration (Administration) to accompany fishing vessels "for the purpose of conducting research and observing operations, including collecting information which may be used in civil or criminal penalty proceedings, forfeiture actions, or permit or certificate sanctions." * * *

The Administrator's new policy of hiring female, as well as male, observers to accompany selected fishing vessels on their voyages prompted the present litigation. * * *

The owners were notified in December 1986 and January 1987 that a female observer would be assigned to accompany their vessels, the M/V Mariner and the M/V Apure, on their next voyages.   In two separate actions, the owners and crew filed these actions for declaratory and injunctive relief.   In each action, the owners and crew alleged that the Administrator's directive requiring the presence of female observers threatened a violation of the crew members' constitutional privacy rights and a violation of regulations requiring the observer to carry out his duties so as to minimize interference with fishing operations, 50 C.F.R. § 216.24(f)(2) (1986).   The owners and crew sought and obtained temporary restraining orders prohibiting the government from implementing its new directive.   The owners and crew then moved for preliminary injunctive relief.   They supplemented their motions with various declarations describing the living and working condition on the vessels.   We now summarize these declarations.

A fishing voyage may last three months or longer, depending upon fishing conditions.   During this period, the crew members work together on the deck of the boat, eat and drink together in the small galley, and are otherwise forced to interact with one another in their bunkrooms, in the passageways, and in the common showers and toilets.

The crew members allegedly enjoy little or no privacy with respect to intimate bodily functions. They share small, dormitory-style bunkrooms and common toilets and showers. Because the bunkrooms are cramped, the crew members usually undress in the common area of the bunkroom, rather than behind curtains in their bunks. Moreover, because the common toilets and showers lack partitions or curtains, they usually bathe and perform other bodily functions in view of their cabinmates. Though single and double cabins equipped with private bathrooms exist on the vessels, these are assigned to officers. Porpoise observers usually bunk with the crews and share their bathroom facilities; thus, these observers may both observe and be observed by the crew members while undressing or performing bodily functions.

* * *

Finally, the declarations state that the West Coast tuna fishing industry has suffered severe financial losses in the past few years. The declarations contend that the presence of a female observer could destroy morale and distract the crew, thus affecting the crew's efficiency and decreasing the vessel's profits. The declarations also express the owners' concern that the crew members, some of whom are allegedly crude men with little formal education, may harass or sexually assault a female observer. Such tortious conduct could subject the owners to uninsurable liability, and further endanger their profits. To support this allegation, the owners referred to an incident which occurred aboard a foreign vessel involving an assault by a Korean officer upon an American female who served as a foreign fishing observer. Finally, the owners claimed that officers would have to devote time to protecting the female observer from the crew, thus distracting them from their primary duty of locating and catching tuna.

* * *

The owners also contended that declarations stating that the presence of a female would create conflicts that would disrupt fishing operations raised a serious legal question regarding the legality of assigning females as observers under 50 C.F.R. § 216.24(f)(2) (1986). This regulation requires that the duties of the observer be performed in a manner that minimizes interference with fishing operations.   * * *

The government responded to these averments by submitting declarations challenging the owners' and crew's assertion that an invasion of the crew members' privacy interests was unavoidable and that the female observer would disrupt fishing operations. With respect to the crew members' privacy claim, the government submitted declarations pointing out that Administration regulations do not require that observers be placed in shared bunkrooms, that private quarters on tuna vessels may remain vacant throughout a fishing voyage, and that both male and female observers had been assigned private accommodations on boats in the past. Declarations from both male and female observers stated that crew members were always partially dressed while performing their duties, and that they had never observed crew members taking showers on deck.

With respect to the owners' claim that the presence of a female would disrupt fishing operations and provoke jealousy and fights, the government submitted the declaration of Wendy Townsend, a female Administrator observer, who completed a 48–day voyage aboard a tuna seiner, which, like the owners' vessels, is subject to the Administration's directive. * * * Townsend also stated that she established amicable relations with the crew members, that no harassment or other disturbing incidents took place during her voyage, and that the crew members succeeded in capturing a hold-full of fish during the voyage.

* * * The government also submitted the declaration of Janet Wall, a foreign fisheries observer since 1978, who stated that approximately one-third, or about 150, of the observers serving on foreign vessels each year are women, and that in the past ten years there had been only six instances of physical or verbal abuse of female observers on these vessels. * * *

The district court granted the motions of the owners and crew for preliminary injunctions in each case. The district court found that the parties raised serious privacy questions, and a serious question concerning the legality of placing women on the vessels under 50 C.F.R. § 216.24(f)(2) (1986). The district court determined that the balance of hardships tipped sharply in favor of the owners and crew. The court decided that the injunction would merely preserve the status quo, and this was important considering "the fact that the tuna industry is not as viable as it once was." In addition, the court concluded that maintenance of the status quo allowing only male observers "will not adversely effect the purpose of the [Act], namely the preservation of porpoise."

* * *

Because our review of the district court's decision is generally limited to whether the district court abused its discretion, our disposition of an appeal from a preliminary injunction ordinarily will not dispose of the merits of the litigation. "Because of the limited scope of our review of the law applied by the district court and because the fully developed factual record may be materially different from that initially before the district court, our disposition of appeals from most preliminary injunctions may provide little guidance as to the appropriate disposition on the merits."

* * * [U]nder the "traditional test" typically used in cases involving the public interest, the district court should consider (1) the likelihood that the moving party will prevail on the merits, (2) whether the balance of irreparable harm favors the plaintiff, and (3) whether the public interest favors the moving party. [Citation.] We have allowed the

district court some latitude in assessing the first two factors as it fashions appropriate relief. In some cases, we have stated that a plaintiff may meet its burden by demonstrating a combination of probable success on the merits and a possibility of irreparable injury. *E.g.,* Los Angeles Memorial Coliseum Commission v. National Football League, 634 F.2d 1197, 1201 (9th Cir.1980) (*L.A. Coliseum*). At other times, we have stated that where the balance of hardships tips decidedly toward the plaintiff, the district court need not require a robust showing of likelihood of success on the merits, and may grant preliminary injunctive relief if the plaintiff's moving papers raise "serious questions" on the merits. This latter formulation is known as the "alternative test." Under either test, however, the district court must consider the public interest as a factor in balancing the hardships when the public interest may be affected. [Citations.]

In the case before us, the district court did not find that the owners and crew were likely to prevail on the merits. Instead, it only considered the seriousness of the questions raised and the balance of the hardships between the parties. After examining the moving papers, the court concluded that the owners and crew raised serious questions on the merits and that the balance of hardships tipped sharply in their favor. The government urges us to find that the district court erred in each of these determinations. However, we need not reach the question whether the owners and crew raised serious questions on the merits before the district court. Our review of the legal questions, as important as they are, will need to await a trial on the merits of this case and any subsequent appeal. We may properly dispose of the appeal before us by considering whether the district court properly evaluated and weighed the relevant harms in this case.

In his Memorandum Decision, the district judge cited four findings in support of his conclusion that the balance of harm tipped sharply in favor of the owners and crew: (1) the preliminary injunction would do no more than "preserve the status quo"; (2) the tuna industry "has been plagued with financial problems"; (3) the female observer would "disturb the domestic aspect of the tuna seiner"; and (4) the declarations submitted by the owners and crew "speculate that accommodation of a female federal observer may be costly."

These findings do not support the district court's conclusion that the balance of harm tipped decidedly in favor of the owners and crew. First, and perhaps most important, the owners and crew did not demonstrate, and the district court did not find, that the alleged harms will be irreparable. At a minimum, a plaintiff seeking preliminary injunctive relief must demonstrate that it will be exposed to irreparable harm. [Citation.] Speculative injury does not constitute irreparable injury sufficient to warrant granting a preliminary injunction. [Citation.] A plaintiff must do more than merely allege imminent harm sufficient to establish standing; a plaintiff must *demonstrate* immediate threatened injury as a prerequisite to preliminary injunctive relief. [Citation.]

The district court did not require a showing that the harms alleged by the owners and crew were imminent or likely. For example, the district court did not require them to demonstrate that the economic losses they alleged would result from a female observer's presence were likely to occur. Instead, the court merely stated that "the declarations submitted by the [owners] *speculate* that accommodation of a female observer *may be costly*" (emphasis added). * * *

The owners' and crew's claim that they will catch fewer fish if a woman is on board is similarly unsupported. The only materials submitted to the district court describing the impact of women on fishing operations were declarations the government filed stating that women have served successfully on numerous voyages on both foreign and American fishing vessels. Subjective apprehensions and unsupported predictions of revenue loss are not sufficient to satisfy a plaintiff's burden of demonstrating an immediate threat of irreparable harm. Moreover, there was no showing that the threat to the owners' revenues constituted an irreparable injury. No consideration was given to whether any lost revenues might be compensable in a damage award, and thus not irreparable. * * *

The district court similarly failed to find a threat of immediate, irreparable harm to the privacy interests alleged by the crew. The district court did not find, for example, that the female observer would have to bunk in the crew's quarters or observe their intimate bodily activities. Instead, the district judge stated in conclusory fashion that though a "male federal observer did not disturb the domestic aspect of the tuna seiner, a female would." It is unclear from this description whether the "harm" the court found consisted of an invasion of any constitutionally protected privacy interests or mere inconvenience to the crew members. * * *

Finally, the district court failed to identify and weigh the public interests at stake in its balance of harms analysis. * * *

The owners and crew argue that delaying either temporarily or permanently the use of women in the Act's observer program would not have any impact on the interests of the public. This argument rests on two premises: first, that the only public interest implicated by this dispute is the interest in preserving marine mammals, and second, that excluding qualified women from the observer program will not negatively affect that interest. * * *

The argument that the injunction would have no impact on the interests of the public fails to take into account both the government's and the public's interest in ensuring equal employment opportunities for women. This interest, as well as the interest in protecting and preserving marine mammals, is clearly implicated by the issuance of the preliminary injunction in this case. * * *

When the governmental and public interest in gender neutral hiring is balanced against the privacy interests asserted in this case, it is by no means apparent that the balance tips decidedly in the crew members' favor. Some courts have held that the privacy interest in remaining free from involuntary viewing of private parts of the body by members of the opposite sex should not impair employment rights unless the threatened invasion of privacy is serious and there are no means by which both interests can be reasonably accommodated. * * *

In conclusion, after careful review of the record and the district court's decision, we hold that the district court abused its discretion by ordering preliminary relief in this case. Under the alternate approach articulated in *L.A. Coliseum,* the moving party must first demonstrate an immediate threat of irreparable injury to itself and that the balance of hardships tips decidedly in its favor. The district court did not determine that the injuries alleged by the owners and crew were serious, immediate, and irreparable. Moreover, it failed to identify the harm which a preliminary injunction might cause to the government, its employees, and the public and to weigh this harm against any irreparable injuries alleged by the owners and crew. We therefore reverse the orders granting preliminary injunctions.

––––––––

1. How often is the alternative test likely to alter the outcome of a motion for a preliminary injunction? Contrast the principal case and *Cassim v. Bowen, supra,* with Chalk v. U.S. District Court, 840 F.2d 701 (9th Cir.1988). In *Chalk* a teacher who was reassigned to an administrative position successfully obtained a preliminary injunction for reinstatement with a classroom assignment. The teacher's removal from the classroom occurred after a medical leave when he was diagnosed with AIDS (Acquired Immune Deficiency Syndrome).

The alternative test for preliminary injunctions governed the motion in *Chalk* as it did in the principal case because both arose in the same federal circuit. The district court denied the order, and the Court of Appeals reversed. The plaintiff had established a strong likelihood of success on the merits because medical testimony established that there was little risk of his infecting the children with the virus in the classroom setting.

The trial court had found that the teacher suffered no irreparable harm because the administrative position paid the same salary as the classroom assignment. On appeal this finding was reversed as clearly erroneous. The appellate opinion said that the focus should not be on the potential monetary loss alone but on the nature of the alternative work. The teacher's original employment was in the area of his special skills, teaching hearing-impaired children. He derived great personal satisfaction from working closely with his small class. The reassigned administrative work involved writing grant proposals and he had no special training nor interest in this work.

The Court of Appeals for the Ninth Circuit further addressed the balance of hardships in this case. Although it was unnecessary under the alternative test to find that the balance of hardships favored the plaintiff after the strong showing of success on the merits and irreparable harm, the court nonetheless found this other element satisfied.

The public expressed fear about the risk of AIDS exposure in schools. The Court of Appeals held that the public interest factor could not be grounded on unreasonable fears without frustrating the legislative purpose behind the act on which the claim was founded. The trial court could retain jurisdiction to remove the teacher from student contact at whatever point qualified medical opinion might determine that his condition poses a risk to the children. For example, as the teacher's immune system deteriorates, he may contract some opportunistic infection capable of transmission. Until then, the preliminary injunction should preserve the *status quo* with the classroom teaching assignment pending the full trial on the merits of the case.

How do this teacher's case and the principal case differ from *Cassim v. Bowen, supra,* involving the Medicare doctor? Was the interpretation of the public interest controlling in each case? Are the different results best explained by the differences in the tests for preliminary injunctions?

2. The public interest factor in the standard for interlocutory relief is an elusive one. The opposing parties often can make reasonable arguments that the public interest favors each side of the dispute. Consider the case of Adams v. Vance, 570 F.2d 950 (D.C.Cir.1978). In this case the Inupiat Eskimos challenged a decision by the Secretary of State. The International Whaling Commission (IWC) had banned Eskimo hunting of the bowhead whale, but the United States could stay the ban by timely objection. The Commission was concerned about the survival of the whale, but subsistence hunting of the bowhead had been the vital element of a millenia-old Eskimo culture.

The Secretary of State decided against making an objection to the IWC just four days before the deadline. Plaintiffs sued the Secretary and, after a short hearing one afternoon, the district court issued a temporary restraining order requiring the Secretary to file an objection. The judge accepted the plaintiffs' contention that an objection would not substantially harm the United States' efforts at international environmental cooperation because the International Whaling Convention allows objections to be withdrawn freely any time after they are made. Without the objection, however, the plaintiffs would be subject to criminal penalties if they continued their subsistence fishing.

The Court of Appeals held an emergency session on a federal holiday to reverse the order. The per curiam opinion characterized the district court's order as an unwarranted intrusion on executive discretion in the field of foreign policy. It criticized the lower court for treating this application for immediate injunctive relief as an ordinary one because it deeply intruded into the core concerns of the executive branch. The opinion observed that no other nation has entered an objection to an IWC action since 1973, so that the symbolic impact of the United States being the first nation to break that pattern could be grave. Therefore, it was clear error for the district court to find that an objection, provisional or otherwise, would not substantially endanger the interests of the United States.

B. PROCEDURAL REQUIREMENTS

Section Coverage:

Federal Rule of Civil Procedure 65 contains specific procedural provisions that have been interpreted strictly. Most notable are the differences in the time limitations and notice requirements for temporary restraining orders (TRO) and preliminary injunctions.

A TRO can be entered *ex parte,* but only upon a specific showing that immediate and irreparable harm will result before the opposing party could be notified and heard. The order can last only ten days, with a second ten-day extension for good cause. The preliminary injunction hearing is expedited on the calendar, and both sides must have a reasonable opportunity to present some evidence. A preliminary injunction then lasts until the full trial on the merits of the case.

Model Case:

Able is a professional athlete under contract with a team named the Reps in Washington, D.C. The contract between Able and the Reps provides, in addition to the usual contractual terms, that Able's services are exclusive to the Reps such that he may not play for any other professional team in that sport during the duration of the contract. The term of the contract is three years.

Although the contract with the Reps is still in effect, Able has received an irresistible offer from a team in nearby Baltimore. That team is part of a newly formed competitive league in the same sport. Able accepted the Baltimore offer and started practicing yesterday with the Baltimore team in anticipation of the opening of the new season today.

The Reps want to enjoin Able from violating the exclusivity of services provision of his contract. The first game of the season for the Baltimore team is only hours away. The Reps' season does not begin for a few more days. The new league is trying to capture publicity by having the first games before the old league starts its season.

The attorney for the Reps seeks a temporary restraining order to prevent Able from breaching the negative covenant in the contract. Able should be notified of the motion if possible. The Reps' theory of irreparable harm should focus on the immediate loss of fans to the nearby Baltimore franchise. The strength of that showing probably will determine the availability of the TRO.

If the court issues the TRO, it can last only a few days. As soon as possible the court must hold a hearing for the preliminary injunction. Since such an injunction would last until trial on the merits—probably after the season—the hearing would be crucial to both parties. Although it is not clear whether the *status quo* is best described as Able playing for the Reps or practicing with the Baltimore team, the last uncontested status was when Able was with the Reps. If the Reps can make a substantial showing of irreparable harm and the probable enforceability of the contract, the court may grant this preliminary injunction to enforce the exclusivity portion of the contract between Able and the Reps. A preliminary injunction is appealable whereas a TRO is not.

SIMS v. GREENE

160 F.2d 512 (3d Cir.1947).

BIGGS, CIRCUIT JUDGE.

On December 2, 1946, the plaintiff, David H. Sims, filed a complaint against the defendant, Sherman L. Greene, alleging that he, Sims, is a citizen of Pennsylvania and a bishop of the African Methodist Episcopal Church and that he was assigned by a General Conference of the AME Church held in 1944 to the First Episcopal District to serve as the presiding bishop of that district until the next General Conference to be held in 1948; that the defendant, another bishop of the same church, has appeared in the First Episcopal District and within the jurisdiction of the court below and has proclaimed that he is the presiding bishop of the First District and is attempting to function as such; that by reason of the foregoing the plaintiff's office and functions as presiding bishop and his salary and emoluments are threatened as is the administration of the church and its conferences in the district; and that irreparable injury will result to the church, to its property and to the plaintiff unless the defendant is enjoined from pursuing the course complained of. An affidavit supporting the allegations of the complaint was filed with it.

On December 2, 1946, the court below, *ex parte*, issued an order restraining the defendant from interfering with the plaintiff as the presiding bishop of the district. The restraint originally imposed was continued by order for an additional ten days, to expire on December 22, 1946. On December 20 the defendant consented to the restraint being extended until January 14, 1947 and the court made an order to such effect on December 20, 1946.

On December 24, 1946 the defendant filed his answer and with it a counterclaim containing prayers for affirmative relief. He * * * asserted that the plaintiff was no longer a bishop of the AME Church because he had been unfrocked by an extra session of the General Conference and by the Episcopal Committee meeting in Little Rock, Arkansas, about November 20, 1946; that he, the defendant, had been assigned by the extra session of the General Conference and by the Bishops' Council to the First Episcopal District as its presiding bishop; that by virtue of the foregoing he is the lawful presiding bishop of the district and his right to that office and its emoluments and his administration of the church and its property within the district are imperiled by the plaintiff's actions. The counterclaim ends with a prayer that the plaintiff be enjoined from interfering with the defendant.

On January 13, 1947 the court below extended the restraining order until January 24 and proceeded to a hearing on the question of whether or not a preliminary injunction should be granted. This hearing continued from January 13 to January 17, inclusive, and twelve hundred pages of argument, colloquy and testimony were taken down and have been transcribed. On January 17, at the close of the day the defendant's counsel made a motion to dissolve the restraint. The court directed him to withhold his motion, stating that he would renew the order "in due time." * * *

On January 23, 1947, the defendant appealed to this court from the restraining order and moved for a stay of all proceedings in the District Court. We stayed the proceedings in the District Court and restrained the defendant from acting as the presiding bishop of the First Episcopal District pending the disposition of the appeal, setting February 13 as the day for argument.

* * * [The defendant contends] that the temporary restraining order, continued without the consent of the defendant after January 14, is in substance a temporary injunction issued illegally since no findings of fact and conclusions of law were made by the court below as required by Rule 52(a) of the Federal Rules of Civil Procedure, 28 U.S.C.A. following section 723c. * * *

We come * * * to questions respecting the nature and effect of the restraining order issued first upon December 2, 1946 and still in force. In extending the restraint the court below did not observe that provision of Rule 65(b) of the [Federal] Rules of Civil Procedure, 28 U.S.C.A. following section 723c, which states, "The reasons for the extension shall be entered of record." The court also disregarded the following provision of Rule 65(b), "In case a temporary restraining order is granted without notice, the motion for a preliminary injunction shall be set down for hearing at the earliest possible time * * *." It is settled that no temporary restraining order may be continued beyond twenty days unless the party against whom the order is directed consents that it may be extended for a longer period. *See* Section 381 or 28 U.S.C.A. and Rule 65(b). The consent of the defendant in the instant case to the extension of the restraining order was not continued past January 14, 1947. It is also the law that the relief to be afforded by Section 129 of the Judicial Code, 28 U.S.C.A. § 227, providing for appeals from injunctions, is not limited by the terminology employed by the trial court. The relief to be afforded by the section looks to the substantial effect of the order made. [Citation.]

When a restraining order, purporting to be "temporary" is continued for a substantial length of time past the period prescribed by Section 381 of 28 U.S.C.A. without the consent of the party against which it issued and without the safeguards prescribed by Rule 65(b) it ceases to be a "temporary restraining order" within the purview of that section and becomes a preliminary injunction which cannot be maintained unless the court issuing it sets out the findings of fact and the conclusions of law which constitute the grounds for its action as required by Rule 52(a).

In our opinion the restraining order now in effect in the District Court must be treated as a temporary injunction, issued without the consent of the defendant, in the face of his motion to dissolve it, and contrary to the provisions of Rule 52(a). It is clear that an appeal lies from a temporary injunction. * * *

In view of the fact that the defendant has filed an answer and a counterclaim we can perceive no reason why the court below should not, as it itself suggested, proceed to final hearing. A prompt disposition of the cause is necessary in the public interest. The witnesses should not be permitted to give extended irrelevant testimony. Counsel should be restricted to relevant examination and cross-examination. The proceedings in the court below, as the record shows, were repeatedly interrupted by demonstrations by the spectators and the learned trial judge took no strong step to prevent such demonstrations. The dignity and decorum of a court of the United States must be maintained at all times.

The court below should sit from day to day and without unnecessary interruptions until the hearing is concluded.

The motion to dismiss the appeal will be denied. The order appealed from will be reversed. The stay order entered by this court on January 31, 1947 will be vacated. The court below will be directed to sit from day to day until the hearing is concluded.

----

1.   Federal Rule of Civil Procedure 65 provides in its first two parts:

(a) *Preliminary Injunction.*

(1) *Notice.* No preliminary injunction shall be issued without notice to the adverse party.

(2) *Consolidation of Hearing with Trial on Merits.* Before or after the commencement of the hearing of an application for a preliminary injunction, the court may order the trial of the action on the merits to be advanced and consolidated with the hearing of the application. Even when this consolidation is not ordered, any evidence received upon an application for a preliminary injunction which would be admissible upon the trial on the merits becomes part of the record on the trial and need not be repeated upon the trial. * * *

(b) *Temporary Restraining Order; Notice; Hearing; Duration.* A temporary restraining order may be granted without written or oral notice to the adverse party or his attorney only if (1) it clearly appears from specific facts shown by affidavit or by the verified complaint that immediate and irreparable injury, loss, or damage will result to the applicant before the adverse party or that party's attorney can be heard in opposition, and (2) the applicant's attorney certifies to the court in writing the efforts, if any, which have been made to give the notice and the reasons supporting the claim that notice should not be required. Every temporary restraining order granted without notice shall be indorsed with the date and hour of issuance; shall be filed forthwith in the clerk's office and entered of record; shall define the injury and state why it is irreparable and why the order was granted without notice; and shall expire by its terms within such time after entry, not to exceed 10 days, as the court fixes, unless within the time so fixed the order, for good cause shown, is extended for a like period or unless the party against whom the order is directed consents that it may be extended for a longer period. The reasons for the extension shall be entered of record. In case a temporary restraining order is granted without notice, the motion for a preliminary injunction shall be set down for hearing at the earliest possible time and takes precedence of all matters except older matters of the same character; and when the motion comes on for hearing the party who obtained the temporary restraining order shall proceed with the application for a preliminary injunction and, if the party does not do so, the court shall dissolve the temporary restraining order. On 2 days' notice to the party who obtained the temporary restraining order without notice or on such shorter notice to that party as the court may prescribe, the adverse party may appear and move its dissolution or modification and in that event the court shall proceed to hear and determine such motion as expeditiously as the ends of justice require.

2. The remainder of Federal Rule of Civil Procedure 65 addresses issues covered in future sections. Section (c) concerns the injunction bond, covered in section C of this chapter. Section (d) specifies who is bound by an injunction, covered in the next chapter.

PROBLEM: FENDING OFF THE FENCE

Your office receives a call from a longstanding client, Thompson, who is distressed that a neighbor is about to erect a fence on the wrong side of the property line. The neighbor was "sure" about the property line and therefore did not have the land surveyed. Thompson believes the neighbor is wrong and is about to erect the fence in Thompson's yard.

This error is particularly disturbing because near the disputed line Thompson has a tree that is one hundred years old and in poor health. A specialist has been giving the tree an expensive nursing treatment. Thompson fears that digging for the fence posts would disturb the roots and jeopardize the life of the tree. The tree is far enough away from the real property line, Thompson believes, that a properly located fence would pose no danger.

The fencing crew arrived this morning and was about to begin work near the tree when your client spotted the activity. An immediate conference with the neighbor revealed the dispute about the boundary. The neighbor said that the crew has been hired to work for two days, and the contract requires that they be paid unless delayed by the weather. The neighbor agreed to start the fence at the other end of the property if Thompson wants to get a surveyor today, but the crew will put the fence along the tree side tomorrow. The neighbor is positive about the property line and insists that a surveyor is unnecessary.

Thompson cannot get a surveyor to come until next week. Is there any legal action that can be taken today?

FENGLER v. NUMISMATIC AMERICANA, INC.

832 F.2d 745 (2d Cir.1987).

Altimari, Circuit Judge:

Stuart Bochner and his law firm, Bochner and Berg ("Bochner"), appeal from an order of the United States District Court for the Southern District of New York, Kevin Thomas Duffy, Judge, which preliminarily enjoined all defendants from engaging in any business transactions with respect to Stationers Supply Co., Inc. ("Stationers"). Because this preliminary injunction was issued without holding an evidentiary hearing and was not supported by any findings of fact, we vacate the injunction and remand to the district court with instructions to hold an evidentiary hearing.

In December 1986, appellee Iris Fengler ("Fengler") contracted to sell 60% of the stock in her financially-troubled office supply company, Stationers, to defendant Numismatic Americana, Inc. ("Numismatic"). Defendant John Cameron ("Cameron") was the president of Numismatic. Preliminary negotiations for the sale had been conducted by defendant Jerry Simon ("Simon"), who was the Senior Acquisitions Director of U.S. Rare Gold Eagles, Inc.

According to Fengler, Simon orally promised that his company would invest $50,000 into Stationers; would pay Fengler a salary of $1,100 weekly; would satisfy all of Stationers' outstanding checks issued to creditors; and would conduct an audit of Stationers so that the business could be restored to financial health.

The contract which was ultimately signed provided for the audit, for the investment of $50,000 into Stationers, and for the payment of a $1,100 weekly salary to Fengler. The contract was executed on December 24, 1986. Both Simon and Cameron were present, and were represented by counsel. Fengler was unrepresented by counsel. She had not retained her own counsel, and she alleges that Simon assured her that his own attorney, Bochner, would adequately represent the interests of all parties to the transaction. Fengler further alleges that Bochner informed her it would be very difficult to obtain her own counsel on the day before Christmas.

Fengler contends that within two weeks after the contract was executed, defendants removed all the inventory, business records and furnishings of Stationers, leaving Fengler with only a desk, chair, and telephone. Defendants also allegedly converted all the cash assets of Stationers to their personal use, and refused to satisfy the claims of Stationers' creditors. Fengler herself received only one weekly salary check, and needless to say, was unable to get defendants to return her phone calls.

In February 1987, Fengler commenced the present action, asserting claims under the federal securities laws, RICO, and common-law fraud, and requesting both monetary and injunctive relief. Defendants Simon and Cameron disappeared to parts unknown before they could be served with process. The two corporate defendants were served, but did not appear and are currently in default. Bochner and Bochner and Berg were also properly served and are the only defendants appealing the district court's grant of injunctive relief.

Fengler alleged in her complaint that Bochner breached his duty of care to her by failing to advise her to obtain independent counsel. She claimed that "Bochner and Bochner and Berg participated in such a plan or scheme with the other defendants to knowingly and maliciously engage in acts of fraud and deceit against plaintiffs...." Fengler did not claim, however, that Bochner actively participated in the looting of the corporate assets.

On February 11, Judge Robert Ward issued an *ex parte* temporary restraining order against defendants, enjoining them from engaging in any business dealings on behalf of Stationers. The return date on plaintiffs' motion for preliminary injunction was set for February 17, 1987. On that date, counsel for Fengler and Bochner appeared to argue the motion before Judge Duffy; these proceedings were not transcribed. Prior to the arguments, Bochner had not submitted any papers to the court. Immediately following argument, however, Bochner submitted an affidavit which stated that his firm no longer represented the corporate defendants, and that neither he nor his firm was in a position to engage in any acts on behalf of Stationers. The affidavit concluded:

> [T]here is no reason to issue the preliminary injunction as against me or my law firm.... *Absent an evidentiary hearing,* the court should not do an unnecessary act, which can have no effect, might yet have damaging implications and might be used by plaintiff at a later date to cast a light on these proceedings that were (sic) never intended (emphasis added).

The district court did not hold the requested evidentiary hearing. Instead, the court issued a preliminary injunction, unsupported by any factual findings, which restrained all defendants from engaging in the following activities with respect to Stationers: "Checking transactions, solicitation of customers, collection of outstanding corporate obligations, payment of corporate accounts receivable, sale or purchase of inventory, and sale and purchase of any securities."

Bochner contends that the preliminary injunction must be vacated because of the district court's failure to hold an evidentiary hearing, as well as its failure to make findings of fact. We agree with appellants on both counts.

On a motion for preliminary injunction, where "essential facts are in dispute, there must be a hearing . . . and appropriate findings of fact must be made." Visual Sciences, Inc. v. Integrated Communications, Inc., 660 F.2d 56, 58 (2d Cir.1981) (Citing Forts v. Ward, 566 F.2d 849 (2d Cir.1977)).

In the present case, "essential facts" were unquestionably in dispute with respect to Bochner. Although Fengler alleged that Bochner was a participant in the scheme to defraud her, Bochner denied any knowledge of his codefendants' intentions. He contended, rather, that his firm's relationship with Numismatic and the other codefendants consisted solely of drafting the contract of sale and attending the closing. He claimed, moreover, that his firm no longer represented the codefendants and was not in a position to exercise any control over the assets of Stationers. Because the material facts were clearly in dispute, the district court erred by not holding an evidentiary hearing before granting the injunction.

Fengler argues that Bochner waived any right to an evidentiary hearing by failing to demand one during argument of the motion. We will never know, of course, if Bochner in fact failed to request a hearing at that time, since there is no transcript of the oral argument. Nevertheless, Bochner submitted an affidavit on the day of argument, in which he expressly urged the court not to order injunctive relief without holding a hearing.

A party against whom an injunction is sought will be found to have waived its right to a hearing only where that party was demonstrably "content to rest" on affidavits submitted to the court. [Citations.]

In this case, Bochner did not opt to wage a battle of affidavits. Indeed, the first (and only) affidavit which Bochner submitted to the court contained an explicit request for a hearing. Bochner did not, therefore, waive his right to an evidentiary hearing.

Finally, the district court's failure to make findings of fact is also reversible error. Fed.R.Civ.P. 52(a) provides that "in granting or refusing interlocutory injunctions the court *shall* . . . set forth the findings of fact and conclusions of law which constitute the grounds of its action" (emphasis added).

In a recent decision this court stated emphatically that "Rule 52(a)'s requirement that the trial court find facts specifically and state its conclusions of law is mandatory and cannot be waived." * * *

The preliminary injunction granted by the district court is hereby vacated. The case is remanded with instructions that the district court hold an evidentiary hearing regarding the propriety of injunctive relief. The district court's ultimate decision following the outcome of this hearing must be supported by adequate findings of fact, in compliance with Fed.R.Civ.P. 52(a).

———

1.   Rule 52(a) requires the court, in all actions "tried upon the facts without a jury," to state separately its conclusions of law and "in granting or refusing interlocutory injunctions" and "similarly [to] set forth the findings of fact and conclusions of law which constitute the grounds of its action."

2.   Compare the principal case with the second appeal in the case of the defrocked bishop, *Sims v. Greene, supra.* After the case was remanded to the district court, the trial judge entered a preliminary injunction that was substantially identical to the previously invalidated temporary restraining order. On appeal from that order the Court of Appeals again set aside the new order as an insufficient preliminary injunction. Sims v. Greene, 161 F.2d 87 (3d Cir.1947). The deficiency this time was with the hearing required under Rule 65(b) for a preliminary injunction. The court observed:

> * * * The preliminary injunction was issued on the identical record which was before this court on the prior appeal. The allegations of the pleadings and affidavits filed in the cause are conflicting. Such conflicts must be resolved by oral testimony since only by hearing the witnesses and observing their demeanor on the stand can the trier of fact determine the veracity of the allegations made by the respective parties. If witnesses are not heard the trial court will be left in the position of preferring one piece of paper to another. Greene was given no opportunity to present oral testimony on his behalf except for one witness whose testimony was immaterial to any issue presented by the pleading. * * * The truth of the matter is that Greene was given no fair opportunity to present testimony prior to the issuance of the preliminary injunction.
>
> The issuance of a preliminary injunction under such circumstances is contrary not only to the Rules of Civil Procedure but also to the spirit which imbues our judicial tribunals prohibiting decision without hearing. Rule 65(a) provides that no preliminary injunction shall be issued without notice to the adverse party. Notice implies an opportunity to be heard. Hearing requires trial of an issue or issues of fact. Trial of an issue of fact necessitates opportunity to present evidence and not by only one side to the controversy. * * *

CARROLL v. PRESIDENT AND COM'RS OF PRINCESS ANNE

393 U.S. 175, 89 S.Ct. 347, 21 L.Ed.2d 325 (1968).

MR. JUSTICE FORTAS delivered the opinion of the Court.

Petitioners are identified with a "white supremacist" organization called the National States Rights Party. They held a public assembly or rally near the courthouse steps in the town of Princess Anne, the county seat of Somerset County, Maryland, in the evening of August 6, 1966. The authorities did not attempt to interfere with the rally. Because of the tense atmosphere which developed as the meeting progressed, about 60 state policemen were brought in, including some from a nearby county. They were held in readiness, but for tactical reasons only a few were in evidence at the scene of the rally.

Petitioners' speeches, amplified by a public address system so that they could be heard for several blocks, were aggressively and militantly racist. Their target was primarily Negroes and, secondarily, Jews. It is sufficient to observe with the court below, that the speakers engaged in deliberately derogatory, insulting, and threatening language, scarcely disguised by protestations of peaceful purposes; and that listeners might well have construed their words as both a provocation to the Negroes in the crowd and an incitement to the whites. The rally continued for something more than an hour, concluding at about 8:25 p.m. The crowd listening to the speeches increased from about 50 at the beginning to about 150, of whom 25% were Negroes.

In the course of the proceedings it was announced that the rally would be resumed the following night, August 7.

On that day, the respondents, officials of Princess Anne and of Somerset County, applied for and obtained a restraining order from the Circuit Court for Somerset County. The proceedings were *ex parte,* no notice being given to petitioners and, so far as appears, no effort being made informally to communicate with them, although this is expressly contemplated under Maryland procedure. The order restrained petitioners for 10 days from holding rallies or meetings in the county "which will tend to disturb and endanger the citizens of the County." As a result, the rally scheduled for August 7 was not held. * * *

* * * We turn to the constitutional problems raised by the 10–day injunctive order.

* * *

We need not decide the thorny problem of whether, on the facts of this case, an injunction against the announced rally could be justified. The 10–day order here must be set aside because of a basic infirmity in the procedure by which it was obtained. It was issued *ex parte,* without notice to petitioners and without any effort, however informal, to invite or permit their participation in the proceedings. There is a place in our jurisprudence for *ex parte* issuance, without notice, of temporary restraining orders of short duration; but there is no place within the area of basic freedoms guaranteed by the First Amendment for such orders where no showing is made that it is impossible to serve or to notify the opposing parties and to give them an opportunity to participate.

* * *

In the present case, the record discloses no reason why petitioners were not notified of the application for injunction. They were apparently present in Princess Anne. They had held a rally there on the night preceding the application for an issuance of the injunction. They were scheduled to have another rally on the very evening of the day when the injunction was issued. And some of them were actually served with the writ of injunction at 6:10 that evening. In these circumstances, there is no justification for the *ex parte* character of the proceedings in the sensitive area of First Amendment rights.

The value of a judicial proceeding, as against self-help by the police, is substantially diluted where the process is *ex parte,* because the Court does not have available the fundamental instrument for judicial judgment: an adversary proceeding in which both parties may participate. The facts in any case involving a public demonstration are difficult to ascertain and even more difficult to evaluate. Judgment as to whether the facts justify the use of the drastic power of injunction necessarily turns on subtle and controversial considerations and upon a delicate assessment of the particular situation in light of legal standards which are inescapably imprecise. In the absence of evidence and argument offered by both sides and of their participation in the formulation of value judgments, there is insufficient assurance of the balanced analysis and careful conclusions which are essential in the area of First Amendment adjudication.

The same is true of the fashioning of the order. An order issued in the area of First Amendment rights must be couched in the narrowest terms that will accomplish the pin-pointed objective permitted by constitutional mandate and the essential needs of the public order. * * * In other words, the order must be tailored as precisely as possible to the exact needs of the case. The participation of both sides is necessary for this purpose. Certainly, the failure to invite participation of the party seeking to exercise First Amendment rights reduces the possibility of a narrowly drawn order, and substantially imperils the protection which the Amendment seeks to assure.

* * *

We need not here decide that it is impossible for circumstances to arise in which the issuance of an *ex parte* restraining order for a minimum period could be justified because of the unavailability of the adverse parties or their counsel, or perhaps for other reasons. In the present case, it is clear that the failure to give notice, formal or informal, and to provide an opportunity for an adversary proceeding before the holding of the rally was restrained, is incompatible with the First

Amendment. Because we reverse the judgment below on this basis, we need not and do not decide whether the facts in this case provided a constitutionally permissible basis for temporarily enjoining the holding of the August 7 rally.

Reversed.

C.   INJUNCTION BONDS AND APPEALS

Section Coverage:

Federal Rule of Civil Procedure 65(c) provides for security to be provided by the applicant before a court issues a restraining order or preliminary injunction. The amount of a bond is in the discretion of the court, but the enjoined party has an opportunity to request an increase in the bond. Since a plaintiff may obtain interlocutory relief based upon a showing of probabilities, the bond serves an important role in ensuring fairness to the enjoined party and to check the zeal of the movant.

The bond assures that the defendant will be compensated for any losses occasioned by the TRO or preliminary injunction in the event that the plaintiff does not ultimately prevail in the underlying case. It functions as an exception to the general rule that litigation losses and expenses are borne by the parties themselves.

The bond requirement indirectly preserves the dignity of the court. Judges dislike acting in haste, as they must for interlocutory orders, because of the greater danger of injustice. Through the bond requirement a plaintiff guarantees to compensate for losses caused by that hasty decision.

Compensable losses include measurable harms caused specifically by the wrongful order but not including distress and humiliation. Recovery is usually limited to the amount of the bond; "open bonds" do not limit recovery. The bond provides a convenient repository of funds against which the wrongfully enjoined party can collect actual damages. Thus, the enjoined party does not have to run the risk of nonrecovery if the plaintiff is judgment proof.

Model Case:

The A–1 Sales Corp. employs many sales representatives to market its product. The employment contract contains an anti-competition clause that prohibits a former employee from selling a similar product in the same geographical area for a certain period of time.

B.J. Babb is a former A–1 sales representative who promptly took employment with a nearby competitor. A–1 seeks a preliminary injunction to prohibit Babb from working for the competitor. A–1 argues that it will be irreparably harmed without the injunction because customers will follow Babb to the competitor and, even if Babb is eventually enjoined from competition, the customers may not return to A–1.

If the court grants the preliminary injunction, A–1 should post a bond to assure a source of payment to Babb if A–1 loses on the merits of the case. If A–1 is a substantial corporation in financially sound condition, the bond may be waived. If the court ultimately holds the anti-competition clause is not enforceable, Babb can recover under the bond for lost income during the period of the injunction.

COQUINA OIL CORP. v. TRANSWESTERN PIPELINE CO.

825 F.2d 1461 (10th Cir.1987).

MOORE, CIRCUIT JUDGE.

This interlocutory appeal challenges a preliminary injunction issued in favor of Coquina Oil Corporation, Flag–Redfern Oil Company, and Yates Petroleum Corporation mandatorily enjoining Transwestern Pipeline Company's purchase of certain gas. At oral argument, counsel for the parties agreed that the trial court has yet to set bond to secure the injunctive order pursuant to Fed.R.Civ.P. 65(c), or to otherwise rule despite the appellant's motion to set bond. As we are given to understand, that motion is pending the outcome of this appeal. We conclude that the consequence of this hiatus is an unenforceable injunction and an absence of an appealable interlocutory order, depriving us of jurisdiction. We dismiss for that reason.

Rule 65(c) quite clearly states: "No ... preliminary injunction shall issue except upon the giving of security by the applicant." As we analyze the significance of the rule in light of what has transpired thus far in this case, the trial judge's consideration of the imposition of bond is a necessary ingredient of an enforceable order for injunctive relief. The plain language of the rule permits no other analysis.

Nonetheless, at this point we do not decide, nor do we even suggest, whether a bond is mandatory to validate the preliminary injunction in this case. Indeed, we have held that a trial court may, in the exercise of discretion, determine a bond is unnecessary to secure a preliminary injunction "if there is an absence of proof showing a likelihood of harm." Continental Oil Co. v. Frontier Refining Co., 338 F.2d 780, 782 (10th Cir.1964). Nevertheless, the *Continental* holding implies the trial court will comply with Rule 65(c) by at least giving consideration to whether the circumstances of a particular case justify the unusual practice of leaving the enjoined party bereft of security. Moreover, until such consideration is given, the trial court has not completed the task mandated by Rule 65.

In this case, the trial court has effectively violated this aspect of Rule 65(c) by refusing to act upon Transwestern's motion to set a preliminary injunction bond. [Citations.] Thus, unlike the case in which a bond is denied as unnecessary after full consideration, when a trial court fails to contemplate the imposition of the bond, its order granting a preliminary injunction is unsupportable. [Citation.]

Appellees would have us avoid dismissal by presuming the district court decided a bond was unnecessary. We cannot accept this invitation. A trial court decision to waive a Rule 65(c) bond is subject to an abuse of discretion test on appeal. That test cannot be employed in the absence of specific findings.

We therefore find ourselves given nothing to review; hence, we must dismiss this case for want of jurisdiction. [Citation.] We arrive at this conclusion even though we recognize other courts have apparently presumed the existence of jurisdiction and approved the issuance of the injunction on the merits but then remanded for consideration of the bond issue under Rule 65(c). [Citations.]

Dismissed.

————

1. Federal Rule of Civil Procedure 65(c) provides:

(c) *Security.* No restraining order or preliminary injunction shall issue except upon the giving of security by the applicant, in such sum as the court deems proper, for the payment of such costs and damages as may be incurred or suffered by any party who is found to have been wrongfully enjoined or restrained. * * *.

2. Is the language of Rule 65(c) jurisdictional? Although the language "no order shall issue" sounds jurisdictional, most courts have held that it is not.

3. If a defendant demands that a bond be set, must the judge accede to the demand? Most courts have interpreted the force of the language in Rule 65(c) to require the district court judge at least to make a decision on the propriety of the bond in the case and not to ignore the demand entirely. *See* Reinders Bros. v. Rain Bird Eastern Sales Corp., 627 F.2d 44 (7th Cir.1980). *See also* System Operations Inc. v. Scientific Games Dev. Corp., 555 F.2d 1131 (3d Cir.1977) (although the trial judge has substantial discretion in setting the amount of the bond, it is reversible error to refuse a bond unless there is no risk of monetary loss).

PROBLEM: THE DEAF GRADUATE STUDENT

Martin Gorden, a recent graduate of the State University, has a case pending in federal district court against the University. He entered the University last year to study for a master's degree. Gorden is hearing impaired, so he requested the University to provide him with sign language interpreter services. The University refused on the ground that Gorden did not meet the University's established criteria for financial assistance to graduate students.

There are substantial questions of law and of fact in this case. The act upon which Gorden bases his suit is unclear on several substantive points, and the actual necessity of the interpreter is medically uncertain because Gorden has some hearing. Preliminary motions are being made and discovery is underway. An association for advancement of the hearing impaired is interested in the case and has provided Gorden some financial assistance.

The case has not yet come to trial. Immediately after filing suit, Gorden sought and obtained a preliminary injunction against the University. The court ordered the University to provide the interpreter and required Gorden to post a $5000 security bond under Federal Rule of Civil Procedure 65(c). With the benefit of the interpreter provided under the preliminary injunction, Gorden successfully completed the degree he sought. He is now gainfully employed and he is no longer associated with the University.

Consider the following possible outcomes of this case:

    1. Given that Gorden has graduated, is the case now moot?

    2. Assume that Gorden wins the case. Should he be able to recover from the University the cost of posting the bond?

    3. Assume that Gorden fails to establish his case under the act. How should his liability under the bond be measured?

    4. Was the preliminary injunction properly issued in this case? Assume that on appeal the preliminary injunction is reversed because there was no showing of irreparable injury. Should Gorden be liable under the bond? Does it matter whether Gorden prevails ultimately in the case?

COYNE–DELANY CO., v. CAPITAL DEVELOPMENT BOARD

717 F.2d 385 (7th Cir.1983).

POSNER, CIRCUIT JUDGE. * * *

[The State of Illinois Capital Development Board (Board) contracted to replace plumbing fixtures in one of the state prisons. A portion of the contract which involved valves was subcontracted to the Coyne–Delany Company. The valves installed in the first phase of the project malfunctioned and replacement valves also proved unsatisfactory. The Board decided to solicit bids from other contractors to complete the project.]

Bids were received, but on May 7, 1979, two days before they were to be opened, Coyne–Delany sued the Board under section 1 of the Civil Rights Act of 1871, 42 U.S.C. § 1983, and on May 8 it obtained a temporary restraining order against the Board's opening the bids. The state asked that Coyne–Delany be ordered to post a $50,000 bond, pointing out that the temporary restraining order was preventing it from proceeding with the entire project and that indefinite delay could be extremely costly. But Judge Perry, the emergency motions judge, required a bond of only $5,000, in the belief that the temporary restraining order would be in effect for only a week until Judge Bua could hear the motion for a preliminary injunction. However, at the preliminary-injunction hearing Judge Bua issued the injunction but refused to increase the bond.

[The court issued the preliminary injunction upon determining that Coyne–Delany, under existing state law, was likely to prevail on its civil rights claim. Subsequently the state law precedent favoring the plaintiff was appealed to the state supreme court and reversed. Accordingly, the Court of Appeals reversed in this case because the law no longer allowed such claims against the Board. The delay from the preliminary injunction resulted in the Board awarding a replacement contract for a $56,000 higher amount than the original bid.] * * *

The Board then joined Hanover Insurance Company, the surety on the injunction bond, as an additional defendant in Coyne–Delany's civil rights suit, pursuant to Rule 65.1 of the Federal Rules of Civil Procedure, and moved the district court to award the Board damages of $56,000 for the wrongfully issued preliminary injunction and statutory costs (filing fees and the like, *see* 28 U.S.C. § 1920) of $523 which the Board had incurred in the district court. Judge Bua refused to award either costs or damages. His opinion states, "the Court must weigh the equitable factors of the case, including whether the case was filed in good faith or is frivolous. . . . [T]he parties have stipulated that the case was filed in good faith and without malice. Further, it is apparent that the case was not frivolous. The law as it existed at the time the case was filed clearly favored the plaintiffs. It would be unreasonable to require a party to anticipate a change in the law and would be unconscionable to label a suit filed in good faith as frivolous where there is such a subsequent change."

There is no dispute over the amount of costs claimed by the Board; and while Coyne–Delany has not conceded that the Board incurred damages of $56,000 as a result of the delay of the project and the district court made no finding with respect to those damages, they undoubtedly exceeded $5,000, the amount of the injunction bond. * * *

Although the district court has unquestioned power in an appropriate case not to award costs to the prevailing party and not to award damages on an injunction bond even though the grant of the injunction was reversed, the district court's opinion suggests that the court may have believed it had to deny both costs and damages because the lawsuit had not been brought in bad faith and was not frivolous. This would be the proper standard if the question were whether to award a prevailing defendant his attorney's fees. * * * In the absence of statute, an award of attorney's fees is proper only where the losing party has been guilty of bad faith, as by bringing a frivolous suit—frivolousness connoting not just a lack of merit but so great a lack as to suggest that the suit must have been brought to harass rather than to win. [Citations.]

The rule is different for costs. Rule 54(d) of the Federal Rules of Civil Procedure provides that "costs shall be allowed as of course to the prevailing party unless the court otherwise directs. . . ." This language creates a presumption in favor of awarding costs. * * *

The language of Rule 65(c), governing damages on an injunction bond, is only a little less clear than that of Rule 54(d): "No restraining order or preliminary injunction shall issue except upon the giving of security by the applicant, in such sum as the court deems proper, for the payment of such costs and damages as may be incurred or suffered by any party who is found to have been wrongfully enjoined or restrained." The court is not told in so many words to order the applicant to pay the wrongfully enjoined party's damages. But it is told to require a bond or equivalent security in order to ensure that the plaintiff will be able to pay all or at least some of the damages that the defendant incurs from the preliminary injunction if it turns out to have been wrongfully issued. The draftsmen must have intended that when such damages were incurred the plaintiff or his surety, pursuant to Rule 65.1's summary procedure, which despite its wording is applicable to the principal as well as the surety on the bond, would normally be required to pay the damages, at least up to the limit of the bond.

Yet some courts treat the district court's discretion to award or deny damages under an injunction bond as completely open-ended unless the plaintiff acted in bad faith in seeking the preliminary injunction. * * *

Most cases hold * * * that a prevailing defendant is entitled to damages on the injunction bond unless there is a good reason for not requiring the plaintiff to pay in the particular case. [Citations.] We agree with the majority approach. Not only is it implied by the text of Rule 65(c) but it makes the law more predictable and discourages the seeking of preliminary injunctions on flimsy (though not necessarily frivolous) grounds.

When rules prescribe a course of action as the norm but allow the district court to deviate from it, the court's discretion is more limited than it would be if the rules were nondirective. Rules 54(d) and 65(c) establish what Judge Friendly recently called "a principle of preference" guiding the exercise of the district judge's discretion. [Citation.] The judge must have a good reason for departing from such a principle in a particular case. It is not a sufficient reason for denying costs or damages on an injunction bond that the suit had as in this case been brought in good faith. That would be sufficient only if the presumption were against rather than in favor of awarding costs and damages on the bond to the prevailing party, as it would be if the issue were attorney's fees under the American rule, which in the absence of bad faith leaves each party to bear his own attorney's fees. The award of damages on the bond is not punitive but compensatory.

A good reason for not awarding such damages would be that the defendant had failed to mitigate damages. The district court made no reference to any such failure in this case and we can find no evidence that there was any; the Board's requesting and obtaining a 30–day extension of time for filing its appeal brief, the factor stressed by Coyne–Delany, did not create material or unreasonable delay. A good reason not for denying but for awarding damages in this case, unmentioned by the district court, was that the bond covered only a small fraction of the defendant's damages. The Board asked for and should have been granted a much larger bond; and when the heavy damages that the Board had predicted in asking for the larger bond materialized, it had a strong equitable claim to recover its damages up to the limit of the bond. Nor could $5,000 be regarded as excessive because the plaintiff was a poor person. The plaintiff is not a poor person but a substantial corporation that will not be crushed by having to pay $5,523 in damages and costs. It is particularly difficult in the circumstances of this case to understand the judge's refusal to award *any* damages, or the trivial amount of costs, conceded to be reasonable in amount, asked by the defendant.

In deciding whether to withhold costs or injunction damages, not only is the district court to be guided by the implicit presumption in Rules 54(d) and 65(c) in favor of awarding them, but the ingredients of a proper decision are objective factors—such as the resources of the parties, the defendant's efforts or lack thereof to mitigate his damages, and the outcome of the underlying suit—accessible to the judgment of a reviewing court.   * * *

Although the district court's decision cannot stand, both because it applies an incorrect standard and because it fails to consider and evaluate the full range of factors (which might in an appropriate case include, but is not exhausted by, the plaintiff's good faith) that would be relevant under the proper standard, we are not prepared to hold that the Board is entitled as a matter of law to its costs and to its injunction damages up to the limit of the bond. The district court did allude to one factor, besides mere absence of bad faith, that supported its ruling—the change in the applicable law after the preliminary injunction was issued. The law on which the court had relied in issuing the injunction was contained in an intermediate state appellate court decision and of course such decisions are reversed with some frequency. We do not believe that a change in the law is always a good ground for denying costs and injunction damages to a prevailing party, but it is a legitimate consideration, perhaps especially where the prevailing party is a state agency that benefited from a change in the law of its state.   * * * In any event, a remand is necessary to allow Judge Bua to consider and weigh all the relevant factors identified in this opinion—bearing in mind the principle of preference that we have indicated should guide his equitable determination.

It remains to consider whether on remand the Board should be allowed to seek injunction damages above the limit of the bond. The surety cannot be required to pay more than the face amount of the bond, but it is a separate question whether the plaintiff can be. However, the Ninth Circuit has held in a scholarly opinion that the bond is the limit of the damages the defendant can obtain for a wrongful injunction, even from the plaintiff, provided the plaintiff was acting in good faith, which is not questioned here. Buddy Systems, Inc. v. Exer–Genie, Inc., 545 F.2d 1164, 1167–68 (9th Cir.1976).   * * * Although there was a bond in the present case, it states unequivocally: "The obligation of this bond is limited to $5,000.00." * * *

Rightly or wrongly, American common law, state and federal, does not attempt to make the winner of a lawsuit whole by making the loser reimburse the winner's full legal expenses, even when the winner is the defendant, who unlike a prevailing plaintiff does not have the consolation of a damage recovery. In noninjunctive suits, except those brought (or defended) in bad faith, the winner can recover only his statutory costs, invariably but a small fraction of his expenses of suit. It would be incongruous if a prevailing defendant could obtain the full, and potentially the staggering, consequential damages caused by a preliminary injunction. The preliminary injunction in this case halted work on a major construction project for a year; it could easily have been two or three years, and the expenses imposed on the defendant not $56,000 but $560,000. * * * [I]f the plaintiff's damages are limited to the amount of the bond, at least he knows just what his exposure is when the bond is set by the district court. It is not unlimited. If the bond is too high he can drop the suit.

A defendant's inability to obtain damages in excess of the bond * * * can have unfortunate results, which are well illustrated by this case where the district court required too small a bond. But a defendant dissatisfied with the amount of bond set by the district court can, on appeal from the preliminary injunction, ask the court of appeals to increase the bond, which the defendant here did not do. * * *

Reversed and Remanded.

––––––––––

1. Neither Fed. R. Civ. P. 65(c) nor 65.1 specify what damages may be recovered by an improperly enjoined party in an action on a preliminary injunction bond. Even when the court allows recovery on the bond, damages are not awarded automatically; the wrongfully enjoined party must prove injury resulted from the issuance of the injunction. Attorney's fees, absent statutory authorization, are generally not recoverable in federal court in an action on the bond. See Fireman's Fund Ins. Co., v. S.E.K. Constr. Co., 436 F.2d 1345 (10th Cir.1971). In Matek v. Murat, 862 F.2d 720 (9th Cir.1988), the court noted that interest on the money held for the duration of the injunction may be a recoverable item of damages, provided that the total damages did not exceed the amount of the surety bond.

2. A court may dispense with the requirement of posting a preliminary injunction bond if the party seeking injunctive relief has sufficient assets to assure its ability to pay damages. In Monroe Division, Litton Business Sys. v. De Bari, 562 F.2d 30 (10th Cir.1977), for example, a large corporation obtained a preliminary injunction against a former employee and the court did not order the posting of security. When the defendant later sought to enforce liability on the wrongfully issued

injunction, the plaintiff argued that no liability existed because there was no bond. The court disagreed and held that Fed. R. Civ. P. 65(c) creates a cause of action for damages suffered by a wrongfully enjoined party. The defendant, who had convinced the trial court to waive security because of its corporate solvency, could not later argue that there is no liability without a bond.

3. For additional commentary on injunction bonds, *see* Dobbs, Should Security Be Required as a Pre–Condition to Provisional Injunctive Relief?, 52 N.C.L.Rev. 1091 (1974); Friendly, Indiscretion About Discretion, 31 Emory L.J. 747 (1982); Comment, The Triggering of Liability on Injunction Bonds, 52 N.C.L.Rev. 1252 (1974); Note, Interlocutory Injunctions and the Injunction Bond, 73 Harv.L.Rev. 333 (1959).

Chapter 7

CONTEMPT

Contempt is the method by which courts enforce equitable orders. The maxim "equity acts in personam" refers to the nature of an equitable decree as a personal directive. When a defendant fails to comply with an order, the disobedience is punishable as contempt. The defendant must have disobeyed a specifically detailed, unequivocal judicial command and the defendant must have had the ability to obey the order. Thus, a defendant who lacks the financial resources to pay child support cannot be jailed for disobeying the support decree.

Contempt proceedings may be characterized as either civil or criminal depending principally on their function. A civil contempt order is analogous to a civil tort claim. It is instituted by a private party, as part of an underlying action, to recover damages occasioned by the disobedience of the equitable order or to coerce the opposing party into compliance with the order. In contrast, the criminal contempt proceeding is like any criminal action brought by the government to punish errant behavior. Its purpose is to vindicate the integrity of the court which was offended by the defendant's contumacious conduct.

Another significant difference between the types of contempt orders is that civil contempt will fall if the underlying order is vacated, whereas a criminal contempt decree will stand even if the order was erroneously issued. Significant differences also appear in the nature and extent of the procedural safeguards given to the defendant, including rights to jury trial, right to counsel, and the burden of proof. The process and principles involved in that characterization are explored in the following materials.

A. CRIMINAL CONTEMPT

Section Coverage:

A criminal contempt proceeding is brought by a state or federal prosecutor to vindicate society's interest in the obedience of lawful orders. A defendant who is capable of complying with an order but who nonetheless fails to obey it can be punished criminally for that failure. The function of criminal contempt is to uphold the dignity of the court.

Like all criminal cases, a defendant in a criminal contempt proceeding is entitled to the full panoply of Constitutional safeguards. The same standards and requirements of criminal procedure are applicable.

If a defendant is found guilty of criminal contempt, the court can draw upon the usual punishments for criminal behavior: imprisonment or fine. Any fine paid by the defendant goes to the public coffers; courts give plaintiffs compensation only under civil contempt.

Criminal contempt may be further classified as direct or indirect depending upon where the defendant's offensive conduct takes place. If the defendant shows disrespect in the presence of the court, in most cases the judge may punish the conduct summarily without according all the traditional Constitutional protections, such as the right to counsel. The purpose of granting judges such extraordinary power is to ensure the proper administration of the judicial process.

Model Case:

Pat Boyle is a political activist fighting for the rights of oppressed youth. A dispute over the nature of some new proficiency exams in the local high school caught Boyle's attention. In protest, Boyle pitched a tent on the lawn of the school superintendent's personal residence and stayed there.

The superintendent obtained an injunction against this continuing trespass. Boyle disobeyed the order. During one point of the criminal contempt hearing Boyle shouted to the judge, "You are a cowardly tyrant! Try to face the truth for once!"

Boyle's outburst in the presence of the court can be punished immediately as summary criminal contempt. The disobedience of the injunction is indirect criminal contempt. It is punishable by fine or imprisonment if there are no Constitutional infirmities in the criminal hearing.

WALKER v. CITY OF BIRMINGHAM

388 U.S. 307, 87 S.Ct. 1824, 18 L.Ed.2d 1210 (1967).

MR. JUSTICE STEWART delivered the opinion of the Court.

On Wednesday, April 10, 1963, officials of Birmingham, Alabama, filed a bill of complaint in a state circuit court asking for injunctive relief against 139 individuals and two organizations. The bill and accompanying affidavits stated that during the preceding seven days:

> "[R]espondents [had] sponsored and/or participated in and/or conspired to commit and/or to encourage and/or to participate in certain movements, plans or projects commonly called 'sit-in' demonstrations, 'kneel-in' demonstrations, mass street parades, trespasses on private property after being warned to leave the premises by the owners of said property, congregating in mobs upon the public streets and other public places, unlawfully picketing private places of business in the City of Birmingham, Alabama; violation of numerous ordinances and statutes of the City of Birmingham and State of Alabama. * * * "

It was alleged that this conduct was "calculated to provoke breaches of the peace," "threaten[ed] the safety, peace and tranquility of the City," and placed "an undue burden and strain upon the manpower of the Police Department."

The bill stated that these infractions of the law were expected to continue and would "lead to further imminent danger to the lives, safety, peace, tranquility and general welfare of the people of the City of Birmingham," and that the "remedy by law [was] inadequate." The circuit judge granted a temporary injunction as prayed in the bill, enjoining the petitioners from, among other things, participating in or encouraging mass street parades or mass processions without a permit as required by a Birmingham ordinance.

Five of the eight petitioners were served with copies of the writ early the next morning. Several hours later four of them held a press conference. There a statement was distributed, declaring their intention to disobey the injunction because it was "raw tyranny under the guise of maintaining law and order." At this press conference one of the petitioners stated: "That they had respect for the Federal Courts, or Federal Injunctions, but in the past the State Courts had favored local law enforcement, and if the police couldn't handle it, the mob would."

That night a meeting took place at which one of the petitioners announced that "[i]njunction or no injunction we are going to march tomorrow." The next afternoon, Good Friday, a large crowd gathered in the vicinity of Sixteenth Street and Six Avenue North in Birmingham. A group of about 50 or 60 proceeded to parade along the sidewalk while a crowd of 1,000 to 1,500 onlookers stood by "clapping and hollering, and [w]hooping." Some of the crowd followed the marchers and spilled out into the street. At least three of the petitioners participated in this march.

Meetings sponsored by some of the petitioners were held that night and the following night, where calls for volunteers to "walk" and go to jail were made. On Easter Sunday, April 14, a crowd of between 1,500 and 2,000 people congregated in the midafternoon in the vicinity of Seventh Avenue and Eleventh Street North in Birmingham. One of the petitioners was seen organizing members of the crowd in formation. A group of about 50, headed by three other petitioners, started down the sidewalk two abreast. At least one other petitioner was among the marchers. Some 300 or 400 people from among the onlookers followed in a crowd that occupied the entire width of the street and overflowed onto the sidewalks. Violence occurred. Members of the crowd threw rocks that injured a newspaperman and damaged a police motorcycle.

The next day the city officials who had requested the injunction applied to the state circuit court for an order to show cause why the petitioners should not be held in contempt for violating it. At the ensuing hearing the petitioners sought to attack the constitutionality of the injunction on the ground that it was vague and overbroad, and restrained free speech. They also sought to attack the Birmingham parade ordinance upon similar grounds, and upon the further ground that the ordinance had previously been administered in an arbitrary and discriminatory manner.

The circuit judge refused to consider any of these contentions, pointing out that there had been neither a motion to dissolve the injunction, nor an effort to comply with it by applying for a permit from the city commission before engaging in the Good Friday and Easter Sunday parades. Consequently, the court held that the only issues before it were whether it had jurisdiction to issue the temporary injunction, and whether thereafter the petitioners had knowingly violated it. Upon these issues the court found against the petitioners, and imposed upon each of them a sentence of five days in jail and a $50 fine, in accord with an Alabama statute.

The Supreme Court of Alabama affirmed.   * * *

Howat v. State of Kansas, 258 U.S. 181, 42 S.Ct. 277, 66 L.Ed. 550, was decided by this Court almost 50 years ago. That was a case in which people had been punished by a Kansas trial court for refusing to obey an antistrike injunction issued under the state industrial relations act. They had claimed a right to disobey the court's order upon the ground that the state statute and the injunction based upon it were invalid under the Federal Constitution. The Supreme Court of Kansas had affirmed the judgment.   * * *

This Court, in dismissing the writ of error, * * * [held]:

"An injunction duly issuing out of a court of general jurisdiction with equity powers, upon pleadings properly invoking its action, and served upon persons made parties therein and within the jurisdiction, must be obeyed by them, however erroneous the action of the court may be, even if the error be in the assumption of the validity of a seeming, but void law going to the merits of the case. It is for the court of first instance to determine the question of the validity of the law, and until its decision is reversed for error by orderly review, either by itself or by a higher court, its orders based on its decision are to be respected, and disobedience of them is contempt of its lawful authority, to be punished." 258 U.S., at 189–190, 42 S.Ct. at 280.

The rule of state law accepted and approved in *Howat v. Kansas* is consistent with the rule of law followed by the federal courts.

In the present case, however, we are asked to hold that this rule of law, upon which the Alabama courts relied, was constitutionally impermissible. We are asked to say that the Constitution compelled Alabama to allow the petitioners to violate this injunction, to organize and engage in these mass street parades and demonstrations, without any previous effort on their part to have the injunction dissolved or modified, or any attempt to secure a parade permit in accordance with its terms. Whatever the limits of *Howat v. Kansas,* we cannot accept the petitioners' contentions in the circumstances of this case.

Without question the state court that issued the injunction had, as a court of equity, jurisdiction over the petitioners and over the subject matter of the controversy. And this is not a case where the injunction was transparently invalid or had only a frivolous pretense to validity. * * *

The generality of the language contained in the Birmingham parade ordinance upon which the injunction was based would unquestionably raise substantial constitutional issues concerning some of its provisions. [Citations.] The petitioners, however, did not even attempt to apply to the Alabama courts for an authoritative construction of the ordinance. Had they done so, those courts might have given the licensing authority granted in the ordinance a narrow and precise scope. * * *

The breadth and vagueness of the injunction itself would also unquestionably be subject to substantial constitutional question. But the way to raise that question was to apply to the Alabama courts to have the injunction modified or dissolved. The injunction in all events clearly prohibited mass parading without a permit, and the evidence shows that the petitioners fully understood that prohibition when they violated it.

The petitioners also claim that they were free to disobey the injunction because the parade ordinance on which it was based had been administered in the past in an arbitrary and discriminatory fashion. In support of this claim they sought to introduce evidence that, a few days before the injunction issued, requests for permits to picket had been made to a member of the city commission. One request had been rudely rebuffed, and this same official had later made clear that he was without power to grant the permit alone, since the issuance of such permits was the responsibility of the entire city commission. Assuming the truth of this proffered evidence, it does not follow that the parade ordinance was void on its face. The petitioners, moreover, did not apply for a permit either to the commission itself or to any commissioner after the injunction issued. Had they done so, and had the permit been refused, it is clear that their claim of arbitrary or discriminatory administration of the ordinance would have been considered by the state circuit court upon a motion to dissolve the injunction.

This case would arise in quite a different constitutional posture if the petitioners, before disobeying the injunction, had challenged it in the Alabama courts, and had been met with delay or frustration of their constitutional claims. But there is no showing that such would have been the fate of a timely motion to modify or dissolve the injunction. There was an interim of two days between the issuance of the injunction and the Good Friday march. The petitioners give absolutely no explanation of why they did not make some application to the state court during that period. The injunction had issued *ex parte;* if the court had been presented with the petitioners' contentions, it might have dissolved or at least modified its order in some respects. If it had not done so, Alabama procedure would have provided for an expedited process of appellate review. It cannot be presumed that the Alabama courts would have ignored the petitioners' constitutional claims. * * *

The rule of law that Alabama followed in this case reflects a belief that in the fair administration of justice no man can be judge in his own case, however exalted his station, however righteous his motives, and irrespective of his race, color, politics, or religion. This Court cannot hold that the petitioners were constitutionally free to ignore all the procedures of the law and carry their battle to the streets. One may sympathize with the petitioners' impatient commitment to their cause. But respect for judicial process is a small price to pay for the civilizing hand of law, which alone can give abiding meaning to constitutional freedom.

Affirmed.

———

1. *Criminal Contempt as "Crime".* The Supreme Court has frequently affirmed the principle that criminal contempt is a "crime in the ordinary sense." Bloom v. Illinois, 391 U.S. 194, 201, 88 S.Ct. 1477, 1481, 20 L.Ed.2d 522 (1968). Therefore, "criminal penalties may not be imposed on someone who has not been afforded the protections that the Constitution requires of such criminal proceedings." Hicks v. Feiock, 485 U.S. 624, 632, 108 S.Ct. 1423, 1429–30, 99 L.Ed.2d 721 (1988).

Those Constitutional protections for crimes that also apply to criminal contempts include privilege against self-incrimination, right to proof beyond a reasonable doubt, right to a jury trial, double jeopardy, rights to notice of charges, assistance of counsel, summary process, and to present a defense. *See* In re Bradley, 318 U.S. 50, 63 S.Ct. 470, 87 L.Ed. 608 (1943); Cooke v. United States, 267 U.S. 517, 537, 45 S.Ct. 390, 395, 69 L.Ed. 767 (1925); Gompers v. Bucks Stove & Range Co., 221 U.S. 418, 444, 31 S.Ct. 492, 499, 55 L.Ed. 797 (1911).

The Constitutional protections for criminal contempt apply only to disobedience of a court's order outside the presence of the court. These contempts are known as indirect contempts. Direct contempts that occur in the court's presence may be immediately adjudged and sanctioned summarily. *See* Ex parte Terry, 128 U.S. 289, 9 S.Ct. 77, 32 L.Ed. 405 (1888). If a court delays punishing a direct contempt until the completion of trial, however, due process requires notice and a hearing. Taylor v. Hayes, 418 U.S. 488, 94 S.Ct. 2697, 41 L.Ed.2d 897 (1974).

2. *Jury Trial Rights in Contempt Cases.* In contempt cases the right to a jury trial depends upon the type of contempt. There is no right to a jury trial in a civil contempt case because the plaintiff receives this remedy as a part of the underlying equitable remedy, such as a specific performance order. For criminal contempts the Supreme Court held in *Bloom v. Illinois, supra,* that the sixth amendment right to jury trial applies to serious criminal contempts. This Constitutional requirement was also applied to the states through the Fourteenth Amendment.

Serious criminal contempts are ones where the penalty actually imposed exceeds six months' imprisonment.   391 U.S. at 199, 88 S.Ct. at 1481. See also Taylor v. Hayes, 418 U.S. 488, 495, 94 S.Ct. 2697, 2701–02, 41 L.Ed.2d 897 (1974).

The consecutive imposition of shorter sentences that aggregate to more than six months' imprisonment also triggers the jury trial right. *See* United States v. Seale, 461 F.2d 345 (7th Cir.1972) (three months' imprisonment sentenced for each of sixteen acts of misbehavior in the presence of the court).

Where a defendant at the end of a trial is further tried for contempt concerning his personal attacks on the integrity of the judge during the trial, the trial judge should avoid the possibility of prejudice by not presiding over the contempt hearing.   *Id.* In a typical summary contempt imposed during the course of a trial, however, the contempt is imposed immediately by the trial judge who witnesses the acts.

3. *Willfulness.* Criminal contempt requires intentional conduct violating the court order.   For a good discussion of the principles of willfulness, *see* United States v. Greyhound Corp., 508 F.2d 529 (7th Cir.1974).

In contrast, willfulness or intentional disobedience is not a necessary element of civil contempt.   The court in Morales Feliciano v. Hernandez Colon, 697 F.Supp. 26 (D. Puerto Rico 1987), explained the distinction:

> [T]he absence of willfulness does not relieve a party from civil contempt.   Civil, as distinguished from criminal contempt, is a sanction to enforce compliance with an order of the court or to compensate for losses for damages sustained by reason of noncompliance.   Since the purpose is remedial, it matters not with what intent the defendant did the prohibited act.

It is not an absolute defense to civil contempt that an unsuccessful effort to obey a court's order was done in good faith.   Impossibility or incapacity to comply with the order are defenses, but the burden of proof rests with the defendant.   United States v. Rylander, 460 U.S. 752, 103 S.Ct. 1548, 75 L.Ed.2d 521 (1983).

IN RE STEWART
571 F.2d 958 (5th Cir.1978).

GODBOLD, CIRCUIT JUDGE.

The appellant Murray Stewart was adjudged guilty of civil contempt by the district court and sentenced to a fine and a period of probation. The fine has been paid and the period of probation has run its course. The judgment of contempt is invalid and is reversed.

* * *

Stewart is county engineer for Hinds County, Mississippi.   Thomas Stubblefield was a county employee working as a laborer on the bridge crew. Stubblefield was summoned to serve as a civil juror in the United States District Court for the Southern District of Mississippi, sitting at Jackson, Hinds County, and was selected to sit on a case which ended January 13. On January 13 an unidentified member of the court personnel told District Judge Harold Cox, presiding, that Stubblefield was having some difficulty with his employer because he was serving on the jury. Judge Cox talked with Stubblefield. * * *

* * * Judge Cox's position is clear from the comments which he directed to Stewart during the hearing:

> * * * I told him [Stubblefield] to tell you when I had some word that there was some irregularity about whether or not he had been demoted—I understood that yesterday, and I told him to tell you that I didn't want anything like that to happen, that he was on the jury up here. * * *

When Stubblefield reported for work on January 14, he was told by the overseer of the solid waste crew that he (Stubblefield) had been transferred to the solid waste crew. Stubblefield went at once to see Stewart and objected, as Stubblefield phrased it, to being put on jury duty and coming back and finding his job gone. In the contempt hearing Stubblefield was asked if he had told Stewart what Judge Cox had told him to say, and he answered affirmatively, but at no time did Stubblefield testify to the content of either the message given to him or his restatement of it to Stewart. In answer to more specific questions Stubblefield testified as follows. He asked Stewart if being on the jury had any bearing on the transfer, and Stewart said it did not. Stubblefield inquired whether the transfer had any relation to a rumor that he had been loafing and hauling firewood while off work for jury duty, and Stewart stated it did not. Stewart told Stubblefield that the pay for the two jobs was the same. Finally Stewart told Stubblefield that he could accept the transfer or be dismissed. Stubblefield told Stewart he would call Judge Cox and get the matter straightened out. To this Stewart responded that Judge Cox had nothing to do with him or with running the county.

* * *

Stewart was arrested during the morning and held in custody until his trial. Judge Cox directed the U.S. Attorney to serve as prosecutor. A hearing was conducted during the afternoon of the 14th. Stewart had no counsel. The record does not show that he was advised that he had a right to counsel nor does it reveal a waiver of right to counsel. Stewart subpoenaed no witnesses, and nothing in the record shows that he was told he could do so. Stubblefield testified and Stewart cross-examined him. Stewart gave his testimony, and both the U.S. Attorney and Judge Cox cross-examined Stewart.

At the conclusion of the brief testimony Judge Cox announced that he found Stewart guilty of contempt. He gave oral findings and reasons. * * *

The judge orally imposed a sentence of $100 fine and costs and put Stewart on probation for six months conditioned upon his paying the fine and costs, upon his restoring Stubblefield to his former position, and upon Stewart's not violating any law of the state, county or municipality and "any rules or regulations of this court like this particular regulation." The judge ordered Stewart committed until the fine and costs were paid. A formal order was entered the same day adjudging Stewart to be in civil contempt and setting out the sentence, except that the condition on probation of Stewart's obeying the law and the rules and regulations of the court was omitted. A few days later Judge Cox amended the sentence by changing the probation to three months unsupervised probation but leaving the other terms in effect.

We understand a district judge's concern if he has evidence that a juror has been treated adversely by his employer because he has served on the jury. But judicial concern cannot explain the injustice that permeates this case. The proceedings did not meet rudimentary standards of due process guaranteed by our Constitution. They did not comply with the Federal Rules of Criminal Procedure. The court erroneously handled the case as a civil contempt case when in fact it was a criminal contempt proceeding. There was no proof that Stewart transferred Stubblefield because Stubblefield had been on the jury. Even if there had been such proof, Stewart's action would not have been contempt of court.

The beginning point is to determine whether the nature of the contempt proceeding was civil or criminal. [Citation.] The district judge's order recited that Stewart was found in civil contempt of the court, but the judge's characterization is not conclusive.[2] [Citation.] The nature of the proceeding may be determined from the purpose of the penalty. Civil contempt is remedial; the penalty serves to enforce compliance with a court order or to compensate an injured party. Criminal contempt is punitive; the penalty serves to vindicate the authority of the court and does not terminate upon compliance with a court order. [Citations.] Further, civil contempt is a facet of a principal suit, while criminal contempt is a separate action brought in the name of the United States. [Citation.] In this case the district judge imposed a penalty that was unconditional[3] and not subject to being lifted if Stewart purged himself. The penalty was meant to punish defiance of the court and deter similar actions.[4] The district judge's statements,

---

2. A reviewing court's inability to determine whether a proceeding is civil or criminal is in itself a ground for reversal. *In re Monroe,* 532 F.2d 424 (5th Cir.1976); *Skinner v. White,* 505 F.2d 685 (5th Cir.1974).

3. The probation had conditions attached, but this is another matter.

4. Part of the penalty, the reinstatement of Stubblefield, was remedial. In *Nye v. U.S.,* 313 U.S. 33, 42–43, 61 S.Ct. 810, 813, 85 L.Ed. 1172, 1177 (1941), the Su-

preme Court said that a contempt proceeding is considered civil only when the punishment is wholly remedial. When the punishment is partly remedial and partly punitive, "the criminal feature of the order is dominant and fixes its character for purposes of review." *Id., quoting Union Tool Co. v. Wilson,* 259 U.S. 107, 110, 42 S.Ct. 427, 428, 66 L.Ed. 848, 850 (1922).

particularly "I haven't had this to contend with too much, but I think I might as well just make an example out of this fellow so I won't have to bother with this matter again," make crystal clear the intent to impose punishment. Finally, while the proceeding was tangentially related to the civil suit on which Stubblefield had sat as juror and nominally did not involve the United States, it was docketed, captioned and treated as a separate case and on order of the court was prosecuted by the U.S. Attorney. The contempt proceeding against Stewart was criminal in nature.

The contempt proceeding did not comply with basic and elementary constitutional requirements of due process. The Supreme Court spelled out the procedural due process protections required in contempt proceedings in Re Oliver, 333 U.S. 257, 275, 68 S.Ct. 499, 508, 92 L.Ed. 682, 695 (1948).

> Except for a narrowly limited category of contempts, due process of law * * * requires that one charged with contempt of court be advised of the charges against him, have a reasonable opportunity to meet them by way of defense or explanation, have the right to be represented by counsel, and have a chance to testify and call other witnesses in his behalf, either by way of defense or explanation.

This proceeding does not fall within the narrow exception where summary disposition is constitutionally permissible.

> The narrow exception to these due process requirements includes only charges of misconduct, in open court, in the presence of the judge, which disturbs the court's business, where all of the essential elements of the misconduct are under the eye of the court, are actually observed by the court, and where immediate punishment is essential to prevent 'demoralization of the court's authority before the public'. If some essential elements of the offense are not personally observed by the judge, so that he must depend upon statements made by others for his knowledge about these essential elements, due process requires, * * * that the accused be accorded notice and a fair hearing as above set out.

Re Oliver, 333 U.S. at 275, 68 S.Ct. at 509, 92 L.Ed. at 695.

Stewart was tried without counsel and without being informed by the court that he had a right to counsel. He was not given a meaningful opportunity to call witnesses or advised of his right to do so. * * *

The proceeding also failed to comply with Federal Rule of Criminal Procedure 42(b), governing criminal contempts. This rule requires that, except for conduct committed in the presence of and seen or heard by the judge, a criminal contempt shall be prosecuted on notice given to the alleged contemnor. The notice "shall state the time and place of hearing, allow a reasonable time for the preparation of the defense, and shall state the essential facts constituting the criminal contempt charged and describe it as such." Here the judge issued a show cause and arrest order, which under 42(b) may be the means of notice. It did not allow a reasonable time for preparation of a defense. It did not even state the time and place of hearing.

* * *

Turning to the merits of the case, Stewart's contempt conviction was clearly erroneous. As in any other criminal case, proof of guilt beyond reasonable doubt is required. [Citations.] The evidence did not even come close to sustaining the district judge's factual conclusion that Stewart demoted or mistreated Stubblefield because he was serving on the jury. * * *

Finally, even if the foregoing gaps in the evidence had been filled, Stewart would not have been guilty of contempt under 18 U.S.C. § 401. That section provides:

A court of the United States shall have power to punish by fine or imprisonment, at its discretion, such contempt of its authority, and none other, as—

(1) Misbehavior of any person in its presence or so near thereto as to obstruct the administration of justice;

(2) Misbehavior of any of its officers in their official transactions;

(3) Disobedience or resistance to its lawful writ, process, order, rule, decree, or command.

Subsection (1) does not apply. Stewart's acts were outside the presence of the court, and they were not "so near thereto as to obstruct the administration of justice." The words "so near thereto" are meant as geographic terms that limit the subsection's application to acts within the immediate vicinity of the courtroom, such as the adjoining hallway or the jury room. *Nye v. U.S.,* 313 U.S. 33, 48–49, 61 S.Ct. 810, 815– 816, 85 L.Ed. 1172, 1180 (1941).

Subsection (2) is obviously inapplicable. Stewart is not an officer of the court.

Subsection (3) was not violated. Stewart disobeyed no writ, process, or decree of the district court. Even if the proof had established the content of Judge Cox's message to Stubblefield and had established that Stubblefield accurately relayed it, an oral "message" such as this, not stated in open court where it could be taken down by a court reporter, addressed to a person not before the court, never entered upon the records of the court, and relayed by word of mouth through a person without official status, is not an "order" or "command" within the meaning of subsection (3). * * *

The conviction is reversed and the cause remanded with directions that the clerk be ordered to repay Stewart the fine he paid and that the proceedings be dismissed.

1. *Criminal/civil contempt distinction.* As the principal case illustrates, the difference between criminal and civil contempt is essential, but often elusive. Scholars have criticized the distinction as unworkable, but the Supreme Court has adhered to the distinction. *See* Dudley, Getting Beyond the Civil/Criminal Distinction: A New Approach to Regulation of Indirect Contempts, 79 Va.L.Rev. 1025, 1033 (1993); Martineau, Contempt of Court: Eliminating the Confusion between Civil and Criminal Contempt, 50 U.Cin.L.Rev. 677 (1981); Moskovitz, Contempt of Injunctions, Civil and Criminal, 43 Colum.L.Rev. 780 (1943); R. Goldfarb, The Contempt Power 58 (1963).

2. *Specificity of the Order.* As the principal case demonstrates, a criminal contempt conviction based upon 18 U.S.C. § 401(3) must be premised upon the violation of an identifiable court order. That order must be sufficiently specific that the defendant has an opportunity to know that his behavior is disobedience.

The specificity requirement for the framing of injunctive orders is contained in F.R.Civ.P. 65(d): "Every order granting an injunction * * * shall be specific in terms [and] shall describe in reasonable detail, and not by reference to the complaint or other document, the act or acts sought to be restrained * * * "

The necessity of careful compliance with the specificity requirement is noted as follows in H.K. Porter Co. v. National Friction Products, 568 F.2d 24, 27 (7th Cir.1977):

> Rule 65(d) is no mere extract from a manual of procedural practice. It is a page from the book of liberty.

> * * * Because of the risks of contempt proceedings, civil or criminal, paramount interests of liberty and due process make it indispensable for the chancellor or his surrogate to speak clearly, explicitly, and specifically if violation of his direction is to subject a litigant * * * to coercive or penal measures, as well as to payment of damages.

One of the problems in the principal case is the uncertainty of the "message" that Judge Cox apparently sent to Stewart through the juror Stubblefield. What could Judge Cox have done instead?

3. *Who Is Bound by Injunctions?* The contempt power is premised upon the disobedience of a binding court order. F.R.Civ.P. 65(d) provides that an injunction is "binding only upon the parties to the action, their officers, agents, servants, employees, and attorneys, and upon those persons in active concert or participation with them who receive actual notice of the order by personal service or otherwise." The Supreme Court has interpreted this rule to include not only party defendants but those in "privity" with them, at least to the extent that they are in "active concert" with the defendants. Regal Knitwear Co. v. NLRB, 324 U.S. 9, 65 S.Ct. 478, 89 L.Ed. 661 (1945). *See also* Golden State Bottling Co. v. NLRB, 414 U.S. 168, 94 S.Ct. 414, 38 L.Ed.2d 388 (1973) (a bona fide purchaser of a company who acquired it with knowledge that an

order to remedy an unfair labor practice had not been fulfilled may be considered in privity with its predecessor for purposes of Rule 65(d)).

4.   Many state courts have been historically more willing to bind nonparties to an injunction and to find them in contempt for violation of the order when they have notice. *See* Silvers v. Traverse, 82 Iowa 52, 47 N.W. 888 (1891) (injunction barring sale of alcohol on certain property bound a nonparty who sold liquor on the premises).

Similarly, a few other courts have taken the extreme position that once jurisdiction is acquired over the *res,* an order can protect the *res* against all, such as an injunction against trespass on a parcel of land. *See* State v. Porter, 76 Kan. 411, 91 P. 1073 (1907); State v. Terry, 99 Wash. 1, 168 P. 513 (1917). *But see* Kean v. Hurley, 179 F.2d 888 (8th Cir.1950) (trespass injunction against world at large impermissible under Rule 65(d)). The *res* approach has been justly criticized as an over-extension of the court's powers. An injunction that binds all the world would be functionally indistinguishable from a statute, thus allowing the court to usurp legislative functions and to punish with a minimal check on its power. *See* discussions in Dobbs, Contempt of Court: A Survey, 56 Cornell L.Rev. 183, 249–52 (1971); Note, Binding Nonparties to Injunction Decrees, 49 Minn.L.Rev. 719, 729–31 (1965).

5.   A related problem has appeared in some cases involving school desegregation decrees where the court has wanted to bind nonparties to an order not to interfere with an orderly desegregation process. The Fifth Circuit has upheld a contempt conviction of a nonparty, Hall, who was served with a noninterference order that purported to bind anyone with notice not to obstruct school entrances. Hall was arrested for blocking a high school entrance in express defiance of the court order. The district court found him in criminal contempt, and the Fifth Circuit upheld the court's "inherent power" to preserve its judgment. The opinion states that Rule 65(d) acts as a "codification rather than a limitation of courts' common-law powers [and] cannot be read to restrict the inherent power of a court to protect its ability to render a binding judgment." United States v. Hall, 472 F.2d 261, 267 (5th Cir.1972). This case is criticized in Rendleman, "Beyond Contempt: Obligors to Injunctions," 53 Tex.L.Rev. 873 (1975). *See also* on this general topic Dobbyn, Contempt Power of the Equity Court Over Outside Agitators, 8 St. Mary's L.J. 1 (1976).

EX PARTE DANIELS

722 S.W.2d 707 (Tex.Cr.App.1987).

McCORMICK, JUDGE.

This is an application for writ of habeas corpus filed pursuant to the provisions of Article 11.06, V.A.C.C.P.

Applicant was held to be in direct criminal contempt of court by the Honorable Max W. Boyer, sitting by assignment in the 308th District

Court in Harris County. The contempt order was the result of an incident which occurred on January 22, 1985, while applicant was appearing pro se.

In the course of the proceedings, applicant became involved in an argument with Judge Boyer. The judge ordered applicant to leave the courtroom and to not return until she obtained counsel. When applicant failed to leave the courtroom immediately, the bailiff was ordered to escort her out.

Applicant apparently went peacefully with the bailiff until they reached the doorway of the courtroom. At that point, applicant is alleged to have physically attacked the master of the court. The bailiff then moved to restrain applicant and a general disturbance erupted in which several people were involved.

The record indicates that at some point after this occurrence the trial judge ordered applicant brought before him for a summary contempt proceeding. During the course of this hearing, applicant did not have the benefit of retained counsel but instead continued to act in a pro se capacity. Applicant was found to be in direct criminal contempt and ordered to be confined in jail for a period of thirty days. No fine was imposed. Applicant was ordered to pay thirty-three dollars in court costs.

Applicant, now represented by retained counsel, * * * argues that her confinement is illegal because she was denied due process of law in that she was denied counsel during the contempt proceedings. * * *

Contempt power is a necessary and integral component of judicial authority. [Citation.] While it is clear the exercise of this authority should be tempered with common sense and sound discretion, contempt power is accorded wide latitude because it is essential to judicial independence and authority. [Citations.]

At the outset of any discussion or judicial determination of the right of due process in a contempt case, it is necessary to distinguish "direct" contempt from "constructive" contempt. Direct contempt is contempt which is committed or occurs in the presence of the court. In direct contempt cases the court has direct knowledge of the facts which constitute contempt. Constructive or indirect contempt involves actions outside of the presence of the court. Constructive contempt refers to acts which require testimony or the production of evidence to establish their existence.

The distinction is important because due process imposes different standards for the proceedings in which the contempt is adjudicated. In cases of constructive contempt in which factual issues relating to activities outside the court's presence must be resolved, due process requires the accused be afforded notice and a hearing. [Citations.] In a situation involving indirect or constructive contempt, the contemner cannot be legally confined without a reasonable opportunity to obtain counsel. [Citations.]

In cases of direct contempt, however, the behavior constituting contempt has occurred in the presence of the court. The judge has personal knowledge of the events in question and the court is allowed to conduct a summary proceeding in which the contemner is not accorded notice nor a hearing in the usual sense of the word. [Citations.]

Furthermore, in cases of direct contempt, the accused has no right to counsel. [Citation.] The right to counsel is, of course, one of the most fundamental protections guaranteed under the United States Constitution. The rationale for this very limited exception to the basic principle of the right to counsel was explained in the case of *Cooke v. United States:*

> "To preserve order in the courtroom for the proper conduct of business, the court must act instantly to suppress disturbance or violence or physical obstruction or disrespect to the court, when occurring in open court. There is no need of evidence or assistance of counsel before punishment, because the court has seen the offense. Such summary vindication of the court's dignity and authority is necessary. It has always been so in the courts of the common law, and the punishment imposed is due process of law...." 267 U.S. at 394, 45 S.Ct. at 534.

* * *

Applicant has argued that the acts of contempt which she is accused of having committed did not take place in the judge's presence. Applicant states that the judge did not actually see much of the activity which took place at the door of the courtroom. Applicant states that the judge required testimony before he could make a complete determination that contemptuous actions occurred. Therefore, applicant argues her contempt was constructive rather than direct and applicant therefore argues that she was denied due process because she was denied the right of counsel.

The record reflects that the activities which gave rise to applicant's being held in contempt occurred in the 308th District Court while Judge Boyer was present and seated at the bench. Applicant states in effect that due to the rapid and confusing sequence of events the judge did not actually see everything that occurred, but only witnessed a general disturbance. Applicant urges this Court to accept the proposition that this means the actions constituting contempt did not occur in the presence of the court.

Applicant overlooks the fact that "in the presence of the court" does not necessarily mean in the immediate presence of the trial judge. Ex parte Aldridge, 169 Tex.Cr.R. 395, 334 S.W.2d 161, 168 (1959). As we stated above, the rationale justifying the harsh remedy of direct contempt adjudications is that the authority and ability of the courts to conduct the peoples' business is compromised by the disruptive actions of the alleged contemner. [Citations.] It is for this reason that this Court has held that the court is present whenever any of its constituent parts, the courtroom, the jury and the jury room are engaged in pursuing the work of the court. It was for this reason that the applicant in *Ex parte Aldridge, supra,* was properly determined to have committed direct contempt when he placed contemptuous publications in the corridors of the courthouse where prospective jurors would necessarily see them.

In the case before us, it is clear that applicant's behavior was sufficiently "before the court" to justify a determination that she was in direct contempt of the court. Her actions took place in the presence of the trial judge. Even though some details of the disturbance were not noted by the trial judge due to the confusion and rapid sequence of the events, that does not mean the incident did not occur in the presence of the court. It is undisputed that the judge witnessed what he considered a disturbance and felt compelled to interrupt court business and intervene in the activities which took place at the courtroom entrance. The judge felt it was necessary to further interrupt the court's business by calling a recess.

The bailiff and the master of the court are court officers. The ability of the 308th District Court to conduct its duties was compromised by the direct physical attack on one of its officers in the courtroom and in the physical presence of the trial judge. As such, applicant's actions constitute direct contempt.

* * *

CLINTON, JUDGE, DISSENTING. * * *

The written order of contempt recites, *inter alia,* that after a hearing in the family law matter applicant "was ordered by this Court to be removed from the Courtroom for causing a disturbance at the bench." [3] According to the brief on behalf of the judge, at the courtroom

---

3. An exchange immediately preceding that order went to a stated determination by the court to pass the case until applicant retained counsel; she objected and announced she would "refuse to leave until I get justice," only to be told by the judge that she would be taken bodily from the courtroom; applicant rejoined that she could not afford to hire an attorney and said, "I appeal right now." Then came the following:

"THE COURT: From what you were saying, you don't think you will get justice from me, do you, the way I am acting?

[APPLICANT]: I thought I would.

[APPLICANT]: Is this a democratic court?

THE COURT: There is no politics in this court.

[APPLICANT]: I pay my taxes.

THE COURT: This Court tries to deal in dispatch and there is no way I can deal in dispatch with a person like you.

Remove her from the courtroom. I order you to remove this woman from the courtroom and don't permit her to come back in. The only way you can permit her to come back in is to have counsel with her.

[The bailiff asked applicant to leave with him; she protested that 'he can't do that to me,' but was informed 'he can;' the judge told the bailiff to get help if needed and to 'remove her without further activity.']

[APPLICANT]: I want to take a picture of this. I don't believe this and I object. This is not justice and I don't accept it.

* * *

THE BAILIFF: Let's go.

THE COURT: And don't let her back in this courtroom unless she has counsel.

(Mrs. Daniels took a picture of the Judge.)

(Recess)."

door applicant "tried to strike the Master of the Court in the head with her purse or briefcase at which time the bailiff threw [applicant] against the wall and had to tackle [applicant]."

* * *

In her brief applicant contends "that it was only after being *told* of an alleged incident in the doorway to the courtroom—only after relying on the word of the bailiff, the Master, and possibly others—that the judge found Applicant in contempt." [emphasis by applicant]. To that the brief for the judge correctly responds that the record does not reflect he had any discussion with anyone, but elsewhere states:

> "Although Judge Boyer expressed *no knowledge* of the attempt to assault the Master of the Court, Judge Boyer was aware that Applicant had done *something* at the courtroom door which disrupted the Court's business."

* * *

In the instant cause alleged contemptuous conduct took on a form that is not susceptible to easy classification as either constructive contempt or direct contempt. Clearly a "disturbance" occurred at an entrance to the courtroom in which applicant was involved. While the majority opinion says that the judge felt "compelled to interrupt court business and intervene in the activities which took place at the courtroom entrance," and that "it was necessary to further interrupt the court's business by calling a recess," I find no support for that conclusion—unless the majority means that the judge recessed to investigate the matter by speaking to the bailiff and others and then prepared his order of contempt. After a lapse of time the judge did reconvene court, state his findings of fact and conclusions of law and order of contempt he rendered for the court. What is presented here is at best a hybrid form of contempt, and a proceeding which the brief for the judge concedes was not "a hearing as to the issue of contempt."

Regardless of its label, the ultimate question is whether the proceeding comported with requisites of due process in the premises. *Codispoti v. Pennsylvania,* 418 U.S. 506, 94 S.Ct. 2687, 41 L.Ed.2d 912 (1974) and *Taylor v. Hayes,* 418 U.S. 488, 94 S.Ct. 2697, 41 L.Ed.2d 897 (1974), have taught us that when a trial judge does not convict and sentence for various disruptive acts "as they occur," "there is no overriding necessity for instant action to preserve order and no justification for dispensing with the ordinary rudiments of due process," *Codispoti, supra,* 418 U.S. at 513, 515, 94 S.Ct. at 1692. "On the other hand, where conviction and punishment are delayed, 'it is difficult to argue that action without notice or hearing of any kind is necessary to preserve order and enable [the court] to proceed with its business.'" [Citations.]

* * *

Applicant was not convicted and sentenced for creating the second disturbance "as it occurred." The bailiff had been ordered by the judge only to remove her from the courtroom, and that was done. Though the majority says the judge "witnessed what he considered to be a disturbance," clearly the judge did not then and there summarily hold her in contempt. Rather, under authority not revealed by this record, she was detained elsewhere for an extended period—four hours, according to her brief, or the time taken while the court was in recess in order for the judge to prepare and include written findings and conclusions in the order of contempt, according to the brief for the judge—before being taken back into court. By then "action without notice or hearing of any kind [was not] necessary to preserve order and enable [the court] to proceed with its business."

* * *

Accordingly, I respectfully dissent.

MATTER OF CONTEMPT OF GREENBERG

849 F.2d 1251 (9th Cir.1988).

PREGERSON, CIRCUIT JUDGE:

Stanley I. Greenberg was counsel for the defendant in a criminal trial in the district court. The district judge summarily convicted Greenberg of criminal contempt and fined him $500 pursuant to 18 U.S.C. § 401. Two issues are presented on appeal: first, whether the district judge certified that he "saw or heard" the alleged contemptuous conduct as required by Fed.R.Crim.P. 42(a); second, whether Greenberg's courtroom conduct constituted sufficient grounds for a summary criminal contempt conviction.

The district court convicted Stanley I. Greenberg of criminal contempt for his courtroom behavior in defending former FBI agent Richard W. Miller, who was convicted on charges of espionage. The verbal exchange for which the district judge held Greenberg in contempt occurred during the government's rebuttal to the defendant's closing argument. The exchange appears in the transcript of June 13, 1986 as follows:

Mr. Bonner: ... And up got Mr. Greenberg and he objected, "No, we're not going into that."

Mr. Greenberg: I object to that. I didn't say that. I said that's not proper opening statement.

The Court: Sit down, Mr. Greenberg. Please, sit down. That's improper Mr. Greenberg.

Mr. Greenberg: I respectfully disagree.

The Court: You're not being respectful and you're going to be very, very much in trouble.

Mr. Greenberg: May I have a ruling on my objection? That misstated the opening statement.

The Court: You sit down Mr. Greenberg, period.

Mr. Bonner: Ladies and Gentlemen—Your honor, may I continue?

Mr. Greenberg: May we have a ruling, your honor?

The Court: I told you to sit down. I'm now going to tell you to be quiet, period.

Mr. Greenberg: I'm sitting, your honor.

The Court: Now, you proceed.

After a recess, the district judge stated the following for the record:

There was an outburst in the courtroom. And again, unfortunately one of the lawyers, Mr. Greenberg, lost his composure. The court finds that Mr. Greenberg was in contempt, after having had time to consider it through this short while.

The Court had warned Mr. Greenberg, and all the lawyers, that the court was not going to tolerate one more outburst of the temper. It was a slamming of something and Mr. Greenberg shouted out at the court in anger and it was very disruptive. And no matter whether Mr. Bonner's argument was correct or not, the court had on more than one occasion warned all lawyers, and specifically Mr. Greenberg.

The court hereby finds Mr. Greenberg for interrupting the court and disrupting the proceedings in an unethical manner, finds him in contempt and a fine of $500 is imposed at this time payable within the next 48 hours.

On July 8, 1986, the district judge filed an order of contempt memorializing the summary proceeding in which Greenberg was convicted of contempt. The order stated that on June 13, 1986, during the government's rebuttal argument before the jury, Greenberg

suddenly interrupted the proceedings by stating, at the top of his voice, an objection to something government counsel had said. The court ordered Mr. Greenberg to be seated and also stated that Mr. Greenberg was acting improperly. Mr. Greenberg then slammed his hand on the counsel table in an angry manner, demanding a ruling from the court. The court then told Mr. Greenberg that he was not being respectful and that he was going to find himself in trouble with the court. Mr. Greenberg then again asked for a ruling from the court, and the court again told Mr. Greenberg to sit down "period." When government counsel attempted to continue its argument, Mr. Greenberg again asked for a ruling, and the court told Mr. Greenberg to be quiet "period." Government counsel then resumed his argument.

We review summary contempt convictions for abuse of discretion. [Citation.]

The district court convicted Greenberg in a summary contempt proceeding under Fed.R.Crim.P. 42(a). Rule 42(a) states in full:

A criminal contempt may be punished summarily if the *judge certifies that the judge saw or heard the conduct constituting the contempt* and that it was committed in the actual presence of the court. The order of contempt shall recite the facts and shall be signed by the judge and entered of record.

(Emphasis added.)

Greenberg argues that the district judge erred by not certifying that the judge "saw or heard" the conduct held to be contemptuous. The July 8 order of contempt, which constitutes the certificate required by Rule 42(a), describes Greenberg as stating an objection "at the top of his voice," slamming "his hand on the counsel table in an angry manner," twice asking for a ruling on his objection, and not sitting down until asked to do so twice. The order, however, does not certify that the district judge "saw or heard" the conduct constituting the contempt. Thus, under Rule 42(a), the order cannot serve as a basis for a summary criminal contempt conviction.

The government contends that if the July 8 order itself does not fulfill the certification requirement of Rule 42(a), then the trial transcript could serve as a certification of the district court's actual knowledge. The trial transcript in this case, however, does not fulfill the function of the certificate. Although the transcript casts some light on the proceedings, to be valid a summary contempt conviction under Rule 42(a) must be supported by a certificate that satisfies the requirements of the rule by clearly identifying the specific facts constituting the contempt and by stating that the judge "saw or heard" the contemptuous conduct. [Citation.] The transcript fails to meet these requirements.

Additionally, the government urges in its brief that even without the explicit certification of first hand knowledge required in Rule 42(a), this court may affirm the conviction because "there can be [no] serious question that the district court *saw* appellant's behavior. The outburst occurred in a courtroom in which the district court was then present and presiding over an ongoing jury trial." Appellee's brief at 24 (emphasis in original).

This argument is unpersuasive for two reasons. First, it appears that the district court judge did not see or hear at least part of the behavior giving rise to the summary contempt conviction. The judge's recounting of the incident immediately following the recess was that "[i]t was a slamming of something and Mr. Greenberg shouted out at the court in anger and it was very disruptive." Arguably from that statement it does not appear that the court knew precisely what was slammed or who slammed it.

More importantly, the government's contention ignores the importance of procedural safeguards mandated in summary criminal contempt proceedings. The summary criminal contempt procedure in Rule 42(a) dispenses with the hearing and notice requirements mandated by the general contempt scheme set forth in Fed.R.Crim.P. 42(b).[1] Rule 42(a) combines the "otherwise inconsistent functions of prosecutor, jury and judge ... in one individual." [Citation.] This procedure "represents a significant departure from the accepted standards of due process," and is to be used only "where instant action is necessary to protect the judicial institution itself." Harris v. United States, 382 U.S. 162, 167, 86 S.Ct. 352, 355–56, 15 L.Ed.2d 240 (1965).

The certification requirement in Rule 42(a) is essential to safeguard the proper use of summary criminal contempt procedure. The requirement is not simply a legal formality. Rather, the certificate provides the basis for informed appellate review. We see no reason to depart from existing Ninth Circuit law requiring "that the procedural safeguards that [Rule 42(a)]provides must be strictly adhered to lest the drastic power authorized escape the permissible limits of reason and fairness." [Citation.]

Greenberg also argues that the acts referred to in the July 8 contempt order do not constitute an "open, serious tnreat to orderly procedure" justifying "instant and summary punishment." [Citation.] As noted above, the July 8 order describes the improper conduct as Greenberg stating an objection "at the top of his voice," slamming "his hand on the counsel table in an angry manner," twice asking for a ruling on his objection, and refusing to sit down until asked to do so twice. Although we recognize the importance of maintaining courtroom decorum, we find that the acts attributed to Greenberg do not standing alone constitute sufficient basis for a summary criminal contempt conviction.

"Rule 42(a) was reserved for 'exceptional circumstances,' such as acts threatening the judge or disrupting a hearing or obstructing court proceedings." [Citation.] Using summary criminal contempt proceedings to punish attorneys for overzealous advocacy is contrary to the important principle of maintaining an independent and assertive bar. * * * Thus summary criminal contempt procedure should be used only in exceptional circumstances where there is an immediate threat to the judicial process. Otherwise the procedure may deter vigorous represen-

---

1. Rule 42(b) states:

(b) Disposition upon Notice and Hearing. A criminal contempt except as provided in subdivision (a) of this rule shall be prosecuted on notice. The notice shall state the time and place of hearing, allowing a reasonable time for the preparation of the defense, and shall state the essential facts constituting the criminal contempt charged and describe it as such. The notice shall be given orally by the judge in open court in the presence of the defendant or, on application of the United States attorney or of an attorney appointed by the court for that purpose, by an order to show cause or an order of arrest. The defendant is entitled to a trial by jury in any case in which an act of Congress so provides. The defendant is entitled to admission to bail as provided in these rules. If the contempt charged involves disrespect to or criticism of a judge, that judge is disqualified from presiding at the trial or hearing except with the defendant's consent. Upon a verdict or finding of guilt the court shall enter an order fixing the punishment.

tation by conscientious attorneys. Accordingly, a district court should not summarily convict an attorney of criminal contempt unless that attorney "create[s] an obstruction which blocks the judge in the performance of his judicial duty." [Citation.]

In this case, the acts of counsel did not cause an obstruction of the judicial process serious enough to justify a summary criminal contempt conviction. We agree with the Seventh Circuit that "where the line between vigorous advocacy and actual obstruction defie[s] strict delineation, doubts should be resolved in favor of vigorous advocacy." [Citation.] That Greenberg twice asked for a ruling on his objection is not a threat to orderly judicial procedure. Greenberg's client had a right to a ruling on the objection. [Citation.] Although the court arguably overruled the objection by asking Greenberg to sit down, Greenberg was entitled to a formal ruling for the record. Moreover, Greenberg's other acts were insufficient to support a summary criminal contempt conviction. That Greenberg continued to stand is not inconsistent with the custom of attorneys in the federal courts to stand when making an objection or addressing the court. Similarly, Greenberg's loud voice and hand slamming during the heat of a long and hard fought trial, although annoying and not condoned by this court, do not constitute the type of "exceptional circumstances" that pose an immediate threat to the judicial process, thereby justifying a summary criminal contempt conviction. [Citation.]

Accordingly, the judgment of the district court holding Greenberg in criminal contempt is reversed.

———

1. The concept of the court's "presence" has been variously interpreted. In *In re Adams*, 421 F.Supp. 1027 (E.D.Mich.1976), an employer was held in contempt by the trial court for threatening to fire a juror. Relying on the provision in 18 U.S.C. § 401(1) for contempt to punish misbehavior in the presence of the court, the court found such threats to be in the "presence" of the court even though not occurring in the vicinity of the courtroom.

The United States Supreme Court had previously held that geographical proximity to the court is necessary under § 401(1) in Nye v. United States, 313 U.S. 33, 61 S.Ct. 810, 85 L.Ed. 1172 (1941). The district court in *Adams* nonetheless found the proximity rule satisfied on the theory that a juror carries a part of the court with him wherever he goes. A threat to a juror anywhere is thus "in the presence of the court." The case was not appealed.

Compare *Adams* with the preceding two summary contempt cases and with *In re Stewart, supra,* which involved firing a juror. Should the judge in *Stewart* have used summary criminal contempt powers instead of either regular criminal contempt or civil contempt? If he had, what arguments would you make on appeal if you represented Stewart?

2. Another curious construction of "the presence of the court" is found in *People v. Higgins,* 173 Misc. 96, 16 N.Y.S.2d 302 (1939). In that case a male deputy sheriff and a woman juror had a private sexual encounter that interfered with jury deliberations. This act was found to be a criminal contempt in the "immediate view and presence" of the court.

3. Are these various interpretations of "presence" justifiable? What power is necessary to assure the integrity of the court and the jury system? Is contempt the appropriate tool for judges to use to avoid courtroom disruptions? To avoid an obstruction of justice by interference with jurors?

PROBLEM: THE ENJOINED CONSTRUCTION PROJECT

An active environmentalist group known as SAVE has been protesting construction projects that commit new land to concrete. When a project threatens to convert an area with existing vegetation to concrete, SAVE attempts to stop the construction. SAVE uses a variety of tactics, some of which the group intends as "headline grabbers," such as sit-ins in front of bulldozers. Other methods are legal maneuvers to get projects enjoined, at least temporarily, while the group tries to attract public attention to the cause. Most of the projects targeted by SAVE are state construction. A few state projects even have been cancelled after the SAVE campaign called the public attention to particularly bad situations. The perception of state legislators, however, is that the overall effect of SAVE's tactics has been simply to delay and increase the cost of many projects.

The state legislature therefore passed a statute designed to prevent SAVE from delaying costly projects. The statute provided that no court in the state has "jurisdiction" to issue an injunction against a state "construction project."

After passage of this statute, SAVE targeted another construction project and sued to enjoin it. The defendant moved to dismiss under the statute. SAVE argued to the court that the statute does not apply in this case because this project is not financed entirely with public funds and therefore is not a "state" construction project. The judge has enjoined the project pending determination of the statute's applicability. Consider:

(1) If the trial judge finds the statute does apply to this project, the injunction will be dissolved. What if the defendant contractors disobeyed the injunction before its dissolution? Is that disobedience contempt?

(2) What if the trial judge finds the statute does not apply and continues the injunction against the project? Must the defendant obey pending appeal? Can the defendant contractor "take its chances" and continue building pending appeal with the hope of winning ultimately?

(3) The statute deprived the court of "jurisdiction" to enjoin state construction projects. Who has jurisdiction to decide the jurisdictional issue whether the construction is a state project?

UNITED STATES v. UNITED MINE WORKERS OF AMERICA

330 U.S. 258, 67 S.Ct. 677, 91 L.Ed. 884 (1947).

MR. CHIEF JUSTICE VINSON delivered the opinion of the Court.

[The President ordered the seizure of the bituminous coal mines pursuant to his constitutional and statutory powers during a national emergency. A dispute arose between the Government and the union over interpretation of the labor contract, and the union threatened to strike. The Government obtained from the federal district court a temporary restraining order against the United Mine Workers and its president, John L. Lewis, to prevent the strike. A walk-out nonetheless occurred and mines producing the major part of the country's bituminous coal were idle. The United States petitioned the court to punish the defendants for contempt because of their willful disobedience of the restraining order. The defendants were found guilty of both civil and criminal contempt, and they appealed.

The defendants challenged the district court's jurisdiction to issue the restraining order under Section 4 of the Norris–LaGuardia Act which provides: "No court of the United States shall have jurisdiction to issue any restraining order or temporary or permanent injunction in any case involving or growing out of any labor dispute to prohibit any person or persons participating in such dispute from doing [any of several enumerated acts] * * *."

The first part of the Supreme Court's opinion held that the United States was not an "employer" within the meaning of the Act in this situation, so the district court did have the power to issue the order. The remainder of the opinion, from which excerpts follow, concerned alternative grounds for upholding the criminal contempt, but not the civil contempt, even if the Court had found the Norris–LaGuardia Act to apply.]

* * *

Although we have held that the Norris–LaGuardia Act did not render injunctive relief beyond the jurisdiction of the District Court, there are alternative grounds which support the power of the District Court to punish violations of its orders as criminal contempt.

* * *

In the case before us, the District Court had the power to preserve existing conditions while it was determining its own authority to grant injunctive relief. The defendants, in making their private determination of the law, acted at their peril. Their disobedience is punishable as criminal contempt.

Although a different result would follow were the question of jurisdiction frivolous and not substantial, such contention would be idle here. * * *

* * * [A]n order issued by a court with jurisdiction over the subject matter and person must be obeyed by the parties until it is reversed by orderly and proper proceedings. This is true without regard even for the constitutionality of the Act under which the order is issued. * * * Violations of an order are punishable as criminal contempt even though the order is set aside on appeal, or though the basic action has become moot. [Citations.]

We insist upon the same duty of obedience where, as here, the subject matter of the suit, as well as the parties, was properly before the court; where the elements of federal jurisdiction were clearly shown; and where the authority of the court of first instance to issue an order ancillary to the main suit depended upon a statute, the scope and applicability of which were subject to substantial doubt. The District Court on November 29 affirmatively decided that the Norris–LaGuardia Act was of no force in this case and that injunctive relief was therefore authorized. Orders outstanding or issued after that date were to be obeyed until they expired or were set aside by appropriate proceedings, appellate or otherwise. Convictions for criminal contempt intervening before that time may stand.

It does not follow, of course, that simply because a defendant may be punished for criminal contempt for disobedience of an order later set aside on appeal, that the plaintiff in the action may profit by way of a fine imposed in a simultaneous proceeding for civil contempt based upon a violation of the same order. The right to remedial relief falls with an injunction which events prove was erroneously issued, and *a fortiori* when the injunction or restraining order was beyond the jurisdiction of the court. * * * If the Norris–LaGuardia Act were applicable in this case, the conviction for civil contempt would be reversed in its entirety.

Assuming, then, that the Norris–LaGuardia Act applied to this case and prohibited injunctive relief at the request of the United States, we would set aside the preliminary injunction of December 4 and the judgment for civil contempt; but we would, subject to any infirmities in the contempt proceedings or in the fines imposed, affirm the judgments for criminal contempt as validly punishing violations of an order then outstanding and unreversed. * * *

———

As *United Mine Workers* reveals, the importance of the distinction between civil and criminal contempt is not just the difference in constitutional protections. The dependence of the contempt penalties on the validity of the underlying order also depends upon whether the contempt is civil or criminal. Recall the problem of void orders and the duty to obey erroneous orders, especially *Walker v. City of Birmingham, supra.*

B. CIVIL CONTEMPT AND COERCIVE CIVIL CONTEMPT

Section Coverage:

The primary function of civil contempt is not to vindicate the authority of the court, although such vindication is a derivative benefit. The purpose of civil contempt is to benefit the plaintiff who received the original equitable order. When the defendant disobeyed that order, the plaintiff no longer had the protection from harm that the original remedy was designed to provide. Civil contempt is available to compensate for the resulting losses if any occur, and sometimes to coerce the defendant into compliance to prevent any further losses.

There are two kinds of civil contempt: compensatory and coercive. The compensatory form of civil contempt is damages. The damages must be specifically caused by the defendant's disobedience of the court order. The losses must be actual ones and the plaintiff must prove them with reasonable certainty. In most jurisdictions such losses may include the attorneys' fees incurred by the plaintiff to enforce the order.

The second kind of civil contempt is coercive civil contempt. This form is a close cousin of criminal contempt because under coercive civil contempt judges impose fines paid to the state or order imprisonment. The distinction between criminal and coercive civil contempts lies in their different purposes. Whereas criminal contempt punishes defendants for past disobedience, coercive civil contempt seeks to compel present and future compliance with the court's order. Plaintiffs can seek coercive civil contempt sanctions to protect from future losses.

Model Case:

A court determines in a divorce proceeding that certain out-of-state property held in the husband's name should be deeded to the wife. The husband refuses to obey the order directing him to make the conveyance.

The court may jail the husband until he complies. The imprisonment is not punishment for past disobedience; it is to compel an act in the present for the benefit of the wife. The husband has the "jail keys in his pocket" because he will be out of jail as soon as he makes the conveyance. This imprisonment is coercive civil contempt.

The wife can recover in a civil contempt claim any losses occasioned by the disobedience. In most jurisdictions such damages would include reasonable attorneys' fees to enforce the order, but not fees incurred in the underlying divorce action.

TIME–SHARE SYSTEMS, INC. v. SCHMIDT

397 N.W.2d 438 (Minn.App.1986).

NIERENGARTEN, JUDGE.

Time–Share Systems, Inc. (Time–Share) and Gary Schmidt were engaged in litigation over the ownership and rights to computer software. During the course of litigation the trial court ordered Schmidt to allow Time–Share access to Schmidt's computer in order to do a file save.[1] Schmidt also was ordered not to delete any data prior to the file save. A file save was done but the trial court found that Schmidt deleted, or allowed to be deleted certain files. The trial court found that Schmidt, his companies, and the officers of his companies had violated the court order and were in contempt. The court levied fines, costs, and attorney's fees. Schmidt appeals. We affirm in part, reverse in part and remand for proof of damages.

In late 1983 Gary Schmidt began using the services of Time–Share Systems, Inc. to manage the inventory and accounting aspects of his business, known at that time as The Wooden Bird. Services provided by Time–Share included the creation of software programs as well as the purchase or lease of computer equipment. Over the year Time–Share and Schmidt had extensive dealings with each other as the computer system was expanded.

In 1984 the relationship between the two companies began to break down. Schmidt did not feel he was getting the service he expected and paid for. Time–Share made an effort to remedy the situation but was unable to do so to Schmidt's satisfaction. Schmidt terminated the agreement, Time–Share sued for damages and Schmidt counterclaimed. The parties agreed that Schmidt owned the computer equipment and the dispute revolved around the ownership of certain software designated as "Ease" software.

In December of 1985 Time–Share's motion to replevin the "Ease" software was granted and Schmidt was ordered to turn "Ease" over to Time–Share. This order specifically provided that Schmidt must appear in court to show why he was not in contempt if he failed to deliver the property. The property was not delivered and the parties appeared in court on January 24, 1986. Schmidt's attorney indicated that there was a problem in identifying which software belonged to Time–Share and which software belonged to Schmidt. At that time, the court ordered, *inter alia,* that:

> 1. Time–Share was to have access to Schmidt's computers for the purpose of obtaining a file save of all the information on the computer.

---

1. A file save is a procedure which copies software and data contained in a computer onto a disk or tape.

2. Schmidt "shall not delete any data or programs from the computer" prior to the file save.

3. If any information has been deleted, Schmidt was to provide Time–Share with its most recent file save.

Once this was accomplished there would be another hearing to determine what should be deleted from Schmidt's computers.

Between noon and 1:00 p.m. on January 24, 1986, Time–Share's representative arrived at Schmidt's place of business to carry out the court order. He was not given access to the computer until approximately 5:00 p.m., at which time the file save was done.

An examination of the file save and other evidence indicated that data was deleted from the computer on the same day the court order was issued. Schmidt contended that the deletion was by a computer programmer [Steven Fenn], formerly employed by Time–Share, without Schmidt's knowledge. The programmer is presently employed by Schmidt's company, as an independent contractor, to develop software to replace the unsatisfactory software they bought from Time–Share. The programmer and Time–Share also are engaged in litigation concerning the programmer's program development. Schmidt's employees had notified the programmer by phone of the court ordered file save. The programmer proceeded to delete certain programs which he claimed were his and not Time–Share's.

On April 9, 1986 the court found Schmidt in contempt of court and ordered him to pay Time–Share $3,000 in costs and attorney's fees and $2,500 in damages for violating the court order.

* * *

Civil contempt is defined as the failure to obey a court order which benefits an opposing party in a civil proceeding. The sanction imposed for such failure is ordered primarily to encourage future compliance with the order and to vindicate the rights of the opposing party. [Citation.] The rationale for such power is to provide the trial court with the means to enforce its orders. The trial court has inherently broad discretion to hold an individual in contempt when "the contemnor has acted 'contumaciously, in bad faith, and out of disrespect for the judicial process.' "
* * *

When reviewing a contempt order, the appellate court may reverse or modify only if it finds the trial court abused its discretion. [Citation.] There is evidence to support the trial court's findings. The record shows that appellant notified Fenn of the imminent court order and that Fenn began his deletion process shortly thereafter. The record also shows that Schmidt prevented Time–Share from gaining access to the computer while the deletions were occurring. Additional testimony indicated that Schmidt's employees undertook certain activities with respect to the computer which allowed the deletions to occur.

The trial court awarded $3,000 to cover the costs and attorney's fees incurred in the prosecution of the contempt. The record supports the reasonableness of this award and we affirm this award. The trial court also awarded $2,500 to indemnify Time–Share for the contemnors' wrongful activities. However, "indemnity must be based on proof of damages actually suffered or it cannot be sustained." [Citation.] There is no evidence to show the amount of damages Time–Share suffered as a result of Schmidt's activities. This award cannot be sustained without proof.

* * *

Affirmed in part, reversed in part and remanded for proof of damages.

———

1. Contempt is a broad remedy with varying functions. Acts that interfere directly with the judicial process or affront the dignity of the court are punishable as summary criminal contempt. Failure to comply with a court order, such as an injunctive order to convey a certain parcel of land, is punishable as criminal contempt for disobedience. The same act can also be subject to civil contempt, a private remedy to the wronged plaintiff who is entitled to have the land conveyed to him. The civil contempt can be either in the form of money damages for the delay or a coercive fine or imprisonment until the disobedient defendant complies.

2. The plaintiff must prove the amount of loss with reasonable certainty. In *Allied Materials Corp. v. Superior Products Co.,* for example, the Court of Appeals upheld the district court's refusal to allow $12,000 in compensatory damages because of insufficient proof. The defendant had violated the terms of a consent decree, but the plaintiff presented no proof of the cost of that noncompliance to its company except for the testimony of one manager who said the damages were "probably" $10,000 to $12,000. The court made an award of $7000 in attorneys' fees because it was the only definite sum. 620 F.2d 224 (10th Cir.1980). If the loss to a business is the time of salaried employees, how could such loss be substantiated? What kind of proof should the company in this case have submitted?

3. Civil contempts are appealable when they are final orders. The contempt in the principal case was appealable because the trial court had ordered an unconditional award. A conditional order is not appealable because the contempt can be purged by the defendant's voluntary conduct. *See* Tell v. Tell, 383 N.W.2d 678 (Minn.1986).

UNITED STATES v. DARWIN CONSTRUCTION CO.

680 F.Supp. 739 (D.Md.1988).

YOUNG, DISTRICT JUDGE.

On the date its payment was due on the civil contempt fine levied by this Court, respondent Darwin Construction Company filed a motion to set aside or reduce the fine. * * * This memorandum will resolve respondent's doubts that the Court carefully considered appropriate factors in determining that respondent was in contempt of the Court's order to comply with the IRS summons for six days. * * *

On June 23, 1986, the Court ordered respondent to comply with the IRS summons or face penalties of $5000 per day for noncompliance. The order was not designed to compensate the petitioner for its expenses in bringing the suit, nor has the petitioner ever pled or proven such expenses. Rather the purpose of this second-stage contempt order was coercive, but not punitive: it was chosen to encourage respondent to produce documents which they continued to withhold even after this Court's initial order was affirmed on interlocutory appeal. * * * The Court based its determination of contempt upon the respondent's preferred theory of substantial compliance, but also made a finding upon respondent's good faith defense.

The essence of respondent's argument is that "it is clear that Darwin did everything it possibly could after the order was entered" and that the "order served its purpose, and Darwin should not now be subject to an inordinately severe fine that in effect punishes Darwin for what the Court feels Darwin failed to do prior to the entry of the contempt order." The Court rejects both assertions.

* * * Specifically, Darwin claims that the items produced six days late were "lost" and that "considering only the period from the contempt order forward, immediate production of the lost items was impossible." * * *

Darwin was required to comply substantially with the Court's order. Substantial compliance is found where "all reasonable steps" have been taken to ensure compliance: inadvertent omissions are excused only if such steps were taken. [Citation.] Darwin argues only that there were "difficulties in arranging compliance. . . . Darwin could not reasonably be expected to find financial records that were labelled with the wrong year or that were located in a closed box of engineering materials buried behind dozens of other boxes in Darwin's cramped quarters." But Darwin does not assert that the documents missing from the first production on June 24, 1986, were beyond its possession or control. * * * It is clear that Darwin did not take "all reasonable steps" to ensure complete production until *after* it was notified by Agent Kohorst [on June 27] that some documents were still unproduced and additional efforts to find the missing documents were made. Darwin's efforts to achieve complete production between June 27 and June 30 do not transform its initial failure to make substantial compliance at the time of the first production. Thus, compliance was insubstantial until the second production occurred on June 30, 1986. This finding is based solely upon Darwin's inattentiveness after the June 23 order was issued.

Darwin's good faith defense is also rejected on the basis of its indifference regarding the completeness of the initial production, but particularly in light of the opportunity it had to prepare for production before the Court's order on June 23, 1986. * * * The evidence produced at the assessment hearing leaves no doubt that Darwin either knew that documents were missing or took no special steps to find out before the June 23 hearing. Darwin's initial production, grounded in indifference and ignorance as to the completeness, did not show good faith where Darwin had over one year to ensure that all the documents listed in the summons were located and more than eight weeks' notice that this Court's contempt order would be enforced. * * *

The $5000 per day penalty was pre-specified at a rate determined by the Court to be reasonable based upon the non-complying party's previous reluctance to obey the Court's directives, the corporate character of the non-complying party, and the injury to justice which further contempt would invite. * * * The Court found that substantial compliance occurred only after six days of insubstantial compliance.

The subject of a conditional contempt order cannot expect the Court to threaten to fine the party for non-compliance with a court order at a certain rate and then later find that party to be non-complying but yet deserving of a lesser penalty. The coercive power of a threatened penalty is nullified if the Court is unable to enforce the penalty later at the pre-specified rate. That the factual circumstances under which the Court will find compliance or non-compliance are unclear *ex ante* does not necessitate *ex post* adjustment of the penalty at the assessment stage of the proceedings. The object of the order is to encourage full compliance by setting a known cost for non-compliance. If the Court were required to adjust the cost downward according to the degree of compliance, then the $5000 per day penalty would be indeterminant and therefore less effective in encouraging compliance.

* * *

The Court today rules that a pre-specified daily contempt fine for non-compliance need not be adjusted at the assessment stage. The only mitigating factors are the defenses raised by respondent: substantial compliance and, perhaps, good faith. These defenses were rejected in the Court's February 4, 1988 memorandum and order and are rejected again today. The Court will not consider reduction of the fine, nor, does it find that a $5000 per day fine was then, or is now, unreasonable in light of the appropriate considerations. * * *

———

1. Compare coercive civil contempt fines with criminal contempt fines. Whereas a criminal contempt fine for past disobedience is a fixed sum determined after the acts are complete, a coercive civil contempt fine is pre-determined by the court as a daily penalty for future non-compliance. The coercive civil contempt fine is not specified, however, until after the defendant has manifested a reluctance to obey the court's initial order. Would it be a good idea for every equitable order to indicate a date for compliance and a coercive contempt fine for each day thereafter? Why should a court wait until a defendant shows recalcitrance?

2. The United States Supreme Court has held that determination of the amount of the daily civil contempt fine should be guided by certain factors: "the character and magnitude of the harm threatened by continued contumacy, and the probable effectiveness of any suggested sanctions in bringing about the result desired." United States v. United Mine Workers, 330 U.S. 258, 304, 67 S.Ct. 677, 701, 91 L.Ed. 884 (1947). *See also* Dole Fresh Fruit Co. v. United Banana Co., 821 F.2d 106 (2d Cir.1987); General Signal Corp. v. Donallco, 787 F.2d 1376 (9th Cir. 1986).

3. The court in the principal case refused to adjust the amount of the pre-set fine after the disobedience. A Court of Appeals decision from the District of Columbia indicated that in cases with "complicating factors" such an adjustment is appropriate. Such factors in a back-to-work labor dispute include the complexity of the outstanding order, possible ambiguities, and difficulties in arranging compliance. Brotherhood of Locomotive Firemen and Enginemen v. Bangor & Aroostock Railroad Co., 380 F.2d 570 (D.C.Cir.), *cert. denied*, 389 U.S. 327, 88 S.Ct. 437, 19 L.Ed.2d 560 (1967).

PROBLEM: THE PERSISTENT PROTESTER

Jim Lofton is a college student who is an activist on environmental issues. You represent him in a case where the Newprod Company has obtained an injunction against Lofton to prohibit him from trespassing and interfering with Newprod employees in the company parking lot. Lofton had been going there every night to hand to the employees leaflets about the company's pollution. On occasion Lofton has been sufficiently pushy and argumentative with some individuals that they complained to the company. One night Lofton blocked the president's car and would not get out of the way until the president had read through the leaflet. The company then sought and obtained against Lofton an injunction prohibiting further trespass on the company's property.

Lofton ignored the injunction and returned to distribute new flyers in the company's parking lot. After a hearing, the judge found him in contempt and fined him $100. The episode was repeated a second time, and contempt was again found. This time the fine was $200. The judge told Lofton that if he again defied the court order, the fine would be $500 the next time *and* Lofton would go to jail for thirty days.

Lofton, undaunted, again violated the order. The judge imposed the fine and jail term as previously indicated. When the sentence was announced, Lofton looked straight in the judge's eye and muttered an obscene reference to the judge's ancestry. For this offense the judge summarily sentenced Lofton to six months in jail for contempt of the court.

Throughout these events you have advised Lofton to obey the court's orders, but your advice has not been heeded. The question now is whether you can appeal successfully any of these contempts. Lofton has protested all along that he wanted a jury to hear his case because he believes a jury would be sympathetic. There have been many complaints in the community about Newprod's unresponsiveness to the problem of the factory odor. Lofton also believes that his First Amendment right to free speech has been violated because the parking lot is used in part by the public as well as the company employees. Assuming that the First Amendment argument is a substantial claim, and that a jury trial would be desirable, what can you do for Lofton?

UNITED MINE WORKERS v. BAGWELL

___ U.S. ___, 114 S.Ct. 2552, 129 L.Ed.2d 642 (1994).

JUSTICE BLACKMUN delivered the opinion of the Court.

We are called upon once again to consider the distinction between civil and criminal contempt. Specifically, we address whether contempt fines levied against a union for violations of a labor injunction are coercive civil fines, or are criminal fines that constitutionally could be imposed only through a jury trial. We conclude that the fines are criminal and, accordingly, we reverse the judgment of the Supreme Court of Virginia.

I

Petitioners, the International Union, United Mine Workers of America and United Mine Workers of America, District 28 (collectively, the union) engaged in a protracted labor dispute with the Clinchfield Coal Company and Sea "B" Mining Company (collectively, the companies) over alleged unfair labor practices. In April 1989, the companies filed suit in the Circuit Court of Russell County, Virginia, to enjoin the union from conducting unlawful strike-related activities. The trial court entered an injunction which, as later amended, prohibited the union and its members from, among other things, obstructing ingress and egress to company facilities, throwing objects at and physically threatening company employees, placing tire-damaging "jackrocks" on roads used by company vehicles, and picketing with more than a specified number of people at designated sites. The court additionally ordered the union to take all steps necessary to ensure compliance with the injunction, to place supervisors at picket sites, and to report all violations to the court.

On May 16, 1989, the trial court held a contempt hearing and found that petitioners had committed 72 violations of the injunction. After fining the union $642,000 for its disobedience, the court announced that it would fine the union $100,000 for any future violent breach of the injunction and $20,000 for any future nonviolent infraction, "such as exceeding picket numbers, [or] blocking entrances or exits." The Court early stated that its purpose was to "impos[e] prospective civil fines[,] the payment of which would only be required if it were shown the defendants disobeyed the Court's orders."

In seven subsequent contempt hearings held between June and December 1989, the court found the union in contempt for more than 400 separate violations of the injunction, many of them violent. Based on the court's stated "intention that these fines are civil and coercive," each contempt hearing was conducted as a civil proceeding before the trial judge, in which the parties conducted discovery, introduced evidence, and called and cross-examined witnesses. The trial court required that contumacious acts be proved beyond a reasonable doubt, but did not afford the union a right to jury trial.

As a result of these contempt proceedings, the court levied over $64,000,000 in fines against the union, approximately $12,000,000 of which was ordered payable to the companies. Because the union objected to payment of any fines to the companies and in light of the law enforcement burdens posed by the strike, the court ordered that the remaining roughly $52,000,000 in fines be paid to the Commonwealth of Virginia and Russell and Dickenson Counties, "the two counties most heavily affected by the unlawful activity."

While appeals from the contempt orders were pending, the union and the companies settled the underlying labor dispute, agreed to vacate the contempt fines, and jointly moved to dismiss the case. * * * The trial court granted the motion to dismiss, dissolved the injunction, and vacated the $12,000,000 in fines payable to the companies. After reiterating its belief that the remaining $52,000,000 owed to the counties and the Commonwealth were coercive, civil fines, the trial court refused to vacate these fines, concluding they were "payable in effect to the public."

* * * [T]he court appointed respondent John L. Bagwell to act as Special Commissioner to collect the unpaid contempt fines on behalf of the counties and the Commonwealth.

The Court of Appeals of Virginia reversed and ordered that the contempt fines be vacated pursuant to the settlement agreement. Assuming for the purposes of argument that the fines were civil, the court concluded "that civil contempt fines imposed during or as a part of a civil proceeding between private parties are settled when the underlying litigation is settled by the parties and the court is without discretion to refuse to vacate such fines."

On consolidated appeals, the Supreme Court of Virginia reversed. The court held that whether coercive, civil contempt sanctions could be settled by private parties was a question of state law, and that Virginia public policy disfavored such a rule, "if the dignity of the law and public respect for the judiciary are to be maintained." The court also rejected petitioners' contention that the outstanding fines were criminal and could not be imposed absent a criminal trial. * * * This Court granted certiorari.

II

A

"Criminal contempt is a crime in the ordinary sense," Bloom v. Illinois, 391 U.S. 194, 201, 88 S.Ct. 1477, 1481, 20 L.Ed.2d 522 (1968), and "criminal penalties may not be imposed on someone who has not been afforded the protections that the Constitution requires of such criminal proceedings." [Citations.] In contrast, civil contempt sanctions, or those penalties designed to compel future compliance with a court order, are considered to be coercive and avoidable through obedience, and thus may be imposed in an ordinary civil proceeding upon notice and opportunity to be heard. Neither a jury trial nor proof beyond a reasonable doubt is required.

Although the procedural contours of the two forms of contempt are well established, the distinguishing characteristics of civil versus criminal contempts are somewhat less clear. In the leading early case addressing this issue in the context of imprisonment, Gompers v. Bucks Stove & Range Co., 221 U.S., at 441, 31 S.Ct., at 498, the Court emphasized that whether a contempt is civil or criminal turns on the "character and purpose" of the sanction involved. Thus, a contempt sanction is considered civil if it "is remedial, and for the benefit of the complainant. But if it is for criminal contempt the sentence is punitive, to vindicate the authority of the court." * * *

The paradigmatic coercive, civil contempt sanction, as set forth in Gompers, involves confining a contemnor indefinitely until he complies with an affirmative command such as an order "to pay alimony, or to surrender property ordered to be turned over to a receiver, or to make a conveyance." Gompers, 221 U.S., at 442, 31 S.Ct., at 498[.] * * *

By contrast, a fixed sentence of imprisonment is punitive and criminal if it is imposed retrospectively for a "completed act of disobedience," Gompers, 221 U.S., at 443, 31 S.Ct., at 498, such that the contemnor cannot avoid or abbreviate the confinement through later compliance. * * *

This dichotomy between coercive and punitive imprisonment has been extended to the fine context. A contempt fine accordingly is considered civil and remedial if it either "coerce[s] the defendant into compliance with the court's order, [or] . . . compensate[s] the complainant for losses sustained." United States v. United Mine Workers of America, 330 U.S. 258, 303–304, 67 S.Ct. 677, 701, 91 L.Ed. 884 (1947).

Where a fine is not compensatory, it is civil only if the contemnor is afforded an opportunity to purge. [Citation.] Thus, a "flat, unconditional fine" totalling even as little as $50 announced after a finding of contempt is criminal if the contemnor has no subsequent opportunity to reduce or avoid the fine through compliance.

A close analogy to coercive imprisonment is a per diem fine imposed for each day a contemnor fails to comply with an affirmative court order. Like civil imprisonment, such fines exert a constant coercive pressure, and once the jural command is obeyed, the future, indefinite, daily fines are purged. Less comfortable is the analogy between coercive imprisonment and suspended, determinate fines. In this Court's sole prior decision squarely addressing the judicial power to impose coercive civil contempt fines, *United Mine Workers*, *supra*, it held that fixed fines also may be considered purgable and civil when imposed and suspended pending future compliance. * * *

This Court has not revisited the issue of coercive civil contempt fines addressed in *United Mine Workers*. Since that decision, the Court has erected substantial procedural protections in other areas of contempt law, such as criminal contempts. [Citations.] Lower federal courts and state courts such as the trial court here nevertheless have relied on *United Mine Workers* to authorize a relatively unlimited judicial power to impose noncompensatory civil contempt fines.

B

Underlying the somewhat elusive distinction between civil and criminal contempt fines, and the ultimate question posed in this case, is what procedural protections are due before any particular contempt penalty may be imposed. Because civil contempt sanctions are viewed as nonpunitive and avoidable, fewer procedural protections for such sanctions have been required. To the extent that such contempts take on a punitive character, however, and are not justified by other considerations central to the contempt power, criminal procedural protections may be in order.

* * *

For a discrete category of indirect contempts, civil procedural protections may be insufficient. Contempts involving out-of-court disobedience to complex injunctions often require elaborate and reliable factfinding. [Citation.] Such contempts do not obstruct the court's ability to adjudicate the proceedings before it, and the risk of erroneous deprivation from the lack of a neutral factfinder may be substantial. Under these circumstances, criminal procedural protections such as the rights to counsel and proof beyond a reasonable doubt are both necessary and appropriate to protect the due process rights of parties and prevent the arbitrary exercise of judicial power.

C

In the instant case, neither any party nor any court of the Commonwealth has suggested that the challenged fines are compensatory. * * *

The issue before us is limited to whether these fines, despite their noncompensatory character, are coercive civil or criminal sanctions.

* * *

Despite respondent's urging, we are not persuaded that dispositive significance should be accorded to the fact that the trial court prospectively announced the sanctions it would impose. Had the trial court simply levied the fines after finding the union guilty of contempt, the resulting determinate and unconditional fines would be considered solely and exclusively punitive. [Citation.] Respondent nevertheless contends that the trial court's announcement of a prospective fine schedule allowed the union to avoid paying the fines simply by performing the act required by the court's order, [citations], and thus transformed these fines into coercive, civil ones. Respondent maintains here, as the Virginia Supreme Court held below, that the trial court could have imposed a daily civil fine to coerce the union into compliance, and that a prospective fine schedule is indistinguishable from such a sanction.

Respondent's argument highlights the difficulties encountered in parsing coercive civil and criminal contempt fines. * * * The trial court here simply announced the penalty—determinate fines of $20,000 or $100,000 per violation—that would be imposed for future contempts. The union's ability to avoid the contempt fines was indistinguishable from the ability of any ordinary citizen to avoid a criminal sanction by conforming his behavior to the law. The fines are not coercive day fines, or even suspended fines, but are more closely analogous to fixed, determinate, retrospective criminal fines which petitioners had no opportunity to purge once imposed. We therefore decline to conclude that the mere fact that the sanctions were announced in advance rendered them coercive and civil as a matter of constitutional law.

* * *

III

Our decision concededly imposes some procedural burdens on courts' ability to sanction widespread, indirect contempts of complex injunctions through noncompensatory fines. Our holding, however, leaves unaltered the longstanding authority of judges to adjudicate direct contempts summarily, and to enter broad compensatory awards for all contempts through civil proceedings. [Citation.] Because the right to trial by jury applies only to serious criminal sanctions, courts still may impose noncompensatory, petty fines for contempts such as the present ones without conducting a jury trial. We also do not disturb a court's ability to levy, albeit through the criminal contempt process, serious fines like those in this case.

Ultimately, whatever slight burden our holding may impose on the judicial contempt power cannot be controlling. * * * Where, as here, "a serious contempt is at issue, considerations of efficiency must give way to the more fundamental interest of ensuring the even-handed exercise of judicial power." [citing *Bloom*] at 209, 88 S.Ct., at 1486.

The judgment of the Supreme Court of Virginia is reversed.

JUSTICE SCALIA, concurring.

I join the Court's opinion classifying the $52,000,000 in contempt fines levied against petitioners as criminal. As the Court's opinion demonstrates, our cases have employed a variety of not easily reconcilable tests for differentiating between civil and criminal contempts. Since all of those tests would yield the same result here, there is no need to decide which is the correct one—and a case so extreme on its facts is not the best case in which to make that decision. I wish to suggest, however, that when we come to making it, a careful examination of historical practice will ultimately yield the answer.

That one and the same person should be able to make the rule, to adjudicate its violation, and to assess its penalty is out of accord with our usual notions of fairness and separation of powers. [Citations.] And it is worse still for that person to conduct the adjudication without affording the protections usually given in criminal trials. Only the clearest of historical practice could establish that such a departure from the procedures that the Constitution normally requires is not a denial of due process of law. * * *

The order at issue here provides a relatively tame example of the modern, complex decree. The amended injunction prohibited, inter alia, rock-throwing, the puncturing of tires, threatening, following or interfering with respondents' employees, placing pickets in other than specified locations, and roving picketing; and it required, inter alia, that petitioners provide a list of names of designated supervisors. Although it would seem quite in accord with historical practice to enforce, by conditional incarceration or per diem fines, compliance with the last provision—a discrete command, observance of which is readily ascertained—using that same means to enforce the remainder of the order would be a novelty.

* * * We will have to decide at some point which modern injunctions sufficiently resemble their historical namesakes to warrant the same extraordinary means of enforcement. We need not draw that line in the present case, and so I am content to join the opinion of the Court.

JUSTICE GINSBURG, with whom THE CHIEF JUSTICE joins, concurring in part and concurring in the judgment.

The issue in this case is whether the contempt proceedings brought against the petitioner unions are to be classified as "civil" or "criminal." As the Court explains, if those proceedings were "criminal," then the unions were entitled under our precedents to a jury trial, and the disputed fines, imposed in bench proceedings, could not stand.

* * *

Two considerations persuade me that the contempt proceedings in this case should be classified as "criminal" rather than "civil." First, were we to accept the logic of Bagwell's argument that the fines here were civil, because "conditional" and "coercive," no fine would elude that categorization. * * *

Second, the Virginia courts' refusal to vacate the fines, despite the parties' settlement and joint motion, is characteristic of criminal, not civil proceedings. In explaining why the fines outlived the underlying civil dispute, the Supreme Court of Virginia stated: "Courts of the Commonwealth must have the authority to enforce their orders by employing coercive, civil sanctions if the dignity of the law and public respect for the judiciary are to be maintained." * * *

Concluding that the fines at issue "are more closely analogous to . . . criminal fines" [citation], than to civil fines, I join the Court's judgment and all but Part II–B of its opinion.

––––––

1. What policy reason can justify treating any coercive order to compel obedience as civil rather than criminal? Is there a meaningful distinction between a routine injunction against trespass and a daily fine for continued trespass? If so, should criminal procedure safeguards attach only to the latter? Both? Neither? Does the principal case answer these questions?

2. The Court in the principal case found it unnecessary to define a "serious contempt" when the punishment is by fine rather than imprisonment. In a previous case the Court found that a $10,000 criminal fine imposed upon a union with 13,000 dues paying members was a petty punishment that did not warrant a jury trial. Muniz v. Hoffman, 422 U.S. 454, 95 S.Ct. 2178, 45 L.Ed.2d 319 (1975).

LATROBE STEEL CO. v. UNITED STEELWORKERS OF AMERICA
545 F.2d 1336 (3d Cir.1976).

ADAMS, CIRCUIT JUDGE.

This appeal presents two principal issues. First, we must decide whether the district court had jurisdiction to enjoin the appellant union from refusing to cross a "stranger picket line." [1] Then, if that question is answered in the negative, we must determine whether a coercive civil contempt decree, based on a violation of the injunction, can survive the invalidation of the underlying order.

United Steelworkers of America and its Local Union No. 1537 have for many years represented the production and maintenance employees of the Latrobe Steel Company. Local 1537 and Latrobe Steel were signatories to a collective bargaining agreement that contained a broad no-strike clause and an expansive grievance-arbitration provision.

1. A "stranger picket line" is a picket line established by a union other than the   one against which the injunction is sought.

The Steelworkers and another local union have been the certified representatives of the office, clerical and technical employees at the Latrobe plant since 1974. After efforts to negotiate a collective bargaining agreement between the office workers local and Latrobe Steel proved unsuccessful, the office employees established a picket line outside of the Latrobe facility at about 11:00 P.M. on September 4, 1975. As a result of the picket line, the production workers on the midnight shift refused to enter the plant.

Early the next morning, September 5th, Latrobe Steel brought an action in the district court under section 301 of the Labor Management Relations Act of 1947 [29 U.S.C. § 185 (1970)], seeking a temporary restraining order against the refusal of the production employees to cross the picket line. * * *

When the production workers did not report for work on September 10th, Latrobe Steel moved the district court to hold Local 1537 and certain of its officers and members in "civil contempt." Following a full hearing the district court ruled that the union was "adjudged in civil contempt." * * *

The district court's contempt order levied a two-part fine on the union. An assessment of $10,000 was imposed, payable to the United States, if the production employees did not report for work at the next shift beginning midnight, September 12th. The court's adjudication also provided that the union would have to pay an additional $10,000, again to the United States, for each subsequent day the union failed to comply with the preliminary injunction. * * *

After a careful review of the facts and the authorities, we conclude that the preliminary injunction as well as the contempt judgment in this case must be vacated.

[The court concludes that the anti-injunction provision of the Norris–LaGuardia Act is applicable and "the district court was without jurisdiction to enter a preliminary injunction." The court further determined that the contempt was coercive civil contempt rather than indirect criminal contempt.] * * *

The remaining issue, whether a civil contempt order that is coercive in nature falls with the underlying injunction, is one which has received scant judicial consideration. The paucity of analysis of this problem, which is critical to the disposition of this case, is particularly surprising, given the wealth of precedent on the effect generally of the invalidation of a prior injunction on subsequent criminal and compensatory civil contempts.

With regard to criminal contempt, the Supreme Court's opinions in *Walker v. Birmingham* [388 U.S. 307, 87 S.Ct. 1824 (1967) reproduced *supra*] and *United States v. United Mine Workers* [330 U.S. 258, 67 S.Ct. 677 (1947) reproduced *supra*] clearly hold that a criminal contempt judgment does survive the voiding of an injunction. * * *

Although the cases do not fully explicate the reasoning behind the general principle that compensatory civil contempt does not survive the abrogation of the underlying decree, the precept is, in our opinion, a sound one. A compensatory contempt proceeding is similar in several particulars to an ordinary damage action, since it is in essence an action between private parties, with rights created by the injunctive order rather than by a statute or the common law. The invalidation of an injunction in such a setting is equivalent to a holding that the plaintiff never had a legally cognizable interest which the defendant was obliged to respect, a conclusion which should be distinguished from the nearly unconditional duty of obedience owed by a defendant to a court. The *United Mine Workers'* doctrine thus recognizes that a private party should not profit as a result of an order to which a court determines, in retrospect, he was never entitled.

* * *

* * * [O]ur task, as often the case in litigation, is to reconcile two legal principles, in order to prevent either from destroying the other. Here, the importance of each of the principles can be acknowledged by recognizing that a court may uphold respect for law through the utilization of the criminal contempt process, while preventing litigants from benefiting from void court orders through the medium of either remedial or coercive civil contempt.

* * *

Accordingly, the injunction and the order of contempt will be vacated and the cause remanded for proceedings consistent with this opinion.

————

1. The reversal of a civil contempt upon the reversal of the underlying injunctive order has been explained as follows:

> It is true that the reversal of the decree does not retroactively obliterate the past existence of the violation; yet on the other hand it does more than destroy the future sanction of the decree. It adjudges that it never should have passed; that the right which it affected to create was no right at all. To let the liability stand for past contumacy would be to give the plaintiff a remedy not for a right but for a wrong, which the law should not do.

Salvage Process Corp. v. ACME Tank Cleaning Process Corp., 86 F.2d 727, 727 (2d Cir.1936).

2. The United States Supreme Court once suggested that a test to distinguish the nature of contempt penalties is whether the conduct was "refusing to do an act commanded" or "doing an act prohibited." The former contempts are civil whereas the latter ones are criminal. Gompers v. Bucks Stove & Range Co., 221 U.S. 418, 443, 31 S.Ct. 492, 55 L.Ed. 797 (1911).

Is this distinction useful? Is the conduct in the principal case best characterized as refusing the commanded act to return to work or as doing the prohibited act of striking?

The Supreme Court subsequently rejected this simply dichotomy in complex cases:

* * * The distinction between mandatory and prohibitory orders is easily applied in the classic contempt scenario, where contempt sanctions are used to enforce orders compelling or forbidding a single, discrete act. In such cases, orders commanding an affirmative act simply designate those actions that are capable of being coerced.

But the distinction between coercion of affirmative acts and punishment of prohibited conduct is difficult to apply when conduct that can recur is involved, or when an injunction contains both mandatory and prohibitory provisions. Moreover, in borderline cases injunctive provisions containing essentially the same command can be phrased either in mandatory or prohibitory terms. Under a literal application of petitioners' theory, an injunction ordering the union: "Do not strike," would appear to be prohibitory and criminal, while an injunction ordering the union: "Continue working," would be mandatory and civil. Dobbs, Contempt of Court: A Survey, 56 Cornell L.Rev. 183, 239 (1971). United Mine Workers v. Bagwell, ___ U.S. ___, 114 S.Ct. 2552, 129 L.Ed.2d 642 (1994).

3. Consider the usefulness of the following attempt to distinguish between contempts:

Contempts may be civil or criminal. In a civil contempt the contemnor violates a decree or order of the court made for the benefit of an adverse party litigant. In a criminal contempt a court's process is violated or disobeyed and disrespect of the court is manifested.

State *ex rel.* Oregon State Bar v. Lenske, 243 Or. 477, 480, 405 P.2d 510, 512 (1965), *cert. denied,* 384 U.S. 943, 86 S.Ct. 1460, 16 L.Ed.2d 541 (1966). A helpful discussion is in Dobbs, Contempt of Court: A Survey, 56 Cornell L.Rev. 183, 239–41 (1971).

4. Does *United Mine Workers,* reproduced *supra,* compel the result reached by the court in the principal case? *United Mine Workers* phrased the issue addressed by that opinion as whether "the plaintiff may profit by way of a fine imposed" for violation of an order erroneously issued. 330 U.S. 258, 294–5, 67 S.Ct. 677, 696, 91 L.Ed. 884 (1947). Should "profit" be interpreted broadly?

Should the Court's reasoning in *United Mine Workers v. Bagwell,* reproduced *supra,* affect the result in cases posing the issue in the principal case?

PRO–CHOICE NETWORK v. WALKER

994 F.2d 989 (2d Cir.1993).

MESKILL, CHIEF JUDGE:

These two appeals involve contempt judgments resulting from violations of the same Temporary Restraining Order (TRO)[.] * * *

Appellants Bonnie Behn and Carla Rainero appeal a judgment of the same court entered on August 14, 1992 which granted Pro–Choice Network's petition for civil contempt against them, entered judgment against them in the amount of $10,000 each and granted Pro–Choice Network's request for reasonable attorney's fees and costs associated with prosecuting the contempt.

Although the district judge labeled the contempt proceedings civil, appellants argue that the unconditional fines he imposed are immediately appealable as orders of criminal contempt because they were neither compensatory nor coercive. * * * Behn and Rainero argue that the portion of the order they allegedly violated was not legally valid because the mere act of speaking to unwilling listeners does not create any legally actionable threat of irreparable injury. Furthermore, Behn and Rainero contend that their conduct was protected under the First Amendment and therefore was not a violation of the court's order. * * *

Pro–Choice Network commenced an action in the district court on September 24, 1990 alleging that the defendants had been engaging in a consistent pattern of illegal conduct at the appellees' health care facilities including blocking access to and egress from their facilities, trespassing, and harassing and intimidating their staffs and patients. The complaint stated causes of action under 42 U.S.C. § 1985(3) as well as under several state laws.

Immediately upon filing its complaint, Pro–Choice Network moved for a TRO to enjoin a blockade that defendants had announced for September 28, 1990. After conducting a hearing and hearing argument on the motion, the district court issued a TRO on September 27, 1990 enjoining appellants from conducting any blockade of the appellees abortion facilities and from harassing patients and staff entering or exiting these facilities.[4] Although the defendants held a demonstration

---

4. The TRO stated in pertinent part: ORDERED THAT Defendants ... are: 1. Temporarily enjoined and restrained in any manner or by any means from: (a) trespassing on, sitting in, blocking, impeding or obstructing access to, ingress into or egress from any facility at which abortions are performed in the Western District of New York, including demonstrating within 15 feet of any person seeking access to or leaving such facilities, except that sidewalk counseling by no more than two persons as specified in paragraph (b) shall be allowed; (b) physically abusing or tortiously harassing persons entering or leaving, working at or using any services at any facility at which abortions are performed; Provided, however, that sidewalk counseling, consisting of a conversation of a nonthreatening nature by not more than two people with each person they are seeking to counsel shall not be prohibited. Also provided that no one is required to accept or listen to

on September 28, 1990, they complied with the terms of the TRO. After having previously extended the TRO several times, on November 2, 1990, with the consent of the appellants, the district court ordered that the TRO would remain in effect until the motion for a preliminary injunction was decided. The court granted the preliminary injunction on February 14, 1992. Only two of the defendants appealed the preliminary injunction; none of the appellants now before us was part of that appeal.

* * *

The TRO provides that failure to comply with it will subject the contemnor to civil damages of $10,000 per day for the first violation and to a civil contempt fine double that of the previous fines for successive violations.[6] * * *

On October 22, 1990, Pro–Choice Network petitioned for civil contempt against Behn and Rainero claiming that on October 20, 1990 Behn and Rainero violated the TRO. The district court held hearings on Pro–Choice Network's petition over the course of several days from June 18, 1991 to July 12, 1991. The court issued a decision and order on August 14, 1992 finding Behn and Rainero in contempt of court based on the events of October 20, 1990. The following facts are taken from the district court's opinion.

On that day, Behn and Rainero were in the vicinity of the Buffalo GYN Womenservices' clinic with, according to the district court, the intent "to dissuade women entering the clinic from obtaining abortions by offering them 'sidewalk counseling.' " Behn and Rainero approached two young men and a young woman who were apparently headed toward the clinic. They began talking to the woman and offering her literature and assistance. After three "pro-choice" escorts came to escort the three to the clinic, Behn and Rainero continued to walk alongside the group. When the young woman began to get upset, the escorts told her there was a TRO in effect and that Behn and Rainero would have to stop talking to her if she asked them. The district court found that the

sidewalk counseling and that if anyone who wants to, or who is sought to be counseled who wants to not have counseling, wants to leave, or walk away, they shall have the absolute right to do that, and in such event the persons seeking to counsel that person shall cease and desist from such counseling of that person.

. . .

(c) making any excessively loud sound which disturbs, injures, or endangers the health or safety of any patient or employee of a health care facility where abortions are performed in the Western District of New York, nor shall any person make such sounds which interferes [sic] with the rights of anyone not in violation of this Order; (d)

attempting, or inducing, encouraging, directing, aiding, or abetting in any manner, others to take any of the actions described in paragraphs (a), (b) and (c) above.

6. The TRO specifically provides, in pertinent part: ORDERED that the failure to comply with this Order by any Project Rescue participant or participant in any of the activities enjoined in paragraphs (a) through (d) above with actual notice of the provisions of this Order shall subject him or her to civil damages of $10,000 per day for the first violation of this Order; and it is further ORDERED that each successive violation of this Order shall subject the contemnor to a civil contempt fine double that of the previous fines.

young woman turned to Behn and Rainero and asked them to leave her alone. Despite Behn's and Rainero's testimony to the contrary, the district court also found that it was clear that the young woman was asking both Behn and Rainero to leave her alone. The woman later repeated her request to be left alone.

[The district court] found that the collateral bar rule precluded Behn and Rainero from challenging the validity of the TRO as a defense, that both Behn and Rainero were in civil contempt of the TRO on October 20, 1990, that the TRO was clear and unambiguous, that the proof of noncompliance was clear and convincing, that Behn and Rainero were not reasonably diligent and energetic in attempting to achieve compliance with the TRO and that their violation was willful.

In accordance with the provisions of the TRO, the district court ordered Behn and Rainero each to pay $10,000 in damages to Buffalo GYN Womenservices which had "made an uncontested showing of both actual injury, in the form of disrupted daily operations and patients rendered upset and distressed, and compensable loss, consisting of the cost of extra security measures and additional staff." The court also ordered them to pay attorney's fees and costs.

[Appellants] now appeal the district court's findings of contempt.

We address first our jurisdiction to hear these appeals. All parties to these appeals agree that a party to a pending proceeding may not appeal from an order of civil contempt except as part of an appeal from a final judgment, whereas an adjudication of criminal contempt is a final order appealable prior to final judgment. * * *

We find it unnecessary to address the arguments concerning whether the contempt sanctions were also compensatory in nature. The sanctions were imposed on each of the appellants in this case to compel obedience to a lawful court order. Under our [precedents] these awards are clearly ones for civil, not criminal, contempt. Therefore, we are without jurisdiction to hear this appeal.

Appellants contend that, even if we hold that these are orders of civil contempt, we should vacate the amount and disposition of the sanctions. We disagree. Because we lack jurisdiction over these appeals we cannot consider the merits of this contention or of any of appellants' other arguments. Appellants could have challenged the merits of these contempt orders on an appeal from the preliminary injunction. However, their counsel indicated during oral argument that for financial reasons they chose not to do so.

* * *

We dismiss both appeals for lack of appellate jurisdiction.

———

1. Another consequence of the distinction between civil and criminal contempt is the timing of the appeal. Criminal contempts are

immediately appealable, whereas civil contempts are appealable with the underlying claim.

Would the plaintiffs in the principal case have a good argument under *Bagwell* that their contempts are criminal?

2. Indefinite jail terms or continuing fines under coercive civil contempt pose particular difficulty with respect of contemnors who have demonstrated that they will never comply with the court's order. Recalcitrant witnesses, for example, may demonstrate by their continued silence that they will never testify. Typically such witnesses fear for their physical safety or for the safety of their families. When coercion is impossible, is it permissible for the court to continue to try to coerce?

Some courts have accepted the idea of "exhausted coercion" and have permitted contemnors to demonstrate that their continued incarceration is punitive because there is no meaningful possibility of compliance. Others have refused to allow such a demonstration because future compliance is always theoretically possible. *Compare* Lambert v. Montana, 545 F.2d 87 (9th Cir.1976), *with* In re Grand Jury Investigation, 600 F.2d 420 (3d Cir.1979). *See also* In re Grand Jury Proceedings, 894 F.2d 881 (7th Cir.1989); Catena v. Seidl, 65 N.J. 257, 321 A.2d 225 (1974). One celebrated case of this type involved Dr. Elizabeth Morgan, who refused to reveal the location of her child for the father to have visitation rights because she was convinced that the father had sexually molested the child. She remained imprisoned for two years before her release under a special statutory provision enacted for her benefit. *See* Morgan v. Foretich, 564 A.2d 1 (D.C.App.1989).

Chapter 8

MODERN INJUNCTION FORMS
AND FUNCTIONS

In modern law there are four types of injunctions: preventive, restorative, prophylactic, and structural. The last three have become common enough to receive labels only in the latter part of this century. The preventive injunction, previously studied in Chapter 3, has roots deep in the common law. Its purpose is to prevent the defendant from inflicting future injury on the plaintiff. The plaintiff must prove that the defendant was likely to do harm absent the order, that legal remedies would be inadequate, and that such harm would be irreparable.

The other types of injunctions are similar in the sense that in all of them the court makes an order that the defendant must do some act or refrain from doing some act. It is their different functions that distinguish them. This chapter explores those differences.

A. RESTORATIVE AND PROPHYLACTIC INJUNCTIONS

Section Coverage:

Restorative and prophylactic injunctions are close cousins of preventive injunctions. A restorative injunction principally operates to correct the present by undoing the effects of a past wrong. The notion of "restoring" means that it focuses not only prospectively, as does the traditional preventive injunction, but also retroactively. For example, a tainted election process affects future governance; the wrong can only be corrected by turning back time, in some sense, and redoing the election.

A prophylactic injunction seeks to safeguard the plaintiff's rights by directing the defendant's behavior so as to minimize the chance that wrongs might recur in the future. For example, if an employer maintains an integrated work force where the social atmosphere is so pervasively prejudiced that it violates federal law, the court may order the employer to take specific steps to monitor complaints and to educate the employees on their responsibility not to harass co-workers on the basis of race. The lack of such procedures are not themselves a violation of federal law in the absence of a court order. The court would order the measures only if it seemed that future infractions of the plaintiffs' rights are likely without extra protections. Violation of a prophylactic injunction is not necessarily a legal wrong in itself, except that the injunction makes it so.

Model Case:

Officials in a small town are prejudiced against the members of a new group that has started a utopian community on the outskirts of town. The founders of community, known as The Kolony, force members to adhere to strict rules of dress and behavior. They do not believe in private ownership of property as a general principle, although they own the land where The Kolony is situated.

During the last election the town officials adopted unusually strict voting procedures. The ballots in this small town are hand-counted. Election judges can declare as "spoiled" any ballot where the marks in the boxes exceed the printed bounds sufficient to raise an ambiguity about the vote. In the election in question, election judges in the precinct exclusively containing The Kolony found ninety percent of the ballots were "spoiled." In all the other precincts only one ballot was declared "spoiled."

The Kolony sued and the judge found the behavior of the election judges was founded in prejudice. The court declared the election so tainted that it was invalid. An injunction against election officials required a new election. This order is a restorative injunction.

Because of the pervasive prejudice against members of The Kolony, the court issued additional orders to safeguard their right to vote. The order mandated certain registration practices that were not otherwise required by law. The court also ordered that precincts be drawn such that The Kolony is not exclusively in one. These orders are prophylactic injunctive measures.

VASQUEZ v. BANNWORTHS, INC.

707 S.W.2d 886 (Tex.1986).

McGee, Justice.

This is a suit for wrongful discharge brought by an employee, Maria Guadalupe Vasquez, against her employer, Bannworths, Inc. The issue on this appeal is whether the district court abused its discretion in failing to order Bannworths, Inc. to rehire Mrs. Vasquez, who was wrongfully discharged because of her union affiliation. Although the trial court awarded Mrs. Vasquez lost wages and enjoined Bannworths, Inc. from discriminating against Mrs. Vasquez if she was ever employed by Bannworths again, the trial court refused to order Bannworths to rehire Mrs. Vasquez. The court of appeals, in an unpublished opinion, affirmed the judgment of the trial court. We hold that the trial court abused its discretion and, therefore, we reverse the judgment of the court of appeals. The cause is remanded to the trial court to reform its judgment to include a mandatory injunction ordering Bannworths, Inc. to rehire Mrs. Vasquez in the same or similar capacity to the one she held prior to her unlawful discharge.

Mrs. Vasquez was first employed by Bannworths, Inc. as a farm worker in 1973. Although the nature of the work does not provide for permanent employment, Mrs. Vasquez worked for Bannworths for several different seasons each year for nine consecutive years. While employed by Bannworths, she usually worked five to six days a week for up to ten hours a day at minimum wage.

In January 1982, while employed by Bannworths, Mrs. Vasquez sought assistance through the local United Farm Workers office to obtain permanent resident status in the United States. She became an active member in the UFW, a labor union, about a month later. Subsequently, Mrs. Vasquez began to complain to UFW representatives about the lack of sanitation at Bannworth's facilities. Mrs. Vasquez charged that all employees were required to share a common drinking cup and that the portable restroom facilities provided for the workers in the fields were filthy and did not comply with certain minimum health and sanitation standards which had been promulgated by the Texas Health Commissioner. On November 5, 1982, two Hidalgo County Health Department sanitation engineers came to Bannworth's fields where Mrs. Vasquez's crew was working to inspect the bathroom facilities. Later that same day, Mrs. Vasquez was fired from her job with Bannworths.

Mrs. Vasquez brought this suit seeking damages for lost wages and an injunction to refrain Bannworths from violating the Texas Right-to-Work Law (hereinafter the Act). Tex.Rev.Civ.Stat.Ann. art. 5154g (Vernon 1971). That statute prohibits an employer from denying a person the right to work on account of membership or non-membership in a labor union. Tex.Rev.Civ.Stat.Ann. art. 5154g, sec. 1 (Vernon 1971). A jury found that Mrs. Vasquez had been fired by Bannworths because of her union membership and her complaints concerning the restroom facilities. Although the jury failed to find that Bannworths's act of firing Mrs. Vasquez was done with malice or in gross disregard of her rights, the jury did find that Bannworths would not hire Mrs. Vasquez again because of her union membership. The jury awarded Mrs. Vasquez $3000 in lost wages from the time she was fired until suit was filed.

Based on the jury's finding of probable, continuing, future injury and recognizing that the plaintiff would suffer continuing, immediate and irreparable harm without an adequate remedy at law, the trial court awarded injunctive relief. That relief, however, falls short of remedying the harm recognized by the court. While the trial court enjoined Bannworths from terminating, suspending, discriminating against, or threatening to terminate, suspend or discriminate against the plaintiff because of her union membership, the court conditioned the injunction on Bannworth's voluntary reemployment of Mrs. Vasquez. In other words, unless Mrs. Vasquez actually began working for Bannworths again, the injunction was of no consequence because it neither required Bannworths to rehire Mrs. Vasquez nor required Bannworths to not discriminate against Mrs. Vasquez if she chose to reapply for employment with Bannworths. Considering the jury's finding in this case, that Bannworths would continue to discriminate against Mrs. Vasquez because of her union membership, it became mandatory for the trial court to issue an injunction which would remedy the violation of the Act.

Section 4 of article 5154g mandates that the trial court enjoin an employer whenever it is shown that the employer has violated the Act. Tex.Rev.Civ.Stat.Ann. art. 5154g, sec. 4 (Vernon 1971).

Although a trial court may have some discretion in fashioning the relief to be granted by the injunction, we hold that article 5154g, section 4 limits that discretion by requiring that the remedy devised be one which will effectuate the policy of the Act and which will undo the effects of violations of the Act.   Tex.Rev.Civ.Stat.Ann. art. 5154g, sec. 4 (Vernon 1971).   The injunction issued by the trial court does not alleviate the violation that occurred in this case.   The violation to be enjoined in this case was Bannworths's firing of Mrs. Vasquez because of her union membership.   The trial court failed to address this violation in the injunction it issued.

* * *

The right to injunctive relief, when such is necessary to afford a party full protection of his established right, is clear under Texas decisions.   [Citations.]   When faced with the twin findings of firing because of impermissible discrimination and a refusal to rehire on that basis, as well as a request by the plaintiff for reinstatement, we can see no reason which would justify a court's refusal to order reemployment. [Citation.]   Based on the findings in this case and plaintiff's request to be rehired, there was only one remedy available to the trial court which would rectify the harm caused by Bannworths's violation of the Act. The remedy was to order Bannworths to rehire Mrs. Vasquez.   The trial court abused its discretion in failing to order Mrs. Vasquez's rehiring because, in effect, the court's order allows Bannworths to continue to discriminate against Mrs. Vasquez by refusing to hire her because of her union membership.

The cause is remanded to the trial court to reform its judgment to include a mandatory injunction ordering Bannworths, Inc. to rehire Mrs. Vasquez in the same or similar capacity to the one she held prior to her unlawful discharge.

PROBLEM: THE FALSIFIED TEST RESULTS

Genstore Company has a chain of retail stores marketing general merchandise.   It is a regional chain employing hundreds of non-unionized employees.   The top level Genstore management decided three years ago to require all applicants and current employees to submit to a "personality" test.

One of the purposes of testing current employees was to probe the loyalty of each to the company.   Management believed that indications of disloyalty would be relevant in determining which employees should be promoted.   The policy was that only employees displaying a high degree of loyalty to the company should be promoted.

A top manager unknowingly hired a disreputable company to conduct these tests.   The operator was dishonest and took bribes from some employees to falsify their test results. Moreover, part of the bribery scheme involved falsifying the test results of some rival employees to reflect disloyalty. The bribers' purpose was to eliminate those individuals for future promotions. As a result of this bribery, the records of some two dozen employees were altered to show disloyalty.

The victims of this scheme had no immediate knowledge of their test results. The company kept all results private and fired no one. When the company did not choose any of the victims for promotions, each assumed it was for other reasons. The bribers fared better, but not all of them were promoted. Some promotions went to employees who became contenders after the bribery scheme was completed.

The bribery was recently discovered. Genstore immediately fired all the bribers. Although the bribers told the company managers which records were falsified, Genstore has refused all demands of the victims. The victims want the removal of the adverse loyalty notation from their files or retesting. They also want priority for the next promotions.

Rebuffed by management, the victims now wish to sue. They have a cause of action under state law for the violation of a statute that limits the questions an employer can ask in personality tests. The restrictive list of acceptable questions includes honesty but not loyalty. The remedy provision in this statute allows damages and "such relief as the court deems appropriate."

Is there any "appropriate relief" for the court to give these individual plaintiffs? Should the court order Genstore to take steps to prevent future violations of the act? Genstore has continued to administer personality tests, although now with a different company. Given that Genstore once failed to adhere to the statute's limited list of permissible questions, would it be appropriate for the court to prevent future violations by ordering Genstore to educate its managers concerning the requirements of the statute? In the case that follows, note the type of relief given to right the wrong. Consider whether the court went beyond the specific wrong to order broad relief to prevent future wrongs to unknown individuals.

BUNDY v. JACKSON

641 F.2d 934 (D.C.Cir.1981).

J. Skelly Wright, Chief Judge:

* * *

Appellant Sandra Bundy is now, and was at the time she filed her lawsuit, a Vocational Rehabilitation Specialist, level GS–9, with the District of Columbia Department of Corrections (the agency). * * * In recent years Bundy's chief task has been to find jobs for former criminal offenders.

The District Court's finding that sexual intimidation was a "normal condition of employment" in Bundy's agency finds ample support in the

District Court's own chronology of Bundy's experiences there. Those experiences began in 1972 when Bundy, still a GS–5, received and rejected sexual propositions from Delbert Jackson, then a fellow employee at the agency but now its Director and the named defendant in this lawsuit in his official capacity. It was two years later, however, that the sexual intimidation Bundy suffered began to intertwine directly with her employment, when she received propositions from two of her supervisors, Arthur Burton and James Gainey.

* * * Burton began sexually harassing Bundy in June 1974, continually calling her into his office to request that she spend the workday afternoon with him at his apartment and to question her about her sexual proclivities. Shortly after becoming her first-line supervisor Gainey also began making sexual advances to Bundy, asking her to join him at a motel and on a trip to the Bahamas. Bundy complained about these advances to Lawrence Swain, who supervised both Burton and Gainey. Swain casually dismissed Bundy's complaints, telling her that "any man in his right mind would want to rape you," and then proceeding himself to request that she begin a sexual relationship with him in his apartment. Bundy rejected his request.

We add that, although the District Court made no explicit findings as to harassment of other female employees, its finding that harassment was "standard operating procedure" finds ample support in record evidence that Bundy was not the only woman subjected to sexual intimidation by male supervisors.[3]

In denying Bundy any relief, the District Court found that Bundy's supervisors did not take the "game" of sexually propositioning female employees "seriously," and that Bundy's rejection of their advances did not evoke in them any motive to take any action against her. The record, however, contains nothing to support this view, and indeed some evidence directly belies it. For example, after Bundy complained to Swain, Burton began to derogate her for alleged malingering and poor work performance, though she had not previously received any such criticism.   * * *

The relevance of * * * "discriminatory environment" cases to sexual harassment is beyond serious dispute. Racial or ethnic discrimination

---

3. Carolyn Epps, who worked for the agency between 1967 and 1974, testified that after she asked her supervisor, Lawrence Swain, about the possibility of a promotion he began making unsolicited physical and verbal advances toward her, and that she received verbal sexual advances from supervisor Claude Burgin after she discussed her promotion with him. Epps also testified that she heard Swain ask other female employees to come to his apartment for drinks and saw him pressing his body against their bodies in his office. In 1974 Epps applied to become an administrative aide-stenographer, which would have meant a promotion from GS–6 to GS–

7. She testified that, although she was qualified for the job, it went instead to another female employee who had received sexual advances from Swain and who, unlike Epps, did not know stenography.

Ann Blanchard worked for the agency from 1971 to 1973, supervised by James Gainey and Arthur Burton. Burton made sexual advances toward her and also apparently intimidated her by stating that another employee whom he would not identify had told Burton that Blanchard had been conducting a sexual relationship with one of her clients.

against a company's minority clients may reflect no intent to discriminate directly against the company's minority employees, but in poisoning the atmosphere of employment it violates Title VII. Sexual stereotyping through discriminatory dress requirements may be benign in intent, and may offend women only in a general, atmospheric manner, yet it violates Title VII. Racial slurs, though intentional and directed at individuals, may still be just verbal insults, yet they too may create Title VII liability. How then can sexual harassment, which injects the most demeaning sexual stereotypes into the general work environment and which always represents an intentional assault on an individual's innermost privacy, not be illegal?

* * *

Indeed, so long as women remain inferiors in the employment hierarchy, they may have little recourse against harassment beyond the legal recourse Bundy seeks in this case. The law may allow a woman to prove that her resistance to the harassment cost her her job or some economic benefit, but this will do her no good if the employer never takes such tangible actions against her.

* * *

The employer can thus implicitly and effectively make the employee's endurance of sexual intimidation a "condition" of her employment. The woman then faces a "cruel trilemma." She can endure the harassment. She can attempt to oppose it, with little hope of success, either legal or practical, but with every prospect of making the job even less tolerable for her. Or she can leave her job, with little hope of legal relief and the likely prospect of another job where she will face harassment anew.

Bundy proved that she was the victim of a practice of sexual harassment and a discriminatory work environment permitted by her employer. Her rights under Title VII were therefore violated. We thus reverse the District Court's holding on this issue and remand it to that court so it can fashion appropriate injunctive relief.[12] And on this novel issue, we think it advisable to offer the District Court guidance in framing its decree.[13]

12. Title VII allows the courts to award a victorious plaintiff reinstatement, back pay, or "any other equitable relief as the court deems appropriate." 42 U.S.C. § 2000e-5(g) (1976). Back pay and reinstatement are, of course, irrelevant to the discriminatory environment issue, and we follow the great majority of the federal courts in construing "equitable relief" to preclude any award of damages for emotional harm resulting from a Title VII violation. [Citations.] We add that, since our holding makes Bundy a prevailing party in this suit, the District Court on remand may entertain a request for attorney's fees. 42 U.S.C. § 2000e-5(k) (1976).

13. Appellee has argued that an injunction is improper and unnecessary in this case since Bundy has complained of no instances of sexual harassment since 1975 and there is therefore no reason to think further harassment will occur. Common sense tells us that the men who harassed Bundy may well have ceased their actions solely because of the pendency of her complaint and lawsuit. Moreover, the law tells us that a suit for injunctive relief does not become moot simply because the offending

The Final Guidelines on Sexual Harassment in the Workplace (Guidelines) issued by the Equal Employment Opportunity Commission on November 10, 1980, 45 Fed.Reg. 74676–74677 (1980) (to be codified at 29 C.F.R. § 1604.11(a)–(f)), offer a useful basis for injunctive relief in this case. Those Guidelines define sexual harassment broadly:

> Unwelcome sexual advances, requests for sexual favors, and other verbal or physical conduct of a sexual nature constitute sexual harassment when (1) submission to such conduct is made either explicitly or implicitly a term or condition of an individual's employment, (2) submission to or rejection of such conduct by an individual is used as the basis for employment decisions affecting such individual, or (3) such conduct has the purpose or effect of unreasonably interfering with an individual's work performance or creating an intimidating, hostile, or offensive work environment.

* * * The general goal of these Guidelines is *preventive*. An employer may negate liability by taking "immediate and appropriate corrective action" when it learns of any illegal harassment, but the employer should fashion rules within its firm or agency to ensure that such corrective action never becomes necessary.

Applying these Guidelines to the present case, we believe that the Director of the agency should be ordered to raise affirmatively the subject of sexual harassment with all his employees and inform all employees that sexual harassment violates Title VII of the Civil Rights Act of 1964, the Guidelines of the EEOC, the express orders of the Mayor of the District of Columbia, and the policy of the agency itself. The Director should also establish and publicize a scheme whereby harassed employees may complain to the Director immediately and confidentially. The Director should promptly take all necessary steps to investigate and correct any harassment, including warnings and appropriate discipline directed at the offending party, and should generally develop other means of preventing harassment within the agency.

Perhaps the most important part of the preventive remedy will be a prompt and effective procedure for hearing, adjudicating, and remedying complaints of sexual harassment within the agency. Fortunately, the District Court need not establish an entire new procedural mechanism for harassment complaints. Under regulations promulgated by the Equal Employment Opportunity Commission, 29 C.F.R. §§ 1613.201–1613.283 (1979), the Department of Corrections, like all other federal and District of Columbia agencies, is required to establish procedures for adjudication of complaints of denial of equal employment opportunity,

party has ceased the offending conduct, since the offending party might be free otherwise to renew that conduct once the court denied the relief, [citation]. The request for injunctive relief will be moot only where there is no reasonable expectation that the conduct will recur, [citation] or where interim events have "completely and irrevocably eradicated the effects of the alleged violation" [citation.] We perceive no such certainty here, most obviously because Bundy's agency has taken no affirmative steps to prevent recurrence of the harassment, and because all the harassing employees still work for the agency. * * *

whether the ground of discrimination is race, color, religion, sex, or national origin. The required procedures guarantee the complainant a prompt and effective investigation, an opportunity for informal adjustment of the discrimination, and, if necessary, a formal evidentiary hearing. Moreover, if the complaint proves meritorious the agency may be required to take disciplinary action against any employee found to have committed discriminatory acts. Finally, the agency must inform any employee denied relief within the agency of his or her right to file a civil action in the District Court.

Since we have held that sexual harassment, even if it does not result in loss of tangible job benefits, is illegal sex discrimination, the District Court may simply order the Director of the agency to ensure that complaints of sexual harassment receive thorough and effective treatment within the formal process the agency has already established to comply with the Civil Service Commission regulations. Finally, we believe the District Court should retain jurisdiction of the case so that it may review the Director's plans for complying with the injunction.

* * *

[Remanded to the district court.]

The court in the principal case further suggested the following language for the district court to consider "as appropriate for the injunction":

The court decrees that the defendant Delbert Jackson, Director of the District of Columbia Department of Corrections, along with his supervising employees, agents, and all those subject to his control or acting in concert with him, are enjoined from causing, encouraging, condoning, or permitting the practice of sexual harassment of female employees by male supervisors and employees within the Department: to wit, any unwelcome sexual advances, requests for sexual favors, or other verbal or physical conduct of a sexual nature when submission to such conduct is explicitly or implicitly a requirement of the individual's employment, or used as a basis for any employment decision concerning that individual, or when such conduct has the purpose or effect of unreasonably interfering with the individual's work performance or creating an intimidating or hostile or offensive work environment.

Defendant is further required:

1. To notify all employees and supervisors in the Department, through individual letters and permanent posting in prominent locations throughout Department offices, that sexual harassment, as explicitly defined in the previous paragraph, violates Title VII of the Civil Rights Act of 1964, regulatory guidelines of the Equal Employment Opportunity Commission, the express orders of the Mayor of

the District of Columbia, and the policy of the Department of Corrections.

2.   To ensure that employees complaining of sexual harassment can avail themselves of the full and effective use of the complaint, hearing, adjudication, and appeals procedures for complaints of discrimination established by the Department of Corrections pursuant to Equal Employment Opportunity Commission regulations 29 C.F.R. §§ 1613–201–1613.283 (1979).

3.   To develop appropriate sanctions or disciplinary measures for supervisors or other employees who are found to have sexually harassed female employees, including warnings to the offending person and notations in that person's employment record for reference in the event future complaints are directed against that person.

4.   To develop other appropriate means of instructing employees of the Department of the harmful nature of sexual harassment.

Defendant shall return to this court within 60 days to report on the steps he has taken in compliance with this order and to present his plans for the additional measures required by Paragraph 4 above.   The court shall retain jurisdiction of this case.

B.   STRUCTURAL INJUNCTIONS

Section Coverage:

Structural injunctions are a modern phenomenon born of necessity from developments in Constitutional law.   The United States Supreme Court has identified substantive rights whose enforcement requires substantial judicial supervision.   These rights concern the treatment of individuals by institutions, such as the right not to suffer inhumane treatment in a prison or public mental hospital.   Enforcement of such rights by injunction has become an implicit part of the Constitutional guarantee.

Such injunctions are categorized "structural" because courts undertake supervision over the institutional policies and practices.   If defendants do not respond cooperatively to orders requiring reform proposals, then judges often undertake to mandate particular changes.   Structural injunctions are often long and costly battles with persistent class plaintiffs, recalcitrant defendants, and frustrated judges.

Model Case:

The city of Springdale has a public school system that serves children of many racial and ethnic identities.   Twenty-five years ago the city voluntarily ended its policy of neighborhood schools because officials perceived that the effect was legally impermissible racial and ethnic segregation.   There were also noticeable differences in the quality and conditions of the schools.   Although this effect had long existed with apparent community approval by the majority who benefitted from it, officials were mindful of the Constitutional rights of the minority students. The Supreme Court declared in *Brown v. Board of Education* that segregated schools violated the equal protection guarantee. Its 1955 decree in the same case required district courts to make orders as necessary in school cases to end segregation "with all deliberate speed."

In the decade following the decision, the Springdale officials became aware that districts failing to take voluntary action often became defendants in school desegregation actions. The Springdale School Board adopted a busing plan that produced some integration, and some schools that previously were populated with only minority children became new magnet schools. The magnet schools specialized in particular programs and required application; they attracted a racial and ethnic mix of children.

In the years since these changes the neighborhoods have correspondingly changed and the magnet schools were less successful. "Special talents" programs within other schools replaced interest in the magnet schools, and the effect was new racial and ethnic segregation within programs and disproportionate representation within schools. The School Board discussed these effects but made no changes.

A suit is filed against the School Board. After a lengthy trial the court finds unlawful segregation. The Board is ordered to propose a plan to correct the Constitutional violations. Months pass and the Board submits only one half-hearted plan to the court. The judge rejects the plan as inadequate and orders the Board to produce a plan addressing specific issues. A temporary plan allowing some voluntary transfers is adopted for the immediate school year. The court receives complaints from individuals who believe the plan was not administered in good faith.

The Board fails to satisfy the court. The judge begins to take a more active role in monitoring school policies and practices. The affirmative orders that result are structural injunctions.

O. FISS, THE CIVIL RIGHTS INJUNCTION*

8–10 (1978) footnotes omitted.

Justice Story described the unique office of the injunction as preventive justice: the injunction is an instrument designed to prevent a wrong from occurring in the future.

[Story's description] misleads in suggesting that prevention is the only concern of the injunction. Prevention may have been the exclusive office of the property, labor, and anti-Progressivism injunctions, but not of the civil rights injunction. Many civil rights injunctions are preventive: they decree that the defendant not discriminate in the future. But there are at least two species, two important species, that are more backward-looking.

* Reprinted with permission by the Indiana University Press.

The first is the structural injunction—the injunction seeking to effectuate the reform of a social institution. The most notable example is a decree seeking to bring about the reorganization of a school system from a "dual system" to a "unitary nonracial school system." * * * [I]t was school desegregation, I maintain, that gave these types of injunctions their contemporary saliency and legitimacy; in the wake of this experience, courts have attempted the structural reorganization of other institutions, such as hospitals and prisons, not just to vindicate a claim of racial equality, but also to vindicate other claims, such as the right against cruel and unusual punishment or the right to treatment.

The other backward-looking injunction is the reparative injunction—an injunction that seeks to eliminate the effects of a past wrong, in this instance conceived as some discrete act or course of conduct. To see how it works, let us assume that a wrong has occurred (such as an act of discrimination). Then the mission of an injunction—classically conceived as a preventive instrument—would be to prevent the recurrence of the wrongful conduct in the future (stop discriminating and do not discriminate again). But in United States v. Louisiana [380 U.S. 145 (1965)], a voting discrimination case, Justice Black identified still another mission for the injunction—the elimination of the effects of the past wrong (the past discrimination). The reparative injunction—long thought by the nineteenth-century textbook writers, such as High, to be an analytical impossibility—was thereby legitimated. And in the same vein, election officials have been ordered not only to stop discriminating in future elections, but also to set aside a past election and to run a new election as a means of removing the taint of discrimination that infected the first one. Similarly, public housing officials have been ordered both to cease discriminating on the basis of race in their future choices of sites and to build units in the white areas as a means of eliminating the effects of the past segregative policy (placing public housing projects only in the black areas of the city).

BROWN v. BOARD OF EDUCATION

349 U.S. 294, 75 S.Ct. 753, 99 L.Ed. 1083 (1955).

[The Supreme Court in 1954 decided in *Brown v. Board of Education* and companion cases that racial segregation in public schools violated the Constitution. That liability decision is known as *Brown I.* The following term the Court addressed the appropriate remedy for this Constitutional wrong. This opinion, known as *Brown II,* is reprinted in part below.]

MR. CHIEF JUSTICE WARREN delivered the opinion of the Court.

These cases were decided on May 17, 1954. The opinions of that date,[1] declaring the fundamental principle that racial discrimination in public education is unconstitutional, are incorporated herein by refer-

---

1. 347 U.S. 483; 347 U.S. 497.

ence. All provisions of federal, state, or local law requiring or permitting such discrimination must yield to this principle. There remains for consideration the manner in which relief is to be accorded.

Because these cases arose under different local conditions and their disposition will involve a variety of local problems, we requested further argument on the question of relief.[2] * * *

Full implementation of these constitutional principles may require solution of varied local school problems. School authorities have the primary responsibility for elucidating, assessing, and solving these problems; courts will have to consider whether the action of school authorities constitutes good faith implementation of the governing constitutional principles. Because of their proximity to local conditions and the possible need for further hearings, the courts which originally heard these cases can best perform this judicial appraisal. Accordingly, we believe it appropriate to remand the cases to those courts.

In fashioning and effectuating the decrees, the courts will be guided by equitable principles. Traditionally, equity has been characterized by a practical flexibility in shaping its remedies and by a facility for adjusting and reconciling public and private needs. These cases call for the exercise of these traditional attributes of equity power. At stake is the personal interest of the plaintiffs in admission to public schools as soon as practicable on a nondiscriminatory basis. To effectuate this interest may call for elimination of a variety of obstacles in making the transition to school systems operated in accordance with the constitutional principles set forth in our May 17, 1954, decision. Courts of equity may properly take into account the public interest in the elimination of such obstacles in a systematic and effective manner. But it should go without saying that the vitality of these constitutional principles cannot be allowed to yield simply because of disagreement with them.

---

2. Further argument was requested on the following questions, 347 U.S. 483, 495–496, n.13, previously propounded by the Court:

"4. Assuming it is decided that segregation in public schools violates the Fourteenth Amendment

"(a) would a decree necessarily follow providing that, within the limits set by normal geographic school districting, Negro children should forthwith be admitted to schools of their choice, or

"(b) may this Court, in the exercise of its equity powers, permit an effective gradual adjustment to be brought about from existing segregated systems to a system not based on color distinctions?

"5. On the assumption on which questions 4(a) and (b) are based, and assuming further that this Court will exercise its equity powers to the end described in question 4(b),

"(a) should this Court formulate detailed decrees in these cases;

"(b) if so, what specific issues should the decrees reach;

"(c) should this Court appoint a special master to hear evidence with a view to recommending specific terms for such decrees;

"(d) should this Court remand to the courts of first instance with directions to frame decrees in these cases, and if so what general directions should the decrees of this Court include and what procedures should the courts of first instance follow in arriving at the specific terms of more detailed decrees?"

While giving weight to these public and private considerations, the courts will require that the defendants make a prompt and reasonable start toward full compliance with our May 17, 1954, ruling. Once such a start has been made, the courts may find that additional time is necessary to carry out the ruling in an effective manner. The burden rests upon the defendants to establish that such time is necessary in the public interest and is consistent with good faith compliance at the earliest practicable date. To that end, the courts may consider problems related to administration, arising from the physical condition of the school plant, the school transportation system, personnel, revision of school districts and attendance areas into compact units to achieve a system of determining admission to the public schools on a nonracial basis, and revision of local laws and regulations which may be necessary in solving the foregoing problems. They will also consider the adequacy of any plans the defendants may propose to meet these problems and to effectuate a transition to a racially nondiscriminatory school system. During this period of transition, the courts will retain jurisdiction of these cases.

The judgments below * * * are accordingly reversed and the cases are remanded to the District Courts to take such proceedings and enter such orders and decrees consistent with this opinion as are necessary and proper to admit to public schools on a racially nondiscriminatory basis with all deliberate speed the parties to these cases.   * * *

It is so ordered.

———

1. Historically courts of equity frequently said that equitable relief would not be granted if the enforcement of the injunction would require extensive supervision by the court. Thus it is still common to refuse an injunction requiring the specific performance of a construction contract on the ground that supervision would be too complex.

2. In the second half of the twentieth century there has been a major departure from that principle in the area of the civil rights injunction. Beginning with the school desegregation cases, courts have frequently responded to the necessity of issuing and supervising a complex injunction despite the many hours of judicial time necessary for the task.

Professor Philip Kurland considered the effect of the *Brown II* decision in his article " '*Brown v. Board of Education* Was the Beginning'—The School Desegregation Cases in the United States Supreme Court: 1954–1979," 1979 Washington University Law Quarterly 309. He characterized the question in *Brown II* as whether the Court should act in its ordinary judicial mode or in a novel legislative mode to respond to the special problem. Rather than grant the plaintiff's request for an order immediately ending all school segregation by race, the Court accepted the defendants' premise that such a fundamental change could not be accomplished immediately. Therefore, the opinion emphasized the breadth of equity powers available to the district court judges as well as the wide range of issues that they could consider in effecting the social revolution required by the *Brown I* decision. The essence of *Brown II*, Professor Kurland argues, is that the federal courts were to substitute themselves for the local governing bodies with regard to the management of schools. As a result, every one of the Court's list of relevant factors, such as transportation and redistricting, led to lengthy and complex litigation. *Brown II* was thus the first case to make the federal courts the "overseers" of local government, which today is not regarded as unusual.

PROBLEM: THE MERGED CITIES

Plaintiffs are minority city residents who have proven that the city of Metroside discriminated against the minority community in the allocation of city services. The trial judge has found this discrimination to be a denial of equal protection under the state and federal Constitutions. The dilemma facing the judge is how to fashion an order to remedy this unconstitutional condition.

The present city of Metroside developed from the merger of two smaller cities. A dozen years ago the two cities voted to merge into one larger city. It was provided in the proposition accepted by the voters that the city services for each of the old cities would remain separate with no centralized control for a period of ten years. This provision was politically necessary to avoid the opposition of the separate city workers. The proposition further provided that after ten years a commission appointed by the mayor of the new city would determine whether to merge the two city-services departments or to leave them separate.

The two old cities originally developed side by side when a railroad was built through the area in the 19th century. By the time of the merger one of the old cities, Riverside, was dominated by one major factory employer. Most of the workers at this shoe factory, both blue collar and white collar workers, lived in Riverside. The other city, Arborside, contained office buildings and some light industry. The residents of Arborside were generally wealthier than those of Riverside, but Riverside had the advantage of the shoe factory in its tax base.

A few years after the merger, however, the shoe factory closed. This unforeseen development dramatically changed the character of Riverside. The white collar workers moved elsewhere to new jobs. There were fewer opportunities for the blue collar workers, and unemployment rose in Riverside. At the end of the ten year period Riverside's population declined, and the percentage of minority residents was much larger than it had been before. Arborside, on the other hand, prospered. New high-technology industries were attracted there and the population grew with affluent, and predominately non-minority, residents.

The city services budget of Riverside at the time of the merger was a small one but the Arborside budget was fairly large. Riverside had no separate Park District; the city parks were simply included in the general public maintenance division. Arborside, in contrast, had a separate Park District with extensive recreational programs for residents of all ages. Similarly, the library in Arborside had always had a large budget with funds for various programs; the Riverside library was poorer. During the ten years after the merger, the Metroside government increased the budget of the Arborside city services in response to the growth in its population. The Riverside budget was not increased and did not even keep up with the high inflation present in the economy at the time. Accordingly, the differences in city services between the two communities grew more disparate. When the Mayor appointed a commission at the end of the ten years to determine whether to merge the city services, the vote was no. The trial judge found that the commission had discriminated racially in this decision, following the city's pattern of racial discrimination in the budget allocation of city services in recent years.

The problem is how to fashion a remedy for this violation. There is no simple way to achieve equality by ordering an increase in the Riverside budget, even if the judge has the power to make such an order to a city government. Only unification of the city services could result in equality, and then only if done in a way to provide all residents with all services. How can the court order the city to achieve this goal without having the judge virtually become the administrator of the city services? Consider the cases that follow.

HUTTO v. FINNEY

437 U.S. 678, 98 S.Ct. 2565, 57 L.Ed.2d 522 (1978).

Mr. Justice Stevens delivered the opinion of the Court.

After finding that conditions in the Arkansas penal system constituted cruel and unusual punishment, the District Court entered a series of detailed remedial orders. On appeal to the United States Court of Appeals for the Eighth Circuit, petitioners [Commissioner of Correction and members of the Arkansas Board of Correction] challenged * * * an order placing a maximum limit of 30 days on confinement in punitive isolation. * * *

This litigation began in 1969; it is a sequel to two earlier cases holding that conditions in the Arkansas prison system violated the Eighth and Fourteenth Amendments. Only a brief summary of the facts is necessary to explain the basis for the remedial orders.

The routine conditions that the ordinary Arkansas convict had to endure were characterized by the District Court as "a dark and evil world completely alien to the free world." That characterization was amply supported by the evidence.[3] The punishments for misconduct not serious enough to result in punitive isolation were cruel,[4] unusual,[5] and unpredictable.[6] It is the discipline known as "punitive isolation" that is most relevant for present purposes.

Confinement in punitive isolation was for an indeterminate period of time. An average of 4, and sometimes as many as 10 or 11, prisoners were crowded into windowless 8′ × 10′ cells containing no furniture other than a source of water and a toilet that could only be flushed from outside the cell. At night the prisoners were given mattresses to spread on the floor. Although some prisoners suffered from infectious diseases such as hepatitis and venereal disease, mattresses were removed and jumbled together each morning, then returned to the cells at random in the evening. Prisoners in isolation received fewer than 1,000 calories a day;[7] their meals consisted primarily of 4–inch squares of "grue," a substance created by mashing meat, potatoes, oleo, syrup, vegetables, eggs, and seasoning into a paste and baking the mixture in a pan.

3. The administrators of Arkansas' prison system evidently tried to operate their prisons at a profit. *See* Talley v. Stephens, *supra*, at 688. Cummins Farm, the institution at the center of this litigation, required its 1,000 inmates to work in the fields 10 hours a day, six days a week, using mule-drawn tools and tending crops by hand. 247 F.Supp., at 688. The inmates were sometimes required to run to and from the field, with a guard in an automobile or on horseback driving them on. Holt v. Hutto, 363 F.Supp. 194, 213 (ED Ark.1973) (Holt III). They worked in all sorts of weather, so long as the temperature was above freezing, sometimes in unsuitably light clothing or without shoes. Holt II, 309 F.Supp., at 370.

The inmates slept together in large, 100–man barracks, and some convicts, known as "creepers," would slip from their beds to crawl along the floor, stalking their sleeping enemies. In one 18–month period, there were 17 stabbings, all but 1 occurring in the barracks. *Holt I, supra,* at 830–831. Homosexual rape was so common and uncontrolled that some potential victims dared not sleep; instead they would leave their beds and spend the night clinging to the bars nearest the guards' station. *Holt II, supra,* at 377.

4. Inmates were lashed with a wooden-handled leather strap five feet long and four inches wide. *Talley v. Stephens, supra,* at 687. Although it was not official policy to do so, some inmates were apparently whipped for minor offenses until their skin was bloody and bruised. *Jackson v. Bishop, supra,* at 810–811.

5. The "Tucker telephone," a hand-cranked device, was used to administer electrical shocks to various sensitive parts of an inmate's body. *Jackson v. Bishop, supra,* at 812.

6. Most of the guards were simply inmates who had been issued guns. *Holt II, supra,* at 373. Although it had 1,000 prisoners, Cummins employed only eight guards who were not themselves convicts. Only two nonconvict guards kept watch over the 1,000 men at night. 309 F.Supp., at 373. While the "trusties" maintained an appearance of order, they took a high toll from the other prisoners. Inmates could obtain access to medical treatment only if they bribed the trusty in charge of sick call. As the District Court found, it was "within the power of a trusty guard to murder another inmate with practical impunity," because trusties with weapons were authorized to use deadly force against escapees. *Id.,* at 374. "Accidental shootings" also occurred; and one trusty fired his shotgun into a crowded barracks because the inmates would not turn off their TV. *Ibid.* Another trusty beat an inmate so badly the victim required partial dentures. *Talley v. Stephens, supra,* at 689.

7. A daily allowance of 2,700 calories is recommended for the average male between 23 and 50. National Academy of Sciences, Recommended Dietary Allowances, Appendix (8th rev. ed. 1974). Prisoners in punitive isolation are less active than the average person; but a mature man who spends 12 hours a day lying down and 12 hours a day simply sitting or standing consumes approximately 2,000 calories a day.

After finding the conditions of confinement unconstitutional, the District Court did not immediately impose a detailed remedy of its own. Instead, it directed the Department of Correction to "make a substantial start" on improving conditions and to file reports on its progress. When the Department's progress proved unsatisfactory, a second hearing was held. The District Court found some improvements, but concluded that prison conditions remained unconstitutional. Again the court offered prison administrators an opportunity to devise a plan of their own for remedying the constitutional violations, but this time the court issued guidelines, identifying four areas of change that would cure the worst evils: improving conditions in the isolation cells, increasing inmate safety, eliminating the barracks sleeping arrangements, and putting an end to the trusty system. The Department was ordered to move as rapidly as funds became available.

After this order was affirmed on appeal, more hearings were held in 1972 and 1973 to review the Department's progress. Finding substantial improvements, the District Court concluded that continuing supervision was no longer necessary. The court held, however, that its prior decrees would remain in effect and noted that sanctions, as well as an award of costs and attorney's fees, would be imposed if violations occurred.

The Court of Appeals reversed the District Court's decision to withdraw its supervisory jurisdiction, and the District Court held a fourth set of hearings. It found that, in some respects, conditions had seriously deteriorated since 1973, when the court had withdrawn its supervisory jurisdiction. Cummins Farm, which the court had condemned as overcrowded in 1970 because it housed 1,000 inmates, now had a population of about 1,500. The situation in the punitive isolation cells was particularly disturbing. The court concluded that either it had misjudged conditions in these cells in 1973 or conditions had become much worse since then. There were twice as many prisoners as beds in some cells. And because inmates in punitive isolation are often violently antisocial, overcrowding led to persecution of the weaker prisoners. The "grue" diet was still in use, and practically all inmates were losing weight on it. The cells had been vandalized to a "very substantial" extent. Because of their inadequate numbers, guards assigned to the punitive isolation cells frequently resorted to physical violence, using nightsticks and Mace in their efforts to maintain order. Prisoners were sometimes left in isolation for months, their release depending on "their attitudes as appraised by prison personnel."

The court concluded that the constitutional violations identified earlier had not been cured. It entered an order that placed limits on the number of men that could be confined in one cell, required that each have a bunk, discontinued the "grue" diet, and set 30 days as the maximum isolation sentence. * * *

* * * Confinement in a prison or in an isolation cell is a form of punishment subject to scrutiny under Eighth Amendment standards.

Petitioners do not challenge * * * the District Court's original conclusion that conditions in Arkansas' prisons, including its punitive isolation cells, constituted cruel and unusual punishment. Rather, petitioners single out that portion of the District Court's most recent order that forbids the Department to sentence inmates to more than 30 days in punitive isolation. Petitioners assume that the District Court held that indeterminate sentences to punitive isolation always constitute cruel and unusual punishment. This assumption misreads the District Court's holding.

Read in its entirety, the District Court's opinion makes it abundantly clear that the length of isolation sentences was not considered in a vacuum. * * * If new conditions of [solitary] confinement are not materially different from those affecting other prisoners, a transfer for the duration of a prisoner's sentence might be completely unobjectionable and well within the authority of the prison administration. [Citation.] It is equally plain, however, that the length of confinement cannot be ignored in deciding whether the confinement meets constitutional standards. A filthy, overcrowded cell with a diet of "grue" might be tolerable for a few days and intolerably cruel for weeks or months.

The question before the trial court was whether past constitutional violations had been remedied. The court was entitled to consider the severity of those violations in assessing the constitutionality of conditions in the isolation cells. The court took note of the inmates' diet, the continued overcrowding, the rampant violence, the vandalized cells, and the "lack of professionalism and good judgment on the part of maximum security personnel." The length of time each inmate spent in isolation was simply one consideration among many. We find no error in the court's conclusion that, taken as a whole, conditions in the isolation cells continued to violate the prohibition against cruel and unusual punishment.

In fashioning a remedy, the District Court had ample authority to go beyond earlier orders and to address each element contributing to the violation. The District Court had given the Department repeated opportunities to remedy the cruel and unusual conditions in the isolation cells. If petitioners had fully complied with the court's earlier order, the present time limit might well have been unnecessary. But taking the long and unhappy history of the litigation into account, the court was justified in entering a comprehensive order to insure against the risk of inadequate compliance.[9]

---

9. As we explained in Milliken v. Bradley, 433 U.S. 267, 281, state and local authorities have primary responsibility for curing constitutional violations. "If, however, '[those] authorities fail in their affirmative obligations ... judicial authority may be invoked.' Swann [v. Charlotte–Mecklenburg Board of Education, 402 U.S. 1,] 15. Once invoked, 'the scope of a district court's equitable powers to remedy past wrongs is broad, for breadth and flexibility are inherent in equitable remedies.' " *Ibid.* In this case, the District Court was not remedying the present effects of a violation in the past. It was seeking to bring an ongoing violation to an immediate halt. Cooperation on the part of Department officials and compliance with other aspects of their decree may justify elimination of this added safeguard in the future, but it is

The order is supported by the interdependence of the conditions producing the violation. * * * [W]e find no error in the inclusion of a 30–day limitation on sentences to punitive isolation as part of the District Court's comprehensive remedy.

* * * [Affirmed.]

MR. JUSTICE REHNQUIST, dissenting.

The Court's affirmance of a District Court's injunction against a prison practice which has not been shown to violate the Constitution can only be considered an aberration in light of decisions as recently as last Term carefully defining the remedial discretion of the federal courts. Dayton Board of Education v. Brinkman, 433 U.S. 406 (1977); Milliken v. Bradley, 433 U.S. 267 (1977) (*Milliken II*). * * * Accordingly, I dissent.

No person of ordinary feeling could fail to be moved by the Court's recitation of the conditions formerly prevailing in the Arkansas prison system. Yet I fear that the Court has allowed itself to be moved beyond the well-established bounds limiting the exercise of remedial authority by the federal district courts. The purpose and extent of that discretion in another context were carefully defined by the Court's opinion last Term in *Milliken II, supra,* at 280–281:

"In the first place, like other equitable remedies, the nature of the desegregation remedy is to be determined by the nature and scope of the constitutional violation. Swann v. Charlotte–Mecklenburg Board of Education, 402 U.S. [1,] 16 [(1971)]. The remedy must therefore be related to 'the *condition* alleged to offend the Constitution. . . .' Milliken [v. Bradley], 418 U.S. [717,] 738 [(1974)]. Second, the decree must indeed be *remedial* in nature, that is, it must be designed as nearly as possible 'to restore the victims of discriminatory conduct to the position they would have occupied in the absence of such conduct.' *Id.,* at 746. Third, the federal courts in devising a remedy must take into account the interests of states and local authorities in managing their own affairs, consistent with the Constitution." (Footnotes omitted.) [1]

entirely appropriate for the District Court to postpone any such determination until the Department's progress can be evaluated.

1. The Court suggests ante, at 687 n.9, that its holding is consistent with *Milliken II,* because it "was not remedying the present effects of a violation in the past. It was seeking to bring an ongoing violation to an immediate halt." This suggestion is wide of the mark. Whether exercising its authority to "remedy the present effects of a violation in the past," or "seeking to bring an ongoing violation to an immediate halt," the court's remedial authority remains circumscribed by the language quoted in the text from *Milliken II.* If anything, less ingenuity and discretion would appear to be required to "bring an ongoing violation to an immediate halt" than in "remedying the present effects of a violation in the past." The difficulty with the Court's position is that it quite properly refrains from characterizing solitary confinement for a period in excess of 30 days as a cruel and unusual punishment; but given this position, a "remedial" order that no such solitary confinement may take place is necessarily of a prophylactic nature, and not essential to "bring an ongoing violation to an immediate halt."

The District Court's order limiting the maximum period of punitive isolation to 30 days in no way relates to any condition found offensive to the Constitution. It is, when stripped of descriptive verbiage, a prophylactic rule, doubtless well designed to assure a more humane prison system in Arkansas, but not complying with the limitations set forth in *Milliken II, supra.* * * *

––––––

1. The litigation concerning the prison in this 1978 Supreme Court opinion began with a 1965 district court opinion. Many times the court continued the cases that arose from the conditions there. The judge who heard the first case was Judge Henley. He became quite an expert on the litigation that stretched over a period of many years. Even when he was appointed to the Court of Appeals, he was specially designated to continue to hear this case as a district judge because of his familiarity with its extensive history.

2. What determines which rights are sufficiently important to consume such an enormous amount of judicial energy and societal expense? Would one solution be to consider the remedy at law adequate and to give the wrongfully treated prisoners damages? Would a damages approach be likely to change conditions in the future or not?

3. Professor Owen Fiss offers some provocative thoughts on the subordination of equity to law in general. Read the following excerpts from Fiss, *The Civil Rights Injunction* 38–45 (1978) *, and consider his discussion in the context of cases such as *Brown II* and *Holt*, as well as the *Thurston v. Baldi* decision *supra* in Chapter 3:

> I begin with the legacy of the property injunction—the view that in our legal system the relationship among remedies is hierarchical and that in this hierarchy the injunction is disfavored, ranked low. This hierarchical relationship and the subordination of the injunction is, we recall, primarily the handiwork of the irreparable injury requirement. That requirement makes the issuance of an injunction conditional upon a showing that the plaintiff has no alternative remedy that will adequately repair his injury. * * *

> * * * I am concerned with the unmistakable general effect of the doctrine: it creates a remedial hierarchy and relegates the injunction to a subordinate place in that hierarchy. The inadequacy of alternative remedies must be demonstrated before the injunction can be utilized, but there is no reciprocal requirement on those alternative remedies. The plaintiff in a damage action or a criminal prosecution, for example, need not establish the inadequacy of the injunction before those remedies come available.

> This hierarchical relationship among remedies is not exclusively the product of the irreparable injury requirement. It derives from

––––––
* Reprinted with permission by the Indiana University Press.

several other doctrines as well, although they are of less general scope. One is the prior restraint doctrine, applicable to injunctions against speech. This doctrine does not altogether preclude the issuance of an injunction aimed at speech, but rather places a burden on such injunctions that is not placed on other legal instruments aimed at speech, such as damage judgments, criminal convictions, liability rules, or criminal prohibitions. * * *

Finally, there is the doctrine that transformed the usual province of the classical injunction—the property injunction—into an exclusive domain: equity will intervene only to protect property rights. The injunctive plaintiff is put to the task of convincing the court that the interest he wishes to protect is a property interest; that hurdle is not encountered in the request for other remedies[.] * * * [This historical rule] is so devoid of justification—indeed I cannot think of a single argument in support of it—that we may treat is as having already been repudiated. No one takes it seriously. The only point worth noting is that the repudiation was so long in coming[.] * * *

The other subordinating doctrines are of continuing vitality. This is obviously true of the prior restraint doctrine, which seems to be invoked with increasing frequency, * * * and the more generalized irreparable injury requirement [is] alive and well. They continue to be invoked and affirmed. * * *

The subordinating doctrines can be traced back to English Chancery practice, and thus it is not surprising that they were primarily addressed to the traditional form of the injunction, the preventive one. Some of the doctrines, such as prior restraint, are confined to those injunctions. Other of the subordinating doctrines, however, have not been so confined, but have been applied to the newer types of injunctions, those linked to the more recent civil rights experience. The irreparable injury requirement has, for example, been applied to the structural injunction in *O'Shea v. Littleton* [414 U.S. 488 (1974).] The plaintiffs there sought, in part, an injunction against the state judges prohibiting them from determining bail on a mass basis and from discriminating on the basis of race in sentencing; they were in effect seeking a reorganization of the criminal justice system in Cairo, Illinois. The Supreme Court denied relief and rationalized this result in terms of the irreparable injury requirement. The plaintiffs had not established the requisite irreparable injury, the Court complained; they had not demonstrated the inadequacy of a host of alternative remedies—damage actions, criminal prosecutions, change of venue, removal proceedings, appellate review, habeas corpus. * * *

* * * [S]ome might point to history to explain the remedial hierarchy and the place of the injunction in it. They might remind us of the fact that the injunction evolved as a legal instrument belonging to a system of justice—administered by the Chancellor—

that was intended to be a supplementary system, to provide relief when the common law system failed. * * * [E]ven if the familiar historical account is complete as an *explanation,* it must fail my purpose—to inquire into the *justification* of the remedial hierarchy. I am asking normative questions—whether it is *correct* to conceive of remedies in a hierarchical fashion and to assign the injunction a subordinate position in that hierarchy.

Chapter 9

SPECIAL ISSUES IN EQUITY
A. STATUTORY LIMITATIONS ON DISCRETION

Section Coverage:

A statute may affect equitable discretion in several ways: (1) by enumerating some remedies but not others, leaving a question of interpretation whether additional remedies may be implied; or (2) by prohibiting courts from issuing injunctions in a narrowly defined type of dispute; or (3) by requiring a court to enjoin certain types of conduct upon a showing that the statutory elements are met. The materials in Chapter 2 explored the first two of these restraints; this section focuses on the third—statutes mandating injunctions.

A statute may mandate explicitly that a court issue an injunction upon the plaintiff's showing that the defendant's conduct has contravened the statutory prohibitions. Because such statutes dramatically alter equitable remedies by removing the judge's discretion in awarding them, courts do not readily impute a legislative intent to do so. If the statute is clear that the legislature has already balanced the equities in favor of injunctive relief, however, the court will enjoin conduct upon a demonstration of statutory conditions. The court's traditional equitable discretion in determining entitlement to injunctive relief is withdrawn by the legislative action. The court nevertheless retains its discretion in fashioning the injunction to implement the intent of the legislature and to accommodate the respective interests of the parties.

Model Case:

Congress enacts a statute that creates a new federal right for private sector employees in service or industry affecting interstate commerce. That new right in this hypothetical act is to receive upon termination a "service letter" indicating the length and nature of employment and the reason for severance. The Secretary of Labor is empowered to make regulations concerning the form of the letter, its contents, and similar matters. The Secretary is further empowered to investigate complaints and to make findings of noncompliance when an employer demonstrates a pattern or practice of violating the act.

This hypothetical new act further provides that whenever the Secretary makes a finding of "wilful noncompliance" by an employer, the Secretary will bring an action in federal district court to compel compliance. The act specifies that in such an action the court "will enter an injunction" requiring the employer to comply with the act once the Secretary establishes the fact of "noncompliance."

In a suit brought by the Secretary under this act, the federal district court has a problem of interpretation. Although the Secretary found the defendant employer to be willfully in noncompliance, the judge found the noncompliance not willful. The judge, unlike the Secretary, found credible the employer's excuses and believed that there would be compliance in the future without an injunction to require it. Ordinarily the judge would not grant an order under such findings, but the statute appears to mandate an injunction.

Congress may not have contemplated that if the judge confirmed the Secretary's finding of noncompliance the two could disagree on willfulness. The act requires only the Secretary to find noncompliance willful. Was this an oversight, or did Congress mean that it had already weighed the equities in such a situation and the injunction is mandatory?

Courts do not interpret statutes to remove the judge's traditional equitable discretion unless the intent of Congress to do so is clear. The problem under this new hypothetical act would be to determine the Congressional intent. The court would consult legislative history, other portions of the act, and opinions interpreting similar wording in other acts.

TENNESSEE VALLEY AUTHORITY v. HILL

437 U.S. 153, 98 S.Ct. 2279, 57 L.Ed.2d 117 (1978).

MR. CHIEF JUSTICE BURGER delivered the opinion of the Court.

The questions presented in this case are (a) whether the Endangered Species Act of 1973 requires a court to enjoin the operation of a virtually completed federal dam—which had been authorized prior to 1973—when, pursuant to authority vested in him by Congress, the Secretary of the Interior has determined that operation of the dam would eradicate an endangered species. * * *

* * * [T]he Tennessee Valley Authority, a wholly owned public corporation of the United States, began constructing the Tellico Dam and Reservoir Project in 1967, shortly after Congress appropriated initial funds for its development. Tellico is a multipurpose regional development project designed principally to stimulate shoreline development, generate sufficient electric current to heat 20,000 homes, and provide flatwater recreation and flood control, as well as improve economic conditions in "an area characterized by underutilization of human resources and outmigration of young people." [Citation.] Of particular relevance to this case is one aspect of the project, a dam which TVA determined to place on the Little Tennessee, a short distance from where the river's waters meet with the Big Tennessee. When fully operational, the dam would impound water covering some 16,500 acres—much of which represents valuable and productive farmland—thereby converting the river's shallow, fast-flowing waters into a deep reservoir over 30 miles in length.

The Tellico Dam has never opened, however, despite the fact that construction has been virtually completed and the dam is essentially ready for operation. Although Congress has appropriated monies for Tellico every year since 1967, progress was delayed, and ultimately stopped, by a tangle of lawsuits and administrative proceedings. * * *

* * * [A] discovery was made in the waters of the Little Tennessee which would profoundly affect the Tellico Project. Exploring the area around Coytee Springs, which is about seven miles from the mouth of the river, a University of Tennessee ichthyologist, Dr. David A. Etnier, found a previously unknown species of perch, the snail darter, or *Percina (Imostoma) tanasi*. This three-inch, tannish-colored fish, whose numbers are estimated to be in the range of 10,000 to 15,000, would soon engage the attention of environmentalists, the TVA, the Department of the Interior, the Congress of the United States, and ultimately the federal courts, as a new and additional basis to halt construction of the dam.

Until recently the finding of a new species of animal life would hardly generate a cause célèbre. This is particularly so in the case of darters, of which there are approximately 130 known species, 8 to 10 of these having been identified only in the last five years. The moving force behind the snail darter's sudden fame came some four months after its discovery, when the Congress passed the Endangered Species Act of 1973 (Act), 87 Stat. 884, 16 U.S.C. § 1531 *et seq.* (1976 ed.). This legislation, among other things, authorizes the Secretary of the Interior to declare species of animal life "endangered" and to identify the "critical habitat" of these creatures. * * *

* * * After receiving comments from various interested parties, including TVA and the State of Tennessee, the Secretary formally listed the snail darter as an endangered species on October 8, 1975. 40 Fed.Reg. 47505–47506; *see* 50 CFR § 17.11(i) (1976). In so acting, it was noted that "the snail darter is a living entity which is genetically distinct and reproductively isolated from other fishes." More important for the purposes of this case, the Secretary determined that the snail darter apparently lives only in that portion of the Little Tennessee River which would be completely inundated by the reservoir created as a consequence of the Tellico Dam's completion. * * *

In February 1976, pursuant to § 11(g) of the Endangered Species Act, 87 Stat. 900, 16 U.S.C. § 1540(g) (1976 ed.), respondents filed the case now under review, seeking to enjoin completion of the dam and impoundment of the reservoir on the ground that those actions would violate the Act by directly causing the extinction of the species *Percina (Imostoma) tanasi*. The District Court denied respondents' request for a preliminary injunction and set the matter for trial. * * *

Trial was held in the District Court on April 29 and 30, 1976, and on May 25, 1976, the court entered its memorandum opinion and order denying respondents their requested relief and dismissing the complaint. The District Court found that closure of the dam and the consequent impoundment of the reservoir would "result in the adverse modification, if not complete destruction, of the snail darter's critical habitat," making it "highly probable" that "the continued existence of the snail darter" would be "jeopardize[d]." Despite these findings, the District Court declined to embrace the plaintiffs' position on the merits: that once a federal project was shown to jeopardize an endangered species, a court of equity is compelled to issue an injunction restraining violation of the Endangered Species Act.

In reaching this result, the District Court stressed that the entire project was then about 80% complete and, based on available evidence, "there [were] no alternatives to impoundment of the reservoir, short of scrapping the entire project." The District Court also found that if the Tellico Project was permanently enjoined, "some $53 million would be lost in nonrecoverable obligations," meaning that a large portion of the $78 million already expended would be wasted. The court also noted that the Endangered Species Act of 1973 was passed some seven years after construction on the dam commenced and that Congress had continued appropriations for Tellico, with full awareness of the snail darter problem. Assessing these various factors, the District Court concluded:

> "At some point in time a federal project becomes so near completion and so incapable of modification that a court of equity should not apply a statute enacted long after inception of the project to produce an unreasonable result.... Where there has been an irreversible and irretrievable commitment of resources by Congress to a project over a span of almost a decade, the Court should proceed with a great deal of circumspection." * * *

Thereafter, in the Court of Appeals, respondents argued that the District Court had abused its discretion by not issuing an injunction in the face of "a blatant statutory violation." The Court of Appeals agreed, and on January 31, 1977, it reversed, remanding "with instructions that a permanent injunction issue halting all activities incident to the Tellico Project which may destroy or modify the critical habitat of the snail darter." The Court of Appeals directed that the injunction "remain in effect until Congress, by appropriate legislation, exempts Tellico from compliance with the Act or the snail darter has been deleted from the list of endangered species or its critical habitat materially redefined."

* * *

We granted certiorari, 434 U.S. 954 (1977), to review the judgment of the Court of Appeals.

* * * [T]wo questions are presented: (a) would TVA be in violation of the Act if it completed and operated the Tellico Dam as planned? (b) if TVA's actions would offend the Act, is an injunction the appropriate remedy for the violation? For the reasons stated hereinafter, we hold that both questions must be answered in the affirmative.

It may seem curious to some that the survival of a relatively small number of three-inch fish among all the countless millions of species extant would require the permanent halting of a virtually completed dam for which Congress has expended more than $100 million. The paradox is not minimized by the fact that Congress continued to appropriate large sums of public money for the project, even after congressional Appropriations Committees were apprised of its apparent impact upon the survival of the snail darter. We conclude, however, that the explicit provisions of the Endangered Species Act require precisely that result.

One would be hard pressed to find a statutory provision whose terms were any plainer than those in § 7 of the Endangered Species Act. Its very words affirmatively command all federal agencies "to *insure* that actions *authorized, funded,* or *carried out* by them do not *jeopardize* the continued existence" of an endangered species or "*result* in the destruction or modification of habitat of such species...." 16 U.S.C. § 1536 (1976 ed.). (Emphasis added.) This language admits of no exception. * * *

Concededly, this view of the Act will produce results requiring the sacrifice of the anticipated benefits of the project and of many millions of dollars in public funds. But examination of the language, history, and structure of the legislation under review here indicates beyond doubt that Congress intended endangered species to be afforded the highest of priorities.

* * * [T]he totality of congressional action makes it abundantly clear that the result we reach today is wholly in accord with both the words of the statute and the intent of Congress. The plain intent of Congress in enacting this statute was to halt and reverse the trend toward species extinction, whatever the cost. This is reflected not only in the stated policies of the Act, but in literally every section of the statute. * * *

It is not for us to speculate, much less act, on whether Congress would have altered its stance had the specific events of this case been anticipated. In any event, we discern no hint in the deliberations of Congress relating to the 1973 Act that would compel a different result than we reach here.

* * *

One might dispute the applicability of these examples to the Tellico Dam by saying that in this case the burden on the public through the loss of millions of unrecoverable dollars would greatly outweigh the loss of the snail darter. But neither the Endangered Species Act nor Art. III of the Constitution provides federal courts with authority to make such fine utilitarian calculations. On the contrary, the plain language of the Act, buttressed by its legislative history, shows clearly that Congress viewed the value of endangered species as "incalculable." Quite obviously, it would be difficult for a court to balance the loss of a sum certain—even $100 million—against a congressionally declared "incalculable" value, even assuming we had the power to engage in such a weighing process, which we emphatically do not.

* * *

Having determined that there is an irreconcilable conflict between operation of the Tellico Dam and the explicit provisions of § 7 of the Endangered Species Act, we must now consider what remedy, if any, is appropriate. It is correct, of course, that a federal judge sitting as a chancellor is not mechanically obligated to grant an injunction for every violation of law. This Court made plain in Hecht Co. v. Bowles, 321 U.S. 321, 329 (1944), that "[a] grant of *jurisdiction* to issue compliance orders hardly suggests an absolute duty to do so under any and all circumstances." As a general matter it may be said that "[s]ince all or almost all equitable remedies are discretionary, the balancing of equities and hardships is appropriate in almost any case as a guide to the chancellor's discretion." [Citation.] Thus, in Hecht Co. the Court refused to grant an injunction when it appeared from the District Court findings that "the issuance of an injunction would have 'no effect by way of insuring better compliance in the future' and would [have been] 'unjust' to [the] petitioner and not 'in the public interest.' "

But these principles take a court only so far. Our system of government is, after all, a tripartite one, with each branch having certain defined functions delegated to it by the Constitution. While "[i]t is emphatically the province and duty of the judicial department to say what the law is," Marbury v. Madison, 1 Cranch 137, 177 (1803), it is equally—and emphatically—the exclusive province of the Congress not only to formulate legislative policies and mandate programs and projects, but also to establish their relative priority for the Nation. Once Congress, exercising its delegated powers, has decided the order of priorities in a given area, it is for the Executive to administer the laws and for the courts to enforce them when enforcement is sought.

Here we are urged to view the Endangered Species Act "reasonably," and hence shape a remedy "that accords with some modicum of common sense and the public weal." [Citation.] But is that our function? We have no expert knowledge on the subject of endangered species, much less do we have a mandate from the people to strike a balance of equities on the side of the Tellico Dam. Congress has spoken in the plainest of words, making it abundantly clear that the balance has been struck in favor of affording endangered species the highest of priorities, thereby adopting a policy which it described as "institutionalized caution."

Our individual appraisal of the wisdom or unwisdom of a particular course consciously selected by the Congress is to be put aside in the process of interpreting a statute. Once the meaning of an enactment is discerned and its constitutionality determined, the judicial process comes to an end. We do not sit as a committee of review, nor are we vested with the power of veto. The lines ascribed to Sir Thomas Moore by Robert Bolt are not without relevance here:

"The law, Roper, the law. I know what's legal, not what's right. And I'll stick to what's legal.... I'm *not* God. The currents and eddies of right and wrong, which you find such plain-sailing, I can't navigate, I'm no voyager. But in the thickets of the law, oh there I'm a forester.... What would you do? Cut a great road through the law to get after the Devil? ... And when the last law was down, and the Devil turned round on you—where would you hide, Roper, the laws all being flat? ... This country's planted thick with laws from coast to coast—Man's laws, not God's—and if you cut them down ... d'you really think you could stand upright in the winds that would blow them? ... Yes, I'd give the Devil benefit of law, for my own safety's sake." R. Bolt, A Man for All Seasons, Act I, p. 147 (Three Plays, Heinemann ed. 1967).

We agree with the Court of Appeals that in our constitutional system the commitment to the separation of powers is too fundamental for us to pre-empt congressional action by judicially decreeing what accords with "common sense and the public weal." Our Constitution vests such responsibilities in the political branches.

Affirmed.

———

1. Prior to *TVA v. Hill,* the Supreme Court had previously considered similar statutory wording in the Emergency Price Control Act of 1942. The Act concerned maximum price control of commodities and services during World War II. It provided:

Whenever in the judgment of the Administrator any person has engaged or is about to engage in any acts or practices which constitute a violation of any provision [of this Act] * * * he may make application to the appropriate court for an order enjoining such acts or practices * * * and upon a showing by the Administrator that such person has engaged or is about to engage in any such acts or practices a permanent or temporary injunction, restraining order, or other order shall be granted without bond.

The question before the Supreme Court in Hecht Co. v. Bowles, 321 U.S. 321, 64 S.Ct. 587, 88 L.Ed. 754 (1944), was whether the Administrator was automatically entitled to an injunction upon a showing of a violation, or whether the court had some discretion to grant or withhold relief. The case concerned the Hecht Company's violations found during a spot check. The regulations under the Act were complex and confusing to apply, and the good faith effort of the defendant to comply with the Act was not questioned. The violations were corrected immediately and voluntarily by the store and vigorous steps were taken to prevent further mistakes. The district court had concluded that an injunction against the store would be pointless and unjust, and dismissed the complaint. The Court of Appeals reversed because it construed the Act as requiring the issuance of the injunction as a matter of course once violations were found.

The Administrator argued to the Supreme Court that the language "shall be granted" is not permissive. The Court nonetheless found that there is room for discretion under the statute. The reference in the Act to the possibility of some type of "other order" suggests that a court may conclude that it is more appropriate to issue some type of order other than the type sought by the Administrator. Therefore an injunction was not mandatory simply because the Administrator asked for it.

Moreover, the Court found unlikely an intent by Congress to make a drastic departure from the traditions of equity practice by removing discretion in the issuance of an injunction. Justice Douglas' opinion for the Court observed: "The historic injunctive process was designed to deter, not to punish. The essence of equity jurisdiction has been the power of the Chancellor to do equity and to mould each decree to the necessities of the particular case. Flexibility rather than rigidity have distinguished it. * * * We do not believe that such a major departure from that long tradition as is here proposed should be lightly implied." The Court of Appeals was therefore reversed.

2. How did the Court handle *Hecht* in *TVA v. Hill?* Was *Hecht* distinguished or implicitly overruled?

3. Statutes affect remedies in many ways. They more typically limit remedies than mandate relief. Recall Orloff v. Los Angeles Turf Club, 30 Cal.2d 110, 180 P.2d 321 (1947), reprinted *supra* in Chapter 2, where the court considered a statute that provided only a small and specific damages remedy. Is it permissible for a court to grant equitable relief if the statute provides only for damages? When the statutory remedies are limited, a court must decide whether the legislature intended to foreclose other remedies or whether an additional remedy, such as an injunction, may be properly implied to carry out the purposes of the statute.

4. In contrast to the statutes that mandate injunctions, some statutes completely prohibit them in certain circumstances. For example, one such anti-injunction provision is Internal Revenue Code § 7421(a), which effectively prohibits injunctions against the Internal Revenue Service from collecting taxes. Another example is the Norris–LaGuardia Act, 29 U.S.C. § 104, reprinted in part *supra* in Chapter 2. This Act prevents federal courts from enjoining labor disputes by removing federal "jurisdiction" over such issues. Recall the problems with interpreting this prohibition in United States v. United Mine Workers of America, 330 U.S. 258, 67 S.Ct. 677, 91 L.Ed. 884 (1947), reprinted *supra* in Chapter 7.

PROBLEM: THE HOSPITAL DISCLOSING PATIENT RECORDS

Assume that Congress passed legislation designed to protect the privacy of medical records in all clinics and hospitals receiving federal funds. The Act provides that no records concerning the health of any individual can be released by such an institution without the express written consent of the patient. The Act further provides that such consent must be obtained for each specific request for release, such as for a scientific study, and that the patient's rights under the statute cannot be otherwise waived. For minors the consent of parent or guardian is needed.

Penalties for violation of the hypothetical Act include compensatory and punitive damages, plus attorneys' fees to prevailing plaintiffs. The Act gives jurisdiction in federal district court without regard to the amount in controversy. Moreover, the Act provides that if a hospital or clinic threatens to release information without the proper authorization from the patient, the federal district court "shall issue" an injunction prohibiting such disclosure until the Act has been complied with. The only exception to the Act is that proper local or national health authorities may seek information concerning "any communicable disease that seriously threatens the health and welfare of the surrounding community" without consent of the patients.

There is a controversy in one community with respect to health studies following a radiation leak from a nearby nuclear power plant last year. Local and national health officials wish to study the effects of the leak on babies who were *in utero* at the time of the leak. The local newspaper, which has followed all aspects of the leak incident closely, reported that these health authorities were going to obtain data from the local hospital. The article quoted a hospital official who said that although the hospital generally respects the privacy of its patients, it intends to continue full cooperation with the authorities on this matter of profound public importance.

Several parents who had babies born in the hospital during the time in question object to the threatened release of their babies' records. They have sued under the Act in federal district court to prohibit the hospital, a recipient of federal funds, from releasing the information without their consent. The complaint does not indicate the reason why the parents object; it simply invokes the language of the Act that an injunction "shall issue" to prevent unauthorized disclosure.

The question is whether the judge may use discretion in the issuance of an injunction in this case. Is it proper to balance the equities between the individuals' right of privacy and the public need? The communicable disease exception to the Act does not apply. Should the court nonetheless use traditional equitable principles to decide the case or is the order mandatory upon the plaintiffs' proof of threatened disclosure in violation of the Act? Should the court dismiss the complaint unless the plaintiffs reveal the reasons for their objections, at least *in camera?*

NORTHERN CHEYENNE TRIBE v. HODEL

851 F.2d 1152 (9th Cir.1988).

NOONAN, CIRCUIT JUDGE:

The Northern Cheyenne Tribe (the Tribe) appeals from an amended injunction against the Secretary of the Interior (Secretary). * * * We hold that the injunction should be modified further and remand for this purpose.

In the aftermath of the Battle of Little Bighorn, the Northern Cheyenne moved to Montana. Virtually no white men inhabited the country. The land lay along no migration routes "and remained physically isolated until the 1950's." Then the first paved highway across the reservation was laid. E. Adamson Hoebel, *The Cheyenne Indians of the Great Plains* (1978) 124–125. In this beautiful environment, the Northern Cheyenne "retained much of their identity" as the people of the Morning Star. The discovery of extensive coal deposits in the region produced a crisis for the Tribe.

In 1982 the Secretary decided to offer to lease 2.24 billion tons of federal coal in the Powder River region of Montana and Wyoming. The eight Montana tracts border the Tribe's reservation on the north, east and south. The Tribe occupies 445,000 acres. The population of the reservation is approximately 4,300, of whom 85% are Indian. The predominant use of the land is cattle grazing.

The Secretary's decision was based on a final Environmental Impact Statement (EIS) which, except for occasional peripheral references, did not mention any impact on the Tribe. On April 15, 1982 the Tribe brought this action to enjoin the Secretary from proceeding with the leases without complying with federal law in such a way as to avoid, minimize, or mitigate adverse impacts of the leases on the Tribe.

On April 28, 1982 the Secretary proceeded with sale of the leases. The bidders were notified of the Tribe's suit and went ahead nonetheless. * * *

On May 28, 1985 the district court granted the Tribe summary judgment and held that the decision to make the Montana leases violated the National Environmental Policy Act, 42 U.S.C. §§ 4321 *et seq.;* the Federal Coal Leasing Amendments Act of 1976, 30 U.S.C. § 201 *et seq.;* and the responsibilities of the United States as trustee of the Tribe. The court held all leases issued as a result of the sale void.

* * *

On October 6, 1986 the district court amended its injunction to suspend but not void the leases to Thermal and Wesco. The suspension was to last until the Secretary prepared a supplemental EIS "addressing the cultural, social and economic impact of issuing coal leases near the Northern Cheyenne Indian Reservation." The lessees were relieved of their obligations under the leases. Western Energy was permitted to go forward with mining on its leases, subject to the caveat that mining should immediately be halted if the Secretary found that it caused "significant socioeconomic impacts." The Secretary was directed at the completion of the supplemental EIS to decide whether or not to rescind all of the leases and whether to impose additional measures of mitigation if the leases stayed in force. The Tribe appeals from this amendment of the original injunction.

* * * The Tribe argues that under the principles enunciated in TVA v. Hill, 437 U.S. 153, 98 S.Ct. 2279, 57 L.Ed.2d 117 (1978), we should conclude that Congress has balanced the equities under the Federal Coal Leasing Amendments Act and thereby mandated that district courts issue an injunction upon finding that the government is in violation. The Tribe seeks to have this court extend the principles of *Hill* and conclude that Congress has not only mandated that an injunction issue whenever the Coal Leasing Act is violated, but also that Congress has mandated that the injunction void all activities, such as the leasing of federal land containing coal, undertaken in violation of the Act. The Secretary and the intervenors disagree and contend that Congress has not balanced the equities under the statute and that, therefore, the district retained its traditional equitable power to vindicate the objectives and requirements of the statute. Amoco Production Co. v. Village of Gambell, 480 U.S. 531, 107 S.Ct. 1396, 94 L.Ed.2d 542 (1987); Weinberger v. Romero–Barcelo, 456 U.S. 305, 102 S.Ct. 1798, 72 L.Ed.2d 91 (1982).

Hill, Romero–Barcelo, and *Village of Gambell* provide significant guidance in deciding whether Congress has balanced the equities under the statute and mandated an injunction. In *Hill,* the Court stated that generally courts retain discretion to fashion appropriate relief unless Congress has clearly demonstrated explicitly or implicitly that it has balanced the equities and mandated an injunction. In *Romero–Barcelo,* the plaintiff sued the Secretary of Defense and claimed that the Navy, while using an island off Puerto Rico's coast for weapons training, violated the Federal Water Pollution Control Act, 33 U.S.C. § 1251. The plaintiff argued that, as in *Hill,* Congress had balanced the equities under that act and, therefore, that the district court had to issue an injunction once it found the government in violation. The Court disagreed, stating that the "purpose and language of the statute under consideration in *Hill,* not the bare fact of a statutory violation, compelled" the conclusion that an injunction was mandatory in *Hill. Romero–Barcelo,* 456 U.S. at 314, 102 S.Ct. at 1804. In contrast, the Court pointed out that the statutory scheme now before it demonstrated that Congress did not intend to limit a court's remedy to an immediate prohibiting injunction upon finding a violation. The Court concluded that the district court retained the equitable discretion to grant or deny injunctive relief.

In *Village of Gambell,* the plaintiff argued that the defendant violated the Alaska National Interest Lands Conservation Act, 16 U.S.C.

§ 3120, when it sold oil and gas leases for federally owned lands on Alaska's continental shelf, and, that, therefore, it was automatically entitled to injunctive relief. The Court examined the statutory scheme and held that the act did not remove the district court's traditional equitable power in fashioning a remedy once a violation is established.

We accordingly focus "on the underlying substantive policy" that Congress designed the statute to effect. [Citation.] Nothing in the Act indicates that Congress intended to restrict the court's jurisdiction in equity. "The basic purpose" of the Act is "to provide a more orderly procedure for the leasing and development" of coal the United States owns, while ensuring its development "in a manner compatible with the public interest." [Citation.] Congress's underlying substantive policy concern was to develop the coal resources in an environmentally sound manner. This purpose lays as much stress on developing the coal resources as it does on the environmental effects of development. It is a purpose served without imposing an iron rule that an injunction will issue if the Act is violated. As Congress has not divested the district courts of their traditional equitable power, it logically follows that district courts have the discretion to deny or grant injunctive relief. [Citation.]

The Tribe argues that the district court abused its discretion in amending the injunction to suspend, rather than to void, the leases. The Tribe contends that merely suspending the leases leads to the danger of "bureaucratic commitment" to the leases. *See Massachusetts v. Watt*, 716 F.2d 946 (1st Cir.1983). The Tribe essentially contends that the danger of bureaucratic commitment presents a type of irreparable harm that warrants an injunction voiding, not merely suspending, the leases.

Bureaucratic rationalization and bureaucratic momentum are real dangers, to be anticipated and avoided by the Secretary. But the difference between voiding the leases and suspending them does not create any major difference in the process that must now go on. We see no reason to suppose that the Secretary will feel greater commitment to the original project if the leases are not voided but held in abeyance until a new evaluation is made, especially as the injunction will now specifically direct the Secretary not to consider prior investments by the lessees when he reconsiders the lease sale. The decision based on a legally insufficient EIS counts for nothing. We assume the Secretary will comply with the law. As the Tribe failed to demonstrate any significant difference between voiding and suspending the leases, the district court did not abuse its discretion in amending the injunction to provide for the suspension of the leases. *Cf.* Village of False Pass v. Clark, 733 F.2d 605, 614–616 (9th Cir.1984).

The Tribe also contends that the district court abused its discretion in failing to consider the public interest before amending the injunction to suspend rather than void the leases. The record reveals no such consideration. The Tribe's point is well-taken.

In deciding whether to issue an injunction in which public interest is affected, a district court must expressly consider the public interest on the record. [Citations.] The failure to do so constitutes an abuse of discretion. The district court should now rehear arguments and expressly consider the public interest in deciding whether to issue an injunction suspending rather than voiding the leases.

There are two other defects in the injunction. First, the district court did not order the Secretary to comply with his own regulations concerning the competitive leasing of federal coal rights. Under the Secretary's regulations on the competitive leasing of federal coal rights, coal deposits are to be "developed in consultation, cooperation, and coordination with ... Indian tribes...." 43 C.F.R. § 3420.0–2 (1987). Regional coal teams are to be "the forum through which initial leasing recommendations" are to be transmitted to the Secretary. The regional coal team in this case did not have input from the Tribe. A supplemental EIS will not cure this radical defect. The process was spoiled. It was an abuse of discretion not to order the Secretary to follow his own rules. Consequently, if the court decides to re-issue an injunction, the injunction must require the Secretary to follow his present own regulations and engage again in "activity planning" by which lease tracts are identified, ranked, analyzed, and selected. The Secretary must equally be ordered to analyze the "site-specific potential environmental impacts" of each tract.

Second, the injunction should have expressly prohibited the Secretary from considering the intervenors' financial interests completing the EIS. In analogous circumstances we have specifically directed the Secretary not to consider the investments made on the basis of a defective EIS. A fortiori the investments should not be considered here when the lessees made their bids with full awareness of the Tribe's suit and chose to gamble on the EIS being adequate. Consequently, if the court decides to re-issue an injunction, the injunction should direct the Secretary not to consider the fact that the leases have been made and to direct him not to consider the investments made by the lessees.

The Tribe also contends that it is entitled to a present injunction preventing the presently-permitted mining operations of Western Energy. Here the considerations are different because mining is going forward on the basis of a fundamentally flawed EIS. Even in these circumstances, however, we do not believe that the court is compelled to issue an injunction without a balancing of the equities. A court's decision not to enjoin may not threaten the very existence of what Congress intended to preserve. *See* TVA v. Hill, 437 U.S. 153, 98 S.Ct. 2279, 57 L.Ed.2d 117 (1978) (injunction necessary to preserve habitat of the snail darter). But unless a statute "in so many words, or by a necessary and inescapable inference" has limited a court's equitable discretion, an injunction does not issue automatically on a showing that an environmental impact statement is defective. Amoco v. Village of Gambell, 480 U.S. 531, 107 S.Ct. 1396, 1403, 94 L.Ed.2d 542 (1987). Nothing in the Federal Coal Leasing Amendments Act of 1976, as we earlier concluded, imposes such a restriction on judicial discretion. The same conclusion holds as to the more general National Environmental Policy Act, 42 U.S.C. § 4321 *et seq.* Its high aim "to create and maintain conditions under which man and nature can exist in productive harmony," 42 U.S.C. § 4331, does not show a congressional intent to foreclose equitable balancing by a court enforcing its requirements.

The district court, however, engaged in its balancing of the equities on an inadequate record and to that extent abused its discretion. We cannot tell from that record what the costs would be to the Tribe, the public, and Western Energy from any particular resolution of the issue. The district court should now promptly hold an evidentiary hearing to determine these costs and then decide whether or not an injunction is appropriate. If the district court should determine that the threatened harm to the environment, including the cultural, social and economic cost to the Tribe, would be irreparable and that the balance of equities favors the Tribe, all mining shall be stayed until the Secretary completes his new review.

REVERSED and REMANDED with instructions to amend the judgment consistently with this Opinion and to hold an evidentiary hearing.

FARBER, EQUITABLE DISCRETION, LEGAL DUTIES AND ENVIRONMENTAL INJUNCTIONS

45 U.Pitt.L.Rev. 513 (1984). *

* * *

The critical factors in determining the nature of a statutory injunction are its relationship to a defendant's underlying legal duty and the nature of that duty. Based on this analysis, injunctions can be divided into four groups.

1. *The Enforcement Injunction.* This category involves direct enforcement of an absolute legal duty. In these cases, the defendant is under a legal duty, but refuses to carry out actions that a law-abiding citizen would perform voluntarily. The purpose of the injunction is to force the defendant to do that which the defendant ought to have done without legal compulsion. *TVA v. Hill* is a clear example of this type of injunction. Since the purpose of the injunction is simply to put the defendant in the same position as the law-abiding citizen, balancing the equities is inappropriate. Asking a court to balance the virtues of obedience to the law against the benefits of violating the law is wholly inappropriate.

2. *The Compliance Injunction.* This category involves cases like *Weinberger* [*Weinberger v. Romero–Barcelo,* 456 U.S. 305, 102 S.Ct. 1798, 72 L.Ed.2d 91 (1982)], in which the defendant is in breach of a qualified duty. Once again, the purpose of the injunction is to force the defendant

to act as law-abiding citizens voluntarily do, but here the duty does not amount to immediate compliance. Congress did not intend that citizens shut plants as a routine method of meeting permit deadlines. For the same reason, Congress did not expect courts to make this a routine remedy. As before, the remedy tracks the underlying legal duty. In this category, however, there is more room for consideration of burden in defining the underlying duty itself.

3. *The Ancillary Injunction.* In the preceding two categories, the hypothetical defendant was in breach of a legal duty that was the basis of the injunction. Often, however, the defendant is in breach of a procedural duty. Obviously, the court can order the defendant to apply for a permit, issue an environmental impact statement or comply with some other procedure. The question is the extent to which a court should also enjoin the activity to which the procedure relates. For example, Congress requires agencies engaging in major federal actions with substantial environmental impacts to issue environmental impact statements. The relevant statute does not, however, expressly create a legal duty to refrain from implementing a project until the impact statement is prepared. But it would be futile for a court simply to issue an order to prepare an impact statement while allowing the underlying federal action to proceed. In *Weinberger,* the Navy was not under a direct duty to refrain from discharges while its permit application was pending. Nevertheless, if those discharges had been causing ecological harm, allowing the activity to continue until the permit proceeding had been completed would have undermined the function of the permit process.

Injunctions falling into this category, in which the underlying activity is enjoined because of the breach of a procedural duty, can be classified as ancillary injunctions. Ancillary injunctions can be found in many other contexts: for example, where an agency seeks injunctive relief pending the outcome of an administrative proceeding. Courts have discretion in this situation, but must carefully avoid undermining the integrity of the procedures mandated by Congress. Typically, the merits of the underlying dispute have been committed to another forum, but the injunctive proceeding requires at least some examination of the merits. Resolution of these cases depends upon the particular statutory scheme. In general, the court's task is (1) to avoid intrusion into the domain of the agency considering the merits, and (2) to preserve that agency's power to effectuate its later decision. At the same time, the court must protect the defendant from unnecessary injunctive relief.

4. The *Freestanding Injunction.* In each of the previous categories, the injunction was used as a means of enforcing, either directly or indirectly, an underlying statutory duty. Congress sometimes provides, however, for an injunctive proceeding without creating any separate statutory duties to be enforced in the proceeding, as in the emergency provision under the Clean Water Act. Three possible interpretations of such provisions are possible. First, Congress may simply intend that the provision create a federal forum in which state law will be applied.

Second, Congress's aim might be that federal courts create a body of federal common law governing these disputes. Third, such provisions may signify that Congress intends injunctive relief to be mandatory once statutory threshold requirements are met. Environmental emergency provisions arguably are intended to trigger creation of a federal common law, but they actually seem to come closer to the mandatory injunction category. The discretion a court has in issuing emergency injunctions relates more to fashioning the most effective form of relief than to balancing the public health against hardship to the defendant.

One of the reasons for the considerable confusion in the area of statutory injunctions seems to have been a failure to distinguish clearly between these various varieties of statutory injunction. While the typology given here certainly will not resolve all disputes about statutory injunctions, it may provide a clearer framework for settling these disputes.

* * *

B. ENJOINING SPEECH OR LITIGATION

Section Coverage:

Special problems arise when the object of an injunction is to inhibit free speech, to restrict access to civil courts, or to interfere with the function of the criminal law system. A judge should not lightly enjoin conduct involving any of these important aspects of a free society.

Such restraints are sometimes necessary. When freedom of speech is exercised in a way that seriously interferes with other important rights, a court may restrain it with a narrowly tailored order. Similarly, when a defendant greatly abuses the civil litigation system with harassing litigation, the judge may restrict access to the normal court process with a limited order.

Injunctions against criminal prosecutions are very rare. A state civil court will enjoin a threatened or existing criminal case in its jurisdiction only upon a strong showing of improper prosecutorial motivation. When the prosecution is in another state, only a showing of greatest urgency will support an injunction against it because the court has no practical means of enforcing an order against the out-of-state parties.

Federal court plaintiffs face further difficulties when they seek an injunction against a state prosecution. The Supreme Court has held that principles of "our Federalism" caution against the exercise of this power except in cases where the state officials' clearly improper motivation threatens fundamental freedoms. Otherwise plaintiffs must seek their remedies at law by defending themselves in the criminal cases.

Model Case:

A city ordinance provides that vendors, in order to sell food and beverages either at retail or wholesale, must obtain a license by paying a fee of $300. The ordinance further provides that violators would be subject to a fine of $50. Marty Mitchell sells popcorn from a moveable cart on the streets of the city without a license. Like other street vendors, Mitchell had sold on the street for years without a license on the assumption that the ordinance applied only to stores.

The city prosecuting attorney recently decided to interpret the ordinance to apply to the city's increasing number of street vendors. Marty Mitchell became the test case. Rather than pursue criminal penalties against Mitchell, however, the city instead sought an injunction to prohibit any future business transactions in violation of the ordinance. The case is pending, but the court is unlikely to grant the injunction because the city has an adequate remedy at law, namely criminal prosecution under the ordinance. Because the ordinance did not specifically provide for injunctive relief, the court would need either to imply the remedy from the ordinance or to rely upon common law nuisance. Even if the court finds such a source of injunctive power, however, it is unlikely to grant the relief. Not only is the legal remedy adequate, but equity will not ordinarily enjoin a crime without proof that the defendant's conduct is a public nuisance.

Mitchell is supported by a civil rights group that fears the city wants to reduce the number of vendors on the street because recently their numbers have swelled with immigrants from an ethnic minority. This group arranged legal representation for Mitchell by a young attorney named Alexis Rosch. Rosch's theory is that the city wants to discourage the vendors with a highly public case and that Mitchell, a non-minority and long-established vendor, was targeted to hide the city official's prejudiced motives. Rosch further theorizes that the official's purpose in seeking an injunction was twofold: If it is granted, the contempt penalties for continued violations by Mitchell on principle can be much larger than the fine provided by statute. If it is not granted, the case will get daily publicity for a while as the city then seeks a criminal prosecution.

Rosch therefore files a claim for Mitchell in federal district court seeking an injunction against the civil suit and against the threatened criminal prosecution. The court is unlikely to grant either request. The remedy at law is adequate for the civil suit; Mitchell cannot show that the court would act improperly in the matter. Mitchell also cannot show irreparable harm because the harm normally incident to prosecution is not sufficient. The threatened criminal prosecution does not seriously endanger important rights to allow a federal court to interfere with the state's process. Principles of federalism require abstention under these facts. The state court will be left to rectify any injustice that may occur if the city officials are indeed acting with wrongful motives.

WILLING v. MAZZOCONE

482 Pa. 377, 393 A.2d 1155 (1978).

MANDERINO, JUSTICE.

On Monday, September 29, and Wednesday, October 1, 1975, appellant, Helen Willing, demonstrated in the pedestrian plaza between building number two and building number three, Penn Center Plaza, downtown Philadelphia, Pennsylvania. The plaza is bounded by 15th and 16th Streets, Market Street, and John F. Kennedy Boulevard, and is a well traveled pedestrian pathway between the two court buildings located at City Hall and at Five Penn Center Plaza. While engaged in this activity, which lasted for several hours each day, appellant wore a "sandwich-board" sign around her neck. On the sign she had hand lettered the following:

LAW—FIRM

of

QUINN—MAZZOCONE

Stole money from me—and

Sold-me-out-to-the

INSURANCE COMPANY

As she marched back and forth, appellant also pushed a shopping cart on which she had placed an American flag. She continuously rang a cow bell and blew on a whistle to further attract attention.

Appellees in this case are two members of the legal profession, Carl M. Mazzocone and Charles F. Quinn, who are associated in the two member law firm of Mazzocone and Quinn, p.c. When appellant refused appellees' efforts to amicably dissuade her from further activity such as that described above, appellees filed a suit in equity in the Court of Common Pleas of Philadelphia County seeking to enjoin her from further demonstration. Three hearings were held at which the following factual history emerged.

In 1968, appellees, who have specialized in the trial of workmen's compensation matters for several years, represented appellant in such a case. Pursuant to appellees' representation, appellant was awarded permanent/partial disability benefits which she collected for a number of years. At the time of the initial settlement distribution with appellant, appellees deducted the sum of $150.00 as costs of the case. This sum, according to appellees' evidence, was paid in full to Robert DeSilverio, M.D., a treating psychiatrist who testified on appellant's behalf in the Workmen's Compensation matter. Appellees presented copies of their records covering the transaction with Dr. DeSilverio. A cancelled check for the amount of the payment, and the testimony of Dr. DeSilverio himself, confirmed appellees' account of the transaction. Appellant offered no evidence other than her testimony that the cause of her antagonism towards appellees was not any dissatisfaction with the settlement, but rather, her belief that appellees had wrongfully diverted to themselves $25.00 of the $150.00 that was supposed to have been paid to Dr. DeSilverio.

Based on this evidence, the equity court concluded that appellant was " ... a woman firmly on the thrall of the belief that [appellees] defrauded her, an *idee fixe* which, either by reason of eccentricity or an even more serious mental instability, refuses to be dislodged by the most convincing proof to the contrary." The Court then enjoined appellant from

> " ... further unlawful demonstration, picketing, carrying placards which contain defamatory and libelous statements and or uttering, publishing and declaring defamatory statements against the [appellees] herein."

On appeal, the Superior Court modified the trial court's order to read,

> "Helen R. Willing, be and is permanently enjoined from further demonstrating against and/or picketing Mazzocone and Quinn, Attorneys–at–Law, by uttering or publishing statements to the effect that Mazzocone and Quinn, Attorneys–at–Law stole money from her and sold her out to the insurance company." [Citation.]

We granted appellant's petition for allowance of appeal, and now reverse.

[The majority opinion reversed on the ground that the injunction was an unconstitutional prior restraint on rights of free speech under the Pennsylvania Constitution. The court also said that the indigency of the appellant was irrelevant to the consideration of whether the remedy at law was adequate. The following concurrence of Justice Roberts elaborates on the indigency consideration and considers the prior restraint question under federal constitutional law.]

ROBERTS, JUSTICE, concurring.

I agree with the opinion of Mr. Justice Manderino that appellant's indigency does not justify the Superior Court's radical departure from the long-standing general rule that equity will not enjoin a defamation. In Heilman v. Union Canal Company, 37 Pa. 100, 104 (1860), this Court said:

> "The fact, if it be so, that this remedy may not be successful in realizing the fruits of a recovery at law, on account of the insolvency of the defendants, is not of itself a ground of equitable interference. The remedy is what is to be looked at. If it exist [sic], and is ordinarily adequate, its possible want of success is not a consideration."

[Citations.] Money damages are adequate to recompense the plaintiffs for any losses they have suffered as a consequence of the defendant's defamatory publication. Thus, it was improper to grant equitable relief based on appellant's presumed inability to pay a money judgment.

As a consequence of holding that the defendant's indigency creates equitable jurisdiction, the Superior Court conditions appellant's right to trial by jury on her economic status. One of the underlying justifications for equity's traditional refusal to enjoin defamatory speech is that in equity all questions of fact are resolved by the trial court, rather than the jury. Thus, it deprives appellant of her right to a jury trial on the issue of the truth or falsity of her speech. [Citations.] The right to trial by jury is more than mere form. * * *

Furthermore, despite this Court's traditional practice of avoiding constitutional questions where a non-constitutional ground is dispositive [citation], it is appropriate in this case to reaffirm expressly the settled law governing the first amendment issue before us. The injunction in this case is a classic example of a prior restraint on speech. Protection of the citizenry from prior restraints is one of the leading principles on which the first amendment is based. [Citations.] Thus, there is a heavy presumption against the constitutional validity of any prior restraint on speech. [Citations.]

In *Organization for a Better Austin* [402 U.S. 415 (1971)], the Supreme Court held unconstitutional an injunction restraining members of a citizen group from leafletting and picketing outside a real estate broker's home. In doing so the Court stated:

> "Respondent thus carries a heavy burden of showing justification for the imposition of such a restraint. He has not met that burden. No prior decisions support the claim that the interest of an individual in being free from public criticism of his business practices in pamphlets or leaflets warrants use of the injunctive power of a court."

Id., 402 U.S. at 419. That rationale is equally applicable here. Appellees' interest in protecting their reputations is insufficient to justify enjoining appellant's speech, particularly where there is a legal remedy available. Thus, under the first amendment and the Supreme Court cases involving prior restraints, no basis exists for permitting the injunction in this case to stand.

———

1. Note that the intermediate appellate court in the principal case found it necessary to modify the trial court's order even though the intermediate court believed the restraint was constitutional. Is the trial court's wording overly broad? Is the modified wording too narrow? The intermediate appellate court has a good discussion at 246 Pa.Super. 98, 369 A.2d 829.

2. Compare the principal case to the result in *Martin v. Reynolds Metals Company*, 224 F.Supp. 978 (D.Or.1963). In *Martin* a rancher believed that a nearby alumina reduction plant was damaging human and animal health by allowing large quantities of fluorides to escape from the plant. He erected a billboard that said the company had

contaminated his ranch and killed 831 cattle in the past six years. The district court judge found the allegations were actionable libel and a jury trial was scheduled for the company's past damages claim. The court held further that pending adjudication of the damage claim the rancher would be enjoined to take down the sign. The court noted that the legal remedy was inadequate because "the mere existence of a concurrent legal remedy does not bar equitable relief. Rather ' * * * the legal remedy must be equally effectual with the equitable remedy, as to all the rights of the complainant.' " Lewis v. Cocks, 90 U.S. 466, 23 L.Ed. 70, 23 Wall. 466 (1874)." 224 F.Supp. at 984.

The injunction against the rancher was in effect only until the adjudication of the damages claim. What if the rancher erects the billboard again immediately after paying damages? Would a permanent injunction be appropriate?

3. In the exceptional cases where courts grant prior restraints of speech, the injunctions must be narrowly tailored not only to withstand Constitutional scrutiny but also to meet due process standards to enforce them with contempt. The specificity of an order was challenged recently in *Portland Feminist Women's Health Center v. Advocates for Life, Inc.* In that case a woman's clinic obtained a preliminary injunction against right-to-life demonstrators. The order provided that the defendants were prohibited from "shouting, screaming, chanting, or yelling during on-site demonstrations." They were further enjoined from "producing noise by any other means which substantially interferes with the provision of medical services within the Center." The Court of Appeals found that the injunction was not impermissibly vague even though the order did not include a specific decibel level or other objective standard. The court observed:

> The vagueness doctrine is based on due process principles that require fair notice and warning. [Citation.] It also incorporates a requirement that specificity be sufficient to avoid arbitrary and discriminatory enforcement. The doctrine's goal is to avoid "allow[ing] policemen, prosecutors, and juries to pursue their personal predilection," by requiring legislators to promulgate specific standards in criminal statutes. [Citation.] These concerns arise in a different context here, where enforcement lies entirely in judicial hands. So viewed, the injunction is not unconstitutionally vague, for reasons we have already set forth. Those subject to its strictures have adequate notice of what is required of them, and sufficient assurance of the direction enforcement will take. 859 F.2d 681 (9th Cir.1988).

Is it appropriate to apply the vagueness doctrine differently for injunctions than for statutes? Are judges less likely to follow their own predilections than are police officers, prosecutors, and juries?

MABE v. GALVESTON

687 S.W.2d 769 (Tex.App.1985).

EVANS, CHIEF JUSTICE.

The appellant, James Mabe, appeals from a temporary injunction entered in favor of appellees, The City of Galveston and Park Board of Trustees, prohibiting him from distributing pamphlets that list the names and phone numbers of certain members of the City Council and Park Board. The City and Park Board petitioned for injunctive relief, claiming that Mabe's publication of his pamphlet invaded the privacy of the individual members of the Council and Park Board. * * * The trial court * * * issued an injunction prohibiting Mabe from directly or indirectly publishing in writing any list of the names of members of the City Council or Park Board, coupled with their home telephone numbers. We reverse and render, directing that the temporary injunction be dissolved.

In his one point of error, Mabe challenges the constitutionality of the trial court's action, arguing that the injunction is void because it operates as a prior restraint of the exercise of his first amendment right to freedom of speech. * * *

Mabe owns a gift shop on Seawall Boulevard, the beachfront in Galveston. He is a Galveston native and has been in business on the island for seven years. Because of comments made by his customers and other visitors, he became concerned that there were no public restroom facilities on the Seawall. On a number of occasions, he appeared before the Galveston City Council and the Park Board and made his complaints known to those governmental bodies. Mabe finally reached the conclusion that the City Council and Park Board officials lacked concern about the matter, and in midsummer 1984, he printed and distributed 2000 pamphlets, which read:

THE BUSINESS OPERATORS ON SEAWALL BOULEVARD APOLOGIZE FOR NO PUBLIC RESTROOM FACILITIES ON OUR BEACHFRONT.

The Persons to Contact Are:

Council Members:
Lou Muller (409) 744–7444
John L. Sullivan (409) 744–5632
Mayor:
Jan Coggeshall (409) 744–5918

Park Board Members:
Mrs. Marilyn Schwartz (409) 744–3531
Mr. Meyer Reiswerg (409) 762–7540
Mr. Roby Burkett (409) 744–3686
Mr. Tom Wiseheart (409) 762–8434

Shortly after these pamphlets were distributed, the named members of City Council and Park Board of Trustees began receiving phone calls at home from persons who complained about the lack of restroom facilities. Some of the calls were received during the day, some in the evening, and three or four calls were received in the very late evening or early morning hours. The phone numbers of each person listed on the pamphlet could be found in the Galveston telephone directory, and some were also listed in documents published by the Park Board.

Any system of prior restraints bears a heavy presumption against its constitutional validity. [Citations.] Although in exceptional cases prior restraints may be constitutionally permissible, [citation] prior restraint against distribution of pamphlets is particularly suspect. [Citation.]

In 1973, the Supreme Court of Texas followed the practice of most other American jurisdictions and recognized a legally enforceable right of privacy. [Citation.] However, this right of privacy has never been considered unlimited. In certain circumstances, an individual's right of privacy must yield to other overriding constitutional mandates. [Citations.] This is particularly true where an individual is a public official, and the distributed information is critical of the conduct of public business or bears on some matter of public concern. In such an instance, the interest in privacy is outweighed by the larger, fundamental interest in free discussion and the dissemination of truth. [Citations.] Thus, courts are extremely reluctant to allow a prior restraint on free speech merely to protect a perceived threat to a public official's limited right of privacy.

In the case at bar, the pamphlets merely published the names and telephone numbers of certain public officials. These same telephone numbers were listed in the telephone directory and in other public documents. The pamphlets had a direct relationship to the public interest, *i.e.,* the lack of public restroom facilities on the Seawall. Thus, Mabe had the constitutional right to publish the pamphlets, regardless of whether the particular public officials were, in fact, empowered to take corrective action with respect to his complaint. [Citation.] The evidence does not suggest that Mabe's actions were taken solely to harass the public officials, nor was there evidence that the officials could not have taken measures, such as having their phone numbers unlisted, to protect themselves against unwanted telephone calls. We conclude that the trial court's injunctive order constituted an unwarranted prior restraint on the exercise of Mabe's first amendment right of freedom of speech, and we accordingly sustain his point of error.

The trial court's temporary injunctive order is reversed, and the injunction is ordered dissolved.

PROBLEM: THE LITIGIOUS NEIGHBOR

Cotter and a neighbor named Baxter had a dispute one night during a card game. Since then they have not spoken to each other. Baxter, knowing that Cotter hated to have cars parked on the street in this suburban neighborhood, began parking his car on the street in front of Cotter's house for the purpose of annoying Cotter. It was otherwise permissible to park there.

Cotter, an attorney, filed a civil complaint against Baxter for parking in front of the house. Baxter was a dentist and therefore needed to hire an attorney to get the complaint dismissed for failure to state a cause of action. Baxter has learned from neighbors that Cotter plans to repeat this procedure if Baxter continues to park in front of Cotter's house.

Baxter wants to get a court order against Cotter to prohibit such future complaints from being filed against Baxter. Is a court likely to protect Baxter from Cotter's harassment with such an injunction?

PAVILONIS v. KING

626 F.2d 1075 (1st Cir.1980).

BOWNES, CIRCUIT JUDGE.

Anne M. Pavilonis appeals from the dismissal of two civil rights actions she filed against various people connected with the Boston schools. She also challenges the district court's entry of an order enjoining her from filing any lawsuit in the federal district court of Massachusetts—and prohibiting the clerk of court from accepting for filing any paper submitted by her—without authorization by a district judge.

Pavilonis' first lawsuit was commenced on December 9, 1977, by a complaint against the then Governor Michael Dukakis, Boston School Committee President Kathleen Sullivan, and Solomon Lewenberg School Principal William I. O'Connell. The body of the complaint read, in its entirety, as follows:

1.   This is an action to redress the deprivation under color of a law of the state of Massachusetts of a right secured to plaintiff by Article V Amendment 14 of the Constitution of the United States. Jurisdiction is conferred on this Court by 28 U.S.C. Section 1343.

2.   Plaintiff brings this action under 42 U.S.C. Section 1986 to recover damages for defendant's failure to prevent a wrong mentioned in 42 U.S.C. Section 1985, which defendant knew was about to occur and which defendants had the power to prevent, as hereinafter more fully appears. Jurisdiction is conferred on this Court by 28 [U.S.C.] Section 1343.

The second complaint, filed on December 19, 1977, was nearly identical, but named Northeastern University President Kenneth G. Ryder as an additional defendant.

When Pavilonis moved for appointment of counsel, these cases were referred to a magistrate. Consulting the district court docket, the magistrate found five other complaints filed by Pavilonis, against various defendants including Michael Dukakis and Kenneth Ryder, in which the language contained in paragraph 2 of the instant complaints was used, apparently without significant elaboration. Of the opinion that the two complaints before him, even read liberally, were "completely devoid of any information that would assist the defendants ... [in] answer[ing]," were "completely violative of Rule 8 of the Federal Rules of Civil Procedure," and "appear[ed] frivolous," the magistrate denied the motions for appointment of counsel. Finding that Pavilonis had filed "numerous unsupported actions" that placed an undue burden on the court and deprived other legitimate litigants of a hearing, the magistrate also recommended that she be restricted from filing new actions without permission of a district judge.

* * *

The district judge approved the magistrate's recommendation and, on April 12, 1978, issued an order enjoining Pavilonis from filing new lawsuits without permission of a judge of the District Court of Massachusetts, and ordering the clerk to refuse to file additional papers submitted by her without such permission. * * *

We have little difficulty upholding the district court's dismissal of the complaints. Although pro se complaints are to be read liberally, [citations], these complaints are so hopelessly general that they could give no notice of Pavilonis' claims. * * *

Whether Pavilonis was properly enjoined from filing additional pleadings or new lawsuits without permission from a district judge is a closer question. In recommending an injunction against her filing new actions without permission, the magistrate relied on *Rudnicki v. McCormack,* 210 F.Supp. 905 (D.R.I.1962), *appeal dismissed sub nom.* Rudnicki v. Cox, 372 U.S. 226, 83 S.Ct. 679, 9 L.Ed.2d 714 (1963), and Rudnicki v. Department of Massachusetts Attorney General, 362 F.2d 337 (1st Cir.1966). In *Rudnicki v. McCormack,* such an injunction was entered against a plaintiff who had filed "baseless, vexatious, and repetitive" suits against judges, judicial officers, and attorneys, in an effort to relitigate cases that had been dismissed. The court ruled that it had equitable and supervisory power to protect the defendants from harassment and the court itself from the burden of processing frivolous and unimportant papers. In *Rudnicki v. Department of Massachusetts Attorney General,* we noted the existence of the injunction against Rudnicki and upheld the district court's denial of leave to file a new action. More recently, a similar injunction was entered against another litigant who had filed complaints comprised of vituperative attacks against judges who had ruled against him; upholding the district court's refusal to allow a new complaint of a similar ilk to be filed, we said, "The law is well established that it is proper and necessary for an injunction to issue barring a party, such as appellant, from filing and processing frivolous and vexatious lawsuits." *Gordon v. United States Department of Justice,* 558 F.2d 618 (1st Cir.1977).

While we reject Pavilonis' argument that enjoining litigation is unconstitutional, we do not think her case fits into the classic *Rudnicki–Gordon* mold. Those cases, like many others from other jurisdictions, involved plaintiffs bent on reopening closed cases and evidently also intent on harassing defendants, often judges who had ruled against them. Here, the magistrate determined only that Pavilonis had filed "numerous unsupported" actions, using the same deficient complaints. It does not appear that Pavilonis was attempting to reopen closed cases; according to the magistrate's report, when injunctive relief was recommended at least four of Pavilonis' five other lawsuits were still pending. Likewise, although Pavilonis is obviously dissatisfied with the Boston school system and certain individuals connected with it, it is not clear that her litigation was malicious and designed to harass. Furthermore, it is possible that her use of the same complaint in several cases resulted from a misunderstanding of Rule 8, rather than a desire to mask repetitive litigation or to make response by the defendants difficult.

Nevertheless, Pavilonis' lawsuits were at least to some extent duplicative; for example, in the two cases now on appeal, she sued certain defendants twice in two weeks and there is no apparent difference between the actions. In addition, all her complaints suffered from the same deficiencies. Faced with a situation where its docket was being burdened and defendants were being called upon to answer multiple, impenetrable complaints, the district court was justified in taking action. * * *

Affirmed.

NORCISA v. BOARD OF SELECTMEN OF PROVINCETOWN
368 Mass. 161, 330 N.E.2d 830 (1975).

QUIRICO, JUSTICE.

This is an appeal by the defendants, the board of selectmen of Provincetown (selectmen) and their agent, from a decree entered by the judge of the Probate Court * * * declaring that the plaintiff and her retail clothing business in the town of Provincetown (town) are not within the scope of G.L. c. 101, §§ 1–12, the Transient Vendor Statute, and ordering that the town and its agents, servants, and employees "are hereby restrained and permanently enjoined from enforcing . . . any of the provisions of Mass. G.L. c. 101, §§ 1–12, against the Petitioner or the retail business she operates." * * * Prior to the commencement of this suit in equity, a criminal complaint had issued in the Second District Court of Barnstable County charging the plaintiff with violating G.L. c. 101, §§ 6, 8. This criminal complaint was still pending when the decree appealed from issued. The obvious purpose and effect of the decree was to enjoin the pending criminal prosecution. We reverse.

* * * [I]n 1973 the plaintiff, who was a resident of Provincetown, opened a retail clothing business in that town under the name of The Town Crier Wearhouse. At the time she opened her business, the plaintiff was informed by the agent for the selectmen "that she would not be able to open and operate her business unless she paid to Provincetown a license fee of two hundred dollars ($200.00), furnished a bond of five hundred dollars ($500.00) to the Commonwealth, and applied for both a state and town Transient Vendor's License, all of the above pursuant to and authorized by G.L. c. 101, § 3."

General Laws c. 101, § 3, requires that anyone "before commencing business in the commonwealth as a transient vendor" shall apply for a

State license, good for one year, to do business as a transient vendor, subject to local rules and regulations. * * *.

The plaintiff's position as stated in the "Agreed Statement of Facts" is that she was not a transient vendor at the time the selectment sought to categorize her as one, that she had not been a transient vendor in the past, and that she would not be a transient vendor in the future. She further asserted that she had performed no acts which could be construed as classifying her as anything except a retailer of clothes, that she intended to conduct her business as a full time retail clothing shop, and that she would take no action inconsistent with these assertions. * * * The defendants' position, in the court below as well as in their brief here, has been "that under the terms of the statute petitioner is required to take out a transient vendor's license unless she *has been* 'open for business during usual business hours for a period of at least twelve consecutive months' "(emphasis added).

* * * [W]e conclude that the judge should not have enjoined the pending criminal prosecution.

At one time, it was common for courts to express the view that an equity court had no "jurisdiction" to enjoin a criminal prosecution. In In re Sawyer, 124 U.S. 200, 8 S.Ct. 482, 31 L.Ed. 402 (1888), the court said, "The office and jurisdiction of a court of equity, unless enlarged by express statute, are limited to the protection of rights of property. It has no jurisdiction over the prosecution, the punishment, or the pardon of crimes or misdemeanors.... To assume such a jurisdiction, or to sustain a bill in equity to restrain or relieve against proceedings for the punishment of offences, ... is to invade the domain of the courts of common law, or of the executive and administrative department of the government." * * *

In this Commonwealth, however, it was early established that courts with general equity powers have the power to restrain criminal prosecutions. In Shuman v. Gilbert, 229 Mass. 225, 118 N.E. 254 (1918), for example, this court recognized the "general rule" that criminal prosecutions are not to be enjoined, but pointed out, "[T]here is an exception to this comprehensive statement. Jurisdiction in equity to restrain the institution of prosecutions under unconstitutional or void statutes or local ordinances has been upheld by this court when property rights would be injured irreparably, and when other elements necessary to support cognizance by equity are present." [Citations.]

As pointed out in the *Shuman* case, the occasions when an equity court may properly enjoin a criminal prosecution remain the exception to the "general rule" of non-intervention. Some of the basic policy reasons underlying the rule of nonintervention were well-expressed by the Supreme Court of Hawaii: "Courts of equity are not constituted to deal with crimes and criminal proceedings. They have no power to punish admitted offenders of a challenged penal statute after holding it to be valid, or to compensate those injured by the violations thereof while the hands of the officers of the law have been stayed by injunction. To that extent such courts are incapable of affording a complete remedy. Equity, therefore, takes no part in the administration of the criminal law. It neither aids, restrains, nor obstructs criminal courts in the exercise of their jurisdiction. Ordinarily a court of equity deals only with civil cases involving property rights where it can afford a complete remedy by injunctive relief. Hence it does not interfere in the enforcement of penal statutes even though invalid unless there be exceptional circumstances and a clear showing that an injunction is urgently necessary to afford adequate protection to rights of property so as to circumvent great and irreparable injury until the validity of the particular penal statute is sustained." Liu v. Farr, 39 Hawaii 23, 35–36 (1950).

Both the *Shuman* and *Liu* cases quoted above indicated that equity would act only to protect "property rights" from irreparable damage by criminal prosecution. In the leading case of Kenyon v. Chicopee, 320 Mass. 528, 70 N.E.2d 241 (1946), however, we largely rejected the personal rights-property rights distinction as a factor in considering whether an injunction should issue. We considered this question and said at 534, 70 N.E.2d at 244: "We believe the true rule to be that equity will protect personal rights by injunction upon the same conditions upon which it will protect property rights by injunction. In general, these conditions are, [1] that unless relief is granted a substantial right of the plaintiff will be impaired to a material degree; [2] that the remedy at law is inadequate; and [3] that injunctive relief can be applied with practical success and without imposing an impossible burden on the court or bringing its processes into disrepute." This, then, is the test which the probate judge should have applied in considering the request for an injunction, and it is the test which we now apply to the facts before us. In so doing, we assume without deciding that parts (1) and (3) of the *Kenyon* test are satisfied and concentrate on part (2), that is, whether the remedy at law would be adequate in this case.

The plaintiff variously claims that G.L. c. 101, §§ 1–12, is either unconstitutional on its face or as applied, or that the statute, properly construed, does not apply to her at all. In accordance with these claims, she asserts that she cannot be prosecuted for failure to comply with the statute. If we assume, again without deciding the question, that the plaintiff indeed cannot properly be prosecuted under this statute, the issue resolves itself simply to whether the available defenses to the District Court criminal complaint amount to an adequate remedy at law. In the circumstances of this case, we think they plainly do.

In both the *Shuman* and *Kenyon* cases, the question was considered whether, in the circumstances of those cases, the defense to the criminal prosecution provided an adequate remedy at law. Since the injunction was denied in the former case and granted in the latter, it is instructive to compare them.

In the *Shuman* case, six merchants alleged that the defendant chief of police of Northampton threatened to prosecute them for conducting a business without a license, which they claimed they were not obligated to obtain. The plaintiffs' bill sought to make out a case of irreparable damage and inadequacy of legal remedy by alleging, inter alia, that it would take several months to obtain a decision on the case from an appellate court and that in the intervening period the loss of profits and advantageous business relations would cause the plaintiffs great and irreparable damage. To these averments, a demurrer was sustained. This court upheld the sustaining of the demurrer. After noting that in the event of multiple, oppressive, and wrongful prosecutions, an injunction might properly issue, we said: "A possibility that complaints may be lodged against six persons is not enough under these circumstances to make out a case of multiplicity. The allegations as to repeated complaints are not sufficient to warrant the inference that the courts of this commonwealth will countenance continued and oppressive prosecutions when once a genuine test case open to fair question has been presented and is on its way to final decision[.] * * * Simply that one is in business and may be injured in respect of his business by prosecution for an alleged crime, is no sufficient reason for asking a court of equity to ascertain in advance whether the business as conducted is in violation of a penal statute." [Citation.]

In the *Kenyon* case, by contrast, we reversed interlocutory decrees sustaining demurrers where the bill alleged that members of Jehovah's Witnesses had been repeatedly, on different dates, arrested, prosecuted, and convicted under an unconstitutional ordinance, prohibiting distribution of handbills, that on at least two occasions a defendant judge had convicted some of the plaintiffs despite being shown United States Supreme Court decisions holding such an ordinance unconstitutional, that the defendants well knew that the ordinances were unconstitutional and void, that the plaintiffs' means of paying bail fees and of posting bail and appeal bonds were exhausted, and that the defendants had threatened to and would continue to make false arrests, all to the irreparable damage of the plaintiffs' attempts to exercise their constitutional rights. In these circumstances, we held that an injunction against further prosecutions could properly issue, if the allegations were ultimately proved. We observed: "The plaintiffs' rights are of the most fundamental character. According to the bill they have been violated repeatedly. It is plain that the legal remedies by defending against repeated complaints and bringing successive actions for malicious prosecution or false arrest are not adequate." [Citation.]

In the present case, the plaintiff is the subject of a complaint charging a single violation of the statute. She avers that the statute is either unconstitutional on its face or as applied, or that, properly construed, it is inapplicable to her. These averments, of course, would, if established, each constitute a complete defense to the violation charged. We repeat here a passage from a United States Supreme Court case which applies equally to the matter before us: "It is a familiar rule that courts of equity do not ordinarily restrain criminal prosecutions. No person is immune from prosecution in good faith for his alleged criminal acts. Its imminence, even though alleged to be in violation of constitutional guarantees, is not a ground for equity relief since the lawfulness or constitutionality of the statute or ordinance on which the prosecution is based may be determined as readily in the criminal case as in a suit for injunction .... It does not appear from the record that petitioners have been threatened with any injury other than that incidental to every criminal proceeding brought lawfully and in good faith, or that a ... court of equity by withdrawing the determination of guilt from the ... [criminal] courts could rightly afford petitioners any protection which they could not secure by prompt trial and appeal pursued to this Court." [Citation.]

* * *

Our decision would not be different if we were considering only those portions of the proceedings below which involved a request for and grant of declaratory relief under G.L. c. 231A, §§ 1, 2. The fundamental jurisprudential considerations underlying the general prohibition against enjoining a pending criminal prosecution apply with full force to support a prohibition against issuing declaratory decrees concerning a pending criminal prosecution. To conclude otherwise would encourage fragmentation and proliferation of litigation and disrupt the orderly administration of the criminal law.[6]

The rule we adopt today in regard to the issuance of declaratory judgments when criminal litigation is pending is merely a logical extension of our rules which generally proscribe the issuance of such a judgment when an appropriate administrative proceeding is in progress, or when a civil proceeding in which the same issue is or can be raised is already pending between the parties. * * *

For the reasons given above, the injunction and declaratory relief should not have been granted. The final decree is reversed and a new judgment is to be entered dismissing the bill.

So ordered.

C.   ENJOINING CRIMES AND NUISANCES

Section Coverage:

A considerable amount of litigation has dealt with whether a court should enjoin activity which constitutes a public or private nuisance. The threshold inquiry concerns the substantive entitlement to relief; the plaintiff must establish that the defendant's conduct was a substantial

---

6. "The modern declaratory action to construe or invalidate a penal statute bears the important distinction that it does not disrupt a pending prosecution, but seeks to resolve legal issues to prevent prosecution. Whereas prosecution can only follow conduct, the modern declaratory action precedes it, and in that difference lies its cardinal function. Cases do appear in which the plaintiff seeks a declaratory judgment after having acted, either racing to the court ahead of the prosecutor or with prosecution formally pending, but the courts refuse the remedy to prevent needless proliferation of litigation. Once the disputed conduct has taken place, the equities of the statute itself can be at least as well litigated in defense to the prosecution thus ripened." Note, Declaratory Relief in the Criminal Law, 80 Harv.L.Rev. 1490, 1503–1504 (1967).

and unreasonable interference with the use and enjoyment of the plaintiff's property or public interests. The court evaluates "unreasonable interference" by weighing the gravity of the harm against the utility of the conduct. If this standard is met, the plaintiff must further demonstrate (1) that the threatened harm is immediate, (2) that the injury is irreparable, (3) that no adequate remedy at law exists, and (4) that equitable considerations balance in its favor. Two factors are particularly significant in the balancing process: the extent to which a damages award will redress the injury and the public interest. An injunction against a nuisance is never automatic nor a matter of right; it rests within the discretion of the judge sitting in equity.

Nuisance cases sometimes involve activities that also fall within the scope of criminal law. The problem then becomes whether a civil court should issue an injunction to prohibit behavior that could be sanctioned by the criminal justice system. The modern approach generally holds that equity will not enjoin conduct merely because it offends a criminal statute. Conversely, if the activity constitutes a public nuisance, an injunction is not automatically precluded because of potential penal sanctions. The plaintiff who seeks to enjoin activity that is criminal needs to address the adequacy of the remedy at law in terms of both civil and criminal law.

Model Case:

Dunlop, a contractor, is constructing a large building near a college dormitory. The construction is very noisy; pneumatic drills and riveting machines operate 24 hours a day. The noise substantially interferes with the students' studying in the dormitory during the day and with their sleeping at night.

In a suit to enjoin the construction, the court would take evidence on the nature of the construction and on the alternatives available to both parties. It is found as a fact that the operation of the drills and riveting machines could be discontinued during the night without delaying the ultimate construction of the building more than a few days. It is further found that the cost of the delay would not be unduly burdensome to Dunlop. The court also concludes that the students can study in a relatively quiet near-by library during the day.

A court would weigh the competing interests of the parties and determine that a damages award for the past harm would not be effective in curtailing the interference with the plaintiff's use and enjoyment of their property. Accordingly, the court could issue an injunction which would prohibit future construction operations during certain evening and early morning hours. The court would not have difficulties in retaining a supervisory role for the limited duration of the building construction. Potential enforcement of the decree should not present an obstacle since the order could be narrowly tailored to the specific harm.

1. Enjoining Nuisances

HARRISON v. INDIANA AUTO SHREDDERS CO.
528 F.2d 1107 (7th Cir.1975).

CLARK, ASSOCIATE JUSTICE.

This is an appeal from a judgment of the United States District Court for the Southern District of Indiana in a nuisance action, permanently enjoining appellant-Indiana Auto Shredders Company from operating its shredding plant for the recycling of automobiles in the Irish Hill section of Indianapolis, Indiana, and awarding $176,956 in compensatory and $353,912 in punitive damages to plaintiffs and interveners. The suit was filed by appellee-Russell Harrison (d/b/a Indiana Coldweld Company) and some 33 other "claimants" who reside or work in the Irish Hill section, alleging: (1) that the dust, vibration, and noise generated by the company's shredding plant constituted a common law and statutory nuisance under Indiana law by damaging property and endangering the health and safety of residents and workers in the area; and (2) that the company's shredding plant violated various local air pollution regulations.

This case presents the very difficult question of how to balance the legitimate demands of an urban neighborhood for clean air and a comfortable environment against the utility and economic enterprise of a beneficial, but polluting, industry. * * *

In recent years, the abandoned and junked automobile has become recognized as one of this country's major solid waste disposal problems. Auto "graveyards" represent not only an aesthetic blight that mars the natural beauty of the land, but also a scandalous waste of energy and resources that produced those cars. * * *

This case is representative of the new breed of lawsuit spawned by the growing concern for cleaner air and water. The birth and burgeoning growth of environmental litigation have forced the courts into difficult situations where modern hybrids of the traditional concepts of nuisance law and equity must be fashioned. Nuisance has always been a difficult area for the courts; the conflict of precedents and the confusing theoretical foundations of nuisance, led Prosser to tag the area a "legal garbage can." In any case, environmental consciousness may be the saving prescript for our age. Thus the right of environmentally aggrieved parties to obtain redress in the courts serves as a necessary and valuable supplement to legislative efforts to restore the natural ecology of our cities and countryside.

Judicial involvement in solving environmental problems does, however, bring its own hazards. Balancing the interests of a modern urban community like Indianapolis may be very difficult. Weighing the desire for economic and industrial strength against the need for clean and livable surroundings is not easily done, especially because of the graduations in quality as well as quantity that are involved. There is the danger that environmental problems will be inadequately treated by the piecemeal methods of litigation. It is possible that courtroom battles may be used to slow down effective policymaking for the environment. Litigation often fails to provide sufficient opportunities for the expert analysis and broad perspective that such policymaking often requires.

As difficult as environmental balancing may be, however, some forum for aggrieved parties must be made available. If necessary, the courts are qualified to perform the task. The courts are skilled at "balancing the equities," a technique that traditionally has been one of the judicial functions. Courts are insulated from the lobbying that gives strong advantages to industrial polluters when they face administrative or legislative review of their operations. The local state or federal court, because of its proximity to the individual problem, is often in a better position to judge the effect of a pollution nuisance upon a locality. For all of these reasons, the balancing in this case, although difficult, was nonetheless a proper function for the court below to perform. All other forums for obtaining relief were cut-off from the claimants and they understandably turned to the courts for relief.

The problem of balancing the equities in this case, however, was compounded by the fact that the company was not the ordinary industrial polluter. Usually, industrial polluters bring only their proprietary rights to be balanced on the scale opposite the community interests in a cleaner environment. The polluter asks the court to give due weight to the contributions that the business enterprise makes to the community by its economic achievements: payroll, taxes, investment of profits. Although when contrasted with the direct damage caused by uncontrolled pollution, such contributions may seem indirect, they are nonetheless entitled to serious consideration. No court could lightly decide to shut down a business that was the sole or principal livelihood of a community's citizens. Economic and property interests are entitled to significant weight. But here, the Indiana Auto Shredders Company makes more than only those economic contributions to the Indianapolis community; it is making a direct contribution toward improving the environment and conserving its natural resources by the recycling of abandoned automobiles. In curtailing the company's operations, the court below chose a very serious course of action. It is our view that such a course of action must be based upon conspicuous facts and reasonable standards of law.

* * * [E]nvironmental litigation of this type, whether based upon the Indiana nuisance statute or the common law of nuisance, logically will involve two stages of adjudication. First, the court or trier of fact will determine whether the facts alleged actually constitute a nuisance and a nuisance of what type. Second, having determined the nature of the alleged nuisance, the court will fashion relief appropriate to the equities of the case. Each of these two stages implicate their own legal standards.

Some activities, occupations, or structures are so offensive at all times and under all circumstances, regardless of location or surroundings, that they constitute "nuisance per se." Activities that imminently and dangerously threaten the public health fall into this category. It is more often the case, however, that the activities challenged by suitors in a nuisance case fall short of this standard of imminent and dangerous harm. Such activities as cause more remote harm to people or are the source of inconvenience, annoyance, and minor damage to property are labeled "nuisance in fact" or "nuisance per accidens." These latter activities are nuisances primarily because of the circumstances or the location and surrounding of the activities, rather than the nature of the activities themselves. Most air and water pollution, when their effects are only minimally or remotely harmful to the public health, will be nuisances of this second type. Obviously, it is this second type that more frequently occurs. Very often this second type will present the offensive activities of an otherwise lawful business, activities that are being conducted in such a manner so as to become a nuisance.

* * *

If a pollution nuisance has been found to exist, the court must then decide what relief to grant to those suffering the nuisance. In this second stage in the adjudication of environmental nuisance suits, balancing the equities becomes all important. The court must decide whether injunctive relief, damages, or some combination of the two best satisfies the particular demands of the case before it. This is the difficult but necessary work the court must perform.

Of course, where the pollution from a mill or factory creates hazards that imminently and dangerously affect the public health, the appropriate relief is a permanent injunction against the continuation of the polluting activities. It would be unreasonable to allow a private interest in the profits and product of such a polluting menace to outweigh the community's interests in the health of its citizens. However, a permanent injunction that shuts down a mill or factory without consideration of the extent of the harm that its pollution caused would be equally unreasonable. Pollution nuisance cases present no special features that should exempt them from the equitable requirements for injunctive relief, including proof of irreparable harm and inadequate remedy at law. * * * Ordinarily a permanent injunction will not lie unless (1) either the polluter seriously and imminently threatens the public health or (2) he causes non-health injuries that are substantial and the business cannot be operated to avoid the injuries apprehended. Thus the particular situation facts of each pollution nuisance case will determine whether a permanent injunction should be issued. When a business' offensive activities fall short of that standard, only the combination of both reckless disregard of substantial annoyances caused to adjoining property owners plus the impossibility of mitigating the offensive characteristics of the business will justify the granting of permanent injunctive relief.

* * *

We can well appreciate and fully sympathize with the unhappiness of the appellees over their situation. However, the problem of zoning is a local one, governed by local law; it must be solved in local perspective. The appropriate local authority has zoned the property specifically for shredder use; and appellant has been issued a permit to so use the property. After careful and continued tests by reputable experts as well as public officials, appellant's operation has met all the required standards. Under these circumstances and in the absence of an imminent hazard to health or welfare—none of which was established or found present here, the appellant cannot be prevented from continuing to engage in the operation of its shredding. [Citation.] The national environmental policy, as announced by Congress, allows offending industries a reasonable period of time to make adjustments to conform to standards. [Citations.] Appellant is a new undertaking in Irish Hill; it too is entitled to a reasonable period of time to correct any defects not of imminent or substantial harm. If there is damage to property, of course, it is recoverable here as in any other case.

The trial court based its action on the existence of a common nuisance but even if such were present, the drastic remedy of closing down the operation without endeavoring to launder its objectionable features would be impermissible under our law. [Citation.] In applying the test of the cases, we find no ground on which to base a permanent injunction here.

This is not to say that those features of the appellant's operation that are found to be offensive should not be remedied. We only say that the offender shall have time to correct the evil. If the appellant does not correct the infractions presently existing within a reasonable period, the district court may take action that will require the appellant so to do. * * *

The judgment is reversed, the permanent injunction is dissolved, and the case is remanded for further proceedings in accordance herewith.

---

1. As the principal case reflects, a zoning ordinance may affect the availability and the nature of injunctive relief. The defendant's compliance with governmental regulations should be relevant to the reasonableness of the activity and its suitability to the locale.

Compliance with all pertinent regulations is not sufficient to defeat an injunction, however. What about activities that a court finds extremely hazardous and presenting a serious threat to public health? Should such activity be enjoined as a public nuisance if the defendant has obtained all necessary permits? Does it matter how imminent is the threat to health?

2. Some jurisdictions have passed anti-injunction acts affecting nuisance cases. They typically preclude courts from restraining business activities that are being reasonably conducted in compliance with zoning regulations if the only injury is a nuisance to the plaintiff in the operations. Thus, in Kornoff v. Kingsburg Cotton Oil Co., 45 Cal.2d 265, 288 P.2d 507 (1955), the court held that California Code Civ.Proc. § 731a shielded the defendant from an injunction against the operation of its cotton gin because it was conducted in a location properly zoned for business and commercial activity. However, the court found that § 731a did not operate to bar a recovery for damages.

An anti-injunction act does not necessarily end the court's equitable power, but may simply affect its exercise of discretion. Consider Sierra Screw Products v. Azusa Greens, Inc., 88 Cal.App.3d 358, 151 Cal.Rptr. 799 (1979), where landowners sought damages and injunctive relief against the neighboring golf course. The complaint sought abatement of the nuisance caused by stray golf balls damaging the plaintiff's property. The defendants contended that its conditional use permit which authorized operation of the golf course constituted an automatic bar to injunctive relief. The court found that the defendants had employed unnecessary and injurious methods in operating the course and therefore issued an injunction mandating that the defendants redesign two holes.

Compare *Nussbaum v. Lacopo,* 27 N.Y.2d 311, 317 N.Y.S.2d 347, 265 N.E.2d 762 (1970) (no injunction against golf course where errant golf balls landed on neighboring plaintiff's property only once or twice a week).

3. In the absence of statutory restraints on a court's ability to enjoin a nuisance, what kinds of social utility should justify the continued operation of an activity that causes a small but predictable number of personal injuries over time? Consider the following observations about the game of golf in *Gleason v. Hillcrest Golf Course,* a personal injury case awarding damages to a woman injured when a golf ball struck and shattered the windshield of an automobile in which she was traveling.

> The ancient game of golf had its origin in Scotland. It was formerly indulged in by only kings and the nobility. It furnishes a healthy means of exercise and relaxation, and is a sport of the first order. In more modern times, the game spread to England, and its popularity has so increased that the game is now extensively in vogue in this and other countries, among all classes of people.

> A golf ball in itself is an innocent, lawful article, and so is the club which drives it. The game itself, being fundamentally honorable and sportsmanlike, suggests nothing imminently unlawful or hazardous about it.

> But, when driven, though in full compliance with the rules of the game, the ball attains great speed, and may thus become a dangerous and destructive object, and may strike with great violence and force, not unlike a projectile which is propelled from a weapon

by whatever power it be actuated, or a stone thrown by a catapult or by the hand. In the recent case of *Simpson v. Fiero*, 237 App.Div. 62, 64, 260 N.Y.S. 323, 325, Mr. Justice Hagarty, himself an accomplished player, in holding a golf player liable for the injury of a caddy by a ball, writing for a unanimous court, says: "It must be conceded that, although golf may not be deemed a hazardous game, a driven golf ball is a very dangerous missile, and that its flight and direction cannot always be controlled by the player. That uncertainty is a part of the game. The ball when struck is liable to go on down the fairway, or fly off to the right or left at almost any angle."

The element of danger, therefore, though not intrinsic in the game itself, is nevertheless present, according to a given set of circumstances. The situation is not changed by the fact that the act of propelling the ball is in itself not wrongful and is for a lawful purpose, that is, to play the game.

* * *

Like baseball, the golf game is not a nuisance per se. Both games involve the same element; *i.e.,* striking the ball with an instrument with force so as to send it spinning into the air. If, however, the ball playing is attended with a reasonable degree of danger, as to make it likely that it would "work hurt" upon a traveler in the street, a question of fact is presented, and, if it be decided adversely to the parties who are responsible for, or who participated in, or who authorized, the setting of the ball in motion, liability will attach on the theory that the playing was a nuisance.
* * *

This plaintiff had a right to be traveling in the automobile upon the highway. The ball hit the windshield suddenly. She could not be expected to watch out for deflected golf balls in the path of the car, and, even if she were, there is nothing to indicate that she could have reasonably done anything to avert the accident. * * * "The primary purpose of highways is use by the public for travel and transportation, and the general rule is that any one who interferes with such use commits a nuisance." 148 Misc. 246, 265 N.Y.S. 886 (1933).

4. When a court orders abatement of a nuisance, such as requiring the redesign of some holes on a golf course, must the defendant always bear the cost of compliance? If the financial burden of compliance with an extensive injunction is very high, a defendant might choose to cease the activity altogether. If the public interest dictates that the nuisance should be abated but not prohibited, should the court weigh the danger of closure when framing the order?

PROBLEM: THE POLLUTING PLANT

The Browns live with their family on Blackacre and raise wheat and corn crops. They also have a fruit orchard which they cultivate for a small commercial profit each year.

Their neighbors, the Websters, live on Greenacre and operate a chicken processing plant on the premises. The Websters have operated the plant for five years without any significant interference with the Browns' property. Recently the Websters decided to expand the plant by adding another smokestack. Immediately after the new smokestack was installed a large quantity of noxious fumes escaped from a crack caused by improper sealant. The fumes scorched the leaves on the Browns' lemon trees and damaged the majority of the fruit. At harvest they had a significantly reduced yield on the fruit crop, although the other crops were unaffected.

The Browns complained bitterly to the Websters and demanded that they close the plant. The Websters repeatedly promised repairs, but each effort to fix the problem during that summer failed. After the harvest the Websters said that the problem had finally been repaired permanently. The quantity of fumes was indeed reduced, although not eliminated. The Browns are skeptical and worried about next year's lemon crop. They sue to enjoin the operation of the plant as a private nuisance.

(a) What result?

(b) Assume instead that the normal operation of the plant results in the periodic emission of some noxious fumes and feather particles which settle on Blackacre, partially damaging the Browns' crops and the orchard. The estimated damage to the crops and the trees is approximately $10,000 per year. The cost to replace the orchard itself would be $80,000. The chicken plant cost the Websters $100,000, and its only employees are family members. The plant is located outside the city and thus not subject to any zoning ordinances. The Browns called the state environmental protection agency and learned that the state does have an air pollution control statute which prohibits the discharge of toxic pollutants into the air. The agency is overburdened with enforcement of the statute and could not help the Browns any time soon. Meanwhile, the Browns discovered that several of their livestock had become diseased as a result of drinking water contaminated by the plant's discharge of various chemicals. Should a court issue an injunction? If so, how should it be drafted?

VILLAGE OF WILSONVILLE v. SCA SERVICES, INC.
86 Ill.2d 1, 55 Ill.Dec. 499, 426 N.E.2d 824 (1981).

CLARK, JUSTICE:

[The plaintiff Village of Wilsonville sought an injunction against the operation of the defendant's hazardous chemical waste disposal site as a public nuisance. The materials deposited at the site were extremely toxic; exposure to the chemicals could result in pulmonary disease, cancer, brain damage, and birth defects. The defendant had obtained all necessary governmental permits to operate the landfill, but conflicting testimony was presented regarding chemical spills and that dust and noxious odors had emanated from the site. The trial court found that the disposal site constituted a prospective nuisance, and ordered the defendant to remove the toxic waste and to restore and reclaim the site.]

* * * [W]here individual rights are unreasonably interfered with, the public benefit from a particular facility will not outweigh the individual right, and the facility's use will be enjoined or curtailed. Such a conclusion presupposes a balancing process with the greater weight being given to the individual's right to use and enjoy property over a public benefit or convenience from having a business operate at a particular location. In such an instance, the individual's right to noninterference takes precedence.

* * * [T]here is a need for disposal of industrial hazardous wastes. However, where disposal of wastes create a nuisance said disposal site may be closed through legal action.

Substantial sums of money have been expended by the defendant in developing and operating the Earthline site at Wilsonville. Not only is the site convenient to nearby industries but it is a profit producer for the defendant. All of these elements are relevant to our economic system but notwithstanding the same it is the opinion of the Court that nuisances cannot be justified on such grounds when we have substantial injury to individual rights, community rights, substantial damage to human beings and other living things.

* * *

The importance of an industry to the wealth and prosperity of an area does not as a matter of law give to it rights superior to the primary or natural rights of citizens who live nearby. *However, such matters may be considered and have been in this case.*

* * *

A significant inquiry is—was the business established and then persons moved into the business area after it was established and subsequent thereto the business operation moved in and now complaints are made by the citizens who were located in the area before the business was so located. It is the opinion of the Court that if a business is located in a certain area before complainants moved into the area and if the complainants come to the nuisance this may constitute a defense or operate as an estoppel. A person cannot place himself in a position where you suffer and then complain. In this case the defendant established its chemical waste landfill near the area where persons of the Village had resided for many years. Complaints came from residents many of whom lived in the area long before the industrial waste disposal site was ever established. * * *

The defendant's next contention is that the courts below were in error when they failed to require a showing of a substantial risk of certain and extreme future harm before enjoining operation of the defendant's site. We deem it necessary to explain that a *prospective* nuisance is a fit candidate for injunctive relief. Prosser states: "Both public and private nuisances require some substantial interference with the interest involved. Since nuisance is a common subject of equity jurisdiction, the damage against which an injunction is asked is often merely threatened or potential; but even in such cases, there must be at least a threat of a substantial invasion of the plaintiff's interests." [Citation.] The defendant does not dispute this proposition; it does, however, argue that the trial court did not follow the proper standard for determining when a prospective nuisance may be enjoined. The defendant argues that the proper standard to be used is that an injunction is proper only if there is a "dangerous probability" that the threatened or potential injury will occur. (*See* Restatement (Second) of Torts sec. 933(1), at 561, comment *b* (1979).) The defendant further argues that the appellate court looked only at the potential consequences of not enjoining the operation of the site as a nuisance and not at the likelihood of whether harm would occur. * * *

We agree with the defendant's statement of the law, but not with its urged application to the facts of this case. Again, Professor Prosser has offered a concise commentary. He has stated that "[o]ne distinguishing feature of equitable relief is that it may be granted upon the threat of harm which has not yet occurred. The defendant may be restrained from entering upon an activity where it is highly probable that it will lead to a nuisance, although if the possibility is merely uncertain or contingent he may be left to his remedy after the nuisance has occurred." * * *

* * * [I]t is highly probable that the instant site will constitute a public nuisance if, through either an explosive interaction, migration, subsidence, or the "bathtub effect," the highly toxic chemical wastes deposited at the site escape and contaminate the air, water, or ground around the site. That such an event will occur was positively attested to by several expert witnesses. A court does not have to wait for it to happen before it can enjoin such a result. * * *

* * * [T]he gist of this case is that the defendant is engaged in an extremely hazardous undertaking at an unsuitable location, which seriously and imminently poses a threat to the public health. We are acutely aware that the service provided by the defendant is a valuable and necessary one. We also know that it is preferable to have chemical-waste-disposal sites than to have illegal dumping in rivers, streams, and deserted areas. But a site such as defendant's, if it is to do the job it is intended to do, must be located in a secure place, where it will pose no threat to health or life, now, or in the future. This site was intended to be a *permanent* disposal site for the deposit of extremely hazardous chemical-waste materials. Yet this site is located above an abandoned tunneled mine where subsidence is occurring several years ahead of when it was anticipated. Also, the permeability-coefficient samples taken by defendant's experts, though not conclusive alone, indicate that the soil is more permeable at the site than expected. Moreover, the

spillage, odors, and dust caused by the presence of the disposal site indicate why it was inadvisable to locate the site so near the plaintiff village.

Therefore, we conclude that in fashioning relief in this case the trial court did balance relative hardship to be caused to the plaintiffs and defendant, and did fashion reasonable relief when it ordered the exhumation of all material from the site and the reclamation of the surrounding area. The instant site is akin to Mr. Justice Sutherland's observation that "Nuisance may be merely a right thing in a wrong place—like a pig in the parlor instead of the barnyard." [Citations.]

We are also cognizant of *amicus* USEPA's suggestion in its brief and affidavits filed with the appellate court which urge that we remand to the circuit court so that alternatives to closure of the site and exhumation of the waste materials may be considered. The USEPA states: "Heavy equipment may damage drums, releasing wastes and possibly causing gaseous emissions, fires, and explosions. Repackaging and transporting damaged drums also risks releasing wastes. Workers performing the exhumation face dangers from contact with or inhalation of wastes; these risks cannot be completely eliminated with protective clothing and breathing apparatus. Nearby residents may also be endangered." It is ironic that the host of horribles mentioned by the USEPA in support of keeping the site open includes some of the same hazards which the plaintiffs have raised as reasons in favor of closing the site.

* * * We conclude therefore that the relief fashioned by the trial court is reasonable under the precise facts of this case and will not be disturbed.

* * *

Affirmed and remanded.

Ryan, Justice, concurring:

While I agree with both the result reached by the majority and the reasoning employed supporting the opinion, I wish to add a brief comment. In response to the defendant's argument that the trial court failed to apply the proper standard for determining when a prospective nuisance may be enjoined, the majority concluded that the court had in fact applied the correct rule as set out in Fink v. Board of Trustees (1966), 71 Ill.App.2d 276, 218 N.E.2d 240. I am concerned that the holding of *Fink,* quoted by the majority, may be an unnecessarily narrow view of the test for enjoining prospective tortious conduct in general. Any injunction is, by its very nature, the product of a court's balancing of competing interests, with a result equitably obtained. Prosser, in discussing the law of nuisance, quoted by the majority, states:

"[I]f the possibility [of harm] is merely uncertain or contingent [the plaintiff] may be left to his remedy after the nuisance has occurred." Prosser, Torts sec. 90, at 603 (4th ed. 1971).

Prosser thus recognizes that there are cases in which the possibility of inflicting harm is slight and where the plaintiff may be left to his remedy at law. However, I believe that there are situations where the harm that is potential is so devastating that equity should afford relief even though the possibility of the harmful result occurring is uncertain or contingent. The Restatement's position applicable to preventative injunctive relief in general is that "[t]he more serious the impending harm, the less justification there is for taking the chances that are involved in pronouncing the harm too remote." (Restatement (Second) of Torts sec. 933, at 561, comment *b* (1979).) If the harm that may result is severe, a lesser possibility of it occurring should be required to support injunctive relief. Conversely, if the potential harm is less severe, a greater possibility that it will happen should be required. Also, in the balancing of competing interests, a court may find a situation where the potential harm is such that a plaintiff will be left to his remedy at law if the possibility of it occurring is slight. This balancing test allows the court to consider a wider range of factors and avoids the anomalous result possible under a more restrictive alternative where a person engaged in an ultrahazardous activity with potentially catastrophic results would be allowed to continue until he has driven an entire community to the brink of certain disaster. A court of equity need not wait so long to provide relief.

Although the "dangerous probability" test has certainly been met in this case, I would be willing to enjoin the activity on a showing of probability of occurrence substantially less than that which the facts presented to this court reveal, due to the extremely hazardous nature of the chemicals being dumped and the potentially catastrophic results.

---

1. An injunction case always involves some degree of future prediction. The judge must determine both the probability and degree of future threatened harm absent the injunction. The legal consequence of a particular prediction is easily applied only at the two extremes: Equity will not enjoin a completed act, but injunctions are granted to halt clearly continuous invasions of an important interest where the remedy at law is inadequate.

A court is faced with an especially difficult task of prediction when the activity sought to be enjoined is causing no current harm and poses only an uncertain future threat. An injunction is not justified if its basis is solely that a tort may possibly occur. For example, in Nicholson v. Connecticut Half–Way House, Inc., 153 Conn. 507, 218 A.2d 383 (1966), residents sought to enjoin the prospective use of defendant's property as a temporary residence for selected parolees from state prison. The plaintiffs claimed that the parolees might commit criminal acts in their neighborhood and that the half-way house would cause their property values to depreciate. The court denied injunctive relief because unsubstantiated fears could not justify the intervention of equity.

Are there circumstances where prospective harm is so potentially devastating that a lower probability of such injury should suffice to support an injunctive? Are there problems with a sliding scale approach that weighs the seriousness of the harm against the likelihood of its occurrence?

2. What role should the common law of nuisance play in relation to various statutory schemes for environmental protection? In Illinois v. Milwaukee, 406 U.S. 91, 92 S.Ct. 1385, 31 L.Ed.2d 712 (1972) (*Milwaukee I*), the Supreme Court recognized a federal common law of nuisance to abate pollution of interstate or navigable waters. The Court intimated that a comprehensive federal regulatory scheme could preempt the field of federal common law of nuisance. Congress subsequently enacted the Federal Water Pollution Control Act Amendments of 1972.

Almost a decade later the Court then held in Milwaukee v. Illinois, 451 U.S. 304, 101 S.Ct. 1784, 68 L.Ed.2d 114 (1981) (*Milwaukee II*), that the federal legislation occupied the field of water pollution regulation and left no room for federal common law. Most recently a third case concerning the boundaries of statutory and common law completes a trilogy of Supreme Court cases on the subject. In International Paper Company v. Ouellette, 479 U.S. 481, 107 S.Ct. 805, 93 L.Ed.2d 883 (1987), the plaintiffs sought damages and an injunction to require the defendant to restructure part of the water treatment system of its pulp and paper mill. The plaintiffs claimed that the defendant's New York operations had caused a significant interference with their property interests in Vermont through the discharge of waste materials into Lake Champlain. The Court held that the federal Clean Water Act precluded the application of the Vermont state law against an out of state source. However, the Court further held that New York nuisance law would not be preempted by the federal regulation. The opinion observes that states could properly use their own common laws in setting permit standards consistent with the Clean Water Act. The decision effectively rejuvenates the role of state nuisance law to complement federal pollution control regulations.

3. Courts traditionally have accorded a heavy presumption of validity to legislative determinations that certain activities offend the public health, safety, or welfare. Nonetheless, judicial deference to the legislative police power is not without limits. In Ace Tire Co. v. Municipal Officers of Waterville, an operator of a junkyard challenged the constitutionality of a statute concerning junkyard licensing fees. It provided that junkyards and automobile graveyards within 100 feet of a highway must pay a $500 licensing fee, whereas those located farther away had to pay only a $10 fee. The court acknowledged that a legislature may take into account aesthetic values, such as preserving scenic beauty, when enacting measures for the public welfare. However, the court determined that the statutory licensing scheme arbitrarily and unreasonably favored some operators of junkyards over others, and bore no rational relationship to the stated objectives of preventing distractions to highway travelers. The court therefore held it unconstitutional and noted:

"The legislature may not, under the guise of protecting the public interests, arbitrarily interfere with private legitimate businesses or impose unusual and unnecessary restrictions upon lawful occupations by labeling them nuisances." 302 A.2d 90 (Me.1973).

Similarly, Kadash v. City of Williamsport, 19 Pa.Cmwlth. 643, 340 A.2d 617 (1975), held that the legislature could not declare an activity to be a nuisance per se when it did not constitute a nuisance in fact. Accordingly, the court interpreted an ordinance regulating junked automobiles as involving a reasonableness test: Is the defendant's operation reasonable in light of the locale and attendant circumstances?

SPUR INDUSTRIES, INC. v. DEL E. WEBB DEVELOPMENT CO.

108 Ariz. 178, 494 P.2d 700 (1972).

CAMERON, VICE CHIEF JUSTICE.

From a judgment permanently enjoining the defendant, Spur Industries, Inc., from operating a cattle feedlot near the plaintiff Del E. Webb Development Company's Sun City, Spur appeals. Webb cross-appeals. Although numerous issues are raised, we feel that it is necessary to answer only two questions. They are:

1. Where the operation of a business, such as a cattle feedlot is lawful in the first instance, but becomes a nuisance by reason of a nearby residential area, may the feedlot operation be enjoined in an action brought by the developer of the residential area?

2. Assuming that the nuisance may be enjoined, may the developer of a completely new town or urban area in a previously agricultural area be required to indemnify the operator of the feedlot who must move or cease operation because of the presence of the residential area created by the developer?

The facts necessary for a determination of this matter on appeal are as follows. The area in question is located in Maricopa County, Arizona, some 14 to 15 miles west of the urban area of Phoenix, on the Phoenix–Wickenburg Highway, also known as Grand Avenue. About two miles south of Grand Avenue is Olive Avenue which runs east and west. 111th Avenue runs north and south as does the Agua Fria River immediately to the west.

Farming started in this area about 1911. In 1929, with the completion of the Carl Pleasant Dam, gravity flow water became available to the property located to the west of the Agua Fria River, though land to the east remained dependent upon well water for irrigation. By 1950, the only urban areas in the vicinity were the agriculturally related communities of Peoria, El Mirage, and Surprise located along Grand Avenue. Along 111th Avenue, approximately one mile south of Grand Avenue and 1½ miles north of Olive Avenue, the community of Youngtown was commenced in 1954. Youngtown is a retirement community appealing primarily to senior citizens.

In 1956, Spur's predecessors in interest, H. Marion Welborn and the Northside Bay Mill and Trading Company, developed feedlots, about ½ mile south of Olive Avenue, in an area between the confluence of the usually dry Agua Fria and New Rivers. The area is well suited for cattle feeding and in 1959, there were 25 cattle feeding pens or dairy operations within a 7 mile radius of the location developed by Spur's predecessors. In April and May of 1959, the Northside Hay Mill was feeding between 6,000 and 7,000 head of cattle and Welborn approximately 1,500 head on a combined area of 35 acres.

In May of 1959, Del Webb began to plan the development of an urban area to be known as Sun City. For this purpose, the Marinette and the Santa Fe Ranches, some 20,000 acres of farmland, were purchased for $15,000,000 or $750.00 per acre. This price was considerably less than the price of land located near the urban area of Phoenix, and along with the success of Youngtown was a factor influencing the decision to purchase the property in question.

By September 1959, Del Webb had started construction of a golf course south of Grand Avenue and Spur's predecessors had started to level ground for more feedlot area. In 1960, Spur purchased the property in question and began a rebuilding and expansion program extending both to the north and south of the original facilities. By 1962, Spur's expansion program was completed and had expanded from approximately 35 acres to 114 acres.

Accompanied by an extensive advertising campaign, homes were first offered by Del Webb in January 1960 and the first unit to be completed was south of Grand Avenue and approximately 2½ miles north of Spur. By 2 May 1960, there were 450 to 500 houses completed or under construction. At this time, Del Webb did not consider odors from the Spur feed pens a problem and Del Webb continued to develop in a southerly direction, until sales resistance became so great that the parcels were difficult if not impossible to sell. * * *

By December 1967, Del Webb's property had extended south to Olive Avenue and Spur was within 500 feet of Olive Avenue to the north. Del Webb filed its original complaint alleging that in excess of 1,300 lots in the southwest portion were unfit for development for sale as residential lots because of the operation of the Spur feedlot.

Del Webb's suit complained that the Spur feeding operation was a public nuisance because of the flies and the odor which were drifting or being blown by the prevailing south to north wind over the southern portion of Sun City. At the time of the suit, Spur was feeding between 20,000 and 30,000 head of cattle, and the facts amply support the finding of the trial court that the feed pens had become a nuisance to the people who resided in the southern part of Del Webb's development. The testimony indicated that cattle in a commercial feedlot will produce 35 to 40 pounds of wet manure per day, per head, or over a million pounds of wet manure per day for 30,000 head of cattle, and that despite the admittedly good feedlot management and good housekeeping practices by

Spur, the resulting odor and flies produced an annoying if not unhealthy situation as far as the senior citizens of southern Sun City were concerned. There is no doubt that some of the citizens of Sun City were unable to enjoy the outdoor living which Del Webb had advertised and that Del Webb was faced with sales resistance from prospective purchasers as well as strong and persistent complaints from the people who had purchased homes in that area.

* * *

It is noted, however, that neither the citizens of Sun City nor Youngtown are represented in this lawsuit and the suit is solely between Del E. Webb Development Company and Spur Industries, Inc.

The difference between a private nuisance and a public nuisance is generally one of degree. A private nuisance is one affecting a single individual or a definite small number of persons in the enjoyment of private rights not common to the public, while a public nuisance is one affecting the rights enjoyed by citizens as a part of the public. To constitute a public nuisance, the nuisance must affect a considerable number of people or an entire community or neighborhood. [Citation.]

Where the injury is slight, the remedy for minor inconveniences lies in an action for damages rather than in one for an injunction. [Citation.] Moreover, some courts have held, in the "balancing of conveniences" cases, that damages may be the sole remedy. [Citations.]

Thus, it would appear from the admittedly incomplete record as developed in the trial court, that, at most, residents of Youngtown would be entitled to damages rather than injunctive relief.

We have no difficulty, however, in agreeing with the conclusion of the trial court that Spur's operation was an enjoinable public nuisance as far as the people in the southern portion of Del Webb's Sun City were concerned.

§ 36–601, subsec. A reads as follows:

"§ 36–601. Public nuisances dangerous to public health

"A. The following conditions are specifically declared public nuisances dangerous to the public health:

"1. Any condition or place in populous areas which constitutes a breeding place for flies, rodents, mosquitoes and other insects which are capable of carrying and transmitting disease-causing organisms to any person or persons."

By this statute, before an otherwise lawful (and necessary) business may be declared a public nuisance, there must be a "populous" area in which people are injured:

" * * * [I]t hardly admits a doubt that, in determining the question as to whether a lawful occupation is so conducted as to constitute a nuisance as a matter of fact, the locality and surroundings are of the first importance. (citations omitted) A business which is not per se a public nuisance may become such by being carried on at a place where the health, comfort, or convenience of a populous neighborhood is affected. * * * What might amount to a serious nuisance in one locality by reason of the density of the population, or character of the neighborhood affected, may in another place and under different surroundings be deemed proper and unobjectionable. * * * "[Citation.]

It is clear that as to the citizens of Sun City, the operation of Spur's feedlot was both a public and a private nuisance. They could have successfully maintained an action to abate the nuisance. Del Webb, having shown a special injury in the loss of sales, had a standing to bring suit to enjoin the nuisance. [Citations.] The judgment of the trial court permanently enjoining the operation of the feedlot is affirmed.

A suit to enjoin a nuisance sounds in equity and the courts have long recognized a special responsibility to the public when acting as a court of equity:

§ 104. Where public interest is involved.

"Courts of equity may, and frequently do, go much further both to give and withhold relief in furtherance of the public interest than they are accustomed to go when only private interests are involved. Accordingly, the granting or withholding of relief may properly be dependent upon considerations of public interest. * * *." 27 Am. Jur.2d, Equity, page 626.

In addition to protecting the public interest, however, courts of equity are concerned with protecting the operator of a lawfully, albeit noxious, business from the result of a knowing and willful encroachment by others near his business.

In the so-called "coming to the nuisance" cases, the courts have held that the residential landowner may not have relief if he knowingly came into a neighborhood reserved for industrial or agricultural endeavors and has been damaged thereby:

"Plaintiffs chose to live in an area uncontrolled by zoning laws or restrictive covenants and remote from urban development. In such an area plaintiffs cannot complain that legitimate agricultural pursuits are being carried on in the vicinity, nor can plaintiffs, having chosen to build in an agricultural area, complain that the agricultural pursuits carried on in the area depreciate the value of their homes. The area being *primarily agricultural,* any opinion reflecting the value of such property must take this factor into account. The standards affecting the value of residence property in an urban setting, subject to zoning controls and controlled planning techniques, cannot be the standards by which agricultural properties are judged.

"People employed in a city who build their homes in suburban areas of the county beyond the limits of a city and zoning regulations do so for a reason. Some do so to avoid the high taxation rate imposed by cities, or to avoid special assessments for street, sewer and water projects. They usually build on improved or hard surface highways, which have been built either at state or county expense and thereby avoid special assessments for these improvements. It may be that they desire to get away from the congestion of traffic, smoke, noise, foul air and the many other annoyances of city life. But with all these advantages in going beyond the area which is zoned and restricted to protect them in their homes, they must be prepared to take the disadvantages." [Citations.]

And:

"* * * * a party cannot justly call upon the law to make that place suitable for his residence which was not so when he selected it. * * *." [Citation.]

Were Webb the only party injured, we would feel justified in holding that the doctrine of "coming to the nuisance" would have been a bar to the relief asked by Webb, and, on the other hand, had Spur located the feedlot near the outskirts of a city and had the city grown toward the feedlot, Spur would have to suffer the cost of abating the nuisance as to those people locating within the growth pattern of the expanding city:

"The case affords, perhaps, an example where a business established at a place remote from population is gradually surrounded and becomes part of a populous center, so that a business which formerly was not an interference with the rights of others has become so by the encroachment of the population * * *." [Citation.]

We agree, however, with the Massachusetts court that:

"The law of nuisance affords no rigid rule to be applied in all instances. It is elastic. It undertakes to require only that which is fair and reasonable under all the circumstances. In a commonwealth like this, which depends for its material prosperity so largely on the continued growth and enlargement of manufacturing of diverse varieties, 'extreme rights' cannot be enforced. * * *." [Citation.]

There was no indication in the instant case at the time Spur and its predecessors located in western Maricopa County that a new city would spring up, full-blown, alongside the feeding operation and that the developer of that city would ask the court to order Spur to move because of the new city. Spur is required to move not because of any wrongdoing on the part of Spur, but because of a proper and legitimate regard of the courts for the rights and interests of the public.

Del Webb, on the other hand, is entitled to the relief prayed for (a permanent injunction), not because Webb is blameless, but because of the damage to the people who have been encouraged to purchase homes in Sun City. It does not equitably or legally follow, however, that Webb, being entitled to the injunction, is then free of any liability to Spur if Webb has in fact been the cause of the damage Spur has sustained. It does not seem harsh to require a developer, who has taken advantage of the lesser land values in a rural area as well as the availability of large tracts of land on which to build and develop a new town or city in the area, to indemnify those who are forced to leave as a result.

Having brought people to the nuisance to the foreseeable detriment of Spur, Webb must indemnify Spur for a reasonable amount of the cost of moving or shutting down. It should be noted that this relief to Spur is limited to a case wherein a developer has, with foreseeability, brought into a previously agricultural or industrial area the population which makes necessary the granting of an injunction against a lawful business and for which the business has no adequate relief.

It is therefore the decision of this court that the matter be remanded to the trial court for a hearing upon the damages sustained by the defendant Spur as a reasonable and direct result of the granting of the permanent injunction. * * *

---

1. Early authorities denied equitable assistance to parties who chose to locate within close proximity to the operation of an established industry. The rationale was that the later arriving parties either implicitly had consented to the offending trade or they should have foreseen that the business would constitute a nuisance. *See* Rex v. Cross, 2 C. & P. 483, 172 Eng.Rep. 219; Wittman, First Come, First Served: An Economic Analysis of "Coming to the Nuisance," 9 J.Leg. Stud. 557 (1980).

The contrary position, which has become the current trend in the United States, holds that one who arrives in a locale first does not have a prescriptive right to continue the business indefinitely without possible constraint. In one early case, *Wier's Appeal,* the court repudiated the coming to the nuisance doctrine:

> * * * Carrying on an offensive trade for any number of years in a place remote from buildings and public roads, does not entitle the owner to continue it in the same place after houses have been built and roads laid out in the neighborhood, to the occupants of which and travellers upon which it is a nuisance. As the city extends, such nuisances should be removed to the vacant grounds beyond the immediate neighborhood of the residences of the citizens. This, public policy, as well as the health and comfort of the population of the city, demand. 74 Pa. 230 (1873)

The parties' order of arrival nonetheless still serves as a persuasive factor in determining the availability of equitable relief for a nuisance and the scope of the relief granted.

2. The requirement that an activity substantially and unreasonably interfere with the use and enjoyment of another's property for nuisance is a relative concept. The court may properly consider the uses of adjoining land and the general character of the area. In Mahlstadt v. City of Indianola, 251 Iowa 222, 100 N.W.2d 189 (1959), the court

determined that a long-established city trash dump itself partially defined the character of the area. The court held that the dump served a useful public service, and that the long run costs and benefits made it appropriate to remain in existence with some modifications in the manner of its operations.

3. When a nuisance cannot be sufficiently abated, the question becomes whether the court should order the cessation of the offending activity. Requests for such orders pose difficult problems when the defendant operates an established, lawfully conducted business. An order to cease operations in the current location forces the business to relocate or shut down. The order is likely to impose heavy economic losses, to cost some number of jobs, and to defeat the justifiable expectations of those who invested in the business.

Further losses are likely if the order to cease operations requires prompt action. In Pendoley v. Ferreira, 345 Mass. 309, 187 N.E.2d 142 (1963), the court enjoined the operation of a piggery. In drafting the decree, the court gave consideration to alleviating the economic hardship on the defendant by providing a reasonable period of time for the defendant either to liquidate its stock or to find new premises.

4. What should happen if the nuisance activity comes to the plaintiff? In Bove v. Donner–Hanna Coke Corporation, 236 A.D. 37, 258 N.Y.S. 229 (1932), the plaintiff purchased a house and grocery store in a light industrial area and lived there several years before the defendant built a factory nearby. The court denied the plaintiff's request for an injunction against the factory on the basis that the plaintiff should have reasonably foreseen that the area was adapted for industrial purposes rather than residential uses.

5. Preferential treatment for the first property use which is established in a locale appears in areas of property law in addition to nuisance. In the early development of the arid western United States, water rights were determined by "first in time, first in right." This doctrine of prior appropriation protected investments in mining equipment and materials to utilize the water resources. In times of short water supply the first appropriator was entitled to a full share of the water even if that use exhausted the supply for the secondary appropriators. Nine states still follow the prior appropriation scheme in statutory form and ten others in hybrid fashion in combination with other factors. *See* Tex. Water Code § 11.027 (Supp.1988).

6. For additional commentary on the doctrine of coming to the nuisance see the following references: Whittman, First Come, First Served: An Economic Analysis of "Coming to the Nuisance," 9 J.Leg. Stud. 557 (1980); Note, Land Use and Environmental Policy: Litigation of Nuisances as a Land Use Control: The Spur Industries Case, 26 Okla.L.Rev. 583 (1973); Note, Torts–Nuisance–"Coming to the Nuisance," 32 Or.L.Rev. 264 (1953); Note–Torts: Nuisance: Defenses: "Coming to the Nuisance" as a Defense, 41 Calif.L.Rev. 148 (1953).

AKAU v. OLOHANA CORP.

65 Hawaii 383, 652 P.2d 1130 (1982).

RICHARDSON, CHIEF JUSTICE.

Plaintiffs Akau and others brought this class action to enforce alleged rights-of-way along once public trails to the breach that crossed original defendants' property in Kawaihae on the Big Island of Hawaii. The court below ruled that plaintiffs have standing to assert the rights of the public, and certified the suit as a class action. We affirm.

The named plaintiffs have lived or fished in Kawaihae for many years. They represent two subclasses; one contains Hawaii residents who used or were deterred from using the trails, the other contains all persons who own land or reside in the area and used or were deterred from using the trails. The original defendants were landowners or tenants who possess the beachfront land between Spencer Beach Park and Hapuna Beach Park, a span of about two and a half miles along the beach. They had barred all public access across their land to the public beach since acquiring the land in 1954.

Two of the trails in issue run roughly parallel to the beach between the two parks. They have existed since before the turn of this century. The Kamehameha Trail is at most points very close to the water and at others about 100 yards away. The Kawaihae–Puako Road is about 150 yards further upland. There are also eleven intersecting trails that run from the main trails to the shore. Plaintiffs allege that these trails had been used by the public until 1954.

* * *

Plaintiffs claim that the trails have been and are public rights-of-way and ask for declaratory and injunctive relief to that effect. * * *

We address the standing issue first. All of plaintiffs' theories are based on rights that accrue to them as members of the public, except perhaps easement by necessity and prescription. These easements might be public depending on the facts brought out at trial.

Defendant argues that only the State may bring an action against landowners to enforce the public's right of beach access. This proposition can be traced to the general rule in the law of public nuisance that a private individual has no standing to sue for the abatement of a public nuisance if his injury is only that which is shared by the public generally. [Citations.] Obstruction of the public right of way is a public nuisance. [Citation.]

This rule developed in the early common law because harm to the public order, decency or morals was considered a crime against the king. *See* Prosser, *Private Action for Public Nuisance,* 52 Va.L.R. 997 (1966). Only the king, therefore, could bring an action against the perpetrator. The sole exception to this rule was that a member of the public had standing to sue if he suffered a special injury that was different in kind, and not merely in degree, from the general public. [Citation.] The purpose of the rule is to prevent a multiplicity of actions and frivolous suits.

There is a trend in the law, however, away from focusing on whether the injury is shared by the public, to whether the plaintiff was in fact injured.[3] This trend began, not in nuisance, but in taxpayer suits. The general rule had been that a plaintiff had no standing to challenge an improper government act based solely on his status as a taxpayer. [Citation.] In these actions, like nuisance, the harm was considered to be to the public generally and no one suffered any direct harm to himself. In Flast v. Cohen, 392 U.S. 83, 88 S.Ct. 1942, 20 L.Ed.2d 947 (1968), the Court rejected the special injury requirement where the harm was that Congress had violated a specific constitutional limitation on its spending power. Many states have since greatly liberalized taxpayer standing beyond the federal rule and allow taxpayer suits against any improper expenditure of public funds without need to show special injury to the plaintiff. [Citations.] This court has allowed standing for taxpayers who allege an unconstitutional expenditure of public funds. [Citations.]

The courts have also broadened standing in actions challenging administrative decisions. The U.S. Supreme Court has granted standing where plaintiffs allege environmental harm even though plaintiffs' harm is equally shared by a large segment of the public. United States v. SCRAP, 412 U.S. 669, 93 S.Ct. 2405, 37 L.Ed.2d 254 (1973). * * *

Claims of harm to public trust property is another area where courts are expanding standing. [Citations.] In Marks v. Whitney, 6 Cal.3d 251, 98 Cal.Rptr. 790, 491 P.2d 374 (1971), the California Supreme Court granted standing to an individual who sued a private property owner claiming that the owner was obstructing use of public tidelands. In an implied dedication case, Dietz v. King, 2 Cal.3d 29, 84 Cal.Rptr. 162, 465 P.2d 50 (1970), the court granted standing to individuals representing a class who sued a private landowner to enforce a public right to use a beach access route across his property.

This court has been in step with the trend away from the special injury rule towards the view that a plaintiff, if injured, has standing. In *Life of the Land v. Land Use Commission,* we said:

> Standing is that aspect of justiciability focusing on the party seeking a forum rather than on the issues he wants adjudicated. And the crucial inquiry in its determination is "whether the plaintiff has 'alleged such a personal stake in the outcome of the controversy'

---

3. Restatement, Second, Torts § 821C(2) states: "In order to maintain a proceeding to enjoin to abate a public nuisance, one must ... (c) have standing to sue as a representative of the general public, as a citizen in a citizen's action or as a member of a class in a class action." *See* also, Berger, *Standing to Sue in Public Actions: Is It a Constitutional Requirement?,* 78 Yale L.J. 816 (1969); Note, *Public Nuisance: Standing to Sue Without Showing "Special Injury",* 26 U.Fla.L.R. 360 (1974).

as to warrant *his* invocation of . . . [the court's] jurisdiction and to justify exercise of the court's remedial powers on his behalf."

63 Haw. at 172, 623 P.2d at 438.

We concur in this trend because we believe it is unjust to deny members of the public the ability to enforce the public's rights when they are injured. "The very essence of civil liberty certainly consists in the right of every individual to claim the protection of the laws, whenever he receives an injury." Marbury v. Madison, 5 U.S. 137, 163, 2 L.Ed. 60 (1803).

Another reason for allowing liberal standing is that the danger of a multiplicity of suits is greatly alleviated by a proper class action. A judgment in a class action consisting of the people actually injured will bind the members who are all those allowed to sue. This will also prevent inconsistent judgments.

We hold, therefore, that a member of the public has standing to sue to enforce the rights of the public even though his injury is not different in kind from the public's generally, if he can show that he has suffered an injury in fact, and that the concerns of a multiplicity of suits are satisfied by any means, including a class action.

We turn next to whether plaintiffs here have suffered an injury in fact. We first define the term. In *Life of the Land v. Land Use Commission,* we stated:

> There has been an unmistakable parallelism in the substance of our standing decisions involving the particular interests Life of the Land seeks to protect and in the substance of related federal decisions. While the term "injury in fact" may not appear in their text, our decisions have afforded standing on a basis at least coextensive with federal doctrine where harm to such interests has been alleged.

63 Haw. at 176, 623 P.2d at 441. The United States Supreme Court has summarized its decisions on injury in fact as follows:

> Art. III requires the party who invokes the court's authority to "show that he personally has suffered some actual or threatened injury" as a result of the putatively illegal conduct of the defendant, and that the injury "fairly can be traced to the challenged action," and "is likely to be redressed by a favorable decision." [Citations.]

Courts generally examine the injury question by looking at the interest being injured and seeing whether a favorable decision will benefit plaintiffs. Injury in fact has always included harm to economic interests. [Citations.] The Court has recently expanded injury to include harm to aesthetic and recreational values. United States v. SCRAP, 412 U.S. 669, 93 S.Ct. 2405, 37 L.Ed.2d 254 (1973); Sierra Club v. Morton, 405 U.S. 727, 92 S.Ct. 1361, 31 L.Ed.2d 636 (1972). In *SCRAP* the injury was difficult to measure. The Court there explained that it was asked to follow a far more attenuated line of causation to the eventual injury of which the appellees complained—a general rate increase [on railroad freight charges] would allegedly cause increased use of nonrecyclable goods, thus resulting in the need to use more natural resources to produce such goods, some of which resources might be taken from the Washington area, and resulting in more refuse that might be discarded in national parks in the Washington area.

412 U.S. at 688, 93 S.Ct. at 2416.

Although the injury was very slight or attenuated in *SCRAP,* the Court granted standing because the interest to be protected was an accepted one. In *Sierra Club, supra,* the Court held that development in parkland was an injury to a cognizable interest, but denied standing to an environmental organization because it had failed to show that it was among the injured because it did not allege that its members used the endangered area. Thus a plaintiff has standing if he can demonstrate some injury to a recognized interest such as economic or aesthetic, and is himself among the injured and not merely airing a political or intellectual grievance.

In this case, plaintiffs allege that they are prevented from using a public right of way. The resulting difficulty in getting to the beach hampers the use and enjoyment of it and may prevent or discourage use in some instances. This is an injury to a recreational interest similar to the one in *SCRAP* because the ability to get to a recreational area is as vital for enjoying it as having it in its natural condition.

We are convinced, therefore, that plaintiffs have sufficiently alleged that they are among the injured. The class description includes all those who have used or have been deterred from using the trails. Thus all class members have suffered an injury in fact. This meets the requirement of actual injury in *Sierra Club.* The trial court correctly granted plaintiffs' standing. * * *

----

1. The court in the principal case departed from the traditional rule that a private individual lacks standing to maintain an action to abate a public nuisance absent a showing that he has suffered harm of a different kind from members of the general public. The traditional view is reflected, for example, in California Civil Code § 3493; a private person is allowed to bring a public nuisance suit if the activity is "specially injurious to himself, but not otherwise." This approach is followed in the majority of jurisdictions.

Burns Jackson Miller Summit & Spitzer v. Lindner, 464 N.Y.S.2d 712, 59 N.Y.2d 314, 451 N.E.2d 459 (1983), illustrates the effect of the traditional rule. The court held that a law firm lacked standing to assert a public nuisance claim for lost business profits resulting from a mass transit strike because all members of the public had been affected by the strike. The court reasoned that any interference with the law firm's business was only an incidental result of the transit union's conduct rather than a special kind of harm.

The general requirement that a plaintiff suffer special harm, rather than merely a greater degree of harm, has proved troublesome in some cases. For example, in Stop & Shop Companies, Inc. v. Fisher, 387 Mass. 889, 444 N.E.2d 368 (1983), reprinted in Chapter 14 *infra,* the plaintiff claimed it lost profits because the negligent obstruction of a public bridge cut off access to the plaintiff's business premises for customers. The court held that the plaintiff had standing to assert a public nuisance claim. On similar facts, the court in Nebraska Innkeepers, Inc. v. Pittsburgh–Des Moines Corp., 345 N.W.2d 124 (Iowa 1984), denied standing. The plaintiff's claim was made on behalf of the retail business community for losses attributed to a bridge's closing. That court denied the claim because the plaintiff suffered no "special" harm.

2. To what extent in a nuisance case should a court consider subjective factors, such as the motive behind using property in a certain way? In Sundowner, Inc. v. King, 95 Idaho 367, 509 P.2d 785 (1973), the plaintiff sought an injunction to remove an 85 foot long and 18 foot high sign which had been erected between two adjacent hotels. The sign blocked 80 percent of the plaintiff's building and restricted the passage of light and air. The court acknowledged that the so-called English rule, followed by many 19th century American courts, gave a property owner the unfettered right to maintain such structures. The court instead chose to follow the American rule which enjoins "spite" fences that serve no useful purpose and are intended to annoy and inconvenience neighboring landowners.

Similarly, in Hutcherson v. Alexander, 264 Cal.App.2d 126, 70 Cal.Rptr. 366 (1968), the court ordered the defendant restaurant owner to remove a 14 foot high "menu board" which obstructed the public view of a nearby competing business. The court determined that the sign was not essential to the defendant's business but was constructed as part of a general scheme to interfere with the reasonable use and enjoyment of the plaintiff's property.

What if a court finds that a defendant has conducted its business in a manner intended to be offensive to a neighboring use but that the actual interference is insubstantial? Would the activity constitute a nuisance at all? Even if it does, should the court simply decline to enjoin the conduct and award damages?

3. For further commentary regarding enjoining nuisances see the following references: Calabresi & Melamed, Property Rules, Liability Rules, and Inalienability: One View of the Cathedral, 85 Harv.L.Rev. 1089 (1972); Epstein, Nuisance Law: Corrective Justice and Its Utilitarian Constraints, 8 J. Legal Stud. 49 (1979); Keeton, Trespass, Nuisance and Strict Liability, 59 Colum.L.Rev. 457 (1959); Lewin, Compensated Injunctions and the Evolution of Nuisance Law, 71 Iowa L.Rev. 775 (1986); Clintock, Discretion to Deny Injunction Against Trespass and

Nuisance, 12 Minn.L.Rev. 565 (1926); Michelman, Pollution as a Tort; A Non–Accidental Perspective on Calabresi's Costs, 80 Yale L.J. 647 (1971); Morris & Keeton, Notes on Balancing the Equities, 18 Tex. L.Rev. 253 (1940); Note, Injunctive Negotiations: An Economic, Moral and Legal Analysis, 27 Stan.L.Rev. 1563 (1975); Polinski, Resolving Nuisance Disputes: The Simple Economics of Injunctive and Damage Remedies, 32 Stan.L.Rev. 1075 (1980); Prosser, Private Action for Public Nuisance, 52 Va.L.Rev. 997 (1966); Rabin, Nuisance Law: Rethinking Fundamental Assumptions, 63 Va.L.Rev. 1299 (1977).

2.   Enjoining Crimes

MEYER v. SEIFERT
216 Ark. 293, 225 S.W.2d 4 (1949).

Leflar, Justice.

Appellant G.A. Meyer on behalf of himself and other property owners filed this bill in equity for a mandatory injunction to require the removal of a non-fireproof building erected by defendants Seifert and Mahle, under a permit granted by the other defendants (City of Stuttgart, Ark., and the Mayor, City Clerk, and Aldermen of said city, in their official capacities) within a fire zone in which the erection of such buildings was prohibited by city ordinances. The Chancery Court refused to issue the injunction, and plaintiff appeals.

[The court first recognized that the relevant city ordinances (Nos. 277 and 286) flatly prohibited the construction of non-fireproof frame buildings, such as the type built by the defendants Seifert and Mahle. Additionally, the building permit relied upon by the defendants had been invalidly issued by the city council.]

* * *

A second contention urged by the defendants is that equity is without power, or should not exercise the power, to enjoin maintenance of the prohibited structure. The argument is that the ordinance prescribes criminal punishments, making violation a misdemeanor punishable by fine of not less than $10 nor more than $100 for each day of violation, and that this remedy is exclusive. That equity will not act to restrain ordinary violations of the criminal law, but will leave the task of enforcing the criminal laws to courts having criminal jurisdiction, is basic learning in our legal system. But it is equally basic that if grounds for equity jurisdiction exist in a given case, the fact that the act to be enjoined is incidentally violative of a criminal enactment will not preclude equity's action to enjoin it.

In one of the most publicized cases that ever arose in Arkansas, Chancellor Martin enjoined the holding at Hot Springs of a world championship heavyweight prizefight between James J. Corbett and Robert Fitzsimmons. [Citation.] Judge Martin conceded that ordinarily equity does not enjoin the commission of crimes, but pointed out that it

does issue such injunctions where property interests are involved, and emphasized the prospective property injuries threatened by the prize-fight, notably the payment of money by purchasers of tickets of admission to the illegal enterprise, losses by bettors, the use and congestion of some buildings which might be harmful to other adjoining buildings, and the possible loss of property to thieves, pick-pockets and similar gentry who might come to the state for the fight. The most frequently quoted statement of the rule in Arkansas appears in State v. Vaughan, 81 Ark. 117, 126, 98 S.W. 685, 690, 7 L.R.A., N.S., 899, 118 Am.St.Rep. 29, 11 Ann.Cas. 277, where, after denying the injunction in the particular case, Chief Justice Hill added: "On the other hand, if the public nuisance is one touching civil property rights or privileges of the public, or the public health is affected by a physical nuisance, or if any other ground of equity jurisdiction exists calling for an injunction, a chancery court will enjoin, notwithstanding the act enjoined may also be a crime. The criminality of the act will neither give nor oust jurisdiction in chancery."
* * *

It is characteristic of most instances in which injunctions against criminal acts are sustained that the threat of punishment after the event will not have a very strong deterrent effect upon the offender. As to some acts, this is because the criminal punishment is small and unimportant as compared with the benefits or profits expected to be gained from the criminal act. Oftentimes the act is a recurrent or continuing one, necessitating numerous successive petty prosecutions if the regular criminal procedure is to be followed. Frequently the acts are such that it is difficult to get jury convictions, either because local juries are prejudiced against the enforcement of the particular law involved, or for some other equally practical reason. In effect these considerations point to (1) the practical inadequacy of the available legal (criminal) remedy, and (2) interference with property or other equitably protectible interests of the plaintiff or, if he has sued in a representative capacity, of a substantial group of the general public.

The decisions on the specific type of invasion of rights involved in the instant case are in accord with these principles. Many cases hold that a nearby property owner, for himself and others similarly situated, may enjoin the violation of building codes, zoning laws or similar enactments, on showing substantial threat of injury to his and their property. [Citations.] The case of Lewis v. A. Hirsch & Co., 192 Ark. 209, 90 S.W.2d 976, is not contrary to these cases. The *Hirsch* case merely held that one who sued as a citizen and taxpayer only, who did not claim to own any property or show any prospective injury to himself, would not be granted an injunction against construction of a building in violation of a fire zone ordinance. * * * And in Van Hovenberg v. Holman, 201 Ark. 370, 144 S.W.2d 718, 722, this court held squarely that an injunction should be sustained on behalf of a plaintiff property owner restraining defendant's erection of a filling station in a restricted zone in violation of a city ordinance. There we said: "But the primary and fundamental purpose of the ordinance was to prohibit operation—

not to punish. It is definitely settled that equity will not interfere to stay proceedings in a criminal matter. Here, however, the relief sought is abatement of unauthorized conduct. If it should be held that penalty of the ordinance deprived equity of jurisdiction, then any person desiring to proceed in violation of law could pay the maximum fine and become immune thereafter except as to damages. This is not the law."

The plaintiff made a substantial showing of probable damage to his own and other adjoining properties through increased fire hazards arising from maintenance of defendants' building where they have placed it in violation of the Stuttgart fire zone ordinance. This constitutes a proper case for equitable relief, as against defendants Seifert and Mahle. As to them, the decree is reversed and remanded. It is not shown that a decree against the City of Stuttgart, its Mayor, City Clerk and Board of Aldermen would afford any relief to the plaintiff, therefore the decree is affirmed as to them.

———

1. In State v. Red Owl Stores, 253 Minn. 236, 92 N.W.2d 103 (1958), the state sought to enjoin the defendant corporations from continuing to sell and distribute certain drugs without obtaining the necessary registration and licenses required by the state's Pharmacy Act. The trial court had denied the injunctive relief on the grounds that the exclusive remedy in the Act was enforcement by criminal prosecution. The Minnesota Supreme Court reversed because the state lacked an adequate remedy at law to enforce a public health measure. The legal remedy was inadequate because enforcement through the sanctions in the Act would require a multiplicity of actions.

The state in *Red Owl* had not even attempted to enforce the Act by criminal prosecution. Did the court act too hastily in concluding that criminal sanctions would be ineffective? How should equity courts balance public interest concerns with the rights of defendants to the safeguards of trial by jury and the reasonable doubt standard of proof? Would a better alternative have been for the court to defer to the legislature by refusing the injunction simply because the Act failed to offer such a remedy?

2. Should a court use nuisance law to issue an injunction prohibiting the practice of a profession without a license by characterizing the activity as a public nuisance? The cases reach mixed conclusions. *See* The Florida Bar v. Borges–Caignet, 321 So.2d 550 (Fla.1975) (unauthorized practice of law); Arizona State Bd. of Dental Examiners v. Hyder, 114 Ariz. 544, 562 P.2d 717 (1977) (practicing dentistry without a license); People ex rel. Bennett v. Laman, 277 N.Y. 368, 14 N.E.2d 439 (1938) (practicing medicine without a license). *But see* Massachusetts Society of Optometrists v. Waddick, 340 Mass. 581, 165 N.E.2d 394 (1960).

In Missouri Veterinary Medical Ass'n. v. Glisan, 230 S.W.2d 169 (Mo.App.1950), the court denied the Association's request to enjoin the defendant from the unlicensed practice of veterinary medicine. The court stated that equity would not enjoin the commission of a crime absent a showing that the Association had property rights which were being violated by the defendant's conduct. The court further held that the Association was not a proper party to bring a public nuisance action without demonstrating that it suffered a special injury as a consequence of the unlicensed practice.

BATES v. BATES

303 Ark. 89, 793 S.W.2d 788 (1990).

DUDLEY, JUSTICE.

Appellee Michael Bates allegedly abused his wife, appellant Merle Bates. She filed a petition in chancery court pursuant to the Arkansas Domestic Abuse Act of 1989. In the petition she sought an order to restrain appellee from committing future acts of domestic abuse and from entering their residence or her place of work, and to require him to pay child and housemate support. (Housemate support, not alimony or maintenance, because, pursuant to the act, she did not seek a divorce or separate maintenance. Further, it is not necessary that the parties be married to seek the protection of the act.) The petition was denied. The chancellor held that the act created a new cause of action and unconstitutionally placed jurisdiction of the new cause of action in chancery court. We affirm the holding.

The Arkansas Domestic Abuse Act provides that a petition may be filed in chancery court to prevent domestic abuse. "Domestic Abuse" is generally described as causing harm to, or committing a sex offense against, any persons who presently or in the past have resided together. An "order of protection" may include: restraining the abusing party from committing domestic abuse; excluding the offending party from the residence and the place of work of the victim; awarding custody and support of the children and support of the housemate; and awarding an attorney fee. A "temporary order of protection" may be granted upon ex parte application with a hearing to be held after notice. The temporary order shall be effective for a period not to exceed fourteen (14) days. Accordingly, the quintessence of the cause of action is preventing a person from committing acts of domestic abuse. The pivotal issue in this case is whether jurisdiction for such a cause of action lies in chancery court. That issue must be assessed within the narrow confines of equity jurisdiction under the Constitution of Arkansas.

Article 7, section 11 provides: "The circuit court shall have jurisdiction in all civil and criminal cases the exclusive jurisdiction of which may not be vested in some other court provided for by this Constitution." This provision means that unless a cause of action is confided by the Constitution exclusively to another court, it belongs exclusively, or concurrently, to the circuit court. [Citation.] In other words "[a]ll unassigned jurisdiction under the Constitution is vested in the circuit court...." Patterson v. Adcock, 157 Ark. 186, 248 S.W. 904 (1923). Article 7, section 15, provides: "Until the General Assembly shall deem it expedient to establish courts of chancery the circuit court shall have jurisdiction in matters of equity, subject to appeal to the Supreme Court, in such manner as may be prescribed by law." By Act 166 of 1903, Ark.Code Ann. § 16–13–301 (1987), separate courts of chancery were established by the General Assembly. However, the General Assembly is without authority to give chancery courts any jurisdiction other than that which the equity courts could exercise at the time of the adoption of the Constitution of 1874. Patterson v. McKay, 199 Ark. 140, 134 S.W.2d 543 (1939).

Appellant argues that the Domestic Abuse Act did not impermissibly enlarge chancery court jurisdiction. She contends that "equity should take the necessary steps to protect victims of domestic abuse, since equity is intended to be adaptable and fluid to meet the changing needs of society." Certainly, equity does accord new or extraordinary relief in novel situations, but that does not at all mean that its jurisdiction can be enlarged in violation of the Constitution of Arkansas.

The appellant argues that the chancery court has jurisdiction to protect personal and property rights. Her general statement is valid, but equity can only protect personal and property rights when certain conditions are present. [Citation.] One of those conditions is that the remedy at law is inadequate. Thus, the real issue is whether there is an adequate remedy at law. There is.

At law, a wife is entitled to protection from both actual physical abuse, Ark.Code Ann. §§ 5–26–301 to–304 (1987), and the risk or threat of such abuse, Ark.Code Ann. §§ 5–26–305 to–307 (1987). All "housemates" are protected by statutes prohibiting battery, Ark.Code Ann. §§ 5–13–201 to–203 (1987 & Supp.1989); assault, Ark.Code Ann. §§ 5–13–204 to–207 (1987); harassment, Ark.Code Ann. § 5–71–208 (1987); harassing communications, Ark.Code Ann. § 5–71–209 (1987); and terroristic threats, Ark.Code Ann. § 5–13–301 (1987). Property rights are also protected by the burglary statute, Ark.Code Ann. § 5–39–201 (1987); the criminal trespass statute, Ark.Code Ann. § 5–39–203 (1987); and the forcible possession of land statute, Ark.Code Ann. § 5–39–210 (1987).

Appellant argues the above criminal statutes are ineffective because battered housemates are afraid to file criminal charges and prosecutors do not act diligently. Even if the arguments were valid, we would not ignore the jurisdictional language of the Constitution and, in doing so, deprive an accused of his Constitutional right to a trial by jury. Further, we are not convinced either of the arguments are valid. First, if a housemate is afraid to file a complaint in circuit court we cannot see any reason why she would not also be afraid to file it in chancery court.
* * *

Additionally, except in narrow circumstances not present here, equity will not enjoin the commission of a crime because the remedy at law is adequate. The limited exception, articulated in Smith v. Hamm, 207 Ark. 507, 181 S.W.2d 475 (1944), arises when the criminal act is "incidental," and there is a danger of "irreparable pecuniary injury to property or pecuniary rights of the complaining party." If the rule were otherwise, the constitutional right of trial by jury would be infringed.
* * *

In sum, we cannot say the remedy provided at law is inadequate and, accordingly, one of the conditions necessary for equity to act to protect personal and property rights has not been met. Thus, the Chancellor correctly held that the Domestic Abuse Act impermissibly enlarged chancery court jurisdiction.

* * *

Finally, we are certainly aware that domestic abuse does occur and is a serious problem. We applaud the general assembly's concern and hope that a way, consistent with the constitution, can be found to curb this recognized evil. Our duty in this case is not to determine whether domestic abuse occurs and to approve any legislation designed to stop it. Our duty is to determine whether our constitution permits the method selected by the general assembly in the legislation questioned in this case.

If we were to perceive the issue and take the steps the appellant and some of the amici briefs suggest, the jurisdiction of chancery court could be extended almost beyond imagination. For example, drunken driving is a serious problem. * * * The criminal laws have not stopped drunken driving, but we cannot use that fact as a reason to approve extending the jurisdiction of the chancery court to issue an "order of protection" against persons accused of, but not convicted of, drunk driving. Drug sales to children is a comparable problem, as is burglary. We cannot subvert the Constitution of Arkansas and allow the creation of a cause of action totally foreign to the equity jurisdiction of the chancery court just because we perceive and abhor a particular social ill. We are pledged to support the Constitution of Arkansas, and our duty is to follow it in this case as in any other.

Affirmed.

HAYS and GLAZE, JJ., dissent.

GLAZE, JUSTICE, dissenting. * * *

My strong objection with the majority is its conclusion that battered housemates and children have an adequate remedy under the state's criminal statutes which must be enforced in circuit court. The majority does a good job in listing criminal statutes that, indeed, cover a multitude of sins and aggressions. However, none of those laws provide for the removal of the abuser or perpetrator from the residence so as to prevent future violence.

At this point, I should mention that, in divorce cases filed in chancery court, parties routinely request and are given restraining orders or injunctions to prevent their spouses from (1) committing violence, (2) committing harassing acts, (3) going into or about the premises, (4) destroying property and (5) communicating by telephone or otherwise—just to name a few examples. Most importantly, this court, in James v. James, 237 Ark. 764, 375 S.W.2d 793 (1964), recognized that the fact an act enjoined also happens to be a criminal offense does not affect the power of a court of equity to enforce its order and the aspects of an act neither give nor oust equity of jurisdiction. * * *

After today's discussion, only married people, who file for absolute or limited divorce or separate maintenance, will be able to obtain the type relief that the General Assembly attempted to provide for all family or household members by enacting the Domestic Abuse Act of 1989. Such disparate treatment of family or household members seems, to me, to be constitutionally suspect.

* * * In the forty-eight states where a trial court has both equity and law powers, the court has authority to remove abusers of house-mates and children from the home. That being so, where does that court's authority go when a state, like Arkansas, splits its trial court into separate equity (chancery) and law (circuit) courts? Does that authority disappear? Or does that authority still exist and reside in equity courts, as it has existed in divorce cases for nearly a century? I believe the latter is true and, in my view, therein lies the greatest flaw in the majority's rationale and holding.

PEOPLE v. LIM

18 Cal.2d 872, 118 P.2d 472 (1941).

GIBSON, CHIEF JUSTICE.

The district attorney of Monterey county commenced this action on behalf of the People of the State of California to restrain defendants from continuing the operation of a gambling establishment in the city of Monterey. The complaint set forth the manner in which the various games were played and alleged that the operation of this gambling house constituted a public nuisance by encouraging idle and dissolute habits, by disturbing the public peace and by corrupting the public morals. It was further alleged that previous attempts to eradicate this evil by prosecutions under the penal laws had proven ineffective and that the aid of equity was necessary to accomplish its suppression. A preliminary injunction was asked to restrain defendants from conducting and operating gambling games pending a trial of the action. Defendants interposed both general and special demurrers. The trial court sustained the demurrers and denied plaintiff's motion for a temporary injunction. After plaintiff's refusal to amend the complaint, the court entered its judgment in favor of defendants.

Upon this appeal it is contended in behalf of the People that the complaint states a proper cause of action and that it was error on the part of the trial court to sustain the general demurrer. The authority of a district attorney to bring such an action is found in the Code of Civil Procedure, section 731, which provides: "A civil action may be brought in the name of the people of the State of California to abate a public nuisance, as the same is defined in section thirty-four hundred and eighty of the Civil Code, by the district attorney of any county in which such nuisance exists * * *." Civil Code, section 3480 provides: "A public nuisance is one which affects at the same time an entire community or neighborhood, or any considerable number of persons, although the extent of the annoyance or damage inflicted upon individuals may be unequal." The definition of "nuisance", as the term is used in section 3480, is found in the provisions of the preceding section, Civil Code, section 3479: "Anything which is injurious to health, or is indecent or offensive to the senses, or an obstruction to the free use of property, so as to interfere with the comfortable enjoyment of life or property, * * * is a nuisance." It is stated in the allegations of the complaint that the action was instituted under statutory provisions. Thus, it is alleged that the gambling house operated by defendants constitutes a public nuisance "for the reason that it tends to and does in fact debauch and corrupt the public morals, encourage idle and dissolute habits, draws together great numbers of disorderly persons, disturbs the public peace, brings together idle persons and cultivates dissolute habits among them, creates traffic and fire hazards, and is thereby injurious to health, indecent and offensive to the senses and impairs the free enjoyment of life and property."

Although this proceeding purports to have been brought under the code provisions governing such actions, the plaintiff upon this appeal relies rather upon the theory that the statutory definition of "public nuisance" is not intended to be exclusive and that gaming houses, which were recognized as public nuisances at common law, are inherently public nuisances apart from the provisions of our statute. Plaintiff cites those statutes which provide that the common law must be given effect as the rule of decision where not repugnant to or inconsistent with the constitution or laws of the state. Pol.Code, § 4468; Civ.Code, § 5. Thus, it is said, a gambling house constitutes an inherent public nuisance in this state and equity will enjoin such a public nuisance in an action brought on behalf of the People. Defendants argue, however, that the authority conferred upon a district attorney to bring such an action in equity extends only to those nuisances specified by statute and that their activities are not within the terms of our statute.

It must be conceded that the cases cited by plaintiff, as well as many others, demonstrate that a gambling house constituted a public nuisance at common law for the purposes of a criminal prosecution. [Citations.] While these cases indicate that gambling houses were recognized as public nuisances in criminal prosecutions, they do not hold that an equity action on behalf of the state might be maintained at common law to enjoin the operation of a gambling house. On the contrary, it is clear that the jurisdiction of equity was very sparingly exercised on behalf of the sovereign to enjoin public nuisances. The attitude of the early English cases is expressed by Chancellor Kent in a leading case: "I know that the court is in the practice of restraining private nuisances to property, and of quieting persons in the enjoyment of private right; but it is an extremely rare case, and may be considered, if it ever happened, as an anomaly, for a court of equity to interfere at all, and much less, preliminarily, by injunction, to put down a public nuisance which did not violate the rights of property, but only contravened the general policy." [Citation.] The authorities support the conclusion that this statement accurately represents the attitude of the earlier courts of equity where the sovereign sought injunctions against public nuisances. [Citations.] The common law recognized various types of wrongful activity as indictable public nuisances, including such miscellaneous acts as eavesdropping, being a common scold and maintaining for hire a place of amusement which served no useful purpose. [Citation.] The kinds of public nuisance at common law, however, where injunctions were granted on behalf of the sovereign included only those cases of public nuisance in which the sovereign's rights were given the same protection that would have been given to the rights of a private person. An action on behalf of the state, therefore, to enjoin activity which violates general concepts of public policy finds no basis in the doctrines of the common law.

It has been recognized that the tendency to utilize the equity injunction as a means of enforcing public policy is a relatively recent development in the law. [Citations.] Courts have held that public and social interests, as well as the rights of property, are entitled to the protection of equity. [Citations.] This development has resulted in a continuous expansion of the field of public nuisances in which equitable relief is available at the request of the state. It has been held, for example, that the legislature may properly define the term "public nuisance" for the purposes of an equity injunction so as to include activity which was not a nuisance at common law or activity which offends concepts of public policy even though no rights of property are involved. [Citations.] Where particular activity, such as gambling or horse-racing, has been held to come within the language of a statute defining the term "public nuisance" for the purposes of equity jurisdiction on behalf of the state, courts have granted injunctions, or indicated that they would grant them, even though the acts were also criminal. [Citations.] Upon at least two occasions the legislature of this state has passed statutes authorizing an action in equity to enjoin particular activity contrary to the public policy as a "public nuisance". Thus, houses of prostitution and houses where narcotics are illegally sold may be enjoined in an action brought by the district attorney of the county in which they are located. [Citations.]

It must be admitted, however, that the authorities are divided as to whether the expansion of the field of public nuisances in which equity will grant injunctions must be accomplished by an act of the legislature. [Citations.] Some courts have attempted by judicial action alone to define "public nuisance" very broadly in order to grant injunctions on behalf of the state. Thus, it has been said that any place where a public statute is continuously flouted constitutes a public nuisance which may be enjoined by the state. [Citations.] Other courts have flatly stated that a particular form of activity, such as bullfighting, is so objectionable as to constitute a public nuisance for the purposes of an equity injunction without the aid of a statute. [Citations.] The courts of this state, however, have refused to sanction the granting of injunctions on behalf of the state merely by a judicial extension of the definition of "public nuisance". * * * In Weis v. Superior Court, 30 Cal.App. 730, 159 P. 464, it was held that the district attorney of San Diego county was authorized, under Code of Civil Procedure, section 731, to enjoin the performance of a public exhibition which was shown to have been indecent, and thus within the statutory definition of public nuisance in Civil Code, section 3479. In People v. Seccombe, 103 Cal.App. 306, 284 P. 725, however, the court refused to permit the maintenance of a suit in equity on behalf of the state to restrain defendant's continued practice of usury. It was held that though reprehensible, the practice of usury could not be brought within any of the sections of the statute defining public nuisances. The courts have thus refused to grant injunctions on behalf of the state except where the objectionable activity can be brought within the terms of the statutory definition of public nuisance. Where the legislature has felt that the summary power of equity was required to control activity contrary to public policy, it has enacted statutes specifying that such activity constitutes a public nuisance which may be enjoined in an action brought on behalf of the state.

We think the proper rule, therefore, and the one to which this state is committed is expressed in the following language from State v. Ehrlick, 65 W.Va. 700, 64 S.E. 935, 940, 23 L.R.A., N.S., 691: "It is also competent for the Legislature, within the constitutional limits of its powers, to declare any act criminal and make the repetition or continuance thereof a public nuisance * * * or to vest in courts of equity the power to abate them by injunction; but it is not the province of the courts to ordain such jurisdiction for themselves." [Citations.]

In addition to the historical precedents which we have considered, compelling reasons of policy require that the responsibility for establishing those standards of public morality, the violations of which are to constitute public nuisances within equity's jurisdiction, should be left with the legislature. "Nuisance" is a term which does not have a fixed content either at common law or at the present time. [Citations.] Blackstone defined it so broadly as to include almost all types of actionable wrong, that is, "any thing that worketh hurt, inconvenience or damage". 2 Cooley's Blackstone, 4th ed. 1899, p. 1012. We have already referred to those modern definitions which seek to make of equity an additional remedy for the enforcement of the criminal law by defining "public nuisance" for the purposes of an injunction as any repeated and continuous violation of the law. In a field where the meaning of terms is so vague and uncertain it is a proper function of the legislature to define those breaches of public policy which are to be considered public nuisances within the control of equity. Activity which in one period constitutes a public nuisance, such as the sale of liquor or the holding of prize fights, might not be objectionable in another. Such declarations of policy should be left for the legislature.

Conduct against which injunctions are sought in behalf of the public is frequently criminal in nature. While this alone will not prevent the intervention of equity where a clear case justifying equitable relief is present, it is apparent that the equitable remedy has the collateral effect of depriving a defendant of the jury trial to which he would be entitled in a criminal prosecution for violating exactly the same standards of public policy. [Citations.] The defendant also loses the protection of the higher burden of proof required in criminal prosecutions and, after imprisonment and fine for violation of the equity injunction, may be subjected under the criminal law to similar punishment for the same acts. For these reasons equity is loath to interfere where the standards of public policy can be enforced by resort to the criminal law, and in the absence of a legislative declaration to that effect, the courts should not broaden the field in which injunctions against criminal activity will be granted. Thus, for the reasons set forth, the basis for an action such as this must be found in our statutes rather than by reference to the common law definitions of public nuisance.

* * * In support of the court's ruling on the general demurrer, defendants argue that the allegations of the complaint are insufficient because no facts are alleged from which the court could conclude that a nuisance existed under the provisions of Civil Code, sections 3479, 3480, and Code of Civil Procedure, section 731. It is contended that the allegations of the complaint present merely conclusions of the pleader, framed in the language of the statute.

* * *

Although the defendants' contention that particular allegations of fact are required is therefore correct, we think that the allegations of the present complaint are adequate as against a general demurrer. The complaint alleges that the gambling house operated by defendants "draws together great numbers of disorderly persons, disturbs the public peace, brings together idle persons and cultivates dissolute habits among them, creates traffic and fire hazards, and is thereby injurious to health, indecent and offensive to the senses and impairs the free enjoyment of life and property". Crowds of disorderly people who disturb the peace and obstruct the traffic may well impair the free enjoyment of life and property and give rise to the hazards designated in the statute. In cases of a similar nature pleadings which are not essentially different from the one here involved have been held to state facts sufficient to constitute a cause of action. [Citations.] It follows that the trial court was in error in sustaining the general demurrer.

* * *

The judgment is reversed.

———

Compare the principal case with Goose v. Commonwealth, 305 Ky. 644, 205 S.W.2d 326 (1947), where the court issued an injunction against the proprietors of a gambling establishment. The court observed that numerous arrests of the owners and employees on various charges during a five year period had not been effective in abating the criminal conduct. The state thus had no adequate remedy at law which in turn caused irreparable harm to the public. The court stated:

> These men confess a general course of criminality at this place. They have in some way been able to set the law at naught and to continue their criminal project. The processes of the criminal courts seem to have broken down in dealing with this place and these men. At least, they have failed to accomplish their primary purposes of protecting society, reforming the wayward and preventing future offenses of the same kind. As a consequence, the Commonwealth has invoked the processes of the court of equity and obtained an injunction against the named persons to abate their use of the property for the unlawful purposes.

* * *

> Courts of equity will not ordinarily enjoin the commission of a crime. The statutes themselves are standing injunctions. But the mere fact that the act constituting a nuisance is also a crime does not hinder the use of the civil processes to procure its abatement where the use of property is a part. There may also be a remedy by indictment and upon conviction an abatement by order of the criminal court where the nuisance may be of a continuing character. This remedy is sometimes confused with the other. But there is a clear distinction between enjoining an individual from committing a crime and enjoining him from using his or another's property so as to make it a nuisance to others, and between a proceeding in equity to abate a nuisance and a criminal prosecution to punish the offender for maintaining it. [Citations.]

> It is a historic function of courts of equity to grant preventive as well as remedial relief. Irreparable injury to property rights is perhaps the most common of causes for injunctive relief. Surely irreparable injury to public morals and individual character is of as grave concern as mere loss of dollars and cents. The ground of the jurisdiction is the ability of the chancellor to give a more complete and perfect remedy by a perpetual injunction. It is a weapon from the arsenal of equity to be used to protect Society—to meet the social need that continuation of the offenses at a given place shall be repressed. This abatement by injunction, independent of the crimi-

nal prosecution, is supported by ancient precedents and modern instances.

* * *

Stronger and stronger has become the disposition of the legislatures and the courts to extend the law of nuisances to every sort of gambling irrespective of its connection with other offenses, or of its potentiality of spawning them, or of other conditions which brought it within the classification of a nuisance in former days. It long ago ceased to be essential to injunctive redress that the gambling should be in view of the public or that the public be disturbed by noise therefrom. Nor is it requisite to show that dissolute or criminal characters frequent the premises or that respectable citizens have been "forced to come in contact with a lower strata of society", as appellants submit. However, we suspect that none of the habitues of this place wore the halo of a saint or the wings of an angel. * * *

Neither principle nor precedent supports the absolution claimed by these defendants. If the moral fiber of its manhood and womanhood is not a state concern, we may ask, what is? The court does not falter for an answer. 305 Ky. 644, 205 S.W.2d 326 (1947).

UNITED STATES v. BAY MILLS INDIAN COMMUNITY

692 F.Supp. 777 (W.D.Mich.1988).

HILLMAN, CHIEF JUDGE.

The United States filed this suit against five Indian tribes in November of 1985, requesting declaratory relief and a permanent injunction that would prohibit the tribes from operating casinos on tribal land in Michigan. The government alleges that defendants' activities are illegal under two federal criminal statutes: The Organized Crime Control Act of 1970, 18 U.S.C. § 1955 ("OCCA") and the Assimilative Crimes Act, 18 U.S.C. § 13 ("ACA"). * * *

Three of defendants' casinos are open to the public, seven days a week year round. One is open 5 days a week. Most offer blackjack, pull-tabs, poker, and craps games. The tribal casinos generate substantial revenues which are used to fund governmental services. The United States Department of Housing and Urban Development and the Department of Health and Human Services contributed $225,000 to the development of one of the tribes' gaming enterprises. This tribe also received assistance for its gaming operations from the Department of Interior's Bureau of Indian Affairs in the form of a loan guarantee. Several of the tribes' casinos are governed by tribal ordinance. These ordinances impose safeguards such as background checks for employees, annual audits, and bet or winning limits.

The smallest casino in current operation employs about 30 people, over 70 percent of whom are tribal members, the largest employs over 200 people, over 50 percent tribal members. Unemployment for the tribes in 1986 ranged from 32–62 percent. In an affidavit submitted to the court, an anthropologist specializing in Michigan Indian tribes stated that tribal government and tribally owned enterprises probably account for up to one-third of all Indian jobs and that gaming operations account for at least half of all tribal employment. He concludes that the tribal governments are heavily dependent on gaming for their economic welfare. A report of a Michigan House of Representatives Ad Hoc Committee dated May 1986 states that many tribes use gambling as a means of reducing dependence on government funded social welfare programs and that gambling on Indian reservations in Michigan has led to financial benefits for the reservations as well as surrounding Michigan communities.

Before reaching the merits of the dispute, that is, whether or not defendants are violating federal criminal statutes, I feel obligated to consider an issue not raised by the parties: the propriety of enforcing criminal statutes through declaratory judgment and injunction rather than through criminal prosecution.

As a general rule, a court may not enjoin the commission of a crime. [Citations.]

The rule is based on two concerns: First, criminal prosecution generally provides an adequate remedy at law so that equitable relief is unnecessary, and, second, injunctive relief may deny a defendant the procedural rights otherwise available in a criminal prosecution.

At least three exceptions to the rule that courts will not enjoin criminal activity have developed over the years. A court may properly enjoin activity that is in violation of criminal law, if 1) that activity is a widespread public nuisance, 2) a national emergency warrants departure from the rule, or 3) a statute specifically provides for injunctive relief.

Applying these principles to the case before me, I conclude that the United States is not entitled to equitable relief declaring defendants in violation of criminal statutes or enjoining defendants from continuing to violate criminal statutes. Criminal prosecution of defendants under OCCA and the ACA is an adequate remedy at law, readily available to plaintiff. Plaintiff has not shown nor suggested that prosecution of defendants is an inadequate remedy. The government has not argued, nor does the record reflect, for example, that plaintiff would have difficulty instituting a prosecution, or that the sanctions provided for violations of 18 U.S.C. § 13 and § 1955 are too trivial to provide adequate relief. [Citations.] The issue of the applicability of OCCA and the ACA to each defendant's conduct may be raised in the context of a criminal prosecution.

Congress could have, but has not provided for injunctive relief as a remedy for violations of OCCA or the ACA. *Compare* United States v. Odessa Union Warehouse Co-op, 833 F.2d 172 (9th Cir.1987) (enjoining violation of Food, Drug, and Cosmetic Act under 21 U.S.C. § 332(a)); United States v. White, 769 F.2d 511 (8th Cir.1985) (enjoining violations of Internal Revenue Code under 26 U.S.C. § 7408); SEC v. Carriba Air,

Inc., 681 F.2d 1318, 1321 (11th Cir.1982) (enjoining securities violations under 15 U.S.C. § 77t); United States v. Winstead, 421 F.Supp. 295 (N.D.Ill.1976) (injunctive relief available to enjoin gambling in violation of 18 U.S.C. § 1962 under 18 U.S.C. § 1964).

Nowhere in the record do I find any support for a finding of national emergency authorizing injunctive relief in lieu of prosecution. *Compare* Zenon, 711 F.2d at 479 (District court found appellants had interfered substantially with operations vital to the national defense).

The remaining exception for public nuisance is also inapplicable. *Compare* National Assn. of Letter Carriers, AFL–CIO v. Independent Postal System of America, Inc., 336 F.Supp. 804, 811 (W.D.Ok.1971) (illegal operation in 45 cities involving 25 million Christmas cards was "widespread public nuisance"), *aff'd,* 470 F.2d 265 (10th Cir.1972); United States v. McIntire, 365 F.Supp. 618, 623 (D.N.J.1973) (radio broadcasting without a license is the type of public nuisance which may be restrained by injunction). I recognize that the legislature of the State of Michigan has declared that any building used for the purpose of gambling is a nuisance which may be enjoined and abated in state court under certain circumstances. *See* M.C.L.A. §§ 600.3801–3830. [Citation.] However, plaintiff has never suggested to the court that it is seeking an injunctive in order to remedy a public nuisance or to right a civil wrong. The government seeks injunctive relief solely as a means to enforce federal criminal statutes. Moreover, I find nothing in the record to support a finding that defendants' operations constitute a public nuisance. No evidence suggests that defendants' operations have caused or will cause injury to the public or private interests of the United States. Indeed, a report of the Michigan House Ad Hoc Committee concluded that defendants' activity has led to financial benefits for the reservations as well as to surrounding Michigan communities.

Admittedly, in United States v. Dakota, 796 F.2d 186 (6th Cir.1986), the Sixth Circuit upheld the grant of declaratory relief and permanent injunction against defendants for violations of OCCA and the ACA. However, since the propriety of equitable relief was never raised or addressed in either the opinion of the lower court, nor the opinion of the Court of Appeals, I do not consider *Dakota,* either precedential or persuasive authority for granting the equitable relief sought by the government. Aside from *Dakota,* and an unpublished opinion in United States v. Lummi Indian Tribe, No. C83–94C (W.D.Wash.1983, February 17, 1983), I have found no case in which the United States sought to enforce OCCA or the ACA by injunction instead of by indictment.

In addition to the availability of an adequate remedy at law, other equitable considerations persuade me that injunctive relief is inappropriate. First, the record discloses that enjoining defendants' operations would cause substantial financial hardship to the tribes and their members. Nowhere does the government dispute this conclusion. On the other hand, the harm allegedly precipitated by not enjoining defendants consists only of unproved speculation of the possibility that organized crime might infiltrate defendants' operations before the United States could litigate the legality of defendants' operations in criminal prosecutions. I am unmoved by this speculation.

Second, in an equitable proceeding, the court must consider the public interest. While the United States Attorney represents the interests of the citizens of the Western District of Michigan in attempting to close down the tribes' casinos, other Departments and branches in the federal government have considerable interest in encouraging tribal gambling operations. *See* California v. Cabazon Band of Mission Indians, 480 U.S. 202, 107 S.Ct. 1083, 1092–93, 94 L.Ed.2d 244 (1987). The Supreme Court in discussing the "important federal interest" in "encouraging tribal self-sufficiency and economic development" stated:

> The . . . reservations contain no natural resources which can be exploited. The tribal games at present provide the sole source of revenues for the operation of the tribal governments and the provision of tribal services. They are also the major sources of employment on the reservations. Self-determination and economic development are not within reach if the Tribes cannot raise revenues and provide employment for their members.

Certainly the well established federal interest in promoting tribal economic self-sufficiency would be thwarted by granting the requested relief.

Congress has been struggling for years to enact a federal law expressly regulating tribal gambling enterprises. The latest bills currently under consideration attempt to balance the federal and state interests in controlling organized crime with federal and tribal interests in economic self-sufficiency, a balance never considered by those who enacted OCCA or the ACA. [Citations.] Until Congress acts, however, plaintiff is confined to existing code provisions and the remedies those statutes provide.

In sum, Congress did not provide the extraordinary remedy of injunction as a means to enforce OCCA or the ACA, and I will not imply it.

For similar reasons, I decline to issue a declaratory judgment concerning whether or not defendants are violating criminal law. Declaratory relief, like injunctive relief, is discretionary. [Citation.] Although Rule 57 provides that the "existence of another adequate remedy does not preclude a judgment for declaratory relief in cases where it is appropriate," I am satisfied declaratory relief is inappropriate in this case since "more effective relief can and should be obtained by another procedure." [Citations.] The public interest in encouraging tribal self-sufficiency is also a legitimate consideration in deciding whether to grant declaratory relief. [Citation.]

Accordingly, the motions for summary judgment are denied and for the reasons stated the case is dismissed.

———

1.   Compare the principal case with United States v. Menominee Indian Tribe of Wisconsin, a 1988 federal district court opinion concerning gambling activities on an Indian reservation.   The government sought declaratory and injunctive relief under the Organized Crime Control Act to prohibit gambling operations conducted by an Indian tribe.   The court denied the government's request and followed the general rule that equity will not enjoin the commission of a crime.   The court observed:

> To use an analogy: suppose the government wanted to prosecute a bank robber who was using a toy gun to convince tellers to hand over the cash, but first the government wanted to know whether by using a toy gun, the robber committed "armed" rather than simple robbery.   Should a court issue a declaratory judgment that the robber committed an armed robbery, or should that issue be litigated in a criminal case?   I think the latter.   The essence of the request for both declaratory and injunctive relief is that a crime is being committed.   As framed, the issue is not one which should be decided in a civil proceeding.   A criminal proceeding, where proof beyond a reasonable doubt is necessary for a conviction, is the place where these issues should be decided.   694 F.Supp. 1373, 1377 (E.D.Wis.1988).

2.   In West Allis Memorial Hospital, Inc. v. Bowen, 852 F.2d 251 (7th Cir.1988), the plaintiff hospital sought a preliminary injunction against a competitor.   The complaint alleged that the defendant's waiver of deductible and coinsurance program violated the anti-fraud provisions of Medicare and various state and federal antitrust laws.   The plaintiff apparently perceived that it faced a Hobson's choice: implement a similar program and potentially face criminal prosecution for violating the anti-fraud provisions or refrain from acting and lose business to its competitor.   The district court denied the injunction.

The Court of Appeals agreed with the trial judge that the Medicare statute did not create an implied private right of action to give the plaintiff standing to sue and that equity would not enjoin criminal activity.   The court noted that the plaintiff's claims did not fit within one of the three recognized exceptions which would warrant an injunction against crimes: cases of national emergencies, public nuisances, and specific statutory authorization.

The court reversed and remanded to the district court with respect to the plaintiff's antitrust claims and common law claims of unfair competition.   In contrast to the Medicare statute, the relevant statutes did provide for injunctive relief to enjoin criminal activity in violation of the acts.

3.   For further commentary regarding enjoining crimes see the following references: Wharton's Criminal Procedure §§ 22–27 (12th ed. 1974); 11 C. Wright & A. Miller, Federal Practice and Procedure § 2942 (1973); 5 Moore's Federal Practice § 38.24[3] (2d ed. 1987); Developments in the Law—Injunctions, 78 Harv.L.Rev. 994 (1965).

Part III

DAMAGES

Chapter 10

CONTRACT DAMAGES

A. INTRODUCTION

Section Coverage:

The law of damages for breach of contract recognizes and protects an injured party's expectancy, reliance, and restitutionary interests. The measure of recovery often will vary depending upon which remedial interest is asserted. Expectancy damages provide a monetary substitute for the promised but undelivered performance. Therefore, compensation is calculated by the amount necessary to place the injured plaintiff in as good a position financially as that party would have occupied if the defendant had rendered the remaining performance.

In some instances, the plaintiff may seek reliance damages or restitutionary relief as an alternative to expectancy damages. The nature of the circumstances that give rise to the various remedial options varies. In some cases the reliance or restitution measures may be appropriate because the plaintiff cannot prove expectancy damages with reasonable certainty. These alternative measures are also appropriate in cases where the contract ultimately proved to be a losing one for the plaintiff, so there are no expectancy damages. The most fortunate plaintiffs can prove damages under all measures and thus they have a choice.

Model Case:

Clark contracted with American Restaurants, Inc. to buy a franchise of a Ribs & Stuff Restaurant. The principal terms of the franchise agreement required Clark to pay a $25,000 non-refundable franchise fee, including an obligation to purchase from American all of Clark's requirements of certain "secret ribs sauce," and a 6% royalty based on gross sales payable monthly. Clark paid the $25,000 fee and expended another $10,000 for advertising and marketing services in a promotional campaign introducing the opening of the restaurant.

American's senior management decided to terminate the Clark's franchise agreement because they thought that the business had expanded into new geographical areas too quickly to service all of them. Assuming that the cancellation by American constituted a breach of contract, Clark may seek compensatory damages to protect the expectancy, reliance, and restitution interests in the agreement. Clark probably would have difficulty in proving expectancy damages with reasonable certainty because the business had no established track record, thus making claims for lost profits too speculative. A court probably would award the $25,000 franchise fee as restitution, together with the $10,000 expenditures as reliance damages.

EASTLAKE CONSTRUCTION CO. v. HESS

102 Wash.2d 30, 686 P.2d 465 (1984).

PEARSON, JUSTICE.

* * *

Plaintiff Eastlake Construction Company (Eastlake) brought this action in King County Superior Court to recover $13,719 allegedly owing on a construction contract. Eastlake had entered the contract with defendants Leroy and Jean Hess to erect a 5–unit condominium building in Issaquah. Defendants counterclaimed, alleging damages for breach of the contract * * *. The trial court awarded defendants damages for breach of contract, less the amount owing to Eastlake under the contract. * * *

* * * The trial court found that Eastlake had breached the construction contract in a number of respects. These findings, and the damages allowed by the trial court, may be summarized as follows.

A. Breaches for which the trial court allowed damages.

1. Eastlake wrongfully abandoned the project in February 1978, and defendants were allowed the reasonable cost of completing construction to make the condominiums habitable, $7,979.90.

2. Defendants were allowed the reasonable rental value of the condominiums from the time construction should have been completed until the actual completion date, $4,262.50.

3. Defendants were allowed damages for the reasonable cost of work specified in the plans, but not completed by Eastlake: insulating waste pipes, $807.44; installing recirculating fans, $1,031.10.

4. Defendants were allowed damages for the reasonable cost of repairing and replacing work performed by Eastlake which did not conform to the specifications: repairing the roof, $4,414.01; replacing balcony guardrails, $1,580.76; repairing and replacing washer and dryer closets, $751.84; replacing nonvented kitchen hood fans, $926.53; and replacing interior doors, $787.22.

5. Defendants were also allowed $75 for installation of cable television and $200 for light fixture underrun.

6. Defendants were also allowed damages for the installation of kitchen cabinets not in accordance with contract specifications.

The court declined to award the cost of replacement of these cabinets because this would constitute unreasonable economic waste. Instead, the measure of damages was the difference between the value of the specified cabinets ($8,725.50) and the cost of the cabinets actually installed ($3,700): $5,0252.50.

B. *Breaches for which the trial court allowed no damages.*

The trial court found that Eastlake had breached the construction contract in a number of other respects, but that these breaches "did not result in substantial damage to the building nor result in a substantial loss of value to the building". Defendants were not allowed damages for these breaches.

* * *

The trial court found a total of $27,841.70 in damages to defendants, against which was offset the $13,719 owing on the construction contract, for an award on the counterclaim of $14,122.70.

* * *

The general measure of damages for breach of contract is that the injured party is entitled (1) to recovery of all damages that accrue naturally from the breach, and (2) to be put into as good a pecuniary position as he would have had if the contract had been performed. [Citation.] In the case of construction contracts, special problems have been encountered in putting the injured party in the pecuniary position he would have enjoyed had the contract been properly performed by the builder. These special problems have led to the creation of special rules for measuring damages in such cases.

* * * [D]amages should put the injured party in the position which he would have enjoyed without the breach. In many cases this will be achieved by awarding the costs of repairing defective construction so as to conform to the contract. Some defects, however, cannot be remedied without great expense and substantial damage to the rest of the structure (for instance, the cracked foundations in Forrester v. Craddock, 51 Wash.2d 315, 317 P.2d 1077, or the nonconforming insulation beneath the concrete floor in the present case). In such cases, the cost of remedying the defect would far exceed the value to the injured party of the improvement. An award of the cost of repairs in such cases would therefore constitute a substantial windfall to the injured party. The cost of repairs should not be awarded if that cost is clearly disproportionate to the value to the injured party of those repairs.

This idea was recognized by Professor McCormick in his treatise on damages:

> In whatever way the issue arises, the generally approved standards for measuring the owner's loss from defects in the work are two: First, in cases where the defect is one that can be repaired or cured *without undue expense,* so as to make the building conform to the agreed plan, then the owner recovers such amount as he has

reasonably expended, or will reasonably have to spend, to remedy the defect. Second, if, on the other hand, the defect in material or construction is one that cannot be remedied without an *expenditure for reconstruction disproportionate to the end to be attained,* or without endangering unduly other parts of the building, then the damages will be measured not by the cost of remedying the defect, but by the difference between the value of the building as it is and what it would have been worth if it had been built in conformity with the contract.

(Footnotes omitted. Italics ours.) C. McCormick, *Damages* § 168, 648–49 (1935).

The crux of the determination of which measure of damages to apply is therefore the proportionality of the cost to the corresponding benefits. This is a factual question which must be resolved, as Professor Corbin points out, according to "prevailing practices and opinions (the mores) of men, involving their emotions as well as reason and logic". A. Corbin, *Contracts* § 1089, at 492 (1964).

The authors of the Restatement have recently recognized in Restatement (Second) of Contracts (1981) that the concept of unreasonable economic waste is unhelpful in determining damages, and have turned instead to consider the proportionality of the cost of repairs to the value conferred. The second Restatement provides a convenient and effective means of clarifying and regularizing the rules governing this issue.

The general rule of damages is stated in Restatement (Second) of Contracts § 347, at 112:

Subject to the limitations stated in §§ 350–53, the injured party has a right to damages based on his expectation interest as measured by

(a) the loss in the value to him of the other party's performance caused by its failure or deficiency, plus

(b) any other loss, including incidental or consequential loss, caused by the breach, less

(c) any cost or other loss that he has avoided by not having to perform.

Comment *a* to this rule explains the rationale for damages under the second Restatement.

a. Expectation interest. Contract damages are ordinarily based on the injured party's expectation interest and are intended to give him the benefit of his bargain by awarding him a sum of money that will, to the extent possible, put him in as good a position as he would have been in had the contract been performed.

Further comments to section 347 recognize that in some cases it may be difficult to determine with sufficient certainty the damage to the injured party's expectation interest. Comment *b* states, in part:

Where the injured party's expected advantage consists largely or exclusively of the realization of profit, it may be possible to express this loss in value in terms of money with some assurance. In other situations, however, this is not possible and compensation for lost value may be precluded by the limitation of certainty. *See* § 352. In order to facilitate the estimation of loss with sufficient certainty to award damages, the injured party is sometimes given a choice between alternative bases of calculating his loss in value. The most important of these are stated in § 348.

The alternatives set out in Restatement (Second) of Contracts § 348, at 119–20, include measures of damages specifically applicable to construction contracts.

> (1) If a breach delays the use of property and the loss in value to the injured party is not proved with reasonable certainty, he may recover damages based on the rental value of the property or on interest on the value of the property.

> (2) If a breach results in defective or unfinished construction and the loss in value to the injured party is not proved with sufficient certainty, he may recover damages based on

> > (a) the diminution in the market price of the property caused by the breach, or

> > (b) the reasonable cost of completing performance or of remedying the defects if that cost is not clearly disproportionate to the probable loss in value to him.

The comments to section 348 include a helpful discussion of the considerations applicable to a determination of damages for a breach of the construction contract. Comment *c* at 121 is especially relevant to this case and is here set out in full:

> *c. Incomplete or defective performance.* If the contract is one for construction, including repair or similar performance affecting the condition of property, and the work is not finished, the injured party will usually find it easier to prove what it would cost to have the work completed by another contractor than to prove the difference between the values to him of the finished and the unfinished performance. Since the cost to complete is usually less than the loss in value to him, he is limited by the rule on avoidability to damages based on cost to complete. *See* § 350(1). If he has actually had the work completed, damages will be based on his expenditures if he comes within the rule stated in § 350(2).

> Sometimes, especially if the performance is defective as distinguished from incomplete, it may not be possible to prove the loss in value to the injured party with reasonable certainty. In that case he can usually recover damages based on the cost to remedy the defects. Even if this gives him a recovery somewhat in excess of the loss in value to him, it is better that he receive a small windfall than that he be undercompensated by being limited to the resulting diminution in the market price of his property.

Sometimes, however, such a large part of the cost to remedy the defects consists of the cost to undo what has been improperly done that the cost to remedy the defects will be clearly disproportionate to the probable loss in value to the injured party. Damages based on the cost to remedy the defects would then give the injured party a recovery greatly in excess of the loss in value to him and result in a substantial windfall. Such an award will not be made. It is sometimes said that the award would involve "economic waste," but this is a misleading expression since an injured party will not, even if awarded an excessive amount of damages, usually pay to have the defects remedied if to do so will cost him more than the resulting increase in value to him. If an award based on the cost to remedy the defects would clearly be excessive and the injured party does not prove the actual loss in value to him, damages will be based instead on the difference between the market price that the property would have had without the defects and the market price of the property with the defects. This diminution in market price is the least possible loss in value to the injured party, since he could always sell the property on the market even if it had no special value to him.

The Restatement formulation of the rule represents a sensible and workable approach to measuring damages in construction contract cases. It achieves a fair measure of damages while avoiding the potentially confusing concepts of substantial completion and unreasonable economic waste. We therefore adopt Restatement (Second) of Contracts § 348 as the appropriate rule for determining damages in cases such as the present one.

This conclusion requires us to remand the issue of damages to the trial court for reconsideration in light of section 348. The trial court should award defendants the cost of replacing defective items, unless the cost of replacement is "clearly disproportionate" to the value of the benefit conferred by replacement. Section 348(2)(a) and (b).

Of course, we do not disturb the trial court's award of damages for the loss of rental value, the costs of completing the project, and the costs of remedying various defects. These items of damages are clearly recoverable under Section 348. The trial court, therefore, need only apply the "clearly disproportionate" test to the kitchen cabinets and to the 9 breaches for which the trial court allowed no damages.

* * *

---

1. The expectancy interest of the injured party may be measured in a variety of ways. Traditionally, courts have awarded the cost to complete the performance which has been promised. However, as indicated in the principal case, in some circumstances the cost to remedy the defects in performance may be disproportionately greater than the difference in value of what was promised and what was actually received.

In that event, courts may award the diminution in value to the injured party in order to prevent economic waste.

In the leading case of Jacob & Youngs v. Kent, 230 N.Y. 239, 129 N.E. 889 (1921), a contractor built a residence, but mistakenly installed a brand of plumbing pipe which differed from the specifications. Judge Cardozo held that the proper measure of damages would be the difference in value between the pipe specified and the type actually installed because it would be economically wasteful to tear down the house for the small benefit of substituting a different brand of pipe.

Contrast the result in O.W. Grun Roofing & Const. Co. v. Cope, 529 S.W.2d 258 (Tex.Civ.App.1975). In that case the plaintiff sued a roofing company to set aside a mechanic's lien and for damages sustained as a result of the defendant's failure to install properly a new roof on the plaintiff's home. After the defendant had installed the roof, the plaintiff noticed it had "streaks" due to a difference in color of some of the shingles. The defendant's attempts to remedy the problem by replacing certain shingles proved unsuccessful. The court awarded the homeowner damages to compensate for installing a completely new roof.

Can the result in *O.W. Grun Roofing & Const. Co. v. Cope* be reconciled with *Jacob & Youngs v. Kent?* To what extent is the object and purpose of the contract relevant in selecting the appropriate measure of damages?

2. Some courts have awarded damages for the cost to complete performance even where that measure is clearly disproportionate to the diminution in value because the defendant breached the contract willfully or in bad faith. *See* Groves v. John Wunder Co., 205 Minn. 163, 286 N.W. 235 (1939). The majority of courts, though, have rejected the factor of an intentional or willful breach as affecting the remedial consequences. The latter view reflects the philosophy that the goal in contract damages is compensating for losses and that the domain for punishing certain behavior is exemplary damages.

3. Moreover, in some instances a party may choose to breach a contract and pay the resulting damages in order to move goods to a higher bidder. This process accords with traditional notions of economic theory by distributing assets to maximize resources in the most efficient manner. For an examination of the competing interests involved in the economic theory of contract damages *see generally* Macneil, Efficient Breach of Contract: Circle in the Sky, 68 Va.L.Rev. 947 (1982); Linzer, On the Amorality of Contract Remedies—Efficiency, Equity, and the Second Restatement, 81 Colum.L.Rev. 111 (1981); Farber, Reassessing the Economic Efficiency of Compensatory Damages for Breach of Contract, 66 Va.L.Rev. 1443 (1980); Kronman, Specific Performance, 45 U.Chi.L.Rev. 351 (1978); Polinsky, Economic Analysis as a Potentially Defective Product: A Buyer's Guide to Posner's Economic Analysis of Law, 87 Harv.L.Rev. 1655 (1974); Barton, The Economic Basis of Damages for Breach of Contract, 1 J.Leg.Studies 277 (1972); Birming-

ham, Breach of Contract, Damage Measures, and Economic Efficiency, 24 Rutgers L.Rev. 273 (1970).

PROBLEM: THE PORTRAIT CONTRACT

The Anderson family wished to have individual portraits painted for each of seven family members. The portraits were wanted as an integral set with similar style and design so that they may be hung as a group on the living room wall. Cavender, a locally well-known artist, was sought for the job. They contracted to have the seven portraits painted for a total of $14,000. By custom the parties expected Cavender to furnish all supplies.

The Andersons became dissatisfied with Cavender after the completion of two of the portraits. The work was progressing much more slowly than they had been led to expect, and they did not find the two finished portraits sufficiently flattering. They notified Cavender that they did not want to continue the contract. No money had been paid at that point except a $1000 advance, and the Andersons refused to pay any more.

Cavender had expended $300 on each of the two portraits on supplies. The overhead costs in running the commercial studio add another $200 in expenditures attributable to painting each of these portraits.

The Andersons turned the unwanted portraits over to an art auctioneer for sale. An out-of-town art collector who was intrigued by Cavender's refreshing and honest portrait style bid up the price on each. The collector ultimately paid $7000 for one of the portraits and $9000 for the other. The auctioneer's commission was $1600, so the Andersons netted $14,400 from this sale.

Cavendar sues the Andersons. Assuming the court decides that the contract did not require the satisfaction of the Andersons, what should be the measure of damages for their breach?

GRUBER v. S–M NEWS COMPANY

126 F.Supp. 442 (S.D.N.Y.1954).

MURPHY, DISTRICT JUDGE.

[Plaintiffs] seek damages for breach of contract. Plaintiffs allege * * * that a contract between them and defendant was made [whereby plaintiffs] promised to manufacture in conformity with samples approved by defendant, 90,000 sets of twelve Christmas greeting cards for the impending Christmas season; to pack every set in a box of design approved by defendant and be ready for shipment to a list of wholesalers to be furnished by defendant not later than the second week in October; to give defendant exclusive sale and distribution rights to these sets. According to plaintiffs' complaint, in consideration of their promises, defendant bound itself to exercise reasonable diligence to sell all of the sets and use its resources for scientific sales promotion, national advertising, newsstand outlets and sales organization. Defendant further agreed, plaintiffs claim, to pay eighty-four cents for each set f.o.b. its wholesalers' respective places of business where, according to defendant's regular checkup, the cards had been sold at retail. Credit was to be allowed for all sets returned to plaintiffs unsold. It is further alleged that plaintiffs manufactured and packed the sets in accordance with the agreement, notified the defendant to this effect on October 2, 1945, and that defendant then refused its promised performance. Damages for $101,800 are demanded.

* * *

For breach of a contract of exclusive distribution and return, plaintiffs should be entitled to damages measured by the difference between what they actually obtained for their cards and what they would have obtained had defendant exercised its promised reasonable diligence. On this, plaintiffs have the burden of proof to the extent of a reasonably certain and definite factual basis of computation. Under the evidence, such basis in this case is too speculative for an award in a sum certain. The past experience of the defendant in distribution of a high proportion of jig-saw puzzles, maps and cleaning fluids is hardly a basis for prophecy with respect to Christmas cards. And a single retailer's opinion that he would have disposed of 50 boxes of the cards is a precarious foundation for generalization with respect to 90,000 such boxes. Accordingly, plaintiffs have not sustained their burden of proof with respect to their expectation under the breached agreement.

However, alternative to damages for loss of their expectation, plaintiffs have demanded at the close of trial at least their out-of-pocket expenses. The basis for these damages is not plaintiffs' expectation of profits but rather their expenditures made in "essential reliance" upon defendant's promise. Defendant, for its part, insists that there can be no recovery upon this theory of essential reliance because there would have been a loss to plaintiffs had defendant fully performed its promise of distribution.

The few cases in point in New York are apparently not entirely in accord with respect to the relationship between anticipated loss in event of full performance by the defendant, on one hand, and a plaintiff's recovery of his out-of-pocket expenses in reliance on defendant's unperformed promise, on the other. There are situations where there is no such relationship, and a plaintiff may recover his expenditures in reliance upon defendant's promise without regard to profit if that promise had been fully performed by defendant, as in actions for restitution and ones based upon fraud. The Restatement has suggested that if full performance by defendant would have resulted in loss to a plaintiff, then this loss must be deducted from plaintiff's expenditures. * * *

We accept as the rule that plaintiffs' recovery for their out-of-pocket expenses must be diminished by any loss that would result from defendant's full performance. We are not persuaded that defendant has established the probability of such loss. True plaintiffs were able to obtain merely six cents per box on a sale of 40,000 boxes in 1949, rather than the promised eighty-four cents for sale in 1945 under their agreement with defendant. But the Christmas cards had a novelty appeal, designed as they were to exploit a dozen different nations at the time of the newly-formed United Nations in 1945. The glamour of the caricatures may well have been clouded by the worsening world situation that gathered in the succeeding years.

The burden of proving loss in event of performance properly rests on the defendant who by its wrong has made the question relevant to the rights of the plaintiffs. We do not find that defendant has sustained this burden.

Only the amount of plaintiffs' expenditures reasonably made in performance of the contract or in necessary preparation therefore, may be recovered. This does not include, as plaintiffs have requested, the cost of making the plates from which the cards were printed since these had already been fabricated prior to making the contract with defendant. The amount of plaintiffs' expenditures for labor and material reasonably made in essential reliance on defendant's promise was $19,934.44. From this sum must be deducted the *net* amount realized by plaintiffs from sale of 40,000 sets at six cents a set which was $2,080. Accordingly plaintiffs are entitled to $17,854.44 in damages.

Judgment accordingly.

––––––

1. In the principal case, the manufacturer's expectancy interest for breach of the exclusive distributorship agreement would have been measured by the difference in value between the performance promised by the defendant and that which was actually received. However, since the plaintiff could not sustain its burden of proof on expectancy damages with reasonable certainty, the alternative measure of reliance damages was sought. The reliance damages often will be less than the expectancy damages because the profit of the non-breaching party is not included. Moreover, the recovery is further reduced to the extent that the breaching party can prove the plaintiff would have sustained losses in the event of full performance. How difficult would it be for the defendant to demonstrate such losses would have resulted? What information would be relevant as evidence on the issue of the plaintiff's potential losses?

2. Courts will limit the amount of reliance damages recoverable not to exceed the contract price. The rationale for such a limitation is that expenses incurred above the contract price certainly would have been losses sustained by the plaintiff, and therefore are properly deducted from the total recovery.

3. The court in the principal case awarded damages for "essential" reliance. These damages typically include expenses incurred in prepara-

tion for performance or in the actual performance of the contract. "Incidental" reliance damages, in contrast, may be described as expenditures made in preparing for collateral transactions apart from the contract.

The difference in classification may be seen in cases involving new business ventures. For example, assume that O entered into a contract with the XYZ Construction Company to build a restaurant. If O breached the contract after XYZ had partly performed, the builder could recover as essential reliance damages the expenditures made in preparing to perform and in commencing performance. If, on the other hand, the builder breached the contract, purchases made by O toward furnishing the restaurant would be characterized as incidental reliance. The significance of the distinction lies in the role that foreseeability plays as a limitation on incidental reliance damages. *See generally* Fuller and Perdue, The Reliance Interest in Contract Damages, 46 Yale L.J. 52 (1936).

CAMPBELL v. TENNESSEE VALLEY AUTHORITY

421 F.2d 293 (5th Cir.1969).

MORGAN, CIRCUIT JUDGE:

This is an action in *quantum meruit* brought by Raymond Campbell against the Tennessee Valley Authority (hereafter TVA) to recover $30,240 for the microfilming of certain technical trade journals which were a part of TVA's technical library located at Muscle Shoals, Alabama. The District Court entered a judgment upon a verdict for Campbell in the amount of $30,240. We affirm.

Campbell entered into an oral agreement with Earl Daniel, Director of the TVA Technical Library, to reproduce 13 sets of technical trade journals on 16 mm. microfilm at a price of $90 per roll. Mr. Daniel had no authority to make such a purchase for TVA and entered into the agreement with Campbell without the knowledge of his superiors. Campbell photographed, developed and processed 336 rolls of 16 mm. film containing the journals in question, placed the film in cartridges and delivered them to the TVA Technical Library at Muscle Shoals. Under the terms of the oral agreement, the charge for this work was to have been $30,240. The cartridges were placed on the shelves of the library and were available to its patrons for approximately two months.[1] The microfilm cartridges were then returned to Campbell by registered mail along with a letter from Daniel stating that there was no contract for their reproduction, that he had no authority to enter into such a contract, and that the price of the film was excessive. Campbell refused to accept the film and it was returned to the library, where it has since

---

1. There is evidence in the record that in this two-month period three of the cartridges were each used once.

been stored. TVA has refused to pay for the film. The journals reproduced by Campbell were destroyed upon instruction by Daniel.

Campbell's original complaint relied on an express contract with TVA. TVA's motion for summary judgment on the ground that there could be no express contract since its employee Daniel had no authority to enter such a contract was granted. Campbell then amended his complaint to set out a claim for recovery based on *quantum meruit* or a contract implied in law. TVA then moved for and was granted the right to join librarian Daniel (whose employment had since been terminated) as a third-party defendant. Daniel's motion for summary judgment was granted on the ground that he could not be held liable to indemnify TVA in the event that it were held liable to Campbell since for Campbell to recover he had to prove that the microfilm benefited TVA in an economic sense and indemnity by an agent applies only to economic loss or detriment suffered by his principal.

The principal contention made by appellant TVA is that the District Court committed error in instructing the jury that the measure of damages in this case was "the fair market value of the microfilm that benefited TVA." It is TVA's contention that it "is obligated to pay not for the film itself, but only for the 'benefit', or unjust enrichment, if any, which it received by reason of the *use* it made of the film while it was in the library." The first question thus presented to this Court is whether a person who is entitled to recover from an agency of the federal government under a theory of *quantum meruit* is entitled to the reasonable, or fair market, value of the goods or services so provided, or to the reasonable value of the benefit so realized by the Government. In other words, is the measure of recovery to be determined by the amount of money that would be necessary to acquire on the open market the goods or services from which the benefit is derived, or is the measure of recovery how much the benefit has been worth to the person upon whom it was conferred?

* * *

In re Moyer, W.D. Virginia 1960, 190 F.Supp. 867, 873, held that "the measure of recovery * * * on the principle of *quantum meruit* * * * is the reasonable value of the work performed, less the amount of compensation, whether in money or otherwise, already received". Evans v. Mason, 82 Ariz. 40, 308 P.2d 245, 65 A.L.R.2d 936 (1957), an action in *quantum meruit* to recover for services rendered to decedent pursuant to a parol contract barred by the Statute of Frauds held that the measure of damages is the actual value of the services rendered to the decedent. On the other hand, Hill v. Waxberg (9 Cir.1956) 237 F.2d 936, 16 Alaska 477, an action by a contractor to recover for services and expenditures made in contemplation of a proposed building contract, held the "restitution is properly limited to the value of the benefit which was acquired". At 939.

This confusion in the cases is clarified by a statement made in a footnote of the Court's decision in Martin v. Campanaro (2 Cir.1946),

156 F.2d 127, 130 n.5, *cert. den.,* 329 U.S. 759, 67 S.Ct. 112, 91 L.Ed. 654:

> The claimants are entitled to recover on a quantum meruit basis. But "quantum meruit" is ambiguous; it may mean (1) that there is a contract "implied in fact" to pay the reasonable value of the services, or (2) that, to prevent unjust enrichment, the claimant may recover on a quasi contract (an "as if" contract) for that reasonable value. It has been suggested that the latter is a rule-of-thumb measure of damages adopted in quasi contract cases where the actual unjust enrichment or benefit to the defendant is too difficult to prove; *see* Costigan, Implied–In–Fact Contracts, 33 Harv.Law Rev. (1920) 376, 387.

In the present situation the District Court was correct in using the "rule of thumb" measure of damages and in instructing the jury that the measure of damages was "the fair market value of the microfilm that benefited TVA," instead of instructing that the measure of damages was the reasonable value of the benefit realized by TVA from the microfilm, since the actual benefit to TVA would not have been susceptible of proof. The value realized by a library in having a particular reference work available to its patrons cannot be adequately expressed in dollars and cents. The real benefit is realized, not so much by the library itself, as by those who depend upon the library in their research activities, and the benefit is not so much that the books, technical journals and other research sources are actually *used,* on a regular basis, but that they are conveniently *available for use.* If use, rather than availability, were the only test of the benefit conferred by a book in a library, a good university library could be many times smaller than the present day standard and still retain its effectiveness as a center for research.

Furthermore, in view of the fact that the microfilmed technical journals furnished by Campbell had no readily marketable value to anyone except the TVA because of their unique character and the special circumstances[3] of this case, the District Court properly instructed the jury that the measure of recovery was the fair market value, even though the microfilm was available on the library's shelves for only two months.

* * * TVA argues that if the jury could find that the "fair market value of the microfilm that benefited TVA" could be the contract price between the parties, it could not exceed the lowest contract price that would have been obtainable had competitive bidding taken place on the microfilming under 16 U.S.C., Sec. 831h(b) (1964), and that the evidence is uncontradicted that University Microfilming, a division of Xerox Corporation, would have done the microfilming for $10,000. Thus, TVA contends that Campbell could recover no more than $10,000 and that his recovery of $30,240 was contrary to the law and the evidence.

---

3. The journals which had been reproduced had been destroyed, making the microfilm copies the only ones available. Moreover, there was evidence that the journals in question were a necessary part of a technical library. Likewise, it does not appear the microfilm copies had value to anyone other than to the library.

While there is authority for the proposition that the upper limit of recovery in an action of this nature is the amount agreed to by the parties in the unenforceable contract, the testimony of Holladay, the representative from the University Microfilm division of Xerox, that his company would have done the microfilming here in question for $10,000 did not constitute a bid under 16 U.S.C., Sec. 831h(b), and thus can in no way be considered an upper limit on Campbell's recovery. [Citation.] It is also hornbook law that the jury is in no way bound by the testimony of experts. [Citation.]

* * *

The judgment of the District Court is Affirmed.

RIVES, CIRCUIT JUDGE (dissenting): * * *

Under the facts and circumstances of this case, I would hold that TVA is not liable to Campbell in any amount. If mistaken in that view, I would nonetheless hold that the extent of its liability is measured by the benefit it received from the limited use made of the film during the two months it remained in the TVA Technical Library.

This litigation began with the filing of a complaint which alleged that Earl Daniel, as agent of the TVA, acting within the line and scope of his authority, agreed with Campbell for him to produce and deliver microfilm of certain trade journals for which Campbell was to be paid $90.00 per roll; that TVA ordered 336 rolls, all of which were delivered; but that TVA refused to pay to Campbell the agreed amount of the contract, $30,240.00. The district court granted TVA's motion for summary judgment as to that claim.

Campbell then amended his complaint by filing counts in general assumpsit seeking to recover in quantum meruit.

While the amended complaint is broad enough to sustain recovery on a contract implied *in fact*, as well as on one implied *in law*, I repeat that the sole claim is on a contract implied *in law*. Judge Grooms correctly so charged the jury:

> "Members of the jury, this case began as a contract case, but it was determined at the outset that Mr. Earl Daniel had no authority to make a contract; the contract was void for that reason, and the contract aspect went out and then the complaint was amended to claim for work and labor and for goods and chattels, merchandise, goods and chattels sold to the defendant, T.V.A. on the theory of what we know as a quantum meruit. That is an old form of action, and it literally means as much as he deserves. Quantum means quantity, merit [sic], as much as he deserves. The case has proceeded since then on the theory of quantum meruit.

* * *

> "As I stated to you the words quantum meruit, [literally] translated, means as much as he deserves. The basis of a recovery under a quantum meruit is that the defendant has received a benefit

from the plaintiff which it is unjust for him to retain without paying for it. Quantum meruit is a device to prevent unjust enrichment by requiring a recipient of work or services to pay the party furnishing such work and services as much as he reasonably deserves for this work."

I. TVA Is Not Liable to Campbell in Any Amount.

* * *

The jury verdict of $30,240.00 is in the exact amount the plaintiff Campbell claimed that Daniel promised for TVA to pay for the film (336 rolls at $90.00 per roll). A reading of the record makes obvious, I submit, that the unauthorized express contract has simply been enforced under the guise of a quasi contract or quantum meruit. * * *

The underlying principle is that of forbidding unjust enrichment. "A person who has been unjustly enriched at the expense of another is required to make restitution to the other." A.L.I. Restatement, Restitution § 1, p. 12.

Chapter 2 of that text "states the conditions under which there is a right to restitution because of a mistake in the conferring of a benefit." A.L.I. Restatement, Restitution Introductory Note, p. 26. Such a right may arise in the case of a person who has paid money (*Id.* § 16) or transferred property (*Id.* § 39), or rendered services (*Id.* § 40) to another which have inured to the latter's benefit, in the mistaken belief that he is performing a valid contract with the other, although the contract is later avoided. A right to restitution, however, does not arise in such cases unless the recipient of the property or services is *unjustly enriched.*

> "Even where a person has received a benefit from another, he is liable to pay therefor only if the circumstances of its receipt or retention are such that, as between the two persons, it is unjust for him to retain it. The mere fact that a person benefits another is not of itself sufficient to require the other to make restitution therefor."

A.L.I. Restatement, Restitution p. 13.

Under the facts and circumstances of this case, it is doubtful whether TVA was *enriched* or *harmed* by Campbell's services when consideration is given to the fact that Campbell destroyed TVA's original journals. * * *

Assuming arguendo that TVA was benefited by Campbell's services, it was not unjustly enriched: It has been demonstrated that no authorized agent of TVA accepted delivery of the rolls of microfilm; that TVA has not wrongfully retained the microfilm, but has made every reasonable effort to return it to Campbell, and that upon Campbell's refusal to accept the film, TVA has stored it and forbidden its use. The only possible benefit retained by TVA is in the two-month period that the microfilm remained in its Technical Library. In that two months, three of the rolls were each used once. There was no evidence that the person making such limited use of the film knew or had reason to know that he was using film which did not belong to TVA or that he was in any way obligating TVA to pay for the film. Such knowledge is, I submit, necessary for this limited user to impose upon TVA a duty of restitution. *See* A.L.I. Restatement, Restitution §§ 40 and 41. Further, a precedent should not be laid for the public policy requirement of competitive bidding to be frustrated by the application of some principle of restitution or quasi contract. For all of the foregoing reasons, I am firmly of the opinion that TVA is not liable to Campbell in any amount.

II. *If* Liable, What Is the Extent of TVA's Liability.

* * * It is incomprehensible to me that Campbell should be rewarded for *his* destruction of TVA's original trade journals. Perhaps the best precedent is the classic case of the son who murdered his father and mother, but was granted mercy because he was an orphan.

The majority holding measures the extent of TVA's liability by Campbell's loss. That overlooks the fundamental reason for granting restitution or quantum meruit relief, *viz.,* to avoid unjust enrichment. Ordinarily in such cases the benefit to the one and the loss to the other are co-extensive. However, when the benefit is less than the loss, the recovery is limited to the benefit. * * *

I respectfully dissent.

———

1. Restitution may provide an alternative remedy to damages for breach of contract. The determination of the appropriate remedy requires an understanding of the respective interests sought to be protected. The purpose of compensatory damages for breach of contract is to place the non-breaching party in as good a position as if the contract had been performed as promised. In contrast to that expectancy measure, the purpose of restitution is to place the breaching party in the position occupied before a contract was made or, where no contract exists, before benefits were conferred. Although the measurement of recovery may be identical in some instances, sometimes one remedy will produce a higher recovery for the claimant.

2. The different measures between damages and restitution were addressed in Dravo Corporation v. L.W. Moses Company, 6 Wash.App. 74, 492 P.2d 1058 (1971). In that case a subcontractor partly performed a construction contract before termination by the general contractor. The subcontractor alleged wrongful termination of the contract and sought restitution for the value of the services rendered. The general contractor, Dravo, argued that the court should deduct from the subcontractor's recovery the cost of completing the work. The court disagreed, and held that restitution was properly measured by the reasonable value of the subcontractor's services, less any benefits which the subcontractor received. Accordingly, no deductions were made for the cost of comple-

tion nor, conversely, were the subcontractor's profits included. The objective was to return the parties to the *status quo ante*.

3. How should the reasonable value of services be measured in an action for quantum meruit? In *Dravo,* the court suggested that the contract itself may provide evidence of the value of the benefits conferred. Also relevant were the actual expenditures by the subcontractor in performance. The services must be valuable, however, from the perspective of the defendant.

In *Campbell v. TVA,* did the defendant actually benefit from the microfilm of the trade journals or did the defendant suffer a detriment because the plaintiff destroyed the original journals?

4. Some cases have held that the contract price does not impose a ceiling on the amount of restitution available to a nonbreaching party. It serves instead as evidence on the issue of the value of benefits conferred. *See* United States v. Algernon Blair, Inc., 479 F.2d 638 (4th Cir.1973).

Contrast the result when the injured party has fully performed and the breaching party must only pay an ascertainable sum of money. Courts routinely have denied restitution as an alternative basis of recovery because the plaintiff is enforcing a simple debt. Is such a distinction justifiable? Some courts have rejected this distinction and therefore limit restitutionary recovery to the contract price even when the contract has not been fulfilled. These issues are developed further in Chapter 16.

B. SALE OF GOODS CONTRACTS

Section Coverage:

The damages remedies with respect to contracts for the sale of goods are governed by Article 2 of the Uniform Commercial Code. The remedies available to non-breaching buyers mirror in large part those available to non-breaching sellers. An aggrieved buyer may make a reasonable purchase of substitute goods and recover damages measured by the excess of the cost to cover and the contract price, plus any incidental or consequential damages less expenses saved. [*See* U.C.C. § 2–712]. If the buyer declines to purchase replacement goods, the same formula for calculating damages is used by substituting the market price at the time the buyer learned of the breach for the market price actually paid when effecting cover. [*See* U.C.C. § 2–713]. If the buyer chooses to accept the goods, then damages may be recovered for the difference between the value as promised and the value of the goods as accepted. [*See* U.C.C. § 2–714].

Similarly, a seller may seek either the contract price minus the market price at the time and place for tender under U.C.C. § 2–708(1), or the difference in the contract price less the resale price (equivalent to buyer's cover) under U.C.C. § 2–706. Although sellers are not entitled to consequential damages, they may recover lost profits and reasonable overhead if the ordinary measure of damages under § 2–708(1) is "inadequate to put the seller in as good a position as performance." [*See* U.C.C. § 2–708(2)]. The seller may also be entitled to incidental damages, such as expenses incurred in transportation or storage of the goods, with an adjustment for expenses saved as a result of the buyer's breach.

Finally, Article 2 provides buyers and sellers with corresponding remedies of rescission and restitution [U.C.C. §§ 2–702, 2–711] and specific performance (action for the price) [U.C.C. §§ 2–716, 2–709, respectively]. The remedies are considered cumulatively available to the non-breaching party, as the U.C.C. rejects the election of remedies doctrine "as a fundamental policy." [U.C.C. § 2–703, comment 1].

Model Case:

On January 1, Jones contracts to purchase 1,000 widgets from Widget Co. for $1.00 each, and makes a $200 down payment with the balance due at the time of the scheduled delivery on March 1. On February 1, Widget Co. notifies Jones that it is repudiating the contract because the current market value of widgets has skyrocketed to $1.30 each.

Jones "covers" by purchasing substitute widgets on the open market for $1.30 each and also incurs $250 expenses for transportation and storage in connection with the transaction. Assuming that Widget Co. breached the contract without a legally recognized excuse, Jones may claim damages against Widget Co. in the amount of $750. These damages reflect: (a) multiplication of 1,000 times the market price in effecting cover ($1.30) less the contract price ($1.00) = $300 (following U.C.C. § 2–712(2)); (b) the $250 additional expenses as "incidental" damages under U.C.C. § 2–715(1); and (c) restitution of the down payment of $200 pursuant to U.C.C. § 2–711(1).

1. Buyer's Remedies

WILSON v. HAYS
544 S.W.2d 833 (Tex.Civ.App.1976).

JAMES, JUSTICE.

This is a suit by the buyer against the seller for breach of an oral contract to sell and deliver used bricks. Trial was had to a jury, which rendered a verdict favorable to the Plaintiff buyer, pursuant to which verdict the trial court entered judgment. We affirm in part and reverse and render in part.

Plaintiff–Appellee W.D. Hays was in the business of buying and selling used building materials. Defendant–Appellant Bobby Wilson doing business as Wilson Salvage Co. was in the business of wrecking or demolishing buildings. * * * Hays and Wilson entered into an oral agreement whereby Wilson agreed to sell and deliver 600,000 used uncleaned bricks to Hays at a price of one cent per brick, and Hays agreed to buy said bricks at said price. Hays paid Wilson $6,000.00 in advance. Wilson delivered the uncleaned brick to a designated area where Hays had people hired to clean and stack the brick. Wilson delivered a lesser number of brick than 600,000, thereby precipitating this suit.

Plaintiff–Appellee Hays brought this suit for the return of the proportionate part of the purchase price paid for the bricks he did not get, plus damages. In answer to special issues the jury found:

(1) That Bobby Wilson orally agreed with Hays that he, Bobby Wilson, would sell and deliver to Hays at least 600,000 bricks at a price of one cent per brick; * * *

(6) That Bobby Wilson did not deliver 600,000 uncleaned bricks to Hays (but)

(6A) delivered only 400,000 bricks to Hays;

(7) The market value of used bricks in Midland, Texas in April 1972, was five cents per brick;

(8) Hays suffered lost profits in the amount of $6250.00 by virtue of the failure of Bobby Wilson to deliver to Hays at least 600,000 bricks;

(9) That Hays saved $2605.00 in expenses in consequence of the failure of Bobby Wilson to deliver to him (Hays) at least 600,000 bricks.

Pursuant to the jury verdict, the trial court entered judgment in favor of Plaintiff Hays against Defendant Bobby Wilson in the amount of $13,645.00, plus accrued interest at 6% per annum from and after May 15, 1972, up to Jan. 27, 1976, same being the date of the trial court's judgment, plus interest at 9% per annum from and after the date of said judgment. From this judgment, Defendant Wilson appeals.

* * * [Appellant] challenges the $13,645.00 judgment upon the ground, among other things, that there is no evidence to support the jury's findings in answer to Special Issues No. 8 (lost profits) and No. 9 (expenses). We sustain these points of error insofar as they assert no evidence to support the jury's findings concerning lost profits less expenses, and in all other respects we overrule such points.

Plaintiff–Appellee Hays's remedies and measures of damages as a buyer of goods in the case at bar are governed by Sections 2.711, 2.712, 2.713, and 2.715 of the Texas Business and Commerce Code. We herewith quote the portions of said sections that bear upon the case at bar:

"*Sec. 2.711. Buyer's Remedies in General;* * * *.

"(a) Where the seller fails to make delivery or repudiates * * * the buyer may cancel and whether or not he has done so may in addition to recovering so much of the price as has been paid

"(1) 'cover' and have damages under the next section as to all the goods affected whether or not they have been identified to the contract; or

"(2) recover damages for non-delivery as provided in this chapter (Section 2.713)."

* * *

"*Section 2.712.   'Cover'; Buyer's Procurement of Substitute Goods*

"(a) After a breach within the preceding section the buyer may 'cover' by making in good faith and without unreasonable delay any reasonable purchase of or contract to purchase goods in substitution for those due from the seller.

"(b) The buyer may recover from the seller as damages the difference between the cost of cover and the contract price together with any incidental or consequential damages as hereinafter defined (Section 2.715), but less expenses saved in consequence of the seller's breach.

"(c) Failure of the buyer to effect cover within this section does not bar him from any other remedy."

"*Section 2.713.   Buyer's Damages for Non–Delivery or Repudiation*

"(a) * * * the measure of damages for non-delivery or repudiation by the seller is the difference between the market price at the time when the buyer learned of the breach and the contract price together with any incidental and consequential damages provided in this chapter (Sec. 2.715), but less expenses saved in consequence of the seller's breach."

* * *

"*Section 2.715.   Buyer's Incidental and Consequential Damages*

"(a) Incidental damages * * * (not applicable).

"(b) Consequential damages resulting from the seller's breach include

"(1) any loss resulting from general or particular requirements and needs of which the seller at the time of contracting had reason to know and which could not reasonably be prevented by cover or otherwise; * * *."

Let us analyze the verdict and judgment in the light of the foregoing statutory provisions. In the first place, it is established that Plaintiff Hays paid $6000.00 for 600,000 used brick at the rate of one cent per brick, whereas he received only 400,000 brick. Therefore he paid $2000 for 200,000 brick that he never got, and he is thereby entitled to recover $2000.00 under Section 2.711 for "recovering so much of the price as has been paid."

Next, under Section 2.713, he is entitled to damages for "non-delivery or repudiation," and here his measure of damages is the difference between the market price and the contract price. The contract price of the 200,000 brick not delivered is established at $2000.00.

The market price at the appropriate time and place of the undelivered brick was five cents per brick or $10,000.00. This jury finding of market value (five cents per brick) although challenged by Appellant for legal and factual insufficiency, is amply supported by the evidence and is well within the range of probative testimony. Therefore under Section 2.713 and appropriate jury findings, Plaintiff is entitled to $8000.00 damages (or $10,000.00 market price less $2000.00 contract price) for non-delivery.

Now we come to the problem of "consequential damages * * * less expenses saved in consequence of the seller's breach" as mentioned in Sec. 2.713 and which damages are provided for in Sec. 2.715. As stated, the jury found Hays sustained lost profits of $6250.00 (Special Issue No. 8) and saved $2605.00 expenses (No. 9), thereby suffering a lost profits net of $3645.00, which last-named amount was included in the $13,-645.00 judgment total. This $3645.00 lost profits amount has no support in the evidence. Under Sec. 2.715, "consequential damages" includes "any loss * * * which could not reasonably be prevented by cover or otherwise." There is no evidence in the record whatever that Plaintiff Hays at any time made any effort to cover or in any other manner attempt to prevent or mitigate a loss resulting from the Defendant Wilson's non-delivery of the 200,000 brick in question. In the absence of such a showing these consequential damages are unauthorized under Section 2.715. The burden of proving the extent of loss incurred by way of consequential damage is on the buyer. [Citations.] This being so, we are of the opinion that there is no evidence to support these jury findings concerning consequential damages, and that the trial court's judgment insofar as it awarded Plaintiff Hays $3645.00 lost profits is improper and this amount should be deleted from said judgment.

As stated before, the judgment is proper and should be affirmed for the amount of $10,000.00, same being composed of $2000.00 paid by Plaintiff for which he received no bricks plus $8000.00 damages for non-delivery. * * *

---

1. The Uniform Commercial Code, like the common law, attempts to protect the expectancy interests of non-breaching parties. The damages remedy attempts to place them in the same position they would have occupied but for the breach.

The buyer's expectancy interest is accomplished with three principal elements of damages: (1) the difference in value to the non-breaching party between the performance or goods tendered and the performance or goods as promised under the contract; (2) incidental losses incurred in reasonable efforts to avoid losses occasioned by the breach; and (3) consequential losses, including items such as lost profits reasonably foreseeable by the breaching party.

2. An aggrieved buyer may recover consequential damages under 2–715(2) if the seller had reason to know of the buyer's general or particular requirements and needs at the time of contracting, assuming the losses could not have been prevented by cover or otherwise. The "reason to know" test has two elements: an objective inquiry of what a reasonable person in the seller's position would know and a subjective test of what the seller actually knew. *See* R.I. Lampus Co. v. Neville Cement Products Corp., 474 Pa. 199, 378 A.2d 288 (1977).

The adoption of the reasonable foreseeability test in Section 2–715(2) is a rejection of the so-called tacit agreement test; the latter test required a buyer to prove that the seller specifically contemplated and consciously assumed the risk of consequential damages. Globe Refining Co. v. Landa Cotton Oil Co., 190 U.S. 540, 23 S.Ct. 754, 47 L.Ed. 1171 (1903); Keystone Diesel Engine Co. v. Irwin, 411 Pa. 222, 191 A.2d 376 (1963).

3. Consequential damages may be precluded or limited to the extent that the loss could "reasonably be prevented by cover or otherwise." This limitation reflects the principle of mitigation of damages whereby the non-breaching party must take reasonable steps to avoid damages. The buyer need not undertake extraordinary measures in attempting to mitigate, such as incurring substantial expenses or assuming excessive risk.

In R.E.B., Inc. v. Ralston Purina Co., 525 F.2d 749 (10th Cir.1975), a hog farmer sued an animal feed manufacturer for damages for lost profits and diminished value of producing business as result of defective feed which injured or killed numerous animals. The court allowed lost profits for the diminished herd, finding that the farmer satisfied the standard for mitigation by obtaining replacement animals within his financial capability and using reasonable efforts to cull the affected herd.

4. Cover is not the only mitigating option available to an aggrieved buyer who may want to recover consequential damages. In Waters v. Massey–Ferguson, 775 F.2d 587 (4th Cir.1985), for example, a buyer of a defective tractor hired local area farmers to assist in planting his fields. In several other cases buyers have continued to use the defective goods in order to preserve their rights to consequential damages where replacement goods were not readily available or the buyers could not reasonably effect cover. *See, e.g.,* Chatlos Systems, Inc. v. National Cash Register Corp., 479 F.Supp. 738 (D.N.J.1979); Prutch v. Ford Motor Co., 618 P.2d 657 (Colo.1980).

GERWIN v. SOUTHEASTERN CAL. ASS'N OF SEVENTH DAY ADVENTISTS

14 Cal.App.3d 209, 92 Cal.Rptr. 111 (1971).

TAMURA, ASSOCIATE JUSTICE.

Plaintiff brought an action seeking specific performance and damages for breach of an alleged contract for the sale from defendant to plaintiff of certain restaurant and bar equipment. Following a nonjury trial the court found in favor of plaintiff and entered judgment which (1) decreed specific performance, or, in the event defendant fails or is unable to deliver the property, ordered payment of damages in the sum of $15,000 in lieu of specific performance, and (2) awarded plaintiff consequential damages for loss of anticipated profits in the sum of $20,000. Defendant appeals from the judgment.

* * *

The court found that Cunningham's [agent for plaintiff] written bid was received and accepted by defendant; that the bid was definite and certain respecting the items bid upon; * * * that defendant refused to deliver; that plaintiff performed all of the required conditions; * * * that the reasonable value of the equipment as of July 12, 1965, was $25,000; and that plaintiff, in addition, suffered consequential damages of $20,000. The judgment decree ordered specific performance or, in lieu thereof, ordered payment of $25,000, and, in addition, awarded consequential damages of $20,000. Defendant moved for a new trial. The court denied the motion but amended the judgment by reducing the award in lieu of specific performance from $25,000 to $15,000.

[The court concluded that the evidence was sufficient to support the finding that the parties had entered into a contract.] * * *

We next consider the damage issues. As heretofore noted the court awarded $15,000 direct or general damages as an alternative to specific performance and, in addition, $20,000 consequential damages for loss of anticipated profits. Defendant contends that the $15,000 award was excessive and that the award of consequential damages based upon loss of anticipated profits was improper.

* * * Where the seller refuses to deliver, the buyer may "cover" by making, in good faith and without unreasonable delay, a reasonable purchase of goods in substitution for those due from the seller and recover from the seller as damages the difference between the cost of "cover" and the contract price, together with any incidental or consequential damages. (Comm.Code, § 2712.) If the buyer elects not to "cover," he may sue for breach in which event the measure of damages is the difference between market price and the contract price (Comm. Code, § 2713) and any consequential damages "which could not reasonably be prevented by cover or otherwise, * * *" (Comm.Code, § 2715).

Although plaintiff failed to "cover," failure to do so did not bar him from the right to recover damages for the difference between market price and the contract price under section 2713 of the Commercial Code. (Comm.Code, § 2712.)

There was substantial evidence to support the amount of the alternative award of $15,000. Plaintiff testified he had owned and operated bars, was familiar with the cost of bar equipment and cash registers, and that his investigation disclosed that the cost of obtaining "similar type of equipment" ranged from $25,000 to $75,000. His testimony was uncontradicted. Evidence of cost, uncontradicted by other evidence, is sufficient to support a finding of value. * * *

We turn next to the award of \$20,000 for consequential damages for loss of anticipated profits.

As noted earlier herein, if a buyer elects not to "cover" and sues for damages for breach, the measure of damages is the difference between market value and the contract price (Comm.Code, § 2713), and any consequential damage "resulting from general or particular requirements and needs of which the seller at the time of contracting had reason to know and which could not reasonably be prevented by cover or otherwise; * * * "(Comm.Code, § 2715.) Paragraph 2 of the Uniform Commercial Code Comment to section 2715 states: "Although the older rule at common law which made the seller liable for all consequential damages of which he had 'reason to know' in advance is followed, the liberality of that rule is modified by refusing to permit recovery unless the buyer could not reasonably have prevented the loss by cover or otherwise. * * * "Thus, in order to recover consequential damages other than those which could not have been avoided by cover or otherwise, the buyer must have made a good faith attempt to mitigate his losses by "cover." The concept of "cover" thus serves two purposes; it enables the buyer to make reasonable substitute purchases and to recover the cost thereof rather than the difference between market value and contract price and, at the same time, protects the seller from consequential damages which could have been mitigated by the purchase of substitute goods. [Citations.]

In the present case plaintiff did not cover. But it does not follow that he was thereby precluded from recovering consequential damages. Plaintiff was unable to purchase substitute items because of their unavailability at prices within his financial ability. Ordinarily a duty to mitigate does not require an injured party to take measures which are unreasonable or impractical or which require expenditures disproportionate to the loss sought to be avoided or which are beyond his financial means. [Citations.] That principle should govern in determining whether a buyer acted reasonably in failing to cover or otherwise mitigate his losses. [Citation.] In the circumstances here presented plaintiff's failure to purchase substitute goods did not, in and of itself, preclude his recovery of consequential damages. By ordering specific performance, the court impliedly found that after reasonable effort plaintiff was either unable to effect cover or the circumstances reasonably indicated that such effort would be unrewarding. (Comm.Code, § 2716(3).) There was substantial evidence to support such an implied finding.

Nevertheless the evidence in the instant case is insufficient to support the award of damages for loss of prospective profits. The Commercial Code permits recovery of consequential damages for "[a]ny loss resulting from general or particular requirements and needs of which the seller at the time of contracting had reason to know[.]

* * * "(Sec. 2715) Paragraph 3 of Uniform Commercial Code Comment to section 2715 states in part: "Particular needs of the buyer must generally be made known to the seller while general needs must rarely be made known to charge the seller with knowledge." In substance, the section modifies the rule enunciated in Hadley v. Baxendale, 9 Ex. 341, 156 Eng.Rep. 145; the test is one of reasonable foreseeability of probable consequences. [Citations.] Foreseeability, however, is to be determined as of the time the contract was entered into and not as of the time of the breach or some other subsequent event. [Citations.]

In the present case the court found that defendant knew "that plaintiff intended to use the assets to run a restaurant, hotel and cocktail lounge." * * * At the time it accepted the bid, defendant could not reasonably have foreseen the probable consequences of its breach upon plaintiff when it didn't even know it was contracting with him. Although plaintiff made known to defendant his particular need for the equipment when he went to pick up the items on July 12, 1965, knowledge on the part of the seller at the time of breach is insufficient.

Apart from the foregoing, the evidence discloses deficiency in proof of anticipated profits.

It has been frequently stated that if a business is new, it is improper to award damage for loss of profits because absence of income and expense experience renders anticipated profits too speculative to meet the legal standard of reasonable certainty necessary to support an award of such damage. [Citations.] However, the rule is not a hard and fast one and loss of prospective profits may nevertheless be recovered if the evidence shows with reasonable certainty both their occurrence and the extent thereof. [Citations.] In the present case the question is whether the evidence of loss of prospective profits meets that standard.

* * *

[The] evidence fails to measure up to that degree of reasonable certainty required to support the award for loss of anticipated profits. The business being new, plaintiff was obviously unable to produce evidence of operating history of the proposed venture. But neither did he introduce even evidence of operating history of comparable businesses in the locality. Although plaintiff expressed his opinion that the Turners could have paid the $1500 per month rental for the operation of the hotel, bar and restaurant, plaintiff had no prior experience in the operation of a hotel or of a bar in the locality in question. In these circumstances it was speculative and conjectural whether the venture would have generated the business necessary to enable the Turners to pay the $1500 per month.

Moreover, there was no showing that the rental income from the lease would have constituted net profit to plaintiff. Under the terms of the proposed lease plaintiff was required to provide and install the necessary equipment, furniture and furnishings. Amortization of such costs as well as interest on his capital investment, taxes, and cost of maintenance should have been deducted. When loss of anticipated profits is an element of damages, it means net and not gross profits. * * * An award of consequential damages based on loss of anticipated profits, particularly in a new venture, may not be sustained on such evidence.

* * *

For the foregoing reasons that portion of the amended judgment awarding plaintiff $20,000 as consequential damages (Paragraph II of Judgment) is reversed; the remainder of the judgment is affirmed.

---

1. The requirement that damages be established with reasonable certainty has been articulated frequently as a key basis for denying a new or unestablished business any recovery of lost profits for breach of contract. The rationale for precluding recovery simply was the assumption that the lack of sufficient operating history for new businesses necessarily made prospective profits too speculative, contingent, and remote to satisfy the legal standard of reasonable certainty. See Thrift Wholesale v. Malkin–Illion Corp., 50 F.Supp. 998, 1000 (E.D.Pa.1943).

The distinction drawn between new business ventures and existing operations with respect to potential awards of future profits became so prevalent that some courts elevated it to virtually a per se rule. See Evergreen Amusement Corporation v. Milstead, 206 Md. 610, 112 A.2d 901, 905 (1955) ("While this Court has not laid down a flat rule ... nevertheless, no case has permitted recovery of lost profits under comparable circumstances.") A growing number of courts, however, have recognized no sound policy basis to automatically preclude lost profits solely on the characterization that a "new business" was involved and instead have focused on whether the damages were established by sufficient evidence. El Fredo Pizza, Inc. v. Roto–Flex Oven Co., 199 Neb. 697, 261 N.W.2d 358 (1978); Chung v. Kaonohi Center Co., 62 Hawaii 594, 618 P.2d 283 (1980); Fera v. Village Plaza, Inc., 396 Mich. 639, 242 N.W.2d 372 (1976). These courts acknowledge that a new business faces a greater burden of proof in establishing the loss of anticipated profits but allow the claimant an opportunity to produce evidence to meet the reasonable certainty standard. Handi Caddy, Inc. v. American Home Products Corporation, 557 F.2d 136, 139 (8th Cir. 1977). The Restatement (Second) of Contracts § 352 comment b acknowledges this shift in the law by stating that the difficulty of proving lost profits should vary depending upon the nature of the transaction.

Illustrative of the modern trend is In re Merritt Logan, Inc., 901 F.2d 349 (3d Cir.1990), where a buyer of a defective refrigeration system sought lost profits of its grocery store business. The court rejected a per se rule against potential recovery of lost profits simply because the business had a brief operating history.

2. What should be the appropriate measure of damages when the market price of goods changes dramatically? In Sun Maid Raisin Growers of California v. Victor Packing Co., 146 Cal.App.3d 787, 194 Cal.Rptr. 612 (1983), buyers of raisins sought damages for lost profits from the sellers who failed to deliver the contracted quantity when the market price doubled due to "disastrous" rains which caused a 50 percent crop loss. The sellers claimed that the extraordinarily high price of raisins caused by the destruction of crops was unforeseeable. The court disagreed, holding that the breaching party was not required to foresee the *amount* of lost profits at time of entering contract, only that they objectively contemplated that *some* profits could be lost as consequence of non-performance. Further, the court found that the raisin packers should have understood the risk in contracting to sell raisins at a fixed price over a period of time extending into the next crop year, knowing that the market price could change dramatically based on consumer demand and supply and quality of raisins. The court awarded the buyer lost profits, reasoning that otherwise the seller could effectively speculate on the direction of the market price as compared to the contract price.

3. A particularly troublesome problem is determination of the appropriate time to measure a buyer's damages when the seller has anticipatorily repudiated a contract and the buyer does not cover. Section 2–713 provides that the damages for a seller's repudiation are calculated at the time the buyer learned of the breach. Courts have made three interpretations of the phrase "learned of the breach" in this context: (1) when the buyer learns of the breach, (2) when the buyer learns of the breach plus a commercially reasonable time, and (3) when performance is due under the contract.

The interpretation of "time of the breach" is most significant when market prices are rising. The Court of Appeals for the Fifth Circuit explained the problem in Cosden Oil v. Karl O. Helm Aktiengesellschaft, 736 F.2d 1064 (5th Cir.1984):

> Typically, [the] question will arise where parties to an executory contract are in the midst of a rising market. To the extent that market decisions are influenced by a damages rule, measuring market price at the time of seller's repudiation gives seller the ability to fix buyer's damages and may induce seller to repudiate, rather than abide by the contract. By contrast, measuring buyer's damages at the time of performance will tend to dissuade the buyer from covering, in hopes that market price will continue upward until performance time.
>
> Allowing the aggrieved buyer a commercially reasonable time, however, provides him with an opportunity to investigate his cover possibilities in a rising market without fear that, if he is unsuccessful in obtaining cover, he will be relegated to a market-contract damage remedy measured at the time of repudiation. The Code

supports this view. While cover is the preferred remedy, the Code clearly provides the option to seek damages.

The court further recognized that the buyer's option to wait a commercially reasonable time beyond the breach interacts with section 2–611, which allows the seller an opportunity to retract his repudiation.

AM/PM FRANCHISE ASSN. v. ATLANTIC RICHFIELD CO.

526 Pa. 110, 584 A.2d 915 (1990)

Cappy, Judge.

[ARCO entered into franchise agreements with the plaintiffs to operate mini-markets. The contract mandated that the franchisees sell only ARCO petroleum products. Plaintiffs claimed that many of their customers who purchased an oxinol gasoline blend produced by ARCO experienced various engine problems. The franchisees asserted that they suffered a decline in business and attendant loss of profits as a consequence of the defective gasoline. The plaintiff class sought damages for breach of warranty by ARCO. The Superior Court affirmed the trial court's dismissal of the franchisees' complaint, holding that damages for loss of goodwill in a breach of warranty action were not recoverable.]

The point at which we start our inquiry is the Uniform Commercial Code ("the U.C.C."), codified at 13 Pa.C.S. § 1101 *et seq.* Section 2714, entitled "Damages of buyer for breach in regard to accepted goods" is one of the governing provisions in the case before us, and provides, in pertinent part:

(b) Measure of damages for breach of warranty.—The measure of damages for breach of warranty is the difference at the time and place of acceptance between the value of the goods accepted and the value they would have had if they had been as warranted, unless special circumstances show proximate damages of a different amount.

(c) Incidental and consequential damages.—In a proper case any incidental and consequential damages under section 2715 (relating to incidental and consequential damages of buyer) may also be recovered.

Section 2715 is entitled "Incidental and Consequential Damages of Buyer" and provides, in pertinent part:

(a) Incidental damages.—Incidental damages resulting from the breach of the seller include:

(3) any other reasonable expenses incident to the delay or other breach.

(b) Consequential damages.—Consequential damages resulting from the breach of the seller include:

(1) any loss resulting from general or particular requirements and needs of which the seller at the time of contracting had reason to know and which could not reasonably be prevented by cover or otherwise.

Pursuant to the provisions of the U.C.C., plaintiffs are entitled to seek "general" damages, so-called, under section 2714(b), and consequential damages as provided by section 2714(c).

There has been substantial confusion in the courts and among litigants about what consequential damages actually are and what types of consequential damages are available in a breach of warranty case. Where a buyer in the business of reselling goods can prove that a breach by the seller has caused him to lose profitable resales, the buyer's lost profits constitute a form of consequential damages. We now hold that in addition to general damages, there are three types of lost profit recoverable as consequential damages that may flow from a breach of warranty: (1) loss of primary profits; (2) loss of secondary profits; and (3) a loss of good will damages (or prospective damages, as they are sometimes termed). * * *

General damages in the case of accepted goods (such as occurred here) are the actual difference in value between the goods as promised and the goods as received. Thus, suppose a buyer bought five hundred tires from a wholesaler that were to be delivered in good condition, and in that condition would be worth $2,500. The tires were delivered with holes in them which rendered them worthless. The buyer would be entitled to $2,500 from the seller—the difference between the value of the tires as warranted and the value of the tires as received; those would be the general damages.

Consequential damages are generally understood to be other damages which naturally and proximately flow from the breach and include three types of lost profit damages: (1) lost primary profits; (2) lost secondary profits; and (3) loss of prospective profits, also commonly referred to as good will damages.

Lost primary profits are the difference between what the buyer would have earned from reselling the goods in question had there been no breach and what was earned after the breach occurred. Thus, if the buyer of the tires proved that he would have resold the tires for $5,000, he would be able to claim an additional $2,500 for loss of tire profits; the difference between what he would have earned from the sale of the tires and what he actually did earn from the sale (or lack of sales) from the tires.

If the buyer of the tires also sold, for example, hubcaps with every set of tires, he would also suffer a loss of hubcap profits. These types of damages are what we term "loss of secondary profits."

If the buyer's regular customers were so disgruntled about the defective tires that they no longer frequented the buyer's business and began to patronize a competitor's business, the buyer would have suffered a "loss of good will" beyond the direct loss of profits from the nonconforming goods; his future business would be adversely affected as a result of the defective tires. Thus, good will damages refer to profits lost on future sales rather than on sales of the defective goods themselves. * * *

In addition to recognizing general damages under § 2714 of the Code, Pennsylvania allows consequential damages in the form of lost profits to be recovered. [Citations.]

Pennsylvania has, however, disallowed good will damages; finding them to be too speculative to permit recovery. In the cases disallowing good will damages, part of the reason we found them too speculative is that the damages were not contemplated by the parties at the time the contract was made.

In 1977, this court had occasion to re-examine sections 2714 and 2715 of the Uniform Commercial Code in the case of R.I. Lampus Co. v. Neville Cement Products Corp., 474 Pa. 199, 378 A.2d 288 (1977). Before the *Lampus* case, we required the party seeking consequential damages in the form of lost profits to show that there were "special circumstances" indicating that such damages were actually contemplated by the parties at the time they entered into the agreement. This rule, termed the "tacit-agreement" test, "permit[ed] the plaintiff to recover damages arising from special circumstances only if 'the defendant fairly may be supposed to have assumed consciously, or to have warranted the plaintiff reasonably to suppose that it assumed, [such liability] when the contract was made.' " [Citation.]

In *Lampus*, we overruled the restrictive "tacit agreement" test and replaced it with the "reason to know" test; which requires that "[i]f a seller knows of a buyer's general or particular requirements and needs, that seller is liable for the resulting consequential damages whether or not that seller contemplated or agreed to such damages." *Id.*, 474 Pa. at 209, 378 A.2d at 292 (1977) (emphasis supplied).[6] Thus, in order to obtain consequential damages, the plaintiff need only prove that the damages were reasonably foreseeable at the time the agreement was entered into.

Turning to the case at hand, we must determine whether the plaintiffs have alleged sufficient facts to permit them to proceed with a claim for consequential damages.

* * * [T]he plaintiffs have alleged: that ARCO expressly warranted through its agreements, mailgrams and brochures that its oxinol gasoline was of high quality, better for the environment and would not damage new or older automobiles; that the oxinol gasoline was not merchantable because it damaged engines; that it was not fit for the ordinary purpose for which it was intended; that ARCO knew that the

---

6. *Lampus* is in accord with section 2–715 of the U.C.C., comment 2 (1978), which states; "[t]he 'tacit agreement' test for the recovery of consequential damages is rejected."

plaintiffs were relying on the skill of the defendants to select or furnish suitable gasoline; that ARCO's actions constituted a breach of express warranties which resulted in harm to the plaintiffs in the form of lost profits, incidental and consequential damages. [The court found that plaintiffs had shown sufficient facts to state a cause of action under the breach of warranty counts.]

The plaintiffs seek lost profits, incidental and consequential damages.[8] The defendants and the lower courts, however, considered these damages to be lost good will. We believe that the lower courts and the defendants are in error in categorizing all the claimed damages as good will damages. * * *

Loss of Profits for Gasoline Sales

The first claim the plaintiff makes for damages is for the profits lost from the sales of gasoline. The plaintiffs claim that the breach of warranty by the defendant concerning the gasoline caused the plaintiffs to lose sales during a three and one half year period while they received nonconforming gasoline from ARCO. In the case of Kassab v. Central Soya, 432 Pa. 217, 246 A.2d 848 (1968), we permitted lost profits for cattle sales when the plaintiff showed that the defective feed caused harm to their cattle, causing the public to stop buying their cattle. The allegation here is similar. When the gasoline buying public discovered that the gasoline was defective, many stopped purchasing ARCO gasoline.

Employing the reasoning of *Kassab* and taking it one step further, we believe that the plaintiffs here are entitled to show that the gasoline buying community did not buy their gasoline from 1982 through 1985 because of the reasonable belief that the gasoline was defective and would harm their engines. The lost gasoline sales are comparable to the lost cattle sales in *Kassab*. The distinction between the two cases is that the Kassabs had bought the feed all at one time and thus all their livestock was affected. The instant plaintiffs bought their gasoline in regular intervals and could only earn a profit on what they could sell per month. The defendant's argument—that the plaintiffs sold all the gasoline they bought—misses the point. While they may have sold every gallon, they sold significantly fewer gallons during the period that ARCO allegedly delivered nonconforming gasoline. Thus, during this period, the plaintiffs' lost sales were just as directly attributable to the defective gasoline as the lost profits were attributable to the defective tires in the example we used previously.[9]

---

8. The plaintiffs claim "lost profits, incidental and consequential damages." As we noted herein, however, "lost profits" are a type of consequential damage; not a separate category of damages.

9. The current case, unlike the tire example, involves a requirements contract rather than a fixed quantity agreement. In a requirement contract, profits lost during the period of time in which the seller sup-plies nonconforming goods constitute lost primary profits. The Code does not require that the buyer prove he would have purchased the same amount as usually required, for § 2715 permits the buyer to mitigate his damages by "cover or otherwise." Thus the buyer need not buy his usual amount of goods and then be unable to sell them before he can claim a loss of profits.

Thus, if prior to the manufacture of defective gasoline the plaintiffs sold 100,000 gallons per month every month and then as a result of the defective gasoline, they sold only 60,000 gallons per month every month until ARCO discontinued that gasoline, then the plaintiffs have lost the profits they would have received on 40,000 gallons per month for the three year claimed period. Lost profits are, in fact, the difference between what the plaintiff actually earned and what they would have earned had the defendant not committed the breach. Because the gasoline was allegedly not in conformance with the warranties, the plaintiffs may be entitled to lost profits for the gasoline on a breach of warranty theory. The lost gasoline sales are what we have termed "loss of primary profits," and they are recoverable pursuant to § 2715 of the U.C.C. upon proper proof.

We note, furthermore, that the remedy of cover was unavailable to the plaintiffs. Section 2715 of the U.C.C. limits a plaintiff's ability to recover when he could have prevented such damage "by cover or otherwise". Pursuant to the code, cover is defined as the buyer's purchase of substitute goods at a commercially reasonable price. The buyer can recover from the seller the difference between the contract price and the cost of goods bought as cover. 13 Pa.C.S. § 2712, defining "cover" and damages recoverable, provides, in pertinent part:

> (a) Right and manner of cover.—After a breach within section 2711 (relating to remedies of buyer in general; security interest of buyer in rejected goods) the buyer may "cover" by making in good faith and without unreasonable delay any reasonable purchase of or contract to purchase goods in substitution for those due from the seller.

The plaintiffs here, by their allegations, could not "cover;" they were contractually required to purchase all their gasoline from ARCO. In effect, they had to accept the allegedly nonconforming gasoline and had no possible way to avoid the attendant loss of profits. Thus, since they could not cover, the only remedy that was available to them was to file suit. * * *

The Code itself compels us to be liberal in our interpretation of the types of damages we permit. We would therefore allow the plaintiffs to proceed with their claims for lost gasoline profits during the period ARCO supplied allegedly nonconforming gasoline.

Loss of Profits for Items Other Than Gasoline Sales

The plaintiffs allege that in addition to a loss of profits for sales of gasoline, they had a concomitant loss of sales for other items that they sold in their mini-marts during the period of time that ARCO supplied nonconforming gasoline. Their rationale is that when the number of customers buying gasoline decreased, so did the number of customers buying items at the mini-mart. In other words, related facets of their business suffered as a result of the defective gasoline. This type of injury is what we characterize as "loss of secondary profits;" meaning that the sales of other products suffered as a result of the breach of warranty.

* * * [T]he essence of plaintiffs' allegations is that customers frequent the mini-marts because it is convenient to do so at the time they purchase gasoline. Customers of the mini-mart are foremost gasoline buying patrons; gasoline is their primary purchase and sundries are their incidental purchases. Here, the plaintiffs claim that the primary product sales so affected the incidental sales as to create a loss in other aspects of their business. It is reasonable to assume that if the gasoline sales dropped dramatically, there was a ripple effect on the mini-mart sales. Additionally, when a primary product does not conform to the warranty, we believe that it is foreseeable that there will be a loss of secondary profits. Thus, permitting these damages would correspond with the requirement of foreseeability as set forth in *Lampus, supra,* and the Code. It is much less foreseeable to assume there will be a loss of secondary profits when the nonconforming products are not the primary ones. We believe that unless it is a primary product that does not conform to the warranty, the causal relationship between the breach and the loss is too attenuated to permit damages for the loss of secondary profits.

We also find that the fact situation before us presents a further problem in that the plaintiffs were not able to mitigate the harm in any way by buying substitute goods or "cover." Thus, the plaintiffs' primary product was defective and they were unable to remedy the situation by buying gasoline from another supplier.

We find that the present case presents compelling reasons for permitting damages for loss of secondary profits. Henceforth, in a breach of warranty case, when a primary product of the plaintiff is alleged to be nonconforming and the plaintiff is unable to cover by purchasing substitute goods, we hold that upon proper proof, the plaintiff should be entitled to sue for loss of secondary profits.[13]

Loss of Good Will

Historically, Pennsylvania has disallowed recovery for loss of good will damages or prospective profits in breach of warranty cases. [Citations.]

The defendant and the lower courts rely on these cases for the proposition that the plaintiffs claims are for "good will damages" and thus too speculative as a matter of law to permit recovery. * * *

With the advent of the *Lampus* "reason-to-know" test—which is a test of foreseeability—the holdings under each of these cases have much less precedential effect, since the *Lampus* test is much less restrictive than the tacit-agreement test.

---

13. What constitutes a "primary product" will be dependent on the facts of each case. However, we would define a "primary product" as an item upon which the aggrieved party relies for a substantial amount of its revenue. The plaintiff must show that without that product, his business would be severely incapacitated.

Although the plaintiffs do not style their claim as one for good will damages, the Superior Court, the trial court, and the defendant have all characterized the claim for lost profits in this case as good will damages. What actually constitutes good will damages has caused much consternation to the courts and litigants. * * *

As one commentator aptly noted, "[l]oss of good will is a mercurial concept and, as such, is difficult to define. In a broad sense, it refers to a loss of future profits." [Citation.] Other jurisdictions have considered loss of good will to be a loss of profits and reputation among customers. Generally, good will refers to the reputation that businesses have built over the course of time that is reflected by the return of customers to purchase goods and the attendant profits that accompanies such sales. Thus the phrase "good will damages" is coextensive with prospective profits and loss of business reputation.

Secondly, we must decide when good will damages arise in a breach of warranty situation. Essentially, damage to good will in a case in which the seller supplies a quantity dictated by the buyer's requirements arises only after the seller has ceased providing nonconforming goods— or the buyer has purchased substitute goods. Damage to good will in this case would refer to the loss of business sales that occurred after the buyer was able to provide acceptable goods to his customers; it does not refer to the period of time during which he is forced to sell the nonconforming goods.

Thirdly, we must address whether good will damages are too speculative to permit recovery, as we held in [previous cases]. Although we disallowed good will damages in those cases, they are not recent. They were written in a time when business was conducted on a more simple basis, where market studies and economic forecasting were unexplored sciences.

We are now in an era in which computers, economic forecasting, sophisticated marketing studies and demographic studies are widely used and accepted. As such, we believe that the rationale for precluding prospective profits under the rubric of "too speculative" ignores the realities of the marketplace and the science of modern economics. We believe that claims for prospective profits should not be barred *ab initio*. Rather, plaintiffs should be given an opportunity to set forth and attempt to prove their damages. * * *

We believe the time has come to reconsider [our] rule. In doing so, we find our position on recovery for good will damages (or prospective profits) to be out of step with modern day business practices and techniques, as well as the law of other jurisdictions.

* * * In reviewing our case law on the issue of prospective profits, we have not had a significant case come before us since [1968]. Since that time, astronauts have walked on the moon, engineers have developed computers capable of amazing feats and biomedical engineers and physicians have made enormous strides in organ transplantation and replacement. * * * While these rapid technological developments have

not been without their concomitant problems, they have made possible many things that were not possible before; including the calculation of prospective profits. For these reasons, we overrule [previous cases] to the extent they prohibit a plaintiff from alleging a claim for damage to good will as a matter of law.

Inextricably entwined with the issue of speculation is the difficulty in proving the damages are causally related to the breach. As we stated earlier, difficulty in proving causation should not operate as a bar to permitting plaintiffs to claim the damages. Furthermore, we note that pursuant to our case law and the Uniform Commercial Code, damages need not be proved with mathematical certainty. As long as the plaintiffs can provide a reasonable basis from which the jury can calculate damages, they will be permitted to pursue their case.

Thus, we now hold that plaintiffs should be entitled to try to prove good will damages; provided they are able to introduce sufficient evidence (1) to establish that the such profits were causally related to a breach of warranty and (2) to provide the trier of fact with a reasonable basis from which to calculate damages.

Turning to the facts of this case, we note that the plaintiffs have made no claim for good will damages, since none was incurred; ARCO having cured the breach by stopping the supply of the nonconforming gasoline. The damages claimed are only for the period of time that the plaintiffs were forced to purchase the gasoline with oxinol. Thus, we reverse the decision of the lower courts in holding that the plaintiffs' claim was for good will damages.

Conclusion

We now hold that there are three types of lost profits recoverable as consequential damages available under § 2714 and § 2715 of the Uniform Commercial Code: (1) loss of primary profits; (2) loss of secondary profits; and (3) good will damages, defined as a loss of prospective profits or business reputation. While this categorization of damages represents a new direction for the court, we believe it is the better direction.

———

1. As the principal case reflects, recovery of damages for loss of goodwill is inherently difficult because it relates to the future; no actual profit base will be available for evidentiary use at trial. Where the aggrieved party can show the fact of damage, however, uncertainty regarding the amount of lost goodwill does not automatically preclude recovery. *See* Lewis River Golf v. O.M. Scott & Sons, 120 Wash.2d 712, 845 P.2d 987, 989 (1993) (damage to business reputation or goodwill and resulting loss in the value of business properly recoverable as an element of consequential damages); Consolidated Data Terminals v. Applied Digital Data Systems, Inc., 708 F.2d 385 (9th Cir.1983) (loss of goodwill

among customers of distributor caused by problems with defective computer terminals compensable).

2.   In Cole Energy Development Co. v. Ingersoll–Rand Co., 913 F.2d 1194 (7th Cir.1990), a lessee of gas compressors brought a breach of warranty claim against the lessor/manufacturer.   The lessee did not lose actual production as a result of the decreased effectiveness of the equipment, but experienced a delay in its realization of profits.   The court held that the lost opportunity costs in delaying expected profits were properly compensable, measured by the costs of actual production compared to costs the lessee would have incurred if defective equipment had worked as warranted at full capacity.   *See also* Horizons, Inc. v. Avco Corp., 551 F.Supp. 771, 781 (D.C.S.D.1982) (buyer of business equipment could recover lost profits, calculated by the down-time caused by period of equipment failure).

3.   The different treatment of foreseeability with respect to general and special damages has been carried forward from the common law to the Uniform Commercial Code.   Because general damages flow directly and immediately as a natural consequence of the kind of wrongful act by the breaching party, they are conclusively presumed foreseeable.   This approach is reflected in section 2–714(1) which concerns accepted but nonconforming goods, in section 2–712 which pertains to cover, and in section 2–713 which gives the market price-contract price differential to an aggrieved buyer.

Hess Die Mold Inc. v. American Plasti–Plate Corp., 653 S.W.2d 927 (Tex.App.1983), illustrates the treatment of foreseeability with respect to general damages.   The case involved a contract to purchase a plastic mold for use in the buyer's business.   The seller failed to deliver a mold conforming to the contract and the buyer obtained a replacement from another manufacturer at a higher price.   The court found that the cost to cover was equivalent to an item of common law general damages, and therefore did not require specific findings that the breaching seller had contemplated the buyer's losses at the time of entering the contract.

Compare the requirements for special damages in section 2–715(2), which requires reference to the particular character, condition, or circumstances of the non-breaching party and foreseeability by the breaching party.   Accordingly, special damages must be specially pleaded to give the defendant fair notice of the claim and must be specially proved rather than being implied by law.

4.   Although incidental items of damages are usually identifiable, there are often problems with the distinction between difference-in-value losses from consequential damages.   Although this distinction normally would not be critical in contract cases because all expectancy damages are recoverable, it becomes so when the parties have excluded consequential damages by agreement.

For example, in Reynolds Metals Co. v. Westinghouse Electric Corp., 758 F.2d 1073 (5th Cir.1985), Westinghouse contracted to manufacture and install an electric transformer for Reynolds Metals.   The seller breached the contract by improperly installing the equipment and thereby causing extensive harm to the transformer. The court recognized that the damages were a foreseeable consequence of the breach which ordinarily would be recoverable as consequential damages. In this contract, however, the parties had specifically limited such damages. Reynolds could only recover damages under section 2–714 for the difference in value of the performance promised and what had been received.

CANNON v. YANKEE PRODUCTS CO., INC.

59 Mass.App.Dec. 169 (1977).

WALSH, J. In this claim for lost profits a restaurant owner originally brought an action of contract against Yankee Products Co., Inc. (Yankee) for breach of express and breach of implied warranty.　* * *

The plaintiff purchased vegetables from Yankee on a weekly basis and dealt with the same route salesman for three years. The plaintiff had purchased the same brand of canned sweet peas packed by Oco, from Yankee, for a period of six months to one year and on January 7, 1970 had purchased one-half of a case of such peas packed in sealed cans. The salesman told plaintiff that the peas were a good product, a big pea, good tasting, not hard and that he and his customers would be satisfied with them and this is the very best brand you can buy, good flavor, wholesome and will please your customers thus increasing your business.

The plaintiff prepared and sold to his customers some of the canned peas purchased on January 7, 1970 on Friday, January 23, 1970 as part of the ninety-nine cent special. He opened a can of peas, placed the peas in a colander, strained them and washed them off. He then put the peas in a pot which had just been cleaned and wiped dry, heated the peas and put them in another pot designed for use in a steam table. He then served the peas to customers.

A worm was discovered by a customer in the "99 cent special" purchased by him. The plaintiff, having had his attention called to the presence of the worm, saw it in the peas on the customer's plate. The worm was skinny, green, dead and 1⅛ inches in length.

The said male customer "made a stink" thereover in the presence of about fifty-five fellow patrons; that other customers exclaimed "oh! oh!"; that the plaintiff commented that the incident or occurrence was just an accident; that he refunded the price of the specially priced meals which had been served with the peas in question to the respective purchasers but the "word spread" and about thirty patrons walked out and the plaintiff refunded the price of their dinners to them. The plaintiff could neither remember the name of or remember the last time he saw the customer who found the worm on his plate.

After this incident the plaintiff observed a reduction in the number of customers patronizing his restaurant, particularly at the lunch hour. He took a ride around the area and observed many of his former customers eating elsewhere at other dining establishments.

Subsequent to the incident the plaintiff increased the number of hours of doing business. He remained open until 11:00 P.M., hiring a night man to do so. However, all of his efforts to increase the volume of his business were futile. According to the plaintiff "the word spread— the news got around." Consequently, he sold the business on February 1, 1971 and the place has changed hands three times since.

[Plaintiff produced evidence of the gross sales of the plaintiff's business from July, 1969, through November, 1970. The trial court found that the incident caused patrons to remain away from the restaurant, and that Yankee's breaches of warranty rendered it liable for damages for lost profits. The court awarded plaintiff damages of $7,622.80 based upon the average diminution of sales for a twelve month period following the incident.]

It is recognized that loss of profits may be recovered as an element of damages for breach of contract, but it may be difficult to fit the applicable law to a particular case. "The loss of prospective profits may be allowed ... where it appears that the loss was the natural, primary and probable consequence of the breach, that the profits arising from the performance of the contract or the loss likely to result from its non-performance were within the contemplation of the parties, and the profits were not so uncertain or contingent as to be incapable of reasonable proof." [Citation.] They must be the proximate result of the breach and cannot be recovered when they are remote or so uncertain, contingent or speculative as not to be susceptible of trustworthy proof. A claimant cannot prevail when any essential element is left to conjecture, surmise or hypothesis. "The difficulty is not so much in the statement of the general principle as in applying it. A comparatively insignificant incident may be in such combination with others as to lead to a conclusion in one decision apparently at variance with that reached in others. Each case must be decided on its own facts under this necessarily somewhat broad and comprehensive proposition." [Citations.]

A leading case allowing recovery for lost profits involving the sale of food and relied on by the plaintiff is Hawkins v. Jamrog, 277 Mass. 540, 179 N.E. 224 (1931). The plaintiff in that case was the proprietor of a boarding house conducted for college students. The defendant sold dressed turkeys to the plaintiff, knowing their intended use as food in the boarding house. The turkeys were unwholesome and after eating them the plaintiff, all the student waiters and almost all of the boarders were made ill. There was evidence that of the seventy original boarders only thirty returned despite plaintiff's efforts to induce them to do so and also evidence of the average weekly profit per boarder. It was held that an award of loss of prospective profits to the end of the school year was neither too remote to be allowed as an element of damage nor merely speculative or conjectural in nature.

The Uniform Commercial Code is also applicable here and GL § 2–714(3) provides that in addition to damages for loss recoverable from a seller's breach in the ordinary course of events, consequential damages may also be recovered in a proper case under § 2–715. Section 2–715(2) provides that "consequential damages resulting from the seller's breach include (a) any loss resulting from general or particular requirements and needs of which the seller at the time of contracting had reason to know and which could not reasonably be prevented by cover or otherwise; and (b) injury to person or property proximately resulting from any breach of warranty."

We think the case at bar is distinguishable from *Hawkins v. Jamrog, supra.* In both cases the plaintiffs purchased food products for resale and their respective vendors had reason to know it. However, in *Hawkins* the plaintiff's customers ate the unwholesome food and a substantial number became ill. Such was not the case here. The customer who saw the worm probably would not have had a cause of action for personal injury. [Citations.] Certainly those who didn't see it would not have had any such claim.

The fact that the exodus of the customers was caused as much by the utterances of the obviously upset customer as by the presence of the worm and the fact that no one was made ill by the alleged unwholesome food would seem to take the loss of customers out of the natural and probable consequences of the breach. If for no other reason we feel these are incidents, not necessarily insignificant, which render a finding of loss of profits in this case not warranted. On the same grounds we do not think this is, in the words of GS § 2–714(3), "a proper case" for the recovery of consequential damages under the provisions of GS § 2–715.

With respect to the amount of the loss of profit, we do not find in the report any direct evidence of that nature. Prospective profits need not be proved to mathematical certainty, but in order to recover they must be proved. Here there was evidence of diminution of receipts or sales but no evidence of how much of this constituted loss of profit. There was basis for an opinion, perhaps, but no opinion or calculation.

The plaintiff fares no better in his complaint alleging negligence on the part of the canner of the product since he has the burden to establish that the defendant's breach of duty was the proximate cause of his claimed loss of profit. "One is bound to anticipate and provide against what usually happens and what is likely to happen, but is not bound in like manner to guard against what is unusual and unlikely to happen, or what, as is sometimes said, is only remotely and slightly probable." [Citations.]

We find that on the complaint for negligence against the defendant canning company the plaintiff is not entitled to recover damages. Even though negligence may be found, there is no invasion of rights and no right of action unless legal damage is caused. [Citation.] With respect to the counts in contract against the vendor the situation is different. The plaintiff alleged in his declaration loss of customers and business, but apparently offered no evidence on any out-of-pocket loss for the purchase of the goods or money refunded to his customers. However, the breach, once established, entitled the plaintiff to at least nominal damages.

It is our determination that there has been prejudicial error in the denial of defendants' request for ruling relating to loss of profit. Accordingly, the judgments entered in counts 1 and 2 are modified and judgment is to be entered for nominal damages in each count. On the complaint, judgment for the plaintiff is vacated and judgment is to be entered for the defendant.

————

1. It is often difficult to ascertain with reasonable certainty the measure of lost profits which a buyer may recover as consequential damages. Carboline Co. v. B.C.D. Co., 712 S.W.2d 453 (Mo.App.1986), illustrates the nature of proof necessary for a successful claim for plaintiff's lost profits. A contractor purchased paint to perform a contract with the state to repaint a bridge. The paint supplied by the seller was defective and necessitated that the contractor incur extra expenditures for labor and materials to finish the job. The contractor recovered lost profits measured by the difference between what actually was spent reasonably to complete the contract with the state and what the buyer would have expended if the paint had been as warranted.

2. The Uniform Commercial Code specifically addresses the requirement of certainty in the context of a buyer's ability to recover consequential damages for a breach by a seller in the sale of goods. Comment 4 to U.C.C. § 2–715 states, in pertinent part:

> The burden of proving the extent of loss incurred by way of consequential damage is on the buyer, but the section on liberal administration of remedies rejects any doctrine of certainty which requires almost mathematical precision in the proof of loss. Loss may be determined in any manner which is reasonable under the circumstances.

In addition, comment 1 to U.C.C. § 1–106 provides that in order to effectuate the liberal administration of remedies under the code, it rejects the view that "damages must be calculable with mathematical accuracy." Rather, the code's approach favors a flexible policy where compensatory damages need only "be proved with whatever definiteness and accuracy the facts permit, but no more." Finally, the common law doctrinal limitation which demands only "reasonable" certainty may be considered incorporated through U.C.C. § 1–103.

3. Compare the principal case to In Migerobe, Inc. v. Certina USA, Inc., 924 F.2d 1330 (5th Cir.1991), where a buyer that owned and operated jewelry counters at department stores brought an action for lost profits resulting from the seller's refusal to ship orders of watches. The buyer had planned to sell the watches as a "loss leader" item (sold at or below cost) and featured them in a "doorbuster" Thanksgiving advertisement at a 50 percent discount. The buyer claimed losses of

corollary sales of other items at its jewelry counters was a foreseeable consequence of the seller's breach of contract to sell the watches. The court upheld the jury verdict awarding lost profits, finding that historical data showing the buyer's profits made in past promotions of different items was the best evidence available and provided a reasonable basis for estimating the loss.

4. In Kwan v. Mercedes–Benz of North America, Inc., 23 Cal. App.4th 174, 28 Cal.Rptr.2d 371 (Cal.App.1994), a buyer of a new $46,000 Mercedes sought damages under California's consumer protection act for emotional distress associated with difficulties he experienced in getting the dealership to repair the vehicle. The buyer claimed that the operational problems made the car unsafe and made him "frustrated and mad," "sad," "nervous," and "worried about the safety for the family." The categories and principles of measurement of compensatory damages available to a buyer under the consumer act paralleled comparable provisions normally available to a buyer for a seller's breach of a contract for sale of goods under the U.C.C. Although a jury awarded the buyer emotional distress damages, the appellate court reversed, following the general rule disallowing damages for mental suffering in contracts independent of physical injury.

The court found that the case did not fit within an exception awarding distress damages for breach of contracts "very personal in nature," in which emotional concerns are closely linked to the essence of contractual performance. The court observed:

> In our view, a contract for sale of an automobile is not essentially tied to the buyer's mental or emotional well-being. Personal as the choice of a car may be, the central reason for buying one is usually transportation. In the words of the Restatement, a breach of such a contract is not "particularly likely" to result in "serious" emotional distress. (Rest.2d Contracts, § 353.) The purchase of an automobile ordinarily does not "so affect the vital concerns of the individual that severe mental distress is a foreseeable result of breach."

> In spite of America's much-discussed "love affair with the automobile," disruption of an owner's relationship with his or her car is not, in the normal case, comparable to the loss or mistreatment of a family member's remains, an invasion of one's privacy, or the loss of one's spouse to a gambling addiction. In the latter situations, the contract exists primarily to further or protect emotional interests; the direct and foreseeable injuries resulting from a breach are also primarily emotional. In contrast, the undeniable aggravation, irritation and anxiety that may result from breach of an automobile warranty are secondary effects deriving from the decreased usefulness of the car and the frequently frustrating process of having an automobile repaired. While purchase of an automobile may sometimes lead to severe emotional distress, such a result is not ordinarily foreseeable from the nature of the contract.

ARIES v. PALMER JOHNSON, INC.

153 Ariz. 250, 735 P.2d 1373 (1987).

HOWARD, P.J.

This is an action by the purchaser of a yacht (Aries) against the manufacturer/seller [Palmer Johnson, Inc. (PJ)] for breach of contract, breach of warranty, and fraud. * * *

The action was tried to the court, sitting without a jury, which found that PJ breached its contractual promise concerning time of delivery, breached express and implied warranties as to description and quality, and defrauded Aries in regard to the boat's promised delivery date. The court awarded Aries $218,795.58 in damages. * * *

In August of 1982, Aries sent PJ $100,000 as a deposit toward the purchase of an Alden 75 yacht, to be called "Scheherazade." * * * On September 1, 1982, Aries sent a letter to PJ which contained a list of specifications for the new yacht. He also inquired about a queen-size bunk for the master stateroom and asked Kelsey's opinion as to whether it could be done. Fifteen days later, PJ signed and mailed one of its standard form contracts for Aries' signature. The contract price was $1,237,500. The delivery date was "on or about June 25, 1983" in accordance with prior discussions between Aries and Kelsey wherein Aries told Kelsey of his intended use of the yacht for the summer of 1983. One day after mailing the contract, PJ wrote Aries in response to his September 1 letter. PJ did not address the issue of the queen-size bunk, but stated that construction was already under way and that PJ expected no problem in completing the yacht by the scheduled delivery date of June 25, 1983.

* * * Aries paid PJ all sums of money that were due under the contract.

* * *

From the fall of 1982 until early spring of 1983, Aries had regular conversations with Kelsey and Johansen concerning the progress of the construction. It was uncontradicted that in these conversations Aries was advised that construction was proceeding on schedule and that the contract delivery date would be met. * * *

The boat was not delivered until November 23, 1983, five months late, depriving Aries of all use during the summer and fall of 1983. After delivery, it promptly broke down. It was dry-docked in a repair facility for approximately 168 days during the year following delivery. Defects in quality and material were wide ranging, from delaminating paint, to drill holes in the hull, to a jerry-rigged sewage tank system which was vented near the cabin portholes.

Aries informed PJ repeatedly, both before and after executing the contract, of his intended use of the boat during the summer and fall of

1983, which included the "shakedown cruise" in Lake Michigan, attendance at the quadrennial America's Cup races in August and September, and then on to the Caribbean. From the time the contract was executed in the fall of 1982, to the early spring of 1983, PJ's president and construction superintendent repeatedly assured Aries that construction was proceeding in a timely manner and that delivery would be timely. The record shows that Aries relied on those representations to his detriment. For example, he decommissioned the yacht he then owned and did not secure a substitute vessel for his intended use during the summer and fall of 1983.

* * *

Damages for Loss of Use

The trial court awarded Aries $100,000 for loss of use of the yacht before delivery and $20,000 for loss of use after delivery. PJ contends the trial court erred in awarding any damages for loss of use because (1) they were speculative, (2) PJ had no knowledge of Aries' intended use of the boat when it entered into the contract, (3) no substitute vessel was actually rented, and (4) the loss of rental value used to compute the damages for loss of use failed to take into account expenses which were necessary in order to rent the vessel.

Damages for loss of use are appropriate under the Uniform Commercial Code if the seller had knowledge of the buyer's intended use of the goods at the time of contracting and the buyer proves that there are periods when the goods would have been used but were not because of defects that the buyer, in good faith, was waiting for the seller to cure. Damages are recoverable for only those days the goods would have been in use. [Citation.] This would also apply to the failure to deliver the goods on the date promised in the contract. [Citation.] One is entitled to use his property for pleasure as well as business, and a loss of use recovery is allowed as to pleasure vehicles as well as to business vehicles. [Citation.]

Aries' damages for loss of use of his yacht are measured by its reasonable rental value at the time of the loss. [Citation.] His failure to actually rent a substitute yacht does not preclude him from recovering such damages.

An excellent discussion on the loss of use of a motor home and entitlement to damages under the Uniform Commercial Code is contained in the Minnesota case of *Jacobs v. Rosemount Dodge–Winnebago South,* 310 N.W.2d 71, 78 (Minn.1981):

> * * * It is for the trier of fact, in this case the jury, to assess damages for loss of use so long as that assessment is reasonable and not punitive.... Where the measure of damages is not easily amenable to mathematical precision, the trier of fact must consider the general or particular needs of the buyer which the seller could have known at the time of contracting. In considering the needs of

the buyer, the specific buyer's needs and circumstances must be considered, not those of the average buyer. [Citations omitted.]

There was ample evidence of Aries' intended use of the yacht during the five months' period of delayed delivery, and there was evidence that PJ knew of Aries' intended use of the yacht when the contract was entered into. Aries testified that had the ship been delivered on time or reasonably close, he would have used it for a one-month shakedown cruise on Lake Michigan and then a trip up the St. Lawrence Seaway and on to Newport, Rhode Island to attend the quadrennial America's Cup trials and finals in August and September. After the America's Cup, Aries intended to take the yacht to the Caribbean, where it was his habit to spend at least ten days per month. Aries' intended use was consistent with the trial court's finding of his substantial use of his prior yacht, Varuna. Aries testified that he used Varuna approximately ten days per month during the winter season in the Caribbean, took numerous trips from the east to the west coast of the United States through the Panama Canal, as well as cruises in the Mediterranean. He testified that his boat was his sanctuary and refuge and that he intended to use it as much as reasonably possible. The trial court did not award loss of use for all five months; instead, it awarded loss of use for two-thirds of this time.

As for post-delivery loss, the trial court awarded Aries $20,000 for loss of use for 20 of the 168 days that the yacht was being repaired during the year after its delivery. Aries' expert witness, Johnson, testified that 30 days' downtime for repair ("warranty") was normal during the first year, and that 60 days was excessive. PJ's expert estimated that 50 to 80 of the 168 days were attributable to warranty work, as distinguished from items such as owner preference work.

We believe there was sufficient evidence of postdelivery loss of time to support the court's award. Furthermore, as to the predelivery loss, the court did not award damages for the entire five months, but only for two-thirds of that time.

Aries testified that, based on his long experience as the owner of a charter company, $1,500 per day was at the low end of the reasonable range to charter a comparable boat under normal circumstances. He further testified that the cost of a comparable boat during the America's Cup would have been $5,000 to $7,000 per day. Finally, he testified that he would have charged $2,000 per day to charter his boat for business purposes.

Johnson testified that $1,500 per day was a reasonable charter rate for a comparable boat under normal circumstances without consumable and crew expenses. Johnson testified that the minimum charter rate for a comparable vessel during the America's Cup would be $3,000 per day.

PJ's executive vice president, Parsons, testified that the reasonable charter value under normal circumstances was $8,500 per week or $1,200 per day averaged on a weekly rate. He also testified, however, that the loss of use in 1983 could have been $1,500 per day. There was also evidence that Ondine, one of the other boats that was being built, contained a $2,000 per day penalty provision that was personally guaranteed by PJ's shareholders. The $2,000 per day rate was a negotiated estimate of loss of daily use for late delivery of that boat. There was evidence as to the daily cost of consumables and crew expenses that would have to be deducted against the rental rate. We presume the trial court took these sums into account, and we find no error in its award of $1,000 per day damages.

* * *

Aries testified that his original intended delivery route was from Lake Michigan out the St. Lawrence Seaway to the North Atlantic and then south, but because of the delay in delivery from early summer to late fall and the prospect of taking an untested pleasure craft into a northern seaway that freezes in winter, the route south was changed to the Mississippi River. This decision was made in consultation with PJ's representatives.

The boat, when finally delivered, had the masts in place, but the masts had to be removed and placed on deck due to the rerouting because they were too tall to pass under some of the bridges on the Mississippi. PJ charged Aries $5,731 to take the masts down, and it cost Aries $2,378.21 to have the masts put up again when he reached New Orleans. This would not have occurred if the boat had been delivered on time. The trial court awarded damages to reimburse him for the cost of the masts' removal and replacement. PJ contends that this was erroneous because there was evidence that the St. Lawrence Seaway did not freeze over and close until December 15, 1983, and there was, therefore, no necessity to remove the masts. We do not agree. The question was whether it was unreasonable for Aries and defendant's employees to change the route at the time they did, not having the power to predict when the St. Lawrence Seaway was going to freeze. The trial court found that Aries acted reasonably in changing the route after delivery; we cannot gainsay the trial court's determination. * * *

———

1. Compare the principal case with McGinnis v. Wentworth Chevrolet Co., 295 Or. 494, 668 P.2d 365 (1983). In this case an aggrieved buyer justifiably revoked acceptance of a nonconforming automobile and then rented a substitute vehicle rather than purchasing a replacement. The buyer then sought damages for her rental expense. The court held that the rental expenses were not recoverable as an expense in effecting "cover" and that loss of bargain damages must be computed by a market price formula.

The court found that the rental expenses did not translate into a comparable figure for loss of bargain. Moreover, the rental expenses were not recoverable as incidental damages because they related to the particular circumstances of this buyer rather than being necessarily incident to the breach of contract. The court ultimately remanded for the trial court to determine if the rental costs were recoverable as consequential damages under these circumstances because the contract contained a limitation of liability clause.

2. Consider when the expense of a rental substitute should be recoverable under a tort theory, such as when the defendant negligently injures the plaintiff's automobile in an accident. Should the same principles apply in tort as in contract? *See* Chapter 11.

3. For additional commentary on damages in contracts for the sale of goods see the following references: Farnsworth, Legal Remedies for Breach of Contract, 70 Colum.L.Rev. 1145 (1970); Harris, A Radical Restatement of the Law of Seller's Damages, 18 Stan.L.Rev. 66 (1965); Peters, Remedies for Breach of Contracts Relating to the Sale of Goods Under the Uniform Commercial Code: A Roadmap for Article Two, 73 Yale L.J. 199 (1963); Macneil, Power of Contract and Agreed Remedies, 47 Cornell L.Q. 495 (1962); Van Hecke, Changing Emphasis in Specific Performance, 40 N.C.L.Rev. 1 (1961); Gilmore, The Commercial Doctrine of Good Faith Purchase, 63 Yale L.J. 1057 (1954); Fuller & Perdue, The Reliance Interest in Contract Damages, 46 Yale L.J. 52 (1936); Llewellyn, What Price Contract?, 40 Yale L.J. 704 (1931).

2. Seller's Remedies

SPRAGUE v. SUMITOMO FORESTRY CO.
104 Wash.2d 751, 709 P.2d 1200 (1985).

Dore, Justice.

This action involves a claim by Clyde Sprague against Sumitomo Forestry Company, Ltd. for breach of contract arising from Sumitomo's unconditional cancellation of a log purchase contract. A jury trial resulted in a judgment of $280,693.03 for Sprague. Except for one element of damages that we hold should have been excluded, we affirm.

Sprague is a logger located in Enumclaw, Washington who has been active in buying, selling, harvesting and milling timber in various capacities. As it relates to the issues involved in this lawsuit, Sprague's business has two distinct aspects: the harvesting of timber on a contract basis for various timberland owners, and the purchase of United States Forest Service timber sales from which Sprague harvests and sells logs.

Sprague purchased a tract of timber, known as the Flip Blowdown from the United States Forest Service (USFS) in June 1979. * * *

[Sprague entered into a written contract to sell timber to the Sumitomo Forestry Company, which was engaged in the purchase and export of logs and lumber to Japan. Sprague commenced performance and delivered approximately 100,000 board feet of logs on the Flip Blowdown site to Sumitomo's specifications. In October, 1980, however, Sumitomo sent a letter to Sprague unequivocally canceling the contract. Sprague brought suit for breach of contract, and attempted to mitigate his damages by reselling the timber to various purchasers at private sales. Sprague sought to recover the difference between the contract price and the resale price of the timber, together with incidental damages.]

Via a special verdict form, the jury found * * * (2) that there was a breach and no waiver; (3) that the contract price was $197,204 and the resale price was $144,924 with net contractual damages of $52,280; (4) that Sprague sustained incidental damages of $216,498 for the following items: (a) cost of refinancing, $39,674; (b) extra transportation cost, $5,612; (c) loss of revenue on Flip Blowdown not covered by contract, $9,121; (d) loss of logging time, 11 weeks, $171,200; and (e) cost of moving tower, $2,115.

The major thrust of Sumitomo's appellate argument here is that Sprague did not give the requisite notice of intention to resell the canceled goods as required by RCW 62W.2–706(3) and, therefore, Sprague is not entitled to recover the difference between the contract price and the resale price.

Resale Price Differential

The catalogue of a seller's remedies in a breach of contract case governed by the sale of goods provisions of the Uniform Commercial Code is found in RCW 62A.2–703. In the present case, the catalogue of available remedies can quickly be reduced to two; these are:

> (1) resale and recovery under RCW 62A.2–706, or
>
> (2) recovery of the difference between the contract price and the market price under RCW 62A.2–708(1).

At trial Sprague apparently proceeded, pursuant to RCW 62A.2–706, to recover as damages the difference between the resale price and contract price. RCW 62A.2–706(1) provides that if the seller acts in good faith and in a commercially reasonable manner, he may recover the difference between the resale price and the contract price, together with any incidental damages allowed under RCW 62A.2–710, less expenses saved.

RCW 62A.2–706(2) goes on to permit resale at public or private sale. Of critical importance here is the requirement of RCW 62A.2–706(3) which provides that where an aggrieved seller resells goods which are the subject of a breach at a private sale, he must give the buyer "reasonable notification of his intention to resell."

In response to his failure to give specific notice of intention to resell, and in support of his judgment, Sprague argues: that the lack of notice was an affirmative defense which the buyer failed to plead, or that the buyer, from all the surrounding facts and circumstances, knew or should have known that the seller was going to resell the logs.

We deal first with whether the buyer needed to plead affirmatively as a defense the admitted lack of actual notice. This issue has not been previously addressed in Washington and only a few courts have reached this issue. Notice has been termed a "prerequisite" and a "condition precedent" to section 2–706 damage claims. [Citations.] The burden of showing compliance with the notice requirement has been placed on the seller. [Citations.]

Williston has analyzed the issue as follows:

Assuming that the seller has an affirmative duty to meet the requirements of § 2–706, a showing by the seller of compliance with this section would make it unnecessary for the buyer to raise a defense of lack of notice. All the buyer need do is show contradictory evidence of seller's statement that he gave notice of his intention to resell.

3 A. Squillante & J. Fonseca, *Williston on Sales* § 24–7, at 418 (4th ed. 1974). This analysis, which finds notice as a prerequisite to bringing the claim, fits well with Washington law on affirmative defenses. CR 8(c) enumerates certain specific affirmative defenses which must be pleaded, but includes a general clause "and any other matter constituting an avoidance or affirmative defense." While this language is very general, it clearly contemplates matters which are in avoidance or are a specific affirmative defense. It would follow, therefore, that if notice of intent to resell is part of the seller's prima facie case, then lack of such notice would not have to be affirmatively denied.

To recover under RCW 62A.2–706, Sprague was required to give notice of intent to resell. This is an element of the seller's right to invoke the remedies of RCW 62A.2–706. Therefore, the buyer need not plead as an affirmative defense those elements which seller must prove.

Next, can the notice requirement be satisfied by the fact that the buyer knew or should have known that the seller intended to resell? From the plain language of RCW 62A.2–706, the giving by the seller of notice of intention to resell is a specific requirement to entitle seller to claim as damages the difference between resale price and the contract price. The words of subsection (3) are precise: "The seller *must* give the buyer reasonable notification of his intention to resell." (Italics ours.) RCW 62A.2–706(3).

Sprague contends Sumitomo knew or should have known that Sprague would make a resale and hold Sumitomo liable for the difference in resulting recovery. Thus, he argues that there was substantial compliance with the notice requirement. Sprague would have us hold that his filing of a lawsuit is sufficient notice. Whether such filing could ever be adequate notice is not before us. Factually, what is before us is a complaint that alleges a breach of contract and subsequent damages. It gives no notice of the remedy claimed other than damages. It was not an adequate substitute for the statutorily required notice of intent to resell.

Market Price Differential

* * * Although the jury verdict cannot be upheld under the resale method of determining damages, we find that the record supports the

verdict under the alternate method of establishing damages, computed by measuring the difference between the market price and the contract price as provided in RCW 62A.2–708. This provision states:

> (1) Subject to subsection (2) and to the provisions of this Article with respect to proof of market price (RCW 62A.2–723), the measure of damages for non-acceptance or repudiation by the buyer is the difference between the market price at the time and place for tender and the unpaid contract price together with any incidental damages provided in this Article (RCW 62A.2–710), but less expenses saved in consequence of the buyer's breach.

> (2) If the measure of damages provided in subsection (1) is inadequate to put the seller in as good a position as performance would have done then the measure of damages is the profit (including reasonable overhead) which the seller would have made from full performance by the buyer, together with any incidental damages provided in this Article (RCW 62A.2–710), due allowance for costs reasonably incurred and due credit for payments or proceeds of resale.

It is fundamental under RCW 62A.2–703 and the sections that follow that an aggrieved seller is not required to elect between damages under RCW 62A.2–706 and 62A.2–708. RCW 62A.2–703 cumulatively sets forth the remedies available to a seller upon the buyer's breach. The pertinent commentary thereto indicates specifically that the remedies provided are cumulative and not exclusive and that as a fundamental policy Article 2 of the U.C.C. rejects any doctrine of election of remedy.

The seller has the burden of proof with respect to market price or market value. A seller cannot avail himself of the benefit of RCW 62A.2–708 when he has not presented evidence of market price or market value. However, the resale price of goods may be considered as appropriate evidence of the market value at the time of tender in determining damages pursuant to RCW 62A.2–708. [Citations.]

While, admittedly, Sprague's resale came after the time for tender, it can still be utilized as a market price. RCW 62A.2–723(2) states:

> (2) If evidence of a price prevailing at the times or places described in this Article is not readily available the price prevailing within any reasonable time before *or after* the time described or at any other place which in commercial judgment or under usage of trade would serve as a reasonable substitute for the one described may be used ... (Italics ours).

The court is granted a "reasonable leeway" (Official Comments to RCWA 62A.2–723) in measuring market price. During the trial of this action, not only was there testimony to the effect that in an effort to mitigate damages, respondent Sprague sold the Flip Blowdown logs to five purchasers at private sales in 1981 and 1982, there was also testimony that the market price remained at the same level as at the time and place of tender in late 1980.

The net contractual damages of \$52,280 (\$197,204 contract price − \$144,924 resale price) which was awarded respondent under the jury verdict thus equaled the measure of damages available under RCW 62A.2–708(1). We affirm this award.

Incidental Damages

Sprague is entitled also to incidental damages. RCW 62A.2–708 provides that the seller is entitled to the difference between the market price and contract price "together with any incidental damages provided in this Article (RCW 62A.2–710), but less expenses saved in consequence of the buyer's breach." Incidental damages are defined in RCW 62A.2–710 as follows:

> Incidental damages to an aggrieved seller include any commercially reasonable charges, expenses or commissions incurred in stopping delivery, in the transportation, care and custody of goods after the buyer's breach, in connection with return or resale of the goods or otherwise resulting from the breach.

At trial, the jury found that respondent sustained incidental damages of \$216,498 for the following items: (a) cost of refinancing, \$39,674; (b) extra transportation cost, \$5,612; (c) loss of revenue on Flip Blowdown not covered by contract, \$9,121; (d) loss of logging time, 11 weeks, \$171,200; and (e) cost of moving tower, \$2,115.

Sumitomo contends that some of these items are not incidental damages but more properly classified as consequential. Consequential damages are *not* allowed except as specifically provided in RCW Title 62A or by other rule of law. RCW 62A.1–106. Washington Comment to section 2–710 indicates that consequential damages are denied to sellers under the Uniform Commercial Code. RCWA 62A.2–710.

The distinction between consequential and incidental damages was made in Petroleo Brasileiro, S.A. Petrobras v. Ameropan Oil Corp., 372 F.Supp. 503, 508 (E.D.N.Y.1974):

> While the distinction between the two is not an obvious one, the Code makes plain that incidental damages are normally incurred when a buyer (or seller) repudiates the contract or wrongfully rejects the goods, causing the other to incur such expenses as transporting, storing, or reselling the goods. On the other hand, *consequential damages* do not arise within the scope of the immediate buyer-seller transaction, but rather *stem from losses incurred by the non-breaching party in its dealings, often with third parties,* which were a proximate result of the breach, and which were reasonably foreseeable by the breaching party at the time of contracting. (Citations omitted. Italics ours.)

We find that the loss of logging time is an inappropriate item of incidental damages. Sprague's damage claim for loss of logging time is essentially a claim for lost profits on a contract with Mt. Baker Plywood.

In *Petroleo Brasileiro*, the court stated that "consequential damages do not arise within the scope of the immediate buyer-seller transaction [as do incidental damages], but rather stem from losses incurred by the nonbreaching party in its dealings, often with third parties . . .". Applying this test to Sprague's claim for loss of logging time, Sprague's loss clearly did not arise within the scope of his contract with Sumitomo; instead, Sprague incurred this loss as a consequence of his delay in performing his contract with Mt. Baker Plywood, a third party. The fact that Sumitomo's conduct proximately caused Sprague's loss is irrelevant to this analysis. The focus is upon losses arising within the scope of the immediate contract. Accordingly, Sprague's loss can only be characterized as consequential. Therefore, the judgment awarded Sprague is reduced by $171,200.

* * *

1. U.C.C. 2–708(1) provides that a seller's benefit of the bargain damages are determined by the differential between the contract price and the market price at the time and place for tender. When proof of prices in the relevant market at tender is lacking, courts have some flexibility in using a reasonable substitute to make the necessary calculations. *See* U.C.C. 2–723(2).

In Buchsteiner Prestige Corp. v. Abraham & Straus, 107 Misc.2d 327, 433 N.Y.S.2d 972 (1980), the contract provided for tender of goods in 1978 for a contract price of $8,764.80. The seller established a market price of $865.20 by offering evidence of a resale offer in July, 1979. The court found the 1979 market figure to be acceptable, reasoning that a "reasonable leeway" should be allowed when proving the market price. Is this result justifiable? What additional facts might be useful in determining what constituted a reasonable substitute market?

2. As indicated in the principal case, a seller's failure to conduct a resale of goods within the requirements of section 2–706 will preclude recovery of the resale-contract price differential as damages. Additionally, courts may place limitations on the amount of damages available under section 2–708(1).

In Coast Trading Co. v. Cudahy Co., 592 F.2d 1074 (9th Cir.1979) the court held that a seller should not be allowed a greater award under 2–708(1) than was actually lost in effecting the resale, but that the burden would be on the buyer to establish the actual loss. This case involved several contracts for the sale of barley in Oregon. The seller had sought damages based on section 2–706 contract price less resale price but was not allowed to do so since the resale was not deemed to be commercially reasonable. The buyer provided evidence of the seller's actual receipts on resale of the barley and the damages award was thus limited.

3. The purpose of the resale provision in section 2–706 is to provide evidence of the market price at the time and place performance should have rendered by the buyer. Consequently, as more time elapses between the breach and the resale, the probative value of the resale price is similarly reduced.

In McMillan v. Meuser Material & Equipment, 260 Ark. 422, 541 S.W.2d 911 (1976), an equipment dealer waited fourteen months after the buyer's breach to resell a bulldozer. The court held that the delay was commercially unreasonable, and therefore precluded recovery of damages under 2–706. A significant fact was that the market had been declining due to a recession in the construction industry and high fuel prices.

Should a seller be forced to resell in a declining market or be given leeway to wait for more favorable market conditions? If the seller does resell in a weak market, can the buyer argue that the seller acted unreasonably by not waiting for a stronger market? How long should a seller wait during a declining market before it should be apparent that the decline is not just a temporary downturn in an otherwise strong market? Should the subjective belief of the seller about the prospect for the market price in the near future be relevant?

NATIONAL CONTROLS v. COMMODORE BUSINESS MACHINES

163 Cal.App.3d 688, 209 Cal.Rptr. 636 (1985).

SCOTT, ASSOCIATE JUSTICE.

Respondent National Controls, Inc. (NCI) brought an action for breach of contract against appellant Commodore Business Machines, Inc. (Commodore). After a court trial, judgment was entered awarding NCI over $280,000 in damages, and Commodore has appealed.

NCI manufactures electronic weighing and measuring devices. Among its products is the model 3221 electronic microprocessor technology load cell scale (the 3221), which is designed to interface with a cash register for use at check-out stands. NCI sells the 3221 to cash register manufacturers, also termed original equipment manufacturers, or O.E.M.s. NCI does not maintain an inventory stock of the scales, but builds them to specific order by an O.E.M. The 3221 is a standard unit, which is modified by NCI to meet the specifications of each O.E.M. with respect to cash register compatibility, paint, and logo.

* * *

On March 31, 1981, in a phone conversation with [NCI], [Commodore] placed a firm order for 900 scales: 50 to be delivered in May, 150 in June, 300 in July, and 400 in August. [The parties] agreed on quantity, price, and delivery schedule. * * *

Delivery was made to Commodore of the first 200 units, and 300 units were ready to ship in June of 1981. As of that date, the remaining 400 units of the order were nearly complete. However, Commodore accepted only the first 50 scales, and did not accept or pay for the remaining 850 units. Thereafter, all of the 850 units were resold to National Semiconductor, an existing O.E.M. customer. NCI's vice president and general manager in charge of its Florida manufacturing facility testified that in 1980 and 1981, the plant had the production capacity to more than double its output of 3221's.

Among its findings and conclusions, the trial court * * * found that NCI was a "lost volume seller" who was entitled to recover the loss of profit it would have made on the sale of the 850 units to Commodore, notwithstanding its subsequent resale of those units to another customer.

* * *

Commodore contends that the trial court erred when it relied on section 2708, subdivision (2), to award NCI damages by way of lost profits. In a related argument, Commodore contends that if lost profits were the proper measure of damages, it was entitled under the plain language of section 2708 to credit for the proceeds of NCI's resale of the contract goods to National Semiconductor.

Damages caused by a buyer's breach or repudiation of a sales contract are usually measured by the difference between the resale price of the goods and the contract price, as provided by Uniform Commercial Code section 2–706. When it is not appropriate to use this difference to measure the seller's loss (as when the goods have not been resold in a commercially reasonable manner), the seller's measure of damages is the difference between the market and the contract prices as provided in Uniform Commercial Code section 2–708, subdivision (1). Ordinarily, this measure will result in recovery equal to the value of the seller's bargain. However, under certain circumstances this formula is also not an adequate means to ascertain that value, and the seller may recover his loss of expected profits on the contract under subdivision (2) of Uniform Commercial Code section 2–708. (3 Hawkland, Uniform Commercial Code Series (1982–1984) §§ 2–708—2–708:04.)

Section 2708 provides: "(1) Subject to subdivision (2) and to the provisions of this division with respect to proof of market price (Section 2723), the measure of damages for nonacceptance or repudiation by the buyer is the difference between the market price at the time and place for tender and the unpaid contract price together with any incidental damages provided in this division (Section 2710), but less expenses saved in consequence of the buyer's breach.

"(2) If the measure of damages provided in subdivision (1) is inadequate to put the seller in as good a position as performance would have done then the measure of damages is the profit (including reasonable overhead) which the seller would have made from full performance by the buyer, together with any incidental damages provided in this division (Section 2710), due allowance for costs reasonably incurred and due credit for payments or proceeds of resale."

When buyers have repudiated a fixed price contract to purchase goods, several courts elsewhere have construed subdivision (2) of Uniform Commercial Code section 2–708 or its state counterpart to permit the award of lost profits under the contract to the seller who establishes that he is a "lost volume seller," *i.e.*, one who proves that even though he resold the contract goods, that sale to the third party would have been made regardless of the buyer's breach. [Citations.] The lost volume seller must establish that had the breaching buyer performed, the seller would have realized profits from two sales. [Citation.]

In Neri v. Retail Marine Corporation, 30 N.Y.2d 393, 334 N.Y.S.2d 165, 285 N.E.2d 311 (1972), seller contracted to sell a new boat, which it ordered and received from its supplier. The buyer then repudiated the contract. Later, seller sold the boat to another buyer, for the same price. The court relied on Uniform Commercial Code section 2–708, subdivision (2), to award the seller its lost profits under the contract, reasoning that the record established that market damages would be inadequate to put the seller in as good a position as performance would have done. The court drew an analogy to an auto dealer with an inexhaustible supply of cars. A breach of an agreement to buy a car at a standard price would cost that dealer a sale even though he was able to resell the car at the same price. In other words, had the breaching buyer performed, seller would have made two sales instead of one.

While the seller in *Neri* was a retailer, the lost volume seller rule is also applicable to manufacturers. [Nederlandse, etc. v. Grand Pre–Stressed Corp., 466 F.Supp. 846 (E.D.N.Y.1979)]. In *Nederlandse,* seller, a manufacturer of steel strand, brought an action against buyer for breach of an agreement to purchase approximately 1,180 metric tons of strand. Defendant had accepted only about 221 tons, and repudiated the remaining 958 tons, of which 317 tons had been already produced by seller. Seller resold the 317 tons to various third party purchasers.

The court held that seller was entitled to lost profits under Uniform Commercial Code section 2–708, subdivision (2), and that no set-off would be allowed for profits earned through the sales to third parties. The evidence established that seller had sufficient production capacity to supply not only the 1,180 tons required by the contract, but also the 317 tons sold to third parties. The fact that seller was a manufacturer rather than a retailer, and that he produced only to order rather than maintaining an inventory, was of no significance in determining the applicability of Uniform Commercial Code section 2–708.

Commodore accurately points out that the lost volume seller rule has been criticized by some commentators as overly simplistic. Nevertheless, those courts considering the question have held that Uniform Commercial Code section 2–708 does allow lost profits to a "lost volume seller" and that criticism has not resulted in any revision of the section.

Commodore also contends that if NCI was entitled to lost profits under the contract, Commodore should have received credit for the proceeds of the resale.

The literal language of section 2708, subdivision (2), does provide some support for that contention: "If the measure of damages provided in subdivision (1) is inadequate to put the seller in as good a position as performance would have done then the measure of damages is the profit (including reasonable overhead) which the seller would have made from full performance by the buyer, *together with . . . due credit for payments or proceeds of resale.*" (Emphasis added.) However, courts elsewhere have uniformly held that the underscored language does not apply to a lost volume seller. [Citations.]

As the court in Snyder v. Herbert Greenbaum & Assoc., Inc., 38 Md.App. 144, 380 A.2d 618 explained, "Logically, lost volume status, which entitles the seller to the § 2–708(2) formula rather than the formula found in § 2–708(1), is inconsistent with a credit for the proceeds of resale. The whole concept of lost volume status is that the sale of the goods to the resale purchaser could have been made with other goods had there been no breach. In essence, the original sale and the second sale are independent events, becoming related only after breach, as the original sale goods are applied to the second sale. To require a credit for the proceeds of resale is to deny the essential element that entitles the lost volume seller to § 2–708(2) in the first place—the mutual independence of the contract and the resale.

"Practically, if the 'due credit' clause is applied to the lost volume seller, his measure of damages is no different from his recovery under § 2–708(1). Under § 2–708(1) he recovers the contract/market differential and the profit he makes on resale. If the 'due credit' provision is applied, the seller recovers only the profit he makes on resale plus the difference between the resale price and the contract price, an almost identical measure to § 2–708(1). If the 'due credit' clause is applied to the lost volume seller, the damage measure of 'lost profits' is rendered nugatory, and he is not put in as good a position as if there had been performance."

In this case, the evidence was undisputed that in 1980 and 1981, NCI's manufacturing plant was operating at approximately 40 percent capacity. The production of the 900 units did not tax that capacity, and the plant could have more than doubled its output of 3221's and still have stayed within its capacity. That evidence was sufficient to support the court's findings that NCI had the capacity to supply both Commodore and National Semiconductor, and that had there been no breach by Commodore, NCI would have had the benefit of both the original contract and the resale contract. Accordingly, the trial court correctly determined that NCI was a lost volume seller, that the usual "contract price minus market price" rule set forth in subdivision (1) of section 2708 was inadequate to put NCI in as good a position as performance would have done, and that NCI was therefore entitled to its lost profits on the contract with Commodore, without any set-off for profits on the resale to National Semiconductor.

Judgment is affirmed.

––––––

1. In Atlantic Paper Box Co. v. Whitman's Chocolates, 844 F.Supp. 1038 (E.D.Pa.1994), a supplier of specialty Valentine's Day candy boxes sought to recover damages for loss of business opportunity resulting from the cancellation of purchase orders by a candy manufacturer. The buyer cancelled its million dollar advance order from the plaintiff when it was acquired by another corporation which also produced similar candy boxes. The court dismissed the claim, characterizing it as an attempt by a seller to recover consequential damages, which are reserved exclusively for buyers under the U.C.C. The court also found that no "other rule of law" independent of the U.C.C. would justify recovery of a lost business opportunity for sellers.

2. In Madsen v. Murrey & Sons Co., Inc., 743 P.2d 1212 (Utah 1987), the seller sought to recover the lost profits under 2–708(2) for customized pool tables which were manufactured in accordance with special electronic features designed by the buyer. The seller had completed the manufacture of the pool tables when the buyer repudiated the agreement. The court found that the seller failed to mitigate damages in a commercially reasonable manner by dismantling the pool tables and using the materials for salvage and firewood, rather than attempting to sell or market tables at a full or discounted price. Since the seller failed to mitigate damages properly by attempting to sell the pool tables on the open market, the court disallowed lost profits and limited damages to the contract price-market price differential under 2–708(1), less restitution to the buyer of amounts paid on the contract.

3. Prospective profits are ordinarily not recoverable for newly established business with no track record or for a business operated at a loss. What if the business is established on the basis of a contract specifically to furnish a particular product? In Fiberlok, Inc. v. LMS Enterprises, Inc., 976 F.2d 958 (5th Cir.1992), a manufacturer of resins initiated a new business which involved output and processing contracts with a buyer for a special product. The seller sought to recover lost profits under 2–708(2) when the buyer failed to purchase goods pursuant to the contracts. The court found that the seller was unable to mitigate damages because the buyer's breach prevented the seller from maintaining its overhead expenses, supplies and materials and caused the seller to cease production entirely of the special items. The seller was awarded lost profits based upon estimates associated with the prior course of dealing of parties.

4. Should a seller be compensated for breach of contract involving a product never produced? In Oral–X Corp. v. Farnam Companies, Inc., 931 F.2d 667 (10th Cir.1991), a manufacturer of horse care products sought to recover lost royalties both for products shipped and destroyed after risk of loss passed to the buyer as well as for orders cancelled by the buyer before manufacture of the remaining goods. The court

awarded the seller lost profits for both the delivered products and for the cancelled orders, reasoning that to do otherwise would defeat the reasonable expectations of the seller of royalties for the entire supply of goods.

NEUMILLER FARMS, INC. v. CORNETT

368 So.2d 272 (Ala.1979).

SHORES, JUSTICE.

[The sellers, Cornett and Moore, entered into a written contract to sell twelve loads of chipping potatoes grown on their farms for $4.25 per hundredweight to Neumiller, a maker of potato chips. The buyer accepted three loads of potatoes without objection when the market price remained at $4.25. However, the buyer refused acceptance of further deliveries when the market price declined to $2.00 per hundredweight, claiming that the potatoes would not "chip" satisfactorily. The sellers subsequently resold four loads of potatoes in local and national markets but their efforts to sell the remainder of their crop were hampered by poor market conditions. The jury awarded the sellers damages of $17,500 for the buyer's breach of contract. On appeal, the court first observed that the buyer's refusal to accept deliveries was not made in good faith and therefore constituted a breach of contract.]

* * *

We next consider the proper measure of damages under the U.C.C. One of the remedies available to aggrieved sellers is the recovery of " . . . damages for nonacceptance (section 7–2–708). . . . " § 7–2–703, Code of Alabama 1975.

The measure of damages available through § 7–2–708, Code of Alabama 1975, is:

> "(1) Subject to subsection (2) and to the provisions of this article with respect to proof of market price (section 7–2–723), the measure of damages for nonacceptance or repudiation by the buyer is the difference between the market price at the time and place for tender and the unpaid contract price together with any incidental damages provided in this article (section 7–2–710), but less expenses saved in consequence of the buyer's breach.

> "(2) If the measure of damages provided in subsection (1) is inadequate to put the seller in as good a position as performance would have done then the measure of damages is the profit (including reasonable overhead) which the seller would have made from full performance by the buyer, together with any incidental damages provided in this article (section 7–2–710), due allowance for costs reasonably incurred and due credit for payments or proceeds of resale."

Buyer contends the jury verdict was excessive in view of § 7–2–708(1), Code of Alabama 1975. Based on a "per hundredweight" calculation, Buyer suggests the proper damage formula would be the difference between the contract price ($4.25 per hundredweight) and the "market price at the time and place for tender" (Stipulated to be $2.00 per hundredweight); netting damages of $2.25 per hundredweight of potatoes in the rejected nine loads. We disagree.

On its face, the Code restricts the use of the subsection (2) measure of damages to those cases in which " ... the measure of damages provided in subsection (1) is inadequate to put the seller in as good a position as performance would have done...." It is implicit within this provision, however, that, in order to employ the damage formula of subsection (1), there must not only exist a market for the contracted goods, but also the aggrieved seller must have a legal obligation to enter that market in his effort to avoid the foreseeable adverse consequences of buyer's breach of contract. Unless there is both a market and an obligation to enter it, the subsection (1) measure of damages is functionally inadequate and the aggrieved seller may seek redress through application of the measure of damages provided in subsection (2). [Citation.]

In the instant case, at least some market for potatoes existed; but we must consider whether Sellers had a legal obligation to sell the rejected nine loads of potatoes in that market. Clearly, if Sellers had such an obligation, subsection (1) will control; and, if no obligation existed, Sellers may look to subsection (2) to provide the formula by which their damages are to be measured.

Generally, the damages recoverable by a nonbreaching party will be measured as though that party had made a reasonable effort to avoid the foreseeable adverse consequences of the breach. In doing so, however, the nonbreaching party is not required to expose himself to undue risk, expense or humiliation. [Citations.] Moreover, the rule does not require an aggrieved party to sacrifice a substantive right or forego an advantageous opportunity for the benefit of the breaching party. [Citations.]

The jury apparently concluded that, although Sellers made reasonable and diligent efforts to sell as many loads as possible, only four loads of potatoes could be sold of the seventeen to twenty-one loads in Sellers' fields, at the time of tender. To expect Sellers to give priority to selling those potatoes allocated to Buyer's contract, rather than selling the unallocated portion of their inventory, would be to require them to forego an advantageous opportunity and sacrifice a substantive right. Such is not the law. Had Sellers' inventory consisted solely of the potatoes allocated to Buyer's contract or had Sellers failed to act reasonably to sell their entire inventory, they would have failed to meet the obligation imposed by the avoidable consequences rule. However, under the circumstances here presented, Sellers had no obligation to enter the market with those potatoes allocated to Buyer's contract. Absent such a legal obligation, the measure of damages provided in § 7–2–708(1), *supra,* is inadequate. Sellers may recover damages as measured by § 7–2–708(2), Code of Alabama 1975.

The contested portion of Sellers' contract calls for the payment of $4.25 per hundred-weight of potatoes contained in nine loads, each of which contained 430 hundred-weight; totaling $16,447.50. Additionally, Sellers claim interest of $1,480.20 for eighteen months, and $62.00 freight expenses incurred due to Buyer's breach. They contend that the total amount which they might have recovered was $17,989.78; and that the jury verdict should stand, because it does not exceed this amount.

The subsection (2) damage formula allows Sellers to recover "... the profit (including reasonable overhead) ... from full performance by the buyer ... incidental damages provided in this article (section 7–2–710), due allowance for costs reasonably incurred and due credit for payments or proceeds of resale." Under the facts of this case, we need not consider the ramification upon the subsection (2) damage formula of "due credit for payments," or "proceeds of resale." We now consider whether the jury's verdict is compatible with a damage award based on Sellers' "profit (including reasonable overhead)," "costs reasonably incurred" and "incidental damages" provided in § 7–2–710, Code of Alabama 1975.

The proper application of the subsection (2) measure of damages has received reflective consideration in *R. Childress & R. Burgess, Seller's Remedies: The Primacy of U.C.C. 2–708(2),* 48 N.Y.U. L.Rev. 833 (1973). The authors define profit as "... an economic term, expressed in dollar amounts, representing the excess of that received [or which ought to have been received] over that expended in the business transactions or operations, the latter being also expressed in dollar amounts."

The total amount expended in performance of a contract is composed of "fixed costs" and "variable costs." The "fixed costs," sometimes called "overhead," are those relatively stable expenses which are essential to performance and which continue even if the performance of a specific contract is temporarily halted. Recovery of overhead, to the extent that it is reasonably incurred, is specifically allowed as part of the award for profit by subsection (2).

The "variable costs" are those expenses, incurred in reliance on the contract, which may be identified to a specific contract and which, if the contract were not to be performed, could be avoided. This element usually includes such items as the costs of material and labor which go directly to the production of the contract goods. If the breach occurs at a time when the aggrieved seller has already incurred variable costs, recovery for these damages is allowable as part of "costs reasonably incurred" under subsection (2). We note, however, that the variable costs which an aggrieved seller might have avoided by diligent and reasonable efforts are not "reasonably incurred" and may not be recovered.

Suffice it to say that there is evidence in the record from which the jury could reasonably conclude that the Sellers substantially performed their part of the bargain and had incurred substantially all of the expenses incidental to performance on their part. This being so, the jury's verdict of $17,500 was within those damages recoverable by Sellers as a consequence of Buyer's breach of contract.

Affirmed.

————

1. In the principal case, the court awarded the seller lost profits because 2–708(1) implicitly requires that a market exists for the contracted goods and the aggrieved seller must have an obligation to enter the market with those goods.

Timber Access Industries v. U.S. Plywood–Champion Papers, Inc., 263 Or. 509, 503 P.2d 482 (1972), illustrates the problem of "loss of market." In this case there was a contract for the sale of timber, but the market price had fallen so low as to not justify the seller's manufacturing the requested product. The court held that this would constitute a loss of market, requiring the use of section 2–708(2) measure of damages.

2. Should courts apply the lost profits measure of damages under section 2–708(2) in cases where the seller would be overcompensated by the traditional damages formula in section 2–708(1)?

In Trans World Metals, Inc. v. Southwire Co., 769 F.2d 902 (2d Cir.1985), the seller sued when the buyer repudiated a long-term commodity supply contract. The seller sought the difference between the contract and market prices but the buyer claimed that the 2–708(1) measure gave the seller an unwarranted windfall. Instead the buyer argued for a limitation of the damages to the seller's lost profits under 2–708(2). The court recognized that the contract-market price differential would seldom be equivalent to the seller's actual economic loss from the breach. Nonetheless, both parties had assumed the risk of market fluctuations, so the court held the seller should not be denied the benefit of its bargain.

Compare Union Carbide Corp. v. Consumers Power Co., 636 F.Supp. 1498 (E.D.Mich.1986), where the court allowed such a limitation. The case involved a contract for fuel oil which the buyer breached after a substantial drop in the price of oil. The seller's damages under section 2–708(1) were limited to a "fair profit" under 2–708(2). The court explained that a windfall to the seller might be appropriate when risks of price fluctuation were assumed in the contract because this would leave the parties with the benefit of their bargain. Here, however, the seller was merely a middleman and the contract was written so that the seller had not assumed any such risks but was guaranteed a profit on the goods accepted by the buyer.

3. Section 2–708(2) has been used in other situations when the contract-market price differential would be inappropriate. For example, in Capital Steel Co. v. Foster and Creighton Co., 264 Ark. 683, 574 S.W.2d 256 (1978), the seller's damages were measured by loss of profits under 2–708(2) when there was an anticipatory repudiation of a contract

for steel and the seller had not fabricated the product. The court held that since the seller could not and did not "tender" actual performance, damages were limited to the contract price less the proposed manufacturing cost as the measure of lost profits.

4. Proof of damages under section 2–708(2) is often more difficult than under other U.C.C. provisions because proving lost profits may be complicated. Lost profits under 2–708(2) are considered an item of special damages and must be pleaded with particularity. *See* Great Western Sugar Co. v. Mrs. Allison's Cookie Co., 563 F.Supp. 430 (E.D.Mo.1983).

Problems arise both from the typical complexity of the accounting and from legal uncertainties. *Compare* Nederlandse Draadindustrie NDI B.V. v. Grand Pre–Stressed Corp., 466 F.Supp. 846 (E.D.N.Y.1979) (calculation of the company's expenses includes only the manufacturer's variable costs and not fixed costs because the contract did not require the seller to incur additional fixed costs) *with* Scullin Steel Co. v. Paccar, Inc., 708 S.W.2d 756 (Mo.App.1986) (overhead expenses were awarded separately from lost profits).

5. Resale under section 2–706 is not limited to the resale of the goods "identified" to the contract when the goods are fungible. For example, in Servbest Foods v. Emessee Ind., 82 Ill.App.3d 662, 37 Ill.Dec. 945, 403 N.E.2d 1 (1980), the buyer rejected a particular lot of beef. In calculating damages from the mitigating resale, the seller was allowed to use the resale price of a different lot of beef because there was no evidence that the lots were not identical in quantity, quality and description.

PROBLEM: THE COINS

A state Centennial Commission contracted to purchase 100,000 silver-colored commemorative coins at $.50 each from the American Manufacturing Company. The Commission planned to distribute the coins in connection with the celebration of the state's one hundredth anniversary.

The Commission ran low on funds and repudiated the contract. American had already manufactured 60,000 coins but the Commission had not yet paid any amounts on the contract.

No ready market exists in which American Manufacturing can resell the coins. The company has also incurred storage charges of $800 for the coins. Assuming the coins cost American $.30 each to manufacture, what would be the proper measure of damages for the seller:

(a) With respect to the 60,000 manufactured coins;

(b) For the remaining 40,000 coins which have not been manufactured?

C.R. DANIELS, INC. v. YAZOO MFG. CO.

641 F.Supp. 205 (S.D.Miss.1986).

Lee, District Judge.

This cause came before the court for trial on the complaint of the plaintiff, C.R. Daniels, Inc. (Daniels), and the counterclaim of the defendant, Yazoo Manufacturing Company, Inc. (Yazoo). * * *

In June 1981, Charles Silvernail, who was then vice president of Daniels, and James Kerr, who was at that time president of Yazoo, began negotiating an agreement whereby Daniels would design and manufacture grass catcher bags for "S" series lawn mowers to be manufactured by Yazoo. Daniels was to begin manufacture upon approval by Yazoo of a design and sample of the proposed bag. * * *

The agreement between Daniels and Yazoo was reduced to writing in the form of a series of purchase orders issued by defendant and signed by Kerr, with each replacing earlier purchase orders. The initial purchase order was issued on October 23, 1981, prior to final approval of the designs, so that Daniels could begin ordering raw materials. In the October 23 purchase order, Yazoo contracted for 20,000 bags. * * *

Kerr testified that in June 1982, he began to see evidence of a problem with cracking chutes on the bags. He sent a damaged bag to Stavinoha who informed Kerr that, based on the presence of tire marks on the bag, Daniels had determined the problem to be caused by abuse.[5] Kerr also testified that he sent two other bags to Stavinoha in 1982 and 1983, apparently without a cover letter. Stavinoha denied receipt and Kerr offered neither physical proof that the bags were sent nor explanation for his failure to contact Stavinoha when no response was forthcoming.

* * * Throughout this time, Daniels continued to manufacture bags and frames. On October 14, 1982, Kerr sent to Daniels a photocopy of the July 5 purchase order with "cancelled" written on its face. Kerr offered no explanation at that time for the attempted cancellation. * * *

Daniels' attorney wrote Yazoo on May 18 demanding payment. Yazoo's counsel responded and notified Daniels for the first time of the specific complaints which Yazoo had with the bags and frames. Following initiation of this suit, Daniels' attorney was invited to view inspection of the bags in Yazoo's inventory. The inspection revealed that ninety-two percent of the bags had cracked chutes. Until this time, Daniels had been unaware that the chutes were defective in a substantial number of bags. Upon learning the results of Yazoo's inspection, Daniels found that approximately seventy-five percent of the bags that it held were also faulty.

---

5. At trial, Kerr testified that the tire marks were the result of his driving over the bag to test it. There was no evidence that he told Stavinoha of this.

Daniels brought this suit to recover the price of the goods pursuant to Miss.Code Ann. § 75–2–709 (1972), which provides in part:

(1) When the buyer fails to pay the price as it becomes due the seller may recover, together with any incidental damages under the next section, the price

   (a) of goods accepted or conforming goods lost or damaged within a commercially reasonable time after risk of their loss is passed to the buyer; and

   (b) of goods identified to the contract if the seller is unable after reasonable effort to resell them at a reasonable price or the circumstances reasonably indicate that such effort will be unavailing.

Yazoo argues that it never accepted the bags and frames. * * * It is undisputed that at least by December 1982, Kerr was aware of the tremendous magnitude of the problem with cracked chutes. Thereafter, however, he continued to indicate to Daniels that Yazoo would attempt to sell the bags it had in stock and anticipated delivery of bags some time in the future. By his action, Kerr signified to Daniels that the bags were accepted in spite of his knowledge of their nonconformity. Additionally, Yazoo's continued attempts to sell the bags, as well as its destruction of the defective bags, were inconsistent with an effective rejection. Accordingly, this court is of the opinion that Yazoo accepted the bags. * * *

The amount of damages to which plaintiff is entitled is governed by Miss.Code Ann. § 75–2–709 (1972) which is set out above. At trial, plaintiff established that the bags and frames were specially designed and manufactured for Yazoo and cannot be used for any other purpose and that the raw materials have no other use and cannot be resold. Plaintiff computed its damages for bags and frames in different stages of production without challenge by defendant. Plaintiff's computations, which include materials cost, labor and overhead, selling and administrative expense and profit relating to manufacture of the bags and frames, and incidental damages, are as follows:

Bags, completed: 6,953 bags @ $12.05	83,783.65
Bags, various stages of production 2,220 units @ $10.68	23,709.60
Bags, raw material 2,459 units @ $7.50	18,442.50
Frames, complete 764 units @ $4.88	3,728.32
Frames, in process 5,270 units @ $4.26	22,450.20
Incidental Damages	2,379.68
TOTAL	$154,493.95

* * *

Daniels contends that Yazoo's action for breach of warranties is foreclosed by failure to give adequate notice of the breach. * * * Daniels had no reason even to suspect that Yazoo considered the contract to be breached. In fact, it was not until initiation of this litigation that Daniels learned of the magnitude of the problem.   Such conduct on the part of Yazoo can hardly be viewed as notification of breach. [Citation.]   Accordingly, this court is of the opinion that Yazoo's counterclaim should be dismissed.   * * *

no notif. of breach

---

1.   In Rheinberg Kellerei GmbH v. Brooksfield National Bank, 901 F.2d 481 (5th Cir.1990) the seller of wine shipped on an international collection order maintained an action on the price under 2–709 where the wine's quality was destroyed by a long delay at the harbor after risk of loss passed to the buyer.   Customs agents subsequently resold the deteriorated wine at auction.   The court allowed damages under 2–709, reasoning that 2–708 was inapplicable because the wine's ultimate sales price bore no resemblance to its market price at the time and place of tender.   Thus, the seller received damages measured by the contract price plus unpaid freight costs, with the buyer credited for any proceeds of resale.

2.   Compare the principal case with City of Louisville v. Rockwell Manufacturing Co., 482 F.2d 159 (6th Cir.1973), where the manufacturer sought damages for breach of contract for the purchase and installation of 7,650 parking meters for the municipality.   The company completed the manufacture of the initial purchase order of 1,000 parking meters when the city repudiated the entire contract.   The court allowed recovery of damages pursuant to 2–709 of the purchase price for the already completed meters which remained "unsold and unsalable" and the loss of profit under 2–708(2) for the remaining meters.   *See also Taft*-Peirce Mfg. v. Seagate Technology, 789 F.Supp. 1220 (D.R.I.1992) (seller of completed custom manufactured machine entitled to action on the price where specialty item with very limited resale market).

C.   LIQUIDATED DAMAGES

Section Coverage:

Contracting parties may stipulate a specified sum of money which would be payable as damages to the non-breaching party for a material breach of the contract.   Liquidated damages serve to remove the uncertainties and difficulties involved in proving actual damages in the event of a breach, and thereby they function to reduce litigation expenses and expedite the trial process.

The principle of freedom of contract is not an absolute concept;   it is limited by the refusal of courts to enforce extortionate or unconscionable bargains.   Therefore, a liquidated damages provision is valid only if it corresponds with general notions of damages as a substitutionary measure for performance in the event of breach.   If the court perceives the purpose of the clause as an attempt to compel performance through the threat of onerous damages, the provision will be considered a penalty and thus unenforceable. Labels applied by the parties to describe the provision as a penalty or an enforceable liquidated damages clause are not controlling.

The law of liquidated damages is consistent with the common law policy of allowing efficient contract breach. This substantive policy is that a contracting party should be permitted to pay compensatory damages for a breach in exchange for the opportunity to shift goods or services to a different source in order to maximize economic resources. To the extent that a contractual damages provision operates to punish a contract breach, the goal of maximizing resources is undermined. Conversely, a liquidated damages provision that specifies a reasonable estimate of actual damages upon breach is consistent with that goal.

The traditional test to evaluate the validity of a liquidated damages provision is whether, at the time the parties entered the contract, (1) damages resulting from a breach would be difficult to determine, and (2) that the stipulated amount had a reasonable relationship to the potential damages if a breach occurred. Some have criticized the requirement that damages be difficult to determine, suggesting that the only essential inquiry is whether the stipulated clause is reasonable in light of the risks and expectations of the parties at the time of contract formation. Others claim that the two criteria are not necessarily inconsistent or contradictory because the reasonableness of the liquidated sum is determined in light of the anticipated harm rather than in hindsight looking at the amount of actual damages. In either event, courts do not require precise estimates; the amount of actual damages will almost certainly vary from that stipulated in the contract. The very uncertainty in predicting future harm militates against requiring a precise matching of actual to liquidated damages.

The Uniform Commercial Code § 2–718(1) and the Restatement (Second) of Contracts § 356(1) carry forward the common law approach in a slightly modified fashion by providing that reasonableness of a liquidated damages clause may be shown based upon either the anticipated or actual harm from the breach. Section 2–718 further provides an insight into the meaning of "reasonableness" by considering the "difficulties of proof of loss, inconvenience or infeasibility of otherwise obtaining an adequate remedy." Under both the U.C.C. and the common law, whether the parties made a good faith pre-estimate of damages should be objectively evaluated rather than inquiring into the subjective intentions of the parties.

Finally, courts may consider whether the parties intended the liquidated damages provision to serve as the exclusive or an alternative remedy in the event of a breach. Unless the contract expressly provides otherwise, courts generally will construe the contract to allow the non-breaching party to pursue other available remedies, such as specific performance. In that regard, however, the party seeking specific performance still must demonstrate the requisite elements for entitlement to equitable relief, including that damages were not an adequate remedy, despite the existence of the liquidated damages clause.

Model Case:

John Harrell, who had fifteen years of experience in the jewelry business working for several companies, decided to open his own jewelry store. He acquired a small tract of land in a developing commercial area of the city and entered into a contract with Parsons Engineering Company to construct a building for the store.

Harrell wanted the building to be completed by September 1 in order to take advantage of the historically strong sales which take place at the end of the year. Accordingly, the parties placed a clause in their construction agreement which provided that Parsons agreed to pay, as liquidated damages, a sum in the amount of $200 per day for every day that the completion of the building was delayed past September 1. Correspondingly, Parsons would receive a bonus payment from Harrell of $1,000 if the building was finished by August 15.

A court would probably uphold the validity of the stipulated damages provision because the loss of business which Harrell would sustain by a delay in opening the new business would be difficult to estimate. Therefore, a liquidated damages clause serves the function of compensating where proof of damages would be otherwise uncertain. Harrell also would need to show a reasonable basis for arriving at the $200 per day figure as a good faith pre-estimate of the anticipated harm which would potentially result from a breach by Parsons. Mathematical precision would not be required; rather the inquiry is whether the stipulated amount was objectively reasonable as a substitute for performance or had an oppressive character to compel performance.

BOYLE v. PETRIE STORES CORPORATION
136 Misc.2d 380, 518 N.Y.S.2d 854 (1985).

GREENFIELD, JUSTICE.

This is an action for wrongful discharge, but unlike many such cases which have besieged the courts of late, this one involves an executive employee who in fact had a carefully worked out written contract, and now, claiming a breach, insists on a literal application of that contract.

* * * Under the contract, Boyle was to become President and Chief Executive Officer of the corporation as of Nov. 1, 1982. * * * The Board approved the agreement, which was duly executed, and amended the corporate by-laws to reflect the fact that Milton Petrie, the Chairman of the Board, was to preside at director's meetings, but that he was no longer to be the Chief Executive Officer. Boyle, as Chief Executive Officer and President was, subject to the control of the Board, to "have general supervision over the business of the corporation."

* * *

Boyle in fact reported for work at the corporate headquarters in Secaucus on Nov. 8, 1982. While Boyle informed the other Petrie executives that he was now the Chief Executive Officer, and they should take their directions from him, Petrie continued to give operating directions just as he always had. * * *

On January 6, a formal real estate meeting and review, with Petrie present, was held. As various items were taken up, Petrie said, "leave it to me, I'll take care of it." When Boyle pressed him for details, Petrie repeated, "I'll take care of it". At the conclusion of the meeting Petrie confronted Boyle in his office. With mounting anger, he said, "Where the hell do you get off to question my authority on these leases and embarrass me in front of all my organization?" He told Boyle he was moving in too fast. Boyle challenged him, and impertinently replied, "If you didn't have 63 percent of this stock, I would take you to the Board of Directors and have you removed as Chairman." This was too much for Petrie. He exploded, "You're fired!"

A special meeting of the Board of Directors was held on January 13, 1983. * * * The Board did not discuss the terms of Boyle's employment agreement or ask to hear Mr. Boyle, but acceded to Mr. Petrie's demand that he be terminated effective immediately. Mr. Petrie retook the titles of Chief Executive Officer and President. A press release announced these changes and stated that "The reason for the change was due to policy differences on the way the business should be run."

Boyle had served but two months of his five year contract. Claiming that the contract had been improperly breached by Petrie Stores Corporation, he brought this action seeking recovery of over $2,000,000 as liquidated damages he is entitled to under the contract. * * *

The employment agreement is quite specific about the damages which are to be payable for termination other than for "material breach or just cause". Section 7(a) of the agreement provides that in the event of a termination other than for "material breach or just cause", the corporation is to pay "in one lump sum the amounts otherwise payable to Employee . . . discounted to present value at the rate of 15 percent per annum." Calculation of the lump sum payable thus works out to $1,439,352.44 in lieu of lost salary, and $166,689.39 in guaranteed bonus claims, for a total of $1,606,041.83.

While this is a very substantial figure to pay a man who was on the job for 8 weeks, and was fired within days after his orientation period, when he tried to take over the reins of management, we are dealing here with a provision for liquidated damages designed to provide some precision for the calculation of otherwise speculative damages.

Parties may properly agree to a dollar figure representing the injuries they agree the plaintiff would sustain if the contract were breached. [Citation.] So long as the liquidated damages provisions are neither unconscionable nor contrary to public policy, they will be enforced as written by a court. [Citations.]

Defendant contends that the contractual provisions for liquidated damages are, in fact, a penalty. Stipulated contractual damages will be

considered a penalty only if the amount provided for is clearly disproportionate to the actual loss, and as an *in terrorem* effort to assure
performance regardless of economic loss. Those cases urged by the
defendant as standing for the proposition that stipulated damages such
as those here involved should be considered a "penalty", are readily
distinguishable. Since courts have traditionally, from the time of the
Merchant of Venice, viewed a forfeiture out of all proportion to the
breach of contract as an unenforceable penalty, our courts have attempted to strike out the clear penalties while upholding agreement which
clarified amounts of damage which could otherwise be in dispute. * * *
In this case, a termination of Boyle's employment contract could result
in damages well over $500,000 a year, and the parties could reasonably
agree that instead of litigating the question of damages after the event,
which would leave uncertainties such as the employee's efforts to mitigate damages by securing other employment, and the question as to how
long the other employment might last, and whether the benefits were
comparable, they could reasonably agree beforehand as to what damages
would be payable. The amounts fixed do not exceed the total compensation provided in the five year contract.

Both parties to the contract were sophisticated and were represented by able counsel. This is a factor to be taken into consideration in
determining whether one side is now exacting an unconscionable penalty. [Citations.]

It is to be recalled that Boyle was aware of Mr. Petrie's mercurial
reputation, and wanted some concrete assurances of security before
giving up the well-paid position he had worked himself up to with
Federated Stores. An involuntary discharge from Petrie Stores would
cast a considerable shadow on Mr. Boyle's reputation as a young super-
achieving executive, and possibly diminish his prospects for the future.
The agreement was carefully negotiated at arms-length by reputable
attorneys for both parties, and it was clearly understood that a precipi-
tate firing of Mr. Boyle could result in very substantial contractual
damages. The fact that the parties agreed to limit liability to $2,100,000
excluding stock options demonstrates a realization that without such a
ceiling the actual damages could go even higher.

* * *

The lump sum payment provision here clearly was a liquidated
damages provision and not a penalty. In the bargaining neither party
had the ability to overreach the other. The sum provided for was not
disproportionate to the damages which could be incurred. * * * The
damage provisions are valid and enforceable pursuant to their terms.

The fact that subsequent to his termination Boyle took a position
with another corporation—General Mills—as one of six executive vice-
presidents rather than as Chief Executive Officer, does not serve to
mitigate the liquidated damages.

Once the parties have provided for valid liquidated damages, the sum payable becomes fixed and there is no further inquiry to be made as to possible mitigation by subsequent employment. * * *

Here, a formula was set forth to calculate damages without regard to subsequent extrinsic facts. At the time the parties could not know how long plaintiff would be unemployed if terminated. We still do not know how long the subsequent employment will continue, or whether it will give the same net to Mr. Boyle as his Petrie Stores contract over a 5 year span, since his subsequent General Mills contract is terminable at will. We need not wait to the conclusion of the five year contract period to find out what Boyle's aggregate loss of earnings might be, because the agreement requires the liquidated damages to be paid "forthwith". That clearly contemplates that damages were to be fixed as of the date of termination, regardless of events thereafter.

* * * [Judgment for the plaintiff.]

----

1. The law of liquidated damages reflects a tension between conflicting goals. It is socially desirable for parties to fix damages in the event of breach when the amount bears a reasonable proportion to the probable loss and the actual loss is difficult to estimate with precision. Such a provision, however, should not have the effect of deterring breach through compulsion because of the potential high economic loss. *See* Leasing Service Corp. v. Justice, 673 F.2d 70, 73 (2d Cir.1982) (liquidated damages may serve a useful purpose, but it cannot have an *in terrorem* effect where the promisee reaps a windfall in excess of just compensation).

2. A threshold requirement for enforceability of a liquidated damages clause is that the terms must be expressly stated in the contract. *See* ABI, Inc. v. City of Los Angeles, 153 Cal.App.3d 669, 200 Cal.Rptr. 563 (1984) (city's claim to retain a developer's fee as liquidated damages not allowed because the contract did not effectively express such a designation). *See also* Polish American Machinery Corp. v. R.D. & D. Corp., 760 F.2d 507 (3d Cir.1985). Also, liquidated damages will not be awarded absent material breach of the contract. *See* Woodbridge Place Apts. v. Washington Square Capital, 965 F.2d 1429 (7th Cir.1992) (liquidated damages provision in loan commitment agreement unenforceable where borrower did not breach contract but rather failed to satisfy conditions precedent to funding of loan).

3. Whether a contractual provision is characterized as a valid liquidated damages clause or a penalty does not depend upon the label given by the parties. A handful of courts, though, will give some weight to the terminology chosen by the parties as a factor in interpreting a provision fixing damages. *See* Zeppenfeld v. Morgan, 185 S.W.2d 898 (Mo.App.1945) (designation as "liquidated damages" was not conclusive

of its character yet was considered very persuasive evidence to that effect).

Although labels do not control, the intention of the parties can be relevant. Some courts have considered the intentions of the parties as a criterion for enforcement in addition to the traditional two-prong test of reasonableness and difficulty in estimating damages. See Higgs v. United States, 212 Ct.Cl. 146, 546 F.2d 373 (Ct.Cl.1976); Walter Motor Truck Co. v. South Dakota, 292 N.W.2d 321 (S.D.1980); Oldis v. Grosse–Rhode, 35 Colo.App. 46, 528 P.2d 944 (1974); ADP–Financial Computer Services v. First National Bank, 703 F.2d 1261 (11th Cir.1983).

The prevailing view, though, rejects the intention element as being surplusage. See Wilmington Housing Authority v. Pan Builders, Inc., 665 F.Supp. 351 (D.Del.1987) (the intention criterion adds nothing because it validates a provision only if the other two criteria are met and invalidates a provision only when they are not). Koenings v. Joseph Schlitz Brewing Co., 126 Wis.2d 349, 377 N.W.2d 593 (1985) (courts should consider the circumstances which give rise to the formation of the contract rather than the intent of the parties). See also Restatement (Second) of Contracts § 356 comment C; Williston, Contracts § 272 (3d ed. 1961); Corbin, Contracts § 1058 (1964); Clarkson, Miller & Muris, Liquidated Damages v. Penalties: Sense or Nonsense, 1978 Wis.L.Rev. 351.

4. Why was Boyle's subsequent employment irrelevant? Consider Musman v. Modern Deb, Inc., 50 A.D.2d 761, 377 N.Y.S.2d 17 (1975), where the plaintiff sued for wrongful termination of a five year employment contract. The contract provided that he would receive full compensation and bonuses to the end of the five year term if he was terminated without cause. The trial court reduced the amount of liquidated damages by the amount plaintiff earned from other employment. This deduction was reversed on appeal and the court restored the full amount of liquidated damages without deduction. Why should a liquidated damages clause remove the ordinary rule requiring an employee to mitigate damages?

5. In *Boyle,* one of the factors which persuaded the court to uphold the validity of the liquidated damages clause was that the parties had negotiated the contract at arms-length, with relatively equal bargaining power and sophistication. Consider Wallace Real Estate Inv. v. Groves, 124 Wash.2d 881, 881 P.2d 1010 (1994), where the court upheld a liquidated damages clause in a real estate contract, relying in part on the fact that the breaching buyer was an experienced businessman who had listed "negotiating and writing purchase and sales agreements" on his resume. The court found that the sophistication of the buyer in real estate transactions supported the enforceability of the liquidated damages clause.

6. Should public interest play a role in determining the validity of a liquidated damages clause? In Space Master International, Inc. v. City of Worcester, 940 F.2d 16 (1st Cir.1991), a contractor entered into an

agreement to install modular classroom buildings at city school sites. The contract specified that if the contractor delayed performance beyond a certain date, the city was entitled to retain $250 per day plus $100 per day per site as liquidated damages. When the contractor failed to meet the stated deadline to build the classrooms, children were forced to attend classes in hallways, gymnasiums, auditoriums and libraries. Morale among teachers, students and administrators suffered as a result of the dislocation. The court upheld the validity of the liquidated damages clause, observing that the injury to the public was inherently difficult to quantify in monetary terms.

TRUCK RENT–A–CENTER, INC. v. PURITAN FARMS 2ND, INC.

41 N.Y.2d 420, 361 N.E.2d 1015, 393 N.Y.S.2d 365 (1977).

JASEN, JUDGE. * * *

Defendant Puritan Farms 2nd, Inc. (Puritan), was in the business of furnishing milk and milk products to customers through home delivery. In January, 1969, Puritan leased a fleet of 25 new milk delivery trucks from plaintiff Truck Rent–A–Center for a term of seven years commencing January 15, 1970. Under the provisions of a truck lease and service agreement entered into by the parties, the plaintiff was to supply the trucks and make all necessary repairs. Puritan was to pay an agreed upon weekly rental fee. * * * The lessee was granted the right to purchase the trucks, at any time after 12 months following commencement of the lease, by paying to the lessor the amount then due and owing on the bank loan, plus an additional $100 per truck purchased.

Article 16 of the lease agreement provided that if the agreement should terminate prior to expiration of the term of the lease as a result of the lessee's breach, the lessor would be entitled to damages, "liquidated for all purposes", in the amount of all rentals that would have come due from the date of termination to the date of normal expiration of the term less the "re-rental value" of the vehicles, which was set at 50% of the rentals that would have become due. In effect, the lessee would be obligated to pay the lessor, as a consequence of breach, one half of all rentals that would have become due had the agreement run its full course. The agreement recited that, in arriving at the settled amount of damages, "the parties hereto have considered, among other factors, Lessor's substantial initial investment in purchasing or reconditioning for Lessee's service the demised motor vehicles, the uncertainty of Lessor's ability to re-enter the said vehicles, the costs to Lessor during any period the vehicles may remain idle until re-rented, or if sold, the uncertainty of the sales price and its possible attendant loss. The parties have also considered, among other factors, in so liquidating the said damages, Lessor's saving in expenditures for gasoline, oil and other service items."

[After three years, the lessee Puritan terminated the lease agreement. Puritan complained that the lessor had failed to repair and maintain the trucks as provided in the lease agreement. The lessor sued for payment of the liquidated damages on the grounds that the lessee had breached the contract. The defendant lessee counterclaimed for return of the security deposit on the basis that the lessor had breached the contract. At the time of termination of the agreement, the plaintiff owed $45,134.17 on the outstanding bank loan.]

* * * The home milk delivery business was on the decline and plaintiff's president testified that efforts to either re-rent or sell the truck fleet to other dairies had not been successful. Even with modifications in the trucks, such as the removal of the milk racks and a change in the floor of the trucks, it was not possible to lease the trucks to other industries, although a few trucks were subsequently sold.

* * *

At the close of the trial, the court found, based on the evidence it found to be credible, that plaintiff had substantially performed its obligations under the lease and that defendant was not justified in terminating the agreement. Further, the court held that the provision for liquidated damages was reasonable and represented a fair estimate of actual damages which would be difficult to ascertain precisely. * * * The court calculated that plaintiff would have been entitled to $177,-355.20 in rent for the period remaining in the lease and, in accordance with the liquidated damages provision, awarded plaintiff half that amount, $88,677.60. * * *

* * * A liquidated damage provision has its basis in the principle of just compensation for loss. A clause which provides for an amount plainly disproportionate to real damage is not intended to provide fair compensation but to secure performance by the compulsion of the very disproportion. A promisor would be compelled, out of fear of economic devastation, to continue performance and his promisee, in the event of default, would reap a windfall well above actual harm sustained. [Citations.] As was stated eloquently long ago, to permit parties, in their unbridled discretion, to utilize penalties as damages, "would lead to the most terrible oppression in pecuniary dealings." [Citations.]

The rule is now well established. A contractual provision fixing damages in the event of breach will be sustained if the amount liquidated bears a reasonable proportion to the probable loss and the amount of actual loss is incapable or difficult of precise estimation. [Citations.] If, however, the amount fixed is plainly or grossly disproportionate to the probable loss, the provision calls for a penalty and will not be enforced. [Citations.] In interpreting a provision fixing damages, it is not material whether the parties themselves have chosen to call the provision one for "liquidated damages", as in this case, or have styled it as a penalty. [Citations.] Such an approach would put too much faith in form and too little in substance. Similarly, the agreement should be interpreted as of the date of its making and not as of the date of its breach. [Citation.]

In applying these principles to the case before us, we conclude that the amount stipulated by the parties as damages bears a reasonable relation to the amount of probable actual harm and is not a penalty. Hence, the provision is enforceable and the order of the Appellate Division should be affirmed.

Looking forward from the date of the lease, the parties could reasonably conclude, as they did, that there might not be an actual market for the sale or re-rental of these specialized vehicles in the event of the lessee's breach. To be sure, plaintiff's lost profit could readily be measured by the amount of the weekly rental fee. However, it was permissible for the parties, in advance, to agree that the re-rental or sale value of the vehicles would be 50% of the weekly rental. Since there was uncertainty as to whether the trucks could be re-rented or sold, the parties could reasonably set, as they did, the value of such mitigation at 50% of the amount the lessee was obligated to pay for rental of the trucks. This could take into consideration the fact that, after being used by the lessee, the vehicles would no longer be "shiny, new trucks", but would be used, possibly battered, trucks, whose value would have declined appreciably. The parties also considered the fact that, although plaintiff, in the event of Puritan's breach, might be spared repair and maintenance costs necessitated by Puritan's use of the trucks, plaintiff would have to assume the cost of storing and maintaining trucks idled by Puritan's refusal to use them. Further, it was by no means certain, at the time of the contract, that lessee would peacefully return the trucks to the lessor after lessee had breached the contract.

* * * [T]he existence of the option clause has absolutely no bearing on the validity of the discrete, liquidated damages provision. The lessee could have elected to purchase the trucks but elected not to do so. In fact, the lessee's letter of termination made a point of the fact that the lessee did not want to purchase the trucks. The reality is that the lessee sought, by its wrongful termination of the lease, to evade all obligations to the plaintiff, whether for rent or for the agreed upon purchase price. Its effort to do so failed. That lessee could have made a better bargain for itself by purchasing the trucks for $48,134.17 pursuant to the option, instead of paying $92,341.79 in damages for wrongful breach of the lease is not availing to it now. Although the lessee might now wish, with the benefit of hindsight, that it had purchased the trucks rather than default on its lease obligations, the simple fact is that it did not do so.

We attach no significance to the fact that the liquidated damages clause appears on the preprinted form portion of the agreement. The agreement was fully negotiated and the provisions of the form, in many other respects, were amended. There is no indication of any disparity of bargaining power or of unconscionability. The provision for liquidated damages related reasonably to potential harm that was difficult to estimate and did not constitute a disguised penalty. * * *

[Affirmed.]

1. The traditional common law test for upholding a liquidated damages clause is that the potential damages which might accrue as a result of a breach must be uncertain and difficult to ascertain. What should "difficulty" mean: Difficulty in forecasting all possible damages that may be caused by breach? Difficulty of producing proof of damages? Difficulty of proving causally the link between the breach and the loss? Difficulty of meeting the foreseeability limitations for contract damages? Difficulty from lack of any standardized measure of the damages for a certain breach? *See* Perlman v. Pioneer Ltd. Partnership, 918 F.2d 1244 (5th Cir.1990) (liquidated damages clause in oil and gas lease giving $1.5 million in damages upon lessee's failure to perform was enforceable as an accurate, reasonable estimate of damages because lost royalties would be difficult to measure). *See* an excellent analysis in Macneil, Power of Contract and Agreed Remedies, 47 Cornell L.Q. 495, 502 (1962).

2. Although courts have tended to apply sparingly the rule that potential damages must be uncertain to enforce liquidated damages clauses, the rule has determined some cases. A case illustrating the force of the rule is Semico, Inc. v. Pipefitters Local No. 195, 538 S.W.2d 273 (Tex.Civ.App.1976). A clause in a collective bargaining agreement provided that if the employer failed to make certain specified union contributions, the employer would be required to pay 15% of the contribution total for each month the payments were delinquent. The court held that the provision was invalid as a penalty because damages for the nonpayment of money could easily be calculated and therefore presented no difficulty in estimation at the time of contracting.

Why should it matter if the damages in the event of breach are difficult to ascertain? Even if the damages are exactly and readily foreseen, why not let the parties agree to the amount in advance? Is there any difference between such a liquidated damages provision and a settlement before trial? *See* McCormick, Damages § 148, at 605 (1935).

3. California has codified the uncertainty element regarding liquidated damages by statute, which provides in pertinent part:

> * * * a provision in a contract liquidating damages for the breach of the contract is void except that the parties to such a contract may agree therein upon an amount which shall be presumed to be the amount of damage sustained by a breach thereof, when, from the nature of the case, it would be impracticable or extremely difficult to fix the actual damage.

California Civil Code § 1671(d). An example of the operation of the California rule may be found in Cook v. King Manor and Convalescent Hospital, 40 Cal.App.3d 782, 115 Cal.Rptr. 471 (1974). A seller sought to recover the stipulated amount of $25,000 for a buyer's breach of a contract to purchase certain real property for approximately $2,000,000. The liquidated damages provision recited that it would be "extremely difficult and impractical to determine the amount and extent of detriment to seller" if the buyer failed to perform its obligations. The court held that the provision constituted a penalty because the seller had failed to plead and prove that the potential damages contemplated by the parties in the event of a breach were in fact difficult of estimation. *See generally* Sweet, Liquidated Damages in California, 60 Calif.L.Rev. 84 (1972).

4. The Restatement (Second) of Contracts § 356 comment b[*] approaches the uncertainty of loss factor with a flexible test:

> The greater the difficulty either of proving that loss has occurred or of establishing its amount with the requisite certainty (*see* § 351), the easier it is to show that the amount fixed is reasonable. To the extent that there is uncertainty as to the harm, the estimate of the court or jury may not accord with the principle of compensation any more than does the advance estimate of the parties. A determination whether the amount fixed is a penalty turns on a combination of these two factors. If the difficulty of proof of loss is slight, less latitude is allowed in that approximation. If, to take an extreme case, it is clear that no loss at all has occurred, a provision fixing a substantial sum as damages is unenforceable.

5. The Uniform Commercial Code test in § 2–718(1) has reduced difficulty of loss from being treated as a separate factor to serving as one consideration regarding the reasonableness of the clause:

> Damages for breach by either party may be liquidated in the agreement but only at an amount which is reasonable in the light of the anticipated or actual harm caused by the breach, the difficulties of proof of loss, and the inconvenience or nonfeasibility of otherwise obtaining an adequate remedy.

The U.C.C. approach has been described by one pair of commentators as a continuum: The latitude of the contracting parties in setting damages for breach increases with the degree of uncertainty facing them. Goetz & Scott, Liquidated Damages, Penalties and the Just Compensation Principle: Some Notes on an Enforcement Model and a Theory of Efficient Breach, 77 Colum.L.Rev. 554, 560 (1977).

6. A valid liquidated damages provision must reflect a *reasonable estimate* of the uncertain damages in the event of breach. In Ryder Truck Lines, Inc. v. Goren Equipment Co., 576 F.Supp. 1348 (N.D.Ga. 1983), the seller of used diesel engines sought to recover $281,250 as liquidated damages for the buyer's breach of contract. The court found that the extent and amount of potential damages were difficult to estimate because at the time of contracting the parties could not accurately calculate the costs of repossession or resale price of the engines. The court concluded, however, that the stipulated amount was a penalty because it was not a reasonable pre-estimate of the probable loss in the event of a breach. Since the liquidated sum actually exceeded the total

amount due under the contract and it appeared that the figure was chosen arbitrarily, the clause was held void and unenforceable.

In Southpace Properties, Inc. v. Acquisition Group, 5 F.3d 500 (11th Cir.1993), the court held that the stipulated damages clause in a real estate listing agreement which provided that the broker was entitled to full 6% commission plus costs and expenses if the property owner breached agreement was considered void under Alabama law as a penalty. The court found that the damages provision was not a reasonable pre-breach estimate of the probable loss because the broker would actually recover more if the contract were breached than if fully performed. *See also* A.V. Consultants, Inc. v. Barnes, 978 F.2d 996 (7th Cir.1992) (liquidated damages clause unenforceable as a penalty where provision would give party expected profit plus the value of its services).

7. What if the stipulated amount of damages for breach of a contract is considered an unreasonably low estimate of the anticipated harm? Some courts focus on the time of contracting to assess the reasonableness of the agreed amount and the uncertainty of damages because that approach is consistent with the traditional test for liquidated damages.

In Better Food Markets v. American Dist. Tel. Co., 40 Cal.2d 179, 253 P.2d 10 (1953), for example, the plaintiff sought actual damages of $35,930 to compensate for merchandise stolen as a result of the defendant security company's failure to properly transmit burglar alarm signals in accordance with its contractual duties. The court nonetheless limited the plaintiff's recovery to the contractually agreed amount of only $50. Following the statutory provision regarding liquidated damages, California Civil Code § 1671, the court found it would have been impracticable or extremely difficult to fix the actual damage in the event of a breach. The court reasoned that the parties had exercised their business judgment that the actual loss resulting from a breach might be greater or lesser than the $50 sum, and therefore it also satisfied the requirement that the sum must bear a reasonable relationship to the losses contemplated.

8. Unreasonably low stipulated damages for breach of contract may reflect overreaching by the favored party. A defense of overreaching requires an inquiry into unconscionability rather than the examination of unreasonableness that is necessary to invalidate a liquidated damages clause. *See* Wedner v. Fidelity Security Systems, Inc., 228 Pa.Super. 67, 307 A.2d 429 (1973).

9. Distinguish a contractual provision that *limits* damages from a provision for liquidated damages. For example, in Tharalson v. Pfizer Genetics, Inc., 728 F.2d 1108 (8th Cir.1984), the buyer's damages for the seller's breach of warranty was limited to the sale price of seed under a limitation of damages provision in the contract of sale. The court relied upon U.C.C. § 2–719(3) which provides, in part, "consequential damages may be limited or excluded unless the limitation or exclusion is unconscionable." The court noted that liquidated damages provisions usually

threaten unjustifiably large recoveries, such that the judicial role is to contain them with a test of reasonableness. There is an opposite concern with limitation of damages provision; the danger is unjustifiably small recoveries. The official comments to Uniform Commercial Code § 2–718 indicate that where the concern is unreasonably small recoveries the proper test is unconscionability.

LAKE RIVER CORP. v. CARBORUNDUM CO.

769 F.2d 1284 (7th Cir.1985).

POSNER, CIRCUIT JUDGE.

This diversity suit between Lake River Corporation and Carborundum Company requires us to consider questions of Illinois commercial law, and in particular to explore the fuzzy line between penalty clauses and liquidated-damages clauses.

Carborundum manufactures "Ferro Carbo," an abrasive powder used in making steel. To serve its midwestern customers better, Carborundum made a contract with Lake River by which the latter agreed to provide distribution services in its warehouse in Illinois. Lake River would receive Ferro Carbo in bulk from Carborundum, "bag" it, and ship the bagged product to Carborundum's customers. The Ferro Carbo would remain Carborundum's property until delivered to the customers.

[Carborundum insisted that Lake River install a new bagging system to handle the contract. In order to be sure of being able to recover the cost of the new system and make a profit, Lake River insisted on a minimum-quantity guarantee and an agreement that if Carborundum had not shipped the minimum quantity in three years, Lake River would receive the full contract price minus the amount already shipped.]

* * *

After the contract was signed in 1979, the demand for domestic steel, and with it the demand for Ferro Carbo, plummeted, and Carborundum failed to ship the guaranteed amount. When the contract expired late in 1982, Carborundum had shipped only 12,000 of the 22,500 tons it had guaranteed. Lake River had bagged the 12,000 tons and had billed Carborundum for this bagging, and Carborundum had paid, but by virtue of the formula in the minimum-guarantee clause Carborundum still owed Lake River $241,000—the contract price of $533,000 if the full amount of Ferro Carbo had been shipped, minus what Carborundum had paid for the bagging of the quantity it had shipped.

* * *

Lake River brought this suit for $241,000, which it claims as liquidated damages. * * *

The hardest issue in the case is whether the formula in the minimum-guarantee clause imposes a penalty for breach of contract or is merely an effort to liquidate damages. Deep as the hostility to penalty clauses runs in the common law, we still might be inclined to question, if we thought ourselves free to do so, whether a modern court should refuse to enforce a penalty clause where the signator is a substantial corporation, well able to avoid improvident commitments. Penalty clauses provide an earnest of performance. The clause here enhanced Carborundum's credibility in promising to ship the minimum amount guaranteed by showing that it was willing to pay the full contract price even if it failed to ship anything. On the other side it can be pointed out that by raising the cost of a breach of contract to the contract breaker, a penalty clause increases the risk to his other creditors; increases (what is the same thing and more, because bankruptcy imposes "deadweight" social costs) the risk of bankruptcy; and could amplify the business cycle by increasing the number of bankruptcies in bad times, which is when contracts are most likely to be broken. But since little effort is made to prevent businessmen from assuming risks, these reasons are no better than makeweights.

A better argument is that a penalty clause may discourage efficient as well as inefficient breaches of contract. Suppose a breach would cost the promisee $12,000 in actual damages but would yield the promisor $20,000 in additional profits. Then there would be a net social gain from breach. After being fully compensated for his loss the promisee would be no worse off than if the contract had been performed, while the promisor would be better off by $8,000. But now suppose the contract contains a penalty clause under which the promisor if he breaks his promise must pay the promisee $25,000. The promisor will be discouraged from breaking the contract, since $25,000, the penalty, is greater than $20,000, the profits of the breach; and a transaction that would have increased value will be foregone.

On this view, since compensatory damages should be sufficient to deter inefficient breaches (that is, breaches that cost the victim more than the gain to the contract breaker), penal damages could have no effect other than to deter some efficient breaches. But this overlooks the earlier point that the willingness to agree to a penalty clause is a way of making the promisor and his promise credible and may therefore be essential to inducing some value-maximizing contracts to be made. It also overlooks the more important point that the parties (always assuming they are fully competent) will, in deciding whether to include a penalty clause in their contract, weigh the gains against the costs—costs that include the possibility of discouraging an efficient breach somewhere down the road—and will include the clause only if the benefits exceed those costs as well as all other costs.

On this view the refusal to enforce penalty clauses is (at best) paternalistic—and it seems odd that courts should display parental solicitude for large corporations. But however this may be, we must be on guard to avoid importing our own ideas of sound public policy into an area where our proper judicial role is more than usually deferential. The responsibility for making innovations in the common law of Illinois rests with the courts of Illinois, and not with the federal courts in Illinois. And like every other state, Illinois, untroubled by academic skepticism of the wisdom of refusing to enforce penalty clauses against sophisticated promisors, continues steadfastly to insist on the distinction between penalties and liquidated damages. * * *

Mindful that Illinois courts resolve doubtful cases in favor of classification as a penalty * * * we conclude that the damage formula in this case is a penalty and not a liquidation of damages, because it is designed always to assure Lake River more than its actual damages. The formula—full contract price minus the amount already invoiced to Carborundum—is invariant to the gravity of the breach. When a contract specifies a single sum in damages for any and all breaches even though it is apparent that all are not of the same gravity, the specification is not a reasonable effort to estimate damages; and when in addition the fixed sum greatly exceeds the actual damages likely to be inflicted by a minor breach, its character as a penalty become unmistakable. [Citations.] This case is within the gravitational field of these principles even though the minimum-guarantee clause does not fix a single sum as damages.

* * *

The fact that the damage formula is invalid does not deprive Lake River of a remedy. The parties did not contract explicitly with reference to the measure of damages if the agreed-on damage formula was invalidated, but all this means is that the victim of the breach is entitled to his common law damages. *See, e.g.*, Restatement, Second, Contracts § 356, comment a (1981). In this case that would be the unpaid contract price of $241,000 minus the costs that Lake River saved by not having to complete the contract (the variable costs on the other 45 percent of the Ferro Carbo that it never had to bag). The case must be remanded to the district judge to fix these damages.

* * *

Affirmed in part, reversed in part, and remanded.

———

1. The principal focus in determining the validity of a liquidated damages clause is the reasonableness of the relationship that the stipulated damages bear to the potential harm which the parties contemplate may accrue as a result of a breach. Another question concerns what relevance the provable actual damages have when measured against the liquidated amount. The Restatement (Second) of Contracts § 356 and Uniform Commercial Code § 2–718(1) both provide that the reasonableness of the liquidated damages clause may be shown either by its proportionality to the anticipated or actual harm. Thus, the amount fixed may be considered valid if it approximates either alternative. *See* Reliance Ins. v. Utah Dept. of Transp., 858 P.2d 1363, 1367 (Utah 1993)

(reasonableness of forecast determined by reference to the time of contract formation, not the date of breach).

2. What if the liquidated sum is characterized as a reasonable approximation of the contemplated losses but the proof of actual harm is significantly less? Most courts have held that the liquidated amount must satisfy only one of the alternative tests, not both. Accordingly, evidence of the actual losses resulting from the breach would be considered irrelevant, assuming damages could reasonably be anticipated at the time of contracting. See Southwest Engineering Co. v. United States, 341 F.2d 998 (8th Cir.1965); Frick Co. v. Rubel Corp., 62 F.2d 765 (2d Cir.1933); Sun Printing & Publishing Ass'n v. Moore, 183 U.S. 642, 22 S.Ct. 240, 46 L.Ed. 366 (1902); United States v. Bethlehem Steel Co., 205 U.S. 105, 27 S.Ct. 450, 51 L.Ed. 731 (1907).

The justification for the enforceability of a liquidated damages clause despite the lack of actual damages has been predicated on freedom of contract principles:

> Courts have now become strongly inclined to allow parties to make their own contracts, and to carry out their intentions, even when it would result in the recovery of an amount stated as liquidated damages, upon proof of the violation of the contract, and without proof of the damages actually sustained.

United States v. Bethlehem Steel Co., 205 U.S. 105, 119, 27 S.Ct. 450, 455, 51 L.Ed. 731 (1907).

For example, in In re Lion Overall Co., 55 F.Supp. 789 (S.D.N.Y. 1943), *aff'd sub nom.* United States v. Walkof, 144 F.2d 75 (2d Cir. 1944), the government sought enforcement of a liquidated damages clause for a contractor's failure to deliver clothing for soldiers in a timely manner. The contract recited that the stipulated damages for each day's delay were necessary because the actual damages which the government might sustain as a result of delays were impossible to calculate. The court upheld as reasonable the $20,000 liquidated damages amount in relation to $53,000 as the total contract price for the goods, despite evidence that the government actually incurred an excess cost of only $3.56 as a result of the breach. The court concluded that the only relevant time to evaluate the reasonableness of the clause was when the contract was entered and that the stipulated damages were "not out of all proportion to any possible loss."

3. Certainly to some extent courts may be influenced by public interest considerations to give particular deference to the validity of liquidated damages provisions in government contracts. *See generally* Gant & Breslauer, Liquidated Damages in Federal Government Contracts, 47 B.U.L.Rev. 71 (1967); Note, The Use and Abuse of Liquidated Damages in Federal Defense Contracts: An Analysis, 8 Okla. City U.L.Rev. 261 (1983); Peckar, Liquidated Damages in Federal Construction Contracts: Time for a New Approach, 5 Pub.Cont.L.J. 129 (1972). Thus, the court in In re Lion Overall Co., 55 F.Supp. 789, 791 (S.D.N.Y. 1943) stated:

The contract was made for an article of military equipment for our troops at a time when the war clouds from Europe were gathering ominously about this country and when it could reasonably be anticipated, certainly by the Army and Navy Departments, that sooner or later we might be embroiled in the conflict. While there were others in the country who were manufacturing similar garments, what damage might result from a delayed delivery could not be ascertained with accuracy. In any event, the agreement was made without any overreaching or fraud, and as an obvious spur to prompt performance.

4. The validation of a liquidated damages clause as reasonably proportionate to the anticipated harm but significantly disproportionate to the provable actual losses is not limited to the context of government contracts. For instance, in Robbins v. Finlay, 645 P.2d 623 (Utah 1982), the court held that an employer was entitled to recover $5,000 as liquidated damages for an employee's breach of a covenant not to misuse customer leads even though the employer had not introduced any direct evidence of actual losses incurred and had shown that only five potential customers were involved.

In contrast, some courts have held that evidence of little or no actual losses may invalidate a liquidated damages clause as a penalty even if the stipulated amount was otherwise reasonably related to the anticipated harm. For example, in Gorco Construction Co. v. Stein, 256 Minn. 476, 99 N.W.2d 69 (1959), the court determined that a contract provision which designated damages in the amount of 15% of the total contract price to cover expenses for advertising, labor, equipment, and commissions was invalid where the plaintiff did not prove any actual loss because of the breach. Similarly, in S.O.G.–San Ore–Gardner v. Missouri Pacific Railroad, 658 F.2d 562, 570 (8th Cir.1981), the court invalidated a clause which stipulated $600 per day liquidated damages to cover estimated losses from delayed performance where the party asserting the claim sustained no actual damages from the breach.

5. A liquidated damages clause which provides for payment of the sum to the non-breaching party in the event of a breach of covenants that have varying degrees of importance typically has been invalidated as an unreasonable forecast of the anticipated harm. McCormick, Damages § 151 (1935); Corbin, Contracts § 1066 (1964). Thus, a liquidated damages clause which fixes a payment of $200 per day for late delivery in the shipment of goods may be justifiable as an appropriate compensation for the contemplated disruption in the purchaser's business operations. However, the $200 figure may be considered invalid as a penalty if sought by the seller for a breach of a covenant requiring certain insurance for the goods. In Coe v. Thermasol, Ltd., 615 F.Supp. 316, 320 (W.D.N.C.1985), though, the court upheld the enforceability of a liquidated damages clause even though it could be triggered by a breach of several covenants because the covenants were "interdependent and call for acts with one primary purpose."

6. For additional commentary on liquidated damages, *see*: Warren, Formal and Operating Rules under Common Law and Code, 30 U.C.L.A.L.Rev. (1983); Linenberger, Liquidated Damages in the Sale of Goods, 14; Clarkson, Miller & Muris, Liquidated Damages v. Penalties: Sense or Nonsense, 1978 Wis.L.Rev. 351; Goetz and Scott, Liquidated Damages, Penalties and the Just Compensation Principle: Some Notes on an Enforcement Model and a Theory of Efficient Breach, 77 Colum.L.Rev. 554 (1977); Sweet, Liquidated Damages in California, 60 Calif.L.Rev. 84 (1972); Farnsworth, Legal Remedies for Breach of Contract, 70 Colum.L.Rev. 1145 (1970); Macneil, Power of Contract and Agreed Remedies, 47 Cornell L.Q. 495 (1962); Dunbar, Drafting the Liquidated Damage Clause—When and How, 20 Ohio St.L.J. 221 (1959); Lloyd, Penalties and Forfeitures, 29 Harv.L.Rev. 117 (1915).

D. LAND SALES CONTRACTS

Section Coverage:

The damages remedy is important to vendors and vendees in contracts for the sale of land even though the equitable remedy of specific performance is generally available. Equity courts historically have deemed that every parcel of land is unique and that an award of damages is therefore inadequate. Nonetheless, the specific performance remedy is not automatic; a court must still evaluate the relative hardships of the parties. Moreover, that remedy is not practical in all cases, depending upon the cause for the breach and changes in the parties' positions between breach and trial.

The usual damages award for breach of a contract to convey land is based upon the expectancy interest. It is measured by the difference between the contract price and the fair market value of the property on the date of the breach. The damages award also includes any consequential damages proved with reasonable certainty. There is a further adjustment for benefits received or expenses saved by the plaintiff.

The majority of jurisdictions follow the "American" rule of damages for a vendor's breach which results from a deficiency in title. This rule provides for an award of the benefit of the bargain to a vendee for a vendor's breach of an executory contract to convey title. A minority of courts follow the "English" rule derived from Flureau v. Thornhill, 2 W.Bl. 1078, 96 Eng.Rep. 635 (C.P.1776). It provides a vendee with restitution of amounts paid on the contract plus reliance expenditures, but denies recovery for the vendee's expectancy interest unless the vendor's breach was characterized as made in bad faith.

Model Case:

The Larsons contracted to purchase from Ross for $80,000 a 100 acre tract of land which contained a small farmhouse and barn. The contract provided for a down payment of $8,000 and monthly installments in the principal amount of $1,000 plus interest for six years. The earnest money of $8,000 was designated by the parties as "liquidated damages in all respects in the event of a material breach by the purchaser, and not as a penalty."

The Larsons paid the $8,000 and moved their family into the farmhouse. Almost immediately after assuming possession the Larsons noticed that the well water had a foul smelling odor and was a greenish-yellow color. They notified the state environmental protection agency. Tests revealed that a dangerous level of toxic chemical waste products had contaminated the water. The agency officials located an open landfill near the well which contained a number of barrels of highly toxic chemicals, many of which were improperly sealed. Cracks in the barrels had allowed chemicals to seep into the water supply. The officials informed the Larsons that the landfill site violated both state and federal environmental statutes.

The Larsons stopped making the monthly payments and instituted suit against Ross demanding rescission and restitution. Ross counter-claimed seeking alternatively the specific performance of the contract or enforcement of the $8,000 liquidated damages clause.

A court would probably find that the contaminated water supply constituted a material breach of the executory contract which justified rescission, restitution of the $8,000 down payment, and compensatory damages for the excess, if any, of the market value of the land versus the contract price.

Alternatively, assume that no toxic chemicals were located on the property, and that the Larsons had stopped making payments for personal reasons. Ross seeks specific performance of the contract or, if equitable relief is denied, enforcement of the liquidated damages clause. Specific performance of the land sale contract may be granted a vendor if the legal remedies are inadequate and if the balance of hardships favor the party requesting relief.

The liquidated damages clause was not designated as the exclusive remedy for breach of the contract; however, a court may still consider it to be an adequate remedy for Ross. The clause would not be automatically enforceable based solely on the parties' description that it was not a penalty. Rather, the court will inquire whether at the time of contracting the potential actual damages in the event of a breach were difficult to determine and the $8,000 sum had a reasonable relationship to the potential damages. An amount of liquidated damages of ten percent of the total contract price may be considered reasonable for a land sale contract, especially if Ross is likely to have difficulty in reselling the tract.

SOUTHEASTERN LAND FUND v. REAL ESTATE WORLD
237 Ga. 227, 227 S.E.2d 340 (1976).

INGRAM, JUSTICE.

Certiorari was granted in this case for this court to consider whether a provision in a real estate sales contract, providing for the payment of earnest money, should be considered as a provision for liquidated damages. The Court of Appeals concluded this provision was a penalty and could not be enforced.

The litigation began when the seller filed suit against the buyer who defaulted under the contract. The buyer had paid $5,000 in cash as earnest money when the contract was signed. Thereafter, a promissory note for $45,000, representing additional earnest money, was executed and delivered by the buyer to the seller pursuant to the contract. The buyer defaulted at closing and the seller sued the buyer to collect the $45,000 note. The seller obtained a summary judgment in the trial court and the buyer's motion for summary judgment and counterclaim for return of the $5,000 earnest money were denied.

On appeal to the Court of Appeals, that court reversed in a 6–3 decision and held the earnest money provision of the contract amounted to a penalty. * * *

The contract provides: "In the event purchaser defaults hereunder after having paid the additional earnest money [$45,000] . . . seller shall be entitled to retain all original earnest money [$5,000] paid hereunder as partial liquidated damages occasioned by such default, to collect the proceeds of the indebtedness owed by purchaser as additional earnest money as further partial liquidated damages occasioned by such default, and to pursue any and all remedies available to him at law or equity including, but not limited to, an action for specific performance of this contract."

If, as the Court of Appeals found, this provision in the contract was a penalty, or is unenforceable as a liquidated damages provision, then the buyer can prevail in asserting a defense to the enforcement of the $45,000 note. If, on the other hand, this is a proper provision for liquidated damages, then the seller can prevail in enforcing the note. Of course, whether a provision represents liquidated damages or a penalty does not depend upon the label the parties place on the payment but rather depends on the effect it was intended to have and whether it was reasonable. [Citation.] Where the parties do not undertake to estimate damages in advance of the breach and instead provide for both a forfeiture [penalty] plus actual damages, the amount, even though called liquidated damages, is instead an unenforceable penalty. [Citation.]

The seller argues that a seller who is not in default may *always* retain the earnest money paid by the buyer and sue for actual damages above the amount of earnest money received under the contract. We do not agree with this argument and the seller cites no authority that supports it. While it is true that the earnest money feature of a real estate contract distinguishes it to some extent from a wholly executory contract, the same basic contract rules are used to determine available remedies for the breach of a real estate sales contract as for the breach of other contracts. The general contract law of remedies for a breach, as well as the intent of the parties in providing specific remedies in the contract, must be used in analyzing and deciding each particular case.

Depending on the language used in the contract and the discernible intent of the parties, the existence of an earnest money provision in a real estate sales contract can have one of three effects in the case of a breach by the buyer. First, the money could be considered as partial payment of any actual damages which can be proven as the result of the buyer's breach. Second, the money could be applied as part payment of the purchase price in the enforcement of the contract in a suit for specific performance by the seller. Third, the money could be liquidated damages for breach of the contract by the buyer. A provision for earnest money cannot, however, under Georgia law, be used for all three results as we shall see.

Of course, if the real estate sales contract is silent on the remedy to be provided, the non-breaching seller is entitled to his proven actual damages. The ordinary measure of damages is the difference between the contract price and the market value of the property at the time of the buyer's breach. [Citation.] If the non-breaching seller sues for actual damages, the earnest money then becomes a fund out of which those damages are partially paid if the proven damages exceed the amount of the earnest money.

Even if the real estate contract is silent as to the remedy of specific performance, it is still available as a remedy unless it is specifically excluded as a remedy. In the cases in which rescission has been used as a remedy the parties are put as nearly as is possible back to the status quo ante. [Citations.]

Of course, Georgia law also recognizes that the parties may agree in their contract to a sum to liquidate their damages. Code Ann. § 20–1402 provides: "Damages are given as compensation for the injury sustained. If the parties agree in their contract what the damages for a breach shall be, they are said to be liquidated, and unless the agreement violates some principle of law, *the parties are bound thereby.*" (Emphasis supplied.) *See also* Code Ann. § 20–1403.

In deciding whether a contract provision is enforceable as liquidated damages, the court makes a tripartite inquiry to determine if the following factors are present:

> "First, the injury caused by the breach must be difficult or impossible of accurate estimation; second, the parties must intend to provide for damages rather than for a penalty; and third, the sum stipulated must be a reasonable pre-estimate of the probable loss." [Citations.]

Another feature implicit in the concept of liquidated damages in addition to the above factors is that both parties are bound by their agreement. [Citations.] A non-breaching party who has agreed to accept liquidated damages cannot elect after a breach to take actual damages should they prove greater than the sum specified. The breaching party cannot complain that the actual damages are less than those specified as liquidated damages. The liquidated damages become the "maximum as well as the minimum sum that can be collected." [Citation.]

The problem that this particular contract provision raises is whether the seller has tried to retain a right to elect to sue for actual damages rather than liquidated damages and in so doing has rendered the purported liquidated damages provision unenforceable. This particular paragraph in the contract provides for "partial" liquidated damages. This can be read that the parties intended for the two "partial" liquidated damages provisions to comprise the whole. However, it is also susceptible to the construction that these two partial liquidated damages were not intended to be the sole damages remedy for this particular breach of contract.

The contract provision that included the retention of the right to elect specific performance as an alternative remedy to damages poses no problem in our analysis as it does not render a valid liquidated damages provision unenforceable. [Citation.] "The law is now well settled that a liquidated damages provision will not in and of itself be construed as barring the remedy of specific performance." [Citation.] To bar specific performance there should be explicit language in the liquidated damages provision that it is to be the sole remedy. *See also* Restatement, Contracts, § 378. Thus the retention of the right to elect specific performance in this contract does not render the purported liquidated damages provision invalid. The answer must be found elsewhere in the construction of these contract provisions.

We think a correct resolution of this issue must be found in the doctrine that "in cases of doubt the courts favor the construction which holds the stipulated sum to be a penalty, and limits the recovery to the amount of damages actually shown, rather than a liquidation of the damages." [Citation.] If the parties intended for the $5,000 and the $45,000 to represent the "maximum as well as the minimum sum that can be collected," from the buyer's breach, the contract should have made it clear that this was the effect intended by these provisions. It is the lingering ambiguity inherent in these provisions of the contract that persuades us to affirm the result reached by the Court of Appeals in construing the contract.

In summary, we hold that these contract provisions are not enforceable under Georgia law as proper liquidated damages provisions in this real estate sales contract. It follows that the trial court erred in granting summary judgment in favor of the seller and we affirm the Court of Appeals reversal of that portion of the trial court's order. However, the existence of the actual damages, if any, to be proven by the non-breaching seller precludes the grant of the buyer's motion for summary judgment. Therefore, that portion of the Court of Appeals opinion directing the grant of the buyer's motion for summary judgment must be reversed.

Judgment affirmed in part; reversed in part.

---

1. In the principal case the intention of the parties is considered an independent requirement for the validity of the liquidated damages clause. Should the intention element be a subjective or an objective inquiry? If objective, is such a requirement distinguishable from the one that the stipulated sum must be a reasonable pre-estimate of damages? If intent is evaluated subjectively, would there be problems of application? The majority trend rejects the intention element as adding little, if anything, beyond the issue of reasonableness.

2. The traditional equitable rule holds that damages provide an inadequate remedy at law in land sales contracts because every parcel of land is considered unique. This traditional approach was not followed in Centex Homes Corp. v. Boag, 128 N.J.Super. 385, 320 A.2d 194 (1974), where the court denied specific performance to a seller of a condominium unit. Equitable relief was denied because (1) the property was virtually identical to hundreds of other units being offered for sale to the public, and (2) the damages resulting from the breach were readily measurable.

In the ordinary land sales case, the traditional assumption of the inadequacy of damages still prevails. Is it appropriate to treat remedies for land contracts unlike other types of contracts? Should the availability and measure of damages for a breach of contract to sell land play a significant role in whether a court will grant or deny specific performance?

3. Under what circumstances, if any, should punitive damages be recovered for breach of a contract to sell land? *See* Hanna v. American International Land Corp., 289 So.2d 756 (Fla.App.1974) (punitive damages allowed because vendor's bad faith breach of contract also amounted to an independent tort of conversion where equitable title had vested in the vendee).

VINES v. ORCHARD HILLS, INC.

181 Conn. 501, 435 A.2d 1022 (1980).

PETERS, ASSOCIATE JUSTICE.

This case concerns the right of purchasers of real property, after their own default, to recover moneys paid at the time of execution of a valid contract of sale.   * * *

The facts underlying this litigation are straightforward and undisputed. When the purchasers contracted to buy their condominium in July, 1973, they paid $7880, a sum which the contract of sale designated as liquidated damages. The purchasers decided not to take title to the condominium because Euel D. Vines was transferred by his employer to New Jersey; the Vines so informed the seller by a letter dated January

4, 1974. There has never been any claim that the seller has failed, in any respect, to conform to his obligations under the contract, nor does the complaint allege that the purchasers are legally excused from their performance under the contract. In short, it is the purchasers and not the seller whose breach precipitated the present cause of action.

In the proceedings below, the purchasers established that the value of the condominium that they had agreed to buy for $78,800 in 1973 had, by the time of the trial in 1979, a fair market value of $160,000. The trial court relied on this figure to conclude that, because the seller had gained what it characterized as a windfall of approximately $80,000, the purchasers were entitled to recover their down payment of $7880. Neither the purchasers nor the seller proffered any evidence at the trial to show the market value of the condominium at the time of the purchasers' breach of their contract or the damages sustained by the seller as a result of that breach.

The seller's principal argument on this appeal is that the trial court improperly disregarded the parties' valid liquidated damages clause. * * *

The ultimate issue on this appeal is the enforceability of a liquidated damages clause as a defense to a claim of restitution by purchasers in default on a land sale contract. Although the parties, both in the trial court and here, have focused on the liquidated damages clause per se, we must first consider when, if ever, purchasers who are themselves in breach of a valid contract of sale may affirmatively invoke the assistance of judicial process to recover back moneys paid to, and withheld by, their seller.

The right of a contracting party, despite his default, to seek restitution for benefits conferred and allegedly unjustly retained has been much disputed in the legal literature and in the case law. [Citations.] Although earlier cases often refused to permit a party to bring an action that could be said to be based on his own breach; many of the more recent cases support restitution in order to prevent unjust enrichment and to avoid forfeiture. [Citations.]

A variety of considerations, some practical and some theoretical, underlie this shift in attitude toward the plaintiff in breach. As Professor Corbin pointed out in his seminal article, "The Right of a Defaulting Vendee to the Restitution of Installments Paid," 40 Yale L.J. 1013 (1931), the anomalous result of denying any remedy to the plaintiff in breach is to punish more severely the person who has partially performed, often in good faith, than the person who has entirely disregarded his contractual obligations from the outset. Only partial performance triggers a claim for restitution, and partial performance will not, in the ordinary course of events, have been more injurious to the innocent party than total nonperformance. Recognition of a claim in restitution is, furthermore, consistent with the economic functions that the law of contracts is designed to serve. The principal purpose of remedies for the breach of contract is to provide compensation for loss; and therefore a party injured by breach of contract is entitled to retain nothing in excess of that sum which compensates him for the loss of his bargain. Indeed, there are those who argue that repudiation of contractual obligations is socially desirable, and should be encouraged, whenever gain to the party in breach exceeds loss to the party injured by breach. [Citations.] To assign such primacy to inferences drawn from economic models requires great confidence that the person injured by breach will encounter no substantial difficulties in establishing the losses for which he is entitled to be compensated. It is not necessary to push the principle of compensatory damages that far, or to disregard entirely the desirability of maintaining some incentives for the performance of promises. A claim in restitution, although legal in form, is equitable in nature, and permits a trial court to balance the equities, to take into account a variety of competing principles to determine whether the defendant has been unjustly enriched. "Even though we adhere to the rule that only compensatory damages are to be awarded, there are other important questions of policy to be considered. One is whether aid is to be given to one who breaches his contract, particularly when the breach is deliberate and without moral justification. Another is whether restitution can be administered without leaving the innocent party with uncompensated damages."

Recognition that there are circumstances under which a defaulting purchaser may be entitled to restitution for benefits conferred upon the innocent seller of land is consistent with parallel developments elsewhere in the law of contracts. Judicial resistance to enforcement of forfeitures has of course long been commonplace, particularly with regard to contract clauses purporting to liquidate damages. * * *

The purchaser's right to recover in restitution requires the purchaser to establish that the seller has been unjustly enriched. The purchaser must show more than that the contract has come to an end and that the seller retains moneys paid pursuant to the contract. To prove unjust enrichment, in the ordinary case, the purchaser, because he is the party in breach, must prove that the damages suffered by his seller are less than the moneys received from the purchaser. [Citations.] It may not be easy for the purchaser to prove the extent of the seller's damages, it may even be strategically advantageous for the seller to come forward with relevant evidence of the losses he has incurred and may expect to incur on account of the buyer's breach. Nonetheless, only if the breaching party satisfies his burden of proof that the innocent party has sustained a net gain may a claim for unjust enrichment be sustained. [Citations.]

In the case before us, the parties themselves stipulated in the contract of sale that the purchasers' down payment of 10 percent of the purchase price represents the damages that would be likely to flow from the purchasers' breach. The question then becomes whether the purchasers have demonstrated the seller's unjust enrichment in the face of the liquidated damages clause to which they agreed.

* * * [W]here the plaintiffs are themselves in default, the plaintiffs bear the burden of showing that the clause is invalid and unenforceable. [Citations.] It is not unreasonable in these circumstances to presume that a liquidated damages clause that is appropriately limited in amount bears a reasonable relationship to the damages that the seller has actually suffered. The seller's damages, as Professor Palmer points out, include not only his expectation damages suffered through loss of his bargain, and his incidental damages such as broker's commissions, but also less quantifiable costs arising out of retention of real property beyond the time of the originally contemplated sale. 1 Palmer, Restitution §§ 5.4, 5.8 (1978). A liquidated damages clause allowing the seller to retain 10 percent of the contract price as earnest money is presumptively a reasonable allocation of the risks associated with default. [Citations.]

The presumption of validity that attaches to a clause liquidating the seller's damages at 10 percent of the contract price in the event of the purchaser's unexcused nonperformance is, like most other presumptions, rebuttable. The purchaser, despite his default, is free to prove that the contract, or any part thereof, was the product of fraud or mistake or unconscionability. [Citation.] In the alternative, the purchaser is free to offer evidence that his breach in fact caused the seller no damages or damages substantially less than the amount stipulated as liquidated damages. [Citation.]

The trial court concluded that the plaintiff purchasers had successfully [met their burden] by presenting evidence of increase in the value of the real property between the date of the contract of sale and the date of the trial. That conclusion was in error. The relevant time at which to measure the seller's damages is the time of breach. [Citations.] Benefits to the seller that are attributable to a rising market subsequent to breach rightfully accrue to the seller. [Citations.] There was no evidence before the court to demonstrate that the seller was not injured at the time of the purchasers' breach by their failure then to consummate the contract. Neither the seller's status as a developer of a condominium project nor the absence of willfulness on the part of the purchasers furnishes a justification for disregarding the liquidated damages clause, although these factors may play some role in the ultimate determination of whether the seller was in fact unjustly enriched by the down payment he retained.

Because the availability of, and the limits on, restitutionary claims by a plaintiff in default have not previously been clearly spelled out in our cases, it is appropriate to afford to the purchasers herein another opportunity to proffer evidence to substantiate their claim. What showing the purchasers must make cannot be spelled out with specificity in view of the sparsity of the present record. The purchasers may be able to demonstrate that the condominium could, at the time of their breach, have been resold at a price sufficiently higher than their contract price to obviate any loss of profits and to compensate the seller for any incidental and consequential damages. Alternatively, the purchasers may be able to present evidence of unconscionability or of excuse, to avoid the applicability of the liquidated damages clause altogether. The plaintiffs' burden of proof is not an easy one to sustain, but they are entitled to their day in court.

There is error, the judgment is set aside, and the case is remanded for further proceedings in conformity with this opinion.

DONOVAN v. BACHSTADT

91 N.J. 434, 453 A.2d 160 (1982).

SCHREIBER, J.

The central legal issue in this case concerns the damages to which a buyer of realty is entitled upon the breach of the executory agreement by the seller. The procedural circumstances under which the question arose are unique. The buyers, Edward Donovan and Donna Donovan, husband and wife, prevailed in a suit for specific performance * * *. When the seller, Carl Bachstadt, could not perform because of a defect in title, the Donovans instituted this action for damages [and] they were awarded reimbursement of their expenditures of $145.00 for a survey and $142.85 for title searches. * * *

The contract recited that the purchase price was $58,900. A deposit of $5,890 was paid to and held by the broker. At the closing scheduled for May 1, 1980, the Donovans were to pay an additional $9,010 in cash and the balance was to consist of a purchase money bond or note and mortgage in the principal amount of $44,000, for 30 years, at an interest rate of 13%. The conveyance was to be made subject to easements and restrictions of record and facts disclosed in an accurate survey, provided that these would not render the title unmarketable. The contract also stated that title "shall be marketable and insurable ... by any reputable title insurance company...." There was no liquidated damage provision.

* * *

When defendant could not obtain marketable title, the Donovans commenced this suit for compensatory and punitive damages. As previously observed the trial court granted plaintiffs' motion for summary judgment. It was indisputable that the defendant had breached the agreement. The only issue was damages. The trial court held that plaintiffs were entitled under N.J.S.A. 2A:29–1 to recovery of their costs for the title search and survey. Plaintiffs had apparently in the interim purchased a home in Middlesex County and obtained a mortgage loan bearing interest at the rate of 13¼% per annum. Plaintiffs sought the difference between 10½% and 13¼% as compensatory damages, representing their loss of the benefit of the bargain. The trial court denied recovery because the contract was for the sale of the property and the financing "was only incidental to the basic concept."

The Appellate Division reversed. * * *

The initial inquiry is whether plaintiffs are entitled to compensatory damages. We had occasion recently to discuss the measure of damages available when a seller breaches an executory contract for the sale of real property. St. Pius X House of Retreats v. Diocese of Camden, 88 N.J. 571, 582–87, 443 A.2d 1052 (1982). We noted that New Jersey follows the English rule, which generally limits a buyer's recovery to the return of his deposit unless the seller wilfully refuses to convey or is guilty of fraud or deceit. The traditional formulation of the English rule has been expressed by T. Cyprian Williams, an English barrister, as follows:

> Where the breach of contract is occasioned by the vendor's inability, without his own fault, to show a good title, the purchaser is entitled to recover as damages his deposit, if any, with interest, and his expenses incurred in connection with the agreement, but not more than nominal damages for the loss of his bargain. [T.C. Williams, *The Contract of Sale of Land* 128 (1930)].

In *St. Pius* we found no need to reexamine the English rule, though we raised the question whether the American rule that permits a buyer to obtain benefit of the bargain damages irrespective of the nature of the reasons for the seller's default might not be more desirable.

* * *

We are satisfied that the American rule is preferable. The English principle developed because of the uncertainties of title due to the complexity of the rules governing title to land during the eighteenth and nineteenth centuries. [Citation.] At that time the only evidence of title was contained in deeds which were in a phrase attributed to Lord Westbury, "difficult to read, disgusting to touch, and impossible to understand." The reason for the English principle that creates an exception to the law governing damages for breaches of executory contracts for the sale of property is no longer valid, and the exception should be eliminated. [Citations.] Indeed in England the rule has been modified by placing the burden of proof on the vendor to establish that he has done everything within his power to carry out the contract. [Citations.]

* * *

There is no sound basis why benefit of the bargain damages should not be awarded whether the subject matter of the contract is realty or personalty. Serious losses should not be borne by the vendee of real estate to the benefit of the defaulting vendor. This is particularly so when an installment purchase contract is involved that extends over a period of years during which the vendee makes substantial payments upon the principal, as well as extensive improvements to the property.

The innocent purchaser should be permitted to recover benefit of the bargain damages irrespective of the good or bad faith of the seller. Contract culpability depends on the breach of the contractual promise. [Citation.] Where, as here, the seller agreed that title would be marketable, the seller's liability should depend upon his breach of that promise.

* * *

The English rule is consistent with the limitation on recovery in suits on a covenant for breach of warranty. The damages for a buyer, who has taken title and is ousted because the title is defective, are limited to the consideration paid and interest thereon. [Citation.] There appears to be no real difference between that situation and one where the vendor who does not have good title refuses to convey. In both cases the buyer loses the property because of a defect in the title. The fact that one sues for breach of a warranty covenant does not justify depriving a buyer of compensatory damages to which he is justly entitled when the seller breaches the contract of sale. Professor Corbin has suggested that any inconsistency in this respect should be resolved by awarding full compensatory damages when the action is for breach of warranty. [Citation.] Moreover, an anomaly already exists, for our courts have acknowledged that a buyer may recover such damages upon a showing of the seller's bad faith. [Citation.]

We are satisfied that a buyer should be permitted to recover benefit of the bargain damages when the seller breaches an executory contract to convey real property. Here the defendant agreed to convey marketable title. He made that bargained-for promise and breached it and is responsible to the plaintiff for the damages occasioned thereby. The next question is how to compute those compensatory damages.

Judicial remedies upon breach of contract fall into three general categories: restitution, compensatory damages and performance. Separate concepts undergird each of these remedial provisions. The rationale for restitution is to return the innocent party to his status before the contract was executed. Compensatory damages are intended to recompense the injured claimant for losses due to the breach, that is, to give the innocent party the benefit of the bargain. Performance is to effect a result, essentially other than in terms of monetary reparation, so that the innocent party is placed in the position of having had the contract performed. We have now adopted the American rule providing for compensatory damages upon the seller's breach of an executory contract to sell realty and we must examine the appropriate elements that should properly be included in an award.

"Compensatory damages are designed 'to put the injured party in as good a position as he would have had if performance had been rendered as promised.' " [Citations.] What that position is depends upon what the parties reasonably expected. It follows that the defendant is not chargeable for loss that he did not have reason to foresee as a probable result of the breach when the contract was made. * * * Further the loss must be a reasonably certain consequence of the breach although the exact amount of the loss need not be certain. [Citations.]

The specific elements to be applied in any given case of a seller's breach of an executory agreement to sell realty may vary in order to achieve the broad purposes of reparations; some items, however, will almost invariably exist. Thus the purchaser will usually be entitled to the return of the amount paid on the purchase price with interest thereon. Costs and expenses incurred in connection with the proposed acquisition, such as for the title search and survey, would fall in the same category. The traditional test is the difference between the market price of the property at the time of the breach and the contract price. * * *

The difference between market and contract price may not be suitable in all situations. Thus where a buyer had in turn contracted to sell the realty, it is reasonable to measure his damages in terms of the actual lost profit. * * * What the proper elements of damage are depend upon the particular circumstances surrounding the transaction, especially the terms, conditions and nature of the agreement.

The plaintiffs here assert that their damages are equivalent to the difference in interest costs incurred by them in purchasing a different home at another location. This claim assumes that the financial provision of the contract concerning the purchase money mortgage that the defendant agreed to accept was independent and divisible from the purchase of the land and house. The defendant contends that he did not agree to loan these funds in connection with the purchase of some other property, but that this provision was incidental to the sale of the house. Neither position is entirely sound. This financing was an integral part of the transaction. It can be neither ignored nor viewed as an isolated element.

The relationship of the financing to the purchase of a home has changed in recent years. As interest rates rose and the availability of first mortgage funds was sharply reduced, potential homeowners, though desirous of purchasing homes, found financing difficult to obtain. * * * In evaluating a contract such a financial arrangement could play an important part in determining price. * * * The interest rate is not sufficiently discrete to calculate damages in terms of it alone under these circumstances.

In some circumstances interest rate differentials are an appropriate measure of damages. Where the buyer has obtained specific performance, but because of the delay has incurred higher mortgage rates, then his loss clearly should include the higher financing cost. Godwin v. Lindbert, 101 Mich.App. 754, 300 N.W.2d 514 (1980), is illustrative. The buyers lost their commitment for a mortgage with an interest rate of 8¾% when the seller refused to convey. The buyers succeeded in obtaining specific performance but were compelled to borrow funds at 11½%. They were awarded the difference reduced to present value. * * * The particular realty might well be a secondary and incidental consideration for the loan. Therefore an interest differential occasioned by the seller's default might be a proper factor in fixing damages where the buyer shortly thereafter purchased another property financed at a higher interest rate.

This is not such a situation. The defendant's motive was to sell a house and not to lend money. In measuring the plaintiffs' loss there should be a determination of the fair market value of the property and house that could be acquired with a purchase money mortgage in the principal amount of $44,000 at an interest rate of 10½% (no appeal was taken from the judgment of reformation) for a 30–year term. The valuation should be at the time the defendant failed to comply with the judgment of specific performance. The plaintiffs would be entitled to the difference between $58,900 and that fair market value. If the fair market value was not more than the contract price, the plaintiffs would not have established any damage ascribable to the loss of the bargain. They are also entitled to their expenditures for the survey, search, and counsel fees for services rendered in preparation of the aborted closing. The plaintiffs have hitherto received the return of the deposit.

The judgment of the Appellate Division is modified and, as so modified, remanded to the trial court for further proceedings consistent with this opinion.

O'HERN, J., dissenting.

I must respectfully dissent from the opinion and judgment of the Court. The issue is whether out of pocket costs or benefit of the bargain damages are to be awarded for breach of an executory contract for the sale of real estate when the contract does not close because of a defect in title unknown to the seller at the time of execution of the contract.

Although commentators advocate the adoption of the "American rule" as suggested by the majority, there remains sufficient flexibility in the rule that would except its application to the circumstances of this case. While both Williston and Corbin suggest that the only rule defensible on principle is allowing the purchaser the difference between the contract price and the market value of the land, it is put this way: the rule "is applied in every case where the vendor *breaks* his contract without legal excuse." [Citations.] Most of the recent American cases cited in both treatises do not sustain a conclusion that such a rule would be applied to a case where the seller was wholly without fault with respect to the existence of a defect in title that prevents closing.

* * *

I would adhere to the rule that an award of damages should be just under the circumstances. * * * As originally stated the English rule would not allow recovery of benefit of the bargain under any circumstances, whether with or without fault on the part of the seller, the seller's liability being limited to recovery in an action at law where fraud or deceit is involved for the loss he may sustain thereby. [Citations.]

* * *

If any modifications of existing law were to be made under the circumstances of this case, I would recommend that the Court follow the recommendations of the Commissioners on Uniform State Laws. They suggest the adoption of a rule that better conforms with prevailing American decisional law and reflects a "just method of determining damages." Zeliff v. Sabatino, 15 N.J. at 74, 104 A.2d 54. That rule is stated as follows:

Section 2–510 [Buyer's Damages for Seller's Failure to Convey]

(a) Except as provided in subsection (b), the measure of damages for a seller's repudiation or wrongful failure to convey is the difference between the fair market value at the time for conveyance and the contract price and any incidental and consequential damages (Section 2–514), less expenses avoided because of the seller's breach.

(b) Unless the title defect is an encumbrance securing an obligation to pay money which could be discharged by application of all or a portion of the purchase price, if a seller is unable to convey because of a title defect of which the seller had no knowledge at the time of entering into the contract, the buyer is entitled only to restitution of any amounts paid on the contract price and incidental damages (Section 2–514). [Unif. Land Transactions Act § 2–510, 13 U.L.A. 638 (1980)].

If I were to reach the issue of increased financing costs, I would agree with the majority that such are appropriate for consideration.

STRATTON v. TEJANI

139 Cal.App.3d 204, 187 Cal.Rptr. 231 (1982).

WIENER, ACTING PRESIDING JUSTICE.

This controversy centers on the attempt by James W. and Patricia M. Stratton (Strattons) to buy the single family residence owned by Nasir and Sabira Tejani (Tejanis). After the escrow between the parties failed to close on March 2, 1981, the Tejanis filed their complaint for unlawful detainer and for damages measured by the reasonable rental value of the residence for the period the Strattons remained in possession. The Strattons sued the Tejanis for specific performance and for incidental damages.

The Strattons prevailed in both actions which were consolidated for trial. The trial court ordered the Tejanis to complete the sale of the residence through the pending escrow within 60 days from notice of entry of judgment at the agreed price of $225,000 with the Strattons to pay interest on that sum at 16 percent per annum from March 2, 1981 until the close of escrow. The court also ordered the Strattons to pay the Tejanis rent at the reasonable monthly rate of $1,250 for the same period. Both parties have appealed. The Tejanis challenge the entire judgment. The Strattons complain only about the award of 16 percent interest on the purchase price and the failure of the court to award incidental damages for the higher interest payments they will have to make on their real estate loan as a result of the Tejanis' breach.

We affirm the judgments for specific performance and unlawful detainer. We decide, however, the court erred in charging the Strattons with both rent and interest on the purchase price. Established equitable principles require the parties be placed in the same positions they would have been in had the contract been timely performed. Accordingly, the Strattons are entitled to credit for rent less the reasonable value of their use of any retained purchase funds. The Tejanis, in turn, are entitled to interest on the entire purchase price less any sums the Strattons committed irrevocably and with notice towards the purchase price, but not in an amount exceeding the total rent. We also decide a buyer in a specific performance action is entitled to incidental damages for increased financing costs caused by the seller's breach. If after this appeal the interest rate on the Strattons' real estate loan is higher than it would have been had the escrow timely closed, the trial court shall have discretion to determine whether those damages are best calculated by (1) computing the difference between interest rates for the term of the loan for the time period the Strattons will reasonably occupy the residence and discounting that sum to its present cash value, (2) the difference in market value of the residence, if any, caused by the higher rate of interest, or (3) another method consistent with the guidelines outlined in this opinion.

* * *

In accordance with the judgment of specific performance, the Tejanis are entitled to receive the full performance of their contract with the Strattons. [Citations.] However, because execution of that judgment will occur at a date substantially after the date of performance provided by the contract, financial adjustments must be made to relate their performance back to the contract date. [Citation.] First, when a buyer is deprived of possession of the property pending resolution of the dispute and the seller receives rents and profits, the buyer is entitled to a credit against the purchase price for the rents and profits from the time the property should have been conveyed to him. [Citations.] "The concept of this monetary award to the buyer is *not* to give the buyer *damages* for the seller's breach of contract. Rather, it is designed to relate the performance back to the contract date of performance and to adjust the equities between the parties because of the delayed performance by the seller." [Citation.] Second, a seller also must be treated as if he had performed in a timely fashion and is entitled to receive the value of his lost use of the purchase money during the period performance was delayed. [Citations.] These adjustments are "more like an accounting between the parties than like an assessment of damages." [Citations.]

There are, however, some limitations on these general rules. First, the buyer may not receive both the profits and reasonable rental value of the property and the value derived from his use of purchase funds which were not irrevocably allocated toward the purchase price. The buyer must reduce his credit for rents and profits by a sum equivalent to the value of his use of the retained purchase funds. [Citation.] Second, if any part of the purchase price has been set aside by the buyer with notice to the seller, the seller may not receive credit for his lost use of those funds. [Citation.] Third, any award to the seller representing the value of his lost use of the purchase money cannot exceed the rents and profits awarded to the buyer, for otherwise the breaching seller would profit from his wrong. [Citations.]

Therefore, the trial court erred in charging the Strattons with both the reasonable monthly rental plus interest on the purchase price. The correct application of the foregoing rules requires the following: the Strattons should receive a credit against the purchase price for the reasonable rental value of the residence from March 5, 1981 until the close of escrow, less the reasonable value of their use of the $36,000 they did not deposit into escrow. The Tejanis are entitled to the reasonable value of their use of the entire purchase price less $9,000, the total of the option price and cash deposited into escrow, but not in an amount exceeding the total rent for the period performance was delayed.

In making these adjustments the trial court is not required to equate the reasonable value of the use of money with interest at the legal rate. Computing the value to the Strattons of their retained purchase funds and to the Tejanis of their lost purchase money should reflect the application of equitable considerations and not an award of legal damages. The proper yield on these sums can best be determined by the trial court in an evidentiary hearing in which each party can present evidence on the rate of interest paid by the Tejanis to maintain the trust deeds on the residence during the delay period, the Strattons' use of their retained purchase funds during this same period and the types of investments available to both parties for that period. Obviously, we cannot anticipate all the evidence the parties may seek to introduce on this issue. We defer to the trial court for the proper exercise of discretion in permitting the introduction of relevant evidence which will result in an equitable accounting for the intervening events during the period performance was delayed. [Citations.]

In addition to the accounting the parties must make to equitably adjust their offsetting claims, the Strattons claim they are also entitled to interest differential damages because they will now be obligated to pay interest on their 30–year real estate loan at a higher rate than they would have had to pay had escrow timely closed.

Obviously, one way of resolving this claim is to presume mortgage loan rates will be lower when this case is finally resolved than they were on March 5, 1981. Another solution is to dismiss this issue summarily as presenting a problem so complex that any effort to determine the damages which might possibly flow from the vagaries of the financing market is too speculative. [Citations.] We are reluctant to accept either approach for we believe a court must acknowledge the economic reality that if a seller's breach causes a buyer to pay interest on a real estate loan higher than the rate initially bargained for, then that buyer sustains damages for each dollar unnecessarily expended. Under such circumstances, the hard question is not whether there are damages, but the correct method to determine that sum so as to make the buyer whole.

Here, if the trial court determines the Strattons' financing costs will be higher after this appeal than they would have been had escrow closed on March 5, 1981, the court must determine the amount of that increase and award damages accordingly. In *Hutton v. Gliksberg* (1982) 128 Cal.App.3d 240, 180 Cal.Rptr. 141 such damages were computed by calculating the difference over the full term of the buyer's loan between interest rates at the time the contract should have been performed and at the time of trial and then discounting that amount to its present cash value. *Hutton* approved a $122,000 damage award for the present cash value of the interest difference between a 14 percent and a 9¼ percent loan of $400,000 extending over 30 years. In our view, however, this approach lacks an underlying factual basis. Residential real property typically is held for only seven to ten years. If, in this case, the Strattons sell the residence shortly after escrow closes, interest differential damages calculated under the *Hutton* formula would amount to a windfall if that differential does not cause them to sell at a reduced price. Accordingly, we believe a preferable solution is to require the trial court to determine factually how long the Strattons will remain in possession. As real estate licensees did they buy the property for investment purposes and now intend to market it within the next year or so? Or, in light of personal circumstances, do they intend to retain it as their permanent residence for the duration of their loan? The resolution of this question is no more onerous than fact determinations in other types of cases. Once answered, the present cash value for the interest differential should be awarded for the Strattons' anticipated time of possession rather than for the life of their loan.

If, however, the trial court is unable to factually resolve this question, other solutions are available. For example, on the basis of evidence presented the court may be able to isolate the difference in market value, if any, caused by the residence bearing a real estate loan at a higher rate of interest. This sum would then be a credit in favor of the Strattons against the purchase price through escrow. In any event, we leave it to the discretion of the trial court to select a method of calculating interest differential damages, if any, consistent with the guidelines outlined in this opinion.

* * *

———

1. Compare the principal case with Smith v. American Motor Inns of Florida, 538 F.2d 1090 (5th Cir.1976), where the court addressed the problems of adjustment in an accounting action following rescission of a contract to sell a motel. The court determined that the seller was entitled to charge the buyer for the rental value for the period during which the buyer had operated the motel. The buyer received a credit for

the actual value of improvements made to the property during occupancy, and received credit for payments made on the motel mortgage and the land lease.

2. When a seller breaches a land sale contract, should courts award damages to compensate for the buyer's increased financing costs such as higher mortgage rates? In *Stratton* the court held that damages for the present cash value for the interest rate differential was appropriate while a similar claim was denied in *Donovan*. Should it matter that in *Stratton* the buyer also was awarded specific performance? Do you agree with the *Donovan* opinion that the financing aspect of a real estate transaction plays only an incidental role? Which view more accurately gives the aggrieved buyer the benefit of the bargain?

3. In Smith v. Mady, 146 Cal.App.3d 129, 194 Cal.Rptr. 42 (1983), the sellers contracted to sell a residence for $205,000 but the buyer defaulted. Within a few days after the breach the sellers entered into a second contract to sell the property to third parties for $215,000. The rapid resale established that the market value of the property at the time of the breach exceeded the contract price, thus precluding the sellers from recovering damages for loss of benefit of the bargain. The sellers also sought consequential damages for miscellaneous costs of insurance, taxes, utilities, and interest payments incurred between the default and the subsequent resale. The court held that defaulting buyer should receive a credit for the higher proceeds received in the resale against the damages liability. The rationale was that the seller otherwise would receive a windfall if the offset was denied. Do you agree?

In order to reach its result the court concluded that the two sales were not inherently separate. What if the resale had taken place six months after the breach instead of just a few days?

4. When a sale of land is in gross, meaning by the tract, the vendor generally will not be liable for a deficiency in acreage absent fraud in the transaction. Conversely, where the sale is on a per acre basis, a court will charge the vendor with damages to reflect the deficiency. In Hagenbuch v. Chapin, 149 Ill.App.3d 572, 102 Ill.Dec. 886, 500 N.E.2d 987 (1986), for example, the purchasers of a farm at auction brought suit for damages against the sellers for a deficiency in acreage. The court noted that the presumption that sales are by the acre could be rebutted only by clear and convincing proof. Although the farm was offered for sale as a single, undivided parcel and the notice of sale at public auction described the land as "129 acres, more or less," the court held that it was not a sale in gross because the bidding was done on a per acre basis. Damages were awarded against the vendors for the 6 acre deficiency. *See also* Boswell v. Bryans, 159 Ga.App. 724, 285 S.E.2d 74 (1981).

Chapter 11

TORT DAMAGES

The function of a damages remedy in tort cases is to make the injured party whole by substituting money for tangible and intangible losses caused by the tort. In contrast, the orientation of restitution is to disgorge those benefits which the law considers it unjust for the defendant to retain. The difference in orientation of these remedies may produce different dollar amounts.

This chapter focuses exclusively on the damages remedy for torts and presents the recurring remedial themes for the most commonly suffered losses. It is divided into sections representing types of injuries to legally protected rights: personal property, real property, personal injury, and wrongful death/survival. These categories do not form an exhaustive list of rights for which tort damages are available, but they are the most common ones. Chapter 14 includes some other types of injuries that present special remedial problems and for which damages in tort are only sometimes available, such as emotional distress without personal injury and economic losses without physical injury.

Although the primary goal of tort damages is adequate compensation, other goals must be considered in choosing the measure of damages. One goal is economic efficiency and the avoidance of waste; another interest is the promotion of out-of-court settlements by fixing a predictable and objective measure of damages. In circumstances where a tension develops between apparently conflicting goals, courts will try to achieve appropriate compromises. Jurisdictions have formulated slightly different rules as a result of the process of resolving these conflicting interests, and the rules are subject to exceptions that constantly evolve. Tort damage law rules are confusing and meaningless without an understanding of the unifying principles that govern them and the conflicts in remedial goals that change them. This chapter addresses those principles and conflicts.

A. DAMAGES FOR INJURIES TO PERSONALTY

Section Coverage:

Tortious injury to personalty presents two major remedial issues. First, what losses are compensable? Second, how should the losses be measured? Resolution of these issues traditionally requires drawing a distinction between property that has been completely destroyed and property that is capable of repair. The difference between these two categories can be a thin line at times. It is a finding of fact whether the chattel can be repaired, and legal consequences follow accordingly.

What losses related to personal property are recoverable? A plaintiff can recover the value of a destroyed chattel at the time and place of its destruction. Injury without destruction also produces compensable losses to the chattel itself. Plaintiffs may or may not recover for the loss of the use of the property, however, before it can be replaced or repaired. Many jurisdictions follow a rule that allows loss of use awards only for injured chattel but not for those which are destroyed.

Courts generally agree that losses associated with personalty must be objective ones; consequently plaintiffs cannot recover for emotional injuries caused by the loss of items with sentimental value. Measurement of objective losses also poses difficulties. For example, should the measure of damages for a reparably injured chattel be the cost of its repair or the diminution in its value? Sometimes these measures produce the same dollar amount, but sometimes they do not. Jurisdictions vary in approach.

Another measurement problem arises with unique, irreplaceable goods such as family papers, photographs, or heirlooms. When there is no readily ascertainable fair market value, the court takes evidence on the personal value of the destroyed chattel to the plaintiff. The evidentiary problem is to establish some reasonable basis for a valuation.

Model Case:

Stuart is a graduate student who was involved in a car accident caused by the negligence of another driver. He was returning to campus in his car for the beginning of the fall semester at the time. Stuart's car was loaded with his personal possessions. The car itself was damaged but capable of repair. Things packed in the trunk survived the accident, but items in the back seat were severely damaged. Most of Stuart's clothes were destroyed; a stereo system was badly damaged; and a handmade quilt was partially damaged.

The clothes cannot be salvaged. The stereo can be fixed, but at a cost greater than the fair market value as a used system. The quilt could be repaired only by hand, at great cost. Even when repaired, the quilt would never be in as good a condition as it was prior to the accident. Nonetheless, Stuart wishes to have the quilt repaired because it was a present from his now deceased grandmother. She had made it while he was in college and presented it to him when he first left for graduate school two years ago.

Car: Courts vary in whether to measure damages for the car by cost of repair or by diminution in value. The difference in orientation often does not produce different results, but sometimes it does. *Clothes:* The general rule of valuation for personal property damaged beyond repair is the fair market value at the time and place of destruction. A few consumer items, such as clothes, escape this rule. Under this exception Stuart may be able to recover the value of the clothing to him personally rather than just its low value as used clothes. *Stereo:* If the stereo cannot be repaired for less than it is worth, then arguably it is in the "destroyed" category rather than the "reparable" one. Even if the court finds it capable of repair, however, the general rule is that damages for a reparable item cannot exceed its pre-tort fair market value as a used chattel. *Quilt:* The ceiling of fair market value presents a greater problem with items that have relatively low market value yet have a significant sentimental value to the owner. Although courts are in agreement that Stuart could not recover separately for the sentimental value of the quilt, should that sentiment at least allow repair damages? This issue is not well resolved in most jurisdictions. Should it matter if the repairs to the quilt are actually made before trial? Under existing rules in most jurisdictions Stuart would receive no more than the fair market value of the quilt.

LONG v. McALLISTER

319 N.W.2d 256 (Iowa 1982).

McCORMICK, JUSTICE.

This tort action arose from a dispute concerning adjustment of motor vehicle property damage under the liability coverage of the tortfeasor's insurance policy. In entering summary judgment for defendants, the trial court limited plaintiff's recovery to the reasonable value of his automobile at the time it was damaged. * * *

Plaintiff Arthur Long's automobile was damaged on October 19, 1978, when a farm wagon of defendants Dan McAllister and McAllister Seed Company, Inc., rolled down an incline and struck it. These defendants had property damage liability insurance covering the loss with defendant I.M.T. Insurance Company and another insurer. Although I.M.T. obtained repair estimates from plaintiff shortly after the occurrence, thirty-three days passed before the insurers agreed between themselves on how the loss would be shared. Eight days later I.M.T. offered plaintiff $1250 to settle the loss in behalf of McAllister and the seed company. No dispute existed concerning liability or the fact the vehicle was damaged beyond repair.

After first agreeing to the settlement, plaintiff later in the same day rejected it as inadequate. Eventually plaintiff employed an attorney who demanded $1500 in settlement. I.M.T. raised its offer to $1300 but received no response. * * *

[Plaintiff sued for $1300 as the fair market value of the car and for $500 as the cost of renting a substitute vehicle during the time he waited for the adjustment. The trial court refused to allow the $500 cost of renting a car on the grounds that loss of use damages were not appropriate.]

Loss of use damages. In denying damages for loss of use of the destroyed automobile, the trial court followed existing precedent. *See, e.g.,* Aetna Casualty and Surety Co. v. Insurance Department of Iowa, 299 N.W.2d 484, 485 (Iowa 1980):

(1) When the automobile is totally destroyed, the measure of damages is its reasonable market value immediately before its destruction.

(2) Where the injury to the car can be repaired, so that, when repaired, it will be in as good condition as it was in before the injury, then the measure of damages is the reasonable value of the use of the car while being repaired, with ordinary diligence, not exceeding the value of the car before the injury.

(3) When the car cannot, by repair, be placed in as good condition as it was in before the injury, then the measure of damages is the difference between its reasonable market value immediately before and immediately after the accident.

These rules were first distilled in Langham v. Chicago, R.I. & P. R., 201 Iowa 897, 901, 208 N.W. 356, 358 (1925). The court expressly held that loss of use damages are not allowed under the first and third rules in Kohl v. Arp, 236 Iowa 31, 33–34, 17 N.W.2d 824, 826 (1945).

The rule denying loss of use damages in these situations has not been specifically discussed in the cases. Because the rule has been challenged in the present case, we must determine its continued viability. We do so against the background "that the principle underlying allowance of damages is that of compensation, the ultimate purpose being to place the injured party in as favorable a position as though no wrong had been committed." Dealers Hobby, Inc. v. Marie Ann Linn Realty Co., 255 N.W.2d 131, 134 (Iowa 1977).

Inherent in our present rules governing damages to motor vehicles is the concept that the market value of the vehicle is the ceiling on recovery whether the vehicle can be repaired or must be replaced. In some cases the owner will be fully compensated despite that limitation. Even when the vehicle is destroyed and delay occurs before compensation is received, interest on the market value of the vehicle from the date of the accident theoretically pays the owner for the delay. The same is true when the vehicle is not destroyed but cannot be restored to its prior condition and the owner receives interest on its depreciated value. Moreover, when the vehicle can be restored by repair to its prior condition, the owner is not only entitled to compensation for the reasonable cost of repair but for reasonable loss of use damages. Although market value is nevertheless a ceiling on recovery even in this situation, full compensation is possible when the cumulated damages do not exceed the limitation.

In other cases, however, the present rules plainly do not permit full compensation. Loss of use damages will be incurred as readily when a vehicle is totally destroyed or when it cannot be restored by repair to its prior condition as when the vehicle can be restored by repair. Just as loss of use damages are necessary for full compensation when the vehicle can be restored to its prior condition, they are warranted when the vehicle is destroyed or cannot be so restored. No logical basis exists for cutting them off when the total reaches the vehicle's market value before the injury.

The origin of the market value limitation lies in history rather than logic. Damages for destruction of chattels were based on analogy to conversion. The reasonable market value of the chattel was viewed as adequate compensation under this concept in the common law action of trover. The rigidity of the analogy obscured any distinction between destruction of chattels generally and destruction of chattels of such utility that the owners incurred loss of use expense. Perhaps this distinction became important only with the advent of the motor vehicle and the practice of motor vehicle leasing and rental.

The historical basis and usual arguments for denying loss of use damages are addressed in D. Dobbs, *Remedies* § 5.11 at 384–85 (1973) (footnotes omitted):

> * * * There was probably some thought that the market value of the chattel—which reflected the right to use it gainfully—plus interest for the time the owner was deprived of it, actually furnished full compensation. Another argument made against granting loss of use where there was total destruction sounds rather strange in modern ears. The authors of Sedgwick on Damages argued that when compensation for the whole value of the property destroyed is sought, "it is upon the theory that the plaintiff's entire interest in the property ceased at the time of the injury, and was replaced by a right to have the value of the property in money. Since therefore, the plaintiff no longer has title to the property he can no longer claim that he might make a future gain from it ....." Such an argument probably would not be accepted, or even thought of, today. It is a conceptual argument that does not interest itself in whether the owner has actually lost something of value beyond the market value of his property; it interests itself only in a legal concept— passage of title—that is not a part of the real world of facts and has no significant relation to important facts of actual loss. * * *

The fallacy in the market value ceiling upon recovery in a destruction case was pinpointed in Bartlett v. Garrett, 130 N.J.Super. 193, 196, 325 A.2d 866, 867 (1974):

> When an automobile is damaged through the negligence of another, temporary loss of the use of such vehicle pending repair or replacement is a reasonably foreseeable consequence of the defendant's tortious conduct. Compensation for the temporary loss of use is directed at plaintiff's *economic loss,* the amount of money plaintiff had to pay for rental of a car. This is an injury different in kind from *property damage,* the amount of money necessary to repair or replace the damaged vehicle. A plaintiff in a total destruction case deprived of his reasonable loss-of-use expenses has simply not been made whole. (emphasis in original).

* * *

We believe our motor vehicle damages rules should be modified to permit full compensation including loss of use damages. The new rules shall apply to this case, any pending case in which error has been preserved on the issue, and all cases tried after the date of filing this opinion. As modified, the rules are as follows:

(1) When the motor vehicle is totally destroyed or the reasonable cost of repair exceeds the difference in reasonable market value before and after the injury, the measure of damages is the lost market value plus the reasonable value of the use of the vehicle for the time reasonably required to obtain a replacement.

(2) When the injury to the motor vehicle can be repaired so that, when repaired, it will be in as good condition as it was in before the injury, and the cost of repair does not exceed the difference in market value of the vehicle before and after the injury, then the measure of damages is the reasonable cost of repair plus the reasonable value of the use of the vehicle for the time reasonably required to complete its repair.

(3) When the motor vehicle cannot by repair be placed in as good condition as it was in before the injury, then the measure of damages is the difference between its reasonable market value before and after the injury, plus the reasonable value of the use of the vehicle for the time reasonably required to repair or replace it.

In the present case, plaintiff alleged loss of use damages but did not get an opportunity to prove them because of the adjudication of law points denying their availability. We reverse the adjudication and order that plaintiff be accorded a trial on the issue upon demand.

* * *

---

1. As the principal case indicates, the usual measure of damages for the total destruction of a chattel is the fair market value at the time and place of destruction. This rule applies both to intentional and negligent destruction, because the focus of damage law is on the loss to the plaintiff rather than upon the degree of the defendant's culpability. If the defendant has behaved outrageously, then punitive damages (*see* Chapter 15) or some form of restitution (*see* Chapter 16) may be appropriate.

2. The fair market value rule for the loss of personal property has been the traditional measure also for conversion cases. In conversion the defendant may or may not actually destroy the property, because the gist of the action is that the defendant deprived the plaintiff of control of the chattel. Loss of control can be by destruction of the chattel when it is wrongfully or accidentally in the defendant's possession, or it can be intentional by theft.

The law of conversion considers the serious interference with possession and control to constitute a "forced sale" of the chattel at the time and place converted. If the defendant subsequently improves the value of the goods and the conversion was deemed "willful" or in bad faith, a court may award the increased value as damages. If a withheld item is not destroyed and the plaintiff wants it back, the appropriate remedy is replevin.

3. Loss of use claims are commonly allowed when a chattel is being repaired. When a consumer item like a car is totally destroyed, a plaintiff typically needs to rent a substitute during the time it takes to buy a replacement car. Traditionally the damage rule was to disallow such loss of use claims when property was totally destroyed rather than injured. Some courts have recognized the similarity between renting substitutes during repair time and during replacement time, especially for automobiles. Since World War II the trend of state courts has been to allow loss of use damages also in destruction cases. *See* Annot., "Recovery for Loss of Use of Motor Vehicle Damaged or Destroyed," 18 A.L.R.3d 497 (1968). The view allowing loss of use damages in destruction cases is endorsed by the *Restatement (Second) of Torts* § 927 (1979).

IRVING PULP & PAPER, LIMITED v. DUNBAR TRANSFER & STORAGE CO.

732 F.2d 511 (6th Cir.1984).

CONTIE, CIRCUIT JUDGE.

Defendant Mid–America Distribution Centers, Inc. (MADC) appeals from a $60,000 judgment in favor of plaintiff Irving Pulp & Paper, Ltd. (Irving Pulp), for damages to plaintiff's wood pulp while in the possession of MADC. MADC also appeals from the award of $14,613.00 to Irving Pulp for storage charges incurred by the plaintiff and the award of prejudgment interest on a portion of the total damage award. * * * [W]e affirm in part, reverse in part, and remand to the district court for further proceedings.

The plaintiff, Irving Pulp, is a manufacturer of wood products and is located in Saint John, New Brunswick, Canada. MADC is a Tennessee corporation and a wholly-owned subsidiary of Dunbar Transfer & Storage Co., Inc. At all relevant times, MADC was engaged in the warehousing business. In November 1976, Irving Pulp contracted with MADC to store approximately 8,640 bales of bleached softwood kraft wood pulp in six interconnected warehouses in Memphis, Tennessee. These warehouses were being leased by MADC from Belz Investment Company, Inc. (Belz), and were located near one of Irving Pulp's major customers, Kimberly Clark Corporation (Kimberly Clark). * * * After the contract was executed, the record indicates that the wood pulp arrived at the warehouses in good condition.

On September 13, 1977, the roof on warehouse No. 4 collapsed during a heavy rainstorm. The record indicates that the 1,320 bales of wood pulp located in warehouse No. 4 came in contact with a great deal of dirt and gravel from the collapsed roof. In addition, the pulp in warehouse No. 4 and the adjacent warehouses suffered additional water damage due to the frequent rainfall which occurred after the collapse. * * *

On September 12, 1977, one day prior to the collapse, Irving Pulp had contracted with Kimberly Clark to sell the wood pulp located in the six warehouses at the then prevailing market price of $340 per ton, less a standard discount. This produced a contract price of $556,607.62. Approximately three and one-half months after the collapse, the sales agreement was renegotiated to take into account the unusable wood pulp and the unexpected drop in market price. Accordingly, the pulp was sold to Kimberly Clark in January 1978 at the new market price of $300 per ton, less the standard discount and an additional 17.5% discount for the unusable pulp. The new contract price was $405,177.64. The record also indicates that Irving Pulp paid MADC a total of $14,613.00 in storage charges for the period from September 1977 to March 1978.

* * *

Having determined that MADC is liable for all the damage to the wood pulp, we now address the issue of damages. Irving Pulp contends that it should recover $151,429.98, or the difference between the September 12, 1977 contract price—$556,607.62—and the January 1978 sale price—$405,177.64. MADC contends that Irving Pulp's damages claim should be reduced by $65,483.29 to account for the January 1978 reduction in market price. MADC explains that it should not be liable for any loss arising from the drop in market price because the wood pulp was available for resale prior to January 1978.

The district court correctly held that the ordinary and basic measure of damages for injury to personalty is the difference between its market value immediately before and immediately after the injury. [Citation.] Application of this rule would preclude Irving Pulp from recovering its losses arising from the January 1978 market price reduction. We believe, however, that this measure of damages would not fully compensate Irving Pulp for the losses which are the proximate result of MADC's negligent conduct. [Citation.] Following the roof collapse, Irving Pulp could not ascertain the extent of the damage to the wood pulp until after the roof had been completely removed from the pulp. The record indicates, however, that MADC did not complete this task until November 29, 1977, or over six weeks after the collapse. Once the roof was removed, Irving Pulp completed its inspection of the wood pulp and quickly negotiated a new sales agreement with Kimberly Clark. Although Irving Pulp acted with due diligence, the new contract was not completed until after the market price had fallen. We believe that Irving Pulp's ability to promptly renegotiate an agreement with Kimberly Clark was significantly hampered by MADC's failure to remove the roof in an expeditious fashion. As a result, we hold that Irving Pulp's loss arising from the January 1978 market price reduction was the proximate result of MADC's negligent conduct in failing to remove the roof sooner and that Irving Pulp is entitled to recover the full $151,-429.98 in damages.

MADC also contends that the district court erred in awarding $14,613.00 to Irving Pulp for storage charges paid by Irving Pulp after the collapse. MADC argues that Irving Pulp is not entitled to receive both its consideration for the bailment contract and compensatory damages for MADC's breach of that contract.

This argument is misleading because it assumes that Irving Pulp would have continued to store its pulp in MADC's warehouses after the date of the collapse. This is simply not true. The record indicates that Irving Pulp had sold the wood pulp to Kimberly Clark and that, had the warehouse roof not collapsed, the pulp would have been shipped from the warehouses shortly after the date of sale. Although we agree that MADC is entitled to receive the entire storage fee for September 1977, the month of the collapse, we hold that MADC is not entitled to retain storage fees for the subsequent months which accrued solely as a result of MADC's negligent conduct. * * *

[Remanded.]

———

1. Why should it matter to the damages calculation that the defendant MADC did not remove the roof in an expeditious fashion to allow Irving Pulp to renegotiate a contract? Should Irving Pulp be foreclosed from recovering the difference in contract price once some period of time has passed after the roof was removed? Why should the risk of a further fall in the market price even be shifted from the defendant back to the plaintiff?

2. Similar valuation issues have occurred in cases involving conversion of chattels with fluctuating value, including stocks and commodities. Jurisdictions have adopted a variety of conventions for valuation, such as highest value between time of conversion and a fixed date like filing suit, trial, or verdict. The "New York rule" focuses upon a reasonable time for replacement; a plaintiff is allowed the highest value between the time of conversion (or notice of conversion) and a reasonable time for replacement. Why should it matter if a plaintiff is diligent about replacement? Should a plaintiff be allowed to wait out the market while the defendant absorbs the risk of a falling market? Should it matter if a plaintiff actually replaces a converted commodity?

LANE v. OIL DELIVERY, INC.

216 N.J.Super. 413, 524 A.2d 405 (1987).

MUIR, JR., J.A.D.

Defendant appeals and plaintiffs cross appeal from a judgment entered on a jury verdict in favor of plaintiffs which was subsequently

molded and corrected by the trial court into a $278,677.20 judgment
* * *.

On August 10, 1983, plaintiffs, William and Betty Lane, and the
American National Fire Insurance Company filed a complaint against
defendant, Oil Delivery, Inc. The complaint and its later amendment
sought damages for losses incurred by the Lanes in a fire at their home.
* * *

The jury set the Lanes' damages at $425,985. This figure repre-
sented the total losses claimed for house reconstruction, living expenses
during reconstruction, loss of jewelry and personalty replacement costs.
The Lanes set out the personalty replacement costs in a 30–page list.
Prior to their testimony on the value of the personalty, the trial judge
ruled the measure of damages should be the market value at the time of
the fire.

The value of personalty the jury accepted came from a total of the
figures on the 30–page list. On that list, the Lanes set forth each item
of personalty and their estimated value or the actual cost of the item. In
their testimony, they did not state how they arrived at the value for each
item. Instead, they selected an apparent cross section of the items.

As to the value of items specifically covered, Mr. Lane set the value
based on his experience in buying the articles in the past, pricing them
at stores or in newspaper ads. Mrs. Lane, who testified essentially on
her clothing and furniture in the house, based her opinion on her
experience as the owner of a retail clothing store and as supervisor of
charity flea markets.

* * *

The measure of damages for personalty destroyed by a tortfeasor,
when there is a market value, is the market value at the time of the loss.
[Citations.]

When, however, the personalty is household furnishings and wearing apparel and the like, where the market value cannot be ascertained,
the better measure of damages and the one we find applicable in this
case, is the actual or intrinsic value of the property to the owner,
excluding sentimental or fanciful value. [Citations.]

The rationale for such a rule is consonant with the goal of tort
damages to fully compensate the injured party, thereby making it
possible to replace the lost property with a comparable substitute. The
market value of wearing apparel and household furnishings cannot
compensate the owner for their loss. While there may be a second-hand
market value, other items of equal value are not interchangeable. As
noted in *4 Damages in Tort Actions* (MB) § 37.22[a]:

> The average owner will not replace lost clothing or furniture
> with secondhand merchandise, but will instead be "forced" to pur-
> chase new substitutes. Consequently, the second hand price does
> not provide adequate compensation for the loss sustained.

That is not to say the plaintiff is entitled to full replacement cost. [Citation.] While the element of original cost is relevant, depreciation, age, wear and tear, condition, cost of replacement and cost of repair are all factors to be considered in assessing the damage sustained. [Citation.]

Where an item is brand new, proof of original cost sustains the owner's burden of proof as to value. [Citation.] Further, while the cost of repair may be the sole proof of damages, depreciation of a repaired object, adequately established, may be an additional relevant factor. [Citation.]

Proof of damages need not be done with exactitude, particularly when dealing with household furnishings and wearing apparel. It is therefore sufficient that the plaintiff prove damages with such certainty as the nature of the case may permit, laying a foundation which will enable the trier of the facts to make a fair and reasonable estimate. [Citation.]

In providing such evidence, the plaintiff, as owner, may give an opinion of worth although he or she is without expert knowledge. [Citation.] The basis for arriving at the opinion must, however, not be a matter of speculation and the witness must be required to establish the grounds for any opinion given. It is for the jury, with appropriate instructions from the court, to ascertain the probative value of the opinion. * * *

[Remanded.]

CAMPINS v. CAPELS

461 N.E.2d 712 (Ind.App.1984).

MILLER, JUDGE.

[The plaintiffs (Capels) brought suit for treble damages pursuant to a state criminal mischief statute against Campins alleging that the defendant's store had unlawfully purchased and subsequently destroyed certain jewelry which had been stolen from the plaintiffs by a third party (Hall). The trial court held Campins liable under the statute and computed the damages as follows:

3 USAC award rings at $1,000 each	=	$ 3,000
1 Free design wedding band at $700 each	=	$ 700
TOTAL		$ 3,700
Application of Treble Damages		× 3
TOTAL		$11,100.

Defendant appealed, asserting that the damages awarded by the trial court were excessive. The court of appeals affirmed the finding of liability and then addressed the measurement of the value of the jewelry.]

* * *

After presenting evidence of Campins's liability, the Capelses presented evidence of the value of their rings. Mrs. Capels's wedding band, having been recently appraised at $700, was easily valuated. The USAC rings, for which the Capelses had requested $350 apiece in their complaint, proved a different matter.

The three USAC rings at issue here had been awarded to Capels in 1972, 1977, and 1978. (He had won five in all.) Each ring signified a national championship earned in a particular automobile category and given to the car's owner and the driver. In 1972, Parnelli Jones gave Capels his owner's ring in appreciation for his work as chief mechanic of Jones's Indy car. Capels later won his 1977 and 1978 rings as the actual owner of championship dirt division cars, driven by Bill Vukovich and Pancho Carter. The 1972 ring signified Capels's work as supervisor of what the media labelled a "super team" after having been instrumental in winning three straight Indy car championships (1970, 1971, 1972). As for his own owner's rings, they represented the large financial investment as well as time required to excel in any division of USAC competition. Sentimentally, Capels described these rings as being enduring symbols of his accomplishments and USAC's recognition thereof. Throughout his testimony, his feelings for these rings were apparent:

* * *

"I paid for them in blood or sweat, more or less.... To me, those rings had a value of being presented before many people at an awards banquet for an accomplishment at the time, and they were personal artifacts, and I would never ever feel the same if I just went down and hired somebody to replace my rings for me."

Record, p. 30.

"Made me feel real well, it meant, it meant that I felt like that at one time, I was good enough to have been the champion mechanic, and I was proud of it."

Record, p. 31. There was also more concrete evidence for use in affixing monetary values to the rings.

Each heavy, gold ring bore a synthetic stone and had been molded to display the USAC emblem, the name of the recipient, the specific achievement being rewarded, and the year of that achievement. They were custom-made annually by Josten's with a different design each year. Capels specifically testified there was no market for these rings: "You can't buy these rings from any gift shop or jewelry store or anything." Record, p. 26. Capels admitted that in 1977, he purchased a duplicate of his 1977 ring for a business associate for $349, and Campins himself testified the price of gold at the time of the theft was double that of at least 1979, from $300 to $580–$600. Capels went on to testify he would not have sold the rings, even for $1,500 or $2,000 apiece. He then estimated their worth as between $700 and $1000, finally settling on $750 when asked to be specific.

* * *

When personal property is the subject of an award, damages are measured by its fair market value at the time of the loss, fair market value being the price a willing seller will accept from a willing buyer. [Citation.] Such appears to be the measure of worth for the twelve-diamond wedding band, appraised at $700. This assessment has never really been contested by Campins; he mainly questions the value placed on the USAC rings. And to our knowledge, the problems raised in valuating them have never been addressed in Indiana.

Both parties have argued this issue in terms of the methods of valuating used household goods and wearing apparel. Such system would appear appropriate because used household goods and clothing have a greater actual value to their owners than they do on the secondhand market, similar to the problem here, where Capels's feelings about the rings as mementos outstrips his feelings for them as jewelry. Instead of allowing only the fair market value of secondhand goods, the court determines "the owner may recover the value of the goods to him, based on his actual money loss resulting from his being deprived of the property, or the difference in actual value caused by the injury *excluding fanciful or sentimental values which he might place on them.*" [Citations.] And, indeed, this standard is prevalent throughout the diverse jurisdictions. [Citation.] We believe that standard is useful but not altogether appropriate to the problem here.

First of all, jewelry is neither a household good, nor wearing apparel. [Citations.] Thus, ordinarily, jewelry is valuated at its fair market value. [Citation.] However, these USAC rings were not ordinary jewelry and could not be bought and sold in a readily available market. Rather, they were coveted awards and symbols of certain achievements accomplished by very few, such awards not having many willing sellers and therefore no real market. These rings should be valued differently than other jewelry. *Cf.*, Alfred Atmore Pope Foundation, Inc. v. New York, New Haven & Hartford Railroad Co., (1927) 106 Conn. 423, 138 A. 444 (woodlands valuated as to their educational function, not for value as timber). This, therefore, is our starting point—how do we find jewelry's actual value to its owner when it has a high value for its extrinsic content but also has a primary function and a consequently raised value based on pure sentimentality?

We find a basis for proceeding in the fundamental reasoning behind awarding higher actual values to owners of used household goods and wearing apparel:

> "The underlying principle of universal application is that of fair and just compensation for the loss or damage sustained.... Where subordinate rules for the measure of damages [fair market value for personal property] run counter to the paramount rule of fair and just compensation, the former must yield to the principle underlying all such rules."

[Citation.]

As explained by a federal court,

> "Sometimes fair market value cannot be determined, or would be inadequate, as when for example, the article destroyed was unique or possessed qualities the special nature of which could only be appreciated by the owner. In such a case additional principles are helpful in determining proper compensation to the injured party."

[Citation.] Our departure from those household goods cases is because there is a presupposed second-hand market for such belongings and an actual value in their practicality and usefulness to the owner. In this case, the rings have *no* real market value, and their sentimental function increases the actual worth beyond the value of the materials. How can we accommodate this difference?

The emphasis in the cases where the actual value of the goods exceeded the market value or where there was no market value at all is upon looking at all the circumstances and the available elements of loss in a rational, reasonable fashion. * * * We believe the best method to ensure fairness to both parties is to receive a wide range of elements for consideration in the actual value. [Citations.] This range of evidence gives the trier of fact sufficient latitude to intelligently determine the amount of damages. Such elements that have been introduced and relied upon are often such typical factors as cost of replacement, original cost, and cost to reproduce. [Citations.] But our courts and juries have also examined elements of a less prosaic nature, such as the proposed use of woodland for a forestry course, uniqueness, the feelings of the owner, and the cost to build and decorate a room to match a single painting. [Citations.] We believe that sentimental value, in limited circumstances, is also such a consideration. [Citations.]

When we refer to sentimental value, we do not mean mawkishly emotional or unreasonable attachments to personal property. [Citation.] Rather, we are referring to the feelings generated by items of almost purely sentimental value, such as heirlooms, family papers and photographs, handicrafts, and trophies. [Citations.] What we are referring to basically are those items *generally* capable of generating sentimental feelings, not just emotions peculiar to the owner. In other words, any owner of these USAC rings would have similar feelings. The most apt analogy to our situation is that of the trophies. In two cases, courts have awarded damages based on the consideration of the "blood, sweat and tears" expended to win these objects. [Citations.] We see no difference in giving special consideration to items such as these and to the three USAC rings, awarded for three years of "blood, sweat and tears" and thus having special sentimental meaning for Capels. The question remains whether Capels's evidence supported the $3000 award.

Capels testified not only to the actual worth of the rings as mere pieces of custom-embossed gold but also to his emotional attachment to each. He described the pride and gratification he felt upon their ownership and elaborated on the effort required to win them. Actual estimates of their worth—to *him*—ranged from $700 to $1000 each;

however, he himself settled upon the $750 figure. Campins alternatively argues each ring was worth $67 (wholesale gold), $135–200 (retail gold), or $349 (replacement in 1977). We believe the evidence justified an award of $750.

The essential point is that the actual decision with regard to damages is a question for the trier of fact. [Citations.] And in establishing proof of loss, the complainant is less compelled to provide certainty in the *amount* of loss as he is to provide certainty in the actual *fact* of loss. [Citations.] In addition, no mathematical exactitude is required in assessing damages, and all uncertainties are resolved in favor of the claimant and against the wrongdoer. [Citation.] Such precepts are essential to keep in mind here because not only are we dealing with a piece of jewelry, but we are also dealing with the computation of a virtually unmeasurable mental process, sentiment. Thus, we are prone to giving greater latitude in the specificity of damages here just as we would in a case demanding an award for mental suffering. In such a case, the elements of the mental suffering are more important to this court than the failure to provide specific evidence of the actual amount awarded. The greatest scrutiny is given in comparing the elements with the award given to ascertain whether the fact-finder was motivated by prejudice, partiality, passion, or corruption and thereby made an excessive determination. [Citation.]

In light of the substantial evidence of the replacement value of the rings, the increase in the price of gold, and Capels's justifiable sentimental feelings, we would see no error in finding damages in the amount of $750 apiece. [Citations.]

However, while we ultimately conclude the court did not act erroneously in allowing an award in excess of the replacement value of the rings (based on the unique circumstances here and special attachment to this property), we can hardly deem it appropriate to fix a value higher than that asserted by the owner. Capels finally settled upon a figure of $750 per ring; the court's award of $1000 apiece could only have been improperly based on speculation. To decide otherwise would be to open a Pandora's box of problems in the computation and proof of actual value. By our decision here, we simply conclude that certain property, by its very nature, has an element of sentiment essential to its existence. In this case, we refer to symbols for achievements of national stature and recognition and the calculation of their actual value. But we must also add the proviso that even for significant awards or mementos we do not intend to permit fanciful speculation as to their worth. We must fashion our remedy within the realm of sensibility, as here, where $750 is only slightly above the established range of replacement values. Such would naturally also be our standard in valuating similar significant awards, such as an Oscar, the Heisman Trophy, or an Olympic medal, where the recipient retains the honor despite the loss of the trophy, such trophy being merely the symbol of the achievement and perhaps replaceable by a surrogate. A certain amount of sentiment is inherent in the value of these objects to the owner, and each case must be based on its own facts. But we must refrain from considering all but reasonable estimates of that element of sentiment. We believe in this case, Capels's $750 figure was just such a reasonable value of each ring with the sentiment included therein. We therefore affirm the judgment but modify the award.

* * *

———

1. In *Campins v. Capels* the court faced the problem of calculating what damages should be recoverable, if any, where personal property is damaged or destroyed as a result of the wrongful conduct of another but the items have no readily ascertainable fair market value. The jewelry, though, at least had some measurable intrinsic value, and the only additional stumbling block was whether to award increased damages for the sentimental value.

In Mieske v. Bartell Drug Co., 92 Wash.2d 40, 593 P.2d 1308 (1979), the court had a more difficult task of attempting to place a value on 32 reels of developed family movies which were negligently lost or destroyed by the defendant retailer's processing agent. The court stated that because the film had no market value and could not be replaced or reproduced, then the intrinsic value to the owner was the proper measure of damages. Although the court acknowledged the inherent imprecision in calculating damages where no market value existed, a jury award of $7,500 to the plaintiffs was affirmed. The court expressly rejected, however, any separate recovery for the sentimental value of the film.

Similarly, in Bond v. A.H. Belo Corp., 602 S.W.2d 105 (Tex.Civ.App. 1980), the court allowed recovery of damages for the negligent destruction of family papers and photographs. Is the distinction between "sentimental value" (non-recoverable) and "value to the owner" (recoverable) a valid one?

2. Plaintiffs may sometimes hold items such as used clothes or used furniture for business purposes. An owner of a second-hand shop, for example, would be fully compensated by an award for the market value of such items destroyed in a store fire. Similarly, an award of fair market value would fully compensate a used car dealer for the destruction of used cars if a large truck jumped the curb and rammed into the dealer's lot.

Consumers of clothes and cars are in a different position. As a practical matter they must replace destroyed items rather than simply adjust their balance sheets. Why not give replacement cost? Is replacement overcompensation for consumers? Could any windfall be eliminated by a deduction for the depreciation of the destroyed item? Is such an approach unmanageable for routine litigation concerning car crashes?

3. Even though consumers use both clothes and cars, the law distinguishes between them for damages; clothes may be valued at the personal value to the owner but cars are valued at fair market value. Why distinguish? Is it a sufficient answer that there is a greater market in used cars than used clothes or that the economic interchangeability may be ascertained with a higher degree of certainty in the used car market? To what extent does the difficulty in valuation affect settlement offers?

4. A litigant wishing to present evidence of fair market value must produce testimony from an expert witness or from someone with special knowledge of the matter from experience. *See* McGovern v. Michael, 62 R.I. 485, 6 A.2d 709 (1939). When the issue is personal value to the owner, however, such expert testimony is not required. How valid is the distinction between allowing recovery for personal value to the owner but disallowing damages for sentimental attachment when family heirlooms are lost or destroyed? The owner may testify as to such matters as the cost of the item when new, its condition and age, its time in use, and expense of replacement by similar used item. The jury determines the weight to attach to the plaintiff's own nonexpert testimony about value. *See, e.g.,* DeSpirito v. Bristol County Water Co., 102 R.I. 50, 227 A.2d 782 (1967).

5. What if a household pet such as a cat or dog perishes in a fire caused by the negligence of the defendant? Some pedigree animals young enough for breeding or show have objective value. Most pets have little or no value in the marketplace, yet the owners of pet "chattel" often attach high personal value to them. In some veterinary malpractice suits judges have allowed juries to consider the sentimental value of pets. If many jurisdictions were to make pets an exception to the rule excluding sentimental value, would such an exception be likely to stand alone or would it signal a significant erosion of the general rule?

PROBLEM: THE COACH'S NOTES

Rod Hank is a junior college football coach who was recently fired after several losing seasons. Hank has coached at various high schools and junior colleges for thirty years. During that time he accumulated many notes on plays and strategies. He kept these notes in files in a cabinet in his office. The notes were made over the years as coach and they represented his ideas with particular teams. Some of the notes were made while he watched football games on television. One file contained notes given to him by his own coach, Coach Allen, when he played quarterback in college. When Coach Allen retired the same year Hank graduated, Allen gave Hank his notes as a present because Hank had just accepted his first high school coaching job.

All these notes were in Hank's four drawer office cabinet along with a list of the junior college's equipment and other miscellaneous files. After Hank was fired he did not come into the office for several days.

He stayed home and made calls in search of another job and then he interviewed for a few days. During this time a janitor removed and destroyed everything in Hank's filing cabinet. Even though school officials had assured Hank that his office would be left alone until he packed his possessions at the end of the month, a supervisor negligently instructed the janitor. Assume that the junior college is liable in tort for the destruction of Hank's personal files.

How should the damages for this destruction be measured? What kind of evidence could Hank present? Should the different types of the destroyed notes be divided into categories?

Hank had planned to coach for a few more years at the new school that hired him. Then he planned to retire and write a book about the coaching experiences of Coach Allen and himself. He did not have a contract for such a book yet. Are the book plans admissible as relevant to the calculation of damages? Consider the case that follows.

TALIFERRO v. AUGLE

757 F.2d 157 (7th Cir.1985).

POSNER, CIRCUIT JUDGE.

Taliferro brought this suit for damages under 42 U.S.C. § 1983 against two Chicago police officers, Augle and Hoffman, alleging that they had stopped him on the street without reason to believe he was engaged in criminal activity, had arrested him without probable cause, had beaten him, and had failed to preserve his property, all in violation of his rights under the Fourteenth Amendment. The jury found that the officers had had a reasonable basis for stopping him, but upheld the other charges in the complaint and awarded Taliferro $47,000 in compensatory damages and $25,000 in punitive damages ($12,500 against each defendant), for a total of $72,000. The defendants appeal, arguing that the judge should have granted their motion for a new trial because the verdict was against the weight of the evidence, or at least should have cut down the damage award as excessive.

Taliferro is black, a working man, and also a writer on the theme of oppression of blacks by whites. At the time of the arrest he was 46 years old. He testified as follows: On the night of the arrest he was crossing a street in downtown Chicago, carrying an attache case and two shopping bags containing miscellaneous personal belongings including several manuscripts, when officers Augle and Hoffman, who are white, accosted him, grabbed him, handcuffed him roughly, and, soon joined by other policemen, beat him. After trundling Taliferro off to the police station with the help of the other officers, Augle and Hoffman again beat him (as did other officers, separately, in an elevator), inflicting serious injuries that included destroying his dental plate and knocking out many of his real teeth. His property was taken from him at the police station; he was never told how he could get it back; and it was destroyed as abandoned property a few weeks later. * * *

[The court reviewed the evidence of the plaintiff's losses associated with his physical injuries and found it insufficient proof of particular losses, such as the plaintiff's failure to present evidence of any dental bill.]

As for the loss of the manuscripts, the author of this opinion, as a sometime author of academic manuscripts, can feel keen sympathy with any author who loses a manuscript of which he has not made a copy; and Taliferro had no copies. Although his loss was not a financial one, since he derived less than $400 in annual income from all his writing and made no attempt to attach a dollar value to the manuscripts that were destroyed, an author may prove nonmarket damages for the tortious destruction of a manuscript. [Citations.] True, these are not civil-rights cases. But federal tort statutes such as 42 U.S.C. § 1983 are not self-contained. They are enacted against a background of common law tort principles governing causation and damages. [Citations.] Those principles are therefore applicable to federal civil-rights tort cases unless unsuitable to them, [citation], and they are not unsuitable here. But the cases dealing with tortious destruction of a manuscript require proof of the value of the manuscript—for example, proof of the cost in time or materials of reconstructing it (the value of the manuscript could not exceed that cost). No proof concerning the value of the manuscripts to Taliferro was presented. His lawyer pulled the figure of $50,000 out of his hat at closing argument.

The other figures are equally fanciful. We have criticized the casual attitude of many tort plaintiffs toward proof of damages, [citation], and like other courts have set aside excessive awards of compensatory damages in cases factually quite like this one. [Citations.] A plaintiff is not permitted to throw himself on the generosity of the jury. If he wants damages, he must prove them. The only effort at proof here, besides the proof of $35 in out-of-pocket medical expenses, was Taliferro's testimony that he was distraught and humiliated by his mistreatment at the hands of the police, as well as suffering physical pain. Although it is a painful experience to be manhandled by the police and to have them take away and destroy personal belongings that have at the least a sentimental value, $47,000 is not a reasonable estimate of such an intangible loss when no effort at all is made to establish an objective basis for quantifying the loss. We consider $25,000 the highest compensatory damages that can be justified on this record, so unless Taliferro agrees to remit the difference between this amount and the $47,000 that the jury awarded as compensatory damages we shall order a new trial limited to damages. * * *

So ordered.

---

1. Distinguish irreplaceable property from difficult to replace property. The principal case indicates that the ceiling on recovery for the nonmarket value of the manuscript is the value of the time and materi-

als to reconstruct it. If Taliferro was not gainfully employed as a writer, how could the value of his time be measured? Is it clear that Taliferro could reconstruct the manuscript? Judge Posner's experience as an author of legal manuscripts may not be the same as the plaintiff's experience as an author about oppression. The process of inspiration may work very differently and may affect the ability to reconstruct previously written work.

2.   Another principle of damage law is that any benefits a plaintiff receives from the defendant's tortious conduct are offset against the damages. *See, e.g.,* Mohr v. Williams, 95 Minn. 261, 104 N.W. 12 (1905) (unconsented operation on diseased ear; damages for battery offset by successful treatment of disease). *See also* Restatement (Second) of Torts § 920 (1979). Could that rule appropriately apply to reduce Taliferro's award? Is it reasonable to argue that the defendants' tortious conduct provided this author of oppression a wealth of new material? Is this experience not a "benefit" to Taliferro, or is it simply offensive to public policy to so label police brutality?

3.   Judge Posner refers to Taliferro's sentimental attachment to his manuscript. Is this case an exception to the rule against awards for the sentimental value of personal property? Alternatively, is the reference here to sentimental value used only in the context of humiliation and distress damages for his civil rights claim?

_____

PROBLEM: THE CAUTIOUS RANCHER

Watt is an old Nevada rancher who has lived through a few difficult winters. He particularly remembers one hard winter years ago when he lost a significant portion of his livestock. Ever since, Watt has grown and stored enough hay to survive even such an extraordinary year. Watt has been growing and storing more hay than he has needed in recent years. Neighboring ranchers believe that his degree of caution is foolish. If Watt had not developed such a concern about exceptionally hard weather, he could have turned a larger profit on his ranch. He persists in his practice nonetheless, and warns that nature will teach a lesson of caution again one of these years. His critics observe that the amount he has lost by hoarding hay is probably equal to the entire value of his present stock. He retorts that "the past is past, but the future is uncertain."

Last fall Watt's hay crop was burned as it lay drying in the field. A negligently driven tanker truck owned by Central Trucking overturned and caught fire on the highway adjacent to Watt's ranch. The fire spread to Watt's field and destroyed the drying hay. Watt sued for this destruction of his personal property.

How should the hay be valued? Assume that the hay had a fair market value as a commodity and that, if Watt had elected to sell his hay at the market, he would have incurred transportation expenses. Conversely, if Watt were to purchase hay at the market to store on his ranch, he would incur transportation expenses.

Should the court grant the fair market value of the hay and add or subtract transportation costs? Should the hay be divided into two categories: (1) an amount reasonable to store for the winter and (2) the extra amount that Watt cautiously adds?

KING FISHER MARINE SERVICE, INC. v. THE NP SUNBONNET
724 F.2d 1181 (5th Cir.1984).

HIGGINBOTHAM, CIRCUIT JUDGE:

Newpark Marine Services, Inc. appeals from a judgment entered after a bench trial in favor of King Fisher Marine Service, Inc. for the value of a King Fisher barge sunk while in tow by Newpark. The district court awarded damages for the total loss of the barge plus interest. * * *

For several years King Fisher, president of King Fisher Marine, had been looking for a barge suitable for use as a platform for a drydock. In early February 1979 King Fisher * * * inspected a barge which had been advertised in the Waterways Journal. Once an undersea mat for a drilling rig, the barge was basically a large steel box with four internal compartments and two attached pontoons. * * *

[King Fisher bought the barge and hired Newpark to tow it. Through the negligence of Newpark, the barge sank and was never located.]

Newpark * * * claims that the district court's damage award of $232,996.75 is excessive. King Fisher purchased the barge on February 13, 1979, for $30,000 although it had been advertised for $35,000. He then contracted with Newpark to tow the barge across the Gulf of Mexico and insured the barge against the perils of the journey for $50,000. The barge was lost on February 15, 1979.

King Fisher did not find a suitable replacement barge until November 1979. There was uncontroverted expert testimony that the first barge was ideally suited as a drydock platform; that only six other similar mats existed in the world; and that none of them had been on the market since the loss of King Fisher's barge. Similarly, there was evidence that a new barge of similar specifications would cost one million dollars to build and that combining smaller barges into a barge similar to the one lost would cost King Fisher approximately $600,000. The replacement barge also cost $30,000 but it had a hole which the court found King Fisher paid $202,996.75 to patch in April 1981. Finally, there was uncontroverted expert testimony that the cost incurred by King Fisher to modify the replacement barge to make it similar to the first was reasonable and that King Fisher's efforts were the most economical way to obtain a drydock base. In sum the district court awarded the cost of a replacement barge capable of the same use as the lost barge.

It is fundamental that when a vessel is lost or damaged "the owner is entitled to its money equivalent, and thereby to be put in as good a position pecuniarily as if his property had not been destroyed." *Standard Oil Company v. Southern Pacific Company*, 268 U.S. 146, 155, 45 S.Ct. 465, 466, 69 L.Ed. 890 (1924). To further this policy courts have long held that where a vessel is a total loss the measure of damages is the market value at the time of the loss. Where there are insufficient sales to establish a market other evidence such as replacement costs, depreciation, expert opinion and the amount of insurance can also be considered to determine the value of the lost vessel. [Citations.]

Newpark claims the evidence establishes that the market value of the barge was $30,000 because that is what King Fisher paid for it in an arm's length sale only two days before it was lost. As far as it goes, the argument is unassailable. The difficulty is that the barge was not purchased to perform as a barge. It was instead purchased for use as a drydock platform. The barge's price in the barge market is not determinative of its value because its unique capabilities made it valuable for use other than as a barge. The district court found that no "accurate market price" could be determined for this barge and uncontroverted expert testimony supported that conclusion. There was testimony that similar barges so readily transformed into drydocks were not then or have since been available. Indeed, King Fisher testified that he looked for several years before he found the now lost barge. King Fisher's expert testified that only one drydock a year is built and although it would cost $1,000,000 to build a new barge similar to the one lost, it might "not sell . . . for a dime." When King Fisher bought the barge he appears to have been the only one in the market for such a drydock platform. That the market did not value the barge's use as a drydock platform was supported by the fact that King Fisher paid $30,000 for a replacement barge that could not be used as the drydock platform without considerable modification. The district court correctly found that the price paid by King Fisher for the now lost barge did not represent its value as a drydock platform.

* * *

Newpark cites United States v. Toronto, Hamilton & Buffalo Navigation Co., 338 U.S. 396, 402, 70 S.Ct. 217, 221, 94 L.Ed. 195 (1949) for the proposition that the value of the drydock is what an "ordinary purchaser" would have paid for the barge. While the Court did not elaborate on its definition of ordinary purchaser it noted that when considering the price that could have been obtained for the lost vessel the court should consider what an ordinary seller *in the trade* would do. The price an ordinary drydock purchaser would have paid is the object of our inquiry. King Fisher established that there was no market for drydock platforms created by ordinary drydock purchasers.

Here the lost barge had special qualities as a base for a drydock that filled legitimate commercial needs that would not be recognized in the "market" price of the barge. While the barge may only have been a large steel box to some, King Fisher recognized and took advantage of an opportunity to purchase a suitable drydock platform at low cost. The value of the barge was not reflected by its cost to King Fisher. The district court was not clearly erroneous in awarding King Fisher the value of its lost barge measured by its cost of replacement.

　　* * * Affirmed.

————

1.　Compare the drydock in *King Fisher* to the manuscript in *Taliferro*. Is each best characterized as irreplaceable or difficult to replace? Does it matter?

2.　If King Fisher was desperate for the original drydock that he bought, how did he get such a low purchase price? Does the low price reflect a lack of other buyers as well as sellers? If a unique buyer was seeking to buy a unique chattel, how does the price get determined without others to make a market? If one party negotiates a good price, should that price be considered the fair market value for purposes of later litigation with an unrelated defendant?

Consider the case of Boston Iron & Metal Co. v. S.S. Winding Gulf. Boston Iron purchased an obsolete ship to use as scrap. Like the drydock in *King Fisher,* it sank in tow. Boston Iron argued that the value of the ship as scrap was much greater than the purchase price. The court awarded more than the purchase price, but less than Boston Iron's claim. The district court judge observed:

> * * * As a practical test I think the evidence fairly leads to the view that considering all of the relevant facts some person engaged in a similar business would fairly have been willing to pay for the destroyer as an entity at the time and place of loss substantially more than what it cost the owner up to that time. It must be remembered that the purchase was made by one skilled in the particular business taking advantage of a particular opportunity not often afforded, and resulting from skill and knowledge of when, why and how to buy. Or, in other words, it may be said that the evidence as a whole fairly indicates that in the purchase the owner made a very good bargain and is entitled under the circumstances of the loss to have the damages fixed at a sum which would fairly pecuniarily reimburse him for the loss incurred. Boston Iron & Metal Co. v. S.S. Winding Gulf, 85 F.Supp. 806, 812 (D.Md.1949), *aff'd* 209 F.2d 410 (4th Cir.1954), *rev'd on other grounds* 349 U.S. 122, 75 S.Ct. 649, 99 L.Ed. 933 (1955).

3.　Why should King Fisher get a replacement barge while an ordinary car owner never gets replacement? Was the court intending to give King Fisher a replacement, or was the judge struggling to find the fair market value of a nonmarket item?

4. What if the situation had involved a breach of contract instead of the tortious destruction of the barge? Consider the issues if the seller of the barge had breached by selling it to a third party instead of to King Fisher. Would damages be inadequate? Should a court grant a decree of specific performance? Can property be "unique" to one contracting party and not to the other?

HEWLETT v. BARGE BERTIE

418 F.2d 654 (4th Cir.1969), *cert. denied*, 397 U.S.
1021, 90 S.Ct. 1261, 25 L.Ed.2d 531 (1970).

BRYAN, CIRCUIT JUDGE:

Computation of pecuniary damages recoverable for a ship's injury in a maritime collision centers this cause. The minim of the injury here, however, obscures and tempts neglect of the importance of the issue.

Without dispute, the facts are that barge BA–1401, afloat and made fast alongside a pier in the Elizabeth River at South Norfolk, Virginia, on September 28, 1960 was struck by another barge. * * *

[Hewlett, owner of BA–1401, sued the barge owner in admiralty. The only issue was damages because liability was confessed. The admiralty court awarded only $1.00 as nominal damages.]

The basis of the decision was that as the BA–1401 had been declared a constructive loss two years before, the District Court was of the opinion that a subsequent injury could not sustain a claim. The declaration followed upon her misfortune on November 11, 1958, when she foundered in Chesapeake Bay near the mouth of the Potomac River. [Citation.] Raised and refloated by the present libelant as contractor-salvor in June, 1959, the repair and recovery cost of the barge was estimated to exceed both her 1958 purchase price of $40,000.00 and current insurance of $45,000.00. In these circumstances she was re-leased to Hewlett in satisfaction of his claim for services. After $1305.76 was expended upon her in temporary repairs, such as leak stoppages, she was brought to Norfolk.

The barge was used or useable for carrying pilings or logs—weather-proof cargo. She was engaged on one occasion as a pontoon or caisson in lifting a steamer from the river bottom. In this task the barge was allowed to fill, settle beside the sunken ship and then attached to her. When pumped out, the barge's buoyancy brought the steamer to the surface.

Admittedly, the barge had no market value as an instrument of navigation and could be sold only for scrap. The skin of the barge was not pierced in the collision, and the only mark of impact was a dent in her starboard side. It produced no harmful effect upon the barge's seaworthiness or carrying capacity.

Our concern is the acceptance by the instant court of the respondent's defense to the damage claim, *i.e.* "the barge was a constructive total loss and that no real or actual damages have been shown, thus restricting the recovery to nominal damages". The decree on review purports to fix "nominal damages", but this is in reality a dismissal of the libel, for admiralty does not recognize nominal damages. [Citation.] Presently, the Court stated, "We find no precedent for allowing damages where a vessel, deemed a constructive total loss, suffers still further damage." Apparently, the award of $1.00 was the product of this proposition. It is, we think, an untenable postulate; if accepted, it could result in unjust deprivations.

Actually, the case does not commence with the barge as a constructive loss, as the admiralty judge believed. True, that was her status more than a year previous, but only as between the owner and the salvor. Even this, however, was not a decree of outlawry. She was not a derelict, to be jostled about with impunity. Indeed, as a sheer-hulk she had a demonstrated utility for the libelant. Slightly more than a year previous, to repeat, $1305.76 had been expended in restoration. The accused tugboat and tow cannot escape liability by recall of the past ill luck of the BA–1401. Nor are they relieved by showing that she has not suffered in utility value or in market value.

To illustrate, although an automobile through age or misfortune may have no value in the market save for scrap, and although still another nick in its paint or shape may not appreciably reduce the usefulness or dollar-value of the car, nevertheless its checkered career and disreputable appearance do not assure absolution to one who negligently further scars the vehicle. The owner is entitled to have the automobile free of even that dent. *De minimis non curat lex* does not, semble, apply to damages but only to injury. [Citation.]

"Restitutio in integrum" is the precept in fixing damages, and "where repairs are practicable the general rule followed by the admiralty courts in such cases is that the damages assessed against the respondent shall be sufficient to restore the injured vessel to the condition in which she was at the time the collision occurred; * * * " The Baltimore, 75 U.S. 377, 385, 19 L.Ed. 463, 8 Wall. 377 (1869).

The workable guides to this end, generally stated, are these. If the ship sinks and is beyond recovery, the damages are her value just before she sank, plus interest thereon until payment. If she is not a complete loss and repossession or repairs are both physically and economically feasible, then the reasonable cost of recovery, including repairs and an allowance for deprivation of use, is the measure. But if the reclamation expense including repairs exceeds the ship's just value at the time of the casualty, or if repairs are not both physically and economically practicable, then it is a constructive total loss, and the limit of compensation is the value plus interest. O'Brien Bros. v. The Helen B. Moran, 160 F.2d 502 (2d Cir.1947).

The case at bar comes closer to the second category—the loss was not complete, repairs were physically practicable, but the question remains whether they were economically so. The answer depends on whether the repair cost was more than the value of the barge. Libelant has shown a fair estimate for the repairs to be between $2895.00 and $3000.00. If this expense was beyond the fair and reasonable monetary value of the vessel to the owner, then the recovery is limited to such value. [Citation.]

When, as here, the tortfeasors assert that the value is less than the cost of repairs, they have the burden to establish that fact. The respondents have failed to do so. Consequently, the case stands on the proof of the repair costs, and the libelant is entitled to a decree in that amount.

The District Court made no finding of value. It merely found that the BA–1401 had no value save for sale as scrap, but this is not the equivalent of fixing a figure of value. Moreover, it is erroneous. It is refuted by the other uncontested findings of her continuing utility.

Apparently, the chief factor influencing the District Judge in this determination was the absence of any market for the sale of the barge. That problem, however, cannot justify withholding all value from libelant's vessel. [Citation.] The special value to the owner is a consideration of substance. [Citation.]

* * * If there is no market value, other indicia of value must be looked to. [Citations.] Among other factors is the use value to the owner. As was said in Bishop v. East Ohio Gas Co., 143 Ohio St. 541, 56 N.E.2d 164, 166 (1944):

> "Market value is the standard which the courts insist on as a measure of direct property loss, where it is available, but that is a standard not a shackle. When market value cannot be feasibly obtained, a more elastic standard is restored to, sometimes called the standard of value to the owner. This doctrine is a recognition that property may have value to the owner in exceptional circumstances which is the basis of a better standard than what the article would bring in the open market."

* * *

The order on appeal will be vacated, and the cause remanded with request to the District Court to enter a decree awarding the appellant Hewlett damages of $2895.00, with interest at 6% per annum from the date of the collision until paid, together with costs in the trial and appellate courts.

Reversed and remanded for entry of judgment.

HAYNSWORTH, CHIEF JUDGE (dissenting):

With respect to my brothers, I must dissent, for I think they misapprehend the record, the issue presented, and the legal principle which should control its resolution.

Clarity may be served if I first lay aside one area in which there is no disagreement between us. The fact that the barge had earlier been declared a total constructive loss gave no subsequent wrongdoer an immunity. The District Judge did not hold otherwise. I readily agree, too, that the fact that she was previously declared a constructive total loss has no legal significance in itself in the assessment of the damages or in the application of the governing legal principles. It has only historical significance as the basis upon which the salvor, the principal libelant, acquired her. The prior physical history of the barge, however, is highly relevant in explanation of her condition, her value and potential uses, with respect to all of which the record is far clearer with much less disagreement than the majority opinion might indicate.

The Barge 1401 had been purchased in 1958 for $40,000 and immediately insured for $45,000. One month later she sank. After salvage operations, the lowest bid for restoration to her former condition was $46,290. That was why she was declared a constructive total loss and surrendered to the salvor.

The salvor effected certain repairs costing only $1305.76, which had the effect of making her hull watertight. She was then usable as a pontoon in other salvage operations, as she was once used. It gave her a theoretical potentiality for hauling deck cargo, though she had never been used for such a purpose, and it is very doubtful that she could have been insured for such use.

The barge in her then condition had a market value of $5,616. This was her scrap value, but it was a ready market value, and it seems to me to be a mistake to approach the case as if there were no market value when everyone agrees there was.

Everyone agrees, too, that the market value of $5,616 was not affected in the slightest by the additional dent inflicted in her side when the Barge Bertie collided with her. The already battered Barge 1401 had a scrap value after the additional dent of $5,616, just as she had before.

The libelant here, of course, claimed that the Barge 1401 had a special value to him for use as a pontoon, as once he used it, and potentially, but highly theoretically, for use in carrying telephone poles or other dry deck cargo, a use in which she had never been engaged. It is true, of course, that the special value, if any, was not determined in the District Court, but everyone agrees that the additional dent placed in her side by the Barge Bertie did not effect any diminution in that value, whatever it was. She was as useful as a pontoon after she sustained this dent as she was before, and whatever potential she had for use in carrying deck cargo was not impaired in the slightest.

Under these circumstances, of course, the owner did not attempt to effect the repair of the barge for the repairs were estimated to cost $2,895, and that expenditure would not enhance the value of the barge or its usefulness to the libelant, or to anyone else, in the slightest. No one claims that any such repairs would ever be attempted. If the libelant prevails on the basis of the opinion of my brothers, his winnings will go as cash into his pocket and will not be applied to any reparation of the barge.   It is thus clear beyond all dispute that repair is not economically practicable or feasible, and in no event will it be attempted.

It is thus settled in the record that the additional dent inflicted by the Barge Bertie occasioned no diminution in the market value of the Barge 1401 of $5,616; it occasioned no diminution in any special value she may have had to the libelant.   Between the parties, there is no dispute about this.   The conclusion is inescapable that the libelant has suffered no economic loss.   The question then is whether the libelant's damages should be measured by his economic loss, as was done in the District Court, or by an estimate of the cost of economically imprudent and senseless repair which has not been and never will be incurred.

I think the damages are to be measured by the economic loss sustained by the libelant and that no different rule can be found in admiralty by looking at isolated statements lifted from their context.

* * *

If my brothers are right, the libelant is unduly enriched.   He must hope greatly that another errant navigator will hit his battered barge again, and still another yet again, so that each time he may happily pocket the estimated cost of theoretical repairs which neither he nor anyone else will ever dream of undertaking while retaining all along a barge as seaworthy and useful to him and of undiminished worth if he chooses to sell it.

---

1.   The conflict between diminution in value and cost of repair represents no problem when the two measures are factually equivalent, as they often are.   When an ordinary car gets a dent in a door, the reduced value of the unrepaired car usually will be the cost of fixing or replacing the door.

Occasionally, as in *Barge Bertie,* there is not an exact equivalence between the measures.   Then jurisdictions must choose one measure or the other.   In the majority opinion in this admiralty case, did the judges choose a measure to predominate, or did they avoid the necessity of choice?

2.   How does BA–1401 in this case differ from the drydock in *King Fisher?*   Can an ordinary vehicle acquire unique status by becoming an old wreck?   Should an old jalopy be treated as unique or is there a sufficient market for old jalopies that its market value—and the diminution in its value from another dent—could be ascertained?   What if it did not run and had value only as scrap, but its owners kept it on the street as "decoration," or as a symbol, or as a means of annoying the neighbors, or as a source of spare parts?   Should a court distinguish among such uses?   Make factual findings concerning the actual personal uses?

How important was it to dissenting Judge Haynsworth that the uses of BA–1401 were highly theoretical except for its one-time use as a pontoon?

3. Has the owner of BA–1401 been unduly enriched?　Compare *Barge Bertie* with cases where contractually promised restoration was economically unfeasible.　*See* Eastlake Construction Co. v. Hess, *supra* Chapter 10, and the notes that follow that case.

4. Should a court ever award damages both for cost of repair and for diminution in value?　These two measures are usually considered inconsistent or duplicative.　Consider, however, that a repaired chattel often has diminished value even after repair.　Is an automobile that has been in a serious accident worth as much after full repair as an otherwise equivalent automobile?　The fact that a chattel has undergone major repair may create doubt in a buyer's mind; the usual fear is that there may be latent problems.　Should any such loss in fair market value be compensable in addition to the full cost of repair?

Consider Brighton Homes, Inc. v. McAdams, 737 S.W.2d 340 (Tex. App.1987), where the plaintiff received damages for the cost of repair as well as for the diminution in value of a house.　The court did not find that the damages were duplicative when damages were necessary to repair the house's foundation and drainage, and there was diminution in the value of the house after repairs were made.　*See also* Unitrust, Inc. v. Jet Fleet Corp., 673 S.W.2d 619 (Tex.App.1984) (the value of an aircraft in its repaired condition was not necessarily the same as its fair market value prior to the crash).

B.　DAMAGES FOR LOSSES TO REAL PROPERTY

Section Coverage:

The practical problems and policy conflicts that affect damages for tortious injury to personal property emerge also in cases involving tortious injury to real property.　For example, is it appropriate to award cost of repair damages greater than the overall diminution in value of the property?　Should a plaintiff be awarded loss of use damages during repairs?

It is useful to distinguish between injuries to the land itself and injuries to structures on the land.　Another important distinction separates permanent injuries from reparable ones.　Land itself is rarely "destroyed," of course, unless it is submerged under water.　Some critical feature of the land, such as its productivity, could be effectively ruined in certain instances.　The leaching of toxic chemicals into the soil and water supply, for example, may permanently render the land unfit for growing crops.　The distinction between temporary and permanent harms is often elusive, however.　If negligent blasting causes a well to run dry such that a new one must be drilled, is the well injured or destroyed?

Model Case:

A negligent truck driver runs into a homeowner's yard and smashes a free-standing garage. The structure is very substantially damaged. Repair estimates are close to the value of an entirely new garage. A real estate appraisal shows a fair market value reduction in the value of the homeowner's property that is less than either the cost of repair or replacement of the garage.

Jurisdictions vary in damage rules. Some would give the cost of repair. Others would limit a cost of repair recovery to the diminution in the fair market value of the overall property unless the plaintiff can prove that the structure has a separate value and that cost of repair does not exceed that separate value. Yet other jurisdictions distinguish between permanent and reparable injuries to improvements on land. If the plaintiff establishes that the injury to the garage is not permanent, even though substantial, then cost of repair is appropriate. Courts typically do not distinguish between a homeowner who needs the garage and a real estate investor who buys and sells property regularly.

MILLER v. CUDAHY CO.

858 F.2d 1449 (10th Cir.1988).

BALDOCK, CIRCUIT JUDGE.

In this diversity action, plaintiffs-appellees claimed that the American Salt Company's (American Salt) salt mining operations caused the pollution of an underground aquifer passing under their farms, resulting in their inability to utilize the water in the aquifer for irrigation. At the time appellees filed their complaint, American Salt was an operating division of defendant-appellant Cudahy Company (Cudahy), which is a wholly-owned subsidiary of defendant-appellant General Host Corporation (General Host). The district court concluded that the pollution emanating from the salt plant constituted a continuing, abatable nuisance causing temporary damages and found appellants liable for $3.06 million in actual damages and $10 million in punitive damages. * * *

Appellees are owners and lessees of real property located in Rice County, Kansas. The land is used primarily for agricultural production. American Salt, along with its predecessor, has operated a salt manufacturing plant near Lyons, Kansas since 1908.

Located two miles south of Lyons is Cow Creek, which flows in a southeasterly direction and is a minor tributary of the Arkansas River. Below Cow Creek is the Cow Creek Valley Aquifer (the aquifer), an underground fresh-water stratum which occupies a width of one to two miles and lies at depths of between approximately ten and seventy feet. The aquifer also flows in a southeasterly direction, at a rate of between one-and-a-half and five feet per day. The water in the aquifer passes under the land owned or leased by appellees after it has passed under American Salt's brine fields and plant.

Salt concentrations of over 30,000 parts per million have been recorded in water samples drawn from the aquifer. Concentrations of 250 parts per million are sufficient to render water unfit for domestic or irrigation use. As found by the district court, the salt present in the aquifer escaped from the property and control of American Salt. The majority of the salt escaped through subsurface leaks, while the remainder percolated downward from surface spills.

Due to insufficient rainfall, farmers in Rice County are unable to grow corn without irrigating their land. Appellees alleged that because of the salt pollution of the aquifer, they are unable to irrigate and therefore can grow only dryland crops such as wheat and milo, which do not produce the revenues generated by corn crops.

The district court, in commenting on the more than half-century of disputes between American Salt and area farmers, described the historical background of this case as "Dickensian" in nature. [Citation.] Final resolution of this lawsuit itself required nearly a decade. * * *

The district court denied appellants' motion for summary judgment, which was predicated on their contention that appellees' claims were barred by the statute of limitations. The court concluded that appellees' showing was sufficient to categorize the American Salt operation as a continuing, abatable nuisance causing temporary damages and giving rise to a continuing series of causes of action. The court also concluded that the two-year statute of limitations did operate to preclude appellees from recovering for injuries sustained more than two years prior to the filing of their complaint. The court stated that appellees were entitled to attempt to prove and recover their damages accruing between a date two years before the complaint was filed (May 31, 1975) and the date of judgment.

Following a bench trial, the court found appellants liable for temporary damages to annual crops and awarded appellees $3.06 million in actual damages for the period of 1975 through 1983. The court arrived at the amount of lost crop profits by calculating the difference between the net value of corn crops and the net value of the wheat and milo crops which were actually grown. The court also awarded $10 million in punitive damages; however, it retained jurisdiction over the award and held final judgment in abeyance, pending appellants' "good-faith efforts to define and remedy the pollution they have caused." Pursuant to Fed.R.Civ.P. 54(b), the court entered final judgment on the issues of liability and actual damages. * * *

Appellants first argue that appellees' claims are time-barred, the primary thrust of their argument being that the injuries suffered by appellees are permanent in nature and were ascertained long before the statute of limitations began to run. * * *

The applicable Kansas statute of limitations, Kan.Stat.Ann. § 60–513 (1983), provides in pertinent part:

(a) The following actions shall be brought within two (2) years: (1) An action for trespass upon real property.

* * *

(4) An action for injury to the rights of another, not arising on contract, and not herein enumerated.

The crucial question in regard to the applicability of the two-year statute of limitations is whether the injuries sustained by appellees are permanent or temporary in nature. Drawing a distinction between permanent and temporary damages resulting from a nuisance is at best problematical.[3] The district court, upon surveying Kansas nuisance law from 1876 to the present, noted that the relevant cases addressing the distinction between permanent and temporary injuries are somewhat unclear and inconsistent.

The Kansas Supreme Court likewise has recognized the rather confused state of the law concerning the distinction between permanent and temporary nuisances. [Citation.] The supreme court recently indicated that the distinction between temporary and permanent damages remains a viable concept, however, while emphasizing that "no hard and fast rule can be adopted as to when the damages are deemed permanent and when they are deemed temporary." Olson v. State Highway Comm'n of Kan., 235 Kan. 20, 679 P.2d 167, 172 (1984). Noting that some cases refer not only to the permanent or temporary nature of the damages, but also to the permanent or temporary nature of the causative factor, the court stressed that "[e]ach case must be considered in its own factual setting."

* * *

Under Kansas law, the plaintiff has the option of suing for either permanent or temporary damages. [Citation.] If permanent damages are sought, an action claiming such damages must be brought within two years. [Citation.] "Permanent damages are given on the theory that the cause of injury is fixed and that the property will always remain subject to that injury." McAlister v. Atlantic Richfield Co., 233 Kan. 252, 662 P.2d 1203, 1211 (1983). They "are damages for the entire injury done—past, present and prospective—and generally speaking [are] those which are practically irremediable."

If the injury or wrong is classified as temporary, the limitation period starts to run only when the plaintiff's land or crops are actually harmed, and for purposes of the statute of limitations, each injury causes a new cause of action to accrue, at least until the injury becomes

---

3. As described in one torts treatise, "[t]here is perhaps no more impenetrable jungle in the entire law than that which surrounds the word 'nuisance.'" W. Keeton, D. Dobbs, R. Keeton & D. Owen, Prosser and Keeton on Torts 616 (5th ed. 1984). In regard to the specific issue presented here, another treatise notes the general confusion surrounding the distinction the courts have drawn between permanent and temporary nuisances. F. Harper, F. James & O. Gray, The Law of Torts § 1.30 (2d ed. 1986).

permanent. [Citations.] This rule is especially applicable if the situation involves elements of uncertainty, "such as the possibility or likelihood of the alteration or abatement of the causative condition." [Citation.] The rule is predicated upon the defendant's ability and duty to abate the existing conditions which constitute the nuisance. [Citations.]

Appellants rely primarily on *McAlister v. Atlantic Richfield Co.* in arguing that the damages caused by their admitted pollution of the aquifer will last indefinitely (at least 200 years) and therefore are permanent for purposes of the statute of limitations. In *McAlister,* the plaintiff sued for temporary damage to his water well caused by the defendant's oil fields. The plaintiff alleged "that not less than 150 nor more than 400 years will pass before the well water will be once again fit for drinking." [Citation.] Under the circumstances of that case, in which there was no indication that the pollution was abatable and the relevant defendants had discontinued oil well operations in the 1940's, the Kansas Supreme Court held that portion of the claim to be barred by the two-year statute of limitations because the injury was "fixed" and "the property will always remain subject to that injury."

* * *

The trial evidence indicates that the damage to the aquifer is remediable if the salt pollution is abated. While it is true that no conclusive time frame for the cleansing of the aquifer has been established, it is apparent to this court that, contrary to appellants' contention, the cleanup process can be accelerated by intervention measures and can be achieved within a reasonable time. Further, appellants' argument focusing solely on the nature of the injuries resulting from the salt pollution of the aquifer disregards the fact that we must look at the nature of the causative factor of the pollution.[7] [Citation.] Appellants do not contend that there is no "possibility or likelihood" that the causative condition, namely American Salt's mining operations, can be altered or abated. [Citation.] The record indicates that the cause of the injuries can be terminated, and indeed appellants state that they have already undertaken measures to do so. [Citation.] Nor do appellants argue that they have no duty to abate the existing conditions which

---

7. In pointing out the inconsistent use of the terms "temporary" and "permanent" in the Kansas cases, the district court notes

> that, when realty is damaged by pollution, the terms "temporary" and "permanent" can be applied to three quite distinct facets of the situation. First, the *pollution itself,* or the causal chemistry of the injury to the land, may be either temporary or permanent. Second, the *damage or loss* caused by the injury may be temporary or permanent. Last, the *source or origin of the pollution,* be it a sewage plant, an oil well, or a salt mine, may be temporary or permanent. The

possibilities for inconsistencies are, of course, multiplied when different labels are applied to these facets, such as, for example, calling the source of the pollution a nuisance and then characterizing the nuisance as temporary or permanent.

Miller I, 567 F.Supp. at 899–900 (emphasis in original). The district court's analysis is helpful to our determination of the legal nature of the nuisance and serves to reinforce our interpretation of the Kansas nuisance cases, namely that appellants' argument is deficient by virtue of focusing solely on the nature of the injuries resulting from the salt pollution of the aquifer.

constitute the nuisance. [Citations.] The conclusion that the damages are temporary is bolstered by the evidence that the salt pollution actually continued during the course of this litigation, further indicating the existence of a continuing nuisance.

The damage to the aquifer is remediable and the cause of the damage is abatable. Upon considering all the facts and circumstances, including the nature of the pollution and the nature of the causative factor, as well as the continuing pollution of the aquifer, we conclude, as did the district court, that American Salt's operation constitutes a continuing nuisance causing temporary damages.

Having rejected appellants' assertion that the damages resulting from their pollution of the aquifer are permanent for statute of limitations purposes, we also reject their claim that *all* of appellees' claims are time-barred. The fact that salt pollution has existed in the aquifer for many years does not negate the district court's limitation of appellees' recovery to temporary damages. By limiting their potential recovery to those damages incurred not more than two years prior to the filing of their complaint, the court implicitly determined that the two-year statute of limitations precluded any claims for permanent damages.

* * *

Arguing that the district court's method of calculating actual damages was erroneous as a matter of law, appellants assert that the amount of temporary damages awarded cannot exceed the potential recovery for permanent damages. They alternatively contend that, assuming the propriety of an award of temporary damages, the proper measure of such damages is the reduced rental value of appellees' land.

* * *

The temporary-permanent distinction which is determinative in regard to the running of the statute of limitations is also relevant to the question of the proper measure of damages resulting from an actionable nuisance. [Citations.] In Kansas, the measure of damages for permanent injury to real property is the difference in the fair market value of the land before and after the injury. [Citations.] Diminished fair market value is not used as the measure of recovery, however, if an injury to real property is temporary in nature. Temporary damages represent the reasonable cost of repairing the property, "which may include the value of the use thereof during the period covered by the suit, or it may be the diminution in the rental value of the property, together with such special damages to crops, improvements, etc." [Citations.]

Appellants' assertion that temporary damages may not exceed the value of the property injured, or essentially that there must be a "cap" on an award of temporary damages, is unsupported by pertinent Kansas authority. Their alternative contention, that the sole measure of such damages is reduced rental value, is likewise unsupported. While reduced rental value of the property injured is indeed one measure of temporary damages, the value of the *use* of the property is also a proper measure of damages. The Kansas Supreme Court has treated the value of the use of property and the diminution of rental value as separate and distinct bases for awarding temporary damages. [Citations.]

The district court found that because irrigated corn crops would be more profitable than the dryland crops appellees were forced to grow because of the salt pollution of the aquifer, appellees "have been damaged by the pollution to the extent of these lost crop profits." In so finding, the court applied the proper legal standard under Kansas law for measuring temporary damages. [Citation.] The court's calculation of actual damages, made upon consideration of the similar formulas presented by the various expert witnesses, was based upon the difference between the net value of the lost corn production and the net value of the wheat and milo crops actually grown. That calculation is supported by the evidence and is not clearly erroneous.

* * *

GENERAL OUTDOOR ADVERTISING CO.
v. LA SALLE REALTY CORP.

141 Ind.App. 247, 218 N.E.2d 141 (1966).

HUNTER, JUDGE.

The appellee brought this action in the lower court to recover damages for injuries to its building alleged to have been caused by the appellant's sign. The appellant had leased the roof of said building on which it erected a large advertising sign. The court tried the case without the intervention of a jury, awarding the appellee an Eight Thousand Five Hundred ($8,500) Dollar judgment. The appellant assigns as error the lower court's overruling its motion for new trial. * * *

[The court found no error in the acceptance of evidence establishing the negligence of the defendant in the erection and maintenance of the sign that damaged the plaintiff's roof.]

The remaining specification of error in the appellant's motion for new trial and argued in its brief on appeal is that the decision of the lower court is contrary to law and not sustained by sufficient evidence as the appellant failed to properly prove damages. The appellee in the lower court submitted the following evidence on damages caused by the appellant's negligence:

(1) That it would cost approximately $20,000 to $25,000 to restore the building; and

(2) that the original cost of the building was $65,000 to Michiana Realty Corp. who sold the building in 1952 to LaSalle Realty Corp.

The appellant contends that under the issues formed there is insufficient evidence to sustain the judgment of the trial court in the amount of damages awarded. In support of this contention, the appellant urges that the measure of damages must be the market value of the real property before the damage complained of less the market value after said damage. The appellant further states that Indiana has no relevant cases in point where there is a value of a building separate from the real estate. The appellant contends that in the absence of controlling authority in Indiana, we should follow those jurisdictions which state that where there is damage to a building which has a value separate from the real estate, the measure of damages should be the cost of restoration (*i.e.,* repair cost) or the market value of the building prior to the injury less the market value of the building after the injury, whichever is less. In accord with this logic, the appellant urges that since the appellee submitted no evidence on the "before and after" value, the lower court's judgment must fail as not being supported by sufficient evidence and contrary to law under either the Indiana authority on real estate damage or under the theory of damages as stated above relating to damage to a building with a value separate and apart from the real estate.

In addition, the appellant contends that unless the building is actually repaired, the estimates of repair costs are not admissible. * * *

It should be noted that this case involves no problems such as loss of use or loss of profits. The judgment was based solely on evidence pertinent to the physical damage to the building.

We are concerned with rules of law which will control the measure of damages to be awarded to the appellee caused by the actionable wrong of the appellant, *i.e.,* an amount necessary to compensate him for the damages sustained. In reviewing the Indiana authorities, we do not agree with the appellant's contention that the general rule for measuring damage to real estate is the market value of the property before the injury less the market value of the property after the injury. * * *

What the courts have been stating is that if the injury to real estate is permanent, then the proper measure of damages is the market value before the injury less the market value after the injury. The cases have not interpreted the meaning of "permanent". However, * * * if the injury is not permanent, we know that the "before and after" test is improper. * * *

From this analysis, we must conclude that in cases of injury to real estate or to that which has no value separate and apart from the real estate, the proper measure of damages is as follows: (1) if the injury is permanent, the measure of damages is the market value of the real estate before the injury, less the market value after the injury; (2) if the injury to real estate is not permanent, then the measure of damages is the cost of restoration. * * *

* * * [T]he appellant states that if a plaintiff is allowed repair costs without the limitation of the "before and after" test, then he might be

placed in a better position than he was before the damage. If a plaintiff is to be allowed repair costs when they exceed the market value of the building before the injury less the market value after the injury, plaintiff could choose not to repair the building and sell it, profiting to the extent of such excess of repair costs.

Although this view seems equitable from a defendant's position, it is rather discriminate against a plaintiff. What if a plaintiff does not desire to sell his property? In this posture the effect of the rule would be that where the restoration costs exceed the "before and after" measure, a plaintiff would receive the latter. Consequently, if he did not desire to sell the building, he would not receive damages sufficient to restore the building to its original condition. The "before and after" test, if used in cases of non-permanent injury, is in reality forcing the plaintiff to sell the building in order to restore himself to the same position enjoyed before the injury. * * *

Therefore, we reject the appellant's theory of damages. By merely extrapolating the Indiana measure of damages for injury to real estate and applying it to injury to property attached to real estate having a value separate from the real estate, we believe a more legally consistent and equitable theory of damages will result. This means that where such property is permanently damaged, the proper measure of damages would be the market value before the injury: whereas if the damage is non-permanent, the proper measure would be the cost of restoration. [Citation.]

As noted above, the cases analyzed in instances of damage to real estate have not propounded a clear definition of permanent or non-permanent damage. However, we realize that the difficulties in defining permanent injury in instances of damage to realty are largely due to the fact that realty can never be completely destroyed. In cases of injury to buildings which have a value separate from the land, the same questions do not exist. In the facts at bar, it would seem reasonable to define permanent injury as being one wherein the cost of restoration exceeds the market value of the building prior to the injury. By adhering to such a definition, we as a matter of law, raise a safeguard against a windfall while additionally protecting the property rights involved. Such a rule is protective of the interests of both parties in their proper perspectives.

* * *

Although we have rejected the appellant's proposed theory of damages, one point which is made under its proposed theory is equally applicable to that adopted by this court. The appellant contends that if it is shown that the building was not repaired or is not to be repaired, then restoration costs are not admissible and the only measure of damages is the "before and after" test. The appellee in the facts at bar chose to demolish the building rather than repair it. * * *

* * * A court of law has no power to oversee the use of damages once they are awarded in action such as in the case at bar. It is our opinion that a plaintiff is entitled to damages regardless of whether anything is done to correct the injury either by repair or by sale. We are concerned with a *measure* of damages only, and not the actual use by the injured party of any damages awarded. * * *

Judgment affirmed.

---

1. The distinction between permanent and reparable injuries is an appealing approach to the problem of real property damages. If a court awards cost of repair to real property even if that cost exceeds the diminution in the fair market value of the property, has the plaintiff received a windfall? The answer depends upon whether the plaintiff is a consumer of the property who, as a practical matter, will want to repair it rather than move. If the plaintiff is in the business of buying and selling real estate, then diminution in fair market value is a more appropriate measure of the actual loss on the asset.

2. As with personal property damages, courts do not generally distinguish between consumers and dealers of real property. Such distinctions add another uncertainty to the litigation process because the court would need a finding of fact whether the plaintiff is a consumer or dealer. For example, how should a homeowner who plans to move to a new job in a new city be characterized? What about an owner of a duplex who lives in half and rents the other half? The remedial goal of judicial efficiency conflicts with litigation uncertainties. The goal to promote settlements is also more distant with added uncertainties in litigation. Is the distinction between consumer and dealer sufficiently important to overcome these objections? How does the principal case resolve the conflict?

3. The debate concerning these rival measures—the cost of repair measure versus the diminution in fair market value measure—turns on the dangers of undercompensation and overcompensation. A plaintiff receiving the diminution measure will be undercompensated if repairs are honestly desired. Conversely, a plaintiff receiving the cost of repair measure will be overcompensated if repairs are not honestly intended.

Would one solution be to award cost of repair only if the plaintiff has already undertaken actual repair? Would such a rule require an innocent plaintiff to borrow money for the repair expense and then to face the uncertainty of any recovery from litigation? What if the plaintiff cannot borrow the cost of repair? Alternatively, if the plaintiff does succeed in obtaining a bank loan, should damages include the interest payable on the loan? *See* Chapter 12 on the limited availability of interest as damages.

Instead of repair, what if the plaintiff has taken steps before trial incompatible with repair, such as demolishing the injured structure? How would the court in the principal case react to this circumstance?

PROBLEM: THE DAMAGED LAWN

Albertson drove his car over the front lawn of the Hudsons' house as a prank late one Saturday night. A neighbor identified Albertson's car, so the Hudsons sued Albertson in small claims court.

Albertson's car left ruts in the lawn that were six inches deep and twenty-five feet long. The Hudsons, a couple with modest means, restored the lawn themselves by filling in the ruts and replanting. The work was substantial and time-consuming with daily monitoring of the growth, but the out-of-pocket expense was $50.

What should be the measure of damages and what evidence should plaintiffs produce on the issue of damages? What if one professional landscaping company in the city would ordinarily charge $300 for performing a similar job and another company had quoted $450 to restore the yard?

LAUBE v. THOMAS

376 N.W.2d 108 (Iowa 1985).

HARRIS, JUSTICE.

This appeal presents a straightforward damages question. What is the proper measure of damages for the wrongful destruction of walnut trees? The trial court, rejecting plaintiffs' claim for their future productive value, fixed the award on the basis of their current market value as lumber. We affirm.

In 1983 defendants contracted to sell a farm in Floyd County to plaintiffs. Possession was to pass on March 1, 1984. Although no timber rights were reserved to the sellers, they cut down and removed about one hundred walnut trees from the tract during August and September 1983. This suit followed. There is no question of liability; at trial defendants offered to confess judgment for $1,000. The offer was refused.

Plaintiffs conceded the trees were timber or forest. They were not a part of any windbreak or used for any ornamental purposes. The trees had stood at two sites on the farm, one a low-level area near a stream and the other in a permanent pasture. Both sites had been timbered, that is, other trees had been removed from the area some five years previously. According to plaintiffs' expert witness, the prior removal of the other trees is significant because it indicates the one hundred trees in question were smaller, presumably inferior for marketing purposes.

Plaintiffs' expert made a strong showing that it was not a practical marketing time for the trees in question. At an age of twenty years they would not mature so as to reach their reasonable marketing potential for another twenty years. Plaintiffs' damages estimate was computed by taking the current market price, considering the size and quality of trees twenty years hence, then discounting the figure appropriately to reach the present value.

On these facts, especially the showing of the inappropriateness of cutting the trees at their stage of semi-maturity, there is at first blush an attractiveness in plaintiffs' contention that a routine allowance of only log value is inadequate. On the other hand their suggested recovery does not conform with any recognized measure of damages for loss of trees.

It is impossible to state a simple, all-purpose measure of recovery for loss of trees. Because of the wide variety in their uses the law has devised a number of alternative measures, to be applied according to the location and use of the loss of trees. [Citations.] These authorities and our own cases provide rather standard recoveries.

Where the trees were put to a special purpose, such as for windbreaks, shade or ornamental use, the measure is usually the difference in value of the realty before and after the destruction of the trees. [Citation.] Where the trees had no such special use the measure is the commercial market value of the trees at the time of taking. *Grell v. Lumsden,* 206 Iowa 166, 169, 220 N.W. 123, 125 (1928) (ordinary forest trees on hillside). Another measure mentioned in *Grell* applies where the trees can be replaced. It is the reasonable cost of replacement. [Citation.] That measure would obviously be inappropriate here and neither party urges its application. We do not consider fruit trees, which produce a marketable crop. Neither do we consider trees with special aesthetic value.

We have already explained plaintiffs' assertion that the standard measure of damages was inadequate to compensate them for their full loss. It was perhaps to address this criticism that the legislature provided for treble damages in Iowa Code section 658.4 (1985), [citations.] In an appropriate case either punitive damages or treble damages can be sought, though not both. We find no basis to disturb the measure of recovery allowed by the trial court.

* * *

AFFIRMED.

KROULIK v. KNUPPEL
634 P.2d 1027 (Colo.App.1981).

KIRSHBAUM, JUDGE.

Defendants, Raymond F. Knuppel, Jr. and Burnett Construction Co. (Burnett), appeal from a judgment entered by the trial court granting title to plaintiffs, Charles W. Kroulik and Claire L. Kroulik, and plaintiffs cross-appeal the trial court's award of damages and assessment of costs. We modify the trial court's judgment in part and, as modified, affirm.

* * *

[Defendant Knuppel in 1973 purchased property adjoining plaintiffs' land. The gravel bar between them was part of the land purchased by Knuppel, but the court held that it belonged to plaintiffs by adverse possession. In the meantime, Knuppel had leased the gravel bar to Burnett, who conducted mining operations for two years.]

The trial court concluded * * * that defendants had damaged plaintiffs' property by removing gravel and by destroying certain vegetation, including a 73–year old pine tree. Defendants were ordered to render an accounting of the gravel removed from the property, and the parties subsequently stipulated as to the amount of gravel removed and the royalty payments received by Knuppel from Burnett.

At the commencement of the hearing on damages, the trial court ruled that the amount of royalties received by Knuppel was the proper measure of damages. Plaintiffs then made an offer of proof of evidence to support their theory that they were entitled to an award of damages based on the value of the gravel extracted less the extraction costs. The trial court entered judgment for plaintiffs in the amount of $14,189.54 for the gravel extraction, $1,500 for destruction of the pine tree, $10 for damage to real property, and costs of $114.35.

* * * [Defendants] contend that the trial court erred in awarding damages for the destruction of the pine tree on the basis of the aesthetic value of the tree. We agree in part, and modify the damages awarded for the loss of the tree.

Damage to growing trees is generally measured by the diminution in the market value of the real property. [Citations.] However, aesthetic value may be considered in establishing the replacement cost of certain unique property. * * *

The tree here involved was a 50–foot–tall pine tree located on a promontory overlooking the river. No other trees of that size were visible in that locale. Several witnesses testified with respect to the particular grace, majesty and beauty of this isolated tree in that setting. We conclude that the trial court did not commit error here by considering aesthetic value to determine the amount of damages to which plaintiffs were entitled as a result of the defendants' uprooting of the pine tree.

However, the only evidence of the value of the tree introduced at trial was the uncontroverted testimony of an expert witness who valued the pine at $8.40 for lumber and $229.63 for aesthetic value. There is no evidence to support the trial court's award of $1,500 as damages for the destruction of the pine tree. Findings not supported by any evidence cannot stand on appeal. [Citation.] As the only evidence offered respecting the pine tree's value was not contradicted * * * the judgment shall be modified to reflect the damages of $238.03 for such loss.

Plaintiffs assert that the trial court erred in ruling that the royalties received by Knuppel constituted the proper measure of damages. We disagree.

When a non-willful trespasser appropriates minerals, the measure of damages is the value of the minerals in place. [Citations.] Such value may be calculated by ascertaining the amount of royalties the landowner would receive or could have received from the trespassing appropriator. [Citations.] Use of a royalty-based valuation permits the landowner to recover the amount the landowner would have realized by contracting for removal of the minerals, without unduly penalizing the merely negligent trespasser. However, this damages measure permits the extractor to retain the profit, if any, realized from the mining venture.

Another means for determining the value of the minerals in place—calculation of the value at the surface less the direct costs of extracting them—does not allow the excavator to retain profits. This measure of value has been employed in trespasser cases. [Citations.] Furthermore, a willful or intentional trespasser may be required to recompense the landowner for the value of the minerals at the surface without deductions for extraction costs. [Citation.]

Here, the trial court concluded that defendants were not willful trespassers. * * * Plaintiffs at no time attempted to mine the gravel pit, and had themselves previously obtained royalty payments pursuant to a mineral lease. Under all the circumstances of this case, we find no error in the trial court's conclusion that the royalty payments received by Knuppel constituted the appropriate measure of plaintiffs' damages.

* * *

The judgment of the trial court is modified to reflect the sum of $238.03 as the damage to which plaintiffs are entitled for the loss of the pine tree, and, as modified, the judgment is affirmed.

———

1. *Removal of Property with Commercial Value:* Many cases have presented the problem of valuing commercially marketable property taken from land by trespass (intentional, negligent, or innocent invasions of real property without legal right) or through other wrongs, as in the principal case. Courts have not been in agreement on the proper method of valuation. Measures used have included diminution in value of the land, the value of the item removed, or in some cases the cost of replacement. *See, e.g.,* Ghione v. State, 26 Wash.2d 635, 175 P.2d 955 (1946) (diminution in value of the land awarded for wrongful governmental removal of large amount of earth and gravel); Brinkmeyer v. Bethea, 139 Ala. 376, 35 So. 996 (1903) (diminution in value of land from $500 to $250 after deliberate removal of topsoil); Hunt v. Boston, 183 Mass. 303, 67 N.E. 244 (1903) (market value of gravel awarded for wrongful governmental removal); Worrall v. Munn, 53 N.Y. 185 (1873) (removal of timber and sand by vendor, like principal case, gave award of

market value of removed items even without diminution in value of the land); Patterson v. Waldman, 20 Ky. L. Rptr. 514, 46 S.W. 17 (1898) (awarding both market value of removed earth and clay and diminution in value of land measures because the defendant's innocent excavation left the land injured); Gene B. Glick Co., Inc. v. Marion Construction Corp., 165 Ind.App. 72, 331 N.E.2d 26 (1975) (cost of restoration of land proper measure for wrongful removal of earth to dig ditch); Kelly v. Fine, 354 Mich. 384, 92 N.W.2d 511 (1958) (cost of restoration of removed topsoil awarded).

When the property removed is minerals or oil, other measures have also been used. The lowest award usually results if the court uses a royalty measure. The highest award ordinarily results from a measure of market value without any deduction for expenditures. In between these extremes a court might award market value with deductions for some or all expenses. *See, e.g.,* Hughett v. Caldwell County, 313 Ky. 85, 230 S.W.2d 92 (1950) (reversed trial court's award of royalty measure against innocent trespassers and awarded market value minus expenses).

As *Knuppel* indicates, the measure of damages in this area sometimes reflects the defendant's good or bad faith. If a defendant is completely innocent and believes in good faith to have the legal right to remove the commercially valuable items from the land, the court may choose a low measure such as reasonable royalty or value of the mineral in the ground. If the defendant acted wilfully and in knowing disregard of the plaintiff's rights, the court may award a high measure. The highest measure of the removed property's value is its market value without deductions for the defendant's expenditures to remove and market it. *See* Mineral Resources, Inc. v. Mahnomen Construction Co., 289 Minn. 412, 184 N.W.2d 780 (1971); Schafer v. Schnabel, 494 P.2d 802 (Alaska 1972); Dethloff v. Zeigler Coal Co., 69 Ill.App.3d 133, 25 Ill.Dec. 525, 386 N.E.2d 1373 (1979), *modified,* 82 Ill.2d 393, 45 Ill.Dec. 175, 412 N.E.2d 526, *cert. denied* 451 U.S. 910, 101 S.Ct. 1980, 68 L.Ed.2d 299 (1981).

Why should the nature of the defendant's conduct affect the measure of damages in this context but not in others? Since the goal of compensatory damages is to focus upon the plaintiff's loss rather than the defendant's gain, why should it matter if the defendant acted in good faith or bad faith?

2. *Multiple Damage Statutes:* As *Laube* indicates, some states give landowners a special statutory right to double or treble damages for trespass under some circumstances, such as where a defendant recklessly or willfully disregards the plaintiff's rights. The standard in a state's statute is not necessarily the same as its standard for punitive damages. *See* Denoyer v. Lamb, 22 Ohio App.3d 136, 490 N.E.2d 615 (1984) ("recklessness" standard in trespass treble damage statute for injuries to trees and shrubs is lower standard than "actual malice" required for punitive damages); Auburn Harpswell Assoc. v. Day, 438 A.2d 234 (Me.1981) (double damage statute for willfully and knowingly cutting

tree is remedial in nature rather than punitive and need not be specially pleaded).

3. *Damage to Property Without Commercial Value:* Courts similarly lack agreement on the measure of damages for destruction or injury to trees or shrubs without commercial value. It is agreed that the loss of a tree in a homeowner's front yard cannot reasonably be measured by the timber value of the tree because that value is usually close to zero. *See e.g.,* Manitou & Pike's Peak Ry. v. Harris, 45 Colo. 185, 101 P. 61 (1909).

4. The general rule for injuries to trees and shrubs is to measure damages by the diminution in the market value of the land. This measure often produces a low award. Some cases have used the cost of reasonable replacement or the cost of reasonable restoration of land held for personal use. Sometimes courts have allowed juries to consider the aesthetic value of ornamental trees or shrubs, or the shade value of trees or the use of trees as a sound barrier from a highway. A few decisions have considered the comfort or convenience of the owner who holds land for personal use. *See* Kapcsos v. Hammond, 13 Ohio App.3d 140, 468 N.E.2d 325 (1983) (measure for trees indigenous to area is diminution in fair market value of the land; measure for ornamental trees can be replacement cost); Porras v. Craig, 675 S.W.2d 503 (Tex.1984) (usual measure is diminution in fair market value but, if none, recovery can be for intrinsic value of trees); Annot., 95 A.L.R.3d 508.

5. Injury to an ornamental tree in a car accident was the subject of the humorous decision in Fisher v. Lowe, 122 Mich.App. 418, 333 N.W.2d 67 (1983). Judge Gillis wrote the opinion in verse, beginning:

"We thought that we would never

see a suit to compensate a tree.

"A suit whose claim in tort is prest

upon a mangled tree's behest."

In a footnote the court explained that the Michigan no-fault insurance act provided the exclusive remedy for the landowner's tree.

COMMONWEALTH OF PUERTO RICO
v. THE SS ZOE COLOCOTRONI

628 F.2d 652 (1st Cir.1980), *cert. denied* 450 U.S. 912, 101 S.Ct. 1350, 67 L.Ed.2d 336 (1981).

CAMPBELL, CIRCUIT JUDGE.

In the early morning hours of March 18, 1973, the SS ZOE COLOCOTRONI, a tramp oil tanker, ran aground on a reef three and a half miles off the south coast of Puerto Rico. To refloat the vessel, the captain ordered the dumping of more than 5,000 tons of crude oil into the surrounding waters. An oil slick four miles long, and a tenth of a mile wide, floated towards the coast and came ashore at an isolated peninsula on the southwestern tip of the island—a place called Bahia Sucia. The present appeal concerns an action in admiralty brought by the Commonwealth of Puerto Rico and the local Environmental Quality Board (EQB) to recover damages for harm done to the coastal environment by the spilled oil.

Defendants have raised numerous objections to the district court's judgment awarding plaintiffs $6,164,192.09 in damages for cleanup costs and environmental harm. * * *

The following facts found by the district court are not in serious dispute. On March 15, 1973, the ZOE COLOCOTRONI departed La Salina, Venezuela, carrying 187,670 barrels of crude oil en route to Guayanilla, Puerto Rico. * * * As the vessel approached the south coast of Puerto Rico, it was, the district court stated, "hopelessly lost." At 0300 hours on March 18, the ship grounded on a reef. Efforts to free the tanker by alternately running the engines in forward and reverse were unsuccessful. After ten minutes, the captain ordered the crew to lighten ship by emptying the cargo of crude oil into the sea. By the time the vessel refloated, some 1.5 million gallons of crude oil—5,170.1 tons— had poured into the surrounding waters.

The oil floated westward from the site of the spill throughout the daylight hours of March 18, and began coming ashore after nightfall. Bahia Sucia is a crescent-shaped bay facing southeastward from the Cabo Rojo peninsula, which forms the southwest tip of Puerto Rico. The oil entered Bahia Sucia, washed onto the beaches, and penetrated the mangrove forests that line the western edge of the bay. The oil was particularly thick in three areas: around the rocky tip of the peninsula, in a section of mangroves known as West Mangrove between a point called "Hermit One" and an inlet called "Dogman's Cove," [5] and on the open beach area stretching along the northern edge of the bay. In addition, as the tide ebbed and flowed, oil entered the tidal flats behind the mangrove fringe, coating the roots of mangroves growing deeper in the forest and soaking into the sediments.

A massive cleanup operation, coordinated by the United States Coast Guard and several Commonwealth agencies, commenced on the morning of March 19. Cleanup crews, hampered to some extent by variable winds that blew oil back and forth across the bay, used booms to attempt to contain oil floating on the surface. Much of this oil was pumped out, either directly from the water or from large holes dug in the beach into which oil was channeled by the cleanup crews. By March 29, approximately 755,000 gallons of oil, or about half the amount spilled, had been recovered. * * *

By April, cleanup activities had switched from large-scale removal of oil to small-scale activities such as manual beach cleanup and bailing of oil from tidal pockets with buckets and small boats. Large amounts of

---

5. Two hermits—Hermit One and the Dogman—lived in the West Mangrove area at the time of trial, the Dogman being so called because of his large collection of canine acquaintances. Neither hermit claimed any legal interest in the property. Various local topographical features were identified in court by reference to these two eponymous individuals.

contaminated sands—totalling about 4,500 cubic yards—were removed from the beach area by bulldozer and by hand. At the end of April, the major remaining cleanup efforts were halted, and all further efforts were discontinued after September 24. Despite the cleanup, oil continued to be present in Bahia Sucia, especially in the stand of mangroves on the west side of the bay.

One of plaintiffs' expert witnesses, Dr. Ariel Lugo Garces, a wetlands specialist, testified that the ecological functions of a mangrove forest such as that at Bahia Sucia included: (1) protecting the shoreline from erosion, storms, tides, and high winds; (2) providing a habitat for wildlife, especially birds; (3) providing a protected breeding ground for fish and shellfish; and (4) acting as a food source for aquatic creatures of all kinds. * * *

Finally, Dr. Philip E. Sorenson, an economist specializing in natural resources, discussed the economic theory that shippers of oil should be required to bear such external social costs as oil spill damages in order to prevent underpricing of their product. "If the producers and consumers of oil are able to conduct their affairs in such a way as to transfer to society a large part of the real cost of producing and consuming their product." Dr. Sorenson said, "we'll be in an inefficient economic situation: one in which the market price of the commodity will be less than the full social cost of producing it." Dr. Sorenson also presented a summary of plaintiff's claims for damages, including *inter alia* the Commonwealth's uncontested claim for cleanup expenses of $78,108.89, the $7.5 million for sediment removal and mangrove replanting, and Dr. Sorenson's own estimate of $5,526,583 as the replacement value of the invertebrate organisms killed by the oil spill.

Dr. Sorenson testified he arrived at the latter figure by * * * [extrapolating] the differences in number of organisms found in the ten—centimeter core samples over a square meter area to determine the net difference in creatures per square meter. * * * The net difference was calculated to be 1,138 creatures per square meter. This figure in turn yielded the sum of 4,605,486 creatures per acre, and a total of 92,109,720 creatures of the 20 acres of mangroves allegedly impacted by oil. * * *

To arrive at an estimate of damages, Dr. Sorenson testified he consulted catalogs from biological supply houses. From these catalogs he determined that "[m]any of these species sell at prices ranging from $1 to $4.50" and "that no animal on the list sold for less than 10 cents." [10] Dr. Sorenson assigned an average replacement value to each creature, regardless of species, of six cents. Multiplying 92,109,720 times .06 resulted in an estimate of $5,526,583 as the replacement value of the organisms "missing" from the Bahia Sucia sediments. * * *

---

10. Dr. Sorenson did not testify that the biological supply houses actually procured specimens at Bahia Sucia or that the Bahia Sucia animals were marketable through such outlets. He only stated that creatures similar to those killed could be replaced by purchasing them from the catalogs.

[The Commonwealth of Puerto Rico held the land in trust for the people. Pursuant to statutory powers, the Commonwealth sued the SS ZOE COLOCOTRONI. The statute provides that the Commonwealth may sue to recover "the total value of the damages caused to the environment and/or natural resources."]

The district court made the following findings on the issue of damages:

"1. Plaintiffs' proven claim of damage to marine organisms covers an approximate area of about 20 acres in and around the West Mangrove. The surveys conducted by Plaintiffs reliably establish that there was a decline of approximately 4,605,486 organisms per acre as a direct result of the oil spill. This means that 92,109,720 marine animals were killed by the COLOCOTRONI oil spill. The uncontradicted evidence establishes that there is a ready market with reference to biological supply laboratories, thus allowing a reliable calculation of the cost of replacing these organisms. The lowest possible replacement cost figure is $.06 per animal, with many species selling from $1.00 to $4.50 per individual. Accepting the lowest replacement cost, and attaching damages only to the lost marine animals in the West Mangrove area, we find the damages caused by Defendants to amount to $5,526,583.20.

2. The evidence is overwhelming to the effect that the sediments in and around the West Mangrove continue to be impregnated with oil. * * * The most affected spots in the West Mangrove cover an area of approximately 23 acres. It is the Court's opinion that these areas can best be reestablished by the intensive planting of mangrove and restoration of this area to its condition before the oil spill. The evidence shows that the planting of mangrove runs at about $16,500 per acre, thus bringing the cost of replanting 23 acres to $379,500. The evidence further demonstrates that the planting will require a five year monitoring and fertilizing program which will cost $36,000 per year or $180,000 for five years. The total damages thus suffered by Plaintiffs by reason of the pollution of the mangrove in the West Mangrove amount to $559,500.

3. Plaintiffs incurred in cleanup costs in the amount of $78,-108.89 which were not reimbursed from any source, and they are entitled to recover said damages from Defendants.

* * * [Defendants] argue the district court erred in failing to apply the common law "diminution in value" rule in calculating damages. Under the traditional rule, the measure of damages for tortious injury to real property is the difference in the commercial or market value of the property before and after the event causing injury. *See* Restatement (Second) of Torts § 929(1)(a) (1979). Where the property can be restored to its original condition for a sum less than the diminution in value, however, the cost of restoration may be substituted as a measure of damages. [Citation.] Defendants introduced evidence at trial tending to show that the market value of comparable property in the vicinity of

Bahia Sucia was less than $5,000 per acre, based on recent sales. Thus, defendants contend, damages here could not have exceeded $5,000 per affected acre even if the land were shown to have lost all value.

We believe that defendants have misconceived the character of the remedy created [by the statute]. The EQB is not concerned with any loss in the market or other commercial value of the Commonwealth's land. In point of fact, the EQB concedes the land has no significant commercial or market value. The claim, rather, is for the injury— broadly conceived—that has been caused to the natural environment by the spilled oil. The question before us is not whether in a typical land damage case a claim of this sort could be successfully advanced—we assume it could not—but rather whether Puerto Rico's statute * * * envisions the awarding of damages on a different basis than would have been traditionally allowed.

* * * Many unspoiled natural areas of considerable ecological value have little or no commercial or market value. Indeed, to the extent such areas have a commercial value, it is logical to assume they will not long remain unspoiled, absent some governmental or philanthropic protection. A strict application of the diminution in value rule would deny the state any right to recover meaningful damages for harm to such areas, and would frustrate appropriate measures to restore or rehabilitate the environment.

* * * [W]e think that limitation of recovery to those damages recoverable under the common law "diminution in value" rule would be inconsistent with the manifest intent of Puerto Rico's environmental statute. In enacting section 1131, Puerto Rico obviously meant to sanction the difficult, but perhaps not impossible, task of putting a price tag on resources whose value cannot always be measured by the rules of the market place. Although the diminution rule is appropriate in most contexts, and may indeed be appropriate in certain cases under section 1131, it does not measure the loss which the statute seeks to redress in a context such as the present. No market exists in which Puerto Rico can readily replace what it has lost. The loss is not only to certain plant and animal life but, perhaps more importantly, to the capacity of the now polluted segments of the environment to regenerate and sustain such life for some time into the future. That the Commonwealth did not intend, and perhaps was unable, to exploit these life forms, and the coastal areas which supported them, for commercial purposes should not prevent a damages remedy in the face of the clearly stated legislative intent to compensate for "the total value of the damages caused to the environment and/or natural resources." 12 L.P.R.A. § 1131(29). In recent times, mankind has become increasingly aware that the planet's resources are finite and that portions of the land and sea which at first glance seem useless, like salt marshes, barrier reefs, and other coastal areas, often contribute in subtle but critical ways to an environment capable of supporting both human life and the other forms of life on which we all depend. The Puerto Rico statute is obviously aimed at providing a damages remedy with sufficient scope to compensate for, and

deter, the destruction of such resources; and while we can see many problems in fashioning such a remedy, we see no reason to try to frustrate that endeavor. We therefore do not limit damages herein to the loss of market value of the real estate affected.

We turn now to whether the damages awarded by the district court were appropriate. To review the court's award, we must ascertain what a fair and equitable damages measure would be in these circumstances. * * *

* * * [W]e think the appropriate primary standard for determining damages in a case such as this is the cost reasonably to be incurred by the sovereign or its designated agency to restore or rehabilitate the environment in the affected area to its pre-existing condition, or as close thereto as is feasible without grossly disproportionate expenditures. The focus in determining such a remedy should be on the steps a reasonable and prudent sovereign or agency would take to mitigate the harm done by the pollution, with attention to such factors as technical feasibility, harmful side effects, compatibility with or duplication of such regeneration as is naturally to be expected, and the extent to which efforts beyond a certain point would become either redundant or disproportionately expensive. Admittedly, such a remedy cannot be calculated with the degree of certainty usually possible when the issue is, for example, damages on a commercial contract. On the other hand, a district court can surely calculate damages under the foregoing standard with as much or more certainty and accuracy as a jury determining damages for pain and suffering or mental anguish.

There may be circumstances where direct restoration of the affected area is either physically impossible or so disproportionately expensive that it would not be reasonable to undertake such a remedy. Some other measure of damages might be reasonable in such cases, at least where the process of natural regeneration will be too slow to ensure restoration within a reasonable period. * * * Alternatives might include acquisition of comparable lands for public parks or, as suggested by defendants below, reforestation of a similar proximate site where the presence of oil would not pose the same hazard to ultimate success. As with the remedy of restoration, the damages awarded for such alternative measures should be reasonable and not grossly disproportionate to the harm caused and the ecological values involved. The ultimate purpose of any such remedy should be to protect the public interest in a healthy, functioning environment, and not to provide a windfall to the public treasury. In emphasizing the above measures, we do not mean to rule out others in appropriate circumstances. There may indeed be cases where traditional commercial valuation rules will afford the best yardstick, as where there is a market in which the damaged resource could have been sold that reflects its actual value. Much must necessarily be left to the discretion of courts, especially before a body of precedent has arisen.

But while the district court's discretion is extensive, we are unable to agree with the approach taken by the court here in placing a value on the damaged resources. Plaintiffs presented two principal theories of damages to the court. The first theory was somewhat analogous to the primary standard we have enunciated above, focusing on plaintiffs' plan to remove the damaged mangrove trees and oil-impregnated sediments from a large area and replace them with clean sediment and container-grown mangrove plants. This plan was estimated to cost approximately $7 million. The district court sensibly and correctly rejected this plan as impractical, inordinately expensive, and unjustifiably dangerous to the healthy mangroves and marine animals still present in the area to be restored. We can find no fault with the district court's conclusion that this draconian plan was not a step that a reasonable trustee of the natural environment would be expected to take as a means of protecting the corpus of the trust.

Plaintiffs' second theory, which the court accepted, focused on the supposed replacement value of the living creatures—the epibenthic and infaunal animals—alleged to have been permanently destroyed or damaged by the oil spill. Plaintiffs repeatedly disavowed any connection between this theory and an actual restoration plan. In other words, plaintiffs did not represent that they proposed to purchase 92 million invertebrate animals for actual introduction into the sediments (which, being contaminated with oil, would hardly support them), but rather wished to use the alleged replacement value of these animals as a yardstick for estimating the quantum of harm caused to the Commonwealth. * * * [Replacement cost is an appropriate recovery only] as a component in a practicable plan for actual restoration. Thus, for example, if a state were seeking to restore a damaged area of forest, a portion of the damages sought might be allocated to replacement of wild birds or game animals or such other creatures as would not be expected to regenerate naturally within a relatively finite period of time even with appropriate restoration. This is a far different matter from permitting the state to recover money damages for the loss of small, commercially valueless creatures which assertedly would perish if returned to the oil-soaked sands, yet probably would replenish themselves naturally if and when restoration—either artificial or natural—took place.

* * * We thus hold that it was error to award $5,526,583.20 for the replacement value of the destroyed organisms.

We come finally to the disposition of this case. Defendants argue that, having rejected plaintiffs' damages theories, we should reverse the district court's judgment, except as to the Commonwealth's undisputed cleanup costs. While this is superficially an attractive course, we do not think the matter is quite so simple. To say that the law on this question is unsettled is vastly to understate the situation. The parties in this lawsuit, and we ourselves, have ventured far into uncharted waters. We do not think plaintiffs could reasonably have been expected to anticipate where this journey would take us. Though we have affirmed the district court's rejection of the Commonwealth's original, rather grandiose restoration plan, we believe the EQB should still have an opportunity to show, if it can, that some lesser steps are feasible that would have a beneficial effect on the West Mangrove ecosystem without excessive destruction of existing natural resources or disproportionate cost. The costs projected for carrying out of such reasonable lesser steps would be an appropriate award of damages. Plaintiffs may wish, at the same time, to reopen the question of alternative-site restoration, as to which the district court initially declined to take evidence, although we hasten to add that we do not now rule on whether the concept of alternative site restoration would make sense in this case as a measure of damages. We therefore, remand the case to the district court with instructions to reopen the record for further evidence on the issue of damages in line with our discussion of the principles governing recovery in cases of this sort.

* * * [Reversed and remanded.]

1. If the Bahia Sucia had been privately owned, the landowner would have a common law tort action in which recovery would probably be limited to the value of the land. Assume as correct the evidence that such value was $5,000 per acre. Why should a private owner be restricted by the economic value of the land? Do the prior cases in this section support an extension of common law to allow more creative measures, such as the ones discussed in this case? Why does it matter that the harm is covered by an environmental statute?

2. Many environmental statutes provide for specific types of recovery like the ones discussed in the case. *See, e.g.,* The Clean Water Act, 22 U.S.C. § 1321(f)(4) (as amended 1977); Outer Continental Shelf Lands Act, 43 U.S.C. § 1813(b)(3) (as amended 1978).

3. The criminal law also seeks to deter oil dumping by providing statutory penalties. The captain of the SS ZOE COLOCOTRONI was tried and convicted of violating 33 U.S.C. § 1321(b)(5) in connection with the dumping of the oil. 456 F.Supp. at 1333 n.9. Does the deterrent effect of criminal sanctions affect the goals of civil damages remedies?

C. PERSONAL INJURY DAMAGES

Section Coverage:

Personal injury tort claims involve bodily injury to the person of the plaintiff proximately resulting from the defendant's tortious conduct. Chapter 13 explores the foreseeability limitation represented by proximate cause; this section examines the basic elements of personal injury damages.

Damage rules for personal injury are independent of the basis of the claim. The focus is upon the plaintiff's condition, without regard to whether the injuries resulted from a bar-room fight or a defective product. The tort may be based upon negligence, strict liability, or intentional conduct. It is only with respect to punitive damages (Chapter 15) that the nature of the defendant's conduct affects personal injury recovery. The cases in the section concern the elements of damages for physical injuries. Not included are shock cases, such as the suits by accident bystanders who suffer injuries from watching tortious harm to loved ones. (Chapter 14) Distress, even with physical consequences, is distinguished from physical harm.

There is a distress component, however, in damages for physical harm. Recovery for bodily injury includes compensation for the plaintiff's physical pain and mental suffering. Pain and suffering are characterized as general damages in personal injury cases because bodily injury necessarily involves some degree of physical pain and suffering. Therefore, the complaint does not need to allege pain and suffering in order to present evidence of it. All other losses are considered special damages, and require special pleading, because they are the particular losses of each plaintiff.

It is helpful to distinguish between past (pre-trial) losses and future losses, if any. Elements of personal injury damages include: loss of earnings or of earning capacity, medical expenses, pain and suffering, and special expenses attributable to the injury. Most states require future losses to be reduced to their present value. This topic is covered in the chapter immediately following this one, Chapter 12, concerning the use and value of money.

A derivative action for loss of consortium with a personal injury victim is available for spouses. There is no uniformity among jurisdictions on the availability of consortium claims for other family relationships, such as for parents whose child is personally injured or for children whose parents have suffered personal injury. Loss of consortium should not be confused with other emotional intangibles, such as grief or distress.

Several state legislatures have enacted statutes affecting personal injury damages, especially in the area of medical malpractice. A common provision is to limit the dollar amount of the pain and suffering component. Some statutes alter the collateral source rule (Chapter 13) or limit the availability of punitive damages. (Chapter 15).

Model case:

A speeding motorist negligently injured a young child on a bicycle. The child's damages for permanent personal injury can include the following components for both past losses and reasonably established future expenses: medical expenses, pain and suffering, rehabilitation costs, special education costs, lost earning capacity, and psychiatric expense to recover from the trauma.

The parents might separately claim damages for loss of society with their child from the injuries. Such a claim for loss of consortium is a derivative action from the child's personal injury suit. It should not be confused with any claims the parents may have as shock victims if they witnessed the accident. Claims for loss of society with a child are an outgrowth of the consortium claims allowed when a husband or wife is injured. Although jurisdictions widely recognize loss of consortium with an injured spouse, only a few state courts have recently accepted parents' loss of consortium with a child.

FRANKEL v. UNITED STATES

321 F.Supp. 1331 (E.D.Pa.1970).

SHERIDAN, CHIEF JUDGE.

[As a result of an automobile collision with a car driven by an employee of the Department of the Army, Marilyn Heym sustained serious, irreversible personal injuries. Her guardian instituted a negligence suit against the United States pursuant to the Federal Tort Claims Act, 28 U.S.C. §§ 1346(b), 2671 *et seq.* seeking damages for her medical expenses and personal injuries.]

The hospital and medical bills to the time of trial totaled $17,325.69. These expenses were fair, reasonable and necessary for the treatment of her injuries. Under Pennsylvania law, her father is entitled to recover for the expenses incurred before she reached the age of 21. * * *

At the time of the accident, Marilyn, born November 6, 1946, was 19 years of age, had completed two years of a four year course in commercial art at the Academy of Fine Arts in Philadelphia and intended and was expected to continue to graduation, after which she intended to enter upon a career as a commercial artist. She did generally well in school, and excelled in art. Before the accident she was normal, accident free and in good health, and enjoyed the usual activities of persons in her social and economic situation, including membership in the Girl Scouts, 4–H activities and the like. She was an accomplished and a well-known rider of horses, and an instructress in all phases of horsemanship. * * *

Plaintiff claims past loss of earning capacity from shortly after the time Marilyn would have completed school, or July 1, 1968, to the time of the award. She would have been 21 years of age in July of 1968. The evidence showed that she would have completed school and embarked on a career as a commercial artist. Her progress in school, her family background and her paintings indicated that she was making excellent progress. The evidence convincingly demonstrated that she would have earned an average of $5,000.00 a year commencing July 1, 1968. * * *

* * * [Her earning capacity] to age 65 is $125,000.00 which when reduced to present worth at 6% simple interest under the Pennsylvania rule is $62,000.00, which will be awarded for this item.

Other items of damage are physical and mental pain and suffering, loss of enjoyment of life's pleasures, inconvenience, disfigurement, and permanent injuries. The Government argues that a large part of Marilyn's pain and suffering was not conscious because she was in a coma or semi-coma. Even while in a coma she responded to painful stimuli. For many weeks when she was in a semi-coma she recognized members of her family but could not communicate with them. During this time she undoubtedly appreciated pain. In the future she will experience pain from her arm, the use of the prosthesis and from the therapy that she must undergo for the rest of her life. She frequently falls "with a thud," making no attempt to break her fall. She is suffering and will continue to suffer mentally. * * * She realizes that her sudden and uncontrollable outbursts are wrong and she feels badly that she cannot explain her actions and apologizes for them. In addition, she has lost the ability to engage in those activities which normally contribute to the enjoyment of life. The possibility of marriage and motherhood are gone. [Citation.] She cannot continue in the art career that she so enjoyed, or engage in horseback riding. She has lost peace of mind and well-being. * * * In short, she has lost almost every enjoyment that life can offer. An award of $650,000.00 will be made for these items. [Citations.]

A final item of damage is what plaintiff has characterized as future hospitalization and related medical and incidental expense. Plaintiff contends that: Marilyn is reasonably expected to live out her life expectancy of 54.7 years; she will need constant care for life, both physical and psychiatric; this care cannot be provided at home; only one private institution, Fairmount Farm, near Marilyn's residence, is prepared to accept her and to render this care; and at the present rate of $75.00 a day and taking into account projected increases, an award of at least $8,046,379.00 should be made for this item. A much larger amount is requested if any part is taxable.

* * * While Marilyn is presently being maintained at home, there is no doubt that her parents will not be able to cope with her much longer, much less give her the physical and emotional therapy she needs. Fairmount Farm has 130 employees, including 40 nurses, nurses aides and attendants, servicing 114 patients. In addition, there are 50 doctors on the staff. If Marilyn were admitted to this hospital, she would have the individual attention and help she needs in her everyday activities such as washing, dressing, bathing and the like. While there is no hope for improvement in her mentality, emotional improvement is possible. This will require close individual attention. Public and most private institutions are not equipped to give this attention. Her program in these institutions would consist largely of sedation in an effort to control her outbursts. The medical testimony clearly shows that heavy sedation is not the proper course of treatment of Marilyn. There is no evidence that the regime in a public institution would be adequate or comparable to that of Fairmount Farm. There is no evidence of the costs of other private institutions, or of the comparative costs of private and public institutions. Plaintiff's claim for private institutional care is a proper item of damage.

The Government suggests that the traditional lump-sum award should not be made because of the uncertainties in forecasting the cost of long-term institutional care, and the large amount of money necessary to pay for this care; it suggests that the court order the Government to establish a $500,000.00 trust fund under the control of a fiduciary which would pay all the institutional costs, and that the court retain jurisdiction to resolve any questions of administration of the trust and order the Government to replenish the corpus if the occasion should arise. Upon Marilyn's death, the balance in the fund would revert to the United States.

The common law provides for a single lump-sum judgment. [Citation.] There can be no judgment for an indefinite amount, or a judgment payable in installments. [Citation.] The single lump-sum judgment as it relates to future damages has been criticized.[9] On the other hand, if the single recovery rule were discarded, final disposition of cases could be delayed for years, and the courts would have to assume the added burden of supervision of their awards. In ordinary cases involving private parties there are practical considerations of insurance policy limits and the ability of defendants to pay. Frequently, cases are settled or disposed of for less than they are worth because of these. In Federal Tort Claims Act actions the ability of the Government to pay is never in question. An amendment to the Federal Tort Claims Act to provide for periodic payments when future, long range damages are significant seems desirable. If such an amendment were passed, the Government would pay more in some cases and less in others, than it would under a single recovery. In all cases justice through just compensation, no more—no less, would be achieved. Such drastic changes must come from the Congress, however, and not from the courts. The Government's suggestion is rejected.

* * *

Plaintiff presented evidence that institutionalization costs have been increasing, and that the cost of mental institutional care in the Philadelphia area has increased about 5¼ percent each year over the past ten years. Thus, plaintiff's original request for damages of $1,497,412.50 ($75.00 a day × 365 days = $27,375.00 per year × life expectancy of 54.7 years = $1,497,412.50) becomes $8,046,071.00 with the application

---

9. Schreiber, Damages in Personal Injury and Wrongful Death Cases (Practicing Law Institute, 1965) at page 21:

"There are two important practical consequences of the single recovery rule. For one thing it means that all damages, future as well as past, must be taken account of at the time of trial. This in turn faces the tribunal with the difficult and uncertain task of prophesy, with no chance for second-guessing where the prophesy turns out to be mistaken or where the parties have failed to present all items of their claims.

"Another important aspect of a single recovery is the burden it casts on the successful plaintiff of wise investment and of providence, wherever the recovery must be relied on to take care of future needs.

" * * *

"These features mean that the single recovery rule is often both capricious and inflexible in its operation so that damages in accident cases, even where they are awarded and actually paid, often fail to do the job they should if accident law is to perform its function of administering accident losses efficiently in the public interest."

of a factor for future cost increases. Inflationary considerations have most commonly been used in the justification of awards. In many instances the consideration has been an evaluation of an award considering present inflationary trends as compared to awards *in the past.* * * *

The projected inflationary trend is speculation. Plaintiff has used the decade of the 1960's, one of the more inflationary times in the history of our country, as the basis for a projection of over fifty years. It is common knowledge that our Government is and has been attempting to control inflation, even to the point of considering wage and price controls. Economists differ on their predictions. Moreover, plaintiff will have money that can be invested and if inflation continues, the return on the money will be greater, and this would have an offsetting effect. Increased costs for institutional care will not be considered.

The Government urges that an award for private institutional care must be reduced to present worth. Plaintiff relies on *Yost v. West Penn Railways Co.,* 1939, 336 Pa. 407, 9 A.2d 368, for the proposition that present worth does not apply to future medical expenses, and that the institutionalization required for Marilyn falls into this category. Many of the costs which make up the daily rate of care and maintenance are not future medical expenses but rather are custodial in nature. The Pennsylvania rule that future medical expenses are not to be reduced to present worth is based on the theory as expressed in *Yost* that:

> " * * * Future medical attention presupposes an out-of-pocket expenditure by the plaintiff. She was entitled to have defendant presently place in her hands the money necessary to meet her future medical expenses, as estimated by the jury based upon the testimony heard, so that she will have it ready to lay out when the service is rendered. * * * "

Yost expresses a sound general rule, although the kind of medical attention to be rendered does not appear from the facts. In the usual case, future medical expenses are sought to remedy a specific malady. If an accident victim will be required to undergo surgery, he should have the money to pay for the service if it is rendered shortly after the verdict. To apply the present worth rule to future medical expenses in most instances would necessitate the resolution of many collateral, variable and imponderable factors such as whether the victim intended to have medical attention immediately or whether his health would permit immediate treatment and if not, when it would permit it. Clearly, there would be no workable way in which to apply the present worth rule.

Here, the expenses of institutionalization will recur periodically in the same manner as future earnings are payable periodically. If the rule of *Yost* were applied and the sum not reduced to present worth, plaintiff would have the money to "lay out" *far before* "the service is rendered." Moreover, the return on any non-reduced sum, properly invested, would exceed the cost of the institutional care. Thus, Marilyn would not only be compensated for her institutionalization, but would reap a windfall. Damages means compensation for a legal injury sustained. [Citation.]

The purpose of damages is not to make people wealthy. * * * The general rule of *Yost*, as in the case with many general rules, must yield to exceptional circumstances. The award for institutionalization will be reduced to present worth. The amount so computed is $461,084.00 ($75.00 a day × 365 days = $27,375.00 per year × 30 years = $821,250.00 reduced to present worth = $461,084.00).

* * *

To summarize, the damages to be awarded for the injuries suffered by Marilyn are $1,202,909.69:

To Alvin H. Frankel, Guardian of Marilyn Heym, an incompetent:

Past medical and related expenses	$ 1,414.00
Loss of earning capacity, past and future	74,500.00
Pain, suffering, inconvenience, disfigurement and loss of life's pleasures	650,000.00
Future institutionalization expense	461,084.00
	$1,186,998.00

To Herbert Heym, her father:

Medical and other expenses incurred during Marilyn's minority	$ 15,911.69

* * *

———

1. Note that the principal case was decided in 1970. We thus have the benefit of hindsight to evaluate the judge's comments about the future. We now know that the court's refusal to consider inflation with respect to the plaintiff's future medical care left her badly undercompensated. Since 1970, inflation in medical costs has been even greater than in the overall cost of living. Every $1 of medical costs in 1970 now costs approximately $4. In the overall cost of living, goods and services purchased with every $1 now cost approximately $3.

The judge was hopeful that the inflationary trend during the decade of the 1960s was over, but his prediction was wrong. He referred to governmental efforts to control inflation "even to the point of considering wage and price controls." Ironically, the Nixon administration began wage and price controls shortly after this opinion. Inflation was nonetheless rampant. By 1975 prices were up 38 percent.

The judge further commented that even if inflation continued, the plaintiff would be protected by a greater return on her money. This reassuring statement depends upon how her father, the guardian, invested the award. If her father shared the judge's sanguine view of future trends, he would have purchased long term investments in order to take advantage of existing interest rates before they would fall with lower inflation. If the award was put in such investments, the plaintiff's money was not "protected" because their value fell rapidly during the ensuing high inflation. These issues are developed further in Chapter 12.

Future economic trends cannot be predicted with certainty today any more than in 1970. What is the solution for personal injury victims?

2. An alternative to the lump sum payment of a personal injury award is periodic payments. For a seriously injured person there may be many advantages to receiving smaller sums of money over a longer period of time. One important advantage is that the lump sum of money cannot be lost completely through mismanagement or misfortune. The injured recipients are assured a constant stream of payments even if they outlive their normal life expectancy; payments for each injured party stop only at death. Certain tax advantages may accompany periodic payments as well. Although a lump sum personal injury award itself is not taxable, the interest it earns upon investment is fully taxable.

To date, periodic payments are used more in private structured settlements than in judgments. By way of settlement the parties can agree to periodic payments, with or without adjustments for changes in the plaintiff's condition.

The Uniform Laws Commissioners have written a Model Periodic Payment of Judgments Act, 14 Uniform Laws Ann. 2 (West Supp.1981). The Act is explained by the Reporter in Henderson, "Periodic Payments of Bodily Injury Awards," 66 Amer.Bar Ass'n J. 301 (1980). *See generally* Hindert, Dehner & Hindert, Structured Settlements and Periodic Payment Judgments (1986).

3. Public dissatisfaction with the operation of the tort system has produced a variety of reforms. Some changes are directed at the substantive law, others at remedies.

Fundamental substantive changes began with the workers' compensation movement at the beginning of the century. *See* Weinstein, The Corporate Ideal in the Liberal State, 1900–1918 (1968). In every state there is now a no-fault compensation scheme for workers' injuries. An injured worker no longer needs to prove that the employer was negligent, and is no longer barred by any defense such as assumption of the risk. In exchange for the substantive changes favorable to workers, the damage scheme provides for lower recoveries than a successful personal injury tort claimant ordinarily would recover. The merits of this trade-off and any effect the workers' compensation scheme may have on overall industrial safety are the subject of debate. For a critical view of the history of workers' compensation acts in the context of injuries from asbestos *see* M. Brodeur, Outrageous Misconduct (1985).

In the second half of this century public attention turned to injuries from automobile accidents. Responding to dissatisfaction with the tort system, scholars advocated no-fault auto accident legislation. Particularly notable is the 1965 book by R. Keeton & J. O'Connell, Basic

Protection for Accident Victims—A Blueprint for Reforming Automobile Insurance. Central to this reform movement is recognition of the role of insurance. Potential defendants seek "third party" insurance to protect them from losses occasioned by tort liability. The no-fault scheme for auto accidents relies upon a "first party" insurance whereby insureds recover directly from their own insurers.

Proponents of no-fault plans identify as major advantages the guaranteed recoveries for injury victims and savings in the transactional costs of litigation. Opponents question the amount of savings and argue that traditional tort law has a deterrent effect on drivers.

About half of the states have passed some form of automobile no-fault legislation. There is wide variation among them. Unlike workers' compensation acts, the no-fault plans for auto accidents replace only part of the tort system. *See* U.S. Dept. of Transportation, Compensating Auto Victims: A Follow-up Report on No–Fault Auto Insurance Experiences (1985).

CATES v. BROWN

278 Ark. 242, 645 S.W.2d 658 (1983).

DUDLEY, JUSTICE. * * *

Appellee Roy Brown was the operator of a logging truck belonging to appellee Gaylor Thomas. The truck held a full cargo of pulpwood logs on its bed and was parked unattended on a descending slope in a line of trucks to be unloaded at the Arkansas Kraft Corporation in Conway. One of the appellants, Billy H. Cates, a carpenter, was engaged in construction work downhill from the unloading area. Either the gear became disengaged or the braking mechanism failed, or both, and the truck rolled toward Cates. He was injured while attempting to avoid being hit. He and his wife, Sandra, filed suit in tort. The jury awarded $2,000 to Billy Cates and $300 to Sandra Cates. They appeal. * * *

Loss of earnings and loss of earning capacity are two separate elements of damage. * * * Briefly stated, damage resulting from loss of earning capacity is the loss of the ability to earn in the future. The impairment of the capacity to earn is the gravamen of the element. It is sometimes confused with permanency of the injury but is a separate element. However, an instruction on this element is normally given only in the event of a permanent injury. Proof of this element does not require the same specificity or detail as does proof of loss of future wages. [Citation.] The reason is that a jury can observe the appearance of the plaintiff, his age and the nature of the injuries which will impair his capacity to earn. In addition, proof of specific pecuniary loss is not indispensable to recovery for this element.

Conversely, the element of loss of future earnings must be proven with reasonable certainty. [Citation.] An instruction on this element is normally given only when the plaintiff will lose wages in the future but has sustained no injury which will impair his earning capacity. In the case before us, the damage from loss of future earnings would be the loss of wages from the date of the trial until the plaintiff is able to return to full employment. * * *

Here, appellant Cates asked for the instruction on the loss of future wages. He was entitled to the instruction only if he proved this element with reasonable certainty. Loss of future earnings is proved with reasonable certainty by evidence involving two basic factors: (1) the amount of wages lost for some determinable period, for example, $100 per month; and (2) the future period over which wages will be lost, for example, 18 months. The jury is able, then, to calculate the product of the two factors which, reduced to its present value, represents the loss of future earnings.

Even though his testimony was controverted, appellant Cates supplied the first factor for the jury's consideration. He testified that from the date of the accident until the date of the trial, a period of 20 months, he had been unable to work for 684 hours as a result of his injuries, which amounted to lost wages of $5,745.37. However, he did not testify about a period of lost future wages. His supervisor testified that because of the injury appellant was unable to perform as well as he had in the past and that because of the injury Cates, while injured, would be the last hired on a new job and the first discharged on an existing job. Thus, his supervisor's testimony on the second factor was that there was some undetermined period of loss of future wages, but that testimony still allows only sheer speculation on the second factor. This failure of proof was not supplied by any of the other witnesses who testified on the subject. The three other witnesses were physicians and not one of them testified that appellant Cates would suffer any future loss of wages. Indeed, two of the orthopedic surgeons testified that Cates had no disability and could return to full work whenever he chose. The third testified that appellee's figure of physical impairment would not exceed five percent of the body as a whole but he offered no testimony about a future loss of wages. He stated: "A test of time is the only thing that would answer that accurately." We need not decide whether this testimony would have been sufficient to require an instruction on loss of future earning capacity because appellant did not request such an instruction and does not raise the issue on appeal. We need only determine whether the jury should have been instructed on the loss of future earnings and that, in turn, is determined by whether the jury could have reached a conclusion, without speculation, on a future period of time over which wages would be lost. The answer is obvious. The second factor was not proven. Conjecture and speculation cannot be permitted to replace proof. Thus, the trial court was correct in refusing to give the requested instruction on loss of future earnings.

* * *

Appellant Billy Cates' last point is that the trial court erred in allowing questions about deductions from wages. The contention has merit. Cates' employer was called to the stand to dispute Cates' prior testimony about the loss of wages up until the time of trial. He testified three times that he had given the gross amount of wages paid to Cates. Even after that, the following took place:

> Q. [Appellees' attorney]. That does not include the necessary deductions that would come out of a man's hourly wages?
>
> A. No, sir.
>
> Q. No taxes; no social security?

Appellants' attorney then objected on the specific ground that an award for lost wages should not be reduced by taxes or social security. The trial court overruled the objection and allowed the witness to answer: "It does not include any deductions for taxes and Social Security and so forth."

Curiously, we were not presented the issue of deducting taxes in computing any type of personal injury awards until this year. We then held that the trial court should not instruct the jury that the plaintiff's recovery for personal injury is tax free. [Citations.] This case presents a corollary issue in computing awards for lost wages. We adopt the preferable rule which is that the measure of damages for a wage loss is the gross amount of wages. [Citations.] Therefore, taxes, Social Security, retirement contributions or other withholdings may not be used to reduce a plaintiff's recovery for lost wages. * * * The loss of earnings should have been decided solely on material issues and taxation is not such an issue. * * *

[Reversed and remanded.]

---

1. A plaintiff must prove separately claims for past losses of income and future ones reasonably certain to occur from the personal injury. A worker with a fixed wage and secure employment at the time of injury will find it easier than an unemployed or underemployed worker to prove loss of wages between the time of injury and trial. Even so, it is a difficult task to construct hypothetically how a plaintiff's post-injury life would have developed had the injury not occurred. Would the plaintiff have been laid off work? Promoted? Transferred? This task is impossible to do in an exact way, but testimony with respect to the history of similarly situated workers during the time frame is very helpful.

If the past is difficult to calculate, it is clear why there are even greater problems predicting future lost income. As the principal case indicates, it is helpful to distinguish between future lost earnings and loss of earning capacity. An employed worker with a predictable income at the time of injury can use expert testimony to project what similarly situated workers are likely to earn for some reasonable distance in the future. *See, e.g.,* Knight v. Texaco, Inc., 786 F.2d 1296 (5th Cir.1986) (defendant employed injured roustabout at another job with higher wage, but testimony suggested job was to be eliminated after trial and expert testimony established future losses based on probable future wages of a successful roustabout).

2.   Loss of earning capacity is distinguishable from lost income in specific employment.   The capacity to work refers generally to one's marketability in the workplace.   Factors affecting employment include education, age, experience, talents, general health and physical capacity. A permanently injured person may have lost future earning capacity even if unemployed at the time of the injury.   *See, e.g.,* Bishop v. Poore, 475 So.2d 486 (Ala.1985) (unemployed worker alleging permanent injury may present evidence of lost earning capacity).

3.   A student may present proof of reasonably anticipated future employment.   In *Hodges v. Plasky,* for example, the plaintiff was a rehabilitated polio victim who had returned to college when he was involved in a car accident that totally incapacitated him.   His damages from the negligent driver included compensation for his future lost earning capacity.   The court noted that Mr. Plasky was a person of "unusual energy, drive, ambition, and the possessor of undaunted courage and determination."   The jury verdict for approximately $85,000 in 1957 was upheld.   300 S.W.2d 955 (Tex.Civ.App.1957).   *See also* Wells v. Colorado College, 478 F.2d 158 (10th Cir.1973) (sufficient basis of student's athletic prowess prior to injury).

4.   Personal injury damage awards are exempt from federal tax and from most state income taxes.   Interest from awards is taxable, however, and adversely affects the calculation of the present value of awards for future losses, studied in Chapter 12.

5.   In the principal case the court considered whether tax liability on wages should affect the calculation of lost past and future income. Should lost income be measured by gross earnings or net earnings after taxes?   Jurisdictions are divided.   Many courts have held that tax deductions from income are improper and that gross earnings are the proper measure because the estimation of taxes is too speculative.   For example, in Hoge v. Anderson, 200 Va. 364, 106 S.E.2d 121 (1958), the court held that loss of wages means gross pay, not "take home" pay. The defendant's attorney was not allowed to cross-examine the plaintiff's witness about deductions on the payroll slips because only the gross earnings were pertinent.

Other courts have allowed tax deductions from gross lost earnings. These opinions reason that even though the tax estimation is uncertain, it is necessary to prevent a windfall to the plaintiff.   For example, in Floyd v. Fruit Industries, Inc., 144 Conn. 659, 136 A.2d 918 (1957), the court allowed a deduction for the probable income taxes on the lost wages.   The opinion noted that any rule based on the hypothesis that no income taxes would be paid is unjust, unrealistic and unfair.   The court rejected the argument that an income tax factor was too speculative. That factor was held no more conjectural than many others admitted to the consideration of the jury.

Some cases have distinguished types of income in formulating a tax rule. For example, in Beaulieu v. Elliott, 434 P.2d 665 (Alaska 1967), the court held that past lost income should be adjusted for probable tax liability, but that future lost income should not include an estimate for taxes.

GRAEFF v. BAPTIST TEMPLE OF SPRINGFIELD

576 S.W.2d 291 (Mo.1978).

SIMEONE, SPECIAL JUDGE.

[An eight-year-old boy was injured when he alighted from a bus and was struck by a motorist. The jury found in favor of the boy in his suit against the bus owner and awarded $97,100. The trial court ordered a new trial and the plaintiff appealed.]

* * *

During the opening portion of plaintiff's argument, the plaintiff's attorney argued the following:

> "All right, what are those damages,.... This boy was in the hospital for 40 days and we think, and we suggest this, for this 40 days in the hospital, we think $4,000 to $4,500 is a modest sum for the kind of agony Frankie underwent with five operations.... Now, after he came home from the hospital he was in a cast.... And for that period of time, being in that cast for 34 days, we say somewhere in the range of $3,400 to $3,600 is a modest sum.... Then excluding all this up to the present time, 413 days have elapsed, and in that period of time this is the way Frankie's leg has looked,.... For those to the present time, 413 days, we say eight to nine thousand dollars is a modest sum.

> "What about the future? ... You can see the way he has to take care of his leg when he has done nothing but sit in the courtroom. Your verdict must be for life and for the future, these 23,701 days [64.89 years] we think a fair amount would be $71,103 to $80,000, and either column you use (writing on large paper before the jury)—it ranges from $86,503 to $97,100, and we say that this is a small amount for a lifetime of injury."

* * *

On this appeal, plaintiff-Graeff makes several points: he contends that the court erred in granting a new trial to Baptist Temple on the issue of plaintiff's argument concerning damages because (a) the argument of plaintiff's counsel was in accordance with Ricketts v. Kansas City Stock Yards of Maine, 537 S.W.2d 613 (Mo.App.1976), (b) such argument did not contain any mathematical formula, (c) the jury's verdict does not reflect that a per diem formula was used, and (d) error in the argument, if any, was harmless because the verdict was not excessive and found by the court to be so. * * *

One of the most difficult decisions facing the jury in a personal injury action is to decide the amount of monetary award, if any, that the plaintiff is entitled to be awarded as compensation for past, present and future pain and suffering. The measure of damages for pain and suffering in this state is and has been what is fair and reasonable. * * * No method is available to the jury by which it can objectively evaluate such damages, and no witness may express his subjective opinion concerning the matter. "From time immemorial, the judicial measure of damages for pain and suffering has been fair and reasonable compensation ... because there is and can be no established standard, fixed basis, or mathematical rule by which such damages may be calculated." *Faught v. Washam,* 329 S.W.2d 588, 602 (Mo.1959). In a very real sense, the jury is required to evaluate in terms of monetary compensation the injuries and pain and suffering sustained. In guiding the jury in this difficult task, the courts, including those in this state, permit counsel to suggest a "lump sum", and the "mere argumentative suggestion" of a lump sum is not error. It is proper to inform the jury of the total amount of damages sought and this technique does not seem to be questioned. * * *

The controversy which has raged over the past several decades has been the propriety of the so-called "per diem" argument made by plaintiff's counsel to the jury.

The "pure" "per diem" argument discussed in the numerous judicial decisions reduces the physical and mental suffering down into units of years, days, hours or minutes, and then sets a value on each such unit. Each unit is multiplied by the total number of such units which gives a total value of compensation.

* * *

The "pure" per diem argument—whether an attorney may argue to the jury that his client's damages for pain and suffering may be measured in terms of dollars for a specific unit of time—has been debated and discussed for years. Few issues have evoked more controversy. There is no unanimity among the states. * * * The weight of authority favors the use of such an argument.

Botta v. Brunner, 26 N.J. 82, 138 A.2d 713, 60 A.L.R.2d 1331 (1958) is the leading decision prohibiting such an argument. In *Botta,* the Supreme Court of New Jersey upheld the trial court's refusal to allow plaintiff's attorney to suggest that the client's damages for pain and suffering be measured by units. Such statements are not evidence and such statements substitute unproven, speculative and fanciful standards of evaluation for evidence. Such argument instills in the minds of the jurors impressions, figures and amounts not in evidence. Such valuations have no foundation in the evidence. "In the final analysis, ... [such] suggestions ... constitute an unwarranted intrusion into the domain of the jury.... 'Jurors know the nature of the pain, embarrassment and inconvenience, and they also know the nature of money....' " *Botta,* 138 A.2d at 725, 60 A.L.R.2d at 1345–1346.

* * *

The leading case in Missouri is *Faught v. Washam, supra.* * * * Recognizing a "sharp cleavage" among the decisions, it was held that the "considerations advanced by the authorities disapproving the mathematical formula argument are more persuasive."

> "Whatever may be the cold logic or academic theory of the matter, the ungilded reality is that such argument is calculated and designed to implant in the juror's minds definite figures and amounts not theretofore in the record ... and to influence the jurors to adopt those figures and amounts in evaluating pain and suffering and in measuring damages therefor." *Faught,* 320 S.W.2d at 603.

* * * The posture in which the plaintiff's counsel in this case offered the figures is such that he did not refer to any per day or per hour amount but merely suggested a lump sum for the specific periods of hospitalization, the time in the cast, the pain and suffering for the period from injury to trial, and for future life expectancy. The argument was not broken down into minutes, hours or days. * * *

We therefore conclude on this point that the argument of counsel for plaintiff was not within the limitations and objections of *Faught.*

We are not persuaded that because the jury reached a verdict identical to the maximum amount suggested by plaintiff's counsel, that such an argument is to be condemned. *Faught* stated the "proof of the pudding is in the eating," by referring to Braddock v. Seaboard Air Line R. Co., 80 So.2d 662 (Fla.1955), aff'd. 96 So.2d 127 (Fla. banc 1957) when the jury returned a verdict in the exact amount requested. But despite such isolated instances there can be little doubt that in the vast majority of cases the jury does not follow counsel's suggestions. [Citation.] Such an argument places little faith in the jury. The jury is still bound by the court's instructions and is presumed to do its duty and award damages that are just and reasonable. We therefore rule this point against respondent Temple and conclude that the trial court erred in finding the argument of plaintiff's counsel prejudicial.

* * *

Baptist Temple contends that the jury verdict against it in the amount of $97,100.00 was "clearly" excessive. * * * We rule this point adversely to the respondent Baptist Temple.

There is no precise formula for determining whether a verdict is excessive; each case must be considered on its own facts. Consideration is given to the nature and extent of the injuries and the diminished earning capacity, economic conditions, plaintiff's age, and a comparison of the compensation awarded and permitted in cases of comparable injuries. [Citations.] The ultimate test is what fairly and reasonably compensates plaintiff for the injuries sustained.

The injuries received by Frankie were serious; Frankie had to undergo five operations, scar tissue developed, the scar tissue was permanent, there is a likelihood of future operations, his life expectancy was lengthy, he cannot engage in several occupations which would be detrimental to his leg; he suffered a 10% disability of the leg. Under all these circumstances we agree with the trial court that the verdict was not excessive. The jury is vested with a broad discretion in fixing the amount of damages. The verdict is comparable to other situations.

* * * [Remanded to reinstate the verdict and enter judgment.]

———

1. Per diem arguments take many forms. In addition to the "pure" per diem and lump sum ones discussed in the principal case, there is also a "job offer" per diem approach. The argument to the jury goes something like this: "I want to offer you a job. You will get paid just (some dollar figure) a day for this job and you must work 24 hours a day and never get a day off. Your job is to suffer the disability of the plaintiff." Courts generally have held that this variation of the per diem argument is subject to the same rules as the "pure" per diem argument: "How much is it worth to suffer the pain this plaintiff has endured and continues to suffer? A dollar a (minute/hour/day)? Two dollars? Three? If we say just three dollars a day, then (multiplication times number of minutes, hours, or days) is a modest award."

2. A related form of argument, often combined with per diem, is called the "golden rule" approach. Plaintiff's attorney asks jurors to award damages in an amount they would want for their own suffering, or conversely its avoidance. For example, the following argument is not permitted in New Jersey:

> Remember the wisdom tooth, a little canker sore in your mouth. You can't get rid of it. You may take Tylenol. Or take a fractured tooth, finger, a cut, a burn. What is the pain worth for one hour? You've gone to doctors and dentists. An anesthesiologist, you know how much he charges just to limit or prevent pain during the course of an operation. You know how much a dentist charges to give a shot of Novocain so you don't feel pain for ten, fifteen minutes. How much is that pain worth for one hour? When you get that hour, think about the thousands of hours that Ken Henker has suffered pain just the last three years ... The jury is going to tell how much is owed him for that pain, thousands of hours in the past and thousands of hours in the future.

See Henker v. Preybylowski, 216 N.J.Super. 513, 524 A.2d 455 (1987); Cox v. Valley Fair Corp., 83 N.J. 381, 416 A.2d 809 (1980).

3. Should a pain and suffering award be only for pain that any person would feel, or should it reflect this particular plaintiff's pain? Some individuals have a higher or lower threshold for pain than most people. Consider also phantom pain. In Jarrell v. Ft. Worth Steel &

Mfg. Co., 666 S.W.2d 828 (Mo.App.1984), a man lost his right arm to an ice conveyor. In the violent accident the machine totally and traumatically tore off the arm and part of the back at the shoulder. He later suffered phantom limb pain at the stump, in addition to other emotional disorders from the trauma.

4. What are the most persuasive arguments for prohibiting per diem arguments? Consider the following:

(1) The attorney is giving impermissible testimony by suggesting a formula for pain and suffering;

(2) There is no evidentiary basis for the formula;

(3) Juries are misled and tricked by the effect of multiplication;

(4) Defendant's counsel is placed in a very difficult position following such an argument.

Are there other reasons that the per diem arguments should not be allowed? Are the arguments fundamentally unfair, even if one cannot articulate a reason why?

5. Compare the reasons commonly given for allowing the per diem arguments:

(1) The judge can explain to the jury the difference between evidence and argument;

(2) The jury needs some practical guidance in making pain and suffering awards;

(3) The jury instructions guide the jury to estimate a proper amount based upon the evidence;

(4) Defense attorneys can anticipate per diem arguments and be prepared to counter them.

Are there other reasons why the majority of jurisdictions are correct when they allow per diem arguments? Does the debate really turn on one's opinions about civil juries in general?

6. Is pain and suffering an appropriate component of personal injury damages? Is it possible to fix a dollar amount on an intangible loss? Are large verdicts justifiable? Insurance coverage for defendants in many personal injury cases is the source of the money paid to plaintiffs. The cost is thus spread throughout the insureds in defendant's class by the cost of the insurance premium. Self-insured corporations spread the cost of personal injury awards through the price of their goods or services. Much recent debate has centered on whether society is best served by compensating some of its injured by large personal injury awards. Limiting pain and suffering is one means of reducing awards.

Such limitations have appeared in numerous tort reform acts. The constitutionality of such limitations on medical malpractice awards was upheld in Fein v. Permanente Medical Group, 38 Cal.3d 137, 695 P.2d

665, 211 Cal.Rptr. 368 (1985), *cert. denied* with dissenting opinion by Justice White, 474 U.S. 892, 106 S.Ct. 214, 88 L.Ed.2d 215 (1985).

Plaintiffs have had some success with attacking statutory damages limitations on state constitutional grounds. In Lucas v. United States, 757 S.W.2d 687 (Tex.1988), for example, the Texas Supreme Court held that the medical malpractice statutory cap on damages violated the Texas Constitution. *See also* Wright v. Central Du Page Hospital Association, 63 Ill.2d 313, 347 N.E.2d 736 (1976); Carson v. Maurer, 120 N.H. 925, 424 A.2d 825 (1980). *But see* Johnson v. St. Vincent Hospital, Inc., 273 Ind. 374, 404 N.E.2d 585 (1980).

7. What if a jury finds "for the plaintiff" but assesses damages at "no" dollars? Should judgment be entered for plaintiff? For defendant? Should the court order an entirely new trial? A new trial limited to damages? *See* Klein v. Miller, 159 Or. 27, 77 P.2d 1103 (1938). *See also* Freshwater v. Booth, 160 W.Va. 156, 233 S.E.2d 312 (1977) (typology of cases involving inadequate verdicts).

8. What if the jury agreed that liability was established but could not resolve conflicting evidence on the extent to which there were injuries attributable to the defendant? Would an award equal to the amount of medical bills, but nothing for pain and suffering, be permissible? *See* Miller v. San Diego Gas & Electric Co., 212 Cal.App.2d 555, 28 Cal.Rptr. 126 (1963) (out of pocket losses awarded by a sympathetic jury when liability proven but not injury).

9. What if a jury finds both negligence by the defendant and contributory negligence by the plaintiff in a comparative negligence jurisdiction? Could the verdict for only special damages without pain and suffering be upheld as an adjustment to liability? *See* Benton v. B.F. Walker Truck Line, Inc., 410 S.W.2d 822 (Tex.Civ.App.1967).

10. What if an unsegregated verdict by the jury awards the exact amount of disputed special damages? *See* Wheeler v. Huston, 288 Or. 467, 605 P.2d 1339 (1980).

PROBLEM: BABY ALISSA AND THE CONFUSED DOCTOR

Jim and Anna Pegman were expecting their first child to be born on August 6, but the due date passed uneventfully. The obstetrician explained that first babies are often late and assured them that all was normal. When the baby was eleven days late, Anna Pegman awoke with excruciating pain. Her husband rushed her to the hospital, but she was sent home again after examination by the physician in charge, Dr. Hill. Although the nurse had attached a fetal monitor and the instrument recorded a heartbeat indicating infant distress, Dr. Hill did not undertake the necessary surgical delivery. The reason the patient was sent home instead was that Dr. Hill, a medical resident, did not know how to read the fetal monitor and was too embarrassed to call the supervising physician or to make an inquiry of the experienced nurse.

When Anna Pegman delivered by normal birth the next day, a baby girl named Alissa was born. Baby Alissa was not normal, however. The failure to deliver her the preceding day caused brain damage from insufficient oxygen. As a result she has cerebral palsy. She is expected to live a normal life span as a severely retarded and partially paralyzed person who will suffer constant physical discomfort. Experts testify that she will never be able to walk, talk, or feed herself, nor will she gain bladder and bowel control. Otherwise she will grow to normal adult size.

By the time of the malpractice trial on these facts, Alissa is three. She is unable to lift her head, turn herself over, or lift a bottle. She requires special chairs, special swings, and special toys. Assuming liability is established, how should damages be measured?

HEALY v. WHITE

173 Conn. 438, 378 A.2d 540 (1977).

SPEZIALE, ASSOCIATE JUSTICE.

This personal injury action was tried to the jury as a hearing in damages, the issue of the defendants' liability having been determined by summary judgment. The defendants have appealed from the judgments rendered on the verdicts for the plaintiffs.

On July 24, 1973, the plaintiff Brian Healy, then seven and a half years old, was riding as a passenger in an automobile operated by his mother, Mary Jane Healy. At the intersection of Routes 25 and 202 in Newtown, their automobile was struck by a tractor-trailer truck owned by the defendant Silliman Company and operated by its employee, the defendant Allen H. White. As a result of the impact, Brian was thrown from the car onto the pavement. He was taken by ambulance to Danbury Hospital and, subsequently, to Yale–New Haven Hospital.

On July 11, 1974, the present negligence action was begun. After summary judgment on liability was rendered against the defendants, the plaintiffs filed a substituted complaint in two counts. The first count, claiming $750,000 in damages, was in behalf of Brian Healy and alleged, inter alia, that, as a result of the defendants' negligence, Brian had been violently thrown from his car and had suffered various physical injuries which included the "aggravation and worsening of a specific learning disability" and resulted in a "permanent minimal brain dysfunction syndrome [brain damage] with associated multiple psychomotor seizures [permanent epilepsy]." The second count was on behalf of Brian's father, Bartholomew Healy. It alleged that, as a result of the injuries sustained by his minor son, he had incurred and would in the future incur expenses for Brian's hospitalization, physicians' care and other medical needs, as well as expenses for private tutors and teaching specialists. The ad damnum to this second count claimed $125,000 damages.

In answering the substituted complaint, the defendants admitted their negligence and the allegations that Brian had suffered "fractured ribs, and multiple contusions and abrasions." The granting of the plaintiffs' motion for summary judgment eliminated any consideration of liability during the trial. The jury returned a verdict of $350,000 damages on the first count and $60,000 on the second count. Thereafter, the court denied the defendants' motion to set aside the verdicts, judgments were entered, and the defendants appealed.

* * * [The court reviewed the medical evidence on the permanency of the epilepsy and found sufficient evidence in expert testimony that the odds of permanency were greater than fifty percent.]

Our final consideration is whether the evidence was sufficient to support the verdict on the second count insofar as Brian's father claimed damages for future medical and educational expenses to be incurred because of Brian's injuries. There was sufficient qualified and undisputed testimony from which the jury could conclude that it was reasonably probable that Brian's conditions would, for a long time, necessitate future treatment, medications, medical therapy and supervision and would even require neurosurgery.

There was also evidence from which the jury could find that following his accident, Brian received a lower score in his I.Q. testing; his school work deteriorated badly; the epilepsy medications would continue to affect his learning adversely; these medications, combined with the problems from his brain damage, would severely limit his functioning in school; and special education would be essential for a very long time. [A medical expert] specifically testified that Brian "certainly is doing very poorly. The only hope that this youngster has to at least gain enough academic skills to make him competitive is for him to get special education." * * *

There was strong evidence that Brian would need special schooling for a long time; the actual cost of such education in private schools was established by testimony; and the defendants took no exception to the court's charge to the jury on this item of damages. From this evidence the jury could reach a valid conclusion as to (1) the reasonable probability of Brian's continued need for special schooling and (2) the reasonable value of such schooling. This evidence alone, without regard to Brian's future medical needs, fully supports the jury's award of damages to his father for future expenses during Brian's minority.

The defendants make no claim that the amount of damages on either count is excessively high in and of itself. The claim is, rather, one of insufficient evidence. The jurors could reasonably have found in accordance with the verdicts as rendered on both counts, giving the evidence the most favorable construction in support of the verdicts to which it is reasonably entitled. The verdicts could, therefore, not be set aside as being against the evidence and should stand. [Citations.]

There is no error.

———

1. Prediction of future disability, such as Brian's future epilepsy in the principal case, is often difficult. What if there is a fifty-fifty chance of a future medical condition? Consider the observation of the Oregon Supreme Court in *Crawford v. Seufert:* "For medical testimony to have any probative value, it must at least advise the jury that the inference drawn by the doctor is more probably correct than incorrect. If the probabilities are in balance, the matter is left to speculation. Speculation filtered through a jury is still speculation." 236 Or. 369, 388 P.2d 456, 459 (1964).

What if the testimony had been that only ten percent of the people in Brian's position still have epilepsy by the age of sixteen? No damages for this unlikely occurrence would be awarded, but what if Brian was one of the unlucky ten percent? Should judgments not be final? Should plaintiffs be able to reopen cases years later and seek more damages? If the issue were to arise in a child support suit against a parent in a domestic relations case, the court would retain jurisdiction and allow a change in support to meet changing conditions. Is it desirable to treat personal injury claims differently?

Conversely, reconsider the fact that Brian actually did receive damages for the future condition because the odds were greater than fifty percent. If Brian turns out to be among the lucky minority that are cured, should the defendant be able to reopen the case to recover the excess compensation?

2. What about future medical conditions that the plaintiff does not currently suffer but probably will later? Consider a plaintiff who was negligently exposed to toxic chemicals and who has some probability of developing cancer sometime in the future. Should there be an award for the fear and distress about the prospective cancer? For the increased risk itself? For regular check-ups to attempt early detection of any cancer?

In Hagerty v. L & L Marine Services, Inc., 788 F.2d 315 (5th Cir.1986), a seaman was accidentally soaked with toxic chemicals. He suffered no great harm at the time except dizziness, leg cramps, and a stinging sensation in his extremities. In the suit that was allowed against his employer, the court found sufficient actual physical injury to support the cause of action. His damages included an award for his mental anguish and cancerphobia. He was also allowed medical expenses for continued check-ups. No damages were allowed for the increased risk of cancer. Instead, any latent cancer could be the basis of a subsequent suit; the statute of limitations would begin upon diagnosis. The court noted the rule requiring all damages for a "single injury" to be tried at one time, but held that later suit for latent disease does not necessarily isolate that rule.

3. What about shortened life expectancy? Some courts have allowed shortened life expectancy as a separate compensable element of damages. In Morrison v. Stallworth, 73 N.C.App. 196, 326 S.E.2d 387 (1985), for example, a 45-year-old woman went to her gynecologist with

a lump in her breast. Two negative examinations by the doctor served as the basis of her malpractice suit when a subsequent biopsy revealed a malignancy. The case was remanded because the trial court improperly excluded evidence of shortened life expectancy as an element of damages.

4. A federal district court is authorized by Federal Rule of Evidence 706 to appoint expert witnesses of its own selection. In Reilly v. United States the Court of Appeals for the First Circuit recognized an inherent judicial power to appoint technical advisors, apart from the statutory authorization. The court cautioned:

> [S]uch appointments should be the exception and not the rule, and should be reserved for truly extraordinary cases where the introduction of outside skills and expertise, not possessed by the judge, will hasten the just adjudication of a dispute without dislodging the delicate balance of the juristic role.

> * * * Appropriate instances, we suspect, will be hen's teeth rare. The modality is, if not a last, a near-to-last resort, to be engaged only where the trial court is faced with problems of unusual difficulty, sophistication, and complexity, involving something well beyond the regular questions of fact and law with which judges routinely grapple. Although a technical advisor can be valuable in an appropriate case, the judge must not be eager to lighten his load without the best of cause. 863 F.2d 149 (1st Cir.1988).

See generally, Sink, "The Unused Power of a Federal Judge to Call His Own Expert Witnesses," 29 S.Cal.L.Rev. 195 (1956).

5. As the principal case indicates, prospective loss of earning capacity and future health care expenses are separate items of compensation in personal injury cases. Are they ever duplicative? The amount for lost earning capacity compensates the plaintiff for money that could have been earned for self-support as well as for the support of others. To the extent that a personal injury victim receives medical costs that include items of self-support, such as institutional housing and meals, there is a potential for some duplication.

In Flannery v. United States, 718 F.2d 108 (4th Cir.1983), the court partially offset these two items of damages because the plaintiff was permanently comatose and the medical expenses included all the plaintiff's personal expenses. The court reasoned that, without the offset, the defendant would in effect be required to pay the plaintiff's living expenses twice.

The *Flannery* rationale was criticized in a recent decision by the Court of Appeals for the First Circuit in *Reilly v. United States*. As the court explained:

> To be sure, the prudential policies which underlie the law of torts are uncomfortable with the prospect of windfalls: compensatory damages are meant to compensate, and duplicative recoveries, which by definition overcompensate, are disfavored. Yet, duplication cannot entirely be avoided. Every time that a tort claimant is hospital-

ized for treatment of injuries, she "saves" on certain personal expenditures. Her meals are provided by the hospital, thus reducing her food budget; she spends her time in a hospital gown, thus reducing her dry cleaning expense; utilities come with the accommodations, thus minimizing the costs of heat, light, and power at her residence. Despite this 'duplications,' it has never been suggested that the tortfeasor should be allowed to insist that his victim account for these savings and deduct them from the amount of the hospital bill when proving her damages.

The reasons why such offsets are not accepted practice, we suggest, have both pragmatic and equitable roots. From a practical standpoint, the difficulties in attempting to prove such offsets are enormous. Unless we are prepared to say that damages must now be proved with sliderule precision—an approach which this court has never adopted—it makes very little sense to devote the over-taxed resources of court, jury, and litigants to a search designed to sanitize every penny of consequential expense and certify it as altogether free from the taint of duplication. Once that rationale is accepted, equity comes into play. As a matter of simple justice, it is far fairer to give the injured plaintiff the benefit of what small duplication may inevitably occur than to confer the trouvaille upon the wrongdoer.

In view of these concerns, we find *Flannery* to rest on very shaky underpinnings and decline to adopt it as a model for this circuit. 863 F.2d 149 (1st Cir.1988).

Which view is the better one? How does this issue of duplication relate to the collateral source rule? If the plaintiff has health insurance that covers the hospital costs, those costs can still be recovered from the tortfeasor. *See* Chapter 13. How many times can a plaintiff recover the expense of the same meal?

If the plaintiff is hospitalized for a year, how much money is likely to be involved in such a setoff? What proportion is it likely to be to the damages as a whole for someone hospitalized that long? Would it be useful to distinguish between plaintiffs who are temporarily hospitalized and plaintiffs who are permanently institutionalized because of the injuries? If that distinction is useful, is it nonetheless offensive to our sense of justice to allow the setoff only for the more injured plaintiffs, or is it a logical and justifiable ground for reducing some plaintiffs' awards for the savings in personal expenses?

6. When an unemancipated minor is injured, both the parents and the child have a cause of action. Courts generally divide the elements of damages between the actions appropriately. For example, when parents have paid medical expenses, those losses can be part of their damages. Parrott v. Mallett, 262 Ark. 525, 558 S.W.2d 152 (1977) (two distinct actions; parent entitled to recover expenses incurred and to be incurred by parent on account of injury to child). If the child actually pays the medical expenses personally, only the child is entitled to recover those

damages. Sommers v. Hartford Accident & Indemnity Co., 277 S.W.2d 645 (Mo.App.1955). If the parents do not bring a separate action, the child's action may include medical expenses paid by the parents because the child is also liable for them. White v. Moreno Valley Unified School Dist., 181 Cal.App.3d 1024, 226 Cal.Rptr. 742 (1986). Courts do not allow double recovery for the same expenses in two actions, however. Alaskan Village, Inc. v. Smalley, 720 P.2d 945 (Alaska 1986) (mother waived right to recover damages for past medical expenses incurred by allowing child to assert claim and testifying on her behalf).

7. When both minors and parents have claims, some elements of damages are not shared and require separate actions. The child's pain and suffering and lost adult earning capacity belong only to the child's action. The parent's action claims loss of services or earnings of a child during minority. Emanuel v. Clewis, 272 N.C. 505, 158 S.E.2d 587 (1968). Parents may have special damages, such as travel, lodging, and telephone expenses to establish contact with the injured child. Mancino v. Webb, 274 A.2d 711 (Del.Super.1971) (allowing those elements but not parents' mental anguish or lost wages). Punitive damage claims belong to the child rather than the parent. Hughey v. Ausborn, 249 S.C. 470, 154 S.E.2d 839 (1967).

WHITE CONSTRUCTION CO. v. DUPONT

430 So.2d 915 (Fla.App.1983), *modified on other grounds* 455 So.2d 1026 (1984).

ERVIN, JUDGE

Appellants, White Construction Company, Inc. (White) and Limerock Industries, Inc. (Limerock) appeal a jury verdict awarding $5,550,-000.00 in compensatory and punitive damages to appellees, Nathaniel and Janey Dupont, in an action for personal injuries and loss of consortium. Of the five points raised on appeal, we find merit only with point two, challenging the award of $1,025,000.00 to Janey Dupont, Nathaniel's wife, for loss of consortium as excessive. * * *

The record discloses that Nathaniel Dupont, a 55–year old independent truck owner/operator, arrived at Limerock's mine on September 13, 1977 to pick up a load of rock. Dupont parked his four-axle tractor-trailer, with the motor running, to wait his turn for loading, and he stepped out of the cab and went between the trailer and the cab for the purpose of cleaning the cab. A Limerock employee, driving a CAT 988 loader, weighing some forty tons and standing approximately 22 feet high, proceeded to *back* the loader around a large pile of limerock toward Dupont's trailer. As the loader, proceeding at top speed, approached Dupont's trailer, the driver looked back, and realizing he was going to hit the trailer, shouted a warning to Dupont. The loader struck the back end of the trailer and the impact apparently caused its gear to pop into forward position, forcing the trailer to advance about one and half times its length, and in the process to roll over Dupont, who in turn suffered permanent disability as a result of his injuries.

Dupont brought an action against Limerock, the corporation that owns the mine, and White, the corporation that owns the loader which was then leased to Limerock, seeking compensatory and punitive damages for his personal injuries. Janey Dupont joined in the action, seeking damages for her loss of consortium. The jury returned a verdict in favor of the Duponts for the following damages: $1,025,000.00 in compensatory damaged to Nathaniel Dupont, $1,025,000.00 in damages to Janey Dupont for loss of consortium, $2,000,000.00 in punitive damages against Limerock, and $1,500,000.00 in punitive damages against White.

Appellants contend that the award of $1,025,000.00 for loss of consortium must be reversed as excessive because the jury could only have arrived at that figure through motivations of passion or prejudice, or because the award amounts to a double recovery of damages properly awarded to Mr. Dupont. Although we find nothing in the record substantiating the former argument, we find that the record supports appellants' claim of double recovery, requiring that the award be reversed. * * *

Before 1971 a wife could not maintain an action for loss of consortium in Florida when her husband was injured due to the negligent or intentional acts of another. In *Gates v. Foley,* 247 So.2d 40 (Fla.1971), the Florida Supreme Court, rejecting precedent and the common law rule, elected to follow the trend in other jurisdictions by recognizing that a wife is entitled to recover for loss of consortium in the same manner as her husband if she were injured. [Citations.]

An action for loss of consortium is, of course, a derivative action and the jury must first find that the husband has sustained compensable injuries at the hands of another before the wife's action may be considered. If that threshold is met, the wife must then "present competent testimony concerning the impact which the accident had on the marital relationship and, more specifically, evidence concerning her loss of consortium." [Citation.] Upon such a showing, the wife is thus entitled to, at the very minimum, nominal damages. [Citations.]

We are not confronted with a situation in which only nominal damages were awarded, but rather with an award which appellants contend is excessive and amounts to a double recovery. In Florida, because the types of losses which the spouse may recover have not been clearly defined, the potential danger of a double recovery is always lurking. One commentator has observed that "[t]he concept of 'consortium' embraces two contrasting types of elements. The *tangible* elements include support and services provided by the other spouse, while *intangible* elements encompass such items as love, companionship, affection, society, sexual relations, comfort, and solace." [Citation.] In Florida, there is no question that recovery may be had for the intangible elements of loss of consortium, which, as defined by *Gates,* consist of

> the companionship and fellowship of husband and wife and the right of each to the company, cooperation and aid of the other in every

conjugal relation. Consortium means much more than mere sexual relation and consists, also, of that affection, solace, comfort, companionship, conjugal life, fellowship, society and assistance so necessary to a successful marriage.

247 So.2d at 43. Contrasted against these elements, *Gates* forbids, however, recovery by the wife for the tangible loss of "support or earnings which the husband might recover in his own right." The law of consortium in Florida is less clear as to the wife's right to recover for "services" which the husband is no longer able to perform.

In an earlier decision addressing the issue of what services the jury may consider in an action for wrongful death and loss of consortium brought by a husband after the death of his wife, it was held that the composition of this element includes the

pecuniary value of services which the husband might reasonably expect to have received from the deceased wife if she had not been killed, less maintenance costs, of course; this includes the value of such services as the wife was accustomed to perform in the household and which will have to be replaced by hiring services; services ordinarily performed by the deceased wife in the care and moral training of the minor children in the household; and any special service which the wife was accustomed to perform for the husband in the household, and in his business without compensation, which will have to be replaced by hired services.

Lithgow v. Hamilton, 69 So.2d 776, 778 (Fla.1954). Because the plaintiff in *Lithgow* was able to substantiate the actual cost of obtaining the services of a "combination housekeeper-governess-counsellor", the award of damages, including those for loss of services, was affirmed.

* * *

In this case we find that there was insufficient evidence to justify the $1,025,000.00 award for loss of consortium. Although Mrs. Dupont has undoubtedly suffered a loss of the intangible elements of consortium as defined in *Gates,* that loss alone cannot explain or justify an award of this magnitude. Nor can the award be sustained on the theory of loss of services, since the only evidence to support such loss consists of Mrs. Dupont's statement that her husband was no longer able to help her with routine household chores. Because no evidence was presented as to the reasonable value of such services or to show that it was necessary to hire someone else to perform such services, the award may not be justified on the basis of such unsubstantiated, non-pecuniary loss.

Our review of the record causes us to conclude that the jury's award does in fact amount to a double recovery of the sums included in the jury's verdict of damages to the husband. Mrs. Dupont was allowed to testify at length concerning financial losses incurred by her husband's trucking business since the accident and the fact that she had been forced to take a more active role in the operation of that business as a result of her husband's injuries. Because any losses relating to the business were properly recoverable by Mr. Dupont, his wife's testimony as to such losses could only have served to confuse the jury as to the proper measure of damages in considering her claim for loss of consortium. Because we find insufficient evidence in the record to support the award of $1,025,000.00 for loss of consortium, we reverse the trial court's judgment as to that award only.

Accordingly, we REVERSE in part, AFFIRM in part, and REMAND this cause for purposes of a new trial on the issue only of Mrs. Dupont's damages for loss of consortium.

---

1. Loss of consortium was historically a claim held only by men for injuries to wives. As the principal case indicates, the modern approach allows claims by women for injuries to their husbands. *See* Annot. 36 A.L.R.3d 900.

The first change occurred with the passage of the Married Women's Acts. Courts then allowed a wife to recover for loss of consortium when her husband was intentionally injured by third parties. The major case to establish the claim for negligent injuries was not until 1950. Hitaffer v. Argonne Co., 183 F.2d 811 (D.C.Cir.1950), *cert. denied,* 340 U.S. 852, 71 S.Ct. 80, 95 L.Ed. 624 (1950). In the decades since then, especially the 1970's, virtually all jurisdictions recognized the claim of the wife as identical to the claim of the husband.

2. Some jurisdictions have expanded loss of consortium claims beyond the spousal relationship. The parent-child relationship has provided the greatest litigation. Should a parent recover for loss of society with an injured child? Should a child recover for loss of society with an injured parent? The jurisdictions are not in agreement with either answer. *See* Annot. 69 A.L.R.3d 553; Annot. 11 A.L.R.4th 549.

3. There is no easy test for the excessiveness of consortium awards, as with other intangible losses. One common test is whether the amount "shocks" the court. *See, e.g.,* Jackson v. Magnolia Brokerage Co., 742 F.2d 1305 (11th Cir.1984); Clissold v. St. Louis–S.F.R., 600 F.2d 35 (6th Cir.1979).

An award generally should be in some reasonable proportion to the damages of the injured spouse, but there is no fixed rule. In *General Electric Co. v. Bush,* for example, a wife was awarded half a million dollars for loss of consortium with her husband after a mining accident. The husband was awarded over three million dollars for his injuries, and there was evidence that the accident had left him "among the living dead." 88 Nev. 360, 498 P.2d 366 (1972).

4. The principal case lists the usual elements of a consortium claim, but the list is not exhaustive. For example, in one case a wife properly presented evidence that she shared with her husband embarrassment over scars on his upper body. Dolinger v. Scott & Fetzer Co., 405 A.2d 690 (Del.1979).

The change in an injured party's personality and interests or ability to enjoy sexual relations can lead to dissolution of the marriage. If the destruction of the marriage was caused by the injuries rather than by pre-existing conflict, it is relevant to the loss of consortium claim. *See* Togstad v. Vesely, Otto, Miller & Keefe, 291 N.W.2d 686 (Minn.1980).

D. WRONGFUL DEATH AND SURVIVAL

Section Coverage:

Wrongful death and survival actions are almost exclusively statutory actions with limited damages. There is little agreement among jurisdictions on appropriate damages when a tortfeasor's conduct results in death rather than personal injury short of death.

Two old common law rules with little justification explain modern developments. First, the death of a person was not considered an actionable injury. Second, personal tort actions died with the plaintiff. The result of these rules was harsh for dependents who consequently had no claim for the tortious death of a family member. In modern law these rules have been changed, usually by statutes. The odd patchwork of current law is attributable to this history.

Most state legislatures now have provided Survival Acts that allow the decedent's estate to bring at least some tort actions. Many jurisdictions allow the victim's personal injury claims to survive under these acts. The orientation of these actions is upon the decedent's losses rather than upon the family's losses. The estate recovers the damages and distribution is by will or intestacy.

Many state and federal statutes provide for wrongful death actions in addition to or as an alternative to the survival of personal injury claims. A typical Wrongful Death Act names specific beneficiaries with some relationship to the decedent who may sue and limits the types of recoverable damages, such as to "pecuniary" losses sustained by the statutory beneficiaries. Jurisdictions with both a Survival Act and a Wrongful Death Act allow both actions and use rules such as collateral estoppel to avoid double recovery by family members.

Model Case:

A speeding motorist negligently injured and killed a young child on a bicycle. In some jurisdictions the child's estate has a cause of action against the motorist. In other jurisdictions the wrongful death act would name close relatives, such as the child's parents, who could sue the motorist for the loss of the family member.

Damages in the survival or wrongful death actions vary by jurisdiction. Some or all of the following elements may be permitted: loss of future income, loss of child's services in minority and support of parents in their elderly years, the child's pain and suffering before death, medical expenses, funeral expenses, loss of society with the child, and parents' grief.

MORAGNE v. STATES MARINE LINES, INC.

398 U.S. 375, 90 S.Ct. 1772, 26 L.Ed.2d 339 (1970).

MR. JUSTICE HARLAN delivered the opinion of the Court.

We brought this case here to consider whether *The Harrisburg,* 119 U.S. 199, 7 S.Ct. 140 30 L.Ed. 358, in which this Court held in 1886 that maritime law does not afford a cause of action for wrongful death, should any longer be regarded as acceptable law.

The complaint sets forth that Edward Moragne, a longshoreman, was killed while working aboard the vessel *Palmetto State* in navigable waters within the State of Florida. Petitioner, as his widow and representative of his estate, brought this suit in a state court against respondent States Marine Lines, Inc., the owner of the vessel, to recover damages for wrongful death and for the pain and suffering experienced by the decedent prior to his death. The claims were predicated upon both negligence and the unseaworthiness of the vessel.

States Marine removed the case to the Federal District Court for the Middle District of Florida on the basis of diversity of citizenship, *see* 28 U.S.C. §§ 133, 1441, and there filed a third-party complaint against respondent Gulf Florida Terminal Company, the decedent's employer, asserting that Gulf had contracted to perform stevedoring services on the vessel in a workmanlike manner and that any negligence or unseaworthiness causing the accident resulted from Gulf's operations.

Both States Marine and Gulf sought dismissal of the portion of petitioner's complaint that requested damages for wrongful death on the basis of unseaworthiness. They contended that maritime law provided no recovery for wrongful death within a State's territorial waters. * * *

* * * We granted certiorari * * * to reconsider the important question of remedies under federal maritime law for tortious deaths on state territorial waters.

* * *

The first explicit statement of the common-law rule against recovery for wrongful death came in the opinion of Lord Ellenborough, sitting at *nisi prius,* in *Baker v. Bolton,* 1 Camp. 493, 170 Eng.Rep. 1033 (1808). That opinion did not cite authority, or give supporting reasoning, or refer to the felony-merger doctrine in announcing that "[i]n a Civil court, the death of a human being could not be complained of as an injury."

* * * [D]espite some early cases in which the rule was rejected as "incapable of vindication," [citations], American courts generally adopted the English rule as the common law of this country as well. Throughout the period of this adoption, * * * the courts failed to produce any satisfactory justification for applying the rule in this country.

Some courts explained that their holdings were prompted by an asserted difficulty in computation of damages for wrongful death or by a "repugnance * * * to setting a price upon human life." [Citations.] However, other courts have recognized that calculation of the loss sustained by dependents or by the estate of the deceased * * * does not present difficulties more insurmountable than assessment of damages for many nonfatal personal injuries. * * *

We need not, however, pronounce a verdict on whether *The Harrisburg,* when decided, was a correct extrapolation of the principles of decisional law then in existence. A development of major significance has intervened, making clear that the rule against recovery for wrongful death is sharply out of keeping with the policies of modern American maritime law. This development is the wholesale abandonment of the rule in most of the areas where it once held sway, quite evidently prompted by the same sense of the rule's injustice that generated so much criticism of its original promulgation.

* * * [L]egislatures both here and in England began to evidence unanimous disapproval of the rule against recovery for wrongful death. The first statute partially abrogating the rule was Lord Campbell's Act, 9 & 10 Vict., c. 93 (1846), which granted recovery to the families of persons killed by tortious conduct, "although the Death shall have been caused under such Circumstances as amount in Law to Felony."

In the United States, every State today had enacted a wrongful-death statute. [Citation.] The Congress has created actions for wrongful deaths of railroad employees, Federal Employers' Liability Act, 45 U.S.C. §§ 51–59; of merchant seamen, Jones Act, 46 U.S.C. § 688; and of persons on the high seas, Death on the High Seas Act, 46 U.S.C. §§ 761, 762. Congress has also, in the Federal Tort Claims Act, 28 U.S.C. § 1346(b), made the United States subject to liability in certain circumstances for negligently caused wrongful death to the same extent as a private person. [Citation.]

These numerous and broadly applicable statutes, taken as a whole, make it clear that there is no present public policy against allowing recovery for wrongful death. The statutes evidence a wide rejection by the legislatures of whatever justifications may once have existed for a general refusal to allow such recovery. This legislative establishment of policy carries significance beyond the particular scope of each of the statutes involved. The policy thus established has become itself a part of our law, to be given its appropriate weight not only in matters of statutory construction but also in those of decisional law. * * *

Respondents argue that overruling *The Harrisburg* will necessitate a long course of decisions to spell out the elements of the new "cause of action." We believe these fears are exaggerated, because our decision does not require the fashioning of a whole new body of federal law, but merely removes a bar to access to the existing general maritime law. In most respects the law applied in personal-injury cases will answer all questions that arise in death cases.

Respondents argue, for example, that a statute of limitations must be devised or "borrowed" for the new wrongful-death claim. However, petitioner and the United States respond that since we have simply removed the barrier to general maritime actions for fatal injuries, there is no reason—in federal admiralty suits at least—that such actions should not share the doctrine of laches immemorially applied to admiralty claims.   * * *

The one aspect of a claim for wrongful death that has no precise counterpart in the established law governing nonfatal injuries is the determination of the beneficiaries who are entitled to recover. General maritime law, which denied any recovery for wrongful death, found no need to specify which dependents should receive such recovery.   * * *

We do not determine this issue now, for we think its final resolution should await further sifting through the lower courts in future litigation. For present purposes we conclude only that its existence affords no sufficient reason for not coming to grips with *The Harrisburg.* If still other subsidiary issues should require resolution, such as particular questions of the measure of damages, the courts will not be without persuasive analogy for guidance. Both the Death on the High Seas Act and the numerous state wrongful-death acts have been implemented with success for decades. The experience thus built up counsels that a suit for wrongful death raises no problems unlike those that have long been grist for the judicial mill.

* * *

We accordingly overrule *The Harrisburg,* and hold that an action does lie under general maritime law for death caused by violation of maritime duties.   * * *

Reversed and remanded.

———

1. The common law rule that "the death of a human being could not be complained of as an injury" originated as a comment by Lord Ellenborough in Baker v. Bolton, 1 Camp. 493, 170 Eng.Rep. 1033 (1908). The source of change of this restrictive rule was legislative action. *Moragne* was highly unusual in that the Supreme Court made the change in admiralty by common law. Lord Campbell's Act, mentioned in the opinion, was the model for most statutes.

2. Beneficiaries under the original Lord Campbell's Act were the decedent's husband or wife, parent, or child. Many American wrongful death acts list the same beneficiaries; some expand the group. If no beneficiary is alive to bring the action, there is no claim against the tortfeasor unless the state has a Survival Act. A statutory survival action for death may be initiated by the representative of the decedent's estate.

Problems in interpreting the family terms arise in Wrongful Death Acts. For example, is an illegitimate child a "child" within the meaning of a Wrongful Death Act's designated beneficiaries? A Louisiana act precluded illegitimate children, as did many other states, until the United States Supreme Court held that exclusion to be a denial of equal protection. Levy v. Louisiana, 391 U.S. 68, 88 S.Ct. 1509, 20 L.Ed.2d 436 (1968). The Court found no constitutional infirmity, however, with a Georgia statute that precluded a father from suing for the tortious death of an illegitimate child while allowing a mother to sue. Parham v. Hughes, 441 U.S. 347, 99 S.Ct. 1742, 60 L.Ed.2d 269 (1979).

3. Some states do not have Wrongful Death Acts, but provide survival statutes that preserve personal injury claims for the estate of the decedent. A primary difference between the two approaches is that Wrongful Death Acts create a new action in favor of the statutory beneficiaries whereas Survival Acts only preserve the actions which victims would have otherwise been entitled to bring had they survived. Named beneficiaries recover under Wrongful Death Acts whereas recovery to the estate under a Survival Act is distributed like any other property. The ability of the decedent's creditors to share in the recovery also varies.

Some jurisdictions have both Survival Acts and Wrongful Death Acts. Problems of allocation between the two claims are resolved to avoid double recovery. There is disagreement, however, as to the allocation of the decedent's future lost earnings between the Wrongful Death and the Survival Acts. If the recipients happen to be identical, such as where a valid will distributes to all surviving family members in the exact manner the death act does, then allocation makes no difference. In the usual case, however, there are differences in recipients. Other circumstances also can make allocation important, such as when the statute of limitations has run for only one claim, or where there are no beneficiaries to sue under the Wrongful Death act. See generally Annot., 76 A.L.R.3d 125.

4. Defenses that could be asserted against the decedent preclude recovery under either Wrongful Death Acts or Survival Acts. Problems arise with respect to defenses against beneficiaries of the death action. In an auto accident, for example, a negligent tortfeasor may kill a passenger in another car driven by the decedent's spouse or parent, whose negligence may also contribute to the accident.

PROBLEM: THE GRIEVING MOTHER

Timothy Hart was an eighteen-year-old college freshman when he was fatally injured by a drunk driver whose car jumped the curb and hit him on the sidewalk. Hart had been an outstanding athlete in high school as well as an accomplished scholar. He attended the university on a full scholarship and had tentative plans to become an attorney.

His mother, Dolores Hart, was in her forties at the time of the accident. She was in excellent health and had a thirty-five year life expectancy. She was employed at a low salary at a retreat house operated by her church. Her husband had abandoned her and Tim several years before and his whereabouts were unknown. Hart had announced his intention to support his mother so that she could retire as soon as he finished his education.

The Wrongful Death Act in the jurisdiction provides a cause of action for immediate family members. The damages permitted under the Act are simply described as "pecuniary losses."

Dolores Hart is devastated over the loss of her son. She continues to work to earn enough to live, but she is severely depressed. She is also worried about her financial security in her aging years. Her deep religious faith alone has sustained her. Members of her church helped her with the funeral expenses by establishing a special fund for contributions.

What damages for her son's death should Dolores Hart receive from the drunk driver under the state's Wrongful Death Act?

SANCHEZ v. SCHINDLER

651 S.W.2d 249 (Tex.1983).

SPEARS, JUSTICE.

Eugene and Angelica Sanchez brought this wrongful death action against Charles Schindler and his parents for the death of their minor son, Johnny Sanchez, arising from a collision between Johnny's motorcycle and Schindler's pick-up truck. The jury found for plaintiffs on the liability issues. On the damages issues, however, they found that Mr. and Mrs. Sanchez sustained no pecuniary loss, but awarded $102,500.00 in damages for the mental anguish suffered by Mrs. Sanchez. The trial court disregarded the jury's answers to the special issues on mental anguish. The court of appeals affirmed the trial court's denial of recovery for mental anguish. We reverse in part and render judgment for Sanchez for the damages found for mental anguish.

Johnny Sanchez, age fourteen, was severely injured in a motorcycle-pickup truck collision in Key Allegro, Texas in 1979. Paramedics treated him on the scene and transported him to Memorial Medical Center in Corpus Christi. His parents were at home at the time of the accident, and were told of the collision by a neighbor. At the hospital, they were prevented from seeing their son, but caught glimpses of his bloody legs through the doorway. He died several hours later.

Mr. and Mrs. Sanchez brought suit for the damages they sustained, individually and as heirs of Johnny Sanchez, against Charles J. Schindler, Jr., a minor, and Charles J. and Jean Schindler, his parents. The jury awarded $50,000 for the pain and suffering endured by Johnny Sanchez prior to his death, $7,187.41 for Johnny's medical treatment, $4,000 for funeral and burial expenses, and $450 for damages to his motorcycle. The jury found that Mr. and Mrs. Sanchez sustained no pecuniary loss resulting from their son's death; however, they awarded $102,500 damages for the mental anguish suffered by Mrs. Sanchez. Upon defendants' motion, the trial court disregarded the answers to the special issues on mental anguish. Angelica Sanchez has appealed, seeking the jury award of $102,500 for her injuries.

The seminal question presented is whether damages for mental anguish are recoverable under the Texas Wrongful Death Act for the death of a child. Tex.Rev.Civ.Stat.Ann. art. 4671. More specifically, we must determine whether Texas should continue to follow the pecuniary loss rule as the proper measure of damages for the death of a child.

In the past a surviving parent's damages in an action for the death of a child under the Texas Wrongful Death Act have been limited to the pecuniary value of the child's services and financial contributions, minus the cost of his care, support and education. The Texas statute does not expressly limit recovery to pecuniary loss. Tex.Rev.Civ.Stat.Ann. article 4671 creates a cause of action for "actual damages on account of the injuries causing the death...." Article 4677 provides that "[t]he jury may give such damages as they may think proportionate to the injury resulting from such death." Like most states, Texas patterned its wrongful death statutes after Lord Campbell's Act. The Fatal Accident Act, 9 & 10 Vict., ch. 93 § 1 (1846). The English court ruled that Lord Campbell's Act limited recovery to pecuniary loss. [Citation.] In March v. Walker, 48 Tex. 372, 375 (1877), this court held that since the language of the Texas Wrongful Death Act was based on Lord Campbell's Act, the measure of damages under the Texas statute would also be restricted to pecuniary loss.

Sanchez argues the pecuniary loss rule is based on an antiquated concept of the child as an economic asset, and should be rejected. We agree. It is time for this court to revise its interpretation of the Texas Wrongful Death statutes in light of present social realities and expand recovery beyond the antiquated and inequitable pecuniary loss rule. If the rule is literally followed, the average child would have a negative worth. [Citations.] Strict adherence to the pecuniary loss rule could lead to the negligent tortfeasor being rewarded for having saved the parents the cost and expense of rearing a child. The real loss sustained by a parent is not the loss of any financial benefit to be gained from the child, but is the loss of love, advice, comfort, companionship and society. [Citations.] We, therefore, reject the pecuniary loss limitation and allow a plaintiff to recover damages for loss of companionship and society and damages for mental anguish for the death of his or her child. In this case, Mrs. Sanchez pleaded for the recovery of damages for mental anguish, and the jury awarded her $102,500 pursuant to the special issues on mental anguish. She has preserved her argument on appeal to this court.

Schindler argues that the responsibility of changing the recovery under the Wrongful Death statute belongs to the Texas Legislature. This court originally imposed the pecuniary loss rule as a limitation of the damages recoverable under the Texas Wrongful Death Act. *March v. Walker*, 48 Tex. 372, 375 (1877). It is, therefore, logical for this court to now act in response to the needs of a modern society, and abolish the antiquated rule in favor of recovery of loss of society and mental anguish.

This court has always endeavored to interpret the laws of Texas to avoid inequity. As a result, the court has abolished other antiquated doctrines. [Citations.]

The legislature has attempted to amend the Texas Wrongful Death Act to allow damages for loss of society and mental anguish; however, none of the bills have passed. This court should not be bound by the prior legislative inaction in an area like tort law which has traditionally been developed primarily through the judicial process. * * *

This court has recognized previously that injuries to the familial relationship are significant injuries and are worthy of compensation. In *Whittlesey v. Miller*, 572 S.W.2d 665, 668 (Tex.1978), we held that either spouse has a cause of action for loss of consortium suffered as a result of an injury to the other spouse by a tortfeasor's negligence. We held that loss of affection, solace, comfort, companionship, society, assistance, and sexual relations were real, direct, and personal losses and said that these losses were not too intangible or conjectural to be measured in pecuniary terms. A parent's claim for damages for the loss of companionship of a child is closely analogous to the loss of consortium cause of action created in *Whittlesey*. * * *

The jurisdictions that do not limit recovery to pecuniary loss realize that damages for loss of companionship and society of a child are not too uncertain to be measured in pecuniary terms in an attempt to redress the actual loss which a parent suffers. These elements of damage are not too speculative to be given a monetary value. Recovery is allowed in other tort areas for injuries which are equally intangible; *e.g.*, pain and suffering. The fear of excessive verdicts is not a sufficient justification for denying recovery for loss of companionship. The judicial system has adequate safeguards to prevent recovery of damages based on sympathy or prejudice rather than fair and just compensation for the plaintiff's injuries.

A parent's recovery under the Wrongful Death Statute includes the mental anguish suffered as a result of the child's wrongful death. The destruction of the parent-child relationship results in mental anguish, and it would be unrealistic to separate injury to the familial relationship from emotional injury. [Citation.] Injuries resulting from mental anguish may actually be less nebulous than pain and suffering, or injuries resulting from loss of companionship and consortium. * * *

In this case Mrs. Sanchez proved she is suffering from traumatic depressive neurosis. She presented testimony that she is despondent and disoriented, has been forced to seek medical attention for her neurosis and has frequent neck and shoulder pains and headaches. Mrs. Sanchez has proved that she suffered mental anguish, and therefore, is entitled to recover the $102,500 awarded to her by the jury for her mental anguish.

* * *

It is within our discretion to determine whether our reinterpretation of damages under the Wrongful Death Act will be given prospective or retrospective application. [Citations.] The general rule is that a decision of a supreme court is to be retrospective in its operation. [Citation.] However, exceptions are recognized when considerations of fairness and policy preclude full retroactivity. Resolution of the issue turns primarily on the extent of public reliance on the former rule and the ability to foresee a coming change in the law. [Citations.] In wrongful death cases it seems very unlikely that the negligent party would be influenced by the earlier interpretation of damages. Therefore, our holding that a plaintiff may recover under the Wrongful Death Statute for loss of society and companionship and damages for mental anguish for the death of his or her minor child applies to all future causes as well as those still in the judicial process. * * *

We, therefore, reverse the judgment of the court of appeals, and render judgment that Mrs. Angelica Sanchez recover $102,500 for the mental anguish she suffered as a result of her son's death in additional to the other damages awarded by the jury which have not been appealed.

Pope, Chief Justice, dissenting.

I respectfully dissent because I believe the court should not overturn its longstanding decisions and reinterpret the Texas Wrongful Death Statute to authorize recovery for mental anguish. In 1877, this court ruled that since the Texas Wrongful Death Statute was borrowed from Lord Campbell's Act, the measure of damages under the Texas statute was the same as the English act—pecuniary loss only. * * *

The majority reverses this well-established rule. If we were dealing with the common law rather than the statute, I might be persuaded by the majority's reasoning. There is strong evidence, however, that the Texas Legislature intended to limit recovery to pecuniary losses when it enacted the Texas Wrongful Death Statute. The Texas statute was patterned after the English statute. Both statutes provided that "the jury may give such damages as they may think proportioned to the injury resulting from such death ..." [Citations.] When the Texas Legislature adopted the statute in 1860, the English statute and every American statute patterned after it had already been interpreted to limit recovery to pecuniary losses. * * *

The Texas Wrongful Death Statute created a right that did not exist at common law. We are now dealing with that statute—not the common law. * * *

The majority opinion does not clearly delineate the proof required to recover its newly created damages for mental anguish. Some of the language in the opinion suggests that any mental anguish, however slight, is compensable. The established threshold for recovering mental anguish damages requires proof of willful tort, gross negligence, willful and wanton disregard, or physical injury resulting from the mental anguish. This threshold is universally applied in the common law and statutory law of this state. * * *

I would affirm the judgments of the courts below.

RAY, JUSTICE, concurring. [On motion for rehearing.]

I concur with the majority in overruling the Schindlers' motion for rehearing. I further concur with the majority of the court in rejecting the pecuniary loss limitation in actions for the wrongful death of a child. In doing so, we join the modern trend in allowing recovery for loss of companionship, society, emotional support, love and felicity.

The opinion speaks only to recovery by a parent for the death of a *minor* child. Legal symmetry mandates that the class of beneficiaries affected by this decision not be limited to parents of minor children. The majority has aptly noted that "injuries to the familial relationship are significant injuries and are worthy of compensation." In future cases brought under the Texas Wrongful Death Act, I would permit recovery for the social losses and emotional injuries inflicted upon any beneficiary designated by statute.

We have permitted Mrs. Sanchez to recover damages for mental anguish, recognizing that "[a] plaintiff should be permitted to prove the damage resulting from a tortfeasor's negligent infliction of emotional trauma." Mrs. Sanchez introduced evidence that she is suffering from traumatic depressive neurosis and as a result must seek medical care for physical pains associated with her neurosis. While the majority opinion does not address the issue, I do not believe that proof of such physical manifestations should be a necessary predicate for recovery for mental anguish. [Citation.]

Mr. Chief Justice Pope, in his dissent to the majority opinion, states that "[s]ome of that language in the opinion suggests that any mental anguish, however slight, is compensable." While I agree with his observation, I disagree with his objection. The focus should be on compensating the bereaved for their harrowing experience resulting from the untimely, preventable and otherwise unnecessary death of one with whom they have shared a special emotional relationship. * * *

The concurring opinion in Bedgood v. Madalin, 600 S.W.2d 773, 776–80 (Tex.1980) (Spears, J.), was the harbinger of the present majority opinion. Mr. Justice Spears concluded his concurrence by stating: "It is time for Texas to take this step into the 20th Century." The majority has initiated that step; we should now complete the evolution.

––––––––

1. The damages provisions in Wrongful Death Acts are generally one of three types: (1) the all-inclusive type lists particular elements of damages, (2) the pecuniary loss type that restricts recoveries to economic

losses, and (3) the general loss type that provides for damages in a vague way, such as "damages as are just."

2. Commentators have harshly criticized the jurisdictions that limit recoveries to pecuniary loss. *See, e.g.,* Strong & Jacobsen, Such Damages as are Just: A Proposal for More Realistic Compensation in Wrongful Death Cases, 43 Mont.L.Rev. 55 (1982); Belfance, The Inadequacy of Pecuniary Loss as a Measure of Damages in Actions for the Wrongful Death of Children, 6 Ohio Northern U.L.Rev. 543 (1979); Speiser & Malawer, An American Tragedy: Damages for Mental Anguish of Bereaved Relatives in Wrongful Death Actions, 51 Tulane L.Rev. 1 Death of Children: A Nonparametric Statistical Analysis of Compensation for Anguish, 74 Colum.L.Rev. 884 (1974).

3. In wrongful death actions the beneficiaries can recover the value of the decedent's support and services in the home. Evidence of the decedent's work history, if any, and contribution to household is relevant. Such contributions can include wages from work outside the home, performance of routine household tasks, and advice, counsel, or guidance for other family members, especially children. The amount that would have been spent from earnings toward the personal support of the decedent are deducted. *See, e.g.,* Wentling v. Medical Anesthesia Services, P.A., 237 Kan. 503, 701 P.2d 939 (1985) (assistance in spouse's work and care of handicapped child); Henneman v. McCalla, 260 Iowa 60, 148 N.W.2d 447 (1967) (housework, care of minor child, assistant to husband in farm work, income outside home as nurse's aide).

4. The "pecuniary loss" or "actual loss" limitation in many Wrongful Death Acts has posed a problem in claims of mental anguish and grief by surviving family members. Such limitations create particular problems with the death of a child, because the value of a child's services and support to family is usually low. Although solace damages, often called solatium, are allowed in many civil law countries, the influence of Lord Campbell's Act made such recovery rare in common law jurisdictions. The modern trend has been to reconsider this exclusion, as the principal case reflects.

Mental suffering is distinguished from loss of society in many jurisdictions following the modern trend. Reform by statute or judicial interpretation has liberalized recovery for intangible losses, but mental anguish and grief is often excluded as an element of damages. Some jurisdictions that allow recovery for loss of society, comfort and affection nonetheless prohibit grief damages as likely to produce unjustifiably high awards. Other jurisdictions allow the mental element because it is no less intangible than other non-economic losses.

See, e.g., Wilson v. Lund, 80 Wash.2d 91, 491 P.2d 1287 (1971) (statute permits recovery for loss of love; mental anguish damages allowed if established by expert testimony); Dawson v. Hill & Hill Truck Lines, 206 Mont. 325, 671 P.2d 589 (1983) (grief damages allowed under statute providing for "just" damages); Smith v. Hub Manufacturing, Inc., 634 F.Supp. 1505 (N.D.N.Y.1986) (no grief damages under New

York pecuniary loss statute); Pagitt v. Keokuk, 206 N.W.2d 700 (Iowa 1973) (allowing mental suffering under pecuniary loss statute).

The orientation of the death statute toward the survivors or the decedent also affects intangible losses. For example, New Hampshire refused to allow parents to recover for loss of society with an injured or killed child. The court reasoned that the state's wrongful death statute is not based on loss to survivors but focuses on losses suffered by decedent. The court further invoked public policy reasons: (1) the emotional nature of intangible, nonpecuniary losses could lead to disproportionate awards; (2) multiple claims hinder settlements; and (3) consortium claims increase expenses ultimately to be borne by the public through increased insurance premiums. Siciliano v. Capitol City Shows, Inc., 124 N.H. 719, 475 A.2d 19 (1984).

5. Some jurisdictions allow damages for decedent's pain and suffering in survival actions. The usual requirement is that the victim be consciously in pain before death. *See, e.g.,* Murphy v. Martin Oil Co., 56 Ill.2d 423, 308 N.E.2d 583 (1974); Schlichte v. Franklin Troy Trucks, 265 N.W.2d 725 (Iowa 1978).

One noteworthy case involving pre-death mental and physical suffering is *DeLong v. Erie County.* A woman who heard a prowler outside called the police 911 emergency number, but the operator negligently dispatched the near-by patrol car to the wrong address. She died of multiple knife wounds in a savage attack. The court upheld a $200,000 pain and suffering award. 89 A.D.2d 376, 455 N.Y.S.2d 887 (1982).

6. What about the decedent's loss of the pleasure of life as an element in survival actions equivalent to such elements in personal injury actions? A few jurisdictions have recognized these damages, which are sometimes called hedonic damages. Sherrod v. Berry, 827 F.2d 195 (7th Cir.1987) ($850,000 for the loss of the pleasure of life supported by expert witness who testified on the measurable value of life apart from the $300,000 in lost earnings); Katsetos v. Nolan, 170 Conn. 637, 368 A.2d 172 (1976) ($400,000 general award for loss of ability to enjoy life's activities, pain and suffering, and lost future earnings). Should an award of hedonic damages in a survival action be allowed only if there is no wrongful death action available with an intangible component for beneficiaries, such as a beneficiary's mental anguish or loss of society? Are such losses equivalent, parallel, or independent of one another? Is the logical answer different than the practical one?

Chapter 12

ADJUSTMENTS TO COMPENSATORY DAMAGES

A. PRESENT VALUE AND INFLATION

Section Coverage:

The purpose of compensatory damages in personal injury actions is to restore the injured party, as nearly as practicable, to the position held prior to incurring the harm. A principal component of the damages awarded often will be to replace projected lost wages, calculated by the injured party's diminished earning capacity over the period of their work life expectancy. Typically, the future earning stream is awarded in a lump sum rather than in periodic payments.

An adjustment to the damages awarded is necessary to take into consideration the amount of interest that an investment of the lump sum itself will earn over time. The task confronting the trier of fact is to calculate what amount of money at the date of the judgment will equal the lost wages when placed in safe investments. Several critical issues play a role in making the appropriate adjustments to the final total of damages given.

First, determining which percentage rate should be used for discounting the damages has evoked considerable controversy among courts, commentators, and experts. A high discount rate functions to the defendant's advantage by lowering the total liability; conversely, the plaintiff benefits from applying the lowest possible percentage rate.

Second, no consensus has developed regarding the extent, if any, to consider the impact of inflation on the projected earning stream. Proponents of including it as an adjustment factor contend that, unless the damages award reflects estimated future inflationary trends, a plaintiff will be undercompensated because inflation will erode the purchasing power of the substituted wages. Critics of adjusting damages for inflation argue that predicting future inflation is akin to crystal ball gazing; it is too speculative and unreliable to be fairly applied. Moreover, forecasting such trends is too complex for accurate assessment by jurors, even with the aid of expert testimony.

The inflation factor must be distinguished from other individualized and societal factors which may affect the computation of damages. For example, apart from inflation, estimated wage increases may be entirely attributable to projected job promotions or industry growth.

In the final analysis, predicting future inflationary trends, future market interest rates, and future industrial trends is an inexact science.

The final lump sum damages award almost certainly will, in hindsight, turn out to be either overcompensation or undercompensation. Consequently, there is a growing interest in periodic payment of damages in a series of installments rather than in a lump sum.

Model Case:

Smith sustained personal injuries in an automobile accident, including a partial but permanent disability in Smith's arms. Prior to the accident Smith had been employed in a skilled position as a machine press operator earning $18,000 per year. As a result of the injuries, however, Smith could be expected to earn approximately $12,000 annually as an unskilled laborer.

The jury accepted expert evidence showing the difference in earning capacity, including projected job promotions and societal factors, over Smith's work life expectancy at a total of $140,000. A special verdict showed this amount of damages for the lost wages.

Courts have employed numerous methods to evaluate the respective roles of the discount rate and future inflation rate. One approach acknowledges that both the discount and inflation factors are relevant yet not susceptible of being accurately predicted. Therefore, both factors are simply offset and cancel each other out. Another method allows the introduction of expert testimony with respect to each factor, leaving the trier of fact to evaluate the evidence and make any adjustments as deemed appropriate. Other courts have disregarded inflation but have adjusted the damages award downward by some discount rate. Many courts are now following the lead of the United States Supreme Court with a varied offset approach. Under this method courts discount the damages award only by the "real" rate of interest. This method considers that market interest rates include two components: an estimate of anticipated inflation and the lender's desired real return on investment. The first element concerning inflation is offset against projected future inflation. The real interest rate, which essentially remains constant over time (between 1 and 3%), is then applied to reduce the damages award into present value.

BUDGE v. POST

643 F.2d 372 (5th Cir.1981).

Before GOLDBERG, AINSWORTH and RUBIN, CIRCUIT JUDGES.

PER CURIAM:

This [is a] diversity suit for breach of contract. * * *

Don Budge, a former Wimbeldon tennis champion and winner of the Davis Cup, contracted with Troy Post to serve as tennis professional at Post's clubs, resorts and hotels for five years working for seven months each year. * * * Post discontinued payments to Budge under the contract and notified Budge that he was terminating their business relationship, claiming that Budge had violated the contract by failing properly to perform the duties required of the tennis professional under the agreement. Budge subsequently instituted this action contending that Post, not he, had breached the contract by failing to pay him the agreed compensation and by terminating the contract.

After a three-day trial, the jury returned a verdict in Budge's favor awarding him $353,800 as the compensation he would have received under the contract for the remaining fifty-eight months after Post discontinued payments to Budge, plus $85,500 for the value of the living accommodations and meals that Post had contracted to provide to Budge. To an interrogatory asking the jury what amount of money Budge had earned or, in the exercise of due diligence, could earn in similar employment during the contract period after Post terminated the agreement, the jury responded $1,500. The court entered a judgment for a total of $455,041, the sum of the amounts awarded for compensation and living expenses, minus the $1,500. * * *

In a diversity case, the determination of damages is substantive and is, therefore, governed by state law. [Citations.] Thus, whether an award of future damages must be reduced to its present value is an issue controlled by state law. [Citations.]

The Texas cases are not ambiguous. Discounting of future damage awards is adequately handled by the trial judge if he simply instructs the jury that damages are equal to the "sum of money, if any, if paid now in cash" that would compensate the plaintiff. [Citations.] Texas courts refuse to amplify this simple instruction because they believe that further explanation would confuse the jury. [Citation.] We might think an instruction further explaining the theory of discount would clarify the matter, but we are obliged to accept the decision of the Texas courts. Moreover, no evidence was presented at trial from which a discount rate could be computed. Therefore, the trial court's instruction to the jury to measure damages as the "present cash value" of the contract was an adequate charge under Texas law.

However, although the instruction was correct, the jury evidently did not follow it. The award patently reflected that, to arrive at the figure for earnings due, the jury simply multiplied the monthly compensation contracted for by the parties times the number of months of the contract period for which Budge was not paid. * * * The jury's failure to discount the award of earnings under the contract is an obvious oversight that must be corrected to prevent a manifest miscarriage of justice. Accordingly, we remand the case so that the trial judge, after considering such evidence as he may deem appropriate, may determine an appropriate discount rate and compute the present value of the award for contract earnings.

[Affirmed and remanded for recomputation.]

———

1. *Discounting Future Losses.* The calculation of future lost income requires first a determination of the amount of income that would have been earned each future year. Then that amount is reduced to present value. The present value of a sum is the amount of money that the plaintiff must have today in order to have the amount equal to the loss at the future date. It is assumed that the plaintiff will invest the money prudently and that it will compound annually until it equals the correct sum at the right time in the future.

2. Discounting is difficult arithmetically, but there are present value tables available to simplify the task. *See, e.g.,* 1 Speiser § 8:4. When a sum is discounted to present value, the interest rate determines the result. If a low interest rate is used, the discounted result will be more money than if a high interest rate is used. For example, consider a plaintiff who will need $1000 at the end of next year. If this sum is discounted by 10%, then the plaintiff must have approximately $909 this year to equal $1000 with simple interest in a year. If, however, the sum is discounted by 20%, then the plaintiff must have approximately $833 this year to equal $1000 with simple interest in a year.

3. *Lost Future Wages.* The starting place for calculating each annual installment in the lost stream of income is the actual wage or base salary. The worker may have fringe benefits to add, or work related expenses and taxes to subtract. For simplicity the parties often agree that the elements affecting the basic wage cancel out each other.

The major adjustment in wages that is not related to merit or productivity is inflation. As inflation makes dollars worth less, wages tend to increase an equal amount to preserve the worker's buying power. It is this adjustment that has attracted the greatest legal debate, as reflected in the following landmark case.

JONES & LAUGHLIN STEEL CORP. v. PFEIFER

462 U.S. 523, 103 S.Ct. 2541, 76 L.Ed.2d 768 (1983).

JUSTICE STEVENS delivered the opinion of the Court.

Respondent was injured in the course of his employment as a loading helper on a coal barge. As his employer, petitioner was required to compensate him for his injury under § 4 of the Longshoremen's and Harbor Workers' Compensation Act (Act). 44 Stat. 1426, 33 U.S.C. § 904. * * * We granted certiorari to decide * * * whether the Court of Appeals correctly upheld the trial court's computation of respondent's damages.

* * *

The District Court's calculation of damages was predicated on a few undisputed facts. At the time of his injury respondent was earning an annual wage of $26,025. He had a remaining work expectancy of 12½ years. On the date of trial (October 1, 1980), respondent had received compensation payments of $33,079.14. If he had obtained light work and earned the legal minimum hourly wage from July 1, 1979, until his 65th birthday, he would have earned $66,352.

The District Court arrived at its final award by taking 12½ years of earnings at respondent's wage at the time of injury ($325,312.50), subtracting his projected hypothetical earnings at the minimum wage ($66,352) and the compensation payments he had received under § 4 ($33,079.14), and adding $50,000 for pain and suffering. The court did not increase the award to take inflation into account, and it did not discount the award to reflect the present value of the future stream of income. The court instead decided to follow a decision of the Supreme Court of Pennsylvania, which had held "as a matter of law that future inflation shall be presumed equal to future interest rates with these factors offsetting." Kaczkowski v. Bolubasz, 491 Pa. 561, 583, 421 A.2d 1027, 1038–1039 (1980). * * *

The District Court found that respondent was permanently disabled as a result of petitioner's negligence. He therefore was entitled to an award of damages to compensate him for his probable pecuniary loss over the duration of his career, reduced to its present value. It is useful at the outset to review the way in which damages should be measured in a hypothetical inflation-free economy. We shall then consider how price inflation alters the analysis. Finally, we shall decide whether the District Court committed reversible error in this case.

In calculating damages, it is assumed that if the injured party had not been disabled, he would have continued to work, and to receive wages at periodic intervals until retirement, disability, or death. An award for impaired earning capacity is intended to compensate the worker for the diminution in that stream of income. The award could in theory take the form of periodic payments, but in this country it has traditionally taken the form of a lump sum, paid at the conclusion of the litigation. The appropriate lump sum cannot be computed without first examining the stream of income it purports to replace.

The lost stream's length cannot be known with certainty; the worker could have been disabled or even killed in a different, non-work-related accident at any time. The probability that he would still be working at a given date is constantly diminishing. Given the complexity of trying to make an exact calculation, litigants frequently follow the relatively simple course of assuming that the worker would have continued to work up until a specific date certain. In this case, for example, both parties agreed that the petitioner would have continued to work until age 65 (12½ more years) if he had not been injured.

* * * [T]he first stage in calculating an appropriate award for lost earnings involves an estimate of what the lost stream of income would have been. The stream may be approximated as a series of after-tax payments, one in each year of the worker's expected remaining career. In estimating what those payments would have been in an inflation-free economy, the trier of fact may begin with the worker's annual wage at the time of injury. If sufficient proof is offered, the trier of fact may

increase that figure to reflect the appropriate influence of individualized factors (such as foreseeable promotions) and societal factors (such as foreseeable productivity growth within the worker's industry).

Of course, even in an inflation-free economy the award of damages to replace the lost stream of income cannot be computed simply by totaling up the sum of the periodic payments. For the damages award is paid in a lump sum at the conclusion of the litigation, and when it—or even a part of it—is invested, it will earn additional money. It has been settled since our decision in *Chesapeake & Ohio R. Co. v. Kelly*, 241 U.S. 485, 36 S.Ct. 630, 60 L.Ed. 1117 (1916), that "in all cases where it is reasonable to suppose that interest may safely be earned upon the amount that is awarded, the ascertained future benefits ought to be discounted in the making up of the award."

The discount rate should be based on the rate of interest that would be earned on "the best and safest investments." Once it is assumed that the injured worker would definitely have worked for a specific term of years, he is entitled to a risk-free stream of future income to replace his lost wages; therefore, the discount rate should not reflect the market's premium for investors who are willing to accept some risk of default. * * *

Thus, although the notion of a damages award representing the present value of a lost stream of earnings in an inflation-free economy rests on some fairly sophisticated economic concepts, the two elements that determine its calculation can be stated fairly easily. They are: (1) the amount that the employee would have earned during each year that he could have been expected to work after the injury; and (2) the appropriate discount rate, reflecting the safest available investment. The trier of fact should apply the discount rate to each of the estimated installments in the lost stream of income, and then add up the discounted installments to determine the total award.

Unfortunately for triers of fact, ours is not an inflation-free economy. Inflation has been a permanent fixture in our economy for many decades, and there can be no doubt that it ideally should affect both stages of the calculation described in the previous section. The difficult problem is how it can do so in the practical context of civil litigation under § 5(b) of the Act.

The first stage of the calculation requires an estimate of the shape of the lost stream of future income. For many workers, including respondent, a contractual "cost-of-living adjustment" automatically increases wages each year by the percentage change during the previous year in the consumer price index calculated by the Bureau of Labor Statistics. Such a contract provides a basis for taking into account an additional societal factor—price inflation—in estimating the worker's lost future earnings.

The second stage of the calculation requires the selection of an appropriate discount rate. Price inflation—or more precisely, anticipated price inflation—certainly affects market rates of return. If a lender knows that his loan is to be repaid a year later with dollars that are less valuable than those he has advanced, he will charge an interest rate that is high enough both to compensate him for the temporary use of the loan proceeds and also to make up for their shrinkage in value.

* * *

Our sister common-law nations generally continue to adhere to the position that inflation is too speculative to be considered in estimating the lost stream of future earnings; they have sought to counteract the danger of systematically undercompensating plaintiffs by applying a discount rate that is below the current market rate. Nevertheless, they have each chosen different rates, applying slightly different economic theories. * * *

In this country, some courts have taken the same "real interest rate" approach as Australia. [Citations.] They have endorsed the economic theory suggesting that market interest rates include two components—an estimate of anticipated inflation, and a desired "real" rate of return on investment—and that the latter component is essentially constant over time. They have concluded that the inflationary increase in the estimated lost stream of future earnings will therefore be perfectly "offset" by all but the "real" component of the market interest rate.

Still other courts have preferred to continue relying on market interest rates. To avoid undercompensation, they have shown at least tentative willingness to permit evidence of what future price inflation will be in estimating the lost stream of future income. * * *

Within the past year, two Federal Courts of Appeals have decided to allow litigants a choice of methods. Sitting *en banc*, the Court of Appeals for the Fifth Circuit has overruled its prior decision in Johnson v. Penrod Drilling Co., 510 F.2d 234 (1975), and held it acceptable either to exclude evidence of future price inflation and discount by a "real" interest rate, or to attempt to predict the effects of future price inflation on future wages and then discount by the market interest rate. Culver v. Slater Boat Co., 688 F.2d 280, 308–310 (1982). A panel of the Court of Appeals for the Seventh Circuit has taken a substantially similar position. O'Shea v. Riverway Towing Co., 677 F.2d 1194, 1200 (1982).

Finally, some courts have applied a number of techniques that have loosely been termed "total offset" methods. What these methods have in common is that they presume that the ideal discount rate—the after-tax market interest rate on a safe investment—is (to a legally tolerable degree of precision) completely offset by certain elements in the ideal computation of the estimated lost stream of future income. They all assume that the effects of future price inflation on wages are part of what offsets the market interest rate. The methods differ, however, in their assumptions regarding which if any other elements in the first stage of the damages calculation contribute to the offset.

* * *

The litigants and the *amici* in this case urge us to select one of the many rules that have been proposed and establish it for all time as the exclusive method in all federal trials for calculating an award for lost earnings in an inflationary economy. We are not persuaded, however, that such an approach is warranted. [Citation.] For our review of the foregoing cases leads us to draw three conclusions. First, by its very nature the calculation of an award for lost earnings must be a rough approximation. Because the lost stream can never be predicted with complete confidence, any lump sum represents only a "rough and ready" effort to put the plaintiff in the position he would have been in had he not been injured. Second, sustained price inflation can make the award substantially less precise. Inflation's current magnitude and unpredictability create a substantial risk that the damages award will prove to have little relation to the lost wages it purports to replace. Third, the question of lost earnings can arise in many different contexts. In some sectors of the economy, it is far easier to assemble evidence of an individual's most likely career path than in others.

These conclusions all counsel hesitation. Having surveyed the multitude of options available, we will do no more than is necessary to resolve the case before us. We limit our attention to suits under § 5(b) of the Act, noting that Congress has provided generally for an award of damages but has not given specific guidance regarding how they are to be calculated. Within that narrow context, we shall define the general boundaries within which a particular award will be considered legally acceptable.

The Court of Appeals correctly noted that respondent's cause of action "is rooted in federal maritime law." [Citations.] The fact that Pennsylvania has adopted the total offset rule for all negligence cases in that forum is therefore not of controlling importance in this case. * * *

In calculating an award for a longshoreman's lost earnings caused by the negligence of a vessel, the discount rate should be chosen on the basis of the factors that are used to estimate the lost stream of future earnings. If the trier of fact relies on a specific forecast of the future rate of price inflation, and if the estimated lost stream of future earnings is calculated to include price inflation along with individual factors and other societal factors, then the proper discount rate would be the after-tax market interest rate. But since specific forecasts of future price inflation remain too unreliable to be useful in many cases, it will normally be a costly and ultimately unproductive waste of longshoremen's resources to make such forecasts the centerpiece of litigation under § 5(b). As Judge Newman has warned: "The average accident trial should not be converted into a graduate seminar on economic forecasting." Doca v. Marina Mercante Nicaraguense, S.A., 634 F.2d, at 39. For that reason, both plaintiffs and trial courts should be discouraged from pursuing that approach.

On the other hand, if forecasts of future price inflation are not used, it is necessary to choose an appropriate below-market discount rate. As long as inflation continues, one must ask how much should be "offset" against the market rate. Once again, that amount should be chosen on the basis of the same factors that are used to estimate the lost stream of future earnings. If full account is taken of the individual and societal factors (excepting price inflation) that can be expected to have resulted in wage increases, then all that should be set off against the market interest rate is an estimate of future price inflation. This would result in one of the "real interest rate" approaches described above. Although we find the economic evidence distinctly inconclusive regarding an essential premise of those approaches, we do not believe a trial court adopting such an approach in a suit under § 5(b) should be reversed if it adopts a rate between 1 and 3% and explains its choice.

* * *

We do not suggest that the trial judge should embark on a search for "delusive exactness." It is perfectly obvious that the most detailed inquiry can at best produce an approximate result. And one cannot ignore the fact that in many instances the award for impaired earning capacity may be overshadowed by a highly impressionistic award for pain and suffering. But we are satisfied that whatever rate the District Court may choose to discount the estimated stream of future earnings, it must make a deliberate choice, rather than assuming that it is bound by a rule of state law.

The judgment of the Court of Appeals is vacated, and the case is remanded for further proceedings consistent with this opinion.

It is so ordered.

————

1. At one time many courts refused to adjust future lost wages for anticipated inflation or deflation because of the speculative nature of such adjustment. The problem was that the same courts used current market interest rates to reduce future losses to their present value. To the extent that the current market interest rate reflects anticipated inflation reducing the value of the dollar upon maturity, plaintiffs were disadvantaged. Such rules incorporated inflation into only one stage of the calculation but not the other. *See* Johnson v. Penrod Drilling Co., 510 F.2d 234 (5th Cir.1975); Sleeman v. Chesapeake and Ohio R. Co., 414 F.2d 305 (6th Cir.1969).

The effect of this rule was to deny the plaintiff the benefit of inflationary increases to calculate future earnings, while giving the defendant the benefit of inflation's impact on the interest rate that is used to discount those earnings to present value. This inequity was not serious during periods of relatively low rates of inflation. The nation's economic history since the middle of the 1960's has forced courts to reevaluate this policy. A personal injury victim who received a judgment in 1967 now has dollars worth approximately one third as much in purchasing power.

2. *Merit Increases in Wages:* An individual worker may receive "real" wage increases, beyond inflationary adjustments. Such increases are usually reflected in "seniority" or "experience" raises, "merit" raises, or promotions. It is difficult to prove whether a particular injured worker might have received such increases, or when they might occur. Some types of employment lend themselves to such proof more easily than others. There has been little dispute that such adjustments should be included in the stream if they can be established with reasonable certainty. *See* State v. Guinn, 555 P.2d 530 (Alaska 1976).

3. *Societal Factors:* A plaintiff's wages may change for societal reasons unrelated to price inflation or the individual worker's advancement on merit. The wages of workers in plaintiff's class may increase or decrease over time. Changes in society bring about such adjustments. New technology, growth in industrial productivity, and successful collective bargaining are all factors that can contribute to changes in wages. Some cases have allowed evidence of the probable effect of such societal factors. *See* Kaczkowski v. Bolubasz, 491 Pa. 561, 421 A.2d 1027 (1980).

4. *Future Price Inflation:* Persistently high inflation rates during a period of recent history convinced many courts that plaintiffs were being seriously undercompensated. Judicial refusal to acknowledge price inflation left many personal injury victims and wrongful death dependents with reduced purchasing power. The problem was that courts refused to allow evidence of future inflation to compute lost future income, yet allowed discounting with current interest rates that reflected anticipated future price inflation.

Judge Posner explained this problem in O'Shea v. Riverway Towing Co.: "[I]f there is inflation it will affect wages as well as prices. Therefore to give Mrs. O'Shea $2318 today because that is the present value of $7200 10 years hence, computed at a discount rate—12 percent—that consists mainly of an allowance for anticipated inflation, is in fact to give her less than she would have been earning then if she was earning $7200 on the date of the accident, even if the only wage increases she would have received would have been those necessary to keep pace with inflation." 677 F.2d 1194, 1199 (7th Cir.1982).

5. *Methods of Adjustment for Inflation:* As the Supreme Court noted in the principal case, there are several ways to adjust damages awards to account for the effect of wage and price inflation. Courts have generally used one of three methods.

(1) In the "case-by-case" method, the fact-finder first predicts all of the wage increases a plaintiff would have received during each future year of work lost by the injury. These wage increases include expected adjustments for future inflation. These predictions allow calculation of the future income stream the plaintiff has lost. The fact-finder then discounts that income stream to present value using the market interest

rate, which reflects future predicted price inflation. The resulting figure is the plaintiff's damages for lost wages.

(2) Another approach is the "real interest rate" method, also called the below-market-discount method. The fact-finder predicts wage increases attributed to merit or industry productivity, but does not attempt to predict the wage increases that might result from inflationary pressures on wages. Then the resulting income stream is discounted by a below-market discount rate between 1% and 3%. The "real interest rate" subtracts the amount attributable to future price inflation. This is the method used in *Pfeifer*.

(3) Another method is based on the "total-offset" theory. In this approach future wage increases, including the effects of future inflation, are presumed to offset exactly the interest a plaintiff would earn by investing the lump-sum damage award. A court thus awards a plaintiff the amount of estimated lost wages. The fact-finder neither discounts the award nor adjusts it for inflation.

6. *Taxes:* The United States Supreme Court had said previous to *Pfeifer* that the lost stream of income in a Federal Employers' Liability Act (FELA) case should be estimated in after-tax dollars and that the discount rate should also represent the after-tax rate of return to the injured worker. Norfolk & Western R. Co. v. Liepelt, 444 U.S. 490, 100 S.Ct. 755, 62 L.Ed.2d 689 (1980).

7. Should courts be addressing these damages adjustments issues or are legislatures better equipped to resolve them? If the legislative branch does not provide guidance, should appellate courts give clear mandates to the trial courts, or leave them wide discretion?

PROBLEM: THE FRUSTRATED JUDGE

You are a clerk for a federal district court judge who is hearing without a jury a wrongful death case under federal jurisdiction. The decedent was a privately employed pilot who crashed over the ocean because of a defect in the manufacture of the aircraft.

The plaintiff presented evidence on the future lost earnings of the pilot, B.J. Raull. At the time of death, Raull was earning only $7,680, not including certain benefits supplied by the employer, such as food and shelter while Raull was on the job. An econometrist testified about projected pilot earnings compounded on a 6% basis and on an 8% basis, and discounted at a 4% basis. There were two models: one projected continued work with the same employer; the other assumed that after five years Raull would enter the more lucrative profession of commercial pilots. The expert testified that all projections were based upon several conservative assumptions: employment was assumed only to age sixty; no fringe benefits were included in the calculations; and the value of personal household services and future inheritances were not included.

The expert had several charts showing the projections. The district court judge was very upset with the testimony and with the charts. One in particular showed very high damages:

Growth rate	Future Earnings	Personal Consumption	Pecuniary Loss
8%	$3,764,029.00	1,129,209.00	2,634,820.00
Present Value	1,199,983.00		

The judge tells you privately that this testimony is useless. You listen to the following lecture:

"I am unconvinced that anyone can foretell economic conditions years down the road; it is nothing but crystal ball gazing. When I was born we were at the bottom of the Great Depression. In 1931, a transcontinental telephone call cost about $20, and for that same $20 one could mail 1,000 letters. Today, the call can be made for less than $1.50, but only 155 letters can be mailed for $20.00. In other words, some costs go up and some go down. Fifty years ago, one of the largest of the building trades was that of the plasterers. Today plasterers are almost a curiosity.

"These charts assume that there will be a continuing and a growing demand for ever more high priced airline pilots. With the rapid development of automation, who is to say that by the year 2030 commercial airline pilots will not be an occupation of the past. During this decade coal miners have found out a lot about automation just as have the members of many other trades.

"I don't enjoy reading that *Pfeifer* case either, but it controls here. Go read the thing again and tell me if I have to hear any more of this testimony."

What will you report?

CULVER v. SLATER BOAT CO.

722 F.2d 114 (5th Cir.1983).

ALVIN B. RUBIN and FRANK M. JOHNSON, JR., CIRCUIT JUDGES:

In Johnson v. Penrod Drilling Co., 510 F.2d 234 (5th Cir.) (en banc), *cert. denied,* 423 U.S. 839, 96 S.Ct. 68–69, 46 L.Ed.2d 58 (1975), this court held that juries "should not be instructed to take into account future inflationary or deflationary trends in computing lost earnings ..." Reviewing that decision in our first *en banc* consideration of these two cases, we overruled *Penrod* and held admissible evidence of inflation's probable effect on damage awards. Culver v. Slater Boat Co., 688 F.2d 280 (5th Cir.1982) (en banc) (Culver I). Concluding that the jury should resolve the issue on a case-by-case basis, we disclaimed any intention to establish a "single method" for considering future economic conditions. Instead, we discussed several permissible methods the district courts and parties could use.

While we were considering an application for rehearing in *Culver I,* the Supreme Court decided Jones & Laughlin Steel Corp. v. Pfeifer, 462 U.S. 523, 103 S.Ct. 2541, 76 L.Ed.2d 768 (1983). The Court's opinion in

Pfeifer cites *Culver I* and confirms our holding that the fact-finder should consider inflation in determining an appropriate damage award. The Court's opinion also emphasizes, however, a fundamental point that we did not fully consider in *Culver I:* that courts must not allow the adjustment for inflation to convert " '[t]he average accident trial . . . into a graduate seminar on economic forecasting.' "

Reconsideration of *Culver I* in light of *Pfeifer* has convinced us that our failure to identify a single method as the one trial courts should use in adjusting damage awards for inflation, particularly in jury trials, would extend an invitation to litigants to engage in just such a seminar. We, therefore, withdraw the opinion in *Culver I* insofar as it goes beyond overruling *Johnson,* and hold that, in the absence of a stipulation by the parties concerning the method to be used, fact-finders shall determine and apply an appropriate below-market discount rate as the sole method to adjust loss-of-future-earnings awards to present value to account for the effect of inflation. While expert testimony and jury instructions must be based on this method, juries may be instructed either to return a general verdict or to answer special interrogatories concerning the computation of damages.

* * *

The calculation of damages suffered either by a person whose personal injuries will result in extended future disability or by the representatives of a deceased person involves four steps: estimating the loss of work life resulting from the injury or death, calculating the lost income stream, computing the total damage, and discounting that amount to its present value.

The procedures necessary to determine the impact of future price inflation on a particular plaintiff on a year-by-year basis are complex and time consuming. Elaborate expert testimony is required. The battle of economic experts is apt to shift the trial's emphasis from the determination of liability and the estimation of basic damages into the formulation of predictions concerning the national, indeed, global, economic future, including the likelihood of future increases or decreases in oil prices and the stability of foreign governments. Under *Culver I,* defendants were free not only to controvert the plaintiffs' damage calculations; they could also dispute the validity of the method by which the plaintiffs' experts calculated damages. If such a dispute evolved, the fact-finder would be required to decide which of at least two competing methods, each avouched by an expert, it would use to determine discount before applying the method it chose to determine the rate of discount, yet another determination to be based on contradictory expert testimony.

Different formulae, each thought to be theoretically accurate, might be applied in literally hundreds of individual cases because of the conclusions reached by different fact-finders. The results in otherwise similar cases would vary widely depending on the particular expert witnesses called, on the fact-finders' agreement or disagreement with the methods they advocated, and on the different fact-finders' evaluations of their testimony. The voyage in search of mathematical certainty would discover instead a continent of conflict and conjecture.

Anticipating these problems to some degree in *Culver I,* we expressed hope that the parties would, by agreement, eliminate the need to litigate many of these confusing issues. * * * We continue to express that hope. Nothing in this opinion prevents the parties from stipulating to any of these matters or to anything else that may affect the determination of damages. We cannot ignore the possibility, however, that in many, perhaps most, cases such stipulations will not be possible. This opinion determines only the method to be followed when the parties cannot agree.

In such cases, litigating in every instance the amount and the effect of future price inflation is not likely to produce the result that would have been obtained had the plaintiff not been injured. No one can accurately predict the course of future inflation. A survey of the general literature for the past several years illustrates a sorry tale of repeated confusion, contradiction and uncertainty in economic forecasts.[15] Current complaints about economic forecasting generally concern relatively short-term forecasts. Over a longer term, events as diverse—and unpredictable—as spending to finance a Southeast Asian war, an oil embargo, disagreement between members of the oil cartel, or a drought causing wide-spread agricultural failures could profoundly increase inflation. A major depression or the discovery of significant and inexpensive fuel resources might reduce its present impact.

Whether or not the science of economics continues to be dismal, it is assuredly in this regard conjectural. The case-by-case method sacrifices efficiency and simplicity for pursuit of a "delusive exactness." * * *

We hold that fact-finders in this Circuit must adjust damage awards to account for inflation according to the below-market discount rate method. The parties may, if they wish, stipulate the below-market discount rate, as they may stipulate any other disputed issue. If they are unable to do so, they may introduce expert opinion concerning the appropriate rate. Other evidence about the effect of price inflation is inadmissible. Evidence about the likelihood that the earnings of an injured worker would increase due to personal merit, increased experience and other individual and societal factors continue, of course, to be admissible. We recognize that the Supreme Court declined in *Pfeifer* to select a single method of accounting for inflation. We are confronted, however, with the need to adapt that opinion to jury trials. We also think it desirable to afford litigants and the courts the opportunity to determine the actual operation of this less complex method in order that its efficacy for national use can be determined.

---

15. On September 14, 1981, the date we heard oral argument *en banc* in *Culver I,* the prime lending rate was 20.5 percent and the annual rate of inflation was 14.8 percent. On August 1, 1983, the prime lending rate was 10.5 percent. For the first six months of 1983, the annual rate of inflation has been only 2.9 percent.

As we have noted, the discount rate may be affected by the fact-finder's assumption about the type of investment the plaintiff will choose, for long-term investments usually yield higher nominal interest rate returns than short-term investments of the same quality. The Supreme Court having said in *Pfeifer* that it perceives "no intrinsic reason to prefer one assumption over the other," we mandate neither. However, the fact-finder should not consider the plaintiff's possible need for emergency funds as a factor in favor of short-term investments; the injured wage-earner should have no greater right to a resource against future emergencies than he would have had if he had continued to work.

In judge-tried cases, a trial court adopting a pre-tax discount rate between one and three percent will not be reversed if it explains the reasons for its choice. This guideline, however, goes only to the reasonableness of the correlation between the pre-tax market rate of interest and the inflation rate. As discussed above, this pre-tax discount rate must then be adjusted for tax effects. If supported by appropriate expert opinion, the trial judge might make no discount or even adopt a negative rate not to exceed–1.5% before adjusting for tax effects. In jury trials, the jury should be instructed in the usual fashion concerning the weight to be given expert opinion evidence. The jury may then be permitted to return a single-figure award for damages or it may be required to answer interrogatories stating, among other items, the amount of loss of future earnings for each year for which it makes an award, and the discount rate it chooses to apply. The court will then be able to compute the total award or to require the parties to complete the arithmetic.

* * *

Courts are not prophets and juries are not seers. In making awards to compensate injured plaintiffs or the dependents of deceased workers for loss of future earnings, however, these fact-finders must attempt, in some degree, to gauge future events. Absolute certainty is by the very nature of the effort impossible. It is also impossible to take into account every bit of potentially relevant evidence concerning the tomorrows of a lifetime. The approach we adopt attempts to assure plaintiffs a fair measure of damages, to give defendants a reasonable adjustment for reducing future losses to present value, and to avoid making trials even more complex and their results even more uncertain. It is the product of a balancing of competing values. Ultimately, however, that is the root of all justice.

The judgments in *Culver* are reversed, and the cases are remanded to the district court for further proceedings on the issue of damages. The panel opinions are adopted in all other respects.

JOHN R. BROWN, CIRCUIT JUDGE * * * dissenting:

With the ink scarcely dry on *Pfeifer,* [citation], in which, with remarkable clarity, the High Court chose *not* to pick one of the several methods in its collective economic hat it considered legally sound for calculating lost future wages in civil damage actions and instead chose to leave that crucial decision to the trial judge in that and future cases, a majority of this Court elevates one approach beyond any choice to be the only way, for mandatory application in eighteen federal judicial districts across a half-dozen Southern states, for a broad group of litigants to arrive at fair sums of money to compensate injured parties. Guided by the decision of *Pfeifer,* its approval of *Culver I,* and the direction that the choice of methodology should be left to the district court, not to this Court, I respectfully dissent. * * *

———

1. *Choice of Discount Rate.* The Court in *Pfeifer,* drawing from its previous decision in Chesapeake & Ohio Railway v. Kelly, 241 U.S. 485, 36 S.Ct. 630, 60 L.Ed. 1117 (1916), suggested that the discount rate should be based on the interest rate available on the "best and safest investments" but failed to explain the meaning of that phrase. Certainly United States government issued securities would be considered the only completely "risk-free" investment. Consider the 9.125 percent discount rate based on United States government long term bonds used in the original *Culver* opinion, 644 F.2d 460 (5th Cir.1981), modified on rehearing by the opinion reprinted as the principal case, known as *Culver II.* Compare the 6 percent rate based on short-term government securities used in Espana v. United States, 616 F.2d 41 (2d Cir.1980). Further contrast the approach followed in Hoskie v. United States, 666 F.2d 1353 (10th Cir.1981), where the court applied a 9.5 percent discount rate based on the current yield of triple-A rated corporate bonds as satisfying the court's standard of a "reasonably safe long-term investment available to the average person." How does that test differ from the *Pfeifer* standard?

2. Even securities issued by the federal government are only risk-free in the sense that the debtor is unlikely to default. The holder still will be subject to fluctuations in the current value of the bond which, if the need arises for liquidation of the bond prior to maturity, could result in a net loss. Consider the following illustration:

Plaintiff is a child personal injury victim who has suffered serious internal injuries from swallowing a toxic drain cleaner. At the time of trial the expert medical testimony established that one more operation would probably be necessary, but that it should be postponed as long as possible during the growing years. The testimony further established that the operation would simply have to be done whenever it was absolutely necessary, and that time could be anytime within the next seven years. In the meantime, the child must continue to have expensive treatments until an internal problem can be cured by the operation.

The cost of this future operation was determined to be $10,000. The treatments until the operation are $800 annually. The compensation allowed purchase of a seven year United States government bond with a coupon (yield) of 8% at par ($10,000). Thus the child will receive the necessary $800 interest annually to pay for the treatments and will have $10,000 upon maturity in seven years to pay for the operation.

As the medical expert feared, however, the operation became absolutely necessary after only two years. The bond had to be sold immediately to pay for the operation. The problem is that even though the investment is a conservative one, the change in interest rates in the market during the intervening time period will affect the price of the bond. Consider two possibilities: (1) If interest rates have risen and 11% is the rate for similar bonds, then the bond will sell for approximately $8870. The child will not have enough money from this sale for the $10,000 operation. Moreover, the high interest rate may reflect an inflation rate that is unexpectedly high, which would also be likely to increase the cost of the operation beyond the estimated $10,000. (2) If interest rates have fallen and 5% is the rate for similar bonds, then the bond will sell for approximately $11,310. Then there is more than enough money for the operation. Moreover, the cost of the operation may have been overestimated if this low interest rate reflects low inflation.

3. In Colleen v. United States, 843 F.2d 329 (9th Cir.1987), the court held that the use of a zero discount rate to find the present value of a lump-sum award in a medical malpractice suit, absent support by credible expert testimony, constituted an abuse of the trial court's discretion. Compare that result with Monaghan v. Uiterwyk Lines, Ltd., 607 F.Supp. 1020 (E.D.Pa.1985), where no economic evidence regarding discounting to present value was introduced, but the court took "judicial notice of historical interest and inflation rates" and determined the appropriate discount rate was 2%.

A different approach was used in Fisher v. Danos, 595 F.Supp. 461 (E.D.La.1984), where the court, recognizing that the record was insufficient to support an application of the below market discount rate mandated in *Culver II,* awarded the plaintiff general damages for pain and suffering in lieu of lost future earnings. The court quipped that, "There appear ... to be as many methods of calculating an award of future lost earnings under *Culver II* as there are economists available to perform the calculation."

ALDRIDGE v. BALTIMORE AND OHIO RAILROAD COMPANY

789 F.2d 1061 (4th Cir.1986), rev'd on other grounds, 486
U.S. 1049, 108 S.Ct. 2812, 100 L.Ed.2d 913 (1988).

SPROUSE, CIRCUIT JUDGE:

The Baltimore & Ohio Railroad Company (the Railroad) appeals from a judgment entered against it after a jury verdict in the sum of $196,800 in favor of George Aldridge in this Federal Employers' Liability Act (FELA) suit. 45 U.S.C. §§ 51–60 (1982). Aldridge filed suit after he suffered a neck injury while working for the Railroad as a crossing watchman. * * *

Awards for loss of future earnings in federal actions should be reduced to present value. Jones & Laughlin Steel Corp. v. Pfeifer, 462 U.S. 523, 536–37, 103 S.Ct. 2541, 2550–51, 76 L.Ed.2d 768 (1983). * * *

The Supreme Court has not allocated the burden of proceeding or the burden of persuading the jury as to either the reduction to present value or the increase for inflation. Simply stated then, the issue is whether reduction to present value is an indispensable element of the plaintiff's claim for future lost wages which he must always prove by specific evidence or whether, absent contest by the defendant, the plaintiff sufficiently proves his claim by evidence of the gross amount of these lost wages. This approach, however, overlooks many complicated issues which arise in this amorphous area combining law and economics. As the Supreme Court said in *Pfeifer*, "the question of lost earnings can arise in many different contexts. In some sectors of the economy, it is far easier to assemble evidence of an individual's most likely career path than in others." Added to this obstacle of prediction are the many factors which can complicate the calculation of present value admirably discussed in *Pfeifer*: Should the discount rate be a "market" interest rate or a "real" interest rate adjusted for inflation, and, if the latter, for what period or periods of inflation? [Citation.] To prove that the gross amount of future wages established should be increased because projected inflation is greater than projected interest rates, what type of inflation should a plaintiff use—pure economic inflation or the various types of individual and societal inflation discussed by the Court in *Pfeifer, e.g.,* future production efficiency, increased skills, and differing collective bargaining approaches? [Citation.] These factors make it clear that the question of allocating the burden of proof is not one dimensional.

The Ninth Circuit resolved the problem by holding in effect that the party who would benefit from the application of a particular economic formula has the burden of producing competent evidence to prove it. Alma v. Manufacturers Hanover Trust, 684 F.2d 622, 626 (9th Cir.1982). *Contra* DiSabatino v. National Railroad Passenger Corp., 724 F.2d 394, 395 (3d Cir.1984) (burden of producing evidence of present value of future lost wages rests on plaintiff). If a defendant wishes the fact-finder to reduce the gross amount of future lost wages to present value, he can present evidence probative of an appropriate interest rate and method of discount. The plaintiff, in turn, may offer evidence tending to prove that the award should be increased because inflation will diminish its current value. In that case, the plaintiff must show what kind of and how much inflation. [Citation.] We think this is a sensible approach. In most cases, the factors are simple, and it should be a light burden for the defendant to prove a proper discount rate or for the plaintiff to prove the probable effects of inflation. * * * To the extent that the issue in a given case necessarily becomes difficult, it seems fair to place the burden of procuring and presenting economic evidence on the litigant who would benefit from its acceptance by the factfinder.

* * *

AFFIRMED.

BOYLE, DISTRICT JUDGE, concurring:

I concur in the result reached by the majority and join in their reasoning on all but one issue. That issue is the allocation of the burden of proof for the present value of lost future earnings. In my opinion, that burden must rest with the plaintiff.

* * *

The majority places the burden on the defendant to prove this material element of plaintiff's claim.

A defendant has no burden to prove any of the contested material issues of fact in a plaintiff's cause of action. The present value of lost future earnings is not an affirmative defense but rather a material element of the plaintiff's claim for that special damage.

If the plaintiff fails to offer any evidence of one or more of the elements of this special damage, then as a matter of law, the plaintiff's proof has failed and that claim should not be submitted to the jury.

The plaintiff has the burden at all times to prove by some competent evidence each of the material facts of his claim. Where part of plaintiff's case, as it was here, is for the special damage of lost future earnings, then plaintiff must offer some evidence of the earnings, the future term, and the present worth of this sum.

* * *

———

1. The parties in a private suit may stipulate to the "total offset" method before trial, thus eliminating the need for the production of evidence on inflation and discount rates. The Supreme Court observed in Monessen Southwestern Ry. Co. v. Morgan, 486 U.S. 330, ___ n.11, 108 S.Ct. 1837, 1846 n.11, 100 L.Ed.2d 349 (1988), that Jones & Laughlin Steel Corp. v. Pfeifer, reprinted *supra* in this chapter, allows such stipulation. "[N]othing prevents parties interested in keeping litigation costs under control from stipulating to [the total offset method's] use before trial." 462 U.S. 523, 550, 103 S.Ct. 2541, 2557, 76 L.Ed.2d 768 (1983).

Monessen held that if the parties do not so stipulate, the trial judge in a FELA case may not require the jury to accept one method of calculation, as some state courts do as a matter of common law. The trial court had applied the state rule mandating the total offset method, but the Supreme Court held that the mandatory instruction to the jury was reversible error in a FELA case. The Court reasoned that the judge improperly took from the jury the factual question of the appropriate rate for discounting the award. In *Monessen* the Court explained that its previous decision in *Pfeifer* required that the present value calculation had to be made as a "deliberate choice" by the trier of fact. Since no right to a jury trial existed in the Longshoremen's and Harbor Workers' Compensation Act claim involved in *Pfeifer*, the trier of fact was necessarily the judge. For the FELA claim in *Monessen*, the Court said the judge could not preempt the jury's function by mandating one method of computing present value, although the opinion notes that it is permissible for the judge to assist the jury by recommending a method. 486 U.S. 330, 108 S.Ct. 1837, 1846, 100 L.Ed.2d 349 (1988).

What if the plaintiff and defendant both fail to produce any evidence on inflation or discount rates, as in the principal case? May the judge in a FELA case then refuse to instruct the jury on these matters? *Aldridge* was remanded on this point following *Monessen*. Chesapeake & Ohio Ry. v. Aldridge, 486 U.S. 1049, 108 S.Ct. 2812, 100 L.Ed.2d 913 (1988). The Court of Appeals for the Fourth Circuit then held that the district court erred in refusing a jury instruction on discounting the award to its present value. Aldridge v. Baltimore & Ohio R.R., 866 F.2d 111 (4th Cir.1989).

Is this result correct where the parties have produced no evidence on discount rates or reduction to present value? Is the decision by both parties not to produce evidence on these matters analogous to a permissible stipulation of the total offset method? The opinion upon remand contains no discussion of the point. The court simply reversed its portion of the judgment pertaining to damages and remanded the case to the district court.

2.   The Supreme Court in St. Louis Southwestern Railway Company v. Dickerson, 470 U.S. 409, 105 S.Ct. 1347, 84 L.Ed.2d 303 (1985), held that the refusal to give a present value instruction in a FELA case constituted reversible error. Although FELA cases are adjudicated in state courts and are subject to state procedural rules, the substantive law which governs the actions is federal. In contrast, in Kokesh v. American Steamship Company, 747 F.2d 1092 (6th Cir.1984), the court held that the trial court had not committed plain error by not instructing the jury on reducing future personal injury damages to present value in a negligence action under the Jones Act. The court of appeals noted that one approach acknowledged in *Pfeifer* was to assume that the market interest rate exactly offsets price inflation and productivity gains. Accordingly, the court concluded that the failure to request a present value instruction may have been an intentional trial strategy.

Contra Rodgers v. Fisher Body Division, 739 F.2d 1102 (6th Cir. 1984) (court considered the issue *sua sponte* and held that it was plain error not to give instruction on reducing future damages to present value.)

3.   The approach of awarding damages in a lump sum to compensate for future losses in personal injury and wrongful death cases is, at best, a system of calculated guesswork involving a "battle of the experts." A complex formula which incorporates numerous projections of individual and societal factors will certainly result in a lump-sum total

which will either over or under compensate. An alternative method is to award payments in installments over the time period during which the losses will accrue in the future. The Model Periodic Payment of Judgments Act provides a system for the payment of damages for bodily injury in periodic installments, at the election of any party, subject to certain safeguards. The Model Act is designed to pay damages as losses actually accrue, thus eliminating the need to discount awards of future damages to present value. Also, the Act suggests that the installment method removes the burden of making difficult investment decisions for those claimants who are unsophisticated in financial matters. For a contrary view *see* Conklin, Wrongful Death Damages Expansion, Inflation; Discounts and Taxes—The Numbers Game, 28 Trial Law.Guide 249 (1984).

4. For additional information concerning the roles of inflation and discount rate as adjustments to damages see the following commentary: Mukatis & Widicus, Toward Just Compensation: A Statistical Comparison of the Total Offset Method of Valuing Lost Future Earnings Awards and United States Supreme Court Methods, 59 Temp.L.Q. 1131 (1986); Landsea & Roberts, Inflation and the Present Value of Future Economic Damages, 37 U. Miami L.Rev. 93 (1982); Note, Inflation, Productivity, and the Total Offset Method of Calculating Damages for Lost Future Earnings, 49 U.Chi.L.Rev. 1003 (1982); Sherman, Projection of Economic Loss: Inflation v. Present Value, 14 Creighton L.Rev. 723 (1981); Kolbach, Variable Periodic Payments of Damages: An Alternative to Lump Sum Awards, 64 Iowa L.J. 138 (1978); Formuzis & O'Donnell, Inflation and the Valuation of Future Economic Losses, 38 Mont.L.Rev. 297 (1977); Note, Future Inflation, Prospective Damages, and the Circuit Courts, 63 Va.L.Rev. 105 (1977); Henderson, The Consideration of Increased Productivity and the Discounting of Future Earnings to Present Value, 20 S.D.L.Rev. 307 (1975); Lawless, Computation of Future Damages: A View of the Bench, 54 Geo.L.J. 1131 (1966); Leasure, How to Prove Reduction to Present Worth, 21 Ohio St.L.J. 204 (1960); Immel, Actuarial Tables and Damage Awards, 19 Ohio St.L.J. 240 (1958).

B. PREJUDGMENT INTEREST

Section Coverage:

There are three types or categories of interest: conventional, prejudgment, and postjudgment. Conventional interest, or *eo nomine* ("in name only"), is contractual; an example is the amount payable by a borrower on a home mortgage loan. Postjudgment interest is statutory. All jurisdictions have enacted an interest rate payable on a judgment. Interest accrues at that rate from the date of entry to judgment satisfaction.

Prejudgment interest is somewhat of a mirror-image of its postjudgment counterpart. It too is interest payable upon the judgment, but from the time period running from accrual of a cause of action until entry of the judgment. The basis for imposing prejudgment interest may be pursuant to the agreement of the parties, by statute, or in equity as a restitutionary device to prevent unjust enrichment. Unlike post-judgment interest which accrues automatically, prejudgment interest is not always awarded.

Several competing policies exist with respect to the propriety of prejudgment interest. From the plaintiff's perspective, prejudgment interest provides a form of compensation for the loss of use of money damages until the date of judgment. If a defendant knows that the court will award prejudgment interest, there is no longer any incentive to delay paying a valid claim or to delay engaging in good faith settlement negotiations.

From the defendant's perspective, it is unfair to award interest on a claimed sum when it is uncertain whether the plaintiff would prevail at trial and uncertain as to the size of the ultimate verdict after trial. The threat of prejudgment interest presents a defendant with a Hobson's choice: either pay a contested claim in order to halt accrual of prejudgment interest or wait until judgment and pay interest for the time period from accrual of the claim until satisfaction of the judgment.

Courts, and sometimes legislatures, have resolved this conflict by placing several limitations on the allowability of prejudgment interest. The usual limitations are that prejudgment interest is recoverable when (1) the date the claim accrued was definite and (2) the amount of damages was readily ascertainable at that time. The first requirement recognizes that some damages, such as medical expenses, may be incurred intermittently from the occurrence of the harm until trial. The second criterion provides that prejudgment interest should be assessed only in the event that the damages were "liquidated" or calculable with some precision at the time the cause of action accrued. Consequently, courts historically have denied prejudgment interest in personal injury cases because certain elements, such as pain and suffering, inherently are unliquidated until determined by the trier of fact. Prejudgment interest awards typically have been reserved for breach of contract actions involving a definite sum of money or performance with an ascertainable pecuniary value and for those tort cases involving harm to land or chattels where valuation may be established by market prices.

Model Case:

On January 1 Baker entered into a contract to purchase 1,000 bushels of wheat at $3.00 per bushel from Peterson, payment and delivery to take place on October 1. On September 1 Peterson wrongfully repudiated the contract and Baker immediately obtained replacement wheat in the open market for $4.00 per bushel.

Baker sent a notice to Peterson demanding the $1,000 differential between the cost to cover and the contract price, reimbursement of expenses incidental to effecting cover, and lost profits. Peterson refused to pay any amount and Baker filed suit for breach of contract claiming each of the stated elements as damages.

The trial is concluded two years later and the court awards Baker the $1,000 plus incidental damages and an additional $500 as lost profits. Prejudgment interest would be properly assessed on the $1,000 and the incidental damages but the court, in its discretion, could justifiably deny it with respect to the lost profits. The claim for lost profits would typically be much more difficult to ascertain with certainty at the time of the breach, and therefore less appropriate to expect Peterson to satisfy in advance of trial. The assessment of prejudgment interest on the other two elements of damages serves two functions: Baker is wholly compensated for the damages for the loss of use of his money until the court's order and, the corollary, Peterson is denied the benefits of holding and being able to earn interest on the damages from the date of breach until judgment. Peterson could have tolled the running of prejudgment interest by promptly tendering payment of the $1,000 and the incidental expenses incurred as a result of the breach but should not be penalized for validly contesting the lost profits claim.

ANCHORAGE ASPHALT PAVING CO. v. LEWIS

629 P.2d 65 (Alaska 1981).

MATTHEWS, JUSTICE.

* * *

In 1969, appellee, Lewis, contracted with Anchorage Asphalt to pave seven roads in his mobile home park, the Four Seasons Mobiland. The roads began to deteriorate soon after the paving was completed and after April 1970, Lewis discontinued payments on the paving contract, having paid a total of $30,000.00. The contract price was $57,052.50.

Anchorage Asphalt sued on the contract and Lewis counterclaimed for breach of contract. On the second appeal, this court ruled that Anchorage Asphalt was liable for the pavement failure due to its failure to warn Lewis of the inadequacy of the pavement subsurface and remanded the case for a determination of damages. [Citation.] Damages were to be determined according to the formula established by this court on the first appeal:

If the court below reaches the issue of damages, they should be limited to those necessary to put Lewis in as good a position as that in which he would have been had such warning been given. * * * The amount due and unpaid on the contract will be an offset against those damages, and if the amount due and unpaid exceeds the amount of the damages, Anchorage Asphalt will be entitled to an award for the difference. [Citation.]

At the third trial, Lewis introduced expert testimony that of the total pavement area of 205,464 square feet, 105,474 square feet had failed and needed reconstruction or patching. Total reconstruction would, naturally, give the best result. Bids were introduced from four paving companies on the cost of total reconstruction during the summer of 1979. Using the lowest of these bids, Lewis' expert stated it would cost $114,987.00 to reconstruct and patch the road, to achieve a "good result." The trial court accepted this testimony and awarded damages of $114,987.00. From that amount, the court deducted $28,757.29 which Lewis still owed Anchorage Asphalt on the contract, netting a damage recovery by Lewis of $86,229.71. The court also awarded prejudgment interest on the full amount of the damages from April 9, 1970, plus costs and attorney's fees.

Anchorage Asphalt contends that the proper time to value damages is at the time of breach or a reasonable time thereafter, and the 1979 valuation used by the trial court was thus error. First, it should be noted that in accordance with the measure of damages mandated by this court, "damages should be the reasonable cost of completion in accordance with the contract specifications." [Citations.] The purpose of this rule is to grant the plaintiff what he bargained for under the contract.

As a general rule in contract actions, the date of breach affords the most appropriate time for valuing damages. However, this is not a rule to be applied inflexibly when it undermines the remedial goals of a damage award.

A case such as the one at bar, where litigation has been protracted over the length of a decade and the appropriate remedy is the cost of repair, presents a situation where limiting the plaintiff to the time of breach cost or repair has the potential of subverting the remedial purposes of the damage award. Simply put, where inflation has eroded the time of breach monetary valuation of an injury to a fraction of what is required to remedy the plaintiff's injury, then the time of breach rule may be regarded as inappropriate. Because the circumstances of individual cases differ drastically, it is impractical to adopt a definite point in time to value damages. It has been found preferable to leave the question to the trial court's discretion. [Citations.]

In this case, in view of the substantial inflation which took place between 1972, when the full extent of the breakdown of the streets became apparent, and the time of the trial in 1979,[7] we cannot say that the court abused its discretion using 1979 as the date of damage valuation.

In reaching this conclusion we necessarily reject a suggestion * * * that one may be guilty of an unreasonable failure to minimize costs which have increased due solely to inflation. This question has not been frequently addressed by American courts, and those authorities that

---

7. According to the Bureau of Labor Statistics, United States Department of Labor, the Anchorage Consumer Price Index for October 1972 was 116.9; it had increased to 211.4 as of October of 1979, reflecting an inflation rate over the period of approximately 81%. This far outstripped the allowable rate of prejudgment interest which was 6% until September of 1976 and thereafter 8% for a total prejudgment increase of approximately 48%.

exist are divided. We believe that the better view is that there is no duty to take action simply to avoid an increase in costs due solely to inflation because such an increase is not a real increase in cost to the defendant, who will be paying the award with money which has also decreased in value. Including a rise in costs due solely to inflation within the duty to minimize damages simply means that the claimant rather than the wrongdoer must bear the risk of inflation. Since this allows the wrongdoer to gain by delaying payment, where allowable prejudgment interest is exceeded by inflation, we see nothing to recommend it.

* * *

Anchorage Asphalt urges that the award of prejudgment interest from April 9, 1970, to the date of judgment in the damage award is improper. We agree and reverse the trial court on this point.

One purpose of prejudgment interest is to compensate the plaintiff for the loss of use of money from the date of injury until the date of judgment. [Citations.] A corollary purpose is to deprive the defendant of unjust enrichment resulting from the use of the money from the date of injury, thereby encouraging settlement. [Citations.] But prejudgment interest should not be awarded where it would work an injustice. [Citations.]

* * *

The award of damages at 1979 values suffices, in our view, to give Lewis what he initially bargained for, an acceptable paved road system. Ordinarily his award would be his cost of repair at or near the time of the breach, plus prejudgment interest up to the time of trial. Here, for the reasons previously explained, the court was justified in deviating from this standard method. However, to calculate the cost of repair at 1979 values and award prejudgment interest on that from 1970 strikes us as an unwarranted and unjustifiable compounding of damages.

It is necessary to award Anchorage Asphalt prejudgment interest on the $28,757.29 which Lewis still owes on the paving contract. Prejudgment interest should be calculated from May 1970, when Lewis' next payment was due until September 12, 1976, at six per cent interest, and at eight per cent interest from then until the date of judgment. [Citations.]

* * *

The case is affirmed in part; reversed in part; and remanded to the trial court to issue an order in accordance with this opinion.

———

1. Prejudgment interest awards have at least two purposes: (1) they compensate plaintiffs with the true amount of money damages they have suffered; and (2) they promote settlements and deter defendants in

cases where liability and the amount of damages are fairly certain from attempting to benefit unfairly from the inherent delays of litigation.

2.   The common law has traditionally followed an apparently simple dichotomy for whether to award prejudgment interest—ascertainable and unascertainable damages.   Thus, where the amount of damages is readily calculable, such as the amount due to be paid on a contract claim, courts routinely allow prejudgment interest.   Where the amount of damages is unascertainable, such as for pain and suffering, courts generally have not allowed prejudgment interest.

The Supreme Court of California articulated the rationale for this distinction.   In Greater Westchester Homeowners Assoc. v. City of Los Angeles, 26 Cal.3d 86, 160 Cal.Rptr. 733, 603 P.2d 1329 (1979), the court observed that prejudgment interest represents the accretion of wealth which could have been produced by the money during the period between loss and trial.   A fact-finder can use established techniques for computing with fair accuracy the amount of interest on a specific sum of money or specially valued property when the date of loss is known.

"However," the court observed, "damages for the intangible, non-economic aspects of mental and emotional injury are of a different nature.   They are inherently nonpecuniary, unliquidated and not readily subject to precise calculation.   The amount of such damages is necessarily left to the subjective discretion of the trier of fact.   Retroactive interest on such damages adds uncertain conjecture to speculation."   Moreover, when an injury is of a continuous nature, as many tort claims are, it is difficult to determine when any particular increment of intangible loss has occurred.

3.   The ascertainability requirement is a stumbling block in most tort cases except ones for tangible injury to property.   In a typical car accident case, the court will not award prejudgment interest on the personal injury, but will include this element of damages for any injury to the car.

In contract cases the same distinction occurs, but it less often acts to preclude recovery of prejudgment interest.   The Restatement (Second) of Contracts § 354 reflects the rule for breach of contract cases: Prejudgment interest is permissible when the breach consists of a failure to pay a definite sum of money or a failure to do acts with ascertainable monetary value.   In other circumstances, courts should award interest "as justice requires."

4.   What reasons for the ascertainability rule are most persuasive:

(a) A court should not require payment of interest on an unknowable sum because the defendant could not stop the accrual of that interest by paying the sum immediately to the plaintiff.

(b) In contract cases involving a fixed debt or a performance with an ascertainable value, the purposes of the contract are best met by providing lost interest after the breach.

(c) Where intangible losses occur, the uncertainty in their calculation is so great that adding prejudgment interest is a pretention to precision that never exists.

(d) Prejudgment interest is not really a "loss" suffered by the plaintiff except in cases involving specific debts or other analogous situations.

(e) Interest should never be allowed except where it is clearly an injustice to preclude it; that clear injustice occurs only in cases involving ascertainable sums.

MOORE–McCORMACK LINES, INC. v. RICHARDSON
295 F.2d 583 (2d Cir.1961).

LUMBARD, CHIEF JUDGE.

Moore–McCormack Lines, Inc., appeals from a final decree of the United States District Court for the Southern District of New York in an admiralty proceeding awarding damages against Moore–McCormack to eleven claimants for losses resulting from the capsizing of the steamer "Mormackite" off Cape Hatteras on the morning of October 7, 1954, with the loss of 37 lives and a cargo of iron ore and cocoa beans. The death claimants cross-appeal, challenging the district court's disallowance of interest from the date of death on the four death claims. * * *

In their cross-appeals the four death claimants urge that the district court should have granted interest as damages from the date of death to the date of the decree, June 3, 1960, on the awards for pecuniary loss to the decedents' dependents [5]* * *. The district court refused moratory interest (interest as damages), allowing interest only from the date of the decree. We conclude that these claims should be remanded to the district court for the allowance of pre-judgment interest. [Citation.]

Damages for pecuniary loss are recoverable under the Death on the High Seas Act, 46 U.S.C.A. § 761 *et seq.*, Section 761 provides that "the personal representative of the decedent may maintain a suit for damages * * * in admiralty." Under admiralty practice the district court has a measure of discretion in allowing and fixing moratory interest.

Moore–McCormack urges several objections to the allowance of moratory interest: First, it is argued, the failure of the Congress to provide expressly for pre-judgment interest on claims in admiralty indicates an intent to preserve the ancient rule permitting pre-judgment interest on claims termed "liquidated" while denying it as to "unliquidated" claims such as those here in question. Second, it is contended that we should follow decisions in this circuit in actions at law under Jones Act and F.E.L.A. provisions (also not expressly providing for moratory interest) which have recognized that, at least at law, interest is

---

5. No claim is made for interest on damages awarded for the seamen's conscious pain and suffering prior to death. The personal injury claimants have not cross-appealed from the decree which allowed them interest only from the date of the decree, June 3, 1960.

not allowed for the period between occurrence of the tort and entry of judgment. Third, it is urged that this court should as a matter of policy, hold that pre-judgment interest may not be given on damages for pecuniary loss resulting from a tortious death.

If it was the intention of Congress to bar recovery of moratory interest on "unliquidated" death claims, we are of course bound. But the hoary distinction between "liquidated" and "unliquidated" claims, criticized by eminent authority well before the enactment in 1920 of the Death on the High Seas Act, has never become so firmly entrenched in admiralty as it has been at law. The trend in admiralty prior to enactment of the statute had been toward allowance of pre-judgment interest on claims for negligent or wrongful death. The Death on the High Seas Act merely instructs that "the recovery * * * shall be a fair and just compensation for the pecuniary loss sustained." 46 U.S.C.A. § 762. We see nothing in this language to indicate that the Congress did not intend that the damages should give full compensation for *all* pecuniary loss sustained including that resulting from delay in being compensated. [Citation.]

Awards for financial loss to dependents, as distinguished from damages for pain and suffering, are intended to compensate for a pecuniary deprivation. McCormick, Damages, § 56 (1935). There would seem to be no reason why the delay in receipt of compensation for pecuniary loss should not likewise constitute a "pecuniary loss." [Citation.] There is surely considerable loss in having to wait over seven years before the judgment is entered and paid; this is the kind of loss for which compensation is customarily given by the payment of interest.

* * *

The first F.E.L.A. was enacted in 1906, when pre-judgment interest was generally limited to liquidated claims. This distinction was carried over into decisions under the Jones Act, perhaps with good reason in view of the latter statute's express incorporation of F.E.L.A. provisions. Both statutes provided for an action at law, with right to trial by jury, although Jones Act suits could also be brought in admiralty. Both statutes envisaged a recovery for pain and suffering and for injuries to the date of trial and thereafter, the computation of interest on which might well be far more confusing to the average jury than to a judge. [Citation.] In any event, no one would be so naive as to suppose that juries do not throw into the scales the years that a plaintiff may have had to wait before his case can be heard by a jury. The practical reason why the courts in jury cases have refused to grant moratory interest may therefore be found in the judicial recognition that a jury usually makes some allowance for loss caused by delay. Likewise judges doubtless make some allowance for loss because of the law's delay. It would seem to us to be better to recognize this and have the computation made on a basis which is known and understood.

Interest was never refused on unliquidated claims from any doubt that some financial loss is actually suffered from delay in receiving money. Theoretically, refusal was based on the concept that interest was payable only on a "debt" and that no debt could be due until the liability had been fixed. [Citation.] McCormick traces the distinction to a survival of the medieval distaste for interest as "usurious." McCormick, Damages §§ 51, 55 (1935 Ed.). A further explanation sometimes advanced is that a debtor should not be burdened with pre-judgment interest upon an obligation so nebulous that he must necessarily look to the courts to fix its scope. Similar considerations would, however, seem to support the disallowance of pre-judgment interest where liability is in doubt as to a "liquidated" claim. But since the courts have not seen fit to deny pre-judgment interest in the latter case, we see no reason why they should not grant it in the former.

We think, therefore, that when a court fixes damages to compensate for a loss which occurred in the past, there should be some allowance for the period between the date of the loss and the date of the judgment. Recompense may thus be given for the further loss in the postponement of the receipt of compensation. In all too many instances the delay in reaching cases for trial brings suffering and privation to those who were dependent on the deceased. Even the more fortunate of the bereaved may have been forced to borrow money at interest to meet their expenses.

As ancient as the injured's plaint of "the law's delay," is the use of that delay as a means by which a defendant may obtain a more favorable settlement. But whether an action has been deliberately prolonged or not, the defendants who are ultimately directed to pay have had the use of the money declared to be due. If it be only fair to discount sums paid now on account of future loss which would not be due until some years in the future [citation] it is, by the same token, inequitable not to make appropriate compensation for delay in discharging the obligation. McCormick, Damages, § 56 (1935 Ed.). Here the delay is not the fault of the plaintiffs and while it may equally not be the fault of the defendant, the plaintiffs have lost and the defendant has benefited.

We do not think, however, that the claimants are necessarily entitled to pre-judgment interest at the full legal rate. Although the claimants are entitled to compensation for delay, the conduct of Moore–McCormack has not been, so far as we can now determine, either so reckless or so wanton as to justify imposition of a penalty. An allowance of interest at the full legal rate would seem based on the unrealistic assumption that the claimants would have invested all they received so skillfully as to yield a return above that given by prudent investments not requiring special skill and attention by the investor. It would thus appear that interest should properly be allowed at a rate, within the discretion of the district judge, which may well be something less than the full legal rate. [Citations.] Since the allowance for loss of future benefits to the dependents of the four deceased men are discounted at 4%, it would seem appropriate for the district judge also to compute interest at a 4% rate on allowances for pecuniary losses sustained prior to decree. Of course interest on sums past due will not run from the date of death, but from the several dates at which the sums would have accrued.

* * *

————

1.   The distinction between ascertainable and unascertainable sums generally controls recovery of prejudgment interest in tort as it does in contract.   The situations in which courts usually find a tort loss ascertainable include: taking of land, taking or detention of personal property, and destruction of personal property or some part of real property.

Unascertainable losses in tort include: pain and suffering, emotional distress, and injury to reputation.   Amounts due for lost wages or medical expenses in personal injury cases lose their ascertainability by the uncertainty about the specific time each loss occurs.

The Restatement (Second) of Torts § 913 accepts this distinction. It further states that except for cases where prejudgment interest should never be allowed—bodily injury, emotional distress, or injury to reputation—the court should allow interest if it is required "to avoid an injustice."

Does this provision add any predictability for litigants or guidance for courts?   Would it serve to promote good faith settlement discussions?

2.   The general rules on prejudgment interest do not apply in every jurisdiction or in every circumstance.   Significant conflict of laws problems thus can occur.   In Draper v. Airco, Inc., 580 F.2d 91 (3d Cir.1978), for example, there was a conflicts issue concerning prejudgment interest in a wrongful death and survival action.   This diversity case was brought in a federal district court in New Jersey.   The judge determined that Pennsylvania substantive law governed in accordance with the choice of law rules but that New Jersey Law should control prejudgment interest. As a result, the jury verdict of $430,000 was increased to $585,000.   The Third Circuit Court of Appeals disagreed and held that, as a matter of conflicts law, Pennsylvania law should govern the issue of prejudgment interest.   Consequently, the award of prejudgment interest was reversed because Pennsylvania law disallows it in tort actions claiming unliquidated damages.

3.   Should courts use a simple or compound interest method for prejudgment interest awards?   Generally courts have assessed just simple interest.   *See* Restatement (Second) of Contracts § 354; Restatement (Second) of Torts § 913.   Would compound interest more closely approximate the loss of investment opportunity in the market?   Are there any reasons to chose simple interest over compound as a matter of policy?

In Stovall v. Illinois Central Gulf R.R. Co., 722 F.2d 190 (5th Cir.1984), the court compounded the prejudgment interest but computed postjudgment interest on a simple interest basis. The second choice was based upon certain amendments to Mississippi's legal interest statutes.

The Court Improvement Act of 1982, 28 U.S.C. § 1961 (Supp. I 1988) provides for compound interest for postjudgment interest but is silent regarding prejudgment interest. Is there any policy reason for distinguishing the two?

In restitution cases involving a wrongdoer who wrongfully acquired proceeds and acquired compound interest on them, a court of equity may disgorge such compound interest to prevent unjust enrichment. This result is reached under restitution rather than under law. *See* Restatement of Restitution § 157.

PROBLEM: THE BARGE COLLISION

Oilco is an oil company engaged in a variety of operations relating to petroleum production and marketing. It operates a barge-loading facility for use by its own barges and, for a fee, for use by independently operated barges.

Marine Service, which owns and operates barges, periodically uses Oilco's barge-loading facility. One stormy night there was a collision of one of Marine Service's barges into Oilco's docks. The Marine Service employees in charge of the errant barge had been drinking heavily on the job that day. They abandoned the barge during the storm and otherwise failed to take regular safety precautions. The barge broke loose from its moorings and crashed into the dock.

As a result of the collision, Oilco sustained several losses. First, the facility needed repairs. Second, Oilco incurred expenses when it made arrangements with other barge facilities to cover its contractual obligations with several other independent barges.

Oilco and Marine Service failed to settle this case. Marine Service admitted liability for the dock damage, but denied liability for the other expenses.

A full trial was held. The trier of fact found the conduct of Marine Service's employees sufficiently reckless to support punitive damages. Moreover, Oilco received damages for the additional expenses to honor its contractual obligations as well as the dock repair cost. The relevant substantive law allows prejudgment interest on ascertainable sums. Which of Oilco's damages should include prejudgment interest under this rule?

POLETO v. CONSOLIDATED RAIL CORP.

826 F.2d 1270 (3d Cir.1987).

BECKER, CIRCUIT JUDGE.

[Poleto instituted suit under the Federal Employer's Liability Act (FELA) against his employer, Conrail, to recover damages and prejudgment interest for personal injuries sustained in the course of employment. The district court entered judgment for Poleto against Conrail for $120,000 but denied the motion for prejudgment interest. Both parties appealed.]

* * *

The district court declined to award Poleto prejudgment interest on the amount of the jury award. Poleto concedes that the great weight of authority favors the district court's position. [Citations.] However, the question remains open in this circuit notwithstanding the approach of the eightieth anniversary of the FELA, and Poleto argues that we should find that the statute authorizes the award of prejudgment interest. He argues that such an award would be consistent with the FELA and would further Congress' purposes in enacting the statute. He also invokes the equitable powers of federal courts and argues that, in not mentioning prejudgment interest, the general federal interest statute, 28 U.S.C. § 1961, does not prohibit a court from making such a prejudgment interest award in pursuit of FELA's general purpose of "provid[ing] liberal recovery for injured workers." [Citations.] Finally, Poleto presses us to apply Pennsylvania Rule of Civil Procedure 238, which allows prejudgment interest.

We note at the outset of our analysis that the availability of interest in an action arising under a federal statute is governed by federal law, not the law of the forum state.[6] [Citations.] Because Poleto's claim against Conrail is predicated upon a violation of a federal statute, state substantive law, particularly Pennsylvania Rule of Civil Procedure 238, is not implicated. [Citation.] Any claim to prejudgment interest must therefore be derived from federal statutory sources.

Both the general federal interest statute, 28 U.S.C. § 1961, and the FELA are silent on the issue of prejudgment interest. The silence of neither statute is controlling, however. Absent an express prohibition within 28 U.S.C. § 1961, Congress has not by its silence ruled out the award of prejudgment interest. [Citations.] The absence of an FELA provision concerning prejudgment interest similarly does not end our inquiry. As the Supreme Court has instructed,

> the failure to mention interest in statutes which create obligations has not been interpreted by this Court as manifesting an unequivocal congressional purpose that the obligation shall not bear interest. For in the absence of an unequivocal prohibition of interest on such obligations, this Court has fashioned rules which granted or denied interest on particular statutory obligations by an appraisal of the congressional purpose in imposing them and in the light of general principles deemed relevant by the Court.

6. This is to be contrasted with the situation where federal jurisdiction is predicated upon diversity of citizenship; there, matters of prejudgment interest are considered substantive and are governed by state law. *See* Jarvis v. Johnson, 668 F.2d 740, 746–47 (3d Cir.1982).

Rodgers v. United States, 332 U.S. 371, 373, 68 S.Ct. 5, 7, 92 L.Ed. 3 (1947) (citations omitted).

In general, Congressional intent must guide our determination of whether we should imply a statutory provision that was not explicitly enacted; in particular, it must guide our determination of the availability of prejudgment interest under the FELA. [Citations.] Absent special circumstances, when Congress has been silent, we look to the purposes behind a statute as a general indication of Congressional purpose. [Citations.] We therefore turn to an examination of the Congressional purposes in exercising the FELA to determine whether those purposes would be furthered by imposition of prejudgment interest.

For us to award prejudgment interest, we must find that it would advance Congress' purpose in enacting "liberal recovery" under the FELA. In this regard, Poleto is aided by the Supreme Court's recent acknowledgment that the FELA is expansive in securing full recompense for injured railroad workers:

> The coverage of the statute is defined in broad language, which has been construed even more broadly. We have recognized generally that the FELA is a broad remedial statute, and have adopted a "standard of liberal construction in order to accomplish [Congress'] objects."

Atchison, T. & S.F. Ry. v. Buell, 480 U.S. 557, 107 S.Ct. 1410, 94 L.Ed.2d 563 (1987) (citation omitted). In the face of the adverse weight of the caselaw addressing the prejudgment interest issue, Poleto seeks his own caselaw support. He finds it only in *Garcia,* 597 F.Supp. 1304 [(D.Colo. 1984)], a case that has been rejected by the court of appeals of its own circuit, *see* Wilson v. Burlington Northern Ry., 803 F.2d 563 (10th Cir.1986), but which nonetheless forcefully articulates the ways in which prejudgment interest would contribute to full recompense.

In *Garcia,* the district court suggested two ways in which prejudgment interest would further the purposes of the FELA. "First, full compensation to an injured worker requires compensation from the date of injury." Because an injured worker must pay out-of-pocket expenses despite a debilitating injury that interrupts the flow of income, reasons *Garcia,* interest on a jury award should run from injury, which is the point from which income is first interrupted. "Second ... an injured worker's damages should not depend on the mere fortuity of when the case goes to trial." Where jury verdicts are returned at different times, "[t]wo railroad employees suffering identical injuries on the same day could recover significantly different actual economic benefits even if their respective jury verdicts were for identical dollar amounts." [10]

---

10. The district court in *Garcia* also offered a third reason for awarding prejudgment interest. It found that the availability of prejudgment interest would discourage defendants from pursuing the tactical delay that prompts plaintiffs to settle on more favorable terms (a rationale, we note, that is similar to that underlying Pennsylvania Rule of Civil Procedure 238). "Depriving an injured worker of the right to interest on the debt created with his injury merely encourages defendants to put off the day of

This holding represents the culmination of a trend in the relevant jurisprudence. The common law had been hostile to the award of prejudgment interest, an attitude that commentators have considered a vestige of the medieval view that considered all forms of interest usurious. This attitude, it should be noted, prevailed at the turn of the century, when the FELA was enacted and court cases first contemplated the availability of prejudgment interest. Subsequent cases have relied on these early cases as authority for denying prejudgment interest. [Citation.]

As this hostility ebbed, it was replaced by "the hoary distinction between 'liquidated' [*i.e.,* not reduced to a dollar amount] and 'unliquidated' claims," the former being entitled to prejudgment interest, whereas the latter was not. [Citations.] The distinction has survived, primarily in those jurisdictions that limit prejudgment interest to claims whose amount can be ascertained before trial and disallow it when a claim is not only unliquidated, but is also considered unascertainable. [Citations.]

Some courts have suggested that the liquidated/unliquidated distinction should be abandoned in cases where the economic character of the damages being awarded is apparent. For example, in Turner v. Japan Lines, Inc., 702 F.2d 752 (9th Cir.1983), the Ninth Circuit made the following observation in *dicta*:

> [E]ven where a claim is not based on a liquidated sum or the prejudgment interest statute is otherwise inapplicable, courts have nonetheless permitted in proper cases the recovery of interest by way of damages, as a means of making the plaintiff whole. The recovery includes as an item of damages compensation for the delay between the time of injury and the awarding of damages.

Notwithstanding this movement toward the award of prejudgment interest for economic harm in all cases, it cannot be gainsaid that the prevailing rule is to deny prejudgment interest except when damages can be easily ascertained prior to trial. Because the question nonetheless remains open in this circuit, however, we must independently assess Poleto's argument and, insofar as it principally relies on that case, the district court's opinion in *Garcia.*

The district court in *Garcia* looked to the policy of liberal recovery that underlies the FELA, *see, e.g.,* Atchison Topeka, 480 U.S. 557, 107 S.Ct. 1410, 94 L.Ed.2d 563 (1987), and found that it would be furthered by awarding prejudgment interest. [Citations.] Because the FELA seeks fully to compensate injured railroad employees, denying prejudgment interest would seem to work against the statutory scheme—"[t]he interest foregone on lost income or on money spent for out-of-pocket expenses from the date of loss to the time of compensation is as much a part of making an injured party whole as is the calculation of her wage rate." [Citation.] Because a proper criterion for determining Congres-

judgment as long as possible," reasoned the court. 597 F.Supp. at 1309.

sional intent is the policy of the statute, *Garcia* makes a strong case that the award of prejudgment interest would further the statutory purpose.[11]

Although not an affirmative reason for granting prejudgment interest, we note that Poleto's case would allow for the practical application of prejudgment interest. This is because, unlike the situation in *Wilson*, the district court submitted carefully crafted special interrogatories to the jury that segregated past economic damages from non-economic and future economic damages. It has been suggested that when a jury has been asked to render only a general verdict, it might be presumed to have included prejudgment interest in its calculation of damages. "[N]o one would be so naive as to suppose that juries do not throw into the scales the years that a plaintiff may have had to wait before his case can be heard by a jury." Restatement (Second) Torts § 913(2) (not allowing interest, but allowing "the time that has elapsed between the harm and the trial [to] be considered in determining the amount of damages"). However, the situation differs where carefully crafted interrogatories have been submitted to the jury. Special interrogatories constrain the jury to determining the dollar amount of the damage only, leaving to the court the task of adding prejudgment interest to account for the consequence of delay. Additionally, by submitting special interrogatories to the jury, the district court segregated the portion of Poleto's award that represents past economic harms from that which represents the non-economic and the future economic portion of his loss.[14]

---

11. We find *Garcia* unconvincing to the extent that it relies on interest as a way to rectify litigation delay, as does Pennsylvania's Rule 238, which is relied on by Poleto. Although Congress did enact the FELA for compensatory purposes, nothing in the statute, its legislative history, or the jurisprudence surrounding its application lends support to the conclusion that the Congress sought to rectify litigation delays when it enacted the statute. Similarly, the general federal interest statute does not attempt to rectify this problem; to the contrary, Congress did not adopt the amendments that would have provided for prejudgment interest, intended in part as delay damages, *supra* at 1274, n.7; *cf.* Fed.R.Civ.P. 68 (shifting costs onto party who rejects a settlement offer and does not obtain a more favorable judgment at trial).

14. Not all portions of a verdict are economic in character, and only the sum that represents past economic loss is properly adjusted to present value through an interest calculation. Non-economic awards, such as pain and suffering or punitive damages, do not compensate for market-induced harms, so they do not require the adjustment for the time the successful plaintiff's money was out of the market which prejudgment interest provides. *See Wilson*, 803 F.2d at 567 (McKay, J., concurring);

see also 22 Am.Jur.2d, Damages § 191 (1965) (suggesting that delay in paying for all but pain and suffering compensation should be adjusted through an award of interest). For example, as the Supreme Court of California has noted, "damages for the intangible, noneconomic aspects of mental and emotional injury are of a different nature. They are inherently nonpecuniary ... [and] necessarily left to the subjective discretion of the trier of fact. Retroactive interest on such damages adds uncertain conjecture to speculation." Greater Westchester Homeowners Assoc. v. City of Los Angeles, 26 Cal.3d 86, 160 Cal.Rptr. 733, 603 P.2d 1329, 1338 (1979).

Future economic harms must similarly be excluded from the adjustment of prejudgment interest, for interest adjustment would be antithetical to adjusting such a future stream of money to its present value. The Supreme Court requires that, for example, the portion of the verdict that is awarded to compensate for the loss of earning power must be reduced to present value dollars. *See* Chesapeake & Ohio R.R. v. Kelly, 241 U.S. 485, 489, 36 S.Ct. 630, 632, 60 L.Ed. 1117 (1916). Significantly, the Court recognized that the reason for reducing future earnings to present dollars is to "tak[e] account of the earning power of the money that is presently to be awarded." *Id.*

In sum, there is an excellent case that an award of prejudgment interest for past economic loss would further the goal of liberal recovery that underlies the FELA. An injured worker forgoes income, yet must meet the expenses of daily life before compensation for his injury is reduced to judgment. Prejudgment interest for economic losses accounts for this period between the date of the loss and the date of its ascertainment, thereby contributing to making the plaintiff whole. As the Supreme Court has explained in the context of holding that prejudgment interest should generally be awarded in patent cases, "[a]n award of interest from the time that the royalty payments would have been received merely serves to make the patent owner whole, since his damages consist not only of the value of the royalty payments but also of the forgone use of the money between the time of infringement and the date of the judgment." [Citation.] The case for prejudgment interest appears at least as strong in FELA as in patent cases.

Despite the apparent wisdom of an award of prejudgment interest in the case before us, we are compelled by other considerations to uphold the district court's denial of its award. The FELA has been in existence since the turn of the century, yet none of the circuits award prejudgment interest in cases that arise under the statute. Few of the cases contain any extensive discussion of the subject, and, as we have suggested, many of the recent cases simply note that the issue was settled in an older case that disposed of the point summarily. [Citations.] Despite the apparent weakness, however, we find the prior holdings of these courts significant for two reasons.

First, they reflect the view that at the time of passage, Congress did not intend prejudgment interest in the FELA. * * * The FELA represented a radical change from the common law in an attempt to assure workers a more sure recovery by abolishing many traditional defenses. Additionally, as Judge Seth's majority opinion in *Wilson* notes, at the time the FELA was enacted in 1908 the common law uniformly rejected the imposition of prejudgment interest. In view of Congress' conscious focus on the manner in which the FELA should differ from common law, it is not insignificant that Congress failed to abrogate the prejudgment interest principle. Judge Seth found "some indication of legislative intent in Congress' failure to expressly abrogate that principle in passing the FELA when it did so to other well established doctrines," and he concluded:

> The omission by Congress in the FELA of such an express statement indicates to us that Congress did not intend to provide for prejudgment interest. Congress, in our view, reached a balance as to the many considerations before it on this then novel legislation and this we should not disturb.

803 F.2d at 565. Similarly, Judge Rambo in *Camplese* found that

> it is evident that Congress, by enacting FELA, has adjusted the equities between the railroad employer and the injured employee.

To grant prejudgment interest would undermine the equities that have been balanced by the Act itself.

594 F.Supp. at 47–48.

The "balance" of which Judges Seth and Rambo speak is obviously the trade-off of employer and employee rights implicit in the FELA compensation scheme. It is far from certain that interest was a conscious factor in the striking of that balance; hence the argument is not without flaw. * * * However, notwithstanding the acknowledged force of plaintiff's argument, and like the other courts of appeals that have recently dealt with the issue, we are not sufficiently persuaded to depart from eighty years of precedent consistently interpreting the FELA as not permitting prejudgment interest. We simply find evidence lacking that Congress intended prejudgment interest to accompany FELA awards.

Second, whether the early judicial decisions were or were not proper, their view has continued to prevail with virtual unanimity until the present day. While Congressional silence in the face of judicial interpretation is not normally a sufficient indication of Congressional approval, a consistent judicial approach of many years may become enough. [Citation.] In this case, Congress has failed to upset the careful balance of employer and employee rights. While that inaction might be insufficient if the law had moved so far as to make the denial of prejudgment interest an aberration, we consider it a sufficient expression of Congressional approval to require that change come from Congress.

If Congress wished to change the consistent result of the courts, it could have amended the statute. It has not. We shall therefore uphold the district court in its denial of prejudgment interest to Poleto.

* * *

---

1. A minority of jurisdictions have found the ascertainability distinction illogical. A few cases have held that the rule inappropriately prevents personal injury claimants from receiving full compensation.

The district court in In re Air Crash Disaster Near Chicago, 480 F.Supp. 1280 (N.D.Ill.1979), held that prejudgment interest must be allowed in the wrongful death cases relating to a mass disaster air crash in order to eliminate the defendants' incentive to delay settlements. There was little doubt about the liability of the defendants, the air carrier, and the aircraft manufacturer. The issues for trial centered on damages. The district court judge noted:

[I]t is inequitable to have one plaintiff receive substantially more or less than another even though the amount of the judgment or settlement is the same solely because months or years intervene between the judgments or settlements. As previously indicated, estimates as to the aggregate damages resulting from the approximately 275 deaths and injuries range from 110 to 500 million dollars. The average claim will probably be at least $1,000,000. The monthly interest on $1,000,000 at 10% is over $8,333 or $100,000 per annum. 480 F.Supp. 1280 (N.D.Ill.1979)

The district court's approach to prejudgment interest in these air disaster cases was reversed subsequently by the Court of Appeals for the Seventh Circuit. The wrongful death actions were brought as diversity cases and therefore state law applied. There was no provision for prejudgment interest under the applicable Wrongful Death Act. Ironically, the district court's award was upheld in the first appealed case because the amount of the verdict was arithmetically correct; there were offsetting errors in the jury instructions. The court explained:

> [P]resent case value is to be calculated at the date of *trial*. But in this case, the jury was instructed to calculate present value as of the date of Craig Valladares' *death*. The parties agreed to use the date of death, rather than date of trial, to calculate present value because the evidence in the trial gave life expectancy and income estimates based on the date of death. It is not surprising that the defendants readily agreed to the date of death instruction, since it gave them an extra thirteen months of discount on the decedent's future income stream. This formulation is equivalent to actually subtracting interest from what the total award would have been if future income had been discounted to trial instead of death.

* * *

> The question then becomes how to adjust an award that represents "present value at date of death" when it is actually received at the date of judgment. The answer is to add one year of "interest" to "present value at death" in order to reverse the extra year of discounting (assuming, as we do, that the "interest rate" and "discount rate" are the same). * * * 644 F.2d 633 (7th Cir.1981)

The judgment of the district court was thus affirmed despite the incorrect jury instruction on prejudgment interest.

2. A notable recent decision allowing prejudgment interest on a personal injury claim was Cavnar v. Quality Control Parking, Inc., 696 S.W.2d 549 (Tex.1985). The Texas legislature immediately responded with a statute that pre-empts the common law. The statute is provided below because of its extensive and creative response to the issue.

SECTION 1. Article 1.05, Title 79, Revised Statutes, as amended (Article 5069–1.05, Vernon's Texas Civil Statutes), is amended by adding Section 6 to read as follows:

Sec. 6. (a) Judgments in wrongful death, personal injury, and property damage cases must include prejudgment interest. Except as provided by Subsections (b), (c), and (d) of this section, prejudgment interest accrues on the amount of the judgment during the period beginning on the 180th day after the date the defendant receives written notice of a claim or on the day the suit is filed, whichever occurs first, and ending on the day preceding the date judgment is rendered.

(b) If judgment for a claimant is less than the amount of a settlement offer by the defendant, prejudgment interest does not accrue on the amount of the judgment for the period during which the offer may be accepted.

(c) If judgment for a claimant is more than the amount of the settlement offer by the defendant, prejudgment interest does not include prejudgment interest on the amount of the settlement offer for the period during which the offer may be accepted.

(d) In addition to the exceptions provided under Subsections (b) and (c) of this section, the court in its discretion may order that prejudgment interest does or does not accrue during periods of delay in the trial, taking into consideration:

(1) periods of delay caused by a defendant; and

(2) periods of delay caused by a claimant.

(e) In order for a settlement offer to toll the running of prejudgment interest in accordance with the provisions of this section, the offer must be communicated to a party or his attorney or representative in writing.

(f) If a settlement offer is made for other than present cash payment at the time of settlement, prejudgment interest on the amount of the settlement offer is computed on the basis of cost or fair market value of the settlement offer at the time it is made.

(g) The rate of prejudgment interest shall be the same as the rate of postjudgment interest at the time of judgment and shall be computed as simple interest.

3.   Similarly, California added § 3291 to its Civil Code which provides that prejudgment interest will be awarded in personal injury actions at the legal rate of 10 percent per annum on the portion of the judgment which exceeds the plaintiff's settlement offer. The interest is calculated from the date of the plaintiff's initial offer and accrues until judgment is satisfied. *See generally* Clark, Prejudgment Interest after *Cavnar*: What Rate Applies?, 50 Tex.B.J. 126 (1987); Note, Prejudgment Interest Available on Accrued Damages in Personal Injury, Wrongful Death and Survival Actions, 17 Tex.Tech L.Rev. 293 (1986); Note, Prejudgment Interest is Now Recoverable in Personal Injury, Wrongful Death and Survival Action Cases, 38 Baylor L.Rev. 385 (1986); Note, Prejudgment Interest in Personal Injury Litigation; California's Long–Awaited Remedy in Civil Code Section 3291, 11 W.St.U.L.Rev. 85 (1983).

4.   Distinguish between past harms and future harms with respect to awards of prejudgment interest. The purpose of prejudgment interest is to compensate for the loss of the use of money from losses that accrued before trial. Therefore prejudgment interest is appropriate only for past losses and not for future ones.

This distinction can be important for personal injury awards in those few instances where prejudgment interest is allowed, such as in maritime law. For example, in Verdin v. C & B Boat Co., Inc., 860 F.2d

150 (5th Cir.1988), the district court erred in an admiralty case by allowing prejudgment interest on future losses as well as on past ones. The action was against a barge owner for the wrongful death of a tugboat captain.   On appeal the court denied prejudgment interest for future losses and allowed it only on damages for past ones: the past loss of support, the pain and suffering of the decedent before death, and the medical and funeral expenses for the decedent.

BLAKE v. CALIFANO

626 F.2d 891 (D.C.Cir.1980).

Davis, Judge:

Appellants are federal employees who have received retroactive promotions and back pay because they were victims of sex discrimination prohibited by the Equal Employment Opportunity Act of 1972, Pub.L. No. 92–261, 86 Stat. 103.   The issue is whether their back pay awards should have reflected an award of prejudgment interest or should have been adjusted by an inflation factor to account for the decline of the purchasing power of the dollar between the time of the discrimination and the time of the award.   In the District Court, on cross-motions for summary judgment on this point, Chief Judge Bryant held that the court did not have authority to order the United States to pay either prejudgment interest or a sum in addition to back pay to reflect inflation.   We affirm.

The plaintiffs are five women who were employed as nursing assistants at the Clinical Center, National Institutes of Health.   They brought this sex-discrimination action in March 1976, but no trial on the merits was held in the District Court.   As the result of administrative decision or agreement of the parties, it was determined that they had each been denied promotion from a GS–4 to a GS–5 position as the result of sex discrimination.   The parties settled the complaint that they were also discriminated against in consideration for promotion from GS–3 to GS–4.   By the winter of 1976 each of the plaintiffs had received retroactive promotion and back pay.   The only question remaining for decision by the District Court was that now before us—addition of prejudgment interest or, alternatively, of an inflation factor.

Without such a supplement, appellants say, their awards give them an incomplete remedy, especially in view of the considerable time elapsed since their injuries occurred.   They note that prejudgment interest has been awarded by some courts under Title VII in private-sector cases, and urge that to deny this remedy to federal employees is to relegate them to second-class status.   They argue that the automatic preclusion of an award of interest or an adjustment for inflation is contrary to the remedial provision of Title VII referring to "any other equitable relief as the court deems appropriate," [4] as well as to the Congressional purpose,

---

4.   42 U.S.C. § 2000e–5(g) reads in pertinent part:

in adopting the Equal Employment Opportunity Act of 1972, to extend the protections of Title VII to federal personnel.

We take the other view because (a) there is a long-established, deeply-imbedded principle that interest is not allowed on monetary claims against the Federal Government unless Congress (or a contract) plainly authorizes such an addition, and (b) in the light of this traditional doctrine we are not persuaded by the text, legislative history, or purposes of the 1972 extension of Title VII to federal workers that Congress has provided for this kind of relief to such employees.

There is no doubt as to the historical existence of an entrenched immunity of the Government from prejudgment interest, in the absence of authorization by Congress (or, in the case of a contract, the contracting parties). The Supreme Court has reiterated it many times for about a century. [Citations.] And Congress has declared in 28 U.S.C. § 2516(a) that "Interest on a claim against the United States shall be allowed in a judgment of the Court of Claims only under a contract or Act of Congress expressly providing for payment thereof."

For this case it makes no difference whether one phrases this firmly-established rule as calling in all cases for some specific or express legislation authorizing interest, or more simply for a statute evincing the intention to allow interest. [Citations.] Under either formulation there is here no statute which overcomes the traditional principle. Appellants rely on the broad authorization for "other equitable relief" in 42 U.S.C. § 2000e–5(g). We agree, however, with the two Courts of Appeals which have ruled on the issue and have held that this language is insufficient to constitute the necessary statutory authority where the complainant is a federal employee. [Citations.] While it may not be unreasonable to infer that "equitable relief" can cover an award of interest in private-sector cases, there is nothing to indicate that Congress affirmatively intended this for the federal sector. The legislative history is wholly silent on the propriety of awarding interest in Title VII cases. Without some further indication in statutory language or in legislative history, "equitable relief" is too wide and general a category to outbalance, by itself, the specific entrenched immunity of the Government from prejudgment interest. * * * Moreover, while an award of prejudgment interest would be consistent with the remedial policies of Title VII, mere consistency with statutory purposes is not enough. In *Fitzgerald v. Staats,* 188 U.S.App.D.C. 193, 578 F.2d 435, *cert. denied,* 439 U.S. 1004, 99 S.Ct. 616, 58 L.Ed.2d 680 (1978), we considered whether prejudgment interest could be assessed against the United States under the Back Pay Act or the Veterans Preference Act. In holding that it could not, we

If the court finds that the respondent has intentionally engaged in or is intentionally engaging in an unlawful employment practice charged in the complaint, the court may enjoin the respondent from engaging in such unlawful employment practice, and order such affirmative action as may be appropriate, which may include, but is not limited to, reinstatement or hiring of employees, with or without back pay * * *, *or any other equitable relief as the court deems appropriate* (emphasis added).

concluded that we were not free to make a decision to allow interest based on the remedial purposes of those statutes. [Citation.] We can give no greater weight to the comparable remedial purposes of Title VII.[8]

The same result must be reached for appellants' alternative contention that they are entitled to increases in their back-pay awards to compensate for the loss of the dollar's value due to inflation. We assume arguendo that interest and an inflation adjustment are distinct remedies, but the settled governmental immunity from interest counsels against this similar supplementation (in the absence of clear Congressional authorization). Both interest and an inflation adjustment serve the same general end of compensating the recipient for differences in the worth of her award between the date of actual receipt and the date as of which the money should have been paid. If one is barred the other should also be; the same considerations govern. [Citations.] In addition, appellants have been unable to offer any example of a back-pay award under Title VII being augmented to account for inflation, even in a private case. In the light of the special need for a waiver of sovereign immunity in suits against the Government [citations], this case is *a fortiori.*

Affirmed.

---

1. Courts may award prejudgment interest in restitution to prevent the unjust enrichment of the defendant. For example, the court in *Sack v. Feinman* held that prejudgment interest may be allowed on a constructive trust. In that case, one sister sought to impress a constructive trust on savings bonds allegedly converted fraudulently by another sister from their mother. The Pennsylvania Supreme Court reversed the trial court's denial of prejudgment interest and noted that pre-verdict interest may be necessary in order to disgorge completely any profits which a fiduciary might otherwise gain from abusing a confidential relationship. The decision whether to grant or deny prejudgment interest in such a restitution case rests within the court's sound discretion to prevent unjust enrichment. 489 Pa. 152, 413 A.2d 1059 (1980).

2. The back pay in the principal case is a restitutionary award to accompany equitable reinstatement orders. Is it appropriate to award prejudgment interest on back-pay awards generally in order to prevent unjust enrichment? Are such cases distinguishable from the unjust enrichment of a fiduciary who holds fraudulently converted property in a constructive trust?

3. Consider the prejudgment interest award on back pay that the court awarded for violation of the Fair Labor Standards Act in *Donovan*

---

8. In extending Title VII to federal employees, Congress contemplated that there could be differences between the cases of private-sector employees and of federal workers. 42 U.S.C. § 2000e–16(d) (added by the 1972 Act) provides that "[t]he provisions of section 2000–5(f) through (k) of this title, *as applicable,* shall govern civil actions brought hereunder" (emphasis added).

v. Sovereign Security, Ltd. The case concerned a violation of the Act by a private sector employer. The court allowed the interest award as part of a restitutionary injunction provided under section 17. The court reasoned that the purposes of the restitutionary injunction are to make whole employees who have been underpaid. The Act was intended to eliminate the competitive advantage of employers who violate the federal wage restrictions. The court continued, "Pre-judgment interest also serves to remedy the competitive disadvantage inflicted on law-abiding businesses by denying the errant employer the free use of the money it should have paid out in wages. Failure to award interest would create an incentive to violate the FLSA, because violators in effect would enjoy an interest-free loan for as long as they could delay paying out back wages." 726 F.2d 55 (2d Cir.1984).

Would the same rationale apply to a common law claim of wrongful discharge? If the defendant employer discharges the plaintiff for refusing to decline jury duty, for example, the court may order reinstatement and back pay. Should prejudgment interest be awarded under the unjust enrichment theory? Under the competitive edge theory? Under the ascertainability rule? *See* Diggs v. Pepsi–Cola Metropolitan Bottling Co., 861 F.2d 914 (6th Cir.1988) (wrongfully discharged employee entitled to prejudgment interest on back pay award).

In response to the perceived inequity between employees of the public and private sector with respect to prejudgment interest, Congress amended the Back Pay Act. It now specifically provides for prejudgment interest in suits by federal agency employees covered by the Act. 5 U.S.C. § 5596(b)(1)(A).

4. Courts almost universally deny prejudgment interest on punitive damages. The typical rationale is that the purpose behind prejudgment interest is to compensate for the loss of the use of the compensatory damages rather than to punish or deter the defendant. *See* Restatement (Second) of Torts § 913, comment d; Cavnar v. Quality Control Parking, Inc., 696 S.W.2d 549 (Tex.1985).

5. The court may exercise its discretion to limit or deny prejudgment interest if the plaintiff has delayed unduly in pursuing the lawsuit. General Motors Corp. v. Devex Corp., 461 U.S. 648, 103 S.Ct. 2058, 76 L.Ed.2d 211 (1983). The court may require that the defendant be prejudiced by the delay before denying prejudgment interest. *See* Lummus Industries, Inc. v. D. M. & E. Corp., 862 F.2d 267 (Fed.Cir.1988) (prejudgment interest should not be denied in a patent infringement claim absent a showing that the plaintiff's delay prejudiced the defendant).

Should a court consider the cause for the plaintiff's delay or the relative hardship to the parties with respect to an award of prejudgment interest? In United States v. Ottati & Goss, 694 F.Supp. 977 (D.N.H. 1988), the court denied prejudgment interest to the Environmental Protection Agency for environmental cleanup costs incurred at a hazardous waste site. The trial judge found that the government had delayed unduly the progress of the case.   Should a governmental plaintiff be treated like any private plaintiff in this context?   If not, should the delay rule be applied more or less strictly for the government's recovery of prejudgment interest?

6.   For additional commentary on developments in the law of prejudgment interest see the following references: Mann, On Interest, Compound Interest and Damages, 101 Law Q.Rev. 30 (1985); Bowles, Interest on Damages for Non–Economic Loss, 100 Law Q.Rev. 197 (1984); Note, Prejudgment Interest: Survey and Suggestion, 77 Nw. U.L.Rev. 192 (1982); Note, Prejudgment Interest: An Element of Full Compensation in Wrongful Death Cases, 1981 U.Ill.L.Rev. 453 (1981).

Chapter 13

LIMITATIONS ON COMPENSATORY DAMAGES
A. FORESEEABILITY

Section Coverage:

A significant limitation on the extent of compensatory damages recoverable for breach of contract is that the loss must be reasonably "foreseeable" from the perspective of the breaching party at the time the contract was formed. The requirement of foreseeability reflects a policy that a party should be held accountable only for those risks that were foreseeable at the time of making contractual promises.

The role of foreseeability in tort differs significantly from its function in contracts. It affects first the nature of the duty imposed by law upon the actors. Once that duty is established, the actor is responsible for all the ensuing harm proximately caused by conduct in breach of that duty. The limitation of "proximate cause" is also defined by foreseeability, although jurisdictions differ on when and what injuries must be foreseeable for this "legal cause" concept.

As a result, the recoverable damages in tort are usually greater than in contract once the tortfeasor's duty has been established. This difference has received criticism because it invites characterization of certain conduct as tortious simply to gain greater damages than if couched as a breach of contract. Despite the different treatment of foreseeability in tort and contract, the shared underlying policy goal is limiting or excluding recovery of damages that are too remote.

Model Case:

On January 1 Baker contracted to purchase 10,000 gallons of high-grade aircraft fuel oil from the Energon Company for $100 per gallon with delivery scheduled for July 1. In April Energon repudiated the contract, asserting that new government tariffs had increased its costs dramatically, making it commercially impracticable to perform under the contract. The market price for fuel oil at the time of Energon's repudiation had risen to $150 per gallon.

Baker, prior to entering its contract with Energon, had effected a resale contract of the fuel oil to Industri–Chem for $200 per gallon. Assuming that the repudiation constituted a breach of contract which was not excused, Baker would be entitled to recover damages measured by the cost to cover or the difference between the market price and the contract price for the oil in April. However, Baker would not be allowed to recover damages for lost profits under its resale contract to Industri–

Chem absent a showing that Energon would have reasonably foreseen those consequences of its potential breach on January 1.

REDGRAVE v. BOSTON SYMPHONY ORCHESTRA

855 F.2d 888 (1st Cir.1988).

Coffin, Circuit Judge. * * *

The plaintiffs, actress Vanessa Redgrave and Vanessa Redgrave Enterprises, Ltd. (hereinafter Redgrave), brought suit against the Boston Symphony Orchestra (hereinafter the BSO) for cancelling a contract for Redgrave's appearance as narrator in a performance of Stravinsky's "Oedipus Rex." The cancellation occurred in the wake of protests over Redgrave's participation because of her support of the Palestine Liberation Organization. * * * [A jury awarded Redgrave $100,000 in consequential damages caused by the BSO's breach of contract, but the district court granted the BSO's motion for judgment notwithstanding the verdict.]

In response to special interrogatories, the jury found that the BSO's cancellation of the "Oedipus Rex" concerts caused consequential harm to Redgrave's professional career and that this harm was a foreseeable consequence within the contemplation of the parties at the time they entered the contract. A threshold question is whether Massachusetts contract law allows the award of such consequential damages for harm to a claimant's professional career.

Redgrave's consequential damages claim is based on the proposition that a significant number of movie and theater offers that she would ordinarily have received in the years 1982 and following were in fact not offered to her as a result of the BSO's cancellation in April 1982. The BSO characterizes this claim as one for damage to Redgrave's reputation, and argues that the recent Massachusetts state court decisions in McCone v. New England Telephone & Telegraph Co., 393 Mass. 231, 471 N.E.2d 47 (1984), and Daley v. Town of West Brookfield, 19 Mass.App. Ct.1019, 476 N.E.2d 980 (1985), establish that Massachusetts law does not permit plaintiffs in breach of contract actions to recover consequential damages for harm to reputation.

In *McCone v. New England Telephone & Telegraph Co.*, plaintiffs alleged that their employer's breach of an implied covenant of good faith had caused them loss of salary increases, loss of pension benefits, and "damage to their professional reputations, disruption of their personal lives, and great pain of body and mind." The Massachusetts Supreme Judicial Court held that the claims for damages to reputation and other emotional injury could not be sustained in the suit because "these additional damages are not contract damages." In *Daley v. Town of West Brookfield,* a Massachusetts appellate court observed that "[d]amages for injury to reputation are usually not available in contract actions," noting that the rationale most often given is that "such

damages are remote and not within the contemplation of the parties."
[Citation.]

The BSO notes that Massachusetts is in agreement with virtually all
other jurisdictions in holding that damages for reputation are not
available in contract actions. * * *

In cases that have analyzed the reasons for disallowing a contract
claim for reputation damages, courts have identified two determinative
factors. First, courts have observed that attempting to calculate damages for injury to reputation is "unduly speculative." [Citations.] In
many cases, the courts have viewed the claims for damages to reputation
as analogous to claims for physical or emotional distress and have noted
the difficulty in ascertaining such damages for contract purposes. * * *

The second factor that courts identify is that damages for injury to
reputation "cannot reasonably be presumed to have been within the
contemplation of the parties when they entered into the contract."
These courts state that the basic rule of Hadley v. Baxendale, 9 Ex. 341,
156 Eng.Rep. 145 (1854), which requires that contract damages be of the
kind that arise naturally from the breach of a contract or be of a kind
that reasonably may have been in the contemplation of the parties when
they entered the contract, cannot possibly be met in a claim for general
damages to reputation occurring as the result of a breach of contract.
[Citations.] The Massachusetts Supreme Judicial Court seems to have
accepted this rationale as a legitimate one for disallowing claims for
injury to reputation as a contract damage. * * *

The claim advanced by Redgrave is significantly different, however,
from a general claim of damage to reputation. Redgrave is not claiming
that her general reputation as a professional actress has been tarnished
by the BSO's cancellation. Rather, she claims that a number of specific
movie and theater performances that would have been offered to her in
the usual course of events were not offered to her as a result of the
BSO's cancellation. This is the type of specific claim that, with appropriate evidence, can meet the *Hadley v. Baxendale* rule, as adopted by
the Massachusetts Supreme Judicial Court in John Hetherington &
Sons, Ltd. v. William Firth Co., 210 Mass. 8, 21, 95 N.E. 961, 964 (1911)
(in breach of contract action, injured party receives compensation for any
loss that follows as a natural consequence from the breach, was within
the contemplation of reasonable parties as a probable result of breach,
and may be computed by "rational methods upon a firm basis of facts").
* * *

The jury was given appropriate instructions to help it determine
whether Redgrave had suffered consequential damages through loss of
future professional opportunities. They were told to find that the BSO's
cancellation was a proximate cause of harm to Redgrave's professional
career only if they determined that "harm would not have occurred but
for the cancellation and that the harm was a natural and probable
consequence of the cancellation." *Redgrave v. BSO,* 602 F.Supp. at
1211. In addition, they were told that damages should be allowed for

consequential harm "only if the harm was a foreseeable consequence within the contemplation of the parties to the contract when it was made." In response to special interrogatories, the jury found that the BSO's cancellation caused consequential harm to Redgrave's career and that the harm was a foreseeable consequence within the contemplation of the parties.

Although we find that Redgrave did not present sufficient evidence to establish that the BSO's cancellation caused consequential harm to her professional career in the amount of $100,000, we hold that, as a matter of Massachusetts contract law, a plaintiff may receive consequential damages if the plaintiff proves with sufficient evidence that a breach of contract proximately caused the loss of identifiable professional opportunities. This type of claim is sufficiently different from a nonspecific allegation of damage to reputation that it appropriately falls outside the general rule that reputation damages are not an acceptable form of contract damage.

* * *

The requirements for awarding consequential damages for breach of contract are designed to ensure that a breaching party pays only those damages that have resulted from its breach. Thus, to receive consequential damages, the plaintiff must establish a "basis for an inference of fact" that the plaintiff has actually been damaged, and the factfinder must be able to compute the compensation "by rational methods upon a firm basis of facts." * * *

In order for Redgrave to prove that the BSO's cancellation resulted in the loss of other professional opportunities, she must present sufficient facts for a jury reasonably to infer that Redgrave lost wages and professional opportunities subsequent to April 1982, that such losses were the result of the BSO's cancellation rather than the result of other, independent factors, and that damages for such losses are capable of being ascertained "by reference to some definite standard, either market value, established experience or direct inference from known circumstances." [Citation.] During trial, evidence was presented regarding losses Redgrave allegedly suffered in film offers and American theater offers. Based on this testimony, the jury found that the BSO's cancellation of its contract with Redgrave caused Redgrave $100,000 in consequential damages. We find that the evidence presented by Redgrave was not sufficient to support a finding of damages greater than $12,000, less expenses.

Most of Redgrave's annual earnings prior to April 1982 were derived from appearances in films and the English theater. Redgrave presented evidence at trial that she earned more than $200,000 on the average since her company's fiscal year 1976, and she testified that she had a constant stream of offers from which she could choose films that had secure financial backing. After the BSO's cancellation in April 1982, Redgrave contended, her career underwent a "startling turnabout." Redgrave testified that she did not work at all for the fourteen months following the cancellation and that the only offers she received during that time were for films with insufficient financial backing.

The evidence demonstrates that Redgrave accepted three firm film offers in the fourteen months following the BSO cancellation. If these three films had been produced, Redgrave would have earned $850,000 during that period. The first offer, for a film entitled *Annie's Coming Out,* was for a role in which Redgrave had expressed interest in February 1982, two months prior to the BSO cancellation. The offer for the role was made in July 1982, a short time after the BSO's cancellation, and was finalized in August 1982. The film was to be financed by Film Australia, a government production company, and no evidence was presented that Redgrave believed the film might experience financial difficulties. Redgrave's fee for the film was to be $250,000.

From July 1982 until approximately the end of October 1982, Redgrave believed that she would be filming *Annie's Coming Out* sometime during the fall. Because of that commitment, Redgrave turned down other firm offers that had secure financial backing. These included an offer received in July 1982 to do a cameo appearance in a Monty Python film entitled *Yellowbeard* for $10,000 and an offer received in September 1982 to star in the television film *Who Will Love My Children?* for $150,000. In late October or early November 1982, Redgrave was informed that *Annie's Coming Out* would not be produced because of financial difficulties. No evidence was presented that the film's financial failure was related to the BSO cancellation.

* * *

Although there is no doubt that Redgrave did not have a successful financial year following the BSO cancellation, we cannot say that she presented sufficient evidence to prove that her financial difficulties were caused by the BSO cancellation. No evidence was presented that, at the time she accepted the offer for *Annie's Coming Out,* Redgrave believed the film would experience financial difficulties. In addition, there was no allegation that the offers Redgrave turned down because of her commitment to *Annie's Coming Out,* such as offers to appear in *Yellowbeard* and *Who Will Love My Children?,* did not have firm financial backing. If *Annie's Coming Out* had been produced, Redgrave would have earned $250,000 in the year following the BSO cancellation—an amount equal to Redgrave's average earnings before April 1982.

Redgrave contends, however, that the film offers she received following the BSO cancellation lacked secure financial backing and were thus significantly different from offers she had received prior to the cancellation. Thus, although Redgrave would have received $600,000 had *No Alternatives* and *Track 39* been produced, she argues that the fact that she had to accept two films that ultimately were not produced was itself a result of the BSO cancellation.

* * *

Even if we accept, however, that Redgrave proved she had experienced a drop in the quality of film offers following the BSO cancellation, Redgrave must also prove that the drop was proximately caused by the BSO cancellation and not by other, independent factors. Redgrave failed to carry her burden of presenting evidence sufficient to allow a jury reasonably to infer this causal connection.

The defense introduced evidence that Redgrave's political activities and statements had generated much media attention prior to the incident with the BSO. Redgrave conceded that her agents had informed her, prior to April 1982, that certain producers were hesitant to hire her because of the controversy she generated. And, in a newspaper interview in February 1982, Redgrave stated that she "had lost a lot of work because of her political beliefs" but that every time there had been a move to stop her working, "an equally terrific response [came] forward condemning any witch hunts."

To the extent that Redgrave may have experienced a decline in the quality of film offers received subsequent to April 1982, that decline could have been the result of Redgrave's political views and not the result of the BSO's cancellation. Even if the cancellation highlighted for producers the potential problems in hiring Redgrave, it was Redgrave's burden to establish that, in some way, the cancellation itself caused the difference in film offers rather than the problems as highlighted by the cancellation. Redgrave produced no direct evidence from film producers who were influenced by the cancellation. Thus, the jury's inference that the BSO cancellation had caused Redgrave consequential damages was one based more on "conjecture and speculation" than on a sufficient factual basis.

* * *

Redgrave contends that, as a result of the BSO cancellation, she no longer received offers to appear on Broadway. She testified that in April 1983 she was appearing in a successful English theater production of *The Aspern Papers* and was led to believe by the producers that the show would move to New York. Although it was Redgrave's opinion that the reason the play did not move to Broadway was because of the "situation" caused by the BSO cancellation, there was no testimony from the producers or others as to why the production did not go to Broadway. * * * Finally, Redgrave testified that Theodore Mann had considered offering her a role in *Heartbreak House* at Circle in the Square, but decided not to extend the offer because of the ramifications of the BSO cancellation.

Theodore Mann was the one producer who testified regarding his decision not to employ Redgrave in a Broadway production. He explained that

> the Boston Symphony Orchestra had cancelled, terminated Ms. Redgrave's contract. This had a—this is the premier or one of the

premier arts organizations in America who, like ourselves, seeks support from foundations, corporations, individuals; have subscribers; sell individual tickets. I was afraid ... and those in my organization were afraid that this termination would have a negative effect on us if we hired her. And so we had conferences about this. We were also concerned about if there would be any physical disturbances to the performance.... And it was finally decided ... that we would not hire [Redgrave] because of all the events that had happened, the cancellation by the Boston Symphony and the effects that we felt it would have on us by hiring her.

The evidence presented by Redgrave concerning her drop in Broadway offers after April 1982, apart from Mann's testimony, is not sufficient to support a finding of consequential damages. We do not, of course, question Redgrave's credibility in any way. Our concern is with the meager factual evidence. Redgrave had to introduce enough facts for a jury reasonably to infer that any drop in Broadway offers was proximately caused by the BSO cancellation and not by the fact that producers independently were concerned with the same factors that had motivated the BSO. Mann's testimony itself reflects that fact that many producers in New York may have been hesitant about hiring Redgrave because of a feared drop in subscription support or problems of physical disturbances. Apart from Mann's testimony, Redgrave presented nothing other than the fact that three expected offers or productions did not materialize. This type of circumstantial evidence is not sufficient to support a finding of consequential damages.

* * *

Mann's testimony reveals that, in considering whether to hire Redgrave, he and his partners were concerned about losing support from foundations and subscribers, having difficulty selling tickets, and dealing with possible physical disruptions. These are factors that result from the community response to Redgrave's political views. They are the same factors that apparently motivated the BSO to cancel its contract with Redgrave and are not the result of that cancellation. Thus, one possibly could infer from Mann's testimony that the BSO cancellation was not a proximate cause of the damage suffered by Redgrave in being denied the part in *Heartbreak House.*

Mann also testified, however, that he and his partners were affected by the BSO cancellation because the BSO was a premier arts organization and was dependent on the same type of support as Circle in the Square. A jury reasonably could infer that the BSO's cancellation did more than just highlight for Mann the potential problems that hiring Redgrave would cause but was actually a cause of Mann's decision, perhaps because Mann's theater support was similar to that of the BSO or because Mann felt influenced to follow the example of a "premier arts organization." Because this is a possible inference that a jury could draw from Mann's testimony, we defer to that inference. We therefore find that Redgrave presented sufficient evidence to prove consequential damages of $12,000, the fee arrangement contemplated by Mann for Redgrave's appearance in *Heartbreak House,* minus expenses she personally would have incurred had she appeared in the play.

* * *

———

1.   The principle that the breaching party bears responsibility for damages contemplated when the contract was made found early expression in *Hadley v. Baxendale,* 156 Eng.Rep. 145, 151 (1854):

> Where two parties have made a contract which one of them had broken, the damages which the other party ought to receive in respect of such breach of contract should be such as may fairly and reasonably be considered either arising naturally, *i.e.,* according to the usual course of things, from such breach of contract itself, or such as may reasonably be supposed to have been in the contemplation of both parties, at the time they made the contract, as the probable result of the breach of it.

The *Hadley* formulation, adopted by the Restatement (Second) of Contracts § 351, sets forth an objective test for determining the recoverability of damages based upon what the breaching party had reason to foresee as the probable result of the breach.

2.   The *Hadley* rule has been applied with varying degrees of restrictiveness. The strictest application requires that the defendant "tacitly agreed," by implication or expressly at the time of contracting, to accept the risk of the particular type of loss. Most courts, however, have used the concept for foreseeability from *Hadley* more generally and have rejected the tacit agreement test for the recovery of consequential damages. *See* Restatement (Second) of Contracts § 351 comment a; U.C.C. § 2–715 comment 2.

3.   The foreseeability principle has varied application with respect to determining "general" and "special" or "consequential" damages. General damages, according to *Hadley,* are those which flow directly and immediately as a natural consequence of the kind of wrongful act by the breaching party; therefore, the law conclusively presumes them to be foreseen or contemplated by the defendant. Special damages, in contrast, although actually caused by the defendant's acts, would not necessarily always follow from such conduct. Accordingly, liability attaches only by reference to the special character, condition or circumstances of the non-breaching party, and the loss must be foreseen by the breaching party rather than implied by law. The least restrictive interpretation of the *Hadley* foreseeability requirement is that the loss must have been "foreseeable" at the time of contracting even if it was not actually "foreseen."

Although the terms "general" and "special" damages have fallen gradually out of favor in some jurisdictions, the essence of the special damages criteria has been embraced by the Uniform Commercial Code § 2–715(2) with respect to the availability of consequential damages to an aggrieved buyer of goods. Section 2–715(2) determines recoverability of damages depending upon whether the seller, at the time of contracting, had "reason to know" of general or particular requirements of the buyer.

SPANG INDUSTRIES, INC. v. THE AETNA CASUALTY AND SURETY CO.

512 F.2d 365 (2d Cir.1975).

MULLIGAN, CIRCUIT JUDGE:

[Torrington Construction Co. (Torrington) successfully bid to reconstruct a highway in New York. Prior to submitting its bid, Torrington received a quotation from Spang Industries, Inc., Fort Pitt Bridge Division (Fort Pitt) for the fabrication, furnishing and erection of structural steel to construct a bridge. The delivery date was "to be mutually agreed upon", and Torrington subsequently notified Fort Pitt of the required delivery schedule. Fort Pitt subcontracted the unloading and erection of the steel to Syracuse Rigging Co. (Syracuse) but neglected to notify it of the delivery schedule. As a result, Syracuse delayed in unloading and Torrington did the work itself. The delays also resulted in completion of the structure during the winter. Since the job site was in northern New York and the danger of freezing temperatures was imminent, Torrington arranged for the pouring of concrete on an expedited basis at increased expense.

Fort Pitt instituted suit in federal court against Torrington's surety, Aetna, to recover the balance due on the subcontract. Torrington commenced suit in state court against Fort Pitt for damages caused by the delays in performance. The suit was removed to federal court, and in the consolidated action the district court held that Fort Pitt was entitled to recover the contract balance of $23,290.12, reduced by $7,653.57 in damages sustained by Torrington caused by the delays in performance.]

Fort Pitt on this appeal does not take issue with any of the findings of fact of the court below but contends that the recovery by Torrington of its increased expenses constitutes special damages which were not reasonably within the contemplation of the parties when they entered into the contract.

While the damages awarded Torrington are relatively modest ($7,653.57) in comparison with the subcontract price ($132,274.37), Fort Pitt urges that an affirmance of the award will do violence to the rule of Hadley v. Baxendale, 156 Eng.Rep. 145 (Ex.1854), and create a precedent which will have a severe impact on the business of all subcontractors and suppliers.

While it is evident that the function of the award of damages for a breach of contract is to put the plaintiff in the same position he would have been in had there been no breach, *Hadley v. Baxendale* limits the recovery to those injuries which the parties could reasonably have anticipated at the time the contract was entered into. If the damages suffered do not usually flow from the breach, then it must be established that the special circumstances giving rise to them should reasonably have been anticipated at the time the contract was made.

* * *

The gist of Fort Pitt's argument is that, when it entered into the subcontract to fabricate, furnish and erect the steel in September, 1969, it had received a copy of the specifications which indicated that the total work was to be completed by December 15, 1971. It could not reasonably have anticipated that Torrington would so expedite the work (which was accepted by the State on January 21, 1971) that steel delivery would be called for in 1970 rather than in 1971. Whatever knowledge Fort Pitt received after the contract was entered into, it argues, cannot expand its liability, since it is essential under *Hadley v. Baxendale* and its Yankee progeny that the notice of the facts which would give rise to special damages in case of breach be given at or before the time the contract was made. The principle urged cannot be disputed. [Citations.] We do not, however, agree that any violence to the doctrine was done here.

* * * [A]t the time when the parties, pursuant to their initial agreement, fixed the date for performance which is crucial here, Fort Pitt knew that a June, 1970 delivery was required. It would be a strained and unpalatable interpretation of *Hadley v. Baxendale* to now hold that, although the parties left to further agreement the time for delivery, the supplier could reasonably rely upon a 1971 delivery date rather than one the parties later fixed. * * *

We conclude that, when the parties enter into a contract which, by its terms, provides that the time of performance is to be fixed at a later date, the knowledge of the consequences of a failure to perform is to be imputed to the defaulting party as of the time the parties agreed upon the date of performance. This comports, in our view, with both the logic and the spirit of *Hadley v. Baxendale*. * * * At the time Fort Pitt did become committed to a delivery date, it was aware that a June, 1970 performance was required by virtue of its own acceptance. * * *

Having proceeded thus far, we do not think it follows automatically that Torrington is entitled to recover the damages it seeks here; further consideration of the facts before us is warranted. Fort Pitt maintains that, under the *Hadley v. Baxendale* rubric, the damages flowing from its conceded breach are "special" or "consequential" and were not reasonably to be contemplated by the parties. Since Torrington has not proved any "general" or "direct" damages, Fort Pitt urges that the contractor is entitled to nothing. We cannot agree. * * *

It must be taken as a reasonable assumption that, when the delivery date of June, 1970 was set, Torrington planned the bridge erection within a reasonable time thereafter. It is normal construction procedure that the erection of the steel girders would be followed by the installation of a poured concrete platform and whatever railings or superstructure the platform would require. Fort Pitt was an experienced bridge fabricator supplying contractors and the sequence of the work is hardly arcane. Moreover, any delay beyond June or August would assuredly have jeopardized the pouring of the concrete and have forced the postponement of the work until the spring. The work here, as was well known to Fort Pitt, was to be performed in northern New York near the Vermont border. The court below found that continuing freezing weather would have forced the pouring to be delayed until June, 1971. Had Torrington refused delivery or had it been compelled to delay the completion of the work until the spring of 1971, the potential damages claim would have been substantial. Instead, in a good faith effort to mitigate damages, Torrington embarked upon the crash program we have described. It appears to us that this eventuality should have reasonably been anticipated by Fort Pitt as it was experienced in the trade and was supplying bridge steel in northern climes on a project requiring a concrete roadway.

Torrington's recovery under the circumstances is not substantial or cataclysmic from Fort Pitt's point of view. It represents the expenses of unloading steel from the gondola due to Fort Pitt's admitted failure to notify its erection subcontractor, Syracuse Rigging, that the steel had been shipped, plus the costs of premium time, extra equipment and the cost of protecting the work, all occasioned by the realities Torrington faced in the wake of Fort Pitt's breach. In fact, Torrington's original claim of $23,290.81 was whittled down by the court below because of Torrington's failure to establish that its supervisory costs, overhead and certain equipment costs were directly attributable to the delay in delivery of the steel.

Professor Williston has commented:

> The true reason why notice to the defendant of the plaintiff's special circumstances is important is because, just as a court of equity under circumstances of hardship arising after the formation of a contract may deny specific performance, so a court of law may deny damages for unusual consequences where the defendant was not aware when he entered into the contract *how serious an injury would result from its breach.*

11 S. Williston, *supra,* at 295 (Footnote omitted) (emphasis added).

In this case, serious or catastrophic injury was avoided by prompt, effective and reasonable mitigation at modest cost. Had Torrington not acted, had it been forced to wait until the following spring to complete the entire job and then sued to recover the profits it would have made had there been performance by Fort Pitt according to the terms of its agreement, then we might well have an appropriate setting for a classical *Hadley v. Baxendale* controversy. As this case comes to us, it hardly presents that situation. We therefore affirm the judgment below permitting Torrington to offset its damages against the contract price.

* * *

EVRA CORP. v. SWISS BANK CORP.

673 F.2d 951 (7th Cir.1982).

POSNER, CIRCUIT JUDGE.

The question—one of first impression—in this diversity case is the extent of a bank's liability for failure to make a transfer of funds when requested by wire to do so. The essential facts are undisputed. In 1972 Hyman–Michaels Company, a large Chicago dealer in scrap metal, entered into a two-year contract to supply steel scrap to a Brazilian corporation. Hyman–Michaels chartered a ship, the *Pandora,* to carry the scrap to Brazil. The charter was for one year, with an option to extend the charter for a second year; specified a fixed daily rate of pay for the hire of the ship during both the initial and the option period, payable semi-monthly "in advance"; and provided that if payment was not made on time the *Pandora's* owner could cancel the charter. Payment was to be made by deposit to the owner's account in the Banque de Paris et des Pays–Bas (Suisse) in Geneva, Switzerland.

The usual method by which Hyman–Michaels, in Chicago, got the payments to the Banque de Paris in Geneva was to request the Continental Illinois National Bank and Trust Company of Chicago, where it had an account, to make a wire transfer of funds. Continental would debit Hyman–Michaels' account by the amount of the payment and then send a telex to its London office for retransmission to its correspondent bank in Geneva—Swiss Bank Corporation—asking Swiss Bank to deposit this amount in the Banque de Paris account of the *Pandora's* owner. The transaction was completed by the crediting of Swiss Bank's account at Continental by the same amount.

When Hyman–Michaels chartered the *Pandora* in June 1972, market charter rates were fixed in the charter for its entire term—two years if Hyman–Michaels exercised its option. Shortly after the agreement was signed, however, charter rates began to climb and by October 1972 they were much higher than they had been in June. The *Pandora's* owners were eager to get out of the charter if they could.   * * *

* * * On the morning of April 25, 1973, [Hyman–Michaels] telephoned Continental Bank and requested it to transfer $27,000 to the Banque de Paris account of the *Pandora's* owner in payment for the charter hire period from April 27 to May 11, 1973. Since the charter provided for payment "in advance," this payment arguably was due by the close of business on April 26. The requested telex went out to Continental's London office on the afternoon of April 25, which was nighttime in England. Early the next morning a telex operator in Continental's London office dialed, as Continental's Chicago office had instructed him to do, Swiss Bank's general telex number, which rings in the bank's cable department. But that number was busy, and after trying unsuccessfully for an hour to engage it the Continental telex

operator dialed another number, that of a machine in Swiss Bank's foreign exchange department which he had used in the past when the general number was engaged. We know this machine received the telexed message because it signaled the sending machine at both the beginning and end of the transmission that the telex was being received. Yet Swiss Bank failed to comply with the payment order, and no transfer of funds was made to the account of the *Pandora's* owner in the Banque of Paris.

No one knows exactly what went wrong. One possibility is that the receiving telex machine had simply run out of paper, in which event it would not print the message although it had received it. Another is that whoever took the message out of the machine after it was printed failed to deliver it to the banking department. Unlike the machine in the cable department that the Continental telex operator had originally tried to reach, the machines in the foreign exchange department were operated by junior foreign exchange dealers rather than by professional telex operators, although Swiss Bank knew that messages intended for other departments were sometimes diverted to the telex machines in the foreign exchange department.

At 8:30 a.m. the next day, April 27, Hyman–Michaels in Chicago received a telex from the *Pandora's* owner stating that the charter was canceled because payment for the April 27–May 11 charter period had not been made. Hyman–Michaels called over to Continental and told them to keep trying to effect payment through Swiss Bank even if the *Pandora's* owner rejected it. * * * Days passed while the missing telex message was hunted unsuccessfully. Finally Swiss Bank suggested to Continental that it retransmit the telex message to the machine in the cable department and this was done on May 1. The next day Swiss Bank attempted to deposit the $27,000 in the account of the *Pandora's* owner at the Banque de Paris but the payment was refused.

[The matter was referred to arbitration, in accordance with the charter. The arbitrators agreed that this delay was sufficient to entitle *Pandora's* owner to cancel the agreement.]

Hyman–Michaels then brought this diversity action against Swiss Bank seeking to recover its expenses in the * * * arbitration proceeding plus the profits that it lost because of the cancellation of the charter. The contract by which Hyman–Michaels had agreed to ship scrap steel to Brazil had been terminated by the buyer in March 1973 and Hyman–Michaels had promptly subchartered the *Pandora* at market rates, which by April 1973 were double the rates fixed in the charter. Its lost profits are based on the difference between the charter and subcharter rates.

* * *

The case was tried to a district judge without a jury. * * * [He ruled] that Swiss Bank had been negligent and under Illinois law was liable to Hyman–Michaels for $2.1 million in damages. This figure was made up of about $16,000 in arbitration expenses and the rest in lost profits on the subcharter of the *Pandora*. * * * The case comes to us on Swiss Bank's appeal from the judgment. * * *

When a bank fails to make a requested transfer of funds, this can cause two kinds of loss. First, the funds themselves or interest on them may be lost, and of course the fee paid for the transfer, having bought nothing, becomes a loss item. These are "direct" (sometimes called "general") damages. Hyman–Michaels is not seeking any direct damages in this case and apparently sustained none. It did not lose any part of the $27,000; although its account with Continental Bank was debited by this amount prematurely, it was not an interest-bearing account so Hyman–Michaels lost no interest; and Hyman–Michaels paid no fee either to Continental or to Swiss Bank for the aborted transfer. A second type of loss, which either the payor or the payee may suffer, is a dislocation in one's business triggered by the failure to pay. Swiss Bank's failure to transfer funds to the Banque de Paris when requested to do so by Continental Bank set off a chain reaction which resulted in an arbitration proceeding that was costly to Hyman–Michaels and in the cancellation of a highly profitable contract. It is those costs and lost profits—"consequential" or, as they are sometimes called, "special" damages—that Hyman–Michaels seeks in this lawsuit, and recovered below. It is conceded that if Hyman–Michaels was entitled to consequential damages, the district court measured them correctly. The only issue is whether it was entitled to consequential damages.

* * *

Hadley v. Baxendale, 9 Ex. 341, 156 Eng.Rep. 145 (1854), is the leading common law case on liability for consequential damages caused by failure or delay in carrying out a commercial undertaking. The engine shaft in plaintiffs' corn mill had broken and they hired the defendants, a common carrier, to transport the shaft to the manufacturer, who was to make a new one using the broken shaft as a model. The carrier failed to deliver the shaft within the time promised. With the engine shaft out of service the mill was shut down. The plaintiffs sued the defendants for the lost profits of the mill during the additional period that it was shut down because of the defendants' breach of their promise. The court held that the lost profits were not a proper item of damages, because "in the great multitude of cases of millers sending off broken shafts to third persons by a carrier under ordinary circumstances, such consequences [the stoppage of the mill and resulting loss of profits] would not, in all probability, have occurred; and these special circumstances were here never communicated by the plaintiffs to the defendants." 9 Ex. at 356, 156 Eng.Rep. at 151.

The rule of *Hadley v. Baxendale*—that consequential damages will not be awarded unless the defendant was put on notice of the special circumstances giving rise to them—has been applied in many Illinois cases, and *Hadley* cited approvingly. [Citations.] In *Siegel* [*Siegel v. Western Union Tel. Co.,* 312 Ill.App. 86, 92–93, 37 N.E.2d 868, 871 (1941)], the plaintiff had delivered $200 to Western Union with instructions to transmit it to a friend of the plaintiff's. The money was to be bet (legally) on a horse, but this was not disclosed in the instructions. Western Union misdirected the money order and it did not reach the friend until several hours after the race had taken place. The horse that the plaintiff had intended to bet on won and would have paid $1650 on the plaintiff's $200 bet if the bet had been placed. He sued Western Union for his $1450 lost profit, but the court held that under the rule of *Hadley v. Baxendale* Western Union was not liable, because it "had no notice or knowledge of the purpose for which the money was being transmitted." [Citation.]

The present case is similar, though Swiss Bank knew more than Western Union knew in *Siegel;* it knew or should have known, from Continental Bank's previous telexes, that Hyman–Michaels was paying the Pandora Shipping Company for the hire of a motor vessel named *Pandora.* But it did not know when payment was due, what the terms of the charter were, or that they had turned out to be extremely favorable to Hyman–Michaels. And it did not know that Hyman–Michaels knew the *Pandora's* owner would try to cancel the charter, and probably would succeed, if Hyman–Michaels was * * * late in making payment, or that despite this peril Hyman–Michaels would not try to pay until the last possible moment and in the event of a delay in transmission would not do everything in its power to minimize the consequences of the delay. Electronic funds transfers are not so unusual as to automatically place a bank on notice of extraordinary consequences if such a transfer goes awry. Swiss Bank did not have enough information to infer that if it lost a $27,000 payment order it would face a liability in excess of $2 million. [Citations.]

It is true that in both *Hadley* and *Siegel* there was a contract between the parties and here there was none. * * * We must therefore ask what difference it should make whether the parties are or are not bound to each other by a contract. On the one hand, it seems odd that the absence of a contract would enlarge rather than limit the extent of liability. * * * Privity is not a wholly artificial concept. It is one thing to imply a duty to one with whom one has a contract and another to imply it to the entire world.

On the other hand, contract liability is strict. A breach of contract does not connote wrongdoing; it may have been caused by circumstances beyond the promisor's control—a strike, a fire, the failure of a supplier to deliver an essential input. [Citation.] And while such contract doctrines as impossibility, impracticability, and frustration relieve promisors from liability for some failures to perform that are beyond their control, many other such failures are actionable although they could not have been prevented by the exercise of due care. The district judge found that Swiss Bank had been negligent in losing Continental Bank's telex message and it can be argued that Swiss Bank should therefore be liable for a broader set of consequences than if it had only broken a contract. But *Siegel* implicitly rejects this distinction. Western Union had not merely broken its contract to deliver the plaintiff's money order;

it had "negligently misdirected" the money order. "The company's negligence is conceded." Yet it was not liable for the consequences.

Siegel, we conclude, is authority for holding that Swiss Bank is not liable for the consequences of negligently failing to transfer Hyman–Michaels' funds to Banque de Paris; reason for such a holding is found in the animating principle of *Hadley v. Baxendale,* which is that the costs of the untoward consequence of a course of dealings should be borne by that party who was able to avert the consequence at least cost and failed to do so. In *Hadley* the untoward consequence was the shutting down of the mill. The carrier could have avoided it by delivering the engine shaft on time. But the mill owners, as the court noted, could have avoided it simply by having a spare shaft. Prudence required that they have a spare shaft anyway, since a replacement could not be obtained at once even if there was no undue delay in carting the broken shaft to and the replacement shaft from the manufacturer. The court refused to imply a duty on the part of the carrier to guarantee the mill owners against the consequences of their own lack of prudence, though of course if the parties had stipulated for such a guarantee the court would have enforced it. The notice requirement of *Hadley v. Baxendale* is designed to assure that such an improbable guarantee really is intended.

This case is much the same, though it arises in a tort rather than a contract setting. Hyman–Michaels showed a lack of prudence throughout. * * * It was imprudent for Hyman–Michaels * * * to wait till arguably the last day before payment was due to instruct its bank to transfer the necessary funds overseas. And it was imprudent in the last degree for Hyman–Michaels, when it received notice of cancellation on the last possible day payment was due, to fail to pull out all the stops to get payment to the Banque de Paris on that day, and instead to dither while Continental and Swiss Bank wasted five days looking for the lost telex message. * * *

This is not to condone the sloppy handling of incoming telex messages in Swiss Bank's foreign department. But Hyman–Michaels is a sophisticated business enterprise. It knew or should have known that even the Swiss are not infallible; that messages sometimes get lost or delayed in transit among three banks, two of them located 5000 miles apart, even when all the banks are using reasonable care; and that therefore it should take its own precautions against the consequences— best known to itself—of a mishap that might not be due to anyone's negligence.

* * *

The rule of *Hadley v. Baxendale* links up with tort concepts. * * * The rule is sometimes stated in the form that only foreseeable damages are recoverable in a breach of contract action. *E.g.,* Restatement (Second) of Contracts § 351 (1979). So expressed, it corresponds to the tort principle that limits liability to the foreseeable consequence of the defendant's carelessness. * * * To estimate the extent of its probable liability in order to know how many and how elaborate fail-safe features to install in its telex rooms or how much insurance to buy against the inevitable failures, Swiss Bank would have to collect reams of information about firms that are not even its regular customers. It had no banking relationship with Hyman–Michaels. It did not know or have reason to know how at once precious and fragile Hyman–Michaels' contract with the *Pandora's* owner was. These were circumstances too remote from Swiss Bank's practical range of knowledge to have affected its decisions as to who should man the telex machines in the foreign department or whether it should have more intelligent machines or should install more machines in the cable department, any more than the falling of a platform scale because a conductor jostled a passenger who was carrying fireworks was a prospect that could have influenced the amount of care taken by the Long Island Railroad. *See Palsgraf v. Long Island R.R.*, 248 N.Y. 339, 162 N.E. 99 (1928).

In short, Swiss Bank was not required in the absence of a contractual undertaking to take precautions or insure against a harm that it could not measure but that was known with precision to Hyman–Michaels, which could by the exercise of common prudence have averted it completely. * * *

* * * The undisputed facts, recited in this opinion, show as a matter of law that Hyman–Michaels is not entitled to recover consequential damages from Swiss Bank.

* * *

So Ordered.

———

1. In tort law, foreseeability operates in the initial determination of liability for negligence. A reasonably prudent person acts in accordance with the foreseeable consequences of voluntary conduct. If an injury occurs as a result of an unforeseeable consequence from an otherwise prudent act, there is no liability for negligence. Once liability is found, however, the tortfeasor is liable for all damage that is "proximate."

2. The role of foreseeability in tort to determine what injuries are "proximate" is a continuing subject of debate. It is universally agreed that foreseeability does not limit damages in cases where the extent of a personal injury is greater than anticipated. This is the "thin-skulled plaintiff" rule, based on the frequent illustration in the case law that if a negligent defendant injures a person with an eggshell skull so that death results, the tortfeasor is liable for all the loss even though a normal person would only have a bump on the head. This example originated in Dulieu v. White, 2 K.B. 669 (1901).

For other types of unforeseeable consequences, however, courts have not been in agreement on the role of foreseeability in proximate cause. The famous case *In re Polemis*, 3 K.B. 560 (1921), articulates the extreme position that all direct consequences of negligence are compensable regardless of the unforeseeability of the consequences. The contrary position is represented in the case known as The Wagon Mound, No. 1, [1961] A.C. 388. Viscount Simmons noted there that "it does not seem consonant with current ideas of justice or morality for an act of negligence . . . which results in some trivial foreseeable damage, the actor should be liable for all consequences however unforeseeable and however unforeseeable and however grave, so long as they can be said to be 'direct.' "

Justice Cardozo approached the issue of foreseeability in terms of liability analysis rather than damages limitation in his celebrated opinion Palsgraf v. Long Island R.R. Co., 248 N.Y. 339, 162 N.E. 99 (1928). There must be a duty established toward the injured party first, *Palsgraf* holds, and that duty arises from the foreseeability of harm to that person. In the absence of such foreseeability, there is no duty and thus no liability. In *Palsgraf* the plaintiff was injured by a firecracker explosion on a railway platform. The defendant railroad's employees had acted negligently toward another passenger by helping him board a moving train. A package that passenger was carrying dropped and the fireworks inside went off. Plaintiff Palsgraf, standing several feet away, was injured. She was denied recovery on the grounds that the negligent act endangered only the boarding passenger and did not foreseeably threaten someone remote. She was an "unforeseen plaintiff" and thus there was no liability to her.

The *Palsgraf* approach uses foreseeability in negligence analysis to determine liability, but it does not settle the problem of when to deny damages for unseen losses caused to foreseen plaintiffs. *See* Petition of Kinsman Transit Co., 338 F.2d 708 (2d Cir.1964).

3. For additional commentary on the role of foreseeability in contracts and torts see the following references: Landa, Hadley v. Baxendale and the Expansion of the Middleman Economy, 16 J. Legal Stud. 455 (1987); McDowell, Foreseeability in Contract and Tort: The Problems of Responsibility and Remoteness, 36 Case W.Res. 286 (1985); Perloff, Breach of Contract and the Foreseeability Doctrine of Hadley v. Baxendale, 10 J. Legal Stud. 39 (1981); Danzig, Hadley v. Baxendale: A Study in the Industrialization of the Law, 4 J. Legal Stud. 249 (1975); Barton, The Economic Basis of Damages for Breach of Contract, 1 J. Legal Stud. 277 (1972); Calabresi & Hirchoff, Toward a Test for Strict Liability in Torts, 81 Yale L.J. 1055 (1972); Payne, Foreseeability and Remoteness of Damage in Negligence, 25 Mod.L.Rev. 1 (1962); Green, Foreseeability in Negligence Law, 61 Colum.L.Rev. 1401 (1961); Keeton, Conditional Fault in the Law of Torts, 72 Harv.L.Rev. 401 (1959); Goodhart, The Imaginary Necktie and the Rule in Re Polemis, 68 L.Q.Rev. 514 (1952).

B. CERTAINTY

Section Coverage:

A limiting factor on the compensatory damages recoverable in contract or tort is the requirement that the injured party must prove damages with reasonable certainty. The first facet of the certainty limitation pertains to substantive entitlement to damages. Has the plaintiff shown with sufficient definiteness that the defendant acted in a manner which invaded a legally protected duty and caused resulting harm? If so, the certainty requirement secondarily functions to determine the extent to which the defendant should be held accountable for the consequences of the misconduct. A plaintiff may satisfy this burden upon producing a reasonable evidentiary basis that would allow damages to be calculated without speculation or conjecture. Mathematical exactitude is not required. An injured party who fails to meet the requisite burden of proof with reasonable certainty may be entitled to nominal damages.

Traditionally courts have demanded a higher level of certainty with respect to damages for breach of contract than for torts. One explanation for the differentiation is that certain elements of tort awards, such as pain and suffering or emotional distress, are inherently difficult to quantify into dollar amounts, while loss of earnings may be more precisely determined. The Restatement (Second) of Torts § 912 suggests a flexible test for certainty "as the nature of the tort and the circumstances permit."

Model Case:

Carter planned to open a new restaurant to be named Pizzatown. He contracted to purchase furnishings for the restaurant from the Interior Supply Company with delivery and installation scheduled in time for the grand opening on September 1. Carter expended $5,000 for promotional materials which advertised the September 1 opening.

The furnishings did not arrive when scheduled, resulting in the delay of the restaurant opening until January 1. Carter brings suit for breach of contract against Interior Supply. Carter seeks reliance damages for the advertising expenditures and also requests prospective lost profits for the four month period during which the restaurant could not operate.

A court would typically find that the promotional expenses would be a compensable item of damages capable of being reasonably ascertained. The claim for lost profits would be viewed as speculative or conjectural, even if the foreseeability test is passed, because Carter had no prior operating history to satisfy the requirement of certainty. Consider, in light of the following materials, whether it should make a difference if Carter could introduce evidence of operating histories of comparable restaurants at similar stages of development. What if Carter could produce such evidence of other Pizzatown restaurants in similar locales?

STORY PARCHMENT CO. v. PATERSON PARCHMENT PAPER CO.

282 U.S. 555, 51 S.Ct. 248, 75 L.Ed. 544 (1931).

MR. JUSTICE SUTHERLAND delivered the opinion of the Court.

This is an action arising under the Sherman Anti–Trust Act to recover damages resulting from an alleged conspiracy between respondents and West Carrollton Parchment Company, not joined for lack of jurisdiction, to monopolize interstate trade and commerce in vegetable parchment, exclude the petitioner therefrom, and destroy its business in such trade and commerce. A jury returned a verdict for petitioner in the sum of $65,000, but in the alternative for the respondents "if, as a matter of law, the plaintiff is not entitled to a verdict." The trial court approved the verdict and rendered judgment for treble the amount of the damages in accordance with § 7 of the act. On appeal to the circuit court of appeals, the judgment was vacated and the case remanded to the trial court with directions to enter judgment for respondents upon the ground that petitioner had not sustained the burden of proving that it had suffered recoverable damages.

[The Court found sufficient evidence in the record to justify the jury verdict that the respondents combined and conspired to monopolize interstate trade in violation of the federal antitrust laws.] Questions in respect of the liability of the wrongdoers to respond in damages alone remain to be considered.

The trial court submitted to the jury for consideration only two items of damages, (1) the difference, if any, between the amounts actually realized by petitioner and what would have been realized by it from sales at reasonable prices except for the unlawful acts of the respondents; and (2) the extent to which the value of petitioner's property had been diminished as the result of such acts.

The view of the court of appeals that no recovery could be had in respect of the first item apparently rests upon its conclusions that there was no basis for a reasonable inference that prices in excess of those actually realized would have prevailed if there had been no combination; and that, in any event, there was no damage which could be measured and expressed in figures not based on speculation and conjecture.

There was evidence from which the jury reasonably could have found that in pursuance of the conspiracy respondents sold their goods below the point of fair profit, and finally below the cost of production; that petitioner had an efficient plant and sales organization, and was producing a quality of paper superior to that produced by either of the three companies; and that current prices, shown in detail, were higher during a period antedating the unlawful combination and price cutting in pursuance of it than afterward. It does not necessarily follow, of course, that these higher prices would have continued except for the conspiracy, but it is fair to say that the natural and probable effect of the combination and price cutting would be to destroy normal prices; and there was evidence of the prices received by petitioner before the cut prices were put into operation, and those received after, showing actual and substantial reductions, and evidence from which the probable amount of the loss could be approximated. The trial court fairly instructed the jury in substance that if they were satisfied that the old prices were reasonable and that they would not have changed by reason of any economic condition, but would have been maintained except for the unlawful acts of the respondents, the jury might consider as an element of damages the difference between the prices actually received and what would have been received but for the unlawful conspiracy.

Upon a consideration of the evidence we are of the opinion that it was open to the jury to find that the price cutting and the resulting lower prices were directly attributable to the unlawful combination; and that the assumption indulged by the court below, that respondents' acts would have been the same if they had been acting independently of one another, with the same resulting curtailment of prices, must be rejected as unsound.

Nor can we accept the view of that court that the verdict of the jury, in so far as it included damages for the first item, cannot stand because it was based upon mere speculation and conjecture. This characterization of the basis for the verdict is unwarranted. It is true that there was uncertainty as to the extent of the damage, but there was none as to the fact of damage; and there is a clear distinction between the measure of proof necessary to establish the fact that petitioner had sustained some damage, and the measure of proof necessary to enable the jury to fix the amount. The rule which precludes the recovery of uncertain damages applies to such as are not the certain result of the wrong, not to those damages which are definitely attributable to the wrong and only uncertain in respect of their amount. [Citation.]

"It is sometimes said that speculative damages cannot be recovered, because the amount is uncertain; but such remarks will generally be found applicable to such damages as it is uncertain whether sustained at all from the breach. Sometimes the claim is rejected as being too remote. This is another mode of saying that it is uncertain whether such damages resulted necessarily and immediately from the breach complained of.

* * *

Where the tort itself is of such a nature as to preclude the ascertainment of the amount of damages with certainty, it would be a perversion of fundamental principles of justice to deny all relief to the injured person, and thereby relieve the wrongdoer from making any amend for his acts. In such case, while the damages may not be determined by mere speculation or guess, it will be enough if the evidence show the extent of the damages as a matter of just and reasonable inference, although the result be only approximate. The wrongdoer is not entitled to complain that they cannot be measured with the exactness and precision that would be possible if the case, which he alone is responsible for making, were otherwise. [Citation.] As the Supreme Court of Michigan has forcefully declared, the risk of the uncertainty should be thrown upon the wrongdoer instead of upon the injured party. Allison v. Chandler, 11 Mich. 542, 550–556. * * *

* * * [I]n Gilbert v. Kennedy, 22 Mich. 117, 129 *et seq.,* also a tort action, the court, through the same eminent judge, pointed out that cases will often occur in which it is evident that large damages have resulted, but where no reliable data or element of certainty can be found by which to measure with accuracy the amount. Rejecting the view that in such cases the jury should give only nominal, that is, in effect, no damages, leaving the injured party without redress, the court said (p. 130):

> "To deny the injured party the right to recover any actual damages in such cases, because they are of a nature which cannot be thus certainly measured, would be to enable parties to profit by, and speculate upon, their own wrongs, encourage violence and invite depredation. Such is not, and cannot be the law, though cases may be found where courts have laid down artificial and arbitrary rules which have produced such a result."

* * * Numerous decisions are there cited in support of the statement, that "The constant tendency of the courts is to find some way in which damages can be awarded where a wrong has been done. Difficulty of ascertainment is no longer confused with right of recovery."

* * *

There was evidence to the effect that petitioner's plant had cost $235,000, of which $90,000 had been used to purchase and install a parchmentizing machine. After petitioner had been compelled to close its business, as a result, we must now assume, of the unlawful acts of the respondents, this property for the purpose of that business was abandoned. That some depreciation in the value of the plant must have resulted is obvious. The treasurer of petitioner estimated the market value of the plant after it had been closed down at $75,000. If this estimate be accepted, the depreciation was far more than the entire amount of the verdict, which included both items of damages. It is true that the treasurer was an interested witness and that he was not an expert; and the court in its charge expressly directed the attention of the jury to those facts. But it was for the jury to determine the weight of the evidence, the credit to be given the witness, and the extent to which his testimony should be acted upon. That there was actual damage due to depreciation in value was not a matter of speculation, but a fact which could not be gainsaid. The amount alone was in doubt; and, in the light of the foregoing discussion as to the first item of damages, the proof is sufficiently certain and definite to support the verdict of the jury in that respect.

* * *

The judgment of the court of appeals is reversed and that of the district court affirmed.

———

1. The limitation that damages be established with reasonable certainty is consistent with the policy that compensatory damages should be awarded to make an injured party whole but not to punish. Just as the notion of what constitutes fair compensation is variable with the circumstances of the nature and extent of harm, the sort of evidence which satisfies the burden of "reasonable certainty" similarly must be flexible and pragmatic. In order to accommodate the differences in torts and contracts, and within those broad categories the range of harms, courts have recognized modifications of the rule of certainty:

> Courts have modified the "certainty" rule into a more flexible one of "reasonable certainty." In such instances, recovery may often be based on opinion evidence, in the legal sense of that term, from which liberal inferences may be drawn. Generally, proof of actual or even estimated costs is all that is required with certainty.

M & R Contractors & Builders v. Michael, 215 Md. 340, 138 A.2d 350 (1958).

2. As recognized in *Story Parchment,* where sufficient evidence of the fact of damage exists courts will not allow a tortfeasor to escape liability because the amount of damages cannot be ascertained with precision. In the torts context, the rationale for such a differentiation often is stated as being that the wrongdoer should bear the risk of uncertainty. Bastian v. King, 661 P.2d 953 (Utah 1983). That does not mean, however, that the burden of proving damages with certainty is actually shifted to the wrongdoer. One court explained the justification for relaxing the certainty limitation by observing: "It is the height of hypocrisy that a wrongdoer complain about inaccuracies or uncertainty in a jury system. One whose actions hurt another is in an extremely poor position to demand precision in measuring damages, and will have to bear whatever risk of uncertainty exists in our system of settling differences." Creason v. Myers, 217 Neb. 551, 350 N.W.2d 526 (1984) (difficulty in assessing damages did not justify abolishing the cause of action for alienation of affections).

3. Professor McCormick has observed that there are various modifications of the rule of certainty which enable courts to hold up a high standard of certainty as an ideal, but also to avoid harsh applications of it. Among them are:

> Extent: The extent or amount may be left to reasonable inference as long as the fact of damage is reasonably certain.

> Defendant's fault: A defendant who has caused the difficulty of proof of damage cannot complain of the resulting uncertainty.

Imprecision: Courts do not require precision in fixing the exact amount of damages. Mere difficulty in ascertaining the amount of damages does not preclude recovery.

Best evidence: It is sufficient to supply the best evidence of the damage sustained by the plaintiff.

See McCormick, Damages § 27, at 101–102 (1935). *See also* Fortune v. First Union Nat. Bank, 323 N.C. 146, 371 S.E.2d 483 (1988) (breach of fiduciary duty by trustee; plaintiff need only prove "the extent of the harm and the amount of money representing adequate compensation with as much certainty as the nature of the tort and the circumstances permit"); Fera v. Village Plaza, Inc., 396 Mich. 639, 242 N.W.2d 372 (1976) (recovery not precluded where precision is unattainable, especially when defendant has caused the imprecision).

YOUST v. LONGO

43 Cal.3d 64, 729 P.2d 728, 233 Cal.Rptr. 294 (1987).

LUCAS, JUSTICE.

Is a racehorse owner entitled to tort damages when the harness driver of another horse negligently or intentionally interferes with the owner's horse during a race, thereby preventing the owner from the chance of winning a particular cash prize? It is a well-settled general tort principle that interference with the chance of winning a contest, such as the horserace at issue here, usually presents a situation too uncertain upon which to base tort liability. We agree that application of this principle should govern here. * * *

Plaintiff Harlan Youst entered his standardbred trotter horse, Bat Champ, in the eighth harness race at Hollywood Park in Inglewood, California. Also entered in the race was The Thilly Brudder, driven by defendant, Gerald Longo. During the race, defendant allegedly drove The Thilly Brudder into Bat Champ's path and struck Bat Champ with his whip, thereby causing the horse to break stride. Bat Champ finished sixth while The Thilly Brudder finished second. The Board reviewed the events of the race and disqualified The Thilly Brudder, which moved Bat Champ into fifth place, entitling plaintiff to a purse of only $5,000.[2]

Plaintiff filed a complaint for damages against defendant in the Los Angeles Superior Court, asserting three causes of action: (1) defendant *negligently* interfered with Bat Champ's progress in the race; (2) defendant *intentionally* interfered therewith; and (3) defendant and unidentified individuals (Does I through X) *conspired to interfere.* Plaintiff sought as compensatory damages the difference in prize money between Bat Champ's actual finish and the finish which allegedly would have occurred but for defendant's interference. Plaintiff requested compensatory damages in three alternative amounts, namely, the purse amount

---

2. The purse for the race was $100,000 distributed as follows: the winner received $50,000; second place received $25,000; third place received $12,000; fourth place received $8,000, and fifth place received $5,000.

for either first, second or third place (less the fifth place prize of $5,000 which Bat Champ has already received). Ascertainment of the amount of actual damages apparently would require a finding as to the position in which Bat Champ would have finished but for defendant's interference. Punitive damages of $250,000 were also sought.

[The trial court sustained the defendant's demurrer and the court of appeal affirmed.]

* * * [T]he Court of Appeal failed to apply the threshold requirement of a probability of the prospective economic benefit. That requirement is especially appropriate to evaluate a lost economic expectancy where the facts involve a competitive contest of one kind or another. To require less of a showing would open the proverbial floodgates to a surge of litigation based on alleged missed opportunities to win various types of contests, despite the speculative outcome of many of them. In fact, it is the very "speculativeness" of the outcome that makes such competitions interesting. Further, to allow recovery without proof of probable loss would essentially eliminate the tort's element of causation, which links the wrongful act with the damages suffered.

Scholarly authority and cases from other jurisdictions agree that an application of the threshold requirement of probable expectancy to the area of contests in general will usually result in a denial of recovery. Prosser has generally remarked that "since a large part of what is most valuable in modern life depends on 'probable expectancies,' as social and industrial life becomes more complex the courts must do more to discover, define and protect them from undue interference." (*See* Prosser & Keeton, Torts (5th ed. 1984) § 130, p. 1006, fn. omitted.) Prosser, however, has specifically addressed the area of interference with contests: "When the attempt has been made to carry liability for interference . . . into such areas as . . . *deprivation of the chance of winning a contest,* the courts have been disturbed by a feeling that they were embarking upon uncharted seas, and recovery has been denied; and *it is significant that the reason usually given is that there is no sufficient degree of certainty that the plaintiff ever would have received the anticipated benefits.*"

Notwithstanding rare cases where public policies are compelling, the tort of interference with prospective economic advantage traditionally has not protected speculative expectancies such as the particular outcome of a contest. Prosser instructs that the true source of the modern law on interference with prospective relations is the principle that tort liability exists for interference with *existing* contractual relations. (Prosser & Keeton, *supra,* at p. 1006.) "For the most part the 'expectancies' thus protected have been those of future contractual relations. . . . In such cases there is a background of business experience on the basis of which it is *possible to estimate with some fair amount of success both the value of what has been lost and the likelihood that the plaintiff would have received it if the defendant had not interfered.*"

* * *

Determining the probable expectancy of winning a *sporting* contest but for the defendant's interference seems impossible in most if not all cases, including the instant case. Sports generally involve the application of various unique or unpredictable skills and techniques, together with instances of luck or chance occurring at different times during the event, any one of which factors can drastically change the event's outcome. In fact, certain intentional acts of interference by various potential "defendant" players may, through imposition of penalties or increased motivation, actually allow the "victim" player or team to prevail. Usually, it is impossible to predict the outcome of most sporting events without awaiting the actual conclusion.

The Restatement Second of Torts specifically addresses the speculative nature of the outcome of a horse race. The relevant comment is contained in a "Special Note on Liability for Interference With Other Prospective Benefits of a Noncontractual Nature." The comment states that various possible situations may justify liability for interference with prospective economic benefits of a noncommercial character. Special mention is given to "[c]ases in which the plaintiff is wrongfully deprived of the expectancy of winning a race or a contest, when he has had *a substantial certainty or at least a high probability of success.* For example, the plaintiff is entered in a contest for a large cash prize to be awarded to the person who, during a given time limit, obtains the largest number of subscriptions to a magazine. At a time when the contest has one week more to run and the plaintiff is leading all other competitors by a margin of two to one, the defendant unjustifiably strikes the plaintiff out of the contest and rules him ineligible. In such a case there may be sufficient certainty established so that the plaintiff may successfully maintain an action for loss of the prospective benefits. *On the other hand, if the plaintiff has a horse entered in a race and the defendant wrongfully prevents him from running, there may well not be sufficient certainty to entitle the plaintiff to recover. . . .*" (Rest.2d Torts, § 774B, special note, pp. 59–60, italics added.)

As indicated by the Restatement comment, certain contests may have a higher probability of ultimate success than others. To this end, the cases cited by the Court of Appeal here, awarding damages to competitors in contests, are distinguishable because in each case there was a high probability of winning.[8] In addition to the Restatement position, one older case has specifically held that the loss of a chance to

---

8. Nor are we persuaded by the Court of Appeal's argument that damages should be allowed for the value of the lost chance of benefit. (*See* Schaefer, *Uncertainty and the Law of Damages* (1978) 19 Wm. & Mary L.Rev. 719.) Under this approach, plaintiff would not recover the full value of the lost prize but that value discounted by the probability of winning in the absence of defendant's interference. We believe this calculation is incorporated in the basic analysis for interference with prospective economic advantage; the speculative nature of the chance of winning is examined in establishing the first element of the tort as opposed to determining specific damages after recognizing a cause of action. In the instant case, the potential economic advantage is simply too speculative to allow *any recovery.*

win a prize purse at a trotting horse race was too speculative to support tort liability. (*See* Western Union Tel. Co. v. Crall (1888) 39 Kan. 580, 18 P. 719.)

Applying the foregoing analysis to the instant case, it seems clear that plaintiff's complaint fails adequately to allege facts showing interference with a *probable* economic gain, *i.e.*, that Bat Champ would have won this horse race, or at least won a larger prize, if defendant had not interfered. Here, the complaint only alleged in conclusory terms that defendant's wrongful interference resulted in a lost "opportunity" to finish higher in the money. The complaint merely indicated that defendant's maneuvers and whipping forced Bat Champ to break stride and fall out of contention.[9]

We conclude, as a matter of law, that the threshold element of probability for interference with prospective economic advantage was not met by the facts alleged, whether or not some "conspiracy" between a competitor and noncompetitor may have existed. It was not reasonably *probable*, on the facts alleged, that Bat Champ would have finished in a better position. Indeed, we may take judicial notice of the impossibility of predicting such matters; the winner of a horserace is not always the leader throughout the race for a horse can "break the pack" at any point in the race, even as a matter of strategy. Further, many races are won by a "nose." Thus, no cause of action exists for interference with this horseracing event.

* * *

Deprivation of the *chance* of winning a horserace or any sporting event does not present a basis for tort liability for interference with prospective economic advantage. Here, the probability that plaintiff's horse would have won the race is simply too speculative a basis for tort liability. * * *

The judgment of the Court of Appeal is affirmed.

———

1.   Should courts recognize that the reasonable certainty limitation is met when placing a value on a chance, such as to win a contest? In Locke v. United States, 151 Ct.Cl. 262, 283 F.2d 521 (Ct.Cl.1960) an operator of a typewriter repair business sought lost profits resulting from a breach of a requirements contract with the government. The plaintiff, together with three other unaffiliated local companies, were

---

9. Presented in plaintiff's opposition to the demurrer were the following additional facts: "As the horses entered in the eighth race rounded the last turn, Bat Champ *began to make his move* to the lead of the group. As his move progressed, Defendant drove his horse into Bat Champ's path and thereafter whipped Bat Champ with his whip. Bat Champ's advance was halted, his stride broken and his *chances* at finishing 'in the money' ended." (Italics added.) Further, at oral argument, plaintiff asserted that the alleged interference took place 100 yards from the finish line. However, despite these asserted facts, Bat Champ's chance of placing higher in the purse money remained highly speculative.

awarded typewriter repair contracts which entitled the contractor's names to be placed on a federal supply schedule for distribution to government installations in the area. Although the various government offices were free to select any of the four contractors, the court held that it was proper for the lower court to assess the value of the plaintiff's chance at the lost business opportunities. The court stated:

> We are here concerned with the value of a chance for obtaining business and profits.... Here it appears that the plaintiff did have a chance of obtaining at least one-fourth of the total typewriter-repair business let by the Government.... We believe that where the value of a chance for profit is not outweighed by a countervailing risk of loss, and where it is fairly measurable by calculable odds and by evidence bearing specifically on the probabilities that the court should be allowed to value that lost opportunity.

What limitations, from a policy standpoint, should be placed on the ability to recover for damages based on the value of a chance? *See generally* Schaefer, Uncertainty and the Law of Damages, 19 Wm. & Mary L.Rev. 719 (1978) (suggesting that uncertainty in estimating the value of lost earnings may be overcome by combining an expected-value deduction and a discount for risk).

2. The requirement that damages be established with reasonable certainty has generally presented less of an obstacle to recovery for torts than for breaches of contract. In Grayson v. Irvmar Realty Corp., 184 N.Y.S.2d 33, 7 A.D.2d 436 (1959), for example, a young musician sustained a fractured leg and hearing impairment as a result of the defendant's negligence in failing to light properly a construction sidewalk. Although the plaintiff had never earned any money as an opera singer, the court permitted the recovery of damages based upon impaired future earning capacity because credible evidence was introduced that she had a "bright future." The court recognized the tension between denying recovery because of the difficulty in quantifying the harm balanced against the policy of compensating for the injury:

> The would-be operatic singer, or the would-be violin virtuoso, or the would-be actor, are not assured of achieving their objectives merely because they have some gifts and complete the customary periods of training. Their future is a highly speculative one, namely, whether they will ever receive recognition or the financial prerequisites that result from such recognition. Nevertheless, the opportunities exist and those opportunities have an economic value which can be assessed, although, obviously, without any precision. But a jury may not assume that a young student of the opera who has certain gifts will earn the income of an operatic singer, even in the median group.
>
> In determining, therefore, the amount to be recovered, the jury may consider the gifts attributed to plaintiff; the training she has received; the training she is likely to receive; the opportunities and the recognition she already has had; the opportunities she is likely

to have in the future; the fact that even though the opportunities may be many, that the full realization of those opportunities is limited to the very few; the fact that there are many other risks and contingencies, other than accidents, which may divert a would-be vocal artist from her career; and, finally, that it is assessing directly not so much future earning capacity as the opportunities for a practical chance at such future earning capacity.

The foregoing factors to be considered must reflect substantial development in the would-be artist's career. Every gleam in a doting parent's eye and every self-delusion as to one's potentialities must be skeptically eradicated. The jury is not to assess within the limits of wishful thinking but is to assess the genuine potentialities, although not yet realized, as evidenced by objective circumstances. Thus viewed, plaintiff here was undoubtedly serious about her operatic career; but, except from her teachers, she had not achieved any spectacular or extraordinary recognition for her talents. It is not the dilettante interest that has a pecuniary value, but the genuine opportunity to engage in a serious artistic career. In this context no effort has been made to consider the possible issues, sometimes tendered, as to the compensability for artistic pursuits indulged in solely for self-enjoyment, but impaired as a result of tortious injury. 184 N.Y.S.2d 33, 7 A.D.2d 436 (1959).

3. Simply because the cause of action sounds in tort, though, does not automatically eliminate the certainty limitation on the damages recoverable. Where courts determine that no rational basis exists to measure damages, then the task of calculating any potential recovery is considered insurmountable. For example, in Procanik v. Cillo, 97 N.J. 339, 478 A.2d 755 (1984), the Supreme Court of New Jersey denied recovery of general damages for emotional distress or for impaired childhood in a claim for wrongful life brought on behalf of a birth-defective child. The court stated:

> The crux of the problem is that there is no rational way to measure non-existence or to compare non-existence with pain and suffering of his impaired existence. Whatever theoretical appeal one might find in recognizing a claim for pain and suffering is out-weighed by the essentially irrational and unpredictable nature of that claim. Although damages in a personal injury action need not be calculated with mathematical precision, they require at their base some modicum of rationality.

> Underlying our conclusion is an evaluation of the capability of the judicial system, often proceeding in these cases through trial by jury, to appraise such a claim. Also at work is an appraisal of the role of tort law in compensating injured parties, involving as that role does, not only reason, but also fairness, predictability, and even deterrence of future wrongful acts. In brief, the ultimate decision is a policy choice summoning the most sensitive and careful judgment.

From that perspective it is simply too speculative to permit an infant plaintiff to recover for emotional distress attendant on birth defects when that plaintiff claims he would be better off if he had not been born.

On the other hand, the court allowed recovery of extraordinary medical expenses associated with the birth-defects as special damages because they were susceptible of calculation. Also *see* Goldberg v. Ruskin, 113 Ill.2d 482, 101 Ill.Dec. 818, 499 N.E.2d 406 (1986); Harbeson v. Parke–Davis, Inc., 98 Wash.2d 460, 656 P.2d 483 (1983); Turpin v. Sortini, 31 Cal.3d 220, 182 Cal.Rptr. 337, 643 P.2d 954 (1982).

LAKOTA GIRL SCOUT COUNCIL, INC. v. HAVEY FUND–RAISING MANAGEMENT, INC.

519 F.2d 634 (8th Cir.1975).

WEBSTER, CIRCUIT JUDGE. * * *

In 1968, the Lakota Girl Scout Council decided to hold a fund-raising drive, the proceeds of which would be used to develop year-around facilities at its 175–acre campsite near Dayton, Iowa. Four professional fund-raising firms, including Havey Fund–Raising, Inc., were considered to coordinate the campaign. Havey Fund–Raising conducted a survey and informed the Council that it was feasible to raise $325,000–$350,000 for the project. The Council thereupon set its goal at $345,000 and selected Havey Fund–Raising, Inc., to assist it.

On October 1, 1968, the parties executed a contract: Havey Fund–Raising was to provide professional assistance to help the Council reach its goal in return for a fee of $28,000; the Havey firm did not guarantee that any money would in fact be raised. When Havey Fund–Raising failed to perform in accordance with the contract and the campaign fell far short of its goal, the Council instituted this action, seeking various enumerated damages.

[The case was tried and submitted to a jury, which awarded the Council $35,000 in damages.] * * *

The evidence submitted by the Council to prove breach of contract centered upon the failure of Havey Fund–Raising to provide the degree of assistance and supervision promised. Shifting personnel, inadequate consultation and direction, and failure to provide follow-up assistance on collections were the principal derelictions. The campaign was in shambles throughout the period of the drive and fell far short of its goal of $345,000. The drive grossed $88,842.32; the Council paid $24,000 to Havey Fund–Raising, Inc., and incurred $10,000 in additional expenses.

In its complaint, the Council sought to recover for many specific items of damages.[5] The District Court submitted the damage issue to

---

5. Its prayer was broken down as follows:

(a) No Cookie Sale in 1969 ...$ 11,000

(b) Total payment to defendant   24,000
(c) Extra office expense.......   10,000

the jury only upon the theory of lost profits: "what the plaintiff would have made if the contract had been performed minus a deduction for savings made possible by the breach."

Appellants contend that there was no liability under Iowa law since the receipts from the drive exceeded the expenses. This argument assumes, however, that the fact of the Council's claimed lost profits was "too uncertain for recovery," since an "expense" approach to damages is recognized as appropriate only when other measures of damages are inappropriate. [Citation.] Our first consideration must therefore be the propriety of an award based upon lost profits under the circumstances of this case.

Under Iowa law, when a contract has been breached, the innocent party is generally entitled to be placed in the position he would have occupied had there been performance. [Citation.] Lost profits are recoverable under Iowa law, provided: (1) there is proof that some loss occurred, (2) that such loss flowed directly from the agreement breached and was foreseeable, and (3) there is proof of a rational basis from which the amount can be inferred or approximated. * * *

Fact of Loss. At trial, evidence was admitted which tended to show that the capital fund drive, as planned and programmed by Havey Fund–Raising, with a goal of $345,000 was feasible. Indeed, Francis P. Havey himself so testified. Instead, due to the derelictions which constituted the breach, the Council grossed only $88,842.32 in a campaign which cost it at least $34,000. We think the District Judge had a sufficient basis from which to conclude as a matter of law that some damage resulted from the breach and thus properly submitted the question of lost profits to the jury for the purpose of computing damages.

Proximate Cause. While Iowa law does recognize the "new business rule" under which potential profits from an untried enterprise are deemed too speculative to afford a basis for recovery [citations], the campaign in this case differs materially from a general business enterprise. The campaign was a single venture, conducted apart from the general business operations of the Girl Scout Council. It had a specific goal to be achieved within a reasonably clear time frame. It was certainly foreseeable to defendants that a goal reasonably believed by the parties to be capable of achievement would be prejudiced by the failure of Havey Fund–Raising to provide the services contemplated by the agreement, and that such a diminished return would be the "immediate fruit" of the breach. [Citation.] Of special significance here is the case of Wachtel v. National Alfalfa Journal Co. [190 Iowa 1293, 176 N.W. 801 (1920)]. Therein the Iowa Supreme Court ruled that the value of a

(d) Deprived of 1969 operating funds	8,000	$29,000 in cash of a total of $160,000 pledged, as reported in defendant's Final Report, rather than $325,000 to $350,000 269,000
(e) Deprived of the use of the Lakota Girl Scout Camp ...	50,000	
(f) Deprived of an effective Campaign Drive for ten years, and secured only		TOTAL ....$399,000.

chance to win a specific prize already in existence was not so speculative, contingent or uncertain as to limit a plaintiff's recovery to a minimal amount where defendant had deprived her of that chance by breaching its contract with her.

* * *

Basis for Computation. Under Iowa law, the jury need not make the computation of damages with mathematical exactness. It is enough if there is proof of a rational basis for computation. [Citations.] Expert testimony was adduced at trial from which a jury might determine how much less the Council netted than it would have received with full performance by Havey Fund–Raising.

Ed Breen, a long-time resident of the area in which the campaign was conducted, who served as the campaign's general chairman, testified that he had previously worked on United Fund campaigns and chaired a Y.M.C.A. drive which netted $850,000 in the area and that the general feeling of the people involved with the campaign was that the goal would be achieved. He added that it was reasonable to expect considerable help from all the Girl Scout families in the area since Girl Scouting was not new to the area and since the camp had been in existence a long time. Breen also stated that there was a general public interest in the development of the camp.

James D. Harrison, a former campaign director and director of sales for Havey Fund–Raising, Inc., who had worked on the Lakota drive, was deposed before trial. In his deposition, which was read to the jury, he stated that in 1967 he had helped direct a Boy Scout campaign in Joliet, Illinois, which had raised over $426,000; that he had been co-director of a drive in Tacoma, Washington, which had raised its goal of about $1.5 million; and that he had directed a Boy Scout drive in Springfield, Illinois, and nine surrounding counties which had raised $18,000 more than its goal of $350,000. He added that he had indirectly participated in other drives. It was Harrison's opinion that the outcome of the campaign would have been much different if it had been handled properly. * * *

Where lost profits is an issue, we have expressly approved the use of expert testimony to establish the amount of the loss. * * *

Finally, we note that expert opinion testimony has been deemed competent in at least one other case where a unique promotional venture did not lend itself to any other reasonable basis for computing damages. In Riley v. General Mills, Inc., 226 F.Supp. 780 (E.D.Pa.1964), *rev'd on other grounds,* 346 F.2d 68 (3d Cir.1965), insurance agents brought an action against General Mills, claiming that the abortive termination of a free gift promotional program had cost them profits which would otherwise have been earned. Damages for lost profits were assessed by the district court which held:

Therefore, *considering the nature of the instant transaction* which was a *unique* promotional venture we find that one reasonable source for computing the damages rests with the opinion testimony of expert witnesses. Where there is no other "reasonably safe basis" for measuring the substantial damages which the plaintiff has suffered by reason of the defendant's breach of his contract, expert testimony may be utilized for the purpose. Western Show Company Inc. v. Mix, 315 Pa. 139, 141, 173 A. 183 (1934).

226 F.Supp. at 783. While reversing the district court (on the basis of insurance laws), the Third Circuit expressly approved the trial court's approach to computation of damages. 346 F.2d at 72. We think this approach was warranted in the instant case. "[A] defendant whose wrongful conduct has rendered difficult the ascertainment of the precise damages suffered by the plaintiff, is not entitled to complain that they cannot be measured with the same exactness and precision as would otherwise be possible. * * * The wrongdoer should bear the risk of uncertainty that his own conduct has created." [Citations.]

As summarized by Professor Corbin:

It is not possible to state the precise degree of approach to certainty required by the recovery of profits as damages for breach of contract. If the mind of the court is certain that profits would have been made if there had been no breach by the defendant, there will be a greater degree of liberality in allowing the jury to bring in a verdict for the plaintiff, even though the amount of profits prevented is scarcely subject to proof at all. In this respect, at least, doubts will generally be resolved in favor of the party who has certainly been injured and against the party committing the breach. The trial court has a large amount of discretion in determining whether to submit the question of profits to the jury; and when it is so submitted, the jury will also have a large amount of discretion in determining the amount of its verdict.

5 Corbin on Contracts § 1022 (1964).

Instructions. Having concluded that there was sufficient evidence and that it was permissible under Iowa law to submit the issue of lost profits to the jury, we must finally consider whether the instructions allowed the jury to speculate or permit a recovery under an erroneous standard. The District Judge instructed that before damages for lost profits could be awarded the jury must first find (1) that the injury was foreseeable as a probable result of the breach when the contract was made, (2) that the evidence afforded a sufficient basis for estimating the amount with reasonable certainty, although exact proof was not required, and (3) that lost profits must not be speculative or conjectural. * * *

We have dealt at length with the issue of damages because it is important to understand the narrow holding upon which this opinion rests. Not every promotional venture gone astray may be redeemed by resort to lost profits as a measure of damages. In this case we hold for the reasons stated that the District Court did not err in submitting the issue to the jury. Since the award was within the range of the evidence and the limiting instructions, the verdict and the judgment must stand.

BRIGHT, CIRCUIT JUDGE (dissenting).

I respectfully dissent. The claim for lost profits in a case of this kind rests upon pure speculation alone. The trial court should not, for at least two reasons, have submitted this issue to the jury.

First, the expert testimony in the instant case was conjectural and speculative. Two experts, whose qualifications to offer an opinion on the matter were, at best, dubious, testified as to lost profits. Ed Breen, the general chairman of the Girl Scouts' campaign, testified that, based upon his experience in United Fund campaigns and a Y.M.C.A. drive and upon his belief that the community generally supported the Girl Scouts, the goal of $345,000 was attainable. He grounded his opinion that widespread public support existed for the drive principally upon his view that the families of Girl Scouts would contribute and that "supporting the Girl Scouts * * * [is] like supporting motherhood." The record shows that local sponsors of the fund campaign were less than generous in their contributions, however, and that Breen admitted to no prior experience with drives in support of Girl Scouts.

Moreover, the deposition of James D. Harrison, which was read to the jury, discloses that Harrison, as the only other expert witness on the question of damages, had never participated in any fund-raising drives in the Fort Dodge area and had never participated in such drives for the Girl Scouts anywhere. His opinion as to what might have been raised in this community was extrapolated from his experience in communities in Illinois and Washington.

In short, the conclusion of both Breen and Harrison that the Lakota Girl Scout Council campaign could gross $345,000 if properly managed reflected a hoped-for result and rested entirely upon speculation about the receptiveness of the Fort Dodge community to such a campaign. No such campaign had been undertaken in the community previously, and it was consequently, impossible for any witness, including Breen or Harrison, to testify with any degree of accuracy to its likelihood of success.

Second, Iowa adheres to the "new business rule," which precludes recovery of lost profits by an enterprise that has no operating history from which profits may be accurately projected. [Citations.] There is no justification for importing authority from other jurisdictions in support of the position that the Iowa courts, if this diversity case had been brought before them, would waive the "new business rule" on these facts. The opposite is more likely true, for, in contradistinction to Wachtel v. National Alfalfa Journal Co., 190 Iowa 1293, 176 N.W. 801 (1920), a case, cited by the majority, in which the Iowa Supreme Court allowed recovery of prize money where the amount of the prize was fixed in advance of the plaintiff's participation in the contest and the plaintiff's entitlement to the prize was established to a virtual certainty, the very existence of damages in the form of lost profits is, in the instant case, highly questionable. Where "it is speculative and uncertain whether damages have been sustained, recovery * * * [should be] denied." [Citation.]

The amount of the jury award demonstrates the speculative nature of the damages. Although the award does not, in light of the damages actually proved but not submitted to the jury, appear wholly unreasonable, it cannot be reconciled with the testimony relied upon to support the judgment, for, if that testimony had been believed or given credence, the award would have been at least $96,000—the difference between the campaign goal of $345,000 and $160,000 pledged plus $89,000 realized.

I would reverse and remand this case for a new trial on the issue of damages.

----

1. In order to satisfy the requirement of reasonable certainty, new businesses have drawn from several methods suggested by the Supreme Court in Bigelow v. RKO Radio Pictures, 327 U.S. 251, 66 S.Ct. 574, 90 L.Ed. 652 (1946), in an antitrust context to establish lost profits for breach of contract. One court explained as follows:

> There are two generally recognized methods of proving lost profits: (1) the before and after theory; and (2) the yardstick test. The before and after theory compares the plaintiff's profit record prior to the violation with that subsequent to it. The before and after theory is not easily adaptable to a plaintiff who is driven out of business before he is able to compile an earnings record sufficient to allow estimation of lost profits. Therefore, the yardstick test is sometimes employed. It consists of a study of the profits of business operations that are closely comparable to the plaintiff's. Although allowances can be made for differences between the firms, the business used as a standard must be as nearly identical to the plaintiff's as possible. Lehrman v. Gulf Oil Corp., 500 F.2d 659, 667 (5th Cir.1974).

Also see Guard v. P & R Enterprises, Inc., 631 P.2d 1068 (Alaska 1981); Chung v. Kaonohi Center Co., 62 Hawaii 594, 618 P.2d 283 (1980); El Fredo Pizza, Inc. v. Roto–Flex Oven Co., 199 Neb. 697, 261 N.W.2d 358 (1978); Comment, Remedies—Lost Profits as Contract Damages for an Unestablished Business: The New Business Rule Becomes Outdated, 56 N.C.L.Rev. 693 (1978).

2. The Uniform Commercial Code specifically addresses the requirement of certainty in the context of a buyer's ability to recover consequential damages for a breach by a seller in the sale of goods. Comment 4 to U.C.C. § 2–715 states, in pertinent part:

> The burden of proving the extent of loss incurred by way of consequential damage is on the buyer, but the section on liberal administration of remedies rejects any doctrine of certainty which requires almost mathematical precision in the proof of loss. Loss

may be determined in any manner which is reasonable under the circumstances.

In addition, comment 1 to U.C.C. § 1–106 provides that in order to effectuate the liberal administration of remedies under the code, it rejects the view that "damages must be calculable with mathematical accuracy." Rather, the code's approach favors a flexible policy where compensatory damages need only "be proved with whatever definiteness and accuracy the facts permit, but no more." Finally, the common law doctrinal limitation which demands only "reasonable" certainty may be considered incorporated through U.C.C. § 1–103.

3. For additional commentary on the requirement of certainty in the law of damages see the following references: King, Causation, Valuation and Chance in Personal Injury Torts Involving Preexisting Conditions and Future Consequences, 90 Yale L.J. 1353 (1981); Leubsdorf, Remedies for Uncertainty, 61 B.U.L.Rev. 132 (1981); Note, Remedies—Lost Profits as Contract Damages for Unestablished Business: The New Business Rule Becomes Outdated, 56 N.C.L.Rev. 693 (1978); Schaefer, Uncertainty and the Law of Damages, 19 Wm. & Mary L.Rev. 719 (1978); Note, Lost Profits as Contract Damage: Problems of Proof and Limitations on Recovery, 65 Yale L.J. 922 (1956); Note, Speculative Profits as Damages for Breach of Contract, 46 Harv.L.Rev. 696 (1933); Note, The Requirement of Certainty in the Proof of Lost Profits, 64 Harv.L.Rev. 317 (1950); McCormick, The Recovery of Damages For Loss of Expected Profits, 7 N.C.L.Rev. 231 (1929).

C. AVOIDABLE CONSEQUENCES

Section Coverage:

The rule of avoidable consequences has two components, one negative and one affirmative. The affirmative side allows damages reasonably incurred to mitigate damages. The negative side precludes an injured party from recovering damages that could have been averted by taking reasonable steps following accrual of the harm.

The negative doctrine does not impose a restriction on a party's substantive entitlement to damages; instead it serves as a limitation on the measure of damages recoverable for a tort or contract breach. Although the rule sometimes is labeled as a "duty," that characterization is inartful because the injured party has no true legal obligation to act. Rather, the rule only operates to exclude the damages that result from a failure to minimize losses. Moreover, the avoidable consequences rule becomes operative only after the wrongdoer has caused the harm. It does not require that a party take avoidance measures in anticipation of the harm.

The avoidable consequences rule encourages an injured party to take reasonable steps to mitigate the loss caused by the defendant's tortious wrong or breach of contract. An injured party is not expected to undertake extraordinary measures or suffer undue hardship; the rule

policy: to avoid unnecessary loss *fairness, to tortfeasor*

not a complete
the lack of
due care
after
injury

requires reasonable attempts to <u>avoid incurring additional</u> losses. For example, if P is injured in an automobile accident caused by the negligence of D, P is obliged to seek medical attention as reasonably necessary. Similarly, if an employer discharges an employee in breach of contract, the employee is obligated to mitigate damages by taking reasonable steps to secure equivalent employment. <u>The principle is to avoid unnecessary losses.</u> It reflects a public policy of fairness to <u>breaching parties or tortfeasors</u> by not holding them accountable to the extent <u>that the injured party has evidenced a lack of due care after</u> sustaining the harm.

The same principle guides the affirmative rule that any expenditures reasonably incurred to mitigate damages are recoverable. For example, if the plaintiff's doctor reasonably orders x-ray photographs after an accident, their cost is recoverable even if the results show no fractures. Similarly, a discharged employee may recover costs reasonably incurred in seeking equivalent employment after the breach of the employment contract.

Model Case:

Jones, a machine press operator, suffered minor cuts and bruises in an automobile accident caused by the negligence of an employee of ABC Trucking Company in the scope of employment. Jones unreasonably delayed in seeking medical treatment, however, and the wounds became infected. As a result, Jones missed six weeks of work. Jones sued ABC claiming damages for pain and suffering, medical expenses, and the loss of six weeks' wages. ABC filed an answer contending that Jones failed to exercise due care by delaying in taking antiseptic measures.

The avoidable consequences rule would not be a complete defense to ABC's liability, but it would serve to deny Jones' recovery for those damages which could have been averted after the accident by the exercise of reasonable care. In that regard, the lost wages would not be compensable if ABC could establish that prompt medical attention would have meant Jones would not have missed any work. In contrast, the medical expenses and the pain and suffering caused by ABC's negligence should be recoverable elements of damages to the extent that Jones could not have avoided them by reasonable measures.

ROCKINGHAM COUNTY v. LUTEN BRIDGE CO.

35 F.2d 301 (4th Cir.1929).

PARKER, CIRCUIT JUDGE.

[The Board of Commissioners of Rockingham county awarded a contract to the Luten Bridge Company for the construction of a bridge. Shortly after entering the contract, however, the board adopted a series of resolutions which declared the contract invalid and gave notice of cancellation to Luten. Although Luten had barely commenced performance when it received the initial notice from the county repudiating the contract, the company proceeded with construction of the bridge. Luten then instituted suit against the county to recover amounts allegedly due under the contract. The trial court excluded evidence offered by the county concerning its notice of cancellation and damages, and instructed a verdict for Luten for the full amount of its claim. The county appealed.]

* * *

As the county now admits the execution and validity of the contract, and the breach on its part, the ultimate question in the case is one as to the measure of plaintiff's recovery, and * * * whether plaintiff, if the notices are to be deemed action by the county, can recover under the contract for work done after they were received, or is limited to the recovery of damages for breach of contract as of that date.

* * *

[W]e do not think that, after the county had given notice, while the contract was still executory, that it did not desire the bridge built and would not pay for it, plaintiff could proceed to build it and recover the contract price. It is true that the county had no right to rescind the contract, and the notice given plaintiff amounted to a breach on its part; but, after plaintiff had received notice of the breach, it was its duty to do nothing to increase the damages flowing therefrom. If A enters into a binding contract to build a house for B, B, of course, has no right to rescind the contract without A's consent. But if, before the house is built, he decides that he does not want it, and notifies A to that effect, A has no right to proceed with the building and thus pile up damages. His remedy is to treat the contract as broken when he receives the notice, and sue for the recovery of such damages as he may have sustained from the breach, including any profit which he would have realized upon performance, as well as any other losses which may have resulted to him. In the case at bar, the county decided not to build the road of which the bridge was to be a part, and did not build it. The bridge, built in the midst of the forest, is of no value to the county because of this change of circumstances. When, therefore, the county gave notice to the plaintiff that it would not proceed with the project, plaintiff should have desisted from further work. It had no right thus to pile up damages by proceeding with the erection of a useless bridge.

* * * The American rule and the reasons supporting it are well stated by Prof. Williston as follows:

"There is a line of cases running back to 1845 which holds that, after an absolute repudiation or refusal to perform by one party to a contract, the other party cannot continue to perform and recover damages based on full performance. * * * If a man engages to have work done, and afterwards repudiates his contract before the work has been begun or when it has been only partially done, it is inflicting damage on the defendant without benefit to the plaintiff to allow the latter to insist on proceeding with the contract. The work may be useless to the defendant, and yet he would be forced to pay the full contract price. On the other hand, the plaintiff is interested only in the profit he will make out of the contract. If he receives this it is equally advantageous for him to use his time otherwise."

The leading case on the subject in this country is the New York case of *Clark v. Marsiglia,* 1 Denio (N.Y.) 317, 43 Am.Dec. 670. In that case defendant had employed plaintiff to paint certain pictures for him, but countermanded the order before the work was finished. Plaintiff, however, went on and completed the work and sued for the contract price. In reversing a judgment for plaintiff, the court said:

"The plaintiff was allowed to recover as though there had been no countermand of the order; and in this the court erred. The defendant, by requiring the plaintiff to stop work upon the paintings, violated his contract, and thereby incurred a liability to pay such damages as the plaintiff should sustain. Such damages would include a recompense for the labor done and materials used, and such further sum in damages as might, upon legal principles, be assessed for the breach of the contract; but the plaintiff had no right, by obstinately persisting in the work, to make the penalty upon the defendant greater than it would otherwise have been."

* * * It follows that there was error in directing a verdict for plaintiff for the full amount of its claim. The measure of plaintiff's damage, upon its appearing that notice was duly given not to build the bridge, is an amount sufficient to compensate plaintiff for labor and materials expended and expense incurred in the part performance of the contract, prior to its repudiation, plus the profit which would have been realized if it had been carried out in accordance with its terms.

* * * [Reversed]

———

1. The avoidable consequences doctrine precludes the recovery of damages which could have been averted by the injured party undertaking reasonable steps following the harm. This avoidance principle occasionally is expressed as a "duty" on the part of a claimant to minimize damages, or as an "obligation" to take reasonable action to avoid enhancing the damages attributable to the defendant. Such characterizations are inaccurate expressions of the doctrine, however, because the failure to make reasonable efforts to limit damages creates no affirmative right in the defendant to assert an action for breach of that duty. Rock v. Vandine, 106 Kan. 588, 189 P. 157 (1920); Restatement (Second) of Torts § 918 comment a.

The only result of a failure to mitigate properly is that the court will not allow damages for those consequences of the breach of contract or tort which the injured party could have reasonably avoided. Thus, the doctrine should be viewed as a disability on the recovery of reasonably avoidable damages.   Gideon v. Johns–Manville Sales Corp., 761 F.2d 1129 (5th Cir.1985).

2.   Expenditures reasonably incurred by an injured party in attempting to mitigate losses are recoverable even if the mitigation efforts prove to be unsuccessful.   Thus, commercially reasonable expenses incurred by an aggrieved buyer in effecting cover are recoverable as incidental damages under U.C.C. § 2–715(1).   In Women's Federal Sav. & Loan v. Nevada National Bank, 607 F.Supp. 1129 (D.Nev.1985), the court identified the following factors to evaluate the mitigation effort: (1) good faith, (2) reasonable skill, prudence and efficiency, (3) reasonably proportioned to the injury and consequences to be averted, and (4) reasonably justified belief that it will avoid or reduce the damage otherwise expected.

PARKER v. TWENTIETH CENTURY–FOX FILM CORPORATION

3 Cal.3d 176, 474 P.2d 689, 89 Cal.Rptr. 737 (1970).

BURKE, JUSTICE.

Defendant Twentieth Century–Fox Film Corporation appeals from a summary judgment granting to plaintiff the recovery of agreed compensation under a written contract for her services as an actress in a motion picture.   * * *

Plaintiff is well known as an actress, and in the contract between plaintiff and defendant is sometimes referred to as the "Artist."   Under the contract, dated August 6, 1965, plaintiff was to play the female lead in defendant's contemplated production of a motion picture entitled "Bloomer Girl."   The contract provided that defendant would pay plaintiff a minimum "guaranteed compensation" of $53,571.42 per week for 14 weeks commencing May 23, 1966, for a total of $750,000.   Prior to May 1966 defendant decided not to produce the picture and by a letter dated April 4, 1966, it notified plaintiff of that decision and that it would not "comply with our obligations to you under" the written contract.

By the same letter and with the professed purpose "to avoid any damage to you," defendant instead offered to employ plaintiff as the leading actress in another film tentatively entitled "Big Country, Big Man" (hereinafter, "Big Country").   The compensation offered was identical, as were 31 of the 34 numbered provisions or articles of the original contract.   Unlike "Bloomer Girl," however, which was to have been a musical production, "Big Country" was a dramatic "western type" movie.   "Bloomer Girl" was to have been filmed in California; "Big Country" was to be produced in Australia.   Also, certain terms in the proffered contract varied from those of the original.   Plaintiff was given one week within which to accept; she did not and the offer lapsed. Plaintiff then commenced this action seeking recovery of the agreed guaranteed compensation.

The complaint sets forth two causes of action.   The first is for money due under the contract;   the second, based upon the same allegations as the first, is for damages resulting from defendant's breach of contract. Defendant in its answer admits the existence and validity of the contract, that plaintiff complied with all the conditions, covenants and promises and stood ready to complete the performance, and that defendant breached and "anticipatorily repudiated" the contract. It denies, however, that any money is due to plaintiff either under the contract or as a result of its breach, and pleads as an affirmative defense to both causes of action plaintiff's allegedly deliberate failure to mitigate damages, asserting that she unreasonably refused to accept its offer of the leading role in "Big Country."

* * * [S]ummary judgment for $750,000 plus interest was entered in plaintiff's favor. This appeal by defendant followed.

* * *

As stated, defendant's sole defense to this action which resulted from its deliberate breach of contract is that in rejecting defendant's substitute offer of employment plaintiff unreasonably refused to mitigate damages.

The general rule is that the measure of recovery by a wrongfully discharged employee is the amount of salary agreed upon for the period of service, less the amount which the employer affirmatively proves the employee has earned or with reasonable effort might have earned from other employment. [Citations.] However, before projected earnings from other employment opportunities not sought or accepted by the discharged employee can be applied in mitigation, the employer must show that the other employment was comparable, or substantially similar, to that of which the employee has been deprived; the employee's rejection of or failure to seek other available employment of a different or inferior kind may not be resorted to in order to mitigate damages. [Citations.]

In the present case defendant has raised no issue of *reasonableness of efforts* by plaintiff to obtain other employment; the sole issue is whether plaintiff's refusal of defendant's substitute offer of "Big Country" may be used in mitigation. Nor, if the "Big Country" offer was of employment different or inferior when compared with the original "Bloomer Girl" employment, is there an issue as to whether or not plaintiff acted reasonably in refusing the substitute offer. Despite defendant's arguments to the contrary, no case cited or which our research has discovered holds or suggests that reasonableness is an element of a wrongfully discharged employee's option to reject, or fail to seek, different or inferior employment lest the possible earnings therefrom be charged against him in mitigation of damages.

* * * [I]t is clear that the trial court correctly ruled that plaintiff's failure to accept defendant's tended substitute employment could not be applied in mitigation of damages because the offer of the "Big Country" lead was of employment both different and inferior, and that no factual dispute was presented on that issue. The mere circumstance that

"Bloomer Girl" was to be a musical review calling upon plaintiff's talents as a dancer as well as an actress, and was to be produced in the City of Los Angeles, whereas "Big Country" was a straight dramatic role in a "Western Type" story taking place in an opal mine in Australia, demonstrates the difference in kind between the two employments; the female lead as a dramatic actress in a western style motion picture can by no stretch of imagination be considered the equivalent of or substantially similar to the lead in a song-and-dance production.

Additionally, the substitute "Big Country" offer proposed to eliminate or impair the director and screenplay approvals accorded to plaintiff under the original "Bloomer Girl" contract and thus constituted an offer of inferior employment. No expertise or judicial notice is required in order to hold that the deprivation or infringement of an employee's rights held under an original employment contract converts the available "other employment" relied upon by the employer to mitigate damages, into inferior employment which the employee need not seek or accept.
* * *

The judgment is affirmed.

SULLIVAN, ACTING CHIEF JUSTICE (dissenting).

The basic question in this case is whether or not plaintiff acted reasonably in rejecting defendant's offer of alternate employment. The answer depends upon whether that offer (starring in "Big Country, Big Man") was an offer of work that was substantially similar to her former employment (starring in "Bloomer Girl") or of work that was of a different or inferior kind. To my mind this is a factual issue which the trial court should not have determined on a motion for summary judgment. The majority have not only repeated this error but have compounded it by applying the rules governing mitigation of damages in the employer-employee context in a misleading fashion. Accordingly, I respectfully dissent.

The familiar rule requiring a plaintiff in a tort or contract action to mitigate damages embodies notions of fairness and socially responsible behavior which are fundamental to our jurisprudence. Most broadly stated, it precludes the recovery of damages which, through the exercise of due diligence, could have been avoided. Thus, in essence, it is a rule requiring reasonable conduct in commercial affairs. This general principle governs the obligations of an employee after his employer has wrongfully repudiated or terminated the employment contract. Rather than permitting the employee simply to remain idle during the balance of the contract period, the law requires him to make a reasonable effort to secure other employment. He is not obliged, however, to seek or accept any and all types of work which may be available. Only work which is in the same field and which is of the same quality need be accepted.

* * * The inquiry in cases such as this should not be whether differences between the two jobs exist (there will always be differences) but whether the differences which are present are substantial enough to

constitute differences in the *kind* of employment or, alternatively, whether they render the substitute work employment of an *inferior kind.*

* * *

I believe that the judgment should be reversed so that the issue of whether or not the offer of the lead role in "Big Country, Big Man" was of employment comparable to that of the lead role in "Bloomer Girl" may be determined at trial.

———

1. The general rule for breach of contract is that the party injured must make every reasonable effort to minimize damages and may not recover for damages which could have been avoided by reasonable efforts under existing circumstances. However, where the offer of a substitute contract is conditioned on surrender by the injured party of its claim for breach, one is not required to mitigate losses by accepting an arrangement with the repudiator which is made conditional on the surrender of rights under the repudiated contract. Teradyne, Inc. v. Teledyne Industries, Inc., 676 F.2d 865 (1st Cir.1982).

can't recover damage which could have been avoided by reas. effort

2. In *Ford Motor Co. v. EEOC,* the Supreme Court held that an employer charged with sex discrimination could toll the continuing accrual of back pay liability by unconditionally offering Title VII claimants the job previously denied. The Court stated:

> An unemployed or underemployed claimant, like all other Title VII claimants, is subject to the statutory duty to minimize damages set out in § 706(g). This duty, rooted in an ancient principle of law, requires the claimant to use reasonable diligence in finding other suitable employment. Although the unemployed or underemployed claimant need not go into another line of work, accept a demotion, or take a demeaning position, he forfeits his right to backpay if he refuses a job substantially equivalent to the one he was denied. Consequently, an employer charged with unlawful discrimination often can toll the accrual of backpay liability by unconditionally offering the claimant the job he sought, and thereby providing him with an opportunity to minimize damages.

Although the Court's statements accorded with traditional notions of mitigation principles, its application with respect to the particular claimants was highly questionable. The majority held that Ford was not liable for wages lost after the date on which it offered jobs to the plaintiffs even though they had already obtained comparable positions with better seniority benefits at General Motors. As pointed out by the dissent, allowing an employer to limit its liability by making a "cheap offer" with a seniority disadvantage does not effectuate the policies of Title VII to make victims of discrimination whole and to eradicate discriminatory practices. 458 U.S. 219, 102 S.Ct. 3057, 73 L.Ed.2d 721 (1982).

PROBLEM: THE DAMAGED FENCE

The Potters are professional breeders of show dogs. Their dogs are kept in their rural home and they are allowed to exercise in the large, fenced yard.

Davis, a neighbor, negligently damages a portion of the Potters' fence. Three puppies discover the hole in the fence and escape; they are never found again. The Potters learn of the damage to the fence after the loss of the three puppies. They take no immediate action to mend the fence, but instruct the children to keep the dogs in the house. The next day a young Potter child forgets the restriction and allows a puppy to go outside. That puppy also escapes and is found injured in the road. After a $400 treatment by the veterinarian that puppy recovers.

The Potters then erect a temporary barricade to cover the hole in the fence. The temporary materials cost $50 and have no use once the fence is permanently mended.

Davis admits liability to creating the hole in the fence and agrees to pay the permanent repair cost. The Potters and Davis dispute several other points:

1. The Potters claim that Davis should pay the value of the three lost puppies. Davis argues that the Potters should have discovered the hole as soon as it was made.

2. The Potters claim Davis should pay the $400 veterinarian's bill, but Davis maintains that the Potters should have blocked the hole in the fence immediately.

3. The Potters claim $50 for the cost of the temporary barricade, whereas Davis argues there is liability only for the permanent repair.

How should the principles of avoidable consequences apply to these facts?

LOBERMEIER v. GENERAL TELEPHONE COMPANY OF WISCONSIN

119 Wis.2d 129, 349 N.W.2d 466 (1984).

HEFFERNAN, CHIEF JUSTICE. * * *

On July 19, 1976, the plaintiff sustained a ruptured eardrum, with a resulting hearing loss, while talking on a telephone in his parents' home. The phone was installed and maintained by the defendant, General Telephone Company of Wisconsin. The plaintiff was treated for the injury by Doctors Ruben T. Aguas and Gurdon Hamilton. The doctors determined that the plaintiff sustained a traumatic tympanic membrane perforation of the left ear caused by a lightning-induced electrical charge. For the first four months after the injury, the doctors prescribed a conservative treatment of antibiotics and ear drops. On October 28, 1976, Dr. Aguas felt the tympanic membrane was not going to heal spontaneously and recommended the plaintiff have surgery on the left ear.

On November 24, 1976, Dr. Aguas performed a tympanoplasty of the left ear, which involved the grafting of a substitute membrane over the eardrum. Doctor Aguas last saw the plaintiff on June 27, 1977. The plaintiff's subsequent treating doctor, Dr. Richard L. Dobbs, first saw him on February 6, 1979, at which time the plaintiff complained of a hearing loss in the left ear since July of 1976 and of ringing in the ear. After examining the plaintiff, Dr. Dobbs concluded, to a reasonable degree of medical certainty, that the graft done in November of 1976 had lateralized, there was severe conductive hearing loss in the left ear, and there was a possibility of a cholesteatoma. A cholesteatoma is disquamated skin and tissue which collected behind the eardrum. It is a potentially threatening disease because, as it slowly enlarges, it erodes into the inner ear and may cause vertigo or deafness, or may erode the covering of the brain and cause a brain abscess, or may erode into the facial nerve canal and cause a facial paralysis.

On June 7, 1979, the plaintiff filed a complaint alleging the defendant was negligent in that the telephone system on the Lobermeier premises was inadequately grounded and that, while the plaintiff was using the telephone service, he suffered a severe shock of atmospheric electricity conducted by the telephone lines to the telephone handset into the left ear and through the eardrum, causing the plaintiff's injuries. In its answer of July 3, 1979, the defendant denied negligence in failing to ground adequately the telephone or to maintain adequately such telephone service and raised, as one of its affirmative defenses, that the plaintiff failed to mitigate his damages.

* * *

The trial court erred * * * when it ruled, as a matter of law, that the defendant had no duty to mitigate damages by undergoing a second ear operation. We agree with the conclusion of the court of appeals that it was a matter of fact to be determined by the jury whether a reasonable person under the circumstances would submit to a second surgical procedure. Because it appears that this conclusion, reached as a matter of law by the trial judge, that the defendant's damages were not to be reduced by reason of his refusal to submit to surgery had a substantial impact upon the award of damages, a new trial upon the question of damages is necessary.

The facts show that, upon objection by plaintiff, the court refused to permit a physician, hired by the telephone company, to examine the defendant and to testify in respect to the damage to the plaintiff if second surgery were not performed and the improvement in hearing that probably would result if further surgical procedures were undertaken. The court also held that the deposition of Lobermeier's treating physician could not be produced either in respect to risks for or against future surgery. The court stated:

> "[I]n all fairness to a person who is injured, if there is a risk of either further harm or death, that decision should be left up to him without penalty."

The court concluded that, once it reached the conclusion based on the reasoning above that a second operation was not required, the jury had nothing to weigh in respect to further mitigation of damages by reason of not having further surgery.

It instructed the jury, "[P]laintiff's damages are not to be diminished because he did not have a second operation." Because of this instruction, the defendant objected and moved for a mistrial. The balance of the instruction included the usual admonitions in respect to mitigation of damages:

> "[D]uty of plaintiff to exercise ordinary care to mitigate his damages and if you find that he did not do so, you should not include in your answer to this question any amount for consequences of his injuries which could have been averted by the exercise of such care."

The court also instructed that, in fixing damages, the jury could consider Lobermeier's failure to use a hearing aid.

The general instruction of the trial court in respect to the duty to mitigate damages was correct. Its specific ruling as a matter of law that there was no duty to submit to a second operation was not.

The duty to mitigate damages has long been standard personal injury law. McCormick, *Damages* (hornbook series, 1935), sec. 36, p. 136, states as a matter of black letter law:

> "Any suffering or disability incurred by one who has sustained personal injury, when the same could have been avoided by submitting to treatment by a physician selected with reasonable care, must be excluded as a ground of recovery. It is held, however, that the victim may use his own judgment about submitting to a dangerous or serious operation."

McCormick goes on to explain that:

> "If the operation is simple and not dangerous, a failure to submit when advised to do so will be deemed unreasonable." *Id.* at 137.

Nevertheless, at the time McCormick wrote, 1935, there was a considerable body of law supportive of the trial judge here that held that:

> "[A] 'major,' 'dangerous,' or 'serious' operation, especially where the results are 'problematical,' involves so critical a choice between the danger of the operation and the danger of the injury ... that most courts seem to hold as a matter of law that a refusal to undergo such a danger is not ground for reducing damages." *Id.* at 137.

McCormick then went on to note that, as surgical science progresses and becomes more predictable, reasonable conduct in the future may require that the advice of physicians be followed even in respect to serious operations.

Question for jury:
what is reasonable
course of conduct?

We conclude that Wisconsin law has set its course midway between these two extremes. The question is one of fact for the jury—what was a reasonable course of conduct, under the circumstances, to mitigate the injuries or damages.

* * *

Failure to mitigate damages if affirm. Def. (for raised by D) Δ must meet BOP: reduce damages could have been mitig.

Failure to mitigate damages is an affirmative defense which must be raised by the defendant in its answer. [Citations.] When the defense is properly raised, the burden of proving failure to mitigate is upon the party asserting it. [Citation.] If the defendant asserts failure to mitigate on the part of the injured party, he must prove that a person of ordinary intelligence and prudence under the same or similar circumstances would have elected to undergo the recommended medical procedure. If the defendant meets the burden of proof, the consequence of the injured party's failure to mitigate damages is that the fact finder will not allow damages for those consequences of the injury which the plaintiff could have avoided by the exercise of ordinary care.

not req. surgery only that reas'd would have done

To summarize Wisconsin law on mitigation of damages in tort actions: An injured party is obligated to exercise that care usually exercised by a person of ordinary intelligence and prudence, under the same or similar circumstances; to seek medical or surgical treatment; and to submit to and undergo recommended surgical or medical treatment, within a reasonable time, which is not hazardous and is reasonably within his means, to minimize his damages. The injured party is not *required* to submit to surgery or medical treatment but is only required to submit to those treatments to which the "reasonable person" would have submitted. Although the injured party is not required to undergo recommended treatment, a tortfeasor is not expected to pay for disability or pain if medical treatment could reasonably correct the ailment. The proper period for which damages are allowed is only for the length of time reasonably required to effect a cure.

In the instant case, the defendant attempted to assume the burden of proving that the plaintiff, if acting reasonably under the circumstances, would have followed the advice of physicians and undergone the elective surgery. The trial court erred when it refused to allow the question to go to the jury, rejected evidence on the point, and ruled as a matter of law that the plaintiff's damages were not to be diminished for the failure to have surgery. The trial judge erroneously excluded surgery from the general rule, stating that an injured person was required to seek treatment that was not hazardous, would probably improve the condition, and was within his means.

Δ denied full jury Trial on issue of damages, remand.

The defendant was denied a full jury trial on the question of damages. Accordingly, the cause must be remanded for retrial on damages. * * *

———

1. The policy underlying the doctrine of mitigation of damages is to encourage injured parties to use reasonable efforts and expense to avert further losses.   The policy applies equally to tort and contract cases.

Should that policy of conserving economic and social interests apply with equal force in cases of intentional torts?   A recent New York decision, Clark Operating Corp. v. Yokley, 120 Misc.2d 631, 466 N.Y.S.2d 204 (1983), held that a tenant was not required to mitigate damages by terminating a tenancy and vacating premises when the landlord's conduct constituted intentional infliction of emotional distress.   The court acknowledged the potential problem of economic waste if a tort victim unreasonably increases damages following the harm, but justified its result by applying the Restatement (Second) of Torts § 918(2) which distinguishes intentional or reckless conduct, provided that the plaintiff's failure to mitigate is not itself intentional or reckless.

2. The injured party is required only to pursue reasonable measures in attempting to mitigate losses.   Accordingly, a person is not required to commit a tort in order to lessen the damage.   For example, in J.M. Huber Petroleum Co. v. Yake, 121 S.W.2d 670 (Tex.Civ.App. 1938), the defendant excavated a deep ditch, pursuant to its right-of-way deed, for the purpose of installing a pipeline.   The ditch, however, wrongfully obstructed the access of the plaintiff-lessee's cattle to certain portions of the leasehold.   Consequently the plaintiff sustained losses through "shrinkage" of his herd and incurred higher labor costs in repairing fences and in preventing the cattle from falling into the ditch. The court held that the plaintiff had no duty to fill in the ditch in mitigation because that action would have constituted an unlawful trespass upon the defendant's right-of-way.   Should the same result obtain if the trespass is only technical, yet the potential losses avoided would be significant?

3. Should a claimant's failure to wear an available seat belt limit the amount of damages recoverable from an automobile accident by application of the doctrine of avoidable consequences?   The minority view, articulated in Spier v. Barker, 35 N.Y.2d 444, 363 N.Y.S.2d 916, 323 N.E.2d 164 (1974), holds that the jury can properly consider the non-use of a seat belt in determining whether the plaintiff exercised due care in mitigating damages.   A different approach was followed in Thomas v. Henson, 102 N.M. 417, 696 P.2d 1010 (1984), where the court acknowledged the merit in the avoidable consequences approach of *Spier* but decided that the factfinder could consider evidence of the failure to wear a seat belt in apportioning damages.   This result was supported by the Restatement (Second) of Torts § 465 comment c.

SOMMER v. KRIDEL
74 N.J. 446, 378 A.2d 767 (1977).

PASHMAN, J.

We granted certification in these cases to consider whether a landlord seeking damages from a defaulting tenant is under a duty to

is landlord req. to mitig. dam, by re-letting apts, wrongfully vacated?

622   *DAMAGES*   Pt. 3

mitigate damages by making reasonable efforts to re-let an apartment wrongfully vacated by the tenant. Separate parts of the Appellate Division held that, in accordance with their respective leases, the land-lords in both cases could recover rents due under the leases regardless of whether they had attempted to re-let the vacated apartments. * * *

This case was tried on stipulated facts. On March 10, 1972 the defendant, James Kridel, entered into a lease with the plaintiff, Abra-ham Sommer, owner of the "Pierre Apartments" in Hackensack, to rent apartment 6–L in that building. The term of the lease was from May 1, 1972 until April 30, 1974, with a rent concession for the first six weeks, so that the first month's rent was not due until June 15, 1972.

One week after signing the agreement, Kridel paid Sommer $690. Half of that sum was used to satisfy the first month's rent. The remainder was paid under the lease provision requiring a security deposit of $345. Although defendant had expected to begin occupancy around May 1, his plans were changed. He wrote to Sommer on May 19, 1972, explaining

> I was to be married on June 3, 1972. Unhappily the engage-ment was broken and the wedding plans cancelled. Both parents were to assume responsibility for the rent after our marriage. I was discharged from the U.S. Army in October 1971 and am now a student. I have no funds of my own, and am supported by my stepfather.
>
> In view of the above, I cannot take possession of the apartment and am surrendering all rights to it. Never having received a key, I cannot return same to you.
>
> I beg your understanding and compassion in releasing me from the lease, and will of course, in consideration thereof, forfeit the 2 month's rent already paid.
>
> Please notify me at your earliest convenience.

Plaintiff did not answer the letter.

Subsequently, a third party went to the apartment house and inquired about renting apartment 6–L. Although the parties agreed that she was ready, willing and able to rent the apartment, the person in charge told her that the apartment was not being shown since it was already rented to Kridel. In fact, the landlord did not re-enter the apartment or exhibit it to anyone until August 1, 1973. At that time it was rented to a new tenant for a term beginning on September 1, 1973. The new rental was for $345 per month and a six week concession similar to that granted Kridel.

Prior to re-letting the new premises, plaintiff sued Kridel in August 1972, demanding $7,590, the total amount due for the full two-year term of the lease. Following a mistrial, plaintiff filed an amended complaint asking for $5,865, the amount due between May 1, 1972 and September 1, 1973. The amended complaint included no reduction in the claim to reflect the six week concession provided for in the lease or the $690 payment made to plaintiff after signing the agreement. Defendant filed an amended answer to the complaint, alleging that plaintiff breached the contract, failed to mitigate damages and accepted defendant's surrender of the premises. He also counterclaimed to demand repayment of the $345 paid as a security deposit.

The trial judge ruled in favor of defendant. Despite his conclusion that the lease had been drawn to reflect "the 'settled law' of this state," he found that "justice and fair dealing" imposed upon the landlord the duty to attempt to re-let the premises and thereby mitigate damages. He also held that plaintiff's failure to make any response to defendant's unequivocal offer of surrender was tantamount to an acceptance, thereby terminating the tenancy and any obligation to pay rent. As a result, he dismissed both the complaint and the counterclaim. The Appellate Division reversed in a *per curiam* opinion, 153 N.J.Super. 1, 378 A.2d 774 (1975), and we granted certification.

* * * [T]he weight of authority in this State supports the rule that a landlord is under no duty to mitigate damages caused by a defaulting tenant. [Citations.] This rule has been followed in a majority of states and has been tentatively adopted in the American Law Institute's Restatement of Property. *Restatement (Second) of Property,* § 11.1(3) (Tent.Draft No. 3, 1975).

Nevertheless, while there is still a split of authority over this question, the trend among recent cases appears to be in favor of a mitigation requirement. [Citations.]

The majority rule is based on principles of property law which equate a lease with a transfer of a property interest in the owner's estate. Under this rationale the lease conveys to a tenant an interest in the property which forecloses any control by the landlord; thus, it would be anomalous to require the landlord to concern himself with the tenant's abandonment of his own property. * * *

Yet the distinction between a lease for ordinary residential purposes and an ordinary contract can no longer be considered viable. As Professor Powell observed, evolving "social factors have exerted increasing influence on the law of estates for years." 2 *Powell on Real Property* (1977 ed.), § 221[1] at 180–81. The result has been that

> [t]he complexities of city life, and the proliferated problems of modern society in general, have created new problems for lessors and lessees and these have been commonly handled by specific clauses in leases. This growth in the number and detail of specific lease covenants has reintroduced into the law of estates for years a predominantly contractual ingredient.

* * *

Application of the contract rule requiring mitigation of damages to a residential lease may be justified as a matter of basic fairness. Professor McCormick first commented upon the inequity under the majority rule when he predicted in 1925 that eventually the logic, inescapable according to the standards of a "jurisprudence of conceptions" which permits the landlord to stand idly by the vacant, abandoned premises and treat them as the property of the tenant and recover full rent, will yield to the more realistic notions of social advantage which in other fields of the law have forbidden a recovery for damages which the plaintiff by reasonable efforts could have avoided. [McCormick, "The Rights of the Landlord Upon Abandonment of the Premises by the Tenant," 23 *Mich.L.Rev.* 211, 221–22 (1925)].

Various courts have adopted this position.

The pre-existing rule cannot be predicated upon the possibility that a landlord may lose the opportunity to rent another empty apartment because he must first rent the apartment vacated by the defaulting tenant. Even where the breach occurs in a multi-dwelling building, each apartment may have unique qualities which make it attractive to certain individuals. Significantly, in *Sommer v. Kridel,* there was a specific request to rent the apartment vacated by the defendant; there is no reason to believe that absent this vacancy the landlord could have succeeded in renting a different apartment to this individual.

We therefore hold that antiquated real property concepts which served as the basis for the pre-existing rule, shall no longer be controlling where there is a claim for damages under a residential lease. Such claims must be governed by more modern notions of fairness and equity. A landlord has a duty to mitigate damages where he seeks to recover rents due from a defaulting tenant.

If the landlord has other vacant apartments besides the one which the tenant has abandoned, the landlord's duty to mitigate consists of making reasonable efforts to re-let the apartment. In such cases he must treat the apartment in question as if it was one of his vacant stock.

As part of his cause of action, the landlord shall be required to carry the burden of proving that he used reasonable diligence in attempting to re-let the premises. We note that there has been a divergence of opinion concerning the allocation of the burden of proof on this issue. While generally in contract actions the breaching party has the burden of proving that damages are capable of mitigation [Citations], here the landlord will be in a better position to demonstrate whether he exercised reasonable diligence in attempting to re-let the premises. * * *

In assessing whether the landlord has satisfactorily carried his burden, the trial court shall consider, among other factors, whether the landlord, either personally or through an agency, offered or showed the apartment to any prospective tenants, or advertised it in local newspapers. Additionally, the tenant may attempt to rebut such evidence by showing that he proffered suitable tenants who were rejected. However, there is no standard formula for measuring whether the landlord has utilized satisfactory efforts in attempting to mitigate damages, and each case must be judged upon its own facts. * * *

[Reversed.]

CARNATION CO. v. OLIVET EGG RANCH

189 Cal.App.3d 809, 229 Cal.Rptr. 261 (1986).

KLINE, P.J.

* * * Appellant Kristal, through the Olivet Egg Ranch Limited Partnership and a network of other partnerships and joint ventures, controlled and managed an egg producing operation in Northern California.

For approximately five years, Olivet or its predecessors in interest purchased chicken feed from Albers, which operated a mill in Santa Rosa. After unsuccessfully seeking payment of its bills, Carnation advised appellants they would no longer be allowed to purchase on credit. Appellants executed a note for the $606,382 balance owed to Carnation. When appellants defaulted on the note Carnation commenced this litigation. Appellants cross-complained on various theories, all premised on their assertion that the feed sold them was "misformulated, misproduced and nutritionally substandard" and, therefore, breached a variety of express and implied warranties made to appellants by Carnation and its employees. Appellants alleged that the feed's nutritional deficiencies had caused a decrease in Olivet's egg production revenues and sought to offset such losses against the amount due Carnation on the note.

[The court granted Carnation's motion for a nonsuit on Olivet's claim seeking damages for loss of goodwill flowing from the loss of their retail egg marketing accounts. The court based its decision on the premise that Olivet had not met its burden of proving, under California Commercial Code § 2715, that it had made reasonable efforts to mitigate damages.]

The non-suit as to the $309,000 loss in goodwill appellants claimed due to their inability to service their egg marketing accounts was granted upon the theory that California Commercial Code § 2715(2)(a) places on the aggrieved party the burden of showing it took reasonable steps to mitigate its consequential damages. In granting non-suit the court necessarily determined that, as a matter of law, Olivet failed to present evidence sufficient to meet its burden. It will be necessary to consider whether Olivet presented evidence sufficient to withstand nonsuit on this issue only if we first determine that the court's imposition of the burden on Olivet was legally correct. Olivet could not be penalized for failing to meet a burden which actually rested with Carnation. Thus, we are squarely faced with a question of first impression in California: which party bears the burden of proving the adequacy or inadequacy of efforts to mitigate consequential damages under California Commercial Code § 2715(2)(a)?

Section 2715(2)(a), which was adopted without change from the Uniform Commercial Code (U.C.C.), simply declares that "[c]onsequential damages resulting from the seller's breach include ... [a]ny loss resulting from general or particular requirements and needs of which the seller at the time of contracting had reason to know and which could not reasonably be prevented by cover or otherwise."

The official comment to the parallel provision of the U.C.C. does not shed much light on allocation of the burden of proof. Paragraph 2 of the pertinent U.C.C. Comment provides in material part that: "The 'tacit agreement' test for the recovery of consequential damages is rejected. Although the older rule at common law which made the seller liable for all consequential damages of which he had 'reason to know' in advance is followed, *the liberality of that rule is modified by refusing to permit recovery unless the buyer could not reasonably have prevented the loss by cover or otherwise.* Subparagraph (2) [of the statute] carries forward the provision of the prior uniform statutory provision as to consequential damages resulting from breach of warranty, but modifies the rule by requiring first that the buyer attempt to minimize his damages in good faith, either by cover or otherwise." (Italics added.) This comment does not demonstrate, as respondent asserts, that § 2715(2)(a) was intended to act as "a restraint on the liberality of the common law."

Paragraph 4 of the U.C.C. comment makes specific reference to the U.C.C.'s section on the liberal administration of remedies, indicating that the right to consequential damages should be *broadly,* not narrowly, construed. Furthermore, while paragraph 4 states that "[t]he burden of proving the extent of loss incurred by way of consequential damage is on the buyer ...," this statement does not determine the allocation of the burden of proof on the mitigation issue. It is entirely possible for the injured party to bear the burden of proving the *extent* of consequential damages while the breaching party has the duty of proving those items which *limit* the award of consequential damages.

The U.C.C.'s failure to allocate unambiguously the burden of proving mitigation has resulted in conflicting interpretations among those jurisdictions that have considered the question. Unfortunately, these cases are of little value to us since they do not analyze the problem nor explain why the burden should rest with one party or the other. By and large the cases merely state the unembellished conclusion that one or the other party has the burden of proof on this issue.

Paragraph 3 of the California Code Comment to § 2715 provides that "[t]he consequential damages provided for in subdivision (2) were recoverable under prior California law." [Citations.] Similarly, another California court of appeal has concluded that § 2715(2)(a) "is merely a codification of the rule that the buyer must attempt to minimize damages." [Citations.] Thus, adoption of the U.C.C. did nothing to alter pre-existing California law on the right to recover consequential damages and the duty to mitigate such losses. We have discovered no pre-U.C.C. California goods cases (which now would be governed by the U.C.C.) which deal with the issue before us. However, there is abundant California authority on the question as it arises in other contract cases.

In those cases, the established rule is the "[t]he burden of proof is on the party whose breach caused damage, to establish matters relied on to mitigate damage." [Citations.] Thus, to the extent adoption of the U.C.C. was intended to leave undisturbed pre-existing law on this question, we should continue to place the burden on the breaching party. Moreover, the interest in consistency supports a option of a rule placing on the breaching party the burden of proof under California Commercial Code § 2715(2)(a).

While the commentators do not unanimously support allocating the burden to the breaching party, there is substantial support among them for this position. Corbin, for example, declares that "[t]he burden of proving that losses have been avoided by reasonable effort and expense must always be borne by the party who has broken the contract." (5 Corbin on Contracts (1964), § 1039). White and Summers stated that "consequential damages that the *defendant* proves the buyer could have avoided will not be allowed ...." (J. White and R. Summers, Uniform Commercial Code (2d ed. 1980) §§ 6–7, p. 250, italics added.)

Placing on the party who breaches the burden of showing that consequential losses could have been avoided is intuitively attractive, since proof that there has been a failure to mitigate adequately will reduce the damages awarded and, therefore, seems more in the nature of a defense than an element of the plaintiff's affirmative case. In this sense, proof of failure to mitigate is analogous to evidence showing comparative negligence in tort law, which must be alleged and proved by the defendant. Moreover, it is sensible to require the defendant to prove those items which go to reduce the plaintiff's recovery, as plaintiffs would have little incentive to do so.

Respondent maintains that "[i]t makes more sense to place the burden of proving efforts to mitigate on the party best able to adduce evidence of such efforts." While this argument is on its surface appealing it does not stand up to closer scrutiny. As has been noted "[v]ery often one must plead and prove matters as to which his adversary has superior access to the proof. Nearly all required allegations of the plaintiff in actions for tort or breach of contract relating to the defendant's acts or omissions described matters peculiarly in the defendant's knowledge. Correspondingly, when the defendant is required to plead contributory negligence, he pleads facts specially known to the plaintiff." (McCormick on Evidence (3d ed. 1984) Ch. 36, § 337 at p. 950.)

Moreover, in cases such as this defendants do not genuinely lack the ability to ascertain the pertinent facts. A carefully drafted set of interrogatories could have provided Carnation with all the information it required about Olivet's efforts to mitigate its consequential damages. Since it therefore had access to the relevant evidence we see no reason why this consideration should prevent allocation to Carnation of the burden of showing that appellants failed to adequately mitigate their consequential damages.

Carnation was orig. of proving lack of ming. of damages (handwritten marginalia)

For the foregoing reasons, we hold that while the burden of proving the extent of loss incurred by way of consequential damages rests with the injured party, § 2715(2)(a) imposes upon the allegedly breaching party the burden of proving the inadequacy of efforts to mitigate consequential damages. Thus, Carnation, not Olivet, properly had the burden of proof on the issue of Olivet's mitigation of the consequential damages arising from Carnation's breach. Olivet therefore had no duty to present evidence of mitigation and the granting of the non-suit on the basis of Olivet's asserted failure to produce such evidence was error. The non-suit removed from the jury's consideration a $309,000 damage claim. Since Carnation never presented evidence on this issue there is no way of knowing whether appellants likely would have prevailed if the court had placed the burden of proof on Carnation. Accordingly, the judgment must be reversed.

Due to the trial court's improper allocation of the burden of proof under Commercial Code § 2715(2)(a), the judgment is reversed. Each party to bear its own costs on appeal.

Judg. reversed (handwritten marginalia)

---

1. In contracts for the sale of goods the failure of the aggrieved party to take reasonable measures to mitigate damages following a material breach will limit the amount of damages potentially recoverable. *See* U.C.C. §§ 2–708; 2–713; 2–610 comment 1. For example, in Oloffson v. Coomer, 11 Ill.App.3d 918, 296 N.E.2d 871 (1973), a grain dealer who unreasonably delayed in effecting cover after the seller repudiated was denied damages which could have been avoided by promptly procuring substitute goods. Similarly, the court in Whewell v. Dobson, 227 N.W.2d 115 (Iowa 1975), held that a seller of Christmas trees should have mitigated damages by reselling the trees in a commercially reasonable time following repudiation by the buyer. The seller's damages were not reduced, however, because the buyer failed to plead mitigation as a special defense.

2. For additional commentary on the doctrine of avoidable consequences see the following references: Simon, A Critique of the Treatment of Market Damages in the Restatement (Second) of Contracts, 81 Colum.L.Rev. 80 (1981); Weissenberger, The Landlord's Duty to Mitigate Damages on the Tenant's Abandonment: A Survey of Old Law and New Trends, 53 Temp.L.Q. 1 (1980); Simon & Novak, Limiting the Buyer's Market Damages to Lost Profits: A Challenge to the Enforceability of Market Contracts, 92 Harv.L.Rev. 1395 (1979); Goetz & Scott, Measuring Seller's Damages: The Lost Profits Puzzle, 31 Stan.L.Rev. 323 (1979); Childress, Buyer's Remedies: The Danger of Section 2–713, 72 Nw.U.L.Rev. 837 (1978); Jackson, "Anticipatory Repudiation" and the Temporal Element of Contract Law: An Economic Inquiry into Contract Damages in Cases of Prospective Nonperformance, 31 Stan. L.Rev. 69 (1978); Hillman, Keeping the Deal Together after Material Breach—Common Law Mitigation Rules, the UCC, and the Restatement

(Second) of Contracts, 47 U.Colo.L.Rev. 553 (1976); Leibson, Anticipatory Repudiation and Buyer's Damages—A Look Into How the UCC Has Changed the Common Law, 7 UCCLJ 272 (1975); Farnsworth, Legal Remedies for Breach of Contract, 70 Colum.L.Rev. 115 (1970); Summers, "Good Faith" in General Contract Law and the Sales Provisions of the Uniform Commercial Code, 54 Va.L.Rev. 195 (1968); Nordstrom, Seller's Damages Following Resale Under Article Two of the Uniform Commercial Code, 65 Mich.L.Rev. 1299 (1967); Peters, Remedies for Breach of Contracts Relating to the Sale of Goods under the Uniform Commercial Code: A Roadmap for Article Two, 73 Yale L.J. 199 (1963); Schmitthoff, The Duty to Mitigate, 1961 J.Bus.L. 361.

D. COLLATERAL SOURCE RULE

Section Coverage:

Defendants sometimes make payments of undisputed sums before trial. Such pre-trial payments to a plaintiff are then credited against the wrongdoer's ultimate liability. The collateral source rule states a negative corollary to that principle: compensation or other benefits which an injured party receives from a source unaffiliated or independent of the responsible party are *not* deducted from the defendant's liability. A second facet to the rule is that it serves as an evidentiary preclusion device; the defendant may not introduce evidence that the plaintiff has insurance coverage or has received gifts or benefits from some other source. Although the rule principally finds application in the tort context, it also may surface in cases of breach of contract.

Critics have attacked the collateral source rule on the basis that in certain instances an injured party actually receives double compensation for a single harm. Because the rule operates to allow a plaintiff to keep the benefits from a collateral source and to assess the wrongdoer for the same damages, it stands as an exception to the traditional goal of compensatory damages to place plaintiffs as nearly as practicable in the position they held prior to the harm.

Proponents of the rule have justified it with several arguments. First, if insurance benefits were viewed as an offset to tort liability, then a plaintiff would have less incentive to obtain insurance; without the rule plaintiffs actually would be net losers because they paid the insurance premiums. Second, an injured party may not in fact receive a double recovery if the insurance policy provided for subrogation rights. Third, apart from subrogation, the collateral source rule serves as a rough offset for the attorney's contingency fee. Finally, proponents argue that as between the tortfeasor and the plaintiff, any windfall should be enjoyed by the innocent party.

The principal legal difficulty in applying the collateral source rule is determining when a source is truly "independent" from the tortfeasor. Some jurisdictions have narrowed the effect of the rule by shifting the focus away from the wrongdoer and analyzing whether the source is affiliated in some manner with the plaintiff. The private sector sources, such as personal medical insurance, are fairly easy to characterize under either approach. The more complex questions have involved trying to classify whether certain types of public sector social benefits, such as medicare or unemployment benefits, should be viewed as "collateral" for purposes of the rule.

Model Case:

Baker drove through a red light and hit a pedestrian named Penn who was attempting to cross an intersection. Penn consequently incurred various medical expenses and was forced to miss several weeks of work. The claim against Baker prays for compensatory damages, including lost wages, medical expenses, and pain and suffering. A trial court applying the collateral source rule would refuse to allow the introduction of evidence of disability payments and medical benefits which Penn received under the terms of a union contract. The union benefits would be characterized as a source wholly independent from the interests of Baker. If the union contract did not provide for subrogation rights, Penn would effectively receive a double compensation for the injuries sustained.

HELFEND v. SOUTHERN CALIFORNIA RAPID TRANSIT DIST.

2 Cal.3d 1, 465 P.2d 61, 84 Cal.Rptr. 173 (1970).

TOBRINER, ACTING CHIEF JUSTICE.

Defendants appeal from a judgment of the Los Angeles Superior Court entered on a verdict in favor of plaintiff, Julius J. Helfend, for $16,400 in general and special damages for injuries sustained in a bus-auto collision that occurred on July 19, 1965, in the City of Los Angeles.

We have concluded that the judgment for plaintiff in this tort action against the defendant governmental entity should be affirmed. The trial court properly followed the collateral source rule in excluding evidence that a portion of plaintiff's medical bills had been paid through a medical insurance plan that requires the refund of benefits from tort recoveries.

* * *

Plaintiff filed a tort action against the Southern California Rapid Transit District, a public entity, and Mitchell an employee of the transit district. At trial plaintiff claimed slightly more than $2,700 in special damages, including $921 in doctor's bills, a $336.99 hospital bill, and about $45 for medicines. Defendant requested permission to show that about 80 percent of the plaintiff's hospital bill had been paid by plaintiff's Blue Cross insurance carrier and that some of his other medical expenses may have been paid by other insurance. The superior court thoroughly considered the then very recent case of City of Salinas v. Souza & McCue Construction Company (1967) 66 Cal.2d 217, 57 Cal. Rptr. 337, 424 P.2d 921, distinguished the *Souza* case on the ground that *Souza* involved a contract setting, and concluded that the judgment should not be reduced to the extent of the amount of insurance payments which plaintiff received. The court ruled that defendants should not be permitted to show that plaintiff had received medical coverage from any collateral source.

After the jury verdict in favor of plaintiff in the sum of $16,300, defendants appealed. * * *

We must decide whether the collateral source rule applies to tort actions involving public entities and public employees in which the plaintiff has received benefits from his medical insurance coverage.

The Supreme Court of California has long adhered to the doctrine that if an injured party received some compensation for his injuries from a source wholly independent of the tortfeasor, such payment should not be deducted from the damages which the plaintiff would otherwise collect from the tortfeasor. * * *

Although the collateral source rule remains generally accepted in the United States, nevertheless many other jurisdictions have restricted or repealed it. In this country most commentators have criticized the rule and called for its early demise. In *Souza* we took note of the academic criticism of the rule, characterized the rule as "punitive," and held it inapplicable to the governmental entity involved in that case.

* * *

The collateral source rule as applied here embodies the venerable concept that a person who has invested years of insurance premiums to assure his medical case should receive the benefits of his thrift. The tortfeasor should not garner the benefits of his victim's providence.

The collateral source rule expresses a policy judgment in favor of encouraging citizens to purchase and maintain insurance for personal injuries and for other eventualities. Courts consider insurance a form of investment, the benefits of which become payable without respect to any other possible source of funds. If we were to permit a tortfeasor to mitigate damages with payments from plaintiff's insurance, plaintiff would be in a position inferior to that of having bought no insurance, because his payment of premiums would have earned no benefit. Defendant should not be able to avoid payment of full compensation for the injury inflicted merely because the victim has had the foresight to provide himself with insurance.

Some commentators object that the above approach to the collateral source rule provides plaintiff with a "double recovery," rewards him for the injury, and defeats the principle that damages should compensate the victim but not punish the tortfeasor. We agree with Professor Fleming's observation, however, that "double recovery is justified only in the face of some exceptional, supervening reason, as in the case of accident or life insurance, where it is felt unjust that the tortfeasor should take advantage of the thrift and prescience of the victim in having paid the premiums." (Fleming, Introduction to the Law of Torts (1967) p. 131.) * * *

no
double
jeop

Furthermore, insurance policies increasingly provide for either sub-rogation or refund of benefits upon a tort recovery, and such refund is indeed called for the present case. [Citation.] Hence, the plaintiff receives no double recovery; the collateral source rule simply serves as a means of by-passing the antiquated doctrine of non-assignment of tor-tious actions and permits a proper transfer of risk from the plaintiff's insurer to the tortfeasor by way of the victim's tort recovery. The double shift from the tortfeasor to the victim and then from the victim to his insurance carrier can normally occur with little cost in that the insurance carrier is often intimately involved in the initial litigation and quite automatically receives its part of the tort settlement or verdict.

Even in cases in which the contract or the law precludes subrogation or refund of benefits, or in situations in which the collateral source waives such subrogation or refund, the rule performs entirely necessary functions in the computation of damages. For example, the cost of medical care often provides both attorneys and juries in tort cases with an important measure for assessing the plaintiff's general damages. [Citation.] To permit the defendant to tell the jury that the plaintiff has been recompensed by a collateral source for his medical costs might irretrievably upset the complex, delicate, and somewhat indefinable calculations which result in the normal jury verdict. [Citations.]

upset
jury
decis.

take into
account
atty.
fees

We also note that generally the jury is not informed that plaintiff's attorney will receive a large portion of the plaintiff's recovery in contin-gent fees or that personal injury damages are not taxable to the plaintiff and are normally deductible by the defendant. Hence, the plaintiff rarely actually receives full compensation for his injuries as computed by the jury. The collateral source rule partially serves to compensate for the attorney's share and does not actually render "double recovery" for the plaintiff. Indeed, many jurisdictions that have abolished or limited the collateral source rule have also established a means for assessing the plaintiff's costs for counsel directly against the defendant rather than imposing the contingent fee system. In sum, the plaintiff's recovery for his medical expenses from both the tortfeasor and his medical insurance program will not usually give him "double recovery," but partially provides a somewhat closer approximation to full compensation for his injuries.

If we consider the collateral source rule as applied here in the context of the entire American approach to the law of torts and damages, we find that the rule presently performs a number of legitimate and even indispensable functions. Without a thorough revolution in the American approach to torts and the consequent damages, the rule at least with respect to medical insurance benefits has become so integrated within our present system that its precipitous judicial nullification would work hardship. In this case the collateral source rule lies between two systems for the compensation of accident victims: the traditional tort recovery based on fault and the increasingly prevalent coverage based on non-fault insurance. Neither system possesses such universality of coverage or completeness of compensation that we can easily dispense with the collateral source rule's approach to meshing the two systems. [Citations.] The reforms which many academicians propose cannot easily be achieved through piecemeal common law development; the proposed changes, if desirable, would be more effectively accomplished through legislative reform. * * *

* * * Hence, we conclude that in a case in which a tort victim has received partial compensation from medical insurance coverage entirely independent of the tortfeasor the trial court properly followed the collateral source rule and foreclosed defendant from mitigating damages by means of the collateral payments.

* * *

Defendants would have this court create a special form of sovereign immunity as a novel exception to the collateral source rule for tortfeasors who are public entities or public employees. [Citations.] We see no justification for such special treatment. In the present case the nullification of the collateral source rule would simply frustrate the transfer of the medical costs from the medical insurance carrier, Blue Cross, to the public entity. The public entity or its insurance carrier is in at least as advantageous a position to spread the risk of loss as is the plaintiff's medical insurance carrier. To deprive Blue Cross of repayment for its expenditures on plaintiff's behalf merely because he was injured by a public entity rather than a private individual would constitute an unwarranted and arbitrary discrimination.

* * *

The judgment is affirmed.

———

1. The common law collateral source rule has been abolished or modified with respect to certain types of cases, such as ones involving medical malpractice, in a number of jurisdictions. For example, Cal.Civ. Code § 3333.1 (West 1984) abrogates the rule in negligence actions for personal injuries against health care providers:

(a) In the event the defendant so elects, in an action for personal injury against a health care provider based upon professional negligence, he may introduce evidence of any amount payable as a benefit to the plaintiff as a result of the personal injury pursuant to the United States Social Security Act, any state or federal income disability or worker's compensation act, any health, sickness or income-disability insurance, accident insurance that provides health benefits or income-disability coverage, and any contract or agreement of any group, organization, partnership, or corporation to provide, pay for, or reimburse the cost of medical, hospital, dental, or other health care services. Where the defendant elects to introduce such evidence, the plaintiff may introduce evidence of any amount which the plaintiff has paid or contributed to secure his right to any insurance benefits concerning which the defendant has introduced evidence.

2.   In Miller v. Sciaroni, 172 Cal.App.3d 306, 218 Cal.Rptr. 219 (1985), the court upheld the constitutionality of California Civil Code § 3333.1.   The court found that because the legislation affected only economic interests of indemnitors, rather than fundamental rights, it should be scrutinized according to whether the statutory evidentiary distinctions bore a rational relationship to a legitimate state purpose.   In applying the rational basis test, the court found a legitimate state interest in "the protection of a viable state health care system," and that it was not the judiciary's role to reweigh or second-guess the facts involved in the legislative determination.   Also, in Barme v. Wood, 37 Cal.3d 174, 207 Cal.Rptr. 816, 689 P.2d 446 (1984), the court held that another provision of the California collateral source statute which eliminated certain subrogation rights against a malpractice defendant was rationally related to the legislative purpose because it reduced costs on those defendants by shifting them to other insurers.   Finally, in Fein v. Permanente Medical Group, 38 Cal.3d 137, 211 Cal.Rptr. 368, 695 P.2d 665 (1985), the California Supreme Court held that the statutory modification of the common law collateral source rule satisfied constitutional due process objections, even though the provision admittedly affects the measure of a plaintiff's damage award, because a plaintiff has no vested property right in a particular measure of damages.   *See also* Eastin v. Broomfield, 116 Ariz. 576, 570 P.2d 744 (1977) (Arizona's statutory abrogation of collateral source rule with respect to medical malpractice actions did not deprive claimants of any property interest protected by constitutional due process, nor was it arbitrary and unreasonable to deny claimants equal protection of the laws).

3.   The majority of cases that have addressed the issue have upheld the constitutionality of provisions modifying or abolishing the collateral source rule in medical malpractice cases.   *See* Rudolph v. Iowa Methodist Medical Ctr., 293 N.W.2d 550 (1980); Baker v. Vanderbilt Univ., 616 F.Supp. 330 (M.D.Tenn.1985).   *See generally* McDowell, The Collateral Source Rule—The American Medical Association and Tort Reform, 24 Washburn L.J. 205 (1985).

Some decisions have struck down statutory abolitions of the collateral source rule on constitutional grounds.   In Graley v. Satayatham, 74 Ohio Op.2d 316, 343 N.E.2d 832 (1976), the court held that an Ohio statute abrogating the collateral source rule only with respect to medical malpractice actions was violative of the equal protection guarantees in both the state and federal Constitutions.   The statutory classification scheme which differentiated between medical malpractice claims and other tort actions failed the compelling governmental interest test.

Similarly, in Doran v. Priddy, 534 F.Supp. 30 (D.Kan.1981), the court upheld an equal protection challenge to a Kansas statute which applied only if the putative tortfeasor was a health care provider.   The statute permitted the introduction into evidence of collateral benefits received by a plaintiff from gratuitous sources and disallowed evidence of benefits received from a plaintiff's insurance or employment. The court held that this new statutory rule did not bear a reasonable and substantial relation to the avowed legislative purpose of reducing medical costs.

4. Who should bear the burden of proving the amount received from a collateral source when a statute abrogates the common law rule? In Reilly v. United States, 863 F.2d 149 (1st Cir.1988), the court found that burden rested with the defendant under the statute. The defendant's general allusions to the plaintiff's possible eligibility to receive benefits failed to satisfy evidentiary requirements.

CRAIG v. Y & Y SNACKS, INC.
721 F.2d 77 (3d Cir.1983).

SLOVITER, CIRCUIT JUDGE.

Before us are cross-appeals following a judgment for the employee in an action alleging sexual harassment in violation of Title VII of the Civil Rights Act of 1964. * * * On the separate issue of damages, the employee cross-appeals from the deduction of unemployment compensation from her gross back pay award.

* * *

In her cross-appeal, Craig contends the district court erroneously deducted unemployment benefits from her back pay award under Title VII. This issue, which we have not previously addressed, has divided the circuits that have considered it.

The Eleventh, Ninth and Fourth Circuits have recently adopted the rule that there should be no deduction for unemployment benefits from a Title VII back pay award. [Citations.]

The district court here, after concluding that the proper remedy was reinstatement and back pay, including 10% prejudgment interest, reduced this amount by unemployment compensation to avoid "something that would be in the neighborhood of unjust enrichment." The court reasoned, "I see no reason in the statute and the equitable principles that inform it that should require the defendant to reimburse the plaintiff for sums which he has, by society's other devices, already received."

Nothing in the statutory language, the legislative history, or the case law is clearly dispositive of the issue raised by plaintiff Craig on cross-appeal. The statute does provide for a deduction from a back pay award for "interim earnings" or "amounts earnable with reasonable diligence." 42 U.S.C. § 2000e–5(g). Thus, a duty to mitigate damages is incorporated. But the statute makes no mention of unemployment compensation, and the legislative history does not specifically discuss such benefits.

* * *

Although the issue is extremely close and one over which reasonable persons could differ, we conclude that unemployment benefits should not be deducted from a Title VII back pay award for the following reasons:

(1) We begin with the statutory language. Section 2000e–5(g) explicitly provides that interim earnings and amounts earnable with reasonable diligence must be deducted from back pay otherwise allowable. If Congress intended other deductions, it could have so provided. Its failure to do so must be given some effect by the courts.

(2) Although the legislative history of Title VII does not specifically address whether unemployment compensation is to be regarded as deductible "interim earnings", Congress was undoubtedly aware that under the National Labor Relations Act (NLRA) unemployment benefits are not deducted from back pay awards. The Supreme Court in Albemarle Paper Co. v. Moody, 422 U.S. 405, 419–22, 95 S.Ct. 2362, 2372–2374, 45 L.Ed.2d 280 (1975), noted that Congress modeled Title VII's back pay provision on that of the NLRA. Indeed, it was for that reason that the Court held back pay was normally to be awarded under Title VII absent special circumstances, relying on the NLRB's practice of awarding back pay. Thus, in analyzing the deductibility of unemployment benefits, we may reasonably turn for guidance to the practice under the NLRA.

* * *

(3) Unemployment compensation most clearly resembles a collateral benefit which is ordinarily not deducted from a plaintiff's recovery. Under the collateral benefit rule, payment which a plaintiff receives for his or her loss from another source is not credited against the defendant's liability for all damages resulting from its wrongful or negligent act. * * *

The collateral benefits rationale was one of the bases for the Supreme Court's decision in *Gullett Gin* [NLRB v. Gullett Gin Co., 340 U.S. 361, 71 S.Ct. 337, 95 L.Ed. 337 (1951)]. The Court expressly categorized unemployment compensation benefits as "collateral", and stated that "failure to take them into account in ordering back pay does not make the employees more than 'whole' as that phrase has been understood and applied." The Court explained that "[s]ince no consideration has been given to collateral *losses* in framing an order to reimburse employees for their lost earnings, manifestly no consideration need be given to collateral benefits which employees may have received."

In *Gullett Gin,* the Court also rejected the employer's argument that unemployment benefits are direct rather than collateral benefits because they are financed partially through employer taxation. The Court stated:

Payments of unemployment compensation were not made to the employees by respondent but by the state out of state funds derived from taxation. True, these taxes were paid by employers, and thus to some extent respondent helped to create the fund. However, the payments to the employees were not made to discharge any liability or obligation of respondent, but to carry out a policy of social betterment for the benefit of the entire state.

(4) A rule precluding deduction of unemployment benefits from a back pay award would further the two key objectives of Title VII's back pay provision, which have been described by the Supreme Court as primarily to end employment discrimination and secondarily to compensate injured victims in a make whole fashion. * * * To the extent that a back pay award is reduced by unemployment benefits, this purpose is diluted.

The above considerations persuaded the Eleventh, Ninth, and Fourth Circuits to reach the conclusion that unemployment benefits should not be deducted from Title VII back pay awards. * * *

In summary, we adopt the rule of nondeductibility of unemployment benefits. * * *

SEITZ, CHIEF JUDGE, dissenting in part:

I fully agree with the majority that the district court correctly found the defendant liable under Title VII and that an award of back pay was an appropriate remedy. I dissent from part III of the opinion, however, because I do not agree that unemployment compensation may never be deducted from a back pay award under Title VII.

One of the purposes of a back pay award is to deter future discrimination. [Citation.] A second purpose is to place the victim of discrimination in the same position as if the discrimination had not occurred. Thus, Congress has determined that the economic sanction contained in a make-whole remedy is a sufficient deterrent to future discrimination. "[B]ack pay is not a penalty imposed as a sanction for moral turpitude; it is compensation for the tangible economic loss resulting from an unlawful employment practice." [Citation.] Since the plaintiff is only entitled to reimbursement for her economic loss, and the back pay award has no punitive character, the collateral source rule does not apply and does not compel the partial double recovery here. *See* Restatement (Second) of Torts §§ 901, 920A and comment b (1977) (theory of tort damages generally and collateral source rule in particular includes punitive aspect).

The plaintiff's "tangible economic loss" has already been partially offset by her unemployment benefits. In my view the deterrent purpose of Title VII does not require that the victim of discrimination be compensated again for that portion of the economic loss already offset. * * * The majority holds that deducting unemployment benefits gives a windfall to the employer because it reduces the damages which he would otherwise have to pay. However, by providing only a make-whole remedy Congress has made the windfall issue irrelevant. The remedy is measured by the amount needed to make the plaintiff whole, and only if the employer paid less than that amount would there be a windfall.

There is no suggestion that plaintiff has not been made whole by the district court's order.

Prior case law under both Title VII and the NLRA does not compel a rule that unemployment benefits may never be deducted from an award of back pay. All that the Supreme Court held in *Gullett Gin* was that it was within the NLRB's discretion not to deduct unemployment benefits from an award of back pay. Since Title VII was modeled on the NLRA, presumably deductions are similarly discretionary under that statute as well. * * *

My disagreement with the majority is not over the purposes of Title VII, but with how those purposes—deterrence of further discrimination and making victims whole—are to be effectuated. I believe that Congress has determined that compelling an employer to make victims of discrimination whole will deter the employer from future similar acts. The employer cannot be compelled to pay more damages than this, however much greater the deterrent effect of such a payment might be.

* * *

————

1. In Hassan v. United States Postal Service, 842 F.2d 260 (11th Cir.1988), the claimant in a Federal Tort Claims Act suit asserted that the trial court had erred by allowing the government to introduce evidence that its liability should be reduced by collateral social security and insurance payments received by the plaintiff. The state statute applicable in assessing damages under the Act had abrogated the collateral source rule in personal injury or wrongful death actions involving motor vehicles. The plaintiff argued that the government's attempt to reduce its liability by the collateral source payments was an affirmative defense which was waived when not raised in the government's pleadings. The court held that the issue did fall within the scope of Federal Rule of Civil Procedure 8(c) as an affirmative defense, but nonetheless upheld its admission into evidence. The court noted that the underlying purpose of Rule 8(c) is to guarantee the opposing party notice of an issue to avoid prejudice, and in this case the claimant knew about the government's plans to raise the issue at trial.

2. The line between affiliated and collateral sources is often blurry. This difficulty is highlighted when one government agency has liability under the Federal Tort Claims Act while a separate branch or agency of the government renders medical services to the injured party or supplies other benefits. Courts typically have resolved the issue by allowing an offset to liability when the benefits come from unfunded general government revenues and not deducting benefits from a special fund. *See* United States v. Gray, 199 F.2d 239 (10th Cir.1952) (disability payments under Veterans Act deductible); United States v. Harue Hayashi, 282 F.2d 599 (9th Cir.1960) (social security payments not deductible because funded in part by the beneficiary or a relative upon whom the beneficia-

ry was dependent); United States v. Price, 288 F.2d 448 (4th Cir.1961) (benefits under the Civil Service Retirement Act were a collateral source); United States v. Brooks, 176 F.2d 482 (4th Cir.1949) (National Service Life Insurance Policy benefits not deductible from an FTCA damages award).

3.   The rationales for distinguishing special government funds for collateral source treatment are twofold: the source itself is considered independent of other federal agencies and the plaintiffs deserve any additional compensation because they have effectively contracted for it in the nature of social insurance. *See* Overton v. United States, 619 F.2d 1299 (8th Cir.1980). A more restrictive approach was taken in Steckler v. United States, 549 F.2d 1372 (10th Cir.1977), where the court held that Social Security payments constituted a non-deductible collateral source only to the extent that the claimant succeeded in tracing his contributions to the fund.

4.   Courts have had particular problems applying the collateral source rule to Medicare, a federal program originally enacted as an amendment to the Social Security Act. In Overton v. United States, 619 F.2d 1299 (8th Cir.1980), the court held that Medicare payments were deductible from the government's liability because the Medicare Part A trust fund was not wholly independent from the general revenues of the federal treasury and the plaintiff did not show contributions to the source of the payments. In contrast, in Siverson v. United States, 710 F.2d 557 (9th Cir.1983), the court held that the government was not entitled to offset Medicare payments against an FTCA award where the claimant had shown that he contributed to the Medicare fund through social security payments while employed. *Accord,* Titchnell v. United States, 681 F.2d 165 (3d Cir.1982) (Medicare payments deemed collateral source because plaintiff had contributed to fund).

PROBLEM: THE GOOD SAMARITAN

Carlton was driving down a quiet two lane country road when a cement-mixer truck barreled around the corner and forced Carlton's car into a ditch. The driver of the truck sped away from the scene of the accident, leaving Carlton injured and helpless.

Fortunately, kindly Doc Miller and his teenage son, Butch, drove past just a few minutes later, saw the overturned vehicle, and stopped to render aid. Doc and Butch pulled Carlton from the car and rushed to the hospital. Doc performed emergency surgery on Carlton to stop internal hemorrhaging and he also stitched and bandaged several cuts. Carlton recovered in the hospital for three days and was then discharged.

1.   Assume that Carlton had been paying premiums on a medical insurance policy for a number of years. The policy, apart from a small deductible, provided coverage for the hospital charges as well as for surgical fees. Ignorant of this fact, Doc decided not to send Carlton a

bill for the operation but considered his services to be a "favor for a friend." Meanwhile, the company that owned the cement truck, Pavco, was identified. Assume that Pavco would be liable for the tort of its driver in this instance. Should Carlton be entitled to receive payment from the insurance company for a "reasonable surgical fee" as expressly provided in the policy and to recover such fees also from Pavco?

2. What if Doc instead sent Carlton a bill for the operation and the insurance company paid the fee. Under the collateral source rule, can Carlton claim the surgical fee as a compensable item of damages against Pavco? Should the jury be instructed that the plaintiff had medical insurance which would cover the various hospital charges and doctor's fees?

HUEPER v. GOODRICH

314 N.W.2d 828 (Minn.1982).

TODD, JUSTICE.

Bruce Hueper, a minor, was seriously injured in an auto accident. A lawsuit was commenced on his behalf for his injuries and his father brought action for his medical expenses. The trial was bifurcated as to liability and damages. Following the damages trial, the court allowed the father full recovery of the reasonable value of medical expenses, including hospital services furnished without charge, under the collateral source rule. * * *

The jury award of $37,270 to Emil Hueper was for special damages arising out of medical and hospital care provided to his son Bruce before Bruce's 18th birthday. Of that sum, $25,977 reflected the reasonable value of the medical care provided to Bruce Hueper while he was a patient at Shriner's Hospital. A physician at Shriner's Hospital testified that it was the policy of the hospital not to charge patients for care provided or to accept insurance proceeds from a third party.

* * *

The issues presented are:

I. Did the trial court err in applying the collateral source rule to allow the father of a minor son to recover the reasonable value of medical and hospital services provided free of charge by a charitable institution?

* * *

Under the collateral source rule, a plaintiff may recover damages from a tortfeasor, although the plaintiff has received money or services in reparation of the injury from a source other than the tortfeasor. [Citation.] The benefit conferred on the injured person from the collateral source is not credited against the tortfeasor's liability, although it may partially or completely reimburse the plaintiff for his injuries. Restatement (Second) of Torts, § 920A (1979). The rule has been applied where the plaintiff has received insurance proceeds, employment benefits, gifts of money or medical services, welfare benefits or tax advantages. [Citation.]

Various justifications have been given for applying the rule. Where the plaintiff has paid for the benefit such as by buying an insurance policy, the rationale is that the plaintiff should be reimbursed and the tortfeasor should not get a windfall. *See* Restatement (Second) of Torts, § 920A, comment b (1979). If the benefit is a gift from a third party, such as an employer, a relative or a charity, the argument is that the donor intended that the injured party receive the gift and not that the benefit be shifted to the tortfeasor. Other reasons for applying the rule are that the wrongdoer should be punished by being made to take full responsibility for his negligence and that the plaintiff will be more fully compensated if he is allowed to recover from the tortfeasor.

Minnesota has adopted the collateral source rule and the cases applying the rule have relied upon the policy reasons discussed above. *See* Hubbard Broadcasting, Inc. v. Loescher, 291 N.W.2d 216 (1980) (purpose of rule is punitive); Van Tassel v. Horace Mann Ins. Co., 296 Minn. 181, 207 N.W.2d 348 (1973) (insurance paid for by plaintiff should not benefit tortfeasor); Local 1140, Int'l Union of Elec., Radio & Mach. Workers, 282 Minn. 455, 165 N.W.2d 234 (1969) (benefit of reimbursement by hospital when blood was replaced by donor group to which injured plaintiffs belonged goes to plaintiffs.)

In this case the trial court correctly followed Minnesota case law in applying the collateral source rule. Emil Hueper, as the father of Bruce Hueper, a minor, had a right to recover special damages for medical expenses from the defendants. [Citations.] He could still recover the reasonable value of those medical expenses although Shriner's Hospital did not charge the Huepers anything for Bruce's medical care. In Dahlin v. Kron, 232 Minn. 312, 45 N.W.2d 833 (1950), this court held that the plaintiff could recover the reasonable value of medical services provided by a hospital even though those services were rendered gratuitously by the hospital.

We are being asked to review the policy considerations involved in our long-standing support of the collateral source rule. The facts of this case present this issue in a light most favorable to those advocating abandonment of the collateral source rule. However, the rule in its application is broader than the facts of this case. To begin limiting the application of the rule is to invite an unlimited flow of litigation seeking ad hoc determinations with the confusion that would necessarily follow. Considering the rule in its broadest sense and reviewing all of the considerations involved in such an evaluation, we decline to abandon the collateral source rule or to create limitations on its application.

* * *

Simonett, Justice (dissenting in part).

* * *

Mr. Hueper has been compensated for his own personal injuries. He settled for $85,000. Before us is his claim for hospital and medical expenses incurred by him for his son Bruce's care during Bruce's minority. This claim is separate from, although derivative of, Bruce's claim. The jury awarded Mr. Hueper $43,847.34. This was reduced by 15% for Mr. Hueper's own fault to $37,370.24. This figure includes $24,977.14, representing the reasonable value of the services rendered by Shriners Hospital. Mr. Hueper keeps this money, since the hospital made no charge and accepts no payment for its services. The $24,977.14 is to be paid by defendants Dean Goodrich and John M. Neubauer, the owner and driver, respectively, of the other truck involved in the accident. Mr. Goodrich is not personally at fault. He is liable to Mr. Hueper for the unincurred hospital bill of $24,977.14 by reason of his vicarious liability as owner of the truck.

The collateral source rule is usually justified on one or more of the following rationales: (1) the injured party has *paid for* the collateral source benefit and deserves what he paid for; (2) a collateral source benefit is sometimes a *gift intended* by the donor to benefit the injured donee and not the tortfeasor; (3) only cumulation of collateral source benefits with amounts assessed the tortfeasor will *fully compensate* the injured person; (4) a tortfeasor deserves to be *punished,* a purpose which would be foiled if he were relieved from "total responsibility" for his wrong; and (5) since a *windfall* payment is inevitable, better it go to the injured person than the tortfeasor.

None of these reasons, it seems to me, applies in this case, or, to the extent any does, it applies with very little persuasive force.

First, Mr. Hueper did not pay for the Shriner's care in any way. He paid no insurance premium; there was no surrender of sick leave or other fringe benefits. No "consideration" was given * * *.

Second, in providing its care, the Shriners Hospital was indifferent as to whether Bruce Hueper had been in a compensable auto accident or not. He was afforded no different care than other patients. No specific gift was intended, such as where fellow employees donate blood to one of their number, as in Local 1140 v. Massachusetts Mutual Life Insurance Co., 282 Minn. 455, 165 N.W.2d 234 (1969), or where one spouse renders nursing care to the other.

Third, it cannot be said deduction of the Shriners Hospital bill will leave Mr. Hueper less than fully compensated. It is said that pain and suffering are more likely to be completely compensated if collateral source benefits are recoverable. Here, however, plaintiff's entire claim is for specific expense items; no general damages, difficult to measure, are involved. The claim is more akin to a property damage claim where often the collateral source rule is disallowed.

Fourth, there would seem to be little reason to punish the defendants. If the defendants deserve punishment, punitive damages should be the route. If the jurors had known the hospital bill was not actually incurred, it is doubtful they would have punished defendants by making them pay it nevertheless. In any event, there seems to be little need to punish defendant Goodrich, who was not personally at fault.

Fifth, the windfall rationale lacks persuasive force here. Ordinarily, other things being equal, if someone is to benefit by the generosity of the Shriners Hospital, it is better that it be the injured party rather than the wrongdoer. What this means is that it is better to assure that plaintiff is made whole than that the defendant pay less than he ought to. Here, however, "other things" are not equal. Since plaintiff's damages relate solely to "out-of-pocket" expenses, it cannot be said plaintiff is not made whole even with the collateral source benefit deducted. To say defendant should not pay less than he ought to is only another way of saying the defendant should be punished, a rationale which, as we have seen, is inappropriate in this factual setting.

While the collateral source rule has been strongly criticized, it is still true no one has really offered a better alternative. Perhaps this is the strongest rationale for its continued use. In most cases there is simply no way of knowing what is the fairest way to handle the collateral source benefit "windfall." To try and find this "equality" by admitting a multitude of collateral sources would be most confusing, prejudicial and unfair.[2] It is probably better, arbitrarily, to keep collateral source benefits out of the lawsuit and then allow the windfall to plaintiff.

But having said this, I see no need to extend this somewhat arbitrary rule to a fact situation where the policy considerations favoring it clearly do not apply. I would be willing to hold that in a parent's derivative claim for out-of-pocket expenses the parent may not recover for hospital or medical care furnished his or her minor child gratuitously and not as a specific gift. At the very least, I would hold, in this case, that plaintiff is not entitled to recover against defendant Goodrich who is not personally at fault. It should be plaintiff's option whether to prove up the reasonable value of the gratuitous services and then have the court, after the verdict, make the reduction, or to choose not to include the services in his claim.

---

2. If one starts recognizing collateral sources, where does one stop? Studies indicate that about 55% of auto accident tort victims' compensation comes from tort recoveries, the remainder being supplied by collateral sources. Birmingham, *The Theory of Economic Policy and the Law of Torts,* 55 Minn.L.Rev. 1, 9 (1970); United States Department of Transportation, *Automobile Insurance and Compensation Study,* March 1971, "Motor Vehicle Crash Losses and their Compensation in the United States." What about health insurance benefits, pensions, social security, sick leave, disability insurance and, in the case of a decedent, life insurance? And if these items are recognizable, then what about defendant's liability insurance or lack of it? Here, for example, the Goodrich truck had only $100,000 coverage for any one claim and the insurer paid the $100,000 to Bruce, so apparently the defendants have personal exposure for Mr. Hueper's verdict of $37,370.24.

1. Courts have split over the issue whether the collateral source rule should be applied to allow an injured party to recover the reasonable value of gratuitously supplied medical services. In Oddo v. Cardi, 100 R.I. 578, 218 A.2d 373 (1966), the court adopted the same approach as in the principal case; the amount of recovery from a party responsible for an injury is not affected by the plaintiff's receipt of free medical care from sources collateral to the defendant. *See also* Banks v. Crowner, 694 P.2d 101 (Wyo.1985); Restatement (Second) of Torts § 920A, comment c (1979).

2. Consider the court's support of the collateral source rule in Hudson v. Lazarus, 217 F.2d 344 (D.C.Cir.1954):

> Usually the collateral contribution necessarily benefits either the injured person or the wrongdoer. Whether it is a gift or the product of a contract of employment or of insurance, the purposes of the parties to it are obviously better served and the interests of society are likely to be better served if the injured person is benefitted than if the wrongdoer is benefitted. Legal "compensation" for personal injuries does not actually compensate. Not many people would sell an arm for the average or even the maximum amount that juries award for the loss of an arm. Moreover the injured person seldom gets the compensation he "recovers," for a substantial attorney's fee usually comes out of it.

The court, then, is justifying the potential overcompensation attributed to the collateral source rule by saying that an injured party cannot truly be compensated in monetary equivalents for personal injuries. Does that answer beg the question?

3. Compare Coyne v. Campbell, 11 N.Y.2d 372, 230 N.Y.S.2d 1, 183 N.E.2d 891 (1962), where the court held that the rationale underlying the collateral source rule did not allow an injured physician to recover as special damages the reasonable value of medical and nursing care and treatment which were gratuitously rendered. The court reasoned that the goal of tort law is merely compensatory rather than of a punitive character, and if the rule were otherwise applied it "would involve odd consequences, and in the end simply require a defendant to pay a plaintiff the value of a gift." *Accord* Peterson v. Lou Bachrodt Chevrolet Co., 76 Ill.2d 353, 29 Ill.Dec. 444, 392 N.E.2d 1 (1979).

4. For additional commentary on the collateral source rule *see*: Branton, The Collateral Source Rule, 18 St. Mary's L.J. 883 (1987); Schwartz, Tort Law Reform: Strict Liability and the Collateral Source Rule Do Not Mix, 39 Vand.L.Rev. 569 (1986); McDowell, The Collateral Source Rule—The American Medical Association and Tort Reform, 24 Washburn L.J. 205 (1985); Fleming, The Collateral Source Rule and Contract Damages, 71 Calif.L.Rev. 56 (1983); Hogan, The Collateral Source Rule: Its Justification and its Defense, 19 Trial Law Q. 58 (1983); Sedler, The Collateral Source Rule and Personal Injury Damages: The Irrelevant Principle and the Functional Approach, 58 Ky.L.J. 36 (1969); Fleming, The Collateral Source Rule and Loss Allocation in

Tort Law, 54 Calif.L.Rev. 1478 (1966); Note, Unreason in the La
Damages: The Collateral Source Rule, 77 Harv.L.Rev. 741 (1964); West,
The Collateral Source Rule Sans Subrogation: A Plaintiff's Windfall, 16
Okla.L.Rev. 395 (1963); Maxwell, The Collateral Source Rule in the
American Law of Damages, 46 Minn.L.Rev. 669 (1962); Schwartz, The
Collateral Source Rule, 41 B.U.L.Rev. 348 (1961); Averbach, The Collat-
eral Source Rule, 21 Ohio St.L.J. 231 (1960); James, Social Insurance
and Tort Liability: The Problem of Alternative Remedies, 27
N.Y.U.L.Rev. 537 (1952).

Chapter 14

SPECIAL ISSUES IN DAMAGES
A. LIQUIDATED DAMAGES

Section Coverage:

Contracting parties may stipulate a specified sum of money which would be payable as damages to the non-breaching party for a material breach of the contract. Liquidated damages serve to remove the uncertainties and difficulties involved in proving actual damages in the event of a breach, and they thereby function to reduce litigation expenses and expedite the trial process.

The principle of freedom of contract is not an absolute concept; it is limited by the refusal of courts to enforce extortionate or unconscionable bargains. Therefore, a liquidated damages provision is valid only if it corresponds with general notions of damages as a substitutionary measure for performance in the event of breach. If the court perceives the purpose of the clause as an attempt to compel performance through the threat of onerous damages, the provision will be considered a penalty and thus unenforceable. Labels applied by the parties to describe the provision as a penalty or an enforceable liquidated damages clause are not controlling.

The law of liquidated damages is consistent with the common law policy of allowing efficient contract breach. This substantive policy is that a contracting party should be permitted to pay compensatory damages for a breach in exchange for the opportunity to shift goods or services to a different source in order to maximize economic resources. To the extent that a contractual damages provision operates to punish a contract breach, the goal of maximizing resources is undermined. Conversely, a liquidated damages provision that specifies a reasonable estimate of actual damages upon breach is consistent with that goal.

The traditional test to evaluate the validity of a liquidated damages provision is whether, at the time the parties entered the contract, (1) damages resulting from a breach would be difficult to determine, and (2) the stipulated amount had a reasonable relationship to the potential damages if a breach occurred. The two criteria are not necessarily inconsistent or contradictory because the reasonableness of the liquidated sum is determined in light of the anticipated harm rather than in hindsight looking at the amount of actual damages. Thus, courts do not require precise estimates; the amount of actual damages will almost certainly vary from that stipulated in the contract. The very uncertainty in predicting future harm militates against requiring a precise matching of actual to liquidated damages.

The Uniform Commercial Code § 2–718(1) and the Restatement (Second) of Contracts § 356(1) carry forward the common law approach in a slightly modified fashion by providing that reasonableness of a liquidated damages clause may be shown based upon either the anticipated or actual harm from the breach. Section 2–718 further provides an insight into the meaning of "reasonableness" by considering the "difficulties of proof of loss, inconvenience or infeasibility of otherwise obtaining an adequate remedy." Under both the U.C.C. and the common law, whether the parties made a good faith pre-estimate of damages should be objectively evaluated rather than inquiring into the subjective intentions of the parties.

Finally, courts may consider whether the parties intended the liquidated damages provision to serve as the exclusive or an alternative remedy in the event of a breach. Unless the contract expressly provides otherwise, courts generally will construe the contract to allow the non-breaching party to pursue other available remedies, such as specific performance. In that regard, however, the party seeking specific performance still must demonstrate the requisite elements for entitlement to equitable relief, including that damages were not an adequate remedy, despite the existence of the liquidated damages clause.

Model Case:

John Harrell, who had fifteen years of experience in the jewelry business working for several companies, decided to open his own jewelry store. He acquired a small tract of land in a developing commercial area of the city and entered into a contract with Parsons' Engineering Company to construct a building for the store.

Harrell wanted the building to be completed by September 1 in order to take advantage of the historically strong sales which take place at the end of the year. Accordingly, the parties placed a clause in their construction agreement which provided that Parsons agreed to pay, as liquidated damages, a sum in the amount of $200 per day for every day that the completion of the building was delayed past September 1. Correspondingly, Parsons would receive a bonus payment from Harrell of $1,000 if the building was finished by August 15.

A court would probably uphold the validity of the stipulated damages provision because the loss of business which Harrell would sustain by a delay in opening the new business would be difficult to estimate. Therefore, a liquidated damages clause serves the function of compensating where proof of damages would be otherwise uncertain. Harrell also would need to show a reasonable basis for arriving at the $200 per day figure as a good faith pre-estimate of the anticipated harm which would potentially result from a breach by Parsons. Mathematical precision would not be required; rather the inquiry is whether the stipulated amount was objectively reasonable as a substitute for performance or had an oppressive character to compel performance.

BOYLE v. PETRIE STORES CORPORATION

136 Misc.2d 380, 518 N.Y.S.2d 854 (1985).

GREENFIELD, JUSTICE.

This is an action for wrongful discharge, but unlike many such cases which have besieged the courts of late, this one involves an executive employee who in fact had a carefully worked out written contract, and now, claiming a breach, insists on a literal application of that contract.

* * * Under the contract, Boyle was to become President and Chief Executive Officer of the corporation as of Nov. 1, 1982. * * * The Board approved the agreement, which was duly executed, and amended the corporate by-laws to reflect the fact that Milton Petrie, the Chairman of the Board, was to preside at director's meetings, but that he was no longer to be the Chief Executive Officer. Boyle, as Chief Executive Officer and President was, subject to the control of the Board, to "have general supervision over the business of the corporation."

* * *

Boyle in fact reported for work at the corporate headquarters in Secaucus on Nov. 8, 1982. While Boyle informed the other Petrie executives that he was now the Chief Executive Officer, and they should take their directions from him, Petrie continued to give operating directions just as he always had. * * *

On January 6, a formal real estate meeting and review, with Petrie present, was held. As various items were taken up, Petrie said, "leave it to me, I'll take care of it." When Boyle pressed him for details, Petrie repeated, "I'll take care of it". At the conclusion of the meeting Petrie confronted Boyle in his office. With mounting anger, he said, "Where the hell do you get off to question my authority on these leases and embarrass me in front of all my organization?" He told Boyle he was moving in too fast. Boyle challenged him, and impertinently replied, "If you didn't have 63 percent of this stock, I would take you to the Board of Directors and have you removed as Chairman." This was too much for Petrie. He exploded, "You're fired!"

A special meeting of the Board of Directors was held on January 13, 1983. * * * The Board did not discuss the terms of Boyle's employment agreement or ask to hear Mr. Boyle, but acceded to Mr. Petrie's demand that he be terminated effective immediately. Mr. Petrie retook the titles of Chief Executive Officer and President. A press release announced these changes and stated that "The reason for the change was due to policy differences on the way the business should be run."

Boyle had served but two months of his five year contract. Claiming that the contract had been improperly breached by Petrie Stores Corporation, he brought this action seeking recovery of over $2,000,000 as liquidated damages he is entitled to under the contract. * * *

The employment agreement is quite specific about the damages which are to be payable for termination other than for "material breach or just cause". Section 7(a) of the agreement provides that in the event of a termination other than for "material breach or just cause", the corporation is to pay "in one lump sum the amounts otherwise payable to Employee ... discounted to present value at the rate of 15 percent per annum." Calculation of the lump sum payable thus works out to $1,439,352.44 in lieu of lost salary, and $166,689.39 in guaranteed bonus claims, for a total of $1,606,041.83.

While this is a very substantial figure to pay a man who was on the job for 8 weeks, and was fired within days after his orientation period, when he tried to take over the reins of management, we are dealing here with a provision for liquidated damages designed to provide some precision for the calculation of otherwise speculative damages.

Parties may properly agree to a dollar figure representing the injuries they agree the plaintiff would sustain if the contract were breached. [Citation.] So long as the liquidated damages provisions are neither unconscionable nor contrary to public policy, they will be enforced as written by a court. [Citations.]

Defendant contends that the contractual provisions for liquidated damages are, in fact, a penalty. Stipulated contractual damages will be considered a penalty only if the amount provided for is clearly disproportionate to the actual loss, and as an *in terrorem* effort to assure performance regardless of economic loss. Those cases urged by the defendant as standing for the proposition that stipulated damages such as those here involved should be considered a "penalty", are readily distinguishable. Since courts have traditionally, from the time of the Merchant of Venice, viewed a forfeiture out of all proportion to the breach of contract as an unenforceable penalty, our courts have attempted to strike out the clear penalties while upholding agreement which clarified amounts of damage which could otherwise be in dispute. * * * In this case, a termination of Boyle's employment contract could result in damages well over $500,000 a year, and the parties could reasonably agree that instead of litigating the question of damages after the event, which would leave uncertainties such as the employee's efforts to mitigate damages by securing other employment, and the question as to how long the other employment might last, and whether the benefits were comparable, they could reasonably agree beforehand as to what damages would be payable. The amounts fixed do not exceed the total compensation provided in the five year contract.

Both parties to the contract were sophisticated and were represented by able counsel. This is a factor to be taken into consideration in determining whether one side is now exacting an unconscionable penalty. [Citations.]

It is to be recalled that Boyle was aware of Mr. Petrie's mercurial reputation, and wanted some concrete assurances of security before giving up the well-paid position he had worked himself up to with

Federated Stores. An involuntary discharge from Petrie Stores would cast a considerable shadow on Mr. Boyle's reputation as a young super-achieving executive, and possibly diminish his prospects for the future. The agreement was carefully negotiated at arms-length by reputable attorneys for both parties, and it was clearly understood that a precipi-tate firing of Mr. Boyle could result in very substantial contractual damages. The fact that the parties agreed to limit liability to $2,100,000 excluding stock options demonstrates a realization that without such a ceiling the actual damages could go even higher.

* * *

The lump sum payment provision here clearly was a liquidated damages provision and not a penalty. In the bargaining neither party had the ability to overreach the other. The sum provided for was not disproportionate to the damages which could be incurred. * * * The damage provisions are valid and enforceable pursuant to their terms.

The fact that subsequent to his termination Boyle took a position with another corporation—General Mills—as one of six executive vice-presidents rather than as Chief Executive Officer, does not serve to mitigate the liquidated damages.

Once the parties have provided for valid liquidated damages, the sum payable becomes fixed and there is no further inquiry to be made as to possible mitigation by subsequent employment. * * *

Here, a formula was set forth to calculate damages without regard to subsequent extrinsic facts. At the time the parties could not know how long plaintiff would be unemployed if terminated. We still do not know how long the subsequent employment will continue, or whether it will give the same net to Mr. Boyle as his Petrie Stores contract over a 5 year span, since his subsequent General Mills contract is terminable at will. We need not wait to the conclusion of the five year contract period to find out what Boyle's aggregate loss of earnings might be, because the agreement requires the liquidated damages to be paid "forthwith". That clearly contemplates that damages were to be fixed as of the date of termination, regardless of events thereafter.

* * * [Judgment for the plaintiff.]

---

1. The law of liquidated damages reflects a tension between con-flicting goals. It is socially desirable for parties to fix damages in the event of breach when the amount bears a reasonable proportion to the probable loss and the actual loss is difficult to estimate with precision. Such a provision, however, should not have the effect of deterring breach through compulsion because of the potential high economic loss. *See* Leasing Service Corp. v. Justice, 673 F.2d 70, 73 (2d Cir.1982) (liqui-dated damages may serve useful purpose, but cannot have an *in terrorem*

effect and the promisee may reap a windfall well in excess of his just compensation).

2. A threshold requirement for enforceability of a liquidated damages clause is that the terms must be expressly stated in the contract. *See* Abi, Inc. v. City of Los Angeles, 153 Cal.App.3d 669, 200 Cal.Rptr. 563 (1984) (city's claim to retain a developer's fee as liquidated damages not allowed because the contract did not effectively express such a designation). *See also* Polish American Machinery Corp. v. R.D. & D. Corp., 760 F.2d 507 (3d Cir.1985). Also, liquidated damages will not be awarded absent material breach of the contract. *See* Woodbridge Place Apts. v. Washington Square Capital, 965 F.2d 1429 (7th Cir.1992) (liquidated damages provision in loan commitment agreement unenforceable where borrower did not breach contract but rather failed to satisfy conditions precedent to funding of loan).

3. Whether a contractual provision is characterized as a valid liquidated damages clause or a penalty does not depend upon the label given by the parties. Southeastern Land Fund, Inc. v. Real Estate World, Inc., reprinted in Chapter 10, *supra*. A handful of courts, though, will give some weight to the terminology chosen by the parties as a factor in interpreting a provision fixing damages. Thus, in Zeppenfeld v. Morgan, 185 S.W.2d 898 (Mo.App.1945), the court recognized that the mere fact that the parties styled the sum "liquidated damages" was not conclusive of its character yet was considered very persuasive evidence to that effect.

4. Although labels do not control, the intention of the parties can be relevant. Some courts have considered the intentions of the parties as a criterion for enforcement in addition to the traditional two-prong test of reasonableness and difficulty in estimating damages. Higgs v. United States, 212 Ct.Cl. 146, 546 F.2d 373 (Ct.Cl.1976); Walter Motor Truck Co. v. South Dakota, 292 N.W.2d 321 (S.D.1980); Oldis v. Grosse–Rhode, 35 Colo.App. 46, 528 P.2d 944 (1974); ADP–Financial Computer Services v. First National Bank, 703 F.2d 1261 (11th Cir.1983).

The prevailing view, though, rejects the intention element as being surplusage. *See* Wilmington Housing Authority v. Pan Builders, Inc., 665 F.Supp. 351 (D.Del.1987) (the intention criterion adds nothing because it validates a provision only if the other two criteria are met and invalidates a provision only when they are not). Koenings v. Joseph Schlitz Brewing Co., 126 Wis.2d 349, 377 N.W.2d 593 (1985) (courts should consider the circumstances which give rise to the formation of the contract rather than the intent of the parties). *See also* Restatement (Second) of Contracts § 356 comment C; Williston, Contracts § 272 (3d ed. 1961); Corbin, Contracts § 1058 (1964); Clarkson, Miller & Muris, Liquidated Damages v. Penalties: Sense or Nonsense, 1978 Wis.L.Rev. 351.

5. Consider the common practice of college campuses to restrict parking rights and to impose a fine system for violations. The fines typically increase with the number of violations. Are these fines valid as

liquidated damages? *See* Donow v. Board of Trustees of Southern Illinois University, 21 Ill.App.3d 139, 314 N.E.2d 704 (1974) (University could not withhold parking fines from salaries as liquidated damages because no sum certain was stipulated for specific offenses and fines were penalties to compel performance or to punish for offenses rather than to be paid in lieu of performance).

6. Why was Boyle's subsequent employment irrelevant? Consider also Musman v. Modern Deb, Inc., 50 A.D.2d 761, 377 N.Y.S.2d 17 (1975), where the plaintiff sued for wrongful termination of a five year employment contract. The contract provided that he would receive full compensation and bonuses to the end of the five year term if he was terminated without cause. The trial court reduced the amount of liquidated damages by the amount plaintiff earned from other employment. This deduction was reversed on appeal and the court restored the full amount of liquidated damages without deduction. Why should a liquidated damages clause remove the ordinary rule requiring an employee to mitigate damages?

7. In Space Master International, Inc. v. City of Worcester, 940 F.2d 16 (1st Cir.1991), a contractor entered into an agreement to install modular classroom buildings at city school sites. The contract specified that if the contractor delayed performance beyond a certain date, the city was entitled to retain $250 per day plus $100 per day per site as liquidated damages. When the contractor failed to meet the stated deadline to build the classrooms, children were forced to attend classes in hallways, gymnasiums, auditoriums and libraries. Morale among teachers, students and administrators suffered as a result of the dislocation. The court upheld the validity of the liquidated damages clause, observing that the injury to the public was inherently difficult to quantify in monetary terms.

TRUCK RENT–A–CENTER, INC. v. PURITAN FARMS 2ND, INC.

41 N.Y.2d 420, 361 N.E.2d 1015, 393 N.Y.S.2d 365 (1977).

Jasen, Judge. * * *

Defendant Puritan Farms 2nd, Inc. (Puritan), was in the business of furnishing milk and milk products to customers through home delivery. In January, 1969, Puritan leased a fleet of 25 new milk delivery trucks from plaintiff Truck Rent–A–Center for a term of seven years commencing January 15, 1970. Under the provisions of a truck lease and service agreement entered into by the parties, the plaintiff was to supply the trucks and make all necessary repairs. Puritan was to pay an agreed upon weekly rental fee. * * * The lessee was granted the right to purchase the trucks, at any time after 12 months following commencement of the lease, by paying to the lessor the amount then due and owing on the bank loan, plus an additional $100 per truck purchased.

Article 16 of the lease agreement provided that if the agreement should terminate prior to expiration of the term of the lease as a result of the lessee's breach, the lessor would be entitled to damages, "liquidated for all purposes", in the amount of all rentals that would have come due from the date of termination to the date of normal expiration of the term less the "re-rental value" of the vehicles, which was set at 50% of the rentals that would have become due. In effect, the lessee would be obligated to pay the lessor, as a consequence of breach, one half of all rentals that would have become due had the agreement run its full course. The agreement recited that, in arriving at the settled amount of damages, "the parties hereto have considered, among other factors, Lessor's substantial initial investment in purchasing or reconditioning for Lessee's service the demised motor vehicles, the uncertainty of Lessor's ability to re-enter the said vehicles, the costs to Lessor during any period the vehicles may remain idle until re-rented, or if sold, the uncertainty of the sales price and its possible attendant loss. The parties have also considered, among other factors, in so liquidating the said damages, Lessor's saving in expenditures for gasoline, oil and other service items."

[After three years, the lessee Puritan terminated the lease agreement. Puritan complained that the lessor had failed to repair and maintain the trucks as provided in the lease agreement. The lessor sued for payment of the liquidated damages on the grounds that the lessee had breached the contract. The defendant lessee counterclaimed for return of the security deposit on the basis that the lessor had breached the contract. At the time of termination of the agreement, the plaintiff owed $45,134.17 on the outstanding bank loan.]

* * * The home milk delivery business was on the decline and plaintiff's president testified that efforts to either re-rent or sell the truck fleet to other dairies had not been successful. Even with modifications in the trucks, such as the removal of the milk racks and a change in the floor of the trucks, it was not possible to lease the trucks to other industries, although a few trucks were subsequently sold.

* * *

At the close of the trial, the court found, based on the evidence it found to be credible, that plaintiff had substantially performed its obligations under the lease and that defendant was not justified in terminating the agreement. Further, the court held that the provision for liquidated damages was reasonable and represented a fair estimate of actual damages which would be difficult to ascertain precisely. * * * The court calculated that plaintiff would have been entitled to $177,-355.20 in rent for the period remaining in the lease and, in accordance with the liquidated damages provision, awarded plaintiff half that amount, $88,677.60. * * *

* * * A liquidated damage provision has its basis in the principle of just compensation for loss. A clause which provides for an amount plainly disproportionate to real damage is not intended to provide fair compensation but to secure performance by the compulsion of the very disproportion. A promisor would be compelled, out of fear of economic

devastation, to continue performance and his promisee, in the event of default, would reap a windfall well above actual harm sustained. [Citations.] As was stated eloquently long ago, to permit parties, in their unbridled discretion, to utilize penalties as damages, "would lead to the most terrible oppression in pecuniary dealings." [Citations.]

The rule is now well established. A contractual provision fixing damages in the event of breach will be sustained if the amount liquidated bears a reasonable proportion to the probable loss and the amount of actual loss is incapable or difficult of precise estimation. [Citations.] If, however, the amount fixed is plainly or grossly disproportionate to the probable loss, the provision calls for a penalty and will not be enforced. [Citations.] In interpreting a provision fixing damages, it is not material whether the parties themselves have chosen to call the provision one for "liquidated damages", as in this case, or have styled it as a penalty. [Citations.] Such an approach would put too much faith in form and too little in substance. Similarly, the agreement should be interpreted as of the date of its making and not as of the date of its breach. [Citation.]

In applying these principles to the case before us, we conclude that the amount stipulated by the parties as damages bears a reasonable relation to the amount of probable actual harm and is not a penalty. Hence, the provision is enforceable and the order of the Appellate Division should be affirmed.

Looking forward from the date of the lease, the parties could reasonably conclude, as they did, that there might not be an actual market for the sale or re-rental of these specialized vehicles in the event of the lessee's breach. To be sure, plaintiff's lost profit could readily be measured by the amount of the weekly rental fee. However, it was permissible for the parties, in advance, to agree that the re-rental or sale value of the vehicles would be 50% of the weekly rental. Since there was uncertainty as to whether the trucks could be re-rented or sold, the parties could reasonably set, as they did, the value of such mitigation at 50% of the amount the lessee was obligated to pay for rental of the trucks. This could take into consideration the fact that, after being used by the lessee, the vehicles would no longer be "shiny, new trucks", but would be used, possibly battered, trucks, whose value would have declined appreciably. The parties also considered the fact that, although plaintiff, in the event of Puritan's breach, might be spared repair and maintenance costs necessitated by Puritan's use of the trucks, plaintiff would have to assume the cost of storing and maintaining trucks idled by Puritan's refusal to use them. Further, it was by no means certain, at the time of the contract, that lessee would peacefully return the trucks to the lessor after lessee had breached the contract.

* * * [T]he existence of the option clause has absolutely no bearing on the validity of the discrete, liquidated damages provision. The lessee could have elected to purchase the trucks but elected not to do so. In fact, the lessee's letter of termination made a point of the fact that the lessee did not want to purchase the trucks. The reality is that the lessee

sought, by its wrongful termination of the lease, to evade all obligations to the plaintiff, whether for rent or for the agreed upon purchase price. Its effort to do so failed. That lessee could have made a better bargain for itself by purchasing the trucks for $48,134.17 pursuant to the option, instead of paying $92,341.79 in damages for wrongful breach of the lease is not availing to it now. Although the lessee might now wish, with the benefit of hindsight, that it had purchased the trucks rather than default on its lease obligations, the simple fact is that it did not do so.

We attach no significance to the fact that the liquidated damages clause appears on the preprinted form portion of the agreement. The agreement was fully negotiated and the provisions of the form, in many other respects, were amended. There is no indication of any disparity of bargaining power or of unconscionability. The provision for liquidated damages related reasonably to potential harm that was difficult to estimate and did not constitute a disguised penalty. * * *

[Affirmed.]

---

1. The traditional common law test for upholding a liquidated damages clause is that the potential damages which might accrue as a result of a breach must be uncertain and difficult to ascertain. What should "difficulty" mean: Difficulty in forecasting all possible damages that may be caused by breach? Difficulty of producing proof of damages? Difficulty of proving causally the link between the breach and the loss? Difficulty of meeting the foreseeability limitations for contract damages? Difficulty from lack of any standardized measure of the damages for a certain breach? *See* an excellent analysis in Macneil, Power of Contract and Agreed Remedies, 47 Cornell L.Q. 495, 502 (1962).

2. Although courts have tended to apply sparingly the rule that potential damages must be uncertain to enforce liquidated damages clauses, the rule has determined some cases. A case illustrating the force of the rule is Semico, Inc. v. Pipefitters Local No. 195, 538 S.W.2d 273 (Tex.Civ.App.1976). A clause in a collective bargaining agreement provided that if the employer failed to make certain specified union contributions, the employer would be required to pay 15% of the contribution total for each month the payments were delinquent. The court held that the provision was invalid as a penalty because damages for the nonpayment of money could easily be calculated and therefore presented no difficulty in estimation at the time of contracting.

Why should it matter if the damages in the event of breach are difficult to ascertain? Even if the damages are exactly and readily foreseen, why not let the parties agree to the amount in advance? Is there any difference between such a liquidated damages provision and a settlement before trial? *See* McCormick, Damages § 148, at 605 (1935).

3. California has codified the uncertainty element regarding liquidated damages by statute, which provides in pertinent part:

> * * * a provision in a contract liquidating damages for the breach of the contract is void except that the parties to such a contract may agree therein upon an amount which shall be presumed to be the amount of damage sustained by a breach thereof, when, from the nature of the case, it would be impracticable or extremely difficult to fix the actual damage.

California Civil Code § 1671(d). An example of the operation of the California rule may be found in Cook v. King Manor and Convalescent Hospital, 40 Cal.App.3d 782, 115 Cal.Rptr. 471 (1974). A seller sought to recover the stipulated amount of $25,000 for a buyer's breach of a contract to purchase certain real property for approximately $2,000,000. The liquidated damages provision recited that it would be "extremely difficult and impractical to determine the amount and extent of detriment to seller" if the buyer failed to perform its obligations. The court held that the provision constituted a penalty because the seller had failed to plead and prove that the potential damages contemplated by the parties in the event of a breach were in fact difficult of estimation. *See generally* Sweet, Liquidated Damages in California, 60 Calif.L.Rev. 84 (1972).

4. The Restatement (Second) of Contracts § 356 comment b * approaches the uncertainty of loss factor with a flexible test:

> The greater the difficulty either of proving that loss has occurred or of establishing its amount with the requisite certainty (*see* § 351), the easier it is to show that the amount fixed is reasonable. To the extent that there is uncertainty as to the harm, the estimate of the court or jury may not accord with the principle of compensation any more than does the advance estimate of the parties. A determination whether the amount fixed is a penalty turns on a combination of these two factors. If the difficulty of proof of loss is slight, less latitude is allowed in that approximation. If, to take an extreme case, it is clear that no loss at all has occurred, a provision fixing a substantial sum as damages is unenforceable.

5. The Uniform Commercial Code test in § 2–718(1) has reduced difficulty of loss from being treated as a separate factor to serving as one consideration regarding the reasonableness of the clause:

> Damages for breach by either party may be liquidated in the agreement but only at an amount which is reasonable in the light of the anticipated or actual harm caused by the breach, the difficulties of proof of loss, and the inconvenience or nonfeasibility of otherwise obtaining an adequate remedy.

The U.C.C. approach has been described by one pair of commentators as a continuum: The latitude of the contracting parties in setting damages for breach increases with the degree of uncertainty facing them. Goetz & Scott, Liquidated Damages, Penalties and the Just Compensation Principle: Some Notes on an Enforcement Model and a Theory of Efficient Breach, 77 Colum.L.Rev. 554, 560 (1977).

6. A valid liquidated damages provision must reflect a *reasonable estimate* of the uncertain damages in the event of breach. In Ryder Truck Lines, Inc. v. Goren Equipment Co., 576 F.Supp. 1348 (N.D.Ga. 1983), the seller of used diesel engines sought to recover $281,250 as liquidated damages for the buyer's breach of contract. The court found that the extent and amount of potential damages were difficult to estimate because at the time of contracting the parties could not accurately calculate the costs of repossession or resale price of the engines. The court concluded, however, that the stipulated amount was a penalty because it was not a reasonable pre-estimate of the probable loss in the event of a breach. Since the liquidated sum actually exceeded the total amount due under the contract and it appeared that the figure was chosen arbitrarily, the clause was held void and unenforceable.

In Southpace Properties, Inc. v. Acquisition Group, 5 F.3d 500 (11th Cir.1993), the court held that a stipulated damages clause in a real estate listing agreement which provided that the broker was entitled to full 6% commission plus costs and expenses if the property owner breached the agreement was void under Alabama law as a penalty. The court found that the damages provision was not a reasonable pre-breach estimate of the probable loss because the broker would actually recover *more* if the contract were breached than if fully performed. *Also see* A.V. Consultants, Inc. v. Barnes, 978 F.2d 996 (7th Cir.1992) (liquidated damages clause unenforceable as a penalty where provision would give party expected profit plus the value of its services).

7. What if the stipulated amount of damages for breach of a contract is considered an unreasonably low estimate of the anticipated harm? Some courts focus on the time of contracting to assess the reasonableness of the agreed amount and the uncertainty of damages because that approach is consistent with the traditional test for liquidated damages.

In Better Food Markets v. American Dist. Tel. Co., 40 Cal.2d 179, 253 P.2d 10 (1953), for example, the plaintiff sought actual damages of $35,930 to compensate for merchandise stolen as a result of the defendant security company's failure to properly transmit burglar alarm signals in accordance with its contractual duties. The court nonetheless limited the plaintiff's recovery to the contractually agreed amount of only $50. Following the statutory provision regarding liquidated damages, California Civil Code § 1671, the court found it would have been impracticable or extremely difficult to fix the actual damage in the event of a breach. The court reasoned that the parties had exercised their business judgment that the actual loss resulting from a breach might be greater or lesser than the $50 sum, and therefore it also satisfied the requirement that the sum must bear a reasonable relationship to the losses contemplated.

8.   Unreasonably low stipulated damages for breach of contract may reflect overreaching by the favored party.   A defense of overreaching requires an inquiry into unconscionability rather than the examination of unreasonableness that is necessary to invalidate a liquidated damages clause.   *See* Wedner v. Fidelity Security Systems, Inc., 228 Pa.Super. 67, 307 A.2d 429 (1973).

9.   Distinguish a contractual provision that *limits* damages from a provision for liquidated damages.   For example, in Tharalson v. Pfizer Genetics, Inc., 728 F.2d 1108 (8th Cir.1984), the buyer's damages for the seller's breach of warranty was limited to the sale price of seed under a limitation of damages provision in the contract of sale.   The court relied upon U.C.C. § 2–719(3) which provides, in part, "consequential damages may be limited or excluded unless the limitation or exclusion is unconscionable."   The court noted that liquidated damages provisions usually threaten unjustifiably large recoveries, such that the judicial role is to contain them with a test of reasonableness.   There is an opposite concern with limitation of damages provision;   the danger is unjustifiably small recoveries.   The official comments to Uniform Commercial Code § 2–718 indicate that where the concern is unreasonably small recoveries the proper test is unconscionability.

LAKE RIVER CORP. v. CARBORUNDUM CO.

769 F.2d 1284 (7th Cir.1985).

POSNER, CIRCUIT JUDGE.

This diversity suit between Lake River Corporation and Carborundum Company requires us to consider questions of Illinois commercial law, and in particular to explore the fuzzy line between penalty clauses and liquidated-damages clauses.

Carborundum manufactures "Ferro Carbo," an abrasive powder used in making steel.   To serve its midwestern customers better, Carborundum made a contract with Lake River by which the latter agreed to provide distribution services in its warehouse in Illinois.   Lake River would receive Ferro Carbo in bulk from Carborundum, "bag" it, and ship the bagged product to Carborundum's customers.   The Ferro Carbo would remain Carborundum's property until delivered to the customers.

[Carborundum insisted that Lake River install a new bagging system to handle the contract.   In order to be sure of being able to recover the cost of the new system and make a profit, Lake River insisted on a minimum-quantity guarantee and an agreement that if Carborundum had not shipped the minimum quantity in three years, Lake River would receive the full contract price minus the amount already shipped.]

* * *

After the contract was signed in 1979, the demand for domestic steel, and with it the demand for Ferro Carbo, plummeted, and Carborundum failed to ship the guaranteed amount. When the contract expired late in 1982, Carborundum had shipped only 12,000 of the 22,500 tons it had guaranteed. Lake River had bagged the 12,000 tons and had billed Carborundum for this bagging, and Carborundum had paid, but by virtue of the formula in the minimum-guarantee clause Carborundum still owed Lake River $241,000—the contract price of $533,000 if the full amount of Ferro Carbo had been shipped, minus what Carborundum had paid for the bagging of the quantity it had shipped.

* * *

Lake River brought this suit for $241,000, which it claims as liquidated damages. * * *

The hardest issue in the case is whether the formula in the minimum-guarantee clause imposes a penalty for breach of contract or is merely an effort to liquidate damages. Deep as the hostility to penalty clauses runs in the common law, we still might be inclined to question, if we thought ourselves free to do so, whether a modern court should refuse to enforce a penalty clause where the signator is a substantial corporation, well able to avoid improvident commitments. Penalty clauses provide an earnest of performance. The clause here enhanced Carborundum's credibility in promising to ship the minimum amount guaranteed by showing that it was willing to pay the full contract price even if it failed to ship anything. On the other side it can be pointed out that by raising the cost of a breach of contract to the contract breaker, a penalty clause increases the risk to his other creditors; increases (what is the same thing and more, because bankruptcy imposes "deadweight" social costs) the risk of bankruptcy; and could amplify the business cycle by increasing the number of bankruptcies in bad times, which is when contracts are most likely to be broken. But since little effort is made to prevent businessmen from assuming risks, these reasons are no better than makeweights.

A better argument is that a penalty clause may discourage efficient as well as inefficient breaches of contract. Suppose a breach would cost the promisee $12,000 in actual damages but would yield the promisor $20,000 in additional profits. Then there would be a net social gain from breach. After being fully compensated for his loss the promisee would be no worse off than if the contract had been performed, while the promisor would be better off by $8,000. But now suppose the contract contains a penalty clause under which the promisor if he breaks his promise must pay the promisee $25,000. The promisor will be discouraged from breaking the contract, since $25,000, the penalty, is greater than $20,000, the profits of the breach; and a transaction that would have increased value will be foregone.

On this view, since compensatory damages should be sufficient to deter inefficient breaches (that is, breaches that cost the victim more than the gain to the contract breaker), penal damages could have no effect other than to deter some efficient breaches. But this overlooks the earlier point that the willingness to agree to a penalty clause is a way of making the promisor and his promise credible and may therefore be essential to inducing some value-maximizing contracts to be made. It also overlooks the more important point that the parties (always assuming they are fully competent) will, in deciding whether to include a penalty clause in their contract, weigh the gains against the costs—costs that include the possibility of discouraging an efficient breach somewhere down the road—and will include the clause only if the benefits exceed those costs as well as all other costs.

On this view the refusal to enforce penalty clauses is (at best) paternalistic—and it seems odd that courts should display parental solicitude for large corporations. But however this may be, we must be on guard to avoid importing our own ideas of sound public policy into an area where our proper judicial role is more than usually deferential. The responsibility for making innovations in the common law of Illinois rests with the courts of Illinois, and not with the federal courts in Illinois. And like every other state, Illinois, untroubled by academic skepticism of the wisdom of refusing to enforce penalty clauses against sophisticated promisors, continues steadfastly to insist on the distinction between penalties and liquidated damages. * * *

Mindful that Illinois courts resolve doubtful cases in favor of classification as a penalty * * * we conclude that the damage formula in this case is a penalty and not a liquidation of damages, because it is designed always to assure Lake River more than its actual damages. The formula—full contract price minus the amount already invoiced to Carborundum—is invariant to the gravity of the breach. When a contract specifies a single sum in damages for any and all breaches even though it is apparent that all are not of the same gravity, the specification is not a reasonable effort to estimate damages; and when in addition the fixed sum greatly exceeds the actual damages likely to be inflicted by a minor breach, its character as a penalty become unmistakable. [Citations.] This case is within the gravitational field of these principles even though the minimum-guarantee clause does not fix a single sum as damages.

* * *

The fact that the damage formula is invalid does not deprive Lake River of a remedy. The parties did not contract explicitly with reference to the measure of damages if the agreed-on damage formula was invalidated, but all this means is that the victim of the breach is entitled to his common law damages. *See, e.g.*, Restatement, Second, Contracts § 356, comment a (1981). In this case that would be the unpaid contract price of $241,000 minus the costs that Lake River saved by not having to complete the contract (the variable costs on the other 45 percent of the

Ferro Carbo that it never had to bag). The case must be remanded to the district judge to fix these damages.

* * *

AFFIRMED IN PART, REVERSED IN PART, AND REMANDED.

---

1. The principal focus in determining the validity of a liquidated damages clause is the reasonableness of the relationship that the stipulated damages bear to the potential harm which the parties contemplate may accrue as a result of a breach. Another question concerns what relevance the provable actual damages have when measured against the liquidated amount. The Restatement (Second) of Contracts § 356 and Uniform Commercial Code § 2–718(1) both provide that the reasonableness of the liquidated damages clause may be shown either by its proportionality to the anticipated or actual harm. Thus, the amount fixed may be considered valid if it approximates either alternative. *See* Reliance Ins. v. Utah Dept. of Transp., 858 P.2d 1363, 1367 (Utah 1993) (Whether an amount constitutes a reasonable forecast is determined by reference to the time of contract formation, not the date of breach).

2. What if the liquidated sum is characterized as a reasonable approximation of the contemplated losses but the proof of actual harm is significantly less? Most courts have held that the liquidated amount must satisfy only one of the alternative tests, not both. Accordingly, evidence of the actual losses resulting from the breach would be considered irrelevant, assuming damages could reasonably be anticipated at the time of contracting. Southwest Engineering Co. v. United States, 341 F.2d 998 (8th Cir.1965); Frick Co. v. Rubel Corp., 62 F.2d 765 (2d Cir.1933); Sun Printing & Publishing Ass'n v. Moore, 183 U.S. 642, 22 S.Ct. 240, 46 L.Ed. 366 (1902); United States v. Bethlehem Steel Co., 205 U.S. 105, 27 S.Ct. 450, 51 L.Ed. 731 (1907).

The justification for the enforceability of a liquidated damages clause despite the lack of actual damages has been predicated on freedom of contract principles:

> Courts have now become strongly inclined to allow parties to make their own contracts, and to carry out their intentions, even when it would result in the recovery of an amount stated as liquidated damages, upon proof of the violation of the contract, and without proof of the damages actually sustained.

United States v. Bethlehem Steel Co., 205 U.S. 105, 119, 27 S.Ct. 450, 455, 51 L.Ed. 731 (1907).

For example, in In re Lion Overall Co., 55 F.Supp. 789 (S.D.N.Y. 1943), *aff'd sub nom.* United States v. Walkof, 144 F.2d 75 (2d Cir.1944), the government sought enforcement of a liquidated damages clause for a contractor's failure to deliver clothing for soldiers in a timely manner. The contract recited that the stipulated damages for each day's delay were necessary because the actual damages which the government might sustain as a result of delays were impossible to calculate. The court upheld as reasonable the $20,000 liquidated damages amount in relation to $53,000 as the total contract price for the goods, despite evidence that the government actually incurred an excess cost of only $3.56 as a result of the breach. The court concluded that the only relevant time to evaluate the reasonableness of the clause was when the contract was entered and that the stipulated damages were "not out of all proportion to any possible loss."

3. Certainly to some extent courts may be influenced by public interest considerations to give particular deference to the validity of liquidated damages provisions in government contracts. *See generally* Gant & Breslauer, Liquidated Damages in Federal Government Contracts, 47 B.U.L.Rev. 71 (1967); Note, The Use and Abuse of Liquidated Damages in Federal Defense Contracts: An Analysis, 8 Okla. City U.L.Rev. 261 (1983); Peckar, Liquidated Damages in Federal Construction Contracts: Time for a New Approach, 5 Pub.Cont.L.J. 129 (1972). Thus, the court in In re Lion Overall Co., 55 F.Supp. 789, 791 (S.D.N.Y. 1943) stated:

> The contract was made for an article of military equipment for our troops at a time when the war clouds from Europe were gathering ominously about this country and when it could reasonably be anticipated, certainly by the Army and Navy Departments, that sooner or later we might be embroiled in the conflict. While there were others in the country who were manufacturing similar garments, what damage might result from a delayed delivery could not be ascertained with accuracy. In any event, the agreement was made without any overreaching or fraud, and as an obvious spur to prompt performance.

4. The validation of a liquidated damages clause as reasonably proportionate to the anticipated harm but significantly disproportionate to the provable actual losses is not limited to the context of government contracts. For instance, in Robbins v. Finlay, 645 P.2d 623 (Utah 1982), the court held that an employer was entitled to recover $5,000 as liquidated damages for an employee's breach of a covenant not to misuse customer leads even though the employer had not introduced any direct evidence of actual losses incurred and had shown that only five potential customers were involved.

In contrast, some courts have held that evidence of little or no actual losses may invalidate a liquidated damages clause as a penalty even if the stipulated amount was otherwise reasonably related to the anticipated harm. For example, in Gorco Construction Co. v. Stein, 256 Minn. 476, 99 N.W.2d 69 (1959), the court determined that a contract provision which designated damages in the amount of 15% of the total contract price to cover expenses for advertising, labor, equipment, and commissions was invalid where the plaintiff did not prove any actual loss because of the breach. Similarly, in S.O.G.–San Ore–Gardner v. Missouri Pacific Railroad, 658 F.2d 562, 570 (8th Cir.1981), the court invalidated a clause which stipulated $600 per day liquidated damages to cover estimated losses from delayed performance where the party asserting the claim sustained no actual damages from the breach.

5.   A liquidated damages clause which provides for payment of the sum to the non-breaching party in the event of a breach of covenants that have varying degrees of importance typically has been invalidated as an unreasonable forecast of the anticipated harm.   McCormick, Damages § 151 (1935);   Corbin, Contracts § 1066 (1964).   Thus, a liquidated damages clause which fixes a payment of $200 per day for late delivery in the shipment of goods may be justifiable as an appropriate compensation for the contemplated disruption in the purchaser's business operations.   However, the $200 figure may be considered invalid as a penalty if sought by the seller for a breach of a covenant requiring certain insurance for the goods.   In Coe v. Thermasol, Ltd., 615 F.Supp. 316, 320 (W.D.N.C.1985), though, the court upheld the enforceability of a liquidated damages clause even though it could be triggered by a breach of several covenants because the covenants were "interdependent and call for acts with one primary purpose."

6.   For additional commentary on liquidated damages see the following references: Warren, Formal and Operating Rules under Common Law and Code, 30 U.C.L.A.L.Rev. (1983); Linenberger, Liquidated Damages in the Sale of Goods, 14; Clarkson, Miller & Muris, Liquidated Damages v. Penalties: Sense or Nonsense, 1978 Wis.L.Rev. 351; Goetz and Scott, Liquidated Damages, Penalties and the Just Compensation Principle: Some Notes on an Enforcement Model and a Theory of Efficient Breach, 77 Colum.L.Rev. 554 (1977); Sweet, Liquidated Damages in California, 60 Calif.L.Rev. 84 (1972); Farnsworth, Legal Remedies for Breach of Contract, 70 Colum.L.Rev. 1145 (1970); Macneil, Power of Contract and Agreed Remedies, 47 Cornell L.Q. 495 (1962); Dunbar, Drafting the Liquidated Damage Clause—When and How, 20 Ohio St.L.J. 221 (1959); Lloyd, Penalties and Forfeitures, 29 Harv. L.Rev. 117 (1915).

B.   DISTRESS DAMAGES

Judicial reluctance to award damages for mental distress has been reflected in both substantive and remedial law.   Substantive law restrictions appear when the plaintiff suffers mental distress in the absence of other injury.   In tort claims this issue arises frequently when a plaintiff is distressed by witnessing an accident involving a loved one, or when a plaintiff is terrorized by a situation threatening serious injury but none results.

In contract, a party may suffer distress if a breach is anticipated but does not occur.   If, for example, a photographic studio has promised to deliver wedding photos on Wednesday, and delivery does occur on Wednesday, there is no contract breach.   The couple may be greatly distressed, however, if the studio indicated on Monday that the photos could not be located and may be lost. Timely location and delivery by Wednesday fulfills the contract, but the couple will have suffered non-compensable distress for two days.

The general rule is that a contract claim will not support distress damages, although there are a few exceptions. The general rule in tort is that there is no substantive claim for negligently caused distress without physical injury. There are also exceptions to the tort rule, the major one being the "witness" cases where plaintiffs suffer distress from viewing an injury to a loved one. Witness plaintiffs who were in the zone of danger of the accident may recover for distress in most states. Some states allow recovery to distressed witnesses even if the claimant is not in the zone of danger if certain specific criteria are met.

Remedial issues with distress damages arise when the plaintiff has established an action for the invasion of another interest, such as personal injury or breach of contract. When a plaintiff has established a claim for invasion of an interest in person or property, distress damages are recoverable as "parasitic damages." The limits on such recovery are governed by the remedial limitations of foreseeability and certainty. Foreseeable distress and its consequences are usually traced quite liberally in personal injury cases, whereas in fraud cases courts generally interpret foreseeability restrictively or prohibit such damages altogether.

Model Case:

Defendant Driver negligently lost control of the car and jumped the curb. A child who was riding a tricycle on the sidewalk was seriously injured. The child's parents were both near-by and witnessed the accident.

The child's personal injury damages will include the mental distress suffered as a result of this trauma. In most jurisdictions such distress is included in the instruction on pain and suffering. Sometimes courts will consider elements of the distress separately. If, for example, the child needed psychological counselling to overcome a phobia resulting from the accident, these damages would be in a separate instruction. The child's distress damages, including subsequent problems caused by the distress, are restricted only by foreseeability and certainty limitations. A subsequent teen-age suicide from the childhood trauma, for example, would not be compensable.

One of the parents witnessing the accident suffered a nervous breakdown with physical manifestations as a result of the experience. Many jurisdictions would allow a claim as a matter of substantive law, but only if this parent was in the "zone of danger" at the time of the accident. A few states would allow this action if the parent was just near-by yet outside the zone of danger.

The other parent who witnessed the accident suffered extreme distress but without any physical manifestations. The great majority of jurisdictions deny any action to this parent.

The parents would both be able to recover if the conduct of the driver was malicious rather than negligent. As a matter of substantive law, most states would allow claims by all these victims if the driver was aiming for the sidewalk to hurt this family.

CRINKLEY v. HOLIDAY INNS, INC.

844 F.2d 156 (4th Cir.1988).

PHILLIPS, CIRCUIT JUDGE:

This is a civil action in which various defendants associated with the Holiday Inns enterprise appeal from jury verdicts finding them liable for personal injuries inflicted by third persons upon the plaintiffs Crinkley, while the Crinkleys were guests in a Holiday Inn Motel. * * *

Sometime before the weekend of February 27–28, 1981, the Crinkleys decided to attend a function being held during that weekend at the Charlotte, North Carolina Civic Center. * * * [T]hey selected the Holiday Inn–Concord and reserved a room for the nights of February 27 and 28. The Holiday Inn–Concord is located some twenty-odd miles north of Charlotte, just off Highway 29, which runs directly south into downtown Charlotte, and Interstate 85, which runs to and around the northern edge of Charlotte.

During the approximately two weeks preceding the weekend of February 27, guests at several Charlotte area motels had been assaulted and robbed on the premises by a group later dubbed the "Motel Bandits" in media reports. The motels involved were located throughout the metropolitan Charlotte area, and many of them were located close to Interstate 85. The assistant manager of the Holiday Inn–Concord, Brian McRorie, was aware of the Motel Bandits from the various news media. He was contacted by several unidentified members of the local County Sheriff's Office who wanted to know if McRorie was aware of the Motel Bandits and what plans he had for security at the motel while the Motel Bandits were at large. Some of these officers also offered to serve for a fee as security guards during their off duty hours, a security measure that the motel had used in the past, but did not avail itself of in this instance.

As a result of this information, McRorie contacted Jim Van Over about the possibility of hiring security guards to patrol the motel. Van Over was the manager of the Holiday Inn on Woodlawn Road in Charlotte, and had some supervisory responsibility over the Holiday Inn–Concord as an employee of defendant Travelers Management Corporation (TRAVCO), the entity in operational control of the Holiday Inn–Concord. Van Over was also the president of the Metrolina Innkeepers Association and had been interviewed for a newspaper story covering the Motel Bandits. In that article, he noted that his hotel had added security personnel for night patrols. As to McRorie's requests for additional security at the Concord property, however, Van Over concluded that extra security measures were not justified. McRorie did instruct his employees to be particularly alert for anything suspicious and he periodically patrolled the premises on February 27, the last time being sometime between 8:00 and 8:30 p.m. The motel also continued its program to encourage local law enforcement personnel to frequent the premises by offering a free snack tray and discount meals in the restaurant though it did not employ any as security guards.

At approximately 8:00 p.m. on February 27, the Crinkleys arrived at the Holiday Inn–Concord. After spending a short time checking in, they parked their car in front of their room and began unloading their baggage. As James Crinkley was bringing in the last of their items, Sarah Crinkley, who was standing in the doorway to their room, noticed a man come around the corner of the motel and begin walking toward them. When the man reached the Crinkleys' room, he stopped and asked to speak with James Crinkley. Almost immediately, the man began trying to push the Crinkleys into their room. Despite James Crinkley's efforts to resist him, the man succeeded in getting the Crinkleys into their room. The man was armed with a gun, and once inside he beat James Crinkley, turned on the television and called for his accomplices. He was joined in the room by two men who again beat James Crinkley, bound and gagged him, and put a mattress on top of him. After going through the Crinkleys' possessions, the men approached Sarah Crinkley. They pushed her down and asked for her money and her engagement ring. When she told them that the ring would not come off, one of the men put a gun to her head and told her that if she did not take it off, he would "blow her brains out." She got the ring off and gave it to the men. They then bound and gagged her before fleeing. She was able to free herself after a short time. She removed the mattress and gag from her husband and called the front desk for help. The desk clerk notified the Cabarras County Sheriff's Office and a deputy arrived at the Crinkleys' room within minutes.

The Crinkleys were taken to an area hospital for emergency medical care. James Crinkley sustained multiple bruises to his head and upper body region, as well as a severely broken jaw. His broken jaw was wired, a condition which lasted approximately six weeks. Sarah Crinkley's subsequent condition was more complicated. Before the assault she was under a doctor's care for hypertension and obesity. In April of 1982—approximately fourteen months after the assault—she suffered a heart attack. A balloon angioplasty was performed in an effort to clear the blockage in her arteries, but was not successful. After consulting with her doctors, she opted for heart by-pass surgery to treat her condition. In addition to her cardiac problems, friends and family noted that Sarah Crinkley's personality changed drastically after the assault. She became fearful, anxious and withdrawn. Her activities also were observed to be much more restricted. In early 1984, she began seeking a psychiatrist who diagnosed her as suffering from posttraumatic stress disorder and major affective disorder.

The Crinkleys brought suit against several defendants variously associated with the Holiday Inn–Concord alleging, *inter alia,* that the defendants were negligent by providing them inadequate security and that such negligence was the proximate cause of their injuries.   * * *

At trial, the Crinkleys relied primarily on the testimony of Brian McRorie to show that the assault was reasonably foreseeable. They introduced testimony from a security expert that the measures in effect at the Holiday Inn–Concord were inadequate to deal with the potential threat. The main deficiencies identified were inadequate fencing around the perimeter of the property, and the lack of no trespassing signs and of any security patrols. Medical experts opined that both Sarah Crinkley's heart attack and her psychological problems were due to the stress she continued to experience in the wake of the assault.

Following the denial of motions for directed verdict, the jury returned verdicts in favor of the Crinkleys against all the defendants above identified, finding in special verdicts that the criminal acts were reasonably foreseeable by the motel owners and TRAVCO, that those defendants were negligent in providing inadequate security, and that such negligence caused the Crinkleys' injuries. Holiday Inns was found vicariously liable on the basis of apparent agency. The jury awarded Sarah Crinkley $400,000 and James Crinkley $100,000 in compensatory damages.

* * *

Defendants * * * contend that there was insufficient evidence to prove the necessary causal link between the assault and Sarah Crinkley's heart attack and psychological problems and her related medical expenses, so that these should not have been submitted to the jury as potentially compensable items of damage. * * *

We are satisfied that there was sufficient evidence of a causal link between the assault and Sarah Crinkley's heart attack and psychological condition to permit the jury to award damages related to those conditions.

* * * [N]umerous witnesses testified that Sarah Crinkley showed marked personality and emotional changes following the assault. Observations included notable anxiety, fearfulness, withdrawal, sadness, lack of activity, and an inability to work. This evidence is corroborative of the medical testimony that Sarah Crinkley was suffering from a significant amount of stress caused as a result of the assault.

The Crinkleys presented expert testimony that it was medically and scientifically plausible that significant stress could produce or accelerate atherosclerosis to the point of heart attack. Further, they removed the cause of Sarah Crinkley's own heart attack from the realm of conjecture by providing competent medical testimony from which the jury would conclude that the stress from the assault was the prime causal factor. They also produced expert testimony, that the assault produced severe stress in Sarah Crinkley.

We are also satisfied that the evidence was sufficient to connect the disputed medical expenses to the assault. As noted above, there was evidence that linked the assault to Sarah Crinkley's heart attack. The evidence also showed that the heart attack itself resulted from the occlusion of an artery in her heart and that the resulting added stress on her remaining "good" arteries necessitated invasive treatment. A balloon angioplasty was attempted as a means of opening the closed artery; however, the procedure was unsuccessful. The record indicates that after this unsuccessful treatment, by-pass surgery was recommended and ultimately performed. From this evidence alone, the jury could infer that all of Sarah Crinkley's heart-related medical procedures for which expenses were claimed were linked to the assault. The district court therefore properly submitted this damages issue to the jury.

* * *

WILKINSON, CIRCUIT JUDGE, concurring in part and dissenting in part:

Like the majority, I am saddened by the sequence of events that has befallen Sarah Crinkley. The assault suffered by the Crinkleys was absolutely dreadful. No one disputes that the circumstances are poignant, yet there remains the need to remember that wrenching facts may wrest a body of law from its moorings and foundations. That is what had happened to North Carolina tort law in this case.

The law of tort performs important functions: it has compensated the victims of wrongful acts and enhanced, through deterrence, or basic sense of safety. It cannot, however, provide an answer to every personal misfortune and it is not intended to replace the role of non-liability insurance, private pensions, public assistance, and the like in promoting the well being of our citizens.

* * *

Plaintiff is now to recover damages, not only for the trauma and injuries that she sustained in the assault, but also for a heart attack she suffered fourteen months later as well as for hospital and medical expenses incurred in treating her heart condition for a period extending up to five and one-half years after the assault. This is highly problematic. The evidence indicates that Sarah Crinkley was sixty-six years old at the time of the assault. She was overweight and had a history of arteriosclerosis, chest pains, and high blood pressure for which she had been under a physician's care since 1978. She was clearly exposed to alternate sources of stress with the closing of the family hardware store where she worked. Although North Carolina recognizes the "thin skull" rule, making tortfeasors liable for the "unusually extensive" damages resulting from their negligence to persons of "peculiar susceptibility," see *Lockwood v. McCaskill*, 262 N.C. 663, 138 S.E.2d 541, 546 (1964), the North Carolina Supreme Court has clearly articulated the limits of a tortfeasor's liability for injuries suffered by persons with such preexisting susceptibilities.

* * *

I understand and appreciate that the expansion of this field of law owes much to genuine concern for the plight of injured persons. It is no easy thing to draw lines in the face of visible personal misfortune. However, there are claims of justice on both sides of these hard cases which find expression in the limits of state law. With all respect for the sympathetic circumstances presented here, I would reverse and remand for a new trial on damages.

---

1. In personal injury cases damages for mental distress are routinely allowed. Even if the plaintiff is unusually susceptible to suffering distress, the "thin-skulled plaintiff" rule allows recovery on the theory that the defendant takes the plaintiff as found. Such damages include any physical or psychological consequences of the distress even if any ordinary person would not have suffered the additional injuries. *See, e.g.,* Bartolone v. Jeckovich, 103 A.D.2d 632, 481 N.Y.S.2d 545 (1984) (back injuries in car accident aggravated a pre-existing paranoid schizophrenic condition). Is there any reason to distinguish physical injuries triggered by distress, as in the principal case, from profound injuries entirely psychological in nature?

2. Distinguish physical manifestations of distress and psychological effects from "mere" distress without such complications. In negligence law the rule has long been that distress without physical manifestations is not compensable. The interpretation of "physical" often includes severe psychological conditions, however. *See, e.g.,* Daley v. LaCroix, 384 Mich. 4, 179 N.W.2d 390 (1970).

California repudiated the physical consequences rule in Molien v. Kaiser Foundation Hosp. In this 1980 case the defendant negligently diagnosed the plaintiff's wife with syphilis and instructed her to notify her husband. The misdiagnosis caused the couple great distress and ultimately ended their marriage. The plaintiff recovered under a negligence theory even though he suffered no physical harm. 27 Cal.3d 916, 167 Cal.Rptr. 831, 616 P.2d 813 (1980). *See also* St. Elizabeth Hospital v. Garrard, 730 S.W.2d 649 (Tex.1987); Rodrigues v. State, 52 Hawaii 156, 472 P.2d 509 (1970).

3. Intentional infliction of emotional distress claims are not subject to the same physical harm requirement. When defendants have acted recklessly or maliciously to inflict mental distress in outrageous and socially intolerable circumstances, plaintiffs may recover if they suffer "severe distress" without physical manifestations. The distress must be severe in quality, however. *See, e.g.,* Harris v. Jones, 281 Md. 560, 380 A.2d 611 (1977).

GOLDBERG v. MALLINCKRODT, INC.

792 F.2d 305 (2d Cir.1986).

WINTER, CIRCUIT JUDGE:

Dr. Donald Goldberg appeals from a grant of summary judgment in favor of Mallinckrodt, Inc., the manufacturer of an allegedly unsafe medical dye. Dr. Goldberg's complaint alleged that defendant had fraudulently misrepresented the safety of its product with the result that two of his patients were injured when he administered the dye. He claimed damages for his emotional distress and for his loss of income as a result of spending time defending malpractice actions. The district court granted summary judgment with respect to both claims. We affirm.

The facts as alleged are as follows: In October, 1976, Dr. Goldberg, an orthopedic surgeon, attended a physicians' conference at which he learned for the first time about "Dimeray," a new product manufactured by defendant Mallinckrodt. Dimeray is a dye injected into a patient's spinal cord during a procedure known as a myelogram. The dye acts as a "contrast medium" that makes the spinal cord more visible, apparently during an X-ray. Defendant touted Dimeray as an improvement of the dye then in general use, as it provided clearer myelograms and would pass naturally out of a patient's system. The ability to pass naturally out of the body was significant, for the dye then in general use had to be withdrawn from the body by needle after it was used. Defendant represented that more than three thousand tests indicated that Dimeray had no adverse side effects involving serious neurological damage. This representation allegedly was false and known to be so when made.

Impressed by the claims made about Dimeray at the conference, Dr. Goldberg used the product on a patient, who shortly thereafter suffered severe pain, paralysis, and other symptoms of nerve damage. Relying on the prior assurances of defendant as to Dimeray's safety, the doctor did not associate this adverse reaction with the product. One month later he administered the product to another patient, who also developed severe pain, lower body paralysis, and other symptoms of nerve damage. Both reactions are typical of a condition known as "cauda equina syndrome," allegedly represented by defendant not to be a side effect of Dimeray. The doctor notified Mallinckrodt of the adverse reactions. Shortly thereafter, Mallinckrodt voluntarily withdrew Dimeray from the market based on reports it had received of similar adverse reactions associated with use of the product.

* * *

Dr. Goldberg brought this diversity action in July, 1982. His first complaint did not allege a cause of action for fraud and was dismissed. An amended complaint alleged that Mallinckrodt had fraudulently misrepresented the safety of its product by failing to disclose knowledge of adverse reactions to Dimeray. * * *

Both sides moved for summary judgment. On June 21, 1985, the district court granted partial summary judgment for defendant, dismissing Dr. Goldberg's claim for "damages based on or arising out of mental and emotion distress." * * *

Plaintiff [claims] that the district court erred in dismissing his claim for damages based on the fact that he no longer performs myelograms.

It is not clear whether the emotional trauma of witnessing the serious injuries to his two patients has left plaintiff emotionally unable to perform the procedure, or whether plaintiff has simply made a personal decision to refrain from the procedure because of the inherent danger associated with it, as illustrated by the Dimeray incidents.

To the extent that plaintiff's lost income is the result of a personal choice, it is beyond question not a direct result of defendant's alleged fraud. Moreover, even if he is disabled by the emotional trauma flowing from the past incidents, such emotional distress is not compensable under New York law. In Bovsun v. Sanperi, 61 N.Y.2d 219, 461 N.E.2d 843, 473 N.Y.S.2d 357 (1984), the New York Court of Appeals held that bystanders may recover for emotional distress damage only under very limited circumstances. The emotional disturbance suffered must be "serious and verifiable," and "must be tied, as a matter of proximate causation, to the observation of the serious injury or death of [an immediate] family member." [Citations.] Finally, the plaintiff must himself have been in the "zone of danger"—that is, he must himself have been exposed to a risk of bodily harm by the conduct of the defendant. [Citation.]

Dr. Goldberg clearly does not meet two of these requirements. First, the persons whose injuries have allegedly caused the emotional distress and subsequent refusal to perform myelograms were patients, not immediate family members. Second, plaintiff was never himself exposed to risk of serious bodily injury from Dimeray, and thus was outside the "zone of danger." Indeed, *Bovsun* expressly reaffirmed Kennedy v. McKesson, 58 N.Y.2d 500, 448 N.E.2d 1332, 462 N.Y.S.2d 421, a case similar to the present one which held that a dentist could not recover for emotional distress suffered as a result of the death of his patient. [Citation.]

Plaintiff attempts to avoid the *Bovsun* rule by relying on several cases involving more intentional or outrageous conduct in which recovery for emotional distress has been allowed. *See, e.g.,* Johnson v. State, 37 N.Y.2d 378, 334 N.E.2d 590, 372 N.Y.S.2d 638 (1975) (recovery for emotional distress allowed where hospital misidentified body and negligently transmitted telegram announcing death of plaintiff's mother, who was actually alive and well in the hospital, with the mistake only being discovered after plaintiff closely examined the corpse at the wake). Such cases are factually inapposite. The district court was thus correct in dismissing the claim for emotional distress.

Affirmed.

———

1. Early English and American law rejected entirely the idea of emotional distress recoveries except as parasitic damages. *See* Magruder, Mental and Emotional Distress in the Law of Torts, 49 Harv.L.Rev. 1033 (1936); Lynch v. Knight, 9 H.L.Cas. 577 (1861) (the law cannot

value mental pain and anxiety and does not pretend to redress it when standing alone).

2.   The general rule continues to disallow claims for distress alone, with a few exceptions.   Intentional infliction of emotional distress and negligent infliction of emotional distress are both torts allowing recovery for distress without other harm, but each tort has strict substantive limitations.   *See* Prosser & Keeton on Torts § 9 (5th ed. 1985).

3.   What reasons are most persuasive for denying distress damages in the absence of other harm?   Consider:

(a) The subjective nature of the injury makes measurement too speculative;

(b) Allowing such actions would open the courts to a "floodgate" of litigation;

(c) The causal connection between distress and other injuries is too tenuous;

(d) The inherent difficulties of proof in such cases requires an excessive reliance on plaintiffs' testimony;

(e) Such claims are simply too speculative.

4.   Compare the principal case with *Cavanaugh v. United States* where the parents of an Air Force lieutenant sued because of the perceived failure of the government to investigate thoroughly the death of their son.   Among their several unsuccessful claims was one for misrepresentation.   This claim failed because the Federal Tort Claims Act excludes misrepresentation from its waiver of sovereign immunity. 640 F.Supp. 437 (D.Mass.1986).

POTTER v. FIRESTONE TIRE AND RUBBER CO.

6 Cal.4th 965, 863 P.2d 795, 25 Cal.Rptr.2d 550 (1993).

Baxter, Justice.

We granted review in this case to consider whether emotional distress engendered by a fear of cancer or other serious physical illness or injury following exposure to a carcinogen or other toxic substance is an injury for which damages may be recovered in a negligence action in the absence of physical injury[.]   * * *

Our analysis of existing case law and policy considerations relevant to the availability of damages for emotional distress leads us to conclude that, generally, in the absence of a present physical injury or illness, recovery of damages for fear of cancer in a negligence action should be allowed only if the plaintiff pleads and proves that the fear stems from a knowledge, corroborated by reliable medical and scientific opinion, that it is more likely than not that the feared cancer will develop in the future due to the toxic exposure.

This is a toxic exposure case brought by four landowners living adjacent to a landfill.   As a result of defendant Firestone's practice of disposing of its toxic wastes at the landfill, the landowners were subjected to prolonged exposure to certain carcinogens. While none of the landowners currently suffers from any cancerous or precancerous condition, each faces an enhanced but unquantified risk of developing cancer in the future due to the exposure.

The following background facts are contained in the trial court's statement of decision following trial.

From 1963 until 1980, Firestone operated a tire manufacturing plant near Salinas. In 1967, Firestone contracted with Salinas Disposal Service and Rural Disposal (hereafter SDS), two refuse collection companies operating the Crazy Horse landfill (hereafter Crazy Horse), for disposal of its industrial waste. Firestone agreed to deposit its waste in dumpsters provided by SDS located at the plant site. SDS agreed to haul the waste to Crazy Horse and deposit it there.

Crazy Horse, a class II sanitary landfill owned by the City of Salinas, covers approximately 125 acres suitable for the disposal of household and commercial solid waste. Unlike dump sites that are classified class I, class II landfills such as Crazy Horse prohibit toxic substances and liquids because of the danger that they will leach into the groundwater and cause contamination.

At the outset of their contractual relationship, SDS informed Firestone that no solvents, cleaning fluids, oils or liquids were permitted at Crazy Horse. Firestone provided assurances that these types of waste would not be sent to the landfill.

Notwithstanding its assurances, Firestone sent large quantities of liquid waste to Crazy Horse, including banbury drippings (a by-product of the tire manufacturing process) containing a combination of semiliquid toxic chemicals. Firestone also sent liquid waste oils, liquid tread end cements, and solvents to the landfill.

In May 1977, Firestone's plant engineer, who was in charge of all environmental matters, sent a memorandum to Firestone's plant managers and department heads. The memorandum, reflecting official plant policy, explained liquid waste disposal procedures and described the particular waste materials involved and the proper method of handling them.

In order to comply with this policy, Firestone initially made efforts to take the waste materials to a class I dump site. However, Firestone accumulated more waste than had been anticipated and disposing of the waste proved costly. When noncompliance with the policy became widespread, the plant engineer sent another memorandum to plant management complaining about the lack of compliance and pointing out that the policy was required by California law.

During this time, the Salinas plant operated under a production manager who had been sent from Firestone's company headquarters in Akron, Ohio for the purpose of "turning the plant around" and making it more profitable. This manager became angered over the costs of the waste disposal program and decided to discontinue it. As a consequence, Firestone's hazardous waste materials were once again deposited at Crazy Horse.

Frank and Shirley Potter owned property and lived adjacent to Crazy Horse. Joe and Linda Plescia were their neighbors.

In 1984, the Potters and the Plescias (hereafter plaintiffs) discovered that toxic chemicals had contaminated their domestic water wells. The chemicals included: benzene; toluene; chloroform; 1,1–dichloroethene; methylene chloride; tetrachloroethene; 1,1,1–trichloroethane; trichloroethene; and vinyl chloride. Of these, both benzene and vinyl chloride are known to be human carcinogens. Many of the others are strongly suspected to be carcinogens.

In 1985, plaintiffs filed separate suits against Firestone for damages and declaratory relief.   * * *

In its statement of decision, the trial court concluded that Firestone's waste disposal practices from 1967 until 1974 constituted actionable negligence.   * * *

In finding liability, the trial court determined that the toxic chemicals in plaintiffs' drinking water were the same chemicals or "daughter" chemicals as those used at the Firestone plant. Firestone was the heaviest single contributor of waste at Crazy Horse and the only contributor with the identical "suite" of chemicals to those found in the water. The court also noted the expert testimony established that the chemicals that migrated off the Firestone plant site so closely resembled those in the water that the comparison constituted a virtual "fingerprint" identifying Firestone as the source of the contaminants.

* * *

The court also stated that although plaintiffs testified to a constellation of physical symptoms which they attributed to the toxic chemicals, it was "not possible to demonstrate with sufficient certainty a causal connection between these symptoms and the well water contamination. Nevertheless, plaintiffs will always fear, and reasonably so, that physical impairments they experience are the result of the well water and are the precursors of life threatening disease. Their fears are not merely subjective but are corroborated by substantial medical and scientific opinion." Based on these findings, plaintiffs were awarded damages totalling $800,000 for their lifelong fear of cancer and resultant emotional distress.

The court further concluded that since plaintiffs now live with an increased vulnerability to serious disease, it was axiomatic that they should receive periodic medical monitoring to detect the onset of disease at the earliest possible time and that early diagnosis was unquestionably important to increase the chances of effective treatment. Accordingly, the court awarded damages totalling $142,975 as the present value of the costs of such monitoring, based on plaintiffs' life expectancies.

The court also awarded plaintiffs damages totalling $269,500 for psychiatric illness and the cost of treating such illness,[2] as well as damages totalling $108,100 for the general disruption of their lives and the invasion of their privacy.[3] Finally, the court awarded punitive damages totalling $2.6 million based on Firestone's conscious disregard for the rights and safety of others in dumping its toxic wastes at the landfill after 1977.

Firestone appealed, arguing that the damage awards were not supported by any of the legal theories relied on by the trial court and that the evidence was insufficient to support the trial court's findings. It claimed that the award for "fear of cancer" in the absence of physical injury was an unwarranted extension of liability for negligent infliction of emotional distress, that if such fear is compensable it should not be so where the plaintiff cannot establish that he or she has a "probability" of developing cancer, and that the amount of damages awarded each plaintiff was not based on proof of individualized injury. The award for "psychiatric injury" was challenged on the ground that the injury was indistinguishable from fear of cancer and was not supported by the evidence.

* * *

The Court of Appeal reversed the awards for medical monitoring costs, as well as a postjudgment order directing Firestone to pay costs and interest, but otherwise affirmed the judgment. * * *

"Fear of cancer" is a term generally used to describe a present anxiety over developing cancer in the future.[5] Claims for fear of cancer have been increasingly asserted in toxic tort cases as more and more substances have been linked with cancer. Typically, a person's likelihood of developing cancer as a result of a toxic exposure is difficult to predict because many forms of cancer are characterized by long latency periods (anywhere from 20 to 30 years), and presentation is dependent upon the interrelation of myriad factors.

2. The court determined that these damages were separate and distinct from plaintiffs' basic fear of developing cancer or other serious physical illnesses in the future.

3. This award reflected the necessity for plaintiffs to shower elsewhere, use bottled water, and submit to intrusions by numerous agencies involved in testing water and soil.

5. Some commentators and courts have referred to claims for "fear of cancer" as "cancerphobia" claims. (*See* Sterling v. Velsicol Chemical Corp. (6th Cir.1988) 855 F.2d 1188, 1206, fn. 24 [hereafter Sterling]; Gale & Goyer, Recovery for Cancerphobia and Increased Risk of Cancer (1985) 15 Cumb.L.Rev. 723, 724–725.) Strictly speaking, however, there is a distinction between fear of cancer and cancerphobia. Cancerphobia, as a "phobic reaction," is a mental illness that is the recurrent experience of dread of a cancer in the absence of objective danger. In contrast, the fear of cancer is a claimed anxiety caused by the fear of developing cancer and is not a mental illness. (*See ibid.*) This opinion is concerned only with fear of cancer as a form of emotional distress and not with cancerphobia. Furthermore, while plaintiffs identified fear of cancer as the principal basis for the emotional distress claim at issue, our discussion is equally relevant to emotional distress engendered by fear that other types of serious physical illness or injury may result from toxic exposure.

The availability of damages for fear of cancer as a result of exposure to carcinogens or other toxins in negligence actions is a relatively novel issue for California courts. Other jurisdictions, however, have considered such claims and the appropriate limits on recovery. Factors deemed important to the compensability of such fear have included proof of a discernible physical injury (*e.g.*, Wisniewski v. Johns–Manville Corp. (3d Cir.1985) 759 F.2d 271, 274; Eagle–Picher Industries, Inc. v. Cox (Fla.Dist.Ct.App.1985) 481 So.2d 517, 528–529; Payton v. Abbott Labs (1982) 386 Mass. 540, 437 N.E.2d 171, 180–181 [hereafter Payton]), proof of a physical impact or physical invasion (*e.g.*, Herber v. Johns–Manville Corp. (3d Cir.1986) 785 F.2d 79, 85; Wilson v. Key Tronic Corp. (1985) 40 Wash.App. 802, 701 P.2d 518, 524 [hereafter Wilson]; Wetherill v. University of Chicago (N.D.Ill.1983) 565 F.Supp. 1553, 1560 [hereafter Wetherill]), or objective proof of mental distress (*e.g.*, Stites v. Sundstrand Heat Transfer, Inc. (W.D.Mich.1987) 660 F.Supp. 1516, 1526, 1527; Daley v. LaCroix (1970) 384 Mich. 4, 179 N.W.2d 390, 395).

* * *

We must determine whether the absence of a present physical injury precludes recovery for emotional distress engendered by fear of cancer. Firestone argues that California should not recognize a duty to avoid negligently causing emotional distress to another, but, if such a duty is recognized, recovery should be permitted in the absence of physical injury only on proof that the plaintiff's emotional distress or fear is caused by knowledge that future physical injury or illness is more likely than not to occur as a direct result of the defendant's conduct. * * *

* * * As we observed more than a decade ago, "[t]he primary justification for the requirement of physical injury appears to be that it serves as a screening device to minimize a presumed risk of feigned injuries and false claims. [Citations.]" (Molien v. Kaiser Foundation Hospitals (1980) 27 Cal.3d 916, 925–926, 167 Cal.Rptr. 831, 616 P.2d 813) [hereafter *Molien*]. Such harm was "believed to be susceptible of objective ascertainment and hence to corroborate the authenticity of the claim."

In *Molien*, we perceived two significant difficulties with the physical injury requirement. First, "the classification is both overinclusive and underinclusive when viewed in the light of its purported purpose of screening false claims." It is overinclusive in that it permits recovery whenever the suffering accompanies or results in physical injury, no matter how trivial (*ibid.*), yet underinclusive in that it mechanically denies court access to potentially valid claims that could be proved if the plaintiffs were permitted to go to trial. * * *

Our reasons for discarding the physical injury requirement in *Molien*, remain valid today and are equally applicable in a toxic exposure case. That is, the physical injury requirement is a hopelessly imprecise screening device—it would allow recovery for fear of cancer whenever such distress accompanies or results in any physical injury, no matter how trivial, yet would disallow recovery in all cases where the fear is both serious and genuine but no physical injury has yet manifested itself. While we agree with amici curiae that meaningful limits on the class of potential plaintiffs and clear guidelines for resolving disputes in advance of trial are necessary, imposing a physical injury requirement represents an inherently flawed and inferior means of attempting to achieve these goals.

We next consider whether recovery of damages for emotional distress caused by fear of cancer should depend upon a showing that the plaintiff's fears stem from a knowledge that there is a probable likelihood of developing cancer in the future due to the toxic exposure. This is a matter of hot debate among the parties and amici curiae. Firestone and numerous amici curiae argue that because fear of cancer claims are linked to a future harm which may or may not materialize, such claims raise concerns about speculation and uncertainty and therefore warrant a requirement that the plaintiff show the feared cancer is more likely than not to occur.   * * *

A carcinogenic or other toxic ingestion or exposure, without more, does not provide a basis for fearing future physical injury or illness which the law is prepared to recognize as reasonable. The fact that one is aware that he or she has ingested or been otherwise exposed to a carcinogen or other toxin, without any regard to the nature, magnitude and proportion of the exposure or its likely consequences, provides no meaningful basis upon which to evaluate the reasonableness of one's fear. For example, nearly everybody is exposed to carcinogens which appear naturally in all types of foods. Yet ordinary consumption of such foods is not substantially likely to result in cancer. (*See* Ames & Gold, Too Many Rodent Carcinogens: Mitogenesis Increases Mutagenesis (1990) 249 Science 970, 971, fn. 10 [observing that apples, celery, coffee, carrots, cauliflower, grapes, honey, orange juice, potatoes and many other common foods naturally produce carcinogenic pesticides that have been found to induce tumors when administered to rodents in large doses].) Nor is the knowledge of such consumption likely to result in a reasonable fear of cancer.

Moreover, permitting recovery for fear of cancer damages based solely upon a plaintiff's knowledge that his or her risk of cancer has been significantly increased by a toxic exposure, without requiring any further showing of the actual likelihood of the feared cancer due to the exposure, provides no protection against unreasonable claims based upon wholly speculative fears. For example, a plaintiff's risk of contracting cancer might be significantly increased by 100 or more percent due to a particular toxic exposure, yet the actual risk of the feared cancer might itself be insignificant and no more than a mere possibility.   * * *

We turn now to Firestone's argument that fear of cancer should be compensable only where the fear is based upon knowledge that cancer is probable, *i.e.*, that it is more likely than not that cancer will develop. In evaluating this argument, we first consider whether it is reasonable for a person to genuinely and seriously fear a disease that is not probable, and if so, whether the emotional distress engendered by such fear warrants recognition as a compensable harm.

We cannot say that it would never be reasonable for a person who has ingested toxic substances to harbor a genuine and serious fear of cancer where reliable medical or scientific opinion indicates that such ingestion has significantly increased his or her risk of cancer, but not to a probable likelihood. Indeed, we would be very hard pressed to find that, as a matter of law, a plaintiff faced with a 20 percent or 30 percent chance of developing cancer cannot genuinely, seriously and reasonably fear the prospect of cancer. Nonetheless, we conclude, for the public policy reasons identified below, that emotional distress caused by the fear of a cancer that is not probable should generally not be compensable in a negligence action.

As a starting point in our analysis, we recognize the indisputable fact that all of us are exposed to carcinogens every day. As one commentator has observed, "[i]t is difficult to go a week without news of toxic exposure. Virtually everyone in society is conscious of the fact that the air they breathe, water, food and drugs they ingest, land on which they live, or products to which they are exposed are potential health hazards. Although few are exposed to all, few also can escape exposure to any." (Dworkin, Fear Of Disease And Delayed Manifestation Injuries: A Solution Or A Pandora's Box? (1984) 53 Fordham L.Rev. 527, 576, fns. omitted.)

Thus, all of us are potential fear of cancer plaintiffs, provided we are sufficiently aware of and worried about the possibility of developing cancer from exposure to or ingestion of a carcinogenic substance. The enormity of the class of potential plaintiffs cannot be overstated; indeed, a single class action may easily involve hundreds, if not thousands, of fear of cancer claims. (*See* Willmore, In Fear of Cancerphobia (Sept. 28, 1988) 3 Toxics L.Rptr. (Bur.Nat. Affairs) 559, 563 [hereafter Willmore].)

With this consideration in mind, we believe the tremendous societal cost of otherwise allowing emotional distress compensation to a potentially unrestricted plaintiff class demonstrates the necessity of imposing some limit on the class. [Citations.] Proliferation of fear of cancer claims in California in the absence of meaningful restrictions might compromise the availability and affordability of liability insurance for toxic liability risks. * * *

[W]e hold with respect to negligent infliction of emotional distress claims arising out of exposure to carcinogens and/or other toxic substances: Unless an express exception to this general rule is recognized: in the absence of a present physical injury or illness, damages for fear of cancer may be recovered only if the plaintiff pleads and proves that (1) as a result of the defendant's negligent breach of a duty owed to the plaintiff, the plaintiff is exposed to a toxic substance which threatens cancer; and (2) the plaintiff's fear stems from a knowledge, corroborated by reliable medical or scientific opinion, that it is more likely than not that the plaintiff will develop the cancer in the future due to the toxic exposure. Under this rule, a plaintiff must do more than simply establish knowledge of a toxic ingestion or exposure and a significant increased risk of cancer. The plaintiff must further show that based upon reliable medical or scientific opinion, the plaintiff harbors a serious fear that the toxic ingestion or exposure was of such magnitude and proportion as to likely result in the feared cancer.

* * *

In the context of a toxic exposure action, a claim for medical monitoring seeks to recover the cost of future periodic medical examinations intended to facilitate early detection and treatment of disease caused by a plaintiff's exposure to toxic substances. [Citation.] We shall now undertake to decide whether and under what circumstances a toxic exposure plaintiff may recover medical monitoring damages in a negligence action.

* * *

That medical monitoring may be called for as a result of a defendant's tortious conduct, even in the absence of actual physical injury, was compellingly demonstrated in the case of Friends For All Children, Inc. v. Lockheed Aircraft Corp. (D.C.Cir.1984) 746 F.2d 816 [hereafter Friends For All Children]. There, suit was instituted on behalf of 149 Vietnamese orphaned children who survived a plane crash during the evacuation of Vietnam in 1975. The complaint alleged that because of decompression, as well as the impact of the crash, the children suffered from a neurological disorder generically classified as minimal brain dysfunction. In that case, the Court of Appeals affirmed the imposition of liability on Lockheed for diagnostic examination expenses because the crash proximately caused the need for a comprehensive diagnostic examination. * * * When a defendant negligently invades this interest, the injury to which is neither speculative nor resistant to proof, it is elementary that the defendant should make the plaintiff whole by paying for the examinations.[10]

[Accordingly,] we hold that the cost of medical monitoring is a compensable item of damages where the proofs demonstrate, through reliable medical expert testimony, that the need for future monitoring is a reasonably certain consequence of a plaintiff's toxic exposure and that

---

10. The court in Friends For All Children posed the following hypothetical situation to illustrate the true nature of medical monitoring damages. "Jones is knocked down by a motorbike which Smith is riding through a red light. Jones lands on his head with some force. Understandably shaken, Jones enters a hospital where doctors recommend that he undergo a battery of tests to determine whether he has suffered any internal head injuries. The tests prove negative, but Jones sues Smith solely for what turns out to be the substantial cost of the diagnostic examinations. [P]

From our example, it is clear that even in the absence of physical injury Jones ought to be able to recover the cost for the various diagnostic examinations proximately caused by Smith's negligent action.... The motorbike rider, through his negligence, caused the plaintiff, in the opinion of medical experts, to need specific medical services—a cost that is neither inconsequential nor of a kind the community generally accepts as part of the wear and tear of daily life. Under these principles of tort law, the motorbiker should pay." (746 F.2d at p. 825.)

the recommended monitoring is reasonable. In determining the reasonableness and necessity of monitoring, the following factors are relevant: (1) the significance and extent of the plaintiff's exposure to chemicals; (2) the toxicity of the chemicals; (3) the relative increase in the chance of onset of disease in the exposed plaintiff as a result of the exposure, when compared to (a) the plaintiff's chances of developing the disease had he or she not been exposed, and (b) the chances of the members of the public at large of developing the disease; (4) the seriousness of the disease for which the plaintiff is at risk; and (5) the clinical value of early detection and diagnosis. Under this holding, it is for the trier of fact to decide, on the basis of competent medical testimony, whether and to what extent the particular plaintiff's exposure to toxic chemicals in a given situation justifies future periodic medical monitoring.

We are confident that our holding will not, as Firestone and amici curiae warn, open the floodgates of litigation. The five factors provide substantial evidentiary burdens for toxic exposure plaintiffs and do not, as Firestone insists, allow medical monitoring damages to be based "solely upon a showing of an increased but unquantified risk resulting from exposure to toxic chemicals." Moreover, toxic exposure plaintiffs may recover "only if the evidence establishes the necessity, as a direct consequence of the exposure in issue, for specific monitoring beyond that which an individual should pursue as a matter of general good sense and foresight." [Citation.] Thus there can be no recovery for preventative medical care and checkups to which members of the public at large should prudently submit. * * *

The judgment of the Court of Appeal is reversed insofar as it affirms the award of punitive damages and the award of damages for plaintiffs' fear of cancer, and reverses the award for future medical monitoring. The cause is remanded to the Court of Appeal for further proceedings consistent with this opinion[.] * * *

RUBIN v. MATTHEWS INTERNATIONAL CORP.

503 A.2d 694 (Me.1986).

SCOLNIK, JUSTICE.

* * * The plaintiff sought to recover damages for the emotional or mental distress she claims to have suffered as the result of the defendant's failure to make timely delivery of a memorial stone. Her complaint asserts four claims: breach of contract, negligence, negligent infliction of mental distress and intentional infliction of mental distress. On the defendant's motion, the Superior Court dismissed Rubin's complaint for failure to state a claim upon which relief could be granted. We vacate only the court's dismissal of that portion of the complaint that alleges the intentional infliction of mental distress.

In determining whether the lower court erred in granting the defendant's motion to dismiss, we consider all well-pleaded material allegations of the complaint as admitted. [Citations.] Those allegations reveal that on February 2, 1984, Donna L. Rubin placed an order with the Memorial Division of Matthews for the design and provision of a memorial stone for her mother's grave. Matthews was notified that the stone was to be provided for an unveiling ceremony scheduled to occur on May 5, 1984. Representatives of Matthews were aware of the religious significance of the event and agreed to have the memorial stone delivered prior to the time for the unveiling. They repeatedly represented in the weeks prior to May 5, 1984, that the memorial stone had been shipped and would be delivered on time to Rubin through Brooklawn Memorial Park in Portland. Matthews was further aware that the delivery of the memorial stone would take at least one week. The stone was in fact not shipped until April 30, 1984, just five days before the scheduled date of the ceremony, and did not arrive on time.

The first issue presented by this appeal is whether a cause of action exists for the recovery of damages for mental or emotional distress suffered solely as the result of a breach of contract. In a breach of contract action, those damages that were "reasonably within the contemplation of the contracting parties when the agreement was made and which would naturally flow from a breach thereof" may be recovered. [Citations.] As a general rule, courts in other jurisdictions have denied recovery for mental or emotional distress suffered as a result of breach of contract unaccompanied by physical injury. [Citations.] On the facts of this case, we decline to adopt a broad exception, as urged by the plaintiff, to the general rule precluding damages for mental and emotional distress in a contract case. We also do not find that the untimely delivery of a memorial stone falls within the existing narrow exceptions to the general rule.

The judicial reluctance to award damages for emotional distress in contract actions is reflected in *Restatement (Second) of Contracts* § 353:

> Recovery for emotional disturbance will be excluded unless the breach also caused bodily harm or the contract or the breach is of such a kind that serious emotional disturbance was a particularly likely result.

Common examples of the second exceptional situation are contracts 1) between carriers and innkeepers and their passengers and guests; 2) for the carriage or proper disposition of dead bodies; and 3) for the delivery of messages concerning death. [Citations.]

Rubin contends that the untimely delivery of a memorial stone falls within the second or third exception concerning death. Assuming without deciding that we recognize these narrow exceptions, the present case does not fall within their parameters. It would strain the exception for disposition of bodies and delivery of death messages to include untimely delivery of a memorial stone. * * *

Rubin alternatively proposes that we not limit ourselves to the narrow exceptions discussed above but that we adopt a broad exception to the general rule precluding such damages in contract actions. * * *

California early allowed recovery for mental distress damages in contract actions. *See, e.g.,* Westervelt v. McCullough, 68 Cal.App. 198, 228 P. 734 (1924) (plaintiff allowed mental distress damages suffered as a result of defendant's breach of promise to provide plaintiff a home for duration of plaintiff's life). Although *Westervelt* involved physical suffering resulting from mental distress, the California court, relying on contract cases from other jurisdictions in which recovery for mental distress alone was allowed, held:

> Whenever the terms of a contract relate to matters which concern directly the comfort, happiness, or personal welfare of one of the parties, or the subject-matter of which is such as directly to affect or move the affection, self-esteem, or tender feelings of that party, he may recover damages for physical suffering or illness proximately caused by its breach.

[Citation.] Subsequent California cases have applied this principle to allow recovery of mental distress damages alone in a contract action. [Citation.] However, we agree with the North Carolina Court that the California standard is overly broad and "imposes too great a burden on parties to a contract." *See* Stanback v. Stanback, 297 N.C. at 194, 254 S.E.2d at 620.

Accordingly, we are not persuaded, on the facts of this case, that the general rule precluding damages for emotional or mental distress for breach of contract should be abandoned.

Rubin argues that the tort of negligent infliction of emotional distress may rest on the underlying tort of negligence where the sole harm suffered is emotional distress. We disagree.

We stated in Packard v. Central Maine Power Co., 477 A.2d 264, 268 (Me.1984) that

> no recovery can be had on a claim for infliction of emotional distress unless the defendant is found liable on the underlying tort.

Contrary to Rubin's contention, mental distress is insufficient in and of itself to establish the harm necessary to make negligence actionable, without either accompanying physical consequences, or an independent underlying tort. *See Prosser and Keeton on Torts,* § 54, at 361–62 (5th ed. 1984); 2 F. Harper & F. James, *The Law of Torts* § 18.4, at 1031–32 (1956) (mental or emotional distress standing alone will not constitute the kind of legal damage needed to support an action for negligence).
* * *

Rubin asserts finally that because reasonable men could differ as to the outrageousness of the defendant's conduct, it was for the jury to determine whether the conduct was sufficiently extreme and outrageous to result in liability. Because we agree, we vacate the order of dismissal as to this count.

We recognized the tort of intentional infliction of emotional distress in Vicnire v. Ford Motor Credit Co., 401 A.2d 148 (Me.1979). We held there that a defendant is subject to liability if he intentionally or recklessly inflicts severe emotional distress upon another by engaging in extreme or outrageous conduct. Accepting as true the allegations here that the defendant's conduct was intentional and the emotional distress suffered by the plaintiff was severe, the issue becomes whether Matthews' misrepresentations and failure to make a timely delivery of the monument rise to the level of "extreme and outrageous" conduct.

* * *

In *Hanke* [Hanke v. Global Van Lines, Inc., 533 F.2d 396 (8th Cir.1976)]the defendant moving company firmly promised an August 13 delivery date for the plaintiff's goods. The moving company repeatedly misrepresented the delivery date to the plaintiff, a local newspaper publisher, a United States government agency, and two United States Senators, finally making three partial deliveries in October and November. The court found that a jury could infer that the repeated misrepresentations, absent an explanation, were knowing falsehoods made for the purpose of "stringing her along." The court concluded that reasonable persons might differ as to whether the facts supported a conclusion that the defendant was liable for intentional infliction of emotional distress.

Although Matthew's misrepresentations in this case were not so extensive, given the allegations of repeated misrepresentation of a timely delivery of the monument for the unveiling ceremony and the circumstances in which they were made, we conclude that the complaint states a cause of action for intentional infliction of emotional distress. *See Restatement (Second) of Torts* § 46 comment d, at 73. Our conclusion draws further support from the alleged contractual nature of the relationship between the parties. *See* D. Givelber, *The Right to Minimum Social Recovery and the Limits of Evenhandedness: Intentional Infliction of Emotional Distress by Outrageous Conduct*, 82 Col.L.Rev. 42, 69 (1982) (courts most likely to recognize a claim of outrageousness when the parties are "apparently bound by contracts regulating an economic relationship"). Thus, the allegations of this complaint sufficiently set forth conduct upon which liability for intentional infliction of emotional distress may be predicated.

[Remanded.]

C. ECONOMIC LOSS DAMAGES

Section Coverage:

Recovery of purely economic losses such as lost profits has been in general the province of contract law and special statutory areas like antitrust law. In tort, the traditional view would preclude any recovery for negligently inflicted economic losses absent physical harm to person or property.

Courts have advanced two principal rationales for the per se foreclosure of recovery in negligence for economic losses unaccompanied by harm to person or property: (1) the rule provides predictability in an otherwise uncertain area of law, and it places a reasonable limit on the tortfeasor's potential liability; and (2) the rule is justifiable because such pecuniary losses are too remote. This rationale takes several forms. Courts sometimes say that there was no duty owed to the class of persons seeking recovery, or that there was no proximate cause because the economic losses are only indirectly related to the tortfeasor's negligence or not foreseeable at the time of the injury. On a more pragmatic level, the rule has been justified on the theory that it encourages settlements.

Although unquestionably the bright-line bar to recovery of such losses has the advantage of predictability and administrative convenience, it has produced some harsh results. There has been a critical perception of past inequities, and courts have begun to recognize exceptions. Some recent law has allowed compensation by finding the parties had a "special relationship" that created a duty to protect from economic harm. Some courts have simply reconsidered the application of foreseeability and remoteness. Despite these inroads on the rule denying economic losses for negligent interference with contracts in the absence of physical harm, this traditional rule remains the prevailing one.

Model Case:

The Hawkins Dredging Company, while conducting excavation operations, negligently damaged a natural gas pipeline owned by the National Pipeline Co. The resulting closure of the pipeline for repairs forced Rexall Industries, a contract purchaser of natural gas from National, to obtain fuel from another source during the repair period at an increased cost.

Hawkins would be liable to National for both the cost of repairs and any direct economic losses it sustained. In contrast, an action brought by Rexall would be unlikely to succeed. Although Hawkins' negligence prevented National from performing its contract to supply gas to Rexall, a court typically would preclude Rexall from recovering damages for its increased fuel costs. The rationale for the disparate treatment of the pipeline company and the contract purchaser would be that the latter was outside the class of persons to whom the dredging company owed a duty of care. On the other hand, if the court found that Hawkins intentionally interfered with National's performance of its contract, then Rexall would be permitted to recover its pecuniary losses.

CLARK v. INTERNATIONAL HARVESTER CO.

99 Idaho 326, 581 P.2d 784 (1978).

BAKES, JUSTICE.

This is a products liability case in which the plaintiffs seek to recover consequential damages for economic losses resulting from an allegedly defective tractor manufactured by defendant International Harvester Company and sold to the plaintiffs by defendant McVey's, Inc., an

International Harvester Co. dealer. The plaintiffs alleged a breach of implied and express warranties and negligent design and manufacture of the tractor. Prior to trial the district court granted partial summary judgments in favor of the defendants on the warranty claims. After trial the district court, sitting without a jury, entered judgment against the defendants on the negligence claim and awarded the plaintiffs $26,-950.15 in damages.

[The plaintiff Clark is a "custom" farmer who contracts to plow or preplant farmland for compensation related to the number of acres involved. Clark purchased a tractor from the defendant McVey's, Inc., manufactured by International Harvester, for use in his custom farming business. The plaintiff claimed damages allegedly attributable to downtime when the equipment was being repaired and asserted that the tractor failed to function as warranted.]

* * *

The defendants separately moved for summary judgment alleging that when Clark purchased the tractor he signed a sales form which provided for a 12 month warranty and which limited the buyer's remedies to the repair or replacement of defective parts by the defendant and disclaimed all other warranties. The trial court granted the motion for summary judgment on the warranty claims but ruled that the disclaimer provisions in the form did not exclude liability for negligence.

* * *

In a memorandum opinion the trial court found that "[p]laintiffs' consequential damages due to 'down' time in their operation were caused by design defect in the valve train of the engine and negligent manufacture or assembly in the torque amplifier, ... Plaintiffs are entitled to recover $24,246.00 for their down time and $2,112.00 for repair of the tractor." The trial court denied the plaintiffs' claims for damages due to loss of "present and future" business and decreased value of the tractor.
* * *

The defendant on appeal has made numerous assignments of error. They can be summarized as follows: * * *

4. The trial court erred in awarding consequential damages for purely economic loss in a tort action. * * *

We first consider assignment of error No. 4, which concerns the recovery of damages for economic loss in a negligence action, because, in our view, that is dispositive of the negligence issue. The specific question presented by this assignment of error is best demonstrated by distinguishing this case from those of our earlier and somewhat related cases. This case is not like Shields v. Morton Chemical Co., 95 Idaho 674, 518 P.2d 857 (1974), in which the plaintiff sought damages for economic loss as a result of seeds which were damaged by the defendant's chemicals. In the instant case the plaintiffs have not alleged that their economic losses were the result of any property damage caused by the defendants. This case is not like Rindlisbaker v. Wilson, 95 Idaho 752, 519 P.2d 421 (1974), in which the plaintiff sought damages for profits lost as a result of a personal injury. In the instant case the plaintiffs have not alleged any personal injury. The negligence issue in this case is not like Salmon Rivers Sportsman Camps, Inc. v. Cessna Aircraft Co., 97 Idaho 348, 544 P.2d 306 (1975), in which the plaintiffs sought damages for economic loss for breach of an implied warranty. In that case we did not rule whether such damages were recoverable in a negligence action, but held that a plaintiff who was not in privity of contract with the defendant could not recover economic losses based on a breach of an implied warranty. In this case it is conceded that there is privity.

In this action the plaintiffs seek recovery only of lost profits due to alleged "down time" and the costs of repairing and replacing allegedly defective parts. The instant case presents the very narrow question whether the purchaser of a defective product who has not sustained any property damage or personal injury, but only suffered economic losses, can recover those losses in a negligence action against the manufacturer.

This Court has not previously considered this issue. The majority of jurisdictions which have considered the issue have not permitted the recovery of purely economic loss in a products liability action sounding in tort. [Citations.] However, a small minority of jurisdictions allow the recovery of purely economic losses in strict liability actions. [Citations.]

Dean Prosser summarized this majority rule with respect to recovery of economic losses in a products liability case sounding in negligence as follows:

> "There can be no doubt that the seller's liability for negligence covers any kind of physical harm, including not only personal injuries, but also property damage to the defective chattel itself, as where an automobile is wrecked by reason of its own bad brakes, as well as damage to any other property in the vicinity. But where there is no accident, and no physical damage, and the only loss is a pecuniary one, through loss of the value or use of the thing sold, or the cost of repairing it, the courts have adhered to the rule, to be encountered later, that purely economic interests are not entitled to protection against mere negligence, and so have denied the recovery." W. Prosser, Handbook on the Law of Torts, § 101 at 665 (4th ed. 1971).

The Restatement (Second) of Torts, § 395 (1965), states that a manufacturer is to be liable for "physical harm" caused by its negligence in the manufacture of a chattel dangerous unless carefully made, but that Restatement section does not extend the manufacturer's liability to encompass purely economic loss.

Similarly, Restatement (Second) of Torts, § 402A (1965), which states the rule of strict liability in tort adopted by this Court in *Shields v. Morton Chemical Co., supra,* provides:

"One who sells any product in a defective condition unreasonably dangerous to the user or consumer or to his property is subject to liability for physical harm thereby caused to the ultimate user or consumer, or to his property...."

Like the Restatement section concerning the manufacturer's liability for negligence, § 402A does not extend a seller's tort liability to include purely economic losses.

One of the most fully articulated discussions of the considerations underlying this rule is found in Justice Traynor's majority opinion in Seely v. White Motor Co., 63 Cal.2d 9, 45 Cal.Rptr. 17, 403 P.2d 145 (1965), [where] * * * the plaintiff sought to recover lost profits and a refund of the purchase price of a defective truck. The California Supreme Court ruled that such damages, although recoverable in a breach of warranty action, were not recoverable in strict liability in tort. The following passage from the majority opinion is pertinent to this case:

"The distinction that the law has drawn between tort recovery for physical injuries and warranty recovery for economic loss is not arbitrary and does not rest on the 'luck' of one plaintiff in having an accident causing physical injury. The distinction rests, rather, on an understanding of the nature of the responsibility a manufacturer must undertake in distributing his products. He can appropriately be held liable for physical injuries caused by defects by requiring his goods to match a standard of safety defined in terms of conditions that create unreasonable risks of harm. He cannot be held for the level of performance of his products in the consumer's business unless he agrees that the product was designed to meet the consumer's demands. A consumer should not be charged at the will of the manufacturer with bearing the risk of physical injury when he buys a product on the market. He can, however, be fairly charged with the risk that the product will not match his economic expectations unless the manufacturer agrees that it will. Even in actions for negligence, a manufacturer's liability is limited to damages for physical injuries and there is no recovery for economic loss alone. [Citations omitted]." 45 Cal.Rptr. at 23, 403 P.2d at 151.

We believe the rule advanced by the majority of the jurisdictions and by the Restatement is sound for the reasons articulated by Justice Traynor in *Seely*. * * * The Idaho legislature, and indeed the legislatures of nearly every state in the Union, have adopted the U.C.C. which carefully and painstakingly sets forth the rights between parties in a sales transaction with regard to economic loss. This Court, in the common law evolution of the tort law of this state, must recognize the legislature's action in this area of commercial law and should accommodate when possible the evolution of tort law with the principles laid down in the U.C.C.

The economic expectations of parties have not traditionally been protected by the law concerning unintentional torts. [Citations.] We do not believe that any good purpose would be achieved by undermining the operation of the U.C.C. provisions by extending tort law to embrace purely economic losses in product liability cases. Moreover, the U.C.C. provisions provide the Court with ample room for the exercise of wide judicial discretion to ensure that substantial justice results in particular cases. *See, e.g.,* I.C. §§ 28–2–302 and–2–719(3) (concerning unconscionable clauses and contracts), and I.C. § 28–1–203 (imposing a general obligation of good faith).

* * *

The plaintiffs further argue that, in many of the cases which refused to permit the recovery of damages for economic loss in negligence actions and which are cited by the defendants, the absence of privity of contract between the parties was the determinative factor, not the nature of the damages. There is language in some cases suggesting that the absence of privity may have played a role in the reasoning of some courts which have denied the recovery of purely economic losses in negligence. [Citation.] The requirement of privity in negligence actions, an unfortunate amalgam of tort and contract principles, was for the most part laid to rest by Justice Cardozo's famous opinion in MacPherson v. Buick Motor Co., 217 N.Y. 382, 111 N.E. 1050 (1916), and we are not disposed to resurrect it in this case. Rather than obscure fundamental tort concepts with contract notions of privity, we believe it is analytically more useful to focus on the precise duty of care that the law of negligence, not the law of contract or an agreement by the parties, has imposed on the defendant International Harvester. The law of negligence requires the defendant to exercise due care to build a tractor that does not harm person or property. If the defendant fails to exercise such due care it is of course liable for the resulting injury to person or property as well as other losses which naturally follow from that injury. However, the law of negligence does not impose on International Harvester a duty to build a tractor that plows fast enough and breaks down infrequently enough for Clark to make a profit in his custom farming business. This is not to say that such a duty could not arise by a warranty—express or implied— by agreement of the parties or by representations of the defendant, but the law of negligence imposes no such duty. Accordingly the trial court erred in granting a judgment to the plaintiffs on their negligence count.

* * * [Reversed and remanded.]

---

1. Distinguish purely economic loss from other types of harm that can be caused by a defective product:

(a) *Physical injury to person.* A defective product may cause personal injury, such as when an automobile manufactured with defective brakes is responsible for a traffic accident. A victim can recover losses under a theory of negligence, if any, or under a strict liability theory following § 402A of the Restatement (Second) of Torts.

(b) *Physical injury to property.* A defective product may cause losses to property, such as when a misdesigned room heater causes a fire. Most courts allow recovery either under a theory of negligence, if any, or under the strict liability theory of § 402A of the Restatement (Second) of Torts. Some courts have distinguished injury to the defective product itself from injury to other property.

(c) *Economic injury from loss of bargain.* The buyer of a defective product has an economic loss because a defective product is worth less than the nondefective one that the buyer contracted to purchase. The buyer may have claims in express or implied warranty under state and federal law, but most jurisdictions do not allow an action in tort without proof of actionable misrepresentation, such as fraud. Absent such exception, remedies are governed by warranty law.

(d) *Other economic injury.* There may be other pecuniary losses besides the loss of the bargain when a defective product fails to perform as expected. When equipment is needed for a business, profits may be lost if a defect in the equipment prevents its normal use. As the principal case illustrates, most jurisdictions follow the general negligence rule in this area as in others and deny recovery.

Economic losses similarly are not recoverable under strict products liability. The leading case is Seely v. White Motor Co., 63 Cal.2d 9, 403 P.2d 145, 45 Cal.Rptr. 17 (1965). Jurisdictions are split on this issue, but most follow *Seely*. Plaintiffs may recover purely economic losses under theories of express or implied warranty, although they are often barred by contract limitations or substantive limitations such as privity of contract, depending on the rules of the jurisdiction.

2. Compare the economic loss suffered when an attorney commits malpractice. This tort allows recovery of provable losses even though they are only economic ones without accompanying physical harm to person or property. *See* Smith v. Lewis, 13 Cal.3d 349, 530 P.2d 589, 118 Cal.Rptr. 621 (1975) ($100,000 award against attorney who represented wife in divorce proceeding and failed to claim her interest in the husband's retirement benefits). Why should purely economic losses caused by legal malpractice be compensable when ones from a defective product are not? Why distinguish between them?

3. In *Clark*, the plaintiff's economic loss resulted not just from an inability to seek business, but from an inability to perform existing contracts with third parties. This distinction was not fruitful.

An absolute bar to recovery for negligent interferences with contracts found an early expression in the United States in Robins Dry Dock & Repair Co. v. Flint, 275 U.S. 303, 309, 48 S.Ct. 134, 135, 72 L.Ed. 290 (1927), where Justice Holmes, writing for the Court stated:

[W]hile intentionally to bring about a breach of contract may give rise to a cause of action ... a tort to the person or property of one man does not make the tortfeasor liable to another merely because the injured person was under a contract with that other, unknown to the doer of the wrong. The law does not spread its protection so far. [Citations.]

The Restatement (Second) of Torts adopts the distinction made by Justice Holmes by denying recovery for pecuniary losses resulting from a negligent interference with contractual performance (§ 766C), but allowing compensation if the tortfeasor intentionally interfered with performance (§ 766A) or with prospective contractual relations (§ 766B).

4. The *Robins* approach of flatly denying recovery for economic losses in negligent interference with contract cases has shown continued vitality among several federal circuit courts. Barber Lines A/S v. M/V Donau Maru, 764 F.2d 50 (1st Cir.1985); Getty Refining and Mktg. Co. v. MT Fadi B, 766 F.2d 829 (3d Cir.1985); Louisiana ex rel. Guste v. M/V Testbank, 752 F.2d 1019 (5th Cir.1985). In *Testbank,* the court justified its reaffirmation of the per se rule against recovery for pecuniary harm on the dual basis that a pragmatic limit was necessary to avoid disproportionate damages relative to the defendant's fault, "liability in an indeterminate amount for an indeterminate time to an indeterminate class." (Quoting Justice Cardozo in Ultramares Corp. v. Touche, 255 N.Y. 170, 174 N.E. 441 (1931).)

Does the result in *Robins* and its progeny really devolve into a policy question of where to allocate losses in the most economically efficient manner from an insurance perspective? *See Testbank,* 752 F.2d at 1029.

5. Even those courts which apply the strict bar rule of *Robins* recognize recovery of lost profits or other pecuniary losses which are "parasitic to an injury to person or property." Restatement (Second) of Torts § 766C comment b. Reconsider the justification for this distinction made in Clark v. International Harvester. Do you find the court's analysis persuasive?

PEOPLE EXPRESS AIRLINES v. CONSOLIDATED RAIL CORP.

100 N.J. 246, 495 A.2d 107 (1985).

HANDLER, J.

This appeal presents a question that has not previously been directly considered: whether a defendant's negligent conduct that interferes with a plaintiff's business resulting in purely economic losses, unaccompanied by property damage or personal injury, is compensable in tort. The appeal poses this issue in the context of the defendants' alleged negligence that caused a dangerous chemical to escape from a railway tank car, resulting in the evacuation from the surrounding area of persons whose safety and health were threatened. The plaintiff, a commercial airline, was forced to evacuate its premises and suffered an interruption of its business operations with resultant economic losses.

Because of the posture of the case—an appeal taken from the grant of summary judgment for the defendant railroad, subsequently reversed by the Appellant Division, we must accept plaintiff's version of the facts as alleged. The facts are straight-forward.

On July 22, 1981, a fire began in the Port Newark freight yard of defendant Consolidated Rail Corporation (Conrail) when ethylene oxide manufactured by defendant BASF Wyandotte Company (BASF) escaped from a tank car, punctured during a "coupling" operation with another rail car, and ignited. The tank car was owned by defendant Union Tank Car Company (Union Car) and was leased to defendant BASF.

The plaintiff asserted at oral argument that at least some of the defendants were aware from prior experiences that ethylene oxide is a highly volatile substance; further, that emergency response plans in case of an accident had been prepared. When the fire occurred that gave rise to this lawsuit, some of the defendants' consultants helped determine how much of the surrounding area to evacuate. The municipal authorities then evacuated the area within a one-mile radius surrounding the fire to lessen the risk to persons within the area should the burning tank car explode. The evacuation area included the adjacent North Terminal building of Newark International Airport, where plaintiff People Express Airlines' (People Express) business operations are based. Although the feared explosion never occurred, People Express employees were prohibited from using the North Terminal for twelve hours.

The plaintiff contends that it suffered business-interruption losses as a result of the evacuation. These losses consist of cancelled scheduled flights and lost reservations because employees were unable to answer the telephones to accept bookings; also, certain fixed operating expenses allocable to the evacuation time period were incurred and paid despite the fact that plaintiff's offices were closed. No physical damage to airline property and no personal injury occurred as a result of the fire.

According to People Express' original complaint, each defendant acted negligently and these acts of negligence proximately caused the plaintiff's harm. * * *

The single characteristic that distinguishes parties in negligence suits whose claims for economic losses have been regularly denied by American and English courts from those who have recovered economic losses is, with respect to the successful claimants, the fortuitous occurrence of physical harm or property damage, however slight. It is well-accepted that a defendant who negligently injures a plaintiff or his property may be liable for all proximately caused harm, including economic losses. *See* Palsgraf v. Long Island R.R., 248 N.Y. 339, 162 N.E. 99 (1928); W. Prosser & W. Keeton, *The Law of Torts* § 129, at 997 (5th ed. 1984) (Prosser & Keeton). Nevertheless, a virtually *per se* rule barring recovery for economic loss unless the negligent conduct also caused physical harm has evolved throughout this century, based, in part, on Robins Dry Dock & Repair Co. v. Flint, 275 U.S. 303, 48 S.Ct. 134, 72 L.Ed. 290 (1927) and Cattle v. Stockton Waterworks Co., 10 Q.B. 453 (1875). * * *

The reasons that have been advanced to explain the divergent results for litigants seeking economic losses are varied. Some courts have viewed the general rule against recovery as necessary to limit damages to reasonably foreseeable consequences of negligent conduct. This concern in a given case is often manifested as an issue of causation and has led to the requirement of physical harm as an element of proximate cause. In this context, the physical harm requirement functions as part of the definition of the causal relationship between the defendant's negligent act and the plaintiff's economic damages; it acts as a convenient clamp on otherwise boundless liability. [Citations.] The physical harm rule also reflects certain deep-seated concerns that underlie courts' denial of recovery for purely economic losses occasioned by a defendant's negligence. These concerns include the fear of fraudulent claims, mass litigation, and limitless liability, or liability out of proportion to the defendant's fault. * * *

It is understandable that courts, fearing that if even one deserving plaintiff suffering purely economic loss were allowed to recover, all such plaintiffs could recover, have anchored their rulings to the physical harm requirement. While the rationale is understandable, it supports only a limitation on, not a denial of, liability. The physical harm requirement capriciously showers compensation along the path of physical destruction, regardless of the status or circumstances of individual claimants. Purely economic losses are borne by innocent victims, who may not be able to absorb their losses. [Citation.] In the end, the challenge is to fashion a rule that limits liability but permits adjudication of meritorious claims. The asserted inability to fix chrystalline formulae for recovery on the differing facts of future cases simply does not justify the wholesale rejection of recovery in all cases.

* * *

We may appropriately consider two relevant avenues of analysis in defining a cause of action for negligently-caused economic loss. The first examines the evolution of various exceptions to the rule of nonrecovery for purely economic losses, and suggests that the exceptions have cast considerable doubt on the validity of the current rule and, indeed, have laid the foundation for a rule that would allow recovery. The second explores the elements of a suitable rule and adopts the traditional approach of foreseeability as it relates to duty and proximate cause molded to circumstances involving a claim only for negligently-caused economic injury.

Judicial discomfiture with the rule of nonrecovery for purely economic loss throughout the last several decades has led to numerous exceptions in the general rule. Although the rationalizations for these exceptions differ among courts and cases, two common threads run throughout the exceptions. The first is that the element of foreseeability emerges as a more appropriate analytical standard to determine the question of liability than a *per se* prohibitory rule. The second is that the extent to which the defendant knew or should have known the particular consequences of his negligence, including the economic loss of a particularly foreseeable plaintiff, is dispositive of the issues of duty and fault.

One group of exceptions is based on the "special relationship" between the tortfeasor and the individual or business deprived of economic expectations. Many of these cases are recognized as involving the tort of negligent misrepresentation, resulting in liability for specially foreseeable economic losses. Importantly, the cases do not involve a breach of contract claim between parties in privity; rather, they involve tort claims by innocent third parties who suffered purely economic losses at the hands of negligent defendants with whom no direct relationship existed. Courts have justified their finding of liability in these negligence cases based on notions of a special relationship between the negligent tortfeasors and the foreseeable plaintiffs who relied on the quality of defendants' work or services, to their detriment. The special relationship, in reality, is an expression of the courts' satisfaction that a duty of care existed because the plaintiffs were particularly foreseeable and the injury was proximately caused by the defendant's negligence.

The special relationship exception has been extended to auditors, surveyors, termite inspectors, engineers, attorneys, notaries public, architects, weighers, and telegraph companies. [Citations given for each category.]

A related exception in which courts have allowed recovery for purely economic losses has been extended to plaintiffs belonging to a particularly foreseeable group, such as sailors and seamen, for whom the law has traditionally shown great solicitude. [Citations.]

Courts have found it fair and just in all of these exceptional cases to impose liability on defendants who, by virtue of their special activities, professional training or other unique preparation for their work, had particular knowledge or reason to know that others, such as the intended beneficiaries of wills [citation] or the purchasers of stock who were expected to rely on the company's financial statement in the prospectus [citation] would be economically harmed by negligent conduct. In this group of cases, even though the particular plaintiff was not always foreseeable, the particular class of plaintiffs was foreseeable as was the particular type of injury.

A very solid exception allowing recovery for economic losses has also been created in cases akin to private actions for public nuisance. Where a plaintiff's business is based in part upon the exercise of a public right, the plaintiff has been able to recover purely economic losses caused by a defendant's negligence. [Citations.] The theory running throughout these cases, in which the plaintiffs depend on the exercise of the public or riparian right to clean water as a natural resource, is that the pecuniary losses suffered by those who make direct use of the resource are particularly foreseeable because they are so closely linked, through the resource, to the defendants' behavior.

Particular knowledge of the economic consequences has sufficed to establish duty and proximate cause in contexts other than those already considered. In Clay v. Jersey City, 74 N.J.Super. 490, 181 A.2d 545 (Ch.Div.1962), aff'd, 84 N.J.Super. 9, 200 A.2d 787 (App.Div.1964), for example, a lessee-manufacturer had to vacate the building in which its business was located because of the defendant city's negligent failure to maintain its sewer line while the line was repaired. While there was some property damage, the court treated the tenant's and owner's claims separately; the tenant's claims were purely economic, stemming from the loss of use of its property right, as in the instant case. Further, the city had had notice of the leak since 1957 and should have known about it even earlier. Duty, breach and proximate cause were found to exist; the plaintiff-tenant recovered lost profits and expenses incurred during the shut-down. [Citation.]

These exceptions expose the hopeless artificiality of the *per se* rule against recovery for purely economic losses. When the plaintiffs are reasonably foreseeable, the injury is directly and proximately caused by defendant's negligence, and liability can be limited fairly, courts have endeavored to create exceptions to allow recovery. The scope and number of exceptions, while independently justified on various grounds, have nonetheless created lasting doubt as to the wisdom of the *per se* rule of nonrecovery for purely economic losses. Indeed, it has been fashionable for commentators to state that the rule has been giving way for nearly fifty years, although the cases have not always kept pace with the hypothesis. [Citations.]

One thematic motif that may be extrapolated from these decisions to differentiate between those cases in which recovery for economic losses was allowed and denied is that of foreseeability as it related to both the duty owed and proximate cause. The traditional test of negligence is what a reasonably prudent person would foresee and do in the circumstances; duty is clearly defined by knowledge of the risk of harm or the reasonable apprehension of that risk. * * *

The further theme that may be extracted from these decisions rests on the specificity and strictness that are infused into the definitional standard of foreseeability. The foreseeability standard that may be synthesized from these cases is one that posits liability in terms of where, along a spectrum ranging from the general to the particular, foreseeability is ultimately found. [Citations.] A broad view of these cases reasonably permits the conclusion that the extent of liability and degree of foreseeability stand in direct proportion to one another. The more particular is the foreseeability that economic loss will be suffered by the plaintiff as a result of defendant's negligence, the more just is it that liability be imposed and recovery allowed.

We hold therefore that a defendant owes a duty of care to take reasonable measures to avoid the risk of causing economic damages, aside from physical injury, to particular plaintiffs or plaintiffs comprising an identifiable class with respect to whom defendant knows or has reason to know are likely to suffer such damages from its conduct. A defendant failing to adhere to this duty of care may be found liable for such economic damages proximately caused by its breach of duty.

We stress that an identifiable class of plaintiffs is not simply a foreseeable class of plaintiffs. For example, members of the general public, or invitees such as sales and service persons at a particular plaintiff's business premises, or persons travelling on a highway near the scene of a negligently-caused accident, such as the one at bar, who are delayed in the conduct of their affairs and suffer varied economic losses, are certainly a foreseeable class of plaintiffs. Yet their presence within the area would be fortuitous, and the particular type of economic injury that could be suffered by such persons would be hopelessly unpredictable and not realistically foreseeable. Thus, the class itself would not be sufficiently ascertainable. An identifiable class of plaintiffs must be particularly foreseeable in terms of the type of persons or entities comprising the class, the certainty or predictability of their presence, the approximate numbers of those in the class, as well as the type of economic expectations disrupted. [Citations.]

[The court reviews the role of proximate cause to restrict recoveries and concludes that the economic losses must be reasonably foreseeable, not just generally foreseeable.] * * * If negligence is the failure to take precautions that cost less than the damage wrought by the ensuing accident, it would be unfair and socially inefficient to assign liability for harm that no reasonably-undertaken precaution could have avoided. [Citations.]

We conclude therefore that a defendant who has breached his duty of care to avoid the risk of economic injury to particularly foreseeable plaintiffs may be held liable for actual economic losses that are proximately caused by its breach of duty. In this context, those economic losses are recoverable as damages when they are the natural and probable consequence of a defendant's negligence in the sense that they are reasonably to be anticipated in view of defendant's capacity to have foreseen that the particular plaintiff or identifiable class of plaintiffs, as defined *infra,* is demonstrably within the risk created by defendant's negligence.

We are satisfied that our holding today is fully applicable to the facts that we have considered on this appeal. Plaintiff has set forth a cause of action under our decision, and it is entitled to have the matter proceed to a plenary trial. Among the facts that persuade us that a cause of action has been established is the close proximity of the North Terminal and People Express Airlines to the Conrail freight yard; the obvious nature of the plaintiff's operations and particular foreseeability of economic losses resulting from a accident and evacuation; the defendants' actual or constructive knowledge of the volatile properties of ethylene oxide; and the existence of an emergency response plan prepared by some of the defendants (alluded to in the course of oral argument), which apparently called for the nearby area to be evacuated to avoid the risk of harm in case of an explosion. We do not mean to suggest by our recitation of these facts that actual knowledge of the eventual economic losses is necessary to the cause of action; rather, particular foreseeability will suffice. The plaintiff still faces a difficult task in proving damages, particularly lost profits, to the degree of certainty required in other negligence cases. The trial court's examination of these proofs must be exacting to ensure that damages recovered are those reasonably to have been anticipated in view of the defendants' capacity to have foreseen that this particular plaintiff was within the risk created by their negligence.

* * * [Remanded.]

PRUITT v. ALLIED CHEMICAL CORP.

523 F.Supp. 975 (E.D.Va.1981).

MERHIGE, DISTRICT JUDGE.

Plaintiffs bring the instant action against Allied Chemical Corporation ("Allied") for Allied's alleged pollution of the James River and Chesapeake Bay with the chemical agent commonly known as Kepone.

* * *

Plaintiffs allegedly engage in a variety of different businesses and professions related to the harvesting and sale of marine life from the Chesapeake Bay ("Bay").[1] All claim to have suffered economic harm from defendant's alleged discharges of Kepone into the James River and thence into the Bay. * * * [Defendant moved to dismiss the claims of all plaintiffs except the fishermen.]

All plaintiffs, subject to defendant's motion, claim as damages lost profits resulting from their inability to sell seafood allegedly contaminated by defendant's discharges, and from a drop in price resulting from a decline in demand for seafood coming from areas affected by Kepone. These plaintiffs can generally be described as parties suffering only indirect harm to their property or businesses as the result of Kepone pollution. They or their possessions have not been caused direct, physical damage by defendant. Instead, plaintiffs allege that the stream of profits they previously received from their businesses or employment has been interrupted, and they seek compensation for the loss of the prospective profits they have been denied. * * *

The Virginia Supreme Court has, to the Court's knowledge, never directly considered the question of recovery for loss of prospective economic benefits. It is commonly stated that the general rule both in admiralty and at common law has been that a plaintiff cannot recover for indirect economic harm. The logical basis for this rule is obscure. Although Courts have frequently stated that economic losses are "not

---

1. Plaintiffs include commercial fishermen; seafood wholesalers, retailers, distributors and processors; restaurateurs; mari- na, boat tackle and baitshop owners; and employees or all the above groups.

foreseeable" or "too remote", these explanations alone are rarely apposite. * * *

The Court frankly acknowledges the fact that there exist a substantial number of cases that may be construed to establish a general rule favorable to plaintiffs. As noted by the Ninth Circuit in Union Oil Co. v. Oppen, 501 F.2d 558 (9th Cir.1974), the general rule has found application in a wide variety of contexts:

> [T]he negligent destruction of a bridge connecting the mainland with an island, which caused a loss of business to the plaintiff who was a merchant on the island, has been held not to be actionable. . . . A plaintiff engaged in commercial printing has been held unable to recover against a negligent contractor who, while engaged in excavation pursuant to a contract with a third party, cut the power line upon which the plaintiff's presses depended. . . . A defendant who negligently injures a third person entitled to life-care medical services by the plaintiff is liable to the third person but not to the plaintiff. . . . The operators of a dry dock are not liable in admiralty to charterers of a ship, placed by its owners in the dry dock, for negligent injury to the ship's propeller where the injury deprived the charterer of the use of the ship.

501 F.2d at 563–64 (citations omitted).

Nevertheless, there also exist cases that conflict with this broadly recognized general rule. At least two of the minority cases deal with precisely the case present here: the loss of business opportunities due to pollution of streams adjoining a plaintiff's property. * * *

Given the conflicting case law from other jurisdictions, together with the fact that there exists no Virginia law on indirect, economic damages, the Court has considered more theoretical sources in order to find a principled basis for its decision. There now exists a considerable amount of literature on the economic rationale for tort law. In general, scholars in the field rely on Judge Learned Hand's classic statement of negligence [11] to argue that a principal purpose of tort law is to maximize social utility: where the costs of accidents exceeds the costs of preventing them, the law will impose liability.

The difficulty in the present case is how to measure the cost of Kepone pollution. In the instant action, those costs were borne most directly by the wildlife of the Chesapeake Bay. The fact that no one individual claims property rights to the Bay's wildlife could arguably preclude liability. The Court doubts, however, whether such a result would be just. Nor would a denial of liability serve social utility: many citizens, both directly and indirectly, derive benefit from the Bay and its

---

11. *See* United States v. Carroll Towing Co., 159 F.2d 169, 173 (2d Cir.1947), in which Judge Hand stated that a person's duty to prevent injuries from an accident "is a function of three variables: (1) The probability that [the accident will occur]; (2) the gravity of the resulting injury, if [it] does; (3) the burden of adequate precautions."

marine life. Destruction of the Bay's wildlife should not be a costless activity.

In fact, even defendant in the present action admits that commercial fishermen are entitled to compensation for any loss of profits they may prove to have been caused by defendant's negligence. The entitlement given these fishermen presumably arises from what might be called a constructive property interest in the Bay's harvestable species. These professional watermen are entitled to recover despite any direct physical damage to their own property. Presumably, sportsfishermen share the same entitlement to legal redress for damage to the Bay's ecology. The Court perceives no valid distinction between recognition of commercial damages suffered by those who fish for profit and personal harm suffered by those who fish for sport.

The claims now considered by the Court, however, are not those of direct users of the Bay, commercial or personal. Instead, defendant has challenged the right of those who buy and sell to direct users of the Bay, to maintain a suit.

Defendant would have the Court draw a sharp and impregnable distinction between parties who exploited the Bay directly, and those who relied on it indirectly. * * *

None of the plaintiffs here—including commercial fishermen—has suffered any direct damage to his private property. All have allegedly suffered economic loss as a result of harm to the Bay's ecology. Apart from these similarities, the different categories of plaintiffs depend on the Bay in varying degrees of immediacy. The commercial fishermen here fit within a category established in *Union Oil:* they "lawfully and directly make use of a resource of the sea." The use that marina and charterboat owners make of the water, though hardly less legal, is slightly less direct. (And indeed, businesses in similar situations have been held entitled to recover in other courts.) Still less direct, but far from nonexistent, is the link between the Bay and the seafood dealers, restaurateurs, and tackle shops that seek relief (as do the employees of these establishments).

One meaningful distinction to be made among the various categories of plaintiffs here arises from a desire to avoid double-counting in calculating damages. Any seafood harvested by the commercial fishermen here would have been bought and sold several times before finally being purchased for consumption. Considerations both of equity and social utility suggest that just as defendant should not be able to escape liability for destruction of publicly owned marine life entirely, it should not be caused to pay repeatedly for the same damage.

The Court notes, however, that allowance for recovery of plaintiffs' lost profits here would not in all cases result in double-counting of damages. Plaintiffs in categories B, C, D, E, and F [20] allegedly lost

---

20. Respectively, seafood wholesalers, retailers, processors, distributors and restaurateurs.

profits when deprived of supplies of seafood. Those profits represented a return on the investment of *each* of the plaintiffs in material and labor in their businesses, and thus the independent loss to each would not amount to double-counting. Conversely, defendants could not be expected to pay, as a maximum, more than the replacement value of a plaintiff's actual investment, even if the stream of profits lost when extra-polated into the future, would yield greater damages.

Tracing the stream of profits flowing from the Bay's seafood, however, involves the Court in other complexities. The employees of the enterprises named in categories B through F, for example, had no physical investment in their employers' businesses. Yet if plaintiffs' allegations are proven, these employees undoubtedly lost wages and faced a less favorable job market than they would have, but for defendant's acts, and they have thus been harmed by defendant. What is more, the number of parties with a potential cause of action against defendant is hardly exhausted in plaintiffs' complaint. In theory, parties who bought and sold to and from the plaintiffs named here also suffered losses in business, as did their employees. In short, the set of potential plaintiffs seems almost infinite.

* * *

The Court thus finds itself with a perceived need to limit liability, without any articulable reason for excluding any particular set of plaintiffs. Other courts have had to make similar decisions.[22] The Court concludes that plaintiffs who purchased and marketed seafood from commercial fishermen suffered damages that are not legally cognizable, because insufficiently direct. This does not mean that the Court finds that defendant's alleged acts were not the cause of plaintiffs' losses, or that plaintiffs' losses were in any sense unforeseeable. In fact, in part because the damages alleged by plaintiffs here were so foreseeable, the Court holds that those plaintiffs in categories G, H and I [23] have suffered legally cognizable damages. The Court does so for several reasons. The United States Court of Appeals for the Fourth Circuit has held, in admiralty, that a defendant should "pay ... once, but no more" for damages inflicted. While commercial fishing interests are protected by allowing the fishermen themselves to recover, it is unlikely that sports-fishing interests would be equally protected. Because the damages each

---

22. *See e.g.,* Judge Kaufmann's opinion in Petitions of Kinsman Transit Co., 388 F.2d 821, 824–25 (2d Cir.1968) (hereinafter cited as *Kinsman II*), where the court noted that

in the final analysis, the circumlocution whether posed in terms of "foreseeability," "duty," "proximate [sic] cause," "remoteness," etc. seems unavoidable.

and then turned to Judge Andrews well-known statement in Palsgraf v. Long I.R.

Co., 248 N.Y. 339, 162 N.E. 99, 104 (N.Y. 1928):

It is all a question of expediency ... of fair judgment, always keeping in mind the fact that we endeavor to make a rule in each case that will be practical and in keeping with the general understanding of mankind.

23. Boat, tackle and bait shop, and marina owners respectively.

sportsman suffered are likely to be both small[25] and difficult to establish, it is unlikely that a significant proportion of such fishermen will seek legal redress. Only if some set of surrogate plaintiffs is entitled to press its own claims which flow from the damage to the Bay's sportsfishing industry will the proper balance of social forces be preserved. Accordingly, the Court holds that to the extent plaintiffs in categories G, H and I suffered losses in sales of goods and services to sportsfishermen as a result of defendant's tortious behavior, they have stated a legally cognizable claim.

Defendant hardly has reason to complain of the equity of the Court's holding. First, it benefited above from the Court's exclusion of the claims of innocent businessmen in categories B through F who are probable victims of their alleged acts. Here, the Court applies different restrictions on liability for reasons of equity and efficiency previously addressed. Second, the "directness" of the harm, at least to plaintiffs in categories G and I,[27] is high here. Both operate on the water or at its edge. * * *

Plaintiffs' Count VIII alleges that defendant may be held liable under the law of admiralty. Defendant moves to dismiss this claim on the same ground previously discussed: that indirect damage to economic expectancies cannot serve as a basis of liability. Defendant argues that this case is governed by the holding of the Supreme Court in Robins Dry Dock & Repair Co. v. Flint, 275 U.S. 303, 48 S.Ct. 134, 72 L.Ed. 290 (1927). The Court is not convinced that *Robins* itself is dispositive here. Nevertheless, in light of *Robins* and subsequent cases thereunder, the Court concludes that the challenged claims of plaintiffs should be dismissed.

In *Robins,* a plaintiff had chartered a ship that was negligently damaged while in dry dock. As a result of the damage and consequent delay, plaintiff suffered losses. Rather than sue the ship's owner for breach of contract, the charter-party sued the dry dock. Justice Holmes, for the Court, held that "the law does not spread its protection so far" as to protect a party from economic loss caused by unintentional torts by third parties against those with whom the original party has continued to do business.

Robins is consistent with defendant's position. It is, however, arguably less than dispositive here, because it essentially involved questions of the law of third party contracts not necessarily applicable in the instant case. * * *

---

25. The net loss to any sportsman would have to take into account any enjoyment received from natural areas visited as a substitute to the Chesapeake Bay.

27. Generally boat and marina owners.

1. In Union Oil Co. v. Oppen, 501 F.2d 558 (9th Cir.1974), the Ninth Circuit recognized a narrow exception to the bright-line rule of *Robins Dry Dock* that precludes recovery of economic losses for negligent interference with contractual relations absent physical harm. The court held that commercial fishermen could recover lost profits attributable to an oil spill caused by the defendants because there was a special duty owed to this particular class of plaintiffs. The court relied upon case law which allowed recovery of economic losses against defendants engaged in certain professions, businesses or trades: pension consultants, accountants, architects, attorneys, notaries public, test hole drillers, title abstractors, termite inspectors, soil engineers, surveyors, real estate brokers, drawers of checks, director of corporations, trustees, bailees and public weighers.

The court further justified its decision with an economic analysis. The rule would effectuate maximum allocation of resources by charging such pecuniary losses against parties that are in the best position to take cost-avoidance measures. In this situation that party was the defendant oil companies.

2. The preclusion of economic losses in negligent interference with contracts is sometimes accomplished through a per se rule and sometimes through the tort concepts of proximate cause and duty. A leading proximate cause case concerning economic losses is *In re Kinsman Transit Co.* (*Kinsman II*), where Judge Kaufman noted:

> In the final analysis, the circumlocution whether posed in terms of "foreseeability," "duty," "proximate cause," "remoteness," etc. seems unavoidable. As we have previously noted, 338 F.2d at 725, we return to Judge Andrews' frequently quoted statement in Palsgraf v. Long Island R.R., 248 N.Y. 339, 354–355, 162 N.E. 99, 104, 59 A.L.R. 1253 (1928) (dissenting opinion): "It is all a question of expediency * * * of fair judgment, always keeping in mind the fact that we endeavor to make a rule in each case that will be practical and in keeping with the general understanding of mankind." 388 F.2d 821 (2d Cir.1968)

In *Kinsman II* the plaintiffs sought recovery for transportation and storage costs resulting from the defendant's negligent collision with a bridge. The court denied recovery on the grounds that the injuries were too remote or indirect a consequence of the defendant's negligence rather than by applying the absolute bar rule of *Robins*. *Accord,* In re Bethlehem Steel Corp., 631 F.2d 441 (6th Cir.1980), *cert. denied,* 450 U.S. 921, 101 S.Ct. 1370, 67 L.Ed.2d 349 (1981); Venore Transportation Co. v. M/V Struma, 583 F.2d 708 (4th Cir.1978).

STOP & SHOP COMPANIES, INC. v. FISHER
387 Mass. 889, 444 N.E.2d 368 (1983).

HENNESSEY, CHIEF JUDGE.

The Stop & Shop Companies, Inc. (Stop & Shop), filed a complaint in Superior Court seeking damages for the loss of business revenues allegedly caused by the defendants' negligent collision with a drawbridge resulting in the obstruction of the bridge. After hearings before a special master, a judge of the Superior Court granted summary judgment for the defendants and dismissed the complaint. * * *

The relevant facts as alleged in the complaint are as follows. Stop & Shop owns and operates a supermarket and a Bradlees retail store in Somerset, Massachusetts. Substantial numbers of customers from Fall River travel across the Brightman Street bridge (bridge) to shop at these stores. On or about September 2, 1979, the seagoing barge Irving Sea Lion, owned and operated by the defendant J.D. Irving, Limited, negligently struck the bridge. * * * As a result of the collision, the bridge was closed to traffic for approximately two months, causing a substantial decline in the number of customers who patronized Stop & Shop's stores, which were located at one end of the bridge. Based on these facts, Stop & Shop sought damages for the injury to its business on two theories: the defendants' negligence was the direct cause of Stop & Shop's economic harm, and the defendants' actions contributed to the creation of a nuisance which caused it substantial injury in the use and enjoyment of its property.

* * *

Stop & Shop relies on Newlin v. New England Tel. & Tel. Co., 316 Mass. 234, 235, 54 N.E.2d 929 (1944), to support its claim in negligence. The plaintiff in *Newlin* alleged that the defendant maintained a pole in a defective condition, by reason of which it fell, cutting off a power line to the plaintiff's mushroom plant. As a result, the mushrooms overheated, the crop was destroyed, and the plaintiff sought to recover for his economic loss. The court held that the plaintiff stated a cause of action.

Stop & Shop's reliance on *Newlin* is misplaced. The economic loss in *Newlin* arose from physical harm to the plaintiff's crop. Stop & Shop's losses, by contrast, were not associated with any physical damage to its property.

Those cases relying on *Newlin* have involved physical harm to the plaintiff or his property. [Citations.] Moreover, the Restatement (Second) of Torts, § 766C (1977) denies recovery for "pecuniary harm not deriving from physical harm ... [which] results from the [defendant's] negligently ... interfering with the [plaintiff's] acquiring a contractual relation with a third person." Although some commentators have criticized this position, it remains the general view. [Citations.] Under these circumstances, we see no reason to apply the negligence analysis of *Newlin* to Stop & Shop's purely economic harm.

Stop & Shop's primary claim is that it is entitled to recover because the defendants' conduct created a nuisance which caused Stop & Shop economic loss. Accepting Stop & Shop's allegations as true, the defendants' negligence closed the bridge for approximately two months. This was an obstruction of a public way, and as such constituted a public nuisance. [Citations.] It is firmly established that an individual cannot recover for damages caused by a public nuisance "unless ... he has sustained some special and peculiar damage thereby, different in kind, and not merely in degree, from that which is occasioned to other persons by the alleged nuisance." [Citations.] The difficulty has been to determine whether a given plaintiff's damages are different in kind, so as to support recovery.

Our older cases held that, absent physical harm to the plaintiff's property, obstruction of a public way caused special damages only if the obstruction cut off immediate access to a public highway or river. [Citations.] Thus, in French v. Connecticut River Lumber Co., 145 Mass. 261, 14 N.E. 113 (1887), an innkeeper was allowed to recover for lost profits caused by the defendant's obstructing a river at the plaintiff's landing place, which cut off the plaintiff's access to the river. [Citations.] In essence, we took the view that use of a public way was a public right, and so a harm stemming from loss of that use, absent loss of direct access, was not different in kind. Thus, harm to Stop & Shop resulting from its customers' loss of the use of a public road would not amount to special damages under these cases. By contrast, physical harm to property, or loss of immediate access from one's property to the system of public roads or rivers, interfered with an individual's right, and hence was a special harm. [Citations.]

Our old rule has the advantage of avoiding a multitude of suits by setting up a clear and restrictive line of demarcation between special and general damages. While such a clear line also has a certain theoretical appeal, we conclude that its clarity does not compensate for the fact that it precludes any claim, even in cases where an established business may have been virtually destroyed. [Citation.] Accordingly, we hold that an established business may state a claim in nuisance for severe economic harm resulting from loss of access to its premises by its customers.

We note that a majority of the Federal courts take the opposite view. Although they use negligence analyses, it is clear that these Federal courts would reach the same result in nuisance, and a few cases have expressly so held. [Citations.] The question is admittedly one of policy; at what point should the tortfeasor's liability stop. [Citations.] We recognize the wisdom of the general rule which denies recovery for negligently caused economic harm. However, not all negligent acts give rise to a public nuisance, or more particularly, to an obstruction of a public way. In light of the degree of harm required for an obstruction to amount to a public nuisance, and the dependence of businesses and their customers on access to business establishments, we conclude that recovery may be warranted in some cases.

The plaintiff must suffer special pecuniary harm from the loss of access. Severe pecuniary loss is usually a special type of harm, but if a whole community suffers such loss, then it becomes a public wrong and the plaintiff cannot recover. [Citations.] Thus, the question becomes whether so many businesses have suffered the same economic harm that the plaintiff's damages are no longer special.

Similarly, the point at which a plaintiff has lost access is not fixed. "Deprivation of immediate access to land ... which is clearly a special kind of harm, shades off by imperceptible degrees into the remote obstruction of a highway, which is just as clearly not." [Citations.] * * *

We express no opinion as to the merits of Stop & Shop's public nuisance claim under these tests; the defendant remains free to challenge the claim on a motion for summary judgment. * * *

In sum, it is clear beyond dispute, and for obvious reasons, that policy rules limiting liability are recommended for application to cases like this one. In negligence cases, recovery has wisely been confined to physical damage to the plaintiff's property. In public nuisance claims we now decide that, absent physical harm or immediate or direct loss of access to the plaintiff's property, relief is warranted only where the plaintiff has suffered special pecuniary harm and substantial impairment of access. Further, these two principal issues are questions of degree.

The judgment of the Superior Court is reversed. * * *

---

1. Compare the result in *Stop & Shop* with Nebraska Innkeepers, Inc. v. Pittsburgh–Des Moines Corp., 345 N.W.2d 124 (Iowa 1984). The plaintiffs, connected with various motel and restaurant establishments, sought recovery for business losses sustained when a public bridge closed due to the negligence of defendants. The court denied recovery of the claimed economic losses because the plaintiffs had suffered no physical harm to their person or property. The court distinguished *Stop & Shop* by noting that the plaintiffs had not demonstrated the special harm required to recover under the theory of public nuisance.

2. For additional references see the following commentary: Gaebler, Negligence, Economic Loss, and the U.C.C., 61 Ind.L.J. 593 (1986); Robertson, Recovery in Louisiana Tort Law for Intangible Economic Loss: Negligence Actions and the Tort of Intentional Interference with Contractual Relations, 46 La.L.Rev. 737 (1986); Solimine, Recovery of Economic Damages in Products Liability Actions and the Reemergence of Contractual Remedies, 51 Mo.L.Rev. 977 (1986); Rabin, Tort Liability for Negligently Inflicted Economic Loss: A Reassessment, 37 Stan.L.Rev. 1513 (1985); McThenia & Ulrich, A Return to Principles of Corrective Justice in Deciding Economic Loss Cases, 69 Va.L.Rev. 1517 (1983); Rizzo, The Theory of Economic Loss in the Law of Torts, 11 J.Legal Stud. 281 (1982); O'Connell, The Interlocking Death and Rebirth of Contract and Tort, 75 Mich.L.Rev. 659 (1977); Note, Interference with Business or Occupation—Commercial Fisherman Can Recover Profits Lost As a Result of Negligently Caused Oil Spill—Union Oil Co. v. Oppen, 501 F.2d 558 (9th Cir.1974), 88 Harv.L.Rev. 444 (1974); Note, Union Oil Co. v. Oppen: Recovery of a Purely Economic Loss in Negligence, 60 Iowa L.Rev. 315 (1974); James, Limitations on Liability

for Economic Loss Caused by Negligence: A Pragmatic Appraisal, 25 Vand.L.Rev. 43 (1972); Note, Manufacturer's Liability to Remote Purchases for "Economic Loss" Damages—Tort or Contract?, 114 U.Pa. L.Rev. 539 (1966); Note, Negligent Interference with Economic Expectancy: The Case for Recovery, 16 Stan.L.Rev. 664 (1964); Harper, Interference with Contractual Relations, 47 Nw.U.L.Rev. 873 (1953).

Chapter 15

PUNITIVE DAMAGES

Section Coverage:

The area of civil damages that overlaps with criminal law is punitive damages, the purpose of which is to punish defendants for past egregious behavior and thus to deter future offenses. Punitive damages are sometimes called "smart money" because they are supposed to hurt the defendant financially. They are also often referred to as "exemplary damages" because they are intended to make the defendant a public example of inappropriate behavior. Despite the quasi-criminal nature of punitive damages, they do not carry the same heightened substantive and procedural safeguards accorded to defendants in criminal prosecutions.

A potential award of punitive damages serves as an incentive for a plaintiff to sue. When a court awards punitive damages, the plaintiff receives a windfall because by definition punitive damages are dollars awarded beyond any compensatory damages. Nonetheless, courts occasionally have justified the imposition of punitive damages as an indirect way of compensating plaintiffs for attorneys' fees or emotional distress where those elements of loss would not otherwise be compensable.

Punitive damages are never awarded automatically or as a matter of right, even in cases of intentional torts. Jurisdictions vary in the standard used for the permissibility of punitive damages. As a general matter, punitive damages are allowed when the defendant's conduct either reflects a subjective malicious intent or objectively indicates gross recklessness or a willful disregard for the rights of others.

Historically, courts did not allow punitive damages for breach of contract regardless of the motive or state of mind of the breaching party. Under modern law punitive damages are permissible at least when the circumstances that gave rise to a contract breach also constituted an independent tort. This exception has been particularly significant where the concept of tort has been expanded, such as in cases involving an insurer's breach of its duty of good faith and fair dealing with the insured. Some cases have gone even further to allow punitive damages when there was a tortious character to the contractual relations even if all the elements of an independent tort were not met.

The practice of awarding damages solely to punish and deter certain modes of behavior has a lengthy heritage in Anglo–American jurisprudence, but has come under sharp attack. Not only are defendants punished for anti-social conduct without benefit of the constitutional safeguards that apply to criminal law, but the result is not in keeping

706

with the traditional compensatory goal of damages law. When courts award punitive damages, the plaintiffs receive compensatory damages for their losses as well as the punitive damages windfall. Further, special problems exist in mass disaster or products liability cases where the same conduct may lead to multiple awards of punitive damages. Courts are challenged in such cases to accommodate principles of punishment and deterrence without imposing ruinous liability. A related problem these cases present is creating a race to judgment among plaintiffs who have filed separate but similar cases where each wishes to be the first, and thus possibly the last, to get a large punitive damages award. A variety of judicial and tort reform measures have sought to restrict punitive awards through various means, including heightening the standards for entitlement as well as placing ceilings on the dollar amounts allowable.

The trier of fact has discretion to determine the proper amount of punitive damages, and the award will stand unless its excessiveness "shocks the judicial conscience." A host of factors are relevant to the measurement of punitive damages, including the nature of the wrong, the relations of the parties, the degree of provocation, and the extent that the conduct offends the public sense of justice and propriety.

The extent of the harm to the plaintiff is relevant in calculating the amount of exemplary damages, although courts are split on the degree to which the harm must be monetary losses. It is generally said that punitive damages need not bear a fixed proportion to compensatory damages, but many jurisdictions require them to have some reasonable relationship to the compensatory damages award. This restriction is often troublesome in cases involving dignitary interests and civil rights where the compensatory damages may be small, yet the tortfeasor has acted in a particularly egregious manner.

The wealth or poverty of the defendant is an appropriate consideration in setting the level of punitive damages because the purpose of the award is to punish and to deter the defendant and others similarly situated from such conduct in the future. In products liability cases the wealth factor is often interpreted to mean the profits earned from marketing an unsafe product in reckless disregard of public safety. Problems arise when multiple cases seek to deprive the defendant of the same profit. At some point the numerous awards of punitive damages exceed the goal of punishment and deterrence and threaten the viability of the enterprise. Measurement restrictions, as well as substantive entitlement ones, have sometimes served to address this growing problem.

Model Case:

Terry Arnold worked for five years as a software design engineer for the High-tech Computer Company. The employment contract contained a non-competition clause which provided that Arnold could not work for any competitor of the company for a period of 18 months following termination of employment with High-tech.

Arnold received a lucrative offer of employment from the Newtech Computer Company and decided to accept the job despite the contractual restriction. High-tech could maintain a suit against Arnold for breach of contract and recover compensatory damages if the contractual noncompetition provision is valid. Moreover, the court might enjoin Arnold from working for any competitor for the term of the restriction.

High-tech might also seek punitive damages for this flagrant disregard of its rights, but it is unlikely to receive them. A contract breach does not generally support a punitive damages unless the plaintiff establishes a tortious basis for them. For instance, if High-tech could demonstrate that Arnold fraudulently misappropriated trade secrets, then exemplary damages might be available. Only a few courts have interpreted such tortious basis to mean less than full proof of the elements of an independent tort. Because the elements of fraud are particularly difficult to prove, High-tech is unlikely to establish a basis for punitive damages in this case.

HODGES v. S.C. TOOF & CO.

833 S.W.2d 896 (Tenn.1992).

DROWOTA. J.

In this retaliatory discharge action, Plaintiff–Appellant Carl E. Hodges alleges Defendant–Appellee S.C. Toof & Company terminated Plaintiff's employment because of his jury service. At trial, the Jury returned a verdict for Plaintiff and awarded him $200,000.00 compensatory and $375,000.00 punitive damages. The Court of Appeals, while upholding the jury's finding of retaliatory discharge, vacated the award of compensatory and punitive damages holding that under T.C.A. § 22–4–108, the exclusive remedy for an employee's discharge because of jury service was reinstatement and lost wages. We granted Plaintiff's application for permission to appeal in order to (1) decide whether the remedy provided by T.C.A. § 22–4–108 is exclusive and (2) reexamine the manner in which punitive damages are awarded in Tennessee.

Plaintiff Carl Hodges had been continuously employed by Defendant S.C. Toof & Company for some 19 years prior to his termination in January 1988. At the time of his firing, Plaintiff's position was that of assistant warehouse supervisor in Defendant's printing business. During his tenure, Plaintiff received 20 merit raises and had never been disciplined. In the summer of 1987 Plaintiff was called for jury service and sat as a juror in a three-month trial from mid-September to December 18, 1987. In early January 1988, Plaintiff was fired.

* * * At trial, Plaintiff claimed he was discharged because of his lengthy jury service; Defendant claimed Plaintiff was discharged because of disobedience. The jury found Plaintiff was terminated because of his jury service. There being material evidence in the record supporting

this verdict, it will not be disturbed on appeal. [The court determined that the statutory remedies of reinstatement and compensation for lost wages and benefits were not exclusive under the state law regarding retaliatory discharge, and then reinstated the jury award of compensatory damages.]

Having found the statutory remedies are not exclusive, we turn to the propriety of the punitive damages award. As early as 1840, this Court stated: "In an action of trespass the jury are not restrained, in their assessment of damages, to the amount of the mere pecuniary loss sustained by the plaintiff, but may award damages in respect of the malicious conduct of the defendant, and the degree of insult with which the trespass had been attended." [Citation.] Shortly thereafter we explained that these damages should operate to punish the defendant and deter others from like offenses. [Citation.] Now termed punitory, vindictive, or exemplary damages, they were legally appropriate "in cases of fraud, malice, gross negligence, or oppression." [Citation.] Exemplary damage awards became proper in two instances: first, if the wrongdoer acted with a fraudulent, malicious, or oppressive intent; and second, if the act, while not done with malicious intent, was done "in a rude, insulting or reckless manner, in disregard of social obligations, or with such gross negligence as to amount to positive misconduct." [Citation.] More recently we stated that punitive damages are available in cases involving fraud, malice, gross negligence, oppression, wrongful acts done with a bad motive or so recklessly as to imply a disregard of social obligations, or where willful misconduct or an entire want of care raises a presumption of conscious indifference to the consequences. [Citation.] The contemporary purpose of punitive damages is not to compensate the plaintiff but to punish the wrongdoer and to deter the wrongdoer and others from committing similar wrongs in the future. [Citation.] With these purposes in mind, and in the interest of fairness, we believe the time has come to reexamine, and modify, the manner in which punitive damages are awarded in Tennessee.

The United States Supreme Court has recently addressed constitutional challenges to punitive damage awards. In *Browning-Ferris Industries v. Kelco Disposal, Inc.*, the Court held that the Excessive Fines Clause of the Eighth Amendment did not apply to civil punitive damages awarded between private parties. 492 U.S. 257, 260, 109 S.Ct. 2909, 106 L.Ed.2d 219 (1989). Rather, the Eighth Amendment is implicated only in cases initiated by the government, either in the criminal process or other direct actions to inflict punishment.

Last Term, the Court considered whether the traditional common law method for assessing punitive damages violated due process under the Fourteenth Amendment. See Pacific Mut. Life Ins. Co. v. Haslip, 499 U.S. 1, 111 S.Ct. 1032, 113 L.Ed.2d 1 (1991). While the Court upheld the particular method employed by the Alabama courts in that case, it was not entirely clear whether the majority was giving its carte blanche approval to the common law scheme. In any event, we agree with the Court's observation that "unlimited jury discretion ... in the fixing of punitive damages may invite extreme results that jar one's constitutional sensibilities." Therefore, today we announce a new procedure aimed at providing specific criteria to guide a jury in deciding whether to award punitive damages and, if so, in what amount.

As stated earlier, Tennessee presently allows punitive damages in cases involving fraud, malice, gross negligence, oppression, evil motives, conscious indifference, and reckless conduct implying "disregard of social obligations." Whatever this may have once meant, by contemporary standards it is both vague ("social obligations") and overbroad ("gross negligence"). We agree with those States that have refined their laws to restrict the awarding of punitive damages to cases involving only the most egregious of wrongs. By thus restricting the availability of punitive damages, we seek to avoid "dull[ing] the potentially keen edge of the doctrine as an effective deterrent of truly reprehensible conduct." In Tennessee, therefore, a court may henceforth award punitive damages only if it finds a defendant has acted either (1) intentionally, (2) fraudulently, (3) maliciously, or (4) recklessly.

A person acts intentionally when it is the person's conscious objective or desire to engage in the conduct or cause the result. A person acts fraudulently when (1) the person intentionally misrepresents an existing, material fact or produces a false impression, in order to mislead another or to obtain an undue advantage, and (2) another is injured because of reasonable reliance upon that representation. [Citation.] A person acts maliciously when the person is motivated by ill will, hatred, or personal spite. A person acts recklessly when the person is aware of, but consciously disregards, a substantial and unjustifiable risk of such a nature that its disregard constitutes a gross deviation from the standard of care that an ordinary person would exercise under all the circumstances.

Further, because punitive damages are to be awarded only in the most egregious of cases, a plaintiff must prove the defendant's intentional, fraudulent, malicious, or reckless conduct by clear and convincing evidence.[3] This higher standard of proof is appropriate given the twin purposes of punishment and deterrence: fairness requires that a defendant's wrong be clearly established before punishment, as such, is imposed; awarding punitive damages only in clearly appropriate cases better effects deterrence.

In a trial where punitive damages are sought, the court, upon motion of defendant, shall bifurcate the trial. During the first phase, the factfinder shall determine (1) liability for, and the amount of, compensatory damages and (2) liability for punitive damages in accordance with the standards announced above. During this phase, evidence of a defendant's financial affairs, financial condition, or net worth is not admissible.

---

3. Clear and convincing evidence means evidence in which there is no serious or substantial doubt about the correctness of the conclusions drawn from the evidence.

If the factfinder finds a defendant liable for punitive damages, the amount of such damages shall then be determined in an immediate, separate proceeding. During this second phase, the factfinder shall consider, to the extent relevant, at least the following:

(1) The defendant's financial affairs, financial condition, and net worth;

(2) The nature and reprehensibility of defendant's wrongdoing, for example

(A) The impact of defendant's conduct on the plaintiff, or

(B) The relationship of defendant to plaintiff;

(3) The defendant's awareness of the amount of harm being caused and defendant's motivation in causing the harm;

(4) The duration of defendant's misconduct and whether defendant attempted to conceal the conduct;

(5) The expense plaintiff has borne in the attempt to recover the losses;

(6) Whether defendant profited from the activity, and if defendant did profit, whether the punitive award should be in excess of the profit in order to deter similar future behavior;

(7) Whether, and the extent to which, defendant has been subjected to previous punitive damage awards based upon the same wrongful act;

(8) Whether, once the misconduct became known to defendant, defendant took remedial action or attempted to make amends by offering a prompt and fair settlement for actual harm caused; and

(9) Any other circumstances shown by the evidence that bear on determining the proper amount of the punitive award.

The trier of fact shall be further instructed that the primary purpose of a punitive award is to deter misconduct, while the purpose of compensatory damages is to make plaintiff whole.

After a jury has made an award of punitive damages, the trial judge shall review the award, giving consideration to all matters on which the jury is required to be instructed. The judge shall clearly set forth the reasons for decreasing or approving all punitive awards in findings of fact and conclusions of law demonstrating a consideration of all factors on which the jury is instructed.

In this case, the jury awarded Plaintiff $200,000.00 compensatory damages and $375,000.00 punitive damages. The compensatory award is affirmed, the punitive award vacated, and the case remanded for a trial on the issue of punitive damages. At this trial, which shall be conducted as a bifurcated proceeding, the jury will be instructed as to the clear and convincing standard of evidence. If the jury finds this standard satisfied, it will then fix the amount of punitive damages after being instructed in accordance with this opinion. * * *

---

1.   The concept of punitive damages has a longstanding meaning and heritage under the common law.   In Molzof v. United States, 502 U.S. 301, 112 S.Ct. 711, 116 L.Ed.2d 731 (1992), the Court interpreted the meaning of the term "punitive damages" under Federal Tort Claims Act, 28 U.S.C. § 2674, in an action against the government for injuries sustained in a negligently performed surgical procedure at a Veteran's Administration hospital.   The government conceded liability but claimed that the damages requested for future medical expenses and loss of enjoyment of life were "punitive in effect" and consequently prohibited under the FTCA.

A unanimous Court rejected the government's contention that any damages that are not strictly compensatory are necessarily characterized as punitive.   The Court stated that "punitive damages" is a "legal term of art" with a "long pedigree in the law."   Thus, although some damages may fall in the "gray zone" for purposes of the FTCA, the Act only explicitly bars the recovery of those damages which are legally considered punitive damages by reference to traditional common-law principles.

2.   *Legislative reform affecting punitive damages.*   State legislatures have sought to regulate the imposition of punitive damages in a variety of measures over the past decade.   One common feature of state regulation involves heightening the plaintiff's burden of proof above the traditional preponderance of the evidence.   *See* Iowa Code Ann. § 668A.1(1)(a) (clear and convincing evidence); *Accord,* Gamma–10 Plastics v. American President Lines, Ltd., 32 F.3d 1244, 1255 (8th Cir.1994) (Minnesota standard for awarding punitive damages is establishing by "clear and convincing evidence" that the defendant acted with deliberate disregard for the rights or safety of others.)   *See also* Colo. Rev. Stat. § 13–25–127(2) (beyond a reasonable doubt).

Another technique is to place a cap or ceiling on punitive damages, either in absolute dollars or by a proportionate ratio to compensatory damages awarded.   *See* Kan. Stat. Ann. § 60–3701(e) (fixed ratio cap); Va. Code Ann. § 8.01–38.1 (1994) ($350,000 ceiling).   Such statutes generally have withstood constitutional challenge.   *See* Wackenhut Applied Technologies Ctr. v. Sygnetron Protection Sys., 979 F.2d 980 (4th Cir.1992); Mack Trucks, Inc. v. Conkle, 263 Ga. 539, 436 S.E.2d 635 (1993) (Upholding on equal protection grounds Georgia's statute which requires 75% of punitive damages awarded in products liability actions to be paid directly to the state treasury.)   *See also* N.H.Rev. Stat. Ann. § 507.16 (abolishing punitive damages unless otherwise authorized by statute).

A further variant on punitive damage reform legislation involves requiring some portion of the exemplary award to be paid directly to the state treasury. These so-called "extraction statutes" are, in essence, revenue-raising laws, that are typically justified on the basis that punitive damages advance the public interest in punishing and deterring conduct which offends societal norms. *See* Fla. Stat. Ann. § 768.73(2) (35% paid to state); Utah Code Ann. § 78–18(3) (50% of punitive damages over $20,000 paid to state); Mo.Rev. Stat. § 537.675(2) (50%, less attorneys fees and expenses payable to Tort Victims' Compensation Fund); Iowa Code Ann. § 668A.1(2)(b) (state's portion of punitive award placed in Civil Reparations Trust fund to aid indigent civil litigation or insurance assistance programs). Illinois gives discretion to the trial judge to apportion punitive damages among the plaintiff, the plaintiff's attorney, and the State Department of Rehabilitative Services Ill.Ann. Stat. ch. 735 pgh. ½–1207.

3. Consider in comparison to *Hodges* the following excerpt from Cal.Civ. Code § 3294, which governs entitlement to exemplary damages:

§ 3294. When permitted.

(a) In an action for the breach of an obligation not arising from contract, where it is proven by clear and convincing evidence that the defendant has been guilty of oppression, fraud, or malice, the plaintiff, in addition to the actual damages, may recover damages for the sake of example and by way of punishing the defendant.

* * *

(c) As used in this section, the following definitions shall apply:

(1) "Malice" means conduct which is intended by the defendant to cause injury to the plaintiff or despicable conduct which is carried on by the defendant with a willful and conscious disregard of the rights or safety of others.

(2) "Oppression" means despicable conduct that subjects a person to cruel and unjust hardship in conscious disregard of that person's rights.

(3) "Fraud" means an intentional misrepresentation, deceit, or concealment of a material fact known to the defendant with the intention on the part of the defendant of thereby depriving a person of property or legal rights or otherwise causing injury.

* * *

See Kanne v. Connecticut General Life Insurance Co., 607 F.Supp. 899 (C.D.Cal.1985), vacated on other grounds 859 F.2d 96 (9th Cir.1988) (punitive damages assessed against an insurance company for breaching its duty of good faith and fair dealing and acting with actual malice where the company "consciously disregarded" the plaintiffs' rights by failing to investigate, process, and pay their medical claims promptly). *Also see* Donald v. Liberty Mutual Ins. Co., 18 F.3d 474, 483 (7th Cir.1994) (recognized cause of action for tortious breach of insurer's duty of dealing with insured in good faith could support punitive damages award). *But see* College Hospital, Inc. v. Superior Court, 8 Cal.4th 704, 34 Cal.Rptr.2d 898, 882 P.2d 894 (1994) (Psychiatric patient failed to show "malice" justifying punitive damages based upon her trauma associated with an extramarital affair with her health care professional).

4. A claim for punitive damages is not considered an independent cause of action but is derivative in character. Therefore, although the elements of proof differ for punitive and compensatory damages, entitlement to an exemplary award is dependent upon success on the underlying claim. *See* Richardson v. Arizona Fuels Corp., 614 P.2d 636, 640 (Utah 1980).

5. *Nominal Damages.* A related question involves whether an award of nominal damages will support recovery of punitive damages. Some courts require actual damages as a predicate for an award of exemplary damages, and further that the punitives bear a reasonable relationship to the compensatory damages. *See, e.g.,* Grand Laboratories, Inc. v. Midcon Labs of Iowa, 32 F.3d 1277, 1286 (8th Cir.1994) (actual damages are necessary to support a claim for punitive damages); Morrissey v. Welsh Co., 821 F.2d 1294 (8th Cir.1987); Cook Industries, Inc. v. Carlson, 334 F.Supp. 809 (N.D.Miss.1971).

A substantial number of jurisdictions have held that nominal damages can support an award of punitive damages. The rationale is that the aims of punitive damages are to punish and deter certain types of misconduct rather than to compensate. *See, e.g.,* Keehr v. Consolidated Freightways of Delaware, Inc., 825 F.2d 133 (7th Cir.1987); Restatement (Second) of Torts § 908 comment c. Further, certain intentional acts do not require showing of actual damages, yet nevertheless may support punitive damages due to the special circumstances surrounding the misconduct. For example, in Lane County v. Wood, 298 Or. 191, 691 P.2d 473 (1984), the court found that a county commissioner's breach of fiduciary and statutory duties to the public in attempting to make personal profits from sale and exchange of public lands was sufficiently egregious that nominal damages would support award of punitive damages.

Jurisdictions that allow nominal damages to support punitive damages focus on the nature and character of the tortfeasor's misconduct rather than the amount of compensatory damages given. This approach has been particularly important in many civil rights cases where the plaintiff has not suffered pecuniary or physical harm from the violation. The Supreme Court held in Carey v. Piphus, 435 U.S. 247, 98 S.Ct. 1042, 55 L.Ed.2d 252 (1978), that nominal damages are an appropriate way to vindicate the deprivation of procedural due process rights where actual damages are not shown. Subsequent cases have allowed punitive damages without actual loss upon a showing of malicious intent or aggravating circumstances or reckless or callous indifference to the plaintiff's rights. *See* Perry v. Larson, 794 F.2d 279 (7th Cir.1986); Sahagian v.

Dickey, 827 F.2d 90 (7th Cir.1987); Endicott v. Huddleston, 644 F.2d 1208 (7th Cir.1980).

6. *Vicarious Liability for Punitive Damages:* A principal may be held vicariously liable for the torts committed by agents acting within the scope of their employment under the doctrine of *respondeat superior*. Such liability of a principal ordinarily allows assessment of compensatory damages, but it generally does not extend to the imposition of exemplary damages absent the principal's authorization, participation, or ratification of the agent's tortious conduct. *See, e.g.,* Samedan Oil Corp. v. Neeld, 91 N.M. 599, 577 P.2d 1245 (1978). These limitations on imposing vicarious liability for punitive damages recognizes that the justification of punishment of egregious conduct loses some force when applied against an entity for indirect accountability. Conversely, exemplary damages awarded against a principal for the tortious behavior of an agent promotes diligence in supervision and advances a deterrent function in society.

The Restatement (Second) of Torts § 909 advances a broader scope of vicarious liability for punitive damages by including situations involving the reckless employment of an unfit agent and acts within the scope of employment by agents serving in a managerial capacity. *Accord* Restatement (Second) of Agency § 217C. The rationale for the Restatement position is twofold: to encourage diligence in the selection and supervision of persons placed in management positions and to serve as a deterrent to the employment of unfit persons for important positions. Restatement (Second) of Torts § 909 comment b. *See* Egan v. Mutual of Omaha Ins. Co., 24 Cal 3d 809, 169 Cal.Rptr. 691, 620 P.2d 141 (1979) (Whether an employee has acted in a "managerial capacity" depends upon the degree of discretion the employee possesses in decision-making which determines corporate policy, not on their level in the corporate hierarchy.) *See also* Mitchell v. Keith, 752 F.2d 385 (9th Cir.1985).

In Albuquerque Concrete Coring Co. v. Pan Am World Services, Inc., 118 N.M. 140, 879 P.2d 772 (N.M.1994), the court held a general contractor vicariously liable for punitive damages for the tortious conduct of its project manager in dealing with a subcontractor. The court examined the meaning and scope of "managerial capacity" for purposes of assessing exemplary damages against a corporation:

In the modern world of multinational corporations, corporate control must be delegated to managing agents who may not possess the requisite upper-level executive authority traditionally considered necessary to trigger imposition of corporate liability for punitive damages. If we were to adopt the position that misconduct by managing agents who actually control daily operations is not sufficient to trigger corporate punitive damages, large corporations that routinely delegate managerial authority to shape corporate policy by making important corporate decisions could unfairly escape liability for punitive damages by virtue of their size. Corporate liability for punitive damages should depend upon corporate responsibility for wrongdoing, not corporate ability to insulate top executives from daily, hands-on management, *i.e.* only though exercising the "whole executive power" of the corporation. Our decision today accommodates modern practicalities. (citations omitted) 879 P.2d at 778.

Should an employer be held vicariously liable for punitive damages for intentional torts committed by an employee? In Rodebush v. Oklahoma Nursing Homes, Ltd., 867 P.2d 1241 (Okla.1993), an intoxicated nurse's aide slapped an elderly Alzheimer's patient while bathing him, causing welts and red marks on the patient's face. The jury awarded $50,000 compensatory damages and $1,200,000 in punitive damages against the nursing home under the principle of vicarious liability. The court found that the aide was acting within the scope of employment because the tortious conduct occurred incident to performing a task assigned by the nursing home.

7. *Punitive Damages in Equity:* The traditional rule that punitive damages are not recoverable in equity derives from the historical limitations on powers of equity courts. The notion was that the equity court lacked the power to award exemplary damages, and was limited in granting compensatory damages as merely incidental to other relief. *See* I.H.P. Corp. v. 210 Central Park South Corp., 16 A.D.2d 461, 228 N.Y.S.2d 883 (1962).

This limitation has lost its vitality following the merger of law and equity courts in most jurisdictions. Courts often quote the observation by Judge Cardozo in *Susquehanna S.S. Co. v. Andersen & Co.:* "The whole body of principles, whether of law or of equity, bearing on the case, becomes the reservoir to be drawn upon by the court in enlightening its judgment." 239 N.Y. 285, 294, 146 N.E. 381, 384.

Courts have diverged in the interpretation of statutes that authorize "equitable relief" as to the permissibility of punitive damages. *Compare* Schoenholtz v. Doniger, 657 F.Supp. 899 (S.D.N.Y.1987) (punitive damages available against fiduciary under ERISA) *with* Whitaker v. Texaco, Inc., 566 F.Supp. 745 (N.D.Ga.1983) (ERISA does not authorize exemplary damages).

8. *Punitive Damages in Arbitration.* Should punitive damages be available in commercial arbitration cases? One view holds that an arbitrator lacks the power to award punitive damages even with the consent of the parties. *See* Garrity v. Lyle Stuart, Inc., 40 N.Y.2d 354, 353 N.E.2d 793, 386 N.Y.S.2d 831 (1976) (Punitive damages disallowed as violative of public policy, intruding on province of jury and court to determine sanctions). In contrast, Willoughby Roofing & Supply Co. v. Kajima Intern., 598 F.Supp. 353 (N.D.Ala.1984), the court sanctioned the authority of commercial arbitrators to make a punitive award. The court recognized arbitration as a viable method of dispute resolution, necessitating a liberal view of an arbitrator's authority and need for flexibility to determine an appropriate remedy commensurate with the harm. *See generally* Stipanowich, Punitive Damages in Arbitration: Garrity v. Lyle Stuart, Inc. Reconsidered, 66 B.U.L.Rev. 953 (1986), for

an excellent expression of the view supportive of heightened deference to arbitral power and flexibility in fashioning relief as consonant with the purposes behind arbitration as an alternative vehicle to litigation.

PROBLEM

A car driven by Chris Durkin jumped the curb and ran into a group of pedestrians on the sidewalk. A young child was severely and permanently injured. At the time of the accident Durkin was drunk, with a blood alcohol level significantly higher than the legal limit. Durkin had been battling alcoholism for a number of years and had been involved in a previous drunk-driving accident. At the time of the accident Durkin's driving license had been suspended because of the previous accident.

On the afternoon of the accident in question, Durkin was too drunk to walk for more than a few steps. The accident occurred only two blocks from where Durkin began to drive.

Consider whether punitive damages should be available in a case of this type. Is it possible to characterize Durkin's behavior as reflecting a callous indifference toward the safety of others? What if the conduct is considered only grossly negligent? Is there a distinction between the conduct at the moment of the accident and at some previous time when the tortfeasor made the (sober?) decision to continue driving with an alcohol problem and without a license? Does that difference matter?

Consider also whether liability insurance should cover punitive damages. If the purpose is to punish certain conduct, then is the purpose defeated by allowing insurance to cover the loss? On the other hand, should the law constrain the ability of parties to contract for such coverage? If insurance coverage is disallowed as a matter of public policy, what is the practical effect of such a rule?

WAUCHOP v. DOMINO'S PIZZA, INC.

832 F.Supp. 1577 (N.D.Ind.1993).

MILLER, DISTRICT JUDGE.

[This factual background is taken from a companion case, 832 F.Supp. 1572. Susan Wauchop died as a result of an automobile accident in Granger, Indiana, when her minivan was struck by a car driven by Christopher Braden. At the time of the accident, Mr. Braden was employed at a Domino's Pizza store that was owned and operated by Scott Halvorsen. Domino's Pizza, Inc. did not own or operate Mr. Halvorsen's store, but the store had a franchise agreement with Domino's. Mr. Braden supplied his own delivery car, which the Halvorsens inspected. Domino's never owned, supplied, maintained, inspected, or saw Mr. Braden's car.

The standard franchise agreement entered into between Domino's and Mr. Halvorsen contained the following language:

[T]he store will not offer delivery service to any customer whose order cannot be delivered within thirty (30) minutes of the time when such order is placed, taking into consideration the least favorable driving conditions and your [the franchisee's] strict compliance with all laws, regulations and rules of the road and due care and caution in the operation of delivery vehicles.

Domino's offers a guarantee to customers that provides:

All Domino's Pizza stores, corporate owned and franchised owned, are to guarantee pizza delivery in 30 minutes or less to every customer serviced. A minimum discount of $3.00 off the sale price, defined as the price normally charged to the customer minus the amount for any advertising special or promotional discount, is to be given to the customer for every order delivered in over 30 minutes. The discount is to be given at the time the late delivery is made and is to apply to all orders of five pizzas or less. Customers are to be informed that the guarantee for orders larger than five pizzas requires a 24 hour notice. The Guarantee Policy is to remain in effect for all stores during all hours of operation with exception given only under the following condition:

During times where extremely severe weather conditions make delivery service in less than 30 minutes impossible, the guarantee may be waived only for such time as conditions prevent proper delivery service. In addition, all customers are to be notified at the time their order is taken of the policy postponement, otherwise, the store will be required to honor the guarantee.

This policy in no way implies that the company expects its employees to act or deliver pizzas in an unsafe manner in order to meet the 30 minute deadline. The Domino's pizza delivery system coupled with limited delivery areas enables drivers to deliver pizzas safely to customers in less than 30 minutes. All delivery personnel are expected to deliver in accordance with company safety policies as well as state and federal traffic laws regardless of the 30 minute delivery guarantee policy.]

This cause comes before the court on the motion of defendant Domino's Pizza, Inc. for summary judgment as to Count XI of the plaintiffs' complaint, which seeks punitive damages. Count XI alleges that, "For years prior to May 25, 1990, ... Domino's willfully and wantonly maintained THE 30 MINUTE RULE although [it] knew or should have known that [the 30–minute guarantee] resulted and would likely continue to result in motor vehicle accidents causing death and serious injuries." * * *

II.

Indiana courts have used one test to describe the standard of conduct required for punitive damages in connection with a breach of contract, and another to describe such conduct in negligence cases. [Citation.] To recover punitive damages for breach of contract, the plaintiff must show, by clear and convincing evidence, that the defendant acted with malice, fraud, gross negligence, or oppressiveness, and that the defendant's actions were "inconsistent with the hypothesis that the tortious conduct was a result of a mistake of law or fact, honest error of judgment, overzealousness, mere negligence or other noniniquitous human failing." [Citations.] Moreover, the Indiana Supreme Court recently held that to recover punitive damages for breach of contract, the "plaintiff must plead and prove the existence of an independent tort of the kind for which Indiana law recognizes that punitive damages may be awarded." [Citation.]

In actions arising under tort, mere negligence will not support an award of punitive damages; failing to act as a reasonable person would have acted does not constitute the type of conduct punishable by punitive damages. [Citations.] Rather, punitive damages may be awarded only upon a showing by clear and convincing evidence that the defendant "subjected other persons to probable injury, with an awareness of such impending danger and with heedless indifference of the consequences." [Citations.] Punitive damages may be awarded upon a showing of Domino's willful and wanton misconduct, even absent malice, ill will, or intent to injure. [Citations.]

The Indiana Supreme Court has stated:

The perverseness that public policy will permit the courts to punish is conscious and intentional misconduct which, under the existing conditions, the actor knows will probably result in injury.

As examples of such misconduct, our decision in [Orkin Exterminating Co. v.] Traina [486 N.E.2d at 1023] recognized the following: conscious indifference, heedless indifference, reckless disregard for the safety of others, reprehensible conduct, and heedless disregard of the consequences. [Citations.]

Both the plaintiffs and Domino's agree that the award of punitive damages turns upon Domino's state of mind: whether Domino's knew of, but consciously disregarded, the danger of the 30–minute guarantee. [Citations.]

State of mind, however, is a fact to be inferred from the surrounding circumstances, and caution should be employed before granting summary judgment:

Knowledge on the part of [a] company can be proved only by showing the state of mind of its employees. The court should be cautious in granting a motion for summary judgment when resolution of the dispositive issue requires a determination of state of mind. Much depends upon the credibility of witnesses testifying as to their own states of mind. In these circumstances, the jury should be given the opportunity to observe the demeanor, during direct and cross-examination, of the witnesses whose states of mind are at issue. [Citations.]

The Seventh Circuit has provided that "where the defendant's motive or state of mind is an essential element of a plaintiff's case, a court must be circumspect in granting summary judgment based solely on the defendant's categorical denial that the requisite mental state existed." [Citations.] It is also well-settled, however, that a movant is entitled to summary judgment if the burden is on the non-movant to establish the state of mind, and the nonmovant fails to present even circumstantial evidence from which a jury could infer the requisite state of mind. [Citations.]

At bottom, the question of punitive damages ordinarily is for the jury to decide. [Citations.]

III.

To prevail, Domino's must demonstrate that there is no genuine issue of material fact as to Domino's state of mind, and that no reasonable jury could conclude that Domino's knew of the danger of the 30–minute guarantee, yet consciously disregarded it. The plaintiffs have presented the following evidence, as well as reasonable inferences therefrom, to establish that Domino's had knowledge of the danger of the 30–minute guarantee, but consciously disregarded such danger.

Domino's employees testified that they knew that some franchisees and employees within the company believed that the 30–minute guarantee was a safety hazard. Domino's acknowledged that it received information from outside concerns that the 30–minute guarantee was hazardous. Domino's was aware of media criticism concerning the safety of the 30–minute guarantee, including essays by a Seattle news station, and national programs such as Inside Edition and Good Morning America. There is evidence that Domino's believed that insurance underwriters regarded the 30–minute guarantee as unsafe and a cause for claims. As a result, many franchisees had difficulty in obtaining insurance.

The 30–minute guarantee requires the franchisee, not Domino's Pizza, Inc., to refund $3.00 off the price for each order not delivered within thirty minutes. The approximate profit on each pizza is between $.80 and $2.00. Domino's Divisional Vice–President of Finance testified that he favored elimination of the 30–minute guarantee for corporate stores because it was an economic detriment. This raises an inference that there may be financial consequences for the franchisee if it fails to deliver a pizza within the thirty minute deadline.

The 30–minute guarantee is premised upon Domino's ability to make the pizzas in approximately ten minutes, and to restrict the geographic area in which the franchisee or corporate store delivers its pizzas. However, there is some testimony that Domino's never measured the time that it would take to complete the orders, never measured delivery times, never determined the percentage of deliveries that involved two or more separate orders at separate addresses, and never determined the percentage of deliveries that were more than two miles from the store.

Domino's offered to sell driver training materials to the franchisees, but did not require the franchisees to purchase such materials, and never confirmed whether its franchisees instituted safe driving programs. In the April 14, 1989 edition of Domino's weekly newsletter, Thomas Monaghan stated, "Every pizza should be a matter of life and death to make the delivery in 30 minutes or less. When the rush comes—Hustle."

Domino's never gathered any information to determine the number of accidents or claims involving Domino's drivers. Although Domino's maintained a toll free telephone number to register complaints about late service and the quality of the product, Domino's did not register complaints about reckless driving. Domino's never implemented any quality control risk management principles with respect to delivery drivers, nor undertook safety studies. Domino's has never statistically analyzed accidents in response to the negative publicity it received, or in relation to driver safety. The reason that Domino's did not analyze such accidents was because the 30–minute guarantee was a primarily a marketing program, and the magnitude of such a tabulation was outside the scope of Domino's budget and manpower .

Notwithstanding concern generated about the hazards of the 30–minute guarantee, there is evidence that no discussion regarding the safety of the 30–minute guarantee ever occurred in an "official corporate format". No person on Domino's board of directors or executive team expressed any concern about the 30–minute guarantee policy being a safety hazard. Although Domino's "management people in the field" debated the safety of the 30–minute guarantee, no person higher up in the corporate hierarchy did so.

After reviewing the facts recited above, as well as all reasonable inferences that may be drawn therefrom, the court finds that the plaintiffs have presented evidence from which a jury could find that Domino's had knowledge of the danger of the 30–minute guarantee, but consciously disregarded such danger.

IV.

Domino's argument that summary judgment is proper requires the court to weigh evidence and determine the credibility of witnesses, a role the court cannot undertake in deciding a motion for summary judgment. [Citations.] Rather, the court must construe the facts as favorably to the plaintiffs as the record will permit, and draw any permissible inferences from the materials before it in favor of the non-moving party, as long as the inferences are reasonable. [Citation.]

Instructive on this issue is Reed v. Ford Motor Co., 679 F.Supp. 873, where the plaintiff sued the defendant in tort because the plaintiff's car inadvertently jumped into reverse. To support its motion for summary judgment on the punitive damages issue, Ford introduced deposition testimony of two employees who had investigated and explored the problem of remedying the inadvertent rearward movement with certain Ford transmissions. The court denied Ford's motion, stating in part:

> The major portion of Ford's reply is devoted to a review of the plaintiff's evidence. Ford offers, for much of that evidence, a "noniniquitous" or otherwise innocent hypothesis that a reasonable juror could draw from its conduct. The flaw in this argument for summary judgment purposes is that a conclusion by the court that a reasonable juror could find the positive (that Ford's conduct was innocent) is not the same as a conclusion by the court that a reasonable juror could not find the negative (that there is no innocent hypothesis reasonably to be drawn from Ford's conduct). The plaintiff's evidence should be viewed only in light of the latter question.

Likewise, Domino's presents evidence of a number of "noniniquitous" or otherwise innocent hypotheses from which a reasonable juror could conclude that Domino's conduct was not deserving of punitive damages. For example, Domino's contends that none of its employees whose depositions were taken regarded the 30–minute guarantee as dangerous; thus, Domino's maintains, there is no question of fact as to their state of mind. Domino's evidence does support an inference that it did not possess the requisite state of mind. However, there is also evidence that some of these same individuals, including the president of Domino's, had knowledge of concerns related to the safety of the 30–minute guarantee, yet did nothing to investigate or explore those concerns. Given that reasonable inferences can be raised supporting both Domino's and the plaintiffs' positions, summary judgement is inappropriate. The jury must be given the opportunity to observe the demeanor of the witnesses whose states of mind are at issue. [Citations.]

Domino's also contends that it made a substantial effort to increase driver safety by initiating a safe delivery program for training drivers, a program in effect on May 25, 1990. However, there is also evidence that Domino's did not require the franchisees to purchase driver training materials, and never confirmed whether its franchisees instituted safe driving programs. [Citations.] Resolution of this conflicting evidence, and the inferences therefrom, is the jury's domain, not the court's.

Domino's claims that its "rack time" policy—whereby a pizza still in the store twenty-five minutes after the order was placed was automatically marked late—relieved pressure on the drivers to deliver within thirty minutes. While this may be true, a converse inference may be drawn that a pizza still on the rack twenty-four minutes after the order had to be rushed to the customer within six minutes, or the franchisee would lose money.

Domino's contends that Mr. Monaghan's statement that "every pizza should be a matter of life or death to make the delivery in 30 minutes or less", was clearly a figure of speech. However, whether the statement was a figure of speech, or whether there is an inference that

Mr. Monaghan's statement was Domino's unwritten policy is a question for the jury to decide.

Domino's also contends that Scott Halverson, the independent franchisee who hired Christopher Braden, repeatedly told the drivers to drive safely, and the drivers at Mr. Halverson's store were not penalized for late deliveries. Count XI, however, does not seek punitive damages against Mr. Halverson or Mr. Braden, but is directed solely at Domino's for its willful and wanton maintenance of the 30–minute guarantee although Domino's knew or should have known that the 30–minute guarantee resulted and would continue to result in accidents causing death and serious injuries. Thus, the implementation of the 30–minute guarantee by Mr. Halverson and Mr. Braden is not dispositive of Count XI.

In sum, this motion involves conflicting evidence, as well as conflicting inferences that may be drawn from that evidence. Much depends upon the credibility of witnesses testifying as to their own states of mind. At this stage of the proceedings, the court cannot conclude "that there is no evidence from which reasonable jurors could find, by a clear and convincing, that punitive damages should be awarded." [Citation.]

Accordingly, Domino's motion for summary judgment must be, and is hereby, DENIED.

————

1. *Maliciousness:* Punitive damages may be awarded on the basis that the actor had an "evil mind" in committing a tortious act. The frame of mind of the wrongdoer under this standard is not the same as the "intent" requirement for an intentional tort. Intentional torts are premised upon deliberate conduct that is substantially certain to invade the plaintiff's legally protected interest. The defendant may even have good intentions and yet be liable for an intentional tort. *See, e.g.,* Mohr v. Williams, 95 Minn. 261, 104 N.W. 12 (1905) (physician who performed successful but unconsented surgery on diseased ear in the absence of emergency liable for battery).

In contrast, maliciousness implies a desire to do harm. In Hawkins v. Allstate Insurance Co., 152 Ariz. 490, 733 P.2d 1073 (1987), for example, the plaintiff was able to establish that the defendant insurance company had a company policy designed to harm consumers. The plaintiffs were involved in an accident that demolished their automobile. The car was virtually new at the time it was destroyed. Their insurance policy included a provision limiting the insurer's liability to either replacement or actual cash value at the time of loss. The plaintiff couple experienced numerous problems in the course of dealing with the adjuster assigned to handle the claim. Ultimately they sued the insurer for fraud and bad faith in handling their claim.

At the trial, several former claims representatives testified that the company's procedures for handling total loss claims were designed to "chisel, to calculate offers substantially below fair value" in order to increase company profits. Adjusters were instructed in corporate literature, policy statements, and training school to make certain automatic deductions (such as a "cleaning fee") in ascertaining a car's actual cash value regardless of its applicability in the particular case. Further, the corporate policy evaluated the agent's performance and promotion potential according to a "severity rating" based upon the ratio of total dollars paid per claim.

The court upheld the jury determination that company's pattern of deceptive practices showed a conscious disregard of the plaintiff couple's right to a fair valuation of their property loss. Therefore, the company had acted with an "evil mind" in breaching the implied covenant of good faith and fair dealing in the insurance contract. The court explained that the insurer had "intended to injure the insured or consciously pursued a course of conduct knowing that it created a substantial risk of significant harm to the insured." 733 P.2d at 1080.

2. *Reckless disregard*: Another basis for recovery of punitive damages is the defendant's reckless disregard of the plaintiff's rights. This standard falls short of a malicious desire to harm, but still involves conscious wrongdoing. The Supreme Court explained this basis in Smith v. Wade, 461 U.S. 30, 103 S.Ct. 1625, 75 L.Ed.2d 632 (1983):

> Perhaps not surprisingly, there was significant variation (both terminological and substantive) among American jurisdictions in the latter 19th century on the precise standard to be applied in awarding punitive damages—variation that was exacerbated by the ambiguity and slipperiness of such common terms as "malice" and "gross negligence." Most of the confusion, however, seems to have been over the degree of negligence, recklessness, carelessness, or culpable indifference that should be required—not over whether actual intent was essential. On the contrary, the rule in a large majority of jurisdictions was that punitive damages (also called exemplary damages, vindictive damages, or smart money) could be awarded without a showing of actual ill will, spite, or intent to injure. * * *

> The large majority of state and lower federal courts were in agreement that punitive damages awards did not require a showing of actual malicious intent; they permitted punitive awards on variously stated standards of negligence, recklessness, or other culpable conduct short of actual malicious intent.

> The same rule applies today. The Restatement (Second) of Torts (1979), for example, states: "Punitive damages may be awarded for conduct that is outrageous, because of the defendant's evil motive *or his reckless indifference to the rights of others. "* § 908(2) (emphasis added); *see also id.,* Comment *b.* Most cases under state common law, although varying in their precise terminology, have adopted more or less the same rule, recognizing that punitive damages in tort cases may be awarded not only for actual intent to injure or evil

motive, but also for recklessness, serious indifference to or disregard for the rights of others, or even gross negligence.

3. *Gross negligence:* In some jurisdictions, punitive damages may be awarded based upon gross negligence. This standard differs significantly from maliciousness or reckless indifference because it is not premised upon conscious wrongdoing. It is a level of negligence greater than simple negligence but short of conscious indifference. It is frequently referred to as "entire want of care."

The lines among these standards are not bright ones. Jurisdictions sometimes provide their own definitions of these concepts in ways that blur the distinctions even further. Consider, for example, the definition of "gross negligence" articulated by the Texas Supreme Court in Wal–Mart Stores, Inc. v. Alexander, 868 S.W.2d 322 (Tex.1993):

> Gross negligence, to be the ground for exemplary damages, should be that entire want of care which would raise the belief that the act or omission complained of was the result of a conscious indifference to the right or welfare of the person or persons to be affected by it.

The court further explained:

> This definition, which is unique to Texas, combines the two recognized tests for gross negligence in American jurisprudence: "entire want of care" and "conscious indifference." The "entire want of care" test focuses on the objective nature of defendant's conduct, distinguishing gross negligence as being different in degree or quantity from ordinary negligence. The "conscious indifference" test focuses on the defendant's mental state, and thus "stresses a qualitative distinction from ordinary negligence." Under this approach, the actor, although not actually intending to cause harm, must have proceeded with knowledge that harm was a "highly probable" consequence.

Are there potential difficulties in the application of this "hybrid" test?

4. *Insurability of Punitive Damages:* Several jurisdictions have considered whether, as a matter of public policy, tortfeasors should be permitted to shift the punishment for their egregious acts to insurance companies. The threshold inquiry involves construction of the insurance contract to determine whether the policy provides indemnity coverage for exemplary damages. Some courts have liberally construed phrases such as "for all sums which the insured might become legally obligated to pay" to include potential liability coverage. *See, e.g.,* Dayton Hudson Corp. v. American Mut. Liability Ins. Co., 621 P.2d 1155 (Okl.1980).

Secondly, courts must consider whether the goals of punishment and deterrence would be undermined if a tortfeasor can be indemnified for punitive damages. The leading decision refusing to allow indemnification through insurance is *Northwestern National Casualty Co. v. McNulty.* In that case the Court of Appeals for the Fifth Circuit observed:

Where a person is able to insure himself against punishment he gains a freedom of misconduct inconsistent with the establishment of sanctions against such misconduct. It is not disputed that insurance against criminal fines or penalties would be void as violative of public policy. The same public policy should invalidate any contract of insurance against the civil punishment that punitive damages represent.

The policy considerations in a state where * * * punitive damages are awarded for punishment and deterrence, would seem to require that the damages rest ultimately as well as nominally on the party actually responsible for the wrong. If that person were permitted to shift the burden to an insurance company, punitive damages would serve no useful purpose. Such damages do not compensate the plaintiff for his injury, since compensatory damages already have made the plaintiff whole. And there is no point in punishing the insurance company; it has done no wrong. In actual fact, of course, and considering the extent to which the public is insured, the burden would ultimately come to rest not on the insurance companies but on the public, since the added liability to the insurance companies would be passed along to the premium payers. Society would then be punishing itself for the wrong committed by the insured. 307 F.2d 432 (5th Cir.1962)

Similarly, in Public Service Mutual Ins. Co. v. Goldfarb, 53 N.Y.2d 392, 425 N.E.2d 810, 442 N.Y.S.2d 422 (1981), the court refused to enforce an insurance contract specifically providing indemnity for punitive damages. The claim was for malpractice when a dentist sexually abused a patient. The court found that although the insurance company was in the awkward position of challenging the validity of one of its own contracts, there is an overriding public policy requiring meaningful punishment and deterrence.

Should the insurability of punitive damages turn on the nature of the defendant's conduct? In jurisdictions that allow punitive damages for reckless conduct as well as malicious behavior, would it make sense to distinguish the two for purposes of insurability? *See* Harrell v. Travelers Indemnity Co., 279 Or. 199, 567 P.2d 1013 (1977). Some jurisdictions that otherwise refuse to enforce insurance contracts for punitive damages have allowed enforcement where the insured is only vicariously liable for the exemplary damages. *See, e.g.,* U.S. Concrete Pipe Co. v. Bould, 437 So.2d 1061 (Fla.1983).

WANGEN v. FORD MOTOR CO.
97 Wis.2d 260, 294 N.W.2d 437 (1980).

ABRAHAMSON, JUSTICE.

[Products liability suits for compensatory and punitive damages were commenced against Ford Motor Company based upon an automobile accident which involved a collision between a 1967 Ford Mustang and another car. The Mustang's fuel tank ruptured, a fire ensued, and all the occupants of the Mustang died or sustained severe injuries.

The circuit court denied Ford's motion to dismiss the complaints for failure to state a cause of action. It held that punitive damages may be awarded in products liability cases upon a sufficient evidentiary basis. The court of appeals divided the complaint for punitive damages into various categories of actions and concluded that they were recoverable in a products liability suit for compensatory damages predicated on strict liability in tort but not for negligence. The Wisconsin Supreme Court granted an appeal to address whether punitive damages are recoverable in a products liability suit based on negligence or strict liability. The portion of the supreme court's opinion discussing the availability of punitive damages in wrongful death and survival actions and for a parent's loss of society and companionship of a child have been omitted.]

* * *

Ford Motor Company asserts that punitive damages are recoverable only in actions based on intentional, personal torts, and are not recoverable in product liability actions which are grounded in negligence or strict liability. Ford argues that the concept of punitive damages is antithetical to the theories of negligence and strict liability because punitive damages are based on the defendant's intentional conduct. Ford's argument is premised on two assumptions: that intentional conduct is the only conduct justifying punitive damages and that the same facts which justify compensatory damages must be sufficient to justify punitive damages. This court has never adopted this view of punitive damages.

* * *

This court has rested its analysis of punitive damages not on the classification of the underlying tort justifying compensatory damages but on the nature of the wrongdoer's conduct. Although the usual aggravating circumstances required for the recovery of punitive damages are often found as substantive elements of the tort itself, this court has said a claim for punitive damages may be supported by proof of aggravating circumstances beyond those supporting compensatory damages.

Punitive damages rest on allegations which, if proved, demonstrate a particular kind of conduct on the part of the wrongdoer, which has variously been characterized in our cases as malicious conduct or willful or wanton conduct in reckless disregard of rights or interests.

This court has not required proof of an intentional desire to injure, vex or annoy, or proof of malice, in order to sustain an award for punitive damages. "[M]alice or vindictiveness are not the *sine qua non* of punitive damages." [Citation.] It is sufficient if the injured party shows a reckless indifference to or disregard of the rights of others on the part of the wrongdoer. "Reckless indifference to the rights of others and conscious action in deliberate disregard of them . . . may provide the necessary state of mind to justify punitive damages." 4 Restatement

(Second) of Torts sec. 908, comment b, p. 465 (1977). Some commentators speak of the behavior justifying punitive damages as "flagrant indifference to the public safety." [Citations.] "A governing principle of these cases in allowing punitive damages has been the presence of 'circumstances of aggravation' in the tortious injury." [Citation.] We shall sometimes use the term "outrageous" in this opinion as an abbreviation for the type of conduct which justifies the imposition of punitive damages.

* * *

In Entzminger v. Ford Motor Co., 47 Wis.2d 751, 757–758, 177 N.W.2d 899, 903 (1970) this court made clear that the award of punitive damages depends on the character of the particular conduct in question, not on the mere fact that the defendant's conduct constituted a tort or a crime:

> "Punitive damages are not allowed for a mere breach of contract ... or for all torts or for crimes but generally for those personal torts, which are malicious, outrageous or a wanton disregard of personal rights which require the added sanction of a punitive damage to deter others from committing acts against human dignity. . . ."

* * *

If there is tortious conduct supporting a claim for compensatory damages, we can find no logical or conceptual difficulty in allowing a claim for punitive damages in a negligence or strict liability action if the plaintiff is able to establish the elements of "outrageous" conduct justifying punitive damages. * * *

This court rejects Ford's argument that as a matter of law, punitive damages cannot be recovered in any product liability case based on strict liability or negligence. We hold that punitive damages are recoverable in a product liability suit if there is proof that the defendant's conduct was "outrageous." Awarding punitive damages in a product liability case is a natural, direct outgrowth of basic common law concepts of tort law and punitive damages.

* * *

Although controversy continues to surround the doctrine of punitive damages in the twentieth century, and although some have questioned whether tort law—which is designed to compensate an injured plaintiff— should also serve the function of the criminal law, *i.e.,* to punish a defendant for the purpose of deterring him and others from further offenses, this court has consistently and frequently said that punishment and deterrence are important considerations in the law of torts in Wisconsin. * * *

In light of this court's repeated reaffirmation of the concept of punitive damages as a civil deterrent to "outrageous" behavior, and because apparently some businesses have found it in their interests to operate with reckless disregard to consumer safety, this court cannot, in good conscience, prohibit punitive damages in all product liability cases unless there is a strong showing that such prohibition is in the public interest.

* * *

Ford asserts that in product liability cases compensatory damages operate as a substantial punishment and deterrence against the manufacture and distribution of unreasonably unsafe products and that punitive damages are not necessary. Ford contends that product liability cases differ in nature from the traditional punitive damage tort case in which generally only one plaintiff is involved and in which compensatory damages are relatively small. In product liability cases there are potentially many plaintiffs who will recover compensatory damages. Ford maintains that there has been a substantial increase in the number of product liability cases brought and the amount of damages awarded; that Ford is exposed to multiple, substantial compensatory damage awards; and that the cost of paying products liability claims and buying products liability insurance has become a significant cost of doing business.

The counterargument, which is frequently made to Ford's argument and which we find persuasive, is that the need for punitive damages may be particularly appropriate in a product liability case because mere compensatory damages might be insufficient to deter the defendant from further wrongdoing. Some may think it cheaper to pay damages or a forfeiture than to change a business practice. In Funk v. H. S. Kerbaugh, 222 Pa. 18, 70 A. 953, 954 (1908), the defendant willfully carried out blasting in such a way as to damage buildings belonging to the plaintiff "because it was cheaper to pay damages . . . than to do work in a different way." The possibility of the manufacturer paying out more than compensatory damages might very well deter those who would consciously engage in wrongful practices and who would set aside a certain amount of money to compensate the injured consumer. Punishment of manufacturers guilty of intentional or reckless breaches of their obligation by imposing punitive damages might diminish the profitability of misconduct and any unfair competitive advantages such manufacturers might otherwise have.

* * *

Ford also argues that punitive damages in a product liability case, unlike in the traditional punitive damage tort case, would not serve the purposes of punishment and deterrence because the public, not the manufacturer, would pay the damages through higher prices for goods. We recognize, as did the court of appeals, an inconsistency between the concept of punitive damages as a deterrent and the possibility that punitive damages can be passed on to consumers as a cost of production. This court adopted strict liability in tort in product liability cases partly because "the seller is in the paramount position to distribute the costs of the risks created by the defective product he is selling. He may pass the cost on to the consumer via increased prices." [Citation.] Manufacturers are, however, not always able to pass on to their customers all costs, including multiple punitive damage awards. * * *

Ford observes that a frequently given justification for punitive damages in the traditional punitive damage tort case is that they encourage redress of wrongs that might otherwise go unpunished; punitive damages provide an incentive to the injured party to sue. Ford argued that punitive damages are wholly unnecessary to encourage the bringing of claims in product liability cases, because compensatory damages provide sufficient incentive to the victim of a product accident to proceed with his claim for compensatory damages. Ford may be right for those instances where injuries are very severe, but is probably wrong for the many product liability cases where injuries are moderate or minor. But even if the injury to each individual is not severe, there is a public need to deter the production of unreasonably safe products, and the availability of punitive damages increases the likelihood that the injured customer will sue for recovery.

In summary, we are not persuaded by Ford's argument that punitive damages are unnecessary in product liability cases to effect punishment or deterrence, the objectives of imposing punitive damages in the traditional tort action.

Ford further argues that it is in the public interest for this court to outlaw punitive damages in all product liability cases because allowing the recovery of punitive damages would cause undesirable economic and social consequences.

* * *

Ford argues that if the punitive damages are not passed on to the consumer the innocent shareholder bears the burden. But the loss of investment and the decline in value of investments are risks which investors knowingly undertake, and investors should not enjoy ill-gotten gains. There is a public interest in encouraging shareholders and corporate management to exercise closer control over the operations of the entity, and the imposition of punitive damages may serve this interest.

Ford argues that as a practical matter there will be a limit to the amount of punitive damages a manufacturer can pay and to the number of times a manufacturer will be—or should be—punished for the same product. Thus the injured parties who win the race to the courthouse reap "the bonanza of punitive damages." The later plaintiffs may receive little or no punitive damages. Ford further asserts that punitive damages are a windfall to the injured party and, if they are to be awarded, they should be awarded to the public. Although Ford's arguments have a certain equitable ring to them, we should not be sidetracked by them. Ford would solve the inequity of awarding punitive damages to some plaintiffs by having this court eliminate all punitive damages and by having us allow the wrongdoer to go unpunished. The supposed unfairness Ford attributes to punitive damages ignores the effort and money required of the early plaintiffs to uncover and prove the misconduct. Later plaintiffs will often be able to use the information gathered by the first plaintiffs and benefit from the early favorable verdicts and settlements. The "windfall criterion" overlooks that the payment of punitive damages to the injured party is justifiable as a practical matter, because such damages do serve to compensate the injured party for uncompensated expenses, *e.g.,* attorneys' fees and litigation expenses, and that the windfall motivates reluctant plaintiffs to go forward with their claims. If punitive damages were to be paid to the public treasury, fewer wrongdoers would be punished because the injured would have no inducement to spend the extra time and expense to prove a claim for punitive damages once an action had been brought. The basic question in determining whether punitive damages should be outlawed in product liability cases is not whether some injured party is going to make a profit but whether punitive damages will punish and deter, objectives which are in the public interest.

* * *

On the basis of the facts pleaded and reasonable inferences therefrom the complaint alleges that Ford knew of the defects in the design of the gas tank and filler neck and in the lack of barrier between the gas tank and passenger compartment in the 1967 Mustang and of the fire hazard associated with the design because of tests run by Ford as early as 1964; that for years before this accident Ford knew that these defects were causing serious burn injuries to occupants of these and similar cars; that years before the accident involved in the instant case Ford knew how to correct these defects in ways that would have prevented the plaintiffs' burns, but Ford intentionally concealed this knowledge from the government and the public; that despite this knowledge Ford deliberately chose not to recall its 1967 Mustangs and not to disclose the defects to the public by the issuance of warnings because Ford wanted to avoid paying the costs of recall and repair and wanted to avoid the accompanying bad publicity; and that Ford's conduct was intentional, reckless, willful, wanton, gross and fraudulent. These facts, if proved by the plaintiff, portray conduct which is willful and wanton and in reckless disregard of the plaintiff's rights. We conclude that the complaint alleges facts sufficient to state a claim for punitive damages in a product liability action predicated on negligence or strict liability. * * *

———

1. *Basis of suit*: The requirements for recovery of punitive damages are distinct from those of the underlying claim. Punitive damages are never a matter of right, even if the underlying claim requires malicious or outrageous behavior. The plaintiff must convince the trier of fact that such additional damages are appropriate.

Conversely, may a plaintiff seek punitive damages when the underlying basis of the suit is strict liability, which requires no proof of the defendant's state of mind nor even any proof of fault? In addition to the principal case, *see also* Fischer v. Johns–Manville Corp., 103 N.J. 643, 512 A.2d 466 (1986) (punitive damages allowable in products liability case based upon strict liability). What advantage is it to the plaintiff to seek recovery under strict liability if there is also evidence sufficient to support a claim for punitive damages?

2. *Punitive damages in products liability claims:* The arguments usually advanced in opposition of punitive damages in products liability cases include:

(a) Punitive damages assessed against a corporation are simply passed along to the consumer through higher prices to reflect the greater cost of doing business;

(b) Even if competition makes it impossible to spread the cost of punitive damages through the price of the product, the burden then falls on the innocent shareholder;

(c) When a defective product injures several people and there are large claims for punitive damages in multiple cases, punitive damages cannot be administered fairly to avoid ruinous results to the defendant for a single defect appearing in many products;

(d) Only people can be deterred, not corporations with constantly changing personnel.

3. The arguments usually advanced in support of punitive damages in products liability cases include:

(a) Manufacturers of risky products will price themselves out of the market when they pass along all their costs, including punitive damages;

(b) If innocent shareholders ultimately bear the burden, that result is justifiable because the decline in value of investments is a risk investors knowingly undertake;

(c) Corporations, including their innocent shareholders, should not enjoy ill-gotten gains;

(d) There is a public interest in encouraging shareholders and corporate management to exercise closer control over a manufacturer's operations.

4. In Smith v. Wade, 461 U.S. 30, 103 S.Ct. 1625, 75 L.Ed.2d 632 (1983), a prison inmate sued guards and correctional officials under § 1983 asserting that their failure to take protective measures to prevent his harassment and beatings by other cellmates constituted violations of his Eighth Amendment rights. The defendants, who had qualified immunity, could be held liable only upon a showing of reckless or callous indifference. They challenged the lower court's instruction regarding punitive damages because that instruction permitted the jury to award punitive damages on the same standard. The defendants

contended that the threshold for punitive damages should be higher than for liability. The Court rejected those arguments, stating:

> Smith's argument, which he offers in several forms, is that an actual-intent standard is preferable to a recklessness standard because it is less vague. He points out that punitive damages, by their very nature, are not awarded to compensate the injured party. He concedes, of course, that deterrence of future egregious conduct is a primary purpose of both § 1983, and of punitive damages. But deterrence, he contends, cannot be achieved unless the standard of conduct sought to be deterred is stated with sufficient clarity to enable potential defendants to conform to the law and to avoid the proposed sanction. Recklessness or callous indifference, he argues, is too uncertain a standard to achieve deterrence rationally and fairly. A prison guard, for example, can be expected to know whether he is acting with actual ill will or intent to injure, but not whether he is being reckless or callously indifferent.

> * * * While, *arguendo,* an intent standard may be easier to understand and apply to particular situations than a recklessness standard, we are not persuaded that a recklessness standard is too vague to be fair or useful. * * *

> * * * There has never been any general common-law rule that the threshold for punitive damages must always be higher than that for compensatory liability. On the contrary, both the First and Second Restatements of Torts have pointed out that "in torts like malicious prosecution that require a particular antisocial state of mind, the improper motive of the tortfeasor is both a necessary element in the cause of action and a reason for awarding punitive damages." Accordingly, in situations where the standard for compensatory liability is as high as or higher than the usual threshold for punitive damages, most courts will permit awards of punitive damages without requiring any extra showing. Several courts have so held expressly. Many other courts, not directly addressing the congruence of compensatory and punitive thresholds, have held that punitive damages are available on the same showing of fault as is required by the underlying tort in, for example, intentional infliction of emotional distress, defamation of a public official or public figure, and defamation covered by a common-law qualified immunity.

This common-law rule makes sense in terms of the purposes of punitive damages. Punitive damages are awarded in the jury's discretion "to punish [the defendant] for his outrageous conduct and to deter him and others like him from similar conduct in the future." Restatement (Second) of Torts § 908(1) (1979). The focus is on the character of the tortfeasor's conduct—whether it is of the sort that calls for deterrence and punishment over and above that provided by compensatory awards. If it is of such a character, then it is appropriate to allow a jury to assess punitive damages; and that assessment does not become less appropriate simply because the plaintiff in the case faces a more demanding standard of actionability. To put it differently, society has an interest in deterring and punishing *all* intentional or reckless invasions of the rights of others, even though it sometimes chooses not to impose any liability for lesser degrees of fault.   * * *

We hold that a jury may be permitted to assess punitive damages in an action under § 1983 when the defendant's conduct is shown to be motivated by evil motive or intent, or when it involves reckless or callous indifference to the federally protected rights of others. We further hold that this threshold applies even when the underlying standard of liability for compensatory damages is one of recklessness.

W.R. GRACE & CO. v. WATERS

638 So.2d 502 (Fla.1994).

GRIMES, C.J.

Thomas Waters and his wife filed this action seeking compensatory and punitive damages against several manufacturers of asbestos-containing products, including W.R. Grace & Company (Grace). From the late 1950s until 1988, Waters worked as a tile setter. The complaint alleged that Waters had developed asbestosis as a result of exposure to Grace's products at various job sites.

Prior to trial, Grace filed a motion for summary judgment on the issue of punitive damages asserting that (1) Grace's conduct, as a matter of law, did not rise to the level required for the imposition of punitive damages in Florida; (2) since punitive damage judgments had been entered against it in other jurisdictions, a partial summary judgment should be entered in accordance with a prior "standard ruling" by the trial court; [4] and (3) the punitive damages claim violated Grace's due process rights. The trial court granted Grace's motion and entered a partial summary judgment on the punitive damages issue based on the "standard ruling."

* * * [T]he district court of appeal affirmed the judgment for compensatory damages but held that the trial court erred in striking Waters' punitive damages claim. The court ruled that the fact that a defendant has already had punitive damages assessed against it does not preclude punitive damages in future litigation. The court reinstated Waters' punitive damages claim against Grace and remanded the case. However, the district court of appeal also certified to this Court the question concerning the propriety of imposing successive punitive damage awards against a single defendant for the same course of conduct.

---

4. The "standard ruling" was issued by Judge Harold Vann who administered the asbestos litigation docket in Dade County and elsewhere in Florida pursuant to administrative orders from this Court beginning in 1980. The ruling eliminated claims for punitive damages upon a showing that the defendant had already been subjected to a prior punitive damage award for the same conduct.

Punitive damages are appropriate when a defendant engages in conduct which is fraudulent, malicious, deliberately violent or oppressive, or committed with such gross negligence as to indicate a wanton disregard for the rights of others. [Citations.] Punishment and deterrence are the policies underlying punitive damages. [Citation.]

Grace asks this Court to limit the imposition of punitive damage awards in mass tort litigation, or at least with respect to asbestos cases. The company warns of the likelihood of "overkill" brought about by multiple punitive damage awards against a single defendant for the same course of conduct. Grace argues that, in the context of asbestos litigation, the interests of punishment and deterrence are not advanced by the continued imposition of punitive damages. It contends that multiple awards of exemplary damages will lead to asset depletion threatening the solvency of corporations, and, ultimately, will result in the unavailability of even compensatory damages for future claimants. Grace further points out that it discontinued marketing asbestos-containing products over twenty years ago. Because the company has been assessed punitive damages in previous asbestos cases, Grace asserts that it "has been punished enough."

Roginsky v. Richardson–Merrell, Inc., 378 F.2d 832 (2d Cir.1967), was one of the earliest cases to express concern over multiple punitive damage awards in mass tort litigation. In that case, the manufacturer of MER/29, a drug used to lower cholesterol levels, contested an award of punitive damages for personal injuries allegedly caused by MER/29. This was the first of seventy-five similar cases to be tried in the Southern District of New York. Several hundred other actions had been filed elsewhere, and the company had already sustained several large punitive damage awards in cases involving MER/29.

The court recognized the potentially devastating impact on the company if all plaintiffs in MER/29 cases were awarded punitive damages. However, the court stated:

> We know of no principle whereby the first punitive award exhausts all claims for punitive damages and would thus preclude future judgments.... Neither does it seem either fair or practicable to limit punitive recoveries to an indeterminate number of first-comers, leaving it to some unascertained court to cry, "Hold, enough," in the hope that others would follow.

Ultimately, the court declined to judicially limit successive punitive damage awards in products liability cases.

In the twenty-seven years following the Roginsky opinion, many courts have addressed the issue of multiple punitive damage awards against a single defendant for the same course of conduct. The courts of other jurisdictions have unanimously refused to limit the imposition of successive punitive damage awards in mass tort or products liability litigation. * * *

The solution to the problem which is most often suggested is the so-called "one bite" or "first comer" theory of punitive damages whereby, in successive litigation arising from a continuing episode, the award of exemplary damages to one plaintiff would preclude the recovery of punitive damages for all subsequent plaintiffs. This approach has been uniformly rejected. See State ex rel. Young v. Crookham, 290 Ore. 61, 618 P.2d 1268, 1272 (Or.1980) (This court cannot "endorse a system of awarding punitive damages which threatens to reduce civil justice to a race to the courthouse steps.").[5]

We acknowledge the potential for abuse when a defendant may be subjected to repeated punitive damage awards arising out of the same conduct. Yet, like the many other courts which have addressed the problem, we are unable to devise a fair and effective solution. Were we to adopt the position advocated by Grace, our holding would not be binding on other state courts or federal courts. This would place Floridians injured by asbestos on an unequal footing with the citizens of other states with regard to the right to recover damages from companies who engage in extreme misconduct. Any realistic solution to the problems caused by the asbestos litigation in the United States must be applicable to all fifty states. It is our belief that such a uniform solution can only be effected by federal legislation.

* * * [T]he district court of appeal suggested that Grace could use the fact that it had previously been assessed punitive damages as mitigation before the jury. However, Grace points out that advising the jury of previous punitive damage awards would actually hurt its cause. The introduction of such evidence would be extremely prejudicial to a defendant trying to convince a jury that its conduct is worthy of no punishment at all.

We agree with Grace's position on this point. We recognize that defendants in mass tort litigation who are forced to litigate the issue of liability and punitive damages in the same proceeding are at a severe disadvantage. We also recognize that even those defendants against whom no prior punitive damage awards have been assessed are prejudiced by the current procedure which permits evidence of a defendant's net worth to be introduced when liability for punitive damages has not yet been determined. * * *

We hold that henceforth trial courts, when presented with a timely motion, should bifurcate the determination of the amount of punitive damages from the remaining issues at trial. At the first stage of a trial in which punitive damages are an issue, the jury should hear evidence regarding liability for actual damages, the amount of actual damages,

---

5. To limit recovery to the first punitive damage award would be particularly unfair in Florida which limits the amount of punitive damages to three times the award of compensatory damages. § 768.73, Fla. Stat. (1993). If a slightly injured plaintiff were the first to recover punitive damages, the small award of compensatory damages would limit the amount of punitive damages. Under those circumstances, this amount would not be nearly enough to punish a defendant whose egregious conduct had caused injury to many persons.

and liability for punitive damages, and should make determinations on those issues. If, at the first stage, the jury determines that punitive damages are warranted, the same jury should then hear evidence relevant to the amount of punitive damages and should determine the amount for which the defendant is liable. At this second stage, evidence of previous punitive awards may be introduced by the defendant in mitigation. In this manner, the defendant would also be able to build a record for a due process argument based on the cumulative effect of prior awards. This new procedure, of course, is meant only to supplement, not replace, the limitations on punitive damages set forth by the legislature in sections 768.71–768.74, Florida Statutes (1993).

In conclusion, we hold that prior punitive damages assessed against a defendant do not preclude subsequent awards against the same defendant for injuries arising from the same conduct. We approve the decision below and remand for further proceedings consistent with this opinion.

---

1. The assessment of multiple punitive damage awards against a responsible party arising out of the same incident has sparked considerable controversy. At some level, the imposition of multiple punitive damage awards transcends the goals of punishment and deterrence and may result in bankrupting the offending entity. In that event, obviously the offending party then would probably lack sufficient resources even to pay meritorious compensatory damage claims. Judge Friendly in Roginsky v. Richardson–Merrell, Inc., 378 F.2d 832 (2d Cir.1967), first raised the problem of potentially ruinous liability for a corporation from large claims for punitive damages in multiple product liability cases concerning a single defect appearing in many products. In *Roginsky*, the manufacturer of MER/29, a drug used to lower blood cholesterol levels, faced numerous claims for compensatory and punitive damages for personal injuries allegedly caused by ingestion of the drug.

Although the court in *Roginsky* declined to place judicial constraints on successive punitive awards in products liability cases, Judge Friendly lamented that hundreds of suits in different jurisdictions could lead to overkill where "in an aggregate which, when piled on large compensatory damages, could reach catastrophic amounts." *Id.* at 841.

Is it a sufficient safeguard that punitive damages are never awarded as a matter of right and are always a matter of discretion? Are there better solutions?

2. Consider the following observations of Chief Judge Erickson dissenting in Palmer v. A.H. Robins Co., Inc., 684 P.2d 187 (Colo.1984). He attacks the very imposition of any punitive damages in mass tort cases:

> The remedy of punitive damages, with deep roots in ancient law, and in medieval English statutes, first received explicit recogni-

tion in 1763 in Huckle v. Money, 2 Wils. 205 (K.B.1763). There, the jury was held justified in going beyond the "small injury done to the plaintiff" because of the desirability of taking account of "a most daring public attack made upon the liberty of the subject" through entry and imprisonment pursuant to "a nameless warrant." Later decisions which extended the remedy to situations where the defendant showed a conscious and deliberate disregard of the interests of others, still resembled those first cases in one important respect—a high probability that the number of plaintiffs will be few and that they will join, or can be forced to join, in a single trial.

The punitive damage remedy was transported to America, and by the middle of the nineteenth century, gained substantial acceptance in this country. *See* Owens, *Punitive Damages in Products Liability Litigation,* 74 Mich.L.Rev. 1258 (1976). The purpose behind the imposition of punitive damages was, and continues to be, to punish the defendant for the commission of an aggravated or outrageous act of misconduct and to deter him and others from such conduct in the future. Historically, the torts for which punitive damages were awarded were intentional torts involving a *single* victim.

Although the remedy of punitive damages is now firmly established by statute and as part of the common law, many critics have concluded that the concept is being abused. Any expansion, therefore, of its application to areas of the law which are only now developing and taking on a distinct character of their own, must be carefully scrutinized.

* * *

The unfair financial pyramiding of liability for punitive damage claims on the part of multiple plaintiffs throughout the United States is staggering. * * * Admittedly, I have difficulty in perceiving how claims for punitive damages in such a multiplicity of actions throughout the nation can be administered in such a way as to avoid overkill and unwarranted cumulative financial punishment. One solution is the so-called "one-bite/first comer" proposal which would limit recovery of punitive damages to the first litigant. [Citation.] A second alternative would allow for the introduction of evidence by the defendant of prior awards of punitive damages or of criminal sanctions. A third proposal would require that all related cases be assembled before a single court. Such a consolidation of claims would make it possible for a jury to make one punitive damage award which could then be held in trust for appropriate distribution among all successful plaintiffs. * * *

None of these proposals, however, offers a complete answer to this pressing concern; yet, each recognizes expressly the need for drastic judicial or legislative control of the amount of punitive awards in order to keep the cumulative prospective total within some manageable balance. * * *

3. Are the same policy considerations concerning multiple products liability claims for punitive damages equally applicable to mass disaster or other mass torts cases? *Compare* Jackson v. Johns–Manville Sales Corp., 727 F.2d 506 (5th Cir.1984) (punitive damages not appropriate in mass tort asbestosis cases where exposure to multiple liability is sufficient punishment and deterrence) *with* the same case on rehearing, 781 F.2d 394 (5th Cir.1986) (applicable state law allowed both compensatory and punitive damages in multiple tort cases stemming from same corporate acts).

4. Compare State ex rel Young v. Crookham, 290 Or. 61, 618 P.2d 1268 (1980), cited in the principal case, where the court squarely addressed the issue whether to adopt the "one-bite" or "first-comer" theory of punitive damages which provides that an award of exemplary damages to one plaintiff precludes such awards to all subsequent plaintiffs in multiple litigation arising from the same occurrence. In *Crookman*, raw sewage overflowed and contaminated the public water supply in a national park, causing numerous visitors to contract severe gastrointestinal illnesses.

The court declined to certify a class action and subsequently disallowed consolidation of the individual claims on the issue of liability. The claimants then signed an agreement to prorate and divide any punitive damages recovered by any one of the members. After compensatory and punitive damages were awarded to one plaintiff, the trial judge granted summary judgment to defendants which would prevent additional punitive damages being awarded in the other pending cases. The Supreme Court of Oregon, in an original proceeding for issuance of writ of mandamus, rejected the "one bite/first comer" approach, reasoning that sufficient safeguards existed in the judicial system to prevent excessive damages.

The court recognized the concern raised in the *Roginsky* dictum of corporate destruction through multiple punitive awards but distinguished the MER/29 litigation of *Roginsky* in several respects. First, less danger of overkill existed where a limited and ascertainable number of plaintiffs were involved. Second, that approach, if adopted, would raise another problem by fostering a "race to the courthouse steps." Finally, the court noted that the potential availability of punitive damages serves as an inducement to citizens to act as private attorneys general in seeking redress for matters affecting the public interest. The court noted that the applicable Oregon statute adopted the Restatement (Second) of Torts § 908 Comment e view that one factor influencing the amount of punitive damages should be whether punitive damages had been previously awarded to persons in similar situations. *Also see* Davis v. Celotex, 187 W.Va. 566, 420 S.E.2d 557, 565 (1992) (Court observed that it was "illogical and unfair for courts to determine at what point punitive damages should cease."); 11 A.L.R. 4th 1261.

5. *Punitive damages in toxic tort cases.* Punitive damages have been awarded with increasingly frequency in toxic tort litigation against

parties found responsible for the dumping of hazardous materials and resulting exposure of persons to toxic chemicals. For example, in Sterling v. Velsicol Chemical Corp., 855 F.2d 1188 (6th Cir.1988), the court recognized the validity of an award of punitive damages to the entire plaintiff class where evidence showed that the defendant corporation had continued operating a landfill chemical waste disposal site after receiving notice that highly toxic chemicals had leaked from the site and contaminated a local water supply. The district court determined that the company's failure to cease its dumping activities after receiving warnings from state and federal agencies constituted gross negligence and a willful and wanton disregard for the health and welfare of adjacent landowners and the environment. *See also* Exxon Corp. v. Yarema, 69 Md. App. 124, 516 A.2d 990 (1986) (Punitive damages imposed where corporation failed to minimize health risks and undertake corrective action to abate leakage from underground gasoline storage tanks which had contaminated groundwater). *Accord* Potter v. Firestone Tire and Rubber Co., 6 Cal.4th 965, 25 Cal.Rptr.2d 550, 863 P.2d 795 (1993) (Tire manufacturer which disposed of hazardous waste at landfill acted in conscious disregard of rights and safety of neighboring landowners sufficient to justify imposition of punitive damages; however reversed and remanded on other grounds.)

HONDA MOTOR CO., LTD. v. OBERG
___ U.S. ___, 114 S.Ct. 2331, 129 L.Ed.2d 336 (1994).

JUSTICE STEVENS delivered the opinion of the Court.

An amendment to the Oregon Constitution prohibits judicial review of the amount of punitive damages awarded by a jury "unless the court can affirmatively say there is no evidence to support the verdict." The question presented is whether that prohibition is consistent with the Due Process Clause of the Fourteenth Amendment. We hold that it is not.

I

Petitioner manufactured and sold the three-wheeled all-terrain vehicle that overturned while respondent was driving it, causing him severe and permanent injuries. Respondent brought suit alleging that petitioner knew or should have known that the vehicle had an inherently and unreasonably dangerous design. The jury found petitioner liable and awarded respondent $919,390.39 in compensatory damages and punitive damages of $5,000,000. The compensatory damages, however, were reduced by 20% to $735,512.31, because respondent's own negligence contributed to the accident. On appeal, relying on our then recent decision in Pacific Mut. Life Ins. Co. v. Haslip, 499 U.S. 1 (1991), petitioner argued that the award of punitive damages violated the Due Process Clause of the Fourteenth Amendment, because the punitive damages were excessive and because Oregon courts lacked the power to correct excessive verdicts.

The Oregon Court of Appeals affirmed, as did the Oregon Supreme Court. The latter court relied heavily on the fact that the Oregon statute governing the award of punitive damages in product liability actions and the jury instructions in this case [1] contain substantive criteria that provide at least as much guidance to the factfinders as the Alabama statute and jury instructions that we upheld in Haslip. The Oregon Supreme Court also noted that Oregon law provides an additional protection by requiring the plaintiff to prove entitlement to punitive damages by clear and convincing evidence rather than a mere preponderance. Recognizing that other state courts had interpreted Haslip as including a "clear constitutional mandate for meaningful judicial scrutiny of punitive damage awards," the Court nevertheless declined to "interpret *Haslip* to hold that an award of punitive damages, to comport with the requirements of the Due Process Clause, always must be subject to a form of post-verdict or appellate review that includes the possibility of remittitur." 316 Ore. 263, 284, 851 P.2d 1084, 1096 (1993). It also noted that trial and appellate courts were "not entirely powerless" because a judgment may be vacated if "there is no evidence to support the jury's decision," and because "appellate review is available to test the sufficiency of the jury instructions."

We granted certiorari, 510 U.S. ___ (1994), to consider whether Oregon's limited judicial review of the size of punitive damage awards is consistent with our decision in *Haslip*.

II

Our recent cases have recognized that the Constitution imposes a substantive limit on the size of punitive damage awards. Pacific Mut. Life Ins. Co. v. Haslip, 499 U.S. 1 (1991); TXO Production Corp. v. Alliance Resources, Corp., 509 U.S. ___ (1993). Although they fail to "draw a mathematical bright line between the constitutionally acceptable and the constitutionally unacceptable," a majority of the Justices agreed that the Due Process Clause imposes a limit on punitive damage awards. A plurality in TXO assented to the proposition that "grossly excessive" punitive damages would violate due process, while JUSTICE O'CONNOR, who dissented because she favored more rigorous standards, noted that "it is thus common ground that an award may be so excessive

---

1. The jury instructions, in relevant part, read: " 'Punitive damages' may be awarded to the plaintiff in addition to general damages to punish wrongdoers and to discourage wanton misconduct. In order for plaintiff to recover punitive damages against the defendants, the plaintiff must prove by clear and convincing evidence that defendant[s have] shown wanton disregard for the health, safety, and welfare of others.... If you decide this issue against the defendants, you may award punitive damages, although you are not required to do so, because punitive damages are discretionary. In the exercise of that discretion, you shall consider evidence, if any, of the following: First, the likelihood at the time of the sale [of the three-wheeled vehicle] that serious harm would arise from defendants' misconduct. Number two, the degree of the defendants' awareness of that likelihood. Number three, the duration of the misconduct. Number four, the attitude and conduct of the defendants upon notice of the alleged condition of the vehicle. Number five, the financial condition of the defendants. And the amount of punitive damages may not exceed the sum of $5 million." 316 Ore. 263, 282, n.11, 851 P.2d 1084, 1095, n.11 (1993).

as to violate due process." [Citations.] In the case before us today we are not directly concerned with the character of the standard that will identify unconstitutionally excessive awards; rather we are confronted with the question of what procedures are necessary to ensure that punitive damages are not imposed in an arbitrary manner. More specifically, the question is whether the Due Process Clause requires judicial review of the amount of punitive damage awards.

The opinions in both *Haslip* and *TXO* strongly emphasized the importance of the procedural component of the Due Process Clause. In *Haslip,* the Court held that the common law method of assessing punitive damages did not violate procedural due process. In so holding, the Court stressed the availability of both "meaningful and adequate review by the trial court" and subsequent appellate review. Similarly, in *TXO,* the plurality opinion found that the fact that the "award was reviewed and upheld by the trial judge" and unanimously affirmed on appeal gave rise "to a strong presumption of validity." Concurring in the judgment, JUSTICE SCALIA (joined by JUSTICE THOMAS) considered it sufficient that traditional common law procedures were followed. In particular, he noted that " 'procedural due process' requires judicial review of punitive damages awards for reasonableness...."

All of those opinions suggest that our analysis in this case should focus on Oregon's departure from traditional procedures. We therefore first contrast the relevant common law practice with Oregon's procedure, which that State's Supreme Court once described as "a system of trial by jury in which the judge is reduced to the status of a mere monitor." [Citation.] We then examine the constitutional implications of Oregon's deviation from established common law procedures.

III

Judicial review of the size of punitive damage awards has been a safeguard against excessive verdicts for as long as punitive damages have been awarded. One of the earliest reported cases involving exemplary damages, Huckle v. Money, 2 Wils. 205, 95 Eng.Rep. 768 (C. P. 1763), arose out of King George III's attempt to punish the publishers of the allegedly seditious North Briton, No. 45. The King's agents arrested the plaintiff, a journeyman printer, in his home and detained him for six hours. Although the defendants treated the plaintiff rather well, feeding him "beef-steaks and beer, so that he suffered very little or no damages," 2 Wils., at 205, 95 Eng.Rep., at 768, the jury awarded him $300, an enormous sum almost three hundred times the plaintiff's weekly wage. The defendant's lawyer requested a new trial, arguing that the jury's award was excessive. Plaintiff's counsel, on the other hand, argued that "in cases of tort ... the Court will never interpose in setting aside verdicts for excessive damages." *Id.,* at 206, 95 Eng.Rep., at 768. While the court denied the motion for new trial, the Chief Justice explicitly rejected plaintiff's absolute rule against review of damages amounts. Instead, he noted that when the damages are "outrageous" and "all mankind at first blush must think so," a court may grant a new trial "for excessive damages." *Id.*, at, 207, 95 Eng.Rep., at 769. In accord with his view that the amount of an award was relevant to the motion for a new trial, the Chief Justice noted that "upon the whole, I am of opinion the damages are not excessive." *Ibid.*

Subsequent English cases, while generally deferring to the jury's determination of damages, steadfastly upheld the court's power to order new trials solely on the basis that the damages were too high. * * *

Common law courts in the United States followed their English predecessors in providing judicial review of the size of damage awards. They too emphasized the deference ordinarily afforded jury verdicts, but they recognized that juries sometimes awarded damages so high as to require correction. Thus, in 1822, Justice Story, sitting as Circuit Justice, ordered a new trial unless the plaintiff agreed to a reduction in his damages.[3] * * *

In the 19th century, both before and after the ratification of the Fourteenth Amendment, many American courts reviewed damages for "partiality" or "passion and prejudice." Nevertheless, because of the difficulty of probing juror reasoning, passion and prejudice review was, in fact, review of the amount of awards. Judges would infer passion, prejudice, or partiality from the size of the award. * * *

Modern practice is consistent with these earlier authorities. In the federal courts and in every State, except Oregon, judges review the size of damage awards. [Citations.]

IV

There is a dramatic difference between the judicial review of punitive damages awards under the common law and the scope of review available in Oregon. An Oregon trial judge, or an Oregon Appellate Court, may order a new trial if the jury was not properly instructed, if error occurred during the trial, or if there is no evidence to support any punitive damages at all. But if the defendant's only basis for relief is the amount of punitive damages the jury awarded, Oregon provides no procedure for reducing or setting aside that award. This has been the law in Oregon at least since 1949 when the State Supreme Court announced its opinion in Van Lom v. Schneiderman, 187 Ore. 89, 210 P.2d 461 (1949), definitively construing the 1910 Amendment to the Oregon Constitution.[5]

* * *

Respondent also argues that Oregon provides adequate review, because the trial judge can overturn a punitive damage award if there is no

---

3. While Justice Story's grant of a new trial was clearly in accord with established common law procedure, the remittitur—withdrawal of new trial if the plaintiff agreed to a specific reduction of damages—may have been an innovation. * * *

5. The amended Article VII, § 3, of the Oregon Constitution provides: "In actions at law, where the value in controversy shall exceed twenty dollars, the right of trial by jury shall be preserved, and no fact tried by a jury shall be otherwise re-examined in any court of this State, unless the court can affirmatively say there is no evidence to support the verdict."

substantial evidence to support an award of punitive damages. This argument is unconvincing, because the review provided by Oregon courts ensures only that there is evidence to support some punitive damages, not that there is evidence to support the amount actually awarded. While Oregon's judicial review ensures that punitive damages are not awarded against defendants entirely innocent of conduct warranting exemplary damages, Oregon, unlike the common law, provides no assurance that those whose conduct is sanctionable by punitive damages are not subjected to punitive damages of arbitrary amounts. What we are concerned with is the possibility that a guilty defendant may be unjustly punished; evidence of guilt warranting some punishment is not a substitute for evidence providing at least a rational basis for the particular deprivation of property imposed by the State to deter future wrongdoing.

V

Oregon's abrogation of a well-established common law protection against arbitrary deprivations of property raises a presumption that its procedures violate the Due Process Clause. As this Court has stated from its first Due Process cases, traditional practice provides a touchstone for constitutional analysis. * * *

Punitive damages pose an acute danger of arbitrary deprivation of property. Jury instructions typically leave the jury with wide discretion in choosing amounts, and the presentation of evidence of a defendant's net worth creates the potential that juries will use their verdicts to express biases against big businesses, particularly those without strong local presences. Judicial review of the amount awarded was one of the few procedural safeguards which the common law provided against that danger. Oregon has removed that safeguard without providing any substitute procedure and without any indication that the danger of arbitrary awards has in any way subsided over time. For these reasons, we hold that Oregon's denial of judicial review of the size of punitive damage awards violates the Due Process Clause of the Fourteenth Amendment.

VI

Respondent argues that Oregon has provided other safeguards against arbitrary awards and that, in any event, the exercise of this unreviewable power by the jury is consistent with the jury's historic role in our judicial system.

Respondent points to four safeguards provided in the Oregon courts: the limitation of punitive damages to the amount specified in the complaint, the clear and convincing standard of proof, pre-verdict determination of maximum allowable punitive damages, and detailed jury instructions. The first, limitation of punitive damages to the amount specified, is hardly a constraint at all, because there is no limit to the amount the plaintiff can request, and it is unclear whether an award exceeding the amount requested could be set aside. [Citation.] The second safeguard, the clear and convincing standard of proof, is an important check against unwarranted imposition of punitive damages, but, like the "no substantial evidence" review discussed above it provides no assurance that those whose conduct is sanctionable by punitive damages are not subjected to punitive damages of arbitrary amounts. Regarding the third purported constraint, respondent cites no cases to support the idea that Oregon courts do or can set maximum punitive damage awards in advance of the verdict. Nor are we aware of any court which implements that procedure. Respondent's final safeguard, proper jury instruction, is a well-established and, of course, important check against excessive awards. The problem that concerns us, however, is the possibility that a jury will not follow those instructions and may return a lawless, biased, or arbitrary verdict.

In support of his argument that there is a historic basis for making the jury the final arbiter of the amount of punitive damages, respondent calls our attention to early civil and criminal cases in which the jury was allowed to judge the law as well as the facts. [Citation.] As we have already explained, in civil cases, the jury's discretion to determine the amount of damages was constrained by judicial review. The criminal cases do establish—as does our practice today—that a jury's arbitrary decision to acquit a defendant charged with a crime is completely unreviewable. There is, however, a vast difference between arbitrary grants of freedom and arbitrary deprivations of liberty or property. The Due Process Clause has nothing to say about the former, but its whole purpose is to prevent the latter. A decision to punish a tortfeasor by means of an exaction of exemplary damages is an exercise of state power that must comply with the Due Process Clause of the Fourteenth Amendment. The common law practice, the procedures applied by every other State, the strong presumption favoring judicial review that we have applied in other areas of the law, and elementary considerations of justice, all support the conclusion that such a decision should not be committed to the unreviewable discretion of a jury.

[Reversed and remanded.]

JUSTICE GINSBURG, with whom the CHIEF JUSTICE joins, dissenting.

In product liability cases, Oregon guides and limits the factfinder's discretion on the availability and amount of punitive damages. The plaintiff must establish entitlement to punitive damages, under specific substantive criteria, by clear and convincing evidence. Where the factfinder is a jury, its decision is subject to judicial review to this extent: the trial court, or an appellate court, may nullify the verdict if reversible error occurred during the trial, if the jury was improperly or inadequately instructed, or if there is no evidence to support the verdict. Absent trial error, and if there is evidence to support the award of punitive damages, however, Oregon's Constitution, Article VII, § 3, provides that a properly instructed jury's verdict shall not be reexamined. n1 Oregon's procedures, I conclude, are adequate to pass the Constitution's due process threshold. I therefore dissent from the Court's judgment upsetting Oregon's disposition in this case.

To assess the constitutionality of Oregon's scheme, I turn first to this Court's recent opinions in Pacific Mut. Life Ins. Co. v. Haslip, 499 U.S. 1 (1991), and TXO Production Corp. v. Alliance Resources Corp., 509 U.S. ___ (1993). The Court upheld punitive damage awards in both cases, but indicated that due process imposes an outer limit on remedies of this type. Significantly, neither decision declared any specific procedures or substantive criteria essential to satisfy due process. In *Haslip,* the Court expressed concerns about "unlimited jury discretion—or unlimited judicial discretion for that matter—in the fixing of punitive damages," but refused to "draw a mathematical bright line between the constitutionally acceptable and the constitutionally unacceptable." Regarding the components of "the constitutional calculus," the Court simply referred to "general concerns of reasonableness and [the need for] adequate guidance from the court when the case is tried to a jury."

And in *TXO,* a majority agreed that a punitive damage award may be so grossly excessive as to violate the Due Process Clause. In the plurality's view, however, "a judgment that is a product" of "fair procedures . . . is entitled to a strong presumption of validity"; this presumption, "persuasive reasons" indicated, "should be irrebuttable, . . . or virtually so." The opinion stating the plurality position recalled *Haslip's* touchstone: A "concern [for] reasonableness" is what due process essentially requires. Writing for the plurality, JUSTICE STEVENS explained:

> "We do not suggest that a defendant has a substantive due process right to a correct determination of the 'reasonableness' of a punitive damages award. As JUSTICE O'CONNOR points out, state law generally imposes a requirement that punitive damages be 'reasonable.' A violation of a state law 'reasonableness' requirement would not, however, necessarily establish that the award is so 'grossly excessive' as to violate the Federal Constitution."

The procedures Oregon's courts followed in this case satisfy the due process limits indicated in *Haslip* and *TXO* ; the jurors were adequately guided by the trial court's instructions, and Honda has not maintained, in its full presentation to this Court, that the award in question was "so 'grossly excessive' as to violate the Federal Constitution."

Several preverdict mechanisms channeled the jury's discretion more tightly in this case than in either *Haslip* or *TXO.* First, providing at least some protection against unguided, utterly arbitrary jury awards, respondent Karl Oberg was permitted to recover no more than the amounts specified in the complaint, $919,390.39 in compensatory damages and $5 million in punitive damages. The trial court properly instructed the jury on this damage cap. No provision of Oregon law appears to preclude the defendant from seeking an instruction setting a lower cap, if the evidence at trial cannot support an award in the amount demanded. Additionally, if the trial judge relates the incorrect maximum amount, a defendant who timely objects may gain modification or nullification of the verdict.

Second, Oberg was not allowed to introduce evidence regarding Honda's wealth until he "presented evidence sufficient to justify to the court a prima facie claim of punitive damages." Ore. Rev. Stat. § 41.315(2) (1991); see also § 30.925(2) ("During the course of trial, evidence of the defendant's ability to pay shall not be admitted unless and until the party entitled to recover establishes a prima facie right to recover [punitive damages]."). ·This evidentiary rule is designed to lessen the risk "that juries will use their verdicts to express biases against big businesses."

Third, and more significant, as the trial court instructed the jury, Honda could not be found liable for punitive damages unless Oberg established by "clear and convincing evidence" that Honda "showed wanton disregard for the health, safety and welfare of others." "The clear-and-convincing evidence requirement," which is considerably more rigorous than the standards applied by Alabama in *Haslip* and West Virginia in *TXO,* "constrains the jury's discretion, limiting punitive damages to the more egregious cases." Nothing in Oregon law appears to preclude a new trial order if the trial judge, informed by the jury's verdict, determines that his charge did not adequately explain what the "clear and convincing" standard means.

Fourth, and perhaps most important, in product liability cases, Oregon requires that punitive damages, if any, be awarded based on seven substantive criteria, set forth in Ore. Rev. Stat. § 30.925(3) (1991):

"(a) The likelihood at the time that serious harm would arise from the defendant's misconduct;

"(b) The degree of the defendant's awareness of that likelihood;

"(c) The profitability of the defendant's misconduct;

"(d) The duration of the misconduct and any concealment of it;

"(e) The attitude and conduct of the defendant upon discovery of the misconduct;

"(f) The financial condition of the defendant; and

"(g) The total deterrent effect of other punishment imposed upon the defendant as a result of the misconduct, including, but not limited to, punitive damage awards to persons in situations similar to the claimant's and the severity of criminal penalties to which the defendant has been or may be subjected."

These substantive criteria, and the precise instructions detailing them, gave the jurors "adequate guidance" in making their award, far more guidance than their counterparts in *Haslip* and *TXO* received. In *Haslip,* for example, the jury was told only the purpose of punitive damages (punishment and deterrence) and that an award was discretionary, not compulsory. We deemed those instructions, notable for their generality, constitutionally sufficient.

The Court's opinion in *Haslip* went on to describe the checks Alabama places on the jury's discretion postverdict—through excessiveness review by the trial court, and appellate review, which tests the award against specific substantive criteria. While postverdict review of that character is not available in Oregon, the seven factors against which Alabama's Supreme Court tests punitive awards [9] strongly resemble the statutory criteria Oregon's juries are instructed to apply. And this Court has often acknowledged, and generally respected, the presumption that juries follow the instructions they are given.

As the Supreme Court of Oregon observed, *Haslip* "determined only that the Alabama procedure, as a whole and in its net effect, did not violate the Due Process Clause." The Oregon court also observed, correctly, that the Due Process Clause does not require States to subject punitive damage awards to a form of postverdict review "that includes the possibility of remittitur." Because Oregon requires the factfinder to apply § 30.925's objective criteria, moreover, its procedures are perhaps more likely to prompt rational and fair punitive damage decisions than are the post hoc checks employed in jurisdictions following Alabama's pattern. As the Oregon court concluded, "application of objective criteria ensures that sufficiently definite and meaningful constraints are imposed on the finder of fact." The Oregon court also concluded that the statutory criteria, by adequately guiding the jury, worked to "ensure that the resulting award is not disproportionate to a defendant's conduct and to the need to punish and deter."

The Supreme Court of Oregon's conclusions are buttressed by the availability of at least some postverdict judicial review of punitive damage awards. Oregon's courts ensure that there is evidence to support the verdict. * * *

In addition, punitive damage awards may be set aside because of flaws in jury instructions. * * *

In short, Oregon has enacted legal standards confining punitive damage awards in product liability cases. These state standards are judicially enforced by means of comparatively comprehensive preverdict procedures but markedly limited postverdict review, for Oregon has elected to make factfinding, once supporting evidence is produced, the province of the jury. [Citations.] The Court today invalidates this choice, largely because it concludes that English and early American

---

9. The Alabama factors are:

"(a) whether there is a reasonable relationship between the punitive damages award and the harm likely to result from the defendant's conduct as well as the harm that actually has occurred; (b) the degree of reprehensibility of the defendant's conduct, the duration of that conduct, the defendant's awareness, any concealment, and the existence and frequency of similar past conduct; (c) the profitability to the defendant of the wrongful conduct and the desirability of removing that profit and of having the defendant also sustain a loss; (d) the 'financial position' of the defendant; (e) all the costs of litigation; (f) the imposition of criminal sanctions on the defendant for its conduct, these to be taken in mitigation; and (g) the existence of other civil awards against the defendant for the same conduct, these also to be taken in mitigation." [Citations.]

courts generally provided judicial review of the size of punitive damage awards. The Court's account of the relevant history is not compelling.

I am not as confident as the Court about either the clarity of early American common law, or its import. * * *

More revealing, the Court notably contracts the scope of its inquiry. It asks: Did common law judges claim the power to overturn jury verdicts they viewed as excessive? But full and fair historical inquiry ought to be wider. The Court should inspect, comprehensively and comparatively, the procedures employed—at trial and on appeal—to fix the amount of punitive damages. Evaluated in this manner, Oregon's scheme affords defendants like Honda more procedural safeguards than 19th-century law provided. * * *

---

1. *Constitutional Challenges to Punitive Damages*: As *Honda Motor* reflects, there have been a number of challenges to the constitutionality of punitive damages in the past few years. *Honda Motor* was the first to invalidate an award. The earlier cases established some constitutional constraints in principle, but failed to provide much guidance on the parameters of the constitutional protection. *Honda Motor* is significant because it is the first to find a specific constitutional infirmity.

2. *Failed Eighth Amendment Challenge*: In Browning–Ferris Industries v. Kelco Disposal, Inc., 492 U.S. 257, 109 S.Ct. 2909, 106 L.Ed.2d 219 (1989), the Court held the Excessive Fines Clause of the Eighth Amendment did not apply to a civil jury award of punitive damages in civil cases between private parties. Although the goals of punishment and deterrence underly both civil punitive awards and criminal penalties, the Court did not find the similarity sufficient to impose the same constitutional limitations and safeguards. The Court noted that the Due Process Clause of the Fourteenth Amendment places "outer limits" on civil damages under certain statutory schemes and postponed for "another day" the question whether due process also operates to limit jury discretion in imposing exemplary awards absent an express statutory limit.

3. *Due Process Limitations*: The Court first reached the due process issue left open in *Browning–Ferris* in Pacific Mut. Life Ins. Co. v. Haslip, 499 U.S. 1, 21–22, 111 S.Ct. 1032, 113 L.Ed.2d 1 (1991). The issue in *Haslip* was Alabama's common law method and procedures for assessing and reviewing punitive damages. The case concerned a claim against an insurance company for the fraudulent actions of its agent. The jury awarded $840,000 in punitive damages, which was approximately four times the compensatory damages given and over 200 times the claimant's actual out-of-pocket expenses. The jury instruction was simply that punitive damages served the purposes of punishment and deterrence and that any exemplary award was discretionary. The judge further told the jury that if it chose to impose such damages, it must

take into consideration the character and degree of the wrong and the necessity of preventing such conduct in the future. Alabama employed a common law multi-factor post-verdict method for testing whether a punitive damages award was excessive or inadequate.

A majority of the Court upheld the verdict, over vigorous dissent. Writing for the majority, Justice Blackmun noted:

> One must concede that unlimited jury discretion—or unlimited judicial discretion for that matter—in the fixing of punitive damages may invite extreme results that jar one's constitutional sensibilities. We need not, and indeed we cannot, draw a mathematical bright line between the constitutionally acceptable and the constitutionally unacceptable that would fit every case. We can say, however, that general concerns of reasonableness and adequate guidance from the court when the case is tried to a jury properly enter into the constitutional calculus.

The Court examined both the jury instructions and the post-verdict practices by the state courts and upheld Alabama's standards for punitive damages. The majority observed that due process requirements were satisfied where the discretion was exercised within "reasonable constraints." The Court did not, however, dictate that states should necessarily follow the procedural safeguards contained in the Alabama model for due process considerations.

Subsequently, in TXO Production Corp. v. Alliance Resources Corp., ___ U.S. ___, 113 S.Ct. 2711, 125 L.Ed.2d 366 (1993), the Court again upheld a punitive damage award against a due process challenge. The case involved a $10 million punitive damage award in a common law slander of title action involving only $19,000 in actual damages. The Court declined to adopt any bright line test, but held that where "fair procedures were followed," an exemplary award was entitled to a strong presumption of validity.

Justice Stevens, writing for the plurality, observed that punitive damages awards are "the product of numerous, and sometimes intangible, factors; a jury imposing a punitive damages award must make a qualitative assessment based on a host of facts and circumstances unique to the particular case before it." The Court reaffirmed its approach of "reasonableness" as the touchstone for due process review as announced in Haslip. Although the punitive damage award in TXO was 526 times greater than the compensatory award, the Court refused to embrace a limitation which focused solely on proportionality to actual damages. Instead, the the Court indicated that additional factors to proportionality were relevant, including consideration of the magnitude of the harm that potentially could have occurred and the potential gain to the defendant.

The plurality of the Court approved of the following illustration:

> For instance, a man wildly fires a gun into a crowd. By sheer chance, no one is injured and the only damage is to a $10 pair of glasses. A jury reasonably could find only $10 in compensatory

damages, but thousands of dollars in punitive damages to teach a duty of care. We would allow a jury to impose substantial punitive damages in order to discourage bad acts.

The Court upheld the punitive damage award based upon evidence that the defendant engaged in a pattern of malicious and fraudulent behaviour in an attempt to deprive the plaintiff of royalties.

HERMAN v. SUNSHINE CHEM. SPECIALTIES

133 N.J. 329, 627 A.2d 1081 (1993).

POLLOCK, J.

This case raises the issue whether plaintiffs in a products-liability action presented sufficient evidence of the financial condition of defendant Sunshine Chemical Specialties, Inc. (Sunshine) to sustain an award of punitive damages. Finding the evidence insufficient, the Appellate Division reversed the judgment and remanded the matter to the Law Division. We granted the petition for certification of plaintiff Sandra Herman (plaintiff or Mrs. Herman), reverse the judgment of the Appellate Division, and reinstate the $400,000 award of punitive damages.

In February 1985, Sunshine engaged Sandra Herman as an independent contractor to demonstrate and sell its products. During a two-day training period, Sunshine instructed Mrs. Herman about the company's products and personnel. No part of the training concerned the potential hazards or safe use of the products.

Sunshine's best-selling product was Sun–Clean Concentrate (Sun–Clean), an all-purpose cleaner that generated gross sales of $1 million in 1985 and $1.2 million in 1986. The Sun–Clean label stated: "SUN CLEAN is safe to use." In larger print, the label provided that Sun–Clean "CONTAINS NO ACIDS, CAUSTICS[,] AMMONIA, ALIPHATIC OR AROMATIC SOLVENTS." The label represented that Sun–Clean met the "operating standards" of the Occupational Safety and Health Administration (OSHA). It did not warn of the dangers of inhaling Sun–Clean vapors.

Sunshine did not manufacture Sun–Clean. Instead, it purchased in bulk from Harley Chemical Corp. (Harley) a product called "3–D," which Harley colored orange and transferred to one-and five-gallon containers bearing the Sun–Clean label.

Robert Feldman, the president and sole owner of Sunshine, designed the Sun–Clean label by cutting and pasting together the labels from products of other manufacturers. Although Harley had provided to Sunshine a "safety data sheet" that outlined the hazardous ingredients of its products, Feldman either did not know of the sheet or ignored it. The sheet indicated that 3–D contained sodium hydroxide, a caustic soda. In contrast, the Sun–Clean label specifically stated that the product contained no caustics. Harley placed on 3–D a label warning, "Danger. . . . Avoid breathing vapor. Keep container closed. Use with adequate ventilation." The Sun–Clean label, however, did not warn against breathing Sun–Clean vapors. Furthermore, Sunshine did not submit either the label or the product to OSHA for approval, nor did the company consult "OSHA operating standards" to determine whether the product met those standards. Feldman simply had removed the OSHA seal from another label. * * *

While demonstrating Sun–Clean in July 1985, Mrs. Herman suffered a coughing fit. Shortly thereafter she developed a fever and breathing problems. After two weeks she consulted a doctor, who treated her for a suspected respiratory infection. Her respiratory problems continued, and she consulted a second physician and then an allergist, who were likewise unsuccessful in treating her. The doctors then placed her on steroid-and cortisone-based drugs that improved her breathing, but caused her to gain over sixty pounds.

Mrs. Herman continued to work for Sunshine after she became ill. Not until October 1986 did her doctors suspect a connection between her asthma and her work. Mrs. Herman stopped working for Sunshine the next month. In August 1987 her doctors learned that Sun–Clean contained a caustic, sodium hydroxide. The doctors then diagnosed her as suffering from "occupational asthma," meaning asthma not related to allergies but caused by exposure to chemicals in the workplace.

On September 3, 1987, Mrs. Herman and her husband filed a complaint against Sunshine Chemical and Concord Chemical Corp. (Concord), which had purchased Harley. They asserted claims in strict liability, negligence, and breach of express and implied warranty. Later, they amended the complaint to include a claim for punitive damages. * * *

The Appellate Division found the evidence sufficient to support the jury's findings that Sunshine had been indifferent to, or had disregarded, the known dangers posed by Sun–Clean. It, however, reversed the punitive-damages judgment, finding that plaintiff had failed to present sufficient evidence of Sunshine's wealth. Consequently, it remanded the case to the Law Division for a trial on punitive damages only.

In recent years courts, legislatures, and scholars have resumed the long-standing debate on the legitimacy of punitive-damage awards. The polemic has ranged from calls for the abolition of punitive damages to arguments for controlling them through more definite standards. Both this Court and the Legislature, although recognizing that a punitive-damages award may be appropriate in some products-liability actions, have tried to set standards to assure that any such award is fair and reasonable.

We have proceeded with an appreciation that at the core of punitive damages lurks a volatile dilemma: the same findings necessary for the award of punitive damages can incite a jury to act irrationally. A condition precedent to a punitive-damages award is the finding that the defendant is guilty of actual malice. The purposes of the award—the deterrence of egregious misconduct and the punishment of the offender—when mixed with a finding that the defendant is malicious, can readily inflame an otherwise-dispassionate jury. Essential to a fair and reasonable award therefore is the consideration of all relevant circumstances, including the nature of the defendant's misconduct and the harm to the plaintiff. Stated generally, the award of punitive damages "must bear some reasonable relation to the injury inflicted and the cause of the injury." * * *

As long as punitive-damage awards are strictly confined, they may be appropriate in a failure-to-warn, strict-products-liability action. Fischer v. Johns–Manville Corp., 103 N.J. 643, 652–60, 512 A.2d 466 (1986). *Fischer* identified the factors relevant to the determination of a plaintiff's entitlement to punitive damages, and of the appropriate amount of such damages. In addition to bearing a reasonable relationship to actual injury, the amount of punitive damages should account for the profitability of the defendant's marketing misconduct, the plaintiff's litigation expenses, the punishment the defendant will probably receive from other sources, the defendant's financial condition, and the effect on its condition of a judgment for the plaintiff.

Our case law recognizes the defendant's financial condition as a relevant factor in all punitive-damages awards. The Appellate Division has stated in *McDonough v. Jorda* that "[i]n assessing exemplary damages, a jury must take into consideration the wealth of the defendants." 214 N.J.Super. 338, 349, 519 A.2d 874 (1986), *certif. denied*, 110 N.J. 302, 540 A.2d 1282 (1988), *cert. denied*, 489 U.S. 1065 (1989). In *McDonough*, the court stated that a defendant's financial condition must be considered "because the theory behind punitive damages is to punish for the past event and to prevent future offenses, and the degree of punishment resulting from a judgment must be, to some extent, in proportion to the means of the guilty person." The *McDonough* court concluded that evidence of the ability of the wrongdoers to pay punitives is an "essential" of the plaintiff's burden of proof, the absence of which "precluded the jury from having a proper foundation to assess damages."

When adopting N.J.S.A. 2A:58C–1 to–7, the Legislature substantially codified the judicial standards for the award of punitive damages. [Citations.] The act mandates that in determining the amount of punitive damages in product-liability actions, the trier of fact "shall consider all relevant evidence, including, but not limited to . . . [t]he financial condition of the tortfeasor." N.J.S.A. 2A:58C–5d(4); *see* A. 2068, 205th Leg., 1st Sess., § 1b(4) (1992) (mandating consideration of financial condition of defendant in all actions based on injuries or wrongs done to either persons or property).

Some scholars, however, have challenged the relevance of a defendant's wealth in determining the amount of punitive damages, especially when the defendant is a corporation. [Citations.]

Still other courts and scholars argue in favor of considering the defendant's financial condition. As the author of one law review article states, "the underlying rationale of punitive damages seems to demand consideration of a defendant's wealth, since a sum that would deter a poor person may have little or no impact on a rich person." Consideration of a defendant's wealth is relevant both to preventing the imposition of an especially devastating fine, and to determining the amount that will sufficiently punish and deter. [Citations.]

In a products-liability action, the Legislature has resolved the issue by determining that the trier of fact "shall consider . . . [t]he financial condition of the tortfeasor." N.J.S.A. 2A:58C–5d(4). That mandate comports with prior judicial decisions. We conclude that a jury must consider evidence of a defendant's financial condition in determining the amount of punitive damages.

* * * For whatever reason, the trial did not conform to the act. The act mandates a bifurcated proceeding in which [t]he trier of fact shall first determine whether compensatory damages are to be awarded. Evidence relevant only to punitive damages shall not be admissible in that proceeding. After such determination has been made, the trier of fact shall, in a separate proceeding, determine whether punitive damages are to be awarded. [N.J.S.A. 2A:58C–5b.]

The act provides further that "[i]f the trier of fact determines that punitive damages should be awarded, the trier of fact shall then determine the amount of those damages." N.J.S.A. 2A:58C–5d. Although section 5d could be read to require a further bifurcation of the punitive-damages hearing, neither the words nor the legislative history of the statute compels that result. Unlike its treatment of the trial of compensatory and punitive damages, the Legislature did not require the bifurcation of the liability and damage phases of a punitive-damages claim. * * *

In sum, plaintiff sought no discovery of Sunshine's financial condition. Nor did she introduce any evidence of its financial condition at trial. Sunshine, however, did not move at the close of plaintiff's case to dismiss the punitive-damage claim because of the failure to adduce evidence of defendant's financial condition. Evidence of Sunshine's financial condition emerged on the cross-examination of the company's president. Although the jury ultimately heard the necessary proof, the procedure did not comport with the statutory requirements. To avoid similar problems in the future, we provide the following guidelines for the trial of punitive-damage claims. * * *

Tempering the normal rule favoring wide discovery of relevant issues is a regard for the defendant's interest in maintaining the confidentiality of information about its financial status. We have not previously considered the issue, but in a variety of contexts lower courts have prudently required that a plaintiff may not make discovery of a defendant's financial condition without first establishing a prima facie case of the right to recover punitive damages. Those courts have required the plaintiffs to establish their right to punitive damages in actions for libel, malicious prosecution, and for tortious interference with prospective economic advantage. [Citations.] Judicial review of applications for discovery, like the bifurcation of compensatory and punitive-damage claims, should alleviate concerns about abusive or burdensome discovery. In reviewing requests for discovery of a defendant's financial condition, a trial court should balance the plaintiff's need for the information with the burden on a defendant of disclosure, and with an appreciation that a defendant's finances "are private matters which are normally jealously guarded". [Citation.]

Sensitive balancing by the trial court is essential to the accommodation of a plaintiff's need for discovery and the defendant's right to maintain the confidentiality of information about its financial condition. In many cases, a plaintiff can obtain the needed information through the production of documents. For publicly-held corporate defendants, discovery of annual shareholder reports or reports filed with regulatory bodies should not unreasonably invade the defendant's privacy. Certified financial statements of a privately-held corporation may also be discoverable in an appropriate case. Discovery of income tax returns, however, may go too far. [Citations.] Under some circumstances, depositions or interrogatories may be appropriate. If so, a trial court can accord a defendant some measure of protection by limiting the persons present at the deposition to the defendant and counsel for the parties. Excluding the plaintiff and sealing the deposition or answers to interrogatories may be essential for striking the right balance of the litigants' interests. * * *

Neither the product-liability act nor judicial decisions define "financial condition." From the purposes of punitive damages—punishment and deterrence—we glean that "financial condition" roughly means the ability to pay. Contrary to the Appellate Division, that ability does not necessarily equate with net worth. Depending on the facts of a case, a defendant's income might be a better indicator of the ability to pay. [Citations.] For present purposes, we need not dwell on the subtleties of "net worth," except to note that it can be an elusive concept, a potentially-puzzling indicator of current value, and of questionable utility. Notwithstanding these problems, net worth remains one of the indicia of financial condition.

Although the present case arises in the context of a claim for punitive damages in a products-liability action, the requirements for bifurcation of compensatory and punitive damages, for allocation to a plaintiff of the burden of proving a defendant's financial condition, for proof of a prima facie case as a condition precedent to discovery of a defendant's financial condition, and for limitations on such discovery apply as readily to all such claims. Consequently, we expect those requirements to govern all claims for punitive damages, even those that arise outside the act.

In this case, the cross-examination of Sunshine's president revealed that Sun–Clean was Sunshine's best-selling product, accounting for approximately one-third of the company's gross sales of $3 million.

Feldman also testified that in 1986, when Sunshine's gross sales had grown to $3.5 million, he and his wife sold 100% of Sunshine's stock for $750,000. That evidence, although not overwhelming, is sufficient to support an award of punitive damages. Although the jury did not know of the net profit from the sale of Sun–Clean, it knew the gross sales figures for both the product and the company. It also knew that one year after Mrs. Herman's injury Feldman had sold 100% of the stock of the corporation for $750,000. "A sale of the entire business in the fairly recent past, in an arms-length transaction between sophisticated individuals, is considered practically conclusive evidence of value as of the time of the sale." We find that the evidence is sufficient to sustain the award of punitive damages. As previously indicated, we have not reviewed the amount of the award for excessiveness.

The judgment of the Appellate Division is reversed and the judgment of the Law Division is reinstated.

---

1. *Wealth of the Defendant.* The prevailing view holds that the wealth of the defendant is a relevant, although not necessary, factor in determining the amount of punitive damages. *See* City of Newport v. Fact Concerts, Inc., 453 U.S. 247, 101 S.Ct. 2748, 69 L.Ed.2d 616 (1981); Restatement (Second) of Torts § 908(2); Kan. Stat. Ann. § 60–3701(b)(6) (court may consider financial condition of defendant in calculating amount of punitives).

Consider the following explanation for considering wealth in Lunsford v. Hon. Joseph Morris, 746 S.W.2d 471 (Tex.1988):

A defendant's "ability to pay" bears directly on the question of adequate punishment and deterrence. That which could be an enormous penalty to one may be but a mere annoyance to another. For example, one hundred dollars as a punitive award against a single mother of three small children may be a greater deterrent than one hundred thousand dollars awarded against a major corporation whose directors are shielded from the stark reality of harm done by the paneled walls and plush carpet of the corporate boardroom.

2. *Curtailment of plaintiff abuses in seeking punitive damages:* The potential discovery and admission of the defendant's wealth for measuring punitive damages has led to some abuses. Many jurisdictions bifurcate the trial and determine entitlement to exemplary damages before allowing the jury to consider evidence of the defendant's wealth in calculating the amount of damages. Some jurisdictions mandate bifurcation by statute. *See, e.g.,* Minn. Stat. Ann. § 549.20 subd.4. The rationale for requiring the plaintiff to demonstrate entitlement to punitive damages prior to considering evidence pertaining to the defendant's financial condition is principally to avoid prejudicing the jury with

"punitive" evidence and thus inflating a compensatory award. *See, e.g.,* Curtis v. Partain, 272 Ark. 400, 614 S.W.2d 671 (1981).

3. *Definition of wealth:* A particularly troublesome issue involves interpretation of what sorts of financial data should fall within the definition of "wealth." For example, should the evidence of a wealth of a defendant company be net worth or simply net sales? Some courts favor an inclusive approach, while others have found that it is harassment to subject a defendant to disclosure of all assets. *Compare* Ortega v. City of Kansas City, 659 F.Supp. 1201 (D.Kan.1987) *with* Gierman v. Toman, 77 N.J.Super. 18, 185 A.2d 241 (1962). *See also* Mont. Code Ann. § 27–1–221 (7) (Jury must consider defendant's financial affairs, financial condition, and net worth in determining punitive damages.)

4. *Proportionality:* Some jurisdictions require that punitive damages bear some reasonable ratio to compensatory damages. *See* Miss. Code Ann. § 11–1–65(1)(f) (Reviewing court evaluates whether punitive award bears a reasonable relationship to harm likely to result and harm actually occurred from defendant's conduct); N. Dak. Code § 32–03.2–11(4) (Exemplary damages cannot exceed two times compensatory damages or $250,000, whichever is greater.) The rule is applied flexibly, however, without demanding any particular ratio or formula of punitive to compensatory damages. *See, e.g.,* Professional Seminar Consultants, Inc. v. Sino American Technology Exchange Council, Inc., 727 F.2d 1470 (9th Cir.1984); Ogilvie v. Fotomat Corp., 641 F.2d 581 (8th Cir.1981).

In Pacific Mut. Life Ins. Co. v. Haslip, 499 U.S. 1, 111 S.Ct. 1032, 113 L.Ed.2d 1 (1991), the Court refused to draw a "mathematical bright line" for an appropriate measure of punitive damages. Similarly, in *TXO* the Court declined to impose a proportionality "test" in reviewing a punitive damages award. Instead, the Court has accepted more generalized notions of reasonableness in assessing the issue of excessiveness of exemplary awards. In *Haslip* the Court upheld the following post-verdict considerations as relevant to a determination of whether a punitive damages award was excessive or inadequate:

(a) whether there is a reasonable relationship between the punitive damages award and the harm likely to result from the defendant's conduct as well as the harm that actually has occurred;

(b) the degree of reprehensibility of the defendant's conduct, the duration of that conduct, the defendant's awareness, any concealment, and the existence and frequency of similar past conduct;

(c) the profitability to the defendant of the wrongful conduct and the desirability of removing that profit and of having the defendant also sustain a loss;

(d) the "financial position" of the defendant;

(e) all the costs of litigation;

(f) the imposition of criminal sanctions on the defendant for its conduct, these to be taken in mitigation; and

(g) the existence of other civil awards against the defendant for the same conduct, these also to be taken in mitigation.

5. *Continuing debate:* Scholars and courts continue to consider suitable standards and procedures for punitive awards to satisfy due process. Consider the following excerpt from the dissenting opinion in *TXO* by Justice O'Connor, joined by Justices White and Souter.

> * * * Influences such as caprice, passion, bias, and prejudice are antithetical to the rule of law. If there is a fixture of due process, it is that a verdict based on such influences cannot stand. But fundamental fairness requires that impermissible influences such as bias and prejudice be discovered nonetheless, by inference if not by direct proof. * * *

> Judicial intervention in cases of excessive awards also has the critical function of ensuring that another ancient and fundamental principle of justice is observed—that the punishment be proportionate to the offense. As we have observed, the requirement of proportionality is "deeply rooted and frequently repeated in common-law jurisprudence." Because punitive damages are designed as punishment rather than compensation, courts historically have required that punitive damages awards bear a reasonable relationship to the actual harm imposed. This Court similarly has recognized that the requirement of proportionality is implicit in the notion of due process. * * *

> In my view, due process at least requires judges to engage in searching review where the verdict discloses such great disproportions as to suggest the possibility of bias, caprice, or passion. As JUSTICE STEVENS observed in a different context, "one need not use Justice Stewart's classic definition of obscenity—'I know it when I see it'—as an ultimate standard for judging" the constitutionality of a punitive damages verdict "to recognize that the dramatically irregular" size and nature of an award "may have sufficient probative force to call for an explanation." *Cf.* Karcher v. Daggett, 462 U.S. 725, 755, 103 S.Ct. 2653, 2672, 77 L.Ed.2d 133, (1983) (concurring opinion) (footnotes omitted).

> * * * As I read the record in this case, it seems quite likely that the jury in fact was unduly influenced by the fact that TXO is a very large, out-of-state corporation. * * *

> That a jury might have such inclinations should come as no surprise. Courts long have recognized that jurors may view large corporations with great disfavor. Corporations are mere abstractions and, as such, are unlikely to be viewed with much sympathy. Moreover, they often represent a large accumulation of productive resources; jurors naturally think little of taking an otherwise large sum of money out of what appears to be an enormously larger pool of wealth. Finally, juries may feel privileged to correct perceived social ills stemming from unequal wealth distribution by transfer-

ring money from "wealthy" corporations to comparatively needier plaintiffs. * * *

This is not to say that consideration of a defendant's wealth is unconstitutional. To be sure, there are strong economic arguments that permitting juries to consider wealth is unwise if not irrational, especially where the defendant is a corporation. * * *

The risk of prejudice was especially grave here. The jury repeatedly was told of TXO's extraordinary resources, which respondents estimated at $2 billion. To make matters worse, unlike the jurors or the primary plaintiffs, TXO was not from West Virginia. It was an interloper, from the large State of Texas. As the Supreme Court of Appeals of West Virginia has recognized, the temptation to transfer wealth from out-of-state corporate defendants to in-state plaintiffs can be quite strong. * * *

Counsels' arguments, however, converted that grave risk of prejudice into a near certainty. Repeatedly they reminded the jury that TXO was from another State. Repeatedly they told the jury about TXO's massive wealth. And repeatedly they told the jury that it could do anything it thought "fair." The opening line from rebuttal set the tone. "Ladies and gentleman of the jury," one attorney began, "this greedy bunch from down in Texas still doesn't understand this case." Playing on images of Texans as overrich gamblers who profit by chance rather than work, he referred to TXO shortly thereafter as a bunch of "Texas high rollers, wildcatters." Finally, counsel drove the point home yet one more time, comparing TXO to an obviously wealthy out-of-town visitor who refuses to put money in the parking meter to help pay for community service:

"Well, what is fair? ... If someone comes to town and intentionally doesn't put a quarter in the meter, stays here all day, [in this] town that needs it to pay for the police force and the fire department, they give [him] a fine. And at the end of the day [he] may have to pay a dollar. That person reaches in his billfold at the end of the day and maybe he's got a hundred bucks in there. He doesn't want to have to pay that dollar, but he does, because he knows if he doesn't [he'll have legal problems]. . . . The town didn't take everything from the individual, didn't ruin [him], just took one percent of what that person had in cash. One percent. You can fine TXO one percent if you want, you can fine them one dollar if you want. But I submit to you a one percent fine, the same as John Doe on this street, would be fair. That's twelve and a half million dollars, based on what they had left over. And their earnings were $225,000,000.00 [per year]. I mean, yeah, their cash flow. Their surplus. So anything between twelve and a half million and twenty-two million is only one percent—the same as this poor guy who just tried to cheat a little bit. Now that's a lot of money. I hope, like I said, you don't analyze this on a lot or a little, but fair." (emphases added).

Over and over respondents' lawyers reminded the jury that there were virtually no substantive limits on its discretion. Time and again they told the jury of TXO's great wealth and that it could take away any amount it wanted, as long as it seemed "fair." And each time the argument found solid support in the trial court's instructions, which not only licensed the jury to afford respondents any "additional compensation" they believed appropriate, but also encouraged them to do so based on TXO's wealth alone. * * *

* * * [The Supreme Court of Appeals of West Virginia] refused to consider the possibility of remittitur because TXO "and its agents and servants failed to conduct themselves as gentlemen." 187 W.Va. at 462, 419 S.E.2d at 875. Proceeding to the question whether the award of punitive damages should be stricken as excessive, the court distinguished between two categories of defendants: those who are "really stupid" and those who are "really mean." If the defendant is "really stupid," the court explained, "the outer limit of punitive damages is" generally about "five to one." For the "really mean" defendant, however, "even punitive damages 500 times greater than compensatory damages are not per se unconstitutional." TXO, it seems, was not really stupid but "really mean." The Supreme Court of Appeals affirmed the $10 million punitive award even though it was 526 times greater than compensatory damages.

Reference to categories like "really stupid" and "really mean" are a caricature of the difficult task of determining whether an award may be upheld consistent with due process. It is simply not enough to observe that the conduct was malicious and conclude that, as a result, the sky (or 500 times compensatory damages) is the limit. Instead, post-trial review must be sufficient to "ensure that punitive damages awards are not grossly out of proportion to the severity of the offense and have some understandable relationship to" some measure of harm.

7. Application of the Alabama factors in post-*TXO* and *Haslip* cases in the lower courts has been an imprecise science. Many of the same considerations that justify imposition of punitive damages at all also become relevant in assessing an appropriate measure of those damages. Consider Hopkins v. Dow Corning Corp., 33 F.3d 1116 (9th Cir.1994), where the claimant sought compensatory and punitive damages for injuries resulting from post-operative complications arising from ruptured silicone gel breast implants manufactured by the defendant, Dow Corning. The Ninth Circuit Court of Appeals, employing an abuse of discretion standard of review, upheld the jury award of $840,000 in compensatory damages and $6.5 million in punitive damages on the basis of strict liability.

Dow challenged the punitive damages award as "grossly excessive," and without bearing a rational relationship to actual damages. Evidence produced at trial indicated that Dow, in its haste to market the product, failed to adequately test the implants, ignored information suggesting potential adverse health effects of silicone on the human body, and decided against proposed design modifications that might have reduced the likelihood of problems. Further, the court focused on the evidence that a large number of Dow silicone gel breast implants had been implanted in thousands of women. The court noted:

> Each of these women was at risk of encountering the same fate from which Hopkins suffered. Therefore, Dow's conduct in exposing thousands of women to a painful and debilitating disease, and the evidence that Dow gained financially from its conduct, may properly be considered in imposing an award of punitive damages. Moreover, given the facts that Dow was aware of possible defects in its implants, that Dow knew long-term studies of the implants' safety were needed, that Dow concealed this information as well as the negative results of the few short-term laboratory tests performed, and that Dow continued for several years to market its implants as safe despite this knowledge, a substantial punitive damages award is justified. Coupled with the facts that Dow is a wealthy corporation and that Dow made a considerable amount of money from the sale of its implants, the jury's award of $6.5 million is reasonable in light of *TXO* and *Haslip*.

STRUM v. EXXON CO.

15 F.3d 327 (4th Cir.1994).

WILKINSON, Circuit Judge:

This case requires us to address various rationales for using tort remedies to compensate contract breaches. Because the plaintiff pled fanciful tort theories where redress, if any, lay in the law of contract, we affirm the district court's grant of summary judgment in favor of the defendant.

Plaintiff Matthew Strum operated an Exxon service station in Hillsborough, North Carolina. After leasing the station for many years, Strum purchased it in 1975 and continued to operate it as an Exxon station pursuant to a series of gasoline distribution agreements with the company. In April 1988, Exxon informed Strum that it would not renew his distribution agreement because his station was unprofitable, and Strum ceased selling Exxon gasoline on September 1, 1988. He did, however, continue to operate the station as an automobile repair business.

Once Exxon had terminated its distribution agreement with Strum, it began negotiations with him regarding recovery of its underground storage tanks which were used to hold the station's gasoline. The two parties reached an agreement governing removal of the tanks in March 1989. The agreement provided that Exxon would remove the tanks from Strum's property within three days of starting work "unless any environmental problems develop or unanticipated events arise...."

Removal of the tanks began on May 15, 1989. For reasons which are in dispute, the removal took much longer than three days. The record does make clear that Exxon discovered at least some soil contamination while removing the tanks and was still involved in various remedial actions on Strum's property as late as December 1989. Exxon's activities during this period included the taking of multiple soil samples and the installation of monitoring wells to evaluate any groundwater contamination. Exxon also negotiated a second agreement with Strum in November 1989, which laid out procedures for solving the soil problems and for the restoration of Strum's property.

Strum was ultimately unsatisfied with Exxon's activities at the station and brought suit against the company in North Carolina state court in March 1992. Strum alleged causes of action for fraudulent inducement, negligence, and gross negligence. Strum claimed that during the period when Exxon was removing the tanks, the excavations impeded access to the service and repair bays of his station, making it impossible for him to operate a profitable auto service business. Exxon removed the case to federal district court on diversity grounds and moved for summary judgment. The district court granted Exxon's motion on each of the three counts. It found that Strum could not establish the essential elements of fraud, and could not provide sufficient evidence to ground a cause of action for either negligence or gross negligence. Strum now appeals, contending that each cause of action should have proceeded to trial.

At the outset, it is necessary to place the claims underlying this appeal in the appropriate context. Simply put, this case involves an attempt by the plaintiff to manufacture a tort dispute out of what is, at bottom, a simple breach of contract claim. Whatever injury Strum may have sustained here resulted from the possible breach of a commercial relationship memorialized in contract. However, because plaintiff suffered little, if any, actual damages, he attempted to shoe-horn this case into a tort framework. Each of the counts as now pleaded by Strum holds the prospect of a hefty punitive damages award. This attempt to turn a contract dispute into a tort action with an accompanying punitive dimension is inconsistent both with North Carolina law and sound commercial practice.

Contract law is simply more restrictive than tort law in awarding damages. Indeed, the punitive damages recovery Strum would seek in tort is not generally permitted in the context of a contract breach. *See* 5 Arthur L. Corbin, *Corbin on Contracts* § 1077, at 438 (1964) ("It can be laid down as a general rule that punitive damages are not recoverable for breach of contract.... "); 1 Linda L. Schlueter & Kenneth R. Redden, Punitive Damages § 7.2, at 275 (2d ed. 1989) ("Punitive damages cannot be recovered for a mere breach of contract ... no matter how reprehensible the breach was by the defendant.") (footnotes omitted).

This difference in awarding damages results from the fact that tort and contract law serve different goals. Tort law emerges from duties individuals owe generally to other members of society; it is fault-based and seeks both to compensate the victim and punish the wrong-doer. Accordingly, punitive awards may be appropriate where the requisite standards of culpability under state law have been met. Contract law, by contrast, arises out of the attempt by private individuals to order relationships among themselves. When such relationships collapse, the law has long recognized that compensating the individual only for actual loss will suffice. See Restatement (Second) of Contracts § 355 cmt. a, at 154 (1981) (stating that the purpose of awarding contract damages is to compensate the injured party, not to punish the party in breach).

The distinction between tort and contract possesses more than mere theoretical significance. Parties contract partly to minimize their future risks. Importing tort law principles of punishment into contract undermines their ability to do so. Punitive damages, because they depend heavily on an individual jury's perception of the degree of fault involved, are necessarily uncertain. Their availability would turn every potential contractual relationship into a riskier proposition. Indeed, Corbin cautioned against punitive damages in contract for just this reason, stating that, "in the innumerable cases arising from the breach of an ordinary commercial contract, it has seemed wise to adhere to the general rule excluding the punitive element and to avoid the frequently futile attempt to determine the degree of moral obliquity." Corbin, *supra*, § 1077, at 440.

The parties in this case deserved the chance to lay out their obligations and to limit their liabilities through the medium of contract. The presence of punitive damages claims deprives defendant of the very benefit it bargained for. Exxon did not bargain for the risk of an open-ended jury award, the most palpable risk that punitive damages create. Instead, the company bargained for liability limited to damages that might arise from deficient performance under the agreement. The contractual relationship does make Exxon liable for consequential damages to Strum's business arising out of any unreasonable delay by Exxon during the tank removal process. It does not make Exxon liable, however, for an award unrelated to the actual damages Strum sustained.

Here the actual damages were not significant. Strum's labor and merchandise sales for each month in 1989 when Exxon was engaged in remedial actions either approximated or, as was true in most months, far surpassed the sales for the corresponding month in 1988. The fact that Strum's own financial records indicate that his auto repair business did not suffer appreciably from Exxon's activities does not entitle him to recast his contract claim in tort. A paucity of actual damages affords no basis for a party to seek a punitive award.

We now turn to Strum's particular claims. Only where a breach of contract also constitutes an "independent tort" may tort actions be pursued. See Restatement (Second) of Contracts § 355 (1981). The independent tort exception is the only exception the Restatement recognizes to the general rule that punitive damages are not recoverable for breach of contract. North Carolina law also recognizes the availability of the independent tort exception in breach of contract cases. [Citations.] However, that exception has been carefully circumscribed by state law. The independent tort alleged must be "identifiable," and the tortious conduct must have an aggravating element such as malice or recklessness before any punitive damages may be recovered. None of Strum's counts allege viable independent tort claims.

While Strum's [claim for] fraudulent inducement could constitute an independent tort, that claim lacks both factual and legal support. Strum contends that Exxon fraudulently induced him into entering the March 1989 agreement governing removal of the tanks. Specifically, Strum argues that Exxon knew it could not remove the tanks within three days and that it made this promise only to induce Strum's acquiescence in the March agreement. Strum maintains that because issues of motive and intent are difficult to resolve on summary judgment, he deserves an opportunity to have his fraudulent inducement claim presented to a jury.

We disagree. Strum ignores both the language of the March agreement with Exxon and the elements necessary to make out a fraud claim. The March agreement plainly conditions the three day removal period on the absence of environmental problems, a condition which failed to materialize. Furthermore, while Exxon may have misjudged the time it would take to remove the tanks, misjudgment alone is not fraudulent inducement. At most, Strum may have been able to prove that Exxon did not carry out its promise, not that Exxon never had any intention of doing so. The mere failure to carry out a promise in contract, however, does not support a tort action for fraud. * * *

Strum's final cause of action, which alleges gross negligence, also cannot be encompassed within the independent tort exception. Strum argues that Exxon did not follow various North Carolina Department of Environment, Health, and Natural Resources ("DEHNR") reporting requirements for underground storage tanks. For example, Strum claims that Exxon violated DEHNR regulations requiring that the discovery of a gasoline release from an underground storage tank be reported within twenty days. Strum asserts that Exxon's failure to follow these requirements creates a material issue of fact as to whether Exxon acted in a grossly negligent fashion.

We are not persuaded. For purposes of summary judgment, we accept Strum's contention that Exxon defaulted on its obligations to notify DEHNR of the discovery of a gasoline release at the site. However, any sanction for noncompliance with DEHNR regulations most appropriately lies with that agency, and it has taken no action against Exxon. [Citation.] Moreover, the relationship between the reporting requirements and Exxon's contractual obligations to Strum is tenuous at best. The violations of DEHNR regulations lack connection to the damages Strum points to, namely the inability to use his service station. Indeed, most of Exxon's delays in following DEHNR reporting requirements occurred after the excavations at Strum's station had been filled in.

Additionally, Strum presented no evidence that Exxon's removal procedures were unreasonable. As the district court noted, Strum has provided no evidence of normal industry standards or any expert testimony relevant to Exxon's actual clean-up efforts. Indeed, one of Strum's own witnesses stated that remediation of soil contamination could take over six months. Strum's meager evidentiary showing here would not even be sufficient to sustain a claim for negligence, since such a claim requires a demonstration that defendant failed to exercise due care in performing duties owed to the plaintiff. [Citation.] To sustain the gross negligence claim, Strum would have been required to demonstrate that Exxon's conduct in removing the tanks had been wanton or reckless as well.

There is, however, a more basic deficiency here. Strum's claim for gross negligence really arises out of Exxon's performance on the contract, not out of the type of distinct circumstances necessary to allege an independent tort. We think it unlikely that an independent tort could arise in the course of contractual performance, since those sorts of claims are most appropriately addressed by asking simply whether a party adequately fulfilled its contractual obligations. Finding that the evidence presents no triable issue as to a contractual breach or as to damages sustained therefrom, we affirm the grant of summary judgment for defendant.

Affirmed.

---

1. The prevailing rule is that punitive damages are not recoverable for breach of a contractual obligation, no matter how willful, intentional or malicious the breach, unless the conduct also constitutes an independent tort which would support such an award. Some of the common justifications for that approach include:

(1) Traditional contract theory provides that a contract is simply a set of alternative promises to perform or to pay compensation in lieu of performance. Therefore, courts should not further examine the breaching party's moral culpability or fault because compensatory damages provide an adequate remedy for the harm resulting from the breach.

(2) Compensation for losses resulting from a breach arising out of commercial dealings often are relatively easily calculable, whereas injuries to personal interests typically are more difficult to value (thus justifying non-compensatory recoveries).

(3) An efficient breach of contract, which allows the breaching party to maximize profit even after paying the non-breaching party their expectation interest, is wealth-enhancing and therefore should not only be permitted without sanction but encouraged within a com-

pensatory model. The prospect of imposition of punitive damages would undermine the willingness of parties to pursue taking such beneficial actions.

(4) Breaches of contracts do not cause the same mental anguish, desire for personal vengeance, nor societal resentment as may be associated with a response to certain tortious behavior; thus, the retributive and deterrent purposes of punitive damages would not be applicable in the context of contract breaches.

(5) Contract liability, both in terms of entitlement and measurement of damages, turns on an assessment of risk allocation as determined at the time the parties entered the bargain. An award of punitive damages would be an unforeseeable risk outside the ordinary expectations of the parties and would interject an element of uncertainty into commercial transactions.

(6) The motivation of a party to fail to perform contractual obligations often is immaterial; correspondingly the search for motive introduces unwarranted subjectivity into the evaluation of appropriate remedies for breach.

See generally, Thyssen, Inc. v. S.S. Fortune Star, 777 F.2d 57, 63 (2d Cir.1985); Canderm Pharmacal v. Elder Pharmaceuticals, Inc., 862 F.2d 597 (6th Cir.1988); Globe Ref. Co. v. Landa Cotton Oil Co., 190 U.S. 540, 547, 23 S.Ct. 754, 756, 47 L.Ed. 1171 (1902); Farnsworth, Contracts § 12.8 (1982); Simpson, Punitive Damages for Breach of Contract, 20 Ohio St.L.J. 284 (1959); Sullivan, Punitive Damages in the Law of Contract: The Reality and the Illusion of Legal Change, 61 Minn. L. Rev. 207 (1977). Which of the foregoing policy considerations influenced the court in the principal case? The presence of an independent tort to justify punitive damages for breach of contract is not actually an "exception" to the general rule, but rather a recognition that the same course of conduct can potentially give rise to alternative or cumulative causes of action sounding in contract or tort. In recent years, some courts have displayed an increased willingness to find sufficiently tortious conduct accompanying the contract breach to support an award of punitive damages. *See, e.g.*, Life Insurance Co. of Virginia v. Murray Investment Co., 646 F.2d 224 (5th Cir.1981).

2. One early line of cases allowed punitive damages against common carriers and other enterprises involved in furnishing public services for failing to perform their obligations to the public. Consider Ft. Smith & W. Ry. v. Ford, 34 Okl. 575, 126 P. 745 (1912), where a train carried a passenger with a ticket past the scheduled stop. The conductor ignored the passenger's urgent requests to return to the station and the brakeman exclaimed, "To hell with the station. I've passed it, fall off!" The court noted the passenger's tale as follows:

Plaintiff testified that he jumped off the train while in motion, and fell on his hands and knees, though he was not injured; that it was near 10 o'clock at night, in the month of February, and was raining at the time. Plaintiff's testimony in part is as follows: "I asked him to move me back up to the station, and he said: 'He had been there once and was not going any more.' He says, 'Do you want off,' and I says, 'Yes; I have business to attend to tomorrow, I am not well and I want off.' We slowed up again. We had kept going on until we got to Rain Prairie. It was a very rough place. I was acquainted with the place, so I went down on the step and he went along with me. He says, 'Get off,' and it had slowed up reasonably slow. I am getting old. I am 52 years old, not a real old man, but I have lost my eyesight. It was dark and rainy." The plaintiff then attempted to follow an old cow trail, but missed it, and then followed a wire fence for a guide a distance of a half mile to a neighbor's, when he again followed another wire fence until he reached home.

The court upheld an award of punitive damages against the railroad based upon the actions of its employees in exhibiting neglect, indifference, and reckless disregard of the duty of care owed to the passenger.

3. Punitive damages have been awarded on occasion for breach of a fiduciary duty. In Brown v. Coates, 253 F.2d 36 (D.C. Cir.1958), for example, the court imposed exemplary damages against a real estate agent for engaging in deceitful practices in the course of representing a homeowner. Although the fiduciary relationship derived out of contract, the court found that the agent breached the trust and confidence inherent in the contract but limited its decision to instances where the breach "merges with and assumes the character of a wilful tort, calculated rather than inadvertent, flagrant, and in disregard of obligations of trust punitive damages may be imposed."

4. Some courts have relied upon "fraudulent" conduct accompanying breach of contract to support punitive damages even if the tort elements of fraud are not technically satisfied. Welborn v. Dixon, 70 S.C. 108, 49 S.E. 232 (1904); Wright v. Public Sav. Life Ins. Co., 262 S.C. 285, 204 S.E.2d 57 (1974). *See also* Paiz v. State Farm Fire and Cas. Co., 118 N.M. 203, 880 P.2d 300 (N.M.1994) (punitive damages awarded in breach of contract cases only where the breaching party acted in reckless disregard for the interests of the other or showed bad faith); Ross v. Stouffer Hotel Co., 879 P.2d 1037, 1049 (Hawaii 1994) (punitive damages recoverable only where contract breach in wilful, wanton or reckless manner to result in tortious injury); Smith v. Hawkins, 120 Kan. 518, 243 P. 1018 (1926) (punitive damages justified for claim of breach of contract to marry after seduction).

In Hibschman Pontiac v. Batchelor, 266 Ind. 310, 362 N.E.2d 845 (1977), the court upheld a jury award of punitive damages against a car dealer on the basis that fraud, malice, gross negligence, or oppression *mingled* into the breach of warranty where the dealer had repeatedly failed to correct defects. What legal relevance, for purposes of exemplary damages, would be the introduction of evidence of tortious conduct committed after the breach of contract?

5. A handful of courts have carved out an exception to the rule denying punitive damages for breach of contract where the conduct also

contravenes an important public policy, even if the conduct did not amount to an independent tort. For example, in Vernon Fire & Casualty Insurance Co. v. Sharp, 264 Ind. 599, 349 N.E.2d 173 (1976), the court awarded an insured punitive damages for an insurance company's breach of an obligation to pay for property losses. The court did not find that the insurer had committed an independent tort; rather, the imposition of tort liability was based upon a determination that the public interest in insurance rate-making would be served by the deterrent effect of punitive damages. *See also* Watson v. Blankinship, 20 F.3d 383, 387 (10th Cir.1994) (New Mexico permits punitive damages in contract cases where malicious or wanton conduct, such as bad faith or public interest is involved.)

6. In Jeppesen v. Rust, 8 F.3d 1235, 1239 (7th Cir.1993), the court explained the distinction between allowing punitive damages for tortious conduct rather than for breach of contract:

> **A** agrees to sell tons of turnips to **B**. Breaking its promise, **A** sells the turnips to **C** instead. Contract law requires **A** to compensate **B** for the difference between the contract price and the cost of "cover" in the turnip market, and there are sound reasons for limiting damages to this amount. Yet **B** could recharacterize this breach as the "tort" of interfering with **B**'s business of selling the turnips it had contracted to buy from **A**. Now **A** *could* interfere with **B**'s business in the tort sense by throwing a stick of dynamite into **B**'s premises, or by slandering **B** so that **B**'s customers deserted; these would be torts independent of **A**'s failure to deliver the turnips, properly leading to additional damages.

7. The Nevada Supreme Court in K Mart Corp. v. Ponsock, 103 Nev. 39, 732 P.2d 1364 (Nev.1987), similarly upheld an award of compensatory and punitive damages to an employee for the employer's tortious breach of the covenant of good faith and fair dealing by firing the employee in order to avoid paying retirement benefits. The court observed:

> Mr. Blackstone tells us: "[C]ourts of justice are instituted in every society in order to protect the weak from the insults of the stronger by expounding and enforcing those laws by which rights are defined and wrongs punished." The impression on reading this record is that K Mart's actions can be described in terms of "insults of the stronger" and appear to be inherently wrong and abusive. One gets the impression that a Rawlsian observer looking at this kind of conduct would have to conclude that if such actions were not actionably tortious, they should be.
>
> * * * [Oftentimes] tortious conduct arises out of or is related to a contractual relationship. A tort, however, requires the presence of a duty created by law, not merely a duty created by contract; and, although a duty of good faith and fair dealing is created by law in all cases, it is only in rare and exceptional cases that the duty is of such a nature as to give rise to tort liability. The kind of breach of duty

that brings into play the bad faith tort arises only when there are special relationships between the tort-victim and the tort-feasor as described below.

* * * One of the underlying rationales for extending tort liability in the described kinds of cases is that ordinary contract damages do not adequately compensate the victim because they do not require the party in the superior or entrusted position, such as the insurer, the partner, or the franchiser, to account adequately for grievous and perfidious misconduct; and contract damages do not make the aggrieved, weaker, "trusting" party "whole." * * *

The use of punitive damages in appropriate cases of breach of the duty of good faith and fair dealing expresses society's disapproval of exploitation by a superior power and creates a strong incentive for employers to conform to clearly defined legal duties. Such duties are so explicit and so subject of common understanding as to justify the punitive award.

The court in Slottow v. American Casualty Co., 10 F.3d 1355, 1361 (9th Cir.1993), observed that a factor in cases awarding punitive damages for breach of the covenant of good faith and fair dealing may be the significant difference in the economic power and legal sophistication of the parties. Should such considerations influence a court to characterize conduct as tortious for purposes of awarding exemplary damages? Would the employee in *K Mart Corp. v. Ponsock, supra,* be made whole by an award of contract damages for wrongful discharge? Does the justification lie in compensation or in retribution and deterrence? Is it the province of law to "punish" parties which have committed contract breach in circumstances where the parties have significantly disparate economic bargaining power? Consider whether the application of punitive remedies in contract settings illustrates the continuing congruence of contract and tort law. *See* G. Gilmore, The Death of Contract 83 (1974).

Part IV

RESTITUTIONARY REMEDIES
Chapter 16

UNJUST ENRICHMENT
A. THE UNJUST ENRICHMENT CONCEPT

Section Coverage:

Restitution is civil liability based upon unjust enrichment. An action in restitution is often an additional remedial option for a plaintiff who has a claim in contract or tort, but sometimes it is the sole remedy available to a plaintiff. For example, when someone mistakenly confers a benefit on another, the sole basis of liability is unjust enrichment and the only remedy available is restitution.

Historically restitution developed separately both at law and in equity. The common law courts developed a restitutionary device called "quasi-contract" which was based upon the action of assumpsit. Assumpsit was the action plaintiffs used to recover for breaches of express contracts. The law courts adapted assumpsit for restitution by finding that an unjustly enriched defendant became party to a contract implied by law. The "contract" fashioned by the court was a fiction designed simply to oblige payment to the plaintiff of the amount of unjust enrichment.

One type of implied-in-law contract that developed at law was quantum meruit. This action allows recovery of the reasonable value of beneficial services rendered or materials furnished under circumstances not covered by express contract where retention of the benefit would constitute unjust enrichment. For example, if a contract is unenforceable for some reason such as impossibility, a plaintiff could use quantum meruit to recover the value of any work performed under the mistaken belief that the contract was enforceable. Without the restitutionary action, the defendant would be unjustly enriched at the plaintiff's expense.

The equity courts developed different restitutionary remedies, most notably constructive trusts and equitable liens. Substantive equity had already developed devices for enforcing express trusts, so the constructive trust became the method for disgorging unjust enrichment. Like the quasi-contract development at law, the constructive trust was based upon a fiction; the defendant became an involuntary trustee of the unjust enrichment for the benefit of the plaintiff. For example, if a fiduciary misappropriated money and used it to purchase land, the court of equity would impose a constructive trust to disgorge from the defendant the land and any profits traceable from it.

The common theme between restitutionary actions at law and in equity is that they are all based upon the idea of disgorging unjust enrichment. Sometimes the result may appear punitive in character, such as when a constructive trust is used to disgorge any property purchased with embezzled money even when that property has increased in value. It does not matter that the increase in value is attributable to the wise business judgment of the defendant in making the investment with the misappropriated assets; the wrongdoer must return all profit.

In other instances the defendant may have innocently acquired the unjust enrichment. Whether the defendant is a wrongdoer is not the key; the substantive questions are whether the defendant has been enriched and whether the retention of such enrichment would be unjust. The remedial aspect of restitution focuses on the measurement of the benefit in the hands of the defendant.

This section begins the study of restitution by examining the substantive concept of unjust enrichment. In each case the court first must find an enrichment in the sense that the defendant has received something of value. Then the court must find that the enrichment should be disgorged from the defendant to rectify an unjust result. As with any concept based upon the abstraction of justice, unjust enrichment is not capable of easy definition. The cases in this section struggle both with the concept of enrichment and with the injustice of the defendant's gain.

Model Case:

Owens leased a crane for purposes of performing a subcontract which involved lifting steel girders in the construction of a building. Owens left the crane at the construction site over the weekend, planning to resume operations the following Monday. Owens inadvertently forgot to lock it and left the keys in the ignition.

Joe Adler, owner of Joe's Truckstop and Cafe located adjacent to the construction area, received delivery of a large outdoor sign on Saturday. Joe saw the crane at the nearby site and attempted to inquire if the owner might help him out by lifting the sign into place. He found the construction site deserted, and noticing the keys in the crane he decided to "borrow" it for a few minutes to position the sign.

The next Monday Owens learned about the unauthorized use of the crane from a gas station attendant who had witnessed Joe putting up the sign. Owens sues Joe for unjust enrichment. The court may determine that the benefit enjoyed by Joe constitutes a "form of advantage" which would be unjust to retain without compensation. The restitutionary remedy would not depend upon the existence of a valid contract between Owens and Joe, nor would it be precluded by a showing that Owens in fact suffered no loss corresponding to Joe's gain. Rather, the focus in unjust enrichment is on the defendant's receipt or retention of a benefit rather than on providing compensation for losses incurred by the plaintiff. The court might measure the benefit which Joe received based upon the fair rental value of a crane to perform the job involved.

PYEATTE v. PYEATTE

135 Ariz. 346, 661 P.2d 196 (1982).

CORCORAN, JUDGE.

[A wife (plaintiff-appellee) and husband (defendant-appellant) entered into an oral agreement whereby each spouse agreed to provide in turn the sole support for the marriage while the other spouse was obtaining further education. The wife accordingly supported the husband for three years until his graduation from law school. Approximately one year following graduation, the parties obtained a dissolution of their marriage. Before the dissolution the wife had not yet received any support toward her contemplated continued education. The trial court awarded the wife $23,000 in damages for the husband's breach of express contract. On appeal, the court held that the terms of the spousal agreement were not sufficiently definite to constitute a binding, enforceable contract.]

* * *

Appellee [contends] that the trial court's award should be affirmed as an equitable award of restitution on the basis of unjust enrichment. She argues that appellant's education, which she subsidized and which he obtained through the exhaustion of community assets constitutes a benefit for which he must, in equity, make restitution. This narrow equitable issue is one of first impression in this court. * * *

Restitution is available to a party to an agreement where he performs services for the other believing that there is a binding contract.

When Restitution for Services is Granted.

> A person who has rendered services to another or services which have inured to the benefit of another ... is entitled to restitution therefor if the services were rendered

* * *

> (b) To obtain the performance of an agreement with the other therefor, not operative as a contract, or voidable as a contract and avoided by the other party after the services were rendered, the one performing the services erroneously believing because of a mistake of fact that the agreement was binding upon the other....

Restatement of Restitution § 40(b) at 155 (1937).

In order to be granted restitution, appellee must demonstrate that appellant received a benefit, that by receipt of that benefit he was unjustly enriched at her expense, and that the circumstances were such that in good conscience appellant should make compensation. John A.

Artukovich & Sons v. Reliance Truck Co., 126 Ariz. 246, 614 P.2d 327 (1980); *Restatement of Restitution* § 1 at 13 (1937). In *Artukovich,* the Supreme Court discussed unjust enrichment.

> Contracts implied-in-law or quasi-contracts, also called constructive contracts, are inferred by the law as a matter of reason and justice from the acts and conduct of the parties and circumstances surrounding the transactions ... and are imposed for the purpose of bringing about justice without reference to the intentions of the parties. . . .

> Restatement of Restitution § 1 provides, "A person who has been unjustly enriched at the expense of another is required to make restitution to the other." Comment (a) to that section notes that a person is enriched if he received a benefit and is unjustly enriched if retention of that benefit would be unjust. Comment (b) defines a benefit as being any form of advantage. . . .

> Unjust enrichment does not depend upon the existence of a valid contract, ... nor is it necessary that plaintiff suffer a loss corresponding to the defendant's gain for there to be valid claim for an unjust enrichment ...

126 Ariz. at 248, 614 P.2d at 329.

A benefit may be any type of advantage, including that which saves the recipient from any loss or expense. Appellee's support of appellant during his period of schooling clearly constituted a benefit to appellant. Absent appellee's support, appellant may not have attended law school, may have been forced to prolong his education because of intermittent periods of gainful employment, or may have gone deeply into debt. Relieved of the necessity of supporting himself, he was able to devote full time and attention to his education.

The mere fact that one party confers a benefit on another, however, is not of itself sufficient to require the other to make restitution. Retention of the benefit must be unjust.

Historically, restitution for the value of services rendered has been available upon either an "implied-in-fact" contract or upon quasi-contractual grounds. [Citations.] An implied-in-fact contract is a true contract, differing from an express contract only insofar as it is proved by circumstantial evidence rather than by express written or oral terms. [Citations.] In contrast, a quasi-contract is not a contract at all, but a duty imposed in equity upon a party to repay another to prevent his own unjust enrichment. The intention of the parties to bind themselves contractually in such a case is irrelevant. [Citation.] To support her claim for restitution on the basis of an implied-in-fact contract, appellee must demonstrate the elements of a binding contract. For the reasons we have previously discussed, we cannot find the necessary mutual assent or certainty as to the critical terms of the agreement sufficient to establish such a contract. [Citation.]

Restitution is nevertheless available in quasi-contract absent any showing of mutual assent. While a quasi-contractual obligation may be imposed without regard to the intent of the parties, such an obligation will be imposed only if the circumstances are such that it would be unjust to allow retention of the benefit without compensating the one who conferred it. One circumstance under which a duty to compensate will be imposed is when there was an expectation of payment or compensation for services at the time they were rendered.

> [A]n obligation to pay, ordinarily, will not be implied in fact or by law if it is clear that there was indeed no expectation of payment, that a gratuity was intended to be conferred, that the benefit was conferred officiously, or that the question of payment was left to the unfettered discretion of the recipient.

[Citation.]

Although we found that the spousal agreement failed to meet the requirements of an enforceable contract, the agreement still has importance in considering appellee's claim for unjust enrichment because it both evidences appellee's expectation of compensation and the circumstances which make it unjust to allow appellant to retain the benefits of her extraordinary efforts.

We next address the question of whether restitution on the basis of unjust enrichment is appropriate in the context of the marital relationship. No authority is cited to the court in support of the proposition that restitution as a matter of law is inappropriate in a dissolution proceeding. In *Wisner* [Wisner v. Wisner, 129 Ariz. 333, 631 P.2d 115 (1981)], we observed that "[i]n our opinion, unjust enrichment, as a legal concept, is not properly applied in the setting of a marital relationship." Our observation was directed to the wife's claim in that case for restitution for the value of her *homemaking services* during the couple's 15–year marriage and for the couple's reduced income during the husband's lengthy training period. Where both spouses perform the usual and incidental activities of the marital relationship, upon dissolution there can be no restitution for performance of these activities. Where, however, the facts demonstrate an agreement between the spouses and an extraordinary or unilateral effort by one spouse which inures solely to the benefit of the other by the time of dissolution, the remedy of restitution is appropriate.

* * *

A number of jurisdictions have addressed the issue of restitution in the context of the marital relationship. The cases which have dealt with the issue involve two factual patterns: (1) The first group consists of those cases in which the couples had accumulated substantial marital assets over a period of time from which assets the wife received large awards of property, maintenance and child support. The courts have refused to apply the theory of restitution on the basis of unjust enrichment in each of these cases. (2) The second group consists of those cases in which the parties are divorced soon after the student spouse receives his degree or license and there is little or no marital property from which to order any award to the working spouse.

In the first group the courts have consistently refused to find a property interest in the husband's education, degree, license or earning capacity or to order restitution in favor of the wife. Because restitution is a matter of equity, the circumstances of these cases preclude at the outset any basis for a finding of inequitable circumstances sufficient to support restitution inasmuch as the wife in each case had received substantial awards of the marital assets and was seeking, in addition to those assets, a property interest in the husband's education, degree, license or earning capacity. Because the property award itself is largely the product of the education, degree, license or earning capacity in which the wife sought a monetary interest, the courts hold that the wife realized her "investment" in the husband's education by having received the benefits of his increased earning capacity during marriage and by receipt of an award of property upon its dissolution. * * *

The second group presents the more difficult problem of the "working spouse" claiming entitlement to an equitable recovery where there is little or no marital property to divide and therefore the conventional remedies of property division or spousal maintenance are unavailable. The emerging consensus among those jurisdictions faced with the issue in this factual context is that restitution to the working spouse is appropriate to prevent the unjust enrichment of the student spouse. [Citations.]

Although in *Wisner* we dealt with the first group described above; *i.e.,* a marital community with substantial accumulated assets, we anticipated the second type of case in which (1) the community estate is consumed by the education of the husband which was obtained in substantial measure by the efforts and sacrifices of his wife; (2) the working wife is not entitled to spousal maintenance, having demonstrated an ability to support not only herself but her husband as well; and (3) the divorce follows closely upon the husband's completion of his education before the community realizes any benefit from that education and before the working spouse is able to further her own education and thus increase her own earning capacity. * * *

The Minnesota Supreme Court in *DeLa Rosa* [DeLa Rosa v. DeLa Rosa, 309 N.W.2d 755 (Minn.1981)] similarly affirmed an award of restitution to the wife for the financial support she provided her husband while he attended medical school, in a dissolution which occurred shortly after the husband's graduation.

The case at bar presents the common situation where one spouse has foregone the immediate enjoyment of earned income to enable the other to pursue an advanced education on a full-time basis. Typically, this sacrifice is made with the expectation that the parties will enjoy a higher standard of living in the future. Because the income of the working spouse is used for living expenses, there is usually little accumulated marital property to be divided when the dissolution occurs prior to the attainment of the financial rewards concomitant with the advanced degree or professional license. Furthermore, the working spouse is not entitled to maintenance ... as there has been a demonstrated ability of self-support. The equities weigh heavily in favor of providing a remedy to the working spouse in such a situation, ...

309 N.W.2d at 758.

The Kentucky Court of Appeals held in *Inman v. Inman* [578 S.W.2d 266 (Ky.App.1979)] that the wife was entitled to reimbursement for her monetary contribution to her husband's acquisition of his dentistry license. Although in *Inman* the parties had dissolved their marriage after 17 years and three children and had enjoyed the fruits of the husband's increased earning capacity for a number of years, by the time of the dissolution the couple's debts equalled or exceeded their assets, in large part due to the husband's mismanagement. * * * The Kentucky court relied on the reasoning of the dissent in *Graham* [In re Marriage of Graham, 194 Colo. 429, 574 P.2d 75 (1978)] in which the three dissenting justices stated:

As a matter of economic reality the most valuable asset acquired by either party during this six-year marriage was the husband's increased earning capacity....

The case presents the not-unfamiliar pattern of the wife who, willing to sacrifice for a more secure family financial future, works to educate her husband, only to be awarded a divorce decree shortly after he is awarded his degree....

In cases such as this, equity demands that courts seek extraordinary remedies to prevent extraordinary injustice.

[Citations.]

* * *

The record shows that the appellee conferred benefits on appellant—financial subsidization of appellant's legal education—with the agreement and expectation that she would be compensated therefore by his reciprocal efforts after his graduation and admission to the Bar. Appellant has left the marriage with the only valuable asset acquired during the marriage—his legal education and qualification to practice law. It would be inequitable to allow appellant to retain this benefit without making restitution to appellee. * * * By our decision herein, we reject the view that the economic element necessarily inherent in the marital institution (and particularly apparent in its dissolution) requires us to treat marriage as a strictly financial undertaking upon the dissolution of which each party will be fully compensated for the investment of his various contributions. When the parties have been married for a number of years, the courts cannot and will not strike a balance regarding the contributions of each to the marriage and then translate that into a monetary award. To do so would diminish the individual personalities of the husband and wife to economic entities and reduce the institution of marriage to that of a closely held corporation.

Generally, where claims are made by the working spouse against the student spouse, the trial court in each case must make specific findings as to whether the education, degree or license acquired by the student spouse during marriage involved an unjust enrichment of that spouse, the value of the benefit, and the amount that should be paid to the working spouse. A variety of methods of computing the unjust enrichment may be employed in ascertaining the working spouse's compensable interest in the attainment of the student spouse's education, degree or license.

The award to appellee should be limited to the financial contribution by appellee for appellant's living expenses and direct educational expenses. [Citation.]

Under the agreement between the parties, the anticipated benefit to appellee may involve a monetary benefit in a lesser amount than the benefit conferred by appellee on appellant. In that event, the award to appellee should be limited to the amount of the anticipated benefit to appellee. Appellee should not recover more than the benefit of her bargain. *Restatement of Restitution*, § 107, Comment b, at 449 (1937).

Appellant further objects to the judgment of $23,000 against him on the ground that it directs the payment on terms over a period of time. The terms of payment were of benefit only to appellant. If he wanted to pay the judgment in a lump sum, he certainly could do so. In any event, the trial court, in entering an equitable judgment for money, has the authority to order that it be paid in periodic payments plus interest through the clerk of the court in a certain percentage of appellant's net income, and that appellee have the right to review his records to determine the accuracy of the net income calculations.

The relief granted to appellee is equitable in nature. The rule regarding equitable awards is set forth in Mason v. Ellison, 63 Ariz. 196, 160 P.2d 326 (1945), in which the Arizona supreme court stated:

> In an equity case the court " ... adapts its relief and molds its decrees to satisfy the requirements of the case and to conserve the equities of the parties litigant. The court has such plenary power since its purpose is the accomplishment of justice amid all of the vicissitudes and intricacies of life...."

[Citations.]

* * *

The nature of equity is individual justice. Since the benefit bestowed upon appellant by appellee was periodic in nature and dependent on her income, we find no abuse of the equity power of the court in awarding appellee periodic payments, especially where she can use them periodically to pursue her own education. By our affirmance of an installment method of payment in this case, we do not mean to promulgate a rule that will uniformly govern all awards in subsequent cases of that nature. Each will, by virtue of the equitable nature of the claim, require relief tailored to the facts and circumstances of the individuals. [Citation.]

The portion of the judgment in the amount of $23,000 is reversed and remanded for proceedings in accordance with this opinion.

———

1.   As indicated in the principal case, implied-in-fact contracts must be distinguished from contractual arrangements implied by law. The former is simply another species of express contract which has been inferred from the intentions and conduct of the parties in recognizing the existence of contractual rights and duties. In contrast, a quasi-contract is implied by law without regard to the intentions of the parties, and perhaps even against an expression of dissent. Therefore, it is a fiction created by the court to establish an enforceable obligation. The purpose of implying a contractual duty to pay restitution is to prevent someone from obtaining a benefit of money, services, or property without paying just compensation. In *In Re* Chateaugay Corp., 10 F.3d 944, 957–958 (2d Cir.1993), the court explained:

> A quasi-contract claim for unjust enrichment is based on "an obligation which the law creates, in the absence of any agreement, when and because the acts of the parties or others have placed in the possession of one person money, or its equivalent, under such circumstances that in equity and good conscience he ought not to retain it, and which ex aequo et bono belongs to another."

2.   There are several types of quasi-contract actions which provide restitution at law. An action in quantum meruit, which means in Latin "as much as he deserves," is a frequently employed remedy to compensate a plaintiff for the reasonable value of services rendered to a defendant. A second type of quasi-contract appears where the defendant has used or occupied realty belonging to another under circumstances constituting unjust enrichment.

Another group of quasi-contracts are derived from the common court actions for money had and received or for money paid. The use of the money courts to disgorge unjust enrichment dates back to the landmark decision of Moses v. MacFerlan, 2 Burr. 1005 (K.B.1760), where Lord Mansfield used indebitatus assumpsit as a restitutionary tool.

3.   Substantive entitlement to restitution depends upon whether the defendant has acquired a benefit which is unjust to retain. The concept of "benefit," according to the Restatement formulation, is quite broadly described as "any form of advantage," and generally does not pose a significant obstacle to restitution.

Entitlement also requires that retention of the benefit would be "unjust." In *Pyeatte,* the disenfranchised wife had to show that the husband's retention of the educational benefits would be unjust. She had to demonstrate that the benefits conferred went beyond the ordinary services exchanged in the course of marriage and that the parties understood that no gift was intended. Often, courts employ a presumption that services rendered by one family member to another are gratuitous and therefore noncompensable in restitution.

4. Compare the principal case with Matter of Estate of Zent, 459 N.W.2d 795 (N.D.1990). The claimant was a woman who originally enjoyed a "social" relationship with a man who later developed Alzheimer's disease. As the disease gradually and progressively incapacitated him, the claimant provided various domestic and nursing care until he entered a nursing home and died several weeks later. The court rejected the argument that the services were rendered gratuitously. Salient factors pertaining to the "justice" of recovery in restitution included: the nature of the services provided, the necessity, the absence of a mutual moral or legal obligation, and the nonfamilial relationship. The court characterized the care provided as "menial, tiresome and * * * most unpleasant." As a result, compensation for the reasonable value of the services was compensable in quantum meruit.

5. A troublesome issue in quantum meruit has involved whether an expectation of payment by both parties is an essential element of the action. In In Re De Laurentiis Entertainment Group Inc. v. National Broadcasting Co., 963 F.2d 1269 (9th Cir.1992), a company arranged with an advertising agency to purchase television advertising from NBC on its behalf. When the company failed to pay, NBC sought to recover from the company in quantum meruit the reasonable value of the advertising it had provided. The court awarded recovery based on a quasi-contract, reasoning that the company had requested the advertising and benefitted from it and NBC had not intended to provide its services gratuitously. The court noted that, unlike an express contract, quasi-contracts are not based on intentions of parties to undertake performance or promises, but are created by law to prevent injustice. Also see Bolen v. Paragon Plastics, Inc., 747 F.Supp. 103, 107 (D. Mass.1990) (expectation of payment by holder of benefit determined by reference to objective standard, not subjective belief of party); In re Estate of Krueger, 235 Neb. 518, 455 N.W.2d 809, 814 (Neb.1990) (quantum meruit for labor and materials is grounded upon an implied promise to pay the reasonable value of the benefits received).

6. In Cablevision of Breckenridge v. Tannhauser, 649 P.2d 1093 (Colo.1982), the court considered whether a cable company was entitled to restitution under quasi-contract for the value of its service from unauthorized users. The court explained the basic purpose and requirements of that doctrine:

> To recover under a theory of quasi-contract or unjust enrichment, a plaintiff must show (1) that a benefit was conferred on the defendant by the plaintiff, (2) that the benefit was appreciated by the defendant, and (3) that the benefit was accepted by the defendant

under such circumstances that it would be inequitable for it to be retained without payment of its value. Application of the doctrine does not depend upon the existence of a contract, express or implied in fact, but on the need to avoid unjust enrichment of the defendant notwithstanding the absence of an actual agreement to pay for the benefit conferred. The scope of this remedy is broad, cutting across both contract and tort law, with its application guided by the underlying principle of avoiding the unjust enrichment of one party at the expense of another. * * *

[T]he broad definition of benefit contained in the *Restatement of Restitution* § 1 comment b (1937) [is instructive]:

A person confers a benefit upon another if he gives to the other possession of or some other interest in money, land, chattels, or choses in action, performs services beneficial to or at the request of the other, satisfies a debt or a duty of the other, or in any way adds to the other's security or advantage. He confers a benefit not only where he adds to the property of another, but also where he saves the other from expense or loss. The word "benefit," therefore, denotes any form of advantage.

The court held that restitution was appropriate to prevent unjust enrichment of a condominium association in receiving unauthorized use of cable service without payment for its value.

7. Although jurisdictions vary considerably in their precise formulation of the requirements for recovery under quantum meruit, some common elements include:

(1) the claimant furnished valuable services or materials;

(2) for the person sought to be charged;

(3) the services and materials were accepted, used and enjoyed by the person sought to be charged;

(4) the party who provided the services or materials did so with the reasonable expectation of receiving compensation;

(5) the party who accepted the services had reasonable notice that compensation for the benefits would be expected;

(6) and retention of the benefit without payment of reasonable compensation would constitute unjust enrichment.

See Vortt Exploration v. Chevron U.S.A., 787 S.W.2d 942 (Tex.1990); Midcoast Aviation, Inc. v. General Elec. Credit Corp., 907 F.2d 732 (7th Cir.1990).

MONARCH ACCOUNTING SUPPLIES, INC. v. PREZIOSO
170 Conn. 659, 368 A.2d 6 (1976).

LOISELLE, ASSOCIATE JUSTICE.

[The plaintiff, Monarch Accounting Supplies, Inc. ("Monarch"), leased an office building from the defendant, Prezioso. Prezioso subsequently executed another lease with an outdoor advertising company for purposes of installing a large sign on the roof of the building. Monarch instituted suit against Prezioso for the unauthorized use of the premises, and the trial court awarded $245 for a fee Monarch paid to a structural engineer and $1360 for one-half of the rent already paid and to be paid by the advertising company to Prezioso. The defendant appealed.]

* * *

"A lease transfers an estate in real property to a tenant for a stated period, with a reversion in the owner after the expiration of the lease. Its distinguishing characteristic is the surrender of possession by the landlord to the tenant so that he may occupy the land or tenement leased to the exclusion of the landlord himself." [Citation.] The tenant acquires an interest in the real estate giving him the right to maintain ejectment or trespass against the landlord. [Citation.] And where the entire premises are leased, in the absence of any agreement, either expressed or implied or by covenant to the contrary, the tenant has the right of exclusive possession and control of the entire premises and the landlord or his agents or contractees have no right to enter upon the leased premises. [Citations.]

The instrument of lease demising the property to the plaintiff describes the premises as: "A certain parcel of land with a one story masonry building thereon ... with a second story addition." The instrument does not refer to the "roof." One provision gives the defendant "the right to enter into and upon said premises, or any part thereof, at all reasonable hours for the purpose of examining the same, or making such repairs or alterations therein as may be necessary for the safety and preservation thereof." A subsequent paragraph contains the language that "said premises shall be at all times open to the inspection of said Landlord and Landlord's agents ... for necessary repairs." A following paragraph, however, contains the language that "said Tenant shall also pay for all other utilities and repairs." The only evidence adduced at the trial on the issue of control was that the landlord made a minor repair of the roof in November, 1971, during the tenancy of the original lease.

In construing the instrument the court correctly determined both the leasehold's size and the parties' interests therein. [Citation.] The description of the demised premises, the provisions for repair and the limited nature of the defendant's right to enter only admit of a reversionary interest in the defendant. The fact of the minor repair to the roof does not contradict the implications growing out of the nature of the estate created by the lease. [Citations.] The court was not in error in concluding that, under the terms of the lease, the defendant did not reserve control of the roof of the premises leased and therefore did not have the right to lease the roof of the premises.

The court found that the plaintiff was entitled to receive, on an equitable basis by way of reimbursement, one-half of the total rent received by the defendant from Murphy, Inc. The court also awarded one-half of the rent to be expected from Murphy, Inc., for the remainder of the plaintiff's term. The plaintiff claims the award can be sustained under the doctrine of unjust enrichment. The inquiry then, is whether the plaintiff is entitled to damages for the unjust enrichment of the defendant. The inquiry goes not only to the type of recovery but also to whether recovery of any type was allowable.

The doctrine of unjust enrichment "is based upon the principle that one should not be permitted unjustly to enrich himself at the expense of another but should be required to make restitution of or for property received, retained or appropriated. . . . It is not necessary, in order to create an obligation to make restitution or to compensate, that the party unjustly enriched should have been guilty of any tortious or fraudulent act. The question is: Did he, to the detriment of someone else, obtain something of value to which he was not entitled?" [Citations.] "With no other test than what, under a given set of circumstances, is just or unjust, equitable or inequitable, conscionable or unconscionable, it becomes necessary in any case where the benefit of the doctrine is claimed to examine the circumstances and the conduct of the parties and apply this standard." [Citation.]

The defendant, under its agreement with Murphy, Inc., receives rental payments. That agreement overlooks the plaintiff's possessory interest in the roof, and, in that regard, it is to the detriment of the plaintiff. Although the plaintiff did not show any material physical damage to the premises it has a right either to sublet or assign the roof with the defendant's permission. * * * The facts of the case, therefore, show the defendant's receipt of a benefit, to which he was not entitled, to the detriment of the plaintiff. Furthermore, that showing entitles the plaintiff to an award of money damages. [Citations.]

The measure of recovery in this case focuses on the benefit to the defendant rather than on the loss to the plaintiff. The damages should be the benefit received. [Citation.] The benefit was the rent that was received by the defendant less his expenses, if any, in dealing with Murphy, Inc. The court, therefore, was in error in awarding only one-half of the accrued rent.

The court also erred by awarding a portion of the rent from the date of judgment until the end of the plaintiff's term. That rent has been neither received nor retained by the defendant even though he has the right, under the agreement with Murphy, Inc., to receive it. A prospective award is not properly includable within the concept of damages in this case since the focus of damages in unjust enrichment is not on the damage proximately caused by an injury, but on the benefit unjustly received and retained by the defendant. [Citations.] Whether the defendant will retain the rent from the sign for the period from February, 1975 to May, 1977, the unexpired term of the plaintiff's lease at the time of judgment, cannot be adjudged.

Further, the other item of damages awarded, one-half of the expense of the structural engineer, appears to have been part of an expenditure that was necessary for the proper support of the sign on the roof and as the defendant is not entitled to retain the benefit of the lease to Murphy, Inc., he would not be liable for such expenditures.

There is error in part, the judgment is affirmed except as to the amount of damages awarded and a new trial is ordered limited to that issue.

––––––––

1. In restitution, unlike compensatory damages, the focus is on the defendant's gains rather than on the plaintiff's losses. Note that in the principal case the plaintiff had not directly lost any tangible economic benefits or incurred out-of-pocket expenses. Restitution was nonetheless appropriate to disgorge the extra rental payments received by the landlord.

In many situations the claimant has expended funds or rendered services equivalent to the value received by the defendant; if the enrichment was unjust, its measure is clear. Problems arise in cases where the plaintiff has incurred certain expenses yet the defendant received a lesser amount of benefit. Unless the defendant has acted improperly, such as by fraudulently inducing the plaintiff to build improvements on the defendant's land, restitution will be limited to the measure of the defendant's gains. Recall *Campbell v. T.V.A.,* reprinted *supra* in Chapter 10, where the court awarded restitution for the benefit the plaintiff conferred on the defendant's library with microfilm copies of the trade journals made pursuant to an unenforceable contract. The dissent strenuously argued that restitution should be denied because the defendant received no benefit, had not acted improperly, and in fact might have sustained losses due to the plaintiff's actions.

2. It is not necessary to prove tortious, illegal, or fraudulent conduct by the defendant to establish that the enrichment is unjust. In the principal case the landlord's conduct in re-leasing a portion of the premises without the tenant's consent may have been ill-advised, but it was not tortious. In some circumstances even an innocent party who holds a benefit may be ordered to restore the property to another in order to prevent unjust enrichment. *See Simonds v. Simonds,* reprinted *infra* in section D of this chapter.

3. Restitution often provides an alternative claim in a tort or contract case. Although such cases often refer to restitution as merely an alternative remedy, it is best understood as an independent substantive basis of recovery that is allowed as necessary to avoid unjust enrichment.

4. For additional commentary on unjust enrichment, *see* Dickinson, Mistaken Improvers of Real Estate, 64 N.C.L.Rev. 37 (1985); Levmore, Explaining Restitution, 71 Va.L.Rev. 65 (1985); Dawson, Restitution Without Enrichment, 61 B.U.L.Rev. 563 (1981); Perillo, Restitution in the Second Restatement of Contracts, 81 Colum.L.Rev. 37 (1981); Sulli-

van, The Concept of Benefit in the Law of Quasi–Contract, 64 Geo.L.J. 1 (1975); Wall & Childres, The Law of Restitution and the Federal Government, 66 Nw.U.L.Rev. 587 (1971); Wade, The Literature of the Law of Restitution, 19 Hastings L.J. 1087 (1968); Fornoff, Actions in General Assumpsit, 23 Ohio St.L.J. 401 (1962); Dawson, Restitution or Damages?, 20 Ohio St.L.J. 175 (1959); Macauley, Restitution in Context, 107 U.Pa.L.Rev. 1133 (1959); Patterson, Improvements in the Law of Restitution, 40 Cornell L.Q. 667 (1955); Carlston, Restitution—The Search for a Philosophy, 6 J.Legal Ed. 330 (1954); Seavey, Problems in Restitution, 7 Okla.L.Rev. 257 (1954); Holdsworth, Unjustifiable Enrichment, 55 L.Q.Rev. 37 (1939); Jackson, The Restatement of Restitution, 10 Miss.L.J. 95 (1938); Winfield, The American Restatement of the Law of Restitution, 54 L.Q.Rev. 529 (1938); Patterson, The Scope of Restitution and Unjust Enrichment, 1 Mo.L.Rev. 223 (1936); Bishop, Money Had and Received, An Equitable Action at Law, 18 S.Cal.L.Rev. 41 (1933); Corbin, Quasi–Contractual Obligations, 21 Yale L.J. 533 (1912); Hand, Restitution or Unjust Enrichment, 11 Harv.L.Rev. 249 (1897); Ames, The History of Assumpsit. II.—Implied Assumpsit, 2 Harv.L.Rev. 53 (1888).

B.   BENEFITS ACQUIRED BY AGREEMENT OR MISTAKE

Section Coverage:

Restitution is premised upon the defendant's unjust enrichment without regard to how the benefit was received. Although the manner in which the defendant acquired the benefit is relevant to the justice of its retention, recovery in restitution does not require that the receipt be from wrongful conduct.

The circumstances under which the benefit was acquired originally may even have been by agreement. The parties may have attempted a contractual relationship which ultimately failed. If the plaintiff confers benefits upon the defendant pursuant to a contract that is not in force by the time of trial, the plaintiff can recover the specific benefit or its value in restitution. The failure of the contract can arise because it was unenforceable at its inception, or because it became unenforceable for a reason such as impossibility, or because the defendant materially breached and the plaintiff elected to treat the contract as ended.

Another circumstance in which a defendant may acquire a benefit without wrongful conduct is when the plaintiff confers it by mistake. The substantive question in restitution once again is whether retention of such enrichment would be unjust. The situations in which a mistake may serve as the basis for restitutionary relief are widely varied. Some examples are overpayment of a debt or accidental payment of someone else's debt, improvement of property under the mistaken belief of ownership, and mistakes about the formation or performance of a contract. The restitutionary device used to rectify the mistake varies;

quasi-contract, subrogation, or specific restitution through constructive trust and equitable liens are available under appropriate circumstances.

Model Case:

Pat Denney wanted to acquire some gentle horses suitable for children's rides at carnivals. Mattson had several horses for sale of the type Denney wanted. The two parties negotiated an oral agreement for the sale, and Mattson gave Denney the horses in exchange for a check.

Denney then heard from a friend who was a first year law student that this contract violated the Statute of Frauds. Denney stopped payment on the check and took the horses out of town to a carnival to make money with them. After the carnival Denney concluded that this type of enterprise was not desirable and returned the horses to Mattson. In the meantime Mattson had received a better offer for the horses.

If the contract did violate the Statute of Frauds, Mattson could have rescinded it and received the horses in restitution. If the contract was valid, Mattson could have treated Denney's conduct as a breach of contract. Among the available remedies would be the restitution of the horses. Mattson might receive the profits Denney earned at the carnival under the rule that all profits are disgorged from conscious wrongdoers. The fact that Mattson lost nothing and may now be in a better position is not relevant.

ALDER v. DRUDIS

30 Cal.2d 372, 182 P.2d 195 (1947).

CARTER, JUSTICE. * * *

In 1941 plaintiff William F. Alder, an inventor, was the holder of United States letters patent on a device for producing third dimensional motion pictures, known as a polyscope. Plaintiff McMahon, in return for an interest in the patent, was engaged in efforts to develop and commercialize the device. [Alder and McMahon contracted with Jose Drudis to finance a corporation to develop the device. Drudis' attorney, Marcus Roberts, represented Drudis in the venture. As provided under the contract, Drudis paid $5000 and received the letters patent for safe-keeping pending the formation of the development corporation.]

* * *

Roberts proceeded with steps toward incorporation and about January 6, 1942, filed for record in Los Angeles County, articles of incorporation under the name of Third Dimensional Picture Corporation. The Alders and McMahon claim that they were not told of this action. About January 19th Roberts consulted the attorneys who had procured the letters patent for Alder regarding the contemplated changes in the polyscope. This interview, followed by an adverse report from the attorneys and further inquiry by Roberts indicated to him that he had been misled by fraud and deceit on the part of the Alders and McMahon, in that the basic idea underlying the invention had been the subject of prior patents, of which he was unaware, and the polyscope possibly could be redesigned in such fashion as not to infringe the Alder patent.

About January 20th, at a stormy interview, Roberts gave written notice of rescission. He also telegraphed Alder demanding a return of the $5,000 paid him. On January 23rd, on behalf of himself and Drudis, he gave notice to the attorney for the Alders and McMahon of election to rescind the contract on the ground that plaintiffs were guilty of fraud and deceit in its procurement. * * *

Meanwhile, and on January 26th, and thereafter plaintiffs demanded possession of the polyscopes. In June, 1943, they brought the present action for claim and delivery [count one] and for declaratory relief [count two] against Drudis and Roberts. * * *

At the close of the trial the court entered judgment on the verdict under the first cause of action that plaintiffs recover possession of the polyscopes from defendants, together with $20,000 damages for the unlawful withholding, and costs. On issues joined by the other pleadings, the court made findings in substance as follows:

The court found that after January 20, 1942, defendant Drudis continually failed to perform the written agreement and that it was breached by the two written notices of rescission; that no misrepresentation, deception, or concealment of any material fact was practiced by plaintiffs in their dealings with Drudis and Roberts, and that after January 20th said defendants were in default under the terms of the agreement. The court further found that about December 27, 1941, defendants, having already taken possession of the letters patent, took possession of the only two polyscopes in existence; that the polyscopes were not delivered to defendants because of the payment by Drudis of $5,000 under the written agreement, but were delivered to defendants for safe-keeping and so that they would be conveniently situated for use in carrying out the terms of the agreement; that Drudis and Roberts had the patent and polyscopes in their possession until April, 1943, since which time they have been in the possession of Drudis. * * *

Plaintiffs, in their election of the several remedies open to them, had the choice of accepting defendants' offer of rescission of the contract (which would have given them an immediate return of their property upon their repayment to defendants of the $5000 received), or of treating the offer and the accompanying conduct as an anticipatory breach or repudiation of the contract. [Citations.] * * *

It is well settled in this state that one who had been injured by a breach of contract has an election to pursue any of three remedies, to wit: "He may treat the contract as rescinded and may recover upon a quantum meruit so far as he has performed; or he may keep the contract alive, for the benefit of both parties, being at all times ready and able to perform; or, third, he may treat the repudiation as putting an end to the contract for all purposes of performance, and sue for the profits he would have realized if he had not been prevented from performing." [Citations.]

The first remedy was of no avail to plaintiffs. As to the second remedy, plaintiffs made no effort to keep the contract alive for the benefit of all of the parties, or to procure the $13,000 needed for financing from other sources, or to proceed with the enterprise. It is evident that they elected to treat the anticipatory breach as putting an end to the contract for all purposes of performance. This being so, they were in a position to sue for damages. However, they made no direct claim to damages. * * *

Damages, measured by the prospective profits to be derived from a successful promotion of the enterprise as finally reflected in the amounts which would come to plaintiffs individually as dividends declared in favor of the shareholders of the proposed corporation, were probably too speculative and conjectural for estimation, particularly in view of the evidence of uncertainty as to the commercial possibilities of the polyscope. At any rate they were not satisfactorily proved here. Any award made on this basis, therefore, would have been nominal. * * *

In granting to plaintiffs the remedy of restitution and in ordering the delivery to them of the polyscopes and letters patent, the court should have made its decree for this specific restitution conditional upon the return by plaintiffs to defendants of the $5,000 received. The purpose of restitution as a remedy for breach is the restoration of the status quo ante as far as is practicable, and in the absence of qualifying circumstances, the plaintiff must return any consideration he has received in order to obtain specific restitution. While there is no literal rescission of the contract, the result reached by the restitutionary remedy approximates that reached by rescission. It is not necessary that plaintiff should have made an offer to return the consideration, but the decree for specific restitution may be made conditional upon such return. [Citations.]

For these reasons, the trial court properly limited its judgment on the second cause of action to a return by defendants to plaintiffs of the polyscopes and letters patent, but it erred in failing to condition delivery upon a repayment by plaintiffs to defendants of the $5,000 received.

The remaining question is whether plaintiffs were also entitled to the relief granted by the judgment on their first cause of action— possession of the two polyscopes and $20,000 damages for the unlawful withholding. * * *

This statement makes it clear that plaintiffs' first cause of action was not asserted as an aid to enforcement of the relief sought by their second cause. By their first cause they attempted to bring a simple suit for the recovery of property entrusted by them to another, a voluntary bailment, and asked damages for wrongful withholding, their theory being that the contract was at an end and eliminated from consideration. This theory of voluntary bailment is reflected in a finding of the trial court to the effect that the polyscopes were not delivered to the defendants because of their payment of $5000 under the contract, but were delivered to the defendants "for safe-keeping and so that said polyscopes would be conveniently situated for use in carrying out the terms of the said agreement between the parties."

The fallacy in plaintiffs' reasoning is that the termination of the contract by defendants' anticipatory breach did not, as plaintiffs seem to assume, operate of itself to restore the status which existed prior to the making of the contract. Neither did it convert transfers made by reason of the existence of the contract into transfers made as though no contract had ever existed. Upon the election to treat the attempted rescission as an anticipatory breach, the rights of the parties culminated and the contractual relation ceased to exist, except for the purpose of maintaining an action for the recovery of damages or for restitution.

Although it may be true, as the court found, that the polyscopes were not delivered to the defendants because of their payment of $5,000 under the contract, it is also true, as the court further found, that they were delivered for safe-keeping and so that they would be conveniently situated "for use in carrying out the terms" of the contract. The evidence shows beyond dispute that had there been no contract, there would have been no delivery of the polyscopes to defendants. The delivery was made in pursuance of the joint enterprise, and in fact one of the devices was taken by defendant Roberts to a concern for redesigning in furtherance of the objective sought to be accomplished by the contracts. * * *

Under these facts, as established by the evidence, plaintiffs are not entitled to relief on their first cause of action. There is no showing of a right in plaintiffs to possession of the property except upon the return by them to defendants of the $5,000. Neither is there proof of any wrongful withholding by defendants. * * *

The judgment is reversed.

---

1. Rescission and restitution are equitable remedies available for the breach of a contract or in other appropriate circumstance where benefits are exchanged pursuant to a failed agreement. As the principal case illustrates, the court will condition the availability of these remedies on the mutually equitable conduct of the plaintiff; the order that the defendant give restitution of benefits acquired under the rescinded agreement is conditioned upon the plaintiff's restitution of benefits received under the same agreement. The equitable maxim invoked for this principle is, "He who seeks equity must do equity."

2. The court in the principal case determined that the withholding of the polyscopes was not wrongful in itself. In situations where property is wrongfully withheld, equity will grant relief in appropriate circumstances. When the remedy at law to recover property, replevin, is not adequate, equity will grant specific restitution. Burr v. Bloomsburg,

101 N.J.Eq. 615, 138 A. 876 (1927) (family ring). *See* Van Hecke, Equitable Replevin, 33 N.C.L.Rev. 57 (1964).

KELNER v. 610 LINCOLN ROAD, INC.

328 So.2d 193 (Fla.1976).

OVERTON, JUSTICE.

This cause concerns the method for payment of an attorney [petitioner] employed on a contingency fee contract when he has been discharged [by the respondent client] without cause.

* * *

The client's jewelry store was robbed of approximately $350,000.00 worth of jewelry, of which $150,000.00 was jewelry held on consignment by the client. The loss was covered by an insurance policy issued by Lloyd's of London in the amount of $100,000.00. * * * Lloyd's, however, rejected the client's claim, contending the client's records and proofs of loss did not comply with the provisions of the policy. As a result, the client employed the petitioner-attorney on a 40% contingent fee contract. * * *

[The attorney filed suit against Lloyd's on behalf of the client. Before trial, Lloyd's agreed to pay the full $100,000 face amount of the policy. The attorney negotiated a settlement with the consignors to accept $60,000. Under this plan the consignors' settlement plus the $40,000 to the attorney under the contingency fee, left nothing for the client.]

The client rejected this settlement. The record reflects from the testimony before the jury by the petitioner-attorney that the client had demanded 20% under the table without the knowledge of the consignors. It was unrefuted that the client had taken the position that "If I don't get anything, no one gets anything." The client discharged the attorney and employed a substitute attorney who bettered the consignors' settlement by $9,000.00.

The petitioner-attorney brought this action in the circuit court on the contingency contract. The trial court ruled that this was a valid contract, it was not unconscionable, and there was no overreaching, which holding was affirmed by the District Court.

The real issue concerned the computation of the percentage fee. It was the client's contention that the contingency contract required him to pay 40% of [$40,000] rather than 40% of $100,000.00, as contended by the petitioner-attorney. That issue was submitted to the jury, which resolved the dispute in favor of the attorney.

The following factual and legal conclusions are clearly established in the record: (a) Both the trial court and the District Court found the contingency contract valid and there was no overreaching or unconscionability in its execution; (b) it is uncontroverted that the attorney obtained full recovery of the insurance proceeds under the policy; (c) both the trial court and the District Court found that the attorney was discharged without cause; (d) the jury found that the fee should be computed on the basis of 40% of $100,000.00, as contended by the attorney, rather than 40% of [$40,000], as contended by the client.

Upon these facts the Third District Court reversed the trial court and held that the attorney was limited to recovery on quantum meruit and was not entitled to recover under the contingent fee contract. * * *

The Third District expressed the view that if an attorney is allowed to recover under the contingency contract rather than upon a quantum meruit theory, the practical application "would have a 'chilling' effect on a client exercising his right to discharge an attorney, because he might be liable for fees to the discharged attorney even though he made no recovery on his original claim."

We might agree with this holding if the maximum recovery from the insurance company had not been obtained at the time of the discharge. We recognize that the settlement of the consignors' claims is interwoven with the representation to recover the proceeds of the insurance policy. The attorney was, however, paid separately to represent the client in the consignors' actions. Under the peculiar circumstances of this case, where the proceeds of the insurance policy were fully recovered and the real issue of how the contingency fee was to be computed was settled by a jury, we will not disturb the verdict and restrict the computation of the attorney's fee to quantum meruit. * * *

It is so ordered.

———

1. Distinguish express contracts, implied contracts, and implied-in-law contracts. The last category is not based upon any agreement between the parties at all, but is a fictional contract imposed by the court. For that reason implied-in-law contracts are also called quasi-contracts.

Which kind of contract was involved in the principal case? Consider instead a different result: If the court had refused to enforce the express terms of the agreement between the attorney and client and used quantum meruit as the basis of recovery, what type of "contract" would be involved?

2. Quantum meruit is not available when a contract has been completed and all that remains is the payment of the contract price. When only a liquidated sum is owed, the plaintiff may sue for the debt with the remedy indebitatus assumpsit. As a quasi-contract theory, quantum meruit is available only for partial completion of a contract. The same rule is applied when a contract has divisible parts and the end of the agreement comes at the end of one of the severable parts. The plaintiff may sue for the debt owed for the divisible performance and may not rescind the entire contract and sue in quantum meruit for the

value of the services independent of the contract price. The theory is that the refusal to pay money when it is due is not the repudiation of a contract and therefore the other party cannot rescind an otherwise completed contract. *See* Lynch v. Stebbins, 127 Me. 203, 142 A. 735 (1928).

In Oliver v. Campbell, 43 Cal.2d 298, 273 P.2d 15 (1954), the plaintiff was an attorney for a husband in a contested divorce case. After the completion of the trial, the husband discharged the attorney when the judge indicated an intention to make findings in favor of the wife. The discharged attorney sued for quantum meruit because the contract price was much less than the value of the services actually rendered at an hourly rate. The contract price had been set at $800, whereas the reasonable value of the attorney's services was $5000.

The California Supreme Court considered whether the contract price should be a ceiling to recovery in quantum meruit. The court concluded that the contract price should not be a limit to recovery, but found that this plaintiff was precluded from suing in quantum meruit because the contemplated services were complete. The dissenting opinion agreed with the principle, but argued that the contract services were not complete because the attorney had wanted to appeal the adverse divorce decision.

3. If the attorney in the principal case had failed to recover for the client before the termination of the relationship without cause, would the client have any enrichment whatsoever? Do attorney's services have no value if there is no recovery?

What if a doctor treats a seriously injured person in an emergency, but the person nonetheless dies from the injuries despite the correct medical care. Did the doctor's services have no value? Is there a difference between these examples?

PROBLEM: THE FICKLE POLITICIAN

You are a new attorney in a small town where you and some friends from law school have started a new practice. None of you has an established base here and you are eager for clients and for some standing in the community.

Prominent in the town's current news is an allegation of corruption against a local politician. A few weeks ago the local paper published a story accusing a local politician named Vixon of accepting a bribe. Vixon's response was to declare an intention to sue unless the newspaper printed a retraction. The paper stood by the story even though the source was anonymous.

Vixon approached you and asked if you would take this case for a very low fixed fee. You accepted it solely because you believed that the high publicity attendant to this case would promote the new law practice.

You worked on the case for many hours. If one figured your work at a reasonable hourly rate, its value would far exceed the fixed fee agreed upon for the representation. All was going well in preparation for the trial until the newspaper's anonymous source decided to make the accusation openly public. The evidence of wrongdoing then mounted, and it appeared that the newspaper could successfully defend the defamation suit. Vixon called a press conference on the eve of the trial and announced that the suit is going to be dropped solely because you, Vixon's attorney, were incompetent in preparing the case. Apparently Vixon concluded that the case would be lost and decided to make you the scapegoat.

First you think of suing Vixon for defamation yourself, but you decide against it because of the unlikely success of such a claim. Next you consider the problem of the low fixed fee. The contractual fee is too low to compensate for the work already done, and the publicity sought from the case has now backfired. Is it possible to avoid the contract for the fixed fee because the client fired you? Should you be able to sue Vixon for the reasonable hourly rate?

ROSENBERG v. LEVIN

409 So.2d 1016 (Fla.1982).

OVERTON, JUSTICE. * * *

The facts of this case reflect the following. Levin hired Rosenberg and Pomerantz to perform legal services pursuant to a letter agreement which provided for a $10,000 fixed fee, plus a contingent fee equal to fifty percent of all amounts recovered in excess of $600,000. Levin later discharged Rosenberg and Pomerantz without cause before the legal controversy was resolved and subsequently settled the matter for a net recovery of $500,000. Rosenberg and Pomerantz sued for fees based on a "quantum meruit" evaluation of their services. After lengthy testimony, the trial judge concluded that quantum meruit was indeed the appropriate basis for compensation and awarded Rosenberg and Pomerantz $55,000. The district court also agreed that quantum meruit was the appropriate basis for recovery but lowered the amount awarded to $10,000, stating that recovery could in no event exceed the amount which the attorneys would have received under their contract if not prematurely discharged.

The issue submitted to us for resolution is whether the terms of an attorney employment contract limit the attorney's quantum meruit recovery to the fee set out in the contract. * * *

There are two conflicting interests involved in the determination of the issue presented in this type of attorney-client dispute. The first is the need of the client to have confidence in the integrity and ability of his attorney and, therefore, the need for the client to have the ability to discharge his attorney when he loses that necessary confidence in the attorney. The second is the attorney's right to adequate compensation for work performed. To address these conflicting interests, we must consider three distinct rules.

The traditional contract rule adopted by a number of jurisdictions holds that an attorney discharged without cause may recover damages for breach of contract under traditional contract principles. The measure of damages is usually the full contract price, although some courts deduct a fair allowance for services and expenses not expended by the discharged attorney in performing the balance of the contract. [Citations.] Some jurisdictions following the contract rule also permit an alternative recovery based on quantum meruit so that an attorney can elect between recovery based on the contract or the reasonable value of the performed services. [Citations.]

Support for the traditional contract theory is based on: (1) the full contract price is arguably the most rational measure of damages since it reflects the value that the parties placed on the services; (2) charging the full fee prevents the client from profiting from his own breach of contract; and (3) the contract rule is said to avoid the difficult problem of setting a value on an attorney's partially completed legal work.

To avoid restricting a client's freedom to discharge his attorney, a number of jurisdictions in recent years have held that an attorney discharged without cause can recover only the reasonable value [of] services rendered prior to discharge. [Citation.] This rule was first announced in Martin v. Camp, 219 N.Y. 170, 114 N.E. 46 (1916), where the New York Court of Appeals held that a discharged attorney could not sue his client for damages for breach of contract unless the attorney had completed performance of the contract. The New York court established quantum meruit recovery for the attorney on the theory that the client does not breach the contract by discharging the attorney. Rather, the court reasoned, there is an implied condition in every attorney-client contract that the client may discharge the attorney at any time with or without cause. With this right as part of the contract, traditional contract principles are applied to allow quantum meruit recovery on the basis of services performed to date. Under the New York rule, the attorney's cause of action accrues immediately upon his discharge by the client, under the reasoning that it is unfair to make the attorney's right to compensation dependent on the performance of a successor over whom he has no control. [Citation.]

The California Supreme Court, in Fracasse v. Brent, 6 Cal.3d 784, 494 P.2d 9, 100 Cal.Rptr. 385 (1972), also adopted a quantum meruit rule. That court carefully analyzed those factors which distinguish the attorney-client relationship from other employment situations and concluded that a discharged attorney should be limited to a quantum meruit recovery in order to strike a proper balance between the client's right to discharge his attorney without undue restriction and the attorney's right to fair compensation for work performed. The *Fracasse* court sought both to provide clients greater freedom in substituting counsel and to promote confidence in the legal profession while protecting society's interest in the attorney-client relationship.

Contrary to the New York rule, however, the California court also held that an attorney's cause of action for quantum meruit does not accrue until the happening of the contingency, that is, the client's recovery. If no recovery is forthcoming, the attorney is denied compensation. The California court offered two reasons in support of its position. First, the result obtained and the amount involved, two important factors in determining the reasonableness of a fee, cannot be ascertained until the occurrence of the contingency. Second, the client may be of limited means and it would be unduly burdensome to force him to pay a fee if there was no recovery. The court stated that: "[S]ince the attorney agreed initially to take his chances on recovering any fee whatever, we believe that the fact that the success of the litigation is no longer under his control is insufficient to justify imposing a new and more onerous burden on the client." [Citation.]

The third rule is an extension of the second that limits quantum meruit recovery to the maximum fee set in the contract. This limitation is believed necessary to provide client freedom to substitute attorneys without economic penalty. Without such a limitation, a client's right to discharge an attorney may be illusory and the client may in effect be penalized for exercising a right.

* * *

We have carefully considered all the matters presented, both on the original argument on the merits and on rehearing. It is our opinion that it is in the best interest of clients and the legal profession as a whole that we adopt the modified quantum meruit rule which limits recovery to the maximum amount of the contract fee in all premature discharge cases involving both fixed and contingency employment contracts. The attorney-client relationship is one of special trust and confidence. The client must rely entirely on the good faith efforts of the attorney in representing his interests. This reliance requires that the client have complete confidence in the integrity and ability of the attorney and that absolute fairness and candor characterize all dealings between them. These considerations dictate that clients be given greater freedom to change legal representatives than might be tolerated in other employment relationships. We approve the philosophy that there is an overriding need to allow clients freedom to substitute attorneys without economic penalty as a means of accomplishing the broad objective of fostering public confidence in the legal profession. Failure to limit quantum meruit recovery defeats the policy against penalizing the client for exercising his right to discharge. However, attorneys should not be penalized either and should have the opportunity to recover for services performed.

Accordingly, we hold that an attorney employed under a valid contract who is discharged without cause before the contingency has occurred or before the client's matters have concluded can recover only the reasonable value of his services rendered prior to discharge, limited by the maximum contract fee. We reject both the traditional contract rule and the quantum meruit rule that allow recovery in excess of the maximum contract price because both have a chilling effect on the client's power to discharge an attorney. Under the contract rule in a contingent fee situation, both the discharged attorney and the second attorney may receive a substantial percentage of the client's final recovery. Under the unlimited quantum meruit rule, it is possible, as the instant case illustrates, for the attorney to receive a fee greater than he bargained for under the terms of his contract. Both these results are unacceptable to us.

We further follow the California view that in contingency fee cases, the cause of action for quantum meruit arises only upon the successful occurrence of the contingency. If the client fails in his recovery, the discharged attorney will similarly fail and recover nothing. We recognize that deferring the commencement of a cause of action until the occurrence of the contingency is a view not uniformly accepted. Deferral, however, supports our goal to preserve the client's freedom to discharge, and any resulting harm to the attorney is minimal because the attorney would not have benefited earlier until the contingency's occurrence. There should, of course, be a presumption of regularity and competence in the performance of the services by a successor attorney.

In computing the reasonable value of the discharged attorney's services, the trial court can consider the totality of the circumstances surrounding the professional relationship between the attorney and client. Factors such as time, the recovery sought, the skill demanded, the results obtained, and the attorney-client contract itself will necessarily be relevant considerations.

* * * We find the district court of appeal was correct in limiting the quantum meruit award to the contract price, and its decision is approved.

It is so ordered.

———

1. Consider the observation of the court in *Chambliss, Bahner & Crawford v. Luther,* 531 S.W.2d 108 (Tenn.App.1975). The court rejected the plaintiff-attorney's argument that quantum meruit should be the basis for the recovery even if it exceeds the contract fee and noted:

> To adopt the rule advanced by Plaintiff would, in our view, encourage attorneys less keenly aware of their professional responsibilities than Attorney Chambliss, ... to induce clients to lose confidence in them in cases where the reasonable value of their services has exceeded the original fee and thereby, upon being discharged, reap a greater benefit than that for which they had bargained. 531 S.W.2d at 113.

2. The court in the principal case recites several factors to consider in valuing of the services for quantum meruit recovery. These factors feature also in setting attorney fees in other circumstances, such as recovery by a party for bad faith litigation or pursuant to a statutory allowance for fees to a prevailing party. This area is explored in Chapter 19.

3. What if an attorney quits before completion of a contract with a client? Should the attorney have a quantum meruit recovery for the value of services performed? Consider: (1) Does it matter if those services are useful to the client even without the completion of the contract, and (2) should a plaintiff ever receive restitution when the plaintiff is the defaulting party to the contract? The availability of restitution to a defaulting party has long troubled courts. The early cases framed the issues starkly in the context of hired labor, before the federal preemption of the labor issues. *Compare* Stark v. Parker, 19 Mass. (2 Pick.) 267 (1924) (a farm laborer who quits before completion of a contract may not recover the value of the work actually performed) *with* Britton v. Turner, 6 N.H. 481 (1834) (laborer can recover the value of benefits conferred on employer after nine and a half months work on a year long contract).

4. What if a plaintiff confers benefits on a defendant pursuant to an agreement induced by the defendant's fraud? In addition to the common law tort remedies for fraud, there may be restitutionary remedies. Consider that the loss to the plaintiff may be greater or lesser than the gain of the defendant.

First consider the usual case where the loss to the plaintiff and the gain to the defendant are roughly equal. For example, a defendant car dealer fraudulently represents to the plaintiff buyer that a car is new except for its use as a demonstration model. In fact the car is a used one received by the dealer on a trade-in. The plaintiff discovers this fact after purchase and thus has a car with a "blue book" value less than the purchase price. The common law fraud remedy would allow this loss as damages.

Now consider that the plaintiff further discovers after purchase that the car was previously owned by a young singer who is now a fast-rising star. The fair market value of this car is thus greater than the value of equivalent cars. The dealer was unaware of this fact because the star uses a stage name and the dealer dealt with the star's parents for the trade-in transaction. Common law fraud damages would be zero because the plaintiff does not have a loss. Should there be any restitutionary recovery against the fraudulent dealer in this hypothetical example? If so, how should it be measured? Consider the problem and the case that follow.

PROBLEM: THE EQUIPMENT LOAN

Danzer is an employee of Carter, who owns a furniture store. Pennell, who operates an equipment rental business, has good personal and business relations with Carter. Carter's furniture store attracts as customers people who are moving or remodelling, and Carter frequently refers them to Pennell's rental business.

Danzer contacted Pennell during business hours and asked for the free use of carpet cleaning equipment for a few weeks. Pennell was under the erroneous impression that Carter wanted the equipment to clean carpets in the furniture store and had instructed Danzer to call. Pennell granted the request as a return favor to Carter.

In fact, Carter was not involved in the request. Danzer, acting independently, wanted the cleaning equipment to operate a personal business during the pre-holiday season. Danzer cleaned carpets for private homeowners during evening hours at a rate slightly less than that of professional cleaners. Pennell later discovered these facts and further learned that Danzer earned $500 cleaning carpets. The fair rental value of the equipment is $200. Is restitution appropriate? If so, how should it be measured?

WARD v. TAGGART

51 Cal.2d 736, 336 P.2d 534 (1959).

TRAYNOR, JUSTICE.

At plaintiff William R. Ward's request in February, 1955, LeRoy Thomsen, a real estate broker, undertook to look for properties that might be of interest to Ward for purchase. During a conversation about unrelated matters, defendant Marshall W. Taggart, a real estate broker, told Thomsen that as exclusive agent for Sunset Oil Company he had several acres of land in Los Angeles County for sale. Thomsen said that he had a client who might be interested in acquiring this property. When Thomsen mentioned to Taggart that another broker named Dawson had a "For Sale" sign on the property, Taggart replied that Sunset had taken the listing away from Dawson. With Ward's authorization Thomsen submitted an offer on his behalf to Taggart of $4,000 an acre. Taggart promised to take the offer to Sunset. Taggart later told Thomsen that Sunset had refused the offer and would not take less for the property than $5,000 an acre, one-half in cash. Thomsen conveyed this information to Ward, who directed Thomsen to make an offer on those terms. Thomsen did so in writing. * * *

Plaintiffs did not learn until after they had purchased the property that Taggart had never been given a listing by Sunset and that he had never presented to Sunset and never intended to present plaintiffs' offers of $4,000 and $5,000 per acre. Instead, he presented his own offer of $4,000 per acre, which Sunset accepted. He falsely represented to plaintiffs that the least Sunset would take for the property was $5,000 per acre, because he intended to purchase the property from Sunset himself and resell it to plaintiffs at a profit of $1,000 per acre. All the reasons he gave for the unusual handling of the sale were fabrications. * * *

Plaintiffs brought an action in tort charging fraud on the part of Taggart and Jordan [a Taggart employee]. The case was tried without a jury, and the court entered judgment against both defendants for $72,049.20 compensatory damages, and against Taggart for $36,000 exemplary damages. The judgment also enjoined defendants from transferring notes and trust deeds received from plaintiffs and ordered them to discharge these and thereby reduce the amount of the judgment. Defendants appeal.

Defendants contend that the judgment must be reversed on the ground that there can be no recovery in a tort action for fraud without proof of the actual or "out-of-pocket" losses sustained by the plaintiff and that in the present case there was no evidence that the property was worth less than plaintiffs paid for it. * * * Although, as defendants admit, the evidence is clearly sufficient to support the finding of fraud, the only evidence submitted on the issue of damages was that the property was worth at least $5,000 per acre, the price plaintiffs paid for it. Since there was no proof that plaintiffs suffered "out-of-pocket" loss, there can be no recovery in tort for fraud. [Citation.]

* * *

Even though Taggart was not plaintiff's agent, the public policy of this state does not permit one to "take advantage of his own wrong" (Civ.Code, § 3517), and the law provides a quasi-contractual remedy to prevent one from being unjustly enriched at the expense of another. Section 2224 of the Civil Code provides that one "who gains a thing by fraud * * * or other wrongful act, is, unless he has some other and better right thereto, an involuntary trustee of the thing gained, for the benefit of the person who would otherwise have had it." As a real estate broker, Taggart had the duty to be honest and truthful in his dealings. [Citation.] The evidence is clearly sufficient to support a finding that Taggart violated this duty. Through fraudulent misrepresentations he received money that plaintiffs would otherwise have had. Thus, Taggart is an involuntary trustee for the benefit of plaintiffs on the secret profit of $1,000 per acre that he made from his dealings with them.

* * *

Accordingly, the judgment for $72,092.20, representing the $1,000 per acre secret profit, against defendant Taggart must be affirmed. The judgment against defendant Jordan, however, must be reversed. Although she permitted her name to be used in the dual escrows, she did not share in the illicit profit that Taggart obtained. One cannot be held to be a constructive trustee of something he has not acquired.

Taggart contends that if recovery is based on the theory of unjust enrichment, the judgment of exemplary damages must be reversed. * * *

Courts award exemplary damages to discourage oppression, fraud, or malice by punishing the wrongdoer. [Citations.] Such damages are appropriate in cases like the present one, where restitution would have little or no deterrent effect, for wrongdoers would run no risk of liability to their victims beyond that of returning what they wrongfully obtained. * * *

The judgment against Taggart is affirmed. The judgment against Jordan is reversed.

———

1. Benefits conferred by an agreement that was induced by fraud can be the subject of a claim in tort for misrepresentation or a claim for restitution. Compensatory damages for fraud can be measured in two ways, both of which properly focus upon the plaintiff's loss. The out of pocket loss measure allows the difference between the price paid and the value actually received. For example, if a seller of a house fraudulently represents that a leaky roof was recently repaired, the buyer can recover the difference between the price and the value of the defective house. The benefit of the bargain measure gives the difference between the value received and the value if the representations were true. For example, under this measure the plaintiff could receive the difference between the value of the defective house and the value of the house if the roof were repaired. Jurisdictions vary on the permissibility of these measures for fraud or for negligent misrepresentation. *See* Prosser and Keeton on Torts 765–770 (5th ed. 1984).

A claim for rescission and restitution would return to both parties any benefits conferred in the transaction. Compare the first case in this section, *Alder v. Drudis*, where one party purported to rescind the transaction for fraudulent misrepresentation, but the court found no fraud.

In the principal case, the defendant fraudulently induced the plaintiff to confer on him a benefit, specifically the additional $1000 per acre above the actual price. The tort action was successful substantively, but the remedy produced no recovery. Compensatory damages were not possible because the plaintiff had no actual loss; the value of the land received by the plaintiff was equal to the price paid. The secret profit of $1000 could only be disgorged by a restitutionary theory that the defendant made a "promise" by implication of law to return the secret profit.

2. Compare *Ward* to the following facts: A buyer, Harper, made an offer to purchase a farm for $7000 to an agent for the owner. The agent fraudulently misrepresented that the seller would only convey a portion of it for $6000. In fact the seller was willing to sell it all for $6500, and

the agent purchased the entire farm at that price. The agent then sold Harper a portion of it for $6000 and conveyed the rest to a close relative for $500.

Harper discovered these facts and sued. The original owner of the farm did not sue. How could compensatory damages in tort be measured? Is a restitutionary remedy appropriate under these facts? *See* Harper v. Adametz, 142 Conn. 218, 113 A.2d 136 (1955).

3. If the theory of recovery is an implied-in-law contract, why should the court allow punitive damages as if it were a tort action rather than a contractual one? Is the use of the word "contract" so fictional that it has no meaning? Should it determine the statute of limitations?

WINSLOW, COHU & STETSON, INC. v. SKOWRONEK
136 N.J.Super. 97, 344 A.2d 350 (1975).

GAYNOR, J.C.C.

Plaintiff seeks to recover the value of securities which were erroneously and inadvertently registered in defendant's name and delivered by plaintiff to defendant. The complaint sounds in unjust enrichment, conversion and wrongful possession. Defendant does not deny the receipt of the higher-valued securities but contends that there was no conversion or wrongful possession, that plaintiff's claim is barred by the statute of limitations or laches, and further, that plaintiff's loss is the result of its own mistake and negligence which precludes recovery.

There is no dispute as to the factual pattern giving rise to the present litigation. The uncontroverted facts disclose that in 1967 defendant maintained a brokerage account with plaintiff and in November of that year requested plaintiff to purchase 100 shares of the common stock of Engelhard Minerals and Chemical Corporation. The purchase was made at a price of 41⅞ a share, or a total of $4,187.50, which was paid by defendant. In pursuance of this purchase for defendant, plaintiff sent a 100–share certificate to the transfer agent with instructions to register the certificate in the name of defendant. Through plaintiff's inadvertence the certificate forwarded to the transfer agent was a 100–share certificate of the higher-valued Engelhard Minerals and Chemicals Corporation $4.25 cumulative convertible preferred stock. This certificate was registered in defendant's name, and on December 4, 1967, plaintiff delivered it to defendant. In September 1972, as the result of an independent audit, the error was discovered by plaintiff, and defendant was thereupon requested to return the certificate for the 100 shares of preferred stock or its money equivalent. However, defendant had sold the stock in February 1972 and refused to accede to plaintiff's demand for the return of the stock or its money value. Defendant had sold the stock at a price of $141 a share, thereby realizing the gross amount of $14,100. The dividends paid on the preferred stock while in the possession of defendant totaled $1,806.25. Defendant was notified of the error by a telephone message on or about September 12, 1972, and a confirming letter mailed on September 20, 1972. The market value of the 100 shares of common stock on those dates was $6,077 and the cash dividends paid from December 1967 to that date on the common stock amounted to $390.05. * * *

Plaintiff contends that, under these facts, there was a conversion by defendant of the preferred stock and, as the injured party, it is entitled to recovery of the stock certificate, if defendant still has it, or money damages for the wrongful conversion. If the latter remedy is applicable, plaintiff asserts that the damages recoverable are the highest intermediate value of the securities between the date of delivery of the certificate to defendant, being the alleged date of conversion, and the date of judgment, plus the dividends received by defendant during this period. Plaintiff acknowledges that defendant would be entitled to a setoff for the value of the common stock and accumulated dividends thereon. Alternatively, plaintiff contends that it is entitled to recover under the concept that defendant has been unjustly enriched as a result of the mistake committed by plaintiff, thereby giving rise to a constructive trust in favor of plaintiff as to the money realized from the sale of the securities.

Defendant contends that he was not guilty of converting the subject securities inasmuch as he obtained them lawfully and had divested himself of their possession prior to the demand made by plaintiff. * * *

* * * [In cases in other jurisdictions] refusal of the recipient to return the securities which were mistakenly delivered after notification of the mistake and demand for the return, or the exercise of ownership rights after knowledge of the mistaken transfer, were considered as the factors giving rise to a conversion.

These essential elements are not present in the instant case. The proofs do not disclose knowledge of the error by defendant prior to the notice in September, 1972, at which time the securities were no longer in his possession, nor does the evidence support an inference of prior knowledge on the part of defendant. The demand then made for the return of the securities was thus ineffectual and the action of defendant could not be considered as a refusal to comply with the demand. Under the circumstances of this case, a timely demand and a failure to thereupon return the securities would be necessary requirements to support a claim of conversion. [Citation.] These elements not being present, there was no conversion.

However, it is our opinion that the concepts of undue enrichment and restitution are applicable to the factual situation presented by this case. It is a general rule that a payment of money under a mistake of fact may be recovered, provided that such recovery will not prejudice the payee. This rule is grounded upon considerations of equity and fair dealing. It is considered unjust enrichment to permit a recipient to retain money paid because of a mistake, unless the circumstances are such that it would be inequitable to require its return. [Citations.] This is so notwithstanding that the mistake is unilateral and a consequence of the payor's negligence, or that the payee acted in good faith. [Citation.] While these principles have been applied to cases between stockbrokers and their customers involving payment of the proceeds of a mistaken sale of securities, [citation], we discern no reason why they are not equally applicable to a delivery of stock certificates which were mistakenly purchased or mistakenly transferred. A person who receives a voluntary benefit is liable to make restitution if the circumstances of its receipt or retention are such that, as between the two persons, it would be unjust for the recipient to retain the benefit. [Citations.]

Defendant raises the defenses of laches, waiver and estoppel. The basis of these defenses is the long period of time elapsing between the delivery of the securities and the demand for corrective action, together with the fact that the situation was created by plaintiff's own inadvertence and negligence. Further, that the exercise of reasonable diligence and control by plaintiff in transacting its business should have disclosed the error within a short time after it occurred. Although the error in the transfer and delivery to defendant of the wrong security was not discovered for almost five years, the audit which revealed the mistake had been commenced a year or two prior to the discovery and defendant was notified of the error promptly upon its discovery. The laches claimed by defendant basically relates to the long lapse of time before the error was discovered by plaintiff. Assuming that plaintiff should have known of the error shortly after its occurrence through the exercise of reasonable care and diligence in running its business, there is no evidence that its failure to do so was prejudicial to defendant. The lapse of time, in and of itself, will not give rise to laches unless the failure to assert one's rights within a reasonable period of time results in prejudice to the defending party. [Citations.] In any event, plaintiff acted promptly after it discovered the mistaken transfer and delivery. Additionally, the evidence does not support the defenses of waiver and estoppel. No proof was offered to show any voluntary and intentional relinquishment by plaintiff of its claim, nor of any conduct which would estop it from asserting its claim against defendant.

Inasmuch as we consider that the disposition of this case is governed by the equitable principles of unjust enrichment and restitution, we need not be concerned with the issue of the statute of limitations. * * *

In view of our conclusion that there was no conversion of the mistakenly delivered securities, the measure of damages enunciated in Kaplan v. Cavicchia, 107 N.J.Super. 201, 257 A.2d 739 (App.Div.1969), [for conversion] is not applicable. Rather, the benefit received by defendant resulting from the erroneous transfer and delivery of the securities is the appropriate extent of a recovery by plaintiff. According to our findings, defendant benefitted in the amount of $8,023, being the added amount received from the sale of the preferred stock over that which would have been received from the sale of the common stock, and in the amount of $1,715.30, being the difference between the dividends received and those payable on the common stock.

Judgment will therefore be entered in favor of plaintiff in the sum of $9,738.30, with interest from the date of the judgment to be entered and without costs.

––––––

1. Distinguish mistake in the performance of a contract, as in the principal case, from mistake in the formation of a contract. A mistake in formation will not necessarily justify avoidance of contractual obligations. The mistake also must be considered to be "material" and with respect "to a basic assumption on which the contract was made." *See* Restatement (Second) of Contracts §§ 152, 153. Additionally, the party seeking relief must not be deemed to bear the risk of the mistake either pursuant to the terms of the agreement or as allocated by the court. *See* Restatement (Second) of Contracts § 154.

Mistakes in formation of contracts can be mutual or unilateral. Courts have allowed avoidance for unilateral mistake only in limited circumstances. The mistaken party must further demonstrate either that the enforcement of the contract would be unconscionable or that the other party had reason to know of the mistake or was at fault in causing the mistake. *See* Restatement (Second) of Contracts § 153.

2. A mistake in the performance of a noncontractual obligation may also give rise to a claim for restitution. For example, a plaintiff may pay the debt of another by mistake. The legal question then becomes whether the plaintiff should be treated as a volunteer or whether the circumstances justify restitution. The effect of granting relief in such cases is to force the plaintiff to change creditors. These issues are further explored in Chapter 17.

C. WAIVER OF TORT AND SUIT IN ASSUMPSIT

Section Coverage:

Waiver of tort and suit in assumpsit is a legal restitutionary remedy based on the implication of rights through quasi-contracts. Although the parties have no express or implied contract between them, the common law will imply a contract that requires a defendant to return unjust enrichment to a plaintiff who should more rightfully retain the benefit.

Historically this type of restitution was accomplished by allowing a plaintiff to use one of the old contract writs even in the absence of an express or implied contract. The writ of "money had and received" was thus used to recover under a quasi-contract any profit a wrongdoer received at the expense of the plaintiff. The fiction was that the defendant was acting as the plaintiff's agent. The writ of "goods sold and delivered" was used to recover the fair market value of converted goods on the fiction that the thief had promised to pay for them.

In many states the function of this basis of recovery is to recover profits from wrongdoers when the relationship between the parties does not support the imposition of a constructive trust. A plaintiff can bring an action in assumpsit against even a thief. Another function is to gain the typically longer contract statute of limitations by bringing an action in quasi-contract instead of tort. This result is important for plaintiffs who want to sue for conversion damages but are time-barred. The action in assumpsit based on "goods sold and delivered" allows the same measure of damages—fair market value at time and place of conversion—under a longer period of limitations. Some courts have found this result inappropriate, but most allow it.

Not all torts may be waived in favor of quasi-contract actions. Courts most commonly have permitted waiver of conversion. Waiver of trespass to chattel has been allowed. Jurisdictions have split on the permissibility of waiving trespass. Courts have rejected other torts, such as defamation, as suitable for the implication of a contract implied by law.

Model Case:

Jean Poindexter owns a coin shop in Metropolis. One night a thief defeated the security system and stole the coins that were in the vault. The thief erroneously believed that the most valuable coins would be in the vault. In fact Poindexter guarded the most valuable coins elsewhere and the coins in the vault were only moderately valuable.

The thief, Green, took the coins to an unsophisticated buyer who shared the misconception about their value. Green thus sold the coins for more than their fair market value. When these facts are discovered, Poindexter sues Green. Green has otherwise been a successful burglar and has assets to pay a judgment.

Poindexter has several choices. First, an action for tort would recover the fair market value of the coins at the time and place of conversion. If the conversion statute of limitations has run, the same measure is available with an assumpsit claim based upon the writ of "goods sold and delivered." The fictional contract is based upon an implied promise by the thief to pay for the goods at the moment of stealing them.

Alternatively, an assumpsit action based upon the writ of "money had and received" allows recovery of the resale price on the fiction that Green was acting as Poindexter's agent. Under the facts of this case, this recovery would be greater. The profit earned from the transaction with the unsophisticated buyer is taken from the wrongdoer and given to the plaintiff. Although the plaintiff thus recovers a windfall, the defendant cannot profit from the misdeed.

H. RUSSELL TAYLOR'S FIRE PREVENTION SERVICE, INC. v. COCA COLA BOTTLING CORP.

99 Cal.App.3d 711, 160 Cal.Rptr. 411 (1979).

ZENOVICH, ASSOCIATE JUSTICE.

A complaint filed in Kern County Superior Court alleged that appellant Coca Cola Bottling Corporation (hereafter referred to as Coca Cola) was indebted to appellant H. Russell Taylor's Fire Prevention Service, Inc. (hereafter referred to as Taylor). * * *

By stipulation of the parties, Taylor amended its complaint in the indebitatus assumpsit court, and Coca Cola amended its answer to assert as a separate affirmative defense the bar of the statute of limitations set forth in Code of Civil Procedure section 338, subdivision 3.

Thereafter, the court entered findings of fact and conclusions of law rendering judgment for Taylor in the sum of $7,157. From this judgment Coca Cola appeals. * * *

In 1957, Coca Cola entered into an oral agreement with Taylor. Taylor was to periodically fill some of its own cylinders with carbon dioxide and supply them to Coca Cola's bottling plant in Bakersfield, California, for use as fire extinguishers. * * *

Pursuant to the oral agreement, Taylor made deliveries of cylinders to Coca Cola's plant until September 23, 1971. The trial court found that September 23, 1971, was the termination date for Taylor's services. Within 90 days, employees of Taylor demanded return of several hundred cylinders in Coca Cola's possession. Coca Cola began to return many of the cylinders, although 246 in number were still missing at the time of trial.

* * *

The trial court found that Coca Cola's failure to return the cylinders was a taking and detaining of goods and chattels. In addition, the court determined that Taylor waived the conversion claim and elected to treat the action as a purchase and sale of the cylinders. Having determined that an implied-in-law sale occurred once the tort was waived, the court applied the four-year statute of limitations of Commercial Code section 2725, subdivision (1), and held the suit timely filed. * * *

Procedurally, Taylor filed its complaint on June 4, 1975, more than three years after September 23, 1971, the date upon which demand was made for the outstanding cylinders. The trial court found that the suit was timely filed within the four-year statute of limitations set forth in Commercial Code section 2725, subdivision (1), since the indebitatus assumpsit theory legally transformed the tortious conversion of the cylinders into a *fictional* contract of sale. Coca Cola contends that the trial court erroneously applied the four-year limitations period even though the gravamen of Taylor's claim was for "taking, detaining, or injuring any goods, or chattels," a cause of action governed by the three-year limitations period provided in Code of Civil Procedure section 338, subdivision 3. Under Coca Cola's construction of the action brought by Taylor, the suit would be time barred if the limitations period of the Commercial Code is deemed inapplicable.

In ruling upon the applicability of a statute of limitations, it has been recognized that courts will look to the nature of the rights sued upon rather than to the form of action or to the relief demanded. Neither the caption, form, nor prayer of the complaint will conclusively determine the nature of the liability from which the cause of action flows. Instead, the true nature of the action will be ascertained from the basic facts *a posteriori*. [Citations.] Since the trial court found the four-year limitations period governing sales contracts applicable, it must be determined whether indebitatus assumpsit—Taylor's cause of action—is based on contract or tort. In order to pinpoint the proper nature of the rights sued upon, an examination of the theory underlying indebitatus assumpsit is appropriate.

The general contours of the assumpsit cause of action have been summarized by Professor Corbin as follows:

> The common counts in assumpsit are merely abbreviated and stereo-typed statements that the defendant is indebted to the plaintiff for a variety of commonly recurring reasons, such as ... goods sold and delivered. They are allegations of indebtedness, and the action may be properly described as indebitatus assumpsit.... The common counts could be used for the enforcement of express promises if they were such as to create a money debt, *as well as for the enforcement of implied promises and quasi-contracts.* (1 Corbin, Contracts (1st ed. 1963) § 20, p. 51, emphasis added.)

* * * [T]he California Supreme Court discussed the historical evolution of indebitatus assumpsit. The court stated:

> The action of *assumpsit,* in its development, had an interesting but stormy career at the common law. Although in existence for some years previous to that time, it came into prominence following the decision in Slade's Case in 1603 (Coke's Rep., vol. 2, p. 505; 2 Harvard Law Review, p. 16). It gradually gained prominence and widened in scope until 1760 when Lord Mansfield, in the case of *Moses v. Mcfarlan* (2 Burr, 1005, English Reports, Full Reprint, King's Bench Book 26, vol. 97, p. 676), described its function as follows: 'This kind of equitable action to recover back money, which ought not in justice to be kept, is very beneficial, and therefore much encouraged. It lies only for money which, *ex aequo et bono,* the defendant ought to refund; it does not lie for money paid by the plaintiff, which is claimed of him as payable in point of honor and honesty, although it could not have been recovered from him by any course of law; as in payment of a debt barred by the statute of limitations, or contracted during his infancy, or to the extent of principal and legal interest upon a usurious contract, or for money

fairly lost at play: because in all these cases, the defendant may retain it with a safe conscience, though by positive law he was barred from recovering. But it lies for money paid by mistake; or upon a consideration which happens to fail; or for money got through imposition (express or implied); or extortion; or oppression; or an undue advantage taken of the plaintiff's situation, contrary to laws made for the protection of persons under those circumstances. In one word the gist of this kind of action is, that the defendant, upon the circumstances of the case, is obliged by the ties of natural justice and equity to refund the money.'

Quoting the above, Mr. Holdsworth in his work on the History of English Law, volume 8, page 97, uses this language: 'It was thus in the action of *indebitatus assumpsit* that the larger part of our modern law of *quasi*-contract has originated.'

Authorities in support of the prevalent use of this form of action in the courts of the common law could be multiplied indefinitely, but we will close this branch of the discussion by a quotation from Professor Ames in volume 2 of the Harvard Law Review, page 69: 'The main outlines of the history of *assumpsit* have now been indicated. In its origin an action of tort, it was soon transformed into an action of contract, becoming afterwards a remedy where there was neither tort nor contract. Based at first only upon an express promise, it was afterwards supported upon an implied promise, and even upon a fictitious promise. Introduced as a special manifestation of the action on the case, it soon acquired the dignity of a distinct form of action, which superseded Debt, became concurrent with Account, with Case upon a bailment, a warranty, and bills of exchange, and competed with Equity in the case of essentially equitable *quasi*-contracts growing out of the principle of unjust enrichment. Surely it would be hard to find a better illustration of the flexibility and power of self-development of the Common Law.' (Philpott v. Superior Court, 1 Cal.2d at 518–519, 520–521, 36 P.2d at 638.)

Although recognizing that a tortious act frequently formed the basis for invoking assumpsit, the court determined that "its contractual quality was always its most distinct feature." (*Philpott, supra* at 526, 536 P.2d at 642, quoting 7 Holdsworth, History of English Law, p. 441.)

In the instant case, the trial court found that Coca Cola's failure to return the cylinders was conversion. Nonetheless, the court ruled that Taylor had waived the tort after making its demand for return of the chattels and *elected to treat the transaction as a sale of the cylinders.* This ruling appears to comport with California law, which allows a bailor in Taylor's position to treat the conversion as a *fictional or implied by law* contract of sale. [Citations.] Generally, where there is a waiver of tort and suit in assumpsit, the statute of limitations relating to actions of assumpsit rather than tort applies, although the determination of what limitation period is appropriate may depend on the substance of the action and the nature of the right violated rather than the form of action. [Citation.]

As *Philpott* and other authorities suggest, the nature of rights inherent in the indebitatus assumpsit cause of action appear to be based in *contract* principles. This reasoning is further bolstered by the realization that Taylor had to waive *tort* remedies in order to avail itself of the assumpsit theory. It has been recognized that when a party entitled to enforce two remedies either institutes an action upon one of such remedies or performs any act in pursuit of such remedy, he will be held to have made an election of such remedy and will not be entitled to pursue any other remedy for the enforcement of his right. [Citations.] Given the binding nature of the election made by proceeding under indebitatus assumpsit, we are of the opinion that the trial court correctly found that the gravamen of Taylor's claims was contractual in nature.

After determining that the nature of the rights was based in contract, the trial court applied the four-year statute of limitations governing *sales* contracts in Commercial Code section 2725, subdivision (1). Because Taylor's assumpsit claim created a fictional sale, the novel question presented in this case is whether the limitations period in the Commercial Code applies to sales contracts *implied by operation of law.* If this section is inapposite to implied-in-law contracts, Taylor's claim would be barred under the more restrictive time period of Code of Civil Procedure section 339, subdivision 1.[4]

* * *

In order to determine whether *fictional* sales contracts are governed by the four-year period, it is pertinent to construe the language contained in the Commercial Code's limitation statute.

Commercial Code section 2725 deals with "contract[s] for sale" and, in definitional cross-references at the end of the section, makes reference to Commercial Code section 2106. Commercial Code section 2106 defines "contract for sale" as including "both a present sale of goods and a contract to sell goods at a future time." In addition, the section defines "present sale" as "a sale which is accomplished by the making of the contract." Since "contract" is a key word in Commercial Code section 2106, illumination is provided by consulting Commercial Code section 1201, subdivision (11). This latter provision states that " 'Contract' means the total legal obligation which results from the parties' agreement ..." Further clarity is provided by Commercial Code section 1201, subdivision (3), which defines "Agreement" as "the bargain of the parties in fact as found in their language or by implication from other circumstances including course of dealing or usage of trade or course of performance as provided in this code...."

---

4. Code of Civil Procedure section 339, subdivision 1, provides:

"[The periods prescribed for the commencement of actions other than for the recovery of real property, as follows:]

"Within two years: 1. An action upon a contract, obligation or liability not founded upon an instrument of writing, ..."

Focusing upon Commercial Code section 1201, subdivision (3), it is important to note that the drafters of the Commercial Code defined agreement to mean *"the bargain of the parties ... by implication from other circumstances including...."* The deliberate insertion of the word "including" denotes that the drafters contemplated agreements which could be implied other than in fact. This is further supported by Commercial Code section 1102, which states that the code should be liberally construed. (Comm.Code, § 1102.) Given the fact that indebitatus assumpsit is a well-established contractual theory, there is ample reason for allowing Taylor to employ the limitations period for sales contracts contained in Commercial Code section 2725.

* * *

We therefore find that the trial court did not commit error in determining that the four-year limitation period of Commercial Code section 2725 applied to Taylor's claim. Taylor was not barred from pursuing Coca Cola through the assumpsit cause of action.

* * * [Affirmed.]

———

1. Some courts have refused to allow a waiver of tort and suit in assumpsit unless the defendant made a resale of the plaintiff's goods. This rule is identified with an old Massachusetts case, *Jones v. Hoar*, 22 Mass. 285 (1927), where the court refused to reconsider the resale requirement. Although this old rule is not followed in most jurisdictions today, some still adhere to it. *See* Janiszewski v. Behrmann, 345 Mich. 8, 75 N.W.2d 77 (1956).

2. The advantage of a quasi-contract theory based upon the old writ of money had and received is that the plaintiff could recover the defendant's profits if the resale of plaintiff's goods was for a price greater than their fair market value. The legal fiction is that the defendant acts as the agent of the plaintiff during the resale.

When no resale occurs, the quasi-contract recovery is based upon the old writ of goods sold and delivered. The legal fiction is that the defendant personally purchased the goods from the plaintiff at the price of their fair market value. The measure of recovery under this theory is the same as the measure of damages for the tort of conversion which the plaintiff waives in favor of the recovery in quasi-contract. In such cases there is no advantage to the quasi-contract theory in terms of the amount of money recovered, but there is the advantage of the longer statute of limitations for contract than for tort.

3. The position that no resale of the plaintiff's goods is necessary in order to waive the tort and sue in assumpsit derives from an old North Dakota case, Braithwaite v. Aiken, 3 N.D. 365, 56 N.W. 133 (1893). The court observed: "It is beneath the dignity of any tribunal

to draw a distinction between the receipt of benefits in the shape of cash and the receipt of benefits in the form of property."

Is the *Braithwaite* position persuasive? If the defendant's resale of the plaintiff's goods takes the form of an exchange of the goods for property of value rather than an exchange of the goods for money, the court's position makes perfect sense. Is it equally sensible that restitution is needed to disgorge the benefit held by the defendant if there is no resale? The remedy of damages for conversion is available unless the statute of limitations has run. Should the legislative scheme of limitation be altered by legal fiction? If California had taken the *Jones v. Hoar* position and required a resale, what would have been the result in the principal case?

FELDER v. REETH

34 F.2d 744 (9th Cir.1929).

WILBUR, CIRCUIT JUDGE.

Appellants brought an action in the District Court for the territory of Alaska to recover $5,402.65 for goods, wares, and merchandise sold to the appellee and for appellee's checks cashed by appellant. The appellee admitted the obligations sued upon, and by second amended answer and counterclaim alleged that he was engaged in placer mining upon 1,200 acres of placer mining ground, and that to carry on said mining operations he purchased a certain hydraulic mining plant in San Francisco, and transported the same to a point 40 miles below his placer mining camp, for the reason that because of low water in the stream he could not transport the machinery to the mining camp; that it remained at that point during the seasons of 1919, 1920, and 1921 by reason of low water in the river; that the freight charge for transportation of this plant from San Francisco was $1,045; that during the summer of 1921 the appellants wrongfully took possession of the hydraulic plant, transported the same down the river to Bethel, and converted same to their own use and sold a part thereof. It is further alleged:

"That under the conditions then existing at said Golden Gate Falls and 'Supply Camp' the said mining machinery and equipment was reasonably worth to defendant and were of the value to him of $10,-000.00."

"That defendant elects to waive the tort involved in the said unlawful taking and conversion of said property and to rely upon an implied contract upon the part of the plaintiffs, created by the law, to pay him the said sum of $10,000.00 for said machinery and equipment, the same being the reasonable value therefor by the time it reached the 'Supply Camp'; that the said plaintiffs, by reason of the premises, impliedly agreed, and in law did agree, to pay him the said sum of $10,000.00 for the said machinery and equipment."

Under the Alaska Code, a counterclaim to an action arising out of contract must be either one arising out of the transaction sued upon by the plaintiff, or, "In an action arising on contract, any other cause of action arising also on contract, and existing at the commencement of the action." Comp.Laws Alaska 1913, § 896.

The purpose of the form of pleading adopted by the appellee waiving, or attempting to waive, the tort, and suing upon the implied obligation of the appellant, was to bring his counterclaim within the purview of the statute, authorizing the setting up of a counterclaim.

* * * Appellants admitted taking the property, and alleged that it was taken to avoid a total loss thereof by flood waters of the Riglugalic River, on whose banks it had been placed. Appellants alleged that the property was in an abandoned condition until the fall of 1921; that they took possession of the property, and transported it to Bethel, and notified the defendant; that appellee ignored the entire matter; that they retained possession of the hydraulic plant until 1923, when for the first time they had an opportunity to dispose of the same; and that they sold it for the sum of $550, and that that sum was all the property was worth in Kuskokwin Precinct.

* * * The court found that the appellee was indebted to the appellant in the sum of $8,690.21, and that the appellants were indebted to the appellees in the sum of $8,000, with 8 per cent interest from September 1, 1921, aggregating $12,480, and rendered judgment in favor of appellees for the difference, $3,789.79. With reference to the value of the hydraulic plant, the court found:

"That under the circumstances and conditions as they existed at that time and by reason of the fact that there was no market value for said machinery at that time and place, and by reason of the use that the defendant could have put it to, the said machinery was worth to him the sum of $8,000". * * *

There seems to be no doubt that appellees can assert their claim against the appellants in this action by a counterclaim in the event and because of the fact that they waived the tortious conversion and counted in assumpsit as for goods sold and delivered. [Citation.]

The most serious question in this case is the measure of damages for breach of the implied contract sued upon. At common law, under the older rule, the result of waiving the tort in a case of conversion and sale was a right to recover the amount received upon the sale, as for money had and received, but later cases hold that the action can be maintained as for goods sold and delivered without awaiting sale, or even after sale, and the measure of recovery is the market value of the property. [Citations.] In a case where the owner waives the tort if he accepts the tort-feasor as his agent both in the taking and in the sale, he would necessarily be limited in his recovery to the money received by the agent. There seems, however, to be no good reason why the owner cannot waive the tortious taking and ignore the subsequent sale and recover the reasonable value of the property taken as for goods sold and delivered. [Citations.] This was done by the appellee, who ignored the sale of his property made by the appellants, and sought to recover as upon an implied agreement to pay the value of the hydraulic plant. The complaint, construed more strongly against the pleader, does not allege the market value or reasonable value of the property taken by the appellants. The allegation is of the reasonable value "to him." This allegation is evidently based upon the case of *Swank v. Elwert,* 55 Or. 487, 105 P. 901, 902, par. 11, where it is said (page 906):

The general rule for the measure of damages for the destruction or conversion of personalty is the market value of the property at the time and place of the conversion, if it has such value. [Citations.] But if the property has no market value at the time and place of conversion, either because of its limited production, or because it is of such a nature that there can be no general demand for it, and it is more particularly valuable to the owner than any one else, then it may be estimated with reference to its value to him. [Citation.]

* * * Assuming that this is a proper measure of damages in a suit for conversion under the peculiar circumstances found by the court, it does not follow that the appellee is entitled to recover that amount upon his counterclaim in which he waived the tort. * * *

* * * In view of the fact that this case must be tried again, it should be stated that, as the appellee by his counterclaim seeks to recover the value of the property as upon an implied sale, he should be permitted to amend his counterclaim and allege that value.

If the wrong-doer has not sold the property, but still retains it, the plaintiff has the right to waive the tort, and proceed upon an implied contract of sale to the wrong-doer himself, and in such event he is not charged as for money had and received by him to the use of the plaintiff. The contract implied is one to pay the value of the property as if it had been sold to the wrong-doer by the owner. If the transaction is thus held by the plaintiff as a sale, of course the title to the property passes to the wrong-doer, when the plaintiff elects to so treat it. [Citations.]

If on the trial it appears that there is no market at the point of conversion or implied sale, as from the findings appears to be the case, the value must be determined at the nearest market less the costs of transportation thereto, [citation] for in case of a waiver of a tort in conversion the action ex contractu is sustained rather on the theory of benefit derived by the taker than of damage to the owner. [Citations.] * * *

Judgment reversed.

––––––––

1. The miner in the principal case would have the best recovery under a conversion theory rather than under a quasi-contract theory. The reason that the contract theory was advanced instead of the tort one was procedural; under the old Field Code that governed the case the plaintiff could counterclaim only for the same type of claim. Thus, a

contract counterclaim was permissible on a contract claim, but a counterclaim in tort was impermissible.

On remand in Felder v. Reeth, 62 F.2d 730 (9th Cir.1933), the miner tried to change his counterclaim to one for conversion. The court struck it as procedurally improper and dismissed it without prejudice to maintain a separate action. These difficulties do not trouble modern litigants under procedural rules based upon the Federal Rules of Civil Procedure.

2. The waiver of tort and suit in quasi-contract theory does not apply to all torts. Conversion is the universally accepted tort that may be waived for these purposes. Trespass to chattel also has been waived successfully, as illustrated by the case of *Olwell v. Nye & Nissen, infra*.

The traditional rule allows no quasi-contract recovery for the wrongful use and occupation of land. The case most closely associated with this rule is Phillips v. Homfray, 24 Ch.D. 439 (1883), where no recovery was allowed for the use of a passageway on the plaintiff's land in order to remove coal. Recovery was allowed only for the value of the coal that was improperly taken. The plaintiff argued that the defendant had been saved expense and inconvenience by using the passageway for the operation, but the court held that this use of land did not deprive the plaintiff of anything nor did it enrich the defendant. Although a trespass action might ordinarily be maintained, the defendant in the case had died and the issue was which of the claims would survive against the estate. The court held that the defendant's estate was liable in quasi-contract only for the coal wrongfully taken because the estate had been enriched by the wrong.

A 1946 Virginia Supreme Court case, *Raven Red Ash Coal Co. v. Ball*, rejected the rule that a quasi-contract cannot be used for the use and occupation of land. In this case, the defendant abused an easement for the removal of coal on the other side of the property. The court noted:

> Where a naked trespass is committed, whether upon the person or property, assumpsit will not lie. If one commits an assault and battery upon another, it is absurd to imply a promise by the defendant to pay the victim a reasonable compensation. There is no basis for an implication of a contract where cattle inadvertently invade a neighbor's premises and trample down and destroy his crops. In each instance, a wrong and nothing more and nothing less has been committed. On the other hand, if a trespasser invades the premises of his neighbor, cuts and removes timber or severs minerals from the land and converts them to his own use, the owner may waive the tort and sue in assumpsit for the value of the materials converted. * * *
>
> * * * To hold that a trespasser who benefits himself by cutting and removing trees from another's land is liable on an implied contract, and that another trespasser who benefits himself by the illegal use of another's land is not liable on an implied contract is illogical. The only distinction is that in one case the benefit he

received is the diminution in the other's property. In the other case, he still receives the benefit but does not thereby diminish the value of the owner's property. In both cases, he has received substantial benefit by his own wrong. As the gist of the action is to prevent the unjust enrichment of a wrongdoer from the illegal use of another's property, such wrongdoer should be held on an implied promise in both cases. 185 Va. 534, 39 S.E.2d 231 (1946)

See also Edwards v. Lee's Adm'r, 265 Ky. 418, 96 S.W.2d 1028 (1936) (equitable accounting for profits derived from commercial exploitation of the Great Onyx Cave which extended partly under the plaintiff's property but to which the plaintiff had no access).

3. Recovery in quasi-contract was not allowed when the plaintiff wished to waive the tort of defamation in the 1949 New York case of *Hart v. E.P. Dutton & Co.* The statute of limitations barred the defamation claim against the publisher of a book about war spies. The plaintiff attempted to recover on the theory that profits from the book enriched the defendant at the expense of the plaintiff. The court observed:

> One who publishes a libel, especially if done maliciously, as charged in this complaint, is guilty of conduct which makes him liable for damages. An action for damages affords the plaintiff full compensation for any injuries which he has suffered. In addition to compensatory damages he may recover punitive damages if proper foundation is established by the proof. The law requires that a plaintiff must bring his action to recover such damages within one year. It would seem that it is not equitable and just to permit a person, who has been the subject of a libellous article published in a book, to acquiesce in or permit the sale and distribution of such book to continue for a period of nearly six years without taking any steps whatsoever to protest or stop the sale and distribution of the book and then to maintain an action for the profits derived from the sale and distribution of the book. 197 Misc. 274, 93 N.Y.S.2d 871 (1949)

PROBLEM: THE STOLEN MODEL ENGINE

Dalton owns a hobby shop that sells many items, including model railroad equipment for both child and adult enthusiasts. Tomkins is an adult hobbyist who belongs to a model railroad club.

Dalton has a display containing a few expensive brass engines. Tomkins purchased a small scale brass engine at a price of several hundred dollars in preparation for an upcoming public show sponsored by his club. Dalton had held that engine in inventory for several years. He acquired it when the limited production was made, and he priced it at his cost plus his standard mark-up. He had never reconsidered the price nor paid any attention to this engine as it sat in his display until Tomkins bought it.

The engine had appreciated in value considerably during the years it sat in Dalton's display. The production was limited and the item had become popular nationally among hobbyists. It often commanded a price double what Dalton had charged Tomkins.

Shortly after selling the engine to Tomkins, Dalton received a letter inquiring if he had such an engine in his inventory and, if so, offering to buy it at a price triple what Dalton had charged Tomkins. The letter explained that this model had sentimental value for the writer, who was seeking to replace one that had been stolen. Therefore, the offer was for an exceptionally high price.

Dalton, who was facing high bills at home from the recent hospitalization of a child, was eager for the extra cash. He attended the public show sponsored by Tomkin's club and he put the engine in his pocket at an opportune moment. He promptly sent it to the letter writer in exchange for the triple price offered.

The theft was not discovered until several days later, after the show was over. With the assistance of some friends who had noticed Dalton's strange behavior at the show, Tomkins successfully traced the theft to Dalton. Dalton now admits all these facts. What remedies does Tomkins have against Dalton?

OLWELL v. NYE & NISSEN CO.

26 Wash.2d 282, 173 P.2d 652 (1946).

MALLERY, JUSTICE.

On May 6, 1940, plaintiff, E.L. Olwell, sold and transferred to the defendant corporation his one-half interest in Puget Sound Egg Packers, a Washington corporation having its principal place of business in Tacoma. By the terms of the agreement, the plaintiff was to retain full ownership in an "Eggsact" egg-washing machine, formerly used by Puget Sound Egg Packers. The defendant promised to make it available for delivery to the plaintiff on or before June 15, 1940. It appears that the plaintiff arranged for and had the machine stored in a space adjacent to the premises occupied by the defendant but not covered by its lease. Due to the scarcity of labor immediately after the outbreak of the war, defendant's treasurer, without the knowledge or consent of the plaintiff, ordered the egg washer taken out of storage. The machine was put into operation by defendant on May 31, 1941, and thereafter, for a period of three years, was used approximately one day a week in the regular course of the defendant's business. Plaintiff first discovered this use in January or February of 1945, when he happened to be at the plant on business and heard the machine operating. Thereupon, plaintiff offered to sell the machine to defendant for $600 or half of its original cost in 1929. A counteroffer of $50 was refused, and, approximately one month later, this action was commenced to recover the reasonable value of defendant's use of the machine, and praying for $25 per month from the commencement of the unauthorized use until the time of trial. * * * The court entered judgment for plaintiff in the amount of $10 per week for the period of 156 weeks covered by the statute of limitations, or $1,560, and gave the plaintiff his costs.

Defendant has appealed to this court, assigning error upon the judgment, upon the trial of the cause on the theory of unjust enrichment, upon the amount of damages, and upon the court's refusal to make a finding as to the value of the machine, and in refusing to consider such value in measuring damages.

The theory of the respondent was that the tort of conversion could be "waived" and suit brought in quasi-contract, upon a contract implied in law, to recover, as restitution, the profits which inured to appellant as a result of its wrongful use of the machine. With this the trial court agreed and, in its findings of facts, found that the use of the machine "resulted in a benefit to the users, in that said use saves the users approximately $1.43 per hour of use as against the expense which would be incurred were eggs to be washed by hand; that said machine was used by Puget Sound Egg Packers and defendant, on an average of one day per week from May of 1941, until February of 1945 at an average saving of $10.00 per each day of use."

In substance, the argument presented by the assignments of error is that the principle of unjust enrichment, or quasi-contract, is not of universal application but is imposed only in exceptional cases because of special facts and circumstances and in favor of particular persons; that respondent had an adequate remedy in an action at law for replevin or claim and delivery; that any damages awarded to the plaintiff should be based upon the use or rental value of the machine and should bear some reasonable relation to its market value. Appellant therefore contends that the amount of the judgment is excessive.

It is uniformly held that in cases where the defendant *tortfeasor* has benefited by his wrong, the plaintiff may elect to "waive the tort" and bring an action in assumpsit for restitution. Such an action arises out of a duty imposed by law devolving upon the defendant to repay an unjust and unmerited enrichment. [Citations.]

It is clear that the saving in labor cost which appellant derived from its use of respondent's machine constituted a benefit.

According to the Restatement of Restitution § 1(b), p. 12,

> A person confers a benefit upon another if he gives to the other possession of or some other interest in money, land, chattels, or choses in action, performs services beneficial to or at the request of the other, satisfies a debt or a duty of the other, or in any way adds to the other's security or advantage. *He confers a benefit not only where he adds to the property of another, but also where he saves the* other from expense or loss. The word "benefit," therefore, denotes any form of advantage. (Italics ours)

It is also necessary to show that, while appellant benefited from its use of the egg-washing machine, respondent thereby incurred a loss. It is argued by appellant that, since the machine was put into storage by respondent, who had no present use for it, and for a period of almost three years did not know that appellant was operating it and since it was not injured by its operation and the appellant never adversely claimed any title to it, nor contested respondent's right of repossession upon the latter's discovery of the wrongful operation, that the respondent was not damaged, because he is as well off as if the machine had not been used by appellant.

The very essence of the nature of property is the right to its exclusive use. Without it, no beneficial right remains. However plausible, the appellant cannot be heard to say that its wrongful invasion of the respondent's property right to exclusive use is not a loss compensable in law. To hold otherwise would be subversive of all property rights, since its use was admittedly wrongful and without claim of right. The theory of unjust enrichment is applicable in such a case.

We agree with appellant that respondent could have elected a "common garden variety of action," as he calls it, for the recovery of damages. It is also true that except where provided for by statute, punitive damages are not allowed, the basic measure for the recovery of damages in this state being compensation. If, then, respondent had been *limited* to redress *in tort* for damages, as appellant contends, the court below would be in error in refusing to make a finding as to the value of the machine. In such case the award of damages must bear a reasonable relation to the value of the property. [Citation.]

But respondent here had an election. He chose rather to waive his right of action *in tort* and to sue *in assumpsit* on the implied contract. Having so elected, he is entitled to the measure of restoration which accompanies the remedy.

Actions for restitution have for their primary purpose taking from the defendant and restoring to the plaintiff something to which the plaintiff is entitled, or if this is not done, causing the defendant to pay the plaintiff an amount which will restore the plaintiff to the position in which he was before the defendant received the benefit. If the value of what was received and what was lost were always equal, there would be no substantial problem as to the amount of recovery, since actions of restitution are not punitive. In fact, however, the plaintiff frequently has lost more than the defendant has gained, and sometimes the defendant has gained more than the plaintiff has lost.

In such cases the measure of restitution is determined with reference to the tortiousness of the defendant's conduct or the negligence or other fault of one or both of the parties in creating the situation giving rise to the right to restitution. If the defendant was tortious in his acquisition of the benefit he is required to pay for what the other has lost although that is more than the recipient benefited. *If he was consciously tortious in acquiring the benefit, he is also deprived of any profit derived from his subsequent dealing with it.* If he was no more at fault than the claimant, he is not required to pay for losses in excess of benefit received by him and he is permitted to retain gains which result from his dealing with the property. (Italics ours) Restatement of Restitution, pp. 595, 596.

Respondent may recover the profit derived by the appellant from the use of the machine.

Respondent has prayed "on his first cause of action for the sum of $25.00 per month from the time defendant first commenced to use said machine subsequent to May 1940 (1941) until present time."

In computing judgment, the court below computed recovery on the basis of $10 per week. This makes the judgment excessive, since it cannot exceed the amount prayed for.

* * *

We therefore direct the trial court to reduce the judgment, based upon the prayer of the complaint, to $25 per month for thirty-six months, or $900.

The judgment as modified is affirmed. Appellant will recover its costs.

D.   CONSTRUCTIVE TRUST

Section Coverage:

A constructive trust is a flexible restitutionary device that imposes an equitable duty on a defendant to convey property acquired under certain circumstances to the rightful owner. Those circumstances include acquisition of title to property by fraud, various other wrongdoings, and mistake. Since the remedy of constructive trust is equitable in nature, the court must inquire into the adequacy of available legal remedies to provide redress for the claimant's injury.

The "trust" designation is merely a fictional relationship created by operation of law on the grounds that the constructive trustee would be unjustly enriched if allowed to retain the property. A constructive trust has little in common with an express trust, which is created by the intention of the parties. The only similarity between them is that the trustee holds title to property subject to an equitable duty to hold it for or convey it to the holder of the beneficial interest. Their difference lies in the designation and relationship of the trustee. The trustee for an express trust is appointed pursuant to the intent of the parties and acts in a fiduciary role. The constructive trustee is designated by the court in order to recover the enrichment held by the wrongdoer.

A constructive trust must be distinguished from a resulting trust which may be implied from the facts surrounding a transfer of property. When a transferor of property does not intend the transferee to hold a beneficial interest in the property, the recipient may hold it in trust for the proper beneficiary even in the absence of an express trust. In contrast, a constructive trust is created without reference to the intention of the parties; it is created to meet the goal of preventing unjust enrichment.

Model Case:

A lawyer, Leslie Roberts, held an account on behalf of a client named Carter. One day Roberts hears a "hot tip" on a stock and wishes to purchase some immediately. Lacking any personal funds that were readily available for the transaction, Roberts embezzled $10,000 from the account with the intent of restoring the funds before Carter needed them. The embezzled money was used to purchase stock in Highflyer Corp., which increased in price to a current market value of $14,000. As a result of other poor investments, however, Roberts is now insolvent and the embezzlement is discovered before it could be covered up.

The court would impose a constructive trust on the stock for the benefit of Carter on the grounds that Roberts had abused the fiduciary relationship. Assuming that Carter could trace the misappropriated funds to the stock, a court would require Roberts to disgorge the profits made on the stock purchase in order to prevent unjust enrichment.

Roberts' insolvency affects the case in two ways. First, it makes a damages remedy at law inadequate, although the inadequacy rule has little force in restitution. Second, it means that Carter will have priority over Roberts' other creditors and will receive more than the loss to the account because the good asset is traceable to Carter's funds.

COUNTY OF COOK v. BARRETT

36 Ill.App.3d 623, 344 N.E.2d 540 (1975).

DEMPSEY, JUSTICE.

This is an appeal from the dismissal of the plaintiff's amended complaint for failure to state a cause of action.

The County of Cook filed a complaint and an amended complaint in chancery against former County Clerk, Edward J. Barrett, seeking the declaration of a constructive trust and an accounting for bribes allegedly received by him while he held office. * * *

The amended complaint was composed of three counts. The County represented that Barrett served as the elected Clerk of Cook County from 1956 through 1970, a position of trust imposing obligations to faithfully perform the duties of office in the interest of the people of Cook County and not for the incumbent's personal gain. His salary for the position was fixed by law and was to be his "only compensation for services rendered in the capacity of county clerk, or any other capacity." Ill.Rev.Stat., 1969, ch. 53, par. 49. Throughout the period of Barrett's tenure, the County Board of Commissioners at various times purchased and rented voting machines for use in elections. The board acted on the basis of contracts and proposals submitted and recommended by Barrett. By virtue of his office and influence with the board, his recommendations were "tantamount to the acceptance" of the proposals tendered by him. During this same time, he was also charged with the responsibility to care for voting machines in County custody which included the discretion to award contracts of insurance on the machines.

Count I charged that Barrett abused his position of trust by employing it to seek secret personal gains from the Shoup Voting Machine Corporation, in that he caused Shoup " . . . to secretly pay him money that constituted fees and/or allowances and/or bribes," as a consequence of which the County paid considerably more money for the voting machines purchased and rented from Shoup than it would have otherwise. It was alleged that these payments from Shoup to Barrett amounted to approximately $180,000 for the years 1967–1970 but were unknown for previous years and a detailed accounting was needed to determine the exact figure for the entire period covered by the complaint. The plaintiff prayed that Barrett be declared a constructive trustee for the citizens and taxpayers of the County for the amounts received by him from Shoup, and that he be required to account to the County for those sums.

* * *

Both in that motion [to dismiss] and in his brief on appeal, Barrett has suggested numerous reasons why the County cannot recover from him. He contends that the County is entitled only to fees and allowances which are legally collected, that to allow recovery by a public body of bribes or kickbacks paid to its officers would be against public policy; that the County alleged no damage and suffered none, that no money moved from the County to him, that if any money was paid it was paid by Shoup and Gallagher not by the County, and that since no money moved out of the County treasury it could not have been depleted; that the complaint did not allege that he had been unjustly enriched at the expense of the County or that in the absence of bribery the County would have paid less for voting machines or insurance. Attacking the equitable jurisdiction generally, he suggests that the facts alleged in the amended complaint did not warrant the grant of equitable relief and that there was an adequate remedy at law. Attacking the constructive trust doctrine specifically he contends that its application to one in his position would be unwarranted and unprecedented. * * *

A constructive trust arises not by any agreement or understanding of the parties but by operation of law and is imposed upon grounds of public policy, to prevent a person from holding for his own benefit that which he has gained by reason of a special trust or confidence reposed in him by an innocent party. [Citation.] Stated most succinctly, the purpose of the remedy is to prevent unjust enrichment. [Citation.]

The particular circumstances in which equity will impress a constructive trust are " . . . as numberless as the modes by which property may be obtained through bad faith and unconscientious acts." 4 Pomeroy's Equity Jurisprudence (5th Ed.) sec. 1045, p. 97. The barriers to its effective operation are few. The form of the property claim determines nothing, since a constructive trust will extend to reach real and personal property, choses in action and funds of money. To make out a case a plaintiff must allege facts which disclose either actual or constructive fraud or an abuse of a confidential relationship. It is the latter situation with which this case is concerned.

At all times and for all the transactions pertinent to the complaint Barrett was the fiduciary of the people of Cook County. As an elected public official he held a position of the highest public trust. [Citations.] In the transactions with Shoup and Gallagher, Barrett acted as the County's agent, negotiating terms of purchase and recommending County action. An agent is fiduciary to his principal and the relation is treated generally the same, and with virtually the same strictness, as that of trustee and beneficiary. [Citations.]

In deciding this appeal, it is not necessary to locate the perimeters of the fiduciary obligations due the public from their elected officials. It is sufficient to recognize that, when such an official acts as agent for the public body in business transactions, he owes to his principal duties of loyalty and good faith at least equal to those required of a private fiduciary in like circumstances. [Citations.] The obligations of a person who occupies the latter category are such that he must not place himself in a position which is adverse to that of his principal during the continuance of the agency. [Citations.]

> ... [A]n agent should not unite his personal and his representative characters in the same transaction; and equity will not permit him to be exposed to the temptation, or brought into a situation where his own personal interests conflict with the interests of his principal and with the duties which he owes to his principal. 3 Pomeroy's Equity Jurisprudence (5th Ed.) sec. 959, p. 819.

The remedy for breach of this duty is simple and salutary. Since a fiduciary is bound to act solely for the benefit of his principal, equity will intervene to prevent him from accruing any advantage—however innocently—from transactions conducted in behalf of the principal. So, when a fiduciary, who has acted for his beneficiary or principal, receives a gift, or bonus or commission from a party with whom he has transacted business, that benefit may be recovered from him by the beneficiary of the fiduciary relationship. In Janes v. First Fed. Sav. & Loan Ass'n [57 Ill.2d 398, 312 N.E.2d 605 (1974)], it was alleged that the defendant lending bank procured title insurance for its borrower on mortgaged property and charged the borrower the full price of that insurance, but subsequently received and retained a ten per cent rebate from the title insurance company. The reviewing court ruled that under such facts the bank held the rebate upon a constructive trust from the borrower as beneficiary in the absence of the borrower's express contrary authorization. * * *

In related contentions contained in both his pleadings and brief, Barrett assails the County's complaint for its failure to allege damage. He states that the averments that the County paid excess sums because of his misfeasance are speculative and that there was no averment that he was unjustly enriched at the County's expense. The absence of an allegation of damage is immaterial. A constructive trust is not an action for "recovery" or compensation under any theory of contract or tort. It is a strict equitable doctrine applied to cure a fiduciary's breach of his duty of loyalty by erasing the source of his conflict of interest, and transferring it to the innocent beneficiary. Bad faith is not an essential element of disloyalty and good faith is no defense to the charge. Courts are not interested in a fiduciary's particular motive for accepting a payment or gift, but rather with the general effect of such payments or gifts. Nor are courts concerned with the question of actual damage to the beneficiary. * * *

The defendant argues that since the County seeks only a money judgment and the accounts are not complicated and discovery is unnecessary, it would be improper for chancery to exercise jurisdiction over this controversy and thus deprive him of his constitutional right to a jury trial. This argument minimizes the underlying reason for equity jurisdiction—the trust aspect of the controversy.

The County seeks, first and foremost, a declaration of the people's beneficial interest in and the right to possess the secret profits accrued by Barrett in breach of his fiduciary duty of loyalty. The recognition, execution and control of a trust or equitable interest is a matter exclusively within the jurisdiction of equity. [Citations.] As Barrett himself has argued, the County had no claim at law on money which came to him from third persons as bribes. Nor can Shoup and Gallagher claim these funds. The very conception of an equitable interest requires the simultaneous existence of two estates or ownerships in the same subject matter, the one legal, vested in one person, and recognized by a court of law, the second equitable, in another person, and recognized by a court of equity. Under the circumstances alleged in this case, only equity, applying this doctrine of the divisibility of legal and beneficial ownership, is capable of doing substantial justice between the parties.

When chancery exercises its exclusive jurisdiction to declare the County's equitable interest, it must then afford, as an incident, the complete remedy obtainable through an accounting. Where equity has jurisdiction for the purpose of granting equitable relief, the court may determine all issues of the case, whether legal or equitable. * * *

Reversed and remanded.

McGLOON, PRESIDING JUSTICE (specially concurring):

I concur with the decision of the court to reverse the order of the Circuit Court of Cook County and remand the cause, but would make the following observations.

The majority believes that defendant may be proven to have been a fiduciary of the people of Cook County from the allegations in the complaint that he was an elected public official and the County's agent in its dealings with Shoup and Gallagher. The fact that defendant may have been an elected official is, in my opinion, not crucial to our decision.

The determinative factor is whether the particular facts alleged in the complaint could be proven to show that defendant was a fiduciary.

A fiduciary relationship may be created in many ways; an agency is but one relationship which creates fiduciary duties. The usual test for determining the existence of a fiduciary relationship is whether "confidence is reposed on one side and there is a resulting superiority and influence on the other side. It is not sufficient that confidence be reposed by one party, but the confidence must be actually accepted by the other party in order to constitute a fiduciary relationship." [Citation.] Whether such a relationship exists between the parties depends upon all the facts and circumstances of a particular case. * * *

In my opinion, the complaint contains allegations which may be proven to show that the County Board reposed its confidence in Barrett with regard to the voting machines and insurance contracts, and that Barrett accepted the confidence, thus creating a fiduciary relationship. It would not matter whether Barrett were an elected public official, a public employee, or a private person who had the confidence of the County Board in these matters. The relationship which if abused gives rise to an action for the declaration of a constructive trust involves a confidence reposed and accepted, as herein alleged. At trial upon remand, plaintiff would have to prove that Barrett had the confidence of the County Board, as opposed to being a person who merely made recommendations which may or may not have been followed as the Board saw fit.

The majority believes that every county official has a fiduciary relationship with the county, citing *People v. Bordeaux*, (1909) 242 Ill. 327, 89 N.E. 971. Such a conclusion is warranted, but with the caveat that the relationship exists only when the official performs his statutory duties. * * *

---

1. A primary advantage to the constructive trust remedy is that the rightful owner may compel conveyance of the property in specie. Therefore, by obtaining specific enforcement of the trust, the beneficiary will effectively have a first priority position over other creditors of the defendant. The equitable interest will prevail except against bona fide purchasers for value. Since the device is equitable though, it remains discretionary with the court and may be denied if an adequate remedy at law exists. If the constructive trustee is insolvent, then a money judgment would be an ineffective remedy for the beneficiary and a court would specifically enforce the constructive trust.

2. A second benefit to using a constructive trust is that the beneficiary's equitable interest will be effective to obtain specific restitution of property which has been transferred to a third party who is not a bona fide purchaser. Moreover, if the beneficiary can trace the disposition or exchange of the property, the court will impose a constructive

trust against the property's product in the hands of the defendant. In that regard, unlike an equitable lien which operates as a charge or encumbrance against property in a designated amount, the constructive trust may encompass any increase in value or profits made by the property held by the defendant.

3. Justice Cardozo once described a constructive trust as "the remedial device through which preference of self is made subordinate to loyalty to others." Meinhard v. Salmon, 249 N.Y. 458, 164 N.E. 545 (1928).

STAUFFER v. STAUFFER

465 Pa. 558, 351 A.2d 236 (1976).

EAGEN, JUSTICE.

On April 23, 1970, appellee Donald G. Stauffer joined with his wife, appellant Theresa E. Stauffer, in conveying to appellant alone for the stated consideration of one dollar the land and residence which both owned and had been occupying as tenants by the entireties. Subsequently, he brought this action in equity in the Court of Common Pleas of Chester County to compel a reconveyance. After a trial, the chancellor made his adjudication and entered a decree nisi in favor of Mr. Stauffer which granted the relief sought; on November 29, 1974, the court *en banc* dismissed the exceptions of Mrs. Stauffer and made the decree final. This direct appeal followed.

The record discloses that the parties were married on October 17, 1953, and that they became the owners of the land in question by means of a gift from Mrs. Stauffer's parents on August 3, 1956; their house was subsequently built and paid for primarily, if not entirely, out of the earnings of Mr. Stauffer. Toward the end of March, 1970, Mrs. Stauffer became suspicious that her husband had become involved with another woman, and on March 26 she consulted an attorney for advice about her domestic situation. Shortly thereafter, she confronted her husband with her suspicions, and he admitted to her not only that he had been engaged in an adulterous relationship, but that the "other woman" was Mrs. Stauffer's own sister, Victoria Gavin. Subsequently, Edward Gavin, the husband of Victoria, came to the Stauffer home, and in the presence of Mrs. Stauffer and Mr. Gavin, Mr. Stauffer wrote out a "confession" in which he detailed his involvement with Mrs. Gavin.

* * * [T]he chancellor concluded that appellant held what had been her husband's share in the property as constructive trustee for him because "the transfer of Plaintiff's interest in real property jointly held was fraudulently induced by threats and misrepresentations of the Defendant," and that "Plaintiff is entitled to a reconveyance of his interest in the real property." * * *

Although we have held that ordinarily, when a husband transfers property to his wife, a presumption arises that a gift was intended, such a presumption is, of course, rebuttable, and here the chancellor found that there was sufficient credible evidence to establish a constructive trust rather than a gift. [Citation.] The imposition of a constructive trust, unlike the finding of an express or a resulting trust, does not require that the parties specifically intended to create a trust; it is an equitable remedy designed to prevent unjust enrichment. [Citations.] There is thus no rigid standard for determining whether the facts of a particular case require a court of equity to impose a constructive trust; the test is whether or not unjust enrichment can thereby be avoided. This Court has repeatedly cited with approval the oft-quoted language of Justice (then Judge) Cardozo in Beatty v. Guggenheim Exploration Co., 225 N.Y. 380, 386, 122 N.E. 378, 380–81 (1919):

> A constructive trust is the formula through which the conscience of equity finds expression. When property has been acquired in such circumstances that the holder of the legal title may not in good conscience retain the beneficial interest equity converts him into a trustee.... A court of equity in decreeing a constructive trust is bound by no unyielding formula. The equity of the transaction must shape the measure of relief. [Citations.]

Appellant strenuously argues that in this case no confidential relationship existed between the parties at the time of the transaction, and that therefore there can be no constructive trust; she cites Foster v. Schmitt, 429 Pa. 102, 107, 239 A.2d 471 (1968), for the proposition that a confidential relationship requires that the transferee occupy toward the transferor "such a position of advisor or counselor as reasonably to inspire confidence that he will act in good faith for the other's interest" and maintains that this was not the situation here. Appellant is mistaken, however, in assuming both that the chancellor found a confidential relationship in this case and that he needed to do so in order to impose a constructive trust.

The chancellor's determination was based not on the abuse of a confidential relationship, but on his conclusion that the transfer was "fraudulently induced by threats and misrepresentations of the Defendant." It is well-established that "[w]here the owner of property transfers it, being induced by fraud, duress or undue influence of the transferee, the transferee holds the property upon a constructive trust for the transferor," Restatement of Restitution § 166 (1937), and that where the transfer is so induced, a constructive trust will be imposed without proof of a confidential relationship. [Citations.] Whether or not a confidential relationship exists in a given case is usually a question of fact to be determined by no inflexible rule but by a weighing of the particular factors present in that case. The mere finding of such a relationship does not in itself cause a constructive trust to be imposed; its effect is simply to impose a burden upon the party benefiting from the transaction of proving that he took no unfair advantage of his relationship with the other. By the same token, absent a finding of confidential relationship, the complaining party may still prove unjust enrichment. [Citation.]

But although the chancellor's conclusion in this case did not depend upon a finding of confidential relationship, we must still examine the actual relationship between the parties to determine whether or not the requisite unjust enrichment was present. In doing so, we must focus on the relationship between the parties at the time of the transaction in question. [Citation.] Therefore, although it is a pertinent factor, it is not necessarily a controlling one that the chancellor found "at all times during their marriage, the Plaintiff had made many important financial decisions, upon which the Defendant relied." Mr. Stauffer's decision to turn over to his wife, without meaningful consideration, his share of what the record indicates as by far his largest asset, was not an ordinary "important financial decision" and can only be interpreted in relation to the unique situation in which he found himself at that time. Furthermore, even if the relationship between the parties was not the sort in which our courts have traditionally found a confidential relationship sufficient to shift the burden of proof, we do not have to regard the transaction as merely an arm's-length one. Human relationships are frequently too complex to be classified simply as either "confidential" or "arm's-length," a relationship can have elements of confidentiality without being strictly a "confidential relationship," and less diligence is required of a plaintiff who relies to his detriment on the closeness of his relationship to the defendant than of one who deals on a genuinely arm's-length basis. [Citations.]

The record in this case indicates that when Mrs. Stauffer first became suspicious and later learned of her husband's adultery, her confidence in him was understandably severely undermined, and that her visits to a lawyer during this period were to obtain advice not only about the possibility of straightening out her marital difficulties, but also about securing her rights and those of her children in the event of a separation. We can also infer that she was particularly distressed that the woman her husband had become involved with was her own sister. Yet the chancellor, with sufficient basis in the record, found that up to the time of the conveyance the parties "continued to live together and carry on marital relations" and that at the time of the conveyance "the prevailing mood was that the Plaintiff and Defendant would continue to live together."

As for Mr. Stauffer, the record clearly suggests, whether or not he had formerly been the dominant party in the relationship, that after the discovery of his adultery he was not. His writing out a confession in the presence of his wife and Mr. Gavin suggests a sense of guilt, if not contrition. According to his testimony, his eventual decision to convey the property at his wife's urging came after she had repeatedly told him of her fears of the dire consequences of Mr. Gavin's purported lawsuit, and immediately after "a prolonged hysterical outburst" during which she first drove the family car so recklessly that he pulled the keys out of the ignition in fear and she later drove wildly away from her husband and her father after rejecting her husband's suggestion, agreed to by her father, that the property be conveyed not to her but to the children. He further testified that his only reason for yielding to his wife's urging about the property was the fear, induced by her, of the lawsuit, together with his impression that by agreeing to the transfer, he would "save the house for all of us, the family; not just for my wife and the children, for all of us as a family."

* * * Despite his own prior unfaithfulness, we cannot say that such faith was either implausible or unreasonable, given that his wife had always acted in good faith toward him in the past, he had confessed and terminated his adulterous affair, and—according both to his testimony and the chancellor's finding—the mood at the time of the conveyance was that husband and wife would continue to live together. * * * We cannot therefore find that the conveyance was an arm's-length transaction. * * *

It remains to be determined, nevertheless, whether or not the chancellor erred in his conclusion that Mrs. Stauffer took unfair advantage of Mr. Stauffer and fraudulently obtained his share of the property by means of threats and misrepresentations. * * * The chancellor based his ultimate conclusion of misrepresentation on the contract between the apparently ongoing marital relationship he found before the conveyance and the "total abatement" of the relationship on the part of Mrs. Stauffer that followed shortly after it:

> Immediately after the transfer of April 23, 1970, the Defendant effected a total abatement of family atmosphere toward the Plaintiff in the household, ceased sexual relations with the Plaintiff and moved out of the bedroom. Admittedly, the Plaintiff and Defendant were in the midst of a domestic problem as evidenced by the confession of his adulterous relationship with the Defendant's sister, but this Court is swayed by the severe contrast in Defendant's behavior immediately after the transfer, the "hysterical outbursts" immediately prior to the transfer, and the constant conversation concerning the threat of a lawsuit by Mr. Gavin. These factors lead us to the belief that the Defendant sought to secure complete interest in the property for herself and the Chancellor is satisfied that the means employed to obtain such an interest amounted to such undue influence through misrepresentations and threats as to grant the Plaintiff a reconveyance of his interest in the real property.

It is clear that a fraudulent intention at the time of a transaction can be inferred from the totality of the circumstances surrounding the transaction, including subsequent conduct on the part of the defendant. [Citations.] We cannot, therefore, find that the evidence was insufficient to support the chancellor's conclusion in this case.

Appellant further contends that, regardless of whether the imposition of a constructive trust would ordinarily have been justified, appellee should have been barred from affirmative relief because, as a result both of his attempted fraudulent conveyance and of his adultery, he did not come into a court of equity with clean hands. The clean hands doctrine, however, does not require that a plaintiff be denied equitable relief merely because his conduct has been shown not to have been blameless. The bar of unclean hands is applicable in Pennsylvania only where the wrongdoing of the plaintiff directly affects the equitable relationship subsisting between the parties and is directly connected with the matter in controversy. [The court found that the chancellor had not abused his discretion in declining to apply the clean hands doctrine.]

As for Mr. Stauffer's adulterous relationship with Mrs. Gavin, it is clear that it directly affected the equitable relationship between the parties, but the question remains whether or not it was directly connected with the subject matter in controversy. Certainly there can be not doubt that the transaction in question would not have occurred had there been no adultery, and we therefore cannot say that it was merely collaterally or indirectly connected with it. [Citations.] Nevertheless, we cannot find on the facts of this case that the chancellor abused his discretion in declining to bar appellee from affirmative relief.

This Court has stated that "[e]quity will not stand aside a plaintiff whose rights have been transgressed and permit them to be appropriated because of previous bad conduct, and if the plaintiff offers reparation for what he has done, he may be granted relief, contingent upon repairing the injury he has inflicted." [Citation.] It may well be that the injury appellee has done to his wife and to his marriage is indeed irreparable, yet the record indicates that after the discovery of his adultery he has acted in good faith toward appellant. After confessing and terminating the adulterous relationship, he made the conveyance in question, according to appellant's own pleadings and testimony, for the purpose of securing his wife and children from the consequences of his prior conduct. The record also shows that after the conveyance he continued to make the mortgage payments due on the property. As for his wife, according to the chancellor's findings, after she learned of the adultery, she continued to live with him and maintain a marital relationship until the time of the transfer in issue. The chancellor here found that appellant fraudulently induced appellee to make the transfer after she learned of the adultery and while she continued to live with him as his wife. It would be inequitable to permit her to be unjustly enriched because of his previous adulterous conduct.

The decree is affirmed.

———

1. Some cases have restricted the use of the constructive trust by imposing the following requirements: (1) a confidential or fiduciary relation, (2) a promise, (3) a transfer of legal title to property in reliance on the promise, and (4) unjust enrichment of the transferee. *See, e.g.,* Sharp v. Kosmalski, 40 N.Y.2d 119, 351 N.E.2d 721, 386 N.Y.S.2d 72 (1976). Other courts have used the constructive trust in cases not involving a breach of fiduciary relations. In addition to the principal

case, *see, e.g.,* American Nat'l Bank v. Fed. Dep't Ins. Corp., 710 F.2d 1528 (11th Cir.1983).

2. The constructive trust is a useful device for effecting the transfer of property interests which would be unjust for the fictional trustee to retain. The remedy should not operate to deprive the defendant of property lawfully acquired. In *Ford v. Long,* 713 S.W.2d 798 (Tex.App. 1986), for example, the husband killed his wife and was convicted of murder. The wife's will named her sister, Long, as the sole beneficiary of her estate. The sister sued for partition of certain property which had been jointly owned by the husband and wife. Ford defended by claiming homestead rights, as sole survivor of the community property, in a tract of land. The court imposed a constructive trust for Long as beneficiary on the portion of the property which Ford stood to gain by virtue of the state survivorship laws. The court did not, however, divest Ford of the portion of the tract he previously owned because that interest was neither acquired nor benefitted by the unlawful act.

3. In Snepp v. United States, 444 U.S. 507, 100 S.Ct. 763, 62 L.Ed.2d 704 (1980), the Court examined whether to impose a constructive trust on profits of a book published by a former CIA agent. The agent, Snepp, based the book on his experiences with the CIA in South Vietnam. He had published the book without submitting the manuscript to the Agency for prepublication review, as required by the terms of employment with the Agency. The government brought suit to enforce Snepp's agreement, seeking among other remedies, to impose a constructive trust for the government's benefit on all profits that Snepp might earn from publishing the book in violation of his fiduciary obligations to the Agency. Although the government conceded that the book divulged no classified intelligence information, the Court observed that without the remedy of a constructive trust the government would have "no reliable deterrent against similar breaches of security." 444 U.S. at 514. Consequently, the Court reversed and remanded the case to reinstate the full judgment of the District Court which included imposition of a constructive trust. The Court stated:

> Snepp's employment with the CIA involved an extremely high degree of trust. * * * [H]e exposed the classified information with which he had been entrusted to the risk of disclosure.
>
> A constructive trust * * * protects both the Government and the former agent from unwarranted risks. This remedy is the natural and customary consequence of a breach of trust. It deals fairly with both parties by conforming relief to the dimensions of the wrong. If the agent secures prepublication clearance, he can publish with no fear of liability. If the agent publishes unreviewed material in violation of his fiduciary and contractual obligation, the trust remedy simply requires him to disgorge the benefits of his faithlessness. Since the remedy is swift and sure, it is tailored to deter those who would place sensitive information at risk. And since the remedy reaches only funds attributable to the breach, it cannot saddle the

former agent with exemplary damages out of all proportion to his gain. The decision of the Court of Appeals would deprive the Government of this equitable and effective means of protecting intelligence that may contribute to national security.

Id. at 510–516.

Since the government conceded that the book contained no classified material, was the government's interest in confidentiality compromised by the agent's failure to obtain prepublication clearance? Assuming that Snepp breached a *contractual* duty, not a fiduciary obligation, was the majority correct in imposing a constructive trust? What advantages does a constructive trust hold for the government in contrast to damages for breach of contract?

SIMONDS v. SIMONDS

45 N.Y.2d 233, 380 N.E.2d 189, 408 N.Y.S.2d 359 (1978).

BREITEL, CHIEF JUDGE.

[In 1960 the plaintiff, Mary Simonds, entered into a separation agreement which required her husband, Frederick Simonds, to maintain in effect $7,000 of life insurance policies on his life with plaintiff as the named beneficiary. The agreement further required Frederick to obtain equivalent replacement insurance in the event that the existing policies lapsed or were cancelled. Frederick subsequently remarried, the life insurance policies lapsed, and he acquired several other policies totaling over $55,000 which designated either his second wife or his daughter as beneficiaries.

At the time of his death in 1971 he did not own any life insurance which designated plaintiff as beneficiary, and his estate was insolvent. Plaintiff brought an action against the second wife and daughter seeking to impose a constructive trust on the insurance proceeds to the extent of $7,000. The trial court granted partial summary judgment and imposed a constructive trust on $7,000 of the proceeds paid to the second wife. The appellate division affirmed.] * * *

There is no question that decedent breached his obligation to maintain life insurance with his first wife as beneficiary. Consequently, the first wife would of course be entitled to maintain an action for breach against the estate. The estate's insolvency, however, would make such an action fruitless. Thus, the controversy revolves around plaintiff's right, in equity, to recover $7,000 of the insurance proceeds.

Born out of the extreme rigidity of the early common law, equity in its origins drew heavily on Roman law, where equitable notions had long been accepted (*see* 1 Pomeroy, Equity Jurisprudence [5th ed.], §§ 2–29). "Its great underlying principles, which are the constant sources, the neverfailing roots, of its particular rules, are unquestionably principles of right, justice, and morality, so far as the same can become the elements of a positive human jurisprudence." Law without principle is not law;

law without justice is of limited value. Since adherence to principles of "law" does not invariably produce justice, equity is necessary. [Citation.] Equity arose to soften the impact of legal formalisms; to evolve formalisms narrowing the broad scope of equity is to defeat its essential purpose.

Whatever the legal rights between insurer and insured, the separation agreement vested in the first wife an equitable interest in the insurance policies then in force. An agreement for sufficient consideration, including a separation agreement, to maintain a claimant as a beneficiary of a life insurance policy vests in the claimant an equitable interest in the policies designated. [Citations.] This interest is superior to that of a named beneficiary who has given no consideration, notwithstanding policy provisions permitting the insured to change the designated beneficiary freely.

* * * [T]he policies now at issue are not the same policies in existence at the time of the separation agreement. But it has been held that mere substitution of policies, or even substitution of insurance companies, does not defeat the equitable interest of one who has given sufficient consideration for a promise to be maintained as beneficiary under an insurance policy. [Citations.] The persistence of the promisee's equitable interest is all the more evident where the agreement expressly provides for a change in policies, and in effect provides further that the promisee's right shall attach to the new policies.

For a certainty, the first wife's equitable interest would be easier to trace if the new policies were quid pro quo replacements for the original policies. The record does not reveal whether this was so. But inability to trace plaintiff's equitable rights precisely should not require that they not be recognized, much as in the instance of damages difficult to prove. [Citations.] The separation agreement provides nexus between plaintiff's rights and the later acquired policies. The later policies were expressly contemplated by the parties, and it was agreed that plaintiff would have an interest in them. No reason in equity appears for denying plaintiff that interest, so long as no one who has given value for the policies or otherwise suffered a detriment is involved. The second wife's innocence does not offset the wrong by the now deceased husband.

The conclusion is an application of the general rule that equity regards as done that which should have been done. [Citations.] Thus, if an insured, upon lapse or cancellation of insurance, followed by replacement with new insurance, has a contractual obligation to designate a particular person as beneficiary, equity will consider the obligee as a beneficiary.

In this case, then, the first wife's interest in the original policies extended as well to the later acquired policies. The husband, upon lapse or cancellation of the earlier policies, had by virtue of the separation agreement an obligation to name her as beneficiary on the later policies, an obligation enforceable in equity despite the husband's failure to comply with the terms of the separation agreement. Due to the husband's failure to do what he should have done, the first wife acquired not only a right at law to sue his estate for breach of contract, a right now worthless, but also an equitable right in the policies, a right which, upon the husband's death, attached to the proceeds. [Citations.]

And, since the first wife was entitled to $7,000 of the insurance proceeds at the time of the husband's death, she is no less entitled because the proceeds have already been converted by being paid, erroneously, to the named beneficiaries. [Citations.] Her remedy is imposition of a constructive trust.

In the words of Judge Cardozo, "[a] constructive trust is the formula through which the conscience of equity finds expression. When property has been acquired in such circumstances that the holder of the legal title may not in good conscience retain the beneficial interest, equity converts him into a trustee." [Citation.] Thus, a constructive trust is an equitable remedy. It is perhaps more different from an express trust than it is similar. [Citation.] As put so well by Scott and restated at the Appellate Division, "[the constructive trustee] is not compelled to convey the property because he is a constructive trustee; it is because he can be compelled to convey it that he is a constructive trustee".

More precise definitions of a constructive trust have been termed inadequate because of the failure to recognize the broad scope of constructive trust doctrine. As another leading scholar has said of constructive trusts, "[t]he Court does not restrict itself by describing all the specific forms of inequitable holding which will move it to grant relief, but rather reserves freedom to apply this remedy to whatever knavery human ingenuity can invent." [Citation.]

* * * [T]the purpose of the constructive trust is prevention of unjust enrichment. [Citations.]

Unjust enrichment, however, does not require the performance of any wrongful act by the one enriched. [Citations.] Innocent parties may frequently be unjustly enriched. What is required, generally, is that a party hold property "under such circumstances that in equity and good conscience he ought not to retain it." [Citations.] A bona fide purchaser of property upon which a constructive trust would otherwise be imposed takes free of the constructive trust, but a gratuitous donee, however innocent, does not. [Citations.]

The unjust enrichment in this case is manifest. At a time when decedent was, certainly, anxious to remarry, he entered into a separation agreement with his wife of 14 years. As part of the agreement, he promised to maintain $7,000 in life insurance with the first wife as beneficiary. Later he broke his promise, and died with insurance policies naming only the second wife and daughter as beneficiaries. They have collected the proceeds, amounting to more than $55,000, while the first wife has collected nothing. Had the husband kept his promise, the beneficiaries would have collected $7,000 less in proceeds.

To that extent, the beneficiaries have been unjustly enriched, and the proceeds should be subjected to a constructive trust.

[Affirmed].

---

1. The inadequacy rule, examined in Chapter 3, *supra,* restricts the grant of equitable remedies to cases where the legal remedy is inadequate. It is sometimes applied to deny a constructive trust, although courts usually do not discuss the rule in restitution cases. One recent example of its application is in Hughes Tool Co. v. Fawcett Publications, Inc., 297 A.2d 428 (Del.Ch.1972), *rev'd on other grounds*, 315 A.2d 577 (Del.1974), *aff'd* 350 A.2d 341 (Del.1975). In that case, the plaintiff corporation brought suit against the author and publisher of a book, "Howard, The Amazing Mr. Hughes." The complaint sought an accounting for profits and a constructive trust. It alleged that the defendant's publication was an infringement on literary property in violation of a confidentiality agreement between the plaintiff's sole shareholder and the corporation. The court denied equitable relief by finding that the action was essentially a request for damages "camouflaged" by the prayer for an accounting and constructive trust.

2. Another recent example is in Gilbert v. Meyer, 362 F.Supp. 168 (S.D.N.Y.1973). In that case the court held that a plaintiff requesting an accounting and the imposition of a constructive trust for violation of breach of fiduciary duties under the federal securities laws had an adequate remedy of money damages. Consequently, the claim was governed by a six year statute of limitation rather than a ten year limitations period governing equity actions. The court did not take equity jurisdiction and the legal claim was time-barred.

3. Where the wrongdoer is insolvent, has breached a fiduciary relationship, or has parted with misappropriated property, courts routinely find the legal remedies to be inadequate. Similarly, a constructive trust is available to recover unique property wrongfully withheld.

What if misappropriated chattel is not unique? Should the remedy be an action at law for conversion or a constructive trust? *See* Restatement of Restitution § 160 comment e.

4. In any case where equity takes jurisdiction, the parties' right to a jury trial is affected. *See* Kuhlman v. Cargile, 200 Neb. 150, 262 N.W.2d 454 (1978); *Dick v. Dick*, 167 Conn. 210, 355 A.2d 110 (1974). *See generally* Devlin, Jury Trial of Complex Cases, English Practice at the Time of the Seventh Amendment, 80 Colum.L.Rev. 43 (1980).

5. A particularly vexing but often overlooked problem involves selecting the proper statute of limitations to claims seeking a constructive trust. Since state statutes often do not expressly cover constructive trusts, courts have tended to borrow the limitation period governing the underlying substantive claim of fraud, contract, or mistake. That limitation period then is incorporated into the doctrine of laches or is applied directly.

This approach has caused difficulties. In addition to problems with characterizing the substantive claim, complications develop when the defendant's conduct gives rise to multiple substantive claims with varying limitation periods. In that event, the court must choose which statute of limitations best effectuates the restitutionary goal of preventing unjust enrichment yet satisfies the fairness and evidentiary concerns of the defendant. *See generally* McSwain, Limitations Statutes and the Constructive Trust in Texas, 41 Baylor L.Rev. 429 (1989); Eichengrun, The Statute of Limitations For Constructive Trusts in North Carolina; Note, Developments in the Law—Statutes of Limitations, 63 Harv.L.Rev. 1177 (1950); Dawson, Mistake and Statutes of Limitations, 31 Mich. L.Rev. 591 (1933).

6. For additional commentary on constructive trusts see the following references: Fox, Constructive Trusts in a Company Setting, 1986 J.Bus.L. 23; Frankel, Fiduciary Law, 71 Calif.L.Rev. 795 (1983); Jones, The Recovery of Benefits Gained from a Breach of Contract, 99 L.Q.Rev. 443 (1983); McClean, Constructive and Resulting Trusts—Unjust Enrichment in a Common Law Relationship, 16 B.C.L.Rev. 155 (1982); Friedman, Restitution of Benefits Obtained through the Appropriation of Property or the Commission of a Wrong, 80 Colum.L.Rev. 504 (1980); Gegan, Constructive Trusts: A New Basis for Tracing Equities, 53 St. John's L.Rev. 593 (1979); Wade, The Literature of the Law of Restitution, 19 Hastings L.J. 1087 (1968); Monaghan, Constructive Trust and Equitable Lien: Status of the Conscious and the Innocent Wrongdoer in Equity, 38 U.Det.L.Rev. 10 (1960); Scott, Constructive Trusts, 71 L.Q.Rev. 3, 38 (1955); Lenhoff, The Constructive Trust as a Remedy for Corruption in Public Offices, 54 Colum.L.Rev. 214 (1954); Scott, The Fiduciary Principle, 37 Calif.L.Rev. 539 (1949); Scott, The Trustee's Duty of Loyalty, 49 Harv.L.Rev. 521 (1936); Vanneman, The Constructive Trust: A Neglected Remedy in Ohio, 10 U.Cin.L.Rev. 366 (1936); Pound, The Progress of the Law, 1918–19 Equity, 33 Harv.L.Rev. 420 (1920); Costigan, The Classification of Trusts as Express, Resulting, and Constructive, 27 Harv.L.Rev. 437 (1914); Ames, Following Misappropriated Property into Its Product, 19 Harv.L.Rev. 511 (1906).

E.   EQUITABLE LIENS

Section Coverage:

An equitable lien operates as a charge or encumbrance on property. It is available only where the plaintiff can trace misappropriated property to its product. For example, if a fiduciary embezzles a client's money to purchase a car, the client can trace the property and impose an equitable lien on it. An equitable lien is an alternative restitutionary remedy to the constructive trust. The purpose of both these restitutionary remedies is to disgorge benefits unjustly acquired by the defendant.

A constructive trust, unlike an equitable lien, treats the title to the property as belonging to the claimant. The circumstances when an equitable lien is the preferred remedy are: (1) when the property has declined in value and (2) when there is not a severable interest in the defendant's property against which the plaintiff is making the equitable claim. With respect to the car, the plaintiff could seek a constructive trust because there is a severable property interest. The car is likely to have declined in value since purchase, however, so an equitable lien would be preferable. The plaintiff can then claim from other assets of the defendant the differential between the amount embezzled and the car. If the defendant is insolvent, the equitable lien on the car would take priority over other creditors, as the constructive trust does. The plaintiff would be a general creditor for the claim on the differential amount.

Model Case:

Chandler fraudulently induced Baxter to add an addition to Chandler's vacation house. Baxter, a building contractor, had been promised an important contract in connection with Chandler's business if the improvements were made, but the promise was fraudulent. The cost of the labor and materials for the addition was $5,000, but the addition actually enhanced the market value of the house by only $2,000.

If equitable relief is appropriate in this case, a court will allow Baxter to obtain an equitable lien on the property rather than a constructive trust because title to the land belonged to Chandler. The lien operates as an encumbrance against the property which could be satisfied by a foreclosure of the lien through sale of the house.

Baxter would not be entitled to foreclosure automatically. A court would consider the opportunity of Chandler to pay the charge out of other funds and any potential hardship to Chandler as a result of a forced sale. Other alternatives to immediate sale of the house to satisfy Baxter's lien would be to direct that it be mortgaged and Baxter reimbursed from the proceeds, or to appoint a receiver for receipt of any rentals produced from this vacation house.

Most jurisdictions would allow the amount of the lien to be $5,000 because the nature of Chandler's conduct was fraudulent. If Baxter had made the improvements simply by mistake under circumstances that makes retention of this enrichment unjust, then the lien should be limited to $2,000, the amount that the value of the property was actually enhanced.

MIDDLEBROOKS v. LONAS

246 Ga. 720, 272 S.E.2d 687 (1980).

JORDAN, PRESIDING JUSTICE.

Mary Middlebrooks filed a complaint against W.L. Lonas and Elvira Lonas, her parents, alleging that, in reliance on their promise to repay, she had loaned them $25,000 which they had since used to build a home on land which they owned, that they now refused to repay said loan and that, "[t]he above and foregoing transactions, promises, and delays constitute fraud and as such the defendants herein hold the said $25,000 through and by constructive and implied trust in favor of the plaintiff." The plaintiff further alleged that, "[t]he defendants herein have pledged, mortgaged and borrowed money upon the land ... as well as all improvements thereon."

The defendants moved for summary judgment on the ground that the plaintiff's complaint failed to state a claim upon which equitable relief could be granted and on the ground that they had factually pierced the plaintiff's allegation that they had promised to repay the $25,000 without a present intent to do so. The trial court granted said motion and the plaintiff appeals. We reverse.

* * *

2. Code Ann. § 108–106 states that "[t]rusts are implied ... where, from any fraud, one person obtains the title to property which rightly belongs to another."

A promise made without a present intent to perform is a misrepresentation of a material fact and is sufficient to support a cause of action for fraud. [Citation.]

Thus, assuming that the remedies at law are inadequate, if a plaintiff proves that a defendant promised to repay a loan and did so without a present intent to perform, the plaintiff can "enforce either a constructive trust or an equitable lien on the fund," and, further, if a plaintiff proves that the fraudulently procured funds were used by the defendant to purchase other property, the plaintiff can reach the other property "by a proceeding in equity, and ... can enforce a constructive trust or an equitable lien." [Citations.]

In the present case, it is undisputed that the defendants used the $25,000 to build a home on land which they already owned. Accordingly, assuming that the plaintiff's remedies at law are inadequate, if the plaintiff proves that the defendants promised to repay the $25,000 and did so without a present intent to perform, the plaintiff would be entitled to an equitable lien on the home and land. [Citations.]

> A remedy at law, to exclude appropriate relief in equity, must be ... the substantial equivalent of the equitable relief. It is not enough that there is a remedy at law. It must be plain and adequate, or, in other words, as practical and as efficient to the ends of justice and its prompt administration as the remedy in equity. [Citation.]

Regarding the inadequacy of her remedies at law, the plaintiff alleged that the defendants had mortgaged the home and lot. "A creditor of a mortgagor who obtains his judgment [at law] subsequently to the execution of a mortgage which has been duly registered takes it subject to the rights of the mortgagee ..." [Citation.] In contrast, a plaintiff who similarly establishes entitlement to an equitable lien takes subject to the rights of a mortgagee only if the mortgagee is a bona fide purchaser. * * *

Judgment reversed.

———

1. The constructive trust allows the claimant to obtain any increase in value of the embezzled funds, while an equitable lien would only give the aggrieved employer a security interest to the extent of the benefits unjustly held by the defendant. If the traced property has declined in value after being misappropriated or if the wrongdoer has dissipated some of the claimant's funds, an equitable lien typically is more advantageous than a constructive trust. In such instances, the equitable lien claimant has a charge or encumbrance on the identified property and is entitled to a deficiency judgment against the wrongdoer for the balance of the claim.

2. The equitable restitutionary remedies are imposed directly against particular property, such as a parcel of land, a fund of money, or a specific chattel, rather than on the defendant's general assets. Restitution of the traced property may be accomplished in specie through a constructive trust, and the equitable lien holder obtains a priority position over general creditors of the defendant. The equitable lien, though, may be less expedient because it requires foreclosure of the property in order to realize payment of the lien. The equitable interests necessarily yield, however, to legal interests such as may be asserted by a bona fide purchaser for value.

PROBLEM: THE SHARED HOUSE

Walker, a single parent with two young children, lived in an apartment on Main Street. Walker, who is employed full time, arranged for a single friend, Shaw, to care for the children after school in Shaw's home located on nearby Burgandy Avenue. Shaw was a college student at the time. The house had been inherited, and it was mortgaged to pay tuition.

The apartment complex where Walker lived was purchased by a real estate developer who planned to tear it down and replace it with a commercial shopping center. When Walker received a notice from the landlord terminating the lease, Shaw offered to let the three Walkers temporarily move into Shaw's house until another apartment could be located.

The joint living arrangement proved satisfactory to everyone. Shaw was having financial difficulties with daily living expenses at the time. Since they got along well during the temporary stay, they decided to make it permanent. They orally agreed to continue sharing the home and the household expenses. Over a three year period Walker contributed one-half of the mortgage payments and paid $5,000 for adding a bath to the house. The improvement resulted in an increase of approximately $3,000 in the fair market value of the house.

Relations became strained after Shaw graduated. Shaw was employed and became engaged to be married. Walker agreed to move out, but they disputed whether Shaw should reimburse Walker for any of the prior contributions. Walker moved out and now seeks reimbursement for the improvement made to the Shaw home by requesting the court to impress an equitable lien on the property. What result?

ROBINSON v. ROBINSON

100 Ill.App.3d 437, 57 Ill.Dec. 532, 429 N.E.2d 183 (1981).

UNVERZAGT, JUSTICE:

This action was brought by the plaintiff, Ann M. Robinson, to obtain a dissolution of marriage from Wylie Robinson, and against his parents, Earl J. and Alice M. Robinson, to establish her rights in certain property owned by them, known as the Johnson Road property. * * *

The novel question presented by this appeal is whether one who improves real property which she knows to be owned by others, who neither request nor encourage the improvement but merely give their permission for the improvement, is entitled to restitution. * * *

Wylie and Ann began construction of the house in the spring of 1969 and occupied it in 1970. [The house was located on the Johnson Road property owned by Wylie's parents.] The construction work was done mainly by Wylie with substantial help from friends and family including Earl, Alice and Ann's father. Ann sanded and finished woodwork and cabinets. After the home was occupied, additional improvements in the amount of $5,000 were made. These included carpeting, drapes, kitchen cabinets, linoleum and paint.

All of the parties knew that the house was Wylie's and Ann's home and treated it as such. They did all of the landscaping and planted shrubbery. They repaired it and maintained it. They made all of the loan payments and treated the interest thereon as a deduction on tax returns. They insured the house with a homeowner's policy. They had the only keys to the house and never paid or were asked for rent on it. The one connection Earl and Alice had with the house was that it was included on the farm tax bill since the lot was not subdivided. Earl and Alice paid the real estate tax bill. In exchange for that payment, Wylie worked additional time for his parents on their farm. * * *

There was no written agreement between the young and older Robinsons as to a transfer of title to the property. However, Wylie and his parents had many oral dealings over the years. They were very close. * * * The younger Robinsons and the older Robinsons exchanged services and assistance in the old fashioned country manner. Wylie worked for his parents on their farm each year and received a share of the farm income. Over the years he contributed a substantial amount of his time and knowledge to the construction of various farm improvements on his parents' farm.

Marital discord arose in 1977 and Wylie moved to his parents' home where he resided at the time of the hearing. From the relationship of the parties it can thus be seen that the younger Robinsons would have every expectation of eventual ownership of the home they constructed. However, the testimony was in strong disagreement on this point. * * *

The trial judge concluded that it would unjustly enrich Earl and Alice to gain the house without compensation to Ann.

A person who has been unjustly enriched at the expense of another is required to make restitution to the other. A person is enriched if he has received a benefit. A person is unjustly enriched if the retention of the benefit would be unjust. A person obtains restitution when he is restored to the position he formerly occupied either by the return of something he formerly had or by the receipt of its equivalent in money.

After hearing all of the evidence in this case, the trial court determined that Ann had an interest in the improvements made on the Johnson Road property. The court's rationale for the decision was that the evidence established that Earl and Alice had been unjustly enriched by the improvements made on the Johnson Road property. * * *

Earl and Alice argue that the evidence at trial did not establish recovery under a theory of unjust enrichment. They argue that as a general rule, improvements of a permanent character, made upon real estate, and attached thereto, without consent of the owner of the fee, by one having no title or interest, become a part of the realty and vest in the owner of the fee. * * *

In Olin v. Reinecke (1929), 336 Ill. 530, 534, 168 N.E. 676, the court said:

> In equity, however, if the owner stands by and permits another to expend money in improving his land he may be compelled to surrender his rights to the land upon receiving compensation therefor, or he may be compelled to pay for the improvements. In such cases there is always some ingredient which would make it a fraud in the owner to insist upon his legal rights. Such an ingredient may consist in the owner encouraging the stranger to proceed with the improvement, or where one party acts ignorantly and without the means of better information and the other remains silent when it is in his power to prevent the expenditure of the money under a delusion. It has been held in such cases that to permit one to take advantage of the mistake of another would be revolting to every sentiment of justice. [Citations.] The exercise of such a judicial power, however, unless based upon some actual or implied culpability on the part of the party subjected to it, is a violation of constitutional rights.

In Pope v. Speiser (1955), 7 Ill.2d 231, 240, 130 N.E.2d 507, where the plaintiff placed valuable improvements on the defendant's farm with the knowledge and consent of the defendant and after repeated statements by the defendant that the farm would belong to the plaintiff upon the defendant's death, the court granted plaintiff an equitable lien in the land, after the defendant attempted to sell the farm to a third person.

These cases support the trial court's ruling granting Ann an interest in the Johnson Road property. The improvements were made with the knowledge, cooperation and approval of Earl and Alice. * * *

We determine that while he did not denominate it as such, the interest awarded to Ann in the Johnson Road property by the trial judge was an equitable lien. [Citation.] As this court stated in Calacurcio v. Levson (1966), 68 Ill.App.2d 260, 263, 215 N.E.2d 839:

> The trend of modern decisions is to hold that in the absence of an express contract, a lien based upon the fundamental maxims of equity may be implied and declared by a court of equity out of general considerations of right and justice as applied to the relationship of the parties and the circumstances of their dealing, [citation]. An equitable lien is the right to have property subjected in a court of equity to payment of a claim. It is neither a debt nor a right of property, but a remedy for a debt.

The next question posed by this case is the extent or amount of the equitable lien. The trial court ruled that Ann was entitled to one-half of the appraised value of the improvements less the value of the land after making provision for payment of the construction loan.

Earl and Alice argue that if Ann is entitled to restitution her recovery should be measured by the subjective value to them or the value of the labor and materials that went into the house, and not the increased value of the land resulting from the addition of the house.

One scholar has suggested that when one builds a house on another's land, there are at least two feasible objective measures of restitution and one subjective measure. They are (1) the objective value of the labor and materials which went into the house; (2) the increased value of the land resulting from the addition of the house to it; and (3) the personal value to the defendant land-owner for his particular purposes. (See Dobbs, Remedies, § 4.5 at 261 (1973).) We have been supplied no case which has adopted the latter approach perhaps because of the almost impossibility of determining the subjective approach.

The Illinois cases have variously given an equitable lien for (1) the cost of the improvements or (2) the enhanced value of the premises, or (3) a right to purchase the premises if the owner elects to sell. * * *

From the foregoing, we conclude there was an implied promise by Earl and Alice to deed the land in question to Wylie and Ann and that the trial court was correct in imposing an equitable lien on the premises amounting to the value of the improvements that Ann and Wylie constructed thereon, in order to prevent unjust enrichment to Earl and Alice. * * *

It is the opinion of this court that the trial court properly directed defendants Earl and Alice to perform their implied contract to pay the plaintiff one-half of the reasonable value of the permanent improvements placed on the premises by the plaintiff and her husband and on their failure or refusal so to do, the trial court correctly ordered the property sold to foreclose plaintiff's equitable lien. * * *

Earl and Alice next assert that the trial court erred in attaching a lien for Wylie's debts on the Johnson Road property. The trial court placed a lien on one-half of the property for Ann's attorney's fees, child support arrearage and one-half interest in the Teacher's Retirement Plan. We agree that this was erroneous because an equitable lien is a remedy and not a property right. As was said in Watson v. Hobson (1948), 401 Ill. 191, 201, 81 N.E.2d 885, in discussing the nature of an equitable lien:

> An equitable lien is the right to have property subjected, in a court of equity, to the payment of a claim. It is neither a debt nor a right of property but a remedy for a debt. It is simply a right of a special nature over the property which constitutes a charge or encumbrance thereon, so that the very property itself may be proceeded against in an equitable action and either sold or sequestered under a judicial decree, and its proceeds, in one case, or its rents and profits in the other, applied upon the demand of the creditor in whose favor the lien exists.

We have found no case in which a lien was imposed on an equitable lien under such circumstances, as if the latter were a piece of property. Wylie has disclaimed any interest in the Johnson Road property. No matter how obstinate or intractable the trial court may have felt his action was in disclaiming the interest, the trial court cannot create a lien upon an equitable lien where none is sought. That portion of the judgment is reversed. * * *

Affirmed in part; reversed in part and remanded.

———

1. An equitable lien may be imposed on property to the extent necessary to secure a restitutionary claim for the value of labor or materials furnished toward making improvements on another's property. *See* Restatement of Restitution §§ 170, 206 (1937). The basis for granting an equitable lien rather than a constructive trust is that the claimant lacks title to the entire property and the improvements cannot be severed from the realty to effect specific restitution.

2. For additional commentary concerning equitable liens see the following references: Frankel, Fiduciary Law, 71 Calif.L.Rev. 795 (1983); Jones, The Recovery of Benefits Gained from a Breach of Contract, 99 L.Q.Rev. 443 (1983); Friedman, Restitution of Benefits Obtained

through the Appropriation of Property or the Commission of a Wrong, 80 Colum.L.Rev. 504 (1980); Gegan, Constructive Trusts: A New Basis for Tracing Equities, 53 St. John's L.Rev. 593 (1979); Wade, The Literature of the Law of Restitution, 19 Hastings L.J. 1087 (1968); Lauerman, Constructive Trusts and Restitutionary Liens in North Carolina, 45 N.C.L.Rev. 424 (1967); Monaghan, Constructive Trust and Equitable Lien: Status of the Conscious and the Innocent Wrongdoer in Equity, 38 U.Det.L.Rev. 10 (1960); Maudsley, Proprietary Remedies for the Recovery of Money, 75 L.Q.Rev. 234 (1959); Lacy, Constructive Trusts and Equitable Liens in Iowa, 40 Iowa L.Rev. 107 (1954); Note, Equitable Liens as a Remedy in Restitution in Pennsylvania, 56 Dick.L.Rev. 235 (1952); Scott, The Fiduciary Principle, 37 Calif.L.Rev. 539 (1949); Jennings & Shapiro, The Minnesota Law of Constructive Trusts and Analogous Equitable Remedies, 25 Minn.L.Rev. 667 (1941); Scott, The Trustee's Duty of Loyalty, 49 Harv.L.Rev. 521 (1936); Note, Equitable Liens, 31 Colum.L.Rev. 1335 (1931); Pound, The Progress of the Law, 1918–19 Equity, 33 Harv.L.Rev. 420 (1920); Huston, The Enforcement of Decrees in Equity (1915); Ames, Following Misappropriated Property into Its Product, 19 Harv.L.Rev. 511 (1906).

Chapter 17

LIMITATIONS ON RESTITUTIONARY REMEDIES

A. TRACING

Section Coverage:

Equity limits a person's ability to obtain a constructive trust, equitable lien, or right of subrogation against particular property by requiring the claimant to "trace" or follow the misappropriated property into its substituted form. Restitution of traced property may be asserted not only against the wrongdoer but also against a third party holding the exchanged property, provided the latter is not a bona fide purchaser.

Plaintiffs with equitable interests who can trace specific assets into their products enjoy two advantages. First, a claimant may obtain specific restitution of property which has subsequently increased in value through imposition of a constructive trust. The second, and perhaps even more important, advantage is that the holder of the equitable interest may receive a priority over the general creditors of insolvent or unavailable wrongdoers. If the person seeking an equitable restitutionary remedy cannot successfully identify the product of misappropriated money or property, the only remedy is a personal claim against the wrongdoer and the claimant will be forced to stand in line with other creditors.

Model Case:

An attorney named Blair embezzled $20,000 from a client's trust account. Half of the embezzled money went into a bank account that already contained some personal funds. Some but not all of the combined money in the account was spent on daily living expenses. Blair used the balance of the embezzled money to purchase a sailboat. Shortly thereafter Blair sold the sailboat and used the proceeds to pay a builder for some badly needed home repairs. With the cash left over after paying this bill, Blair purchased some jewelry for a family member's birthday. Thereafter the embezzlement was discovered, along with other misdeeds by Blair, who is now insolvent.

Whether the client will be able to assert an equitable lien against some or all of the money remaining in the bank account will depend upon the tracing presumptions followed in that jurisdiction. Jurisdictions follow a variety of approaches for tracing commingled funds in an account.

A constructive trust may be imposed on the jewelry provided the client can trace the various exchanges of property from the embezzled funds to the jewelry. An equitable lien may be placed on the house if the client similarly can demonstrate that the misappropriated assets were used to make the repairs. Because the client did not have title to the house originally, a court would not impose a constructive trust to effect specific restitution of the house to the client.

G & M MOTOR COMPANY v. THOMPSON

567 P.2d 80 (Okl.1977).

BERRY, JUSTICE.

The question to be decided has not heretofore been decided in Oklahoma. Specifically, may a trial court impress a constructive trust upon proceeds of life insurance policies where a portion of the premiums were paid with wrongfully obtained funds? We hold sound reason and interest of justice require an affirmative answer.

The facts, for the purpose of deciding this question, are simple. A. Wayne Thompson was an accountant for G & M Motor Company [motor company] from January 1, 1968, until his death on August 2, 1970. During this period decedent embezzled $78,856.45 from motor company; a portion of which was used to pay premiums of various insurance policies insuring the life of decedent. The trial court impressed a constructive trust upon various items of real and personal property and a portion of the insurance proceeds in possession of decedent's surviving wife, Shirley Thompson, and child.

Court of Appeals, Division 1, upon wife's appeal, affirmed trial court's impressment of a constructive trust on the real and personal property, but modified the trust on insurance proceeds. The court, relying on American National Bank of Okmulgee v. King, 158 Okl. 278, 13 P.2d 164, said "only that part of the funds that the trial court found was used to pay for the payments of the policies while deceased was employed for appellee . . . together with interest at the rate of 10% per annum from date of judgment . . . until paid" are subject to a constructive trust in favor of motor company.

* * *

The proper basis for impressing a constructive trust is to prevent unjust enrichment. Restatement of Restitution § 160, Comment c [1937]. The Restatement of Restitution foresaw that a wrongdoer may exchange misappropriated property for other property; thus, § 202 provides:

> "Where a person wrongfully disposes of property of another knowing that the disposition is wrongful and acquires in exchange other property, the other is entitled . . . to enforce . . . a constructive trust of the property so acquired."

The drafters explained § 202 as follows:

"Where a person by the consciously wrongful disposition of the property of another acquires other property, the person whose property is so used is ... entitled ... to the property so acquired. If the property so acquired is or becomes more valuable than the property used in acquiring it, the profit thus made by the wrongdoer cannot be retained by him; the person whose property was used in making the profit is entitled to it. The result, it is true, is that the claimant obtains more than the amount of which he was deprived, more than restitution for his loss; he is put in a better position than that in which he would have been if no wrong had been done to him. Nevertheless, since the profit is made from his property, it is just that he should have the profit rather than that the wrongdoer should keep it. It is true that if there had been a loss instead of a profit, the wrongdoer would have had to bear the loss, since the wrongdoer would be personally liable to the claimant for the value of the claimant's property wrongfully used by the wrongdoer. If, however, the wrongdoer were permitted to keep the profit, there would be an incentive to wrongdoing, which is removed if he is compelled to surrender the profit. The rule which compels the wrongdoer to bear any losses and to surrender any profits operates as a deterrent upon the wrongful disposition of the property of others. Accordingly, the person whose property is wrongfully used in acquiring other property can by a proceeding in equity reach the other property and compel the wrongdoer to convey it to him. The wrongdoer holds the property so acquired upon a constructive trust for the claimant."

Thus, it is not necessary for a plaintiff to have suffered any loss or suffer a loss as great as the benefit of defendant. *See Id.* § 160, Comment d.

Where the wrongdoer mingles wrongfully and rightfully acquired funds, owner of wrongfully acquired funds is entitled to share proportionately in acquired property to the extent of his involuntary contribution. *Id.* § 210(2). This principle is specifically applicable to life insurance proceeds where a portion of the premiums were paid with wrongfully acquired money. *Id.* § 210, Comment a. The drafters said:

"... Just as the claimant is entitled to enforce a constructive trust upon property which is wholly the product of his property, so he is entitled to enforce a constructive trust upon property which is the product in part of his own property and in part of the property of the wrongdoer. The difference is that where the property is the product of his property only in part, he is not entitled by enforcing a constructive trust to recover the whole of the property, but only a share in such proportion as the value of his property bore to the value of the mingled fund."

More particularly, § 210, Comment d, Illustration 5 addressed the instant matter. Illustration 5 provides:

"A insures his life for $10,000 and pays the premiums half with money wrongfully taken from B and half with money of his own. A dies. B is entitled to half of the proceeds of the policy . . . ."

The record indicates trial court determined extent of premiums paid with wrongfully acquired funds and impressed a constructive trust upon proceeds consistent with Illustration 5.

Having carefully considered the matter, we adopt the Restatement view. However, Motor Company has sought no more than the embezzled monies, interest and costs. Further, the surviving wife is an innocent beneficiary. Therefore, we cannot say trial court's judgment is against the clear weight of evidence. We hold Motor Company is entitled to a pro rata share of insurance proceeds, but not to exceed the total amount of embezzled monies, interest and costs.

* * * Court of Appeals opinion vacated in part. Judgment of trial court affirmed.

———

1. The mechanics of tracing are simplest when the wrongdoer makes a single exchange of property or where embezzled money is deposited in an account which contains no other funds. The task of following property through numerous transactions vastly complicates the proof; however, equity rules permit tracing despite multiple exchanges.

2. *Commingled Funds.* Problems arise when the wrongdoer commingles the misappropriated funds with other funds which rightfully belong to the wrongdoer or to third parties. Although the misappropriated money has lost its separate identity in the commingled account, courts will impose an equitable lien on the account to allow restitution of the amount which rightfully belongs to the plaintiff. The claimant would be unjustly enriched if the court granted restitution of the entire fund; conversely, a wrongdoer should not be able to foreclose restitution simply by the act of commingling funds.

3. *Withdrawals From Commingled Funds.* When a wrongdoer makes withdrawals from a commingled fund, tracing is still possible. The problem is how to identify whose money was removed and whose remains. Courts have created several fictional presumptions to meet the tracing requirement. Courts devised them to operate without regard to the actual intent of the wrongdoer except in the limited circumstance when the wrongdoer replenishes a reduced commingled account with the intent of restoring the claimant's funds. Otherwise the legal fictions for tracing commingled funds reflect sympathy for the claimant's task of satisfying the tracing requirement for restitutionary equitable remedies.

4. *First In, First Out Rule.* The original English solution to withdrawals from commingled accounts was formulated in Devaynes v. Noble, 1 Mer. 572 (1816), known as Clayton's Case. The court created the arbitrary rule that the first money put into the account would be presumed the first money withdrawn. For example, if the wrongdoer

deposited $1,000 of the plaintiff's money in an account where there was already $800, then the law would presume that the first $800 withdrawn belonged to the wrongdoer. On the other hand, if the plaintiff's money was placed in the account first and the wrongdoer's own funds were deposited later, then withdrawals were deemed from the plaintiff's money up to the $1,000.

The plaintiff was either benefitted or hurt under this "first in, first out" rule depending entirely upon the fortuity of how the money was used. If the money that was arbitrarily determined to be the claimant's was dissipated, the equitable remedy was lost. If the money was used to invest in something of value that could still be traced, the plaintiff could follow it further to impress the constructive trust or equitable lien.

5. *"Jessel's Bag" Rule.* A different resolution of the problem of identifying withdrawals from a commingled fund appeared in a later English decision, In re Hallett's Estate (Knatchbull v. Hallett), 13 Ch. Div. 696 (1879). Under this approach, the first withdrawals from a commingled fund are presumed to belong to the wrongdoer and the remaining balance is subject to the equitable interest asserted by the claimant. This rule is known as the rule of Jessel's Bag, named after a member of the court, Sir George Jessel.

The rule of Jessel's Bag has the effect of benefitting the claimant in many cases because money withdrawn by a wrongdoer from a commingled fund is dissipated more typically than it is invested in traceable property. The money left in the account thus remains for the plaintiff's equitable claim.

The rule produces unsatisfactory results, however, when the first funds withdrawn by the wrongdoer are profitably invested but the remaining funds, which presumptively belong to the innocent claimant, are dissipated. A subsequent English decision, In re Oatway (Hertsler v. Oatway), 2 Ch. Div. 356 (1903), modified the rule of Jessel's Bag to give the claimant a choice between the assets traceable to the funds drawn out first or those withdrawn from the account at a later time.

6. *Restatement Approach.* The Restatement of Restitution proposes a systematic application of a modified choice principle. It will usually, but not always, benefit the plaintiff. The Restatement rejects the tracing fictions and gives the claimant a proportionate share in the fund and its traceable products, enforceable either through an equitable lien or constructive trust:

§ 211. Effect of Withdrawals From Mingled Fund.*

(1) Where a person wrongfully mingles money of another with money of his own and subsequently makes withdrawals from the mingled fund, the other is entitled to an equitable lien upon the part

which remains and the part which is withdrawn or upon their product, except as stated in Subsection (3).

(2) If the wrongdoer knew that he was acting wrongfully, the other is entitled at his option to a proportionate share both of the part which remains and of the part which is withdrawn or of their product, except as stated in Subsection (3).

(3) Where the wrongdoer has effectively separated the money of the other from his own money, the other is entitled to, and only to, his own money or its product.

For example, if an embezzler wrongfully takes $1000 and deposits it in a personal bank account containing $1000, the victim has a one half interest in whatever subsequently happens to the account. If $500 is used to invest in valuable property that appreciates in value, the claimant can have a constructive trust for half of it. If $500 is invested in property that depreciates in value, the victim can impose an equitable lien for half its value. If some money is dissipated and some still remains in the account, the plaintiff can have an equitable lien on half of the remainder.

7. American courts have followed all of these rules in various opinions at various times. The Restatement approach, which permits a proportionate equitable interest in the remaining fund and in the withdrawals from it, has been more generally accepted than the alternatives. *See generally* Palmer, The Law of Restitution § 2.17 (1978).

PROBLEM: THE COMMINGLED BANK ACCOUNT

Clark, a trusted employee of CRT Communications, embezzled $10,000 from the company. First Clark used $5,000 to purchase various building supplies to make home improvements. The improvements actually enhanced the fair market value of the home, however, by just $2,000.

Clark took the remaining $5,000 and placed it into a bank account which already contained $2,000 of personal funds. Consider the following sequence of transactions:

T1 Deposit of $5,000 added to original $2,000.
T2 Withdrawal of $2,000 to purchase 100 shares of stock in High-flier Corp. The stock has advanced to a current market value of $4,000.
T3 Withdrawal of $3,000 to pay for miscellaneous living expenses, leaving a balance of $2,000 in the account.
T4 Deposit of $1,000 for a final balance of $3,000.

(a) What would be the equitable interests that CRT could assert against the bank account and the stock according to the rules in *Clayton's Case, Hallett's Estate, Oatway,* and the Restatement? How much would the company recover altogether under each approach?

(b) What would be the appropriate equitable remedy that CRT could assert against the home? In what amount?

REPUBLIC SUPPLY CO. v. RICHFIELD OIL CO.

79 F.2d 375 (9th Cir.1935).

St. Sure, District Judge. * * *

At the time of the commencement of this proceeding Richfield was in equitable receivership. Universal filed a bill in intervention against the receiver and the bank, as trustee under a mortgage and trust indenture of Richfield, whereby it was sought to establish a prior lien upon certain assets of Richfield then in the hands of its receiver. The gist of the bill was that Richfield, with knowledge that Universal had a cash balance in bank amounting to $1,625,000, deliberately purchased sufficient Universal stock to procure control of Universal through the election of Richfield officers and attaches to the board of directors of Universal; misappropriated the amount named and commingled same with Richfield's general checking account in the bank; and thereafter invested the funds in certain assets which had passed into the hands of Richfield's receiver. The prayer was for a prior and superior lien upon the properties purchased in favor of Universal and against the bank and the receiver.

The matter was referred to a special master, who sustained the allegations of the bill in intervention, found that Universal had successfully traced part of its funds into specific properties which passed into the hands of the receiver, and that Universal was entitled to prior liens upon those designated parcels in the sum of $403,993.92. A general claim for the balance of $779,154.31, which the master found had not been properly traced, was allowed Universal.

The proceeding was instituted, and the master and District Court rested their conclusion upon the theory that recovery was limited to the lowest balance reached by the commingled account between the dates of misappropriations and the dates of acquisition of the specified pieces of property.

The question on appeal is whether a trust may be declared upon the low balance theory.

Preliminarily, it is admitted by appellants that Universal's funds were misappropriated, and that the misappropriations constituted Richfield's receiver the trustee of a constructive trust of which Universal was the beneficiary.

* * * It is established beyond debate that no change of form can divest a trust fund of its trust character, and that the cestui may follow and reclaim his funds so long as he is able to trace and identify them, not as his original dollars or necessarily as any dollars, but through and into any form into which his dollars may have been converted. [Citations.] The underlying principle of this rule is that the cestui que trust

has been wrongfully deprived of that which belongs to him; that his right to his funds has not been lost or destroyed by the misappropriation; and that if, and to the extent, the cestui is able to follow and identify the amount of the misappropriated funds as having been used in the acquisition of other property, he may recover.

*   *   *

[The court then found that Universal had sufficiently traced its misappropriated funds into the hands of the receiver, thus shifting the burden to the defendant to show what amounts, if any, its own funds had contributed to the purchase of the property. Since the defendant failed to make that showing, the court concluded that the lien would be imposed on the entire property held by the receiver, but not to exceed the lowest intermediate balance of the fund.]

In attaching the liens, the master had three alternatives or theories before him for computing the amounts thereof:

1. The daily closing balance, after crediting the opening balance and all deposits during the day and charging all withdrawals for the day, without regard to the order in point of time in which deposits and withdrawals were made.

2. The balance shown during the day as a result of periodical posting of deposits and withdrawals, after crediting the opening balance, with or without regard to the order in point of time of the transactions, observing or neglecting to observe the true balance, according to the arbitrary inclination of the posting clerk.

3. The balance shown by deducting all withdrawals posted during the day from the opening balance without crediting deposits for the day; disregarding the true order of transactions and assuming an order in point of time which would produce the lowest possible balance during the day.

The third alternative was used.

It is urged by Universal that the method followed limits its recovery to the lowest possible figure, and that the daily closing balances should have been the basis of recovery; if not that, at least the lowest daily intermediate posted balances.

No case to which we have been cited really answers the question before us, namely: How is the lowest intermediate balance to be determined? We must, therefore, reach our conclusion upon the basis of equity with due regard, however, to the well-established rules of law and known business practices.

If the lowest intermediate balance between the misappropriations and the purchases is to be taken literally, that is to say at any moment of any day, it is obvious that the order in which deposits and withdrawals were made would be indispensable to proof. None of the three alternatives pretend to show sequence of transactions. It is a matter of common knowledge and, indeed, of record, that the volume and complexity of business and banking practice do not permit of keeping an accurate momentary balance current with deposits and withdrawals in large commercial accounts, for the reason that banks have various departments and many tellers, and the credit and debit transactions react upon one another in rapid succession.

The evidence in this case establishes that the daily intermediate posted balances are merely working balances in the bank; that they do not necessarily represent the actual balance resulting from all transactions in the account up to the time of posting. They represent only the balance of the deposits and withdrawals actually posted, and whether all transactions up to the time of posting shall be included in the intermediate balance is left to the arbitrary inclination of the posting clerk.   * * *

We are not persuaded, however, that the method adopted by the master and the District Court is any more applicable, for it assumes an order of transactions which is wholly unsupported by evidence or reason, and disregards entirely a most essential element of any bank account, namely, credits. The adoption of this method was based upon the premise that the order in point of time of deposits and withdrawals was essential to proof, and that the burden was upon claimant; and upon the reasoning that claimant must fail unless there is a minimum situation which "assumes an order of deposits and withdrawals which, at the worst, must have occurred." We are not in accord with that view.

The evidence discloses that the bank itself, which handles both deposits and withdrawals, and the bookkeeping of the account, cannot, in ordinary cases (and in this case did not), prove accurately the chronology of transactions in large commercial accounts. Why, then, should that insuperable burden penalize the cestui que trust whose funds have been wrongfully taken from it?

Notwithstanding the established doctrine that subsequent deposits in a commingled account such as the one herein does not restore a trust fund once exhausted, and that the burden of proof is upon claimant to show that its funds purchased the property upon which it is sought to fasten a lien, [citations], under the facts in this case we are disinclined to follow either rule to the extent of defeating recovery, or even limiting recovery to the lowest possible figure, upon an unwarranted assumption of the chronology of transactions and a disregard of the credit side of the bank account. The facts disclosed by the record prompt the observation that if any assumption is to be indulged in, it should not favor Richfield or its creditors, for the reason that Universal's funds were surreptitiously abstracted and deposited in Richfield's account, out of which, the evidence shows, all of the properties involved were wholly or in part paid for, and the account was completely exhausted prior to receivership. From this it is apparent that Universal's claim is superior in right and in time to the creditors of Richfield. Under these circumstances, we know of no equitable principle which would entitle the creditors to equal or greater consideration than is due Universal.

No citation of authority is necessary to support the statement that the daily closing balance is the one which reflects the actual state of the ordinary commercial bank account, and is the only one accepted and used by both bank and customer in ordinary business transaction. For obvious reasons, heretofore adverted to, it disregards the chronological order of deposits and withdrawals. It does not, however, disregard any transaction on either side of the ledger.

It seems perfectly clear to us that under the prevailing system of bookkeeping in the bank the essential elements for determining the lowest intermediate balances are not ascertainable with accuracy until the close of the banking day, when all transactions for that day are posted. If in the interim between daily closing balances there was a transgression of the rule with reference to subsequent deposits not restoring trust funds once exhausted, and the balance did in fact fall below the amount of the trust funds then in the account, the burden was upon defendants to show that fact with accuracy. Under the evidence in the case before us, such liability as might have resulted therefrom should be borne by the tort-feasor, not the innocent cestui. Concisely stated, the equities not being equal, proof of the lowest daily closing balances between misappropriations and purchases of the identified properties constituted a prima facie showing of the lowest intermediate balances, which, for reasons already stated, was not overcome by defendants' evidence of daily intermediate posted balances.

* * *

———

1. Difficult tracing problems arise when a wrongdoer with a commingled account makes withdrawals which are dissipated but later makes additional deposits of personal funds into the account. Should the court treat the replacement funds as a restoration of the claimant's money? If so, then such money would still be subject to priority treatment. Alternatively, should the additions be deemed part of the wrongdoer's general assets which are subject to the claims of all creditors?

The majority view is that if the wrongdoer manifests an intention to restore the claimant's funds, the equitable lien will be extended to cover the new deposits. Absent such proof, the general rule holds that the claimant's equitable interest in the fund cannot exceed the lowest intermediate balance of the account. *See* Restatement of Restitution § 212.

2. The lowest intermediate balance rule led to the problem in the principal case. Depending on the fortuity of the time transactions were posted in a commercial account during a business day, the claimant's equitable interest in an account might be completely extinguished. The court opted for the pragmatic solution to an otherwise thorny problem by adopting the daily closing balance. Does this pragmatic solution

destroy the integrity of the tracing process, or is it just another fiction added to the admittedly fictional tracing process with commingled accounts? Would a better solution be to abandon all efforts to trace commingled money? What would be the practical effect of a rule that a plaintiff's money is no longer traceable as soon as it is commingled with money not belonging to the plaintiff? Is this result defensible as a matter of public policy if some primary purposes of abolishing the commingled funds rules are to save judicial time and to reduce litigation costs?

3. For additional commentary regarding the role of tracing in restitution, see the following references: Khurshed & Matthews, Tracing Confusion, 95 L.Q.Rev. 78 (1979); Babafemi, Tracing Assets: A Case for the Fusion of Common Law and Equity in English Law, 34 Mod.L.Rev. 12 (1971); Wade, The Literature of the Law of Restitution, 19 Hastings L.J. 1087 (1968); McConville, Tracing and the Rule in Clayton's Case, 79 L.Q.Rev. 388 (1963); Scott, Following the Res and Sharing the Product, 66 Harv.L.Rev. 872 (1953); Taft, A Defense of a Limited Use of the Swollen Assets Theory Where Money Has Wrongly Been Mingled with Other Money, 39 Colum.L.Rev. 172 (1939); Hirsch, Tracing Trust Funds—Modern Doctrine, 11 Temp.L.Q. 11 (1936); Note, Trusts—Tracing Trust Funds—Right of Principal to Constructive Trust Upon Proceeds of Insurance Policy on Life of Agent Who Used Principal's Money to Pay Premiums, 84 U.Pa.L.Rev. 913 (1936); Note, Trusts—Tracing of Assets—Preference, 30 Mich.L.Rev. 441 (1932); Scott, The Right to Follow Money Wrongfully Mingled with Other Money, 27 Harv.L.Rev. 125 (1913); Ames, Following Misappropriated Property Into Its Product, 19 Harv.L.Rev. 511 (1906).

B. BONA FIDE PURCHASER AND CHANGE IN POSITION

Section Coverage:

A person holding an equitable interest in property, such as through a constructive trust or an equitable lien, is precluded from enforcing that interest against a third person who has acquired legal title to the property for value and without notice of the equitable interest. There are two policies that result in the protection of the legal title obtained by a bona fide purchaser: (1) legal title is deemed superior and therefore will defeat equitable title, and (2) between two innocent parties, a court of equity will not impose the loss on the party who has innocently acquired title to the property for value. The bona fide purchaser defense applies with equal force to various property rights; the subject matter may involve realty, personalty, or negotiable instruments.

Consider a typical case where a trustee wrongfully conveys legal title to trust property to a third person who pays value and who has no notice that the transfer is in violation of the trust. The trust beneficiary possesses mere equitable title and therefore may not obtain specific restitution of the property in the hands of the bona fide purchaser who has legal title. The beneficiary's remedy will lie only against the wrongdoer.

Another defense to restitution is known as "change in position." A court may deny a restitutionary remedy if the defendant would be adversely affected by virtue of circumstances which have materially changed after receipt of the benefit. This defense is predicated upon the policy that a court retains discretion to withhold relief or to fashion an order to the extent desirable to achieve an equitable result. A court may appropriately determine that the defendant's change of circumstances should preclude restitution either entirely or only partially. Nonetheless, if the defendant has acted tortiously or was substantially more at fault than the claimant with respect to the subject matter involved, the court may order restitution despite the hardship from a change in position.

A common example of the change of position defense is where a person mistakenly delivers goods to another under circumstances which would constitute unjust enrichment. Ordinarily the recipient would be required to make restitution. If, however, the goods are subsequently destroyed by fire, not as a consequence of tortious conduct by the recipient and the recipient was no more at fault than the claimant for the loss, a court could properly decline to order restitution. One is not charged with a duty to care for the misdelivered goods until the recipient has knowledge of the mistake and had an opportunity to return the goods. The defense of changed circumstances is especially strong if the recipient has not beneficially used the goods and if an order to make restitution would effect an unreasonable hardship.

Model Case:

Cory Douglas was appointed by a court to serve as the guardian of the person and the estate of a minor named Rebecca. According to the terms of the court's order, Douglas had full fiduciary authority to manage Rebecca's assets on her behalf.

Douglas misappropriated several thousand dollars from the assets. Instead of paying the bill for tuition fees and boarding expenses to the private school which Rebecca attended, Douglas purchased a sports car for a favorite cousin. Douglas subsequently left the state and became insolvent.

A court may impose a constructive trust on the sports car, and order specific restitution to protect the equitable interest held by Rebecca as the beneficiary. The cousin, even if lacking knowledge of the breach of Douglas' fiduciary duties, would be characterized as a gratuitous donee. The cousin did not pay value for the sports car and therefore is not a protected bona fide purchaser.

CITY OF HASTINGS v. JERRY SPADY

212 Neb. 137, 322 N.W.2d 369 (1982).

HAMILTON, DISTRICT JUDGE.

This is an action brought by the appellee, City of Hastings, in equity to impress a constructive trust upon real property purchased by appellant, Jerry Spady Pontiac–Cadillac, Inc., from the Missouri Improvement Company, a subsidiary of Missouri Pacific Railroad Company. The District Court found generally for the City of Hastings and imposed a constructive trust.

During 1977 and part of 1978 Duane Stromer was city attorney for the City of Hastings, and during said period was also attorney for Jerry Spady Pontiac–Cadillac, Inc.

In 1976 the planning director for the City of Hastings began the development of the Hastings comprehensive plan. As part of this plan it was contemplated that F Street would be extended along property owned by the Missouri Pacific Railroad Company, but no longer used as railroad right-of-way. This extension of F Street was a material part of the comprehensive plan, since it would provide the city with its only major thoroughfare crossing the city from east to west in the south part of town.

The extension of F Street was clearly shown on the comprehensive plan that was submitted to the Hastings Planning Commission in March of 1977, which was attended by Duane Stromer in his capacity as city attorney. It became obvious at this point in time that the acquisition of the abandoned railroad right-of-way by the City of Hastings was an absolute necessity to accomplish the intent and purposes of the comprehensive plan insofar as it applied to the extension of F Street.

* * *

In August of 1977 Duane Stromer made a written offer to purchase the property for $6,890, which was rejected. In correspondence to the Missouri Pacific on September 6, 1977, Stromer advised the Missouri Pacific that the City of Hastings was not interested in purchasing the property because a decision had been made not to put a street through in that area. Stromer further advised that his offer was made personally without regard to the City of Hastings. The record reflects this to be a deliberate falsehood, for at the very same time the city planning director was, with city approval, obtaining appraisals so as to submit an offer of purchase to the Missouri Pacific.

On September 21, 1977, by letter, Stromer accepted an offer of the Missouri Pacific and agreed to pay $10,900 for the property. On September 22, 1977, the engineering committee of the city council held a meeting. The F Street property was on the agenda. Duane Stromer requested of the committee chairman that he be put on the agenda. At the meeting Stromer informed the committee that he had acquired the property and that he would be willing to transfer the property to the city for what he had in it, which was stated to be approximately $20,000.

It was at this point that the city council first learned of Stromer's conduct and an apparent conflict of interest. The mayor discussed the matter with Stromer and then advised the council that Stromer had agreed to get out of the transaction and to allow the city to proceed with its acquisition of the property.

On October 12, 1977, Stromer wrote to the Missouri Pacific and made the following statement: "Apparently, the City of Hastings, Nebraska is now interested in purchasing the said land which I did not know about at the time we began negotiations in April. To avoid any possible conflict, I must withdraw my offer to purchase the said land."

Before the letter arrived Mr. Henderson of the Missouri Pacific received a telephone call from Stromer advising him to disregard the letter when he received it. Stromer further advised Mr. Henderson that the deal was still on and he wanted the deed to be issued to the Bonnavilla Plaza Corporation. This corporation was wholly owned by Jerry Spady.

During November and December Stromer had advised the Missouri Pacific he was checking the title and that the money would be sent as soon as the title check had been completed. The City of Hastings, during this period, had completed appraisals on the property and had agreed to offer the Missouri Pacific the sum of $18,000. The matter was placed on the agenda for the city council meeting of January 9, 1978. The motion to offer the $18,000 was passed on said date. On that same date Stromer obtained a check from Jerry Spady Pontiac–Cadillac, Inc., in the amount of $10,900 and forwarded the check to the Missouri Pacific, requesting that the property be deeded to Jerry Spady Pontiac–Cadillac, Inc., which was done, and the deed was mailed to Stromer on February 8, 1978.

* * *

The record reflects that at no time had the City of Hastings ever authorized Duane Stromer to negotiate on its behalf, nor had the city any knowledge that Stromer was representing to others that he was negotiating on its behalf.

* * *

It is fundamental law that an attorney must not while representing a client do anything knowingly that is inconsistent with the terms of his employment or contrary to the best interests of his client. "An attorney is by virtue of his office disqualified from representing interests which are adverse in the sense that they are hostile, antagonistic, or in conflict with each other." [Citation.]

The facts in the record show that all negotiations with the Missouri Pacific for the purchase of the property in question were conducted by Duane Stromer representing to the sellers that he was representing the

City of Hastings, himself, or the appellant. At all times during said negotiations Duane Stromer had actual knowledge that his employer, the City of Hastings, was interested in and intended to purchase the subject property. Duane Stromer, as city attorney, had a fiduciary duty to his employer not to act in a manner inconsistent with the employer's best interests. Clearly the action of Duane Stromer to actively participate in the acquisition of property either for himself personally or for a third-party client, when he had actual knowledge that his employer was not only interested in purchasing the property but considered it a necessity to accomplish the intent and purpose of the employer's comprehensive plan, was a breach of his fiduciary duty to his employer.

An attorney cannot purchase or negotiate for an interest in land in which his own client is interested. [Citations.]

The breach of fiduciary duty having been so clearly established, the City of Hastings was required to show only that Jerry Spady Pontiac–Cadillac, Inc., was not a bona fide purchaser for value. The trial court must have concluded that appellant had either actual or constructive knowledge of the City of Hastings' equitable claim to the property. The record before us requires such a finding. The letter of Duane Stromer to the Missouri Pacific on October 12, 1977, specifically refers to the City of Hastings' interest in the property, and although actual knowledge is not necessary, it is inconceivable that with the close personal association of Duane Stromer with Jerry Spady, as reflected in this record, appellant did not have actual knowledge of the equitable claim of the City of Hastings. Jerry Spady had actual knowledge that Duane Stromer was representing the City of Hastings and at the same time representing him.

It is clear that notice to, or knowledge of facts by, an attorney is notice to, or knowledge of, his client. [Citation.]

The actual knowledge of Duane Stromer of the city's interest in that property is imputed to his client, appellant herein, and that knowledge and notice of Stromer's breach of fiduciary duty negates any claim of being a bona fide purchaser for value by the appellant.

A bona fide purchaser exists where the purchaser takes without knowledge or notice of any suspicious circumstances which would put a prudent man upon inquiry. [Citations.]

Where, as here, the titleholder of real estate takes title to property with actual or constructive knowledge of the breach of a fiduciary duty by an attorney to his client amounting to fraud, the court will impose a constructive trust upon the title-holder and require that title be transferred to the defrauded party.

A constructive trust will be imposed against those who knowingly aid or participate in a breach of trust. [Citation.] To rule otherwise would permit wrongdoers to be unjustly enriched or otherwise benefit parties who have obtained property with actual or constructive knowledge of the fraudulent actions of their agent in acquiring the property.

The action and judgment of the trial court was correct and the judgment is affirmed.

———

1.   A transferee must take property without notice of the facts that give rise to equitable restitutionary interests in order to receive protection as a bona fide purchaser.   The notice requirement may be a subjective test: What did the transferee actually know?   For example, a holder of negotiable instruments takes free of equitable claims if value was paid in good faith, even though the holder was negligent in failing to discover fraud.   U.C.C. §§ 1–201(19)(25); 3–304; 8–304.   The defense requires proof only that the transferee of a negotiable instrument is subjectively honest; there is no duty of due care imposing an objective standard of reasonable knowledge.

A person may be chargeable with constructive notice of an equitable restitutionary claim where a deed, will, mortgage, or other instrument has been recorded in a public office.   *See* Restatement of Restitution § 174 comment b. Conversely, a purchaser of real estate may be entitled to rely on recorded titles, and will not be subordinated to unrecorded equities of which the purchaser has no actual or constructive knowledge. *See, e.g.,* Matter of Phillips, 21 B.R. 565 (Bkrtcy.D.Conn.1982).   On the other hand, notice may be imputed to a transferee in instances where a reasonably diligent investigation would have revealed the existence of the beneficiary's equitable interest.

2.   In certain circumstances a principal will be charged with the knowledge of an agent acquired during the agency relationship.   *See* Bronowski v. Magnus Enterprises, Inc., 61 A.D.2d 879, 402 N.Y.S.2d 868 (1978).

In a leading case, Newton v. Porter, 69 N.Y. 133 (1877), thieves stole bearer bonds from the plaintiff, sold them, and used the proceeds to purchase other securities.   The thieves subsequently were arrested and transferred the securities to the lawyers they had employed as payment for their services.   The plaintiff sued the lawyers, seeking to impose a constructive trust on the securities which had been acquired with the proceeds of the stolen bonds.   The court granted the constructive trust after determining that the lawyers had notice of the tainted history of the securities and thus were not bona fide purchasers.   The decision is also noteworthy because the court imposed a constructive trust in a situation of simple theft.

3.   What constitutes giving "value" for purposes of achieving bona fide purchaser status and consequently receiving protection from the interests of beneficiaries of constructive trusts and equitable liens?   The Restatement of Restitution § 173 essentially tracks the rules regarding value pertaining to express trusts as stated in the Restatement (Second) of Trusts §§ 298–309.

Notably, satisfaction of an antecedent debt constitutes giving value sufficient to cut off the beneficial interest in a constructive trust but is not effective against the beneficiary of an express trust. Restatement (Second) of Trusts § 304; Restatement of Restitution § 173 comment a. Despite a division of authority, the modern trend shows some liberalization toward recognizing that a person receiving property as security for or in satisfaction of a pre-existing obligation is a purchaser for value. The opposing view was followed in Meier v. Meyer, 153 Neb. 222, 43 N.W.2d 502 (1950). In that case the plaintiff made a loan induced by fraud to Owens. Owens deposited the money in a bank account and used part of the funds to discharge a pre-existing debt owed to a third party who had no notice of the fraud. The court allowed the plaintiff to impose a constructive trust on the funds traceable to the third party.

4. The requirement of giving value is not governed by the same principles as consideration for formation of a contract; the test for bona fide purchasers is a narrower one. Uniform Commercial Code 1–201(44) defines value as "any consideration sufficient to support a simple contract," which would include the making of a promise. In contrast, a promise to make payment in the future for a transfer of property is not considered a transfer for value sufficient to cut off a beneficiary's equitable interest. Restatement of Restitution § 173 comment e. The present payment of money or furnishing of goods or services may be made either by the transferee or by a third person, and may be made either prior or subsequent to the transfer of property, provided it occurs before notice of the equitable interest.

5. Will a transferee be accorded bona fide purchaser status if the value given in exchange for the property is significantly below the property's fair market value? In Walters v. Calderon, 25 Cal.App.3d 863, 102 Cal.Rptr. 89 (1972), the plaintiff sought to impose a constructive trust on a $60,000 note and deed of trust which had been assigned by the plaintiff's father, Walters, to a friend, Calderon, for $10 and the promise "to provide a home for and considerately care for W.S. Walters, including medical and burial expenses, for the remainder of W.S. Walters' life." The court held that the assignee had given sufficient value to satisfy the requirements of being a bona fide purchaser, and stated: "Generally, some value means any value whatever, even that of a peppercorn, a tomtit, or one dollar in hand." Did the court confuse the adequacy of consideration necessary for contract formation with the requirement of value for purposes of characterizing a transferee as a bona fide purchaser? Compare Restatement of Restitution § 173 comment b, where it is suggested that evidence of below market value paid for property may suffice to put the transferee on notice of the existence of outstanding equitable claims.

6. A transferee, in addition to giving value and acquiring property without notice of equitable claims, must obtain legal title rather than equitable title in order to prevail as a bona fide purchaser over the competing equitable interests. In Snuffin v. Mayo, 6 Wash.App. 525, 494 P.2d 497 (1972), the court held that a vendee had acquired only an

equitable title in an executory contract to purchase land, with legal title remaining in the vendor until the full purchase price had been paid. Consequently, the vendee was not considered a bona fide purchaser, and could not prevail in an unlawful detainer action.

7.   In *In re Marriage of Allen,* 724 P.2d 651 (Colo.1986), a husband misappropriated money from his employer, used the funds to improve his family residence and then subjected the property to division as marital property in a divorce settlement agreement.   The employer sought a constructive trust against the traceable proceeds of property which the embezzler's wife held as part of the settlement arrangement.   The court held that the wife could not claim bona fide purchaser status to defeat the constructive trust claims even though she had acquired the property without knowledge of the embezzlement.   Since she had not given "value" for the property, she was considered an innocent donee or a gratuitous transferee.   The court reasoned that to give the ex-wife legal or equitable title to the products of the husband's wrongdoing by entering into the property settlement would constitute unjust enrichment.   See Restatement of Restitution § 161 comment d.

8.   For additional information on the defense of bona fide purchaser see the following commentary: Ames, Following Misappropriated Property Into Its Product, 19 Harv.L.Rev. 511 (1906); Ames, Purchase for Value Without Notice, 1 Harv.L.Rev. 1 (1887); Ballantine, Purchase for Value and Estoppel, 6 Minn.L.Rev. 87 (1922); Friedman, Payment of Another's Debt, 99 L.Q.Rev. 534 (1983); Gilmore, The Commercial Doctrine of Good Faith Purchase, 63 Yale L.J. 1057 (1954); Kenneson, Purchase for Value Without Notice, 23 Yale L.J. 193 (1914); Note, The Preference Given to the Legal Estate Over the Equitable, 22 Harv.L.Rev. 151 (1908); Scott, Restitution from an Innocent Transferee Who is Not a Purchaser for Value, 62 Harv.L.Rev. 1002 (1949); Searey, Purchase for Value Without Notice, 23 Yale L.J. 447 (1914); Wade, The Literature of Restitution, 19 Hastings L.J. 1087 (1968).

PROBLEM: THE OLD GRAY MARE

Artemis fraudulently induced Gibson to transfer legal title to a horse named "Old Gray Mare."   Artemis subsequently trotted the horse down to kindly Doc Miller's office and told the good doctor that the horse was being delivered as payment for medical bills incurred several months earlier.   Artemis apologized for not having cash to pay the debt, but the doctor took the reins and replied that Artemis's obligations were considered "paid in full."

A month later Gibson discovered the fraud and spotted the Old Gray Mare tied up outside the doctor's office.   Gibson seeks restitution of the horse from the doctor because Artemis is now insolvent.   Would the doctor be considered a bona fide purchaser?

ALEXANDER HAMILTON LIFE INS. CO. v. LEWIS

550 S.W.2d 558 (Ky.1977).

PALMORE, JUSTICE. * * *

The background [of this case] is that after their daughter had disappeared and her whereabouts had been unknown for over seven years the Lewises brought suit against the insurance company for the face amount of two insurance policies on her life, relying on KRS 422.130 (Presumption of Death). A judgment was entered in their favor and was paid by the insurance company. Then the daughter was discovered alive and the company filed its CR 60.02 motion to set the judgment aside. Following a denial of that relief this court held that the company was entitled to it under both CR 60.02(2) [newly discovered evidence] and CR 60.02(6) ["reason of an extraordinary nature justifying relief"].

After setting aside the order denying relief the trial court received evidence bearing on the disposition of the money by the Lewises and upon their present financial condition and entered a "judgment of restitution" directing them to repay $7218.40, being half of the money collected under the original judgment, without interest. The company appeals and the Lewises cross-appeal.

It is an accepted principle that money paid in obedience to a judgment that is later set aside must be repaid. [Citations.]

"A person who has conferred a benefit upon another in compliance with a judgment ... is entitled to restitution if the judgment is reversed or set aside, *unless restitution would be inequitable....*" (Emphasis added.) Restatement, *Restitution,* § 74.

The company insists that it is entitled to restitution in full. The Lewises rely on the portion of the Restatement, *Restitution,* § 74, that we have italicized, contending that in the name of "equity" restitution may be denied wholly or in part, as the circumstances warrant, and that in their situation it should be denied entirely. We see no just reason to deny any part of it.

The theory of restitution as a basis for recovery is about as old as the law itself. Though often assumed to be purely an equitable remedy, some of the earliest proceedings both at common law and in equity were founded upon it and were amplified in the course of time. [Citation.] The obvious justification for it is that one should not be unjustly enriched at the expense of another.

In Bridges v. McAlister, 106 Ky. 791, 51 S.W. 603, 21 KLR 428, 45 LRA 80, 90 Am.St.Rep. 267 (1899), the accountability of a party for actions taken under authority of a judgment later set aside was discussed at some length. Among other things the court concluded as follows: "When a judgment is reversed, restitution must be made of all that has been received under it, but no further liability should in any case be imposed." Our attention has not been directed to any precedent in this jurisdiction for relieving a party of the duty to restore all of the money paid to him under a judgment subsequently vacated. Understandably, of course, the receipt and disbursement of money by someone in a fiduciary capacity could very well present a different case, but when the party who received the money by authority of the judgment has spent some or all of it at his own volition and for his own ends, we find it difficult to accept the proposition that equity diminishes his accountability.

In this instance the Lewises spent $1935 to pay off a note, $1800 for improvements on their house, $3,000 for educating their son, $3155 for automobiles, and about $4800 for medical expenses and care of the returned daughter. They now have only about $6,000 in cash deposits, but their net worth substantially exceeds the amount received under the judgment against the insurance company.

According to § 142(1) of the Restatement, Restitution, "The right of a person to restitution from another because of a benefit received is terminated or diminished if, after the receipt of the benefit, circumstances have so changed that it would be inequitable to require the other to make full restitution." The *Comment* following that section explains that there is no such change in circumstances "where the money is used for the payment of living expenses, or even used to make gifts, unless such expenses were incurred or gifts made because of the receipt of the money and the amount of such payment was of such size that *considering the financial condition of the payee* it would be inequitable to require payment." [Emphasis added.]

The illustrations following that commentary do not reveal to our satisfaction a workable criterion for determining what is "inequitable." "Equity" is a broad term, allowing for as many different definitions as there are people who are familiar with it. Often overlooked, however, is the simple fact that both equity and equality are derived from the same word and have much more in common than a similar sound. We think of equity as an implement of sympathy and compassion, but its real meaning is more akin to equality. What is fair for one must be fair for the other. In this case, is it fair that the stockholders of the insurance company lose $7200 because the Lewises have spent the money? We do not think so. It was not the insurance company, but the Lewises, who claimed their daughter was dead, and it is not at all unjust to hold that when they took the money they had to do so at the risk of having to repay it if their claim proved to be unfounded, as it did. We perceive nothing in this record to raise an equitable defense in mitigation of the demand for restitution.

On the question of interest, there can be no doubt that the insurance company's claim for restitution, though quasi-contractual in nature, was "liquidated" and that interest ordinarily is recoverable as a matter of right on a liquidated claim. [Citation.] Interest may be allowed also on the basis of an implied contract, or quasi-contract, and probably should be if the money or property has been used for profit-making.
* * *

When an innocent party uses the money or property of another in reliance upon a final unappealed judgment that says it is his, it can hardly be said that he is at fault unless and until he is put on notice of circumstances that justify or call for setting the judgment aside.   In this case the Lewises learned on July 25, 1971, that their daughter was still alive.   A private investigator employed by the insurance company discovered it on August 25, 1971.   On the basis of these facts we are of the opinion that interest on the amount recoverable by the insurance company should run from July 25, 1971.

The judgment is reversed on the appeal and affirmed on the cross-appeal, with directions that a new judgment be entered in conformity with this opinion.

----

1.   The Restatement of Restitution § 69 * addresses the defense of change of circumstances:

(1) The right of a person to restitution from another because of a benefit received because of mistake is terminated or diminished if, after the receipt of the benefit, circumstances have so changed that it would be inequitable to require the other to make full restitution.

(2) Change of circumstances may be a defense or a partial defense if the conduct of the recipient was not tortious and he was no more at fault for his receipt, retention or dealing with the subject matter than was the claimant.

(3) Change of circumstances is not a defense if

(a) the conduct of the recipient in obtaining, retaining or dealing with the subject matter was tortious, or

(b) the change occurred after the recipient had knowledge of the facts entitling the other to restitution and had an opportunity to make restitution.

2.   The Restatement of Restitution § 178 comment a * states:

The right to restitution from another for a benefit conferred upon him is terminated if circumstances have so changed that it would be inequitable to require him to make restitution (*see* §§ 69, 142).   Where property is transferred as a result of a mistake of such a character that the transferor is entitled to restitution, the transferee holds the property upon a constructive trust for the transferor (*see* § 163); but if the transferee, having no notice of the mistake, so changes his position that it would be inequitable to compel him to surrender the property, the transferor can no longer enforce the constructive trust.   The same rule is applicable where a transfer is induced by fraud, duress or undue influence of a third person (*see* § 167); in such a case if the transferee before he has notice of the fraud, duress or undue influence so changes his position that it is inequitable to compel him to surrender the property, he no longer holds it upon a constructive trust for the transferor. So also, the rule is applicable where a person holding property upon a constructive trust transfers it to a person who does not give value for the property (*see* § 168); in such a case if the transferee before he has notice of the facts giving rise to the constructive trust so changes his position that it is inequitable to compel him to surrender the property, he no longer holds it upon a constructive trust for the transferor.

3. The defense of change of position is ineffective if the defendant's circumstances or actions take place after receiving notice of the facts giving rise to the restitutionary claim. In Western Casualty & Surety Co. v. Kohm, 638 S.W.2d 798 (Mo.App.1982), for example, the plaintiff insurance company paid the defendant insured the value, less the contractual deductible amount, of an automobile which had sustained significant damage in a collision. Several months later the insurance company discovered that the insurance policy did not provide for collision coverage. The court acknowledged that the mistake in coverage was attributable to the insurer and was not induced by the fraud or misrepresentations of the policyholder but still awarded restitution of the insurance proceeds. The court held that the fact that the insured had purchased a replacement automobile with the funds did not constitute a sufficient change of position to defeat restitution because the insured knew that he had no contractual right to receive the proceeds.

4. The change of position defense has been asserted often in cases involving the mistaken payment of funds where the defendant or third parties in reliance on the payment take action materially affecting the defendant. For example, in Bank Saderat Iran v. Amin Beydoun, Inc., 555 F.Supp. 770 (S.D.N.Y.1983), the plaintiff bank mistakenly overpaid the defendant on behalf of one of its customers. The defendant shipped materials to the customer in exchange for the mistaken payment, and the customer subsequently went out of business. The bank sued for restitution and the court upheld the defendant's change of position defense on the basis that the defendant, if ordered to refund the money, would have no effective remedy against its former customer. *Also see* Alden Auto Parts Warehouse, Inc. v. Dolphin Equipment Leasing Corp., 682 F.2d 330 (2d Cir.1982) (plaintiff denied restitution where third party responsible for fraudulent inducement of equipment lease had gone out of business).

5. For additional commentary on the defense of change of position see the following references: Cohen, Change of Position in Quasi–Contracts, 45 Harv.L.Rev. 1333 (1932); Costigan, Change of Position as a Defense in Quasi–Contracts—The Relation of Implied Warranty and Agency to Quasi–Contract, 20 Harv.L.Rev. 205 (1907); Friedman, Payment of Another's Debt, 99 L.Q.Rev. 534 (1983); Gilmore, The Commer-

cial Doctrine of Good Faith Purchase, 63 Yale L.J. 1057 (1954); Jones, Change of Circumstances in Quasi–Contract, 73 L.Q.Rev. 48 (1957); Langmaid, Quasi–Contract—Change of Position by Receipt of Money in Satisfaction of a Preexisting Obligation, 21 Calif.L.Rev. 311 (1933).

C. VOLUNTEERS

Section Coverage:

The recipients of gifts are not obliged to pay the donors for them. Volunteers cannot force others to become their debtors by providing them with unrequested goods or services and then suing them for the value of the enrichment. The principle applies not only to gratuities but also to other benefits voluntarily bestowed even when a gift is not intended. If a benefit has been officiously conferred on an unwilling defendant who has no choice in its acceptance, a court will deny restitution. Such plaintiffs are called "officious intermeddlers." For example, an organization that decides to raise money by painting house numbers on curbs and then asking each homeowner for a payment for the service is not legally entitled to restitution. Even if uncooperative homeowners like the service, they had no choice of accepting it and thus are not bound to pay for it.

There are some exceptions to this broad rule that restitution is not available to volunteers. The most important one is that there may be restitution to a plaintiff who never intended a gift if the defendant does have a meaningful choice whether to accept the benefit. The principle is that a defendant should compensate an unofficious volunteer who is not acting gratuitously when the defendant could refuse the benefit but instead elects to retain it. For example, if someone takes a lost pet in need of immediate medical attention to a veterinarian when the owner cannot be located, the owner later has a choice whether to accept the return of the saved pet. Restitution is appropriate for the value of emergency treatment reasonably performed if the defendant elects to retain the benefit of the now healthy pet. If not, then the Good Samaritan can keep the abandoned animal.

Courts sometimes give restitution to a volunteer even when the defendant does not have a choice of acceptance. For example, a Good Samaritan who helps a lost child by paying for emergency treatment when the parents cannot be located is not officiously intermeddling; the parents must give restitution for benefit. Although the parent has no choice of acceptance, the fulfillment of the support obligation under circumstances of necessity is a saving to the parents that amounts to unjust enrichment.

Model Case:

Taylor operates an office building which was leased from its owner, Owens. Taylor in turn subleases office space to various businesses.

Owens retained the ground floor office space for the Owens Realty offices, but leased the rest to Taylor.

During the first few months of this arrangement Taylor paid the heating bills for the entire building because the subleases provided that Taylor would supply heating and cooling. Taylor mistakenly believed that this obligation included the floor occupied by Owens, but in fact Owens was responsible for the heat in that portion of the building.

Taylor could recover from Owens the amount mistakenly paid because no gift was intended and the payment was not done officiously. Although some courts would be troubled that Owens had no choice in the substitution of creditors, most would not bar restitution with the volunteer defense under these circumstances. Taylor's innocence and the relative hardship of the parties would be relevant factors.

EVERHART v. MILES

47 Md.App. 131, 422 A.2d 28 (1980).

WEANT, JUDGE.

[Miles (appellee) negotiated to purchase from Everhart (appellant) certain property: 101 acres of land which included barns, silos and a farmhouse, certain equipment and farm machinery, and 75 head of Holstein cattle. The total purchase price was $279,000. The parties' proposed agreement contemplated a $29,000 down payment, installment payments for the balance for most items, and a lease purchase option for the real property at the end of a ten year period.]

* * *

In May of 1978 Bruce Miles and his wife traveled from North Carolina to the Allegany–Garrett Counties area for the purpose of taking over their proposed purchases. They moved onto the farm on or about 1 June 1978, at which time they made a down payment of Ten Thousand Dollars ($10,000.00) in lieu of the originally agreed upon amount of Twenty-nine Thousand Dollars ($29,000.00). On this same date, a contract of sale was to have been executed; however, for various reasons this was never accomplished and negotiations continued. Nevertheless, the appellees lived on the farm, ran the dairy business, and made certain improvements; for example, they fixed the barn roof, renovated the farmhouse, installed a septic system, and replaced the house pump, despite the absence of a written agreement. Further, they made repairs to a tractor, a silo loader, and a field chopper. Also, through their efforts, approximately six hundred tons of silage were put into the silos; this silage remained behind when the appellees vacated the farm on 21 September 1978.

During the appellees' stay on the farm, efforts were made by the parties to have a written contract prepared that was agreeable to all parties but this never came about. Eventually, the appellees lowered their total offer for the purchase of the farm, equipment, and cattle to

One Hundred and Eighty-nine Thousand Dollars ($189,000.00); this offer was flatly rejected by the appellant, thereby causing the appellees to depart forthwith.

[The trial court awarded restitution to the appellees in the amount of $33,794.02 on the ground that the appellant had been unjustly benefitted by the actions of the appellees.]

* * *

Unjust enrichment is defined as the unjust retention of a benefit to the loss of another, or the retention of money or property of another against the fundamental principles of justice or equity and good conscience. A person is enriched if he has received a benefit, and he is unjustly enriched if retention of the benefit would be unjust. Unjust enrichment of a person occurs when he has and retains money or benefits which in justice and equity belong to another. [Citation.]

Similarly, Williston on Contracts § 1479 (3rd ed. 1970) sets forth the three elements that must be established to sustain a claim based on unjust enrichment; these are:

1. A benefit conferred upon the defendant by the plaintiff;

2. An appreciation or knowledge by the defendant of the benefit; and

3. The acceptance for retention by the defendant of the benefit under such circumstances as to make it inequitable for the defendant to retain the benefit without the payment of its value.

Also, in speaking of unjust enrichment Restatement of Restitution § 1 (1937) makes this comment, "[a] person who has been unjustly enriched at the expense of another is required to make restitution to the other." However, these authorities maintain that unjust enrichment does not exist where the benefit has officiously been thrust upon the defendant. With this in mind, we turn to the facts of the instant case.

There is no doubt that the appellant knew and accepted that the appellees were expending substantial amounts of money for repairs and improvements of his real property. Further, the appellant benefited from the conditioning of his farm equipment, as well as from the retention of certain milk checks that monetized as a result of the appellees' labors.

The question then arises as to whether or not there was an officious conference of these benefits. Restatement of Restitution § 2 (1937) indicates that officiousness is constituted by "interference in the affairs of others not justified by the circumstances under which this interference takes place." In this regard the appellant argues that the appellees thrust the benefits in question upon him and thus that he should not be considered to be unjustly enriched. As support he relies on Gould v. American Water Works Service Co., 52 N.J. 226, 245 A.2d 14 (1968), *cert. denied,* 394 U.S. 943, 89 S.Ct. 1274, 22 L.Ed.2d 477 (1969). Specifically, he depends on the holding of the New Jersey court that the plaintiff therein was a volunteer. Accordingly the appellant would have us designate him similarly because in the present case there was no request for what was done and hence the fact that drawn out negotiations were unsuccessfully held was no basis for forcing liability on the appellant. *Gould,* however, is not directly on point. In that case the plaintiff dug a well on his own property without any request from the defendant American Water Works; rather, Mr. Gould did this on sheer speculation, hoping that he would be able to sell the well to the American Water Works at a later date. The negotiations spoken of in that case by the New Jersey court were negotiations carried on a long time after the drilling of the well and entailed the sale of same. Moreover, the unjust enrichment complained of was the alleged benefit that American Water Works Company obtained from Gould's experience in drilling for water across the road from some property later acquired by American Water Works. We can readily agree that in such a situation the plaintiff did occupy the position of a volunteer.

Be that as it may in our case the appellees were told to take over the farm and run it as they saw fit; in essence, they were told that it was theirs. In fact, although the appellant denies visiting the farm after July 1, he does admit that he did see that the appellees were making certain repairs and improvements thereon. Further, much of the work that was done appears to have been necessary in order to operate the farm. We cannot, therefore, hold that this constitutes officiousness, since it was neither thrust upon the appellant nor strictly voluntary on the part of the appellees.

Maryland has recognized the doctrine of unjust enrichment or restitution or melioration as it is sometimes called. * * * Certainly it would not be in equity and good conscience to allow the appellant herein to retain the fruits of the appellees' labors, which were performed without a contract but within the possessive blessing of the appellant and with his knowledge that improvements were being made.

Another case relied on by the appellant is the equity case of Welsh v. Welsh, 254 Md. 681, 255 A.2d 368 (1969). In *Welsh* the Court of Appeals reversed the trial court by finding that the occupiers of the land in question were not *bona fide* possessors when they built a service station notwithstanding the knowledge of the owner's claim to the property. Having so found, the Court held that the occupiers were not entitled to compensation for improvements made thereon. Of significance in the above-cited case is the fact that there was considerable dispute over the ownership of the land; in fact, an ejectment action had been instituted. In spite of knowledge of this, the claimants proceeded with the erection of an addition to the original service station building.

In the instant case, on the other hand, the appellees were in possession of the property in question with the wholehearted approbation of the appellant. In this regard, the lower court found that "[w]ith the consent of the [appellant], the [appellees] took possession of the farm and began to operate it. The parties assumed that a sale's contract would be executed." Furthermore, it is apparent that all of the improvements were made during the time that the negotiations concerning the terms of the contract to be executed were continuing.

One final note in reference to the *Welsh* case: there the Court of Appeals quoted with approval at pages 88–89, 255 A.2d at 372, the equitable doctrine of melioration or compensation for improvements as stated in 2 H. Tiffany, Real Property § 625 (3rd ed. 1939):

> "Since the rule that erections or additions made by one who has no rights to land are fixtures, and therefore not removable by him, even though he made them in the belief that he was the owner of the land, is calculated to cause hardships to an innocent occupant of another's land, by giving the benefit of his labor and expenditures to the landowner, the courts of this country, without either imputing fraud or requiring proof of it, hold it inequitable to allow one to be enriched under such circumstances by the labor and expenditures of another who acted in good faith and in ignorance of any adverse claim or title. Applying this doctrine of 'unjust enrichment,' a court of equity will, on the principle that he who seeks equity must do equity, refuse its assistance to the rightful owner of the land as against an occupant thereof unless he makes compensation for permanent and beneficial improvements, made by the latter without notice of the defect in his title."

At no time during the appellees' stay on the farm did the appellant question their right to possession. In fact, according to the testimony, the appellant did not visit the farm subsequent to July 1 even though he knew of some of the appellees' labor and expenditures. Also, we find no assertion on the part of the appellant that he ever questioned the appellees' right to possession of the property in question or their right to make improvements thereon. * * *

Judgment affirmed.

---

1. Historically courts denied restitution in all cases involving real property improvements that could not be removed. Modern cases have tended to allow recovery if the improvements are not fixtures. The theory is that the defendant has a choice whether to accept the benefit if it is not affixed. For example, a coat of paint on a house cannot be refused even if it is conferred unofficiously. In contrast, a free-standing shed is capable of removal; if the landowner keeps it, restitution may be appropriate.

The principal case allowed restitution for affixed improvements. Was the choice principle violated? Was the result a correct one?

2. Judicial reception to volunteers has changed during the past century. Historically it was very difficult to get restitution for benefits that were conferred without agreement. For example, in Glenn v.

Savage, 14 Or. 567, 13 P. 442 (1887), a large and valuable lot of defendant's lumber accidentally fell into the Columbia River and was about to be lost. The defendant was gone, so the plaintiff saved the lumber at his own expense. The defendant kept the salvaged lumber but refused to pay the plaintiff for the expense. The court denied restitution and said the defendant would only be liable if he had requested the service. The court observed:

> The great and leading rule of law is to deem an act done for the benefit of another, without his request, as a voluntary act of courtesy, for which no action can be sustained. The world abounds with acts of this kind, done upon no request; but would more abound with ruinous litigation, and the overthrow of personal rights and civil freedom, if the law was otherwise. [Citation.] The law will never permit a friendly act, or such as was intended to be an act of kindness or benevolence, to be afterwards converted into a pecuniary demand. It would be doing violence to some of the kindest and best effusions of the heart to suffer them afterwards to be perverted by sordid avarice. Whatever differences may arise afterwards among men, let those meritorious and generous acts remain lasting monuments of the good offices, intended in the days of good neighborhood and friendship; and let no after-circumstances ever tarnish or obliterate them from the recollection of the parties. 14 Or. 567, 13 P. 442 (1887).

Under modern law the plaintiff in *Glenn v. Savage* would be likely to recover. Courts generally allow restitution to a plaintiff if (1) there was an initial intent to charge, (2) the actions were reasonably necessary for the preservation of the property, and (3) the defendant chose to accept the benefit later.

PROBLEM: THE POOR RICH NEIGHBORS

A farmer who owned a family farm was killed in a combine accident during the harvest season. The neighboring individual farmers attended the funeral and then undertook to harvest the crop for the bereaved family.

After this episode the deceased farmer's estate is discovered to be very large, even independent of the value of the farm land. Although the deceased had lived modestly, he was very wealthy. Can the kind neighbors charge the family for the value of the harvesting services provided after the funeral?

JAKO v. PILLING CO.

848 F.2d 318 (1st Cir.1988).

Torruella, Circuit Judge.

Appellant Geza Jako is a physician and professor of otolaryngology. Beginning in 1963 Dr. Jako entered into an informal collaboration relationship with appellee Pilling Company, a manufacturer of specialized medical equipment. Dr. Jako made several recommendations regarding the design of equipment used in microsurgery of the larynx, mainly laryngoscopes. Pilling had manufactured laryngoscopes prior to 1963, but from 1963 to the mid-to-late 1970's, most of Pilling's laryngoscopes, as well as other instruments used in the course of larynx-microsurgery, were developed substantially according to the suggestions of Dr. Jako. Following industry practice, the instruments bore the name of the physician who suggested the modification, in this instance, *e.g.*, the "Jako laryngoscope."

Dr. Jako does not hold, nor has he ever held, a patent on any of the instruments developed as a result of his ideas. Dr. Jako never sought compensation for his services before 1984. Indeed, Pilling has never compensated persons for the use of their names or ideas in relation to product development unless the idea has been patented.

Dr. Jako has repeatedly stated that when he entered into the relationship with Pilling he believed it inappropriate for physicians to receive any money for their ideas. However, after several years with little or no contact between the parties, Dr. Jako sent Pilling a demand letter in December 1984. The letter demanded a one percent royalty payment for all products bearing his name sold within the prior fifteen years, and a three percent royalty payment on all future sales of similar products.

* * *

Dr. Jako then filed a complaint alleging seven causes of action: count 1, breach of contract; count 2, restitution, unjust enrichment. * * *

The court found there was no evidence of an express contract between the parties prior to 1984. Furthermore, the court correctly held that there was no contract implied in fact. The conduct of the parties and the relationship between them showed no basis to find a contract implied in fact. * * *

As to count two, claiming unjust enrichment, the court similarly found the record silent on Dr. Jako's reasonable expectation that he would be paid. [Citation.] Examining the equities of this situation, we also agree that Dr. Jako is not entitled to any restitution. When Dr. Jako entered into this relationship, he sought only to benefit mankind by improving medical equipment. This he achieved. He also received the benefit of a very successful career promoted, in part, by the name recognition that resulted from the relationship. In effect, the relationship benefited both parties, so Pilling was not unfairly enriched.

* * *

To conclude, we affirm the court's granting of summary judgment as to counts one and two. * * *

———

1. In a famous early case, Bartholomew v. Jackson, 20 Johns. 28 (N.Y.Sup.Ct.1922), it was observed: "The plaintiff performed the service without the privity or request of the defendant, and there was, in fact, no promise express or implied. If a man humanely bestows his labor, and even risks his life, in voluntarily aiding to preserve his neighbor's house from destruction by fire, the law considers the service rendered as gratuitous, and it therefore forms no ground of action."

2. Distinguish gifts from mistakenly conferred benefits. A plaintiff can receive restitution for mistaken payments to a defendant if there are no circumstances making such restitution inequitable, such as changed circumstances.

3. Payments to one of the defendant's debtors poses different problems than payments to the defendant personally. When a volunteer discharges another's debt and sues for restitution, the effect is a substitution of the defendant's creditors. Because the defendant is deprived of the choice of creditors, the court may deny restitution, especially if the plaintiff was acting officiously. When plaintiffs act under the mistaken belief that they are personally liable for the debt, or when they are preserving their own interests as they unofficiously affect the debts of others, courts can balance the hardships and allow restitution even if the choice principle is violated.

In Blue Cross v. Wheeler, 93 A.D.2d 995, 461 N.Y.S.2d 624 (1983), the plaintiff insurance company paid the hospital bills of the defendant's wife in the mistaken belief that the health insurance policy was in effect at the time the debt was incurred. In fact the defendant had failed to pay the premiums for a long enough time that the policy had expired. The court allowed restitution because the defendant was unjustly enriched by the plaintiff's payment for necessaries furnished to the wife for which the husband was legally responsible.

Is the result in *Blue Cross* justifiable? The husband plaintiff was denied the choice of creditors, apparently without fraud and through no fault of his own. Does a change in creditors matter? Is the hospital more likely to forgive the debt or to arrange convenient terms than the insurance company?

Reconsider the longstanding rule that provision of necessaries to a defendant's legal dependents is not officious intermeddling. Is there a difference in a situation such as the one in *Blue Cross* between directly furnishing necessaries and indirectly doing so? The court thought not, but would the result have been different if the insurance company had sued the wife instead of the husband? She received the hospital treatment and apparently had no history of a relationship with the insurance company except that she was named as a covered dependent on the expired policy. Might the court then have balanced the hardships to produce a different result since the case would have involved the payment of her personal debt by a stranger?

FELTON v. FINLEY

69 Idaho 381, 209 P.2d 899 (1949).

GIVENS, JUSTICE.

March 1944, Seigle Finley and W.E. or William Finley, two of the three surviving nephews of Seigle Coleman, who died testate December 4, 1943, employed respondent to contest the deceased Coleman's will, which was successfully done. [Citation.] At that time respondent told Seigle and William Finley that he would accept the employment only on condition that the other nephew and brother, Orval Finley, and the three sisters, Ida Davis, Nan Holder, and Rose Finley Nichles, likewise employ respondent as their attorney and that all six of the heirs participate in the contest.

Respondent requested Seigle and William Finley to contact their brother and sisters and secure signed contracts of employment similar to the ones which Seigle and William signed; namely, on a 50 per cent contingent basis. Respondent likewise wrote the other four heirs requesting their execution of such contracts. Such heirs never replied to respondent's initial letter or to subsequent letters written by him continuing to request their execution of such contracts of employment and advising them as to the course of the litigation.

Seigle and William Finely contacted two sisters, Nan Holder and Ida Davis in Pilot Rock, Oregon, with reference to their joining in the employment of respondent and related that:

> " * * * they said they would have nothing to do with it. My oldest sister, Ida Davis, is very religious and she said she didn't feel like protesting. She said, 'What you boys do is your business, but I will have nothing to do with it.' "

* * *

Testifying further that they (Seigle and William Finley) attempted to get the three sisters and the other brother to join with them—that is, in the employment of respondent in the prosecution of the contest, stating further:

> "A. I had quite a time contacting my brother (Orval). He was in Alaska part of the time and I called him in St. Paul, Minnesota, that's his home, and he said, 'I am having nothing whatever to do with a dead man's money.' "

and that he (Orval),

> " * * * would have nothing to do one way or the other, what I did was my business, to forget about him."

and about the same as to Rose Finley Nichles:

> "She said she would have nothing to do with the estate. She said, 'If you and Bill sign, that's your business. I am not going to.

There is no use sending the contract.' I read it to her over the phone and she said, 'No.' ''

* * *

At the conclusion of the contest action, distributive checks were made out to each one of the six heirs jointly with respondent for their respective shares, which the three sisters and Orval refused to accept, taking the position they had never employed respondent and were not obligated to pay him any fee and subsequent conferences between respondent and Mrs. Holder were unavailing.

The present suit to establish the implied contract and to enforce the attorney's lien, resulted with findings, conclusions and decree there was an implied contract of employment, from which decree the present appeal was taken.

By stipulation, the appellants have been paid their distributive shares less the portion thereof claimed by respondent and decreed to him as his fee from them.

These facts are established by the record without dispute: that respondent wrote the appellants to the effect he had been employed by their two brothers and he desired their co-employment; that he wrote them of the progress of the litigation and that they refused to sign the contracts and did not answer his letters; that at least one of them had actual notice of the progress of the litigation and being a matter of public record, and they being parties to the probate proceedings, regardless of the contest because they were devisees under the will, they all had constructive notice of the proceedings; and that they did not repudiate respondent's appearing for them that though appellants did not affirmatively participate in the contest, they did not resist and immediately upon the contest being successfully concluded, claimed the additional shares in their Uncle's estate which had been made available to them by the prosecution of the suit and respondent's services in connection therewith, which resulted in benefits to the appellants, together with the two brothers who did actually employ him.

* * *

It is an elementary rule that, whenever services are rendered and received, a contract of hiring or an obligation to pay what they are reasonably worth will generally be presumed. [Citations.]

* * *

The record herein affirmatively and positively shows the respondent was not undertaking the services herein for anyone gratuitously. It is also held the acceptance of benefits must be voluntary. The acceptance and receipt by appellants of their share of their enhanced inheritance were entirely voluntary, because there is no law which required them to accept the greater amount; they could have taken only the $500.00 which the will initially gave them and refused the additional sum. Whatever scruples or feelings they had about not signing contracts, taking a dead man's money or interfering with his will, had thus evidently disappeared when the money was made available to them, even though without their active participation. Nevertheless, it was solely through respondent's efforts and successful prosecution of the contest case which procured this additional money for them and which, when thus secured to them by respondent's services, they promptly demanded and have pocketed.

Such course of conduct on their part amounts to such ratification and recognition of respondent's actions as to create in law an implied contract of employment and fully justified the decree in respondent's favor. [Citation.]

The decree is, therefore, affirmed. Costs awarded to respondent.

HOLDEN, CHIEF JUSTICE (dissenting).

December 4, 1943, Seigle Coleman died testate. By will he bequeathed $5,000 to Wilbur Coleman and $500 each to certain nieces and nephews, and the remainder of his estate to certain charitable organizations. The will was later offered and admitted to probate. Thereafter, two of the three surviving nephews, Seigle Finley and William Finley, entered into a contract with respondent Felton by which they agreed to pay Felton one-half of all benefits which might be obtained by virtue of a contest of the will. One nephew, Orval Finley, and three nieces, Ida Davis, Nan Holder and Rose Finley Nichles, refused to sign identical contracts or to have anything to do with the contest or the employment of respondent. Then followed a contest of the will in the probate court. That court held the will to be validly executed, but held the clauses attempting to bequeath and devise part of the property to different institutions were void because the institutions were charitable and the will had been executed less than thirty days prior to the decease of Seigle Coleman. An appeal was taken to the district court. That court decreed the will was valid and properly executed; that the clauses attempting to devise the property to charitable organizations were void; that the will should be enforced as to the specific bequests other than those to the charitable institutions, and the balance of the property should be distributed to the heirs of Seigle Coleman; that inasmuch as Seigle Coleman had left no father, mother, wife, brothers or sisters, the property should be distributed in equal parts to the heirs of the deceased brothers and sisters, who are nephews and nieces of Seigle Coleman, deceased. Upon appeal the district court was affirmed.

* * *

It is urged in the case at bar that where one permits another to perform services for him, the law raises an implied promise to pay the reasonable value of the services. But respondent does not bring himself within the rule. Here, appellants, notwithstanding several efforts were made to induce them to employ respondent, refused to do so. It is true respondent performed services in contesting the will, but the services were performed for "S.P. Finley [Seigle]" and William Finley under the

terms of a written contract. He was thus obligated to perform all the services he performed. He could not repudiate his solemn contract without committing a breach. Nor was respondent expected by those who thus employed him to perform such or any services gratuitously. The contract which respondent himself drew provided for the payment of the compensation which he thought his services were worth. The benefits which came to appellants were the result of the performance of the terms of the written contract entered into by respondent with Seigle and William Finley, not the result of any contract with appellants, because they refused to employ him. And, further, the services respondent performed in contesting the will were performed with knowledge appellants would not employ him. In fact, appellants were opposed to the contest and would not, and did not, have anything to do with it. No case has been cited and none can be found holding an implied promise or implied contract to pay for services under such facts and circumstances.
* * *

But it is argued the acceptance of accruing benefits created an implied contract to pay respondent. In resolving that question the above stated facts of this case should be kept in mind. The courts are unanimous in holding an acceptance of benefits does not create an implied contract to pay.

* * *

The judgment should be reversed and the cause remanded with directions to dismiss the action.

ON REHEARING

HOLDEN, CHIEF JUSTICE.

* * * [T]he decree appealed from in the case at bar should be, and it is hereby, reversed and the cause remanded with directions to dismiss the action, in accordance with the views expressed in the fore-going dissenting opinion of Chief Justice Holden. Costs awarded to appellants.

———

1. There is no recovery in restitution for benefits incidentally bestowed upon the defendant while the plaintiff pursues matters of personal benefit. For example, when a homeowner plants a hedge fence on the property line, the neighbor's property may increase in value. This enrichment is incidentally bestowed upon the neighbor by the homeowner's action and it is not unjust to retain it.

This principle applies even if the benefit was tangible. For example, if the neighbor had been saving money to plant a hedge along that line, the homeowner's action would produce a tangible savings. Moreover, the enrichment is not unjust even if the choice principle were not violated. For example, the homeowner might have asked the neighbor's opinion about having a hedge between them and offered to abandon the project upon objection.   This friendly consultation would not make the enrichment unjust to retain unless the neighbor had promised to help with expenses if certain changes in the plans were made.

2.   In Bashara v. Baptist Memorial Hospital System, 685 S.W.2d 307 (Tex.1985), an attorney effected a settlement agreement with an insurance company on behalf of an injured client.   While the suit was pending but before that settlement was achieved, a hospital filed a lien for charges incurred in treating the injured party.   The insurance company subsequently paid the settlement amount and separately paid the hospital to discharge the lien.   The attorney brought an action in quantum meruit against the hospital for services rendered.   The court acknowledged that the attorney's actions benefitted the hospital by creating a "fund", but still disallowed the attorney's fees because quantum meruit requires that the efforts be undertaken "for the person sought to be charged."

3.   Consider the beneficial effect of ground-breaking litigation for others similarly situated.   When a plaintiff brings an individual action that has the effect of making litigation or settlement easier for subsequent claimants, has there been any unjust enrichment?   The plaintiff's substantial litigation expense has helped others who do not share in the cost.   Recall the circumstances in *Gruca v. United States Steel,* reprinted *supra* in Chapter 5.   The aggrieved veteran in that case did not aggressively assert his claim for years until after another similarly situated veteran litigated the matter.

The beneficiaries of ground-breaking litigation do share the cost if the plaintiff brings a class action.   In such a case they each have the option of withdrawing individually from the class, thus eliminating any obligation to assist with costs.   Why does this difference matter?   Is enrichment from the litigation of others best analyzed as an incidentally bestowed benefit or as a matter involving the choice principle?   Is the enrichment of the defendants in the principal case the same as other beneficiaries from litigation?

Part V

CONCLUSION: COMPLETING THE REMEDIAL PICTURE

Chapter 18

JURY TRIALS

A. SUBSTANTIVE EQUITY AND EQUITABLE CLEAN-UP

Section Coverage:

The rule that limits equitable jurisdiction to cases in which the legal remedy is inadequate governs requests for injunctions and specific performance orders. (*See* Chapters 3 and 4) The historical independence of equity courts accounts for the inadequacy rule as well as for a separate basis of equity jurisdiction known as substantive equity. Cases involving trusts and mortgages, for example, were originally brought to the equity courts because the courts at law had no effective way of handling them fairly. Equity devised means of dealing with the special problems created in these areas, and thus any case concerning these substantive matters came under equitable jurisdiction. The inadequacy rule did not control in these limited instances.

The merger of law and equity brought procedural benefits, including that mixed claims of law and equity could be brought before one judge. The merger did not change the substantive differences between law and equity, however. One important difference that remains is that the federal Constitutional right to trial by jury in civil trials is reserved for actions at law; there is no jury right for equitable actions. This guarantee does not apply to the states, but many state constitutions have similar provisions.

When a plaintiff brings a purely legal claim to a merged court, such as an action for damages, there is a right to a jury trial. There is no such right when the claim is purely equitable, such as one for specific performance. Problems arise when the plaintiff brings a mixed claim that seeks both legal and equitable relief, or when a plaintiff brings one type of claim and the defendant counterclaims with a different type. The complex federal approach to these problems is studied in the next section. The most common state approach is the subject of this section.

Model Case:

Darby and Pendleton own adjoining businesses on Main Street in a summer tourist town. They have had a history of various disagree-

878

ments, including perpetual arguments about political matters concerning the downtown businesses.

Another dispute began when Darby's employees had difficulty unloading merchandise through the regular service doors, which needed repairs. They began to use an entrance that required their vans to trespass on a portion of Pendleton's land. When Pendleton called to complain of the practice, Darby provided reassurance that the problem was temporary because the service doors were being repaired.

The practice became a regular one, however, because Darby's employees preferred the alternative entrance even after the service doors were repaired. Moreover, there were several instances when the Darby vans damaged some of Pendleton's landscaping. Pendleton's repeated calls to Darby brought only unfulfilled promises to correct the problem. The tourist season had begun and Darby was distracted by other matters. The increased business made Pendleton all the more eager to stop the annoying and damaging practice.

Pendleton sued Darby. The complaint sought an injunction against further trespasses and damages for the minor landscaping damage. The judge granted the order. In most states the judge would then "cleanup" the damages issue without benefit of a jury. The final judgment on damages for past losses would be entered by the judge who acted as trier of fact on both the legal and equitable claims.

PELFREY v. BANK OF GREER

270 S.C. 691, 244 S.E.2d 315 (1978).

LEWIS, CHIEF JUSTICE:

This is a corporate stockholder's derivative action to recover damages on behalf of the corporation resulting from the alleged negligence and breach of fiduciary duty by the appellant Bank in the handling of the corporation's funds. * * *

The first question involves a determination of whether the stockholder's derivative action is one in equity or at law. It is undisputed that, if the action is in equity, it is to be tried by the court; if at law, it is triable by a jury and the lower court would have been correct in refusing a compulsory order of reference.

* * *

In determining the right to a jury trial, the lower court relied upon Ross v. Bernhard, 396 U.S. 531, 90 S.Ct. 733, 24 L.Ed.2d 729, 733, where the United States Supreme Court held: " ... the right to a jury trial attaches to those issues in derivative actions as to which the corporation, if it had been suing in its own right, would have been entitled to a jury." The lower court apparently concluded that, since the complaint in this action sought the recovery of damages, a legal cause was stated for trial by jury.

Ross was brought under the Seventh Amendment to the United States Constitution, which governs right to trial by jury in Federal courts. This amendment has never been held applicable to the States; and this Court has interpreted Article 1, Section 14, of the South Carolina Constitution, which preserves the right of trial by jury inviolate, to mean that right of jury trial shall be preserved only in those cases in which the parties were entitled to it under the law or practice existing at the time of the adoption of the constitution. [Citations.]

Paraphrasing the rule stated in the last cited cases, the pertinent inquiry is whether, at the time of the adoption of the Constitution of 1868, either party to a stockholder's derivative action had the right, under the existing law or practice, to demand a jury trial of the factual issues. The mode of trial was unaffected by statute in this State and the inquiry thus becomes one of determining the common law with reference to the right to a jury trial. We have found no decision of this court dealing with the present question and none has been cited.

* * *

Historically the shareholder's derivative suit has always been tried exclusively in equity. "Even where the only relief allowable is a recovery of damages the suit is nevertheless one in equity and not an action at law." [Citations.]

The dissenting opinion in Ross v. Bernhard, 396 U.S. p. 545, 90 S.Ct. p. 742, 24 L.Ed. p. 740, gives a concise statement of the development of the shareholder's derivation action:

> . . . a shareholder's suit was not originally viewed in this country, or in England, as a suit to enforce a *corporate* cause of action. Rather, the shareholder's suit was initially permitted only against the managers of the corporation—not third parties—and it was conceived of as an equitable action to enforce the right of a beneficiary against his trustee. The shareholder was not, therefore, in court to enforce indirectly the corporate right of action, but to enforce directly his own equitable right of action against an unfaithful fiduciary. Later the rights of the shareholder were enlarged to encompass suits against third parties harming the corporation,. . . . Indeed the commentators, . . ., recognize that historically the suit has in practice always been treated as a single cause tried exclusively in equity. They agree that there is therefore no constitutional right to a jury trial even where there might have been one had the corporation itself brought the suit.

Since the shareholder's derivative action has historically been considered as one exclusively in equity, a party is not entitled to a trial by jury as a matter of right. The constitutional provision (Art. 1, Section 14), that the right of jury trial shall remain inviolate, does not apply to cases within the equitable jurisdiction of the court. [Citations.]

The lower court was therefore in error in refusing the motion of appellant for an order of reference and in refusing to strike from the amended complaint the phrase "the plaintiff demands a jury trial."

* * * [Remanded.]

---

1. Substantive equity historically developed as a response to deficiencies in the law. The inadequacy rule was not an issue because there simply was no remedy at law. The separate basis of equitable jurisdiction has persisted despite the subsequent development of remedies at law and despite the merger of law and equity.

2. The problem confronting the Supreme Court in Ross v. Bernhard, 396 U.S. 531, 90 S.Ct. 733, 24 L.Ed.2d 729 (1970), was how to reconcile the historical development of substantive equity with the commands of the Seventh Amendment which provides for a right to jury trial in matters "at law." The Court decided to ignore the "historical accident" of the development of substantive equity and to focus instead upon the legal or equitable nature of the remedy sought in the underlying claim. As the principal case illustrates, the Court's decision in *Ross* applies only to federal jury trial rights because the Seventh Amendment does not apply to the states.

THORNBRUGH v. POULIN

679 S.W.2d 416 (Mo.App.1984).

GREENE, JUDGE.

Berniece, Robert and Maxine Thornbrugh sued defendants Poulin and Ozark Concrete Company (Ozark) in a five-count petition, seeking an injunction to prevent defendants from interfering with the use of plaintiffs' property by the operation of a rock quarry, and seeking actual and punitive damages for damage to their property and interference with its use. The Thornbrughs requested a jury trial on the damages issues, which request was denied. After trial by court, findings of fact, conclusions of law and a judgment were filed.

In its findings of fact, the trial court found as follows. Berniece Thornbrugh owned certain real estate in Taney County, Missouri, and Robert and Maxine Thornbrugh resided in their 1971 mobile home that was located on Berniece's property. * * *

Ozark began operating the quarry under their lease in 1978. In the course of Ozark's business of operating the quarry, it was necessary to use explosives to break up rock prior to processing it. These blasting operations were conducted at a distance of approximately 1100 to 1200 feet from Berniece's property except on one occasion when the blasting occurred approximately 600 feet from Berniece's property. * * *

In its conclusions of law, the trial court held Ozark's operation of the quarry did not constitute a nuisance, but that setting off blasts within 600 feet of the trailer and house located on plaintiffs' premises, or setting off explosive charges when the wind was from the west, which created a dust factor, would constitute a nuisance. The trial court further found that the property of the Thornbrughs had not been damaged by the blasting, and that their use and enjoyment of their property had not been interfered with, limited or curtailed as the result of the operation of the quarry by Ozark. In its judgment, the trial court enjoined Ozark from blasting or setting off explosive charges within 600 feet of plaintiffs' "trailer and house," or from throwing rocks or debris on plaintiffs' property, or from setting off explosive charges when the wind was west to east. The trial court found for the defendants and against the plaintiffs on all other issues, and taxed the costs against Ozark. This appeal followed.

In their first point relied on, the Thornbrughs contend that the denial by the trial court of their request for a jury trial on the actual and punitive damages claims * * * violated their constitutional right to a jury trial given them by the Seventh Amendment to the United States Constitution and art. 1, § 22(a) of the Missouri Constitution. Their argument might have had some validity if their request for equitable relief had been denied, as was the case in Sapp v. Garrett, 284 S.W.2d 49, 52 (Mo.App.1955), cited by plaintiffs as authority for their argument on this issue.

Here, plaintiffs asked for both equitable (injunction) and legal (money damages) relief. In the opinion of the trial judge, the "equitable clean-up doctrine" applies in Missouri, which means that where a petition requests both legal and equitable relief, unless the equitable issue is resolved before trial, or unless the trial court, after hearing evidence, determines that an equitable remedy is inappropriate, the trial court, sitting without a jury, has jurisdiction to hear and decide the legal issues, as well as the equitable ones. We agree with the trial judge, as the law of Missouri recognizes the equitable clean-up doctrine, subject to a finding, as was the case here, that some equitable right of the plaintiffs had been violated. [Citations.] The trial court did not err in denying the request for jury trial on the issue of damages.

In their next three points, plaintiffs argue that the trial court's findings * * * were against the greater weight of the evidence.

This was a hotly contested case. Eleven witnesses testified for plaintiffs and nine for the defendants. Over 100 exhibits were admitted into evidence. The transcript of the trial court's proceedings numbers 795 pages. The testimony, understandably, was conflicting. * * *

Our review of the record convinces us that there was substantial evidence to support the findings of the trial court that plaintiffs had not suffered any actual damages by the operation of the quarry and that plaintiffs were not entitled to a judgment enjoining unlimited operation of the quarry. * * *

The trial judge in this case, in addition to hearing the witnesses and viewing the exhibits, went to the areas mentioned in evidence, viewed plaintiffs' property and defendant rock quarry, and inspected the mobile home and house claimed to have been damaged by the blasting. He had the opportunity, based on fact and a determination of what witnesses were credible, to resolve the conflicts in the testimony and enter a judgment based on substantial evidence which was not against the weight of the evidence, and was not based on an incorrect declaration or application of law. The record indicates that he correctly performed that task.

Judgment affirmed.

Why did the plaintiffs perceive that a jury would have changed the outcome of this case? Is there any reason to believe that a group of jurors would decide such a case more sympathetically to the plaintiffs than a single judge? Is a group or one individual more likely to comprehend the extensive evidence involved? Does it matter that the individual judge is more experienced in hearing evidence than the nonprofessional jury? Does it matter that the various individuals on the jury have collectively among them more world experiences and knowledge about varied matters?

ZIEBARTH v. KALENZE
238 N.W.2d 261 (N.D.1976).

VOGEL, JUSTICE.

This case originated in the district court, Ward County, North Dakota, on a claim for equitable relief based upon contract. The plaintiff-appellee, Silver Ziebarth, a cattle buyer, sought specific performance of a contract for the sale of cattle from the defendant-appellant, LeRoy Kalenze, a rancher in the business of selling cattle.

The district court, without a jury, found for Ziebarth. The court awarded damages in the sum of $4,589 plus costs in lieu of specific performance. Kalenze moved under Rule 41(b), N.D.R.Civ.P., at the end of the plaintiff's case, for dismissal of the action on the ground that the pleadings asked for specific performance of the contract, whereas the subject matter of the contract, the cattle, was no longer available, making specific performance impossible. The district court denied the motion.

Kalenze appeals to this court from the judgment entered on October 23, 1974. He demands a new trial at law on the issues of liability and damages. He also appeals from the order of the district court denying his 41(b) motion to dismiss, and asserts that he was deprived of a jury trial on the issue of damages because of the denial of the motion. He never filed a demand for a jury in the trial court.

* * *

The plaintiff Ziebarth brought this case in equity, demanding specific performance of the contract at the agreed price pursuant to the remedies available to a buyer under the Uniform Commercial Code, Section 41–02–95, N.D.C.C. (UCC § 2–716). This section provides, in part:

> "1. Specific performance may be decreed where the goods are unique or in other proper circumstances."

> "2. The decree for specific performance may include such terms and conditions as to payment of the price, damages, or other relief as the court may deem just." [Emphasis supplied.]

The Code clearly allows the court to grant damages in an action by a buyer for specific performance, *in the court's decree* for specific performance. It is not clear, however, whether the Code allows damages to be awarded *in lieu of a decree* in equity. This case presents the unusual circumstance of a case brought in equity in which specific performance was not possible. The subject matter of the contract had been sold to a third party prior to commencement of the suit. It is not apparent from the pleadings or the testimony whether the plaintiff in this case knew that specific performance was impossible at the time he pled his case in equity.[2]

Of course, the defendant knew when he was served with process that specific performance was impossible, but he did not mention that fact in his answer. If the plaintiff had known that damages, and not specific performance, was the proper remedy—in fact, the only remedy available in this case—and had made the appropriate motion to amend, then the trial court should have allowed the plaintiff to amend his pleadings to conform to his remedy at law or dismissed the suit in equity. * * *

The case law on the issue of the court's jurisdiction to grant damages in lieu of the equitable relief prayed for is conflicting. Some courts recognize the doctrine of substituted legal relief in equity. Historically, where the ground for equitable relief failed, the bill in equity was dismissed and the parties were left to seek in the common-law courts whatever legal remedies remained. But in 1786, an equity court did not dismiss the bill, but retained jurisdiction for granting legal relief where specific performance failed only because of the defendant's wrongful conduct after the suit was begun. This became the basis for granting substituted legal relief in equity. James, Right to Jury Trial in Civil Actions, 72 Yale L.J. 655, 659 (1962). In order for the doctrine to be applied in a particular case, however, the plaintiff must first establish his right to equitable relief, to which damages might then be incidental or subsidiary. [Citation.] In Raasch v. Goulet, 57 N.D. 674, 223 N.W. 808 (1928), this court held that the right to recover damages under the doctrine of substituted legal relief (or equity's "clean up" jurisdiction, as it is sometimes referred to) depends on the right to specific performance and is not available until the latter is established.

---

2. The cattle were sold on December 23, 1972; the complaint was filed on January 22, 1973.

It is thus the rule in some jurisdictions, and the traditional view, that the court cannot give judgment for damages in an action brought in equity unless the plaintiff first proves his right to equitable relief. * * * In our view, the fusion of law and equity, which has been the law of North Dakota since Statehood, and the law of the Territory of Dakota from the time of its adoption of the Field Code of Civil Procedure at the first legislative session in 1862, puts the authority to grant equitable or legal relief in courts of general jurisdiction, regardless of technicalities such as the rule of "substituted legal relief." Early judges, trained in common-law pleading, were perhaps unwilling to accept the fusion of law and equity at face value. [Citation.] More recently, however, we have at least followed the "clean up jurisdiction" theory [citation], and we have held that the existence of a remedy at law does not preclude equitable relief if the equitable remedy is better adapted to render more perfect and complete justice than the remedy at law. We believe that a legal remedy should be granted where equity fails. It would involve needless waste of time and money to send the case back for repleading and retrial to accomplish the same result we have now before us. We prefer to follow the rule stated in Livingston v. Krown Chemical Manufacturing, Inc., 50 Mich.App. 153, 212 N.W.2d 775 (1973), and allow damages even though specific performance is denied.

The holding of the two preceding paragraphs, of course, is limited to cases where the rules stated in them do not operate to deprive a litigant of a right to a jury trial. The distinction between law and equity is still of primary importance in determining the right to a jury trial. But a jury trial can be waived by failing to demand it. [Citations.]

In the present case, it is apparent that the defendant knew that specific performance was impossible when the complaint was served on him. He therefore must have known that the only possible remedy, if the plaintiff prevailed, would be damages. If so, he knew he had a right to a jury trial. The right to a jury trial, if demanded under the facts of this case, would be absolute. [Citations.] The defendant could have demanded a jury trial, even though the complaint on its face showed grounds for equitable relief only. * * * But in the absence of a demand, there was no error. * * * We hold today that the right to a jury trial is likewise waived if not demanded in a case where the complaint demands equitable relief but the defendant is aware that only legal relief could be granted if the plaintiff should prevail. * * *

[Reversed and remanded on other grounds.]

B. RIGHT TO JURY TRIAL: FEDERAL APPROACH

Section Coverage:

The Seventh Amendment to the Constitution provides that in "[s]uits at common law, where the value in controversy shall exceed twenty dollars, the right of trial by jury shall be preserved." This Amendment is interpreted to provide the right to a jury trial when the claim is for legal relief, but not where the claim is for equitable relief.

When a case presents mixed questions of law and equity, the Supreme Court has said, the Seventh Amendment prohibits the equitable clean-up doctrine. In a series of opinions in the past thirty years the Court has found a Constitutional guarantee to have all legal matters tried first by a jury. The judge may then decide the equitable matters in a manner not inconsistent with the jury verdict. Because the Seventh Amendment does not apply to the states, these decisions on the Constitutional right to a jury trial do not affect state law.

The Supreme Court also held that the characterization of a matter as legal or equitable depends upon the historical origin of the claim, or the closest analogy if the right is new, as well as the remedy sought. If the complaint historically arose at law and if the plaintiff seeks damages, the claim is legal for purposes of jury trial rights; if it seeks an injunction or specific performance, it is equitable. Not all claims for money are automatically damages claims, however. The Courts of Appeal have agreed that claims for reinstatement and back pay against an employer are entirely equitable, without a right to a jury. Although the Supreme Court has never decided the issue, several opinions have cited these holdings with apparent approval. The Supreme Court has held that a back pay claim against a union for breach of its duty of fair representation is a legal damages claim, however.

Model Case:

Sarah Martin's supervisor, Steve Durvil, made a sexual proposition to her at work one day. When Martin indicated that she was not interested in any personal relationship, Durvil told her to think about it longer. He hinted that her rating on her job performance might suffer if she remained uninterested in sexual relations.

Martin immediately reported the incident to the management, but no action was taken. Durvil repeated his comments a week later and this time he forcibly kissed her. She pushed away from him and left work. She was fired the next day.

Martin's suit in federal district court contains both legal and equitable claims against the employer. She seeks reinstatement, back pay, and distress damages under various sources of federal and state law. The parties have a right to a jury trial on the legal claim for damages first. Afterwards the judge will decide the equitable issues of back pay and reinstatement in a manner not inconsistent with the jury's findings of fact on the legal issues.

If the complaint had sought only the equitable relief of reinstatement and back pay under Title VII of the Civil Rights Act of 1964, neither party would be entitled to demand a jury trial. If the plaintiff prevailed she would be entitled to reasonable attorneys' fees under the Act as well. This award would not create a jury trial right because the fees are awarded as "costs" rather than as legal damages.

DAIRY QUEEN, INC. v. WOOD

369 U.S. 469, 82 S.Ct. 894, 8 L.Ed.2d 44 (1962).

Mr. Justice Black delivered the opinion of the Court.

The United States District Court for the Eastern District of Pennsylvania granted a motion to strike petitioner's demand for a trial by jury in an action now pending before it on the alternative grounds that either the action was "purely equitable" or, if not purely equitable, whatever legal issues that were raised were "incidental" to equitable issues, and, in either case, no right to trial by jury existed. * * *

At the outset, we may dispose of one of the grounds upon which the trial court acted in striking the demand for trial by jury—that based upon the view that the right to trial by jury may be lost as to legal issues where those issues are characterized as "incidental" to equitable issues—for our previous decisions make it plain that no such rule may be applied in the federal courts. * * *

* * * Rule 38(a) expressly reaffirms that constitutional principle, declaring: "The right of trial by jury as declared by the Seventh Amendment to the Constitution or as given by a statute of the United States shall be preserved to the parties inviolate." Nonetheless, after the adoption of the Federal Rules, attempts were made indirectly to undercut that right by having federal courts in which cases involving both legal and equitable claims were filed decide the equitable claim first. The result of this procedure in those cases in which it was followed was that any issue common to both the legal and equitable claims was finally determined by the court and the party seeking trial by jury on the legal claim was deprived of that right as to these common issues. This procedure finally came before us in Beacon Theatres, Inc. v. Westover, [359 U.S. 500, 79 S.Ct. 948 (1959)]a case which, like this one, arose from the denial of a petition for mandamus to compel a district judge to vacate his order striking a demand for trial by jury.

Our decision reversing that case not only emphasizes the responsibility of the Federal Courts of Appeals to grant mandamus where necessary to protect the constitutional right to trial by jury but also limits the issues open for determination here by defining the protection to which that right is entitled in cases involving both legal and equitable claims. The holding in *Beacon Theatres* was that where both legal and equitable issues are presented in a single case, "only under the most imperative circumstances, circumstances which in view of the flexible procedures of the Federal Rules we cannot now anticipate, can the right to a jury trial of legal issues be lost through prior determination of equitable claims." That holding, of course, applies whether the trial judge chooses to characterize the legal issues presented as "incidental" to equitable issues or not. Consequently, in a case such as this where there cannot even be a contention of such "imperative circumstances," *Beacon Theatres* requires that any legal issues for which a trial by jury is timely and properly demanded be submitted to a jury. There being no question of the timeliness or correctness of the demand involved here, the sole question which we must decide is whether the action now pending before the District Court contains legal issues.

The District Court proceeding arises out of a controversy between petitioner and the respondent owners of the trademark "DAIRY QUEEN" with regard to a written licensing contract made by them in December 1949, under which petitioner agreed to pay some $150,000 for the exclusive right to use that trademark in certain portions of Pennsylvania. The terms of the contract provided for a small initial payment with the remaining payments to be made at the rate of 50% of all amounts received by petitioner on sales and franchises to deal with the trademark and, in order to make certain that the $150,000 payment would be completed within a specified period of time, further provided for minimum annual payments regardless of petitioner's receipts. In August 1960, the respondents wrote petitioner a letter in which they claimed that petitioner had committed "a material breach of that contract" by defaulting on the contract's payment provisions and notified petitioner of the termination of the contract and the cancellation of petitioner's right to use the trademark unless this claimed default was remedied immediately. When petitioner continued to deal with the trademark despite the notice of termination, the respondents brought an action based upon their view that a material breach of contract had occurred.

* * * The complaint then prayed for both temporary and permanent relief, including: (1) temporary and permanent injunctions to restrain petitioner from any future use of or dealing in the franchise and the trademark; (2) an accounting to determine the exact amount of money owing by petitioner and a judgment for that amount; and (3) an injunction pending accounting to prevent petitioner from collecting any money from "Dairy Queen" stores in the territory.

* * *

Petitioner's contention, as set forth in its petition for mandamus to the Court of Appeals and reiterated in its briefs before this Court, is that insofar as the complaint requests a money judgment it presents a claim which is unquestionably legal. We agree with that contention. * * *

We conclude therefore that the district judge erred in refusing to grant petitioner's demand for a trial by jury on the factual issues related to the question of whether there has been a breach of contract. Since these issues are common with those upon which respondents' claim to equitable relief is based, the legal claims involved in the action must be determined prior to any final court determination of respondents' equitable claims.[20] The Court of Appeals should have corrected the error of

---

20. This does not of course, interfere with the District Court's power to grant temporary relief pending a final adjudication on the merits. Such temporary relief has already been granted in this case (*see* McCullough v. Dairy Queen, Inc., 290 F.2d

the district judge by granting the petition for mandamus. The judgment is therefore reversed and the cause remanded for further proceedings consistent with this opinion.

Reversed and remanded.

MR. JUSTICE HARLAN, whom MR. JUSTICE DOUGLAS joins, concurring.

I am disposed to accept the view, strongly pressed at the bar, that this complaint seeks an accounting for alleged trademark infringement, rather than contract damages. Even though this leaves the complaint as formally asking only for equitable relief,* this does not end the inquiry. The fact that an "accounting" is sought is not of itself dispositive of the jury trial issue. To render this aspect of the complaint truly "equitable" it must appear that the substantive claim is one cognizable only in equity or that the "accounts between the parties" are of such a "complicated nature" that they can be satisfactorily unraveled only by a court of equity. [Citations.] It is manifest from the face of the complaint that the "accounting" sought in this instance is not of either variety. A jury, under proper instruction from the court, could readily calculate the damages flowing from this alleged trademark infringement, just as courts of law often do in copyright and patent cases. [Citations.]

Consequently what is involved in this case is nothing more than a joinder in one complaint of prayers for both legal and equitable relief. In such circumstances, under principles long since established, [citation], the petitioner cannot be deprived of his constitutional right to a jury trial on the "legal" claim contained in the complaint.

On this basis I concur in the judgment of the Court.

––––––––––

1. The first in the line of cases where the Supreme Court reconsidered the application of the Seventh Amendment was Beacon Theatres, Inc. v. Westover, 359 U.S. 500, 79 S.Ct. 948, 3 L.Ed.2d 988 (1959). The plaintiff in that case sought declaratory relief and the defendant counterclaimed for damages for past violations of the antitrust laws. The trier of fact would confront the same questions under both claims. The Court held that the right to a jury trial must not depend on a race to the courthouse. It held that where equitable and legal claims are joined in the same action, there is a right to jury trial on the legal claims. A court cannot infringe upon this right by having an equitable trial of common issues in the claims or by trying the legal issues as incidental to the equitable ones. The principle was that the Seventh Amendment question depends on the nature of the issue tried.

2. The Supreme Court held in *Tull v. United States* that the Seventh Amendment requires a jury trial in actions that are analogous

871) and is no part of the issues before this Court.

* Except as to the damage claim there is no dispute but that the complaint seeks only equitable relief.

to "suits at common law." The Court observed: "Prior to the Amendment's adoption, a jury trial was customary in suits brought in the English *law* courts. In contrast, those actions that are analogous to 18th-century cases tried in courts of equity or admiralty do not require a jury trial." 481 U.S. 412, 107 S.Ct. 1831, 1835, 95 L.Ed.2d 365 (1987).

For the historical background surrounding the adoption of the Seventh Amendment, *see* Henderson, The Background of the Seventh Amendment, 80 Harv.L.Rev. 289 (1966); Wolfram, The Constitutional History of the Seventh Amendment, 57 Minn.L.Rev. 639 (1973).

HARKLESS v. SWEENY INDEPENDENT SCHOOL DISTRICT
427 F.2d 319 (5th Cir.1970).

BELL, CIRCUIT JUDGE:

This appeal involves an action brought by ten Negro teachers alleging that the failure of the school district to renew their teaching contracts when the school system was desegregated denied them rights secured by the Fourteenth Amendment. They seek reinstatement and back pay. Jurisdiction is premised on 28 U.S.C.A. § 1343(3) and 42 U.S.C.A. § 1983.[1]

* * *

After adopting a plan for complete school desegregation in the spring of 1966, the Sweeny Independent School District was able to reduce the number of its faculty for the school year 1966–67. In the process, 17 of the 25 Negro teachers in the system were not offered reemployment. This suit followed.

* * * Over objection, the district court granted the demand of defendants for jury trial as to the prayer for back pay and exercised its discretion under Rule 39(b), F.R.Civ.P., to also order a jury trial on all other factual issues.[2] * * *

---

1. 28 U.S.C.A. § 1343(3), provides:

"The district courts shall have original jurisdiction of any civil action authorized by law to be commenced by any person:

* * *

"(3) To redress the deprivation, under color of any State law, statute, ordinance, regulation, custom or usage, of any right, privilege or immunity secured by the Constitution of the United States or by any Act of Congress providing for equal rights of citizens or of all persons within the jurisdiction of the United States;"

42 U.S.C.A. § 1983, provides:

"Every person who, under color of any statute, ordinance, regulation, custom, or usage, of any State or Territory, subjects, or causes to be subjected, any citizen of the United States or other person with the jurisdiction thereof the deprivation of any rights, privileges, or immunities secured by the Constitution and laws, shall be liable to the party injured in an action at law, suit in equity, or other proper proceeding for redress."

2. Rule 39(b) provides:

"Issues not demanded for trial by jury as provided in Rule 38 shall be tried by the court; but, notwithstanding the failure of a party to demand a jury in an action in which such a demand might have been made of right, the court in its discretion upon motion may order a trial by a jury of any or all issues."

The memorandum opinion of the district court on the jury question is reported. Harkless v. Sweeny Independent School District, S.D.Tex., 1968, 278 F.Supp. 632.

The case was submitted to the jury on special interrogatories. The jury returned a verdict finding that the decision not to rehire the plaintiffs was made without regard to their race, and that defendants acted in good faith, objectively comparing the qualifications of all teachers. However, the jury found that participation in this litigation was a factor in the decision not to offer re-employment to seven of the plaintiffs.

* * * The district court determined that the back pay and the factual issues involved in the prayer for injunctive relief presented jury issues and, therefore, granted defendants' demand for jury trial. The law seems otherwise.

Section 1983 was designed to provide a comprehensive remedy for the deprivation of federal constitutional and statutory rights. The prayer for back pay is not a claim for damages, but is an integral part of the equitable remedy of injunctive reinstatement. Reinstatement involves a return of the plaintiffs to the positions they held before the alleged unconstitutional failure to renew their contracts. An inextricable part of the restoration to prior status is the payment of back wages properly owing to the plaintiffs, diminished by their earnings, if any, in the interim. Back pay is merely an element of the equitable remedy of reinstatement. [Citations.]

The district court concluded that [prior authorities] were no longer viable in light of the more recent decisions of Beacon Theatres, Inc. v. Westover, 1959, 359 U.S. 500, 79 S.Ct. 948, 3 L.Ed.2d 988; Dairy Queen, Inc. v. Wood, 1962, 369 U.S. 469, 82 S.Ct. 894, 8 L.Ed.2d 44; and Thermo–Stitch, Inc. v. Chemi–Cord Processing Corp., 5 Cir., 1961, 294 F.2d 486, 489. None of these cases involved back pay. Each involved separate equitable and legal claims joined in the same case. The legal claims were for resolution by the jury. The back pay issue here was not a separate legal claim—rather it was a part of the main equitable claim—reinstatement. The same is true as to the underlying factual issues pertaining to the claims to reinstatement.

This circuit has rejected the view " * * * that the trio of Beacon Theatres, Dairy Queen, and Thermo–Stitch is a catalyst which suddenly converts *any* money request into a money claim triable by jury." * * *

In a recent case involving a suit brought because of discrimination in employment, we determined that the employer was not entitled to a jury trial on the issue of back wages. [Citations.]

We conclude that these authorities teach that a claim for back pay presented in an equitable action for reinstatement authorized by § 1983 is not for jury consideration nor are the factual issues which form the basis of the claim for reinstatement. The Seventh Amendment does not so require. The plaintiffs' claim should have been determined by the court. The grant of jury trial was error.

Reversed and remanded for further proceedings not inconsistent herewith.

CURTIS v. LOETHER

415 U.S. 189, 94 S.Ct. 1005, 39 L.Ed.2d 260 (1974).

MR. JUSTICE MARSHALL delivered the opinion of the Court.

Section 812 of the Civil Rights Act of 1968, 82 Stat. 88, 42 U.S.C. § 3612, authorizes private plaintiffs to bring civil actions to redress violations of Title VIII, the fair housing provisions of the Act, and provides that "[t]he court may grant as relief, as it deems appropriate, any permanent or temporary injunction, temporary restraining order, or other order, and may award to the plaintiff actual damages and not more than $1,000 punitive damages, together with court costs and reasonable attorney fees...." The question presented in this case is whether the Civil Rights Act or the Seventh Amendment requires a jury trial upon demand by one of the parties in an action for damages and injunctive relief under this section.

Petitioner, a Negro woman, brought this action under § 812, claiming that respondents, who are white, had refused to rent an apartment to her because of her race, in violation of § 804(a) of the Act, 42 U.S.C. § 3604(a). In her complaint she sought only injunctive relief and punitive damages; a claim for compensatory damages was later added. After an evidentiary hearing, the District Court granted preliminary injunctive relief, enjoining the respondents from renting the apartment in question to anyone else pending the trial on the merits. This injunction was dissolved some five months later with the petitioner's consent, after she had finally obtained other housing, and the case went to trial on the issues of actual and punitive damages.

Respondents made a timely demand for jury trial in their answer. The District Court, however, held that jury trial was neither authorized by Title VIII nor required by the Seventh Amendment, and denied the jury request. After trial on the merits, the District Judge found that respondents had in fact discriminated against petitioner on account of her race. Although he found no actual damages he awarded $250 in punitive damages, denying petitioner's request for attorney's fees and court costs.

The Court of Appeals reversed on the jury trial issue. After an extended analysis, the court concluded essentially that the Seventh Amendment gave respondents the right to a jury trial in this action, and therefore interpreted the statute to authorize jury trials so as to eliminate any question of its constitutionality. In view of the importance of the jury trial issue in the administration and enforcement of Title VIII and the diversity of views in the lower courts on the question, we granted certiorari. We affirm.

The legislative history on the jury trial question is sparse, and what little is available is ambiguous. There seems to be some indication that supporters of Title VIII were concerned that the possibility of racial prejudice on juries might reduce the effectiveness of civil rights damages actions. * * * We see no point to giving extended consideration to these arguments, however, for we think it is clear that the Seventh Amendment entitles either party to demand a jury trial in an action for damages in the federal courts under § 812.

The Seventh Amendment provides that "[i]n suits at common law, where the value in controversy shall exceed twenty dollars, the right of trial by jury shall be preserved." Although the thrust of the Amendment was to preserve the right to jury trial as it existed in 1791, it has long been settled that the right extends beyond the common-law forms of action recognized at that time. Mr. Justice Story established the basic principle in 1830:

> "The phrase 'common law,' found in this clause, is used in contradistinction to equity, and admiralty, and maritime jurisprudence.... By *common law*, [the Framers of the Amendment] meant ... not merely suits, which the *common* law recognized among its old and settled proceedings, but suits in which *legal* rights were to be ascertained and determined, in contradistinction to those where equitable rights alone were recognized, and equitable remedies were administered.... In a just sense, the amendment then may well be construed to embrace all suits which are not of equity and admiralty jurisdiction, whatever might be the peculiar form which they assume to settle legal rights." Parsons v. Bedford, 7 L.Ed. 732, 3 Pet. 433, 446–447 (1830) (emphasis in original).

Petitioner nevertheless argues that the Amendment is inapplicable to new causes of action created by congressional enactment. * * * Whatever doubt may have existed should now be dispelled. The Seventh Amendment does apply to actions enforcing statutory rights, and requires a jury trial upon demand, if the statute creates legal rights and remedies, enforceable in an action for damages in the ordinary courts of law.

* * *

We think it is clear that a damages action under § 812 is an action to enforce "legal rights" within the meaning of our Seventh Amendment decisions. *See, e.g.*, Ross v. Bernhard, 396 U.S., at 533, 542, 90 S.Ct., at 735, 740; Dairy Queen, Inc. v. Wood, 369 U.S., at 476–477, 82 S.Ct., at 899. A damages action under the statute sounds basically in tort—the statute merely defines a new legal duty, and authorizes the courts to compensate a plaintiff for the injury caused by the defendant's wrongful breach. As the Court of Appeals noted, this cause of action is analogous to a number of tort actions recognized at common law. More important, the relief sought here—actual and punitive damages—is the traditional form of relief offered in the courts of law.

We need not, and do not, go so far as to say that any award of monetary relief must necessarily be "legal" relief. [Citations.] A comparison of Title VIII with Title VII of the Civil Rights Act of 1964, where the courts of appeals have held that jury trial is not required in an action for reinstatement and back pay, is instructive, although we of course express no view on the jury trial issue in that context. In Title VII cases the courts of appeals have characterized back pay as an integral part of an equitable remedy, a form of restitution. But the statutory language on which this characterization is based—

> "[T]he court may enjoin the respondent from engaging in such unlawful employment practice, and order such affirmative action as may be appropriate, which may include, but is not limited to, reinstatement or hiring of employees, with or without back pay . . ., or any other equitable relief as the court deems appropriate," 42 U.S.C. § 2000e–5(g) (1970 ed., Supp. II)—

contrasts sharply with § 812's simple authorization of an action for actual and punitive damages. In Title VII cases, also, the courts have relied on the fact that the decision whether to award back pay is committed to the discretion of the trial judge. There is no comparable discretion here: if a plaintiff proves unlawful discrimination and actual damages, he is entitled to judgment for that amount. Nor is there any sense in which the award here can be viewed as requiring the defendant to disgorge funds wrongfully withheld from the plaintiff. Whatever may be the merit of the "equitable" characterization in Title VII cases, there is surely no basis for characterizing the award of compensatory and punitive damages here as equitable relief.

We are not oblivious to the force of petitioner's policy arguments. Jury trials may delay to some extent the disposition of Title VIII damages actions. But Title VIII actions seeking only equitable relief will be unaffected, and preliminary injunctive relief remains available without a jury trial even in damages actions. * * * We recognize, too, the possibility that jury prejudice may deprive a victim of discrimination of the verdict to which he or she is entitled. Of course, the trial judge's power to direct a verdict, to grant judgment notwithstanding the verdict, or to grant a new trial provides substantial protection against this risk, and respondents' suggestion that jury trials will expose a broader segment of the populace to the example of the federal civil rights laws in operation has some force. More fundamentally, however, these considerations are insufficient to overcome the clear command of the Seventh Amendment. The decision at the Court of Appeals must be affirmed.

Affirmed.

————

1. The Supreme Court further considered the Seventh Amendment in Chauffeurs, Teamsters & Helpers, Local N. 391 v. Terry, 494 U.S. 558, 110 S.Ct. 1339, 108 L.Ed.2d 519 (1990). As in the principal case, the issue was the availability of a jury trial to enforce a new statutory right unknown at common law in 1791. *Terry* involved a claim against a union for breach of its duty of fair representation. The plaintiff sought

back pay for time lost as a result of the union's failure to file his grievance against his employer concerning his layoff.

A plurality of the Court agreed to the result that there was a right to a jury trial in this case. Three Justices dissented; two concurred separately and refused to join a central part of the opinion written by Justice Marshall. A majority of the Justices agreed to the following starting point, however:

> To determine whether a particular action will resolve legal rights, we examine both the nature of the issues involved and the remedy sought. "First, we compare the statutory action to 18th-century actions brought in the courts of England prior to the merger of the courts of law and equity. Second, we examine the remedy sought and determine whether it is legal or equitable in nature." *Tull, supra*, 481 U.S., at 417–418, 107 S.Ct., at 1835–1836 (citations omitted). The second inquiry is the more important in our analysis.
> * * *

Applying the first part of this test, Justice Marshall and three other Justices found no clear historical analogy to a claim for the breach of the duty of fair representation. The two closest analogies they found were an equitable claim against a trustee for breach of a fiduciary duty and a legal claim for breach of contract. Thus left in equipose between law and equity Justice Marshall proceeded with the next stage of the analysis, which a majority of the Justices endorsed:

> Our determination under the first part of the Seventh Amendment analysis is only preliminary. Granfinanciera, S.A. v. Nordberg, 492 U.S., at 47, 109 S.Ct., at 2793. In this case, the only remedy sought is a request for compensatory damages representing backpay and benefits. Generally, an action for money damages was "the traditional form of relief offered in the courts of law." Curtis v. Loether, 415 U.S. 189, 196, 94 S.Ct. 1005, 1009, 39 L.Ed.2d 260 (1974). This Court has not, however, held that "any award of monetary relief must necessarily be 'legal' relief." [Citations.] Nonetheless, because we conclude that the remedy respondents seek has none of the attributes that must be present before we will find an exception to the general rule and characterize damages as equitable, we find that the remedy sought by respondents is legal.

> First, we have characterized damages as equitable where they are restitutionary, such as in "action[s] for disgorgement of improper profits," [citations]. The backpay sought by respondents is not money wrongfully held by the Union, but wages and benefits they would have received from McLean had the Union processed the employees' grievances properly. Such relief is not restitutionary.

> Second, a monetary award "incidental to or intertwined with injunctive relief" may be equitable. [Citations.] Because respondents seek only money damages, this characteristic is clearly absent from the case.

The Union argues that the backpay relief sought here must nonetheless be considered equitable because this Court has labeled backpay awarded under Title VII, of the Civil Rights Act of 1964, 42 U.S.C. s 2000e et seq. (1982 ed.), as equitable. See Albemarle Paper Co. v. Moody, 422 U.S. 405, 415–418, 95 S.Ct. 2362, 2370–2372, 45 L.Ed.2d 280 (1975) (characterizing backpay awarded against employer under Title VII as equitable in context of assessing whether judge erred in refusing to award such relief). It contends that the Title VII analogy is compelling in the context of the duty of fair representation because the Title VII backpay provision was based on the NLRA provision governing backpay awards for unfair labor practices, 29 U.S.C. s 160(c) (1982 ed.) ("[W]here an order directs reinstatement of an employee, back pay may be required of the employer or labor organization"). See Albemarle Paper Co. v. Moody, supra, at 419, 95 S.Ct., at 2372. We are not convinced.

The Court has never held that a plaintiff seeking backpay under Title VII has a right to a jury trial. See Lorillard v. Pons, 434 U.S. 575, 581–582, 98 S.Ct. 866, 870–871, 55 L.Ed.2d 40 (1978). Assuming, without deciding, that such a Title VII plaintiff has no right to a jury trial, the Union's argument does not persuade us that respondents are not entitled to a jury trial here. Congress specifically characterized backpay under Title VII as a form of "equitable relief." 42 U.S.C. s 2000e–5(g) (1982 ed.) ("[T]he court may ... order such affirmative action as may be appropriate, which may include, but is not limited to, reinstatement or hiring of employees, with or without back pay ..., or any other equitable relief as the court deems appropriate"). See also Curtis v. Loether, supra, 415 U.S., at 196–197, 94 S.Ct., at 1009–1010 (distinguishing backpay under Title VII from damages under Title VIII, the fair housing provision of the Civil Rights Act, 42 U.S.C. ss 3601–3619 (1982 ed.), which the Court characterized as "legal" for Seventh Amendment purposes). Congress made no similar pronouncement regarding the duty of fair representation. Furthermore, the Court has noted that backpay sought from an employer under Title VII would generally be restitutionary in nature, see Curtis v. Loether, supra, at 197, 94 S.Ct., at 1010, in contrast to the damages sought here from the Union. Thus, the remedy sought in this duty of fair representation case is clearly different from backpay sought for violations of Title VII.

* * *

We hold, then, that the remedy of backpay sought in this duty of fair representation action is legal in nature. Considering both parts of the Seventh Amendment inquiry, we find that respondents are entitled to a jury trial on all issues presented in their suit.

2. Does *Terry, supra,* change the result in *Harkless, supra*? Consider the Court's analysis with respect to whether the defendant has

"withheld" money from the plaintiff to make the claim restitutionary. Is this distinction a meaningful one?

3. The Seventh Amendment has no application to suits against the federal government because of sovereign immunity. Jury trials are available against a federal government defendant only when Congress authorizes them. *See* Lehman v. Nakshian, 453 U.S. 156, 101 S.Ct. 2698, 69 L.Ed.2d 548 (1981).

Chapter 19

ATTORNEY FEES

Section Coverage:

In the United States the prevailing party in a law suit is not ordinarily entitled to recover its costs of litigation, including attorney fees, from the losing party. This "American Rule" that costs shall be borne by each party independently is in contrast to the British Rule which provides that the prevailing party is entitled to receive their litigation expenses as a matter of course. The principal justification in support of the American Rule is that a party should not be "penalized" for instituting or defending meritorious claims. The imposition of attorney fees against the losing party may discourage the willingness of parties to legitimately resort to the judicial process for dispute resolution. The American Rule has been sharply criticized, however, because the failure to reimburse a successful party their litigation expenses results is preventing them from being "made whole" even if entirely successful on the merits. Federal legislation on the issue has been proposed.

In order to alleviate the potential unfairness of the American Rule, a number of exceptions have developed through contract, common law, and statutes. The contractual exception is simply that parties to a contract are free to agree in advance of breach that reasonable attorney fees can be collected by the non-breaching party as necessary to enforce contract rights. Such fee arrangements are common in business, bank loans, and leases. As long as such provisions are not grounded in unconscionability, they are enforceable.

The common law exceptions are several. A major one is that courts will award reasonable attorney fees against a vexatious litigator. This bad faith exception requires more than a showing that the claim, defense, or appeal was weakly supported; the American Rule theory is that even weak cases deserve a day in court without fear of fee obligations upon loss. Attorney fees awards for bad faith litigation are grounded in deterrence of unjustified litigation; a party with a truly frivolous argument is punished. The line between weak claims and frivolous ones is rarely bright, but that distinction is essential for this exception.

Another common law exception is that the plaintiff who acts as a "private attorney general" sometimes receives attorney fees from the defendant. Under this theory, courts award attorney fees to a private party who pursues a matter benefiting the public good, such as a determination of civil rights or effectuating environmental protection.

Courts find the source of power to award fees in this circumstance, and numerous related ones, in their inherent equitable powers to carry out the interests of justice.

In Alyeska Pipeline Service Co. v. Wilderness Society, 421 U.S. 240, 95 S.Ct. 1612, 44 L.Ed.2d 141 (1975), the Supreme Court specifically rejected as a matter of federal law the private attorney general basis for attorney fees except as expressly authorized by Congress.

In *Alyeska* the federal Court of Appeals had awarded attorney fees to environmental organizations which had successfully challenged the issuance of permits necessary for the construction of the trans-Alaska oil pipeline. In response to *Alyeska*, Congress quickly authorized the recovery of attorney fees to prevailing parties under numerous civil rights, environmental, and other statutes involving matters of public interest.

The provision for attorney fees is particularly significant in public interest litigation because often the nature of the remedy sought is an injunction rather than damages. Therefore, no fund would be created to pay the plaintiff's attorney fees absent the statutory grant. The statutory language of these fee-shifting authorizations typically authorizes the federal court to award reasonable fees to the "prevailing party."

A court retains inherent power to regulate attorney fees in a supervisory role. Contractual provisions and settlement arrangements are all subject to judicial scrutiny. Although this power is invoked sparingly, judges staunchly preserve it and exercise it as needed in cases where the integrity of the court system and legal profession are in question.

Assuming that a party has established entitlement to an award of attorney fees, the next question involves determining what constitutes a "reasonable" fee. Many courts have calculated the reasonableness of the statutory fee according to the "lodestar" method which takes into account the number of hours spent on the successful issues in litigation multiplied times a reasonable hourly rate. The following materials will explore issues involving both the entitlement and the measurement of attorney fees to parties under both common law principles and statutory provisions.

Model Case:

Chris Taylor is a doctor who is the director of a division in a university hospital. Dr. Taylor is a strong believer in the desirability of voluntary affirmative action for groups historically excluded from the medical profession.

The Governing Board of the hospital determined that Dr. Taylor's division should have an assistant director. The Board took applications from doctors for this new position and consulted Dr. Taylor on the merits of each candidate. The applicants were narrowed to two final choices for the single position. One doctor was a member of a group historically excluded by the profession; the other was not. The Board chose the latter. Dr. Taylor made a major protest at a stormy Board meeting and, as a result, was fired.

Dr. Taylor's suit for unlawful employment discrimination under federal law is uncertain of success. On the one hand, if the discharge was retaliation for protesting unlawful discrimination, Dr. Taylor's activity may be protected under federal law. If so, a successful civil rights claim will include recovery of attorney fees in addition to any other available remedies. On the other hand, if the board did not engage in unlawful discrimination, then Dr. Taylor's advocacy of voluntary conduct would not be federally protected. At best Dr. Taylor would have a state claim of wrongful or retaliatory discharge. Such a claim would lie in tort or contract and would not include recovery of attorney fees. As a matter of common law there would be no basis for an exception to the American Rule that each party must bear litigation costs.

AUTORAMA CORP. v. STEWART

802 F.2d 1284 (10th Cir.1986).

CHILSON, DISTRICT JUDGE. * * *

On June 7, 1983, appellees, Autorama Corporation and Ronald I. Swanson, as plaintiffs, filed a complaint in the United States District Court for the Northern District of Oklahoma, premised upon federal question jurisdiction. The plaintiffs alleged that in certain transactions with the defendants (appellants), the latter violated the Federal Securities Acts of 1933 and 1934. Plaintiffs prayed for compensatory and exemplary damages.

[The defendants filed a motion to dismiss for lack of federal court jurisdiction; all parties are residents of Oklahoma and diversity jurisdiction did not exist. The plaintiffs failed to respond, and the final court dismissed the action for lack of jurisdiction. The defendants subsequently filed a motion for attorneys' fees and costs, but the court held that each party should bear its own expenses.] * * *

Under the "American Rule", the prevailing litigant is not entitled to collect reasonable attorneys' fees from the loser. Ruckelshaus v. Sierra Club, 463 U.S. 680, 685, 103 S.Ct. 3274, 3277, 77 L.Ed.2d 938 (1983). It is the appellants' contention that (1) the underlying action was decided on the merits and (2) the plaintiffs brought the case frivolously and in bad faith; consequently, they should be entitled to an award of their attorneys' fees under the bad faith exception to the American Rule. * * *

An involuntary dismissal is with prejudice and on the merits, unless the court order "specifies otherwise" or if there is "a dismissal for lack of jurisdiction...." * * *

The appellants also assert the plaintiffs advanced their case frivolously and in bad faith. The Tenth Circuit recognizes a "narrow exception" to the American Rule, which allows the court to award attorneys' fees when that party's opponent acts "in bad faith, vexatiously, wantonly, or for oppressive reasons." [Citation.] Moreover, "this circuit requires more than merely a finding that a claim was frivolous when brought.... [T]he bad faith exception is drawn very narrowly and may be resorted to 'only in exceptional cases and for dominating reasons of justice.'" [Citation.] The Tenth Circuit also insists that the trial judge make a specific finding of bad intent or improper motive by the misbehaving party before there can be an award of attorneys' fees. [Citation.]

Assuming the instant case had reached the merits, the litigation still was not brought vexatiously. The trial court made absolutely no finding of bad faith; to the contrary, the Order of July 16 specifically found (1) there can be no finding of frivolity or bad faith inferred from the May 10 Order of Dismissal, and (2) the litigation expenses were not "necessitated by frivolous or bad faith acts of the plaintiffs or their attorneys." Additionally, the trial court was asked to reconsider the bad faith allegation, after which, it again declined to find vexatious conduct. Clearly, courts are quite hesitant to find claims were pursued in bad faith unless the evidence is remarkably supportive of such a proposition.

The mere fact that plaintiff did not prevail before the district court does not necessarily imply that its conduct was "vexatious" or "wanton." The reviewing court must resist the temptation to engage in post hoc reasoning by concluding that because a plaintiff did not ultimately prevail, the action must have been wholly unreasonable and without proper foundation. In other words, even where the law or facts appear questionable at the outset, a party may have a perfectly legitimate ground for bringing the suit. *See generally* Christiansburg Garment Co. v. EEOC, 434 U.S. 412, 421–22, 98 S.Ct. 694, 700, 54 L.Ed.2d 648 (1978). Further, bad faith requires more than a mere showing of a weak or legally inadequate case, and the exception is not invoked by findings of negligence, frivolity, or improvidence. Hence, it is not surprising that attorneys' fees are awarded only when there is "clear evidence" that challenged actions are taken entirely without color and are pursued for reasons of harassment or delay.

It is well settled, the granting of aggregate attorneys' fees and costs are committed to the sound discretion of the lower court. Further, the appellate court will reverse such determination only if it finds the trial judge abused his discretion. After a careful review of the record, appellants have failed to persuade this Court that the plaintiff acted in bad faith and that the trial court's ruling was an abuse of discretion. Appellants' contentions are simply without merit. Appellants cite no authority for their miscontention that attorneys' fees may be awarded in a case that was dismissed for lack of jurisdiction, and which was neither brought in bad faith, nor decided on the merits. No such authority exists. Also, neither prong of the two tier test was met. First, the decision was not on the merits; second, appellants have not demonstrated bad faith on behalf of the appellees. We therefore affirm the trial court's denial of attorneys fees and costs.

* * *

Therefore, this Court (1) affirms the trial court's denial of attorneys' fees and costs and (2) holds this appeal was both filed in a timely basis and in good faith.

––––––––

1. The "American Rule" that parties pay their own litigation expenses is distinguished from the English rule. The English practice, followed in various forms in other countries tracing legal heritage to England, is that the winning party recovers litigation expenses as a matter of course from the losing party. Such litigation expenses include attorney fees, and the rule applies equally to prevailing plaintiffs and defendants. *See* McCormick, Damages § 60 (1935).

2. The common law has carved out exceptions to the American Rule. In addition to the bad faith exception exemplified by the principal case, there are three others that courts have found in their "equitable power" to award: common fund, substantial benefit, and private attorney general. These theories are all common law exceptions, although they often have statutory counterparts. The major exceptions to the American Rule of litigation expenses are found as specific statutory authorizations in areas such as civil rights, consumer protection, privacy, and environmental statutes.

3. *Common Fund.* Another equitable doctrine recognized as an exception to the American Rule may arise where litigation produces a common fund for the benefit of several claimants, such as produced in a successful class action. *See* Sprague v. Ticonic Nat'l Bank, 307 U.S. 161, 164, 59 S.Ct. 777, 778, 83 L.Ed. 1184, (1939) (fee award from fund generated is within "the historic equity jurisdiction of the federal courts"). The doctrine allows a party who creates, preserves, or increases the value of a fund in which others have a beneficial interest to obtain reimbursement from the fund for their litigation expenses. Under the "common fund" or "equitable fund" approach the defendant pays a specified sum of damages to the court in exchange for a release of liability. The attorney fees are then taken directly out of the damages fund prior to distribution to the plaintiffs. The plaintiff class thus shares its recovery with the attorneys, then, in a manner similar to contingency fee arrangements. The common fund doctrine is based on the rationale that the beneficiaries of litigation should share in its costs. *See* Skelton v. General Motors Corp., 860 F.2d 250, 252 (7th Cir.1988). This method is not technically an "exception" to the American Rule, however, because the attorney fees are not imposed directly against the losing party but rather are drawn from the fund itself. *See generally* Dawson, Lawyers and Involuntary Clients: Attorney Fees from Funds, 87 Harv.L.Rev. 1597 (1974).

4. *Substantial Benefit Theory.* When litigation produces a "substantial benefit" either pecuniary or nonpecuniary in nature, the com-

mon law sometimes allows attorneys' fees. For example, in *Card v. Community Redevelopment Agency* a plaintiff obtained a declaratory judgment that a city ordinance amending a redevelopment plan was invalid. The amendment added new areas to the development; the invalidation resulted in increased taxes available to various city and county taxing agencies. The court awarded as attorney fees a portion of the incremental funds that would now go to the taxing agencies and divided the amount proportionally among them. 61 Cal.App.3d 570, 131 Cal.Rptr. 153 (1976).

The same theory was used in a case invalidating on Constitutional grounds a state government's practice of giving paid release time to workers on Good Friday. Attorney fees were awarded against the state on the theory that there was a future savings of funds formerly paid for work not performed. Mandel v. Hodges, 54 Cal.App.3d 596, 127 Cal. Rptr. 244 (1976).

The United States Supreme Court has characterized the substantial benefit theory as a part of the common fund exception, and therefore concluded that it is necessary for the benefit to accrue to the defendant who must pay the fee. Alyeska Pipeline Service Co., v. Wilderness Society, 421 U.S. 240, 95 S.Ct. 1612, 44 L.Ed.2d 141 (1975). This restriction is not as clear in state law. *See* Serrano v. Priest, 20 Cal.3d 25, 141 Cal.Rptr. 315, 569 P.2d 1303 (1977).

    5. *Private Attorney General.* In *Serrano v. Priest, supra,* the California Supreme Court held that attorney fees could properly be awarded under a state common law theory of private attorney general. The plaintiff had successfully challenged the California public school financing system as being in violation of state constitutional provisions guaranteeing equal protection of the laws. The California Supreme Court held:

> In the complex society in which we live it frequently occurs that citizens in great numbers and across a broad spectrum have interests in common. These, while of enormous significance to the society as a whole, do not involve the fortunes of a single individual to the extent necessary to encourage their private vindication in the courts. Although there are within the executive branch of the government offices and institutions (exemplified by the Attorney General) whose function it is to represent the general public in such matters and to ensure proper enforcement, for various reasons the burden of enforcement is not always adequately carried by those offices and institutions, rendering some sort of private action imperative. Because the issues involved in such litigation are often extremely complex and their presentation time-consuming and costly, the availability of representation of such public interests by private attorneys action *pro bono publico* is limited. Only through the appearance of "public interest" law firms funded by public and foundation monies, argue plaintiffs and amici, has it been possible to secure representation on any large scale. The firms in question, however, are not funded to the extent necessary for the representa-

tion of all such deserving interests, and as a result many worthy causes of this nature are without adequate representation under present circumstances. One solution, so the argument goes, within the equitable powers of the judiciary to provide, is the award of substantial attorneys fees to those public-interest litigants and their attorneys (whether private attorneys acting *pro bono publico* or members of "public interest" law firms) who are successful in such cases, to the end that support may be provided for the representation of interests of similar character in future litigation. 20 Cal.3d 25, 141 Cal.Rptr. 315, 325, 569 P.2d 1303, 1313 (1977).

6.   The private attorney general theory is available only under state common law, not federal. In *Alyeska Pipeline Service Co. v. Wilderness Society,* the Supreme Court held that the awarding of attorney fees on a "private attorney general" theory did not lie within the equitable jurisdiction of the federal courts in the absence of express statutory authorization. Such awards, the court held, "would make major inroads on a policy matter that Congress has reserved for itself." 421 U.S. 240, 269, 95 S.Ct. 1612, 44 L.Ed.2d 141 (1975).

7.   *Bad faith litigation.* A court has inherent power to award reasonable attorney fees to the prevailing party when the losing party has acted in bad faith in the conduct of the litigation. The Supreme Court in Chambers v. NASCO, Inc., 501 U.S. 32, 111 S.Ct. 2123, 115 L.Ed.2d 27 (1991), explained the historical justification for the "bad faith" exception to the American Rule:

> [A] court may assess attorney's fees when a party has " 'acted in bad faith, vexatiously, wantonly, or for oppressive reasons.' " In this regard, if a court finds "that fraud has been practiced upon it, or that the very temple of justice has been defiled," it may assess attorney's fees against the responsible party, as it may when a party "shows bad faith by delaying or disrupting the litigation or by hampering enforcement of a court order." The imposition of sanctions transcends a court's equitable power concerning relationships between the parties and reaches a court's inherent power to police itself, thus serving the dual purpose of "vindicat[ing] judicial authority without resort to the more drastic sanctions available for contempt of court and mak[ing] the prevailing party whole for expenses caused by the opponent's obstinacy." (Citations omitted.)

In *Chambers*, a buyer of a television station brought an action to compel completion of the transaction. The seller engaged in a series of delay and obstruction tactics designed to defraud the court and prevent enforcement of the court's orders. The Supreme Court upheld the district court's imposition of sanctions against the seller's sole shareholder under the purview of the bad faith exception. The Court held that federal courts can invoke their inherent powers to impose attorney fees for bad faith actions even where the conduct was also sanctionable under other rules. Further, the scope of inherent powers exercisable by federal courts sitting in diversity extends to permit sanctions even if the applicable state law did not recognize the bad-faith exception to the American Rule.

8. *Rule 11.* An increasingly significant tool available to courts to police abusive litigation practices is Fed.R.Civ.P.11. The rule allows the court to impose sanctions where pleadings or motions lack sufficient factual or legal basis or are filed for an improper purpose. *See* Cooter & Gell v. Hartmarx Corp., 496 U.S. 384, 110 S.Ct. 2447, 110 L.Ed.2d 359 (1990) (Central purpose of Rule 11 is to deter baseless filings and streamline the administration and procedure of federal courts; therefore attorney fees incurred on appeal were outside scope of the rule.) *See also* In Re Kunstler, 914 F.2d 505, 522 (4th Cir.1990) (Primary purpose of Rule 11 is to deter future litigation abuse, not to shift costs of litigation.)

Consider the following explanation of the policies animating Rule 11 from Thomas v. Capital Sec. Services, Inc., 836 F.2d 866 (5th Cir.1988):

> [W]hether sanctions are viewed as a form of cost-shifting, compensating opposing parties injured by the vexatious or frivolous litigation forbidden by Rule 11, or as a form of punishment imposed on those who violate the rule, the imposition of sanctions pursuant to Rule 11 is meant to deter attorneys from violating the rule. Sanctions should also be educational and rehabilitative in character and, as such, tailored to the particular wrong. To serve these multiple purposes behind Rule 11, the district court should carefully choose sanctions that foster the appropriate purpose of the rule, depending upon the parties, the violation, and the nature of the case.
>
> In sum, a district court must impose sanctions once a violation of Rule 11 is found, but the district court retains broad discretion in determining the "appropriate" sanction under the rule. What is "appropriate" may be a warm friendly discussion on the record, a hard-nosed reprimand in open court, compulsory legal education, monetary sanctions, or other measures appropriate to the circumstances. Whatever the ultimate sanction imposed, the district court should utilize the sanction that furthers the purposes of Rule 11 and is the least severe sanction adequate to such purpose.

9. In addition to Rule 11, several other statutory and procedural provisions are available to a court to deter litigation abuse. 28 U.S.C. § 1927 permits a court to assess litigation costs against an attorney who "multiplies the proceedings" in a case "unreasonably and vexatiously." Fed.R.Civ.P. 37 permits sanctions against parties or persons unjustifiably resisting discovery. Fed.R.App.P. 38 allows appellate courts to impose cost sanctions against an appellant for bringing a frivolous appeal.

KRAUSE v. RHODES

640 F.2d 214 (6th Cir.1981).

EDWARDS, CHIEF JUDGE.

[During the height of public protest over the Vietnam War there were numerous campus protests when President Nixon appeared to be expanding the war with an incursion into neighboring Cambodia. During such protests at Kent State University the Governor of Ohio called the National Guard to campus. The event that led to this lawsuit—and numerous other inquiries and investigations—was on May 4, 1970, when some Guard members shot into a crowd. This suit was the consolidated cases of nine persons injured and the personal representatives of four persons who were killed in that episode. The defendants were the Governor of Ohio, the president of the university and various officers and enlisted members of the Ohio National Guard. The complaint alleged that they "intentionally, recklessly, willfully and wantonly" caused an unnecessary deployment of the Ohio National Guard on the Kent State campus. It further alleged that the defendants ordered the Guard members to perform illegal actions which resulted in this historic tragedy.]

Steven Sindell, the original counsel for 12 of the plaintiffs in the 1970 Kent State shooting cases, appeals from orders entered by Judge William K. Thomas approving a settlement of this lengthy and bitterly fought litigation.

Sindell contends that his 33⅓% contingency fee contracts for representation of these plaintiffs invalidate the limitation and allocation of attorneys' fees occasioned by the District Court's approval of a $675,000 "settlement" between the State of Ohio and the litigants. * * *

The record in this case is a long and tortuous one. The complaints, originally filed in 1970, were dismissed by the District Court on the theory that essentially the action was against the State of Ohio and barred by the Eleventh Amendment. On appeal, this court affirmed these dismissals by a divided panel. *See* Krause v. Rhodes, 471 F.2d 430 (6th Cir.1972). The United States Supreme Court, however, unanimously reversed the judgments below and remanded for trial. Scheuer v. Rhodes, 416 U.S. 232, 94 S.Ct. 1683, 40 L.Ed.2d 90 (1974). After the first trial, the jury returned a verdict for defendants of no cause for action.

Subsequent to this adverse jury verdict, all plaintiffs and their counsel (including Steven Sindell) signed an agreement naming the American Civil Liberties Union (ACLU) as lead counsel "for purposes of all appellate proceedings in this litigation." Sanford Jay Rosen headed a team of ACLU lawyers in prosecuting the successful appeal to this court, which reversed for new trial. Krause v. Rhodes, 570 F.2d 563 (6th Cir.1977), *cert. denied,* 435 U.S. 924, 98 S.Ct. 1488, 55 L.Ed.2d 517 (1978). Rosen and his team also represented plaintiffs in the first four days of the second trial of this case and in the discussions which led to settlement.

This case was settled by an agreement entered into by all parties and lawyers except Sindell. The State of Ohio (not a party to this litigation) voluntarily offered to pay $675,000 in full settlement, provided that $600,000 of this sum be paid directly to plaintiffs undiluted by legal fees or expenses. Judge Thomas entered a settlement and dismissal order providing for payment of $600,000 to plaintiffs, $50,000 as payment in full to the attorneys, and $25,000 to cover out-of-pocket expenses. The ACLU and most of the other attorneys, including lead counsel Rosen, agreed with the settlement and subsequently agreed to Judge Thomas' distribution of the $50,000 attorneys' fees fund. Judge Thomas limited distribution of the $50,000 to contingent fee contract holders and apparently based the fund's allocation upon work performed prior to the first adverse jury verdict, disregarding for this purpose any of the services rendered by counsel in the successful effort to reverse that verdict and the subsequent retrial which produced the settlement agreement. Thus, law firms associated with appellant Sindell received $33,740 of the $50,000 fund, while the ACLU and the lawyers associated therewith received nothing for their services.

Appellant Sindell's argument before this court is a simple contention that a contingent fee agreement is beyond the power of a federal judge to invalidate or modify on any grounds whatsoever. Judge Thomas, however, based his decision to limit attorneys' fees in these cases in part upon the trial court's traditional power to resolve fee disputes between litigants and their counsel. * * *

Certainly, this case is unique in the annals of litigation in the United States Courts. Judge Thomas found no exact controlling precedent for the actions which he felt required to take, nor do we. Nonetheless, we feel that his approval of the "settlement" offered by the State of Ohio, conditioned specifically upon $600,000 going to the individual plaintiffs without reduction by attorneys' fees, was within his judicial discretion.

A federal district judge has broad equity power to supervise the collection of attorneys' fees under contingent fee contracts. * * *

Indeed, the Code of Professional Responsibility (CPR) of the American Bar Association imposes considerable limitations upon the ability of lawyers to contract for contingent fees. *See* DR 2–106 and EC 2–20.[6]

---

6. DR 2–106 Fees for Legal Services

(A) A lawyer shall not enter into an agreement for charge, or collect an illegal or clearly excessive fee.

(B) A fee is clearly excessive when, after a review of the facts, a lawyer of ordinary prudence would be left with a definite and firm conviction that the fee is in excess of a reasonable fee. Factors to be considered as guides in determining the reasonableness of a fee include the following:

(1) The time and labor required, the novelty and difficulty of the questions involved and the skill requisite to perform the legal service properly.

(2) The likelihood, if apparent to the client, that the acceptance of the particular employment will preclude other employment by the lawyer.

As indicated by the drafters' footnotes, the cited CPR provisions are based largely upon Canon 13 of the old ABA Canons of Professional Ethics, adopted in 1908. Canon 13 provided:

Contingent Fees.

A contract for a contingent fee, where sanctioned by law, should be reasonable under all the circumstances of the case, including the risk and uncertainty of the compensation, *but should always be subject to the supervision of a court, as to its reasonableness.*

(Emphasis added.)

Under the facts of this case, to allow Sindell to enforce his contingent fees to the letter would be, as the District Judge obviously agreed, totally unreasonable.[7] At the outset, had the court accepted Sindell's position, it would have been unable to approve the settlement and there would have been no funds to disburse in any manner. The State of Ohio had conditioned its settlement offer upon the plaintiffs' "netting" $600,-000. The State cannot have been motivated by the same reasoning which ordinarily prompts litigants to settle cases; Ohio had a stake not just in disposing of litigation but in calming the bitter conflict over this case which had raged within its borders—as well as throughout the nation. Thus, the limitations imposed on fee recoveries were absolutely essential to a just settlement of this unique case.

* * *

In closing, we note that Steven Sindell failed to produce any monetary benefit for these plaintiffs. We also observe that the ACLU lawyers

(3) The fee customarily charged in the locality for similar legal services.

(4) The amount involved and the results obtained.

(5) The time limitations imposed by the client or by the circumstances.

(6) The nature and length of the professional relationship with the client.

(7) The experience, reputation, and ability of the lawyer or lawyers performing the services.

(8) Whether the fee is fixed or contingent.

(C) A lawyer shall not enter into an arrangement for, charge, or collect a contingent fee for representing a defendant in a criminal case.

EC 2–20 Contingent fee arrangements in civil cases have long been commonly accepted in the United States in proceedings to enforce claims. The historical bases of their acceptance are that (1) they often, and in a variety of circumstances, provide the only practical means by which one having a claim against another can economically afford, finance, and obtain the services of a competent lawyer to prosecute his claim, and (2) a successful prosecution of the claim produces a *res* out of which the fee can be paid. Although a lawyer generally should decline to accept employment on a contingent fee basis by one who is able to pay a reasonable fixed fee, it is not necessarily improper for a lawyer, where justified by the particular circumstances of a case, to enter into a contingent fee contract in a civil case with any client who, after being fully informed of all relevant factors, desires that arrangement. Because of the human relationships involved and the unique character of the proceedings, contingent fee arrangements in domestic relation cases are rarely justified. In administrative agency proceedings contingent fee contracts should be governed by the same consideration as in other civil cases. Public policy properly condemns contingent fee arrangements in criminal cases, largely on the ground that legal services in criminal cases do not produce a *res* with which to pay the fee.

7. Particularly since Sindell's firm took the "lion's share" of the $50,000 fund, despite his failure to produce any monetary benefit for plaintiffs.

who obtained this settlement are receiving nothing for their services. Under these facts, the award of $33,740 to Sindell and his present or former law firms is at least fair compensation.

It is appropriate that we now ring down the curtain on this tragic drama which so bitterly divided our nation in the decade of the '70's.

The judgment of the District Court is affirmed.

———

1. In Democratic Central Committee of D.C. v. WMATC, 38 F.3d 603 (D.C. Cir.1994), the court held that the interest that attorneys had in being paid fees from a common fund never achieved the status of "private property" within the meaning of the takings clause of the Fifth Amendment. Therefore, modification of the fee agreement by the lower court did not amount to a compensable taking. The court observed that an award of fees from a common fund is discretionary and derived from the exercise of the court's inherent equitable power, not as a matter of right. The court reserved power to amend the fee arrangement contained in a compromise agreement consistent with changed circumstances.

2. Since the focus of the fee-shifting statutes is on the prevailing party, does that justify allowing the client to waive or otherwise negotiate fees in the settlement process? Should eligibility for statutory attorney fees be a "bargaining chip" in the settlement process? Evans v. Jeff D., 475 U.S. 717, 106 S.Ct. 1531, 89 L.Ed.2d 747 (1986), involved a class action which alleged civil rights violations of emotionally and mentally handicapped children in health care and educational programs administered by the State of Idaho. The court appointed a legal aid attorney to represent the interests of the class. The parties negotiated a settlement which contained virtually all of the substantive relief sought, yet which was conditioned upon a waiver of attorney fees by the class.

The plaintiff's attorney contended that the conditional fee waiver effectively constituted "coercion" by exploiting his ethical obligation to recommend settlement in order to avoid the defendant's potential statutory liability for fees. The Supreme Court held that the approval of the class action settlement which included a waiver of statutorily authorized fees was within the district court's discretionary power. The Court found no "ethical dilemma", reasoning that a lawyer is always ethically bound to act in the client's best interests. Therefore, the client had the prerogative to waive fees in order to obtain the relief sought, and thus vindicate civil rights.

Justice Brennan, joined by Justices Marshall and Blackmun, strongly dissented, reasoning that fee awards differ from other remedies. The dissenters asserted that it did "not require a sociological study to see that permitting fee waivers will make it more difficult for civil rights plaintiffs to obtain legal assistance." Which is the better view? Does the practice of allowing a fee waiver undermine the ability of plaintiffs in civil rights cases to attract competent counsel?

NEWMAN v. PIGGIE PARK ENTERPRISES, INC.

390 U.S. 400, 88 S.Ct. 964, 19 L.Ed.2d 1263 (1968).

PER CURIAM.

The petitioners instituted this class action under Title II of the Civil Rights Act of 1964, § 204(a), 78 Stat. 244, 42 U.S.C. § 2000a–3(a), to enjoin racial discrimination at five drive-in restaurants and a sandwich shop owned and operated by the respondents in South Carolina. The District Court * * * found, on undisputed evidence, that Negroes had been discriminated against at all six of the restaurants. But the District Court erroneously concluded that Title II does not cover drive-in restaurants of the sort involved in this case. Thus the court enjoined racial discrimination only at the respondents' sandwich shop.

The Court of Appeals reversed the District Court's refusal to enjoin discrimination at the drive-in establishments, and then directed its attention to that section of Title II which provides that "the prevailing party" is entitled to "a reasonable attorney's fee" in the court's "discretion." § 204(b), 78 Stat. 244, 42 U.S.C. § 2000a–3(b).[1] In remanding the case, the Court of Appeals instructed the District Court to award counsel fees only to the extent that the respondents' defenses had been advanced "for purposes of delay and not in good faith." We granted certiorari to decide whether this subjective standard properly effectuates the purposes of the counsel-fee provision of Title II of the Civil Rights Act of 1964. We hold that it does not.

When the Civil Rights Act of 1964 was passed, it was evident that enforcement would prove difficult and that the Nation would have to rely in part upon private litigation as a means of securing broad compliance with the law.[2] A Title II suit is thus private in form only. When a plaintiff brings an action under that Title, he cannot recover damages. If he obtains an injunction, he does so not for himself alone but also as a "private attorney general," vindicating a policy that Congress considered of the highest priority. If successful plaintiffs were routinely forced to bear their own attorneys' fees, few aggrieved parties would be in a position to advance the public interest by invoking the

1. "In any action commenced pursuant to this subchapter, the court, in its discretion, may allow the prevailing party, other than the United States, a reasonable attorney's fee as part of the costs, and the United States shall be liable for costs the same as a private person." 42 U.S.C. § 2000a–3(b).

2. In this connection, it is noteworthy that 42 U.S.C. § 2000a–3(a) permits intervention by the Attorney General in privately initiated Title II suits "of general public importance" and provides that, "in such circumstances as the court may deem just," a district court may "appoint an attorney for [the] complainant and may authorize the commencement of the civil action without the payment of fees, costs, or security." Only where a "pattern or practice" of discrimination is reasonably believed to exist may the Attorney General himself institute a civil action for injunctive relief. 42 U.S.C. § 2000a–5.

injunctive powers of the federal courts. Congress therefore enacted the provision for counsel fees—not simply to penalize litigants who deliberately advance arguments they know to be untenable but, more broadly, to encourage individuals injured by racial discrimination to seek judicial relief under Title II.

It follows that one who succeeds in obtaining an injunction under that Title should ordinarily recover an attorney's fee unless special circumstances would render such an award unjust. Because no such circumstances are present here, the District Court on remand should include reasonable counsel fees as part of the costs to be assessed against the respondents. As so modified, the judgment of the Court of Appeals is *Affirmed.*

---

1. Numerous civil rights, environmental, consumer, and privacy statutes passed by Congress in the past two decades provide for attorney fees. One of the most important statutory provisions for attorney fees is the Civil Rights Attorney's Fees Awards Act of 1976, codified in 42 U.S.C. § 1988 (supp. 1994). The Act declares:

(b) In any action or proceeding to enforce a provision of [42 U.S.C. §§ 1981–1983, 1985, 1986], title IX of Public Law 92–318 [20 U.S.C. §§ 1681 *et seq.*],the Religious Freedom Restoration Act of 1993 [42 U.S.C. § 2000bb *et seq.*], title VI of the Civil Rights Act of 1964 [42 U.S.C. §§ 2000d *et seq.*], or section 13981 of this title, the court, in its discretion, may allow the prevailing party, other than the United States, a reasonable attorney's fee as part of the costs.

(c) In awarding an attorney's fee under subsection (b) of this section in any action or proceeding to enforce a provision of 1981 or 1981a of this title, the court, in its discretion, may include expert fees as part of the attorney's fee.

2. The Congressional allowance for attorney fees has taken different forms. Under the antitrust laws allowance of attorney fees to a plaintiff awarded treble damages is mandatory, whereas in patent law the statute provides for attorney fees in "exceptional cases" to the prevailing party. 35 U.S.C. § 285.

3. Although many federal fee-shifting statutes provide for the recovery of attorney fees to the "prevailing party," many courts have applied a dual standard whereby prevailing plaintiffs are awarded attorney fees as a matter of course, while successful defendants are held to a stricter standard for recovering fees. In Christiansburg Garment Co. v. Equal Employment Opportunity Commission, 434 U.S. 412, 98 S.Ct. 694, 54 L.Ed.2d 648 (1978), the Supreme Court recognized that a prevailing plaintiff in a Title VII discrimination case under the Civil Rights Act of 1964 ordinarily will receive a fee award absent special circumstances, yet a prevailing defendant could recover fees only by showing that the

plaintiff's claim was "frivolous, unreasonable, or without foundation, even though not brought in subjective bad faith."

The Court reasoned that a differing standard was justified in order to accomplish two goals: to encourage private attorney general actions to protect civil rights and, correspondingly, to shield such claimants from potential fee liability when the suit was meritorious yet unsuccessful. The Court cautioned, however:

> [I]t is important that a district court resist the understandable temptation to engage in *post hoc* reasoning by concluding that, because a plaintiff did not ultimately prevail, his action must have been unreasonable or without foundation. This kind of hindsight logic could discourage all but the most airtight claims, for seldom can a prospective plaintiff be sure of ultimate success. No matter how honest one's belief that he has been the victim of discrimination, no matter how meritorious one's claim may appear at the outset, the course of litigation is rarely predictable. Decisive facts may not emerge until discovery or trial. The law may change or clarify in the midst of litigation. Even when the law or the facts appear questionable or unfavorable at the outset, a party may have an entirely reasonable ground for bringing suit. *Id.* at 421–422.

The Court further noted that a groundless suit will support an award of defendant's attorney fees; a suit that goes beyond "groundless" to "vexatious" will justify recovery under the common law bad faith exception to the American Rule.

See also Independent Federation of Flight Attendants v. Zipes, 488 U.S. 1029, 109 S.Ct. 835, 102 L.Ed.2d 968 (1989), (Attorney fees could not be awarded against losing intervenors in a Title VII action absent showing that intervenor's action was frivolous, unreasonable or without foundation.)

4.   In Fogerty v. Fantasy, Inc., ___ U.S. ___, 114 S.Ct. 1023, 127 L.Ed.2d 455 (1994), the Court departed from its traditional practice and held that a prevailing defendant in a copyright infringement action would be awarded fees on the same basis as a prevailing plaintiff. The Court distinguished *Christiansburg Garment* by observing that the public interest concerns in advancing civil rights were not equally present in the goals and objectives of the Copyright Act. The Court did not follow the "British Rule," however, which awards attorney fees as a matter of course to the prevailing party but stated that entitlement still remains within the equitable discretion of the court.

5.   Attorney fees also may be recoverable under the Equal Access to Justice Act ("EAJA"), in limited circumstances where a party prevails in a civil suit against the United States. 28 U.S.C. § 2412. *See* Resolution Trust Corp. v. Eason, 17 F.3d 1126, 1134 (8th Cir.1994) (Act is limited waiver of sovereign immunity and is strictly construed.) The Act eliminates the financial disincentive and disadvantage otherwise faced by private parties in challenging unreasonable government actions. Sulli-

van v. Hudson, 490 U.S. 877, 883, 109 S.Ct. 2248, 2253, 104 L.Ed.2d 941 (1989).

The EAJA authorizes attorney fees to a "prevailing party" unless "the position of the United States was substantially justified or that special circumstances make an award unjust." 28 U.S.C. § 2412(d)(1)(A). *See* Pierce v. Underwood, 487 U.S. 552, 566, 108 S.Ct. 2541, 2550, 101 L.Ed.2d 490 (1988) ("Substantially justified" means being justified in substance or in the main, supported to a degree that could satisfy a reasonable person.) The Act creates a presumption in favor of awarding fees to prevailing parties, thereby shifting the burden to the government to demonstrate that its actions were reasonable. Thomas v. Peterson, 841 F.2d 332, 335 (9th Cir.1988).

The statute also requires the claimant to file an EAJA application within 30 days of final judgment. *See* Melkonyan v. Sullivan, 501 U.S. (1991); Shalala v. Schaefer, ___ U.S. ___, 113 S.Ct. 2625, 125 L.Ed.2d 239 (1993); Sullivan v. Hudson, 490 U.S. 877, 109 S.Ct. 2248, 104 L.Ed.2d 941 (1989) (Fees incurred during administrative proceedings following remand of civil action recoverable under EAJA.)

The EAJA specifies that fees must be based upon "prevailing market rates," but places a ceiling of $75 per hour on fees absent a showing of a "special factor" or an adjustment for inflation. 28 U.S.C. § 2412(d)(2)(A)(ii). Jones v. Espy, 10 F.3d 690, 692 (9th Cir.1993) (EAJA cost of living adjustment provision permits increasing allowable fee rate based on overall purchasing power of money.) *See generally*, Hill, An Analysis and Explanation of the Equal Access to Justice Act, 19 Ariz. St. L.J. 229 (1987).

6. Consider the provision of the Employee Retirement Income Security Act (ERISA), 29 U.S.C. § 1132. ERISA provides that a district court may award reasonable attorney's fees to either party. In *Lawrence v. Westerhaus,* the Court of Appeals for the Eighth Circuit followed the developing practice of the federal appellate courts to provide specific guidance for fees awards to district courts. Noting that the Congressional purpose in enacting ERISA was to protect employee benefit plan participants by providing ready access to the federal courts, the court listed several factors to weigh in determining whether to award fees in ERISA cases:

> (1) the degree of the opposing parties' culpability or bad faith; (2) the ability of the opposing parties to satisfy an award of attorney's fees; (3) whether an award of attorney's fees against the opposing parties could deter other persons acting under similar circumstances; (4) whether the parties requesting attorney's fees sought to benefit all participants and beneficiaries of an ERISA plan or to resolve a significant legal question regarding ERISA itself; and (5) the relative merits of the parties' positions. 749 F.2d 494, 496 (8th Cir.1984).

See also Iron Workers Local No. 272 v. Bowen, 624 F.2d 1255 (5th Cir.1980).

7. A number of jurisdictions will allow the plaintiff's attorney fees to be considered in calculating the amount of punitive damages. Brewer v. Home–Stake Production Co., 200 Kan. 96, 434 P.2d 828 (1967); Keller v. Davis, 694 S.W.2d 355 (Tex.App.1985) (punitive damages may include damages for inconvenience, reasonable attorneys' fees, and losses considered too remote for actual damages); *contra* Cordeco Development Corp. v. Santiago Vasquez, 539 F.2d 256 (1st Cir.1976). Fitting attorney fees under the umbrella of punitive damages is not viewed as an "exception" to the American Rule, but is justified as part of the punishment for the defendant's wrongful conduct. Those courts have further held, however, that attorney fees may not be recoverable as a separate item apart from punitive damages. Fitz v. Toungate, 419 S.W.2d 708 (Tex.Civ.App. 1967). Does such a distinction seem justifiable?

PROBLEM: THE WRONGFUL DETENTION

Plaintiff Lee Hutchins sues for a civil rights violation concerning an unlawful period of detention after arrest. The police made the arrest without a warrant, and then ten days in jail passed before Hutchins was taken to a court for probable cause and bail hearings. The defendant officials had accidentally misfiled the plaintiff's card.

Hutchins' complaint prayed for damages for this incident and for an injunction against future unlawful periods of detention of plaintiff or any similarly situated future arrestees.

After a trial of several days the judge concluded that plaintiff had made a sufficient case of a personal civil rights violation to allow the case to go to the jury. The jury found for the plaintiff in the sum of $300. The court sitting in equity then determined that there was not a sufficient showing that the plaintiff or similarly situated future arrestees were likely to be subjected to the same wrongful detention. Therefore the injunction was denied.

The civil rights act under which plaintiff recovered the $300 damages allows attorney fees to prevailing plaintiffs. Should some or all of the plaintiff's attorney fees be recoverable in this case?

FARRAR v. HOBBY

___ U.S. ___, 113 S.Ct. 566, 121 L.Ed.2d 494 (1992)

JUSTICE THOMAS delivered the opinion of the Court.

We decide today whether a civil rights plaintiff who receives a nominal damages award is a "prevailing party" eligible to receive attorney's fees under 42 U.S.C. § 1988. * * *

I

Joseph Davis Farrar and Dale Lawson Farrar owned and operated Artesia Hall, a school in Liberty County, Texas, for delinquent, disabled, and disturbed teens. After an Artesia Hall student died in 1973, a

Liberty County grand jury returned a murder indictment charging Joseph Farrar with willful failure to administer proper medical treatment and failure to provide timely hospitalization.

[State officials obtained injunctive relief against Artesia Hall and ultimately succeeded in closing the school. Joseph Farrar sued William Hobby, Jr., Lieutenant Governor of Texas, a judge, the county attorney, and the director and two employees of the Department of Public Welfare for monetary and injunctive relief under 42 U.S.C. §§ 1983 and 1985. The complaint alleged deprivation of liberty and property without due process of law by means of conspiracy and malicious prosecution aimed at closing Artesia Hall. Farrar amended the complaint and dropped the claim for injunctive relief but increased the damages sought to $17 million. Joseph Farrar subsequently died and the coadministrators of his estate were substituted as plaintiffs.

A jury found that all of the defendants except Hobby had conspired against the plaintiffs but that the conspiracy was not a proximate cause of any injury suffered by the plaintiffs. The jury also found that Hobby had "committed an act or acts under color of state law that deprived Joseph Farrar of a civil right," but it found that Hobby's conduct was not "a proximate cause of any damages" suffered by Joseph Farrar. Consequently, the District Court dismissed the case and ordered that the parties bear their own costs. The Court of Appeals affirmed the failure to award compensatory or nominal damages against the conspirators because the plaintiffs had not proved an actual deprivation of a constitutional right. Because the jury found that Hobby had deprived Joseph Farrar of a civil right, however, the Fifth Circuit remanded for entry of judgment against Hobby for nominal damages. Based upon 42 U.S.C. § 1988, a federal fee-shifting statute, the District Court awarded the plaintiffs $280,000 in fees, $27,932 in expenses, and $9,730 in prejudgment interest against Hobby. A divided Fifth Circuit panel reversed the fee award, however, on the basis that the plaintiffs were not "prevailing parties" within the meaning of the civil rights fee-shifting statute.]

II.

The Civil Rights Attorney's Fees Award Act of 1976, 90 Stat. 2641, as amended, 42 U.S.C. § 1988, provides in relevant part:

> "In any action or proceeding to enforce a provision of sections 1981, 1982, 1983, 1985, and 1986 of this title, title IX of Public Law 92–318 . . ., or title VI of the Civil Rights Act of 1964 . . ., the court, in its discretion, may allow the prevailing party, other than the United States, a reasonable attorney's fee as part of the costs."

"Congress intended to permit the . . . award of counsel fees only when a party has prevailed on the merits." Therefore, in order to qualify for attorney's fees under § 1988, a plaintiff must be a "prevailing party." Under our "generous formulation" of the term, " 'plaintiffs may be considered "prevailing parties" for attorney's fees purposes if they succeed on any significant issue in litigation which achieves some of the benefit the parties sought in bringing suit.' " * * *

We have elaborated on the definition of prevailing party in three recent cases. In Hewitt v. Helms, 482 U.S. 755 (1987), we addressed "the peculiar-sounding question whether a party who litigates to judgment and loses on all of his claims can nonetheless be a 'prevailing party.' " In his § 1983 action against state prison officials for alleged due process violations, respondent Helms obtained no relief. * * * Observing that "respect for ordinary language requires that a plaintiff receive at least some relief on the merits of his claim before he can be said to prevail," we held that Helms was not a prevailing party. We required the plaintiff to prove "the settling of some dispute which affects the behavior of the defendant towards the plaintiff." (emphasis omitted).

In Rhodes v. Stewart, 488 U.S. 1 (1988) (per curiam), we reversed an award of attorney's fees premised solely on a declaratory judgment that prison officials had violated the plaintiffs' First and Fourteenth Amendment rights. By the time the District Court entered judgment, "one of the plaintiffs had died and the other was no longer in custody." Under these circumstances, we held, neither plaintiff was a prevailing party. We explained that "nothing in [*Hewitt*] suggested that the entry of [a declaratory] judgment in a party's favor automatically renders that party prevailing under § 1988." We reaffirmed that a judgment—declaratory or otherwise—"will constitute relief, for purposes of § 1988, if, and only if, it affects the behavior of the defendant toward the plaintiff." Whatever "modification of prison policies" the declaratory judgment might have effected "could not in any way have benefited either plaintiff, one of whom was dead and the other released."

Finally, in Texas State Teachers Assn. v. Garland Independent School Dist., 489 U.S. 782 (1989), we synthesized the teachings of *Hewitt and Rhodes*. "To be considered a prevailing party within the meaning of § 1988," we held, "the plaintiff must be able to point to a resolution of the dispute which changes the legal relationship between itself and the defendant." 489 U.S., at 792. We reemphasized that "the touchstone of the prevailing party inquiry must be the material alteration of the legal relationship of the parties." *Id.*, at 792–793. Under this test, the plaintiffs in *Garland* were prevailing parties because they "obtained a judgment vindicating [their] First Amendment rights [as] public employees" and "materially altered the [defendant] school district's policy limiting the rights of teachers to communicate with each other concerning employee organizations and union activities."

Therefore, to qualify as a prevailing party, a civil rights plaintiff must obtain at least some relief on the merits of his claim. The plaintiff must obtain an enforceable judgment against the defendant from whom fees are sought, or comparable relief through a consent decree or settlement. Whatever relief the plaintiff secures must directly benefit him at the time of the judgment or settlement. Otherwise the judgment or settlement cannot be said to "affect the behavior of the defendant toward the plaintiff." Only under these circumstances can civil rights litigation effect "the material alteration of the legal relationship of the parties" and thereby transform the plaintiff into a prevailing party. In short, a plaintiff "prevails" when actual relief on the merits of his claim materially alters the legal relationship between the parties by modifying the defendant's behavior in a way that directly benefits the plaintiff.

III

A

Doubtless "the basic purpose of a § 1983 damages award should be to compensate persons for injuries caused by the deprivation of constitutional rights." Carey v. Piphus, 435 U.S. 247, 254 (1978). For this reason, no compensatory damages may be awarded in a § 1983 suit absent proof of actual injury. We have also held, however, that "the denial of procedural due process should be actionable for nominal damages without proof of actual injury." The awarding of nominal damages for the "absolute" right to procedural due process "recognizes the importance to organized society that [this] right be scrupulously observed" while "remaining true to the principle that substantial damages should be awarded only to compensate actual injury." 435 U.S., at 266. Thus, *Carey* obligates a court to award nominal damages when a plaintiff establishes the violation of his right to procedural due process but cannot prove actual injury.

We therefore hold that a plaintiff who wins nominal damages is a prevailing party under § 1988. When a court awards nominal damages, it neither enters judgment for defendant on the merits nor declares the defendant's legal immunity to suit. To be sure, a judicial pronouncement that the defendant has violated the Constitution, unaccompanied by an enforceable judgment on the merits, does not render the plaintiff a prevailing party. Of itself, "the moral satisfaction [that] results from any favorable statement of law" cannot bestow prevailing party status. No material alteration of the legal relationship between the parties occurs until the plaintiff becomes entitled to enforce a judgment, consent decree, or settlement against the defendant. A plaintiff may demand payment for nominal damages no less than he may demand payment for millions of dollars in compensatory damages. A judgment for damages in any amount, whether compensatory or nominal, modifies the defendant's behavior for the plaintiff's benefit by forcing the defendant to pay an amount of money he otherwise would not pay. As a result, the Court of Appeals for the Fifth Circuit erred in holding that petitioners' nominal damages award failed to render them prevailing parties.

* * *

B

Although the "technical" nature of a nominal damages award or any other judgment does not affect the prevailing party inquiry, it does bear on the propriety of fees awarded under § 1988. Once civil rights litigation materially alters the legal relationship between the parties, "the degree of the plaintiff's overall success goes to the reasonableness" of a fee award under *Hensley v. Eckerhart*, 461 U.S. 424 (1983). Indeed, "the most critical factor" in determining the reasonableness of a fee award "is the degree of success obtained." In this case, petitioners received nominal damages instead of the $17 million in compensatory damages that they sought. This litigation accomplished little beyond giving petitioners "the moral satisfaction of knowing that a federal court concluded that [their] rights had been violated" in some unspecified way.

In some circumstances, even a plaintiff who formally "prevails" under § 1988 should receive no attorney's fees at all. A plaintiff who seeks compensatory damages but receives no more than nominal damages is often such a prevailing party. As we have held, a nominal damages award does render a plaintiff a prevailing party by allowing him to vindicate his "absolute" right to procedural due process through enforcement of a judgment against the defendant. In a civil rights suit for damages, however, the awarding of nominal damages also highlights the plaintiff's failure to prove actual, compensable injury. Whatever the constitutional basis for substantive liability, damages awarded in a § 1983 action "must always be designed 'to *compensate injuries* caused by the [constitutional] deprivation.'" When a plaintiff recovers only nominal damages because of his failure to prove an essential element of his claim for monetary relief, the only reasonable fee is usually no fee at all. In an apparent failure to heed our admonition that fee awards under § 1988 were never intended to " 'produce windfalls to attorneys,' " the District Court awarded $280,000 in attorney's fees without "considering the relationship between the extent of success and the amount of the fee award."

Although the Court of Appeals erred in failing to recognize that petitioners were prevailing parties, it correctly reversed the District Court's fee award. We accordingly affirm the judgment of the Court of Appeals.

So ordered.

JUSTICE O'CONNOR, concurring.

If ever there was a plaintiff who deserved no attorney's fees at all, that plaintiff is Joseph Farrar. He filed a lawsuit demanding 17 million dollars from six defendants. After 10 years of litigation and two trips to the Court of Appeals, he got one dollar from one defendant. As the Court holds today, that is simply not the type of victory that merits an award of attorney's fees. * * *

I

Congress has authorized the federal courts to award "a reasonable attorney's fee" in certain civil rights cases, but only to "the prevailing party." To become a prevailing party, a plaintiff must obtain, at an absolute minimum, "actual relief on the merits of [the] claim," which "affects the behavior of the defendant towards the plaintiff." Joseph Farrar met that minimum condition for prevailing party status. Through this lawsuit, he obtained an enforceable judgment for one dollar in nominal damages. One dollar is not exactly a bonanza, but it constitutes relief on the merits. * * *

II

In the context of this litigation, the technical or *de minimis* nature of Joseph Farrar's victory is readily apparent: He asked for a bundle and got a pittance. While we hold today that this pittance is enough to render him a prevailing party, it does not by itself prevent his victory from being purely technical. It is true that Joseph Farrar recovered something. But holding that any award of nominal damages renders the victory material would "render the concept of *de minimis* relief meaningless. *Every* nominal damage award has as its basis a finding of liability, but obviously many such victories are pyrrhic ones." That is not to say that *all* nominal damages awards are *de minimis*. Nominal relief does not necessarily a nominal victory make. But * * * a substantial difference between the judgment recovered and the recovery sought suggests that the victory is in fact purely technical. Here that suggestion is quite strong. Joseph Farrar asked for 17 million dollars; he got one. It is hard to envision a more dramatic difference.

The difference between the amount recovered and the damages sought is not the only consideration, however. Carey v. Piphus, 435 U.S. 247, 254 (1978), makes clear that an award of nominal damages can represent a victory in the sense of vindicating rights even though no actual damages are proved. Accordingly, the courts also must look to other factors. One is the significance of the legal issue on which the plaintiff claims to have prevailed. Petitioners correctly point out that Joseph Farrar in a sense succeeded on a significant issue—liability. But even on that issue he cannot be said to have achieved a true victory. Respondent was just one of six defendants and the only one not found to have engaged in a conspiracy. If recovering one dollar from the least culpable defendant and nothing from the rest legitimately can be labeled a victory—and I doubt that it can—surely it is a hollow one. Joseph Farrar may have won a point, but the game, set, and match all went to the defendants.

Given that Joseph Farrar got *some* of what he wanted—one seventeen millionth, to be precise—his success might be considered material if it also accomplished some public goal other than occupying the time and energy of counsel, court, and client. Section 1988 is not "a relief Act for lawyers." Riverside v. Rivera, 477 U.S. 561, 588 (1986) (REHNQUIST, J., dissenting). Instead, it is a tool that ensures the vindication of important rights, even when large sums of money are not at stake, by making attorney's fees available under a private attorney general theory. Yet one searches these facts in vain for the public purpose this litigation might have served. * * *

III

In this case, the relevant indicia of success—the extent of relief, the significance of the legal issue on which the plaintiff prevailed, and the public purpose served—all point to a single conclusion: Joseph Farrar achieved only a *de minimis* victory. As the Court correctly holds today, the appropriate fee in such a case is no fee at all. Because the Court of Appeals gave Joseph Farrar everything he deserved—nothing—I join the Court's opinion affirming the judgment below.

JUSTICE WHITE, with whom JUSTICE BLACKMUN, JUSTICE STEVENS, and JUSTICE SOUTER join, concurring in part and dissenting in part.

We granted certiorari in this case to decide whether 42 U.S.C. § 1988 entitles a civil rights plaintiff who recovers nominal damages to reasonable attorney's fees. Following our decisions in Texas State Teachers Assn. v. Garland Independent School Dist., 489 U.S. 782 (1989), Hewitt v. Helms, 482 U.S. 755 (1987), Hensley v. Eckerhart, 461 U.S. 424 (1983), and Carey v. Piphus, 435 U.S. 247 (1978), the Court holds that it does. With that aspect of today's decision, I agree. Because Farrar won an enforceable judgment against respondent, he has achieved a "material alteration" of their legal relationship, and thus he is a "prevailing party" under the statute.

However, I see no reason for the Court to reach out and decide what amount of attorney's fees constitutes a reasonable amount in this instance. That issue was neither presented in the petition for certiorari nor briefed by petitioners. The opinion of the Court of Appeals was grounded exclusively in its determination that Farrar had not met the threshold requirement under § 1988. * * *

Litigation in this case lasted for more than a decade, has entailed a 6–week trial and given rise to two appeals. Civil rights cases often are complex, and we therefore have committed the task of calculating attorney's fees to the trial court's discretion for good reason. Estimating what specific amount would be reasonable in this particular situation is not a matter of general importance on which our guidance is needed. Short of holding that recovery of nominal damages never can support the award of attorney's fees—which, clearly, the majority does not—the Court should follow its sensible practice and remand the case for reconsideration of the fee amount. * * *

---

1. The principal case reflects the Court's most recent attempt to clarify the requirement that a claimant for attorney fees must achieve "some degree of success on the merits." The Supreme Court outlined the basic approach for fee eligibility and measurement in Hensley v. Eckerhart, 461 U.S. 424, 103 S.Ct. 1933, 76 L.Ed.2d 40 (1983), as follows:

> A plaintiff must be a "prevailing party" to recover an attorney's fee under § 1988. The standard for making this threshold determi-

nation has been framed in various ways. A typical formulation is that "plaintiffs may be considered 'prevailing parties' for attorney's fees purposes if they succeed on any significant issue in litigation which achieves some of the benefit the parties sought in bringing suit." This is a generous formulation that brings the plaintiff only across the statutory threshold. It remains for the district court to determine what fee is "reasonable."

The most useful starting point for determining the amount of a reasonable fee is the number of hours reasonably expended on the litigation multiplied by a reasonable hourly rate. This calculation provides an objective basis on which to make an initial estimate of the value of a lawyer's services. The party seeking an award of fees should submit evidence supporting the hours worked and rates claimed. Where the documentation of hours is inadequate, the district court may reduce the award accordingly. * * *

The product of reasonable hours times a reasonable rate does not end the inquiry. There remain other considerations that may lead the district court to adjust the fee upward or downward, including the important factor of the "results obtained." This factor is particularly crucial where a plaintiff is deemed "prevailing" even though he succeeded on only some of his claims for relief. In this situation two questions must be addressed. First, did the plaintiff fail to prevail on claims that were unrelated to the claims on which he succeeded? Second, did the plaintiff achieve a level of success that makes the hours reasonably expended a satisfactory basis for making a fee award? In some cases a plaintiff may present in one lawsuit distinctly different claims for relief that are based on different facts and legal theories. In such a suit, even where the claims are brought against the same defendants—often an institution and its officers—counsel's work on one claim will be unrelated to his work on another claim. Accordingly, work on an unsuccessful claim cannot be deemed to have been "expended in pursuit of the ultimate result achieved." The congressional intent to limit awards to prevailing parties requires that these unrelated claims be treated as if they had been raised in separate lawsuits, and therefore no fee may be awarded for services on the unsuccessful claim.

It may well be that cases involving such unrelated claims are unlikely to arise with great frequency. Many civil rights cases will present only a single claim. In other cases the plaintiff's claims for relief will involve a common core of facts or will be based on related legal theories. Much of counsel's time will be devoted generally to the litigation as a whole, making it difficult to divide the hours expended on a claim-by-claim basis. Such a lawsuit cannot be viewed as a series of discrete claims. Instead the district court should focus on the significance of the overall relief obtained by the plaintiff in relation to the hours reasonably expended on the litigation.

Where a plaintiff has obtained excellent results, his attorney should recover a fully compensatory fee. Normally this will encompass all hours reasonably expended on the litigation, and indeed in some cases of exceptional success an enhanced award may be justified. In these circumstances the fee award should not be reduced simply because the plaintiff failed to prevail on every contention raised in the lawsuit. Litigants in good faith may raise alternative legal grounds for a desired outcome, and the court's rejection of or failure to reach certain grounds is not a sufficient reason for reducing a fee. The result is what matters.

If, on the other hand, a plaintiff has achieved only partial or limited success, the product of hours reasonably expended on the litigation as a whole times a reasonable hourly rate may be an excessive amount. This will be true even where the plaintiff's claims were interrelated, nonfrivolous, and raised in good faith. Congress has not authorized an award of fees whenever it was reasonable for a plaintiff to bring a lawsuit or whenever conscientious counsel tried the case with devotion and skill. Again, the most critical factor is the degree of success obtained.

Application of this principle is particularly important in complex civil rights litigation involving numerous challenges to institutional practices or conditions. This type of litigation is lengthy and demands many hours of lawyers' services. Although the plaintiff often may succeed in identifying some unlawful practices or conditions, the range of possible success is vast. That the plaintiff is a "prevailing party" therefore may say little about whether the expenditure of counsel's time was reasonable in relation to the success achieved. * * *

There is no precise rule or formula for making these determinations. The district court may attempt to identify specific hours that should be eliminated, or it may simply reduce the award to account for the limited success. The court necessarily has discretion in making this equitable judgment. * * *

2. The focus on the degree of success obtained has remained as the touchstone for assessing eligibility as well as the measure of fees. In Texas State Teachers Association v. Garland Independent School District, 489 U.S. 782, 109 S.Ct. 1486, 103 L.Ed.2d 866 (1989), discussed in part in *Farrar*, the Court refined the *Hensley* test of the appropriate standard for determining "prevailing part" status for attorney fee awards under the civil rights fee-shifting statute, 42 U.S.C. § 1988, where the plaintiff has achieved only partial success on the merits. In *Garland*, several teachers' unions brought constitutional challenges concerning various school board policies limiting union activities and communications.

The Court resolved a debate in the lower courts and held that fee eligibility was predicated on demonstrating success on a "significant" issue in litigation, but did not require prevailing on the "central" issue in dispute. Justice O'Connor, writing for a unanimous Court, stated that administration of the so-called central issue test would be as difficult as searching for the "Golden Fleece." The Court explained that the principal consideration in establishing entitlement to any fee award is whether the legal relationship of the parties was "materially altered" in a manner consistent with the intentions of Congress in the fee-shifting statute. Beyond that showing, the degree of overall success relates to the *measure* of the fee; therefore, no fees would be given where the plaintiff achieved only technical or *de minimis* success.

3. Federal statutory provisions authorizing an award of attorney fees take many forms. Many federal fee-shifting statutes expressly limit recovery of fees to a "prevailing party" or "prevailing plaintiff." What result regarding fee eligibility where the language provides that the court *may* award costs of litigation, including reasonable attorney fees, whenever it determines that an award would be "appropriate"? *See* 42 U.S.C. § 307(f). This phrase, which is set forth in the citizen suit provision of the Clean Air Act, was examined by the Supreme Court in Ruckelshaus v. Sierra Club, 463 U.S. 680, 103 S.Ct. 3274, 77 L.Ed.2d 938 (1983). In that case the Court denied fees to the *losing* party which had acted as a private attorney general in challenging certain standards promulgated by the EPA under the Act. Although the suit produced some benefits, the majority held that judicial discretion regarding fee entitlement was nevertheless constrained by the American Rule absent explicit statutory language authorizing fees. Should it make any difference in statutory interpretation that the relevant citizen suit provision permitted only equitable relief and not damages?

Congress has embraced the reasoning of the Supreme Court in *Ruckelshaus* by employing the "prevailing or substantially prevailing" standard rather than the "whenever appropriate" language for fee awards in more recent environmental statutes. *See* Clean Water Act, 33 U.S.C. § 1365(d); Resource Conservation and Recovery Act, 42 U.S.C. § 6972(e); and Comprehensive Environmental Response, Compensation, and Liability Act, 42 U.S.C. § 9659(f).

4. What should be the outcome regarding fee awards where the parties voluntarily settle? *See* Atlantic States Legal Foundation, Inc. v. Eastman Kodak, 933 F.2d 124 (2d Cir.1991) (Plaintiff deemed a "prevailing party" entitled to an award of attorney fees and expenses where "reasonable inference" drawn that existence of citizen suit motivated alleged violators of Clean Water Act to settle dispute.)

5. In Kay v. Ehrler, 499 U.S.432, 111 S.Ct. 1435, 113 L.Ed.2d 486 (1991), the Supreme Court held that an attorney, acting *pro se* in a successful civil rights suit, was not entitled to an award of a reasonable attorneys fee under 42 U.S.C. § 1988. The Court acknowledged that Congress had created the fee-shifting statutory model as a means to encourage litigation to protect civil rights, yet the principal consideration was to enable parties to attract independent counsel. The Court also observed that the concept of "attorney" implicitly contemplated an

agency relationship. Additionally, the Court expressed reservations about the potential ethical and strategic disadvantages where a lawyer represents their own interests. Justice Stevens, writing for a unanimous Court, concluded: "The adage that a 'lawyer who represents himself has a fool for a client' is the product of years of experience by seasoned litigators."

6. In Key Tronic Corp. v. United States, ___ U.S. ___, 114 S.Ct. 1960, 128 L.Ed.2d 797 (1994), a private corporation that had incurred cleanup costs under a federal environmental statute (CERCLA) brought a private cost recovery action against the Air Force, another potentially responsible party (PRP). The Court held that litigation-related fees were not recoverable as "response costs" because the relevant statutory provision did not specifically provide for fee awards to a prevailing party.

The Court thus maintained fidelity to its legacy of Alyeska Pipeline Service Co. v. Wilderness Society, 421 U.S. 240, 247, 95 S.Ct. 1612, 1616, 44 L.Ed.2d 141 (1975), in closely following a strict view that costs of litigation may not be awarded in federal enforcement actions absent express congressional authorization. The Court did find, however, that fees pertaining to the corporation's activities performed in identifying other PRPs could be recoverable because the work could have been performed by other professionals (*e.g.* chemists or engineers) and it benefitted the cleanup effort, rather than merely reallocated costs.

CITY OF RIVERSIDE v. RIVERA
477 U.S. 561, 106 S.Ct. 2686, 91 L.Ed.2d 466 (1986).

JUSTICE BRENNAN announced the judgment of the Court:

The issue presented in this case is whether an award of attorney's fees under 42 U.S.C. § 1988 is *per se* "unreasonable" within the meaning of the statute if it exceeds the amount of damages recovered by the plaintiff in the underlying civil rights action.

Respondents, eight Chicano individuals, attended a party on the evening of August 1, 1975, at the Riverside, California, home of respondents Santos and Jennie Rivera. A large number of unidentified police officers, acting without a warrant, broke up the party using tear gas and, as found by the District Court, "unnecessary physical force." Many of the guests, including four of the respondents, were arrested. The District Court later found that "[t]he party was not creating a disturbance in the community at the time of the break-in." Criminal charges against the arrestees were ultimately dismissed for lack of probable cause.

On June 4, 1976, respondents sued the city of Riverside, its chief of police, and 30 individual police officers under 42 U.S.C. §§ 1981, 1983, 1985(3), and 1986 for allegedly violating their First, Fourth, and Fourteenth Amendment rights. The complaint, which also alleged numerous state-law claims, sought damages, and declaratory and injunctive relief. * * * Respondents were awarded $33,350 in compensatory and punitive damages: $13,300 for their federal claims, and $20,050 for their state-law claims.

Respondents also sought attorney's fees and costs under § 1988. They requested compensation for 1,946.75 hours expended by their two attorneys at a rate of $125 per hour, and for 84.5 hours expended by law clerks at a rate of $25.00 per hour, a total of $245,456.25. The District Court found both the hours and rates reasonable, and awarded respondents $245,456.25 in attorney's fees. The court rejected respondents' request for certain additional expenses, and for a multiplier sought by respondents to reflect the contingent nature of their success and the high quality of their attorneys' efforts.

* * * [Petitioners] sought a writ of certiorari from this Court, alleging that the District Court's fee award was not "reasonable" within the meaning of § 1988, because it was disproportionate to the amount of damages recovered by respondents. We granted the writ, 474 U.S. 917, 106 S.Ct. 244, 88 L.Ed.2d 253 (1985), and now affirm the Court of Appeals.

In Alyeska Pipeline Service Co. v. Wilderness Society, 421 U.S. 240, 95 S.Ct. 1612, 44 L.Ed.2d 141 (1975), the Court reaffirmed the "American Rule" that, at least absent express statutory authorization to the contrary, each party to a lawsuit ordinarily shall bear its own attorney's fees. In response to *Alyeska,* Congress enacted the Civil Rights Attorney's Fees Awards Act of 1976, 42 U.S.C. § 1988, which authorized the district courts to award reasonable attorney's fees to prevailing parties in specified civil rights litigation. While the statute itself does not explain what constitutes a reasonable fee, both the House and Senate Reports accompanying § 1988 expressly endorse the analysis set forth in *Johnson v. Georgia Highway Express, Inc.,* 488 F.2d 714 (CA5 1974). *Johnson* identifies 12 factors to be considered in calculating a reasonable attorney's fee.[3]

Hensley v. Eckerhart, 461 U.S. 424, 103 S.Ct. 1933, 76 L.Ed.2d 40 (1983), announced certain guidelines for calculating a reasonable attorney's fee under § 1988. *Hensley* stated that "[t]he most useful starting point for determining the amount of a reasonable fee is the number of hours reasonably expended on the litigation multiplied by a reasonable hourly rate." This figure, commonly referred to as the "lodestar," is presumed to be the reasonable fee contemplated by § 1988. * * *

Hensley then discussed other considerations that might lead the district court to adjust the lodestar figure upward or downward, including the "important factor of the 'results obtained.'" 461 U.S., at 434.

---

3. These factors are: (1) the time and labor required; (2) the novelty and difficulty of the questions; (3) the skill requisite to perform the legal service properly; (4) the preclusion of employment by the attorney due to acceptance of the case; (5) the customary fee; (6) whether the fee is fixed or contingent; (7) time limitations imposed by the client or the circumstances; (8) the amount involved and the results obtained; (9) the experience, reputation, and ability of the attorneys; (10) the "undesirability" of the case; (11) the nature and length of the professional relationship with the client; and (12) awards in similar cases. 488 F.2d, at 717–719.

The opinion noted that where a prevailing plaintiff has succeeded on only some of his claims, an award of fees for time expended on unsuccessful claims may not be appropriate. In these situations, the Court held that the judge should consider whether or not the plaintiff's unsuccessful claims were related to the claims on which he succeeded, and whether the plaintiff achieved a level of success that makes it appropriate to award attorney's fees for hours reasonably expended on unsuccessful claims. * * *

Petitioners argue that the District Court failed properly to follow *Hensley* in calculating respondents' fee award. We disagree. The District Court carefully considered the results obtained by respondents pursuant to the instructions set forth in *Hensley*, and concluded that respondents were entitled to recover attorney's fees for all hours expended on the litigation. First, the court found that "[t]he amount of time expended by counsel in conducting this litigation was reasonable and reflected sound legal judgment under the circumstances." The court also determined that counsels' excellent performances in this case entitled them to be compensated at prevailing market rates, even though they were relatively young when this litigation began. *See Johnson*, 488 F.2d, at 718–719 ("[i]f a young attorney demonstrates the skill and ability, he should not be penalized for only recently being admitted to the bar").

The District Court then concluded that it was inappropriate to adjust respondents' fee award downward to account for the fact that respondents had prevailed only on some of their claims, and against only some of the defendants. * * * The Court remarked:

"I think every one of the claims that were made were related and if you look at the common core of facts that we had here that you had total success.... There was a problem about who was responsible for what and that problem was there all the way through to the time that we concluded the case. * * *"

The court then found that the lawsuit could not "be viewed as a series of discrete claims." * * *

The District Court also considered the amount of damages recovered, and determined that the size of the damages award did not imply that respondents' success was limited:

"[T]he size of the jury award resulted from (a) the general reluctance of jurors to make large awards against police officers, and (b) the dignified restraint which the plaintiffs exercised in describing their injuries to the jury. For example, although some of the actions of the police would clearly have been insulting and humiliating to even the most insensitive person and were, in the opinion of the Court, intentionally so, plaintiffs did not attempt to play up this aspect of the case."

The court paid particular attention to the fact that the case "presented complex and interrelated issues of fact and law," and that "[a] fee award in this civil rights action will . . . advance the public interest." * * *

Based on our review of the record, we agree with the Court of Appeals that the District Court's findings were not clearly erroneous. We conclude that the District Court correctly applied the factors announced in *Hensley* in calculating respondents' fee award, and that the court did not abuse its discretion in awarding attorney's fees for all time reasonably spent litigating the case.

Petitioners, joined by the Solicitor General as *amicus curiae,* maintain that *Hensley's* lodestar approach is inappropriate in civil rights cases where a plaintiff recovers only monetary damages. In these cases, so the argument goes, use of the lodestar may result in fees that exceed the amount of damages recovered and that are therefore unreasonable. Likening such cases to private tort actions, petitioners and the Solicitor General submit that attorney's fees in such cases should be proportionate to the amount of damages a plaintiff recovers. Specifically, they suggest that fee awards in damages cases should be modeled upon the contingent fee arrangements commonly used in personal injury litigation. In this case, assuming a 33% contingency rate, this would entitle respondents to recover approximately $11,000 in attorney's fees.

The amount of damages a plaintiff recovers is certainly relevant to the amount of attorney's fees to be awarded under § 1988. It is, however, only one of many factors that a court should consider in calculating an award of attorney's fees. We reject the proposition that fee awards under § 1988 should necessarily be proportionate to the amount of damages a civil rights plaintiff actually recovers.

As an initial matter, we reject the notion that a civil rights action for damages constitutes nothing more than a private tort suit benefiting only the individual plaintiffs whose rights were violated. Unlike most private tort litigants, a civil rights plaintiff seeks to vindicate important civil and constitutional rights that cannot be valued solely in monetary terms. [Citation.] And, Congress has determined that "the public as a whole has an interest in the vindication of the rights conferred by the statutes enumerated in § 1988, over and above the value of a civil rights remedy to a particular plaintiff. . . ." [Citation.] Regardless of the form of relief he actually obtains, a successful civil rights plaintiff often secures important social benefits that are not reflected in nominal or relatively small damages awards. In this case, for example, the District Court found that many of petitioners' unlawful acts were "motivated by a general hostility to the Chicano community," and that this litigation therefore served the public interest. * * * In addition, the damages a plaintiff recovers contributes significantly to the deterrence of civil rights violations in the future. [Citation.] This deterrent effect is particularly evident in the area of individual police misconduct, where injunctive relief generally is unavailable.

* * *

A rule that limits attorney's fees in civil rights cases to a proportion of the damages awarded would seriously undermine Congress' purpose in enacting § 1988. Congress enacted § 1988 specifically because it found that the private market for legal services failed to provide many victims of civil rights violations with effective access to the judicial process. These victims ordinarily cannot afford to purchase legal services at the rates set by the private market. * * * Moreover, the contingent fee arrangements that make legal services available to many victims of personal injuries would often not encourage lawyers to accept civil rights cases, which frequently involve substantial expenditures of time and effort but produce only small monetary recoveries. * * * Congress enacted § 1988 specifically to enable plaintiffs to enforce the civil rights laws even where the amount of damages at stake would not otherwise make it feasible for them to do so. * * *

A rule of proportionality would make it difficult, if not impossible, for individuals with meritorious civil rights claims but relatively small potential damages to obtain redress from the courts. This is totally inconsistent with the Congress' purpose in enacting § 1988. Congress recognized that private-sector fee arrangements were inadequate to ensure sufficiently vigorous enforcement of civil rights. In order to ensure that lawyers would be willing to represent persons with legitimate civil rights grievances, Congress determined that it would be necessary to compensate lawyers for all time reasonably expended on a case.

This case illustrates why the enforcement of civil rights laws cannot be entrusted to private-sector fee arrangements. The District Court observed that "[g]iven the nature of this lawsuit and the type of defense presented, many attorneys in the community would have been reluctant to institute and to continue to prosecute this action." The court concluded, moreover, that "[c]ounsel for plaintiffs achieved excellent results for their clients, and their accomplishment in this case was outstanding. The amount of time expended by counsel in conducting this litigation was reasonable and reflected sound legal judgment under the circumstances." Nevertheless, petitioners suggest that respondents' counsel should be compensated for only a small fraction of the actual time spent litigating the case. In light of the difficult nature of the issues presented by this lawsuit and the low pecuniary value of the many of the rights respondents sought to vindicate, it is highly unlikely that the prospect of a fee equal to a fraction of the damages respondents might recover would have been sufficient to attract competent counsel. Moreover, since counsel might not have found it economically feasible to expend the amount of time respondents' counsel found necessary to litigate the case properly, it is even less likely that counsel would have achieved the excellent results that respondents' counsel obtained here. Thus, had respondents had to rely on private-sector fee arrangements, they might well have been unable to obtain redress for their grievances. It is precisely for this reason that Congress enacted § 1988.

We agree with petitioners that Congress intended that statutory fee awards be "adequate to attract competent counsel, but ... not produce windfalls to attorneys." However, we find no evidence that Congress intended that, in order to avoid "windfalls to attorneys," attorney's fees be proportionate to the amount of damages a civil rights plaintiff might recover. Rather, there already exists a wide range of safeguards designed to protect civil rights defendants against the possibility of excessive fee awards. Both the House and Senate Reports identify standards for courts to follow in awarding and calculating attorney's fees; these standards are designed to insure that attorneys are compensated only for time *reasonably expended* on a case. The district court has the discretion to deny fees to prevailing plaintiffs under special circumstances, and to award attorney's fees against plaintiffs who litigate frivolous or vexatious claims. [Citations.] Furthermore, we have held that a civil rights defendant is not liable for attorney's fees incurred after a pretrial settlement offer, where the judgment recovered by the plaintiff is less than the offer. [Citation.] We believe that these safeguards adequately protect against the possibility that § 1988 might produce a "windfall" to civil rights attorneys.

In the absence of any indication that Congress intended to adopt a strict rule that attorney's fees under § 1988 be proportionate to damages recovered, we decline to adopt such a rule ourselves. The judgment of the Court of Appeals is hereby

Affirmed.

CHIEF JUSTICE BURGER, dissenting.

I join Justice Rehnquist's dissenting opinion. I write only to add that it would be difficult to find a better example of legal nonsense than the fixing of attorney's fees by a judge at $245,456.25 for the recovery of $33,350 damages.

The two attorneys receiving this nearly quarter-million-dollar fee graduated from law school in 1973 and 1974; they brought this action in 1975, which resulted in the $33,350 jury award in 1980. Their total professional experience when this litigation began consisted of Gerald Lopez' 1–year service as a law clerk to a judge and Roy Cazares' two years' experience as a trial attorney in the Defenders' Program of San Diego County. For their services the District Court found that an hourly rate of $125 per hour was reasonable.

Can anyone doubt that no private party would ever have dreamed of paying these two novice attorneys $125 per hour in 1975, which, considering inflation, would represent perhaps something more nearly a $250 per hour rate today? * * *

* * * The Court's result will unfortunately only add fuel to the fires of public indignation over the costs of litigation.

JUSTICE REHNQUIST, dissenting.

In Hensley v. Eckerhart, 461 U.S. 424, 433, 103 S.Ct. 1933, 76 L.Ed.2d 40 (1983), our leading case dealing with attorney's fees awarded pursuant to 42 U.S.C. § 1988, we said that "[t]he most useful starting point for determining the amount of a reasonable fee is the number of hours reasonably expended on the litigation multiplied by a reasonable hourly rate." As if we had foreseen the case now before us, we went on to emphasize that "[t]he district court ... should exclude from this initial fee calculation hours that were not 'reasonably expended' "on the litigation.　* * *

It is obvious to me that the District Court viewed *Hensley* not as a constraint on its discretion, but instead as a blueprint for justifying, in an after-the-fact fashion, a fee award it had already decided to enter solely on the basis of the "lodestar." In fact, the District Court failed at almost every turn to apply any kind of "billing judgment," or to seriously consider the "results obtained," which we described in *Hensley* as "the important factor" in determining a "reasonable" fee award. A few examples should suffice: (1) The court approved almost 209 hours of "prelitigation time," for a total of $26,118.75. (2) The court approved some 197 hours of time spent in conversations between respondents' two attorneys, for a total of $24,625. (3) The court approved 143 hours for preparation of a pre-trial order, for a total of $17,875.00. (4) Perhaps most egregiously, the court approved 45.50 hours of "standby time," or time spent by one of respondents' attorneys, who was then based in San Diego, to wait in a Los Angeles hotel room for a jury verdict to be rendered in Los Angeles, where his co-counsel was then employed by the U.C.L.A. School of Law, less than 40 minutes' driving time from the courthouse. The award for "stand-by time" totaled $5,687.50. I find it hard to understand how any attorney can be said to have exercised "billing judgment" in spending such huge amounts of time on a case ultimately worth only $33,350.

* * * I think that this analysis, which appears nowhere in the plurality's opinion, leads inexorably to the conclusion that the District Court's fee award of $245,456.25, based on a prevailing hourly rate of $125 multiplied by the number of hours which respondents' attorneys claim to have spent on the case, is not a "reasonable" attorney's fee under § 1988.

Suppose that A offers to sell Blackacre to B for $10,000. It is commonly known and accepted that Blackacre has a fair market value of $10,000. B consults an attorney and requests a determination whether A can convey good title to Blackacre. The attorney writes an elaborate memorandum concluding that A's title to Blackacre is defective, and submits a bill to B for $25,000. B refuses to pay the bill, the attorney sues, and the parties stipulate that the attorney spent 200 hours researching the title issue because of an extraordinarily complex legal and factual situation, and that the prevailing rate at which the attorney billed, which was also a "reasonable" rate, was $125. Does anyone seriously think that a court should award the attorney the full $25,000 which he claims? Surely a court would start from the proposition that, unless special arrangements were made between the client and the attorney, a "reasonable" attorney's fee for researching the title to a piece of property worth $10,000 could not exceed the value of the property. Otherwise the client would have been far better off never going to an attorney in the first place, and simply giving A $10,000 for a worthless deed. The client thereby would have saved himself $15,000.

Obviously the billing situation in a typical litigated case is more complex than in this bedrock example of a defective title claim, but some of the same principles are surely applicable. * * *

The amount of damages which a jury is likely to award in a tort case is of course more difficult to predict than the amount it is likely to award in a contract case. But even in a tort case some measure of the kind of "billing judgment" previously described must be brought to bear in computing a "reasonable" attorney's fee. * * *

---

1. As the principal case reflects, the standard method for determining fees is the "lodestar" method of multiplying a reasonable hourly rate for each attorney times the number of hours reasonably spent on the litigation. The most critical factor in measuring an award of attorneys' fees is the "degree of success obtained." Hensley v. Eckerhart, 461 U.S. 424, 436, 103 S.Ct. 1933, 1941, 76 L.Ed.2d 40 (1983). The Supreme Court has treated the lodestar figure as presumptively reasonable, subject to adjustment only in rare or exceptional circumstances. Thus, the degree of success in the litigation ordinarily will be subsumed within other factors used to calculate a reasonable fee rather than seen as an independent basis for modifying the fee award. The overarching consideration with respect to fee measurement is "reasonableness" based on all the circumstances of the case. *See* Blanchard v. Bergeron, 489 U.S. 87, 109 S.Ct. 939, 103 L.Ed.2d 67 (1989). Any adjustments to the lodestar based on the results obtained must be supported by evidence in the record; inadequate documentation will justify a downward reduction of the fee.

2. What should be the relevance of a pre-existing contractual fee arrangement to determining a fee award pursuant to a fee-shifting statute? In Blanchard v. Bergeron, 489 U.S. 87, 94–95, 109 S.Ct. 939, 944, 103 L.Ed.2d 67 (1989), the Court held that the fees awarded under the fee-shifting statute were not automatically governed by or limited to the amount provided in a contingent fee arrangement. Although the terms of a contingency fee contract were relevant, it was not dispositive in determining what constituted a "reasonable fee" under § 1988. The Court noted that if contingent fee terms served as a strict limitation on an award of attorney fees, it might place an undesirable, artificial emphasis on recovery of damages in lieu of potentially valuable injunctive or declaratory relief in civil rights litigation.

3. In a related vein, in Venegas v. Mitchell, 495 U.S. 82, 110 S.Ct. 1679, 109 L.Ed.2d 74 (1990), an attorney who had successfully represented a client in a civil rights action sought to recover his fee pursuant to a

contingency fee contract which significantly exceeded the amount award-ed under 42 U.S.C. § 1988. The Court upheld the validity of the contractual arrangement, finding that a "reasonable fee" under the fee-shifting statute will not override or replace otherwise valid contractual terms. The Court reasoned that Congress established fee-shifting stat-utes to benefit the party rather than the lawyer, yet clients remain free to contract on whatever terms they choose to obtain counsel of their choice. *Also see* Blum v. Stenson, 465 U.S.886, 894–895, 104 S.Ct. 1541, 1547, 79 L.Ed.2d 891 (1984) (Attorney fees awarded to prevailing parties even though they were represented without cost by a non-profit legal aid organization.)

4.   What types of costs of litigation may be properly assigned to the losing party pursuant to fee-shifting statutes? In West Virginia Univer-sity Hospitals, Inc. v. Casey, 499 U.S. 83, 111 S.Ct. 1138, 113 L.Ed.2d 68 (1991), the Court held that Section 1988 did not grant authority to shift expert witness fees to the losing party in civil rights case. Congress later amended section 1988 to provide for expert fees as part of the litigation costs awarded to a prevailing party. Many other statutes also expressly provide for shifting expert witness fees as a separate cost of litigation item distinct from attorney fees. *See* Toxic Substances Control Act, 15 U.S.C. §§ 2618(d), 2619(c)(2); Resource Conservation and Recov-ery Act, 42 U.S.C. § 6972(e); Administrative Procedure Act, 5 U.S.C. § 504(b)(1)(A); Equal Access to Justice Act, 28 U.S.C. § 2412(d)(2)(A).

5.   Courts generally calculate fees based upon the customary mar-ket rates for attorneys of like competence and experience in the same community doing similar work during the relevant period. Should courts distinguish between commercial for-profit law firms and non-profit public interest law firms in measuring fees? *See* Blum v. Stenson, 465 U.S. 886, 104 S.Ct. 1541, 79 L.Ed.2d 891 (1984) (§ 1988 fee calculations do not vary depending on whether the plaintiff was repre-sented by private counsel or a non-profit legal services organization.)

What should the measure of fees be if a private practicing attorney charges a plaintiff a lower rate than their other clients in a public interest case? *See* Save Our Cumberland Mountains, Inc. v. Hodel, 857 F.2d 1516 (D.C. Cir.1988) (Prevailing market rate awarded to successful environmental interest group under the Surface Mining Control and Reclamation Act even though the attorney had charged the plaintiff a reduced rate.) *See also* Missouri v. Jenkins, 491 U.S. 274, 109 S.Ct. 2463, 105 L.Ed.2d 229 (1989) (Market rates for paralegals and law clerks were the proper measure of costs under 42 U.S.C. § 1988 rather than the cost of their services to the attorney.)

CITY OF BURLINGTON v. DAGUE
___ U.S. ___, 112 S.Ct. 2638, 120 L.Ed.2d 449 (1992).

JUSTICE SCALIA delivered the opinion of the Court.

This case presents the question whether a court, in determining an award of reasonable attorney's fees under § 7002(e) of the Solid Waste

Disposal Act (SWDA), 90 Stat. 2826, as amended, 42 U.S.C. § 6972(e), or § 505(d) of the Federal Water Pollution Control Act (Clean Water Act (CWA)), 86 Stat. 889, as amended, 33 U.S.C. § 1365(d), may enhance the fee award above the "lodestar" amount in order to reflect the fact that the party's attorneys were retained on a contingent-fee basis and thus assumed the risk of receiving no payment at all for their services. Although different fee-shifting statutes are involved, the question is essentially identical to the one we addressed, but did not resolve, in Pennsylvania v. Delaware Valley Citizens' Council for Clean Air, 483 U.S. 711 (1987) (Delaware Valley II).

I

Respondent Dague owns land in Vermont adjacent to a landfill that was owned and operated by petitioner City of Burlington. Represented by attorneys retained on a contingent-fee basis, he sued Burlington over its operation of the landfill. The District Court ruled that Burlington had violated provisions of the SWDA and the CWA, and ordered Burlington to close the landfill by January 1, 1990. It also determined that Dague was a "substantially prevailing party" entitled to an award of attorney's fees under the Acts.

In calculating the attorney's fees award, the District Court first found reasonable the figures advanced by Dague for his attorneys' hourly rates and for the number of hours expended by them, producing a resulting "lodestar" attorney's fee of $198,027.50. Addressing Dague's request for a contingency enhancement, the court looked to Circuit precedent, which provided that "the rationale that should guide the court's discretion is whether 'without the possibility of a fee enhancement ... competent counsel might refuse to represent [environmental] clients thereby denying them effective access to the courts.' " [The District Court enhanced the attorney's fee by 25% and the Court of Appeals affirmed.] * * *

II

* * * Fees for legal services in litigation may be either "certain" or "contingent" (or some hybrid of the two). A fee is certain if it is payable without regard to the outcome of the suit; it is contingent if the obligation to pay depends on a particular result's being obtained. Under the most common contingent-fee contract for litigation, the attorney receives no payment for his services if his client loses. Under this arrangement, the attorney bears a contingent risk of nonpayment that is the inverse of the case's prospects of success: if his client has an 80% chance of winning, the attorney's contingent risk is 20%.

In *Delaware Valley II*, we reversed a judgment that had affirmed enhancement of a fee award to reflect the contingent risk of nonpayment. In the process, we addressed whether the typical federal fee-shifting statute permits an attorney's fees award to be enhanced on account of contingency. In the principal opinion, JUSTICE WHITE, joined on this point by three other Justices, determined that such enhancement is not permitted. 483 U.S., at 723–727. JUSTICE O'CONNOR, in an opinion concurring in part and concurring in the judgment, concluded that no enhancement for contingency is appropriate "unless the applicant can establish that without an adjustment for risk the prevailing party would have faced substantial difficulties in finding counsel in the local or other relevant market," *id.*, at 733, and that any enhancement "must be based on the difference in market treatment of contingent fee cases *as a class*, rather than on an assessment of the riskiness' of any particular case." JUSTICE BLACKMUN's dissenting opinion, joined by three other Justices, concluded that enhancement for contingency is always statutorily required. *Id.*, at 737–742, 754.

We turn again to this same issue.

III

Section 7002(e) of the SWDA and Section 505(d) of the CWA authorize a court to "award costs of litigation (including *reasonable attorney . . . fees*)" to a "prevailing or substantially prevailing party." 42 U.S.C. § 6972(e) (emphasis added); 33 U.S.C. § 1365(d) (emphasis added). This language is similar to that of many other federal fee-shifting statutes; our case law construing what is a "reasonable" fee applies uniformly to all of them.

The "lodestar" figure has, as its name suggests, become the guiding light of our fee-shifting jurisprudence. We have established a "strong presumption" that the lodestar represents the "reasonable" fee, and have placed upon the fee applicant who seeks more than that the burden of showing that "such an adjustment is *necessary* to the determination of a reasonable fee." The Court of Appeals held, and Dague argues here, that a "reasonable" fee for attorneys who have been retained on a contingency-fee basis must go beyond the lodestar, to compensate for risk of loss and of consequent nonpayment. Fee-shifting statutes should be construed, he contends, to replicate the economic incentives that operate in the private legal market, where attorneys working on a contingency-fee basis can be expected to charge some premium over their ordinary hourly rates. Petitioner Burlington argues, by contrast, that the lodestar fee may not be enhanced for contingency.

We note at the outset that an enhancement for contingency would likely duplicate in substantial part factors already subsumed in the lodestar. The risk of loss in a particular case (and, therefore, the attorney's contingent risk) is the product of two factors: (1) the legal and factual merits of the claim, and (2) the difficulty of establishing those merits. The second factor, however, is ordinarily reflected in the lodestar—either in the higher number of hours expended to overcome the difficulty, or in the higher hourly rate of the attorney skilled and experienced enough to do so. Taking account of it again through lodestar enhancement amounts to double-counting.

The first factor (relative merits of the claim) is not reflected in the lodestar, but there are good reasons why it should play no part in the calculation of the award. It is, of course, a factor that *always* exists (no claim has a 100% chance of success), so that computation of the lodestar would never end the court's inquiry in contingent-fee cases. Moreover, the consequence of awarding contingency enhancement to take account of this "merits" factor would be to provide attorneys with the same incentive to bring relatively meritless claims as relatively meritorious ones. Assume, for example, two claims, one with underlying merit of 20%, the other of 80%. Absent any contingency enhancement, a contingent-fee attorney would prefer to take the latter, since he is four times more likely to be paid. But with a contingency enhancement, this preference will disappear: the enhancement for the 20% claim would be a multiplier of 5 ($^{100}\!/\!_{20}$), which is quadruple the 1.25 multiplier ($^{100}\!/\!_{80}$) that would attach to the 80% claim. Thus, enhancement for the contingency risk posed by each case would encourage meritorious claims to be brought, but only at the social cost of indiscriminately encouraging nonmeritorious claims to be brought as well. * * *

Instead of enhancement based upon the contingency risk posed by each case, Dague urges that we adopt the approach set forth in the *Delaware Valley II* concurrence. We decline to do so, first and foremost because we do not see how it can intelligibly be applied. On the one hand, it would require the party seeking contingency enhancement to "establish that without the adjustment for risk [he] would have faced substantial difficulties in finding counsel in the local or other relevant market." 483 U.S., at 733. On the other hand, it would forbid enhancement based "on an assessment of the riskiness' of any particular case." But since the predominant reason that a contingent-fee claimant has difficulty finding counsel in any legal market where the winner's attorney's fees will be paid by the loser is that attorneys view his case as too risky (*i.e.*, too unlikely to succeed), these two propositions, as a practical matter, collide.

A second difficulty with the approach taken by the concurrence in *Delaware Valley II* is that it would base the contingency enhancement on "the difference in market treatment of contingent fee cases *as a class*." 483 U.S., at 731 (emphasis in original). To begin with, for a very large proportion of contingency-fee cases—those seeking not monetary damages but injunctive or other equitable relief—there is no "market treatment." Such cases scarcely exist, except to the extent Congress has created an artificial "market" for them by fee-shifting—and looking to *that* "market" for the meaning of fee-shifting is obviously circular. Our decrees would follow the "market" for the meaning of fee-shifting is obviously circular. Our decrees would follow the "market", which in turn is based on our decrees. But even apart from that difficulty, any approach that applies uniform treatment to the entire class of contingent-fee cases, or to any conceivable subject-matter-based subclass, cannot possibly achieve the supposed goal of mirroring market incentives. As discussed above, the contingent risk of a case (and hence the difficulty of getting contingent-fee lawyers to take it) depends principally upon its particular merits. Contingency enhancement calculated on any class-wide basis, therefore, guarantees at best (leaving aside the double-counting problem described earlier) that those cases within the class that have the class-average chance of success will be compensated according to what the "market" requires to produce the services, and that all cases having above-class-average chance of success will be overcompensated.

* * *[W]e perceive no other basis, fairly derivable from the fee-shifting statutes, by which contingency enhancement, if adopted, could be restricted to fewer than all contingent-fee cases. And we see a number of reasons for concluding that no contingency enhancement whatever is compatible with the fee-shifting statutes at issue. First, just as the statutory language limiting fees to prevailing (or substantially prevailing) parties bars a prevailing plaintiff from recovering fees relating to claims on which he lost, so should it bar a prevailing plaintiff from recovering for the risk of loss. An attorney operating on a contingency-fee basis pools the risks presented by his various cases: cases that turn out to be successful pay for the time he gambled on those that did not. To award a contingency enhancement under a fee-shifting statute would in effect pay for the attorney's time (or anticipated time) in cases where his client does *not* prevail.

Second, both before and since *Delaware Valley II*, "we have generally turned away from the contingent-fee model"—which would make the fee award a percentage of the value of the relief awarded in the primary action—"to the lodestar model." We have done so, it must be noted, even though the lodestar model often (perhaps, generally) results in a larger fee award than the contingent-fee model. For example, in *Blanchard v. Bergeron*, 489 U.S. 87 (1989), we held that the lodestar governed, even though it produced a fee that substantially exceeded the amount provided in the contingent-fee agreement between plaintiff and his counsel (which was self-evidently an amount adequate to attract the needed legal services). Contingency enhancement is a feature inherent in the contingent-fee model (since attorneys factor in the particular risks of a case in negotiating their fee and in deciding whether to accept the case). To engraft this feature onto the lodestar model would be to concoct a hybrid scheme that resorts to the contingent-fee model to increase a fee award but not to reduce it. Contingency enhancement is therefore not consistent with our general rejection of the contingent-fee model for fee awards, nor is it necessary to the determination of a reasonable fee.

And finally, the interest in ready administrability that has underlain our adoption of the lodestar approach, and the related interest in avoiding burdensome satellite litigation, counsel strongly against adoption of contingency enhancement. Contingency enhancement would make the setting of fees more complex and arbitrary, hence more unpredictable, and hence more litigable. It is neither necessary nor even possible for application of the fee-shifting statutes to mimic the intricacies of the fee-paying market in every respect.

Adopting the position set forth in JUSTICE WHITE's opinion in *Delaware Valley II*, we hold that enhancement for contingency is not permitted under the fee-shifting statutes at issue. We reverse the Court of Appeals' judgment insofar as it affirmed the 25% enhancement of the lodestar.

JUSTICE BLACKMUN, with whom JUSTICE STEVENS joins, dissenting.

In language typical of most federal fee-shifting provisions, the statutes involved in this case authorize courts to award the prevailing party a "reasonable" attorney's fee. Two principles, in my view, require the conclusion that the "enhanced" fee awarded to respondents was reasonable. First, this Court consistently has recognized that a "reasonable" fee is to be a "fully compensatory fee," and is to be "calculated on the basis of rates and practices prevailing in the relevant market." Second, it is a fact of the market that an attorney who is paid only when his client prevails will tend to charge a higher fee than one who is paid regardless of outcome, and relevant professional standards long have recognized that this practice is reasonable.

The Court does not deny these principles. It simply refuses to draw the conclusion that follows ineluctably: If a statutory fee consistent with market practices is "reasonable," and if in the private market an attorney who assumes the risk of nonpayment can expect additional compensation, then it follows that a statutory fee may include additional compensation for contingency and still qualify as reasonable. The Court's decision to the contrary violates the principles we have applied consistently in prior cases and will seriously weaken the enforcement of those statutes for which Congress has authorized fee awards—notably, many of our Nation's civil rights laws and environmental laws.

* * *

JUSTICE O'CONNOR, dissenting.

I continue to be of the view that in certain circumstances a "reasonable" attorney's fee should not be computed by the purely retrospective lodestar figure, but also must incorporate a reasonable incentive to an attorney contemplating whether or not to take a case in the first place. As JUSTICE BLACKMUN cogently explains, when an attorney must choose between two cases—one with a client who will pay the attorney's fees win or lose and the other who can only promise the statutory compensation if the case is successful—the attorney will choose the fee-paying client, unless the contingency-client can promise an enhancement of sufficient magnitude to justify the extra risk of nonpayment. * * *

In my view the promised enhancement should be "based on the difference in market treatment of contingent fee cases as a class, rather than on an assessment of the riskiness' of any particular case." * * * Admittedly, the courts called upon to determine the enhancements appropriate for various markets would be required to make economic calculations based on less-than-perfect data. Yet that is also the case, for example, in inverse condemnation and antitrust cases, and the Court has never suggested that the difficulty of the task or possible inexactitude of the result justifies forgoing those calculations altogether. * * *

In this case, the District Court determined that a 25% contingency enhancement was appropriate by reliance on the likelihood of success in the individual case. The Court of Appeals affirmed on the basis of its holding in *Friends of the Earth v. Eastman Kodak Co.*, 834 F.2d 295 (CA2 1987), which asks simply whether, without the possibility of a fee enhancement, the prevailing party would not have been able to obtain competent counsel. Although I believe that inquiry is part of the contingency enhancement determination, I also believe that it was error to base the degree of enhancement on case-specific factors. Because I can find no market-specific support for the 25% enhancement figure in the affidavits submitted by respondents in support of the fee request, I would vacate the judgment affirming the fee award and remand for a market-based assessment of a suitable enhancement for contingency.

---

1. For what circumstances other than risk of nonrecovery should compensation above the lodestar amount ever be appropriate? Keep in mind that the principal argument for increasing the lodestar to account for the contingency of risk of loss was to attract competent counsel to represent claimants in matters affecting public interest. In that vein, should courts adjust the lodestar upward to consider: (1) the preclusion from other valuable employment opportunities, (2) delay in payment after prolonged litigation, or (3) representing a difficult or unpopular client? Why? Some courts have held that factors such as the novelty of the issues, quality of representation, complexity of litigation, or the number of persons benefitted are already subsumed within the lodestar calculation. *See* Blum v. Stenson, 465 U.S. 886, 898–900, 104 S.Ct. 1541, 1549, 79 L.Ed.2d 891 (1984).

2. An interesting twist in determining attorney fee awards arises where a class action is initiated under a statute with a fee-shifting provision but is settled with the creation of a common fund. In such situations, some courts have applied equitable principles governing common fund distribution rather than looking to the fee-shifting statute. *See* Skelton v. General Motors Corp., 860 F.2d 250, 252 (7th Cir.1988).

3. The choice of method can have significant consequences. For instance, in Florin v. Nationsbank of Georgia, N.A., 34 F.3d 560 (7th Cir.1994), the court determined that common fund equitable rules should apply to payment of attorney fees in a successful class action suit under ERISA. The court held that risk multipliers were not only available but mandated in a common fund case if the awarding court finds that lawyers for the class had no certain source of compensation for their services. The court distinguished *Dague* as only applicable to preclude the use of risk multipliers in fee-shifting cases. Further, the court found no injustice in a multiplier because of the fundamentally different approaches in the common fund method of sharing fees from

the pool of damages in contrast with the direct assessment against the losing party in fee-shifting cases. The court stated that the appropriate multiplier should be based upon balancing the competing goals of fairly compensating the attorneys with the interests of the class, assessing the riskiness of litigation by measuring the probability of success of the type of case at the commencement of litigation.

4. Courts also have applied different methods to determine an appropriate amount of attorney fees in common fund cases. A number of jurisdictions continue to follow the lodestar method (*See* Harman v. Lyphomed, Inc., 945 F.2d 969 (7th Cir.1991), while a growing number of courts have adopted a "percentage of recovery" model). *See* Camden I Condominium Assoc., Inc. v. Dunkle, 946 F.2d 768 (11th Cir.1991). In Swedish Hospital Corp. v. Shalala, 1 F.3d 1261 (D.C. Cir.1993), the court gave the following explanation for implementing the percentage of recovery method for measuring fees:

[First] there is often no resulting fund in fee-shifting cases, so the alternative of using a percentage-of-the-fund method is not necessarily available.

Second, and perhaps more importantly, using the lodestar approach in common fund cases encourages significant elements of inefficiency. First, attorneys are given incentive to spend as many hours as possible, billable to a firm's most expensive attorneys. Second, there is a strong incentive against early settlement since attorneys will earn more the longer a litigation lasts. * * *

In the common fund case, by contrast, victory is still the key factor, but the monetary amount of the victory is often the true measure of success, and therefore it is most efficient that it influence the fee award. That is, in the common fund case, if a percentage-of-the-fund calculation controls, inefficiently expended hours only serve to reduce the per hour compensation of the attorney expending them. On the other hand, if we apply the lodestar method to the common fund case, then the attorney inefficiently expending an excess amount of time does stand to gain by that inefficiency if the awarding court does not ultimately recognize the inefficiency in the far-from-exact testing of the fee award hearing. * * *

Furthermore, a percentage-of-the-fund approach more accurately reflects the economics of litigation practice. The district court in Howes v. Atkins, 668 F.Supp. 1021 (E.D.Ky.1987), noted that "plaintiffs' litigation practice, given the uncertainties and hazards of litigation, must necessarily be result-oriented. It matters little to the class how much the attorney spends in time or money to reach a successful result." * * *

Additionally, a percentage-of-the-fund approach is less demanding of scarce judicial resources than the lodestar method. The lodestar method makes considerable demands upon judicial resources since it can be exceptionally difficult for a court to review attorney billing information over the life of a complex litigation and make a determination about whether the time devoted to the litigation was necessary or reasonable. * * * It is much easier to calculate a percentage-of-the-fund fee than to review hourly billing practices over a long, complex litigation.

A related weakness in the lodestar approach is that it often results in a substantial delay in distribution of the common fund to the class. The lodestar procedure requires detailed involvement by the District Court, evaluating the reasonableness of expenditure of attorney time and effort, and making comparative inquiries on reasonable rates for those services. Given the complexity of many class action lawsuits, combined with the degree of detailed review required and considering the heavy workload of most district court judges, lodestar calculation is likely to cause significant delay between the creation of a common fund and remuneration of class counsel. In contrast, the application of a percentage-of-the-fund methodology is relatively straightforward and much less time consuming.

For similar reasons, a percentage-of-the-fund approach is less subjective than the lodestar approach; under the former, the court need not second-guess the judgment of counsel as to whether a task was reasonably undertaken or hours devoted to it reasonably expended.

1 F.3d at 1268–70.

Chapter 20

DECLARATORY RELIEF
A. NOMINAL DAMAGES

Section Coverage:

The relationship between substantive rights and remedies has been a theme throughout the preceding nineteen chapters. In the context of nominal damages, the identity of right and remedy takes particular meaning. The materials in this section concern cases in which there is a clearly established substantive right, but no available remedy except a declaration of that right.

In some of the areas previously studied, the absence of a compensable loss eliminated the substantive right such that the case could be dismissed. For example, if a plaintiff's only prayer is for distress damages or economic losses under circumstances in which the substantive law will not compensate those losses, then the lack of cognizable injury eliminates the claim. The reason is that in negligence cases a particular type of injury is an element of the claim.

In areas of the law where the injury is not an element of the action, proof of the substantive elements of the claim is sufficient to survive dismissal. If the plaintiff cannot establish compensable injury, the court awards nominal damages to vindicate the principle of the claim.

Model Case:

An author and university professor entered into a written contract which gave a publisher the exclusive rights to publish a novel. The publisher promised in exchange to pay the author a nonreturnable sum of $2,000 and royalties based upon a designated percentage of future sales of the book. The contract also provided that the publisher had the right to terminate the contract by giving the author 60 days written notice.

The author performed by delivering the completed manuscript, and the publisher tendered the $2,000 in return. However, the publisher subsequently breached the contract by refusing to publish the novel without giving the required written notice of termination. The author sued for damages resulting from delayed academic promotion and loss of prospective royalties. The court would deny compensatory damages and award nominals instead if the evidence failed to establish lost anticipated royalties with reasonable certainty or that the breach actually caused any delay in the author's promotion.

SPENCE v. HILLIARD

181 Ga.App. 767, 353 S.E.2d 634 (1987).

McMurray, Presiding Judge.

This is a legal malpractice action in which plaintiff was represented by defendants in a previous lawsuit. Plaintiff, a landlord, was sued by his tenant. He engaged defendants to defend the tenant's suit and to pursue a counterclaim against the tenant. The counterclaim was compulsory in nature.

Defendants answered the tenant's lawsuit and they successfully defended it. Defendants did not, however, assert a counterclaim against the tenant. (Instead, defendants filed a claim against the tenant in a separate action. Of course, that claim failed because it should have been raised via counterclaim. OCGA § 9–11–13(a).)

In this malpractice action, plaintiff contends that as a result of defendants' negligence he was damaged to the tune of $59,273.68. The trial court took issue with plaintiff's contention. In the court's view, plaintiff failed to prove that he suffered damages. It took the position that plaintiff failed to demonstrate the amount of damages he was entitled to recover against the tenant and that, moreover, plaintiff failed to demonstrate that a judgment against the tenant was collectible. Accordingly, the trial court directed a verdict in favor of defendants and plaintiff appeals. *Held:*

Assuming, arguendo, there was a fatal failure of proof with regard to actual damages, we must nevertheless reverse the judgment of the trial court. Nominal damages are recoverable in a legal malpractice action provided plaintiff carries the burden of proving that he was wronged. [Citations.] Thus, plaintiff was entitled to submit the issue of nominal damages to the jury whether or not actual damages were proven. [Citations.] It follows that it was error for the trial court to direct a verdict against plaintiff. [Citations.]

Judgment reversed.

––––––

1. Nominal damages reflect legal recognition that a litigant's rights have been violated even though no compensable harm has resulted. For example, a plaintiff may establish a claim for an intentional tort or breach of contract but not be entitled to compensatory damages because the harm is not to a legally protected interest, or it is insignificant, or the losses cannot be proven with reasonable certainty.

These awards are damages "in name only" and consequently they are a trivial sum. Common awards are one dollar or six cents.

2. Nominal damages function as the common law counterpart to declaratory judgment statutes because they declare rights, status, or

legal relations. Historically they were given only in cases involving trespass to land where the trespasser did no harm. The plaintiff sued to establish entitlement to exclusive possession to prevent an easement by prescription or adverse possession.

3. Some jurisdictions will not allow an award of punitive damages without proof of actual damages. An award of nominal damages therefore precludes such recovery.

In the case of Alcorn County v. U.S. Interstate Supplies, Inc., 731 F.2d 1160 (5th Cir.1984), the rule requiring actual damages to support punitive damages was extended to equity. The court held in that case that when a case is in equity for relief such as cancellation or rescission of a contract, there are produced no compensatory damages. Therefore there can be no exemplary damages.

Is it correct that relief such as cancellation or rescission of a contract are also forms of declaratory remedies? Would any similarity justify treating them like nominal damages for purposes such as the rule against punitive damages without actual damages?

CAREY v. PIPHUS

435 U.S. 247, 98 S.Ct. 1042, 55 L.Ed.2d 252 (1978).

MR. JUSTICE POWELL delivered the opinion of the Court.

In this case, brought under 42 U.S.C. § 1983, we consider the elements and prerequisites for recovery of damages by students who were suspended from public elementary and secondary schools without procedural due process. The Court of Appeals for the Seventh Circuit held that the students are entitled to recover substantial nonpunitive damages even if their suspensions were justified, and even if they do not prove that any other actual injury was caused by the denial of procedural due process. We disagree, and hold that in the absence of proof of actual injury, the students are entitled to recover only nominal damages.

Respondent Jarius Piphus was a freshman at Chicago Vocational High school during the 1973–1974 school year. On January 23, 1974, during school hours, the school principal saw Piphus and another student standing outdoors on school property passing back and forth what the principal described as an irregularly shaped cigarette. The principal approached the students unnoticed and smelled what he believed was the strong odor of burning marihuana. He also saw Piphus try to pass a packet of cigarette papers to the other student. When the students became aware of the principal's presence, they threw the cigarette into a nearby hedge.

The principal took the students to the school's disciplinary office and directed the assistant principal to impose the "usual" 20–day suspension for violation of the school rule against the use of drugs. The students protested that they had not been smoking marihuana, but to no avail. Piphus was allowed to remain at school, although not in class, for the remainder of the school day while the assistant principal tried, without success, to reach his mother.

A suspension notice was sent to Piphus' mother, and a few days later two meetings were arranged among Piphus, his mother, his sister, school officials, and representatives from a legal aid clinic. The purpose of the meetings was not to determine whether Piphus had been smoking marihuana, but rather to explain the reasons for the suspension. Following an unfruitful exchange of views, Piphus and his mother, as guardian *ad litem,* filed suit against petitioners in Federal District Court under 42 U.S.C. § 1983 and its jurisdictional counterpart, 28 U.S.C. § 1343, charging that Piphus had been suspended without due process of law in violation of the Fourteenth Amendment. The complaint sought declaratory and injunctive relief, together with actual and punitive damages in the amount of $3,000. Piphus was readmitted to school under a temporary restraining order after eight days of his suspension.

* * *

Title 42 U.S.C. § 1983, Rev.Stat. § 1979, derived from § 1 of the Civil Rights Act of 1871, 17 Stat. 13, provides:

> "Every person who, under color of any statute, ordinance, regulation, custom, or usage, of any State or Territory, subjects, or causes to be subjected, any citizen of the United States or other person within the jurisdiction thereof to the deprivation of any rights, privileges, or immunities secured by the Constitution and laws, shall be liable to the party injured in an action at law, suit in equity, or other proper proceeding for redress."

The legislative history of § 1983 * * * demonstrates that it was intended to "[create] a species of tort liability" in favor of persons who are deprived of "rights, privileges, or immunities secured" to them by the Constitution. Imbler v. Pachtman, 424 U.S. 409, 417 (1976).

Petitioners contend that the elements and prerequisites for recovery of damages under this "species of tort liability" should parallel those for recovery of damages under the common law of torts. In particular, they urge that the purpose of an award of damages under § 1983 should be to compensate persons for injuries that are caused by the deprivation of constitutional rights; and, further, that plaintiffs should be required to prove not only that their rights were violated, but also that injury was caused by the violation, in order to recover substantial damages. Unless respondents prove that they actually were injured by the deprivation of procedural due process, petitioners argue, they are entitled at most to nominal damages.

Respondents seem to make two different arguments in support of the holding below. First, they contend that substantial damages should be awarded under § 1983 for the deprivation of a constitutional right *whether or not* any injury was caused by the deprivation. This, they say, is appropriate both because constitutional rights are valuable in and of themselves, and because of the need to deter violations of constitutional rights. Respondents believe that this view reflects accurately that of the Congress that enacted § 1983. Second, respondents argue that even if the purpose of a § 1983 damages award is, as petitioners contend, primarily to compensate persons for injuries that are caused by the deprivation of constitutional rights, every deprivation of procedural due process may be *presumed* to cause some injury. This presumption, they say, should relieve them from the necessity of proving that injury actually was caused.

Insofar as petitioners contend that the basic purpose of a § 1983 damages award should be to compensate persons for injuries caused by the deprivation of constitutional rights, they have the better of the argument. Rights, constitutional and otherwise, do not exist in a vacuum. Their purpose is to protect persons from injuries to particular interests, and their contours are shaped by the interests they protect.

* * *

It is less difficult to conclude that damages awards under § 1983 should be governed by the principle of compensation than it is to apply this principle to concrete cases. But over the centuries the common law of torts has developed a set of rules to implement the principle that a person should be compensated fairly for injuries caused by the violation of his legal rights. These rules, defining the elements of damages and the prerequisites for their recovery, provide the appropriate starting point for the inquiry under § 1983 as well.

It is not clear, however, that common-law tort rules of damages will provide a complete solution to the damages issue in every § 1983 case. In some cases, the interests protected by a particular branch of the common law of torts may parallel closely the interests protected by a particular constitutional right. In such cases, it may be appropriate to apply the tort rules of damages directly to the § 1983 action. [Citation.] In other cases, the interests protected by a particular constitutional right may not also be protected by an analogous branch of the common law torts. [Citations.] In those cases, the task will be the more difficult one of adapting common-law rules of damages to provide fair compensation for injuries caused by the deprivation of a constitutional right.

* * *

In this case, the Court of Appeals held that if petitioners can prove on remand that "[respondents] would have been suspended even if a proper hearing had been held," 545 F.2d, at 32, then respondents will not be entitled to recover damages to compensate them for injuries caused by the suspensions. The court thought that in such a case, the failure to accord procedural due process could not properly be viewed as the cause of the suspensions. [Citations.] The court suggested that in such circumstances, an award of damages for injuries caused by the suspensions would constitute a windfall, rather than compensation, to respondents. [Citations.] We do not understand the parties to disagree with this conclusion. Nor do we.

The parties do disagree as to the further holding of the Court of Appeals that respondents are entitled to recover substantial—although unspecified—damages to compensate them for "the injury which is 'inherent in the nature of the wrong,'" 545 F.2d, at 31, even if their suspensions were justified and even if they fail to prove that the denial of procedural due process actually caused them some real, if intangible, injury. Respondents, elaborating on this theme, submit that the holding is correct because injury fairly may be "presumed" to flow from every denial of procedural due process. Their argument is that in addition to protecting against unjustified deprivations, the Due Process Clause also guarantees the "feeling of just treatment" by the government. * * *

Petitioners do not deny that a purpose of procedural due process is to convey to the individual a feeling that the government has dealt with him fairly, as well as to minimize the risk of mistaken deprivations of protected interests. They go so far as to concede that, in a proper case, persons in respondents' position might well recover damages for mental and emotional distress caused by the denial of procedural due process. Petitioners' argument is the more limited one that such injury cannot be presumed to occur, and that plaintiffs at least should be put to their proof on the issue, as plaintiffs are in most tort actions.

We agree with petitioners in this respect. * * *

Even if respondents' suspensions were justified, and even if they did not suffer any other actual injury, the fact remains that they were deprived of their right to procedural due process. * * *

Common-law courts traditionally have vindicated deprivations of certain "absolute" rights that are not shown to have caused actual injury through the award of a nominal sum of money. By making the deprivation of such rights actionable for nominal damages without proof of actual injury, the law recognizes the importance to organized society that those rights be scrupulously observed; but at the same time, it remains true to the principle that substantial damages should be awarded only to compensate actual injury or, in the case of exemplary or punitive damages, to deter or punish malicious deprivations of rights.

Because the right to procedural due process is "absolute" in the sense that it does not depend upon the merits of a claimant's substantive assertions, and because of the importance to organized society that procedural due process be observed, [citations] we believe that the denial of procedural due process should be actionable for nominal damages without proof of actual injury. We therefore hold that if, upon remand, the District Court determines that respondents' suspensions were justified, respondents nevertheless will be entitled to recover nominal damages not to exceed one dollar from petitioners.

The judgment of the Court of Appeals is reversed, and the case is remanded for further proceedings consistent with this opinion.

It is so ordered.

––––––

1.   The Supreme Court addressed the availability of attorney fees when the civil rights plaintiff recovers only nominal damages in its 1992 opinion *Farrar v. Hobby*, reproduced *supra* in Chapter 19.   What practical effect is likely to result from the increased uncertainty of recovering attorney fees when the recovery is only nominal?   Do attorneys ever take cases that they expect will not produce actual damages?

2.   In Powell v. Ward, 487 F.Supp. 917 (S.D.N.Y.1980), inmates sought to enjoin prison officials from enforcing disciplinary procedures unless they complied with the guidelines from the Supreme Court.   The court granted an order requiring the institution of procedural safeguards in all disciplinary proceedings that may result in confinement of an inmate in segregation.

The plaintiffs returned to court later and moved for a finding of contempt for failure to comply with the order.   The judge held that the defendant was not reasonably diligent in attempting to comply with the order.

The plaintiffs also sought damages to compensate for injury suffered as a result of violations of the order.   The court observed:

> To recover damages in a civil contempt action, plaintiffs must show that they suffered actual injury.   Damages are not "presumed to flow from every deprivation of procedural due process."   * * *

> Here, a significant portion of the harm to plaintiffs will be remedied by our order requiring the expungement of records of disciplinary proceedings that violated our order.   With respect to the mental and emotional harm allegedly suffered by plaintiffs, there has not been a sufficient showing of injury actually suffered by individuals whose due process rights were violated.   Although plaintiffs argue in their memorandum that such harm occurred, little if any testimony concerning actual injury was presented.   * * *

> Even though plaintiffs have not shown actual injury sufficient to support a substantial damage award, they are entitled to a nominal award to vindicate the deprivation of their rights, because of the "importance to organized society that procedural due process be observed."   Carey v. Piphus, 435 U.S. at 266, 98 S.Ct. at 1054. Respondents are thus entitled to nominal damages not to exceed one dollar from defendant.

> Plaintiffs have requested attorneys fees for services performed in litigating this motion.   Under the Civil Rights Attorney's Fees Awards Act of 1976, 42 U.S.C. § 1988, in an action to enforce a provision of 42 U.S.C. § 1983 "the court, in its discretion, may allow the prevailing party, other than the United States, a reasonable

attorney's fee." We find that plaintiffs' counsel is entitled to recover fees in this case. * * *

3. In Memphis Community School Dist. v. Stachura, 477 U.S. 299, 106 S.Ct. 2537, 91 L.Ed.2d 249 (1986), the Court clarified the damages issues introduced in *Carey v. Piphus*. The issue in this case was whether 42 U.S.C. § 1983 authorizes an award of compensatory damages based upon the value or importance of a substantive constitutional right.

The plaintiff, Edward Stachura, was a tenured public school teacher in Memphis, Michigan. He taught seventh-grade life sciences with an approved textbook that included a chapter on human reproduction. During this part of the course he showed the class pictures of his wife during her pregnancy. He also showed the students two approved films concerning human growth and sexuality. A number of parents complained at an open school board meeting and he was suspended with pay. After he filed a lawsuit, he was reinstated the next fall.

The complaint alleged that Stachura's suspension deprived him of both liberty and property without due process of law and violated his First Amendment right to academic freedom. He sought compensatory and punitive damages under 42 U.S.C. § 1983 for these constitutional violations.

The jury found for the plaintiff and awarded compensatory and punitive damages. The Supreme Court granted certiorari limited to the question whether the trial court correctly instructed on damages for the deprivation of "any constitutional right." The Court held:

> We have repeatedly noted that 42 U.S.C. § 1983 creates " 'a species of tort liability' in favor of persons who are deprived of 'rights, privileges, or immunities secured' to them by the Constitution." [Citations.] Accordingly, when § 1983 plaintiffs seek damages for violations of constitutional rights, the level of damages is ordinarily determined according to principles derived from the common law of torts. [Citations.]
>
> Punitive damages aside, damages in tort cases are designed to provide "*compensation* for the injury caused to plaintiff by defendant's breach of duty." 2 F. Harper & F. James, Law of Torts § 25.1, p. 1299 (1956) (emphasis in original), quoted in *Carey v. Piphus, supra* * * *
>
> The instructions at issue here cannot be squared with *Carey,* or with the principles of tort damages on which *Carey* and § 1983 are grounded. The jurors in this case were told that, in determining how much was necessary to "compensate [respondent] for the deprivation" of his constitutional rights, they should place a money value on the "rights" themselves by considering such factors as the particular right's "importance . . . in our system of government," its role in American history, and its "significance . . . in the context of the activities" in which respondent was engaged. These factors focus, not on compensation for provable injury, but on the jury's

subjective perception of the importance of constitutional rights as an abstract matter. *Carey* establishes that such an approach is impermissible. The constitutional right transgressed in *Carey*—the right to due process of law—is central to our system of ordered liberty. [Citation.] We nevertheless held that *no* compensatory damages could be awarded for violation of that right absent proof of actual injury. *Carey* thus makes clear that the abstract value of a constitutional right may not form the basis for § 1983 damages.

Respondent nevertheless argues that *Carey* does not control here, because in this case a *substantive* constitutional right—respondent's First Amendment right to academic freedom—was infringed. The argument misperceives our analysis in *Carey*. That case does not establish a two-tiered system of constitutional rights, with substantive rights afforded greater protection than "mere" procedural safeguards. We did acknowledge in *Carey* that "the elements and prerequisites for recovery of damages" might vary depending on the interests protected by the constitutional right at issue. But we emphasized that, whatever the constitutional basis for § 1983 liability, such damages must always be designed "to *compensate injuries* caused by the [constitutional] deprivation." [Citations.] That conclusion simply leaves no room for noncompensatory damages measured by the jury's perception of the abstract "importance" of a constitutional right.

Nor do we find such damages necessary to vindicate the constitutional rights that § 1983 protects. Section 1983 presupposes that damages that compensate for actual harm ordinarily suffice to deter constitutional violations. *Carey, supra,* 435 U.S., at 256–257, 98 S.Ct., at 1043 ("To the extent that Congress intended that awards under § 1983 should deter the deprivation of constitutional rights, there is no evidence that it meant to establish a deterrent more formidable than that inherent in the award of compensatory damages"). Moreover, damages based on the "value" of constitutional rights are an unwieldy tool for ensuring compliance with the Constitution. History and tradition do not afford any sound guidance concerning the precise value that juries should place on constitutional protections. Accordingly, were such damages available, juries would be free to award arbitrary amounts without any evidentiary basis, or to use their unbounded discretion to punish unpopular defendants. [Citation.] Such damages would be too uncertain to be of any great value to plaintiffs, and would inject caprice into determinations of damages in § 1983 cases. We therefore hold that damages based on the abstract "value" or "importance" of constitutional rights are not a permissible element of compensatory damages in such cases.

B. DECLARATORY JUDGMENTS

Section Coverage:

The declaratory judgment is a federal and state statutory remedy that declares the rights or legal relations of parties. The statutory authorization for declaratory relief does not create any new rights nor expand the subject matter jurisdiction of courts; rather it enlarges the range of remedies available to litigants. Declaratory judgments are reviewable as final judgments and they have *res judicata* effect. The declaratory judgment is a discretionary remedy which is liberally construed by courts. The declaratory remedy is neither legal nor equitable but sui generis. It does not require that any other remedy be inadequate.

The Federal Declaratory Judgment Act, codified at 28 U.S.C. §§ 2201, 2202, embraces both constitutional and prudential considerations. A federal court's power to grant a declaratory judgment is limited by the requirement that the dispute present an actual "case or controversy" within the confines of Article III of the Constitution. The statute does not replace the traditional requirement of a justiciable controversy. The parties must have genuinely conflicting claims capable of judicial resolution rather than hypothetical concerns. Courts may not give advisory opinions. The difference between an abstract question and a "controversy" contemplated by the Declaratory Judgment Act is a matter of degree, determined by focusing on whether a substantial and immediate controversy exists between parties having adverse legal interests. Maryland Casualty Co. v. Pacific Coal & Oil Co., 312 U.S. 270, 273, 61 S.Ct. 510, 512, 85 L.Ed. 826 (1941). The court in exercising its discretion regarding whether to render declaratory relief also considers various prudential factors, including whether the declaration will serve a useful purpose and will effectively settle the controversy.

There are several advantages to a declaratory judgment over injunctions, damages, or restitution. The principal benefit of seeking declaratory relief is to determine the legal relationships of the parties at an early stage of a dispute before serious harm is done. A declaratory judgment is considered a "milder" remedy than an injunction because it does not command that specific actions be taken and does not bind parties in personam. Although a declaratory judgment is not coercive in the same sense as an injunction, the effect of a determination of rights or legal relations often will strongly influence parties to take steps to avert incurring liability or prosecution. In that regard, a declaratory judgment is a valuable tool for clarifying legal rights and is advantageous in saving the time and expense of protracted litigation. Declaratory judgments can be used in tandem with other remedies, including injunctive relief, to provide complete relief to a party when it would serve a useful purpose and terminate uncertainty.

Consider the following excerpt from Aetna Life Insurance Co. v. Haworth, 300 U.S. 227, 240–241, 57 S.Ct. 461, 464, 81 L.Ed. 617 (1937), where Mr. Chief Justice Hughes outlined the basic function and purpose of declaratory judgments:

> The Declaratory Judgment Act must be deemed to fall within this ambit of congressional power, so far as it authorizes relief which is consonant with the exercise of the judicial function in the determination of controversies to which under the Constitution the judicial power extends.

> A "controversy" * * * must be one that is appropriate for judicial determination. A justiciable controversy is thus distinguished from a difference or dispute of a hypothetical or abstract character; from one that is academic or moot. The controversy must be definite and concrete, touching the legal relations of parties having adverse legal interests. It must be a real and substantial controversy admitting of specific relief through a decree of a conclusive character, as distinguished from an opinion advising what the law would be upon a hypothetical state of facts. Where there is such a concrete case admitting of an immediate and definitive determination of the legal rights of the parties in an adversary proceeding upon the facts alleged, the judicial function may be appropriately exercised although the adjudication of the rights of the litigants may not require the award of process or the payment of damages. And as it is not essential to the exercise of the judicial power that an injunction be sought, allegations that irreparable injury is threatened are not required.

Model Case:

Howell works as regional vice-president for the XYZ Chemical Company which specializes in direct sales of heavy duty cleaning supplies to large industrial plants. XYZ employed Howell pursuant to a written contract which contained a provision prohibiting "competition with the business of the company in any respect for a period of five years following dismissal or termination of employment."

Howell has an aggressive marketing attitude for the company's products. At a business development meeting with key company officers Howell suggested catalogue sales to out-of-state potential customers. The president rebutted the suggestion by responding, "We've always sold XYZ products just one way—direct customer contact. Catalogues are too impersonal."

Howell is dissatisfied with the company's stodgy marketing techniques and is thinking about leaving the job to pursue the idea of catalogue sales. Howell is concerned that the contract would preclude starting such a business.

A court would probably decline to give a declaratory judgment in such a case. Howell's contemplated business venture is not yet a demonstrable intention to compete. A justiciable controversy would arise if Howell resigns from XYZ and announces plans to start the catalogue business. Howell would benefit by obtaining a declaration of rights and obligations under the contract at that preliminary juncture before incurring substantial expenses in developing the new business. If the court determined that Howell's catalogue company in fact would be competing with XYZ within the language of the contract, then Howell could avoid future litigation with XYZ.

———

The Federal Declaratory Judgment statutes provide:

28 U.S.C. § 2201 (*as amended,* 1993). (a) In a case of actual controversy within its jurisdiction, except with respect to Federal taxes * * *, a proceeding under section 505 or 1146 of title 11, or in any civil action involving an antidumping or countervailing duty proceeding regarding a class or kind of merchandise of a free trade area country (as defined in section 516A(f)(10) of the Tariff Act of 1930), as determined by the administering authority, any court of the United States, upon the filing of an appropriate pleading, may declare the rights and other legal relations of any interested party seeking such declaration, whether or not further relief is or could be sought. Any such declaration shall have the force and effect of a final judgment or decree and shall be reviewable as such.

28 U.S.C. § 2202. Further necessary or proper relief based on a declaratory judgment or decree may be granted, after reasonable notice and hearing, against any adverse party whose rights have been determined by such judgment.

F.R.C.P. Rule 57. The procedure for obtaining a declaratory judgment pursuant to Title 28, U.S.C. § 2201, shall be in accordance with these rules, and the right to trial by jury may be demanded under the circumstances and in the manner provided in Rules 38 and 39. The existence of another adequate remedy does not preclude a judgment for declaratory relief in cases where it is appropriate. The court may order a speedy hearing of an action for a declaratory judgment and may advance it on the calendar.

The Uniform Declaratory Judgment Act has been adopted, with some variations, in a large majority of states. The following are selected provisions of the Uniform Act:

§ 1. **Scope**. Courts of record within their respective jurisdictions shall have power to declare rights, status, and other legal relations whether or not further relief is or could be claimed. No action or proceeding shall be open to objection on the ground that a declaratory judgment or decree is prayed for. The declaration may be either affirmative or negative in form and effect; and [it] shall have the force and effect of a final judgment or decree.

§ 2. **Power to Construe**. Any person interested under a deed, will, written contract or other writings constituting a contract, or whose rights, status or other legal relations are affected by a statute, municipal ordinance, contract or franchise, may have determined any question of construction or validity arising under the instrument, statute, ordinance, contract, or franchise and obtain a declaration of rights, status or other legal relations thereunder.

§ 3. **Before Breach**. A contract may be construed either before or after there has been a breach thereof.

§ 4. **Executor**. Any person interested as or through an executor, administrator, trustee, guardian or other fiduciary, creditor, devisee, legatee, heir, next of kin, or cestui que trust, in the administration of a trust, or the estate of a decedent, an infant, lunatic, or insolvent, may have a declaration of rights or legal relations in respect thereto: (a) To ascertain any class of creditors, devisees, legatees, heirs, next of kin or others; or (b) To direct the executors, administrators, or trustees to do or abstain from doing any particular act in their fiduciary capacity; or (c) To determine any question arising in the administration of the estate or trust, including questions of construction of wills and other writings.

§ 5. **Enumeration not exclusive**. The enumeration in sections 2, 3, and 4 does not limit or restrict the exercise of the general powers conferred in section 1, in any proceeding where declaratory relief is sought, in which a judgment or decree will terminate the controversy or remove an uncertainty.

§ 6. **Discretionary**. The court may refuse to render or enter a declaratory judgment or decree where such judgment or decree, if rendered or entered, would not terminate the uncertainty or controversy giving rise to the proceeding.

§ 7. **Review**. All orders, judgments and decrees under this Act may be reviewed as other orders, judgments and decrees.

§ 8. **Supplemental Relief**. Further relief based on a declaratory judgment or decree may be granted whenever necessary or proper. The application therefor shall be by petition to a court having jurisdiction to grant the relief. If the application be deemed sufficient, the court shall, on reasonable notice, require any adverse party whose rights have been adjudicated by the declaratory judgment or decree, to show cause why further relief should not be granted forthwith.

§ 9. **Jury Trial**. When a proceeding under this Act involves the determination of an issue of fact, such issue may be tried and determined in the same manner as issues of fact are tried and determined in other civil actions in the court in which the proceeding is pending.

§ 10. **Costs**. In any proceeding under this Act the court may make such award of costs as may seem equitable and just.

§ 11. **Parties**. When declaratory relief is sought, all persons shall be made parties who have or claim any interest which would be affected by the declaration, and no declaration shall prejudice the rights of persons not parties to the proceeding. In any proceeding which involves the validity of a municipal ordinance or franchise, such municipality shall be made a party, and shall be entitled to be heard, and if the statute, ordinance or franchise is alleged to be unconstitutional, the Attorney–General of the State shall also be served with a copy of the proceeding and be entitled to be heard.

§ 12. **Construction**. This Act is declared to be remedial; its purpose is to settle and to afford relief from uncertainty and insecurity with respect to rights, status and other legal relations; and is to be liberally construed and administered.

PUBLIC SERVICE COMMISSION OF UTAH v. WYCOFF COMPANY

344 U.S. 237, 73 S.Ct. 236, 97 L.Ed. 291 (1952).

MR. JUSTICE JACKSON delivered the opinion of the Court.

[The Public Service Commission of Utah filed suit in state court seeking to prevent the respondent company from transporting motion picture film and newsreels within the State of Utah without first obtaining authorization from the Commission. Respondent then instituted a proceeding in federal court requesting (1) a declaratory judgment that its activities constituted interstate commerce and therefore it would be free to operate without further permission from the Utah Commission and (2) an injunction preventing the Commission from interfering with its transportation over routes authorized by the Interstate Commerce Commission. The District Court sustained the contention of the Commission that the corporation's activities constituted intrastate commerce, and dismissed the complaint. The Court of Appeals reversed and the Supreme Court granted certiorari.]

* * * [I]t is clear that this proceeding cannot result in an injunction on constitutional grounds. In addition to defects that will appear in our discussion of declaratory relief, it is wanting in equity because there is no proof of any threatened or probable act of the defendants which might cause the irreparable injury essential to equitable relief by injunction.

The respondent appears to have abandoned the suit as one for injunction but seeks to support it as one for declaratory judgment, hoping thereby to avoid both the three-judge court requirement and the necessity for proof of threatened injury. Whether declaratory relief is appropriate under the circumstances of this case apparently was not considered by either of the courts below. But that inquiry is one which every grant of this remedy must survive.

The Declaratory Judgment Act of 1934, now 28 U.S.C. § 2201, styled "creation of remedy," provides that in a case of actual controversy a competent court may "declare the rights and other legal relations" of a party "whether or not further relief is or could be sought." This is an enabling Act, which confers a discretion on the courts rather than an absolute right upon the litigant.

Previous to its enactment there were responsible expressions of doubt that constitutional limitations on federal judicial power would permit any federal declaratory judgment procedure. Finally, as the practice extended in the states, we reviewed a declaratory judgment rendered by a state court and held that a controversy which would be justiciable in this Court if presented in a suit for injunction is not the less so because the relief was declaratory. Encouraged by this and guided by the experience of the thirty-four states that had enacted such laws, the Senate Judiciary Committee recommended an adaptation of the principle to federal practice. Its enabling clause was narrower than that of the Uniform Act adopted in 1921 by the Commissioners on Uniform State Laws, which gave comprehensive power to declare rights, status and other legal relations. The Federal Act omits status and limits the declaration to cases of actual controversy.

This Act was adjudged constitutional only by interpreting it to confine the declaratory remedy within conventional "case or controversy" limits. * * *

* * *[T]he propriety of declaratory relief in a particular case will depend upon a circumspect sense of its fitness informed by the teachings and experience concerning the functions and extent of federal judicial power. While the courts should not be reluctant in granting this relief in the cases for which it was designed, they must be alert to avoid imposition upon their jurisdiction through obtaining futile or premature interventions, especially in the field of public law. A maximum of caution is necessary in the type of litigation that we have here, where a ruling is sought that would reach far beyond the particular case. Such differences of opinion or conflicts of interest must be "ripe for determination" as controversies over legal rights. The disagreement must not be nebulous or contingent but must have taken on fixed and final shape so that a court can see what legal issues it is deciding, what effect its decision will have on the adversaries, and some useful purpose to be achieved in deciding them.

The complainant in this case does not request an adjudication that it has a right to do, or to have, anything in particular. It does not ask a judgment that the Commission is without power to enter any specific order or take any concrete regulatory step. It seeks simply to establish that, as presently conducted, respondent's carriage of goods between points within as well as without Utah is all interstate commerce. One naturally asks, "So what?" To that ultimate question no answer is sought.

A multitude of rights and immunities may be predicated upon the premise that a business consists of interstate commerce. What are the specific ones in controversy? The record is silent and counsel little more articulate. * * *

* * * We may conjecture that respondent fears some form of administrative or judicial action to prohibit its service on routes wholly within the State without the Commission's leave. What respondent asks is that

it win any such case before it is commenced. Even if respondent is engaged solely in interstate commerce, we cannot say that there is nothing whatever that the State may require.

A declaratory judgment may be the basis of further relief necessary or proper against the adverse party (28 U.S.C. § 2202). The carrier's idea seems to be that it can now establish the major premise of an exemption, not as an incident of any present declaration of any specific right or immunity, but to hold in readiness for use should the Commission at any future time attempt to apply any part of a complicated regulatory statute to it. If there is any more definite or contemporaneous purpose to this case, neither this record nor the briefs make it clear to us. We think this for several reasons exceeds any permissible discretionary use of the Federal Declaratory Judgment Act.

In the first place, this dispute has not matured to a point where we can see what, if any, concrete controversy will develop. It is much like asking a declaration that the State has no power to enact legislation that may be under consideration but has not yet shaped up into an enactment. If there is any risk of suffering penalty, liability or prosecution, which a declaration would avoid, it is not pointed out to us. If and when the State Commission takes some action that raises an issue of its power, some further declaration would be necessary to any complete relief. The proposed decree cannot end the controversy.

Nor is it apparent that the present proceeding would serve a useful purpose if at some future date the State undertakes regulation of respondent. After a sifting of evidence and a finding of facts as they are today, there is no assurance that changes of significance may not take place before the State decides to move. Of course, the remedy is not to be withheld because it necessitates weighing conflicting evidence or deciding issues of fact as well as law. That is the province of courts. But when the request is not for ultimate determination of rights but for preliminary findings and conclusions intended to fortify the litigant against future regulation, it would be a rare case in which the relief should be granted.

Even when there is no incipient federal-state conflict, the declaratory judgment procedure will not be used to pre-empt and prejudge issues that are committed for initial decision to an administrative body or special tribunal any more than it will be used as a substitute for statutory methods of review. It would not be tolerable, for example, that declaratory judgments establish that an enterprise is not in interstate commerce in order to forestall proceedings by the National Labor Relations Board, the Interstate Commerce Commission or many agencies that are authorized to try and decide such an issue in the first instance. Responsibility for effective functioning of the administrative process cannot be thus transferred from the bodies in which Congress has placed it to the courts.

But, as the declaratory proceeding is here invoked, it is even less appropriate because, in addition to foreclosing an administrative body, it is incompatible with a proper federal-state relationship. The carrier, being in some disagreement with the State Commission, rushed into federal court to get a declaration which either is intended in ways not disclosed to tie the Commission's hands before it can act or it has no purpose at all.

Declaratory proceedings in the federal courts against state officials must be decided with regard for the implications of our federal system. State administrative bodies have the initial right to reduce the general policies of state regulatory statutes into concrete orders and the primary right to take evidence and make findings of fact. It is the state courts which have the first and the last word as to the meaning of state statutes and whether a particular order is within the legislative terms of reference so as to make it the action of the State. We have disapproved anticipatory declarations as to state regulatory statutes, even where the case originated in and was entertained by courts of the State affected. Anticipatory judgment by a federal court to frustrate action by a state agency is even less tolerable to our federalism. Is the declaration contemplated here to be *res judicata*, so that the Commission cannot hear evidence and decide any matter for itself? If so, the federal court has virtually lifted the case out of the State Commission before it could be heard. If not, the federal judgment serves no useful purpose as a final determination of rights.   * * *

In this case, as in many actions for declaratory judgment, the realistic position of the parties is reversed. The plaintiff is seeking to establish a defense against a cause of action which the declaratory defendant may assert in the Utah courts. Respondent here has sought to ward off possible action of the petitioners by seeking a declaratory judgment to the effect that he will have a good defense when and if that cause of action is asserted. Where the complaint in an action for declaratory judgment seeks in essence to assert a defense to an impending or threatened state court action, it is the character of the threatened action, and not of the defense, which will determine whether there is federal-question jurisdiction in the District Court. If the cause of action, which the declaratory defendant threatens to assert, does not itself involve a claim under federal law, it is doubtful if a federal court may entertain an action for a declaratory judgment establishing a defense to that claim. This is dubious even though the declaratory complaint sets forth a claim of federal right, if that right is in reality in the nature of a defense to a threatened cause of action. Federal courts will not seize litigations from state courts merely because one, normally a defendant, goes to federal court to begin his federal-law defense before the state court begins the case under state law.

Since this case should be dismissed in any event, it is not necessary to determine whether, on this record, the alleged controversy over an action that may be begun in state court would be maintainable under the head of federal-question jurisdiction. But we advert to doubts upon that subject to indicate the injury that would be necessary if the case clearly rested merely on threatened suit in state court, as, for all we can learn, it may.

We conclude that this suit cannot be entertained as one for injunction and should not be continued as one for a declaratory judgment. The judgment below should be reversed and modified to direct that the action be dismissed.

Reversed and so ordered.

MR. JUSTICE REED, concurring.

* * * [The Declaratory Judgment] Act was intended by Congress as a means for parties in such controversies as that between this interstate carrier and the Utah Commission to settle their legal responsibilities and powers without the necessity and risk of violation of the rights of one by the other. The controversy here is clear and definite. A decision would settle the issue that creates the uncertainty as to the parties' rights. The Act intended operations to be conducted in the light of knowledge rather than the darkness of ignorance.

However, it was recognized that the Declaratory Judgment Act introduced a new method for determining rights into the body of existing law. Therefore the language of the Act was deliberately cast in terms of permissive, rather than mandatory, authority to the courts to take cognizance of petitions seeking this new relief. This enables federal courts to appraise the threatened injuries to complainant, the necessity and danger of his acting at his peril though incurring heavy damages, the adequacy of state or other remedies, particularly in controversies with administrative bodies. But even in respect to controversies with administrative bodies, the Declaratory Judgment Act exists as an instrument to protect the citizen against the dangers and damages that may result from his erroneous belief as to his rights under state or federal law. [Citation.] It is a matter of discretion with federal courts.

* * * Here, the record does not show any unusual danger of loss or damage to respondent, a suit had already been filed and the record shows no reason why its result would not settle this controversy. Because of these circumstances, I concur with the reversal of the judgment.

————

1. As noted in *Wycoff*, a party may seek declaratory relief in federal court as a strategic measure to anticipate a defense to the defendant's threatened suit in state court. The party may gain a tactical advantage in selecting the forum and in shaping the issues for judicial declaration. In such circumstances, courts will not necessarily decline to render declaratory relief, but will generally consider such tactical maneuvers as one factor in exercising their discretion. *See* Nashoba Communications v. Town of Danvers, 893 F.2d 435 (1st. Cir.1990) (Declaratory judgment denied where viewed as an attempt to engage in a "preemptive strike" aimed at undermining the state suit.). In Alphatronix Inc. v. Pinnacle

Micro, Inc., 814 F.Supp. 455 (M.D.N.C.1993), a company published an advertisement in a trade magazine which contained product comparisons to one of its competitors. When the competitor threatened legal action if the ad was not withdrawn, the company sought a declaration its advertisement was not misleading and did not violate any rights of the competitor. The court dismissed the suit, holding that the action would not settle the entire controversy and was an improper use of declaratory judgment procedure.

2. The Federal Declaratory Judgment Act gives the court the power to determine rights and legal relations of parties with respect to matters within the court's jurisdiction. The Act does not confer subject matter jurisdiction; therefore, a litigant must show an independent basis for the court's power to act. Liberty Mut. Ins. Co. v. Insurance Corp. of Ireland, Ltd., 693 F.Supp. 340 (W.D.Pa.1988). In Federal Express Corp. v. Tennessee Pub. Serv. Comm'n, 693 F.Supp. 598 (M.D.Tenn.1988), a state administrative agency took action against the corporation and ordered it to comply with a state regulatory scheme. The company instituted a suit in federal court for declaratory and injunctive relief on grounds of federal preemption. The court denied the company's request on the basis that federal preemption arose only as a defense to the threatened state action, and therefore did not independently satisfy federal question jurisdiction. On the corporation's motion to reconsider, the court explained the distinction between the subject matter jurisdiction requirement and the requirement of a justiciable controversy: "Subject matter jurisdiction precedes ripeness. Subject matter jurisdiction is the power of a federal court to hear a case properly before it. Without that power, even the most lively controversy simply cannot be heard in federal court."

3. A court will not consider the propriety of a declaratory judgment unless an actual case or controversy exists throughout the litigation. *See* Native Village of Noatak v. Blatchford, 38 F.3d 1505, 1514 (9th Cir.1994) (No declaratory judgment where constitutional challenge to statute and regulatory programs mooted by repeal of laws in issue.)

4. In Marine Equip. Mgmt. Co. v. United States, 4 F.3d 643 (8th Cir.1993), owners of a sunken river barge sought a declaratory judgment that they had successfully "abandoned" the barge within the meaning of the Rivers and Harbors Act and therefore could not be held liable for any future damage attributed to the sunken barge. Although the owners had filed a notice of abandonment with the Corps of Engineers, there were no pending administrative enforcement actions nor private claims asserted with respect to the barge. The court declined declaratory relief, finding no justiciable dispute sufficient to satisfy the case or controversy requirement of Article III. The court stated that the actual controversy prerequisite to the exercise of jurisdiction contemplates that the threat of enforcement must have some immediate coercive consequences, not the hypothetical situation of potential claims by unknown third parties.

5. A declaratory judgment requires a sufficiently concrete controversy that the court's decree would not constitute an advisory opinion. Resolution of the issue of ripeness is particularly difficult when a party seeks a declaration of nonliability with respect to a future claim. In Levin Metals Corp. v. Parr–Richmond Terminal Co., 799 F.2d 1312 (9th Cir.1986), for example, Levin Metals purchased a parcel of land from Parr–Richmond and discovered that it was contaminated with hazardous wastes. The parties subsequently filed claims against each other on various grounds, including a request by Parr–Richmond for a declaration of nonliability under CERCLA, a federal environmental protection statute, for clean-up costs or damages which might be incurred by Levin. The court observed that a declaratory judgment in the nature of a defense to a threatened or pending action would be ripe for adjudication if the declaratory judgment defendant, Levin, could have brought a coercive action to enforce its rights. Since CERCLA allows a party who has incurred cleanup costs to seek recovery from others who caused the offending condition, and Levin had already notified Parr–Richmond of its pending claim for reimbursement, the declaratory judgment concerning the issue of nonliability presented a real and immediate controversy. If the court declared that Parr–Richmond's conduct was outside the coverage of CERCLA, would that determination have binding effect on a government agency and prevent the agency from enforcement action against Parr–Richmond?

Compare *Levin Metals* with Hendrix v. Poonai, 662 F.2d 719 (11th Cir.1981), where two doctors, formerly on staff of appellant, brought suit against the hospital, alleging violations of the Sherman Act and the Civil Rights Act. When the doctors applied for readmission to their former staff positions, the hospital sought a declaration that if the request were delayed or rejected the hospital would not be subject to liability under the federal antitrust laws. The court characterized the hospital's requested declaration of nonliability as an abstract question which was an inadequate and premature basis to satisfy the case or controversy requirement for a declaratory judgment action.

6. A declaratory judgment may be one of several possible avenues for a party seeking resolution of a controversy. In circumstances where a claim for declaratory relief could have been resolved through another form of action that has a specific time limitation, that time period will also govern the declaratory judgment suit. Orangetown v. Gorsuch, 718 F.2d 29, 42 (2d Cir.1983). Thus, a litigant cannot evade the operative statute of limitations governing a damages claim simply by labelling the suit as one for declaratory relief. *Gilbert v. City of Cambridge*, 932 F.2d 51 (1st Cir.1991) (Owners of apartment buildings seeking declaration of unconstitutionality of municipal ordinance were time-barred by running of limitations period governing coexisting damages claim).

PROBLEM: THE CABLE SIGNAL DISPUTE

ABC Enterprises and Video Marketing Cable Co. (collectively, the "Cable Group") have franchise agreements with a national video programming service, Top Box Entertainment ("TBE") authorizing them to distribute TBE's services to individual subscribers in the Boston area. The video programming is transmitted by means of microwave signal which is received through specially tuned antennae and converter equipment. Subscribers pay a monthly fee for the service. However, persons who have a special antenna and converter system can receive the programming directly without paying a subscription fee.

In 1990, the Cable Group undertook a campaign to prevent "signal piracy" in their service area. They published in Boston area newspapers various advertisements which showed a picture of a police van and stated: "If you are illegally receiving TBE, soon this will be the only free ride for TBE thieves." The publications also stated that illegal reception of TBE signals carries a penalty of up to a $50,000 fine and two years in prison, and stated in boldface type: "To Avoid Prosecution, Call Before March 15, 1990." The Cable Group also hired Brown and Walker, Inc. ("B & W") to conduct an anti-theft campaign in the Boston area.

The Cable Group and B & W sought to identify unauthorized users of the TBE signal. The effort involved visual inspection of the exterior of homes in the Boston area and the collection of photographs of homes to which were affixed "unauthorized" antennae apparently capable of receiving the TBE signal. In some instances, electronic devices were employed to determine whether these antennae were being used to receive the signal at the time of observation. They compiled a list of approximately 5,000 names and addresses of persons suspected of receiving TBE programming without a subscription.

On January 10, 1991, approximately 5,000 people, including Jo Abrams, received a letter from B & W. On or through the envelope were visible the following statements: "Open Immediately—Pending Legal Action," and "Violation of Federal Law." The letter read as follows:

> In recent weeks, areas of Boston have been subjected to a photographic and electronic survey in a search for violators of Section 705 of the Federal Communications Act of 1984. Your property is listed as maintaining an unauthorized microwave antenna which is tuned to and receiving the private, home entertainment programming of Top Box Entertainment ("TBE"). This illegal reception can no longer be tolerated. In order to avoid incurring legal liability, we demand that you take the following steps immediately:
>
> 1. Remove the unauthorized equipment.
>
> 2. Sign the enclosed subscription agreement to stop your illegal reception of the TBE signal.

3. Return this agreement with payment of $300 to The Cable Group. This amount is considered to be an out of court settlement of all prior and present claims against you. THIS SETTLEMENT OFFER IS NOT NEGOTIABLE.

Abrams wishes to file a declaratory judgment in federal district court seeking a declaration that The Cable Group had improperly construed the Federal Communications Act, 47 U.S.C. § 605 ("FCA"), to make mere possession of a particular type of antenna a violation of the Act for which Abrams and members of the class might be held criminally or civilly liable. What result?

CARDINAL CHEM. CO. v. MORTON INT'L, INC
___ U.S. ___, 113 S.Ct. 1967, 124 L.Ed.2d 1 (1993).

JUSTICE STEVENS delivered the opinion of the Court.

The question presented is whether the affirmance by the Court of Appeals for the Federal Circuit of a finding that a patent has not been infringed is a sufficient reason for vacating a declaratory judgment holding the patent invalid.

[Respondent, Morton International, Inc. (Morton), owns two patents on chemical compounds used in polyvinyl chloride (PVC). In 1983 Morton filed an action in federal district court in South Carolina alleging that petitioners, Cardinal Chemical Company and its affiliates (Cardinal), had infringed those patents. Cardinal denied infringement and counterclaimed for a declaratory judgment that the patents were invalid. During the pendency of the case, Morton filed two other actions against other alleged infringers of the same patents. In one case, the federal court in Louisiana ruled for the defendant, finding no infringement and declaring the patents invalid. On appeal, the Federal Circuit affirmed the finding of no infringement but vacated the judgment of invalidity. The South Carolina District Court also concluded that the patentee had failed to prove infringement and declared the patents invalid. The Federal Circuit affirmed the dismissal of the infringement claim but vacated the declaratory judgment.

The Court then traced the history of the Federal Circuit's practice of routinely vacating declaratory judgments regarding patent validity following a determination of noninfringement. The basic rationale for vacating the declaratory judgment was that once the lack of infringement is determined, there remained no case or controversy between the parties concerning the validity of the patent itself.]

III

Under its current practice, the Federal Circuit uniformly declares that the issue of patent validity is "moot" if it affirms the District Court's finding of noninfringement and if, as in the usual case, the dispute between the parties does not extend beyond the patentee's particular claim of infringement. That practice, and the issue before us, therefore concerns the jurisdiction of an intermediate appellate court—not the jurisdiction of either a trial court or this Court. In the trial court, of course, a party seeking a declaratory judgment has the burden of establishing the existence of an actual case or controversy.

In patent litigation, a party may satisfy that burden, and seek a declaratory judgment, even if the patentee has not filed an infringement action. Judge Markey has described

> the sad and saddening scenario that led to enactment of the Declaratory Judgment Act (Act), 28 U.S.C. § 2201. In the patent version of that scenario, a patent owner engages in a danse macabre, brandishing a Damoclean threat with a sheathed sword.... Before the Act, competitors victimized by that tactic were rendered helpless and immobile so long as the patent owner refused to grasp the nettle and sue. After the Act, those competitors were no longer restricted to an in terrorem choice between the incurrence of a growing potential liability for patent infringement and abandonment of their enterprises; they could clear the air by suing for a judgment that would settle the conflict of interests. The sole requirement for jurisdiction under the Act is that the conflict be real and immediate, *i.e.*, that there be a true, actual 'controversy' required by the Act.

Arrowhead Industrial Water, Inc. v. Ecolochem, Inc. 846 F.2d 731, 734–735 (CA Fed.1988) (citations omitted). Merely the desire to avoid the threat of a "scarecrow" patent, in Learned Hand's phrase, may therefore be sufficient to establish jurisdiction under the Declaratory Judgment Act. If, in addition to that desire, a party has actually been charged with infringement of the patent, there is, *necessarily*, a case or controversy adequate to support jurisdiction of a complaint, or a counterclaim, under the Act. In this case, therefore, it is perfectly clear that the District Court had jurisdiction to entertain Cardinal's counterclaim for a declaratory judgment of invalidity.

It is equally clear that the Federal Circuit, even after affirming the finding of noninfringement, had *jurisdiction* to consider Morton's appeal from the declaratory judgment of invalidity. A party seeking a declaratory judgment of invalidity presents a claim independent of the patentee's charge of infringement. If the District Court has jurisdiction (established independently from its jurisdiction over the patentee's charge of infringement) to consider that claim, so does (barring any intervening events) the Federal Circuit.

There are two independent bases for this conclusion. First, the Federal Circuit is not a court of last resort. If that court had jurisdiction while the case was pending before it, the case remains alive (barring other changes) when it comes to us. The Federal Circuit's determination that the patents were not infringed is subject to review in this Court, and if we reverse that determination, we are not prevented from considering the question of validity merely because a lower court thought it superfluous. * * *

Second, while the initial burden of establishing the trial court's jurisdiction rests on the party invoking that jurisdiction, once that burden has been met courts are entitled to presume, absent further information, that jurisdiction continues. If a party to an appeal suggests that the controversy has, since the rendering of judgment below, become moot, that party bears the burden of coming forward with the subsequent events that have produced that alleged result. * * * Even if it may be good practice to decide no more than is necessary to determine an appeal, it is clear that the Federal Circuit had jurisdiction to review the declaratory judgment of invalidity. The case did not become moot when that Court affirmed the finding of noninfringement.

IV

The Federal Circuit's practice is therefore neither compelled by our cases nor supported by the "case or controversy" requirement of Article III. Of course, its practice might nevertheless be supported on other grounds. * * * If, for example, the validity issues were generally more difficult and time-consuming to resolve, the interest in the efficient management of the Court's docket might support such a rule.

Although it is often more difficult to determine whether a patent is valid than whether it has been infringed, there are even more important countervailing concerns. Perhaps the most important is the interest of the successful litigant in preserving the value of a declaratory judgment. * * * A company once charged with infringement must remain concerned about the risk of similar charges if it develops and markets similar products in the future. Given that the burden of demonstrating that changed circumstances provide a basis for vacating the judgment of patent invalidity rests on the party that seeks such action, there is no reason why a successful litigant should have any duty to disclose its future plans to justify retention of the value of the judgment that it has obtained.

Moreover, our prior cases have identified a strong public interest in the finality of judgments in patent litigation. * * *

We also emphasized the importance to the public at large of resolving questions of patent validity in Blonder–Tongue Lab., Inc. v. University of Illinois Found., 402 U.S. 313 (1971). * * * We also commented at length on the wasteful consequences of relitigating the validity of a patent after it has once been held invalid in a fair trial, and we noted the danger that the opportunity to relitigate might, as a practical matter, grant monopoly privileges to the holders of invalid patents. As this case demonstrates, the Federal Circuit's practice of routinely vacating judgments of validity after finding noninfringement creates a similar potential for relitigation and imposes ongoing burdens on competitors who are convinced that a patent has been correctly found invalid.

Indeed, as Morton's current predicament illustrates, the Federal Circuit's practice injures not only the alleged infringer, and the public; it also may unfairly deprive the patentee itself of the appellate review that is a component of the one full and fair opportunity to have the validity issue adjudicated correctly. If, following a finding of noninfringement, a declaratory judgment on validity is routinely vacated, whether it invalidated the patent or upheld it, the patentee may have lost the practical value of a patent that should be enforceable against different infringing devices. The Federal Circuit's practice denies the patentee such appellate review, prolongs the life of invalid patents, encourages endless litigation (or at least uncertainty) over the validity of outstanding patents, and thereby vitiates the rule announced in *Blonder–Tongue.*

In rejecting the Federal Circuit's practice we acknowledge that factors in an unusual case might justify that Court's refusal to reach the merits of a validity determination—a determination which it might therefore be appropriate to vacate. A finding of noninfringment alone, however, does not justify such a result. Nor does anything else in the record of this case. The two patents at issue here have been the subject of three separate lawsuits, and both parties have urged the Federal Circuit to resolve their ongoing dispute over the issue of validity; it would be an abuse of discretion not to decide that question in this case. Accordingly, the judgment of the Court of Appeals is vacated, and the case is remanded to that Court for further proceedings consistent with this opinion.

It is so ordered.

---

1. A court, in exercising its discretion as to whether to grant declaratory relief, will consider whether the decree will clarify and settle the controversy in a useful manner. The fact that an interested party is not joined in a declaratory judgment action, and therefore not bound by the order, may prompt a court to decline issuance of a declaratory judgment. Consequently, in order to avoid partial disposition of a controversy, all persons with an interest in the determination of questions raised in a declaratory judgment suit should be parties before the court. Diamond Shamrock Corp. v. Lumbermens Mut. Casualty Co., 416 F.2d 707 (7th Cir.1969).

In Delpro Co. v. National Mediation Board of U.S.A., 509 F.Supp. 468 (D.Del.1981), a union filed an application with the National Mediation Board requesting it to investigate a representation dispute among the employees of Delpro. The company subsequently sought a declaratory judgment that it was not a carrier within the meaning of the Railway Labor Act and therefore was outside the statutory jurisdiction of the Board. The court denied the request for declaratory relief because the union, which had not been joined in the suit, would not be bound by the decree; therefore, the order would not finally resolve the controversy. The court stated that the nonjoinder of an interested party prevented the declaratory judgment from serving a useful purpose, regardless of whether the absent party was indispensable within the meaning of FRCP 19(b).

2.   The nonjoinder of an interested party in a declaratory judgment action also has *res judicata* implications.   In Harris v. Quinones, 507 F.2d 533 (10th Cir.1974), an insurance company obtained a declaratory judgment in state court that an automobile insurance policy it had issued was not in force on the date of an accident involving the daughter of the insured.   The daughter and the other motorist involved in the accident were not named as parties to the state court action, but subsequently requested a declaratory judgment in federal court against the insurance company regarding the issue of coverage.   The federal court determined that the prior state court decision did not have *res judicata* effect with respect to the nonparties.   The court, finding that the policy had been in force, stated that the daughter was not bound by the state court decision where her rights were not solely derivative from the policyholder.   Is this decision consistent with the Supreme Court's policy on "Our Federalism" with respect to federal injunctive orders affecting state courts? *See* Chapter 9.

3.   Many courts recognize an exception to *res judicata* principles where the prior action involved only declaratory relief.   *See* Harborside Refrigerated Serv., Inc. v. Vogel, 959 F.2d 368 (2d Cir.1992).   The preclusive effect of the declaratory judgment is limited to the subject matter of the declaratory relief sought.   The rationale for the limited exception is to limit litigation and to conserve judicial resources; otherwise parties seeking declaratory relief would be forced to litigate all possible claims and counterclaims to avoid preclusion under *res judicata* principles.   A contrary rule would undermine the utility of the declaratory judgment remedy.

4.   Consider the court's statement in Texas Employers' Ins. Assoc. v. Jackson, 862 F.2d 491, 505 (5th Cir.1988), describing the nature and function of declaratory relief:

> One of the main purposes of the Federal Declaratory Judgment Act was to provide a means to grant litigants judicial relief from legal uncertainty in situations that had not developed sufficiently to authorize traditional coercive relief.   Litigants would no longer be put to the Hobson's choice of foregoing their rights or acting at their peril; nor, if they had already acted, would they be forced to wait, for perhaps many years, until the statute of limitations expired, to know whether they had been subjected to some significant liability. In the words of Professor Borchard, in his written statement submitted at the hearings on the Federal Declaratory Judgment Act, with the enactment of that statute the courts would no longer have to tell "the prospective victim that the only way to determine whether the suspect is a mushroom or a toadstool, is to eat it."
> [Citations omitted]

PROBLEM: THE PROPERTY LINE

Green, Baker, and Jones owned parcels of land which adjoined each other at the intersection of the boundary lines of three states. Green decided to erect a fence along the boundary line of his property and began staking off the projected location of the fence. Baker believes that Green's stakes incorrectly identify the boundary line. Therefore Baker brings a suit requesting a declaratory judgment to establish the correct property line and a temporary injunction to restrain construction pending resolution of the dispute.

The tract belonging to Jones would be only partially affected by the court's decision, so Baker decided not to join Jones in the suit. Green claims that (a) the declaratory judgment action is not a justiciable controversy because no construction has actually commenced, (b) a remedy at law for damages would be more appropriate in the event that Baker is correct about the property line, and (c) the claim should be dismissed for failure to join Jones as an indispensable party. What result?

STEFFEL v. THOMPSON

415 U.S. 452, 94 S.Ct. 1209, 39 L.E.2d 505 (1974).

Mr. Justice Brennan delivered the opinion of the Court.

* * * This case presents the important question * * * whether declaratory relief is precluded when a state prosecution has been threatened, but is not pending, and a showing of bad-faith enforcement or other special circumstances has not been made. * * *

The parties stipulated to the relevant facts: On October 8, 1970, while petitioner [Steffel] and other individuals were distributing handbills protesting American involvement in Vietnam on an exterior sidewalk of the North DeKalb Shopping Center, shopping center employees asked them to stop handbilling and leave. They declined to do so, and police officers were summoned. The officers told them that they would be arrested if they did not stop handbilling. The group then left to avoid arrest. Two days later petitioner and a companion returned to the shopping center and again began handbilling. The manager of the center called the police, and petitioner and his companion were once again told that failure to stop their handbilling would result in their arrests. Petitioner left to avoid arrest. His companion [Becker] stayed, however, continued handbilling, and was arrested and subsequently arraigned on a charge of criminal trespass in violation of § 26–1503. Petitioner alleged in his complaint that, although he desired to return to the shopping center to distribute handbills, he had not done so because of his concern that he, too, would be arrested for violation of § 26–1503; the parties stipulated that, if petitioner returned and refused upon request to stop handbilling, a warrant would be sworn out and he might be arrested and charged with a violation of the Georgia statute.

[Petitioner brought a class action in federal court requesting an injunction against enforcement and a declaratory judgment that Georgia's criminal trespass statute [1] was being applied in violation of his first and fourteenth amendment rights. The state court stayed its proceedings against Becker pending resolution of the federal action. Following denial of relief in federal court, Steffel petitioned for certiorari with respect to the declaratory judgment suit.]

I

At the threshold we must consider whether petitioner presents an "actual controversy," a requirement imposed by Art. III of the Constitution and the express terms of the Federal Declaratory Judgment Act, 28 U.S.C. § 2201.

* * * [P]etitioner has alleged threats of prosecution that cannot be characterized as "imaginary or speculative." He has been twice warned to stop handbilling that he claims is constitutionally protected and has been told by the police that if he again handbills at the shopping center and disobeys a warning to stop he will likely be prosecuted. The prosecution of petitioner's handbilling companion is ample demonstration that petitioner's concern with arrest has not been "chimerical." In these circumstances, it is not necessary that petitioner first expose himself to actual arrest or prosecution to be entitled to challenge a statute that he claims deters the exercise of his constitutional rights. * * *

Nonetheless, there remains a question as to the *continuing* existence of a live and acute controversy that must be resolved on the remand we order today. * * * Here, petitioner's complaint indicates that his handbilling activities were directed "against the War in Vietnam and the United States' foreign policy in Southeast Asia." Since we cannot ignore the recent developments reducing the Nation's involvement in that part of the world, it will be for the District Court on remand to determine if subsequent events have so altered petitioner's desire to engage in handbilling at the shopping center that it can no longer be said that this case presents "a substantial controversy, between parties having adverse legal interests, of sufficient immediacy and reality to warrant the issuance of a declaratory judgment."

II

* * * Sensitive to principles of equity, comity, and federalism, we recognized in *Younger v. Harris*, 401 U.S. 37 (1971), that federal courts

---

1. This statute [Ga. Code Ann. § 26–1503 (1972)] provides:

"(a) A person commits criminal trespass when he intentionally damages any property of another without his consent and the damage there to is $100 or less, or knowingly and maliciously interferes with the possession or use of the property of another person without his consent. * * *

"(3) Remains upon the land or premises of another person, or within the vehicle, railroad car, aircraft, or watercraft of another person, after receiving notice from the owner or rightful occupant to depart.

"(c) A person convicted of criminal trespass shall be punished as for a misdemeanor."

should ordinarily refrain from enjoining ongoing state criminal prosecutions. We were cognizant that a pending state proceeding, in all but unusual cases, would provide the federal plaintiff with the necessary vehicle for vindicating his constitutional rights, and, in that circumstance, the restraining of an ongoing prosecution would entail an unseemly failure to give effect to the principle that state courts have the solemn responsibility, equally with the federal courts, "to guard, enforce, and protect every right granted or secured by the Constitution of the United States...." * * *

* * * When no state criminal proceeding is pending at the time the federal complaint is filed, federal intervention does not result in duplicative legal proceedings or disruption of the state criminal justice system; nor can federal intervention, in that circumstance, be interpreted as reflecting negatively upon the state court's ability to enforce constitutional principles. In addition, while a pending state prosecution provides the federal plaintiff with a concrete opportunity to vindicate his constitutional rights, a refusal on the part of the federal courts to intervene when no state proceeding is pending may place the hapless plaintiff between the Scylla of intentionally flouting state law and the Charybdis of foregoing what he believes to be constitutionally protected activity in order to avoid becoming enmeshed in a criminal proceeding.

When no state proceeding is pending and thus considerations of equity, comity, and federalism have little vitality, the propriety of granting federal declaratory relief may properly be considered independently of a request for injunctive relief. Here, the Court of Appeals held that, because injunctive relief would not be appropriate since petitioner failed to demonstrate irreparable injury—a traditional prerequisite to injunctive relief—it followed that declaratory relief was also inappropriate. Even if the Court of Appeals correctly viewed injunctive relief as inappropriate—a question we need not reach today since petitioner has abandoned his request for that remedy— [12]the court erred in treating the requests for injunctive and declaratory relief as a single issue. * * *

* * * Congress in 1934 enacted the Declaratory Judgment Act, 28 U.S.C. §§ 2201–2202. That Congress plainly intended declaratory relief to act as an alternative to the strong medicine of the injunction and to be utilized to test the constitutionality of state criminal statutes in cases where injunctive relief would be unavailable is amply evidenced by the legislative history of the Act. * * *

The "different considerations" entering into a decision whether to grant declaratory relief have their origins in [history]. First, as Congress recognized in 1934, a declaratory judgment will have a less intru-

---

12. We note that, in those cases where injunctive relief has been sought to restrain an imminent, but not yet pending, prosecution for past conduct, sufficient injury has not been found to warrant injunctive relief. [Citations.] There is some question, however, whether a showing of irreparable injury might be made in a case where, although no prosecution is pending or impending, an individual demonstrates that he will be required to forego constitutionally protected activity in order to avoid arrest. [Citations.]

sive effect on the administration of state criminal laws. As was observed in Perez v. Ledesma, 401 U.S. at 124–126 (separate opinion of Brennan, J.):

> Of course, a favorable declaratory judgment may nevertheless be valuable to the plaintiff though it cannot make even an unconstitutional statute disappear. A state statute may be declared unconstitutional *in toto*—that is, incapable of having constitutional applications; or it may be declared unconstitutionally vague or overbroad— that is, incapable of being constitutionally applied to the full extent of its purport. In either case, a federal declaration of unconstitutionality reflects the opinion of the federal court that the statute cannot be fully enforced. If a declaration of total unconstitutionality is affirmed by this Court, it follows that this Court stands ready to reverse any conviction under the statute. If a declaration of partial unconstitutionality is affirmed by this Court, the implication is that this Court will overturn particular applications of the statute, but that if the statute is narrowly construed by the state courts it will not be incapable of constitutional applications. Accordingly, the declaration does not necessarily bar prosecutions under the statute, as a broad injunction would. Thus, where the highest court of a State has had an opportunity to give a statute regulating expression a narrowing or clarifying construction but has failed to do so, and later a federal court declares the statute unconstitutionally vague or overbroad, it may well be open to a state prosecutor, after the federal court decision, to bring a prosecution under the statute if he reasonably believes that the defendant's conduct is not constitutionally protected and that the state courts may give the statute a construction so as to yield a constitutionally valid conviction. Even where a declaration of unconstitutionality is not reviewed by this Court, the declaration may still be able to cut down the deterrent effect of an unconstitutional state statute. The persuasive force of the court's opinion and judgment may lead state prosecutors, courts, and legislators to reconsider their respective responsibilities toward the statute. Enforcement policies or judicial construction may be changed, or the legislature may repeal the statute and start anew. Finally, the federal court judgment may have some *res judicata* effect, though this point is not free from difficulty and the governing rules remain to be developed with a view to the proper workings of a federal system. What is clear, however, is that even though a declaratory judgment has "the force and effect of a final judgment," 28 U.S.C. § 2201, it is a much milder form of relief than an injunction. Though it may be persuasive, it is not ultimately coercive; noncompliance with it may be inappropriate, but is not contempt. (Footnote omitted.)

Second, engrafting upon the Declaratory Judgment Act a requirement that all of the traditional equitable prerequisites to the issuance of an injunction be satisfied before the issuance of a declaratory judgment is considered would defy Congress' intent to make declaratory relief available in cases where an injunction would be inappropriate.   * * *

The only occasions where this Court has disregarded these "different considerations" and found that a preclusion of injunctive relief inevitably led to a denial of declaratory relief have been cases in which principles of federalism militated altogether against federal intervention in a class of adjudications. In the instant case, principles of federalism not only do not preclude federal intervention, they compel it. Requiring the federal courts totally to step aside when no state criminal prosecution is pending against the federal plaintiff would turn federalism on its head.   * * *

III

* * * [T]the State's concern with potential interference in the administration of its criminal laws is of lesser dimension when an attack is made upon the constitutionality of a state statute as applied. A declaratory judgment of a lower federal court that a state statute is invalid *in toto*—and therefore incapable of any valid application—or is overbroad or vague—and therefore no person can properly be convicted under the statute until it is given a narrowing or clarifying construction—will likely have a more significant potential for disruption of state enforcement policies than a declaration specifying a limited number of impermissible applications of the statute.   * * *

We therefore hold that, regardless of whether injunctive relief may be appropriate, federal declaratory relief is not precluded when no state prosecution is pending and a federal plaintiff demonstrates a genuine threat of enforcement of a disputed state criminal statute, whether an attack is made on the constitutionality of the statute on its face or as applied. The judgment of the Court of Appeals is reversed, and the case is remanded for further proceedings consistent with this opinion.

Reversed and remanded.

MR. JUSTICE STEWART, with whom THE CHIEF JUSTICE joins, concurring.

* * * Our decision today must not be understood as authorizing the invocation of federal declaratory judgment jurisdiction by a person who thinks a state criminal law is unconstitutional, even if he genuinely feels "chilled" in his freedom of action by the law's existence, and even if he honestly entertains the subjective belief that he may now or in the future be prosecuted under it.

* * * The petitioner in this case has succeeded in objectively showing that the threat of imminent arrest, corroborated by the actual arrest of his companion, has created an actual concrete controversy between himself and the agents of the State. He has, therefore, demonstrated "a genuine threat of enforcement of a disputed state criminal statute...." * * * Cases where such a "genuine threat" can be demonstrated will, I think, be exceedingly rare.

MR. JUSTICE REHNQUIST, with whom THE CHIEF JUSTICE joins, concurring.

I concur in the opinion of the Court. Although my reading of the legislative history of the Declaratory Judgment Act of 1934 suggests that its primary purpose was to enable persons to obtain a definition of their rights before an actual injury had occurred, rather than to palliate any controversy arising from *Ex parte Young*, 209 U.S. 123, 28 S.Ct. 441, 52 L.Ed. 714 (1908), Congress apparently was aware at the time it passed the Act that persons threatened with state criminal prosecutions might choose to forego the offending conduct and instead seek a federal declaration of their rights. Use of the declaratory judgment procedure in the circumstances presented by this case seems consistent with that congressional expectation.

* * * [T]he Court's decision today deals only with declaratory relief and with threatened prosecutions. The case provides no authority for the granting of any injunctive relief nor does it provide authority for the granting of any relief at all when prosecutions are pending. The Court quite properly leaves for another day whether the granting of a declaratory judgment by a federal court will have any subsequent *res judicata* effect or will perhaps support the issuance of a later federal injunction. But since possible resolutions of those issues would substantially undercut the principles of federalism reaffirmed in *Younger v. Harris*, 401 U.S. 37 (1971), and preserved by the decision today, I feel it appropriate to add a few remarks.

First, the legislative history of the Declaratory Judgment Act and the Court's opinion in this case both recognize that the declaratory judgment procedure is an alternative to pursuit of the arguably illegal activity. There is nothing in the Act's history to suggest that Congress intended to provide persons wishing to violate state laws with a federal shield behind which they could carry on their contemplated conduct. * * * The plaintiff who continues to violate a state statute after the filing of his federal complaint does so both at the risk of state prosecution and at the risk of dismissal of his federal lawsuit. * * *

Second, I do not believe that today's decision can properly be raised to support the issuance of a federal injunction based upon a favorable declaratory judgment. The Court's description of declaratory relief as "a milder alternative to the injunction remedy," having a "less intrusive effect on the administration of state criminal laws" than an injunction, indicates to me critical distinctions which make declaratory relief appropriate where injunctive relief would not be. It would all but totally obscure these important distinctions if a successful application for declaratory relief came to be regarded, not as the conclusion of a lawsuit, but as a giant step toward obtaining an injunction against a subsequent criminal prosecution. * * *

A declaratory judgment is simply a statement of rights, not a binding order supplemented by continuing sanctions. State authorities may choose to be guided by the judgment of a lower federal court, but they are not compelled to follow the decision by threat of contempt or other penalties. If the federal plaintiff pursues the conduct for which he was previously threatened with arrest and is in fact arrested, he may not return the controversy to federal court, although he may, of course, raise the federal declaratory judgment in the state court for whatever value it may prove to have. In any event, the defendant at that point is able to present his case for full consideration by a state court charged, as are the federal courts, to preserve the defendant's constitutional rights. * * *

Third, attempts to circumvent *Younger* by claiming that enforcement of a statute declared unconstitutional by a federal court is *per se* evidence of bad faith should not find support in the Court's decision in this case. * * *

If the declaratory judgment remains, as I think the Declaratory Judgment Act intended, a simple declaration of rights without more, it will not be used merely as a dramatic tactical maneuver on the part of any state defendant seeking extended delays. Nor will it force state officials to try cases time after time, first in the federal courts and then in the state courts. I do not believe Congress desired such unnecessary results, and I do not think that today's decision should be read to sanction them. Rather the Act, and the decision, stand for the sensible proposition that both a potential state defendant, threatened with prosecution but not charged, and the State itself, confronted by a possible violation of its criminal laws, may benefit from a procedure which provides for a declaration of rights without activation of the criminal process. If the federal court finds that the threatened prosecution would depend upon a statute it judges unconstitutional, the State may decide to forego prosecution of similar conduct in the future, believing the judgment persuasive. Should the state prosecutors not find the decision persuasive enough to justify forbearance, the successful federal plaintiff will at least be able to bolster his allegations of unconstitutionality in the state trial with a decision of the federal district court in the immediate locality. The state courts may find the reasoning convincing even though the prosecutors did not. Finally, of course, the state legislature may decide, on the basis of the federal decision, that the statute would be better amended or repealed. All these possible avenues of relief would be reached voluntarily by the States and would be completely consistent with the concepts of federalism discussed above. * * *

———

1. A party may resort to declaratory relief to construe the coverage of a penal statute, and thus to establish legal rights, at an early stage in order to avoid criminal prosecution or to allow compliance with the statutory directive. If the declaratory action is brought too prematurely, however, the court may determine that the prospective application of the criminal statute to the plaintiff does not present a justiciable controversy.

Conversely, a party may wait too long in requesting declaratory relief. Once criminal proceedings are commenced, a court will ordinarily decline to grant a declaratory judgment concerning application of the penal statute because it would promote needless proliferation of litigation. Although a declaratory judgment action is considered an optional rather than an extraordinary remedy, a court in its discretion may determine that the plaintiff's remedy should be defending the criminal charges. *See* Norcisa v. Board of Selectmen of Provincetown, 368 Mass. 161, 330 N.E.2d 830 (1975), reprinted *supra* in Chapter 9. The court in *Norcisa* further noted:

> The fundamental jurisprudential considerations underlying the general prohibition against enjoining a pending criminal prosecution apply with full force to support a prohibition against issuing declaratory decrees concerning a pending criminal prosecution. To conclude otherwise would encourage fragmentation and proliferation of litigation and disrupt the orderly administration of the criminal law.

> The rule we adopt today in regard to the issuance of declaratory judgments when criminal litigation is pending is merely a logical extension of our rules which generally proscribe the issuance of such a judgment when an appropriate administrative proceeding is in progress, or when a civil proceeding in which the same issue is or can be raised is already pending between the parties.

2. *Abstention*: Special considerations of federalism, comity, and equity affect the exercise of discretion by a federal court to issue declaratory relief in situations where a pending state court proceeding involves matters related to the federal controversy. Under the abstention doctrine, a federal court which otherwise would possess the requisite jurisdiction over a dispute may choose to decline to exercise that jurisdiction in favor of the state forum. The Supreme Court has visited the abstention doctrine in a wide variety of contexts. An early application of the abstention doctrine was raised in Railroad Comm'n of Texas v. Pullman, 312 U.S. 496, 61 S.Ct. 643, 85 L.Ed. 971 (1941). In *Pullman*, the Court held that a federal court should exercise discretion by "staying its hand" to permit a state court to decide important unsettled matters of state law. Further, in Burford v. Sun Oil Co., 319 U.S. 315, 334, 63 S.Ct. 1098, 1107, 87 L.Ed. 1424 (1943), the Court applied abstention such that a federal court sitting in equity should not interfere with complex matters involving state administrative processes where the federal decision would be disruptive of important state policy. In Younger v. Harris, 401 U.S. 37, 91 S.Ct. 746, 27 L.Ed.2d 669 (1971), the Court, relying on principles of comity and federalism, held that a federal court should ordinarily refrain from enjoining ongoing state criminal proceedings, even where federal constitutional rights were implicated.

Finally, courts may rely upon the abstention doctrine to decline jurisdiction based upon considerations of judicial economy or "wise judicial administration." Colorado River Water Conservation Dist. v. United States, 424 U.S. 800, 817, 96 S.Ct. 1236, 1246, 47 L.Ed.2d 483 (1976). Under the *Colorado River* abstention analysis, the Court recognized that despite the "virtually unflagging obligation" of federal courts to exercise jurisdiction, if "exceptional circumstances" existed, the court may abstain based upon concurrent state court proceedings.

The Court in *Colorado River* identified four factors that a district court should consider when determining whether "exceptional circumstances" were present: (1) whether another court had assumed jurisdiction over property, (2) if the federal forum is inconvenient, (3) the desirability of avoiding piecemeal litigation, and (4) the order in which jurisdiction was obtained by the concurrent forums. The *Colorado River* factors were later supplemented in Moses H. Cone Memorial Hosp. v. Mercury Constr. Corp., 460 U.S. 1, 25, 103 S.Ct. 927, 941, 74 L.Ed.2d 765 (1983), to also include whether the federal law provides the rule of decision on the merits and whether the state court proceedings were inadequate to protect the federal court plaintiff's rights. In *Moses Cone*, the Court emphasized the limited and exceptional nature of the abstention doctrine, observing that dismissal of the federal suit did "not rest on a mechanical checklist, but on a careful balancing of the important factors as they apply in a given case, with the balance heavily weighted in favor of the exercise of jurisdiction." 460 U.S. at 16.

3. *Discretion and Declaratory Judgments*: A related, but not co-extensive analysis with the abstention doctrine, is the panoply of discretionary factors that a federal court should consider when exercising its jurisdiction under the Declaratory Judgement Act where concurrent state proceedings are pending. Although the abstention doctrine and discretion under the Declaratory Judgment Act have areas of overlap, there are also significant differences in scope. *See* United States v.Commonwealth of Pennsylvania, Dept. of Envir. Resources, 923 F.2d 1071, 1073 (3d Cir.1991). *See also* St. Paul Ins. Co. v. Trejo, 39 F.3d 585, 590 (5th Cir.1994) (Dismissal of a declaratory judgment suit does not have to satisfy the more stringent *Colorado River* abstention test.).

In Brillhart v. Excess Ins. Co., 316 U.S. 491, 62 S.Ct. 1173, 86 L.Ed. 1620 (1942), the Supreme Court provided guidance for the exercise of discretion regarding abstention from a declaratory judgment, as Justice Frankfurter, writing for the majority, stated:

Ordinarily it would be uneconomical as well as vexatious for a federal court to proceed in a declaratory judgment suit where another suit is pending in state court presenting the same issues, not governed by federal law, between the same parties. Gratuitous interference with the orderly and comprehensive disposition of a state court litigation should be avoided.

[A district court] should ascertain whether the questions in controversy between the parties to the federal suit, and which are not foreclosed under the applicable substantive law, can better be settled in the proceeding pending in the state court. This may entail inquiry into the scope of the pending state court proceeding and the nature of the defenses open there. The federal court may have to consider whether the claims of all parties in interest can satisfactorily be adjudicated in that proceeding, whether necessary parties have been joined, whether such parties are amenable to process in that proceeding, etc. 316 U.S. at 495.

In sum, the mere existence of a related state court proceeding does not automatically trigger federal court abstention; instead the court should inquire into the adequacy and scope of the state forum to decide the claims.

In exercising discretion regarding whether to issue a declaratory judgment, courts have considered a variety of factors beyond those enumerated in *Brillhart* including:

(1) Whether declaratory relief would settle the controversy;

(2) Whether the declaratory action would serve a useful purpose in clarifying the legal relations in dispute;

(3) Whether the declaratory remedy is being used merely for the purpose of "procedural fencing" or "to provide an arena for a race for *res judicata* ";

(4) Whether the use of a declaratory action would increase friction between federal and state courts and improperly encroach upon state jurisdiction;

(5) Whether there is an alternative remedy which is better or more effective;

(6) The convenience of the parties and witnesses;

(7) Principles of comity and restraint where the same issues are pending in a state court;

(8) Judicial economy in avoiding duplicative or piecemeal litigation;

(9) Discouraging forum shopping; and

(10) Potential inequities in permitting the plaintiff to gain precedence in time and forum.

Grand Trunk W. R. Co. v. Consolidated Rail Corp., 746 F.2d 323, 326 (6th Cir.1984); ARW Exploration Corp. v. Aguirre, 947 F.2d 450, 454 (10th Cir.1991); Granite State Ins. Co. v. Tandy Corp., 986 F.2d 94, 96 (5th Cir.1992). Consider which of these factors were relevant and significant in deciding the following case.

NAUTILUS INS. CO. v. WINCHESTER HOMES, INC.

15 F.3d 371 (4th Cir.1994).

PHILLIPS, CIRCUIT JUDGE:

[Winchester Homes, Inc. ("Winchester") filed products liability claims in state court against Reliance Wood Preserving, Inc. ("Reliance"). Several months later, Nautilus Insurance Company ("Nautilus") filed an action in federal court based on diversity of citizenship seeking a declaratory judgment that the liability policy it had issued to Reliance did not cover the products liability claims asserted by Winchester. Reliance counterclaimed, seeking a declaration that Nautilus was contractually obligated to defend and indemnify it in the state court actions, and also sought damages for fraudulent misrepresentation. Reliance filed a petition in bankruptcy and assigned its interests to Winchester. The federal district court dismissed Nautilus' action in deference to the pending state court litigation against the insured on the underlying claims for which coverage was sought.]

* * * The appeal raises once again the difficult question of when a federal district court may decline to entertain a declaratory judgment action that is properly within its jurisdiction because of the pendency of related litigation in the state courts. * * *

III.

* * * The Federal Declaratory Judgment Act gives a federal district court the power, in any "case of actual controversy within its jurisdiction," to "declare the rights and other legal relations of any interested party seeking such declaration, whether or not further relief is or could be sought." 28 U.S.C. § 2201. The district court unquestionably had the power to entertain Nautilus's declaratory judgment action, as it was a "case of actual controversy" within the court's diversity jurisdiction.[3] Winchester contends that the district court erred in refusing to exercise this power, and we agree.

It has long been settled that a federal court has some measure of discretion to decline to entertain a declaratory judgment action that is otherwise properly within its jurisdiction. [Citations.] This discretion is not unbounded, however: a district court may not refuse to entertain a declaratory judgment action out of "whim or personal disinclination," but may do so only for "good reason." In reviewing a district court's decision to decline to entertain a declaratory judgment action properly within its jurisdiction, we therefore "do[ ]not approach the case in a wholly deferential posture," but instead "exercise [our] own judgment in reviewing the various interests at stake." Mitcheson v. Harris, 955 F.2d 235, 237 (4th Cir.1992). We have characterized this review, which requires us effectively to "substitute our discretion for that of the district court[ ]," as essentially "de novo." [Citation.]

Because the remedial discretion conferred by the Declaratory Judgment Act must "be liberally exercised to effectuate the purposes of the statute," we have held that a federal district court should normally entertain a declaratory judgment action within its jurisdiction when it finds that the declaratory relief sought (i) "will serve a useful purpose in clarifying and settling the legal relations in issue," and (ii) "will terminate and afford relief from the uncertainty, insecurity, and controversy

---

3. A dispute between a liability insurer, its insured, and a third party with a tort claim against the insured over the extent of the insurer's responsibility for that claim is an "actual controversy" within the meaning of the Federal Declaratory Judgment Act, even though the tort claimant has not yet reduced his claim against the insured to judgment. *See Maryland Casualty Co. v. Pacific Coal & Oil Co.*, 312 U.S. 270, 61 S.Ct. 510, 85 L.Ed. 826 (1941). * * *

giving rise to the proceeding." As we said in Aetna Casualty. & Sur. Co. v. Quarles, 92 F.2d 321 (4th Cir.1937):

> The statute providing for declaratory judgments meets a real need and should be liberally construed to accomplish the purpose intended, *i.e.*, to afford a speedy and inexpensive method of adjudicating legal disputes without invoking the coercive remedies of the old procedure, and to settle legal rights and remove uncertainty and insecurity from legal relationships without awaiting a violation of the rights or a disturbance of the relationships.

Applying this analysis, we have frequently approved the use of federal declaratory judgment actions to resolve disputes over liability insurance coverage, even in advance of a judgment against the insured on the underlying claim for which coverage is sought. As the Third Circuit has explained, the nature of the duties a liability insurer owes its insured makes such disputes particularly appropriate for early resolution in a declaratory action:

> [A] liability insurer's indemnification agreement carries with it not only an obligation to pay judgments against the insured but also, in the real world, to pay settlement amounts. * * * To delay [resolution of this controversy until the underlying suit against the insured proceeds to judgment] ... would prevent the litigants from shaping a settlement strategy and thereby avoiding unnecessary costs. [Federal] declaratory judgment relief was intended to avoid precisely the "accrual of avoidable damages to one not certain of his rights." [Citation.]

In *Mitcheson*, we recognized that when an insurer comes to federal court seeking a declaratory judgment on coverage issues while the underlying litigation against its insured is pending in the state courts, considerations of federalism, efficiency, and comity should also figure into the discretionary balance, and may, in certain circumstances, require the federal court to refuse to entertain the action, even when the declaratory relief sought would serve a useful purpose. But *Mitcheson* did not announce a *per se* rule forbidding a federal court to entertain a declaratory action brought to resolve issues of insurance coverage during the pendency of related litigation against the insured in the state courts. Such a rule would, of course, be flatly inconsistent with controlling Supreme Court precedent approving the use of declaratory judgment actions by insurers in precisely that situation. [Citations.]

Instead, *Mitcheson* held only that when a federal court is confronted with an insurer's request for a declaratory judgment on coverage issues during the pendency of related litigation in the state courts, its discretion must be guided not only by the criteria outlined in *Quarles*, which focus on the general utility of the declaratory relief sought, but also by the same considerations of federalism, efficiency, and comity that traditionally inform a federal court's discretionary decision whether to abstain from exercising jurisdiction over state-law claims in the face of parallel litigation in the state courts. In *Mitcheson*, we suggested that those additional concerns might require the court to consider: (i) the strength of the state's interest in having the issues raised in the federal declaratory action decided in the state courts; (ii) whether the issues raised in the federal action can more efficiently be resolved in the court in which the state action is pending; and (iii) whether permitting the federal action to go forward would result in unnecessary "entanglement" between the federal and state court systems, because of the presence of "overlapping issues of fact or law." To these we now add another related consideration, which figures prominently in the formulations developed by other courts and is, we think, at least implicit in our discussion in *Mitcheson*: whether the declaratory judgment action is being used merely as a device for "procedural fencing"—that is, "to provide another forum in a race for *res judicata*" or "to achieve a federal hearing in a case otherwise not removable." * * *

In *Mitcheson* itself, consideration of these additional factors led us to conclude that the district court should have declined to entertain a liability insurer's action for declaratory relief on coverage issues, despite its obvious utility to the parties, because of the pendency in state court of the underlying tort action for which the insured claimed coverage. We reasoned that the state's interest in having the issues raised in the federal action decided in its own courts was "particularly strong" there, because those issues were all governed by state law, and the issues of state law presented were "close," "problematic," and "difficult[ ]." We also thought that it would "make[ ]no sense as a matter of judicial economy" for the federal court to entertain the declaratory action, since there was already an action pending in state court that "stemmed from the same overall controversy" and "involved overlapping issues," and the state court had the ability to resolve all issues raised in the federal declaratory action. Finally, we thought that permitting the federal declaratory action to go forward might result in unnecessary "entanglement" between the federal and state court systems, because many of the issues of law and fact raised in it were already being litigated in the pending state action between the insured and the tort claimant, both of whom were also parties to the federal declaratory action. We explained that if the federal court reached final judgment before the state court, its resolution of those common issues might be entitled to preclusive effect in the state action, which would " 'frustrate the orderly progress' of [the] state court proceedings by leaving the state court with some parts of [the] case foreclosed from further examination but still other parts in need of full scale resolution." At bottom, then, *Mitcheson* simply applied the long-standing rule that a federal court should "ordinarily" decline, for reasons of efficiency and comity, to grant declaratory relief "where another suit is pending in a state court presenting the *same issues*, not governed by federal law, between the *same parties*."

In this case, a liability insurer and its insured have come to federal court seeking a declaratory judgment on coverage issues during the pendency of related state court litigation against the insured. There is no question but that the declaratory relief sought would "serve a useful purpose in clarifying and settling the legal relations in issue," and that it would "terminate and afford relief from the uncertainty, insecurity, and controversy giving rise to the proceeding." The critical question, then, is whether—on the facts of this case—the additional considerations of federalism, efficiency, and comity discussed above are sufficiently compelling to justify a refusal to exercise jurisdiction, despite the obvious utility of the declaratory relief sought. The district court held that they were and dismissed the action. After making our own independent assessment of the relative weight of the various interests involved, however, we conclude that the district court overstepped the bounds of its discretion in so doing.

In the first place, we do not think there is a compelling state interest in having the particular issues raised in this federal declaratory action decided in the state courts. As the district court noted, all of the issues of insurance coverage raised here are governed by the substantive law of the State of Maryland. But that alone provides no reason for declining to exercise federal jurisdiction. In analogous situations in which a federal court possesses discretionary power to abstain from deciding state-law questions otherwise properly within its jurisdiction, that discretion may be exercised only when the questions of state law involved are difficult, complex, or unsettled.   * * *

In this case, unlike *Mitcheson*, the questions of state law raised in the federal action are not close, difficult, or problematic; instead, they involve the routine application of settled principles of law to particular disputed facts. Maryland's interest in having those issues decided in its own courts, which is thus no stronger than it is in any case in which a federal court has jurisdiction over a claim in which state law provides the rule of decision, is not sufficiently compelling to weigh against the exercise of federal jurisdiction.   * * *

Nor do we think that the issues raised in the federal declaratory action can more efficiently be resolved in the courts in which the state actions are pending.   * * *

After examining the scope of the pending state proceedings, we cannot say with any confidence that the issues raised in this federal declaratory action can better be resolved in those proceedings. The basic dispute here is over which of Reliance's three liability insurers—if any—is contractually obligated to defend and indemnify Reliance against Winchester's claims. That issue is not directly raised in either of the two pending state actions, which involve the entirely separate and independent question of Reliance's liability to Winchester under the tort law of two different states. Nor are all parties with interests in this coverage dispute joined as parties to the pending state proceedings: none of the three insurance companies whose policies are implicated in this dispute is formally a party to either of those actions. Finally, it is not clear to us that the insurers can be brought into those actions at this point. Under these circumstances, we cannot say that the issues raised in this declaratory action can more efficiently be resolved in the pending state proceedings.

That the issues raised here might be resolved in some yet-to-be filed action brought in state court—either another action for declaratory relief or an action for indemnity after entry of judgment against Reliance in the underlying tort suits—is not alone sufficient to justify dismissal of this action.   It is well-settled that the mere availability of another adequate remedy does not preclude federal declaratory relief, *see* Fed. R.Civ. Proc. 57, and that a federal court may properly decline to entertain a declaratory judgment action because of the availability of another adequate remedy only if it finds that the other remedy would be a "more effective or efficient" means of resolving the controversy.   That is plainly not the case here.   * * * It is difficult to imagine a less efficient use of judicial resources than dismissing this action on the eve of its trial and requiring the parties to start over again in a different court.   Under these circumstances, it cannot credibly be argued that some yet-to-be-instituted action in the state courts offers a "more effective or efficient" means of resolving the coverage issues presented here.   * * *

Nor do we think that permitting this federal declaratory action to go forward would result in unnecessary "entanglement" between the federal and state court systems.   Unlike *Mitcheson*, this is not a case where many of the issues of law and fact sought to be adjudicated in the federal declaratory action are already being litigated by the same parties in the related state court actions.   As earlier noted, the basic issue sought to be resolved here is whether Nautilus, GAIC, and PLMIC are contractually obligated, under the contract law of Maryland, to defend and indemnify Reliance against Winchester's claims.   The issues in the pending state court actions are quite different ones having to do only with whether Reliance and/or some 13 other manufacturers and distributors of fire retardant plywood are liable, under the tort law of two different states, for the losses allegedly suffered by Winchester.   We are satisfied that there is no significant overlap in the issues of fact that must be decided to resolve these two separate and independent legal controversies.   [Citations.]

Finally, we are satisfied that this federal declaratory action is not being used merely as a device for procedural fencing.   This is not a case in which a party has raced to federal court in an effort to get certain issues that are already pending before the state courts resolved first in a more favorable forum, for the issues presented in this declaratory action are not the same as those raised in the pending state court proceedings.   Nor is there any indication that this declaratory action was filed in an effort to obtain a federal forum in a case not otherwise removable.   Instead, this action was filed in an entirely proper effort to obtain prompt resolution of a dispute over a liability insurer's obligation to defend and indemnify its insured against certain tort claims then being pressed against it in state court—a dispute that was separate and independent from the ongoing litigation in the state courts, and particularly appropriate for early resolution in a declaratory action.

Though the parties might have filed this declaratory action in state court, they chose to proceed in federal court instead, as they were authorized to do by 28 U.S.C. §§ 1332 and 2201. Having done so, they are entitled to have the federal court issue the declaration of rights and duties that they seek, unless the considerations of federalism, efficiency, and comity outlined in *Mitcheson* are strong enough to overcome the federal policy in favor of awarding declaratory relief where it will "serve a useful purpose in clarifying and settling the legal relations in issue" and "afford relief from the uncertainty, insecurity, and controversy giving rise to the controversy." * * * [W]e find that these additional considerations of federalism, efficiency, and comity are not sufficiently compelling to overcome the strong federal interest in awarding declaratory relief that will serve the salutary purposes of the Declaratory Judgment Act. We therefore conclude that the district court erred in dismissing this declaratory action on the eve of its trial.

V.

* * * [W]e reverse the district court's dismissal of the declaratory judgment action and remand with instructions to render a declaratory judgment on the issue of insurance policy coverage. * * *

---

1. Alsager v. District Court, 518 F.2d 1160 (8th Cir.1975), illustrates some of the prudential considerations that may influence the exercise of discretion of federal courts to issue declaratory relief. In *Alsager*, parents sought a declaratory judgment that their constitutional rights were violated by state court proceedings which resulted in termination of their parental relationship with their six children. The district court had denied declaratory relief without reaching the constitutional issues on the basis that the relief requested would be ineffective— reasoning that it could not order a permanent disposition of all the children since they were in varying situations with respect to foster and institutional care. The Eighth Circuit Court of Appeals reversed, holding that the district court had abused its discretion in declining to issue declaratory relief. Even though some of the details regarding the disposition of each child remained, the court found that a declaratory judgment would be a useful permanent solution because it would "clear the air" and allow the parties to deal with the children in a manner consistent with their legal relationship.

2. *Political Question.* Federal courts will decline issuing declaratory relief for lack of presenting a justiciable case or controversy where the suit raises a political question. In *Smith v. Reagan*, 844 F.2d 195 (4th Cir.1988), the plaintiff class sought a declaration that American prisoners of the Vietnam War continued to be held in captivity by the governments of Vietnam, Laos, and Cambodia, and that those prisoners

were covered by the protections of the Hostage Act (22 U.S.C. § 1732 (1982)). They also sought a writ of mandamus compelling the President to comply with the terms of the Hostage Act, including certain investigatory and possible affirmative actions to secure the release of prisoners. The court dismissed the suit for lack of subject matter jurisdiction, finding that the claims directly raised the political question doctrine. The court observed that the Act prescribed no remedy for presidential noncompliance, so any declaratory relief would be merely advisory. More importantly, a judicial declaration of responsibilities under the Hostage Act would effectively seek to dictate foreign policy, a province constitutionally committed to the executive branch.

3. For additional commentary on the role of declaratory judgment actions in resolving constitutional issues *see* Calhoun, Exhaustion Requirements in Younger–Type Actions: More Mud in Already Clouded Waters, 13 Ind.L.Rev. 521 (1980); Dickson, Declaratory Remedies and Constitutional Change, 24 Vand.L.Rev. 257 (1971); Laycock, Federal Interference with State Prosecutions: The Need for Prospective Relief, 1977 Sup.Ct.Rev. 193; Martin, Binding Effect of Federal Declaratory Judgments on State Courts, 51 Tex.L.Rev. 743 (1973); Note, Federal Jurisdiction over Declaratory Judgment Suits—Federal Preemption of State Law, 1986 U.Ill.L.Rev. 127; Rendlemen, Prospective Remedies in Constitutional Adjudication, 78 U.Va.L.Rev. 155 (1976); Shapiro, State Courts and Federal Declaratory Judgments, 74 Nw.U.L.Rev. 759 (1979); Wilkinson, Anticipatory Vindication of Federal Constitutional Rights, 41 Alb.L.Rev. 459 (1977).

*

INDEX

References are to Pages

†